SELECTED MULTILATERAL TREATIES IN THE FIELD OF THE ENVIRONMENT

UNEP: REFERENCE SERIES

1 Directory of Institutions and Individuals Active in Environmentally-Sound and Appropriate Technologies, (Pergamon Press, Headington Hill Hall, Oxford, England)
2 An Environmental Bibliography: Publications Issued by UNEP or under Its Auspices 1973-1980
3 Recueil des Traités Multilatéraux Relatifs à la Protection de l'Environnement
4 Selected Multilateral Treaties in the Field of the Environment

UNITED NATIONS ENVIRONMENT PROGRAMME

SELECTED

MULTILATERAL TREATIES IN THE FIELD OF THE ENVIRONMENT

VOLUME ONE

EDITED BY
Alexandre Charles Kiss
Director of Research,
National Centre for Scientific Research,
Strasbourg, France

GROTIUS PUBLICATIONS
CAMBRIDGE
UNIVERSITY PRESS

Published by the Press Syndicate of the University of Cambridge
The Pitt Building, Trumpington Street, Cambridge CB2 1RP
40 West 20th Street, New York, NY 10011–4211, USA
10 Stamford Road, Oakleigh, Melbourne 3166, Australia

First published by Grotius Publications Ltd 1983
Reprinted by Cambridge University Press 1994

Printed in Great Britain by Bell & Bain Ltd, Glasgow

A catalogue record for this book is available from the British Library

ISBN 0 521 46310 6 paperback

CONTENTS

FOREWORD

Both the Governing Council of the United Nations Environment Programme and the General Assembly of the United Nations Organization expressed the wish to be kept regularly informed of any new international convention concluded in the field of the environment and of the state of existing conventions. Accordingly, a register of international conventions and protocols in the field of the environment has been prepared and annually updated since 1977, presenting the data and information relating to such conventions systematically.

It has been considered useful to complete this work by publishing the full texts in English and French — and later perhaps in other languages — of the principal international conventions concerning the protection of the environment. This decision is justified by the rapidly increasing number of international conventions in this field. However, a complete publication of both bilateral and multilateral treaties could not be envisaged, since owing to procedural reasons the text of numerous bilateral treaties is not available at all or only after a rather long period of time. It has therefore been decided to focus the present publication on multilateral treaties. Although there are outstanding publications, such as the *International Environment Law: Multilateral Treaties* edited by W.E. Burhenne (Erich Schmidt Verlag), which is the most complete collection in this field and which is regularly updated — or the *International Protection of the Environment — Treaties and Related Documents* by R. Rüster and B. Simma (Oceana Publications, Inc.) reproducing the text of multilateral treaties concerning environmental protection, it is believed that for practical reasons a shorter compilation of the main conventions might be useful. As a matter of fact, various Governments in the world seem to be interested in having a collection of international multilateral conventions which can be easily handled. Participants in meetings may find it useful to take such texts with them for consultation when necessary, and libraries of universities or other scientific institutions and scholars or students may find them helpful.

There are also theoretical reasons which justify the present publication. Like other fields of international law, the international legal rules concerning the protection of the environment progress gradually, and precedents, even if they do not directly concern a given situation or a given region in the world, play an important role. It may be stated that the reciprocal influence of solutions adopted at a universal level and/or at different regional levels was and still is one of the main factors in the development of international law of the environment. Three different sorts of relationships can be observed in this respect: influence of treaty rules drafted at a world-wide level on solutions in a regional framework, impact of regional rules on the authors of universal treaties — in particular in the Conference on the Law of the Sea — and rules included in regional treaties which may be a source of inspiration for those who draft comparable rules for a different region in the world. A relatively short collection of treaties shows such relationships and perhaps might be helpful in promoting them by illustrating what can be considered as the "best available legal solution" in a given field.

The present publication will be published in two separate versions, in English and French. Both are identical as far as their contents are concerned. Each volume is divided into two parts: the first includes summaries of the conventions and protocols and data and information relating to them in a chronological order; the second reproduces the texts of the conventions and protocols in the same order.

In the first part of this book, each entry contains the full official title, the objectives of the agreement, a summary of the provisions, details concerning membership, the name of the depositary, dates of adoption and entry into force, place of adoption, languages used and the dates when different Contracting States become parties to the convention. In principle, the last data correspond to the situation at the beginning of 1980. However, in spite of the efforts of the editor and the assistance of different depositary Governments and international organizations, it cannot be ensured that there are no mistakes or omissions. As a consequence, such lists should be considered as having an informative character.

Political changes also modified certain situations. Some States have adopted new official names since they signed international conventions. In the present collection the name reproduced is the official name used when signing the convention. It is also to be recalled that the People's Republic of China considers that "as from 1 October 1949, the day of founding of the People's Republic of China, the Chiang-Kai-shek clique has no right at all to represent China. Its signature and ratification of, or accession to, any multilateral treaties by usurping the name 'China' are all illegal, and null and void . . ."*

Several conventions have been adopted by the intergovernmental conferences at the same time as various resolutions. Here only legally binding texts have been inserted. Resolutions by international bodies set up by different conventions (such as international commissions) have also been omitted, except when they modified the original convention or its annexes. As a rule, all the amendments to conventions approved after the adoption of the main convention have been incorporated into the original text if these amendments have entered into force. In other cases, the legal instruments modifying a convention have been fully reproduced after the original convention under the same number, thus not at their chronological place.

The present publication could not have been set up without the initiative and the help of the Secretariat of UNEP and in particular of Dr. Borut Bohte, Chief of the Environmental Law Unit, Mr. Ofori Boateng, his predecessor, and Dr. Sachiko Kuwabara, Programme Officer of the Unit. It is a pleasure to thank them here for their co-operation and assistance. The editor is also indebted to other international organizations, such as FAO, IMCO, UNESCO as well as to several Governments, for the information they have been willing to supply. It should be added that the heaviest burden of checking texts and lists and of various technical tasks in general has fallen on Mrs. Brigitte Diot to whom the editor is grateful for her devotedness.

Alexandre Charles Kiss

*Note dated 25 September 1972, addressed to the Secretary-General of the United Nations by the Minister for Foreign Affairs of the People's Republic of China. See also the Resolution 2758 (XXVI) of 25 October 1981 of the General Assembly recognizing the representatives of the People's Republic of China as the only legitimate representative of China to the United Nations.

PART 1

BASIC DATA

CONVENTION RELATIVE TO THE PRESERVATION OF FAUNA AND FLORA IN THEIR NATURAL STATE [1]

Objectives

To preserve the natural fauna and flora of certain parts of the world, particularly of Africa, by means of national parks and reserves, and by regulation of hunting and collection of species.

Provisions

a) Parties to establish national parks and strict natural reserves in their territories (art. 3), and to control all human settlements therein (art. 4);

b) Preservation of forest areas and domestication of economically utilizable wild animals to be encouraged (art. 7);

c) Protection of species listed in Annex to be of special urgency and importance (art. 8);

d) Trade in trophies and manufacture of articles from them to be controlled (art. 9);

e) Certain methods of hunting to be generally prohibited, e.g. poison, explosives, dazzling lights, nets, pits, snares, etc. (art. 10).

Membership

Open for accession to any Government. Instruments of accession to be deposited with the Depositary Government.

Date of adoption	8.11.1933
Place of adoption	London
Date of entry into force	14.1.1936
Languages	English, French
Depositary	United Kingdom of Great Britain and Northern Ireland

Parties and dates of entry into force

Belgium	14. 1.1936
Egypt*	14. 1.1956
India	9. 8.1939
Italy	27. 9.1939
Portugal	13.10.1950
South Africa	14. 1.1936
Sudan	14. 1.1936
United Kingdom of Great Britain and Northern Ireland	14. 1.1936
United Republic of Tanzania	3. 3.1963

* Superseded by the African Convention on the Conservation of Nature and Natural Resources (see No. 37).

CONVENTION ON NATURE PROTECTION AND WILDLIFE PRESERVATION IN THE WESTERN HEMISPHERE [2]

Objectives

To preserve all species and genera of native American fauna and flora from extinction, and to preserve areas of extraordinary beauty, striking geological formation or aesthetic, historic or scientific value.

Provisions

a) Parties to establish national parks, national reserves, nature monuments and strict wilderness reserves (art. 2);

b) National parks to provide recreational and educational facilities to the public (art. 3);

c) Strict wilderness areas to be maintained inviolate (art. 4);

d) Co-operation to be maintained between Governments in the field of research (art. 6);

e) Species listed in annex to be especially protected (art. 8);

f) Control to be imposed on trade in protected fauna and flora and any part thereof (art. 9).

Membership

The Convention is open for signature by American Governments. Instruments of ratification to be deposited with the Organization of American States.

Date of adoption	12.10.1940
Place of adoption	Washington
Date of entry into force	30. 4.1942
Languages	English, French, Spanish, Portuguese
Depositary	Organization of American States

Parties and dates of entry into force

Argentina	27. 9.1946
Brazil	26.11.1965
Chile	4. 3.1967
Costa Rica	12. 4.1967
Dominican Republic	3. 6.1942
Ecuador	20. 1.1945
El Salvador	30. 4.1942
Guatemala	30. 4.1942
Haiti	30. 4.1942
Mexico	27. 6.1942
Nicaragua	22. 8.1946
Panama	16. 6.1972
Peru	22. 2.1947
Trinidad and Tobago	24. 7.1969
United States of America	30. 4.1942
Uruguay	9. 7.1970
Venezuela	30. 4.1942

INTERNATIONAL CONVENTION FOR THE REGULATION OF WHALING (as amended) [3]

Objectives

To protect all species of whales from overfishing and safeguard for future generations the great natural resources represented by whale stocks. To establish a system of international regulation for the whale fisheries to ensure proper conservation and development of whale stocks.

Provisions

a) Establishment of the International Whaling Commission (art. 3);

b) The Commission to encourage research and investigation, to collect and analyse statistical information, and to appraise and disseminate information concerning whaling and whale stocks (art. 4);

c) The Commission to meet annually to adopt regulations for the conservation and utilization of whale stocks, dealing with protected and unprotected species, open and closed seasons, open and closed areas, size limits for species, maximum catches for any one season, types of gear and apparatus to be used (art. 5);

d) Schedule attached containing detailed regulations for whaling (under art. 5);

e) Contracting Governments to take measures to enforce these regulations, and to report any infraction of them to the Commission (art. 9).

Membership

Any Government may adhere to the Convention by notification in writing to the Depositary Government.

Date of adoption	2.12.1946	19.11.1956 (amendment)
Place of adoption	Washington	
Date of entry into force	10.11.1948	4. 5.1959 (amendment)
Language	English	
Depositary	United States of America	

The Regulations to Convention were amended in June 1976. They came into force on 25.10.1977.

Parties and dates of entry into force

Argentina	18. 5.1960
Australia	10.11.1948
Brazil	4. 1.1974
Canada	25. 2.1949
Chile	6. 7.1979
Denmark	23. 5.1950
France	3.12.1948
Iceland	10.11.1948
Italy	3. 2.1979
Japan	21. 4.1951
Korea Republic	29.12.1978
Mexico	30. 6.1949
New Zealand	15. 6.1976
Netherlands	14. 6.1977
Norway	10.11.1948
Panama	10.11.1948
Peru	18. 6.1979
Seychelles	19. 3.1979
South Africa	10.11.1948
Spain	6. 7.1979
Sweden	15. 6.1979
Union of Soviet Socialist Republics	10.11.1948
United Kingdom of Great Britain and Northern Ireland	10.11.1948
United States of America	10.11.1948

CONVENTION FOR THE ESTABLISHMENT OF AN INTER-AMERICAN TROPICAL TUNA COMMISSION [4]

Objectives

To maintain populations of yellow fin and skipjack tuna in the eastern Pacific Ocean to permit maximum sustained catches year after year.

Provisions

a) Establishment of the Inter-American Tropical Tuna Commission (art. 1);

b) The Commission to investigate the abundance, biology and ecology of the tuna, and of fishes used as bait in the tuna fisheries; to collect and analyse information; publish such information and make recommendations for joint action by the parties to maintain tuna stocks (art. 2).

Membership

Any Government whose nationals participate in the fisheries covered by the Convention may adhere to the Convention: notification shall be made to each of the contracting parties, whose unanimous consent is required. Thereafter such Government shall deposit an instrument of adherence with the Depositary Government.

Date of adoption	31.5.1949
Place of adoption	Washington
Date of entry into force	3.3.1950
Languages	English, Spanish
Depositary	United States of America

Parties and dates of entry into force

Canada	1. 4.1968
France	22. 5.1973
Japan	1. 7.1970
Nicaragua	6.11.1973
Panama	21. 9.1953
United States of America	3. 3.1950

AGREEMENT FOR THE ESTABLISHMENT OF A GENERAL FISHERIES COUNCIL FOR THE MEDITERRANEAN (as amended) [5]

Objectives

The development and proper utilization of the resources of the Mediterranean and contiguous waters through international co-operation.

Provisions

a) The establishment, within the framework of FAO, of the General Fisheries Council of the Mediterranean (art. 1);

b) The Council to encourage and co-ordinate research, to undertake research, to publish information, to propose measures regarding standardization of equipment, techniques and nomenclature, and relating to the development and proper utilization of aquatic resources.

Membership

Open to acceptance by member States of FAO, subject to a two-thirds majority of the Council membership. Acceptance to be effected by deposit of an instrument of acceptance with the Director-General of FAO.

Date of adoption	24. 9.1949
Place of adoption	Rome
Date of entry into force	3.12.1963 (as amended)
Languages	English, French, Spanish
Depositary	FAO

Parties and dates of entry into force

Algeria	3.12.1963
Bulgaria	3. 7.1972
Cyprus	10. 6.1965
Egypt	3.12.1963
France	3.12.1963
Greece	3.12.1963
Israel	3.12.1963
Italy	3.12.1963
Lebanon	3.12.1963
Libyan Arab Republic	3.12.1963
Malta	3.12.1963
Monaco	3.12.1963
Morocco	3.12.1963
Romania	19. 2.1971
Spain	3.12.1963
Syrian Arab Republic	12.12.1975
Tunisia	3.12.1963
Turkey	3.12.1963
Yugoslavia	3.12.1963

INTERNATIONAL CONVENTION FOR THE PROTECTION OF BIRDS [6]

Objectives

To protect birds in the wild state, considering that in the interests of science, the protection of nature and the economy of each nation, all birds should as a matter of principle be protected.

Provisions

a) In general, protection to be given to all birds during the breeding season, to migrants during their flight to their breeding grounds, and to endangered species throughout the year (art. 2);

b) In general, the taking of eggs, shells and young birds shall be prohibited (art. 4);

c) Certain methods of hunting birds to be prohibited or restricted, eg. snares, nets, poisoned bait, blinded decoy-birds, motor boats and motor vehicles (art. 5);

d) A species found to be a pest in region may be excepted from protection (art. 6);

e) Exceptions may also be made in the interests of science and education (art. 7);

f) Each party to draw up lists of birds which may be lawfully taken or killed in compliance with this Convention (art. 8);

g) Parties to take measures to prevent destruction of birds by water pollution, electric cables, insecticides and poisons, and to educate children and the public in the need for protection of birds (art. 10);

h) Parties to establish reserves for breeding birds (art. 11).

Membership

Open for accession to any State. Instruments of accession to be deposited with the Ministry for Foreign Affairs of the Depositary Government.

Date of adoption	18.10.1950
Place of adoption	Paris
Date of entry into force	17. 1.1963
Language	French
Depositary	France

Parties and dates of entry into force

Belgium	17. 1.1963
Iceland	17. 1.1963
Italy	8. 6.1979
Luxembourg	17. 1.1963
Netherlands	17. 1.1963
Spain	17. 1.1963
Sweden	23. 7.1963
Switzerland	17. 1.1963
Turkey	12. 9.1967
Yugoslavia	26. 9.1973

CONVENTION FOR THE ESTABLISHMENT OF THE EUROPEAN AND MEDITERRANEAN PLANT PROTECTION ORGANIZATION [7]

Objectives

To prevent the introduction and spread of pests and diseases of plants and plant products.

Provisions

a) Establishment of the European and Mediterranean Plant Protection Organization (art. 1);

b) The Organization to act, with FAO, as a regional plant protection organization under article 8 of the International Plant Protection Convention, 1951;

c) The Organization to advise, assist and co-ordinate Government measures to prevent the introduction and spread of plant pests and diseases (art. 5), and to obtain, exchange, study and publish information relating to the same;

d) Schedule II contains a list of pests and diseases to be given special attention.

Membership

Restricted to those countries listed in Schedule III of the Convention, and any other country the Council of the Organization may invite to become a member.

Date of adoption	18. 4.1951
Place of adoption	Paris
Date of entry into force	1.11.1953
Languages	English, French
Depositary	France

Parties and dates of entry into force

Algeria	4. 8.1962
Austria	1.11.1953
Belgium	1.11.1953
Bulgaria	16. 4.1959
Cyprus	6.11.1961
Czechoslovakia	29. 4.1960
Denmark	1.11.1953
Finland	1. 6.1960
France	1.11.1953
German Democratic Republic	20.12.1974
Germany, Federal Republic of	26. 7.1954
Greece	9. 3.1956
Hungary	5. 5.1960
Iran	6. 5.1976
Ireland	1.11.1953
Israel	1.11.1953
Italy	1.11.1953
Luxembourg	1.11.1953
Morocco	26.11.1972
Netherlands	1.11.1953
Norway	1. 4.1956
Poland	5.10.1958
Portugal	3.11.1953
Romania	5. 4.1959

Spain	1.11.1953
Sweden	1.11.1953
Switzerland	1.11.1953
Turkey	9. 9.1965
Union of Soviet Socialist Republics	17. 7.1957
United Kingdom of Great Britain and Northern Ireland	1.11.1953
Yugoslavia	1.11.1953

INTERNATIONAL PLANT PROTECTION CONVENTION [8]

Objectives

To maintain and increase international co-operation in controlling pests and diseases of plants and plant products, and in preventing their introduction and spread across national boundaries.

Provisions

a) Parties undertake to adopt the legislative, technical and administrative measures specified in the Convention (art. 1);

b) Specific and regional agreements to be made in conjunction with FAO (art. 2);

c) Each party to set up an official plant protection organization to:

(i) Inspect areas under cultivation consignments of plants in international traffic for existence or outbreak of plant pests or diseases;

(ii) Issue certificates relating to phyto-sanitary condition and origin of plants and plant products;

(iii) Carry on research in the field of plant protection (art. 4);

d) Parties to regulate very strictly import and export of plants and plant products, by means, where necessary, of prohibitions, inspections, destruction of consignments (art. 6).

Membership

Open to all Governments for adherence. Instruments of adherence to be deposited with the Director-General of the FAO.

Date of adoption	6.12.1951
Place of adoption	Rome
Date of entry into force	3. 4.1952
Languages	English, French, Spanish
Depositary	FAO

Parties and dates of entry into force

Argentina	23. 9.1954
Australia	27. 8.1952
Austria	22.10.1952
Bahrain	29. 3.1971
Bangladesh	1. 9.1978
Barbados	6.12.1976
Belgium	22. 7.1952
Bolivia	27.10.1960
Brazil	14. 9.1961
Canada	10. 7.1953
Cape Verde	19. 3.1980
Chile	3. 4.1952
Colombia	26. 1.1970
Costa Rica	23. 7.1973
Cuba	12. 4.1976
Democratic Kampuchea	10. 6.1952
Denmark	13. 2.1953
Dominican Republic	20. 6.1952
Ecuador	9. 5.1956
Egypt	22. 7.1953

El Salvador	12. 2.1953
Ethiopia	20. 6.1977
Finland	22. 6.1960
France	20. 8.1957
German Democratic Republic	4.12.1974
Germany, Federal Republic of	3. 5.1957
Greece	9.12.1954
Guatemala	25. 5.1955
Guyana	31. 8.1970
Haiti	6.11.1970
Hungary	17. 5.1960
India	9. 6.1952
Indonesia	21. 6.1977
Iran	18. 9.1972
Iraq	1. 7.1954
Ireland	31. 3.1955
Israel	3. 9.1956
Italy	3. 8.1955
Jamaica	24.11.1969
Japan	11. 8.1952
Jordan	24. 4.1970
Kenya	7. 5.1974
Lao People's Democratic Republic	28. 2.1955
Lebanon	18. 9.1970
Libyan Arab Jamahiriya	9. 7.1970
Luxembourg	13. 1.1955
Malawi	21. 5.1974
Malta	13. 5.1975
Mauritius	11. 6.1971
Mexico	26. 5.1976
Morocco	12.10.1972
Netherlands	29.10.1972
New Zealand	16. 9.1952
Nicaragua	2. 8.1956
Norway	23. 4.1956
Pakistan	10.11.1954
Panama	14. 2.1968
Papua New Guinea	1. 6.1976
Paraguay	5. 4.1968
Peru	1. 7.1975
Philippines	3.12.1953
Portugal	20.10.1955
Republic of Korea	8.12.1953
Romania	17.11.1971
Senegal	3. 3.1975
Solomon Islands	18.10.1978
South Africa	21. 9.1956
Spain	3. 4.1952
Sri Lanka	3. 4.1952
Sudan	16. 7.1971
Suriname	28.11.1954 (through succession)
Sweden	30. 5.1952
Thailand	16. 8.1978
Trinidad and Tobago	30. 6.1970
Tunisia	22. 7.1971
Union of Soviet Socialist Republics	24. 4.1956
United Kingdom of Great Britain and Northern Ireland	7. 9.1953
United States of America	18. 8.1972
Uruguay	7.1970
Venezuela	12. 5.1966
Yugoslavia	11. 2.1955

AGREEMENT CONCERNING MEASURES FOR PROTECTION OF THE STOCKS OF DEEP-SEA PRAWNS (*Pandalus borealis*), EUROPEAN LOBSTERS (*Homarus vulgaris*), NORWAY LOBSTERS (*Nephrops norvegicus*) AND CRABS (*Cancer pagurus*) (as amended) [9]

Objectives

To protect the stocks of the four species of crustacea.

Provisions

a) Covers only the seas lying between Denmark and Sweden and Norway (art. 1);

b) Size of mesh of nets and minimum size of crustaceans to be caught are regulated (arts. 2, 3, 4);

c) Fishery research is excluded from the provisions of articles 2, 3, 4 (art. 5).

Membership

Restricted to the signatory States.

Date of adoption	7. 3.1952 (amending protocol 14.10.1959)
Place of adoption	Oslo
Date of entry into force	26. 1.1953 (amending protocol 14.10.1959)
Language	Norwegian
Depositary	Norway

Parties and dates of entry into force

Denmark	26. 1.1953	(14.10.1959)
Norway	26. 1.1953	(14.10.1959)
Sweden	26. 1.1953	(14.10.1959)

INTERNATIONAL CONVENTION FOR THE HIGH SEAS FISHERIES OF THE NORTH PACIFIC OCEAN [10]

Objectives

To ensure maximum sustained productivity of the fishery resources of the North Pacific Ocean. To co-ordinate research and conservation measures to this end.

Provisions

a) All the waters of the North Pacific Ocean and adjacent seas, other than territorial waters, are included (art. 1);

b) Establishment of the International North Pacific Fisheries Commission (art. 2);

c) Commission to study fish stocks and decide and recommend necessary joint conservation measures (art. 3);

d) Strong enforcement measures are included (arts. 9-10);

e) Annex to Convention contains conservation measures for halibut, herring and salmon.

Membership

Restricted to the signatory States

Date of adoption	9. 5.1952
Place of adoption	Tokyo
Date of entry into force	12. 6.1953
Languages	English, Japanese
Depositary	
Amendments	7.11.1959
	11.11.1961
	17.11.1962
	25. 1.1963

Parties and dates of entry into force

	Convention	last amendment
Canada	12.6.1953	8.5.1963
Japan	12.6.1953	8.5.1963
United States of America	12.6.1953	8.5.1963

INTERNATIONAL CONVENTION FOR THE PREVENTION OF POLLUTION OF THE SEA BY OIL, 1954 (as amended on 11 April 1962 and 21 October 1969) [11]

Objectives

To take action to prevent pollution of the sea by oil discharged from ships.

Provisions

a) Applies to all ships, except tankers of under 150 tons g.t. and other ships of under 500 tons g.t., registered in the territory of, or having the nationality of, a Party. Excepting also naval ships and ships engaged in whaling (art. 2);

b) Prohibition of discharge from a ship (a tanker), except when proceeding en route or the instantaneous rate of discharge does not exceed 60 litres per mile. Prohibition of discharge is not applicable when the following conditions are satisfied: in case of a ship — the oil content of the discharge is less than 100 parts per 1,000,000 parts of the mixture or the discharge is made as far as practicable from land, in case of a tanker — the total quantity of oil discharged on a ballast voyage does not exceed 1/15,000 of the total cargo-carrying capacity or the tanker is more than 50 miles from the nearest land (art. 3);

c) Exceptions to article 3 in cases of necessity to serve safety of ships, save life or prevent damage to cargo, or where leakage is unavoidable and all measures have been taken to minimize it (art. 4);

d) Ships to be fitted within 12 months to prevent escape of oil into the bilges (art. 7);

e) Parties to provide facilities at ports for reception of oily residues and mixtures, and at oil loading terminals (art. 8);

f) All ships covered by the Convention to carry an oil record book, as per Annex, to be completed whenever certain operations take place (art. 9);

g) Parties to send texts of laws, decrees, orders and regulations giving effect to the Convention to the United Nations.

Membership

Open to all States for acceptance; instruments of acceptance to be deposited with the Inter-Governmental Maritime Consultative Organization (IMCO).

Convention

Date of adoption	12.5.1954
Place of adoption	London
Date of entry into force	26.7.1958
Languages	English, French
Depositary	IMCO

Convention as amended in 1962 and 1969

Date of adoption	21.10.1969
Date of entry into force	20. 1.1978

Further amendments, not yet entered into force in 1980

AMENDMENTS TO THE INTERNATIONAL CONVENTION FOR THE PREVENTION OF POLLUTION OF THE SEA BY OIL, 1954 CONCERNING TANK ARRANGEMENTS AND LIMITATION OF TANK SIZE

Objectives

To regulate tank arrangements and limit tank size in oil tankers in order to avoid the possibility of serious environmental pollution resulting from a single accident involving a tanker.

Provisions

a) To apply to all tankers for delivery after 1 January 1977, or for whom the contract was placed after 1 January 1972 (new art. 6b);

b) Tankers built to these specifications to carry a Government-authorized certificate attesting such compliance;

c) Annex C added to the Convention containing detailed specifications for tank arrangements and size.

Membership

Open to all States party to the 1954 Convention. Instruments of acceptance to be deposited with IMCO.

Date of adoption	15.10.1971
Place of adoption	London
Date of entry into force	
Languages	English, French
Depositary	IMCO

AMENDMENTS TO THE INTERNATIONAL CONVENTION FOR THE PREVENTION OF POLLUTION OF THE SEA BY OIL, 1954, CONCERNING THE PROTECTION OF THE GREAT BARRIER REEF OF AUSTRALIA

Objectives

To protect the Great Barrier Reef of Australia from pollution by oil.

Provisions

Amendment of the definition of "Nearest Land" in article 1 of the 1954 Convention, to contain a precise description of the "nearest land" off the north-east coast of Australia.

Membership

Open to all States party to the 1954 Convention. Instruments of acceptance to be deposited with IMCO.

Date of adoption	12.10.1971
Place of adoption	London
Date of entry into force	
Languages	English, French
Depositary	IMCO

Parties and dates of entry into force of the convention as amended in 1962 and 1969

Algeria	20. 4.1964
Argentina	30.12.1976
Australia	29.11.1962
Austria	19. 8.1975
Bahamas	22.10.1976
Belgium	26. 7.1958
Bulgaria	28. 1.1977
Canada	26. 7.1958
Chile	2.11.1977
Cyprus	10. 9.1980
Democratic Yemen	20. 8.1969
Denmark	26. 7.1958
Dominican Republic	29. 8.1963
Egypt	22. 7.1963
Fiji	15.11.1972
Finland	30. 3.1959
France	26. 7.1958
German Democratic Republic	25. 4.1979
Germany, Federal Republic of	26. 7.1958
Ghana	17. 8.1962
Greece	28. 6.1967
Iceland	23. 5.1962
India	4. 6.1974
Ireland	26. 7.1958
Israel	11. 2.1966
Italy	25. 8.1964
Ivory Coast	17. 6.1967
Japan	21.11.1967
Jordan	8. 8.1963
Kenya	12.12.1975
Kuwait	27. 2.1962
Lebanon	31. 8.1967

Libyan Arab Jamahiriya	18. 5.1972
Liberia	28. 6.1962
Madagascar	1. 5.1965
Malta	10. 4.1975
Mexico	26. 7.1958
Monaco	25. 6.1970
Morocco	29. 5.1968
Netherlands	26. 7.1958
New Zealand	1. 9.1971
Nigeria	22. 4.1968
Norway	26. 7.1958
Panama	25.12.1963
Papua New Guinea	12. 6.1980
Philippines	19. 2.1964
Poland	28. 5.1961
Portugal	28. 6.1967
Qatar	1. 5.1980
Republic of Korea	31.10.1978
Saudi Arabia	30. 3.1972
Senegal	27. 6.1972
Spain	22. 4.1964
Suriname	1. 3.1977
Sweden	26. 7.1958
Switzerland	12. 4.1966
Syrian Arab Republic	24. 3.1969
Tunisia	11. 9.1973
Union of Soviet Socialist Republics	3.12.1969
United Kingdom of Great Britain and Northern Ireland	26. 7.1958
United States of America	8.12.1961
Uruguay	9. 3.1976
Venezuela	12. 3.1964
Yemen Arab Republic	6. 6.1979
Yugoslavia	11. 6.1974

The Convention has been extended to:

Netherlands Antilles	20. 7.1962
Puerto Rico, Guam, Canal Zone	9. 9.1975
Virgin Islands, American Samoa	9. 9.1975
Trust Territories of the Pacific Islands	9. 9.1975
Midway Islands, Wake Island, Johnston Island	18. 3.1976

PHYTO-SANITARY CONVENTION FOR AFRICA SOUTH OF THE SAHARA [12]

Objectives

To prevent the introduction of diseases, insect pests and other enemies of plants into any part of Africa south of the Sahara, to eradicate or control them in so far as they are present in the area and to prevent their spread.

Provisions

a) Establishment of the Inter-African Phyto-Sanitary Commission.

b) Each participating Government undertakes to exercise at least such control of plant imports as the Commission shall consider to be necessary; it takes such measures of quarantine, certification, inspection, or prohibition of importation as may be considered necessary by the Commission. It shall take such action as may be desirable to deal effectively with diseases, insect pests and other enemies of plants which the Commission considers have become, or are likely to become, a serious danger.

Membership

Open to all States

Date of adoption	29. 7.1954
Place of adoption	London
Date of entry into force	15. 6.1956
Languages	English, French
Depositary	United Kingdom of Great Britain and Northern Ireland

Parties and dates of entry into force

Cameroon	28.12.1961
Central African Republic	5. 1.1962
Chad	11. 4.1962
Congo	5. 2.1962
Gabon	25. 1.1962
Ghana	28. 3.1958
Guinea	24. 2.1962
Ivory Coast	22. 1.1962
Liberia	5. 2.1962
Malagasy Republic	2. 2.1962
Malawi	1. 4.1965
Mali	14. 1.1963
Mauritania	24. 2.1962
Niger	17.10.1961
Nigeria	8.11.1961
Portugal	16. 7.1957
Rhodesia and Nyassaland, Fed.	15. 6.1956
Senegal	17.10.1961
Sierra Leone	30. 5.1962
Tanganyika	31. 5.1962
Uganda	20. 4.1965
Zaire	21. 9.1962

PLANT PROTECTION AGREEMENT FOR THE SOUTH EAST ASIA AND PACIFIC REGION [13] (as amended)

Objectives

To prevent the introduction into and spread within the region of destructive plant diseases and pests.

Provisions

a) The region stretches from the western border of Pakistan, to the eastern coast of the Socialist Republic of Vietnam along the southern border of China, and includes also all territories in the Pacific and Indian Oceans and the South China Sea wholly or partly within the area bounded by Long. 100° E, Lat. 45° S, Long. 130° W, Lat. 38° N, to its intersection with the coast of the Republic of Korea (art. 1); for the purpose of implementing the objectives of this agreement, Hong-Kong shall also be considered as being within the region;

b) Establishment of the Plant Protection Committee for the South East Asia and Pacific Region (art. 2);

c) Trade in plants and plant products to be regulated by certification, prohibition, inspection, disinfection, quarantine, destruction, etc. as necessary (art. 3);

d) Special measures (in Appendix B) to be taken to exclude South American leaf blight of the Hevea rubber tree from the region (art. 4).

Membership

Open for adherence by any State situated in the region or any Government which is reponsible for the international relations of a territory or territories in the region. Instruments of adherence to be deposited with the Director-General of FAO.

		(amendment)
Date of adoption	27. 2.1956	3.11.1967
Place of adoption	Rome	
Date of entry into force	2. 7.1956	16. 8.1969
Languages	English, French, Spanish	
Depositary	FAO	

Parties and dates of entry into force

Australia	2. 7.1956
Bangladesh	4.12.1974
Burma	4.11.1959
Democratic Kampuchea	27. 1.1969
Fiji	16.12.1970
France	20. 8.1957
India	2. 7.1956
Indonesia	21. 12.1967
Lao People's Democratic Republic	17. 3.1960
Malaysia	20.11.1957
Nepal	12. 8.1965
New Zealand	17.12.1975
Pakistan	8. 1.1958
Papua New Guinea	1. 6.1976
Philippines	11. 6.1962
Portugal	2. 7.1956
Samoa	23.12.1971
Socialist Republic of Vietnam	2. 7.1956
Solomon Islands	20. 6.1979
Sri Lanka	2. 7.1956
Thailand	3.12.1956
United Kingdom of Great Britain and Northern Ireland	3.12.1956

INTERIM CONVENTION ON CONSERVATION OF NORTH PACIFIC FUR SEALS

Washington, 9 February 1957

See Nr. 67.

CONVENTION CONCERNING FISHING IN THE WATERS OF THE DANUBE [14]

Objectives

The rational utilization and expansion of the fish stocks in the Danube, through co-operation on a scientific basis.

Provisions

a) Parties to apply the Regulations for Fishing in the River Danube, annexed to the Convention, relating to prohibited times and places for fishing, prohibited tackle and fishing methods, sizes of mesh of nets (art. 4).

b) Parties to improve natural conditions for fish breeding and, in the event of erecting engineering works, to safeguard the normal migratory movements of fish (art. 5);

c) Artificial breeding to be undertaken as necessary (art. 6);

d) Parties to take measures to prevent contamination and pollution of the river by untreated sewage and industrial/municipal wastes, and to regulate blasting (art. 7);

e) Parties to co-operate in exchange of information, scientific and technical agreements (arts. 8-9);

f) Establishment of a fixed Commission to work out measures for the regulation of fishing and the augmentation of fish stocks, to make proposals to the Parties, to organize exchange of information, to co-ordinate scientific research (arts. 11-12).

Membership

Open for accession to the Danubian States.

Date of adoption	29. 1.1958
Place of adoption	Bucharest
Date of entry into force	20.12.1958
Languages	Romanian, Bulgarian, Serbo-Croat, Russian
Depositary	Romania

Parties and dates of entry into force

Bulgaria	20.12.1958
Czechoslovakia	29. 6.1972
Hungary	18.12.1961
Romania	20.12.1958
Union of Soviet Socialist Republics	20.12.1958
Yugoslavia	20.12.1958

CONVENTION ON THE CONTINENTAL SHELF [15]

Objectives

To define and delimit the rights of States to explore and exploit the natural resources of the continental shelf.

Provisions

a) Coastal States have sovereign and exclusive rights over the continental shelf for the purpose of exploration and exploitation (art. 1);

b) Such exploration or exploitation must not cause unjustifiable interference with navigation, fishing or the conservation of the living resources of the sea, or with oceanographic or other scientific research (art. 5).

Membership

Open for accession to all States Members of the United Nations or members of the specialized agencies. Instruments to be deposited with the Secretary-General of the United Nations.

Date of adoption	29. 4.1958
Place of adoption	Geneva
Date of entry into force	10. 6.1964
Languages	Chinese, English, French, Russian, Spanish
Depositary	Secretary-General of the United Nations

Parties and dates of entry into force

Albania	6. 1.1965
Australia	10. 6.1964
Bulgaria	10. 6.1964
Byelorussian Soviet Socialist Republic	10. 6.1964
Canada	8. 3.1970
China	11.11.1970
Colombia	10. 6.1964
Costa Rica	17. 3.1972
Cyprus	11. 5.1974
Czechoslovakia	10. 6.1964
Democratic Kampuchea	10. 6.1964
Denmark	10. 6.1964
Dominican Republic	10. 9.1964
Fiji	18. 4.1971
Finland	18. 3.1965
France	14. 7.1965
German Democratic Republic	26. 1.1974
Greece	6.12.1972
Guatemala	10, 6.1964
Haiti	10. 6.1964
Israel	10. 6.1964
Jamaica	7.11.1965
Kenya	20. 7.1969
Lesotho	23.10.1973
Madagascar	10. 6.1964
Malawi	3.12.1965
Malaysia	10. 6.1964
Malta	18. 6.1966
Mauritius	4.11.1970
Mexico	1. 9.1966

Netherlands	19. 3.1966
New Zealand	17. 2.1965
Nigeria	28. 5.1971
Norway	9.10.1971
Poland	10. 6.1964
Portugal	10. 6.1964
Romania	10. 6.1964
Senegal	10. 6.1964
Sierra Leone	25.12.1966
South Africa	10. 6.1964
Spain	27. 3.1971
Swaziland	15.11.1970
Sweden	1. 7.1966
Switzerland	17. 6.1966
Thailand	1. 8.1968
Tonga	29. 7.1971
Trinidad and Tobago	10. 8.1968
Uganda	14.10.1964
Ukrainian Soviet Socialist Republic	10. 6.1964
Union of Soviet Socialist Republics	10. 6.1964
United Kingdom of Great Britain and Northern Ireland	10. 6.1964
United States of America	10. 6.1964
Venezuela	10. 6.1964
Yugoslavia	27. 2.1966

CONVENTION ON THE HIGH SEAS [16]

Objectives

To codify the rules of international law relating to the high seas.

Provisions (environmentally related)

a) States to draw up regulations to prevent pollution of the sea by oil from ships and pipelines or resulting from the exploration and exploitation of the seabed (art. 24);

b) States to take measures to prevent pollution of the sea by dumping of radioactive waste, and to co-operate with international agencies in taking measures to prevent pollution of the seas or airspace above them, resulting from radioactive materials or other harmful agents (art. 25).

Membership

Open for accession to all States Members of the United Nations or members of the specialized agencies. Instruments to be deposited with the Secretary-General of the United Nations.

Date of adoption	29. 4.1958
Place of adoption	Geneva
Date of entry into force	30. 9.1962
Languages	Chinese, English, French, Russian, Spanish
Depositary	Secretary-General of the United Nations

Parties and dates of entry into force

Afghanistan	30. 9.1962
Albania	6. 1.1965
Australia	13. 6.1963
Austria	9. 2.1974
Belgium	5. 2.1972
Bulgaria	30. 9.1962
Byelorussian Soviet Socialist Republic	30. 9.1962
Central African Empire	14.11.1962
Costa Rica	17. 3.1972
Czechoslovakia	30. 9.1962
Democratic Kampuchea	30. 9.1962
Denmark	26.10.1968
Dominican Republic	10. 9.1964
Fiji	10.10.1970
Finland	18. 3.1965
German Democratic Republic	26. 1.1974
Germany, Federal Republic of	25. 8.1973
Guatemala	30. 9.1962
Haiti	30. 9.1962
Hungary	30. 9.1962
Indonesia	30. 9.1962
Israel	30. 9.1962
Italy	16. 1.1965
Jamaica	30. 9.1962
Japan	10. 7.1968
Kenya	20. 7.1969
Lesotho	23.10.1973
Madagascar	30. 9.1962
Malawi	3.12.1965
Malaysia	30. 9.1962

Mauritius	12. 3.1968
Mexico	1. 9.1966
Mongolia	14.11.1976
Nepal	27. 1.1963
Netherlands	20. 3.1966
Nigeria	30. 9.1962
Poland	30. 9.1962
Portugal	7. 2.1963
Romania	30. 9.1962
Senegal	30. 9.1962
Sierra Leone	30. 9.1962
South Africa	9. 5.1963
Spain	27. 3.1971
Swaziland	15.11.1970
Switzerland	17. 6.1966
Thailand	1. 8.1968
Tonga	4. 6.1971
Trinidad and Tobago	30. 9.1962
Uganda	14.10.1964
Ukrainian Soviet Socialist Republic	30. 9.1962
Union of Soviet Socialist Republics	30. 9.1962
United Kingdom of Great Britain and Northern Ireland	30. 9.1962
United States of America	20. 3.1966
Upper Volta	20. 3.1966
Venezuela	20. 3.1966
Yugoslavia	20. 3.1966

CONVENTION OF FISHING AND CONSERVATION OF THE LIVING RESOURCES OF THE HIGH SEAS [17]

Objectives

Through international co-operation, to solve the problems involved in the conservation of the living resources of the high seas, considering that through the development of modern techniques some of these resources are in danger of being over-exploited.

Provisions

a) All States have a duty to adopt, or co-operate with other States in adopting, measures for their respective nationals for the conservation of the living resources of the high seas (art. 1);

b) Such measures should be formulated with a view to securing a supply of food for human consumption (art. 2);

c) Coastal States have special interests in the high seas adjacent to their territorial seas and may unilaterally adopt conservation measures for such areas which shall be valid for other States if there is an urgent need for such measures, and the measures are based on scientific findings and do not discriminate against foreign fishermen (arts. 6-7);

d) Disputes to be settled by a special commission of five members whose decision shall be binding on the States concerned (arts. 9 and 11).

Membership

Open for accession to any State. Instruments of accession to be deposited with the Secretary-General of the United Nations.

Date of adoption	29. 4.1958
Place of adoption	Geneva
Date of entry into force	20. 3.1966
Languages	Chinese, English, French Russian, Spanish
Depositary	Secretary-General of the United Nations

Parties and dates of entry into force

Australia	20. 3.1966
Belgium	5. 2.1972
Colombia	20. 3.1966
Democratic Kampuchea	20. 3.1966
Denmark	26.10.1968
Dominican Republic	20. 3.1966
Fiji	18. 4.1971
Finland	20. 3.1966
France	18.10.1970
Haiti	20. 3.1966
Jamaica	20. 3.1966
Kenya	20. 7.1969
Lesotho	23.11.1973
Madagascar	20. 3.1966
Malawi	20. 3.1966
Malaysia	20. 3.1966
Mauritius	4. 11.1970
Mexico	1. 9.1966

Netherlands	20. 3.1966
Nigeria	20. 3.1966
Portugal	20. 3.1966
Sierra Leone	20. 3.1966
South Africa	20. 3.1966
Spain	27. 3.1971
Switzerland	17. 6.1966
Thailand	1. 8.1968
Tonga	28. 8.1971
Trinidad and Tobago	11. 5.1966
Uganda	20. 3.1966
United Kingdom of Great Britain and Northern Ireland	20. 3.1966
United States of America	20. 3.1966
Upper Volta	20. 3.1966
Venezuela	20. 3.1966
Yugoslavia	20. 3.1966

NORTH-EAST ATLANTIC FISHERIES CONVENTION [18]

Objectives

To ensure the conservation and rational exploitation of the fish stocks of the North-East Atlantic Ocean and adjacent waters.

Provisions

a) Includes seas lying between, approximately latitude 36°N, longitude 42° W, and longitude 51° E, but excluding the Mediterranean and the Baltic. The area to be divided into regions (art. 1);

b) Establishment of the North-East Atlantic Fisheries Commission (art. 3);

c) The Commission to consider what measures may be required to conserve fish stocks, and make recommendations to Parties based on the results of scientific research and investigation (art. 6);

d) Such measures to concern size of mesh for fishing nets, size of fish that may be kept on board, open and closed seasons and areas, regulation of fishing gear (art. 7);

e) All sea fish and shell fish are included but not sea mammals (art. 7(3)).

Membership

Open to all States for accession by notification in writing addressed to the Depositary Government.

Date of adoption	24. 1.1959
Place of adoption	London
Date of entry into force	27. 6.1963
Languages	English, French
Depositary	United Kingdom of Great Britain and Northern Ireland

Parties, dates of entry into force and of withdrawals

Belgium	27. 6.1963	30.12.1977
Bulgaria	1. 9.1976	
Cuba	9.12.1976	
Denmark	27. 6.1963	29.12.1977
Finland	21. 6.1976	
France	27. 6.1963	31.12.1977
German Democratic Republic	26. 6.1974	
Germany, Federal Republic of	27. 6.1963	7. 2.1978
Iceland	27. 6.1963	
Ireland	27. 6.1963	24. 2.1978
Netherlands	27. 6.1963	29.12.1977
Norway	27. 6.1963	1. 7.1978
Poland	27. 6.1963	
Portugal	27. 6.1963	
Spain	27. 6.1963	
Sweden	27. 6.1963	13. 9.1979
Union of Soviet Socialist Republics	27. 6.1963	

United Kingdom of Great Britain and Northern Ireland	27. 6.1963	31.12.1977

CONVENTION CONCERNING FISHING IN THE BLACK SEA [19]

Objectives

The rational utilization of the fishery resources and the development of marine fishing in the Black Sea.

Provisions

a) Co-operation between parties in improving fishing techniques and scientific research (art. 1);

b) Ports of refuge from bad weather for fishing boats from the contracting States established in each State (art. 2);

c) Minimum sizes of fish to be taken (art. 5);

d) Parties to exchange information concerning fish migrations, scientific research and fishing techniques (arts. 6-7);

e) A Mixed Commission established to work out measures to regulate fishing, if necessary to amend article 5, to co-ordinate research, and to exchange information (arts. 8-9).

Membership

Open for accession to Black Sea States

Date of adoption	7. 7.1959
Place of adoption	Varna
Date of entry into force	21. 3.1960
Languages	Bulgarian, Romanian, Russian
Depositary	Bulgaria
Amendment	30. 6.1965

Parties and dates of entry into force

Bulgaria	21. 3.1960
Romania	21. 3.1960
Union of Soviet Socialist Republics	21. 3.1960

AGREEMENT FOR THE ESTABLISHMENT ON A PERMANENT BASIS OF A LATIN-AMERICAN FOREST RESEARCH AND TRAINING INSTITUTE [20]

Objectives

To establish the Institute on a permanent basis to assist in the implementation of the programme of FAO in the field of forestry in Latin America.

Provisions

a) The Institute to be at the Forestry School of the University of the Andes, Merida, Venezuela;

b) The Institute to conduct applied research to contribute to proper conservation, utilization and development of the forest resources of Latin America, to give courses of instruction for the training of forestry technicians and to gather, classify and distribute scientific material within its field (art. 3).

Membership

Open to all member States or associate members of FAO.

Date of adoption	18.11.1959
Place of adoption	Rome
Date of entry into force	16.11.1960
Languages	English, French, Spanish
Depositary	FAO

Parties and dates of entry into force

Chile	7.10.1965
Costa Rica	30. 1.1963
Dominican Republic	5. 4.1965
Ecuador	23. 1.1961
France	16.11.1960
Haiti	13. 3.1961
Honduras	14. 8.1962
Netherlands	16.11.1960
Panama	16.11.1960
Suriname	25.11.1975
Trinidad and Tobago	2. 2.1973
United Kingdom of Great Britain and Northern Ireland	17. 3.1961
Venezuela	16.11.1960

THE ANTARCTIC TREATY [21]

Objectives

That Antarctica should be used for peaceful purposes, for international co-operation in scientific research, and not become the scene or subject of international discord.

Provisions

a) No military bases, military manoeuvres or weapon testing in Antarctica (art. 1);

b) Freedom of scientific investigation and co-operation in exchange of information regarding plans for such investigation and of personnel engaged in such investigation, and of information resulting from such investigation (arts. 2-3);

c) Territorial claims in Antarctica not affected by the Convention (art. 4);

d) Observers to inspect stations, installations, equipment to be appointed by each Party (art. 7);

e) Meetings of parties to be held for consultation and to formulate and recommend measures to further the objectives of the Treaty;

f) Detailed agreed measures for the conservation of Antarctic fauna and flora.

Membership

Open for accession by any State Member of the United Nations, or any other State by unanimous invitation of the parties. Instruments of accession to be deposited with the Government of the United States of America.

Date of adoption	1.12.1959
Place of adoption	Washington
Date of entry into force	23. 6.1961
Languages	English, French, Russian, Spanish
Depositary	United States of America

Parties and dates of entry into force

Argentina	23. 6.1961
Australia	23. 6.1961
Belgium	23. 6.1961
Brazil	16. 5.1975
Bulgaria	11. 9.1978
Chile	23. 6.1961
Czechoslovakia	14. 6.1962
Denmark	20. 5.1965
France	23. 6.1961
German Democratic Republic	19.11.1974
Germany, Federal Republic of	5. 2.1979
Japan	23. 6.1961
Netherlands	30. 3.1967
New Zealand	23. 6.1961
Norway	23. 6.1961
Poland	23. 6.1961
Romania	15. 9.1971
South Africa	23. 6.1961

Union of Soviet Socialist Republics	23. 6.1961
United Kingdom of Great Britain and Northern Ireland	23. 6.1961
United States of America	23. 6.1961

AGREEMENT CONCERNING CO-OPERATION IN THE QUARANTINE OF PLANTS AND THEIR PROTECTION AGAINST PESTS AND DISEASES [22]

Objectives

To expand co-operation in the quarantine of plants and their protection from pests, diseases and weeds, and to co-ordinate measures in respect of quarantine of plants, the control of pests and diseases of agricultural plants, and the control of weeds.

Provisions

a) Parties to take necessary measures against pests, weeds and diseases listed in Annex (art. 1);

b) Parties to exchange information concerning plant pests and diseases and their control (art. 2);

c) Parties to give technical assistance in the control of such pests, diseases and weeds (art. 3);

d) Parties to co-operate in applying uniform phyto-sanitary regulations for import/export of plant matter from one country to another (art. 4).

Membership

Open to any State for accession. Instruments of accession to be deposited with the Secretariat of the Council for Mutual Economic Assistance (CMEA).

Date of adoption	14.12.1959
Place of adoption	Sofia
Date of entry into force	19.10.1960
Languages	Russian
Depositary	Secretariat of CMEA

Parties and dates of entry into force

Albania	19.11.1960
Bulgaria	19.10.1960
Czechoslovakia	19.10.1960
Democractic People's Republic of Korea	15.11.1960
German Democratic Republic	17.11.1960
Hungary	19.10.1960
Mongolia	23. 8.1961
Poland	27.10.1960
Romania	19.10.1960
Union of Soviet Socialist Republics	19.10.1960

CONVENTION CONCERNING THE PROTECTION OF WORKERS AGAINST IONIZING RADIATIONS [23]

Objectives

To protect workers, as regards their health and safety, against ionizing radiations.

Provisions

a) Any party to this Convention undertakes to give effect thereto by means of laws or regulations, codes of practice or other appropriate means (art. 1);

b) This Convention applies to all activities involving exposure of workers to ionizing radiations in the course of their work (art. 2);

c) Maximum permissible doses of ionizing radiations shall be fixed for various categories of workers (art. 6).

Membership

Open for accession to all States Members of the International Labour Organisation. Instruments to be deposited with the Director-General of the International Labour Office.

Date of adoption	22. 6.1960
Place of adoption	Geneva
Date of entry into force	17. 6.1962
Languages	English, French
Depositary	Director-General of the International Labour Office

Parties and dates of entry into force

Argentina	15. 6.1979
Barbados	8. 5.1968
Belgium	2. 7.1966
Brazil	5. 9.1967
Byelorussian Soviet Socialist Republic	26. 2.1969
Czechoslovakia	21. 1.1965
Denmark	7. 2.1975
Djibouti	3. 8.1978
Ecuador	9. 3.1971
Egypt	18 3.1965
Finland	16.10.1978
France	18.11.1972
German Democratic Republic	7. 5.1976
Germany, Federal Republic of	26. 9.1974
Ghana	7.11.1962
Guinea	12.12.1967
Guyana	8. 6.1967
Hungary	8. 6.1969
India	17.11.1976
Iraq	26.10.1963
Italy	5. 5.1972
Japan	31. 7.1974
Lebanon	6.12.1978
Netherlands	29.11.1967
Norway	17. 6.1962
Paraguay	10. 7.1968
Poland	23.12.1965

Spain	17. 7.1963
Sweden	17. 6.1962
Switzerland	29. 5.1964
Syrian Arab Republic	15. 1.1965
Turkey	15.11.1969
Ukrainian Soviet Socialist Republic	19. 6.1969
Union of Soviet Socialist Republics	22. 9.1968
United Kingdom of Great Britain and Northern Ireland	9. 3.1963

CONVENTION ON THIRD PARTY LIABILITY IN THE FIELD OF NUCLEAR ENERGY (INCLUDING THE ADDITIONAL PROTOCOL OF 28 JANUARY 1964) [24]

Objectives

To ensure adequate and equitable compensation for persons who suffer damage caused by nuclear incidents, whilst ensuring tnat the development of nuclear energy for peaceful purposes is not thereby hindered. To unify the basic rules in various countries relating to liability incurred for such damage.

Provisions

a) Operator of a nuclear installation to be liable for damage to or loss of life of any person and damage to or loss of any property upon proof that such loss or damage was caused by a nuclear incident involving either nuclear fuel or radioactive products or waste in, or nuclear substances coming from, such an installation (art. 3);

b) Maximum liability of operator defined (art. 7);

c) Actions must be brought within 10 years from the date of the nuclear incident (art. 8);

d) Operator not liable if incident caused by act of armed conflict, invasion, civil war or grave natural disaster of an exceptional character (art. 9);

e) Operator must maintain insurance to cover his liability (art. 10).

Membership

Open for accession by any State, subject to unanimous consent of Parties, by notification in writing to the Secretary-General of the Organization for Economic Co-operation and Development (OECD).

	Convention	amendment
Date of adoption	29. 7.1960	28. 1.1964
Place of adoption	Paris	
Date of entry into force	1. 4.1968	1. 4.1968

Languages	Dutch, English, French, German, Italian, Spanish
Depositary	Secretary-General of OECD

Parties and dates of entry into force

Belgium	1. 4.1968
Denmark	4. 9.1974
Finland	16. 6.1972
France	1. 4.1968
Germany, Federal Republic of	30. 9.1975
Greece	12. 5.1970
Italy	17. 9.1975
Norway	2. 7.1973
Portugal	29. 9.1977
Spain	1. 4.1968
Sweden	1. 4.1968
Turkey	5. 4.1968
United Kingdom of Great Britain and Northern Ireland	1. 4.1968

PROTOCOL CONCERNING THE CONSTITUTION OF AN INTERNATIONAL COMMISSION FOR THE PROTECTION OF THE MOSEL AGAINST POLLUTION [25]

Objective

To protect the Mosel river against pollution.

Provisions

a) Establishment of the International Commission for the Protection of the Mosel against pollution (art. 1);

b) The Commission to be responsible for research into the nature, importance and sources of pollution, and to propose measures to the Parties to protect the Mosel (art. 2);

c) The Commission to establish relations as necessary with other organizations concerned with water pollution (art. 9).

Membership

Restricted to the three riparian signatory States.

Date of adoption	20.12.1961
Place of adoption	Paris
Date of entry into force	1. 7.1962
Languages	German, French
Depositary	

Parties and dates of entry into force

France	1. 7.1962
Germany, Federal Republic of	1. 7.1962
Luxembourg	1. 7.1962

CONVENTION ON THE AFRICAN MIGRATORY LOCUST ORGANIZATION [26]

Objectives

To maintain on an international basis the preventive control of the African migratory locust, and to extend such control to other species of migratory Acrididae.

Provisions

a) Establishment of the International African Locust Organization (art. 1) and of the International Administrative Council for the Surveillance and Preventive Control of the African Migratory Locust (art. 2);

b) The organization to maintain constant surveillance and control in the recognized outbreak area on the Niger, to undertake research into the ecology of the locust, and to develop the most economic methods of control (art. 3).

Membership

Any State may accede to the Convention by depositing an instrument of accession with the Government of Mali, subject to an agreement being reached between the acceding Government and the Contracting Parties relating to contributions.

Date of adoption	25. 5.1962
Place of adoption	Kano
Date of entry into force	13. 4.1963
Languages	English, French
Depositary	Mali
Amendments	25. 7.1968 10. 7.1975

Parties and dates of entry into force

Benin	13. 4.1963
Chad	13. 4.1963
Ghana	28. 5.1963
Ivory Coast	13. 4.1963
Kenya	29.11.1963
Mali	13. 4.1963
Niger	13. 4.1963
Senegal	13.11.1963
Upper Volta	13. 4.1963

AGREEMENT CONCERNING CO-OPERATION IN MARINE FISHING [27]

Objectives

Co-operation in the development of marine fishing, fishing techniques, fish processing technology and scientific research into the condition of living marine resources.

Provisions

a) Parties to co-operate in the development of marine fishing, exchange results of research into fishing grounds and living resources, and to co-ordinate research efforts (art. 1);

b) Establishment of a Mixed Commission to co-ordinate the application of the Agreement (art. 2);

c) Functions of the Commission to include: preparation of plans for scientific and technical co-operation, organization of exchange of research information, submission of proposals for scientific and technical conferences and meetings, and the making of recommendations to the Parties (arts. 3 - 4).

Membership

Notification of approval to be transmitted to the Government of Poland.

Date of adoption	28. 7.1962
Place of adoption	Warsaw
Date of entry into force	22. 2.1963
Languages	German, Polish, Russian
Depositary	Poland

Parties and dates of entry into force

Bulgaria	19. 9.1964
Cuba	24. 4.1978
German Democratic Republic	22. 2.1963
Poland	22. 2.1963
Romania	1. 9.1966
Union of Soviet Socialist Republics	22. 2.1963

CONVENTION SUPPLEMENTARY TO THE PARIS CONVENTION OF 29 JULY 1960 ON THIRD PARTY LIABILITY IN THE FIELD OF NUCLEAR ENERGY (as amended) [28]

Objectives

To supplement the measures provided in the Paris Convention with a view to increasing the amount of compensation for damage which might result from the use of nuclear energy for peaceful purposes.

Provisions

a) Maximum compensation in respect of damage caused by nuclear incidents defined. Such compensation to be provided out of funds created by insurance or other financial security, out of public funds to be made available by the Contracting Party in whose territory the nuclear installation is situated and out of public funds created according to the special formula for contributions. Liability of operator established (art. 3);

b) Formula for contributions according to which the Contracting Parties shall make available the public funds determined (art. 12).

Membership

Restricted to the Contracting Parties to the Paris Convention

		Amendment
Date of adoption	31. 1.1963	28. 1.1964
Place of adoption	Brussels	
Date of entry into force	4.12.1974	16.12.1974
Languages	Dutch, English French, German, Italian, Spanish	
Depositary	Belgium	

Parties and dates of entry into force

Denmark	4.12.1974
Finland	14. 4.1977
France	4.12.1974
Germany, Federal Republic of	1. 1.1976
Italy	3. 5.1976
Norway	4.12.1974
Spain	4.12.1974
Sweden	4.12.1974
United Kingdom of Great Britain and Northern Ireland	4.12.1974

AGREEMENT CONCERNING THE INTERNATIONAL COMMISSION FOR THE PROTECTION OF THE RHINE AGAINST POLLUTION [29]

Objectives

To maintain co-operation between the riparian States in preventing pollution and improving the quality of the waters of the Rhine.

Provisions

a) Continuation of the International Commission for the Protection of the Rhine (art. 1);

b) The Commission to be responsible for research into the nature, importance and sources of pollution, and to propose measures to the Parties to protect the Rhine (art. 2);

c) The Commission to report annually to the Parties on the results of research done, and to collaborate with other organizations concerned with water pollution (art. 11).

Membership

Originally restricted to the five riparian signatory States, the Agreement has been extended to the European Economic Community.

Date of adoption	29. 4.1963
Place of adoption	Berne
Date of entry into force	1. 5.1965
Languages	German, French, Dutch
Depositary	Switzerland
Amendments	Bonn, 3.12.1976

Parties and dates of entry into force

Agreement:

France	1. 5.1965
Germany, Federal Republic of	1. 5.1965
Luxembourg	1. 5.1965
Netherlands	1. 5.1965
Switzerland	1. 5.1965
European Economic Community	1. 2.1979

Amendments:

France	1. 2.1979
Germany, Federal Republic of	1. 2.1979
Luxembourg	1. 2.1979
Netherlands	1. 2.1979
Switzerland	1. 2.1979
European Economic Community	1. 2.1979

VIENNA CONVENTION ON CIVIL LIABILITY FOR NUCLEAR DAMAGE [30]

Objectives

To establish minimum standards to provide financial protection against damage resulting from peaceful uses of nuclear energy.

Provisions

a) Operator of a nuclear installation to be liable for nuclear damage on proof that such damage was caused by an incident within the installation, or involving nuclear material originating therefrom or being sent thereto (art. 2);

b) The liability of the operator in such a case to be absolute, but contributory negligence may be found against the person suffering such damage; and in any case the operator will not be liable if the nuclear incident was due directly to an act of armed conflict, civil war, insurrection or a grave natural disaster of an exceptional character (art. 4);

c) Limits of liability and limitation of action established (arts. 5-6);

d) Operator to maintain insurance or financial security to cover liability (art. 7).

Membership

Open for accession to all States Members of the United Nations, or members of the specialized agencies or the International Atomic Energy Agency (IAEA). Instruments of accession to be deposited with the Director-General of IAEA.

Date of adoption	21. 5.1963
Place of adoption	Vienna
Date of entry into force	12.11.1977
Languages	English, French, Russian, Spanish
Depositary	IAEA Director-General

Parties and dates of entry into force

Argentina	12.11.1977
Bolivia	12.11.1977
Cuba	12.11.1977
Egypt	12.11.1977
Niger	24.10.1979
Peru	26.11.1980
Philippines	12.11.1977
Trinidad and Tobago	12.11.1977
United Republic of Cameroon	12.11.1977
Yugoslavia	12.11.1977

TREATY BANNING NUCLEAR WEAPON TESTS IN THE ATMOSPHERE, IN OUTER SPACE AND UNDER WATER [31]

Objectives

To obtain an agreement on general and complete disarmament under strict international control in accordance with the objectives of the United Nations: to put an end to the armaments race and eliminate the incentive to the production and testing of all kinds of weapons including nuclear weapons.

Provisions

a) Parties to undertake to prohibit, prevent, and not to carry out any nuclear weapon test explosion, or any other nuclear explosion, at any place under its jurisdiction or control

- (i) In the atmosphere beyond its limits including outer space; or under water including territorial waters or high seas; or
- (ii) In any other environment if such explosion causes radioactive debris to be present outside the territorial limits of the State under whose jurisdiction or control such explosion is conducted (art. 1).

Membership

Open to all States.

Date of adoption	5. 8.1963
Place of adoption	Moscow
Date of entry into force	10.10.1963
Languages	English, Russian
Depositaries	Union of Soviet Socialist Republics, United Kingdom of Great Britain and Northern Ireland, United States of America

Parties and dates of entry into force

Afghanistan	12. 3.1964
Australia	12.11.1963
Austria	17. 7.1964
Bahamas	16. 7.1976
Belgium	1. 3.1966
Benin	15.12.1964
Bhutan	8. 6.1978
Bolivia	4. 8.1965
Botswana	5. 1.1968
Brazil	15.12.1964
Bulgaria	13.11.1963
Burma	15.11.1963
Byelorussian Soviet Socialist Republic	16.12.1963
Canada	28. 1.1964
Central African Empire	22.12.1964
Chad	1. 3.1965
Chile	6.10.1965
China	18. 5.1964
Costa Rica	10. 7.1967
Cyprus	15. 4.1965
Czechoslovakia	14.10.1963
Denmark	15. 1.1964
Dominican Republic	3. 6.1964
Ecuador	6. 5.1964
Egypt	10. 1.1964
El Salvador	3.12.1964
Fiji	14. 7.1972
Finland	9. 1.1964
Gabon	20. 2.1964
Gambia	27. 4.1965
German Democratic Republic	30.12.1963
Germany, Federal Republic of	1.12.1964
Ghana	27.11.1963
Greece	18.12.1963
Guatemala	6. 1.1964
Guinea-Bissau	20. 8.1976
Honduras	2.10.1964
Hungary	21.10.1963
Iceland	29. 4.1964
India	10.10.1963
Indonesia	20. 1.1964
Iran	5. 5.1964
Iraq	30.11.1964
Ireland	18.12.1963
Israel	15. 1.1964
Italy	10.12.1964
Ivory Coast	5. 2.1965
Japan	15. 6.1964

Jordan	29. 5.1964
Kenya	10. 6.1965
Kuwait	20. 5.1965
Lao People's Democratic Republic	10. 2.1965
Lebanon	14. 5.1965
Liberia	19. 5.1964
Libyan Arab Republic	15. 7.1968
Luxembourg	10. 2.1965
Madagascar	15. 3.1965
Malawi	7. 1.1965
Malaysia	15. 7.1964
Malta	25.11.1964
Mauritania	6. 4.1964
Mauritius	12. 3.1968
Mexico	27.12.1963
Mongolia	1.11.1963
Morocco	1. 2.1966
Nepal	7.10.1964
Netherlands	14. 9.1964
New Zealand	10.10.1963
Nicaragua	26. 1.1965
Niger	3. 7.1964
Nigeria	17. 2.1967
Norway	21.11.1963
Panama	24. 2.1966
Peru	20. 7.1964
Philippines	10.11.1965
Poland	14.10.1963
Republic of Korea	24. 7.1964
Romania	12.12.1963
Rwanda	22.10.1963
Samoa	15. 1.1965
San Marino	3. 7.1964
Senegal	6. 5.1964
Sierra Leone	21. 2.1964
Singapore	12. 7.1968
South Africa	10.10.1963
Spain	17.12.1964
Sri Lanka	5. 2.1964
Sudan	4. 3.1966
Swaziland	29. 5.1969
Sweden	9.12.1963
Switzerland	16. 1.1964
Syrian Arab Republic	1. 6.1964
Thailand	15.11.1963
Togo	7.12.1964
Tonga	22. 6.1971
Trinidad and Tobago	14. 7.1964
Tunisia	26. 5.1965
Turkey	8. 7.1965
Uganda	24. 3.1964
Ukrainian Soviet Socialist Republic	30.12.1963
Union of Soviet Socialist Republics	10.10.1963
United Kingdom of Great Britain and Northern Ireland	10.10.1963
United Republic of Tanzania	6. 2.1964
United States of America	10.10.1963
Uruguay	25. 2.1969
Venezuela	22. 2.1965
Yugoslavia	15. 1.1964
Zaire	28.10.1965
Zambia	11. 1.1965

ACT REGARDING NAVIGATION AND ECONOMIC CO-OPERATION BETWEEN THE STATES OF THE NIGER BASIN

and

AGREEMENT CONCERNING THE NIGER RIVER COMMISSION AND THE NAVIGATION AND TRANSPORT ON THE RIVER NIGER [32]

Objectives

To develop co-operation for the judicious exploitation of the resources of the River Niger basin and to establish an institution for this purpose.

Provisions

a) Utilization and navigation of the River and its tributaries to be free to all riparian States (Act, arts 1 and 2);

b) States to co-operate in study and execution of projects likely to have an appreciable effect on the navigability, agricultural and industrial exploitation, sanitary condition and pollution of the waters, and biological characteristics of the fauna and flora of the River (Act, art. 4; Agreement, art. 12);

c) Establishment of an intergovernmental organization, the River Niger Commission (Act, art. 5; Agreement, art. 1);

d) The Commission's functions to include: the maintenance of liaison between riparian States to ensure the most effective use of the waters and resources of the river; collection, evaluation and dissemination of data; examination of proposed projects; recommendations to States for common studies and works (Agreement, art. 2).

Membership

Restricted to the riparian States.

	Act	Agreement
Date of adoption	26.10.1963	25.11.1964
Place of adoption	Niamey	Niamey
Date of entry into force	1. 2.1966	12. 4.1966
Languages	English, French	English, French
Depositary	Niger	Niger
Amendments	2. 2.1968	15. 6.1973

Parties and dates of entry into force

	Act	Agreement
Benin	1. 2.1966	12. 4.1966
Cameroon	1. 2.1966	12. 4.1966
Chad	1. 2.1966	12. 4.1966
Dahomey	1. 2.1966	12. 4.1966
Guinea	1. 2.1966	12. 4.1966
Ivory Coast	1. 2.1966	12. 4.1966
Mali	1. 2.1966	12. 4.1966
Niger	1. 2.1966	12. 4.1966
Nigeria	1. 2.1966	12. 4.1966
Upper Volta	1. 2.1966	12. 4.1966

AGREEMENT FOR THE ESTABLISHMENT OF A COMMISSION FOR CONTROLLING THE DESERT LOCUST IN THE EASTERN REGION OF ITS DISTRIBUTION AREA IN SOUTH-WEST ASIA [33]

Objectives

Through the establishment of a commission within the framework of FAO, to promote national and international research and action to control the desert locust in the region (Afghanistan, India, Iran and Pakistan and any territories adjacent to them).

Provisions

a) Establishment of the Commission (art. 1);

b) Parties to maintain locust information and control services; reserves of insecticides and equipment; trailing, survey and research work (art. 21);

c) The Commission to have functions of joint action and assistance, information and co-ordination, and co-operation in the field of research, training and control (art. 4).

Membership

Open for acceptance by States Members of the United Nations situated in the region subject to a two-thirds vote of the Commission members.

Date of adoption	3.12.1963
Place of adoption	Rome
Date of entry into force	15.12.1964
Languages	English, French, Spanish
Depositary	FAO
Amendment	17. 3.1977

Parties and dates of entry into force

Afghanistan	15.12.1964
India	15.12.1964
Iran	15.12.1964
Pakistan	12. 7.1965

CONVENTION FOR THE INTERNATIONAL COUNCIL FOR THE EXPLORATION OF THE SEA (as amended) [34]

Objectives

To provide a new constitution for the International Council for the Exploration of the Sea established at Copenhagen in 1902.

Provisions

a) The Council to promote and encourage research and investigations for the study of the Sea and particularly its living resources, to draw up programmes for this purpose and to disseminate the results of such research (art. 1),

b) The Council to be concerned with the Atlantic Ocean and its adjacent seas, and primarily with the North Atlantic (art. 2);

c) The Council to maintain working arrangements with other international organizations (art. 4).

Membership

Open for accession to any State subject to the approval of three quarters of the parties. Instruments of accession to be deposited with the Government of Denmark.

		Amending protocol
Date of adoption	12. 9.1964	13. 8.1970
Place of adoption	Copenhagen	
Date of entry into force	22. 7.1968	12.11.1975
Languages	English French	
Depositary	Denmark	

Parties and dates of entry into force

Belgium	22. 7.1968
Canada	22. 7.1968
Denmark	22. 7.1968
Finland	22. 7.1968
France	22. 7.1968
German Democratic Republic	17. 2.1975
Germany, Federal Republic of	22. 7.1968
Iceland	22. 7.1968
Ireland	22. 7.1968
Netherlands	22. 7.1968
Norway	22. 7.1968
Poland	22. 7.1968
Portugal	22. 7.1968
Spain	22. 7.1968
Sweden	22. 7.1968
Union of Soviet Socialist Republics	22. 7.1968
United Kingdom of Great Britain and Northern Ireland	22. 7.1968
United States of America	18. 4.1973

AGREEMENT FOR THE ESTABLISHMENT OF A COMMISSION FOR CONTROLLING THE DESERT LOCUST IN THE NEAR EAST [35]

Objectives

Through the establishment of a commission within the framework of FAO, to promote national and international research and action to control the desert locust in the region.

Provisions

As for the Agreement concerning the Commission for controlling the desert locust in the eastern region of its distribution in South-West Asia (see No. 33).

Membership

Open for acceptance by States Members of the United Nations situated in the region, subject to a two-thirds vote of the Commission members.

Date of adoption	2. 7.1965
Place of adoption	Rome
Date of entry into force	21. 2.1967
Languages	English, French, Spanish
Depositary	FAO
Amendment	22.10.1976

Parties and dates of entry into force

Bahrain	24. 2.1969
Democratic Yemen	10.11.1969
Egypt	6. 7.1967
Iraq	9. 1.1970
Jordan	21. 2.1967
Kuwait	10. 8.1967
Lebanon	21. 2.1967
Oman	9.10.1972
Qatar	31.12.1968
Saudi Arabia	17.10.1972
Sudan	21. 2.1967
Syrian Arab Republic	3.12.1968
United Arab Emirates	31. 5.1974
Yemen	20. 3.1969

INTERNATIONAL CONVENTION FOR THE CONSERVATION OF ATLANTIC TUNAS [36]

Objectives

To maintain populations of tuna-like fish in the Atlantic Ocean at levels permitting the maximum sustainable catch for food and other purposes.

Provisions

a) Applies to all waters of the Atlantic Ocean and adjacent seas (art. 1);

b) Establishment of the International Commission for the Conservation of Atlantic Tunas (art. 3);

c) The Commission to be responsible for research into the abundance, ecology and biometry of the fish, the oceanography of their environment, and the effects of human and natural factors on their abundance (art. 4);

d) The Commission, on the basis of scientific evidence, to make recommendations for the maintenance of the populations of tuna and tuna-like fish (art. 8).

Membership

Open for signature by all States Members of the United Nations or members of the specialized agencies, subject to ratification, or open to adherence by any such State at any time. Relevant instruments to be deposited with the Director-General of FAO.

Date of adoption	14. 5.1966
Place of adoption	Rio de Janeiro
Date of entry into force	21. 3.1969
Languages	English, French, Spanish
Depositary	FAO

Parties and dates of entry into force

Angola	29. 7.1976
Benin	9. 1.1978
Brazil	1. 4.1969
Canada	21. 3.1969
Cape Verde	11.10.1979
Cuba	15. 1.1975
France	21. 3.1969
Gabon	19. 9.1977
Ghana	21. 3.1969
Ivory Coast	6.12.1972
Japan	21. 3.1969
Morocco	26. 9.1969
Portugal	3. 9.1969
Republic of Korea	28. 8.1970
Senegal	25 8.1971
South Africa	21. 3.1969
Spain	21. 3.1969
United States of America	21. 3.1969
Union of Soviet Socialist Republics	7. 1.1977

AFRICAN CONVENTION ON THE CONSERVATION OF NATURE AND NATURAL RESOURCES [37]

Objectives

The undertaking of individual and joint action for the conservation, utilization and development of soil, water, flora and faunal resources for the present and future welfare of mankind, from an economic, nutritional, scientific, educational, cultural and aesthetic point of view.

Provisions

a) Fundamental principle: "The Contracting States shall undertake to adopt the measures necessary to ensure conservation, utilization and development of soil, water, flora and faunal resources in accordance with scientific principles and with regard to the best interests of the people" (art. II);

b) Parties to take effective measures to conserve and improve the soil and to control erosion and land use (art. IV);

c) Parties to establish policies to conserve, utilize and develop water resources, prevent pollution and control water use (art. V);

d) Parties to protect flora and ensure best utilization, management of populations and habitats; control of hunting, capture and fishing;

e) Parties to conserve faunal resources and use them wisely: management of populations and habitats; control of hunting, capture and fishing; prohibition of poisons, explosives, automatic weapons in hunting (art. VII);

f) Protected species — those in List A are under total protection, those in List B to be taken only with authorization (art. VIII);

g) Traffic in trophies to be tightly controlled to prevent trade in illegally killed and obtained trophies (art. IX);

h) Conservation areas to be established and maintained (art. X);

i) Customary rights to be reconciled with the Convention (art. XI);

j) Conservation education to be undertaken at all levels (art. XIII);

k) Conservation and ecological factors to be considered in development plans (art. XIV);

l) Parties to co-operate wherever necessary in implementing the Convention (art. XVI).

Membership

Open for accession by any independent African State. Instruments of accession to be deposited with the Secretary-General of OAU.

Date of adoption	15. 9.1968
Place of adoption	Algiers
Date of entry into force	9.10.1969
Languages	English, French
Depositary	Secretary-General of OAU

Parties and dates of entry into force

Burundi	19.12.1979
Central African Empire	16. 4.1970
Djibouti	7. 5.1978
Egypt	12. 5.1972
Ghana	9.10.1969
Ivory Coast	9.10.1969
Kenya	9.10.1969
Liberia	22.12.1978
Madagascar	23.10.1971
Malawi	6. 4.1973
Mali	3. 7.1974
Morocco	11.12.1977
Niger	26. 2.1970
Nigeria	7. 5.1974
Rwanda	4. 3.1980
Senegal	25. 3.1972
Seychelles	14.11.1977
Sudan	30.11.1973
Swaziland	9.10.1969
Togo	24.11.1979
Tunisia	4. 3.1978
Uganda	30.12.1977
United Republic of Cameroon	29.10.1978
United Republic of Tanzania	22.12.1974
Upper Volta	9.10.1969
Zaire	13.11.1976
Zambia	31. 5.1972

EUROPEAN AGREEMENT ON THE RESTRICTION OF THE USE OF CERTAIN DETERGENTS IN WASHING AND CLEANING PRODUCTS [38]

Objectives

To protect:

a) The supply of water for the population, industry, agriculture and other business occupations;

b) The natural aquatic fauna and flora, in particular so far as they contribute to human well-being;

c) The unhindered enjoyment of places devoted to leisure and sport.

Provisions

a) Parties to legislate nationally so that washing or cleaning products containing one or more synthetic detergents are not put on the market unless the detergents are, as a whole, at least 80 per cent susceptible to biological degradation (art. 1);

b) Compliance with the above must not result in the usage of detergents which, under normal use, might adversely affect human or animal health (art. 2).

Membership

Open to signature by member States of the Council of Europe which take part in the activities in the field of public health under resolution (59) 23 of the Council. Instruments of acceptance or ratification to be deposited with the Secretary-General of the Council of Europe.

Date of adoption	16. 9.1968
Place of adoption	Strasbourg
Date of entry into force	16. 2.1971
Languages	English, French
Depositary	Council of Europe

Parties and dates of entry into force

Belgium	16. 2.1971
Denmark	16. 2.1971
France	30. 5.1971
Germany, Federal Republic of	2. 3.1973
Italy	28.12.1978
Luxembourg	11.11.1980
Netherlands	28. 2.1971
Spain	11.10.1975
Switzerland	22.12.1975
United Kingdom of Great Britain and Northern Ireland	16. 2.1971

EUROPEAN CONVENTION FOR THE PROTECTION OF ANIMALS DURING INTERNATIONAL TRANSPORT [39]

Objectives

To safeguard, as far as possible, animals in transport from suffering, through the adoption of common provisions regarding international transport of animals.

Provisions

a) Five categories of animals established: (1) Domestic animals of soliped, bovine, ovine, caprine and porcine species; (2) Domestic birds and domestic rabbits; (3) Domestic dogs and domestic cats; (4) Other mammals and birds; (5) Cold-blooded animals;

b) Animals of class (1) covered by detailed provisions regarding fitness to travel, construction and marketing of containers, means of attachment of animals, feeding and watering in transit, need for attendant and veterinary attention (arts. 3-37);

c) Animals of class (2) covered by most of the same provisions (arts. 38-39), as are animals of class (3) except when accompanied by the owner or his representative (arts. 40-41);

d) Animals of class (4) similarly covered, with special provisions for wild animals (arts. 42-45);

e) Animals of class (5) covered briefly (art. 46).

Membership

Open to signature by member States of the Council of Europe, subject to ratification. Non-member States may be invited to accede.

Date of adoption	13.12.1968
Place of adoption	Paris
Date of entry into force	20. 2.1971
Languages	English, French
Depositary	Council of Europe

Parties and dates of entry into force

Austria	15. 3.1974
Belgium	1. 7.1974
Cyprus	9. 8.1977
Denmark	20. 2.1971
Finland	5. 8.1975
France	1. 7.1974
Germany, Federal Republic of	1. 7.1974
Greece	26.11.1978
Iceland	20. 2.1971
Ireland	15. 9.1975
Italy	4.11.1974
Luxembourg	14.10.1972
Netherlands	5. 3.1981
Norway	20. 2.1971
Spain	3. 2.1975
Sweden	21. 4.1972
Switzerland	20. 2.1971
Turkey	20. 6.1976
United Kingdom of Great Britain and Northern Ireland	1. 7.1974

EUROPEAN CONVENTION ON THE PROTECTION OF THE ARCHAEOLOGICAL HERITAGE [40]

Objectives

To apply stringent scientific methods to archaeological research and discoveries to preserve their full historical significance; to prevent illicit excavation and through education to give archaeological excavation their full scientific significance.

Provisions

a) Parties to delimit and protect sites and areas of archaeological interest (art. 2);

b) Parties to prohibit illicit excavation, to entrust excavation only to qualified persons, and to ensure control and conservation of finds (art. 3);

c) Parties to establish national inventories and scientific catalogues of publicly-, and where possible, privately-owned archaeological objects (art. 4);

d) Circulation of objects for scientific, cultural and educational purposes to be promoted (art. 5).

Membership

Open to signature by member States of the Council of Europe. Instruments of ratification or acceptance to be deposited with the Secretary-General of the Council of Europe.

Date of adoption	6. 5.1969
Place of adoption	London
Date of entry into force	20.11.1970
Languages	English, French
Depositary	Council of Europe

Parties and dates of entry into force

Austria	28. 5.1974
Belgium	20.11.1970
Cyprus	24. 2.1971
Denmark	20.11.1970
France	4.10.1972
Germany, Federal Republic of	22. 4.1975
Holy See	18. 8.1972
Italy	17.12.1974
Liechtenstein	15. 4.1976
Luxembourg	8. 6.1972
Malta	1. 8.1971
Spain	1. 6.1975
Sweden	18. 6.1975
Switzerland	20.11.1970
United Kingdom of Great Britain and Northern Ireland	9. 3.1973

Parties and dates of entry into force

Belgium	9. 8.1969
Denmark	9. 8.1969
France	9. 8.1969
Germany, Federal Republic of	9. 8.1969
Netherlands	8. 3.1974
Norway	28.11.1970
Sweden	9. 8.1969
United Kingdom of Great Britain and Northern Ireland	9. 8.1969

AGREEMENT FOR CO-OPERATION IN DEALING WITH POLLUTION OF THE NORTH SEA BY OIL [41]

Objectives

Co-operation between the coastal States in providing manpower, supplies, equipment and scientific advice at short notice to deal with discharge of oil or other noxious or hazardous substances in the North Sea.

Provisions

a) Covers the North Sea south of latitude 61° N and the English Channel east of a line 50 nautical miles west of a line joining the Scilly Isles and Ushant (art. 2);

b) Parties to co-operate in informing each other of casualties or oil slicks in the area, and in requiring masters of ships and pilots of aircraft registered in their territories to report such incidents (art. 5);

c) Area divided into national zones for each of which the relevant party has prime responsibility (art. 6);

d) Assistance should be requested first from any other State likely to be affected by the pollution (art. 7).

Membership

Open to any Government for signature, ratification or approval: instruments to be deposited with the Government of the Federal Republic of Germany.

Date of adoption	9. 6.1969
Place of adoption	Bonn
Date of entry into force	9. 8.1969
Languages	English, French
Depositary	Federal Republic of Germany

CONVENTION OF THE CONSERVATION OF THE LIVING RESOURCES OF THE SOUTHEAST ATLANTIC [42]

Objectives

To achieve co-operation in the conservation and rational exploitation of the living resources of the southest Atlantic Ocean.

Provisions

a) Establishment of the International Commission for the Southeast Atlantic Fisheries (art. 4);

b) Commission to be responsible for research into ecology, biometry, abundance and environment of all living resources, and to collect, analyse and publish scientific information (art. 6);

c) Commission to establish Regional Committees for each region of the area, and Stock Committees for certain stocks within the area (art. 7);

d) These Committees to draft recommendations, based on scientific investigations, for measures applicable to the region or stock concerned (art. 7);

e) The Commission may make recommendations regarding mesh sizes, size limits of fish, open and closed seasons and areas, regulation of fishing gear, regulation of total catch (art. 8).

Membership

Open for adherence by any State at the invitation of the Commission. Instruments of adherence to be deposited with the Director-General of FAO.

Date of adoption	23.10.1969
Place of adoption	Rome
Date of entry into force	24.10.1971
Languages	English, French, Spanish
Depositary	FAO

Parties and dates of entry into force

Angola	4.11.1976
Belgium	30.11.1973
Bulgaria	24. 5.1972
Cuba	14. 2.1975
France	3.11.1972
German Democratic Republic	19. 7.1974
Germany, Federal Republic of	17.12.1976
Israel	4. 2.1976
Italy	21. 1.1976
Japan	24.10.1971
Poland	1. 4.1972
Portugal	24.10.1971
Romania	18. 9.1977
South Africa	24.10.1971
Spain	5. 1.1972
Union of Soviet Socialist Republics	24.10.1971

INTERNATIONAL CONVENTION RELATING TO INTERVENTION ON THE HIGH SEAS IN CASES OF OIL POLLUTION CASUALTIES [43]

Objectives

To enable countries to take action on the high seas in cases of a maritime casualty resulting in danger of oil pollution of sea and coastlines; to establish that such action would not affect the principle of freedom of the high seas.*

Provisions

a) Parties may take such measures on the high seas as may be necessary to prevent, mitigate or eliminate grave and imminent danger to their coastline or related interests from pollution or threat of pollution of the sea by oil (art. 1);

b) Before taking action a coastal State should notify the flag State of the ship, consult with independent experts, and notify any person whose interests may reasonably be expected to be affected by such action. In cases of extreme urgency measures may be taken at once. In any case the coastal State must endeavour to protect human life and assist persons in distress (art. 3);

c) Such measures shall not go beyond what is reasonably necessary to achieve the end mentioned in article 1 and shall be proportionate to the damage actual or threatened (art. 5).

Membership

Open for accession to all States Members of the United Nations or members of the specialized agencies or IAEA. Instruments of accession to be deposited with the Secretary-General of IMCO

Date of adoption	29.11.1969
Place of adoption	Brussels
Date of entry into force	6. 5.1975
Languages	English, French
Depositary	IMCO

Parties and dates of entry into force

Bahamas	20.10.1976
Belgium	6. 5.1975
Cuba	3. 8.1976
Denmark	6. 5.1975
Dominican Republic	6. 5.1975
Ecuador	23. 3.1977
Fiji	6. 5.1975
Finland	5.12.1976
France	6. 5.1975
German Democratic Republic	21. 3.1979
Germany, Federal Republic of	5. 8.1975
Ghana	19. 7.1978
Italy	28. 5.1979
Japan	6. 5.1975
Lebanon	3. 9.1975
Liberia	6. 5.1975
Mexico	7. 7.1976
Monaco	6. 5.1975
Morocco	6. 5.1975
Netherlands	18.12.1975
New Zealand	6. 5.1975
Norway	6. 5.1975
Panama	6. 4.1976
Papua New Guinea	10. 6.1980
Poland	30. 8.1976
Portugal	15. 5.1980
Senegal	6. 5.1975
Spain	6. 5.1975
Suriname	25.11.1975
Sweden	6. 5.1975
Syrian Arab Republic	6. 5.1975
Tunisia	2. 8.1976
Union of Soviet Socialist Republics	6. 5.1975
United Kingdom of Great Britain and Northern Ireland	6. 5.1975
United States of America	6. 5.1975
Yemen Arab Republic	4. 6.1975
Yugoslavia	3. 5.1976

The Convention has been extended to:

Hong Kong	6. 5.1975
Puerto Rico	6. 5.1975
Guam	6. 5.1975
Canal Zone	6. 5.1975
Virgin Islands	6. 5.1975
American Somoa	6. 5.1975
Trust Territories of the Pacific Islands	6. 5.1975
Netherlands Antilles	18.12.1975

* See the Protocol relating to Intervention on the High Seas in Cases of Marine Pollution by Substances Other than Oil infra Page 305.

INTERNATIONAL CONVENTION ON CIVIL LIABILITY FOR OIL POLLUTION DAMAGE [44]

Objectives

To ensure that adequate compensation is available to persons who suffer damage caused by pollution resulting from the escape or discharge of oil from ships. To standardize international rules and procedures for determining questions of liability and adequate compensation in such cases.

Provisions

a) The owner of a ship at the time of an incident causing oil pollution damage shall be liable for any damage so caused, unless the incident is caused by act of war, exceptional natural phenomenon, malicious act of a third party, or negligence of a Government or other authority in maintaining navigational aids (art. 3);

b) Contributory liability may be found against the plaintiff in certain cases (art. 3);

c) Where two or more ships have caused such damage the owners shall be jointly and severally liable (art. 4);

d) Limits to liability established (art. 5);

e) Ships carrying over 2,000 tons of oil as cargo must maintain insurance (art. 7);

f) Limitations of 3 and 6 years for rights of action (art. 8);

g) Warships are excluded (art. 11).

Membership

Open for accession to all States Members of the United Nations or members of the specialized agencies or IAEA. Instruments of accession to be deposited with the Secretary-General of IMCO.

Date of adoption	29.11.1969
Place of adoption	Brussels
Date of entry into force	19. 6.1975
Languages	English, French
Depositary	IMCO

Parties and dates of entry into force

Algeria	19. 6.1975
Bahamas	20.10.1976
Belgium	12. 4.1977
Brazil	17. 3.1977
Chile	31.10.1977
China	29. 4.1980
Denmark	19. 6.1975
Dominican Republic	19. 6.1975
Ecuador	23. 3.1977
Fiji	19. 6.1975
France	19. 6.1975
German Democratic Republic	11. 6.1978
Germany, Federal Republic of	18. 8.1975
Ghana	19. 7.1978
Greece	27. 9.1976
Iceland	15.10.1980
Ireland	19.11.1980
Indonesia	30.11.1978
Italy	28. 5.1979
Ivory Coast	19. 6.1975
Japan	1. 9.1976
Lebanon	19. 6.1975
Liberia	19. 6.1975
Monaco	19.11.1975
Morocco	19. 6.1975
Netherlands	8.12.1975
New Zealand	26. 7.1976
Norway	19. 6.1975
Panama	6. 4.1976
Papua New Guinea	10. 6.1980
Poland	16. 6.1976
Portugal	24. 2.1977
Republic of Korea	18. 3.1979
Senegal	19. 6.1975
South Africa	15. 6.1976
Spain	7. 3.1976
Sweden	19. 6.1975
Syrian Arab Republic	19. 6.1975
Tunisia	2. 8.1976
Union of Soviet Socialist Republics	22. 9.1975
United Kingdom of Great Britain and Northern Ireland	19. 6.1975
Yemen	4. 6.1979
Yugoslavia	16. 9.1976

The Convention has been extended to:

Bailiwick of Guernsey	1. 2.1976
Bailiwick of Jersey	1. 2.1976
Isle of Man	1. 2.1976
Bermuda	3. 2.1976
British Indian Ocean Territory	1. 5.1976
British Virgin Islands	1. 5.1976
Cayman Islands	1. 5.1976
Falkland Islands (Malvinas) and Dependencies	1. 5.1976
Gibraltar	1. 5.1976
Gilbert Islands	1. 5.1976
Hong Kong	1. 5.1976
Montserrat	1. 5.1976
Pitcairn	1. 5.1976
St. Helena and Dependencies	1. 5.1976
Seychelles	1. 5.1976
Solomon Islands	1. 5.1976
Turks and Caicos Islands	1. 5.1976
Tuvalu	1.10.1978
United Kingdom Sovereign Base Areas of Akrotivi and Dhololia in the Island of Cyprus	1. 5.1976

BENELUX CONVENTION ON THE HUNTING AND THE PROTECTION OF BIRDS [45]

Objectives

To harmonize legislation and regulations relating to hunting and the protection of wild birds in the three contracting States.

Provisions

a) Parties to standardize their classification of different types of game into four categories (art. 1);

b) Parties to harmonize their regulations for open and closed seasons for hunting, and for weapons, ammunition and means of hunting (art. 2 and 4);

c) Areas in which shooting is permitted to have minimum dimensions (art. 3);

d) Regulations concerning the transport and sale of game to be standardized (art. 4);

e) Parties to protect birds, other than those classified as game, their eggs and their nests (art. 7).

Membership

Restricted to the three signatory States.

Date of adoption	10. 6.1970
Place of adoption	Brussels
Date of entry into force	1. 7.1972
Languages	French, Dutch
Depositary	Union economique Benelux

Parties and dates of entry into force

Belgium	1. 7.1972
Luxembourg	1. 7.1972
Netherlands	1. 7.1972

AGREEMENT FOR THE ESTABLISHMENT OF A COMMISSION FOR CONTROLLING THE DESERT LOCUST IN NORTH-WEST AFRICA [46]

Objectives

Through the establishment of a commission within the framework of FAO, to promote national and international research and action to control the desert locust in the region.

Provisions

As for the Agreement concerning the Commission for controlling the desert locust in the eastern region of its distribution in South-West Asia (see No. 33).

Membership

Open for acceptance by States Members of the United Nations situated in the region, subject to a two-thirds vote of the Commission members.

Date of adoption	11.11.1970
Place of adoption	Rome
Date of entry into force	17. 8.1971
Languages	English, French, Spanish
Depositary	FAO

Parties and dates of entry into force

Algeria	17. 8.1971
Libyan Arab Jamahiriya	17. 8.1971
Morocco	1.10.1971
Tunisia	17. 8.1971

CONVENTION ON WETLANDS OF INTERNATIONAL IMPORTANCE ESPECIALLY AS WATERFOWL HABITAT [47]

Objectives

To stem the progressive encroachment on and loss of wetlands now and in the future, recognizing the fundamental ecological functions of wetlands and their economic, cultural, scientific and recreational value.

Provisions

a) Parties to designate at least one national wetland for inclusion in a List of Wetlands of International Importance (art. 2);

b) Parties to consider their international responsibilities for conservation, management and wise use of migratory stocks of wildfowl (art. 2(6));

c) Parties to establish wetland nature reserves, co-operate in exchange of information, train personnel for wetland management (art. 4);

d) Conferences on the Conservation of Wetlands and Waterfowl to be convened as the need arises.

Membership

Open for signature indefinitely and for accession to all States Members of the United Nations or members of the specialized agencies or IAEA: signature may be with or without reservation as to ratification. Ratification or accession to be effected by deposit of an instrument with the Director-General of the United Nations Educational, Scientific and Cultural Organization (UNESCO).

Date of adoption	2. 2.1971
Place of adoption	Ramsar
Date of entry into force	21.12.1975
Languages	English, French, German, Russian
Depositary	UNESCO

Parties and dates of entry into force

Australia	21.12.1975
Bulgaria	24. 1.1976
Denmark	2. 1.1977
Finland	21.12.1975
German Democratic Republic	30.11.1978
Germany, Federal Republic of	26. 6.1976
Greece	21.12.1975
Hungary	11. 4.1979
Iceland	2. 4.1978
Iran	21.12.1975
Italy	14. 4.1977
Japan	17.10.1980
Jordan	10. 5.1977
Morocco	20.10.1980
Netherlands	23. 9.1980
New Zealand	13.12.1976
Norway	21.12.1975
Pakistan	23.11.1976
Poland	22. 3.1978
Senegal	11.11.1977
South Africa	21.12.1975
Sweden	21.12.1975
Switzerland	16. 5.1976
Tunisia	26.10.1980
Union of Soviet Socialist Republics	11. 2.1977
United Kingdom of Great Britain and Northern Ireland	5. 5.1976
Yugoslavia	28. 7.1977

TREATY ON THE PROHIBITION OF THE EMPLACEMENT OF NUCLEAR WEAPONS AND OTHER WEAPONS OF MASS DESTRUCTION ON THE SEA-BED AND THE OCEAN FLOOR AND IN THE SUBSOIL THEREOF [48]

Objectives

To exclude the sea-bed, the ocean floor and the subsoil thereof from the arms race, as a step towards disarmament, the reduction of international tensions and the maintenance of world peace.

Provisions

a) Parties undertake not to emplace on the sea-bed, ocean floor or in the subsoil thereof, nuclear weapons or other weapons of mass destruction, or structures for launching, storing, testing or using such weapons (art. 1);

b) Outer limit of the sea-bed zone to be the 12 mile limit referred to in the Convention on the Territorial Sea and the Contiguous Zone, 1958 (art. 2);

c) Observers from any Party may observe and verify the activities of any other Party on the sea-bed. In case of doubt Parties shall consult and co-operate to remove such doubt by means of inspection and any other agreed procedure. If a serious question still remains concerning fulfilment of the obligations under this Treaty, a Party may refer the matter to the Security Council of the United Nations (art. 3).

Membership

Open for signature subject to ratification or for accession to all States. Instruments of ratification or accession to be deposited with the Depositary Governments.

Date of adoption	11. 2.1971
Place of adoption	London, Moscow, Washington
Date of entry into force	18. 5.1972
Languages	English, French, Chinese, Russian, Spanish
Depositaries	Union of Soviet Socialist Republics, United Kingdom of Great Britain and Northern Ireland, United States of America

Parties and dates of entry into force

Afghanistan	18. 5.1972
Australia	23. 1.1973
Austria	10. 8.1972
Belgium	20.11.1972
Botswana	10.11.1972
Bulgaria	18. 5.1972
Byelorussian Soviet Socialist Republic	18. 5.1972
Canada	18. 5.1972
Cape Verde	24.10.1979
China	18. 5.1972
Congo	23.10.1978
Cuba	3. 6.1977
Cyprus	18. 5.1972
Czechoslovakia	18. 5.1972
Denmark	18. 5.1972
Dominican Republic	18. 5.1972
Ethiopia	12. 7.1977
Finland	18. 5.1972
German Democratic Republic	18. 5.1972
Germany, Federal Republic of	18.11.1975
Ghana	9. 8.1972
Guinea-Bissau	20. 8.1976
Hungary	18. 5.1972
Iceland	30. 5.1972
India	20. 7.1973
Iran	18. 5.1972
Iraq	13. 9.1972
Ireland	18. 5.1972
Italy	3. 9.1974
Ivory Coast	18. 5.1972
Japan	18. 5.1972
Jordan	18. 5.1972
Lao People's Democratic Republic	18. 5.1972
Lesotho	3. 4.1973

Malaysia	21. 6.1972
Malta	18. 5.1972
Mauritius	18. 5.1972
Mongolia	18. 5.1972
Morocco	18. 5.1972
Nepal	18. 5.1972
Netherlands	14. 1.1976
New Zealand	18. 5.1972
Nicaragua	7. 2.1973
Niger	18. 5.1972
Norway	18. 5.1972
Panama	20. 3.1974
Poland	18. 5.1972
Portugal	24. 6.1975
Qatar	12.11.1974
Romania	10. 7.1972
Rwanda	20. 5.1975
Sao Tome and Principe	24. 8.1979
Saudi Arabia	23. 6.1972
Seychelles	28. 6.1976
Singapore	10. 9.1976
South Africa	14. 1.1973
Swaziland	18. 5.1972
Sweden	18. 5.1972
Switzerland	4. 5.1976
Togo	18. 5.1972
Tunisia	18. 5.1972
Turkey	19.10.1972
Ukrainian Soviet Socialist Republic	18. 5.1972
Union of Soviet Socialist Republics	18. 5.1972
United Kingdom of Great Britain and Northern Ireland	18. 5.1972
United States of America	18. 5.1972
Yemen Democratic Republic	1. 6.1979
Yugoslavia	25.10.1973
Zambia	9.10.1972

CONVENTION CONCERNING PROTECTION AGAINST HAZARDS OF POISONING ARISING FROM BENZENE

[49]

Objectives

To protect workers from hazards arising from the production, handling or use of benzene.

Provisions

a) The Convention to apply all activities involving exposure of workers to benzene (the aromatic hydrocarbon-benzene C_6H_6) and products containing benzene (art. 1);

b) Parties to use harmless or less harmful substitute products instead of benzene or products containing benzene, whenever such substitution is possible (art. 2);

c) The use of benzene or of products containing benzene to be prohibited in certain work processes to be specified by national laws and regulations (art. 4);

d) In premises where benzene or products containing benzene are manufactured, handled or used, all necessary measures to be taken to prevent the escape of benzene vapour into the air of places of employment, and the concentration of benzene in no case to exceed 25 ppm (art. 6);

e) Workers who may be exposed to benzene or products containing benzene to be provided with adequate means of personal protection and the duration of exposure to be limited as far as possible. (art. 7).

Membership

Open for accession to all States members of the International Labour Organisation (ILO). Instruments of accession to be deposited with the Director-General of ILO.

Date of adoption	23. 6.1971
Place of adoption	Geneva
Date of entry into force	27. 7.1973
Languages	English, French
Depositary	ILO

Parties and dates of entry into force

Bolivia	31. 1.1978
Colombia	16.11.1977
Cuba	27. 7.1973
Ecuador	27. 3.1976
Finland	13. 1.1977
France	27. 7.1973
Germany, Federal Republic of	26. 9.1974
Greece	24. 1.1978
Guinea	26. 5.1978
Hungary	11. 9.1973
Iraq	27. 7.1973
Israel	21. 6.1980
Ivory Coast	21. 2.1974
Kuwait	29. 3.1975
Morocco	22. 7.1975
Romania	6.11.1976
Spain	8. 5.1974
Switzerland	25. 3.1976
Syrian Arab Republic	7. 2.1978
Uruguay	2. 6.1978
Yugoslavia	24. 6.1976
Zambia	24. 5.1974

CONVENTION RELATING TO CIVIL LIABILITY IN THE FIELD OF MARITIME CARRIAGE OF NUCLEAR MATERIAL [50]

Objectives

Following the Paris Convention of 29 July 1960 and the Vienna Convention of 21 May 1963, to ensure that the operator of a nuclear installation will be exclusively liable for damage caused by a nuclear incident occurring in the course of maritime carriage of nuclear material.

Provisions

a) Any person apart from the operator of a nuclear installation is exonerated from liability for damage caused by a nuclear incident during maritime carriage of such material (art. 1);

b) The operator's liability extended to cover damage to the means of transport and to the installation (reversing the Paris and Vienna Conventions) (art. 2).

Membership

Open for accession to all States Members of the United Nations or members of the specialized agencies. Instruments of accession to be deposited with the Secretary-General of IMCO.

Date of adoption	17.12.1971
Place of adoption	Brussels
Date of entry into force	15. 7.1975
Languages	English, French
Depositary	IMCO

Parties and dates of entry into force

Denmark	15. 7.1975
France	15. 7.1975
Germany, Federal Republic of	30.12.1975
Italy	19.10.1980
Norway	15. 7.1975
Spain	15. 7.1975
Sweden	15. 7.1975
Yemen Arab Republic	4. 6.1979

INTERNATIONAL CONVENTION ON THE ESTABLISHMENT OF AN INTERNATIONAL FUND FOR COMPENSATION FOR OIL POLLUTION DAMAGE [51]

Objectives

To supplement the International Convention on Civil Liability for Oil Pollution Damage, 1969; to ensure that adequate compensation is available to persons who suffer damage caused by pollution resulting from the escape or discharge of oil from ships; and to ensure that the oil cargo interests bear a part of the economic consequences of such oil pollution damage, to the relief of the shipping industry.

Provisions

a) Establishment of the International Oil Pollution Compensation Fund (art. 2);

b) Compensation to be paid by the Fund to any person suffering pollution damage, including the cost of measures reasonably taken to minimize the damage, who is unable to obtain full and adequate compensation under the terms of the 1969 Liability Convention (art. 4(1));

c) The Fund will incur no obligation if the damage was caused by act of war, hostilities or by discharge from a warship (art. 4(2));

d) Limits of the Fund's obligations are set at 450 million francs for any one incident (art. 4(4));

e) The Fund to indemnify shipowners for the amount of liability incurred more than 1,500 francs per ton of ship's tonnage, but not in excess of 2,000 francs per ton or in any case of 210 million francs (art. 5);

f) Contributions to the fund to be made in respect of each Party by any person who, in the calendar year before the entry into force of the Convention for that Party, received quantities of oil exceeding 150,000 tons, such contributions to be calculated on a per ton basis to be determined by the Assembly of the Fund (arts. 10-12).

Membership

Open for accession to States which have ratified, accepted, approved or acceded to the 1969 Convention on Civil Liability for Oil Pollution Damage. Instruments of accession to be deposited with the Secretary-General of IMCO.

Date of adoption	18.12.1971
Place of adoption	Brussels
Date of entry into force	16.10.1978
Languages	English, French
Depositary	IMCO

Parties and dates of entry into force

Algeria	16.10.1978
Bahamas	16.10.1978
Denmark	16.10.1978
France	16.10.1978
Germany, Federal Republic of	16.10.1978
Ghana	16.10.1978
Iceland	15.10.1980
Indonesia	30.11.1978
Italy	28. 5.1979
Japan	16.10.1978
Liberia	16.10.1978
Monaco	21.11.1979
Norway	16.10.1978
Papua New Guinea	10. 6.1980
Sweden	16.10.1978
Syrian Arab Republic	16.10.1978
Tunisia	16.10.1978
United Kingdom of Great Britain and Northern Ireland	16.10.1978
Yugoslavia	16.10.1978

Ratification by the United Kingdom was declared to be effective also in respect of:

Bailiwick of Guernsey
Bailiwick of Jersey
The Isle of Man
Belize
Bermuda
British Indian Ocean Territory
British Virgin Islands
Cayman Islands
Falkland Islands (Malvinas) and Dependencies
Gibraltar
Gilbert Islands

Hong Kong
Montserrat
Pitcairn Group
St. Helena and Dependencies
Seychelles
Solomon Islands
Turks and Caicos Islands
Tuvalu
United Kingdom Sovereign Base Areas of Akrotivi and Dhololia in the Island of Cyprus

CONVENTION FOR THE PREVENTION OF MARINE POLLUTION BY DUMPING FROM SHIPS AND AIRCRAFT [52]

Objectives

To control the dumping of harmful substances from ships and aircraft in the sea.

Provisions

a) Includes the Atlantic and Arctic Oceans north of longitude 36° N east of longitude 42° W and west of longitude 51° E, excluding the Baltic and Mediterranean Sea (art 2);

b) Parties to apply measures so as to prevent dumping being diverted outside the area (art. 3);

c) Dumping of materials listed in Annex I to be prohibited (art. 5);

d) Dumping of materials listed in Annex II to be allowed only with a specific permit in each case (art. 6);

e) No substance or material to be dumped without the approval of the national authority concerned (art. 7);

f) Annex III contains provisions governing the issue of permits and approvals for the dumping of wastes at sea both as to the characteristics of the waste and those of the dumping site and method of dumping;

g) Parties to ensure compliance by ships and aircraft registered in their territories, loading materials to be dumped in their territories, or believed to be engaged in dumping within their territorial sea.

Membership

Open for accession by any State which participated in the Conference on Marine Pollution, Oslo, 19-22 October 1971, or by any State unanimously invited by the Contracting Parties to accede thereto. Instruments to be deposited with the Government of Norway.

Date of adoption	15. 2.1972
Place of adoption	Oslo
Date of entry into force	7. 4.1974
Languages	English, French
Depositary	Norway

Parties and dates of entry into force

Belgium	30. 3.1978
Denmark	7. 4.1974
Finland	1. 6.1979
France	7. 4.1974
Germany, Federal Republic of	8.12.1977
Iceland	7. 4.1974
Netherlands	29.10.1975
Norway	7. 4.1974
Portugal	7. 4.1974
Spain	7. 4.1974
Sweden	7. 4.1974
United Kingdom of Great Britain and Northern Ireland	30. 7.1975

CONVENTION ON THE PROHIBITION OF THE DEVELOPMENT, PRODUCTION AND STOCKPILING OF BACTERIOLOGICAL (BIOLOGICAL) AND TOXIN WEAPONS, AND ON THEIR DESTRUCTION [53]

Objectives

To eliminate, and to prohibit the development of, biological weapons, as a step towards general disarmament for the sake of all mankind.

Provisions

a) Each party undertakes never in any circumstances to develop, produce, stockpile or otherwise acquire or retain (1) biological agents or toxins in quantities that have no justification for prophylactic, protective or other peaceful purposes, (2) weapons, equipment or means of delivery designed to use such agents or toxins for hostile purposes or in armed conflict (art. 1);

b) Parties to destroy any existing stockpiles and means of delivery, taking precautions to protect populations and the environment (art. 2);

c) Parties not to assist any other State or person to develop such agents, toxins or weapons (art. 3);

d) Complaints regarding breach of obligations under this convention to be reported to the Security Council of the United Nations (art. 6);

e) States to continue negotiation for the effective prohibition of chemical weapons (art. 9).

Membership

Open to non-signatory States for accession, and to signatory States for ratification. Instruments of accession or ratification to be deposited with the Depositary Governments.

Date of adoption	10. 4.1972
Place of adoption	London, Moscow, Washington

Date of entry into force	26. 3.1975
Languages	Chinese, English, French, Russian, Spanish
Depositaries	Union of Soviet Socialist Republics, United Kingdom of Great Britain and Northern Ireland, United States of America

Parties and dates of entry into force

Afghanistan	26. 3.1975
Australia	5.10.1977
Austria	26. 3.1975
Barbados	26. 3.1975
Belgium	15. 3.1979
Benin	25. 4.1975
Bhutan	8. 6.1978
Bolivia	30.10.1975
Brazil	26. 3.1975
Bulgaria	26. 3.1975
Byelorussian Soviet Socialist Republic	26. 3.1975
Canada	26. 3.1975
Cape Verde	20.10.1977
Chile	22. 4.1980
China	26. 3.1975
Congo	23.10.1978
Costa Rica	26. 3.1975
Cuba	21. 4.1976
Cyprus	26. 3.1975
Czechoslovakia	26. 3.1975
Denmark	26. 3.1975
Dominican Republic	26. 3.1975
Ecuador	26. 3.1975
Ethiopia	26. 5.1975
Fiji	26. 3.1975
Finland	26. 3.1975
German Democratic Republic	26. 3.1975
Ghana	6. 6.1975
Greece	10.12.1975
Guatemala	26. 3.1975
Guinea-Bissau	20. 8.1976
Honduras	14. 3.1979
Hungary	26. 3.1975
Iceland	26. 3.1975
India	26. 3.1975
Iran	26. 3.1975
Ireland	26. 3.1975
Italy	26. 3.1975
Jamaica	26. 3.1975
Jordan	27. 6.1975
Kenya	7. 1.1976
Kuwait	26. 3.1975
Lao People's Democratic Republic	26. 3.1975
Lebanon	26. 3.1975
Lesotho	10. 9.1977
Luxembourg	23. 3.1976
Malta	7. 4.1975
Mauritius	26. 3.1975
Mexico	26. 3.1975
Mongolia	26. 3.1975
New Zealand	26. 3.1975
Nicaragua	7. 8.1975
Niger	26. 3.1975
Nigeria	26. 3.1975
Norway	26. 3.1975
Pakistan	26. 3.1975
Panama	26. 3.1975
Paraguay	9. 6.1976
Philippines	26. 3.1975
Poland	26. 3.1975
Portugal	15. 5.1975
Qatar	17. 4.1975
Romania	26. 7.1979
Rwanda	20. 5.1975
San Marino	11. 3.1975
Saudi Arabia	26. 3.1975
Senegal	26. 3.1975
Seychelles	11.10.1979
Sierra Leone	29. 6.1976
Singapore	2.12.1975
South Africa	3.11.1975
Spain	20. 6.1979
Sweden	5. 2.1976
Switzerland	4. 5.1976
Thailand	28. 5.1975
Togo	10.11.1976
Tonga	28. 9.1976
Tunisia	26. 3.1975
Turkey	26. 3.1975
Ukrainian Soviet Socialist Republic	26. 3.1975
Union of Soviet Socialist Republics	26. 3.1975
United Kingdom of Great Britain and Northern Ireland*	26. 3.1975
United States of America	26. 3.1975
Venezuela	18.10.1978
Yemen Democratic	1. 6.1979
Yugoslavia	26. 3.1975
Zaire	16. 9.1975

* Ratification in respect of the United Kingdom of Great Britain and Northern Ireland, Dominica and Territories under the territorial sovereignty of the United Kingdom, as well as the State of Brunei, and the British Solomon Islands Protectorate and, within the limits of United Kingdom jurisdiction therein, the Condominium of the New Hebrides.

CONVENTION FOR THE CONSERVATION OF ANTARCTIC SEALS [54]

Objectives

To promote and achieve the protection, scientific study and rational use of Antarctic seals and to maintain a satisfactory balance within the ecological system of the Antarctic.

Provisions

a) Applies to seas south of latitude 60° S to 5 species of seals and to all southern fur seals (art. 1);

b) Annex contains specific measures adopted by the parties. Parties may also take measures relating to permissible catch, protected and unprotected species, open and closed areas and seasons, designated areas where seals are not to be disturbed, types of gear, etc. (art. 3);

c) Parties to exchange information among themselves and through the Scientific Committee on Antarctic Research of ICSU.

Membership

Open for accession by any non-signatory State at the invitation of all Contracting Parties. Instruments to be deposited with the Government of the United Kingdom of Great Britain and Northern Ireland.

Date of adoption	1. 6.1972
Place of adoption	London
Date of entry into force	11. 3.1978
Languages	English, French, Russian, Spanish
Depositary	United Kingdom of Great Britain and Northern Ireland

Parties and dates of entry into force

Argentina	11. 3.1978
Belgium	11. 3.1978
Chile	9. 3.1980
France	11. 3.1978
Japan	28. 8.1980
Norway	11. 3.1978
Poland	14. 9.1980
South Africa	11. 3.1978
Union of Soviet Socialist Republics	8.12.1978
United Kingdom of Great Britain and Northern Ireland	11. 3.1978
United States of America	11. 3.1978

CONVENTION FOR THE PROTECTION OF THE WORLD CULTURAL AND NATURAL HERITAGE [55]

Objectives

To establish an effective system of collective protection of the cultural and natural heritage of outstanding universal value, organized on a permanent basis and in accordance with modern scientific methods.

Provisions

a) Each State Party recognizes that the duty of identification, protection, conservation and transmission to future generations of the cultural and natural heritage belongs primarily to that State (art. 4);

b) Parties to integrate the protection of that heritage into comprehensive planning programmes, to set up services for the protection of their heritage, to develop scientific and technical studies, to take necessary legal, scientific, administrative and financial steps to protect their heritage (art. 5);

c) Parties undertake to assist each other in the protection of the cultural and natural heritage (art. 6);

d) Establishment of the World Heritage Committee, to which each Party will submit an inventory of that national heritage and which will publish "World Heritage List" and "List of World Heritage in Danger" (arts. 8-11);

e) Establishment of the World Heritage Fund to be financed by the Parties and other interested bodies (art. 15);

f) Any Party may request assistance for property forming part of its listed heritage, and such assistance may be granted by the Fund in the form of studies, provision of experts, training of staff, supply of equipment, loans or subsidies (arts. 19-22).

Membership

Open for ratification or acceptance by all States members of UNESCO, and by other States upon invitation. Instruments to be deposited with the Director-General of UNESCO.

Date of adoption	23.11.1972
Place of adoption	Paris
Date of entry into force	17.12.1975
Languages	Arabic, English, French, Russian, Spanish
Depositary	UNESCO

Parties and dates of entry into force

Afghanistan	20. 6.1979
Algeria	17.12.1975
Argentina	23.11.1978
Australia	17.12.1975
Bolivia	4. 1.1977

Brazil	1.12.1977
Bulgaria	17.12.1975
Canada	23.10.1976
Chile	20. 5.1980
Costa Rica	23.11.1977
Cyprus	17.12.1975
Denmark	25.10.1979
Ecuador	17.12.1975
Egypt	17.12.1975
Ethiopia	6.10.1977
France	17.12.1975
Germany, Federal Republic of	23.11.1976
Ghana	17.12.1975
Guatemala	16. 4.1979
Guinea	18. 6.1979
Guyana	20 9.1977
Haiti	18. 4.1980
Honduras	8. 9.1979
India	14. 2.1978
Iran	17.12.1975
Iraq	17.12.1975
Italy	23.11.1978
Jordan	17.12.1975
Libyan Arab Jamahiriya	13. 1.1979
Mali	5. 7.1977
Malta	14. 2.1979
Monaco	7. 2.1979
Morocco	28. 1.1976
Nepal	20. 9.1978
Nicaragua	17. 3.1980
Niger	17.12.1975
Nigeria	17.12.1975
Norway	12. 8.1977
Pakistan	23.10.1976
Panama	3. 6.1978
Poland	29. 9.1976
Saudi Arabia	7.11.1978
Senegal	13. 5.1976
Seychelles	9. 7.1980
Sri Lanka	6. 9.1980
Sudan	17.12.1975
Switzerland	17.12.1975
Syrian Arab Republic	17.12.1975
Tunisia	17.12.1975
United Republic of Tanzania	2.11.1977
United States of America	17.12.1975
Yugoslavia	17.12.1975
Zaire	17.12.1975

CONVENTION ON THE PREVENTION OF MARINE POLLUTION BY DUMPING OF WASTES AND OTHER MATTER [56]

Objectives

To control pollution of the sea by dumping and to encourage regional agreements supplementary to the Convention.

Provisions

a) Covers all seas, and all deliberate disposal of wastes other than that incidental to normal operation of ships, aircraft, etc.;

b) Dumping of matter listed in Annex I is prohibited, of that in Annex II is allowable only by special permit, and of that in Annex III is allowable only by general permit (art. 4);

c) Exceptions only in the case of force majeure or extreme emergency;

d) Parties to establish authorities to issue permits, keep records and monitor the condition of the seas (art. 6);

e) Parties to enforce measures on all flag aircraft and ships, and ships and aircraft loading within their territories/territorial seas (art. 7);

f) Parties with particular interests in certain areas of the sea to enter into regional agreements to prevent marine pollution (art. 8);

g) Parties to collaborate in training personnel, supplying equipment for research and monitoring, disposing of and treating wastes (art. 9);

h) Procedures to be developed for assessment of liability and settlement of disputes regarding dumping (art. 10);

i) Parties to promote measures to prevent pollution by hydrocarbons, other matter transported other than for dumping, wastes generated during operation of ships, etc., radioactive pollutants and matter arising from exploration of the sea-bed (art. 12).

Membership

Open for accession by any State. Instruments of accession shall be deposited with each of the Depositary Governments.

Date of adoption	29.12.1972
Place of adoption	London, Mexico City, Moscow, Washington
Date of entry into force	30. 8.1975
Languages	English, French, Russian, Spanish
Depositaries	Mexico, United States of America, Union of Soviet Socialist Republics, United Kingdom of Great Britain and Northern Ireland

Parties and dates of entry into force

Afghanistan	30. 8.1975
Argentina	12.10.1979
Byelorussian Soviet Socialist Republic	28. 2.1976
Canada	13.12.1975
Cape Verde	25. 6.1977
Chile	3. 9.1977
Cuba	31.12.1975
Denmark	30. 8.1975
Dominican Republic	30. 8.1975
Finland	2. 6.1979
France	5. 3.1977
German Democratic Republic	19. 9.1976
Germany, Federal Republic of	8.12.1977
Guatemala	30. 8.1975
Haiti	27. 9.1975
Hungary	1. 3.1976
Iceland	30. 8.1975
Jordan	30. 8.1975
Kenya	6. 2.1976
Libyan Arab Jamahiriya	22.12.1976
Mexico	30. 8.1975
Monaco	15. 4.1977
Morocco	20. 3.1977
Netherlands	1. 1.1978
New Zealand	30. 8.1975
Nigeria	18. 4.1976
Norway	30. 8.1975
Panama	30. 8.1975
Papua New Guinea	9. 4.1980
Philippines	30. 8.1975
Poland	22. 2.1979
Portugal	14. 5.1978
San Marino	30. 8.1975
Seychelles	29. 6.1976
South Africa	6. 9.1978
Spain	30. 8.1975
Sweden	30. 8.1975
Switzerland	30. 8.1979
Tunisia	13. 5.1976
Ukrainian Soviet Socialist Republic	6. 3.1976
Union of Soviet Socialist Republics	29. 1.1976
United Arab Emirates	30. 8.1975
United Kingdom of Great Britain and Northern Ireland	17.12.1975
United States of America	30. 8.1975
Yugoslavia	25. 7.1976
Zaire	16.10.1975

The Convention has been extended to the

Faroe Islands 15.11.1976

CONVENTION ON INTERNATIONAL TRADE IN ENDANGERED SPECIES OF WILD FAUNA AND FLORA [57]

Objectives

To protect certain endangered species from over-exploitation via a system of import/export permits.

Provisions

a) Includes animals and plants whether dead or alive, and any recognizable parts or derivatives thereof (art. 1);

b) Four appendices — Appendix I, endangered species, trade in which to be tightly controlled; Appendix II, species that may become endangered unless trade is regulated; Appendix III, species that any party wishes to regulate and requires international co-operation to control trade; Appendix IV, model permits;

c) Species in Appendix I and II must have a permit stating that export/import will not be detrimental to the survival of that species (arts. 3-4).

Membership

Open for accession by any State. Instruments of accession to be deposited with the Depositary Government.

Date of adoption	3. 3.1973
Place of adoption	Washington
Date of entry into force	1. 7.1975
Languages	Chinese, English, French, Russian, Spanish
Depositary	Switzerland

Parties and dates of entry into force

Australia	27.10.1976
Bahamas	18. 9.1979
Bolivia	4.10.1979
Botswana	12. 2.1978
Brazil	4.11.1975
Canada	9. 7.1975
Central African Republic	25.11.1980
Chile	1. 7.1975
Costa Rica	28. 9.1975
Cyprus	1. 7.1975
Denmark	24.10.1977
Ecuador	1. 7.1975
Egypt	4. 4.1978
Finland	8. 8.1976
France	9. 8.1978
Gambia	24.11.1977
German Democratic Republic	7. 1.1976
Germany, Federal Republic of	20. 6.1976
Ghana	12. 2.1976
Guatemala	5. 2.1980
Guyana	25. 8.1977
India	18.10.1976

Indonesia	28. 3.1979
Iran	1.11.1976
Israel	17. 3.1980
Italy	31.12.1979
Japan	4.11.1980
Jordan	14. 3.1979
Kenya	13. 3.1979
Liechtenstein	28. 2.1980
Madagascar	18.11.1975
Malaysia	18. 1.1978
Mauritius	27. 7.1975
Monaco	18. 7.1978
Morocco	14. 1.1976
Nepal	16. 9.1975
Nicaragua	4.11.1977
Niger	7.12.1975
Nigeria	1. 7.1975
Norway	25.10.1976
Pakistan	19. 7.1976
Panama	15.11.1978
Papua New Guinea	11. 3.1976
Paraguay	13. 2.1977
Peru	25. 9.1975
Portugal	11. 3.1981
Rwanda	18. 1.1981
Senegal	3.11.1977
Seychelles	9. 5.1977
South Africa	13.10.1975
Sri Lanka	2. 8.1979
Suriname	15. 2.1981
Sweden	1. 7.1975
Switzerland	1. 7.1975
Tanzania	27. 2.1980
Togo	21. 1.1979
Tunisia	1. 7.1975
Union of Soviet Socialist Republics	8.12.1976
United Arab Emirates	1. 7.1975
United Kingdom of Great Britain and Northern Ireland	31.10.1976
United States of America	1. 7.1975
Uruguay	1. 7.1975
Venezuela	22. 1.1978
Zaire	18.10.1976
Zambia	22. 2.1981

CONVENTION ON FISHING AND CONSERVATION OF THE LIVING RESOURCES IN THE BALTIC SEA AND THE BELTS [58]

Objectives

To achieve greater and closer co-operation between the parties in order to maintain the maximum stable productivity of the living resources of the region.

Provisions

a) Parties to co-operate to achieve optimum yield from the living resources, particularly in the field of research, including programmes for the artifical reproduction of valuable fish species (art. 1);

b) Establishment of the International Baltic Sea Fishery Commission (art. 5);

c) The Commission to keep under review the living resources and fisheries of the region by collecting, analysing and disseminating data; to work out proposals to co-ordinate scientific research; to submit recommendations to the Parties based on scientific research (art. 9);

d) Such recommendations to concern: regulation of fishing gear, size limits of fish, closed seasons or areas, improving and increasing the marine resources, total allowable catch and any other measure related to the conservation of these resources (art. 10).

Membership

Open for accession to any State interested in the preservation and national exploitation of living resources in the Baltic Sea and Belts, subject to invitation from the Parties. Instruments to be deposited with the Government of Poland.

Date of adoption	13. 9.1973
Place of adoption	Gdansk
Date of entry into force	28. 7.1974
Languages	Danish, English, Finnish, German, Polish, Russian, Swedish
Depositary	Poland

Parties and dates of entry into force

Denmark	28. 7.1974
Finland	28. 7.1974
German Democratic Republic	28. 7.1974
Germany, Federal Republic of	9. 9.1977
Poland	28. 7.1974
Sweden	28. 7.1974
Union of Soviet Socialist Republics	28. 7.1974

INTERNATIONAL CONVENTION FOR THE PREVENTION OF POLLUTION FROM SHIPS (1973) AND PROTOCOL (1978) [59]

Objectives

To preserve the marine environment by achieving the complete elimination of intentional pollution by oil and other harmful substances and the minimization of accidental discharge of such substances.

Provisions

a) The 1973 Convention itself is a vehicle for enforcement and administration of the detailed provisions in the attached Annexes I-V, the Protocol on Intervention on the High Seas in cases of Marine Pollution by Substances other than Oil, and Protocols I and II;

b) Protocol I contains provisions concerning reports on incidents involving harmful substances;

c) Annex I contains Regulations for the Prevention of Pollution by Oil, including a list of oils;

d) Annex II contains Regulations for the Control of Pollution by Noxious Liquid Substances in Bulk, including lists of such substances;

e) Annex III contains Regulations for the Prevention of Pollution by Harmful Substances Carried by Sea in Packaged Forms, or in Freight Containers, Portable Tanks or Road and Rail Tank Wagons;

f) Annex IV contains Regulations for the Prevention of Pollution by Sewage from Ships;

g) Annex V contains Regulations for the Prevention of Pollution by Garbage from Ships;

h) The 1978 Protocol modifies various provisions of the 1973 London Convention and in particular of its Annex I. It also postpones the entry into force of Annex II of the Convention at least for a period of three years.

Membership

Open for accession, acceptance or approval to all States. Instruments to be deposited with the Secretary-General of IMCO.

Date of adoption	2.11.1973
Place of adoption	London
Date of entry into force	
Languages	English, French, Russian, Spanish
Depositary	IMCO

Dates of deposit of relevant instruments

Kenya	12. 9.1975
Jordan	17. 3.1975
Tunisia	4. 5.1976
United States of America	1.11.1976
Uruguay	30. 4.1979
Yemen	6. 3.1979

The Protocol was deposited with the Secretary-General of IMCO for signature on 1.6.1978 and remained open for signature until 31.5.1979.

Signatories

France	11. 5.1978
Malaysia	20.10.1977
Mexico	1. 6.1978
Monaco	19. 4.1978
Panama	17. 8.1978
Sri Lanka	15.12.1978
United Kingdom of Great Britain and Northern Ireland	24. 3.1978
United States of America	27. 6.1978
Venezuela	24.10.1978

PROTOCOL RELATING TO INTERVENTION ON THE HIGH SEAS IN CASES OF MARINE POLLUTION BY SUBSTANCES OTHER THAN OIL [60]

Objectives

To enable States to take action on the high seas in cases of maritime casualties resulting in grave and imminent danger of pollution to their coastline or related interests by substances other than oil.

Provisions

a) Parties may take such measures as necessary on the high seas to prevent, mitigate or eliminate grave and imminent danger to their coastline or related interests from pollution or threat of pollution by substances other than oil following a maritime casualty (art. 1);

b) Article 1, paragraph 2 and articles II-VIII of the 1969 Convention relating to Intervention on the High Seas in Cases of Oil Pollution Casualties and its annexes are applicable to this Protocol (art. II);

c) List of such substances to be established and maintained by an appropriate body.

Membership

Open for ratification or accession to States who have ratified or acceded to the 1969 Convention relating to Intervention on the High Seas in Cases of Oil Pollution Casualties. Instruments of ratification or accession to be deposited with the Secretary-General of IMCO.

Date of adoption	2.11.1973
Place of adoption	London
Date of entry into force	
Languages	English, French, Russian, Spanish
Depositary	IMCO

Dates of deposit of instruments

Sweden	28. 6.1976
Tunisia	4. 5.1976
United States of America	7. 9.1978
Yemen Arab Republic	6. 3.1979

AGREEMENT ON CONSERVATION OF POLAR BEARS [61]

Objectives

To achieve protection of the polar bear as a significant resource of the Arctic region through the bringing into effect of further conservation and management measures.

Provisions

a) In general, the taking of polar bears to be prohibited (art. 1) except for bona fide scientific or conservation purposes, or to prevent disturbance of the management of other living resources, or by local people using traditional methods in accordance with the laws of the Party concerned (art. 3);

b) Parties to take action to preserve the ecosytems of which the polar bears are part (art. 2);

c) Parties to conduct research into management and conservation of the species, to co-ordinate such research and exchange information (art. 7).

Membership

Restricted to the signatory States.

Date of adoption	15.11.1973
Place of adoption	Oslo
Date of entry into force	26. 5.1976
Languages	English, Russian
Depositary	Norway

Parties and dates of entry into force

Canada	26. 5.1976
Denmark	25. 1.1978
Germany, Federal Republic of	23.12.1977
Norway	26. 5.1976
Union of Soviet Socialist Republics	26. 5.1976
United States of America	1.11.1976

THE NORDIC ENVIRONMENTAL PROTECTION CONVENTION [62]

Objectives

To protect and improve the environment through co-operation to ensure that activities under the jurisdiction of one State do not cause damage to the environment of other States.

Provisions

a) Any person who is affected by environmentally harmful activities in another Contracting State shall have a right of action in that State (art. 3);

b) Each State to establish a special authority to safeguard general environmental interests as regards nuisances arising from environmentally harmful activities in another Contracting State (art. 4);

c) In considering the permissibility of environmentally harmful activities, the nuisance such activities entail in another Contracting State shall be equated with a nuisance in the State where the activities are carried out (art. 2).

Membership

Restricted to the original Contracting Parties: no provision for accession by other States.

Date of adoption	19. 2.1974
Place of adoption	Stockholm
Date of entry into force	5.10.1976
Languages	Danish, Finnish, Norwegian, Swedish
Depositary	Sweden

Parties and dates of entry into force

Denmark	5.10.1976
Finland	5.10.1976
Norway	5.10.1976
Sweden	5.10.1976

CONVENTION ON THE PROTECTION OF THE MARINE ENVIRONMENT OF THE BALTIC SEA AREA [63]

Objectives

To protect and enhance the marine environment of the Baltic Sea area by means of regional co-operation.

Provisions

a) Parties to control and restrict the introduction of hazardous and noxious substances into the area, including pollution from land-based sources (art. 5-6);

b) Parties to prevent pollution from ships, pollution by dumping, and pollution caused by exploitation of the sea-bed (art. 7-10);

c) Parties to co-operate in combating marine pollution (art. 11);

d) Annexes to the Convention contain lists of substances to be controlled;

e) Establishment of the Baltic Marine Environment Protection Commission, to keep under review the implementation of the Convention and the contents of the Annexes (art. 12-15).

Membership

Open for accession to any State invited by all the Contracting Parties. Instruments to be deposited with the Government of Finland.

Date of adoption	22. 3.1974
Place of adoption	Helsinki
Date of entry into force	2. 5.1980
Language	English
Depositary	Finland

Parties and dates of entry into force

Denmark	2. 5.1980
Finland	2. 5.1980
German Democratic Republic	2. 5.1980
Germany, Federal Republic of	2. 5.1980
Poland	2. 5.1980
Sweden	2. 5.1980
Union of Soviet Socialist Republics	2. 5.1980

CONVENTION FOR THE PREVENTION OF MARINE POLLUTION FROM LAND-BASED SOURCES [64]

Objectives

Part of a comprehensive approach involving progressive and coherent measures to protect the marine environment from pollution.

Provisions

a) Covers the Atlantic and Arctic Oceans north of latitude 36° N, east longitude 42° W and west of longitude 51° E, excluding the Baltic and Mediterranean Seas (art. 2);

b) Parties to eliminate pollution of the maritime area from land-based sources by substances listed in Annex A, Part I, and to limit strictly pollution by substances listed in Part II (art. 4);

c) Parties generally to endeavour to reduce existing pollution and to forestall any new pollution from land-based sources (art. 6);

d) In case of serious pollution from land-based sources by a substance not listed in Annex A, Part I, the parties shall consult and negotiate a co-operation agreement (art. 9);

e) Parties to establish complementary scientific and technical research programmes (art. 10);

f) Parties to set up and operate a permanent monitoring system (art. 11);

g) Establishment of a Commission of parties to supervise the implementation of the Convention to review the condition on the seas within the Convention area, to draw up programmes and measures for the elimination or reduction of pollution from land-based sources, to make recommendations for the amendment of the lists of substances in Annex A (art. 16).

Membership

Open to States which participated in the Paris Conference, to States parties to the Convention for the Prevention of Marine Pollution by Dumping from Ships and Aircraft, 1972, and to States located upstream on watercourses crossing the territory of one or more parties and reaching the Convention sea area. Parties may unanimously invite other States to accede. Instruments of accession to be deposited with the Government of the French Republic.

Date of adoption	4. 6.1974
Place of adoption	Paris
Date of entry into force	6. 5.1978
Languages	English, French
Depositary	France

Parties and dates of entry into force

Denmark	6. 5.1978
France	6. 5.1978
Netherlands	6. 5.1978
Norway	6. 5.1978
Portugal	9. 6.1978
Spain	17. 5.1980
Sweden	6. 5.1978
United Kingdom of Great Britain and Northern Ireland	6. 5.1978
European Economic Community	6. 5.1978

AGREEMENT ON AN INTERNATIONAL ENERGY PROGRAMME [65]

Objectives

To carry out a comprehensive programme of energy co-operation within the framework of the International Energy Agency.

Provisions

a) An allocation scheme in times of emergency, including maintenance of emergency reserves and a programme of demand restraint measures (arts. 2-24);

b) An extensive information system on the international oil market (arts. 25-36);

c) A framework for consultation with oil companies (arts. 37-40);

d) A long-term co-operation programme in the areas of energy conservation, the development of alternative sources of energy, research and development of nuclear energy (arts. 41-43);

e) The promotion of co-operative relations with oil-producing and other oil-consuming countries, including developing countries (arts. 44-48).

Membership

Open for accession to States members of OECD.

Date of adoption	18.11.1974
Place of adoption	Paris
Date of entry into force	19. 1.1976
Languages	English, French, German
Depositary	Belgium

Parties and dates of entry into force

Australia	27. 5.1979
Austria	10. 7.1976
Belgium	8. 8.1976
Canada	19. 1.1976
Denmark	19. 1.1976
Germany, Federal Republic of	19. 1.1976
Greece	25. 7.1977
Ireland	19. 1.1976
Italy	13. 2.1978
Luxembourg	19. 1.1976
Netherlands	9. 4.1976
New Zealand	8. 1.1977
Portugal	19. 5.1980
Spain	19. 1.1976
Sweden	19. 1.1976
Switzerland	19. 1.1976
United Kingdom of Great Britain and Northern Ireland	19. 1.1976
United States of America	19. 1.1976

CONVENTION FOR THE PROTECTION OF THE MEDITERRANEAN SEA AGAINST POLLUTION [66]

Objectives

Realizing the special characteristics and vulnerability of the Mediterranean, to achieve international co-operation for a co-ordinated and comprehensive approach to the protection and enhancement of the marine environment in the Mediterranean area.

Provisions

a) Parties to take all appropriate measures to prevent and abate pollution of the Mediterranean caused by dumping from ships and aircraft, or by discharges from ships, or resulting from exploration and exploitation of the sea-bed and subsoil, or from discharges from rivers, coastal establishments or other land-based sources within their territories (arts. 5-8);

b) Parties to co-operate in taking necessary measures to deal with pollution emergencies, whatever the cause of such emergency (art. 9);

c) Parties to co-operate in establishing programmes for monitoring pollution in the area (art. 10);

d) Parties to co-operate in scientific and technical research relating to all types of marine pollution (art. 11);

e) Parties to co-operate in establishing procedures for the determination of liability and compensation for damage resulting from violations of the Convention and Protocols (art. 12);

f) Protocols for the Prevention of Pollution by Dumping from Ships and Aircraft, and for Co-operation in dealing with Pollution Emergencies, have been adopted.

Membership

Open to States which participated in the Barcelona Conference, February 1976. Instruments of ratification or accession to be deposited with the Government of Spain.

Date of adoption	16. 2.1976
Place of adoption	Barcelona
Date of entry into force	12. 2.1978
Languages	Arabic, English, French, Spanish
Depositary	Spain

Parties and dates of entry into force

Cyprus	19.12.1979
Egypt	23. 9.1978
France*	10. 4.1978
Greece	2. 2.1979
Israel	2. 4.1978
Italy	5. 3.1979
Lebanon	12. 2.1978
Libyan Arab Jamahiriya	2. 3.1979
Malta	12. 2.1978
Monaco	12. 2.1978
Morocco	15. 2.1980
Spain	12. 2.1978
Syrian Arab Republic	25. 1.1979
Tunisia	12. 2.1978
Yugoslavia	12. 2.1978
European Economic Community	15. 4.1978

The Protocol for the Prevention of Pollution of the Mediterranean by Dumping from Ships and Aircraft entered into force on the same date as the Convention, and the following States are parties to it:

Parties and dates of entry into force

Cyprus	19.12.1979
Egypt	23. 9.1978
France	10. 4.1978
Greece	2. 2.1979
Italy	5. 3.1979
Lebanon	12. 2.1978
Libyan Arab Jamahiriya	2. 3.1979
Malta	12. 2.1978
Monaco	12. 2.1978
Morocco	15. 2.1979
Spain	12. 2.1978
Syrian Arab Republic	25. 1.1979
Tunisia	12. 2.1978
Yugoslavia	12. 2.1978
European Economic Community	15. 4.1978

The Protocol concerning Co-operation in Combating Pollution of the Mediterranean Sea by Oil and Other Harmful Substances entered into force on the same date as the Convention and the following States are parties to it:

Parties and dates of entry into force

Cyprus	19.12.1979
Egypt	23. 9.1978
France	10. 4.1978
Greece	2. 2.1979
Israel	2. 4.1978
Italy	5. 3.1979
Lebanon	12. 2.1978
Libyan Arab Jamahiriya	2. 3.1979
Malta	12. 2.1978
Monaco	12. 2.1978
Morocco	15. 2.1979
Spain	12. 2.1978
Syrian Arab Republic	25. 1.1979
Tunisia	12. 2.1978
Yugoslavia	12. 2.1978

* With reservation

CONVENTION ON CONSERVATION OF NORTH PACIFIC FUR SEALS (as amended) [67]

Objectives

To achieve maximum sustainable productivity from the fur seal resources of the North Pacific, and to conduct adequate scientific research to this end.

Provisions

a) Parties to co-ordinate scientific research programmes to determine measures necessary to maximize the sustainable yield from the fur seal resources, and to establish the relationship between fur seals and other living marine resources (art. 2);

b) Establishment of the North Pacific Fur Seal Commission to formulate and co-ordinate research programmes, study the results of such research, and make recommendations to the parties on the basis of the findings for measures to achieve the objectives of the Convention (art. 5);

c) Enforcement measures for boarding and arresting boats believed to beoffending against the Convention (art. 6);

d) Indigenous peoples practising traditional sealing methods are exempted from the Convention's provisions (art. 7).

Membership

Restricted to signatory States, no provision for adherence or accession.

Date of adoption	7. 5.1976*
Place of adoption	Washington
Date of entry into force	12.10.1976
Languages	English, Russian, Japanese
Depositary	United States of America

Parties and dates of entry into force

Canada	12.10.1976
Japan	12.10.1976
Union of Soviet Socialist Republics	12.10.1976
United States of America	12.10.1976

* The original Convention was signed on 9.2.1957.

CONVENTION ON CONSERVATION OF NATURE IN THE SOUTH PACIFIC [68]

Objectives

To take action for the conservation, utilization and development of the natural resources of the South Pacific region through careful planning and management for the benefit of present and future generations.

Provisions

a) Parties to create protected areas to safeguard representative samples of natural ecosystems, superlative scenery, striking geological formations and regions and objects of aesthetic, historic, cultural or scientific value (art. 2);

b) National parks not to be altered so as to reduce their area except after the fullest investigation, their resources not to be subject to commercial exploitation, hunting and collection of species to be prohibited, and provision to be made for visitors (art. 3);

c) National reserves to be maintained inviolate as far as is practicable (art. 4);

d) Parties to maintain lists of indigenous flora and fauna in danger of extinction and to give such species as complete protection as possible (art. 5);

e) Provision may be made as appropriate for customary use of areas and species in accordance with traditional cultural practices (art. 6).

Membership

Open to all States members, or eligible to be invited to become members, of the South Pacific Commission, for signature until 31 December 1977, subject to ratification, and thereafter for accession. Instruments of ratification and accession to be deposited with the Government of Samoa.

Date of adoption	12. 6.1976
Place of adoption	Apia
Date of entry into force	
Languages	English, French
Depositary	Samoa

Signatories

France	28.10.1977
Papua New Guinea	27.12.1977
Samoa	23.12.1977

CONVENTION ON THE PROTECTION OF THE ARCHAEOLOGICAL, HISTORICAL AND ARTISTIC HERITAGE OF THE AMERICAN NATIONS (CONVENTION OF SAN SALVADOR) [69]

Objectives

To take steps at the national and international levels for effective protection of cultural treasures, and to fulfil the obligation to transmit such cultural heritage to coming generations.

Provisions

a) The identification, registration, protection and safeguarding of the cultural heritage to prevent its illegal exportation and importation, and to promote co-operation for mutual awareness and appreciation of such heritage (art. 1);

b) Cultural property to include, *inter alia*, monuments, objects, ruins, remains of human beings, fauna and flora of the Pre-Colombian era; monuments, buildings, objects of artistic, utilitarian or ethnological nature from the colonial era and the nineteenth century; libraries, archives, and manuscripts; publications and documents published before 1850; and other post-1850 objects that Parties declare to be within the scope of the Convention (art. 2);

c) Domestic measures to be taken by Parties to register collections of such cultural property, to register transactions involving such property, to prohibit importation of such property from other States without appropriate authorization (art. 7);

d) Parties to prevent unlawful exportation and importation of cultural property and to return such illegally removed property to the State to which it belongs (art. 10);

e) Parties to co-operate in the circulation, exchange and exhibition of cultural property, and in the exchange of information on such property and on archaeological excavations and discoveries (art. 15).

Membership

Open to signature by the member States of the Organization of American States and to adherence by any State.

Date of adoption	16. 6.1976
Place of adoption	Santiago
Date of entry into force	30. 6.1978
Languages	English, French, Portuguese, Spanish
Depositary	Organization of American States

Parties and dates of entry into force

Chile	12. 7.1978
Ecuador	27. 9.1978
El Salvador	5. 4.1979
Guatemala	30. 6.1978
Nicaragua	10. 4.1980
Panama	30. 6.1978
Peru	19. 3.1979

CONVENTION FOR THE PROTECTION OF THE RHINE AGAINST CHEMICAL POLLUTION [70]

Objectives

To protect the Rhine against chemical pollution with the purpose of ameliorating the standards of water for potable and industrial use, for navigation, etc.

Provisions

a) Discharge of substances in the Rhine strictly regulated. Substances subject to regulation are divided into two groups and reproduced in Annex I and II (art. 1);

b) Norms of emission of substances (Annex I) are defined by the International Commission for the Protection of the Rhine against pollution (art. 2);

c) Government authorization for discharge of substances (Annex I) is required (art. 3);

d) Discharge of substances (Annex II) is regulated by Governments under the supervision of the Commission (art. 6).

Membership

Restricted to the Contracting Parties.

Date of adoption	3.12.1976
Place of adoption	Bonn
Date of entry into force	1. 2.1979
Languages	German, French, Dutch
Depositary	Switzerland

Parties and dates of entry into force

France	1. 2.1979
Germany, Federal Republic of	1. 2.1979
Luxembourg	1. 2.1979
Netherlands	1. 2.1979
Switzerland	1. 2.1979
European Economic Community	1. 2.1979

CONVENTION ON CIVIL LIABILITY FOR OIL POLLUTION DAMAGE RESULTING FROM EXPLORATION FOR AND EXPLOITATION OF SEABED MINERAL RESOURCES [71]

Objectives

To ensure that adequate compensation is available to victims of pollution damage from such offshore activities, by means of adoption of uniform rules and procedures for determining questions of liability and for providing such compensation.

Provisions

a) The damage must originate beyond the coastal low-water line of a State Party, and be suffered in the territory, including the internal and territorial waters, of such a State, or in the areas in which it has sovereign rights over natural resources (art. 2);

b) The operator, or joint operators, of the installation from which such damage originates shall be liable for such damage. Liability shall extend for 5 years after the abandonment of such installation if abandoned in accordance with requirements laid down (art. 3);

c) The operator to be exonerated, wholly or in part, if he can prove act or omission done by the victim with intent to cause damage, or negligence by the victim;

d) Liability of the operator under the Convention limited for each installation and each incident, unless damage caused by deliberate act of the operator himself (art. 6);

e) Operators to maintain insurance or other financial security to cover liability (art. 8);

f) Judgements of victims' courts to be enforceable in any other State Party (art. 12);

g) State Party operators shall waive all defences based on status as a sovereign State (art. 13).

Membership

Open for signature from 1.5.1977 to 30.4.1978 by States which participated in the Intergovernmental Conference on the Convention held in London 20.10.1975 - 31.10.1975 and 13.12.1976 - 17.12.1976, and thereafter for accession by such States, subject to ratification. Parties may unanimously invite other States to accede, which have coastlines on the North Sea, the Baltic Sea, or the Atlantic Ocean North of Lat. 36° N.

Date of adoption	1. 5.1977
Place of adoption	London
Date of entry into force	
Languages	English, French
Depositary	United Kingdom of Great Britain and Northern Ireland

Parties and dates of depositing relevant instruments

Germany, Federal Republic of	28. 4.1978
Ireland	27. 4.1978
Netherlands	4. 5.1977
Norway	4. 5.1977
Sweden	11. 5.1978
United Kingdom of Great Britain and Northern Ireland	4. 5.1977

CONVENTION ON THE PROHIBITION OF MILITARY OR ANY OTHER HOSTILE USE OF ENVIRONMENTAL MODIFICATION TECHNIQUES [72]

Objectives

To prohibit the military or other hostile use of such techniques in order to consolidate world peace and trust among nations.

Provisions

a) Parties not to use such techniques having widespread, long-lasting or severe effects as the means of destruction, damage or injury to other Parties, nor to assist, encourage or induce any other State, group of States or international organization to do so (art. 1);

b) "Environmental modification techniques" refers to any technique for changing, through the deliberate manipulation of natural processes, the dynamics, composition or structure (i) of the earth, including its biota, lithosphere, hydrosphere, and atmosphere, or (ii) of outer space (art. 2);

c) The use of such techniques for peaceful purposes not to be hindered, and Parties to exchange scientific and technological information concerning such uses (art. 3);

d) Any complaint of breach by a Party to be lodged with the Security Council of the United Nations, which shall investigate such complaint (art. 5).

Membership

Open to all States for signature, subject to ratification and, subsequent to its entry into force, for accession to any non-signatory State. Instruments to be deposited with the Secretary-General of the United Nations.

Date of adoption	18. 5.1977
Place of adoption	Geneva
Date of entry into force	5.10.1978
Languages	Arabic, Chinese, English, French, Russian, Spanish
Depositary	Secretary-General of the United Nations

Parties and dates of entry into force

Bangla Desh	3.10.1979
Bulgaria	5.10.1978
Byelorussian Soviet Socialist Republic	5.10.1978
Cape Verde	3.10.1979
Cuba	5.10.1978
Cyprus	5.10.1978
Czechoslovakia	5.10.1978
Denmark	5.10.1978
Finland	5.10.1978
German Democratic Republic	5.10.1978
Ghana	5.10.1978
Hungary	5.10.1978
India	15.12.1978
Kuwait	2. 1.1980
Lao People's Democratic Republic	5.10.1978
Malawi	5.10.1978
Mongolia	5.10.1978
Norway	15. 2.1979
Poland	5.10.1978
Sao Tome and Principe	5.10.1979
Spain	5.10.1978
Sri Lanka	5.10.1978
Tunisia	5.10.1978
Ukrainian Socialist Soviet Republic	5.10.1978
Union of Soviet Socialist Republics	5.10.1978
United Kingdom of Great Britain and Northern Ireland	5.10.1978
United States of America	17.10.1980
Yemen	5.10.1978

CONVENTION CONCERNING THE PROTECTION OF WORKERS AGAINST OCCUPATIONAL HAZARDS IN THE WORKING ENVIRONMENT DUE TO AIR POLLUTION, NOISE AND VIBRATION [73]

Objectives

To protect the workers against occupational hazards in the working environment.

Provisions

a) Applies to all branches of economic activity. Exceptions to this provision in cases of existence of special problems of a substantive nature (art. 1);

b) Parties may accept obligations of this Convention separately in respect of air pollution, noise and vibration (art. 2);

c) Measures to be taken for the prevention and control of, and protection against, occupational hazards in the working environment due to air pollution, noise and vibration shall be prescribed by national laws and regulations (art. 4);

d) Criteria for determining the hazards of exposure to air pollution, noise and vibration in the working environment and exposure limits on the basis of these criteria shall be established by the competent authority (art. 8).

Membership

Open for accession to all States members of the International Labour Organisation. Instruments to be deposited with the Director-General of the International Labour Office.

Date of adoption	20. 6.1977
Place of adoption	Geneva
Date of entry into force	11. 7.1979
Languages	English, French
Depositary	Director-General of the International Labour Office

Parties and dates of entry into force

Ecuador	11. 7.1979
Finland	8. 6.1980
Norway	13. 3.1980
Sweden	11. 7.1979
United Kingdom of Great Britain and Northern Ireland	8. 3.1980 (air pollution only)

KUWAIT REGIONAL CONVENTION FOR CO-OPERATION ON THE PROTECTION OF THE MARINE ENVIRONMENT FROM POLLUTION [74]

Objectives

Realizing the state of pollution in their region, by oil and other noxious materials arising from human activities which threaten marine life, human health, recreational uses of beaches and other amenities, the States concerned have bound themselves by the Convention to prevent, abate and combat pollution of the sea environment.

Provisions

a) Parties to take all measures to prevent, abate and combat pollution of the marine environment (arts. III-VIII);

b) Parties to co-operate in taking necessary measures to deal with pollution emergencies (art. IX);

c) Parties to co-operate in scientific and technical research relating to marine pollution (arts. X-XII);

d) Parties to co-operate in establishing appropriate rules and procedures for the determination of civil liability and compensation for damage related to the subject matter of the convention (art. XIII).

e) The Protocol for Combating Oil and Other Harmful Substances in Cases of Emergency was adopted on the same date as the Convention.

Membership

Open to the States which participated in the Kuwait Conference, 15-23 April 1978.

Date of adoption	24. 4.1978
Place of adoption	Kuwait
Date of entry into force	1. 7.1979
Languages	Arabic, English, Persian
Depositary	Kuwait

Parties and dates of entry into force

Bahrain	1. 7.1979
Iraq	1. 7.1979
Kuwait	1. 7.1979
Oman	1. 7.1979
Qatar	1. 7.1979

TREATY FOR AMAZONIAN CO-OPERATION [75]

Objectives

To promote the harmonious development of the Amazonian region and permit an equitable distribution of the benefits of said development among the Contracting Parties as well as the conservation of the environment.

Provisions

a) Parties to undertake joint action and efforts to promote the harmonious development of their respective Amazonian territories in such a way that these joint actions produce equitable and mutually beneficial results and achieve also the preservation of the environment, and the conservation and rational utilization of the natural resources of those territories (art. I);

b) Parties to guarantee complete freedom of commercial navigation on the Amazon and other international Amazonian rivers on the basis of reciprocity, and to undertake national, bilateral or multilateral measures aimed at improving and making the said rivers navigable (art. III);

c) The sovereign right to the exclusive use of and utilization of natural resources within the respective territories of the Parties declared, and Parties to make efforts to achieve rational utilization of hydro-resources (art. IV-V);

d) Scientific research and exchange of information to be promoted to ensure that the exploitation of the flora and fauna of the Amazon region is rationally planned so as to maintain the ecological balance within the region and preserve the species (art. VII);

e) Transportation and communication links among the States of the Amazonian region to be improved and retail trade of products among them to be promoted (art. X);

f) Conservation of ethnological and archaeological wealth of the Amazon to be ensured (art. XIV);

g) The Amazonian Co-operation Council comprising high level diplomatic representatives to be created and meet once a year to supervise the effective implementation of the Treaty under the general guidance of Meetings of the Ministers for Foreign Affairs (art. XXI).

Membership

The Treaty shall not be open to adherence. It has been adopted by: the Republics of Bolivia, Brazil, Colombia, Ecuador, Guyana, Peru, Suriname and Venezuela.

Date of adoption	3. 7.1978
Place of adoption	Brasilia
Date of entry into force	
Languages	English, Dutch, Portuguese, Spanish
Depositary	Brazil

Dates of deposit of relevant instruments

Bolivia	20. 8.1979
Brasil	10.12.1978
Ecuador	14. 3.1979
Guyana	14. 3.1979
Peru	16.10.1979
Suriname	23. 7.1979

CONVENTION ON THE CONSERVATION OF MIGRATORY SPECIES OF WILD ANIMALS [76]

Objectives

To protect those species of wild animals that migrate across or outside national jurisdictional boundaries.

Provisions

a) Endangered migratory species to be listed in Appendix I (art. III);

b) Migratory species to be subject to agreements to be listed in Appendix II (art. IV);

c) Agreements (international) should deal with those aspects of the conservation and management of the migratory species concerned which serve to achieve the object of protection (art. V);

d) A Conference of the Parties, a Scientific Council to provide advice on scientific matters and a Secretariat to be established (arts. VII-IX).

Membership

Open for signature by all States and regional economic integration organizations until 22 June 1980. After this date, the convention shall be open for accession by non-signatory States and any regional economic integration organization.

Date of adoption	23. 6.1979
Place of adoption	Bonn
Date of entry into force	
Languages	English, French, German, Russian, Spanish
Depositary	Federal Republic of Germany

Signatory States

Central African Republic
Chad
Denmark
Egypt
France
Germany, Federal Republic of
Greece
India
Italy
Ivory Coast
Madagascar
Morocco
Niger
Norway
Paraguay
Portugal
Somalia
Spain
Sri Lanka
Sweden
Togo
United Kingdom of Great Britain and Northern Ireland

CONVENTION ON THE CONSERVATION OF EUROPEAN WILDLIFE AND NATURAL HABITATS [77]

Objectives

To conserve wild flora and fauna and their natural habitats, especially those species and habitats whose conservation requires the co-operation of several States, and to promote such co-operation.

Provisions

a) The Contracting Parties shall take requisite measures to maintain the population of wild flora and fauna at, or adapt it to, a level which corresponds in particular to ecological, scientific and cultural requirements and shall take steps to promote national policies for its conservation with particular attention to endangered and vulnerable species and endangered habitats. (arts. 2 and 3);

b) Appropriate and necessary measures shall be taken to ensure the conservation of the habitats of the wild flora and fauna species, especially those specified in Appendices I and II of the Convention; special attention shall be given to the protection of areas that are of importance for the migratory species specified in Appendices II and III (art. 4);

c) Appropriate and necessary measures shall be taken to ensure the special protection of wild flora and wild fauna species specified respectively in Appendices I and II. Wild fauna species specified in Appendix III shall be protected, any exploitation shall be regulated in order to keep the populations out of danger (arts. 5-7);

d) A Standing Committee is set up, it shall be responsible for following the application of the Convention (arts. 13-15).

Membership

The Convention is open for signature by the member States of the Council of Europe, non-member States which have participated in its elaboration and by the European Economic Community. After its entry into force, the Committee of Ministers of the Council of Europe may invite any non-member State of the Council to accede to the Convention.

Date of adoption	19. 9.1979
Place of adoption	Bern
Date of entry into force	
Languages	English, French
Depositary	Secretary-General of the Council of Europe

Dates of deposit of relevant instruments:

Liechtenstein	30.10.1980
Netherlands	28.10.1980

CONVENTION ON LONG-RANGE TRANSBOUNDARY AIR POLLUTION [78]

Objectives

To protect man and his environment against air pollution and to limit and, as far as possible, gradually reduce and prevent air pollution including long-range transboundary air pollution.

Provisions

a) The Contracting Parties undertake to develop the best policies and strategies which shall serve as a means of combating the discharge of air pollutants (arts 3 and 6);

b) The Contracting Parties exchange information on and review their policies, scientific activities and technical measures aimed at combating the discharge of air pollutants which may have adverse effects (arts. 4 and 8);

c) Consultations shall be held between Contracting Parties which are affected by or exposed to a significant risk of long-range transboundary air pollution and Contracting Parties within which a significant contribution to long-range transboundary air pollution originates or could originate (art. 5);

d) The Contracting Parties shall initiate and co-operate in the conduct of research and/or development in the field of air pollution control technologies (art. 7);

e) Implementation of the existing "Co-operative programme for the monitoring and evaluation of the long-range transmission of air pollutants in Europe" shall be promoted, as Executive Body of the Convention is established.

Membership

Open for signature by the Member States of the Economic Commission for Europe as well as States having consultative status with that Commission. Regional economic organizations may also sign it. The same States and organizations can have access to it from 17 November 1979.

Date of adoption	13.11.1979
Place of adoption	Geneva
Date of entry into force	
Languages	English, French, Russian
Depositary	Secretary-General of the United Nations

Dates of deposit of instruments

Sweden	19.12.1980
Ukrainian Socialist Soviet Republic	5. 6.1980
Union of Soviet Socialist Republics	22. 5.1980

PART 2

TEXTS OF TREATIES

CONVENTION RELATIVE TO THE PRESERVATION OF FAUNA AND FLORA IN THEIR NATURAL STATE [1]

London, 8 November 1933

Article 1

1. Save as regards the territories mentioned in paragraph 3 (i) of the present article, any Contracting Government shall be at liberty in accordance with the provisions of article 13, to assume, in respect of any of its territories (including metropolitan territories, colonies, overseas territories, or territories under suzerainty, protection, or mandate), only those obligations of the present Convention which are set out in article 9, paragraph 3, 8 and 9. The term "in part" in the present Convention shall be deemed to refer to those obligations.

2. The expression "territory" or "territories" in relation to any Contracting Government shall, for the purposes of articles 2-12 of the present Convention, denote the territory or territories of that government to which the Convention is applicable in full; and, subject to the provisions of the preceding paragraph and of article 13, the obligations arising under articles 2-12 shall relate only to such territories.

3. The present Convention shall apply and shall be applicable in full to (i) all the territories (i.e., metropolitan territories, colonies, overseas territories, or territories under suzerainty, protection, or mandate) of any Contracting Government which are situated in the continent of Africa, including Madagascar and Zanzibar; (ii) any other territory in respect of which a Contracting Government shall have assumed all the obligations of the present Convention in accordance with the provisions of article 13.

4. For the purposes of the present Convention the British High Commission Territories in South Africa shall be regarded as territory.

5. The present Convention shall not have any application, either in full or in part, to any metropolitan territory not situated in the continent of Africa, except where and to the extent to which a declaration effecting such application is made under article 13.

Article 2

For the purposes of the present Convention —

1. The expression "national park" shall denote an area (a) placed under public control, the boundaries of which shall not be altered or any portion be capable of alienation except by the competent legislative authority, (b) set aside for the propagation, protection and preservation of wild animal life and wild vegetation, and for the preservation of objects of aesthetic, geological, prehistoric, historical, archaeological, or other scientific interest for the benefit, advantage, and enjoyment of the general public, (c) in which the hunting, killing or capturing of fauna and the destruction or collection of flora is prohibited except by or under the direction or control of the park authorities.

In accordance with the above provisions facilities shall, so far as possible, be given to the general public for observing the fauna and flora in national parks.

2. The term "strict natural reserve" shall denote an area placed under public control, throughout which any form of hunting or fishing, any undertakings connected with forestry, agriculture, or mining, any excavations or prospecting, drilling, levelling of the ground, or construction, any work involving the alteration of the configuration of the soil or the character of the vegetation, any act likely to harm or disturb the fauna and flora, and the introduction of any species of fauna and flora, whether indigenous or imported, wild or domesticated, shall be strictly forbidden; which it shall be forbidden to enter, traverse, or camp in without a special written permit from the competent authorities; and in which scientific investigations may only be undertaken by permission of those authorities.

3. The expression "animal" or "species" shall denote all vertebrates and invertebrates (including non-edible fish, but not including edible fish except in a national park or strict natural reserve), their nests, eggs, egg-shells, skins, and plumage.

Article 3

1. The Contracting Government will explore forthwith the possibility of establishing in their territories national parks and strict natural reserves as defined in the preceding article. In all cases where the establishment of such parks or reserves is possible, the necessary work shall be commenced within two years from the date of the entry into force of the present Convention.

2. If in any territory the establishment of a national park or strict natural reserve is found to be impracticable at present, suitable areas shall be selected as early as possible in the development of the territory concerned, and the areas so selected shall be transformed into national parks or strict natural reserves as soon as, in the opinion of the authorities of the territory, circumstances will permit.

Article 4

The Contracting Governments will give consideration in respect of each of their territories to the following administrative arrangements:

1. The control of all white or native settlements in national parks with a view to ensuring that as little disturbance as possible is occasioned to the natural fauna and flora.

2. The establishment round the borders of national parks and strict natural reserves of intermediate zones within which the hunting, killing and capturing of animals may take place under the control of the authorities of the park or reserve; but in which no person who becomes an owner, tenant, or occupier after a date to be determined by the authority of the territory concerned shall have any claim in respect of

depredations caused by animals.

3. The choice in respect of all national parks of areas sufficient in extent to cover, so far as possible, the migrations of the fauna preserved therein.

Article 5

1. The Contracting Governments shall notify the Government of the United Kingdom of Great Britain and Northern Ireland of the establishment of any national parks or strict natural reserves (defining the area of the parks or reserves), and of the legislation, including the methods of administration and control, adopted in connexion therewith.

2. They shall similarly notify any information relevant to the purposes of the present Convention and communicated to them by any national museums or by any societies, national or international, established within their jurisdiction and interested in those purposes.

3. The Government of the United Kingdom will communicate the information so received to the other Governments whether in full or in part.

Article 6

In all cases in which it is proposed to establish in any territory of a Contracting Government a national park or strict natural reserve contiguous to a park or reserve situated in another territory (whether of that Government or of another Contracting Government), or to the boundary of such territory, there shall be prior consultation between the competent authorities of the territories concerned. Similarly, there shall be co-operation between those authorities subsequent to the establishment of the park or reserve, or where such a park or reserve is already established.

Article 7

Irrespective of any action which may be taken under article 3 of the present Convention, the Contracting Governments shall, as measures preliminary and supplementary to the establishment of national parks or strict natural reserves:

1. Set aside in each of their territories suitable areas (to be known as reserves) within which the hunting, killing or capturing of any part of the natural fauna (exclusive of fish) shall be prohibited save (a) by the permission, given for scientific or administrative purposes in exceptional cases by the authorities of the territory or by the central authorities under whom the reserves are placed, or (b) for the protection of life and property. Licences granted under article 8, paragraphs 1 and 3, shall not extend to reserves.

2. Extend to these areas, as far as may be practicable, a similar degree of protection to the natural flora.

3. Consider the possibility of establishing in each of their territories special reserves for the preservation of species of fauna and flora which it is desired to preserve, but which are not otherwise adequately protected, with special reference to species mentioned in the annex to the present Convention.

4. Furnish information regarding the reserves established in accordance with the preceding paragraphs to the Government of the United Kingdom, which will communicate such information to all the Governments mentioned in article 5, paragraph 2.

5. Take, so far as in their power lies, all necessary measures to ensure in each of their territories a sufficient degree of forest country and the preservation of the best native indigenous forest species, and, without prejudice to the provisions of article 2, paragraph 2, give consideration to the desirability of preventing the introduction of exotic trees or plants into national parks or reserves.

6. Establish as close a degree of co-operation as possible between the competent authorities of their respective territories with the object of facilitating the solution of forestry problems in those territories.

7. Take the necessary measures to control and regulate so far as possible the practice of firing the bush on the borders of forests.

8. Encourage the domestication of wild animals susceptible of economic utilisation.

Article 8

1. The protection of the species mentioned in the annex to the present Convention is declared to be of special urgency and importance. Animals belonging to the species mentioned in Class A shall, in each of the territories of the Contracting Governments, be protected as completely as possible, and the hunting, killing or capturing of them shall only take place by special permission of the highest authority in the territory, which shall be given only under special circumstances, solely in order to further important scientific purposes, or when essential for the administration of the territory. Animals belonging to the species mentioned in Class B, whilst not requiring such rigorous protection as those mentioned in Class A, shall not be hunted, killed, or captured, even by natives, except under special licence granted by the competent authorities. For this purpose a special licence shall denote a licence other than an ordinary game licence, granted at the discretion of the competent authority, and giving permission to hunt, kill, or capture one or more specimens of a specified animal or animals. Every such licence shall be limited as regards the period and the area within which hunting, killing or capturing may take place.

2. No hunting or other rights already possessed by native chiefs or tribes or any other persons or bodies, by treaty, concession, or specific agreement or by administrative permission in those areas in which such rights have already been definitely recognised by the authorities of the territory, are to be considered as being in any way prejudiced by the provisions of the preceding paragraph.

3. In each of the territories of the Contracting

Governments the competent authorities shall consider whether it is necessary to apply the provisions of paragraph 1 of the present article to any species not mentioned in the annex, in order to preserve the indigenous fauna and flora in each area, and, if they deem it necessary, shall apply those provisions to any such species to the extent which they consider desirable. They shall similarly consider whether it is necessary in the territory concerned to accord to any of the species mentioned in Class B of the annex the special protection accorded to the species mentioned in Class A.

4. The competent authorities shall also give consideration to the question of protecting species of animals or plants which by general admission are useful to man or of special scientific interest.

5. Nothing in the present article shall (i) prejudice any right which may exist under the local law of any territory to kill animals without a licence in defence of life or property, or (ii) affect the right of the authorities of the territory to permit the hunting, killing, or capturing of any species (a) in time of famine, (b) for the protection of human life, public health, or domestic stock, (c) for any requirement relating to public order.

6. Each Contracting Government shall furnish to the Government of the United Kingdom information on the subject of the measures adopted in each of its territories in regard to the grant of licences, and in regard to the animals, the destruction or capture of which is, in accordance with paragraph 3 of this article, not permitted except under licence. The Government of the United Kingdom will communicate any such information to all the Governments mentioned in article 5, paragraph 2.

Article 9

1. Each Contracting Government shall take the necessary measures to control and regulate in each of its territories the internal, and the import and export, traffic in, and the manufacture of articles from, trophies as defined in paragraph 8 of the present article, with a view to preventing the import or export of, or any dealing in trophies other than such as have been originally killed, captured or collected in accordance with the laws and regulations of the territory concerned.

2. The export of trophies to any destination whatsoever shall be prohibited unless the exporter has been granted a certificate permitting export and issued by a competent authority. Such certificate shall only be issued where the trophies have been lawfully imported or lawfully obtained. In the event of an attempted export without any certificate having been granted, the authorities of the territory where this attempt takes place shall apply such penalties as they may think necessary.

3. The import of trophies which have been exported from any territory to which the present Convention is applicable in full, whether a territory of another Contracting Government or not, shall be prohibited except on production of a certificate or lawful export, failing which the trophy shall be confiscated, but without prejudice to the application of the penalties mentioned in the preceding paragraph.

4. The import and export of trophies, except at places where there is a customs station, shall be prohibited.

5. (*a*) Every trophy consisting of ivory and rhinoceros horn exported in accordance with the provisions of the present article shall be identified by marks which, together with the weight of the trophy, shall be recorded in the certificate of lawful export.

(*b*) Every other trophy shall, if possible, be similarly marked and recorded, but shall in any event be described in the certificate so as to identify it with as much certainty as possible.

(*c*) The Contracting Governments shall take such measures as may be possible by the preparation and circulation of appropriate illustrations or otherwise to instruct their customs officers in the methods of identifying the species mentioned in the annex to the present Convention and the trophies derived therefrom.

6. The measures contemplated in paragraph 1 of the present article shall include provisions that found ivory, rhinoceros horn and all trophies of animals found dead, or accidentally killed, or killed in defence of any persons, shall, in principle, be the property of the Government of the territory concerned, and shall be disposed of according to regulations introduced by that Government, due regard being had to the native rights and customs reserved in the succeeding paragraph.

7. No rights of the kind specified in paragraph 2 of article 8 are to be considered as being prejudiced by the provisions of the preceding paragraphs.

8. For the purposes of the present article the expression "trophy" shall denote any animal, dead or alive, mentioned in the annex to the Convention, or anything part of or produced from any such animal when dead, or the eggs, egg-shells, nests or plumage of any bird so mentioned. The expression "trophy" shall not, however, include any trophy or part of a trophy which by a process of *bona fide* manufacture, as contemplated in paragraph 1 of the present article, has lost its original identity.

9. Each Contracting Government shall furnish to the Government of the United Kingdom information as to the measures taken in order to carry out the obligations of the present article or any part of them. The Government of the United Kingdom will communicate any information so received to all the Governments mentioned in article 5, paragraph 2.

Article 10

1. The use of motor vehicles or aircraft (including aircraft lighter than air) shall be prohibited in the territories of the Contracting Governments, both

(i) for the purpose of hunting, killing, or capturing animals, and (ii) in such manner as to drive, stampede, or disturb them for any purpose whatsoever, including that of filming or photographing; provided, however, that nothing in the present paragraph shall affect the right of occupiers in respect of land occupied by them, or of Governments in respect of land utilised for public purposes, to use motor vehicles or aircraft for the purpose of driving away, capturing or destroying animals found on such land in all cases where such ejection, capture or destruction is not prohibited by any other provision of the present Convention.

2. The Contracting Governments shall prohibit in their territories the surrounding of animals by fires for hunting purposes. Wherever possible, the under-mentioned methods of capturing or destroying animals shall also be generally prohibited:

- (*a*) the use of poison, or explosives for killing fish;
- (*b*) the use of dazzling lights, flares, poison, or poisoned weapons for hunting animals;
- (*c*) the use of nets, pits, or enclosures, gins, traps or snares, or of set guns and missiles containing explosives for hunting animals.

Article 11

It is understood that upon signature, ratification, or accession any Contracting Government may make such express reservations in regard to articles 3-10 of the present Convention as may be considered essential.

Article 12

1. Each Contracting Government shall furnish to the Government of the United Kingdom information as to the measures taken for the purpose of carrying out the provisions of the preceding articles. The Government of the United Kingdom will communicate all the information so furnished to the Governments mentioned in article 5, paragraph 2.

2. The Contracting Governments shall, wherever necessary, co-operate between themselves for the purpose of carrying out the provisions of the preceding articles and to prevent the extinction of fauna and flora.

3. All the Governments which sign or accede to the present Convention shall be deemed to be parties to the Protocol bearing this day's date drawn up to facilitate the co-operation mentioned in the preceding paragraph.

Article 13

1. Any Contracting Government may, at the time of signature, ratification, or accession, or thereafter, make a declaration assuming in respect of any one or more of its territories (including metropolitan territories, colonies, overseas territories, or territories under suzerainty, protection, or mandate) other than those mentioned in paragraph 3 (i) of article 1, either all the obligations of the present Convention, or only those contained in article 9, paragraphs 3, 8 and 9. If such declaration is made subsequent to ratification or accession it shall be effected by means of a notification in writing addressed to the Government of the United Kingdom, and shall take effect on the entry into force of the Convention or, if the Convention is already in force, three months after the date of the receipt of the notification by the Government of the United Kingdom.

2. It is understood that any Contracting Government may, by a single declaration made under the preceding paragraph, assume, in respect of some of its territories mentioned in that paragraph, all the obligations of the present Convention, and in respect of other such territories only the obligations contained in article 9, paragraphs 3, 8 and 9.

3. Any Contracting Government which has made a declaration under the preceding paragraph, assuming, in respect of any territory, only the obligations contained in article 9, paragraphs 3, 8 and 9, may, at any subsequent time, by a notification in writing addressed to the Government of the United Kingdom, declare that such previous declaration shall henceforth be deemed to relate to all the obligations of the Convention in respect of the territory concerned; and such subsequent declaration shall take effect on the entry into force of the Convention or, if the Convention is already in force, three months after the date of the receipt of the notification by the Government of the United Kingdom.

4. Any Contracting Government may at any time, by a notification in writing addressed to the Government of the United Kingdom, determine the application of the Convention to any territory or territories which have been the subject of a declaration under paragraphs 1 and 3 of the present article, and the Convention shall thereupon cease to apply to the territory or territories mentioned in the notification one year after the date of its receipt by the Government of the United Kingdom, provided that such notification shall in no case take effect until the expiry of the period of five years mentioned in article 19, paragraph 1.

5. It is understood that if, as the result of a notification made under the preceding paragraph, there would remain no territories of the Contracting Government concerned to which the Convention would be applicable either in full or in part, such Government shall, instead of making the notification, proceed by way of denunciation under article 19.

6. It is further understood that no notification made under paragraph 4 of the present article, or otherwise, may purport to apply only the provisions of article 9, paragraphs 3, 8 and 9, to any territory to which, at the time of the notification, the Convention applies in full.

7. The Government of the United Kingdom will

inform all the Governments mentioned in article 5, paragraph 2, of any notification received under the preceding paragraphs of the present article, of the date of their receipt of their terms.

Article 14

It is understood that no Government will sign, ratify, or accede to the present Convention unless it either has territories covered by article 1, paragraph 3 (i), or makes or has made a declaration under article 13 assuming in respect of one or more territories the obligations of the Convention either in full or in part.

Article 15

The present Convention, of which the French and English texts shall both be equally authentic, shall bear this day's date and shall be open for signature until the 31st March 1934.

Article 16

The present Convention shall be subject to ratification. The instruments of ratification shall be deposited with the Government of the United Kingdom, which will notify their receipt and the date thereof, and their terms and the terms of any accompanying declarations or reservations to all the Governments mentioned in article 5, paragraph 2.

Article 17

At any time after the 31st March 1934, the present Convention shall be open to accession by any Government of a metropolitan territory, by which it has not been signed, whether it has territories covered by article 1, paragraph 3 (i), or not. Accessions shall be notified to the Government of the United Kingdom, which will inform all the Governments mentioned in article 5, paragraph 2, of all notifications received, their terms and the terms of any accompanying declarations or reservations, and the date of their receipt.

Article 18

1. After the deposit or notification of not less than four ratifications or accessions on the part of Contracting Governments having territories covered by article 1, paragraph 3 (i), the present Convention shall come into force three months after the deposit or notification of the last of such ratifications or accessions, as between the Governments concerned. The Government of the United Kingdom will notify all the Governments mentioned in article 5, paragraph 2, of the date of the coming into force of the Convention.

2. Any ratifications or accessions received after the date of the entry into force of the Convention shall take effect three months after the date of their receipt of the Government of the United Kingdom.

Article 19

1. Any Contracting Government may at any time denounce the present Convention by a notification in writing addressed to the Government of the United Kingdom. Such denunciation shall take effect, as regards the Government making it, and in respect of all the territories of that Government to which the Convention shall then apply, either in full or in part, one year after the date of the receipt of the notification by the Government of the United Kingdom; provided, however, that no denunciation shall take effect until the expiry of five years from the date of the entry into force of the Convention.

2. If, as the result of simultaneous or successive denunciations, the number of Contracting Governments bound, in respect of one or more of their territories, by all the obligations of the present Convention is reduced to less than four, the Convention shall cease to be in force as from the date on which the last of such denunciations shall take effect in accordance with the provisions of the preceding paragraph.

3. The Government of the United Kingdom will notify all the other Governments mentioned in article 5, paragraph 2, of any denunciations so received and the date on which they take effect. The Government of the United Kingdom will also, if occasion arises, similarly notify the date on which the Convention ceases to be in force under the provisions of the preceding paragraph.

In witness whereof the above-named Plenipotentiaries have signed the present Convention.

Done in London, this eighth day of November, 1933, in a single copy, which shall remain deposited in the archives of the Government of the United Kingdom of Great Britain and Northern Ireland, which will transmit certified true copies thereof to all the Governments attending the Conference at which the present Convention has been drawn up, whether as participators or observers, as well as to any other Government to which the Government of the United Kingdom may deem it desirable to communicate a copy.

ANNEX

Class A

1. ANIMALIA

(i) MAMMALIA

Primates

A 1. Gorilla — *Gorilla gorilla* (Savage & Wyman) (all subspecies)

Anthropopithecus gorilla Savage & Wyman, 1847, Bost. Journ. Nat. Hist. 5 : 419

A 2. **All Madagascar Lemurs — Chiromyidae, Lemuridae and Indrisidae**

(Note: These families include numerous genera and species.)

Carnivora

A 3. Aard Wolf—*Proteles cristatus* (Sparrman)

Viverra cristala Sparrman, 1785, Voy. : 177

A 4. *Fossa* Gray (all subspecies).

Fossa Gray, 1964, Proc. Zool. Soc. Lond. 1864 : 518

Ungulata

A 5. Giant Sable Antelope — *Hippotragus niger variani* Thomas

Hippotragus niger variani Thomas, 1916, Proc. Zool. Soc. Lond. 1916 : 298

A 6. Nyala — *Tragelaphus angasi* Angas

Tragelaphus angasi Angas, 1848, Proc. Zool. Soc. Lon. 1848 : 89

A 7. Mountain Nyala or Bushbuck — *Tragelaphus buxtoni* Lydekker

Tragelaphus buxtoni Lydekker, 1910, Nature 84 : 397

A 8. Okapi —*Okapia johnstoni* (Sclater)

Equus (?) johnstoni Sclater, 1901, Proc. Zool. Soc. Lon. 1901 (1) : 50

A 9. Barbary Stag — *Cervus elaphus barbarus* Bennett

Cervus barbarus Bennett, 1837, List Anim. Gardens Zool. Soc. : 31

A10. Pigmy Hippopotamus — *Choeropsis liberiensis* (Morton)

Hippopotamus liberiensis Morton, 1849, J. Acad, Nat. Sci. Philad. (1) 4 : 232

Hippopotamus minor Morton, 1844, Proc. Acad. Nat. Sci. Philad. 2 (1) : 15

A11. Mountain Zebra — ***Hippotigris zebra*** (Linnaeus) (all subspecies)

Equus zebra Linnaeus, 1758, Syst. Nat. ed. 10 1 : 74

A12. Wild Ass — ***Asinus asinus*** (Linnaeus) **(all subspecies)**

Equus asinus; Linnaeus, 1758, Syst. Nat. ed. 10 1 : 73

A13. White Rhinoceros — ***Rhinoceros simus*** Burchell (all subspecies)

Rhinoceros simns Burchell, 1817, Bull. Soc. Philom. 1817 : 96

A14. Northern Hartebeest or **Bubal** — ***Bubalis buselaphus*** **(Pallas)**

Antilope buselaphus Pallas, 1766, Misc. Zool. : 7

A15. Abyssinian Ibex or Wali — *Capra walie* Rüppell

Capra walie, Rüppell 1835, Neue Wirbelthiere Abyssin. 1 : 16

A16. Elephant — *Elephas africanus* Blumenbach

Elphas africanus **Blumenbach, 1779, Handbuch der** Naturgeschichte, ed. 5 : 125

(Note: This species to be included in Class A only in respect of specimens of which the tusks do not exceed 5 kilograms in weight each.)

A17. Water Chevrotain — *Hyemoschus aquaticus* (Ogilby) **(all subspecies)**

Moschus aquaticus Ogilby, 1840, Proc. Zool. Soc. 1840 : 35

(ii) AVES

A18. Whale-headed Stork or Shoe-bill — *Balaeniceps rex* Gould

Balaneniceps rex **Gould, 1851, Proc. Zool. Soc. Lond.** 1851 : 1

A19. Bald-headed Ibis or Waldrapp — *Comatibis eremita* (Linnaeus)

Upupa eremita Linnaeus, 1758, Syst. Nat. ed. 10 1 : 118

A20. White-breasted Guinea Fowl — *Agelastes meleagrides* Bonaparte

Agelastes meleagrides, Bonaparte, 1849, Proc. Zool. Soc. Lond. 1849 : 145

2. VEGETABILIA

A21. Welwitschia — *Welwitschia Bainesii* **(Carrieere)**

Welwitschia Bainesii **(Carrieere)**, 1933, Flora Capensis 5 (2): Suppl. 1-3

(formerly Welwitschia mirabilis Hooker fil.)

Class B

ANIMALIA

(i) MAMMALIA

Primates

B 1. Chimpanzee — *Anthropopithecus* Blainville (all subspecies.)

Anthropopithecus Blainville, 1838, Ann, Franc. et Enitrang d'Anat. et Physiol. 2 : 360

B 2. Colobus Monkey — *Colobus* Illiger (all subspecies)

Colobus Illiger, 1811, Prodomus : 69

Ungulata

B 3. Giant Eland or Lord Derby's Eland — *Taurotragus derbianus* (Gray) (all **subspecies)**

Boselaphus derbianus Gray, 1847, Ann. Mag. Nat. Hist. (1) 20 : 286

Boselaphus orcas, Gray, 1847, List Osteol. Brit. Mus.: 155

B 4. Giraffe — *Giraffa* Zimmermann **(all subspecies)**

Giraffa Zimmermann, 1780, Georg. Gesch. 2 : 125

B 5. White-tailed Gnu — ***Connochaetes gnou*** (Zimmermann)

Bos gnou; Zimmermann, 1772, spess. Zool. Georgr; 372

B 6. Yellow-backed Duiker — *Cephalophus sylvicultrix* **(Afzelius)**

Antilope sylvicultrix, Afzelius, 1815, Nova Acta Soc. Upsala 6 : 265

B 7. Jentink's Duiker — *Cephalophus jentinki* Thomas

Cephalophus jentinki **Thomas, 1892, Proc. Zool. Soc. Lond. 1892 : 417**
Antilope longiceps **Jentink, 1885, Notes Leyden Mus. 7 : 272**

B 8. Beira — *Dorcotragus megalotis* (Menges)

Oreotragus megalotis **Menges, 1894, Zool. Anz. 1894 : 131**

B 9. Dibatag or Clarke's Gazelle — *Ammodorcas clarkei* (Thomas)

Cervicapra clarkei Thomas, 1891, Ann. Mag. Nat. Hist. (6) 7 : 304

B10. Bontebok — ***Damaliscus pygargus*** **(Pallas)**

Antilope pygarga **Pallas, 1767, Spicil. Zool. fasc. 1 : 10**
Antilope dorcas **Pallas, 1766, Misc. Zool. : 6; nee**
Capra dorcas **Linnaeus**

B11. Black Rhinoceros — *Rhinoceros bicornis* Linnaeus

Rhinoceros bicornis, Linnaeus, 1758, Syst. Nat. ed. 10 1 : 56

B12. Elephant — *Elephas africanus* Blumenback

Elephas africanus, Blumenbach, 1779, Handbuch der Naturgeschichte ed. 5 : 125
(The above species to be included in Class B in respect of specimens of which the tusks exceed 5 kilograms in weight each.)

Edentata

B13. Pangolin — *Manis* Linnaeus (all species)

Manis Linnaeus, 1758, Syst. Nat, ed. 10 1 : 36

(ii) Aves

B14. Marabou — *Leptoptilos crumeniferus* (Lesson)

Ciconia crumenifera Lesson, 1831, Traite' d'Orn : 585

B15. **Abyssinian Ground Hornbill —** ***Bucorvus*** *abyssinicus* (Boddaert)

Buceros abyssinicus Boddaert, 1783, Tabl. Planches enluminees : 48

B16. Ground Hornbill — *Bucorvus cafer* (Schlegel)

Buceros caruncùlatus cafer Schlegel, 1862, Mus. Pays-Bas 1 : 20

B17. Wild Ostrich — *Struthio* Linnaeus (all **African subspecies)**

Struthio Linnaeus, 1758, Syst. Nat. ed. 10 1 : 155
Note: The African subspecies are the following:
North African Ostrich — S. *camelus camelus* Linnaues, 1758;
Southern Ostrich — *S.c. australis* Gurney, 1868;
Masai Ostrich — *S.c. massaicus* Neumann, 1898; and
Somali Ostrich — *S.c. molybdophanes* Reichenow, 1883.

B18. Secretary Bird — *Sagitarius serpentarius* (Miller)

Falco serpentarius **Miller, 1779, Icon. Anim. pl. 28**

B19. Little Egret — *Egretta garzetta* (Linnaeus)

Ardea garzetta Linnaeus, 1766, Syst. Nat. ed. 12 1 :237

B.20 African Great White Egret — ***Casmerodius*** *albus melanorchynchus* (Wagler)

Ardea melanorhynchus **Wagler, 1827, Syst. Av. Additamenta (last page)**

B21. **African yellow-billed Egret —** *Mesophoyx intermedius brachyrhynchus* (Brehm)

Herodias (Egretta) brachyrynchus **Brehm, 1858, J. Ornith. : 471**

B.22 Buff-backed Heron — *Bubulcus ibis* (Linnaeus)

Ardea ibis, Linnaeus, 1758, Syst. Nat. ed. 10 1 : 144

PROTOCOL

London, 8 November 1933

At the moment of signature of the Convention relative to the Preservation of Fauna and Flora in their Natural State which bears this day's date, the Undersigned, being duly authorised to that effect by their respective Governments, have agreed on the following provisions:

1. In order to facilitate co-operation for the purpose of preventing the extinction of natural fauna and flora and to examine the working of the above-mentioned Convention, as well as the question of any improvements which might be made to it, periodical international Conferences shall be held at appropriate intervals at which the Governments parties to the Convention or on whose behalf the present Protocol has been signed shall be represented.

2. The first of such Conferences shall take place within four years from this day's date, and the arrangements in connection with it shall be made by the Government of the United Kingdom of Great Britain and Northern Ireland, which shall invite the Governments referred to in article 1 of the present Protocol, together with any other Government whose presence may be considered desirable.

3. It is agreed that the matters to be discussed at the above-mentioned Conference shall include (*a*) the question of the exchange between the Governments of lists of persons known to have been guilty of persistent infringements of game regulations, (*b*) the question of the exchange of information relating to infectious or contagious diseases of importance for the preservation of fauna or flora, or capable of affecting men as well as animals.

4. Subsequent Conferences shall be held at such dates and in accordance with such arrangements as may be made at the first Conference.

5. The present Protocol, of which the French and English texts shall both be equally authentic, shall bear this day's date, and shall come into force upon signature.

CONVENTION ON NATURE PROTECTION AND WILD LIFE PRESERVATION IN THE WESTERN HEMISPHERE [2]

Washington, 12 October 1940

PREAMBLE

The Governments of the American Republics, wishing to protect and preserve in their natural habitat representatives of all species and genera of their native flora and fauna, including migratory birds, in sufficient numbers and over areas extensive enough to assure them from becoming extinct through any agency within man's control; and

Wishing to protect and preserve scenery of extraordinary beauty, unusual and striking geologic formations, regions and natural objects of aesthetic, historic or scientific value, and areas characterized by primitive conditions in those cases covered by this Convention; and

Wishing to conclude a convention on the protection of nature and the preservation of flora and fauna to effectuate the foregoing purposes, have agreed upon the following Articles:

Article I

DESCRIPTION OF TERMS USED IN THE WORDING OF THIS CONVENTION

1. The expression *national parks* shall denote:

Areas established for the protection and preservation of superlative scenery, flora and fauna of national significance which the general public may enjoy and from which it may benefit when placed under public control.

2. The expression *national reserves* shall denote:

Regions established for conservation and utilization of natural resources under government control, on which protection of animal and plant life will be afforded in so far as this may be consistent with the primary purpose of such reserves.

3. The expression *nature monuments* shall denote:

Regions, objects, or living species of flora and fauna of aesthetic, historic or scientific interest to which strict protection is given. The purpose of nature monuments is the protection of a specific object, or a species of flora or fauna, by setting aside an area, an object, or a single species, as an inviolate nature monument, except for duly authorized scientific investigations or government inspection.

4. The expression *strict wilderness reserves* shall denote:

A region under public control characterized by primitive conditions of flora, fauna, transportation and habitation wherein there is no provision for the passage of motorized transportation and all commercial developments are excluded.

5. The expression *migratory birds* shall denote:

Birds of those species, all or some of whose individual members, may at any season cross any of the boundaries between the American countries. Some of the species of the following families are examples of birds characterized as migratory: Charadriidae, Scolopacidae, Caprimulgidae, Hirundinidae.

Article II

1. The Contracting Governments will explore at once the possibility of establishing in their territories national parks, national reserves, nature monuments, and strict wilderness reserves as defined in the preceding article. In all cases where such establishment is feasible, the creation thereof shall be begun as soon as possible after the effective date of the present Convention.

2. If in any country the establishment of national parks, national reserves, nature monuments, or strict wilderness reserves is found to be impractical at present, suitable areas, objects or living species of fauna or flora, as the case may be, shall be selected as early as possible to be transformed into national parks, national reserves, nature monuments or strict wilderness reserves as soon as, in the opinion of the authorities concerned, circumstances will permit.

3. The Contracting Governments shall notify the Pan American Union of the establishment of any national parks, national reserves, nature monuments, or strict wilderness reserves, and of the legislation, including the methods of administrative control, adopted in connection therewith.

Article III

The Contracting Governments agree that the boundaries of national parks shall not be altered, or any portion thereof be capable of alienation, except by the competent legislative authority. The resources of these reserves shall not be subject to exploitation for commercial profit.

The Contracting Governments agree to prohibit hunting, killing and capturing of members of the fauna and destruction or collection of representatives of the flora in national parks except by or under the direction or control of the park authorities, or for duly authorized scientific investigations.

The Contracting Governments further agree to provide facilities for public recreation and education in national parks consistent with the purposes of this Convention.

Article IV

The Contracting Governments agree to maintain the strict wilderness reserves inviolate, as far as practicable, except for duly authorized scientific investigations or government inspection, or such uses as are consistent with the purposes for which the area was established.

Article V

1. The Contracting Governments agree to adopt, or to propose such adoption to their respective appropriate law-making bodies, suitable laws and regulations for the protection and preservation of flora and fauna within their national boundaries, but not included in the national parks, national reserves, nature monuments, or strict wilderness reserves referred to in Article II hereof. Such regulations shall contain proper provisions for the taking of the specimens of flora and fauna for scientific study and investigation by properly accredited individuals and agencies.

2. The Contracting Governments agree to adopt, or to recommend that their respective legislatures adopt, laws which will assure the protection and preservation of the natural scenery, striking geological formations, and regions and natural objects of aesthetic interest or historic or scientific value.

Article VI

The Contracting Governments agree to cooperate among themselves in promoting the objectives of the present Convention. To this end they will lend proper assistance, consistent with national laws, to scientists of the American Republics engaged in research and field study; they may, when circumstances warrant, enter into agreements with one another or with scientific institutions of the Americas in order to increase the effectiveness of this collaboration; and they shall make available to all the American Republics equally through publication or otherwise the scientific knowledge resulting from such cooperative effort.

Article VII

The Contracting Governemnts shall adopt appropriate measures for the protection of migratory birds of economic or aesthetic value or to prevent the threatened extinction of any given species. Adequate measures shall be adopted which will permit, in so far as the respective governments may see fit, a rational utilization of migratory birds for the purpose of sports as well as for food, commerce, and industry, and for scientific study and investigation.

Article VIII

The protection of the species mentioned in the Annex to the present Convention is declared to be of special urgency and importance. Species included therein shall be protected as completely as possible, and their hunting, killing, capturing, or taking, shall be allowed only with the permission of the appropriate government authorities in the country. Such permission shall be granted only under special circumstances, in order to further scientific purposes, or when essential for the administration of the area in which the animal or plant is found.

Article IX

Each Contracting Government shall take the necessary measures to control and regulate the importation, exportation and transit of protected fauna and flora or any part thereof by the following means:

1. The issuing of certificates authorizing the exportation or transit of protected species of flora or fauna, or parts thereof.

2. The prohibition of the importation of any species of fauna or flora or any part thereof protected by the country of origin unless accompanied by a certificate of lawful exportation as provided for in Paragraph 1 of this Article.

Article X

1. The terms of this convention shall in no way be interpreted as replacing international agreements previously entered into by one or more of the High Contracting Powers.

2. The Pan American Union shall notify the Contracting Parties of any information relevant to the purposes of the present Convention communicated to it by any national museums or by any organizations, national or international established within their jurisdiction and interested in the purposes of the Convention.

Article XI

1. The original of the present Convention in Spanish, English, Portuguese and French shall be deposited with the Pan American Union and opened for signature by the American Governments on 12 October 1940.

2. The present Convention shall remain open for signature by the American Governments. The instruments of ratification shall be deposited with the Pan American Union, which shall notify their receipt and the dates thereof, and the terms of any accompanying declarations or reservations, to all participating Governments.

3. The present Convention shall come into force three months after the deposit of not less than five ratifications with the Pan American Union.

4. Any ratification received after the date of the entry into force of the Convention, shall take effect three months after the date of its deposit with the Pan American Union.

Article XII

1. Any Contracting Government may at any time denounce the present Convention by a notification in writing addresed to the Pan American Union. Such denunciation shall take effect one year after the date of the receipt of the notification by the Pan American Union, provided, however, that no denunciation shall take effect until the expiration of five years from the date of the entry into force of this Convention.

2. If, as the result of simultaneous or successive denunciations, the number of Contracting Governments is reduced to less than three, the Convention shall cease to be in force from the date on which the last of such denunciations takes effect in accordance with the provisions of the preceding Paragraph.

3. The Pan American Union shall notify all of the American Governments of any denunciations and the date on which they take effect.

4. Should the Convention cease to be in force under the provisions of Paragraph 2 of this article, the Pan American Union shall notify all of the American Governments, indicating the date on which this will become effective.

In witness whereof, the undersigned Plenipotentiaries, having deposited their full powers found to be in due and proper form, sign this Convention at the Pan American Union, Washington, D.C., on behalf of their respective Governments and affix thereto their seals on the dates appearing opposite their signatures.

INTERNATIONAL CONVENTION FOR THE REGULATION OF WHALING [3]

Washington, 2 December 1946

The Governments whose duly authorized representatives have subscribed hereto,

Recognizing the interest of the nations of the world in safeguarding for future generations the great nature resources represented by the whale stocks;

Considering that the history of whaling has been overfishing of one area after another and of one species of whale after another to such a degree that it is essential to protect all species of whales from further overfishing;

Recognizing that the whale stocks are susceptible of natural increases if whaling is properly regulated, and that increases in the size of whale stocks will permit increases in the numbers of whales which may be captured without endangering these natural resources;

Recognizing that it is in the common interest to achieve the optimum level of whale stocks as rapidly as possible without causing wide-spread economic and nutritional distress;

Recognizing that in the course of achieving these objectives, whaling operations should be confined to those species best able to sustain exploitation in order to give an interval for recovery to certain species of whales now depleted in numbers;

Desiring to establish a system of international regulation for the whale fisheries to ensure proper and effective conservation and development of whale stocks on the basis of the principles embodied in the provisions of the International Agreement for the Regulation of Whaling signed in London on 8 June 1973 and the protocols to that Agreement signed in London on 24 June 1938 and 26 November 1945; and

Having decided to conclude a convention to provide for the proper conservation of whale stocks and thus make possible the orderly development of the whaling industry;

Have agreed as follows:

Article I

1. This Convention includes the Schedule attached thereto which forms an integral part thereof. All references to "Convention" shall be understood as including the said Schedule either in its present terms or as amended in accordance with the provisions of Article V.

2. This Convention applies to factory ships, land stations, and whale catchers under the jurisdiction of the Contracting Governments, and to all waters in which whaling is prosecuted by such factory ships, land stations, and whale catchers.

Article II

As used in this Convention:

1. "factory ship" means a ship in which or on which whales are treated whether wholly or in part;

2. "land stations" means a factory on the land at which whales are treated whether wholly or in part;

3. "whale catcher" means a ship used for the purpose of hunting, taking, towing, holding on to, or scouting for whales;

4. "Contracting Government" means any Government which has deposited an instrument of ratification or has given notice of adherence to this Convention.

Article III

1. The Contracting Governments agree to establish an International Whaling Commission, hereinafter referred to as the Commission, to be composed of one member from each Contracting Government. Each member shall have one vote and may be accompanied by one or more experts and advisers.

2. The Commission shall elect from its own members a Chairman and Vice Chairman and shall determine its own Rules of Procedure. Decisions of the Commission shall be taken by a simple majority of those members voting except that a three-fourths majority of those members voting shall be required for action in pursuance of Article V. The Rules of Procedure may provide for decisions otherwise than at meetings of the Commission.

3. The Commission may appoint its own Secretary and staff.

4. The Commission may set up, from among its own members and experts or advisers, such committees as it considers desirable to perform such functions as it may authorize.

5. The expenses of each member of the Commission and of his experts and advisers shall be determined and paid by his own Government.

6. Recognizing that specialized agencies related to the United Nations will be concerned with the conservation and development of whale fisheries and the products arising therefrom and desiring to avoid duplication of functions, the Contracting Governments will consult among themselves within two years after the coming into force of this Convention to decide whether the Commission shall be brought within the framework of a specialized agency related to the United Nations.

7. In the meantime the Government of the United Kingdom of Great Britian and Northern Ireland shall arrange, in consultation with the other Contracting Governments to convene the first meeting of the Commission, and shall initiate the consultation referred to in paragraph 6 above.

8. Subsequent meetings of the Commission shall be convened as the Commission may determine.

Article IV

1. The Commission may either in collaboration with or through independent agencies of the Contracting Governments or other public or private agencies, establishments, or organizations, or independently

a) encourage, recommend, or if necessary, organize studies and investigations relating to whales and whaling;

b) collect and analyse statistical information concerning the current condition and trend of the whale stocks and the effects of whaling activities thereon;

c) study, appraise, and disseminate information concerning methods of maintaining and increasing the populations of whale stocks.

2. The Commission shall arrange for the publication of reports of its activities, and it may publish independently or in collaboration with the International Bureau for Whaling Statistics at Sandefjord in Norway and other organizations and agencies such reports as it deems appropriate, as well as statistical, scientific, and other pertinent information relating to whales and whaling.

Article V

1. The Commission may amend from time to time the provisions of the Schedule by adopting regulations with respect to the conservation and utilization of whale resources, fixing (*a*) protected and unprotected species; (*b*) open and closed seasons; (*c*) open and closed waters, including the designation of sanctuary areas; (*d*) size limits for each species; (*e*) time, methods, and intensity of whaling (including the maximum catch of whales to be taken in any one season); (*f*) types and specifications of gear and apparatus and appliances which may be used; (*g*) methods of measurement; and (*h*) catch returns and other statistical and biological records.

2. These amendments of the Schedule (*a*) shall be such as are necessary to carry out the objectives and purposes of this Convention and to provide for the conservation, development, and optimum utilization of the whale resources; (*b*) shall be based on scientific findings; (*c*) shall not involve restrictions on the number or nationality of factory ships or land stations, nor allocate specific quotas to any factory ship or land station or to any group of factory ships or land stations; and (*d*) shall take into consideration the interests of the consumers of whale products and the whaling industry.

3. Each of such amendments shall become effective with respect to the Contracting Governments ninety days following notification of the amendment by the Commission to each of the Contracting Governments, except that (*a*) if any Government presents to the Commission objection to any amendment prior to the expiration of this ninety-day period, the amendment shall not become effective with respect to any of the Governments for an additional ninety days; (*b*) thereupon, any other Contracting Government may present objection to the amendment at any time prior to the expiration of the additional ninety-day period, or before the expiration of thirty days from the date of receipt of the last objection received during such additional ninety-day period, whichever date shall be the later; and (*c*) thereafter, the amendment shall become effective with respect to all Contracting Governments which have not presented objection but shall not become effective with respect to any Government which has so objected until such date as the objection is withdrawn. The Commission shall notify each Contracting Government immediately upon receipt of each objection and withdrawal and each Contracting Government shall acknowledge receipt of all notifications of amendments, objections and withdrawals.

4. No amendments shall become effective before 1 July 1949.

Article VI

The Commission may from time to time make recommendations to any or all Contracting Governments on any matters which relate to whales or whaling and to the objectives and purposes of this Convention.

Article VII

The Contracting Governments shall ensure prompt transmission to the International Bureau of Whaling Statistics at Sandefjord in Norway, or to such other body as the Commission may designate, of notifications and statistical and other information required by this Convention in such form and manner as may be prescribed by the Commission.

Article VIII

1. Notwithstanding anything contained in this Convention, any Contracting Government may grant to any of its nationals a special permit authorizing that national to kill, take, and treat whales for purposes of scientific research subject to such restrictions as to number and subject to such other conditions as the Contracting Government thinks fit, and the killing, taking, and treating of whales in accordance with the provisions of this Article shall be exempt from the operations of this Convention. Each Contracting Government shall report at once to the Commission all such authorizations which it has granted. Each Contracting Government may at any time revoke any such special permit which it has granted.

2. Any whales taken under these special permits shall so far as practicable be processed and the proceeds shall be dealt with in accordance with directions issued by the Government by which the permit was granted.

3. Each Contracting Government shall transmit to such body as may be designated by the Commission, in so far as practicable, and at intervals of not more than one year, scientific information available to that Government with respect to whales and whaling, including the results of research conducted pursuant to paragraph 1 of this Article and to Article IV.

4. Recognizing that continuous collection and analysis of biological data in connection with the operations of factory ships and land stations are indispensable to sound and constructive management of the whale fisheries, the Contracting Governments will take all practicable measures to obtain such data.

Article IX

1. Each Contracting Government shall take appropriate measures to ensure the application of the provisions of this Convention and the punishment of infractions against the said provisions in operations carried out by persons or by vessels under its jurisdiction.

2. No bonus or other remuneration calculated with relation to the results of their work shall be paid to the gunners and crews of whale catchers in respect of any whales the taking of which is forbidden by this Convention.

3. Prosecution for infractions against or contraventions of this Convention shall be instituted by the Government having jurisdiction over the offense.

4. Each Contracting Government shall transmit to the Commission full details of each infraction of the provisions of this Convention by persons or vessels under the jurisdiction of that Government as reported by its inspectors. This information shall include a statement of measures taken for dealing with the infraction and of penalties imposed.

Article X

1. This Convention shall be ratified and the instruments of ratification shall be deposited with the Government of the United States of America.

2. Any Government which has not signed this Convention may adhere thereto after it enters into force by a notification in writing to the Government of the United States of America.

3. The Government of the United States of America shall inform all other signatory Governments and all adhering Governments of all ratifications deposited and adherences received.

4. This Convention shall, when instruments of ratification have been deposited by at least six signatory Governments, which shall include the Governments of Netherlands, Norway, the Union of Soviet Socialist Republics, the United Kingdom of Great Britain and Northern Ireland, and the United States of America, enter into force with respect to each Government which subsequently ratifies or adheres on the date of the deposit of its instrument of ratification or the receipt of its notification of adherence.

5. The provisions of the Schedule shall not apply prior to 1 July 1948. Amendments to the Schedule adopted pursuant to Article V shall not apply prior to 1 July 1949.

Article XI

Any Contracting Government may withdraw from this Convention on June thirtieth of any year by giving notice on or before January first of the same year to the depositary Government, which upon receipt of such a notice shall at once communicate it to the other Contracting Governments. Any other Contracting Government may, in like manner, within one month of the receipt of a copy of such a notice from the depositary Government, give notice of withdrawal, so that the Convention shall cease to be in force on June thirtieth of the same year with respect to the Government giving such notice of withdrawal.

This Convention shall bear the date on which it is opened for signature and shall remain open for signature for a period of fourteen days thereafter.

In Witness whereof the undersigned, being duly authorized, have signed this Convention.

Done in Washington this second day of December 1946, in the English language, the original of which shall be deposited in the archives of the Government of the United States of America. The Government of the United States of America shall transmit certified copies thereof to all the other signatory and adhering Governments.

SCHEDULE

On 13 July 1979

I. INTERPRETATION

1. The following expressions have the meanings respectively assigned to them, this is to say:

"baleen whale" means any whale which has baleen or whale bone in the mouth, i.e any whale other than a toothed whale.

"beaked whale" means any whale belonging to the genus *Mesoplodon*, or any whale known as Cuvier's beaked whale (*Ziphius cavirostris*), or Shepherd's beaked whale (*Tasmacetus shepherdi*).

"blue whale" (*Balaenoptera musculus*) means any whale known as blue whale, Sibbald's rorqual, or sulphur bottom, and including pygmy blue whale.

"bottlenose whale" means any whale known as Baird's beaked whale (*Berardius bairdii*), Arnoux's whale (*Berardius arnuxii*), southern bottlenose whale (*Hyperoodon planifrons*), or northern bottlenose whale (*Hyperoodon ampuliatus*).

"bowhead whale" (*Balaena mysticetus*) means any whale known as bowhead, Arctic right whale, great polar whale, Greenland right whale, Greenland whale.

"Bryde's whale" (*Balaenoptera edeni, B. brydei*) means any whale known as Bryde's whale.

"dauhval" means any unclaimed dead whale found floating.

"fin whale" (*Balaenoptera physalus*) means any whale known as common finback, common rorqual, fin whale, herring whale, or true fin whale.

"gray whale" (*Eschrichtius robustus*) means any whale known as gray whale, California gray, devil fish, hard head, mussel digger, gray back, or rip sack.

"humpback whale" (*Megaptera novaeangliae*) means any whale known as bunch, humpback, humpback whale, humpbacked whale, hump whale or hunchbacked whale.

"killer whale" (*Orcinus orca*) means any whale known as killer whale or orca.

"minke whale" (*Balaenoptera acutorostrata, B. bonaerensis*) means any whale known as lesser rorqual, little piked whale, minke whale, pikeheaded whale or sharp headed finner.

"pilot whale" means any whale known as long-finned pilot whale (*Globicephala melaena*) or short-finned pilot whale (*G. macrorhynchus*).

"right whale" (*Eubalaena glacialis, E. australis*) means any whale known as Atlantic right whale, Arctic right whale, Biscayan right whale, Nordkaper, North Atlantic right whale, North Cape whale, Pacific right whale, or southern right whale.

"pygmy right whale" (*Caperea marginata*) means any whale known as southern pygmy right whale, pygmy right whale.

"sei whale" (*Balaenoptera borealis*) means any whale known as sei whale, Rudolphi's rorqual, pollack whale, or coalfish whale.

"sperm whale" (*Physeter macrocephalus*) means any whale known as sperm whale, spermacet whale, cachalot or pot whale.

"toothed whale" means any whale which has teeth in the jaws.

"lost whale" means any whale that has been taken but not delivered to the factory ship or land station.

"whale taken" means whales that have been killed and either flagged or made fast to catchers.

"lactating whale" means (*a*) with respect to baleen whales — a female which has any milk present in a mammary gland, (*b*) with respect to sperm whales — a female which has milk present in a mammary gland the maximum thickness (depth) of which is 10 cm or more. This measurement shall be at the mid ventral point of the mammary gland perpendicular to the body axis, and shall be logged to the nearest centimetre; that is to say, any gland between 9.5 cm and 10.5 cm shall be logged as 10 cm. The measurement of any gland which falls on an exact 0.5 centimetre shall be logged at the next 0.5 centimetre, e.g. 10.5 cm shall be logged as 11.0 cm.

However, notwithstanding the criteria, a whale shall not be considered a lactating whale if scientific (histological or other biological) evidence is presented to the appropriate national authority establishing that the whale could not at this point in its physical cycle have had a calf dependent on it for milk.

"small-type whaling" means catching operations using powered vessels with mounted harpoon guns hunting exclusively for minke, bottlenose, beaked, pilot or killer whales.

II. SEASONS

2. (*a*) It is forbidden to use a factory ship or whale catcher attached thereto for the purpose of taking or treating baleen whales except minke whales, in any water south of 40° South Latitude, except during the period from 12 December to 7 April following, both days inclusive.

b) It is forbidden to use a factory ship or whale catcher attached thereto for the purpose of taking or treating sperm or minke whales, except as permitted by the Contracting Governments in accordance with sub-paragraphs (*c*), (*d*) and (*e*) of this paragraph.

c) Each Contracting Government shall declare for all factory ships and whale catchers attached thereto under its jurisdiction, an open season or seasons not to exceed eight months out of any period of twelve months during which the taking or killing of sperm whales by whale catchers may be permitted; provided that a separate open season may be declared for each factory ship and the whale catchers attached thereto.

d) Each Contracting Government shall declare for all factory ships and whale catchers attached thereto under its jurisdiction one continuous open season not to exceed six months out of any period of twelve months during which the taking or killing of minke whales by the whale catchers may be permitted provided that:

(i) a separate open season may be declared for each factory ship and the whale catchers attached thereto;

(ii) the open season need not necessarily include the whale or any part of the period declared for other baleen whales pursuant to sub-paragraph (*a*) of this paragraph.

e) Each Contracting Government shall declare for all whale catchers under its jurisdiction not operating in conjunction with a factory ship or land station one continuous open season not to exceed six months out of any period of twelve months during which the taking or killing of minke whales by such whale catchers may be permitted. Notwithstanding this paragraph one continuous open season not to exceed nine months may be implemented so far as Greenland is concerned.

3. (*a*) It is forbidden to use a whale catcher attached to a land station for the purpose of killing or attempting to kill baleen and sperm whales except as permitted by the Contracting Government in accordance with sub-paragraphs (*b*), (*c*) and (*d*) of this paragraph

b) Each Contracting Government shall declare for all land stations under its jurisdiction, and whale catchers attached to such land stations, one open season during which the taking or killing of baleen whales, except minke whales, by the whale catchers shall be permitted. Such open season shall be for a period of not more than six consecutive months in any period of twelve months and shall apply to all land stations under the jurisdiction of the Contracting Government; provided that a separate open season may be declared for any land station used for the taking or treating of baleen whales, except minke whales, which is more than 1,000 miles from the nearest land station used for the taking or treating of baleen whales, except minke whales, under the jurisdiction of the same Contracting Government.

c) *Each Contracting Government shall declare for all land stations under its jurisdiction and for whale catchers attached to such land stations, one open season not to exceed eight continuous months in any one period of twelve months, during which the taking or killing of sperm whales by the whale catchers shall be permitted, provided that a separate open season may be declared for any land station used for the taking or treating of sperm whales which is more than 1,000 miles from the nearest land station used for the taking or treating of sperm whales under the jurisdiction of the same Contracting Government.

d) Each Contracting Government shall declare for all land stations under its jurisdiction and for whale catchers attached to such land stations one open season not to exceed six continuous months in any period of twelve months during which the taking or killing of minke whales by the whale catchers shall be permitted (such period not being necessarily concurrent with the period declared for other baleen whales, as provided for in sub-paragraph (*b*) of this paragraph); provided that a separate open season may be declared for any land station used for the taking or treating of minke whales which is more than 1,000 miles from the nearest land stations used for the taking or treating of minke whales under the jurisdiction of the same Contracting Government.

Except that a separate open season may be declared for any land station used for the taking or treating of minke whales which is located in an area having oceanographic conditions clearly distinguishable from those of the area in which are located the other land stations used for the taking or treating of minke whales under the jurisdiction of the same Contracting Government; but the declaration of a separate open season by virtue of the provisions of this sub-paragraph shall not cause thereby the period of time covering the open seasons declared by the same Contracting Government to exceed nine continuous months of any twelve months.

e) The prohibitions contained in this paragraph shall apply to all land stations as defined in Article II of the Whaling Convention of 1946 and to all factory ships which are subject to the regulations governing the operation of land stations under the provisions of paragraph 6 of this Schedule.

4. It is forbidden to use a factory ship which has been used during a season in any waters south of 40° South Latitude for the purpose of treating baleen whales, except minke whales, in any other area except the North Pacific Ocean and its dependent waters north of the Equator for the same purpose within a period of one year from the termination of that season; provided that catch limits in the North Pacific Ocean and dependent waters are established as provided in paragraph 10 and 15 of this Schedule and provided that this paragraph shall not apply to a ship which has been used during the season solely for freezing or salting the meat and entrails of whales intended for human food or feeding animals.

* Note — This sub-paragraph 3 (*c*) came into force as from 21 February 1952, in respect of all Contracting Governments, except the Commonwealth of Australia, who lodged an objection to it within the prescribed period, and this objection was not withdrawn. The provisions of this sub-paragraph are not therefore binding on the Commonwealth of Australia.

III. CAPTURE

Area limits for Factory Ships:

5. *In accordance with Article V (1) (c) of the Convention, commercial whaling, whether by pelagic operations or from land stations, is prohibited in a region designated as the Indian Ocean Sanctuary. This comprises the waters of the Northern Hemisphere from the coast of Africa to 100 degrees East, including the Red and Arabian Seas and the Gulf of Oman; and the waters of the Southern Hemisphere in the sector from 20 degrees East to 130 degrees East, with the Southern boundary set at 55 degrees south. This prohibition applies irrespective of the classifications of baleen or toothed whale stocks in the sanctuary, as may from time to time be determined by the Commission. This provision will apply for ten years, with the provision for a general review after five years, unless the Commission decides otherwise.*

6. It is forbidden to use a factory ship or whale catcher attached thereto, for the purpose of taking or treating baleen whales, except minke whales, in any of the following areas:

a) in the waters north of 66° North Latitude, except that from 150° East Longitude eastwards as far as 140° West Longitude, the taking or killing of baleen whales by a factory ship or whale catcher shall be permitted between 66° North Latitude and 72° North Latitude;

b) in the Atlantic Ocean and its dependent waters north of 40° South Latitude;

c) in the Pacific Ocean and its dependent waters east of 150° West Longitude between 40° South Latitude and 35° North Latitude;

d) in the Pacific Ocean and its dependent waters west of 150° West Longitude between 40° South Latitude and 20° North Latitude;

e) in the Indian Ocean and its dependent waters north of 40° South Latitude.

7. *a*) A factory ship which operates solely within territorial waters in one of the areas specified in sub-paragraph (*c*) of this paragraph, by permission of the Government having jurisdiction over those waters, and which flies the flag of that Government shall, while so operating, be subject to the regulations governing the operations of land stations and not to the regulations governing the operation of factory ships.

b) Such factory ship shall not, within a period of one year from the termination of the season in which she so operated, be used for the purpose of treating baleen whales in any of the other areas specified in sub-paragraph (*c*) of this paragraph or south of 40° South Latitude.

c) The areas referred to in sub-paragraph (*a*) and (*b*) are:

1. On the coasts of Australia, namely on the whole east coast and on the west coast in the area known as Shark Bay and northward to Northwest Cape and including Exmouth Gulf and King George's Sound, including the Port of Albany.

2. On the Pacific coast of the United States of America between 35° North Latitude and 49° North Latitude.

8. *a*) Classification of Areas and Divisions

Areas in the Southern Hemisphere are those waters between the ice-edge and the equator and lying between the meridians of longitude listed in Table 1.

b) Classification of Divisions

Divisions relating to the catch limits for Southern Hemisphere sperm whales are those waters lying between the ice-edge and the equator and between the meridians of longitude listed in Table 2.

c) Geographical boundaries in the North Atlantic.

The geographical boundaries for the fin, sei and minke whale stocks in the North Atlantic are:

Fin whale stocks

1. Nova Scotia

South and West of a line through:

47°N 54°W, 46°N 54° 30′ W,
46°N 42°, 20°N 42°W.

2. Newfoundland — Labrador

West of a line through:
75°N 73° 30′ W, 69°N 59°W, 61°N 59°W,
52° 20′ N 42°W, 46°N 42°W and
North of a line through:
46°N 42°W, 46°N 54° 30′ W 47°N 54°W.

3. West Greenland

East of a line through:

75°N 73° 30′ W, 69°N 59°W, 61°N 59°W,
52° 20′ N 42°W,
and West of a line through:
52° 20′ N 42°W, 59°N 42°W, 59° 44°W,
Kap Farvel.

4. East Greenland — Iceland

East of a line through:
Kap Farvel (South Greenland)
59°N 44°W, 59°N 42°W, 20°N 42°W
and West of a line through:
20°N 18°W, 60°N 18°W, 68°N 3°E, 74°N 3°E, and South of 74°N latitude.

5. North Norway

North and East of a line through:
74°N 22°W, 74°N 3°E, 68°N 3°E, 67° 0°,
67°N 14°E.

6. West Norway and Faroe Islands

South of a line through:
67°N 14°E, 67°N 0°, 60°N 18°W, and
North of a line through:
61°N 16°W, 61°N 0°, Thyboron (western entrance to Limfjorden, Denmark).

7. British Isles — Spain and Portugal

South of a line through:
Thyboron (Denmark), 61°N 0°, 61°N 16°W,
and East of a line through:
63°N 11°W, 60°N 18°W, 22°N 18°W.

Minke whale stocks

1. Canadian East Coast

West of a line through:
75°N 73° 30′ W, 69°N 59°W, 61°N 59°W,
52° 20′ N 42°W, 20°N 42°W.

2. West Greenland

East of line through:
75°N 73° 30′ W, 69°W 59°W, 61°N 59°W,
52° 20′ N 42°W, and
West of a line through:
52° 20′ N 42°W, 59°N 42°W, 59°N 44°W,
Kap Farvel.

3. East Greenland —Iceland— Jan Mayen

East of a line through:
Kap Farvel (South Greenland)
59°N 44°W, 59°N 42°W, 20°N 42°W,
and West of a line through:
20°N 18°W, 60°N 18°W, 68°N 3°E, 74°N 3°E,
and South of 74°N latitude.

4. Svalbard — Norway — British Isles

East of line through:
20°N 18°W, 60°N 18°W, 68°N 3°E, 74°N 3°E,
and North of a line through:
74°N 3°E, 74°N 22°W.

Sei whale stocks

1. Nova Scotia

South and West of a line through:
47°N 54°W, 46°N 54° 30′ W, 46°N 42°W,
20°N 42°W.

2. Iceland — Denmark Strait

East of a line through:
Kap Farvel (South Greenland),
59°N 44°W, 59°N 42°W, 20°N 42°W
and West of a line through:
20°N 28°W, 60°N 18°W, 68°N 3°E, 74°N 3°E,
74°N 3°E, and South of 74°N latitude.

d) Geographical boundaries in the North Pacific. The geographical boundaries for the sperm and Bryde's whale stocks in the North Pacific are:

Sperm whale stocks

1. Western Division

West of a line from the ice-edge south along the 180° meridian of longitude to 280°, 50°N, then east along the 50°N parallel of latitude to 160°W, 50°N, then south along the 160°W meridian of longitude to 160°W, 40°N, then east along the 40°N parallel of latitude to 150°W, 40°N, then south along the 150°W meridian of longitude to the equator.

2. Eastern Division
East of the line described in 1.

Bryde's whale stocks
1. Western Stock
West of the 160°W meridian of longitude.
2. Eastern Stock
East of the 160°W meridian of longitude.

Classification of Stocks

9. All stocks of whales shall be classified in one of three categories according to the advice of the Scientific Committee as follows:

a) A Sustained Management Stock (SMS) is a stock which is not more than 10 per cent of Maximum Sustainable Yield (hereinafter referred to as MSY) stock level below MSY stock level, and not more than 20 per cent above that level; MSY being determined on the basis of the number of whales.

When a stock has remained at a stable level for a considerable period under a regime of approximately constant catches, it shall be classified as a Sustained Management Stock in the absence of any positive evidence that it should be otherwise classified.

Commercial whaling shall be permitted on Sustained Management Stocks according to the advice of the Scientific Committee. These stocks are listed in Tables 1 and 2 of this Schedule.

For the 1978/79 pelagic season and the 1979 coastal season in the Southern Hemisphere and for the 1979 season in all other areas for stocks between the MSY stock level and 10 per cent below that level, the permitted catch shall not exceed the number of whales obtained by taking 90 per cent of the MSY and reducing that number by 10 per cent for every 1 per cent by which the stock falls short of the MSY stock level. For stocks at or above the MSY stock level, the permitted catch shall not exceed 90 per cent of the MSY.

b) An Initial Management Stock (IMS) is a stock more than 20 per cent of MSY stock level above MSY stock level. Commercial whaling shall be permitted on Initial Management Stocks according to the advice of the Scientific Committee as to measures necessary to bring the stocks to the MSY stock level and then optimum level in an efficient manner and without risk of reducing them below this level. The permitted catch for such stocks will be more than 90 per cent of MSY as far as this is known, or, where it will be more appropriate, catching effort shall be limited to that which will take 90 per cent of MSY in a stock at MSY stock level.

In the absence of any positive evidence that a continuing higher percentage will not reduce the stock below the MSY stock level no more than 5 per cent of the estimated initial exploitable stock shall be taken in any one year. Exploitation should not commence until an estimate of stock size has been obtained which is satisfactory in the view of the Scientific Committee. Stocks classified as Initial Management Stock are listed in Tables 1 and 2 of this Schedule.

c) A Protection Stock (PS) is a stock which is below 10 per cent of MSY stock level below MSY stock level.

There shall be no commercial whaling on species or stocks whilst they are classified as Protection Stocks.

Species and stocks so classified are listed in Tables 1 and 2 of this Schedule.

d) Notwithstanding the other provisions of paragraph 9, there shall be a moratorium on the taking, killing or treating of whales, excluding minke whales, by factory ships or whale catchers attached to factory ships.

Areas, Regions, Divisions, Stock Classifications and Quotas.

Baleen Whales. Catch Limits

10. The number of baleen whales taken during the open season in the Southern Hemisphere by factory ships, land stations or whale catchers attached thereto under the jurisdiction of the Contracting Governments shall not exceed 6,221 minke whales and 0 Bryde's whales (pending a satisfactory estimate of stocks size), in the 1978/79 pelagic season and the 1979 coastal season. The total catches taken in any of the Areas I to VI shall not exceed the limits shown in Table 1. However, in no circumstances shall the sum of the Area catches exceed the total quotas for each species.

11. The number of baleen whales taken in the North Pacific Ocean and dependent waters in 1979 and in the North Atlantic Ocean in 1979 shall not exceed the limits shown in Table 1.

12. Notwithstanding the provisions of paragraph 8 the taking of 10 humpback whales not below 35 feet (10.7 metres) in length, per year is permitted in Greenland waters provided that whale catchers of less than 50 gross register tonnage are used for this purpose, and the taking of gray whales, and of bowhead whales from the Bering Sea stock, by aborigines or a Contracting Government on behalf of aborigines is permitted, but only when the meat and products of such whales are to be used exclusively for local consumption by the aborigines and further provided, with respect to the Bering Sea stock of bowhead whales that:

a) in 1978, hunting shall cease when either 20 have been struck or 14 landed,
b) in 1979, hunting shall cease when either 27 have been struck or 18 landed,
c) it is forbidden to strike, take or kill calves or any bowhead whale accompanied by a calf.

13. It is forbidden to take or kill suckling calves or female whales accompanied by calves.

Baleen whales. Size limits.

14. *a*) It is forbidden to take or kill any sei or Bryde's whales below 40 feet (12.2 metres) in length except that sei and Bryde's whales of not less than 35 feet (10.7 metres) may be taken for delivery to land stations, provided that, the meat of such whales is to be used for local consumption as human or animal food.

b) It is forbidden to take or kill any fin whales below 57 feet (17.4 metres) in length in the Southern Hemisphere, and it is forbidden to take or kill fin whales below 55 feet (16.8 metres) in the Northern Hemisphere; except that fin whales of not less than 55 feet (16.8 metres) may be taken for delivery to land stations in the Southern Hemisphere and fin whales of not less than 50 feet (15.2 metres) may be taken for delivery to land stations in the Northern Hemisphere, provided that, in each case the meat of such whales is to be used for local consumption as human or animal food.

Areas, Regions, Divisions, Stock Classifications and Quotas (*continued*)

Sperm whales. Catch limits.

15. The number of sperm whales taken in the Southern Hemisphere in the 1978/79 pelagic season and the 1979 coastal season shall not exceed 3, 820 males and 1,055 females. The total catch in any of the Divisions 1 to 9 shall not exceed the limits shown in Table 2.

16. The number of sperm whales taken in the North Pacific Ocean and dependent waters in 1979 and in the North Atlantic Ocean in 1979 shall not exceed the limits shown in Table 2.

17. It is forbidden to take or kill suckling calves or female whales accompanied by calves.

Sperm whales. Size Limits.

18. *a*) It is forbidden to take or kill any sperm whales below 30 feet (9.2 metres) in length except in the North Atlantic Ocean where it is forbidden to take or kill any sperm whales below 35 feet (10.7 metres).

b) It is forbidden to take or kill any sperm whale over 45 feet (13.7 metres) in length in the Southern Hemsiphere north of 40° South Latitude during the months of October to January inclusive.

c) It is forbidden to take or kill any sperm whale over 45 feet (13.7 metres) in lenth in the North Pacific Ocean and dependent waters south of 40° North Latitude during the months of March to June inclusive.

IV. TREATMENT

19. *a*) It is forbidden to use a factory or a land station for the purpose of treating any whales (whether or not taken by whale catchers under the jurisdiction of a Contracting Government) which are classified as Protection Stocks in paragraph 8 or are taken by whale catchers under the jurisdiction of a Contracting Government in contravention of paragraphs 2, 3, 5, 9, 10, 14 and 15 of this Schedule.

b) All other whales, except minke whales, taken shall be delivered to the factory ship or land station and all parts of such whales shall be processed by boiling or otherwise, except the internal organs, whale bone and flippers of all whales, the meat of sperm whales and of parts of whales intended for human food or feeding animals. A Contracting Government may in less developed regions exceptionally permit treating of whales without use of land stations, provided that such whales are fully utilised in accordance with this paragrpah.

c) Complete treatment of the carcasses of "dauhval" and of whales used as fenders will not be required in cases where the meat or bone of such whales is in bad condition.

20. *a*) The taking of whales for treating by a factory ship shall be so regulated or restricted by the master or person in charge of the factory ship that no whale carcase (except of a whale used as a fender, which shall be processed as soon as is reasonably practicable) shall remain in the sea for a longer period than thirty-three hours from the time of killing to the time when it is hauled up for treatment.

b) Whales taken by all whale catchers, whether for factory ships or land stations, shall be clearly marked so as to identify the catcher and to indicate the order of catching.

V. SUPERVISION AND CONTROL

21. *a*) There shall be maintained on each factory ship at least two inspectors of whaling for the purpose of maintaining twenty-four hour inspection provided that at least one such inspector shall be maintained on each catcher functioning as a factory ship. These inspectors shall be appointed and paid by the Government having jurisdiction over the factory ship; provided that inspectors need not be appointed to ships which, apart from the shortage of products, are used during the season solely for freezing or salting the meat and entrails of whales intended for human food or feeding animals.

b) Adequate inspection shall be maintained at each land station. The inspectors serving at each land station shall be appointed and paid by the Government having jurisdiction over the land station.

c) There shall be received such observers as the member countries may arrange to place on factory ships and land stations or groups of land stations of other member countries. The observers shall be appointed by the Commission acting through its Secretary and paid by the Government nominating them.

22. Gunners and crews of factory ships, land stations, and whale catchers, shall be engaged on such terms that their remuneration shall depend to a considerable extent upon such factors as the species, size and yield of whales taken and not merely upon the number of the whales taken. No bonus or other remuneration shall be paid to the gunners or crews of whale catchers in respect of the taking of lactating whales.

23. Whales must be measured when at rest on deck or platform after the hauling out wire and grasping device have been released, by means of a tape-measure made of non-stretching material. The zero end of the tape-measure shall be attached to a spike or stable device to be positioned on the deck or platform abreast of one end of the whale. Alternatively the spike may be stuck into the tail fluke abreast of the apex of the notch. The tape-measure shall be held taut in a straight line parallel

to the deck and the whale's body, and other than in exceptional circumstances along the whale's back, and read abreast of the other end of the whale. The ends of the whale for measurement purposes shall be the tip of the upper jaw or, in sperm whales, the most forward part of the head and the apex of the notch between the tail flukes.

Measurements shall be logged to the nearest foot or 0.1 metres. That is to say, any whale between 75 feet 6 inches and 76 feet 6 inches shall be logged as 76 feet, and any whale between 76 feet 6 inches and 77 feet 6 inches shall be logged as 77 feet. Similarly, any whale between 10.15 metres and 10.25 metres shall be logged as 10.2 metres, and any whale between 10.25 metres and 10.35 metres shall be logged as 10.3 metres. The measurement of any whale which falls on an exact half foot or 0.05 metre shall be logged at the next half foot or 0.05 metre, e.g. 76 feet 6 inches precisely shall be logged as 77 feet and 10.25 metres precisely shall be logged as 10.3 metres.

VI. INFORMATION REQUIRED

24. *a*) All whale catchers operating in conjunction with a factory ship shall report by radio to the factory ship:

1) The time when each whale is taken
2) Its species, and
3) Its marking effected pursuant to sub-paragraph 19 (*b*).

b) The information specified in sub-paragraph (*a*) of this paragraph shall be entered immediately by a factory ship in a permanent record which shall be available at all times for examination by the whaling inspectors; and in addition there shall be entered in such permanent record the following information as soon as it becomes available:

1) Time of hauling up for treatment
2) Length, measures pursuant to paragraph 22
3) Sex
4) If female, whether lactating
5) Length and sex of foetus, if present, and
6) A full explanation of each infraction.

c) A record similar to that described in sub-paragraph (*b*) of this paragraph shall be maintained by land stations, and all of the information mentioned in the said sub-paragraph shall be entered therein as soon as available.

d) A record similar to that described in sub-paragraph (*b*) of this paragraph shall be maintained by "small-type whaling" operations conducted from shore or by pelagic fleets, and all of this information mentioned in the said sub-paragraph shall be entered therein as soon as available.

25. *a*) All whale catchers operating in conjunction with factory ships and land stations shall report the following information on each whale taken:

(i) Methods used to kill a whale, other than a harpoon, and in particular compressed air.
(ii) Number of whales struck but lost.

b) A record similar to that described in sub-paragraph (*a*) of this paragraph shall be maintained by vessels engaged in "small-type whaling" operations and by native peoples taking species listed in paragraph 1, and all the information mentioned in the said sub-paragraph shall be entered therein as soon as available.

26. *a*) Notification shall be given in accordance with the provision of Article VII of the Convention, within two days after the end of each calendar week, of data on the number of Bryde's and minke whales taken in any waters south of 40° South Latitude by all factory ships or whale catchers attached thereto under the jurisdiction of each Contracting Government, provided that when the number of each of these species taken is deemed by the Bureau of International Whaling Statistics to have reached 85 per cent of whatever total catch limit is imposed by the Commission notification shall be given as aforesaid at the end of each day of data on the number of each of these species taken.

b) If it appears that the maximum catches of whales permitted by paragraph 9 may be reached before 7th April of any year, the Bureau of International Whaling Statistics shall determine, on the basis of the data provided, the date on which the maximum catch of each of these species shall be deemed to have been reached and shall notify the master of each factory ship and each Contracting Government of that date not less than four days in advance thereof. The taking or attempting to take baleen whales, so notified, by factory ships or whale catchers attached thereto shall be illegal in any waters south of 40° South Latitude after midnight of the date so determined.

c) Notification shall be given in accordance with the provisions of Article VII of the Convention of each factory ship intending to engage in whaling operations in any waters south of 40° South Latitude.

27. Notification shall be given in accordance with the provisions of Article VII of the Convention with regard to all factory ships and land stations of statistical information

a) concerning the number of whales of each species taken, the number thereof lost, and the number treated at each factory ship or land station, and

b) as to the aggregate amounts of oil of each grade and quantities of meal, fertilizer (guano), and other products derived from them, together with

c) particulars with respect to each whale treated in the factory ship, land station or "small-type whaling" operations as to the date and approximate latitude and longitude of taking, the species and sex of the whale, its length and, if it contains a foetus, the length and sex, if ascertainable, of the foetus. The data referred to in (*a*) and (*c*) above shall be verified at the time of the tally and there shall also be notification to the Commission of any information which may be collected or obtained concerning the calving grounds and migration of whales.

28. Notification shall be given in accordance with the provisions of Article VII of the Convention with regard to all factory ships and catcher ships of the following statistical information:

a) The name and gross tonnage of each factory ship

b) For each catcher ship attached to a factory ship or land station

(i) the dates on which each is commissioned and ceases whaling for the season

(ii) the number of days on which each is at sea on the whaling grounds each season

(iii) where possible the time spent each day on different components of the catching operation.

(iv) the gross tonnage, horsepower, length and other characteristics of each; vessels used only as tow boats should be specified

(v) Any modifications of the above measures or data from other suitable indicators of fishing effort for "small-type whaling" operations.

c) A list of the land stations which were in operation during the period concerned, and the number of miles searched per day by aircraft, if any.

The information required under paragraph (*b*) (iii) to (*b*) (v) should be recorded in the log book format shown in Appendix A.

29. *a*) Where possible all factory ships and land stations shall collect from each whale taken and report on:

1) both ovaries or the combined weight of both testes.

2) at least one ear plug, or one tooth (preferably first mandibular).

b) Where possible similar collections to those described in sub-paragraph (*a*) of this paragraph shall be undertaken and reported by small-type whaling operations conducted from shore or by pelagic fleets.

c) All specimens collected under sub-paragraph (*a*) and (*b*) shall be properly labelled with the platform or other identification number of the whale and be appropriately preserved.

d) A Contracting Government shall arrange for analysis as soon as possible of the tissue samples and specimens collected under sub-paragraphs (*a*) and (*b*) and report on the results of such analyses.

30. A Contracting Government shall transmit to the Commission copies of all its official laws and regulations relating to whales and whaling and changes in such laws and regulations.

CONVENTION FOR THE ESTABLISHMENT OF AN INTER-AMERICAN TROPICAL TUNA COMMISSION [4]

Washington, 31 May 1949

The United States of America and the Republic of Costa Rica considering their mutual interest in maintaining the populations of yellowfin and skipjack tuna and of other kinds of fish taken by tuna fishing vessels in the eastern Pacific Ocean which by reason of continued use have come to be of common concern and desiring to co-operate in the gathering and interpretation of factual information to facilitate maintaining the populations of these fishes at a level which will permit maximum sustained catches year after year, have agreed to conclude a Convention for these purposes and to that end have named as their Plenipotentiaries:

who, having communicated to each other their full powers, found to be in good and due form, have agreed as follows:

Article I

1. The High Contracting Parties agree to establish and operate a joint Commission, to be known as the Inter-American Tropical Tuna Commission, hereinafter referred to as the Commission, which shall carry out the objectives of this Convention. The Commission shall be composed of national sections, each consisting of from one to four members, appointed by the Governments of the respective High Contracting Parties.

2. The Commission shall submit annually to the Government of each High Contracting Party a report on its investigations and findings, with appropriate recommendations, and shall also inform such Governments, whenever it is deemed advisable, on any matter relating to the objectives of this Convention.

3. Each High Contracting Party shall determine and pay the expenses incurred by its section. Joint expenses incurred by the Commission shall be paid by the High Contracting Parties through contributions in the form and proportion recommended by the Commission and approved by the High Contracting Parties. The proportion of joint expenses to be paid by each High Contracting Party shall be related to the proportion of the total catch from the fisheries covered by this Convention utilized by that High Contracting Party.

4. Both the general annual program of activities and the budget of joint expenses shall be recommended by the Commission and submitted for approval to the High Contracting Parties.

5. The Commission shall decide on the most convenient place or places for its headquarters.

6. The Commission shall meet at least once each year, and at such other times as may be requested by a national section. The date and place of first

meeting shall be determined by agreement between the High Contracting Parties.

7. At its first meeting the Commission shall select a chairman and a secretary from different national sections. The chairman and the secretary shall hold office for a period of one year. During succeeding years, selection of the chairman and the secretary from the national section shall be in such a manner that the chairman and the secretary will be of different nationalities, and as well provide each High Contracting Party in turn, with an opportunity to be represented in those offices.

8. Each national section shall have one vote. Decisions, resolutions, recommendations, and publications of the Commission shall be made only by a unanimous vote.

9. The Commission shall be entitled to adopt and to amend subsequently, as occasion may require, by-laws or rules for the conduct of its meetings.

10. The Commission shall be entitled to employ necessary personnel for the performance of its functions and duties.

11. Each High Contracting Party shall be entitled to establish an Advisory Committee for its section, to be composed of persons who shall be well informed concerning tuna fishery problems of common concern. Each such Advisory Committee shall be invited to attend the non-executive sessions of the Commission.

12. The Commission may hold public hearings. Each national section also may hold public hearings within its own country

13. The Commission shall designate a Director of Investigations who shall be technically competent and who shall be responsible to the Commission and may be freely removed by it. Subject to the instruction of the Commission and with its approval, the Director of Investigations shall have charge of:

a) the drafting of programs of investigations, and the preparation of budget estimates for the Commission;

b) authorizing the disbursement of the funds for the joint expenses of the Commission;

c) the accounting of the funds for the joint expenses of the Commission;

d) the appointment and immediate direction of technical and other personnel required for the functions of the Commission;

e) arrangements for the co-operation with other organizations or individuals in accordance with paragraph 16 of this Article;

f) the co-ordination of the work of the Commission with that of organizations and individuals whose co-operation has been arranged for;

g) the drafting of administrative, scientific and other reports for the Commission;

h) the performance of such other duties as the Commission may require.

14. The official languages of the Commission shall be English and Spanish, and members of the Commission may use either languages during meetings. When requested, translation shall be made to the other language. The minutes, official documents, and publications of the Commission shall be in both languages, but official correspondence of the Commission may be written, at the discretion of the secretary, in either language.

15. Each national section shall be entitled to obtain certified copies of any documents pertaining to the Commission except that the Comission will adopt and may amend subsequently rules to ensure the confidential character of records of statistics of individual catches and individual company operations.

16. In the performance of its duties and functions the Commission may request the technical and scientific services of, and information from, official agencies of the High Contracting Parties, and any international, public, or private institution or organization, or any private individual.

Article II

The Commission shall perform the following functions and duties:

1. Make investigations concerning the abundance, biology, biometry, and ecology of yellowfin (*Neothunnus*) and skipjack (*Kaisuwonus*) tuna in the waters of the eastern Pacific Ocean fished by the nationals of the High Contracting Parties, and the kinds of fishes commonly used as bait in the tuna fisheries, especially the anchovetta, and of other kinds of fish taken by tuna fishing vessels; and the effects of natural factors and human activities on the abundance of the populations of fishes supporting all these fisheries.

2. Collect and analyze information relating to current and past conditions and trends of the populations of fishes covered by this Convention.

3. Study and appraise information concerning methods and procedures for maintaining and increasing the populations of fishes covered by this Convention.

4. Conduct such fishing and other activities, on the high seas and in waters which are under the jurisdiction of the High Contracting Parties, as may be necessary to attain the end referred to in sub-paragraphs 1, 2, and 3 of this Article.

5. Recommend from time to time, on the basis of scientific investigations, proposals for joint action by the High Contracting Parties designed to keep the populations of fishes covered by this Convention at those levels of abundance which will permit the maximum sustained catch.

6. Collect statistics and all kinds of reports concerning catches and the operations of fishing boats, and other information concerning the fishing for fishes covered by this Convention, from vessels or persons engaged in these fisheries.

7. Publish or otherwise disseminate reports relative to the results of its findings and such other reports as fall within the scope of this Convention, as well as scientific, statistical, and other data

relating to the fisheries maintained by the nationals of the High Contracting Parties for the fishes covered by this Convention.

Article III

The High Contracting Parties agree to enact such legislation as may be necessary to carry out the purposes of this Convention.

Article IV

Nothing in this Convention shall be construed to modify any existing treaty or convention with regard to the fisheries of the eastern Pacific Ocean previously concluded by a High Contracting Party, nor to preclude a High Contracting Party from entering into treaties or conventions with other States regarding these fisheries, the terms of which are not incompatible with the present Convention.

Article V

1. The present Convention shall be ratified and the instruments of ratification shall be exchanged at Washington as soon as possible.

2. The present Convention shall enter into force on the date of exchange of ratifications.

3. Any government, whose nationals participate in the fisheries covered by this Convention, desiring to adhere to the present Convention, shall address a communication to that effect to each of the High Contracting Parties. Upon receiving the unanimous consent of the High Contracting Parties to adherence, such government shall deposit with the Government of the United States of America an instrument of adherence which shall stipulate the effective date thereof. The Government of the United States of America shall furnish a certified copy of the Convention to each government desiring to adhere thereto. Each adhering government shall have all the rights and obligations under the Convention as if it had been an original signatory thereof.

4. At any time after the expiration of ten years from the date of entry into force of this Convention any High Contracting Party may give notice of its intention of denouncing the Convention. Such notification shall become effective with respect to such notifying government one year after its receipt by the Government of the United States of America. After the expiration of the said one year period the Convention shall be effective only with respect to the remaining High Contracting Parties.

5. The Government of the United States of America shall inform the other High Contracting Parties of all instruments of adherence and of notifications of denunciation received.

In Witness Whereof the respective Plenipotentiaries have signed the present Convention.

Done at Washington, in duplicate, in the English and Spanish languages, both texts being equally authentic, this 31st day of May 1949.

EXCHANGE OF NOTES

I

The Costa Rican Appointed Ambassador to the Secretary of State

EMBASSY OF COSTA RICA
WASHINGTON

No. 1579 3 March 1950

Excellency:

I have the honor to refer to the Convention between the Republic of Costa Rica and the United States of America for the Establishment of an Inter-American Tropical Tuna Commission, signed at Washington, D.C., on 31 May 1949, which entered into force this day, and to inform Your Excellency of the desire of my Government to place on record the understanding of our two Governments with respect to the manner in which certain provisions of that Convention shall be applied. Accordingly, I take pleasure in informing you that, without prejudice to the provisions and purposes of the Convention under reference, the understanding of my Government in regard to this matter is that which I set forth to you as follows.

With respect to Article I, paragraph 3, of the Convention, which establishes the proportion of joint expenses to be paid by each High Contracting Party, it is understood that "the proportion of the total catch from the fisheries covered by this Convention utilized by that High Contracting Party" shall be the part of the total catch which is used for domestic consumption in the territory of that High Contracting Party or is the object of commercial transactions the financial benefits of which accrue entirely or in their major portion to individuals or firms whose proprietors or stockholders are domiciled in the territory of that High Contracting Party.

With respect to Article II, paragraph 4, of the Convention, it is understood that the Inter-American Tropical Tuna Commission is authorized to engage in fishing and other activities for scientific research exclusively and that no commercial ventures by the Commission are contemplated.

It is further understood that, notwithstanding the specific powers conferred upon the Commission, nothing in the Convention shall be interpreted as a relinquishment of or a limitation upon the sovereignty of a High Contracting Party over waters under its jurisdiction.

My Government also desires to state that it recognizes as the authentic Spanish text of the Convention that contained in the Convention as signed, but at the same time recognizes that certain of its provisions might have been worded more clearly in the following form:

Article I, paragraph 1.

"The High Contracting Parties agree to establish and maintain a Joint Commission to be known as the Inter-American Tropical Tuna Commission. which will hereinafter be called the Commission, which shall carry into effect the objectives of this

Convention. The Commission shall be made up of national sections, each of which shall include from one to four members appointed by the Governments of the respective High Contracting Parties."

Article I, paragraph 3.

"Each of the High Contracting Parties shall determine and pay the expenses incurred by its respective section. The joint expenses incurred by the Commission shall be covered by the High Contracting Parties through contributions in such form and proportion as the Commission may recommend and the High Contracting Parties may approve. The proportion of the joint expenses to be paid by each of the High Contracting Parties shall be in relation to the proportion of the total catch from the fisheries covered by this Convention utilized by that High Contracting Party."

Article I, paragraph 8.

"Each national section shall have the right to one vote. The decisions, resolutions, recommendations and publications of the Commission must be approved by a unanimous vote."

Article IV.

"Nothing in the Convention shall be interpreted as changing any existing treaty or convention relating to the fisheries of the Eastern Pacific previously signed by one of the High Contracting Parties, nor as preventing a High Contracting Party from entering into treaties or conventions with other States relating to such fisheries, provided their terms are not incompatible with this Convention."

I avail myself of this opportunity to express to Your Excellency my highest consideration.

Mario Echandi

His Excellency Dean Acheson
Secretary of State
Washington, D.C.

II

The Secretary of State to the Costa Rican Appointed Ambassador

DEPARTMENT OF STATE
WASHINGTON

March 3, 1950

Excellency:

I have the honor to refer to your note No. 1579 of March 3, 1950 regarding the Convention between the United States of America and the Republic of Costa Rica for the Establishment of an Inter-American Tropical Tuna Commission, signed at Washington May 31 1949, which entered into force this day, and the desire of your Government to place on record the understanding of our Governments with respect to the manner in which certain provisions of that Convention shall be applied. Accordingly, I take pleasure in informing you that, without prejudice to the provisions or purposes of the Convention under reference, my Government concurs in the understanding set forth in your note as follows:

(See note I, second, third and fourth paragraphs)

My Government has also taken note of your statement that certain provisions of the Spanish text might have been more clearly expressed but that your Government recognizes that the authentic Spanish text of the Convention is that contained in the Convention as signed.

Accept, Excellency, the renewed assurances of my highest consideration.

Dean Acheson

His Excellency Senor Don Mario Echandi
Appointed Ambassador of Costa Rica

AGREEMENT FOR THE ESTABLISHMENT OF A GENERAL FISHERIES COUNCIL FOR THE MEDITERRANEAN

[5]

Rome, 24 September 1949

AMENDMENTS TO THE ABOVE-MENTIONED AGREEMENT ADOPTED ON 22 MAY 1963 BY THE GENERAL FISHERIES COUNCIL FOR THE MEDITERRANEAN AT ITS FIRST SPECIAL SESSION, HELD AT ROME, 21-22 MAY 1963, AND APPROVED ON 3 DECEMBER 1963 BY RESOLUTION No. 39/63 OF THE TWELFTH SESSION OF THE CONFERENCE OF THE FOOD AND AGRICULTURE ORGANIZATION FROM 16 NOVEMBER TO 5 DECEMBER 1963*

AGREEMENT FOR THE ESTABLISHMENT OF A GENERAL FISHERIES COUNCIL FOR THE MEDITERRANEAN

(As amended by the First Special Session of the Council, Rome, 21-22 May 1963)

PREAMBLE

The [Governments of France, Greece, Italy, Lebanon, Turkey, the United Kingdom, Yugoslavia, Members of the Food and Agriculture Organization of the United Nation] *Contracting Governments* having a mutual interest in the development and proper utilization of the resources of the Mediterranean and contiguous waters, and desiring to further the attainment of their objectives through international co-operation which would be furthered by the establishment of a General Fisheries Council for the Mediterranean, agree as follows:

Article I

THE COUNCIL

1. [The contracting Governments agree to] *Contracting Governments hereby establish within the framework of the Food and Agriculture Organization of the United Nations (hereinafter referred to as "the Organization")* a Council to be known as the General Fisheries Council for the Mediterranean, (hereinafter referred to as "the Council"), for the purpose of exercising the functions and discharging the responsibilities set forth in Article [III] *IV* below.

2. The Members of the Council shall be [the Governments] *such Member Nations and Associate Members of the Organization and such non-member Nations of the Organization that are Members of the United Nations, which accept this Agreement in accordance with the provisions of Article [VIII] IX below, it being understood that these provisions shall not affect the membership status in the Council of such nations that are not Members of the United Nations as may have become parties to this Agreement prior to 22 May 1963. As regards Associate Members, this Agreement shall, in accordance with the provisions of Article XIV-5 of the Consitution and Rule XXI-3 of the General Rules of the Organization, be submitted by the Organization to the authority having responsibility for the international relations of such Associate Members.*

Article II

ORGANIZATION

1. Each Member [Governments] shall be represented at sessions of the Council by one delegate, who may be accompanied by an alternate and by experts and advisers. Participation in meetings of the Council by alternates, experts, and advisers shall not entail the right to vote, except in the case of an alternate who is acting in the place of a delegate during his absence.

2. Each Member [Governments] shall have one vote. Decisions of the Council shall be taken by a [simple] majority of the votes cast, except as otherwise provided by this Agreement. A majority of the total membership of the Council shall constitute a quorum.

3. The Council shall elect a Chairman and two Vice-Chairmen.

[4. The Council shall determine the frequency, dates, and place of its sessions, from such committees as it deems desirable, and establish rules governing its procedure.]

[5. The Chairman shall call a session of the Council at least once a year, unless directed otherwise by a majority of the Member Governments. The initial session shall be called by the Food and Agriculture Organization of the United Nations within six months after the entry into force of this Agreement and at such place as it may designate.]

4. The Chairman of the Council shall normally convene a regular session of the Council at least once every two years unless otherwise directed by a majority of the Members. The site and date of all sessions shall be determined by the Council in consultation with the Director-General of the Organization.

[6.]5. The seat of the Council shall be at the [seat of the European Regional Office of the Food and Agriculture Organization of the United Nations now at] Headquarters of the Organization in Rome [Italy].

[7.]6. The [Food and Agriculture Organization of the United Nations] shall provide the Secretariat for the Council [.] *and the Director-General shall appoint its Secretary, who shall be administratively responsible to him.*

7. The Council may, by a two-thirds majority of its membership, adopt and amend its own Rules of Procedure which shall be consistent with the General Rules of the Organization. The Rules of the Council and any amendments thereto shall come into force as from the date of approval by the Director-General of

* The text printed herein shows the changes resulting from the above-mentioned amendments as follows: the words which have been added are italicized and the words which have been deleted are reproduced in brackets.

the Organization, subject to confirmation by the Council of the Organization

Article III

COMMITTEES, WORKING PARTIES AND SPECIALISTS

1. The Council may establish temporary, special or standing committees to study and report on matters pertaining to the purposes of the Council and working parties to study and recommend on specific technical problems.

2. The committees and working parties referred to in paragraph 1 above shall be convened by the Chairman of the Council at such times and places as are determined by the Chairman in consultation with the Director-General of the Organization.

3. The Council may suggest to the Organization the recruitment or appointment of specialists at the expense of the Organization, for the consideration of specific questions or problems.

4. The establishment of committees and working parties referred to in paragraph 1 above and the recruitment or appointment of specialists referred to in paragraph 3 above, shall be subject to the availability of the necessary funds in the relevant chapter of the approved budget of the Organization; the determination of such availability shall be made by the Director-General of the Organization. Before taking any decision involving expenditures in connection with the establishment of committees and working parties and the recruitment or appointment of specialists, the Council shall have before it a report from the Director-General of the Organization on the administrative and financial implications thereof.

Article [III] IV

FUNCTIONS

The Council shall have the following functions and responsibilities:

a) To formulate all oceanographical and technical aspects of the problems of development and proper utilization of aquatic resources.

b) To encourage and co-ordinate research and the application of improved methods employed in fishery and allied industries with a view to the utilization of aquatic resources;

c) To assemble, publish, or [otherwise] disseminate all oceanographical and technical information relating to aquatic resources;

d) To recommend to Members [Governments] such national and international research and development projects as may appear necessary or desirable to fill gaps in such knowledge;

e) To undertake, where appropriate, co-operative research and development projects directed to this end;

f) To propose, and where necessary to adopt, measures to bring about the standardization of scientific equipment, techniques, and nomenclature;

g) To make comparative studies of [the] fishery legislation [of different countries] with a view to making recommendations to its Members [Governments] respecting the greatest possible co-ordination;

h) To encourage research into the hygiene and prevention of occupational diseases of fishermen;

i) To extend its good offices in assisting Member(s) [Governments] to secure essential materials and equipment;

j) To report upon such questions relating to all oceanographical and technical problems as may be recommended to it by Members [Governments] or by the [Food and Agriculture] Organization [of the United Nations] and, if it thinks proper to do so, by other international, national, or private organizations with related interests;

[To report annually upon its activities to Member Governments and to the Conference of the Food and Agriculture Organization of the United Nations; and to make such other reports to the Food and Agriculture Organization of the United Nations on matters falling within the competence of the Council as may seem to it necessary and desirable.]

k) ***To transmit, every two years, to the Director-General of the Organization, a report embodying its views, recommendations and decisions, and make such other reports to the Director-General of the Organization as may seem to it necessary or desirable. Reports of the committees and working parties of the Council provided for in Article III of this Agreeemnt shall be transmitted to the Director-General of the Organization through the Council.***

Article [IV] V

[AREA] REGION

The Council shall carry out the functions and responsibilities set forth in Article [III] IV in the [Mediterranean waters as they are geographically described. If, however, the Council contemplates studies outside this area, it shall make the necessary arrangements with the governments and organizations concerned, in conformity with paragraph (*j*) of Article III] region as referred to in the Preamble.

Article [V] VI

CO-OPERATION WITH INTERNATIONAL ORGANIZATIONS

[1.] The Council shall co-operate closely with other international organizations in matters of mutual interest.

[2. The Council shall, if it so deems opportune and useful, entrust to the international bodies referred to above, those responsibilities set forth in Article III which are of a scientific nature.]

Article [VI] VII

EXPENSES

1. The expenses of delegates and their alternates, experts and advisers occasioned by attendance at [meetings] *sessions* of Council *and the expenses of*

representatives sent to committees or working parties established in accordance with Article III of this Agreement shall be determined and paid by their respective governments.

2. The expenses of the Secretariat, including publications and communications and the expenses incurred by the Chairman and Vice-Chairman of the Council when performing duties on behalf of the Council between Council sessions, shall be determined and paid by the [Food and Agriculture] Organization [of the United Nations] ***within the limits of [an annual budget prepared*** and approved in accordance with the current regulations of that Organization] *the relevant appropriations provided for in the budget of the Organization.*

3. The expenses of research and development projects undertaken by individual Members of the Council, whether independently or upon recommendation of the Council, shall be determined and paid by the governments concerned.

4. The expenses incurred in connection with co-operative research or development projects undertaken in accordance with the provisions of Article [III] *IV*, paragraphs (*d*) and (*e*) unless otherwise available shall be determined and paid by the Members [Governments] in the form and proportion to which they shall mutually agree. *Co-operative projects shall be submitted to the Council of the Organization prior to implementation.* ***Contributions for co-operative projects shall be paid into a trust fund to be established by the*** *Organization and shall be administered by the Organization in accordance with the Financial Regulations and rules of the Organization.*

5. The expenses of experts invited, with the concurrence of the Director-General, to attend meetings of the Council, committees or working parties in their individual capacity shall be borne by the budget of the Organization.

Article [VII] VIII

AMENDMENTS

[Any amendment to this Agreement shall require the approval of a two-thirds majority of all the Members of the Council. An exception to this rule is made in the following cases:

a) Amendments to this Agreement enlarging the functions of the Council require the approval of the Conference of the Food and Agriculture Organization of the United Nations in addition to approval by a two-thirds majority of all the Members of the Council;

b) Amendments to the Agreement enlarging the powers of the Council to incur expenses to be borne by the Food and Agriculture Organization of the United Nations, shall require the approval of a two-thirds majority of all the Members of the Council and of the District-General of the Food and Agriculture Organization of the United Nations.]

The General Fisheries Council for the Mediterranean may amend this Agreement by a two- *thirds majority of all the Members of this Council, any amendment becoming effective only after concurrence of the Council of the Organization unless the latter considers it desirable to refer the amendment to the Conference of the Organization for approval. An amendment shall become effective as from the date of the decision of the Council or Conference of the Organization, as appropriate. However, any amendment involving new obligations for Members shall come into force with respect to each Member only on acceptance of it by that Member. The instruments of acceptance of amendments involving new obligations shall be deposited with the Director-General of the Organization who shall inform all the Members of the General Fisheries Council for the Mediterranean, as well as the Secretary-General of the United Nations, of the receipt of acceptances and the entry into force of such amendments. The rights and obligations of any member of the General Fisheries Council for the Mediterranean that has not accepted an amendment involving additional* ***obligations shall continue to be governed by the provisions of this Agreement as they stood prior to the amendment.***

Article [VIII] IX

ACCEPTANCE

1. This Agreement shall be open to acceptance by [Governments which are Members of the Food and Agriculture Organization of the United Nations] *Member Nations or Associate Members of the Organization.*

[2. This Agreement shall also be open to acceptance by governments which are not members of the Food and Agriculture Organization of the United Nations with the approval of its Conference and of two-thirds of the Members of the Council. Participation by such governments in the activities of the Council shall be contingent upon the assumption of a proportionate share in the expenses of the Secretariat, as determined by the Council and approved by the Conference of the Food and Agriculture Organization.]

2. The Council may, by a two-thirds majority of its membership, admit to membership such other nations that are Members of the United Nations as have submitted an application for membership and a declaration made in a formal instrument that they accept this Agreement as in force at the time of admission.

[3. The notifications of acceptance of this Agreement shall be deposited with the Director-General of the Food and Agriculture Organization of the United Nations, who shall immediately inform all the governments concerned of their receipt.]

3. Participation in the activities of the Council by Members of the Council which are not Members or Associate Members of the Organization shall be contingent upon the assumption of such proportionate share in the expenses of the Secretariat as may be determined in the light of the

relevant provisions of the Financial Regulations of the Organization.

4. Acceptance of this Agreement by any Member Nation or Associate Member of the Organization shall be effected by the deposit of an instrument of acceptance with the Director-General of the Organization and shall take effect on receipt of such instrument by the Director-General.

5. Acceptance of this Agreement by non-member nations of the Organization shall be effected by the deposit of an instrument of acceptance with the Director-General of the Organization. Membership shall become effective on the date on which the Council approves the application for membership, in conformity with the provisions of paragraph 2 of this Article.

6. The Director-General of the Organization shall inform all Members of the Council, all Member Nations of the Organization and the Secretary-General of the United Nations of all acceptances that have become effective.

7. Acceptance of this Agreement may be made subject to reservations which shall become effective only upon unanimous approval by the Members of the Council. The Director-General of the Organization shall notify forthwith all Members of the Council of any reservations. Members of the Council not having replied within three months from the date of the notification shall be deemed to have accepted the reservation. Failing such approval, the Nation making the reservation shall not become a party to this Agreement.

Article [IX] X

ENTRY INTO FORCE

[1.] This Agreement shall enter into force as from the date of receipt of the fifth [notification] *instrument* of acceptance.

[2. Notifications of acceptance received after the entry into force of this Agreement shall take effect on the date of their receipt by the Director-General of the Food and Agriculture Organization of the United Nations who shall immediately inform all the governments concerned and the Council of their receipt.]

Article XI

TERRITORIAL APPLICATION

The Members of the Council shall, when accepting this Agreement, state explicitly to which territories their participation shall extend. In the absence of such a declaration, participation shall be deemed to apply to all the territories for the international relations of which the Member is responsible. Subject to the provisions of Article XII below, the scope of the territorial application may be modified by a subsequent declaration.

Article [X] XII

WITHDRAWAL

1. Any Member Government may [denounce] *withdraw from* this Agreement *at any time* after the expiration of two years from the date upon which the Agreement entered into force with respect to that [Government] *Member*, by giving written notice of its withdrawal to the Director-General of the [Food and Agriculture] Organization [of the United Nations] who shall immediately inform all the [governments concerned and] *Members of* the Council *and the Member Nations of the Organization* of such withdrawal. Notice of withdrawal shall become effective three months from the date of its receipt by the Director-General.

2. A Member of the Council may give notice of withdrawal with respect to one or more of the territories for the international relations of which it is responsible. When a Member gives notice of its own withdrawal from the Council it shall state to which territory or territories the withdrawal is to apply. In the absence of such a declaration, the withdrawal shall be deemed to apply to all the territories for the international relations of which the Member of the Council is responsible, with the exception of Associate Members.

3. Any Member of the Council that gives notice of withdrawal from the Organization shall be deemed to have simultaneously withdrawn from the Council, and this withdrawal shall be deemed to apply to all the territories for the international relations of which the Member concerned is responsible, except that such withdrawal shall not be deemed to apply to an Associate Member.

Article XIII

INTERPRETATION AND SETTLEMENT OF DISPUTES

Any disputes regarding the interpretation or application of this Agreement, if not settled by the Council, shall be referred to a committee composed of one member appointed by each of the parties to the dispute, and in addition an independent chairman chosen by the members of the committee. The recommendations of such a committee, while not binding in character, shall become the basis for renewed consideration by the parties concerned of the matter out of which the disagreement arose. If as the result of this procedure the dispute is not settled, it shall be referred to the International Council of Justice in accordance with the Status of the Court, unless the parties to the dispute agree to another method of settlement.

Article XIV

TERMINATION

This Agreement shall be automatically terminated if and when as the result of withdrawals, the number of Members of the Council drops below five, unless the remaining Members unanimously decide otherwise.

Article XV

CERTIFICATION AND REGISTRATION

The text of this Agreement was originally formulated at Rome on the 24th day of September one thousand nine hundred and forty-nine in the

French language. Two copies in the English, French and Spanish languages of this Agreement as amended on the 22nd day of May one thousand nine hundred and sixty-three by the First Special Session of the General Fisheries Council for the Mediterranean, shall after approval by the Council or Conference of the Organization, as appropriate, be certified by the Chairman of the Conference or Council of the Organization and by the Director-General of the Organization. The other copy shall be transmitted to the Secretary-General of the United Nations for registration. In addition, the Director-General shall certify copies of this Agreement and transmit one copy to each Member Nation of the Organization and to such non-member Nations of the Organization that have or may become parties to this Agreement.

[Drafted at Rome this twenty-fourth day of September one thousand nine hundred and forty-nine, in the French language, in a single copy which shall be deposited in the archives of the Food and Agriculture Organization of the United Nations, which shall furnish certified copies thereof to the Member Governments of the Food and Agriculture Organization of the United Nations.]

INTERNATIONAL CONVENTION FOR THE PROTECTION OF BIRDS [6]

Paris, 18 October 1950

The Governments signatory to this Convention,

Realizing the danger of extermination which threatens certain species of birds and concerned about the numerical decrease in other species, particularly migratory species; and

Considering that, in the interests of science, the protection of nature and the economy of each nation, all birds should as a matter of principle be protected;

Have recognized the need to amend the International Convention for the Protection of Birds useful to Agriculture, signed in Paris on 19 March 1902, and have agreed on the following provisions:

Article 1

The purpose of this Convention is to protect birds in the wild state.

Article 2

With the exceptions specified in articles, 6 and 7 of this Convention, protection shall be given:

a) to all birds, at least during their breeding season, and to migrants, during their return flight to their nesting ground, particularly in March, April, May, June and July;

b) to species which are in danger of extinction or are of scientific interest. throughout the year.

Article 3

With the exceptions specified in articles 6 and 7 of this Convention, the import, export, transport, sale, offer for sale, giving or possession of any live or dead bird or any part of a bird killed or captured in contravention of the provisions of this Convention, during the season in which the species concerned is protected, shall be prohibited.

Article 4

With the exceptions specified in articles 6 and 7 of this Convention, the removal or destruction of nests under construction or in use and the taking or damaging, transport, import or export, sale, offer for sale, purchase or destruction of eggs or their shells or broods of young birds in the wild state, during the season in which a particular species is protected and particularly during its breeding season, shall be prohibited.

Nevertheless, these prohibitions shall not apply, on the one hand, to eggs lawfully collected and accompanied by a certificate establishing either that they are to be used for propagating or scientific purposes or that they come from captive birds and, on the other hand, to lapwing eggs, solely in the case of the Netherlands, where exceptional local conditions have already been recognized.

Article 5

With the exceptions specified in articles 6 and 7

of this Convention, the High Contracting Parties undertake to prohibit the methods enumerated below as being of such a nature as to result in the mass killing or capture of birds or to cause them unneccessary suffering.

However, in countries where such methods are at present permitted by law, the High Contracting Parties undertake gradually to introduce into their legislation measures designed to prohibit or restrict their use:

a) snares, bird-line, traps, hooks, nets, poisoned bait, stupefying agents, blinded decoy-birds,

b) decoy-ponds with nets,

c) mirrors, torches, and other artificial lights,

d) fishing nets or tackle for the capture of aquatic birds,

e) magazine or automatic sporting-guns holding more than two cartridges,

f) in general, all firearms, other than shoulder arms,

g) the pursuit and shooting of birds from motorboats, in inland waters and, from 1 March to 1 October, in territorial and off-shore waters,

h) the use of motor vehicles or air-borne machines to shoot or drive birds,

i) the offering of rewards for the capture or killing of birds,

j) the right of unrestricted shooting and netting shall be regulated throughout the year and suspended during the breeding season on the sea and along the banks and coasts,

k) all other methods designed for the mass capture or killing of birds.

Article 6

If, in a particular region, one species is found to be jeopardizing the future of certain agricultural or animal products by damaging fields, vineyards, gardens, orchards, woods, game or fish or threatening to destroy or simply diminish one or more species whose conservation is desirable, the appropriate authorities may issue individual permits, lifting the prohibitions established in articles 2 and 5 in the case of that species. It shall, however, be unlawful to purchase or sell birds killed in this manner or to transport them outside the region where they were killed.

If national laws contain other provisions designed to reduce the damage caused by certain species of birds in such a way as to assure the perpetuation of those species, such provisions may be maintained by the High Contracting Parties.

In view of the special importance of economic conditions in Sweden, Norway, Finland and the Faroe Islands, the appropriate authorities in those countries may make exceptions and permit certain derogations from the provisions of this Convention. If Iceland should accede to this Convention, it shall be entitled to enjoy the benefit of such derogations upon request.

No measures shall be adopted in any country of such a nature as to cause the complete destruction of the indigenous or migratory species referred to in this article.

Article 7

Exceptions to the provisions of this Convention may be permitted by the appropriate authorities in the interests of science and education, the propagation and breeding of game birds and falconry, depending on the circumstances and provided that all necessary precautions are taken to prevent abuses. The provisions concerning transport contained in articles 3 and 4 shall not apply to the United Kingdom.

In each country, the prohibitions enumerated in article 3 shall not apply to the plumage of species of birds which may be killed there.

Article 8

Each Contracting Party undertakes to prepare a list of birds which may lawfully be killed or captured in its own territory, subject to compliance with the conditions laid down in this Convention.

Article 9

Each Contracting Party shall have the right to draw up a list of species of indigenous and migratory birds which may be kept in captivity by individuals and shall establish the permissible methods of capture and the conditions in which birds may be transported or kept in captivity.

Each Contracting Party shall regulate trade in the birds protected by this Convention and take all necessary measures to limit the expansion of such trade.

Article 10

The High Contracting Parties undertake to consider and adopt measures to prevent the destruction of birds by hydrocarbons and other causes of water pollution, by lighthouses, electric cables, insecticides or poisons or by any other means. They shall endeavour to educate children and the public in order to convince them of the need to preserve and protect birds.

Article 11

In order to alleviate the consequences of the rapid disappearance of suitable breeding grounds for birds as a result of human intervention, the High Contracting Parties undertake to encourage and promote immediately, by every possible means, the creation of water or land reserves of suitable size and location where birds can nest and raise their bodies safely and where migratory birds can also rest and find their food undisturbed.

This Convention shall be ratified and the instruments of ratification shall be deposited with the Ministry of Foreign Affairs of the French Republic, which shall notify their receipt to all States that have signed and acceded to the Convention.

Any State not a signatory to this Convention may accede thereto. Accessions shall be notified to the Ministry of Foreign Affairs of the French

Republic, which shall inform all the States that have signed and acceded to the Convention accordingly.

This Convention shall enter into force on the ninetieth day following the date of deposit of the sixth instrument of ratification or accession. For each State ratifying or acceding to the Convention after that date, it shall enter into force on the ninetieth day following the date of deposit by that State of its instrument of ratification or accession.

This Convention shall supersede, between the countries which ratify or accede to it, the provisions of the 1902 International Convention.

In Witness Whereof, the undersigned, duly authorized by their respective Governments, have signed this Convention.

Done at Paris, on 18 October 1950.

CONVENTION FOR THE ESTABLISHMENT OF THE EUROPEAN AND MEDITERRANEAN PLANT PROTECTION ORGANIZATION [7]

of 18 April 1951, as amended by the Council on 27 April 1955

Paris, 27 April 1955

The Governments parties to the present Convention, being conscious of the importance of international co-operation in the prevention of the introduction and spread of pests and disease of plants and plant products, and desiring to continue and extend the work formerly done in this field by the International Committee for the Control of the Colorado Beetle and by the European Working Party or Infestation Control, have agreed as follows:

Article I

ORGANIZATION

There shall be established a European and Mediterranean Plant Protection Organization (hereinafter referred to as the Organization), which takes over the assets and liabilities of the above-mentioned Committee and Working Party.

Article II

DEFINITION

For the purpose of the present Convention the term "plants and plant products" means "living plants and parts of plants, unmanufactured materials of plant origin, and food products milled from plants and parts of plants".

Article III

MEMBERSHIP

a) Membership of the Organization shall be open to the following by adherence to the present Convention according to the provisions of Article XX:

1. the Governments of the countries in Schedule III.

2. the Government of any other country which the Council of the Organization may decide to invite to become a member.

b) The Government of any territory about which a declaration has been made under the terms of Article XXI may be admitted to membership by the Council of the Organization, but only on the proposal of the Member who made the declaration. Any such decision shall require a two-thirds majority of the votes cast. Territories so admitted shall be such as can in the opinion of the Council make a definite and individual contribution to the work of the Organization.

Article IV

SEAT

a) The seat of the Organization shall be in Paris.

b) Meetings of the Organization shall normally take place at its seat.

Article V

FUNCTIONS

a) The functions of the Organization shall be:

1) to act, in agreement with the Food and Agriculture Organization of the United Nations, as a recognised regional plant protection organisation under Article VIII of the International Plant Protection Convention of 6 December 1951;

2) to advise Member Governments on the technical, administrative and legislative measures necessary to prevent the introduction and spread of pests and diseases of plants and plant products;

3) to assist Member Governments where necessary in carrying out such measures;

4) where practicable, to co-ordinate and stimulate international campaigns against pests and diseases of plants and plant products;

5) to obtain information from Member Governments on the existence, outbreak and spread of pests and diseases of plants and plant products, and convey such information to Member Governments;

6) to provide for the exchange of information on national phytosanitary legislation, or other measures affecting the free movements of plants and plant products;

7) to study the possibility of simplification and unification of phytosanitary regulations and certificates;

8) to facilitate co-operation in research on the pests and diseases of plants and plant products and the methods of control and in the exchange of relevant scientific information;

9) to establish a documentation service and publish in an appropriate form material for publicity purposes or for technical or scientific advancement as may be determined by the Organization;

10) to make recommendations to Member Governments or any of the matters referred to in this Article;

11) generally to take all necessary and appropriate action to achieve the purposes of the Organization.

b) The functions of the Organization shall be related principally but not exclusively to the pests and diseases specified in Schedule II.

Article VI

OBLIGATIONS OF MEMBER GOVERNMENTS

Member Governments shall furnish to the Organization so far as is practicable such information as the Organization may reasonably require in order to carry out its functions.

Article VII

RELATIONSHIP WITH OTHER ORGANIZATIONS

The Organization shall co-operate with the Food and Agriculture Organization of the United Nations and with other bodies with related responsibilities and shall use its best endeavours to prevent overlapping of activities.

Article VIII

STRUCTURE OF THE ORGANIZATION

The Organization shall consist of:

a) the Council;

b) the administration, comprising the Executive Committee, the Director-General and the staff;

c) the Accounts Veritification Panel;

d) the technical bodies (working parties and international conferences).

Article IX

THE COUNCIL

a) The Council of the Organization shall consist of representatives of Member Governments.

Each Member Government shall be entitled to appoint one representative to the Council and one alternate.

Representatives and alternates appointed by Member Governments may be accompanied by associates and advisers.

b) Each Member Government shall have one vote in the Council.

Article X

SESSIONS OF THE COUNCIL

a) The Council shall ordinarily meet in regular session once in each year.

b) Extraordinary sessions of the Council shall be called at any time when the Chairman is so requested in writing by at least one third of the Member Governments.

Article XI

RULES

The Council shall establish its Rules of Procedure and the financial Rules of the Organization.

Article XII

OBSERVERS

With the consent of the Council, any non-member Government and any international body whose responsibilities are related to those of the Organization may be represented at any session of the Council by one or more observers without the right to vote.

Article XIII

FUNCTIONS OF THE COUNCIL

The Council shall:

a) consider and decide upon the progress report of the Director-General on the work of the Organization since the preceding regular session of the Council;

b) consider and approve the policies and programme of activity of the Organization;

c) consider and approve the budget;

d) consider and approve the annual accounts and balance-sheet;

e) set up the *ad hoc* or permanent technical bodies;

f) consider and decide upon the reports of such technical bodies;

g) hold the statutory elections;

h) appoint the Director-General on such terms as it may determine;

i) decide upon any proposals submitted by the Executive Committee.

Article XIV

THE CHAIRMAN AND VICE-CHAIRMAN

a) The Council shall elect a Chairman and a Vice-Chairman from amongst representatives of Member Governments serving on the Executive Committee.

b) The Chairman and Vice-Chairman shall be elected for three years or the remainder of their current term on the Executive Committee (whichever is the shorter) and be eligible for re-election if that term should be renewed.

c) The Chairman and Vice-Chairman shall serve in the same capacity within both the Council and the Executive Committee.

Article XV

THE EXECUTIVE COMMITTEE

a) The Executive Committee shall be composed of the Chairman and Vice-Chairman and of seven other representatives of Member Governments elected by the Council.

b) Members of the Executive Committee shall normally hold office for three years and be eligible for re-election.

c) If a vacancy occurs in the Executive Committee before the expiration of the term of appointment, the Executive Committee shall ask a Member Government to appoint a representative to fill the vacancy for the remainder of the term.

d) The Executive Committee shall meet at least twice a year.

Article XVI

FUNCTIONS OF THE EXECUTIVE COMMITTEE

The Executive Committee shall:

a) submit proposal for the Organization's policies and programme of activity to the Council;

b) ensure that the activity of the Organization conforms with the decisions of the Council;

c) submit the draft budget and the annual accounts and the balance-sheet to the Council; the Executive Committee may approve a provisional budget pending its consideration by the Council;

d) undertake such other tasks as may be assigned to it under this Convention or entrusted to it by the Council;

e) adopt its own procedure.

Article XVII

THE DIRECTOR-GENERAL

The Director-General shall:

a) be the head of the secretariat of the Organization, which functions under his responsibility;

b) carry out the programme approved by the Council and such task as may be entrusted to him by the Executive Committee;

c) report at each regular session of the Council on the activity of the Organization and the financial position.

Article XVIII

FINANCE

a) The expenditure of the Organization shall be met by annual contributions from Member Governments according to the scale specified in Schedule 1, and by such other receipts as may be approved by the Council or the Executive Committee.

b) Each Member Government shall determine the amount of its contribution, which shall be in accordance with the provisions of the foregoing paragraph save in exceptional cases approved by the Council.

c) Annual contributions shall be payable at the beginning of the Organization's financial year.

d) The contributions of Member Governments shall be paid in currencies to be determined by the Executive Committee with the approval of the contributing Governments concerned.

e) Supplementary contributions may be paid by an individual Government or group of Governments towards special schemes or campaigns of control, which the Organization may carry out in the interest of that Government or group of Governments.

f) An Accounts Verification Panel composed of representatives of three Member Governments elected by the Council for three years shall each year examine the accounts and the management of the Organization. The Panel shall report to the Council. The Executive Committee may appoint chartered accountants to audit the accounts of the Organization.

Article XIX

AMENDMENTS

a) Texts of proposed amendments to the present Convention and to Schedules I and II thereto shall be communicated by the Director-General to Member Governments at least three months in advance of their consideration by the Council.

b) Amendments to the Convention shall come into effect when adopted by a two thirds majority of the members of the Council present and voting, provided that amendments involving new obligations for Member Governments shall come into force in respect of each such Government only on acceptance by it.

c) Amendments to Schedules I and II shall be made by a majority of members present and voting.

d) Acceptance of amendments shall be deposited with the French Government who shall inform all Member Governments of the receipt of acceptance and the entry into force of amendments.

Article XX

SIGNATURE AND ACCEPTANCE

a) The present Convention shall remain open for signature or acceptance and Governments to which membership of the Organization is open by virtue of the provisions of Article III may become parties to the Convention by:

1) Signature;
2) Signature subject to ratification;
4) Acceptance.

b) Acceptance shall be effected by the deposit of an instrument with the French Government.

c) The French Government shall immediately inform all Governments of the date on which each has signed or accepted the Convention.

Article XXI

TERRITORIAL APPLICATION

a) Any Government may at any time declare that its participation in the Convention includes all or any of the territories for whose international relations it is responsible. Such declaration shall be deposited with the French Government.

b) Any declaration made by a Government under the preceding paragraph shall take effect on the thirtieth day following its receipt by the French Government.

c) The French Government shall immediately inform all Governments parties to the Convention of declarations made under this Article.

Article XXII

WITHDRAWAL

a) Any Member Government may at any time after two years of membership withdraw from this Convention by giving written notice of withdrawal to the French Government. The withdrawal shall take effect one year from the date of receipt of the notification.

b) The non-payment of two consecutive annual contributions shall under normal conditions imply the withdrawal from the Convention of the defaulting Member Government.

c) The application of the Convention to a territory or territories under Article XXI may be terminated by written notificaion to the French Government by the participating Government responsible for the international relations of such territory or territories. The notification shall take effect a year from the date of its receipt.

d) The French Government shall immediately inform all participating Governments of notification given under this Article.

Article XXIII

ENTRY INTO FORCE

a) The present Convention shall enter into force on the date on which five Governments have become parties thereto in accordance with the provisions of Article XX.

b) The French Government shall immediately inform all Governments which have signed or accepted the Convention of the date of entry into force of the Convention.

In faith whereof the undersigned, duly authorised by their Governments, have signed the present Convention and Schedules thereto.

Done in Paris this 18th day of April 1951 in a single copy, which will remain deposited in the archives of the French Government.

SCHEDULES

PESTS AND DISEASES TO BE GIVEN SPECIAL ATTENTION BY THE ORGANIZATION

with the dates of their inclusion in the Schedule (see Article V (b))

1.	Colorado beetle (*Leptinotarsa decemlineata*)	1951
2.	Potato root eelworm (*Heterodera rostochiensis*)	1951
3.	San Jose scale (*Aspidiotus perniciosus*)	1951
4.	Potato wart disease (*Synchytrium endobioticum*)	1951
5.	Insect, fungus and rodent pests of stored foods, and rodent pests of crops (*hitherto the concern of the European Working Party on Infestation Control*)	1951
6.	Fall webworm (*Hyphantria cunea*)	1952

INTERNATIONAL PLANT PROTECTION CONVENTION [8]

Rome, 6 December 1951

PREAMBLE

The contracting Governments, recognizing the usefulness of international co-operation in controlling pests and diseases of plants and plant products and in preventing their introduction and spread across national boundaries, and desiring to ensure close co-ordination of measures directed to these ends, have agreed as follows:

Article I

PURPOSE AND RESPONSIBILITY

1. With the purpose of securing common and effective action to prevent the introduction and spread of pests and diseases of plants and plant products and to promote measures for their control, the contracting Governments undertake to adopt the legislative, technical and administrative measures specified in this Convention and in supplementary agreements pursuant to Article III.

2. Each contracting Government shall assume responsibility for the fulfilment within its territories of all requirements under this Convention.

Article II

SCOPE

1. For the purposes of this Convention the term "plant" shall comprise living plants and parts thereof, including seeds in so far as the supervision of their importation under Article VI of the Convention or the issue of phytosanitary certificates in respect of them under Articles IV(1), (*a*) (iv) and V of this Convention may be deemed necessary by contracting Governments; and the term "plant products" shall comprise unmanufactured and milled material of plant origin, including seeds in so far as they are not included in the term "plants".

2. The provisions of this Convention may be deemed by contracting Governments to extend to storage places, containers, conveyances, packing material and accompanying media of all sorts including soil involved in the international transportation of plants and plant products.

3. This Convention shall have particular reference to pests and diseases of importance to international trade.

Article III

SUPPLEMENTARY AGREEMENTS

1. Supplementary agreements applicable to specific regions, to specific pests and diseases, to specific plants and plant products, to specific methods of international transportation of plants and plant products, or otherwise supplementing the provisions of this Convention, may be proposed by the Food and Agriculture Organization of the United Nations (hereinafter referred to as "FAO") on the recommendation of a contracting Government or on its own initiative, to meet special problems of plant protection which need particular attention or action.

2. Any such supplementary agreements shall come into force for each contracting Government after acceptance in accordance with the provisions of the FAO Constitution and Rules of Procedure.

Article IV

NATIONAL ORGANIZATION FOR PLANT PROTECTION

1. Each contracting Government shall make provision, as soon as possible and to the best of its ability, for

a) an official plant protection organization, with the following main functions:

(i) the inspection of growing plants, of areas under cultivation (including fields, plantations, nurseries, gardens and greenhouses), and of plants and plant products in storage and in transportation particularly with the object of reporting the existence, outbreak and spread of plant diseases and pests and of controlling those pests and diseases;

(ii) the inspection of consignments of plants and plant products moving in international traffic, and, as far as practicable, the inspection of consignments of other articles or commodities moving in international traffic under conditions where they may act incidentally as carriers of pests and diseases of plants and plant products, and the inspection and supervision of storage and transportation facilities of all kinds involved in international traffic whether of plants and plant products or of other commodities, particularly with the object of preventing the dissemination across national boundaries of pests and diseases of plants and plant products;

(iii) the disinfestation or disinfection of consignments of plants and plant products moving in international traffic, and their containers, storage places, or transportation facilities of all kinds employed;

(iv) the issue of certificates relating to phytosanitary condition and origin of consignments of plants and plant products (hereinafter referred to as "phytosanitary certificates");

b) the distribution of information within the country regarding the pests and diseases of plants and plant products and the means of their prevention and control;

c) research and investigation in the field of plant protection.

2. Each contracting Government shall submit a description of the scope of its national organization for plant protection and of changes in such organization to the Director-General of

FAO, who shall circulate such information to all contracting Governments.

Article V

PHYTOSANITARY CERTIFICATES

1. Each contracting Government shall make arrangements for the issue of phytosanitary certificates to accord with the plant protection regulations of other contracting Governments, and in conformity with the following provisions:

a) Inspection shall be carried out and certificates issued only by or under the authority of technically qualified and duly authorized officers and in such circumstances and with such knowledge and information available to those officers that the authorities of importing countries may accept such certificates with confidence as dependable documents.

b) Each certificate covering materials intended for planting or propagation shall be as worded in the Annex to this Convention and shall include such additional declarations as may be required by the importing country. The model certificate may also be used for other plants or plant products where appropriate and not inconsistent with the requirements of the importing country.

c) The certificates shall bear no alterations or erasures.

2. Each contracting Government undertakes not to require consignments of plants intended for planting or propagation imported into its territories to be accompanied by phytosanitary certificates inconsistent with the model set out in the Annex to this Convention.

Article VI

REQUIREMENTS IN RELATION TO IMPORTS

1. With the aim of preventing the introduction of diseases and pests of plants into their territories, contracting Governments shall have full authority to regulate the entry of plants and plant products, and to this end, may:

a) prescribe restrictions or requirements concerning the importation of plants or plant products;

b) prohibit the importation of particular plants or plant products, or of particular consignments of plants or plant products;

c) inspect or detain particular consignments of plants or plant products;

d) treat, destroy or refuse entry to particular consignments of plants or plant products, or require such consignments to be treated or destroyed.

2. In order to minimize interference with international trade, each contracting Government undertakes to carry out the provisions referred to in paragraph 1 of this Article in conformity with the following:

a) Contracting Governments shall not, under this plant protection legislation, take any of the measures specified in paragraph 1 of this Article unless such measures are made necessary by phytosanitary considerations.

b) If a contracting Government prescribes any restrictions or requirements concerning the importation of plants and plant products into its territories, it shall publish the restrictions or requirements and communicate them immediately to the plant protection services of other contracting Governments and to FAO.

c) If a contracting Government prohibits, under the provisions of its plant protection legislation, the importation of any plants or plant products, it shall publish its decision with reasons and shall immediately inform the plant protection services of other contracting Governments and FAO.

d) If a contracting Government requires consignment of particular products to be imported only through specified points of entry, such points shall be so selected as not unnecessarily to impede international commerce. The contracting Government shall publish a list of such points of entry and communicate it to the plant protection services of other contracting Governments and to FAO. Such restrictions on points of entry shall not be made unless the plants or plant products concerned are required to be accompanied by phytosanitary certificates or to be submitted to inspection or treatment.

e) Any inspection by the plant protection service of a contracting Government of consignments of plants offered for importation shall take place as promptly as possible with due regard to the perishability of the plants concerned. If any consignment is found not to conform to the requirements of the plant protection legislation of the importing country, the plant protection service of the exporting country shall be informed. If the consignment is destroyed, in whole or in part, an official report shall be forwarded immediately to the plant protection service of the exporting country.

f) Contracting Governments shall make provisions which, without endangering their own plant production, will reduce to a minimum the number of cases in which a phytosanitary certificate is required on the entry of plants or plant products not intended for planting, such as cereals, fruits, vegetables and cut flowers.

g) Contracting Governments may make provision for the importation for purposes of scientific research of plants and plant products and of specimens of plant pests and disease-causing organisms under conditions affording ample precaution against the risk of spreading plant diseases and pests.

3. The measures specified in this Article shall not be applied to goods in transit throughout the territories of contracting Governments unless such measures are necessary for the protection of their own plants.

Article VII

INTERNATIONAL CO-OPERATION

The contracting Governments shall co-operate with one another to the fullest practicable extent in achieving the aims of this Convention, in particular as follows:

a) Each contracting Government agrees to co-operate with FAO in the establishment of a world reporting service on plant diseases and pests, making full use of the facilities and services of existing organizations for this purpose, and, when this is established, to furnish to FAO periodically the following information:

(i) reports on the occurrence, outbreak and spread of economically important pests and diseases of plants and plant products which may be of immediate or potential danger;

(ii) information on means found to be effective in controlling the pests and diseases of plants and plant products.

b) Each contracting Government shall, as far as is practicable, participate in any special campaigns for combating particular destructive pests or diseases which may seriously threaten crop production and need international action to meet the emergencies.

Article VIII

REGIONAL PLANT PROTECTION ORGANIZATION

1. The contracting Governments undertake to co-operate with one another in establishing regional plant protection organizations in appropriate areas.

2. The regional plant protection organizations shall function as the co-ordinating bodies in the areas covered and shall participate in various activities to achieve the objectives of this Convention.

Article IX

SETTLEMENT OF DISPUTES

1. If there is any dispute regarding the interpretation or application of this Convention, or if a contracting Government considers that any action by another contracting Government is in conflict with the obligations of the latter under Articles V and VI of this Convention, especially regarding the basis of prohibiting or restricting the imports of plants or plant products coming from its territories, the Government or Governments concerned may request the Director-General of FAO to appoint a committee to consider the question in dispute.

2. The Director-General of FAO shall thereupon, after consultation with the Governments concerned, appoint a committee of experts which shall include representatives of those Governments. This committee shall consider the question in dispute, taking into account all documents and other forms of evidence submitted by the Governments concerned. This committee shall submit a report to the Director-General of FAO who shall transmit it to the Governments concerned, and to other contracting Governments.

3. The contracting Governments agree that the recommendations of such a committee, while not binding in character, will become the basis for renewed consideration by the Governments concerned of the matter out of which the disagreement arose.

4. The Governments concerned shall share equally the expenses of the experts.

Article X

SUBSTITUTION OF PRIOR AGREEMENTS

This Convention shall terminate and replace, between contracting Governments, the International Convention respecting measures to be taken against the *Phylloxera vastatrix* of 3 November 1881, the additional Convention signed at Berne on 15 April 1889 and the International Convention for the Protection of Plants signed at Rome on 16 April 1929.

Article XI

TERRITORIAL APPLICATION

1. Any Government may at the time of ratification or adherence or at any time thereafter communicate to the Director-General of FAO a declaration that this Convention shall extend to all or any of the territories for the international relations of which it is responsible, and this Convention shall be applicable to all territories specified in the declaration as from the thirtieth day after the receipt of the declaration by the Director-General.

2. Any Government which has communicated to the Director-General of FAO a declaration in accordance with paragraph 1 of this Article may at any time communicate a further declaration modifying the scope of any former declaration or terminating the application of the provisions of the present Convention in respect of any territory. Such modification or termination shall take effect as from the thirtieth day after the receipt of the declaration by the Director-General.

3. The Director-General of FAO shall inform all signatory and adhering Governments of any declaration received under this Article.

Article XII

RATIFICATION AND ADHERENCE

1. This Convention shall be open for signature by all Governments until 1 May 1952 and shall be ratified at the earliest possible date. The instruments of ratification shall be deposited with the Director-General of FAO, who shall give notice of the date of deposit to each of the signatory Governments.

2. As soon as this Convention has come into force in accordance with Article XIV, it shall be open for adherence by non-signatory Governments. Adherence shall be effected by the

deposit of an instrument of adherence with the Director-General of FAO, who shall notify all signatory and adhering Governments.

Article XIII

AMENDMENT

1. Any proposal by a contracting Government for the amendment of this Convention shall be communicated to the Director-General of FAO.

2. Any proposal amendment of this Convention received by the Director-General of FAO from a contracting Government shall be presented to a regular or special session of the Conference of FAO for approval and, if the amendment involves important technical changes or imposes additional obligations on the contracting Governments, it shall be considered by an advisory committee of specialists convened by FAO prior to the Conference.

3. Notice of any proposed amendment of this Convention shall be transmitted to the contracting Governments by the Director-General of FAO not later than the time when the agenda of the session of the Conference at which the matter is to be considered is dispatched.

4. Any such proposed amendment of this Convention shall require the approval of the Conference of FAO and shall come into force as from the thirtieth day after acceptance by two-thirds of the contracting Governments. Amendments involving new obligations for contracting Governments, however, shall come into force in respect of each contracting Government only on acceptance by it and as from the thirtieth day after such acceptance.

5. The instruments of acceptance of amendments involving new obligations shall be deposited with the Director-General of FAO, who shall inform all contracting Governments of the receipt of acceptances and the entry into force of amendments.

Article XV

DENUNCIATION

1. Any contracting Government may at any time give notice of denunciation of this Convention by notification addresed to the Director-General of FAO. The Director-General shall at once inform all signatory and adhering Governments.

2. Denunciation shall take effect one year from the date of receipt of the notification by the Director-General of FAO.

Done at Rome, Italy on the sixth day of December, one thousand nine hundred and fifty-one, in a single copy in the English, French and Spanish languages, each of which shall be of equal authenticity. The document shall be deposited in the archives of the Food and Agriculture Organization of the United Nations. Certified copies shall be transmitted by the Director-General of the Food and Agriculture to each signatory and adhering Government.

In Witness Whereof the undersigned duly authorized to that effect, have signed this Convention on behalf of their respective Governments on the dates appearing opposite their signatures.

ANNEX

Model Phytosanitary Certificate

Plant Protection Service of ....

No. ....

This is to certify that the plants, parts of plants or plant products described below or representative samples of them were thoroughly examined on (date) ....

....

by (name) ....

an authorized officer of the (service) ....

....

and were found to the best of his knowledge to be substantially free from injurious diseases and pests; and that the consignment is believed to conform with the current phytosanitary regulations of the importing country both as stated in the additional declaration hereon and otherwise.

Fumigation or disinfection treatment (if required by importing country):

Date ....

Duration of exposure ....

Treatment ....

Chemical and concentration ....

....

Additional declaration

.... 19 .....

....
(Signature)

....
(Rank)

(Stamp of
the Service)

Description of the Consignment

Name and address of exporter: ....

....

Name and address of consignee: ....

....

Number and description of packages: ....

....

Distinguishing marks: ....

Origin (if required by importing country):

....

Means of conveyance: ....

Point of entry: ....

Quantity and name of produce: ....

....

Botanical name (if required by importing country):

....

AGREEMENT CONCERNING MEASURES FOR THE PROTECTION OF THE STOCKS OF DEEP-SEA PRAWNS *(Pandalus borealis)*, EUROPEAN LOBSTERS *(Homarus vulgaris)*, NORWAY LOBSTERS *(Nephrops norvegicus)* AND CRABS *(Cancer pagurus)* [9]

Oslo, 7 March 1952

The Governments of Denmark, Norway and Sweden, being desirous of concluding an agreement relating to measures for the protection of stocks of deep-sea prawns *(Pandalus borealis)*, European lobsters (*Homarus vulgaris*), Norway lobsters (*Nephrops norvegicus*) and crabs (*Cancer pagurus*), have agreed as follows:

Article 1

The area to which this Agreement applies shall include all waters bounded on the west by a line from Lindesnes light to Hanstholm light and on the east by the 13th meridian east of Greenwich.

Article 2

No vessel may use or have on board any prawn trawl which does not comply with the provisions of article 3 of this Agreement.

Article 3

The minimum size of the mesh of a prawn trawl shall be such that a flat measure 30 mm. wide and 2 mm. thick can be easily passed between the meshes when the trawl is wet and spread out lengthwise.

Article 4

No vessel shall keep on board any Norway lobsters (*Nephrops norvegicus*) under 15 cm. in length measured from the tip of the frontal horn to the anterior fixed side of the middle swimming appendage.

Article 5

The provisions of this Agreement shall not apply to fishery research conducted by, or with the consent of, the public authorities.

Article 6

The Contracting Governments agree to take such action and make such regulations as are necessary to give effect to the provisions of this Agreement, including the provisions which prohibit the landing or selling in their territories of Norway lobsters under the prescribed minimum size.

Article 7

A commission shall be set up consisting of two representatives (one representative for scientific research in fishing and one for the fishing industry) from each of the Contracting Parties. The purpose of the commission shall be to attempt to co-ordinate the scientific and practical research conducted by the various countries with regard to stocks of prawns, European lobsters, Norway lobsters and crabs in the area to which the Agreement applies. The commission shall also, on the basis of available information, consider whether there are grounds for modifying existing measures for the protection of stocks of the afore-mentioned shell-fish or for introducing other measures, and, as the circumstances require, shall make appropriate recommendations to the Contracting Governments. The commission shall itself determine its procedure and when it shall meet. The first meeting of the commission shall be called by the Norwegian Government.

Article 8

This Agreement shall be ratified and shall come into force two months after the instruments of ratification are deposited with the Norwegian Government, which shall inform the Contracting Governments of the deposit of the ratifications and of the date on which the Agreement is to come into force.

Article 9

After three years from it coming into force, this Agreement may be denounced by a notice in writing addressed to the Norwegian Government. The denunciation shall take effect in respect of the Government concerned six months after the date of receipt. Notice of the denunciation shall be given to all the Contracting Parties by the Norwegian Government.

Done at Oslo on 7 March 1952 in one copy which shall be deposited with the Norwegian Government. The latter shall send certified copies to the Danish and the Swedish Governments.

Protocol

amending the Agreement concerning measures for the protection of the stocks of deep-sea prawns *(Pandalus borealis)*, European lobsters *(Homarus vulgaris)*, Norway lobsters *(Nephrops norvegicus)* and crabs *(Cancer pagurus)*

The Governments of Denmark, Norway and Sweden, upon the recommendation of the Danish-Norwegian-Swedish Crustaceans Commission, have agreed that article 4 of the Agreement of 7 March 1952 concerning measures for the protection of stocks of deep sea prawns (*Pandalus borealis*), European lobsters (*Homarus vulgaris*), Norway lobsters (*Nephrops norvegicus*) and crabs (*Cancer pagurus*) shall be amended by reducing the minimum length for Norway lobsters (*Nephrops norvegicus*) from 15 cm to 13 cm.

This Protocol of amendment shall come into force on the date of signature.

In Witness Whereof the undersigned, being duly authorized thereto, have signed this Protocol in one copy. It shall be deposited with the Norwegian Government, which shall send certified copies to the Danish and Swedish Governments.

Done at Oslo, on 14 October 1959.

INTERNATIONAL CONVENTION FOR THE HIGH SEAS FISHERIES OF THE NORTH PACIFIC OCEAN* [10]

Tokyo, 9 May 1952

The Governments of the United States of America, Canada and Japan, whose respective duly accredited representatives have subscribed hereto,

Acting as sovereign nations in the light of their rights under the principles of international law and custom to exploit the fishery resources of the high seas, and

Believing that it will best serve the common interest of mankind, as well as the interests of the Contracting Parties, to ensure the maximum sustained productivity of the fishery resources of the North Pacific Ocean, and that each of the Parties should assume an obligation, on a free and equal footing, to encourage the conservation of such resources, and

Recognizing that in view of these considerations it is highly desirable (1) to establish an International Commission, representing the three Parties hereto, to promote and co-ordinate the scientific studies necessary to ascertain the conservation measures required to secure the maximum sustained productivity of the fisheries of joint interest to the Contracting Parties and to recommend such measures to such Parties and (2) that each Party carry such conservation recommendations, and provide for necessary restraints on its own nationals and fishing vessels.

Thereafter agree as follows:

Article I

1. The area to which this Convention applies, hereinafter referred to as "the Convention area," shall be all waters, other than territorial waters, of the North Pacific Ocean which for the purposes hereof shall include the adjacent seas.

2. Nothing in this Convention shall be deemed to affect adversely (prejudice) the claims of any Contracting Party in regard to the limits of territorial waters or to the jurisdiction of a coastal state over fisheries.

3. For the purposes of this Convention the term "fishing vessel" shall mean any vessel engaged in catching fish or processing or transporting fish loaded on the high seas, or any vessel outfitted for such activities.

Article II

1. In order to realize the objectives of this Convention, the Contracting Parties shall establish and maintain the International North Pacific Fisheries Commission, hereinafter referred to as "the Commission."

2. The Commission shall be composed of three national sections, each consisting of not more than four members appointed by the governments of the respective Contracting Parties.

3. Each national section shall have one vote. All resolutions, recommendations and other decisions of the Commission shall be made only by a unanimous vote of the three national sections except when under the provisions of article III, section 1 (*c*) (ii) only two participate.

4. The Commission may decide upon and amend, as occasion may require, by-laws or rules for the conduct of its meetings.

5. The Commission shall meet at least once each year and at such other times as may be requested by a majority of the national sections. The date and place of the first meeting shall be determined by agreement between the Contracting Parties.

6. At its first meeting the Commission shall select a Chairman, Vice-Chairman and Secretary from different national sections. The Chairman, Vice-Chairman and Secretary shall hold office for a period of one year. During succeeding years selection of a Chairman, Vice-Chairman and Secretary from the national sections shall be made in such a manner as will provide each Contracting Party in turn with representation in those offices.

7. The Commission shall decide on a convenient place for the establishment of the Commission's headquarters.

8. Each Contracting Party may establish an Advisory Committee for its national section to be composed of persons who shall be well informed concerning North Pacific fishery problems of common concern. Each such Advisory Committee shall be invited to attend all sessions of the Commission except those which the Commission decides to be *in camera*.

9. The Commission may hold public hearings. Each national section may also hold public hearings within its own country.

10. The official languages of the Commission shall be Japanese and English. Proposals and data may be submitted to the Commission in either language.

11. Each Contracting Party shall determine and pay the expenses incurred by its national section. Joint expenses incurred by the Commission shall be paid by the Commission through contributions made by the Contracting Parties in the form and proportion recommended by the Commission and approved by the Contracting Parties.

12. An annual budget of joint expenses shall be recommended by the Commission and submitted to the Contracting Parties for approval.

13. The Commission shall authorize the disbursement of funds for the joint expenses of the Commission and may employ personnel and acquire facilities necessary for the performance of its functions.

* The Annex to this Convention was amended on November 17, 1962, by the International North Pacific Fisheries Commission. The amendments have been accepted by Japan on February 26, 1963, by the United States of America on March 23, 1963 and by Canada on May 8, 1963.

Article III

1. The Commission shall perform the following functions:

a) In regard to any stock of fish specified in the annex, study for the purpose of determining annually whether such stock continues to qualify for abstention under the provisions of article IV. If the Commission determines that such stock no longer meets the conditions of article IV, the Commission shall recommend that it be removed from the annex. Provided, however, that with respect to the stocks of fish originally specified in the Annex, no determination or recommendation as to whether such stock continues to qualify for abstention shall be made for five years after the entry into force of this Convention.

b) To permit later additions to the annex, study, on request of a Contracting Party, any stock of fish of the Convention area, the greater part of which is harvested by one or more of the Contracting Parties, for the purpose of determining whether such stock qualifies for abstention under the provisions of article IV. If the Commission decides that the particular stock fulfills the conditions of article IV it shall recommend (1) that such stock be added to the annex, (2) that the appropriate Party or Parties abstain from fishing such stock and (3) that the Party or Parties participating in the fishing of such stock continue to carry out necessary conservation measures.

c) In regard to any stock of fish in the Convention area:

(i) Study, on request of any Contracting Party concerned, any stock of fish which is under substantial exploitation by two or more of the Contracting Parties, and which is not covered by a conservation agreement between such Parties existing at the time of the conclusion of this Convention, for the purpose of determining need for joint conservation measures;

(ii) Decide and recommend necessary joint conservation measures including any relaxation thereof to be taken as a result of such study. Provided, however that only the national sections of the Contracting Parties engaged in substantial exploitation of such stock of fish may participate in such decision and recommendation. The decisions and recommendations shall be reported regularly to all the Contracting Parties, but shall apply only to the Contracting Parties the national sections of which participated in the decisions and recommendations.

(iii) Request the Contracting Party or Parties concerned to report regularly the conservation measures adopted from time to time with regard to the stocks of fish specified in the Annex, whether or not covered by conservation agreements between the Contracting Parties, and transmit such information to the other Contracting Party or Parties.

d) Consider and make recommendations to the Contracting Parties concerning the enactment of schedules of equivalent penalties for violations of this Convention.

e) Compile and study the records provided by the Contracting Parties pursuant to article VIII.

f) Submit annually to each Contracting Party a report on the Commission's operations, investigations and findings, with appropriate recommendations, and inform each Contracting Party, whenever it is deemed advisable, on any matter relating to the objectives of this Convention.

2. The Commission may take such steps, in agreement with the Parties concerned, as will enable it to determine the extent to which the undertakings agreed to by the Parties under the provisions of article V, section 2 and the measures recommended by the Commission under the provisions of this article and accepted by the Parties concerned have been effective.

3. In the performance of its functions, the Commission shall, insofar as feasible, utilize the technical and scientific services of, and information from, official agencies of the Contracting Parties and their political subdivisions and may, when desirable and if available, utilize the services of, and information from, any public or private institution or organization or any private individual.

Article IV

1. In making its recommendations the Commission shall be guided by the spirit and intent of this Convention and by the considerations below mentioned.

a) Any conservation measures for any stock of fish decided upon under the provisions of this Convention shall be recommended for equal application to all Parties engaged in substantial exploitation of such stock.

b) With regard to any stock of fish which the Commission determines reasonably satisfies all the following conditions, a recommendation shall be made as provided for in article III, section 1, (*b*).

(i) Evidence based upon scientific research indicates that more intensive exploitation of the stock will not provide a substantial increase in yield which can be sustained year after year.

(ii) The exploitation of the stock is limited or otherwise regulated through legal measures by each Party which is substantially engaged in its exploitation, for the purpose of maintaining or increasing its maximum sustained productivity; such limitations and regulations being in accordance with conservation programs based upon scientific research, and

(iii) The stock is the subject of extensive scientific study designed to discover whether the stock is being fully utilized and the conditions necessary for maintaining its maximum sustained productivity.

Provided, however, that no recommendation shall be made for abstention by a Contracting Party concerned with regard to: (1) any stock of fish which at any time during the twenty-five years next preceding the entry into force of this

Convention has been under substantial exploitation by that Party having regard to the conditions referred to in section 2 of this article; (2) any stock of fish which is harvested in greater part by a country or countries not party to this Convention; (3) waters in which there is historic intermingling of fishing operations of the Parties concerned, intermingling of the stocks of fish exploited by these operations, and a long-established history of joint conservation and regulation among the parties concerned so that there is consequent impracticability of segregating the operations and administering control. It is recognized that the conditions specified in subdivision (3) of this proviso apply to Canada and the United States of America in the waters off the Pacific Coasts of the United States of America and Canada from and including the waters of the Gulf of Alaska southward and, therefore, no recommendation shall be made for abstention by either the United States of America or Canada in such waters.

2. In any decision or recommendation allowances shall be made for the effect of strikes, wars, or exceptional economic or biological conditions which may have introduced temporary declines in or suspension of productivity, exploitation, or management of the stock of fish concerned.

Article V

1. The annex attached hereto forms an integral part of this Convention. All references to "Convention" shall be understood as including the said annex either in its present terms or as amended in accordance with the provisions of article VII.

2. The Contracting Parties recognize that any stock of fish originally specified in the annex to this Convention fulfills the conditions prescribed in article IV and accordingly agree that the appropriate Party or Parties shall abstain from fishing such stock and the Party or Parties participating in the fishing of such stock shall continue to carry out necessary conservation measures.

Article VI

In the event that it shall come to the attention of any of the Contracting Parties that the nationals or fishing vessels of any country which is not a Party to this Convention appear to affect adversely the operations of the Commission or the carrying out of the objectives of this Convention, such Party shall call the matter to the attention of other Contracting Parties. All the Contracting Parties agree upon the request of such Party to confer upon the steps to be taken towards obviating such adverse effects or relieving any Contracting Party from such adverse effects.

Article VII

1. The annex to this Convention shall be considered amended from the date upon which the Commission receives notification from all the Contracting Parties of acceptance of a recommendation to amend the annex made by the Commission in accordance with the provisions of article III, section 1 or of the Protocol to this Convention.

2. The Commission shall notify all the Contracting Parties of the date of receipt of each notification of acceptance of an amendment to the annex.

Articel VIII

The Contracting Parties agree to keep as far as practicable all records requested by the Commission and to furnish compilations of such records and other information upon request of the Commission. No Contracting Party shall be required hereunder to provide the records of individual operations.

Article IX

1. The Contracting Parties agree as follows:

a) With regard to a stock of fish from the exploitation of which any Contracting Party has agreed to abstain, the nationals and fishing vessels of such Contracting Party are prohibited from engaging in the exploitation of such stock of fish in waters specified in the annex, and from loading, processing, possessing, or transporting such fish in such waters.

b) With regard to a stock of fish for which a Contracting Party has agreed to continue to carry out conservation measures, the nationals and fishing vessels of such Party are prohibited from engaging in fishing activities in waters specified in the annex in violation of regulations established under such conservation measures.

2. Each Contracting Party agrees, for the purpose of rendering effective the provisions of this Convention, to enact and enforce necessary laws and regulations, with regard to its nationals and fishing vessel, with appropriate penalties against violations thereof and to transmit to the Commission a report on any action taken by it with regard thereto.

Article X

1. The Contracting Parties agree, in order to carry out faithfully the provisions of this Convention, to co-operate with each other in taking appropriate and effective measures and accordingly agree as follows:

a) When a fishing vessel of a Contracting Party has been found in waters in which that Party has agreed to abstain from exploitation in accordance with the provisions of this Convention, the duly authorized officials of any Contracting Party may board such vessel to inspect its equipment, books, documents, and other articles and question the persons on board. Such officials shall present credentials issued by their respective Governments if requested by the master of the vessel.

b) When any such person or fishing vessel is actually engaged in operation in violation of the provisions of this Convention, or there is reasonable ground to believe was obviously so engaged immediately prior to boarding of such vessel by any such official, the latter may arrest or seize such person or vessel. In that case, the Contracting Party to which the official belongs shall notify the Contracting Party to which such person or vessel belongs of such arrest or seizure, and shall deliver such vessel or persons as promptly as practicable to the authorized officials of the Contracting Party to which such vessel or person belongs at a place to be agreed upon by both Parties. Provided, however, that when the Contracting Party which receives such notifications cannot immediately accept delivery and makes request, the Contracting Party which gives such notification may keep such person or vessel under surveillance within its own territory under the conditions agreed upon by both of the Contracting Parties.

c) Only the authorities of the Party to which the above-mentioned person or fishing vessel belongs may try the offence and impose penalties therefor. The witnesses and evidence necessary for establishing the offence, so far as they are under the control of any of the Parties to this Convention, shall be furnished as promptly as possible to the Contracting Party having jurisdiction to try the offence.

2. With regard to the nationals or fishing vessels of one or more Contracting Parties in waters with respect to which they have agreed to continue to carry out conservation measures for certain stocks of fish in accordance with the provisions of this Convention, the Contracting Parties concerned shall carry out enforcement severally or jointly. In that case, the Contracting Parties concerned agree to report periodically through the Commission to the Contracting Party which has agreed to abstain from the exploitation of such stocks of fish on the enforcement conditions, and also, if requested, to provide opportunity for observation of the conduct of enforcement.

3. The Contracting Parties agree to meet, during the sixth year of the operation of this Convention, to review the effectiveness of the enforcement provisions of this article and, if desirable, to consider means by which they may more effectively be carried out.

Article XI

1. This Convention shall be ratified by the Contracting Parties in accordance with their respective constitutional processes and the instruments of ratification shall be exchanged as soon as possible at Tokyo.

2. This Convention shall enter into force on the date of the exchange of ratifications. It shall continue in force for a period of ten years and thereafter until one year from the day on which a Contracting Party shall give notice to the other Contracting Parties of an intention of terminating the Convention, where upon it shall terminate as to all Contracting Parties.

In Witness Whereof, the respective Plenipotentiaries duly authorized, have signed the present Convention.

Done in triplicate, in the English and Japanese languages, both equally authentic, at Tokyo this ninth day of May, one thousand nine hundred fifty-two.

ANNEX

1. With regard to the stocks of fish in the respective waters named below, Japan agrees to abstain from fishing, and Canada and the United States of America agree to continue to carry out necessary conservation measures, in accordance with the provisions of article V, section 2 of this Convention:

a) Halibut (*Hippoglossus stenolepis*)

The Convention area off the coasts of Canada and the United States of America exclusive of the Bering Sea in which commercial fishing for halibut is being or can be prosecuted. Halibut referred to herein shall be those originating along the coast of North America.

b) Herring (*Clupea pallasii*)

The Convention area off the coast of Canada in which commercial fishing for herring of Canadian origin is being or can be prosecuted, exclusive of the waters of the high seas north of 51°56′ North Latitude and west of the Queen Charlotte Islands and west of a line drawn between Langara Point on Langara Islands, Queen Charlotte Islands and Cape Muzon on Dall Island in Southeast Alaska.

c) Salmon (*Oncorhychus gorbuscha, Oncorhynchus keta, Oncorhynchus kisutch, Oncorhynchus nerka, Oncorhynchus tschawytscha*)

The Convention area off the coasts of Canada and the United States of America, exclusive of the Bering Sea and of the waters of the North Pacific Ocean west of a provisional line following the meridian passing through the western extremity of Atka Island; in which commercial fishing for salmon originating in the rivers of Canada and the United States of America is being or can be prosecuted.

2. With regard to the stocks of fish in the waters named below, Canada and Japan agree to abstain from fishing, and the United States of America agrees to continue to carry out necessary conservation measures, in accordance with the provisions of article V, section 2 of this Convention:

Salmon (*Oncorhynchus gorbuscha, Oncorhynchus keta, Oncorhynchus kisutch, Oncohynchus nerka and Oncorhynchus tschawytscha*)

The Convention area of the Bering Sea east of the line starting from Cape Prince of Wales on the west coast of Alaska, running westward to 168°58′22.59″ West Longitude; thence due south to a point 65°15′00″ North Latitude; thence along the great circle course which passes through 51° North Latitude and 167° East Longitude, to its intersection with meridian 175° West Longitude; thence south along a provisional line which follows this meridian to the territorial waters limit of Atka Island; in which commercial fishing for salmon originating in the rivers of the United States of America is being or can be prosecuted.

PROTOCOL TO THE INTERNATIONAL CONVENTION FOR THE HIGH SEAS FISHERIES OF THE NORTH PACIFIC OCEAN

The Governments of the United States of America, Canada and Japan, through their respective Plenipotentiaries, agree upon the following stipulation in regard to the International Convention for the High Seas Fisheries of the North Pacific Ocean, signed at Tokyo on this ninth day of May, nineteen hundred fifty-two.

The Governments of the United States of America, Canada and Japan agree that the line of meridian 175° West Longitude and the line following the meridian passing through the western extremity of Atka Island, which have been adopted for determining the areas in which the exploitation of salmon is abstained or the conservation measures for salmon continue to be enforced in accordance with the provisions of the annex to this Convention, shall be considered as provisional lines which shall continue in effect subject to confirmation or readjustment in accordance with the procedure mentioned below.

The Commission to be established under the Convention shall, as expeditiously as practicable, investigate the waters of the Convention area to determine if there are areas in which salmon originating in the rivers of Canada and of the United States of America intermingle with salmon originating in the rivers of Asia. If such areas are found the Commission shall conduct suitable studies to determine a line or lines which best divide salmon of Asiatic origin and salmon of Canadian and United States of America origin, from which certain Contracting Parties have agreed to abstain in accordance with the provisions of article V, section 2, and whether it can be shown beyond a reasonable doubt that this line or lines more equitably divide such salmon than the provisional line specified in sections 1 (*c*) and 2 of the annex. In accordance with these determinations the Commission shall recommend that such provisional lines be confirmed or that they be changed in accordance with these results, giving due consideration to adjustments required to simplify administration.

In the event, however, the Commission fails within a reasonable period of time to recommend unanimously such line or lines, it is agreed that the matter shall be referred to a special committee of scientists consisting of three competent and disinterested persons, no one of whom shall be a national of a Contracting Party, selected by mutual agreement of all Parties for the determination of this matter.

It is further agreed that when a determination has been made by a majority of such special committee, the Commission shall make a recommendation in accordance therewith.

The Governments of the United States of America, Canada and Japan, in signing this Protocol, desire to make it clear that the procedure set forth herein is designed to cover a special situation. It is not, therefore, to be considered a precedent for the final resolution of any matters which may, in future, come before the Commission.

This Protocol shall become effective from the date of entry into force of the said Convention.

In Witness Whereof, the respective Plenipotentiaries have signed this Protocol.

Done in triplicate at Tokyo this ninth day of May, one thousand nine hundred fifty-two.

INTERNATIONAL CONVENTION FOR THE PREVENTION OF POLLUTION OF THE SEA BY OIL, 1954* [11]

London, 12 May 1954

The Governments represented at the International Conference on Pollution of the Sea by Oil held in London from 26 April 1954 to 12 May 1954.

Desiring to take action by common agreement to prevent pollution of the sea by oil discharged from ships, and considering that this end may best be achieved by the conclusion of a Convention,

Have accordingly appointed the undersigned plenipotentiaries, who, having communicated their full powers, found in good and due form, have agreed as follows:

Article I

1. For the purposes of the present Convention, the following expressions shall (unless the context otherwise requires) have the meanings hereby respectively assigned to them that is to say:

'The Bureau' has the meaning assigned to it by Article XXI;

'Discharge' in relation to oil or to oily mixture means any discharge or escape howsoever caused;

'Heavy diesel oil' means diesel oil, other than those distillates of which more than 50 per cent by volume distils at a temperature not exceeding 340°C when tested by A.S.T.M. Standard Method D.86/59;

'Instantaneous rate of discharge of oil content' means the rate of discharge of oil in litres per hour at any instant divided by the speed of the ship in knots at the same instant;

'Mile' means a nautical mile of 6,080 feet or 1,852 metres;

'Nearest land'. The term 'from the nearest land' means 'from the baseline from which the territorial sea of the territory in question is established in accordance with the Geneva Convention on the Territorial Sea and the Contiguous Zone, 1958';

'Oil' means crude oil, fuel oil, heavy diesel oil and lubricating oil, and 'oily' shall be construed accordingly;

'Oily mixture' means a mixture with any oil content;

'Organization' means the Inter-Governmental Maritime Consultative Organization;

'Ship' means any sea-going vessel of any type whatsoever, including floating craft, whether self-propelled or towed by another vessel, making a sea voyage; and 'tanker' means a ship in which the greater part of the cargo space is constructed or adapted for the carriage of liquid cargoes in bulk and which is not, for the time being, carrying a cargo other than oil in that part of the cargo space.

2. For the purposes of the present Convention, the territories of a Contracting Government means the territory of the country of which it is the Government and any other territory for the international relations of which it is responsible and to which the Convention shall have been extended under Article XVIII.

Article II

1. The present Convention shall apply to ships registered in any of the territories of a Contracting Government and to unregistered ships having the nationality of a Contracting Party, except:

a) tankers of under 150 tons gross tonnage and other ships of under 500 tons gross tonnage, provided that each Contracting Government will take the necessary steps, so far as is reasonable and practicable, to apply the requirements of the Convention to such ships also, having regard to their size, service and the type of fuel used for their propulsion;

b) ships for the time being engaged in the whaling industry when actually employed on whaling operations;

c) ships for the time being navigating the Great Lakes of North America and their connecting and tributary waters as far east as the lower exit of St. Lambert Lock at Montreal in the Province of Quebec, Canada;

d) naval ships and ships for the time being used as naval auxiliaries.

2. Each Contracting Government undertakes to adopt appropriate measures ensuring that requirements equivalent to those of the present Convention are, so far as is reasonable and practicable, applied to the ships referred to in subparagraph (*d*) of paragraph (1) of this Article.

Article III

Subject to the provisions of Articles IV and V:

a) the discharge from a ship to which the present Convention applies, other than a tanker, of oil or oily mixture shall be prohibited except when the following conditions are all satisfied:

(i) the ship is proceeding en route;

(ii) the instantaneous rate of discharge of oil content does not exceed 60 litres per mile;

(iii) the oil content of the discharge is less than 100 parts per 1,000,000 parts of the mixture.

(iv) the discharge is made as far as practicable from land;

b) the discharge from a tanker to which the present Convention applies of oil or oily mixture

* The original text of the Convention, which was done by the International Conference on Pollution of the Sea by Oil in London on 12 May 1954, entered into force on 26 July 1958. The Convention was modified by Amendments adopted by the International Conference on Prevention of Pollution of the Sea by Oil, 1962; these Amendments entered into force on 18 May and 28 June 1967. The Convention was further modified by Amendments adopted by the sixth Assembly of the Inter-Governmental Maritime Consultative Organization on 21 October 1969 (Resolution A. 175 (VI)); these Amendments entered into force on 20 January 1978.

shall be prohibited except when the following conditions are all satisfied:

(i) the tanker is proceeding en route;

(ii) the instantaneous rate of discharge of oil content does not exceed 60 litres per mile;

(iii) the total quantity of oil discharged on a ballast voyage does not exceed 1/15,000 of the total cargo-carrying capacity;

(iv) the tanker is more than 50 miles from the nearest land;

c) the provisions of sub-paragraph (*b*) of this Article shall not apply to:

(i) the discharge of ballast from a cargo tank which, since the cargo was last carried therein, has been so cleaned that any effluent therefrom, if it were discharged from a stationary tanker into clean calm water on a clear day, would produce no visible traces of oil on the surface of the water; or

(ii) the discharge of oil or oily mixture from machinery space bilges, which shall be governed by the provisions of sub-paragraph (*a*) of this Article.

Article IV

Article III shall not apply to:

a) the discharge of oil or of oily mixture from a ship for the purpose of securing the safety of a ship, preventing damage to a ship or cargo, or saving life at sea;

b) the escape of oil or of oily mixture resulting from damage to a ship or unavoidable leakage, if all reasonable precautions have been taken after the occurrence of the damage or discovery of the leakage for the purpose of preventing or minimizing the escape.

Article V

Article III shall not apply to the discharge of oily mixture from the bilges of a ship during the period of twelve months following the date on which the present Convention comes into force for the relevant territory in accordance with paragraph (1) of Article II.

Article VI

1. Any contravention of Articles III and IX shall be an offence punishable under the law of the relevant territory in respect of the ship in accordance with paragraph (1) of Article II.

2. The penalties which may be imposed under the law of any of the territories of a Contracting Government in respect of the unlawful discharge from a ship of oil or oily mixture outside the territorial sea of that territory shall be adequate in severity to discourage any such unlawful discharge and shall not be less than the penalties which may be imposed under the law of that territory in respect of the same infringements within the territorial sea.

3. Each Contracting Government shall report to the Organization the penalties actually imposed for each infringement.

Article VII

1. As from a date twelve months after the present Convention comes into force for the relevant territory in respect of a ship in accordance with paragraph (1) of Article II, such a ship shall be required to be so fitted as to prevent, as far as reasonable and practicable, the escape of oil into bilges, unless effective means are provided to ensure that the oil in the bilges is not discharged in contravention of this Convention.

2. Carrying water ballast in oil fuel tanks shall be avoided if possible.

Article VIII

1. Each Contracting Government shall take all appropriate steps to promote the provision of facilities as follows:

a) according to the needs of ships using them, ports shall be provided with facilities adequate for the reception, without causing undue delay to ships, of such residues and oily mixtures as would remain for disposal from ships other than tankers if the bulk of the water had been separated from the mixture;

b) oil loading terminals shall be provided with facilities, adequate for the reception of such residues and oily mixture as would similarly remain for disposal by tankers;

c) ship repair ports shall be provided with facilities adequate for the reception of such residues and oily mixtures as would similarly remain for disposal by all ships entering for repairs.

2. Each Contracting Government shall determine which are the ports and oil loading terminals in its territories suitable for the purposes of sub-paragraphs (*a*), (*b*) and (*c*) of paragraph (1) of this Article.

3. As regards paragraph (1) of this Article, each Contracting Government shall report to the Organization, for transmission to the Contracting Government concerned, all cases where the facilities are alleged to be inadequate.

Article IX

1. Of the ships to which the present Convention applies, every ship which uses oil fuel and every tanker shall be provided with an oil record book, whether as part of the ship's official log book or otherwise, in the form specified in the Annex to this Convention.

2. The oil record book shall be completed on each occasion, on a tank-to-tank basis, whenever any of the following operations take place in the ship:

a) for tankers:

(i) loading of oil cargo;

(ii) transfer of oil cargo during voyage;

(iii) discharge of oil cargo;

(iv) ballasting of cargo tanks;

(v) cleaning of cargo tanks;

(vi) discharge of dirty ballast;

(vii) discharge of water from slop-tanks;

(viii) disposal of residues;

(ix) discharge overboard of bilge water containing oil which has accumulated in machinery spaces whilst in port, and the routine discharge at sea of bilge water containing oil unless the latter has been entered in the appropriate log book;

b) for ships other than tankers:

(i) ballasting or cleaning of bunker fuel tanks;

(ii) discharge of dirty ballast or cleaning water from tanks referred to under (i) of this sub-paragraph;

(iii) disposal of residues;

(iv) discharge overboard of bilge water containing oil which has accumulated in machinery spaces whilst in port, and the routine discharge at sea of bilge water containing oil unless the latter has been entered in the appropriate log book.

In the event of such discharge or escape of oil or oily mixture as is referred to in Article IV, a statement shall be made in the oil record book of the circumstances of, and the reason for, the discharge or escape.

3. Each operation described in paragraph (2) of this Article shall be fully recorded without delay in the oil record book so that all the entries in the book appropriate to that operation are completed. Each page of the book shall be signed by the officer or officers in charge of the operations concerned and, when the ship is manned, by the master of the ship. The written entries in the oil record book shall be in an official language of the relevant territory in respect of the ship in accordance with paragraph (1) of Article II, or in English or French.

4. Oil record books shall be kept in such a place as to be readily available for inspection at all reasonable times, and, except in the case of unmanned ships under tow, shall be kept on board the ship. They shall be preserved for a period of two years after the last entry has been made.

5. The competent authorities of any of the territories of a Contracting Government may inspect on board any ship to which the present Convention applies, while within a port in that territory, the oil record book required to be carried in the ship in compliance with the provisions of this Article, and may make a true copy of an entry in that book and may require the master of the ship to certify that the copy is a true copy of such entry. Any copy so made which purports to have been certified by the master of the ship as a true copy of an entry in the ship's oil record book shall be made admissible in any judicial proceedings as evidence of the facts stated in the entry. Any action by the competent authorities under this paragraph shall be taken as expeditiously as possible and the ship shall not be delayed.

Article X

1. Any Contracting Government may furnish to the Government of the relevant territory in respect of the ship in accordance with paragraph (1) of Article II particulars in writing of evidence that any provision of the present Convention has been contravened in respect of that ship, wheresoever the alleged contravention may have taken place. If it is practicable to do so, the competent authorities of the former Government shall notify the master of the ship of the alleged contravention.

2. Upon receiving such particulars, the Government so informed shall investigate the matter, and may request the other Government to furnish further or better particulars of the alleged contravention. If the Government so informed is satisfied that sufficient evidence is available in the form required by its law to enable proceedings against the owner or master of the ship to be taken in respect of the alleged contravention, it shall cause such proceedings to be taken as soon as possible. The Government shall promptly inform the Government whose official has reported the alleged contravention, as well as the Organization, of the action taken as a consequence of the information communicated.

Article XI

Nothing in the present Convention shall be construed as derogating from the powers of any Contracting Government to take measures within its jurisdiction in respect of any matter to which the Convention relates or as extending the jurisdiction of any Contracting Government.

Article XII

Each Contracting Government shall send to the Bureau and to the appropriate organ of the United Nations:

a) the text of laws, decrees, orders and regulations in force in its territories which give effect to the present Convention;

b) all official reports or summarises of official reports in so far as they show the results of the application of the provisions of the Convention, provided always that such reports or summaries are not, in the opinion of that Government, of a confidential nature.

Article XIII

Any dispute between Contracting Governments relating to the interpretation or application of the present Convention which cannot be settled by negotiation shall be referred at the request of either party to the International Court of Justice for decision unless the parties in dispute agree to submit it to arbitration.

Article XIV

1. The present Convention shall remain open for signature for three months from this day's date and shall thereafter remain open for acceptance.

2. Subject to Article XV, the Governments of States Members of the United Nations or of any of the Specialized Agencies or parties to the Statute of the International Court of Justice may become parties to the present Convention by:

a) signature without reservation as to acceptance;

b) signature subject to acceptance followed by

acceptance; or

c) acceptance.

3. Acceptance shall be effected by the deposit of an instrument of acceptance with the Bureau, which shall inform all Governments that have already signed or accepted the present Convention of each signature and deposit of an acceptance and of the date of such signature or deposit.

Article XV

1. The present Convention shall come into force twelve months after the date on which not less than ten Governments have become parties to the Convention, including five Governments of countries each with not less than 500,000 gross tons of tanker tonnage.

2. *a*) For each Government which signs the Convention without reservation as to acceptance or accepts the Convention before the date on which the Convention comes into force in accordance with paragraph (1) of this Article it shall come into force on that date. For each Government which accepts the Convention on or after that date, it shall come into force three months after the date of the deposit of that Government's acceptance.

b) The Bureau shall, as soon as possible, inform all Governments which have signed or accepted the Convention of the date on which it will come into force.

Article XVI

1. *a*) The present Convention may be amended by unanimous agreement between the Contracting Governments.

b) Upon request of any Contracting Government a proposed amendment shall be communicated by the Organization to all Contracting Governments for consideration and acceptance under this paragraph.

2. *a*) An amendment to the present Convention may be proposed to the Organization at any time by any Contracting Government, and such proposal if adopted by a two-thirds majority of the Assembly of the Organization upon recommendation adopted by a two-thirds majority of the Maritime Safety Committee of the Organization shall be communicated by the Organization to all Contracting Governments for their acceptance.

b) Any such recommendation by the Maritime Safety Committee shall be communicated by the Organization to all Contracting Governments for their consideration at least six months before it is considered by the Assembly.

3. *a*) A conference of Governments to consider amendments to the present Convention proposed by any Contracting Government shall at any time be convened by the Organization upon the request of one-third of the Contracting Governments.

b) Every amendment adopted by such conference by a two-thirds majority of the Contracting Governments shall be communicated by the Organization to all Contracting Governments for their acceptance.

4. Any amendment communicated to Contracting Governments for their acceptance under paragraph (2) or (3) of this Article shall come into force for all Contracting Governments, except those which before it comes into force make a declaration that they do not accept the amendment, twelve months after the date on which the amendment is accepted by two-thirds of the Contracting Governments.

5. The Assembly, by a two-thirds majority vote, including two-thirds of the Governments represented on the Maritime Safety Committee, and subject to the concurrence of two-thirds of the Contracting Governments to the present Convention, or a conference convened under paragraph (3) of this Article by a two-thirds majority vote, may determine at the time of its adoption that the amendment is of such an important nature that any Contracting Government which makes a declaration under paragraph (4) of this Article and which does not accept the amendment within a period of twelve months after the amendment comes into force, shall, upon the expiry of this period, cease to be a party to the present Convention.

6. The Organization shall inform all Contracting Governments of any amendments which come into force under this Article, together with the date on which such amendments shall come into force.

7. Any acceptance or declaration under this Article shall be made by a notification in writing to the Organization which shall notify all Contracting Governments of the receipt of the acceptance or declaration.

Article XVII

1. The present Convention may be denounced by any Contracting Government at any time after the expiration of a period of five years from the date on which the Convention comes into force for that Government.

2. Denunciation shall be effected by a notification in writing addressed to the Bureau, which shall notify all the Contracting Governments of any denunciation received and of the date of its receipt.

3. A denunciation shall take effect twelve months, or such longer period as may be specified in the notification, after its receipt by the Bureau.

Article XVIII

1. *a*) The United Nations in cases where they are the administering authority for a territory or any Contracting Government responsible for the international relations of a territory shall as soon as possible consult with such territory in an endeavour to extend the present Convention to that territory and may at any time by notification in writing given to the Bureau declare that the Convention shall extend to such territory.

b) The present Convention shall from the date of the receipt of the notification or from such other date as may be specified in the notification extend to the territory named therein.

2. *a*) The United Nations in cases where they are the administering authority for a territory or any Contracting Government which has made a declaration under paragraph (1) of this Article, at any time after the expiry of a period of five years from the date on which the present Convention has been so extended to any territory, may by a notification in writing given to the Bureau after consultation with such territory declare that the Convention shall cease to extend to any such territory named in the notification.

b) The present Convention shall cease to extend to any territory mentioned in such notification one year, or such longer period as may be specified therein, after the date of receipt of the notification by the Bureau.

3. The Bureau shall inform all the Contracting Governments of the extension of the present Convention to any territory under paragraph (1) of this Article, and of the termination of any such extension under the provisions of paragraph (2) stating in each case the date from which the Convention has been or will cease to be so extended.

Article XIX

1. In case of war or other hostilities, a Contracting Government which considers that it is affected, whether as a belligerent or as a neutral, may suspend the operation of the whole or any part of the present Convention in respect of all or any of its territories. The suspending Government shall immediately give notice of any such suspension to the Bureau.

2. The suspending Government may at any time terminate such suspension and shall in any event terminate it as soon as it ceases to be justified under paragraph (1) of this Article. Notice of such termination shall be given immediately to the Bureau by the Government concerned.

3. The Bureau shall notify all the Contracting Governments of any suspension or termination of suspension under this Article.

Article XX

As soon as the present Convention comes into force it shall be registered by the Bureau with the Secretary-General of the United Nations.

Article XXI

The duties of the Bureau shall be carried out by the Government of the United Kingdom of Great Britain and Northern Ireland* unless and until the Inter-Governmental Maritime Consultative Organization comes into being and takes over the duties assigned to it under the Convention signed at Geneva on the 6 March 1948, and thereafter the duties of the Bureau shall be carried out by the said Organization.

In Witness Whereof the undersigned plenipotentiaries have signed the present Convention†

Done in London this twelfth day of May, 1954, in English and French, both texts being equally authoritative, in a single copy, which shall be deposited with the Bureau and of which the Bureau shall transmit certified copies to all signatory and Contracting Governments.

*Transferred to IMCO 15 June 1959 in accordance with Assembly Resolution A. 8(1).

† Signatures omitted.

ANNEX

FORM OF OIL RECORD BOOK

I.—For Tankers

Name of ship ....

Total cargo carrying capacity of ship in cubic metres ....

a) Loading of oil cargo

1. Date and place of loading			
2. Types of oil loaded			
3. Identity of tank(s) loaded			

b) Transfer of oil cargo during voyage

4. Date of transfer					
5. Identity of tank(s)	i	From			
	ii	To			
6. Was (were) tank(s) in 5 (i) emptied?					

c) Discharge of oil cargo

7. Date and place of discharge			
8. Identity of tank(s) discharged			
9. Was (were) tank(s) emptied?			

d) Ballasting of cargo tanks

10. Identity of tank(s) ballasted			
11. Date and position of ship at start of ballasting			

e) Cleaning of cargo tanks

12. Identity of tank(s) cleaned			
13. Date and duration of cleaning			
14. Methods of cleaning*			

* Hand hosing, machine washing or chemical cleaning. Where chemically cleaned, the chemical concerned and the amount used should be stated.

f). Discharge of dirty ballast

15. Identity of tank(s)			
16. Date and position of ship at start of discharge at sea			
17. Date and position of ship at finish of discharge at sea			
18. Ship's speed(s) during discharge			
19. Quantity discharged to sea			
20. Quantity of polluted water transferred to slop tank(s) (identify slop tanks(s))			
21. Date and port of discharge into shore reception facilities (if applicable)			

g) Discharge of water from slop tanks

22. Identity of slop tank(s)			
23. Time of settling from last entry of residues, or			
24. Time of settling from last discharge			
25. Date, time and position of ship at start of discharge			
26. Sounding of total contents at start of discharge			
27. Sounding of interface at start of discharge			
28. Bulk quantity discharged and rate of discharge			
29. Final quantity discharged and rate of discharge			
30. Date, time and position of ship at end of discharge			
31. Ship's speed(s) during discharge			
32. Sounding of interface at end of discharge			

h) Disposal of residues

33. Identity of tank(s)			
34. Quantity disposed from each tank			
35. Method of disposal of residue: (a) Reception facilities (b) Mixed with cargo (c) Transferred to another (other) tank(s) (identify tank(s) (d) Other method			
36. Date and port of disposal of residue			

*i) Discharge overboard of bilge water containing oil which has accumulated in machinery spaces (including pump rooms) whilst in port**

37. Port			
38. Duration of stay			
39. Quantity disposed			
40. Date and place of disposal			
41. Method of disposal (state whether a separator was used)			

j) Accidental or other exceptional discharges of oil

42. Date and time of occurrence			
43. Place or position of ship at time of occurrence			
44. Approximate quantity and type of oil			
45. Circumstances of discharge or escape and general remarks			

.... Signature of officer or officers in charge of operation concerned

.... Signature of Master

* The routine discharge at sea of bilge water containing any oil from machinery spaces including pump room bilges need not be entered in the oil record book but, if not, it must be entered in the appropriate log book, stating whether or not the discharge was made through a separator. Where the pump starts automatically and discharges through a separator at all times it will be sufficient to enter each day, "Automatic discharge from bilges through separator."

II — For Ships Other Than Tankers

Name of ship ....

a) Ballasting or cleaning of bunker fuel tanks

1. Identity of tank(s) ballasted			
2. Whether cleaned since they last contained oil and, if not, type of oil previously carried			
3. Date and position of ship at start of cleaning			
4. Date and position of ship at start of ballasting			

b) Discharge of dirty ballast or cleaning water from tanks referred to under (a)

5. Identity of tank(s)			
6. Date and position of ships at start of cleaning			
7. Date and position of ship at finish of discharge			
8. Ship's speed(s) during discharge			
9. Method of discharge (state whether separator used)			
10. Quantity discharged			

c) Disposal of residues

11. Quantity of residue retained on board			
12. Methods of disposal of residue: (a) reception facilities (b) mixed with next bunkering (c) transferred to another (other) tank			
13. Date and port of disposal of residue			

*d) Discharge overboard of bilge water containing oil which has accumulated in machinery spaces whilst in port**

14. Port			
15. Duration of stay			
16. Quantity disposed			
17. Date and place of disposal			
18. Method of disposal (state whether separator was used)			

e) Accidental or other exceptional discharges of oil

19. Date and time of occurrence			
20. Place or position of ship at time of occurrence			
21. Approximate quantity and type of oil			
22. Circumstances of discharge or escape and general remarks			

.... Signature of Officer or Officers in charge of operations concerned

.... Signature of Master

* The routine discharge at sea of bilge water containing any oil from machinery spaces need not be entered in the oil record book but if not, it must be entered in the appropriate log book, stating whether or not the discharge was made through a separator. Where the pump starts automatically and discharges through a separator at all times it will be sufficient to enter each day "Automatic discharge from bilges through a separator".

AMENDMENTS TO THE INTERNATIONAL CONVENTION FOR THE PREVENTION OF POLLUTION OF THE SEA BY OIL, 1954, CONCERNING THE PROTECTION OF THE GREAT BARRIER REEF

SUPPLEMENT 1

The Seventh IMCO Assembly adopted on 12 October 1971, by Resolution A.232 (VII), and on 15 October 1971, by Resolution A.246 (VII), the following amendments to the International Convention for the Prevention of Pollution of the Sea by Oil, 1954. In accordance with Article XVI (4) of the Convention, the amendments will come into force twelve months after the date on which they are accepted by two-thirds of the Contracting Governments.

(Resolution A.232 (VII) adopted on 12 October 1971)

Article I

The existing text of the definition of "Nearest Land" in Article I (as amended in 1969) is replaced by the following:

"Nearest land". The term "from the nearest land" means from the baseline from which the territorial sea of the territory in question is established in accordance with the Geneva Convention on the Territorial Sea and the Contiguous Zone, 1958, except that, for the purposes of this Convention "from the nearest land" off the north-eastern coast of Australia shall mean from a line drawn from a point on the coast of Australia in latitude 11° south, longitude 142° 08′ east to a point in latitude 10° 35′ south, longitude 141° 55′ east:

thence to a point latitude 10° 00′ south, longitude 142° 00′ east

thence to a point latitude 9° 10′ south, longitude 143° 52′ east

thence to a point latitude 9° 00′ south, longitude 144° 30′ east

thence to a point latitude 13° 00′ south, longitude 144° 00′ east

thence to a point latitude 15° 00′ south, longitude 146° 00′ east

thence to a point latitude 18° 00′ south, longitude 147° 00′ east

thence to a point latitude 21° 00′ south, longitude 153° 00′ east

thence to a point on the coast of Australia in latitude 24° 42° south, longitude 153° 15′ east.

Article III

The existing text of sub-paragraph (iv) of paragraph (a) of Article III (as amended in 1969) is replaced by the following:

(iv) the discharge is made as far as practicable from the nearest land.

AMENDMENTS TO THE INTERNATIONAL CONVENTION FOR THE PREVENTION OF POLLUTION OF THE SEA BY OIL, 1954 CONCERNING TANK ARRANGEMENTS AND LIMITATIONS OF TANK SIZE

(Resolution A.246 (VII) adopted on 15 October 1971)

The Assembly,

Noting Article 16 (i) of the Convention on the Inter-Governmental Maritime Consultative Organization concerning the functions of the Assembly,

Being conscious of the responsibility of the Organization for taking effective measures for the prevention and control of pollution of the marine environment which may arise from maritime activities,

Realizing that notwithstanding the adoption by the Organization of various measures for preventing collisions and strandings of ships, it is not possible to eliminate entirely accidents which may lead to release of oil, but desiring to minimize ensuing damage to the environment,

Recognizing that construction of oil tankers of large size without accompanying control of size or internal arrangement of cargo tanks leads to the possibility, in the event of a single accident, of serious environmental pollution,

Having examined the Recommendations relating to tank arrangements and to the limitation of tank size prepared by the Maritime Safety Committee at its twenty-third session.

Considering that the universal implementation of such requirements can best be achieved by amending the International Convention for the Prevention of Pollution of the Sea by Oil, 1954,

Noting that Article XVI of the International Convention for the Prevention of Pollution of the Sea by Oil 1954 provides for procedures of amendment involving participation by the Organization,

Adopts the following amendments to the Articles and Annexes to that Convention, the texts of which are attached to this Resolution:

a) the addition of a new Article *VIbis*, and

b) the addition of a new Annex C,

Requests the Secretary-General of the Organization, in conformity with sub-paragraph (2) (*a*) of Article XVI to communicate for consideration and acceptance, certified copies of this Resolution and its Annexes, to all Contracting Governments to the International Convention for the Prevention of Pollution of the Sea by Oil, 1954, together with copies to all Members of the Organization,

Invites all governments concerned to accept the amendments at the earliest possible date, and

Determines in accordance with paragraph (5) of Article XVI that these amendments are of such an important nature that any Contracting Government which makes a declaration under paragraph (4) of Article XVI and which does not accept the amendments within a period of 12 months after the amendments come into force, shall, upon the expiry of this period, cease to be a Party to the present Convention.

ANNEX 1

Add new Article VIbis as follows:

Article VIbis

1. Every tanker to which the present Convention applies and for which the building contract is placed on or after the date of coming into force of this Article shall be constructed in accordance with the provisions of Annex C. In addition, every tanker to which the present Convention applies and for which the building contract is placed, or in the absence of a building contract the keel of which is laid or which is at a similar stage of construction, before the date of coming into force of this Article shall be required, within two years after that date, to comply with the provisions of Annex C, where such a tanker falls into either of the following categories:

a) a tanker, the delivery of which is after 1 January 1977; or

b) a tanker to which both the following conditions apply:

(i) delivery is not later than 1 January 1977; and

(ii) the building contract is placed after 1 January 1972, or in cases where no building contract has previously been placed the keel is laid, or the tanker is at a similar stage of construction, after 30 June 1972.

2. A tanker required under paragraph (1) of this Article to be constructed in accordance with Annex C and so constructed shall carry on board a certificate issued or authorized by the responsible Contracting Government attesting such compliance. A tanker which under paragraph (1) of this Article is not required to be constructed in accordance with Annex C shall carry on board a certificate to that effect issued or authorized by the responsible Contracting Government, or if the tanker does comply with Annex C although not required to do so, it may carry on board a certificate issued or authorized by the responsible Contracting Government attesting such compliance. A Contracting Government shall not permit such tankers under its flag to trade unless the appropriate certificate has been issued.

3. Certificates issued under the authority of a Contracting Government shall be accepted by the other Contracting Governments for all purposes covered by the present Convention. They shall be regarded by the other Contracting Governments as having the same force as certificates issued by them.

4. If a Contracting Government has clear grounds for believing that a tanker required under paragraph (1) of this Article to be constructed in accordance with Annex C entering ports in its territory or using off-shore terminals under its control does not in fact comply with Annex C, such Contracting Government may request consultation with the Government with which the tanker is registered. If, after such consultation or otherwise, the Contracting Government is satisfied that the tanker does not comply with Annex C, such Contracting Government may for this reason deny such a tanker access to ports in its territorial waters or to off-shore terminals under its control until such time as the Contracting Government is satisfied that the tanker does comply.

Add new Annex C as follows:

ANNEX C*

REQUIREMENTS RELATING TO TANK ARRANGEMENTS AND TO THE LIMITATION OF TANK SIZE

1. *Assumed extent of damage*

In the following paragraphs three dimensions of the extent of damage of a parallelepiped due to both collision and stranding are assumed. In the case of stranding, two conditions are set forth to be applied individually to the stated portions of the ship. These values represent the maximum assumed damage in such accidents and are to be used to determine by trial at all conceivable locations the worst combination of compartments which would be breached by such an accident.

1.1 *Collision*

Longitudinal extent (l_c)	$\frac{1}{3} l^{\frac{2}{3}}$	or 14.5 metres, whichever is less
Transverse extent (t_c) inboard from the ship's side at right angles to the centreline at the level of the load line	$\frac{B}{5}$	or 11.5 metres, whichever is less
Vertical extent (v_c)		from the base line upwards without limit

1.2 *Stranding*

	For 0.3L from the forward perpendicular of the ship	Any other part of the ship
Longitudinal extent (l_s)	$\frac{L}{10}$	5 metres
Transverse extent (t_s)	$\frac{B}{6}$ or 10.0 metres, whichever is less	5 metres
Vertical extent (v_s) from the base line	$\frac{B}{15}$ or 6 metres, whichever is less, for any part of the ship	

where: L, B in metres and perpendicular are as defined in Regulation 3 of the International Convention on Load Lines, 1966.

2. *Hypothetical oil outflow from tanks assumed to be breached as a result of the accident*

The hypothetical oil outflow in the case of collision (O_c) and stranding (O_s) shall be calculated by the following formulae with respect to compartments breached by each assumed location of damage as defined in Section 1.

2.1 *Collision*

$$O_c = \Sigma W_i + \Sigma K_i C_i \quad \text{..........(1)}$$

2.2 *Stranding*

$$O_s = \frac{1}{3}(\Sigma Z_i W_i + \Sigma Z_i C_i) \quad \text{..........(2)}$$

where:

W_i = volume of a wing tank in cubic metres breached by the damage assumed in Section 1; W_i for a clean ballast tank may be taken equal to zero,

C = volume of a centre tank in cubic metres breached by the damage assumed in Section 1; C_i for a clean ballast tank may be taken equal to zero,

$K_i = 1 - \frac{b_i}{t_c}$; when b_i is equal to or greater than t_c K_1 shall be taken equal to zero,

$Z_i = 1 - \frac{h_i}{v_s}$, when h_i is equal to or greater than v_s, Z_i shall be taken equal to zero,

b_i = width of wing tank in metres under consideration.

h_i = minimum depth of the bottom in metres under consideration; where no double bottom is fitted, shall be taken equal to zero,

wing tank = any tank adjacent to the side shell plating,

centre tank = any tank inboard a longitudinal bulkhead.

2.3. *Special requirements*

2.3.1 If a void space or clean water ballast tank of a length less than l_c as defined in 1.1 is located between wing oil tanks, O_c in formula (1) may be calculated on the basis of volume W_i being the actual volume of one such tank (where they are of equal capacity) or the smaller of the two tanks (if they differ in capacity) adjacent to such space, multiplied by S_i as defined below and taking for all other wing tanks involved in such a collision the value of the actual full volume.

$$S_i = 1 - \frac{l_i}{l_c}$$

where: l_i = length in metres of void space or clean ballast tank under consideration.

2.3.2 *a)* Credit shall only be given in respect of double bottom tanks which are either empty or carrying clean water when cargo is carried in the tanks above.

b) Where the double bottom does not extend for the full length and width of the tank involved, the

* Where these Amendments enter into force, the Annex (Form of Oil Record Book) will become Annex A and this Annex will become Annex B

double bottom is considered non-existent and the volume of the tanks above the area of the stranding damage shall be included in formula (2) even if the tank is not considered breached because of the installation of such a partial double bottom.

c) Suction wells may be neglected in the determination of the value h_i provided such wells are not excessive in area and extend below the tank for a minimum distance and in no case more than half the height of the double bottom. If the depth of such a well exceeds half the height of the double bottom, h_i shall be equal to the double bottom height minus the well height. Piping serving such wells if installed within the double bottom shall be fitted with valves or other closing arrangements located at the point of connection to the tank served to prevent oil outflow in the event of damage of the piping during stranding. Such piping shall be installed as high from the bottom shell as possible.

2.3.3. In the case where stranding damage simultaneously involves four centre tanks, the value of O_s may be calculated according to the formula

$$O_s = \tfrac{1}{4}(\Sigma Z_i W_i + \Sigma Z_i C_i) \quad \text{.............................. (3)}$$

2.3.4 An Administration may credit as reducing oil outflow in case of stranding, an installed cargo transfer system having an emergency high suction in each cargo oil tank, capable of transferring from a breaching tank or tanks to segregated ballast tanks or to available cargo tankage if it can be assured that such tanks will have sufficient ullage. Credit for such a system would be governed by ability to transfer in two hours of operation, oil equal to one half of the largest of the breached tanks involved and by availability of equivalent receiving capacity in ballast or cargo tanks. The credit shall be confined to permitting calculation of O_s according to formula (3). The pipes for such suction shall be installed at least at a height not less than the vertical extent of the stranding damage v_s.

The Administration shall supply the Organization with the information concerning the arrangements accepted by it, for circulation to other governments.

3. *Limitations of size of cargo oil tanks*

3.1 *Limitation of hypothetical oil outflow*

The hypothetical oil outflow O_c or O_s calculated in accordance with the formulae in Section 2 shall not exceed 30,000 cubic metres or $400\sqrt[3]{DW}$, whichever is the greater but subject to a maximum of 40,000 cubic metres, where DW = deadweight of the ship in metric tons.

3.2 *Limitation of volume of single tank*

The volume of a wing tank shall not exceed seventy-five per cent of the limits of hypothetical oil outflow referred to in 3.1. The volume of a centre tank shall not exceed 50,000 cubic metres.

3.3 *Limitation of tank length*

The length of each tank shall not exceed 10 metres or one of the following values, whichever is the greater:

a) where no longitudinal bulkhead is provided:

$0.1L$

b) where a longitudinal bulkhead is provided at the centreline only:

$0.15L$

c) where two or more longitudinal bulkheads are provided:

(i) for wing tanks:

$0.2L$

(ii) for centre tanks:

(1) if $\frac{b_i}{B}$ is equal to or greater than 1/5:

$0.2L$

(2) if $\frac{b_i}{B}$ is less than 1/5:

— where no centreline longitudinal bulkhead is provided:

$\left(0.5\frac{b_i}{B} + 0.1\right)L$,

— where a centreline longitudinal bulkhead is provided:

$\left(0.25\frac{b_i}{B} + 0.15\right)L$

PHYTO-SANITARY CONVENTION FOR AFRICA SOUTH OF THE SAHARA

[12]

London, 29 July 1954*

The Governments of the Kingdom of Belgium, the French Republic, the Republic of Portugal, the Federation of Rhodesia and Nyasaland, the Union of South Africa and the United Kingdom of Great Britain and Northern Ireland:

Considering that all possible steps should be taken:

a) to prevent the introduction of diseases, insect pests and other enemies of plants into any part of Africa South of the Sahara;

b) to eradicate or control them in so far as they are present in the area;

c) and to prevent their spread;

Having regard to the need for full co-operation to this end with the Commission for Technical Co-operation in Africa South of the Sahara;

Recognising the usefulness of the co-operation provided for in the International Plant Protection Convention signed at Rome on 6 December 1951 and the need for the co-ordination of activities in this field;

Have agreed as follows:

Article 1

The present Convention shall apply to any metropolitan territories of the Governments party to the present Convention (hereinafter referred to as "Participating Governments") which are situated in Africa to the south of the Sahara and to the other territories within that area for whose international relations any of the Participating Governments are responsible.

PERMANENT COMMISSION

Article 2

a) There shall be set up a permanent commission (hereinafter referred to as "the Commission"), to be known as the Inter-African Phyto-Sanitary Commission on which each of the Participating Governments shall be represented and shall exercise one vote.

b) The Commission shall determine its own procedure by a majority vote.

c) The Commission shall seek such information and shall recommend such action as will lead to the fulfilment of the objects of the present Convention.

d) The Commission shall meet at least once a year and at other times when requested so to do by any two of the Participating Governments.

e) Any proposal supported by the votes of not less than two-thirds of the Participating Governments shall be deemed to be carried. Such votes shall be given at a meeting of the Commission or shall be communicated in writing when a proposal has been submitted to the Participating Governments other than at a meeting.

* **As amended by a Protocol signed in London on the 11th October 1961**

Article 3

The Commission shall appoint a Scientific Secretary whose duties shall be as follows:

a) To ensure liaison between the Commission, the Participating Governments, and the Commission for Technical Co-operation in Africa South of the Sahara;

b) To prepare an annual report on the work of the Commission, and on his scientific, administrative and financial activities; to submit this report to the Commission for its approval; and to send copies of the approved report to Participating Governments, and the Secretariat of the Commission for Technical Co-operation in Africa South of the Sahara;

c) To transmit to the Commission any observations received on the annual report;

d) To represent the Commission on the Permanent Committee of Information established under Article 9 of the present Convention and at any international meetings at which the Commission deems his presence desirable.

MEASURES OF PROTECTION

Article 4

Each Participating Government shall undertake to exercise at least such control of plant imports as the Commission shall consider to be necessary, and shall take such legislative or administrative measures as may be required for this purpose.

Article 5

Each Participating Government shall take such measures of quarantine, certification or inspection, or such other measures as may be considered necessary by the Commission in respect of any plants, plant material, seed or packing material (including containers) the importation of which has been considered by the Commission to constitute a threat to agriculture in any part of the area defined in Article 1 of the present Convention.

Article 6

Each Participating Government shall prohibit, for such period of time as the Commission may propose, the importation of any plant, plant material, seed or packing material (including containers) which the Commission has considered shall be refused admittance into the area defined in Article 1 of the present Convention.

Article 7

Each Participating Government shall take such action as may be desirable to deal effectively with diseases, insect pests and other enemies of plants which the Commission considers have become, or are likely to become, a serious danger in territories within the area defined in Article 1 of the present Convention.

Article 8

Nothing in the foregoing Articles of the present Convention shall prevent any Participating Governments from importing into the area defined in Article 1 of the present Convention, under adequate safeguards and for scientific purposes, small quantities of plants, plant material or seeds without prior reference to the other Participating Governments. Participating Governments shall however inform the Commission of each importation of otherwise prohibited plants, plant materials or seeds which is made, and the Commission shall so inform all other Participating Governments.

PERMANENT COMMITTEE OF INFORMATION

Article 9

a) There shall be established in London a Permanent Committee of Information which shall consist of the Directors of the Commonwealth Institute of Entomology and the Commonwealth Mycological Institute and of the Scientific Secretary of the Commission appointed under Article 3 of the present Convention, who shall also act as Secretary of the Committee.

b) The Permanent Committee of Information shall act as an intermediary between the Institutes referred to in paragraph (*a*) of this Article and the Commission for the transmission of relevant information regarding the type, nature and extent of diseases, insect pests and other enemies of plants inside and outside the area defined in Article 1 of the present Convention and shall supply the Commission with such information as it may require.

c) Members of the Permanent Committee of Information, may, in that capacity and for the ends of the present Convention, correspond directly on scientific subjects with the specialists of the territories defined in Article 1 of the present Convention.

d) The Scientific Secretary of the Commission shall have access to the Institutes referred to in paragraph (*a*) of this Article and, pursuant to an agreement to be concluded between the Executive Council of the Commonwealth Agricultural Bureaux and the Commission, shall report to the Commission on the work carried on in those Institutes in relation to this Convention.

e) The Permanent Committee of Information shall endeavour to arrange for the exchange of information with the World Reporting Service on plant diseases and pests which is to be established in accordance with the provisions of Article VII of the aforesaid International Plant Protection Convention.

FINANCE

Article 10

a) Each Participating Government shall contribute towards the cost of the Secretariat of the Commission and towards the cost of the work carried out by the Institutes referred to in Article 9 of the present Convention pursuant to the agreement to be concluded between the Executive Council of the Commonwealth Agricultural Bureaux and the Commission.

b) The annual amount to be contributed by the Participating Governments shall be fixed and apportioned among them as they shall from time to time decide.

c) Payment shall be made to the account of the Commission in London. The first payment shall be made within one month of the date of entry into force of the present Convention by those Governments which have, at that date, already deposited their instruments of ratification, and within one month of the date of the deposit of the instrument of ratification or notification of accession by those Governments which subsequently ratify or accede to the Convention. Subsequent payments shall be made on the corresponding date in each succeeding year.

MISCELLANEOUS PROVISIONS

Article 11

Any Government which is not a signatory to the present Convention may at any time after the Convention has entered into force in accordance with paragraph (*b*) of Article 12 accede thereto in respect of its metropolitan territory or any territory or territories for whose international relations it is responsible, situated in Africa to the south of the Sahara, by means of a notification in writing the Government of the United Kingdom. The Government of the United Kingdom shall inform the other Governments party to the present Convention of each accession notified to them and the Convention shall apply to the territory or territories named in the notification from the date of its receipt by the Government of the United Kingdom.

Article 12

a) The present Convention shall be ratified by the signatory Governments, and the instruments of ratification shall be deposited in the archives of the Government of the United Kingdom, which shall notify the other signatory Governments of the date of deposit of each instrument of ratification and of the date on which the present Convention enters into force in accordance with paragraph (*b*) of this Article.

b) The present Convention shall enter into force on the date of deposit of the fourth instrument of ratification. In respect of any signatory Government ratifying subsequently the Convention shall enter into force on the date of the deposit of its instrument of ratification.

Article 13

a) This Convention may be denounced by any Participating Government after the expiration of one year from the date of its entry into force in respect of that Government by a notification in writing addressed to the Government of the United Kingdom. The denunciation shall take effect one year after the date of the receipt of the notification by the Government of the United Kingdom.

b) The Government of the United Kingdom shall inform the other Participating Governments of each such denunciation and of the date of the receipt thereof.

Article 14

If at any time at least half of the Participating Governments have denounced this Convention in accordance with Article 13 of the present Convention, the Commission shall be dissolved, the records shall be lodged at the Commonwealth Institute of Entomology, and the funds shall be divided *pro rata* according to their annual contributions between such remaining Participating Governments as have made all annual contributions due under Article 10 (*b*) of the present Convention.

Article 15

a) Any Participating Government may recommend amendments to the present Convention.

b) Any such recommendations shall be communicated to the Government of the United Kingdom of Great Britain and Northern Ireland who shall submit them to the other Participating Governments for their acceptance.

c) Any amendment to this Convention shall come into force upon the receipt by the Government of the United Kingdom of Great Britain and Northern Ireland of notice of acceptance by all the Participating Governments.

d) The Governments of the United Kingdom of Great Britain and Northern Ireland shall communicate the date of entry into force to all the Participating Governments.

e) After an amendment has entered into force no Government may accede to this Convention unless it also accepts the amendment.

In Witness Whereof the undersigned, duly authorised thereto by their respective Governments, have signed the present Convention.

Done at London the 29th day of July 1954, in the English and French languages, both texts being equally authoritative, in a single copy which shall be deposited in the archives of the Government of the United Kingdom by whom certified copies shall be transmitted to all the other signatory and acceding Governments.

PLANT PROTECTION AGREEMENT FOR THE SOUTH EAST ASIA AND PACIFIC REGION [13]

Rome, 27 February 1956

The Contracting Governments, desiring to prevent, through concerted action, the introduction into and spread within the South East Asia and Pacific Region of destructive plant diseases and pests, have concluded the following Agreement, which is a supplementary agreement under Article III of the International Plant Protection Convention of 1951:

Article I

DEFINITIONS

In this Agreement and in the appendices hereto, the following terms shall have the meaning hereby assigned to them, save as otherwise provided:

a) The South East Asia and Pacific Region, hereinafter called "The Region," comprises the territories in South East Asia east of the western border of Pakistan and south of the Himalayas, the southern border of China and the northern border of the Philippines, and all those territories in the Pacific Ocean, the South China Sea and the Indian Ocean situated wholly or partly in the area bounded by longitudes 100° East and 165° West and latitudes 15° North and 20° South, but excluding Australia;

b) "plant" or "plants" means all species of plants or parts thereof, whether living or dead (including stems, branches, tubers, bulbs, corms, stocks, budwood, cuttings, layers, slips, suckers, roots, leaves, flowers, fruits, seeds and any other parts of plants);

c) "territory" means a State or Territory within the Region defined in (*a*) above;

d) "the Organization" means the Food and Agriculture Organization of the United Nations.

e) "the Committee" means the Plant Protection Committee for the South East Asia and Pacific Region established in pursuance of Article II of this Agreement.

Article II

REGIONAL COMMITTEE

1. The Contracting Governments hereby establish a regional committee, to be known as the Plant Protection Committee for the South East Asia and Pacific Region, whose functions shall include:

a) the determination of procedures and arrangements necessary for the implementation of this Agreement and the making of recommendations to the Contracting Governments accordingly;

b) the review of reports submitted by the Contracting Governments of progress in the implementation of this Agreement;

c) the consideration of problems requiring co-operation on a regional basis and of measures for mutual assistance.

2. Each Contracting Government shall be represented on the Committee and shall have one vote. A majority of the Contracting Governments shall constitute a quorum. Decisions of the Committee shall be taken by a majority of the votes cast except as otherwise provided in this Agreement.

3. The Committee shall meet whenever convened by the Director-General of the Organization after consultation with the Chairman of the Committee. The Director-General of the Organization shall convene the committee at least once every two years or when so requested by at least one third of the Contracting Governments.

4. The Committee shall elect from amongst the delegates a Chairman who shall serve for a period of two years or until the first session of the Committee held after the expiration of the period of two years. The Chairman shall be eligible for re-election.

5. Expenses incurred by delegates of Contracting Governments in attending sessions of the Committee shall be determined and paid by their respective Governments. The Director-General of the Organization shall appoint and provide the secretariat of the Committee from the staff of the Organization who shall serve only during sessions of the Committee. The expenses of the secretariat of the Committee shall be determined and paid by the Organization.

6. The Committee shall establish its own rules of procedure.

Article III

MEASURES REGARDING THE IMPORTATION OF PLANTS FROM OUTSIDE THE REGION

For the purpose of preventing the introduction into its territory or territories of destructive diseases and pests, and in particular those listed in Appendix A to this Agreement, each Contracting Government shall use its best endeavours to apply with respect to the importation of any plants, including their packings and containers, and any packings and containers of plant origin, from anywhere outside the Region, such measures of prohibition, certification, inspection, disinfection, disinfestation, quarantine, destruction or other measures as may be recommended by the Committee, taking into consideration the provisions of Articles V and VI of the International Plant Protection Convention.

Appendix A to this Agreement may be modified by a decision of the Committee.

Article IV

MEASURES TO EXCLUDE SOUTH AMERICAN LEAF BLIGHT OF HEVEA FROM THE REGION

In view of the importance of the Hevea rubber industry in the Region, and of the danger of introducing the destructive South American leaf blight (*Dothidella ulei*) of the Hevea rubber tree, the Contracting Governments shall take the measures specified in Appendix B to this Agreement. Appendix B to this agreement may be modified by a decision of the Committee taken unanimously.

Article V

MEASURES REGARDING MOVEMENT OF PLANTS WITHIN THE REGION

For the purpose of preventing the spread within the Region of destructive diseases and pests, each Contracting Government shall use its best endeavours to apply, with respect to the importation into its territory of any plants, including packings and containers, and any packings and containers of plant origin, from another territory within the Region, such measures or prohibition certification, inspection, disinfection, disinfestation, quarantine, destruction or other measures as may be recommended by the Committee, in addition to measures already adopted by each Contracting Government.

Article VI

GENERAL EXEMPTION

This Agreement shall not apply to the following plants and plant products except insofar as any such plants or plant products are explicitly made subject to specific measures of control provided in this Agreement or recommended by the Committee:

a) any plants imported for food or for analytical, medicinal or manufacturing purposes;

b) all seeds of annual, or biennial field crops or vegetables, and all seeds or cut flowers of annual, biennial or perennial ornamental plants which are essentially herbaceous in character; and

c) any processed plant products.

Article VII

SETTLEMENT OF DISPUTES

If there be any dispute regarding the interpretation or implementation of this Agreement, or regarding action taken by any Contracting Government under this Agreement, and such dispute cannot be resolved by the Committee, the Government or Governments concerned may request the Director-General of the Organization to appoint a committee of experts to consider such dispute.

Article VIII

RIGHTS AND OBLIGATIONS OF CONTRACTING GOVERNMENTS NOT PARTIES TO THE INTERNATIONAL PLANT PROTECTION CONVENTION

Nothing in the International Plant Protection Convention shall affect the rights and obligations of Contracting Governments which are not parties to the Convention.

Article IX

AMENDMENT

1. Any proposal by a Contracting Government for the amendment of this Agreement, except Appendices A and B, shall be communicated, through the Committee, to the Director-General of the Organization.

2. Any proposed amendment of this Agreement received by the Director-General of the Organization shall be presented to a session of the Council of the Organization for approval.

3. Notice of any proposed amendment of this Agreement shall be transmitted to the Contracting Governments by the Director-General of the Organization not later than the time when the agenda of the session of the Council at which the matter is to be considered is despatched.

4. Any such amendment of this Agreement, approved by the Council of the Organization, shall come into force with respect to all Contracting Governments as from the thirtieth day after acceptance by two-thirds of the Contracting Governments. Amendments involving new obligations for Contracting Governments, however, shall come into force in respect of each Contracting Government only on acceptance by it and as from the thirtieth day after such acceptance.

5. The instruments of acceptance of amendment shall be deposited with the Director-General of the Organization. The effective date of acceptance shall be the date of such deposit. The Director-General of the Organization shall inform all Contracting Governments of the receipt of acceptances and the entry into force of amendments.

Article X

SIGNATURE AND ADHERENCE

1. The Government of any State situated in the Region, or any Government which is responsible for the international relations of a territory or territories in the Region, may become a party to this Agreement, by either

a) signature; or

b) signature subject to ratification followed by such ratification; or

c) adherence.

Governments may not subject their signature, ratification or adherence to any reservation.

2. This Agreement, the text of which was approved by the Council of the Organization on 26 November 1955, shall be open for signature until 30 June 1956 or until the date of its entry into force in conformity with the provisions of Article XI, paragraph 1, whichever date is the later. The Director-General of the Organization shall immediately inform all signatory Governments of the signature of this Agreement by any other Government. Ratification shall be effected by the deposit of an instrument of ratification with the Director-General of the Organization and shall become effective as from the date of deposit.

3. This Agreement shall be open for adherence as from 1 July 1965 or from the date of its entry into force in conformity with the provisions of Article XI, paragraph 1, whichever date is the later. Adherence shall be effected by the deposit of an instrument of adherence with the Director-General of the Organization and shall become effective as from the date of deposit.

4. The Director-General of the Organization shall immediately inform all signatory and adhering Governments of the deposit of an instrument of ratification or of adherence.

Article XI

ENTRY INTO FORCE

1. This Agreement shall come into force as soon as three Governments have become parties to it, either by signature, or by signature subject to ratification followed by such ratification.

2. The Director-General of the Organization shall notify all signatory Governments of the date of entry into force of this Agreement.

Article XII

DENUNCIATION AND TERMINATION

1. Any Contracting Government may, at any time after the expiration of one year from the date on which it became a party to the Agreement, or from the date on which the Agreement entered into force, whichever is the later, denounce this Agreement by notification addressed to the Director-General of the Organization who shall at once inform all signatory and adhering Governments of the denunciation.

2. The denunciation shall take effect one year from the date of receipt of the notification by the Director-General of the Organization.

3. This Agreement shall automatically be terminated should the parties to it become fewer than three as the result of denunciations.

APPENDIX A

DESTRUCTIVE PESTS AND DISEASES NOT YET ESTABLISHED IN THE SOUTH EAST ASIA AND PACIFIC REGION

CACAO *(Theobroma cacao)*		*Known Distribution*
Sahlbergella singularis Hagl.	Capsid	West Africa, Belgian Congo
Distantiella theobroma Dist.	Capsid	West Africa, Belgian Congo
Marasmius perniciosus Stahel	Witches broom	West Indies, South America
Monilia roreri Cif.	Monilia pod rot	South America
Trachysphaera fructigena Tabor and Bunting	Trachysphaera pot rot	Africa
Virus		West Africa
Virus diseases	Swollen shoot	Trinidad
CITRUS (*Citrus* spp.)		
Anastrepha spp.,*es. A. ludens* (Loew.)	Mexican fruit fly	Central America
Deuterophoma tracheiphila Petri	Mal Secco	Mediterranean region
COCONUT (*Cocos nucifera*)		
Pachymerus nucleorum (F).	(A Bruchid)	New World
Theraptus sp.	(A Coreid)	East Africa, Zanzibar
Aphelencoides cocophilus (Cobb.) Goodey	Red Ring disease	West Indies
COFFEE (*Coffea* spp.)		
Antestia spp.	A Pentatomid bug	Africa
Leucoptera caffeella (Guer.)	White coffee leat miner	New World, Africa
Planococccus henyae (Le Pelley)	A mealy bug	East and West Africa
Omphalia flavida Maubl. and Rangel	American leaf spot	Mexico, U.S.A., West Indies. Central and South America
Trachysphaera fructigena Tabor and Bunting	Trachsyphaera fruit rot	Africa
COTTON (*Gossypium* spp.)		
Anthonomous grandis Boh.	Mexican cotton boll worm	West Indies, Mexico, Central
Anthonomus spp.	Boll worms	America, Venezuela, U.S.A.
Diparopsis spp.	Red boll worms	New World
Phymatotrichum omnivorum (Shear) Duggar	Texas root rot	Africa Mexico, U.S.A.
Virus	Leaf curl	Africa
RUBBER *(Hevea brasiliensis)*		
Dothidella ulei P. Henn	South American leaf blight•	Mexico, Central America,
Pellicularia filamentosa (Pat.) Rogers	Target leaf spot	Trinidad, South America Central and South America

MAIZE (*Zea mays)*		
Diatraea spp.	Stalk borers	Southern U.S.A., Mexico, West Indies, Central America, South America
Puccinia polysora Underw.	Polysora rust	Africa, Mexico, U.S.A., Central America, West Indies, South America
OIL PALM (*Elaeis guineensis*)		
Pachymerus lacerdae (Chevr.)	(A Bruchid)	Nigeria
Pachymerus nucleorum (F.)	(A Bruchid)	New World
Pimelephila ghesquierii Tams.	(A Pyralid)	West Africa
Fusarium oxysporum	Fusarium Wilt	West Africa
POTATO (*Solanum tuberosum*)		
Leptinotarsa decemlineata Say	Colorado beetle	New World, Europe
Corynebacterium sepedonicum	Bacterial ring rot	New World, Europe
RICE (*Oryza sativa)*		
Diatraea spp.	Stem or stalk borers	Southern U.S.A., Mexico, West Indies, Central America, South America
Mormidea spp., esp. *M. poecila* Dall	Pentatomid bugs	Central America, South America
Virus	Rice dwarf	Japan
SUGAR CANE (*Saccharum* spp.)		
Diatraea spp., esp. *D. saccharalis* (F.)	Stalk borers	Southern U.S.A., Mexico, West Indies, Central America, South America
Dermolepida spp.	White cane grubs	Queensland
Clemora smithi (Arr.)	A white cane grub	Mauritius
SWEET POTATO (*Ipomaea batatas*)		
Virus	Internal Cork	U.S.A.

(This list is tentative and subject to revision by the Regional Committee.)

APPENDIX B

MEASURES TO EXCLUDE SOUTH AMERICAN LEAF BLIGHT OF HEVEA FROM THE REGION

1. In this Appendix:

a) "the American tropics" means those parts of the continent of America, including adjacent islands, which are bounded by the Tropic of Capricorn (latitude 23½°S) and the Tropic of Cancer (latitude 23½°N) and the meridians of longitude 30°W and 120°W, and includes the part of Mexico north of the Tropic of Cancer;

b) "Competent Authority" means the officer or Government Department or other agency, which each Contracting Government recognizes as its authority for the purpose of this Appendix.

2. Each Contracting Government shall prohibit by law the importation into its territory or territories of any plant or plants of the genus *Hevea* from outside the Region, unless:

a) the importation is made for scientific purposes, and

b) written permission has been granted for each consignment of plant or plants by the Competent Authority of the importing territory or territories and the importation is in accordance with such special conditions as may be imposed by the Competent Authority in granting such permission, and

c) the plant or plants have been disinfected and

freed of any original soil in the country of origin in a manner acceptable to the Competent Authority of the importing territory and are free from pests and diseases, and each consignment of plant or plants is accompanied or covered by a certificate to the effect that the above requirements have been fulfilled, and signed by an appropriate authority in the country of origin; and

d) each consignment is addressed to and is received by the Competent Authority of the importing territory.

3. Each Contracting Government shall prohibit by law the importation into its territory or territories of any plant or plants of the genus *Hevea* capable of further growth or propagation (excluding seed) from the American tropics or from any other country in which South American leaf blight (*Dothidella ulei*) is present, unless, in addition to the requirements of paragraph 2 of this Appendix, at a place approved by the Competent Authority of the importing territory and situated outside the Region and outside the American tropics and any other country in which South American leaf blight (*Dothidella ulei*) is present, such plant or plants have been grown for an adequate period at a plant quarantine station for *Hevea* and each consignment of such plant or plants is accompanied or covered by a certificate to the effect that the above requirements have been fulfilled, and signed by the officer-in-charge of such quarantine station.

4. Each Contracting Government shall prohibit by law the importation into its territory or territories of any seed of any plant of the genus *Hevea* from the American tropics or from any other country in which South American leaf blight (*Dothidella ulei*) is present, unless, in addition to the requirements of paragraph 2 of this Appendix, such seed, having been examined and again disinfected at a place approved by the Competent Authority of the importing territory and situated outside the Region and outside the American tropics and any other country in which South American leaf blight (*Dothidella ulei*) is present, has been repacked with new packing materials in new containers, and unless each consignment of such seed is accompanied or covered by a certificate to the effect that the above requirements have been fulfilled, and signed by the officer-in-charge of these operations.

5. Each Contracting Government shall prohibit by law the importation into its territory or territories of any plant or plants of the genus *Hevea* not capable of further growth or propagation (such as fresh or dried herbarium specimens); unless in addition to the requirements of sub-paragraphs (*a*), (*b*) and (*d*) of paragraph 2 of this Appendix, the Competent Authority of the importing country is satisfied that such plant or plants are required for a legitimate special purpose and that such plant or plants have been sterilized in the country of origin by a method satisfactory to the said Competent Authority.

6. Each Contracting Government shall prohibit by law the importation into its territory or territories of any plant or plants, other than the genus *Hevea*, capable of further growth or propagation and originating in the American tropics or in any other country in which South American leaf blight (*Dothidella ulei*) is present, unless consignment of such plant or plants by the Competent Authority of the importing territory or territories and the importation is in accordance with such special conditions as may be imposed by the Competent Authority in granting such permission.

7. The Competent Authority of any territory or territories into which any plant or plants of the genus *Hevea* are imported for further growth or propagation shall ensure that such plant or plants are grown under control for such period as will ensure that such plant or plants are free from all pests and diseases before they are released.

In Witness Whereof the undersigned, duly authorized to that effect, have signed this Agreement on behalf of their respective Governments on the dates appearing opposite their signatures.

Done at Rome on the twenty-seventh day of February one thousand nine hundred and fifty-six in two copies in the English, French and Spanish languages, which languages shall be equally authoritative. The text of this Agreement shall be authenticated by the Chairman of the Council of the Organization and the Director-General of the Organization. After expiry of the period during which the Agreement is open for signature, in accordance with Article X, paragraph 2, one copy of the Agreement shall be deposited with the Secretary-General of the United Nations and the other in the archives of the Organization. Additional copies of this text shall be certified by the Director-General of the Organization and furnished to all Governments parties to the Agreement, with the indication of the date on which it has come into force.

CONVENTION (WITH ANNEX) CONCERNING FISHING IN THE WATERS OF THE DANUBE [14]

Bucharest, 29 January 1958

The Governments of the Romanian People's Republic, the People's Republic of Bulgaria, the Federal People's Republic of Yugoslavia and the Union of Soviet Socialist Republics,

Having a common interest in the rational utilization and expansion of the stocks of fish in the river Danube,

Recognizing the need for co-operation in working out a scientific basis for intensive augmentation of the stocks of fish and the regulation of fishing,

Have decided to conclude this Convention and have for this purpose appointed as their plenipotentiaries:

The Government of the Romanian People's Republic: Constantin Teodoru, Deputy Minister of the Consumer Goods Industry;

The Government of the People's Republic of Bulgaria: Lalyu Ganchev, First Deputy Minister of the Food Industry;

The Government of the Federal People's Republic of Yugoslavia: Nikola Dzuverovic, member of the Executive Council of the People's Republic of Serbia;

The Government of the Union of Soviet Socialist Republics: Aleksandr Akimovich Ishkov, Minister of the USSR;

who, having exchanged their full powers, found in good and due form, have agreed as follows:

Article 1

The Contracting Parties agree to regulate fishing in the waters of the Danube throughout its course within the territory of the Contracting Parties to the point of entry into the Black Sea, including the Danube Delta, in accordance with the provisions of this Convention.

Article 2

Each Contracting Party shall exercise the right of fishing in the Danube in its own waters bounded by the State frontier.

Article 3

This Convention shall apply to the waters of the Danube, including its mouth, to tributaries of the Danube up to the maximum extent of its flood waters, and to lakes, estuaries and pools permanently or temporarily connected with the Danube, in the Danube flood-basin in the territory of the Contracting Parties, including the area adjoining the mouth.

Article 4

The Contracting Parties agree to put into effect and apply on their own sections of the Danube and on the waters referred to in article 3, simultaneously with the entry into force of this Convention, the Regulations for Fishing in the River Danube which are annexed to and form an integral part of this Convention.

Article 5

The Contracting Parties agree to carry out in the river Danube and in the waters referred to in article 3 improvement works and piscicultural operations to ameliorate the natural conditions for the breeding, growth and normal increase in stocks of fish of economic importance.

In the event of the erection on the Danube of water engineering works, in particular dams, which may change the hydrological and hydrobiological regime of the river, those Contracting Parties which construct and use the said works shall prepare in advance and apply jointly a plan of action to safeguard the normal migratory movements of fish.

The Contracting Parties shall at the same time carry out such piscicultural operations as will safeguard the normal breeding and development of economically valuable species of fish, in the sections of the river situated above and below the said works, under the new environmental conditions created by the erection of those works.

The question of payment of the costs of construction and use of piscicultural and water improvement works on the Danube shall be resolved in each individual case by agreement between the States concerned.

Article 6

In order to increase the stocks of economically valuable species of fish in the waters referred to in this Convention, stations for the artificial breeding of such species of fish, in particular the Acipenseridae, shall be established as necessary.

Article 7

The Contracting Parties shall work out and apply measures to prevent the contamination and pollution of the river Danube and of the waters referred to in article 3 by unclarified sewage and other waste from industrial and municipal undertakings which are harmful to fish and other aquatic organisms, and measures to regulate blasting operations.

Article 8

In the interests of rational fishing and in order to ensure the normal breeding and conservation of economically valuable species of fish, the Contracting Parties shall communicate to one another, in good time, information on the catches and migratory movements of fish in all waters to which this Convention applies.

Article 9

In order to strengthen scientific and technical collaboration in matters of fishery economy, fish breeding and hydrobiology in the Danube basin, the Contracting Parties shall co-operate with one another under the appropriate scientific and technical agreements.

Article 10

For purposes of scientific research the Contracting Parties may conduct joint experimental fishing operations in the Danube waters of any of the States Parties to this Convention, on the basis of recommendations by the Mixed Commission and by agreement between the countries concerned in each particular case.

Article 11

With a view to working out and co-ordinating measures for the application of this Convention, a Mixed Commission shall be established. Each Contracting Party shall appoint two representatives to the said Commission within three months after the entry into force of this Convention. The Governments of the Contracting Parties shall communicate to one another through the diplomatic channel the names of their representatives on the Commission.

The Mixed Commission shall meet at least once a year in the territory of each of the Contracting Parties in turn.

The Mixed Commission shall function under a statute which shall be drafted by the Commission at its first meeting after the entry into force of this Convention and approved by the Governments of the Contracting Parties.

The place and date of meeting of the Mixed Commission shall be fixed by the Commission in advance.

Article 12

It shall be the duty of the Mixed Commission:

1. To work out agreed measures, arising out of this Convention, for the regulation of fishing and the augmentation of the stocks of fish in the river Danube;

2. To present proposals to the Contracting Parties with a view to amending or supplementing the Regulations for Fishing in the River Danube and to take decisions on questions which it is authorized under the said Fishing Regulations to resolve;

3. To organize the exchange of information among the Contracting Parties concerning the implementation of this Convention;

4. To co-ordinate the planning of scientific research projects on the study of fishing in the Danube to be conducted jointly or severally by the competent agencies of the Contracting Parties;

5. To determine the nature and scope of the statistical and other data which each Contracting Party shall furnish to the Mixed Commission for the purpose of implementing this Convention;

6. To deal with such other matters as the Contracting Parties may refer to it.

Article 13

The Mixed Commission may make recommendations to the Contracting Parties on the matters within its competence.

The recommendations of the Mixed Commission and its decisions on the matters mentioned in article 12 above shall be deemed adopted by the Commission if they receive the favourable votes of the representatives of all the countries members thereof.

Article 14

In order that the measures to regulate fishing and operations for breeding and increasing the stocks of economically valuable species of fish may be extended to other parts of the Danube, this Convention shall be open for accession by other Danube States.

Article 15

This Convention shall not impede the conclusion of bilateral agreements on matters relating to fishing in the Danube between any two Contracting Parties or between a Contracting Party and any other Danubian State, provided that such agreements do not conflict with the interests of the conservation of stocks of fish or with the Fishing Regulations laid down by this Convention.

Article 16

This Convention shall be ratified and shall enter into force on the date of deposit of the last instrument of ratification with the Government of the Romanian People's Republic, in whose archives the original of the Convention shall be kept.

The Government of the Romanian People's Republic shall notify the Governments of all the Contracting Parties of the date of deposit of the last instrument of ratification.

Article 17

The Convention is concluded for a term of five years.

For those Contracting Parties which do not give notice of termination of this Convention to the Government of the Romanian People's Republic not later than six months before the expiry of this term, it shall remain in force for a further period of five years.

Article 18

The Government of the Romanian People's Republic shall take the necessary action to register this Convention with the Secretariat of the United Nations.

Certified true copies of this Convention shall be transmitted by the Government of the Romanian People's Republic to all the other Parties to the Convention.

Done at Bucharest, on 29 January 1958, in one copy in the Romanian, Bulgarian, Serbo-Croat and Russian languages, all texts being equally authentic.

ANNEX

REGULATIONS FOR FISHING IN THE RIVER DANUBE AND IN THE WATERS REFERRED TO IN ARTICLE 3 OF THE CONVENTION

Part I

PROHIBITED PLACES AND TIMES FOR FISHING

Article 1

Fishing in the waters of the river Danube shall be prohibited each year for a period of thirty days between 15 April and 15 June, according to hydrometeorological conditions.

In 1958 the close period shall be from 15 April to 15 May. Thereafter the dates of the close period shall be determined by the Mixed Commission.

The Contracting Parties may by common agreement stagger the close period by sectors of the Danube, provided that such period is of thirty days' duration and falls between 15 April and 15 June.

The close period for the taking of Acipenseridae and herring shall be as prescribed in article 2 below.

Article 2

For the Acipenseridae the close period, sector by sector, shall be as follows:

— In the sector from the Black Sea to the mouth of the Prut: 15 March to 15 April;

— In the sector from the mouth of the Prut to the mouth of the Timok: 15 April to 15 May;

— In the sector from the mouth of the Timok up to Kladovo: 15 May to 15 June.

For the taking of Danube herring the close period, sector by sector, shall be as follows:

— In the sector from the Black Sea to Ceatalul Ismail: five consecutive days in the period between 15 March and 1 May;

— In the sector from Ceatalul Ismail to Vadul Oii: twenty consecutive days in the period between 1 April and 15 May;

— In the sector from Vadul Oii to the mouth of the Timok: thirty consecutive days in the period between 15 April and 1 July.

The date of each close period shall be recommended by the Fishery Research Institute of the Romanian People's Republic and shall be communicated to the Parties not later than ten days before the start of the close period.

Article 3

In order to safeguard the passage of Danube herring and Acipenseridae in breeding condition into the Danube and the escape of the young of these species to the sea, fishing shall be prohibited throughout the year in the waters adjoining the mouth, in corridors extending laterally one kilometre on either side of the axis of each branch of the river and a distance of five kilometres out to sea.

During the period 1 June to 31 July the corridors referred to in the first paragraph of this article shall be extended laterally one additional kilometre on either side, so that each corridor covers a zone with a total width of four kilometres.

Article 4

The taking of Black Sea salmon (*Salmo trutta labrax*) and Danube salmon (*Salmo hucho*) in the Danube shall be prohibited throughout the year.

The taking of the said salmon may be permitted solely for purposes of pisciculture and scientific research.

Part II

PROHIBITED TACKLE AND METHODS OF FISHING

Article 5

The following shall be prohibited throughout the year:

1. Fishing with anchovy, sardine and herring seines in the system of the Danube and in the waters adjoining the mouth for a distance of ten kilometres out to sea, over a zone extending laterally two kilometres on either side of the axis of each branch of the river;

2. Fishing with drag-nets or trawls in the waters adjoining the mouth of the Danube;

3. The use of explosive, poisonous and narcotic substances and of firearms for the purpose of fishing in the river Danube, in any waters connected therewith (channels, lakes, estuaries or pools) and in the waters adjoining the mouth;

4. Fishing for Acipenseridae with *ahana* nets;

5. Fishing with fish-traps and bag-nets in the waters of the Danube shall henceforth be regulated by the Mixed Commission, which shall set a quota on such devices for each State Party to this Convention.

6. Fishing with sardine nets in lakes and estuaries between 1 March and 31 October.

Article 6

The setting of fish barriers in canals and branches connecting the Danube with lakes in the sector between the mouth of the Danube and Kladovo shall be permitted only after the end of the spring run of fish, from 10 May to 31 October. The interval between the stakes of the barriers shall not be less than three centimetres.

Article 7

It shall be unlawful to fish with fixed or mobile tackle which takes up more than two-thirds of the width of the Danube, its channels or branches, or to cast seines from opposite points on both banks at once.

Part III

SIZE OF MESH OF FISHING-NETS

Article 8

It shall be unlawful to use fishing-nets with a mesh of less than the following size (in millimetres):

1. Purse of fine-meshed seines and

trawls 28
2. Purse of herring-seines and trawls 26
3. Sac of fish-traps 25
4. Nets for catching pike-perch, bream and carp 40
Nets for catching Danube herring 28

Trammel nets may be used provided that the size of the coarse mesh is not less than 50 millimetres, or for Danube herring fishing, not less than 28 millimetres.

Part IV

SIZE OF FISH, CRAYFISH AND MOLLUSCS

Article 9

It shall be unlawful to take, receive, sell, process or preserve fish of less than the following industrial size (in centimetres) in fresh condition:

Beluga (*Huso huso*) 140
Russian sturgeon (*Acipenser guldenstaedti*) ... 80
Sevryuga (*Acipenser stellatus*) 75
Sterlet (*Acipenser ruthenus*) 33
Carp (*Cyprinus carpio*) 25
Pike-perch (*Lucioperca sandra*) 30
Bream (*Abramis brama*) 20
Herring (*Caspialosa pontica*) 16
Crayfish (*Astacus leptodactylus*) 9
Mussel (*Unio pictorum*) 8

Measurements to determine the industrial size of fish must be made from the tip of the snout to the base of the tail fin.

The taking of fish under the prescribed industrial size shall be permissible in a proportion not exceeding 10 per cent by number of the total catch.

The taking of *Acipenser nudiventris* shall be prohibited for five years from the date of entry into force of the Convention.

Part V

GENERAL PROVISIONS

Article 10

The acclimatization and breeding of new species of fish and other animals and of acquatic plants in the waters of the Danube to which the Convention applies may not be carried out save with the consent of the Mixed Commission.

Article 11

The penalties for violation of these Regulations shall be prescribed by the legislation of the Contracting Parties.

Article 12

The Mixed Commission shall have the right to fix the dates of close periods for fishing, to determine the boundaries of the sectors covered by the staggered close period for fishing provided for in articles 1 and 2 of these Regulations, and to revise and adopt decisions under articles 3, 5, 6 and 8 of these Regulations.

With the consent of the Governments of the Contracting Parties, the Mixed Commission may amend and supplement article 9 of these Regulations (on the basis of article 12, paragraph (2), of the Convention concerning fishing in the waters of the Danube).

Article 13

The use of fishing devices harmful to the stocks of fish shall gradually be discontinued; steps to this end shall be taken as soon as possible. Consequently, beginning in 1958, there shall be no increase in the number of such devices.

The introduction of all new fishing devices and methods (use of electric current, etc.) shall be subject to the condition that they have no adverse effect on the stocks of fish.

Article 14

With a view to the uniform interpretation of the provisions of the Convention and the Fishing Regulations, it is understood that the term *"rybolovstvo"* in the Russian text, the term *"ribarstvo"* in the Bulgarian and Serbo-Croat texts and the term *"Pescuit"* in the Romanian text are identical in meaning.

Article 15

These Regulations for fishing in the river Danube shall constitute an annex to and an integral part of the Convention concerning fishing in the waters of the Danube.

CONVENTION ON THE CONTINENTAL SHELF [15]

Geneva, 29 April 1958

The States Parties to this Convention have agreed as follows:

Article 1

For the purpose of these articles, the term "continental shelf" is used as referring (*a*) to the seabed and subsoil of the submarine areas adjacent to the coast but outside the area of the territorial sea, to a depth of 200 metres or, beyond that limit, to where the depth of the superjacent waters admits of the exploitation of the natural resoures of the said areas; (*b*) to the seabed and subsoil of similar submarine areas adjacent to the coasts of islands.

Article 2

1. The coastal State exercises over the continental shelf sovereign rights for the purpose of exploring it and exploiting its natural resources.

2. The rights referred to in paragraph 1 of this article are exclusive in the sense that if the coastal State does not explore the continental shelf or exploit its natural resources, no one may undertake these activities, or make a claim to the continental shelf, without the express consent of the coastal State.

3. The rights of the coastal State over the continental shelf do not depend on occupation, effective or notional, or on any express proclamation.

4. The natural resources referred to in these articles consist of the mineral and other non-living resources of the seabed and subsoil together with living organisms belonging to sedentary species, that is to say, organisms which, at the harvestable stage, either are immobile on or under the seabed or are unable to move except in constant physical contact with the seabed or the subsoil.

Article 3

The rights of the coastal State over the continental shelf do not affect the legal status of the superjacent waters as high seas, or that of the airspace above those waters.

Article 4

Subject to its right to take reasonable measures for the exploration of the continental shelf and the exploitation of its natural resources, the coastal State may not impede the laying or maintenance of submarine cables or pipe lines on the continental shelf.

Article 5

1. The exploration of the continental shelf and the exploitation of its natural resources must not result in any unjustifiable interference with navigation, fishing or the conservation of the living resources of the sea, nor result in any interference with fundamental oceanographic or other scientific research carried out with the intention of open publication.

2. Subject to the provisions of paragraphs 1 and 6 of this article, the coastal State is entitled to construct and maintain or operate on the continental shelf installations and other devices necessary for its exploration and the exploitation of its natural resources, and to establish safety zones around such installations and devices and to take in those zones measures necessary for their protection.

3. The safety zones referred to in paragraph 2 of this article may extend to a distance of 500 metres around the installations and other devices which have been erected, measured from each point of their outer edge. Ships of all nationalities must respect these safety zones.

4. Such installations and devices, though under the jurisdiction of the coastal State, do not possess the status of islands. They have no territorial sea of their own, and their presence does not affect the delimitation of the territorial sea of the coastal State.

5. Due notice must be given of the construction of any such installations, and permanent means for giving warning of their presence must be maintained. Any installations which are abandoned or disused must be entirely removed.

6. Neither the installations or devices, nor the safety zones around them, may be established where interference may be caused to the use of recognized sea lanes essential to international navigation.

7. The coastal State is obliged to undertake, in safety zones, all appropriate measures for the protection of the living resources of the sea from harmful agents.

8. The consent of the coastal State shall be obtained in respect of any research concerning the continental shelf and undertaken there. Nevertheless the coastal State shall not normally withhold its consent if the request is submitted by a qualified institution with a view to purely scientific research into the physical or biological characteristics of the continental shelf, subject to the proviso that the coastal State shall have the right, if it so desires, to participate or to be represented in the research, and that in any event the results shall be published.

Article 6

1. Where the same continental shelf is adjacent to the territories of two or more States whose coasts are opposite each other, the boundary of the continental shelf appertaining to such States shall be determined by agreement between them. In the absence of agreement, and unless another boundary line is justified by special circumstances, the boundary is the median line, every point of which is equidistant from the nearest points of the baselines from which the breadth of the territorial sea of each State is measured.

2. Where the same continental shelf is adjacent to the territories of two adjacent States, the boundary of the continental shelf shall be determined by agreement between them. In the absence of

agreement, and unless another boundary line is justified by special circumstances, the boundary shall be determined by application of the principle of equidistance from the nearest points of the baselines from which the breadth of the territorial sea of each State is measured.

3. In delimiting the boundaries of the continental shelf, any lines which are drawn in accordance with the principles set out in paragraphs 1 and 2 of this article should be defined with reference to charts and geographical features as they exist at a particular date, and reference should be made to fixed permanent identifiable points on the land.

Article 7

The provisions of these articles shall not prejudice the right of the coastal State to exploit the subsoil by means of tunnelling irrespective of the depth of water above the subsoil.

Article 8

This Convention shall, until 31 October 1958, be open for signature by all States Members of the United Nations or of any of the specialized agencies, and by any other State invited by the General Assembly of the United Nations to become a Party to the Convention.

Article 9

This Convention is subject to ratification. The instruments of ratification shall be deposited with the Secretary-General of the United Nations.

Article 10

This Convention shall be open for accession by any States belonging to any of the categories mentioned in article 8. The instruments of accession shall be deposited with the Secretary-General of the United Nations.

Article 11

1. This Convention shall come into force on the thirtieth day following the date of deposit of the twenty-second instrument of ratification or accession with the Secretary-General of the United Nations.

2. For each State ratifying or acceding to the Convention after the deposit of the twenty-second instrumnet of ratification or accession, the Convention shall enter into force on the thirtieth day after deposit by such State of its instrument of ratification or accession.

Article 12

1. At the time of signature, ratification or accession, any State may make reservations to articles of the Convention other than to articles 1 to 3 inclusive.

2. Any Contracting State making a reservation in accordance with the preceding paragraph may at any time withdraw the reservation by a communication to that effect addressed to the Secretary-General of the United Nations.

Article 13

1. After the expiration of a period of five years from the date on which this Convention shall enter into force, a request for the revision of this Convention may be made at any time by any Contracting Party by means of a notification in writing addressed to the Secretary-General of the United Nations.

2. The General Assembly of the United Nations shall decide upon the steps, if any, to be taken in respect of such request.

Article 14

The Secretary-General of the United Nations shall inform all States Members of the United Nations and the other States referred to in article 8:

a) Of signatures to this Convention and of the deposit of instruments of ratification or accession, in accordance with articles 8, 9 and 10:

b) Of the date on which this Convention will come into force, in accordance with article 11;

c) Of requests for revision in accordance with article 13;

d) Of reservations to this Convention, in accordance with article 12.

Article 15

The original of this Convention, of which the Chinese, English, French, Russian and Spanish texts are equally authentic, shall be deposited with the Secretary-General of the United Nations, who shall send certified copies thereof to all States referred to in article 8.

In Witness Whereof the undersigned Plenipotentiaries, being duly authorized thereto by their respective Governments, have signed this Convention.

Done at Geneva, this twenty-ninth day of April one thousand nine hundred and fifty-eight.

CONVENTION ON THE HIGH SEAS [16]

Geneva, 29 April 1958

The States Parties to this Convention,

Desiring to codify the rules of international law relating to the high seas,

Recognizing that the United Nations Conference on the Law of the Sea, held at Geneva from 24 February to 27 April 1958, adopted the following provisions as generally declaratory of established principles of international law,

Have agreed as follows:

Article 1

The term "high seas" means all parts of the sea that are not included in the territorial sea or in the internal waters of a State.

Article 2

The high seas being open to all nations, no State may validly purport to subject any part of them to its sovereignty. Freedom of the high seas is exercised under the conditions laid down by these articles and by the other rules of international law. It comprises, inter alia, both for coastal and non-coastal States:

1. Freedom of navigation;
2. Freedom of fishing;
3. Freedom to lay submarine cables and pipelines;
4. Freedom to fly over the high seas.

These freedoms, and others which are recognized by the general principles of international law, shall be exercised by all States with reasonable regard to the interests of other States in their exercise of the freedom of the high seas.

Article 3

1. In order to enjoy the freedom of the seas on equal terms with coastal States, States having no sea-coast should have free access to the sea. To this end States situated between the sea and a State having no sea-coast shall by common agreement with the latter and in conformity with existing international convention accord:

a) To the State having no sea-coast, on a basis of reciprocity, free transit through their territory; and

b) To ships flying the flag of that State treatment equal to that accorded to their own ships, or to the ships of any other States, as regards access to seaports and the use of such ports.

2. States situated between the sea and a State having no sea-coast shall settle, by mutual agreement with the latter, and taking into account the rights of the coastal State or State of transit and the special conditions of the State having no sea-coast, all matters relating to freedom of transit and equal treatment in ports, in case such States are not already parties to existing international conventions.

Article 4

Every State, whether coastal or not, has the right to sail ships under its flag on the high seas.

Article 5

1. Each State shall fix the conditions for the grant of its nationality to ships, for the registration of ships in its territory, and for the right to fly its flag. Ships have the nationality of the State whose flag they are entitled to fly. There must exist a genuine link between the State and the ship; in particular, the State must effectively exercise its jurisdiction and control in administrative, technical and social matters over ships flying its flag.

2. Each State shall issue to ships to which it has granted the right to fly its flag documents to that effect.

Article 6

1. Ships shall sail under the flag of one State only and, save in exceptional cases expressly provided for in international treaties or in these articles, shall be subject to its exclusive jurisdiction on the high seas. A ship may not change its flag during a voyage or while in a port of call, save in the case of a real transfer of ownership or change of registry.

2. A ship which sails under the flags of two or more States, using them according to convenience, may not claim any of the nationalities in question with respect to any other State, and may be assimilated to a ship without nationality.

Article 7

The provisions of the preceding articles do not prejudice the question of ships employed on the official service of an inter-governmental organization flying the flag of the organization.

Article 8

Warships on the high seas have complete immunity from the jurisdiction of any State other than the flag State.

2. For the purposes of these articles, the term "warship" means a ship belonging to the naval forces of a State and bearing the external marks distinguishing warships of its nationality, under the command of an officer duly commissioned by the government and whose name appears in the Navy List, and manned by a crew who are under regular naval discipline.

Article 9

Ships owned or operated by a State and used only on government non-commercial service shall, on the high seas, have complete immunity from the jurisdiction of any State other than the flag State.

Article 10

1. Every State shall take such measures for ships under its flag as are necessary to ensure safety at sea with regard inter alia to:

a) The use of signals, the maintenance of communications and the prevention of collisions;

b) The manning of ships and labour conditions for crews taking into account the applicable international labour instruments;

c) The construction, equipment and seaworthiness of ships.

2. In taking such measures each State is required to conform to generally accepted international standards and to take any steps which may be necessary to ensure their observance.

Article 11

1. In the event of a collision or of any other incident of navigation concerning a ship on the high seas, involving the penal or disciplinary responsibility of the master or of any other person in the service of the ship, no penal or disciplinary proceedings may be instituted against such persons except before the judicial or administrative authorities either of the flag State or of the State of which such person is a national.

2. In disciplinary matters, the State which has issued a master's certificate or a certificate of competence or licence shall alone be competent, after due legal process, to pronounce the withdrawal of such certificates, even if the holder is not a national of the State which issued them.

3. No arrest or detention of the ship, even as a measure of investigation, shall be ordered by any authorities other than those of the flag State.

Article 12

1. Every State shall require the master of the ship sailing under its flag, in so far as he can do so without serious danger to the ship, the crew or the passengers:

a) To render assistance to any person found at sea in danger of being lost;

b) To proceed with all possible speed to the rescue of persons in distress if informed of their need of assistance, in so far as such action may reasonably be expected of him;

c) After a collision, to render assistance to the other ship, her crew and her passengers and, where possible, to inform the other ship of the name of his own ship, her port of registry and the nearest port at which she will call.

2. Every coastal State shall promote the establishment and maintenance of an adequate and effective search and rescue service regarding safety on and over the sea and — where circumstances so require — by way of mutual regional arrangements co-operate with neighbouring States for this purpose.

Article 13

Every State shall adopt effective measures to prevent and punish the transport of slaves in ships authorized to fly its flag, and to prevent the unlawful use of its flag for that purpose. Any slave taking refuge on board any ship, whatever its flag, shall ipso facto be free.

Article 14

All States shall co-operate to the fullest possible extent in the repression of piracy on the high seas or in any other place outside the jurisdiction of any State.

Article 15

Piracy consists of any of the following acts:

1. Any illegal acts of violence, detention or any act of depredation, committed for private ends by the crew or the passengers of a private ship or a private aircraft, and directed:

a) On the high seas, against another ship or aircraft, or against persons or property on board such ship or aircraft;

b) Against a ship, aircraft, persons or property in a place outside the jurisdiction of any State;

2. Any act of voluntary participation in the operation of a ship or of an aircraft with the knowledge of facts making it a pirate ship or aircraft;

3. Any act of inciting or of intentionally facilitating an act described in sub-paragraph 1 or sub-paragraph 2 of this article.

Article 16

The acts of piracy, as defined in article 15, committed by a warship, government ship or government aircraft whose crew has mutinied and taken control of the ship or aricraft are assimilated to acts committed by a private ship.

Article 17

A ship or aircraft is considered a pirate ship or aircraft if it is intended by the persons in dominant control to be used for the purpose of committing one of the acts referred to in article 15. The same applies if the ship or aircraft has been used to commit any such act, so long as it remains under the control of the persons guilty of that act.

Article 18

A ship or aircraft may retain its nationality although it has become a pirate ship or aircraft. The retention or loss of nationality is determined by the law of the State from which such nationality was derived.

Article 19

On the high seas, or in any other place outside the jurisdiction of any State, every State may seize a pirate ship or aircraft, or a ship taken by piracy and under the control of pirates, and arrest the persons and seize the property on board. The courts of the State which carried out the seizure may decide upon the penalties to be imposed, and may also determine the action to be taken with regard to the ships, aircraft or property, subject to the rights of third parties acting in good faith.

Article 20

Where the seizure of a ship or aircraft on suspicion of piracy has been effected without adequate grounds, the State making the seizure shall be liable to the State the nationality of which is possessed by the ship or aircraft, for any loss or damage caused by the seizure.

Article 21

A seizure on account of piracy may only be carried out by warships or military aircraft, or other ships or aircraft on government service authorized to that effect.

Article 22

1. Except where acts of interference derive from powers conferred by treaty, a warship which encounters a foreign merchant ship on the high seas is not justified in boarding her unless there is reasonable ground for suspecting:

a) That the ship is engaged in piracy; or

b) That the ship is engaged in the slave trade; or

c) That, though flying a foreign flag or refusing to show its flag, the ship is, in reality, of the same nationality as the warship.

2. In the cases provided for in sub-paragraphs (*a*), (*b*) and (*c*) above, the warship may proceed to verify the ship's right to fly its flag. To this end, it may send a boat under the command of an officer to the suspected ship. If suspicion remains after the documents have been checked, it may proceed to a further examination on board the ship, which must be carried out with all possible consideration.

3. If the suspicions prove to be unfounded, and provided that the ship boarded has not committed any act justifying them, it shall be compensated for any loss or damage that may have been sustained.

Article 23

1. The hot pursuit of a foreign ship may be undertaken when the competent authorities of the coastal State have good reason to believe that the ship has violated the laws and regulations of that State. Such pursuit must be commenced when the foreign ship or one of its boats is within the internal waters or the territorial sea or the contiguous zone of the pursuing State, and may only be continued outside the territorial sea or the contiguous zone if the pursuit has not been interrupted. It is not necessary that, at the time when the foreign ship within the territorial sea or the contiguous zone receives the order to stop, the ship giving the order should likewise be within the territorial sea or the contiguous zone. If the foreign ship is within a contiguous zone, as defined in article 24 of the Convention on the Territorial Sea and the Contiguous Zone, the pursuit may only be undertaken if there has been a violation of the rights for the protection of which the zone was established.

2. The right of hot pursuit ceases as soon as the ship pursued enters the territorial sea of its own country or of a third State.

3. Hot pursuit is not deemed to have begun unless the pursuing ship has satisfied itself by such practicable means as may be available that the ship pursued or one of its boats or other craft working as a team and using the ship pursued as a mother ship are within the limits of the territorial sea, or as the case may be within the contiguous zone. The pursuit may only be commenced after a visual or auditory signal to stop has been given at a distance which enables it to be seen or heard by the foreign ship.

4. The right of hot pursuit may be exercised only by warships or military aircraft, or other ships or aircraft on government service specially authorized to that effect.

5. Where hot pursuit is effected by an aircraft:

a) The provisions of paragraph 1 to 3 of this article shall apply mutatis mutandis;

b) The aircraft giving the order to stop must itself actively pursue the ship until a ship or aircraft of the coastal State, summoned by the aircraft, arrives to take over the pursuit, unless the aircraft is itself able to arrest the ship. It does not suffice to justify an arrest on the high seas that the ship was merely sighted by the aircraft as an offender or suspected offender, if it was not both ordered to stop and pursued by the aircraft itself or other aircraft or ships which continue the pursuit without interruption.

6. The release of a ship arrested within the jurisdiction of a State and escorted to a port of that State for the purposes of an enquiry before the competent authorities may not be claimed solely on the ground that the ship, in the course of its voyage, was escorted across a portion of the high seas, if the circumstances rendered this necessary.

7. Where a ship has been stopped or arrested on the high seas in circumstances which do not justify the exercise of the right of hot pursuit, it shall be compensated for any loss or damage that may have been thereby sustained.

Article 24

Every State shall draw up regulations to prevent pollution of the seas by the discharge of oil from ships or pipelines or resulting from the exploitation and exploration of the seabed and its subsoil, taking account of existing treaty provisions on the subject.

Article 25

1. Every State shall take measures to prevent pollution of the seas from the dumping of radio-active waste, taking into account any standards and regulations which may be formulated by the competent international organizations.

2. All States shall co-operate with the competent international organizations in taking measures for the prevention of pollution of the seas or air space above, resulting from any activities with radio-active materials or other harmful agents.

Article 26

1. All States shall be entitled to lay submarine cables and pipelines on the bed of the high seas.

2. Subject to its right to take reasonable measures for the exploration of the continental shelf and the exploitation of its natural resources, the coastal State may not impede the laying or maintenance of such cables or pipelines.

3. When laying such cables or pipelines the State in question shall pay due regard to cables or pipelines already in position on the seabed. In particular, possibilities of repairing existing cables or pipelines shall not be prejudiced.

Article 27

Every State shall take the necessary legislative measures to provide that the breaking or injury by a ship flying its flag or by a person subject to its jurisdiction of a submarine cable beneath the high seas done wilfully or through culpable negligence, in such a manner as to be liable to interrupt or obstruct telegraphic or telephonic communications, and similarly the breaking or injury of a sub-marine pipeline or high-voltage power cable shall be a punishable offence. This provision shall not apply to any break or injury caused by persons who acted merely with the legitimate object of saving their lives or their ships, after having taken all necessary precautions to avoid such break or injury.

Article 28

Every State shall take the necessary legislative measures to provide that if persons subject to its jurisdiction who are the owners of a cable or pipeline beneath the high seas, in laying or repairing that cable or pipeline, cause a break in or injury to another cable or pipeline, they shall bear the cost of the repairs.

Article 29

Every State shall take the necessary legislative measures to ensure that the owners of ships who can prove that they have sacrificed an anchor, a net or any other fishing gear, in order to avoid injuring a submarine cable or pipeline, shall be indemnified by the owner of the cable or pipeline, provided that the owner of the ship has taken all reasonable precautionary measures beforehand.

Article 30

The provisions of this Convention shall not affect conventions or other international agreements already in force, as between States Parties to them.

Article 31

This Convention shall, until 31 October 1958, be open for signature by all States Members of the United Nations or of any of the specialized agencies, and by any other State invited by the General Assembly of the United Nations to become a Party to the Convention.

Article 32

This Convention is subject to ratification. The instruments of ratification shall be deposited with the Secretary-General of the United Nations.

Article 33

This Convention shall be open for accession by any States belonging to any of the categories mentioned in article 31. The instruments of accession shall be deposited with the Secretary-General of the United Nations.

Article 34

1. This Convention shall come into force on the thirtieth day following the date of deposit of the twenty-second instrument of ratification or accession with the Secretary-General of the United Nations.

2. For each State ratifying or acceding to the Convention after the deposit of the twenty-second instrument of ratification or accession, the Convention shall enter into force on the thirtieth day after deposit by such State of its instrument of ratification or accession.

Article 35

1. After the expiration of a period of five years from the date on which this Convention shall enter into force, a request for the revision of this Convention may be made at any time by any Contracting Party by means of a notification in writing addressed to the Secretary-General of the United Nations.

2. The General Assembly of the United Nations shall decide upon the steps, if any, to be taken in respect of such request.

Article 36

The Secretary-General of the United Nations shall inform all States Members of the United Nations and the other States referred to in article 31:

a) Of signatures to this Convention and of the deposit of instruments of ratification or accession, in accordance with articles 31, 32 and 33;

b) Of the date on which this Convention will come into force, in accordance with article 34;

c) Of requests for revision in accordance with article 35.

Article 37

The original of this Convention, of which the Chinese, English, French, Russian and Spanish texts are equally authentic, shall be deposited with the Secretary-General of the United Nations, who shall send certified copies thereof to all States referred to in article 31.

In Witness Whereof the undersigned Plenipotentiaries, being duly authorized thereto by their respective Governments, have signed this Convention.

Done at Geneva, this twenty-ninth day of April one thousand nine hundred and fifty-eight.

CONVENTION ON FISHING AND CONSERVATION OF THE LIVING RESOURCES OF THE HIGH SEAS [17]

Geneva, 29 April 1958

The States Parties to this Convention,

Considering that the development of modern techniques for the exploitation of the living resources of the sea, increasing man's ability to meet the need of the world's expanding population for food, has exposed some of these resources to the danger of being over-exploited,

Considering also that the nature of the problems involved in the conservation of the living resources of the high seas is such that there is a clear necessity that they be solved, whenever possible, on the basis of international co-operating through the concerted action of all the States concerned,

Have agreed as follows:

Article 1

1. All States have the right for their nationals to engage in fishing on the high seas, subject (*a*) to their treaty obligations, (*b*) to the interests and rights of coastal States as provided for in this Convention, and (*c*) to the provisions contained in the following articles concerning conservation of the living resources of the high seas.

2. All States have the duty to adopt, or to co-operate with other States in adopting, such measures for their respective nationals as may be necessary for the conservation of the living resources of the high seas.

Article 2

As employed in this Convention, the expression "conservation of the living resources of the high seas" means the aggregate of the measures rendering possible the optimum sustainable yield from those resources so as to secure a maximum supply of food and other marine products. Conservation programmes should be formulated with a view to securing in the first place a supply of food for human consumption.

Article 3

A State whose nationals are engaged in fishing any stock or stocks of fish or other living marine resources in any area of the high seas where the nationals of other States are not thus engaged shall adopt, for its own nationals, measures in that area when necessary for the purpose of the conservation of the living resources affected.

Article 4

1. If the nationals of the two or more States are engaged in fishing the same stock or stocks of fish or other living marine resources in any area or areas of the high seas, these States shall, at the request of any of them, enter into negotiations with a view to prescribing by agreement for their nationals the necessary measures for the conservation of the living resources affected.

2. If the States concerned do not reach agreement within twelve months, any of the parties may initiate the procedure contemplated by article 9.

Article 5

1. If, subsequent to the adoption of the measures referred to in articles 3 and 4, nationals of other States engage in fishing the same stock or stocks of fish or other living marine resources in any area or areas of the high seas, the other States shall apply the measures, which shall not be discriminatory in form or in fact, to their own nationals not later than seven months after the date on which the measures shall have been notified to the Director-General of the Food and Agriculture Organization of the United Nations. The Director-General shall notify such measures to any State which so requests and, in any case, to any State specified by the State initiating the measure.

2. If these other States do not accept the measures so adopted and if no agreement can be reached within twelve months, any of the interested parties may initiate the procedure contemplated by article 9. Subject to paragraph 2 of article 10, the measures adopted shall remain obligatory pending the decision of the specified commission.

Article 6

1. A coastal State has a special interest in the maintenance of the productivity of the living resources in any area of the high seas adjacent to its territorial sea.

2. A coastal State is entitled to take part on an equal footing in any system of research and regulation for purposes of conservation of the living resources of the high seas in that area, even through its nationals do not carry on fishing there.

3. A State whose nationals are engaged in fishing in any area of the high seas adjacent to the territorial sea of a State shall, at the request of that coastal State, enter into negotiations with a view to prescribing by agreement the measures necessary for the conservation of the living resources of the high seas in that area.

4. A State whose nationals are engaged in fishing in any area of the high seas adjacent to the territorial sea of a coastal State shall not enforce conservation measures in that area which are opposed to those which have been adopted by the coastal State, but may enter into negotiations with the coastal State with a view to prescribing by agreement the measures necessary for the conservation of the living resources of the high seas in that area.

5. If the States concerned do not reach agreement with respect to conservation measures within twelve months, any of the parties may initiate the procedure contemplated by article 9.

Article 7

1. Having regard to the provisions of paragraph 1 of article 6, any coastal State may, with a view to the maintenance of the productivity of the living resources of the sea, adopt unilateral measures of conservation appropriate to any stock of fish or other marine resources in any area of the high seas

adjacent to its territorial sea, provided that negotiations to that effect with the other States concerned have not led to an agreement within six months.

2. The measures which the coastal State adopts under the previous paragraph shall be valid as to other States only if the following requirements are fulfilled:

a) That there is a need for urgent application of conservation measures in the light of the existing knowledge of the fishery;

b) That the measures adopted are based on appropriate scientific findings;

c) That such measures do not discriminate in form or in fact against foreign fishermen.

3. These measures shall remain in force pending the settlement, in accordance with the relevant provisions of this Convention, of any disagreement as to their validity.

4. If the measures are not accepted by the other States concerned, any of the parties may initiate the procedure contemplated by article 9. Subject to paragraph 2 of article 10, the measures adopted shall remain obligatory pending the decision of the special commission.

5. The principles of geographical demarcation as defined in article 12 of the Convention on the Territorial Sea and the Contiguous Zone shall be adopted when coasts of different States are involved.

Article 8

1. Any State which, even if its nationals are not engaged in fishing in an area of the high seas not adjacent to its coast, has a special interest in the conservation of the living resources of the high seas in that area, may request the State or States whose nationals are engaged in fishing there to take the necessary measures of conservation under articles 3 and 4 respectively, at the same time mentioning the scientific reasons which in its opinion make such measures necessary, and indicating its special interest.

2. If no agreement is reached within twelve months, such State may initiate the procedure contemplated by article 9.

Article 9

1. Any dispute which may arise between States under articles 4, 5, 6, 7 and 8 shall, at the requestof any of the parties, be submitted for settlement to a special commission of five members, unless the parties agree to seek a solution by another method of peaceful settlement, as provided for in Article 33 of the Charter of the United Nations.

2. The members of the commission, one of whom shall be designated as chairman, shall be named by agreement between the States in dispute within three months of the request for settlement in accordance with the provisions of this article. Failing agreement they shall, upon the request of any State party, be named by the Secretary-General of the United Nations, within a further three-month period, in consultation with the States in dispute and with the President of the International Court of Justice and the Director-General of the Food and Agriculture Organization of the United Nations, from amongst well-qualified persons being nationals of States not involved in the dispute and specializing in legal, administrative or scientific questions relating to fisheries, depending upon the nature of the dispute to be settled. Any vacancy arising after the original appointment shall be filled in the same manner as provided for the initial selection.

3. Any State party to proceedings under these articles shall have the right to name one of its nationals to the special commission, with the right to participate fully in the proceedings on the same footing as a member of the commission, but without the right to vote or take part in the writing of the commission's decision.

4. The commission shall determine its own procedure, assuring each party to the proceedings a full opportunity to be heard and to present its case. It shall also determine how the costs and expenses shall be divided between the parties to the dispute, failing agreement by the parties on this matter.

5. The special commission shall render its decision within a period of five months from the time it is appointed unless it decides, in case of necessity, to extend the time limit for a period not exceeding three months.

6. The special commission shall, in reaching its decision, adhere to these articles and to any special agreements between the disputing parties regarding settlement of the dsipute.

7. Decisions of the commission shall be by majority vote.

Article 10

1. The special commission shall, in disputes arising under article 7, apply the criteria listed in paragraph 2 of that article. In disputes under articles 4, 5, 6 and 8, the commission shall apply the following criteria, according to the issues involved in the dispute:

a) Common to the determination of disputes arising under articles 4, 5 and 6 are the requirements:

(i) That scientific findings demonstrate the necessity of conservation measures;

(ii) That the specific measures are based on scientific findings and are practicable; and

(iii) That the measures do not discriminate, in form or in fact, against fishermen of other States;

b) Applicable to the determination of disputes arising under article 8 is the requirement that scientific findings demonstrate the necessity for conservation measures, or that the conservation programme is adequate, as the case may be.

2. The special commission may decide that pending its award the measures in dispute shall not be applied, provided that, in the case of disputes under article 7, the measures shall only be suspended when it is apparent to the commission

on the basis of *prima facie* evidence that the need for the urgent application of such measures does not exist.

Article 11

The decisions of the special commission shall be binding on the States concerned and the provisions of paragraph 2 of Article 94 of the Charter of the United Nations shall be applicable to those decisions. If the decisions are accompanied by any recommendations, they shall receive the greatest possible consideration.

Article 12

1. If the factual basis of the award of the special commission is altered by substantial changes in the conditions of the stock or stocks of fish or other living marine resources or in methods of fishing, any of the States concerned may request the other States to enter into negotiations with a view to prescribing by agreement the necessary modifications in the measures of conservation.
2. If no agreement is reached within a reasonable period of time, any of the States concerned may again resort to the procedure contemplated by article 9 provided that at least two years have elapsed from the original award.

Article 13

1. The regulation of fisheries conducted by means of equipment embedded in the floor of the sea in areas of the high seas adjacent to the territorial sea of a State may be undertaken by that State where such fisheries have long been maintained and conducted by its nationals, provided that non-nationals are permitted to participate in such activities on an equal footing with nationals except in areas where such fisheries have by long usage been exclusively enjoyed by such nationals. Such regulations will not, however, affect the general status of the areas as high seas.
2. In this article, the expression "fisheries conducted by means of equipment embedded in the floor of the sea" means those fisheries using gear with supporting members embedded in the sea floor, constructed on a site and left there to operate permanently or, if removed, restored each season on the same site.

Article 14

In articles 1, 3, 4, 5, 6 and 8, the term "nationals" means fishing boats or craft of any size having the nationality of the State concerned, according to the law of that State, irrespective of the nationality of the members of their crews.

Article 15

This Convention shall, until 31 October 1958, be open for signature by all States Members of the United Nations or of any of the specialized agencies and by any other State invited by the General Assembly of the United Nations to become a Party to the Convention.

Article 16

This Convention is subject to ratification. The instruments of ratification shall be deposited with the Secretary-General of the United Nations.

Article 17

This Convention shall be open for accession by any States belonging to any of the categories mentioned in article 15. The instruments of accession shall be deposited with the Secretary-General of the United Nations.

Article 18

1. This Convention shall come into force on the thirtieth day following the date of deposit of the twenty-second instrument of ratification or accession with the Secretary-General of the United Nations.
2. For each State ratifying or acceding to the Convention after the deposit of the twenty-second instrument of ratification or accession, the Convention shall enter into force on the thirtieth day after deposit by such State of its instrument of ratification or accession.

Article 19

1. At the time of signature, ratification or accession, any State may make reservations to articles of the Convention other than to articles 6, 7, 9, 10, 11 and 12.
2. Any contracting State making a reservation in accordance with the preceding paragraph may at any time withdraw the reservation by a communication to that effect addressed to the Secretary-General of the United Nations.

Article 20

1. After expiration of a period of five years from the date on which this Convention shall enter into force, a request for the revision of this Convention may be made at any time by any contracting party by means of a notification in writing addressed to the Secretary-General of the United Nations.
2. The General Assembly of the United Nations shall decide upon the steps, if any, to be taken in respect of such request.

Article 21

The Secretary-General of the United Nations shall inform all States Members of the United Nations and other States referred to in article 15:

a) Of signatures to this Convention and of the deposit of instruments of ratification or accession, in accordance with articles 15, 16 and 17;

b) Of the date on which this Convention will come into force, in accordance with article 18;

c) Of requests for revision in accordance with article 20;

d) Of reservations to this Convention, in accordance with article 19.

Article 22

The original of this Convention, of which the Chinese, English, French, Russian and Spanish texts are equally authentic, shall be deposited with the Secretary-General of the United Nations, who shall send certified copies thereof to all States referred to in article 15.

In Witness Whereof the undersigned plenipotentiaries, being duly authorized thereto by their respective governments, have signed this Convention.

Done at Geneva, this twenty-ninth day of April one thousand nine hundred and fifty-eight.

NORTH-EAST ATLANTIC FISHERIES CONVENTION [18]

London, 24 January 1959

The States Parties to this Convention

Desiring to ensure the conservation of the fish stocks and the rational exploitation of the fisheries of the North-East Atlantic Ocean and adjacent waters, which are of common concern to them;

Have agreed as follows:

Article 1

1. The area to which this Convention applies (hereinafter referred to as "the Convention area") shall be all waters which are situated:

a) within those parts of the Atlantic and Arctic Oceans and their dependent seas which lie north of 36° north latitude and between 42° west longitude and 51° east longitude, but excluding

(i) the Baltic Sea and Belts lying to the south and east of lines drawn from Hasenere Head to Gniben Point, from Korshage to Spodsbierg and from Gilbierg Head to the Kullen, and

(ii) the Mediterranean Sea and its dependent seas as far as the point of intersection of the parallel of 36° latitude and the meridian of 5°36' west longitude.

b) within that part of the Atlantic Ocean north of 59° north latitude and between 44° west longitude and 42° west longitude.

2. The Convention area shall be divided into regions, the boundaries of which shall be those defined in the Annex to this Convention. The regions shall be subject to such alterations as may be made in accordance with the provisions of paragraph (4) of Article 5 of this Convention.

3. For the purposes of this Convention

a) the expression "vessel" means any vessel or boat employed in fishing for sea fish or in the treatment of sea fish which is registered or owned in the territories of, or which flies the flag of, any Contracting States and;

b) the expression "territories" in relation to any Contracting State, extends to

(i) any territory within or adjacent to the Convention area for whose international relations the Contracting State is responsible;

(ii) any other territory, not situated within the Convention area or adjacent to it, for whose international relations the Contracting State is responsible and for which such State shall have made known, by written declaration to the Government of the United Kingdom of Great Britain and Northern Ireland (hereinafter referred to as the Government of the United Kingdom), either at the time of signature, of ratification, or of adherence, or subsequently, that this Convention shall apply to it;

(iii) the waters within the Convention area where the Contracting State has exclusive jurisdiction over fisheries.

Article 2

Nothing in this Convention shall be deemed to affect the rights, claims, or views of any Contracting State in regard to the extent of jurisdiction over fisheries.

Article 3

1. A North-East Atlantic Fisheries Commission (hereinafter referred to as the Commission) is hereby established and shall be maintained for the purposes of this Convention.

2. Each Contracting State may appoint as its Delegation to the Commission not more than two Commissioners and such experts and advisors to assist them as that State may determine.

3. The Commission shall elect its own President and not more than two Vice-Presidents who need not be chosen from the Commissioners or their experts or advisers. If a member of a Delegation has been elected President he shall forthwith cease to act as a member of that Delegation, and if a Commissioner has been elected the State concerned shall have the right to appoint another person to serve in his place.

4. The Office of the Commission shall be in London.

5. Except where the Commission determines otherwise, it shall meet once a year in London at such time as it shall decide: provided, however, that upon the request of a Commissioner of a Contracting State, the President shall, as soon as practicable, summon a meeting at such time and place as he may determine.

6. The Commission shall appoint its own Secretary and may from time to time appoint such other staff as it may require.

7. The Commission may set up such Committees as it considers desirable to perform such functions as it may determine.

8. Each Delegation shall have one vote in the Commission which may be cast only by a Commissioner of the State concerned. Decisions shall be taken by a simple majority except where otherwise specifically provided. If there is an even division of votes on any matter which is subject to a simple majority decision, the proposal shall be regarded as rejected.

9. Subject to the provisions of this Article, the Commission shall draw up its own Rules of Procedure, including provisions for the election of the President and Vice-Presidents and their terms of office.

10. The Government of the United Kingdom shall call the first meeting of the Commission as soon as practicable after the coming into force of this Convention, and shall communicate the provisional agenda to each of the other Contracting States not less than two months before the date of the meeting.

11. Reports of the proceedings of the Commission shall be transmitted and proposals and recommendations shall be notified as soon as possible to all Contracting States in English and in French.

Article 4

1. Each Contracting State shall pay the expense of the Commissioners, experts and advisers appointed by it.

2. The Commission shall prepare an annual budget of the proposed expenditures of the Commission.

3. In any year in which the annual budget amounts to £200 or less for each Contracting State, the total sum shall be shared equally between Contracting States.

4. In any year in which the annual budget exceeds £200 for each Contracting State, the Commission shall calculate the payments due from each Contracting State according to the following formula:

a) from the budget there shall be deducted a sum of £200 for each Contracting State;

b) the remainder shall be divided into such number of equal shares as correspond to the total number of Regional Committee memberships;

c) the payment due from any Contracting State shall be the equivalent of £200 plus the number of shares equal to the number of Regional Committees in which that State participates.

5. The Commission shall notify to each Contracting State the sum due from that State as calculated under paragraph (3) or (4) of this Article and as soon as possible thereafter each Contracting State shall pay to the Commission the sum so notified.

6. Contributions shall be payable in the currency of the country in which the Office of the Commission is located, except that the Commission may accept payment in the currencies in which it may be expected that expenditures of the Commission will be made from time to time, up to an amount established each year by the Commission when preparing the annual budget.

7. At its first meeting the Commission shall approve a budget for the balance of the first financial year in which the Commission functions and shall transmit to the Contracting States copies of that budget together with notices of their respective contributions as assessed under paragraph (3) or (4) of this Article.

8. In subsequent financial years, the Commission shall submit to each Contracting State drafts of annual budgets, together with a schedule of allocations, not less than six weeks before the annual meeting of the Commission at which the budgets are to be considered.

Article 5

1. The Commission shall establish a Regional Committee, with the powers and duties described in Article 6 of this Convention, for each of the regions into which the Convention area is divided.

2. The representation on any Regional

Committee so established shall be determined by the Commission, provided, however, that any Contracting State with a coastline adjacent to that region, or exploiting the fisheries of the region, has automatically the right of representation on the Regional Committee. Contracting States exploiting elsewhere a stock which is also fished in that region shall have the opportunity of being represented on the Regional Committee.

3. Subject to the provisions of Article 6 of this Convention, the Commission shall determine the terms of reference of, and the procedure to be followed by, each Regional Committee.

4. The Commission may at any time alter the boundaries and vary the number of the regions defined in the Annex to this Convention, provided this is by the unanimous decision of the Delegations present and voting and no objection is made within three months thereafter by any Contracting States not represented, or not voting, at the meeting.

Article 6

1. It shall be the duty of the Commission:

a) to keep under review the fisheries in the Convention area;

b) to consider, in the light of the technical information available, what measures may be required for the conservation of the fish stocks and for the rational exploitation of the fisheries in the area;

c) to consider, at the request of any Contracting State, representations made to it by a State which is not a party to this Convention for the opening of negotiations on the conservation of fish stocks in the Convention area or any part thereof; and

d) to make to Contracting States recommendations, based as far as practicable on the results of scientific research and investigation, with regard to any of the measures set out in Article 7 of this Convention.

2. It shall be the duty of a Regional Committee to peform, in relation to its Region, functions of review and consideration similar to those described in paragraph (1) of this Article in relation to the Commission and the Convention area. A Regional Committee may initiate proposals for measures in relation to its region and shall consider any such proposals as may be remitted to it by the Commission.

3. A Regional Committee may prepare draft recommendations for consideration by the Commission, which may adopt any such draft recommendations, with any modifications it may consider desirable, as recommendations for the purpose of Article 7 of this Convention.

4. A Regional Committee may at any time appoint sub-committees to study specific problems affecting parts of the Region and to report thereon to the Regional Committee.

Article 7

1. The measures relating to the objectives and purposes of this Convention which the Commission and Regional Committees may consider, and on which the Commission may make recommendaions to the Contracting States, are

a) any measures for the regulation of the size of mesh of fishing nets;

b) any measures for regulation of the size limits of fish that may be retained on board vessels, or landed, or exposed or offered for sale;

c) any measures for the establishment of closed seasons;

d) any measures for the establishment of closed areas;

e) any measures for the regulation of fishing gear and appliances, other than regulation of the size of mesh of fishing nets;

f) any measures for the improvement and the increase of marine resources, which may include artificial propagation, the transplantation of organisms and the transplantation of young.

2. Measures for regulating the amount of total catch, or the amount of fishing effort in any period, or any other kinds of measures for the purpose of the conservation of the fish stocks in the Convention area, may be added to the measures listed in paragraph (1) of this Article on a proposal adopted by not less than a two-thirds majority of the Delegations present and voting and subsequently accepted by all Contracting States in accordance with their respective constitutional procedures.

3. The measures provided for in paragraphs (1) and (2) of this Article may relate to any or all species of sea fish and shell fish, but not to sea mammals; to any or all methods of fishing; and to any or all parts of the methods of fishing; and to any or all parts of the Convention area.

Article 8

1. Subject to the provisions of this Article, the Contracting States undertake to give effect to any recommendation made by the Commission under Article 7 of this Convention and adopted by not less than a two-thirds majority of the Delegations present and voting.

2. Any Contracting State may, within ninety days of the date of notice of a recommendation to which paragraph (1) of this Article applies, object to it and in that event shall not be under obligation to give effect to the recommendation.

3. In the event of an objection being made within the ninety-day period, any other Contracting State may similarly object at any time within a further period of sixty days, or within thirty days after receiving notice of an objection by another Contracting State made within the further period of sixty days.

4. If objections to a recommendation are made by three or more of the Contracting States, all the other Contracting States shall be relieved forthwith of any obligation to give effect to that recommendation but any or all of them may nevertheless agree among themselves to give effect to it.

5: Any Contracting State which has objected to a recommendation may at any time withdraw that objection and shall then, subject to the provisions of paragraph (4) of this Article, give effect to the recommendation within ninety days, or as from the date determined by the Commission under Article 9 of this Convention, whichever is the later.

6. The Commission shall notify each Contracting State immediately upon receipt of each objection and withdrawal.

Article 9

Any recommendation to which paragraph (1) of Article 8 of this Convention applies shall, subject to the provisions of that Article, become binding on the Contracting States from the date determined by the Commission, which shall not be before the period for objection provided in Article 8 has elapsed

Article 10

At any time after two years from the date on which it has been required to give effect to any recommendation to which paragraph (1) of Article 8 of this Convention applies any Contracting State may give the Commission notice of the termination of its acceptance of the recommendation and, if that notice is not withdrawn, the recommendation shall cease to be binding on that Contracting State at the end of twelve months from the date of the notice.

2. At any time after a recommendation has ceased to be binding on a Contracting State under paragraph (1) of this Article, the recommendation shall cease to be binding on any other State which so desires upon the date of notice to the Commission of withdrawal of acceptance of that recommendation by such other State.

3. The Commission shall notify all Contracting States of every notice under this Article immediately upon the receipt thereof.

Article 11

1. In order that the recommendations made by the Commission for the conservation of the stocks of fish within the Convention area shall be based so far as practicable upon the results of scientific research and investigation, the Commission shall when possible seek the advice of the International Council for the Exploration of the Sea and the co-operation of the Council in carrying out any necessary investigations and, for this purpose, may make such joint arrangements as may be agreed with the International Council for the Exploration of the Sea or may make such other arrangements as it may think fit.

2. The Commission may seek to establish and maintain working arrangements with any other international organization which has related objectives.

Article 12

1. The Contracting States undertake to furnish on the request of the Commission any available statistical and biological information the Commission may need for the purposes of this Convention.

2. The Commission may publish or otherwise disseminate reports of its activities and such other information relating to the fisheries in the Convention area or any part of that area as it may deem appropriate.

Article 13

1. Without prejudice to the sovereign rights of States in regard to their territorial and internal waters, each Contracting State shall take in its territories and in regard to its own nationals and its own vessels appropriate measures to ensure the application of the provisions of this Convention and of the recommendations of the Commission which have become binding on that Contracting State and the punishment of infractions of the said provisions and recommendations.

2. Each Contracting State shall transmit annually to the Commission a statement of the action taken by it for these purposes.

3. The Commission may by a two-thirds majority make recommendations for, on the one hand, measures of national control in the territories of the Contracting States and, on the other hand, national and international measures of control on the high seas, for the purpose of ensuring the application of the Convention and the measures in force thereunder. Such recommendations shall be subject to the provisions of Articles 8, 9 and10.

Article 14

The provisions of this Convention shall not apply to fishing operations conducted solely for the purpose of scientific investigation by vessels authorised by a Contracting State for that purpose, or to fish taken in the course of such operations, but in any of the territories of any Contracting State bound by a recommenation to which paragraph (1) of Article 8 applies, fish so taken shall not be sold or exposed or offered for sale in contravention of any such recommendation.

Article 15

1. This Convention shall be open for signature until 31 March 1959. It shall be ratified as soon as possible and the intruments of ratification shall be deposited with the Government of the United Kingdom.

2. This Convention shall enter into force upon the deposit of instruments of ratification by all signatory States. If, however, after the lapse of one year from 31 March 1959, all the signatory States have not ratified this Convention, but not less than seven of them have deposited intruments of ratification, these latter States may agree among themselves by special protocol on the date on which this Convention shall enter into force; and in that case this Convention shall enter into force with respect to any State that ratifies thereafter on the date of deposit of its instrument of ratification.

3. Any State which has not signed this Convention may accede thereto at any time after it has come into force in accordance with paragraph (2) of this Article. Accession shall be effected by means of a notice in writing addressed to the Government of the United Kingdom and shall take effect on the date of its receipt. Any State which accedes to this Convention shall simultaneously undertake to give effect to those recommendations which are, at the time of its accession, binding on all the other Contracting States as well as to any other recommendations which are, at that time, binding on one or more of the Contracting States and are not specifically excluded by the acceding State in its notice of accession.

4. The Government of the United Kingdom shall inform all signatory and acceding States of all ratifications deposited and accessions received and shall notify signatory States of the date and the States in respect of which this Convention enters into force.

Article 16

1. In respect of each State Party to this Convention, the provisions of Articles 5, 6, 7, 8 and 9 and Annexes I, II and III of the Convention for the Regulation of the Meshes of Fishing Nets and the Size Limits of Fish, signed at London, on 5 April 1946, as amended by decisions made under paragraph (10) of Article 12 of that Convention, shall remain in force but shall be deemed for the purposes of the present Convention to be a recommendation made and given effect without objection under this Convention as from the date of its entry into force in respect of that State within the area covered by the 1946 Convention; provided that in the period of two years after the coming into force of this Convention, any Contracting State may, on giving twelve months' written notice to the Government of the United Kingdom, withdraw from the whole or any part of the said recommendation. If a Contracting State has, in accordance with the provisions of this Article, given notice of its withdrawal from a part of the said recommendation, any other Contracting State may, with effect from the same date, give notice of its withdrawal from the same or any other part of the said recommendation, or from the recommendation as a whole.

2. The provisions of the Convention for the Regulation of the Meshes of Fishing Nets and the Size Limits of Fish signed at London on 5 April 1949, shall, save as provided in paragraph (1) of this Article, cease to apply to each Contracting State to this Convention as from the date of the entry into force of this Convention in respect of that State.

Article 17

At any time after two years from the date on which this Convention has come into force with respect to a Contracting State, that State may denounce the Convention by means of a notice in writing addressed to the Government of the United Kingdom. Any such denunciation shall take effect twelve months after the date of its receipt, and shall be notified to the Contracting States by the Government of the United Kingdom.

In Witness Whereof the undersigned, being duly authorized thereto, have signed this Convention.

Done in London this twenty-fourth day of January nineteen hundred and fifty-nine in two copies, one in the English language, the other in the French language. Both texts shall be deposited in the archives of the Government of the United Kingdom and shall be regarded as equally authentic.

The Government of the United Kingdom shall transmit certified copies of both texts of this Convention in the two languages to all the signatory and acceding States.

ANNEX

The regions provided for by Article 1 of this Convention shall be as follows:

Region 1 — The part of the Convention area bounded on the south by a line running from a point 59° north latitude 44° west longitude due east to the meridian of 42° west longitude; thence due south to the parallel of 48° north latitude; thence due east to the meridian of 18° west longitude; thence due north to the parallel of 60° north latitude; thence due east to the meridian of 5° west longitude; thence due north to the parallel of 60° 30′ north latitude; thence due east to the meridian of 4° west longitude; thence due north to the parallel of 62° north latitude; thence due east to the coast of Norway; thence north and east along the coast of Norway and along the coast of the Union of Soviet Socialist Republics as far as the Meridian of 51° east longitude.

Region 2 — The part of the Convention area not covered by Region 1 and north of 48° north latitude.

Region 3 — The part of the Convention area between 36° and 48° north latitude.

CONVENTION CONCERNING FISHING IN THE BLACK SEA [19]

Varna, 7 July 1959

The Governments of the People's Republic of Bulgaria, the Romanian People's Republic and the Union of Soviet Socialist Republics,

Having a common interest in the rational utilization of the fishery resources of the Black Sea and in the development of marine fishing,

Have decided to conclude this Convention and have for this purpose appointed as their plenipotentiaries:

who, having exchanged their full powers, found in good and due form, have agreed as follows:

Article 1

The Contracting Parties agree to co-operate and to assist one another, in accordance with the provisions of this Convention, in carrying on rational fishing in the Black Sea, in improving fishing technique, and in carrying out research in the field of ichthylogy and hydrobiology for the purpose of maintaining and augmenting the stocks of fish in the Black Sea with a view to increasing the yield.

The provisions of this Convention shall not affect the status of the territorial and inland waters of the Contracting Parties.

Article 2

Fishing vessels of the People's Republic of Bulgaria, the Romanian People's Republic and the Union of Soviet Socialist Republics engaged in fishing in the open sea may enter the following ports of refuge in order to shelter from bad weather or in case of damage:

In the People's Republic of Bulgaria: Balchik, Varna, Nesebŭr, Burgas, Sozopol and Michurin;

In the Romanian People's Republic: Constanta and Sulina;

In the Union of Soviet Socialist Republics: Odessa, Evpatoria, Yalta, Novorossysk, Sochi, Sukhum, Poti and Batum.

The list of ports of refuge may be amended by agreement among the Parties to the Convention.

Article 3

In the cases referred to in article 2 of this Convention, the fishing vessels of the Contracting Parties shall where necessary be given an opportunity to repair the damage and to replenish their supplies of foodstuffs, drinking water, fuel, lubricants and other ship's stores so that the vessel may continue on its route or return to its nearest home port, and an opportunity to dispose of their catch fresh at the ports of refuge if it cannot be preserved on board the vessel.

Article 4

The procedure governing the disposal of fish and payment for services rendered to fishing vessels entering ports of refuge and for fish disposed of in the cases referred to in article 3 of this Convention shall be agreed between the competent authorities of the Parties to the Convention.

Article 5

The following shall be the minimum sizes at which fish may be taken:

Beluga (*Huso huso*)	140 cm
Russian sturgeon (*Acipenser güldenstaedti*)	80 cm
Sevryuga (*Acipenser stellatus*)	75 cm
Turbot (*Rhombus maeoticus*)	35 cm
Shad (*Alosa kessleri pontica*)	16 cm

The size of a fish shall be determined by measuring its length from the tip of the snout to the base of the tail fin.

Any fish taken which is under the prescribed size must be put back in the sea.

The taking of fish under the prescribed minimum size shall be permissible in a proportion not exceeding the following percentage by number of the total catch of each protected species:

8 per cent in the case of shad (*Alosa kessleri pontica*);

5 per cent in the case of turbot (*Rhombus macoticus*); and

5 per cent in the case of Acipenseridae (*Huso huso, Acipenser güldenstaedti, Acipenser stellatus*).

The taking of *Acipenser nudiventris* shall be prohibited for five years from the date of entry into force of this Convention.

Article 6

For the purpose of preparing forecasts for fishing in the Black Sea, the Contracting Parties agree to exchange by any suitable means operational information concerning the migration of industrial fish, indicating the time and place at which they congregate, the direction of movement, the density of the schools, and the hydrometeorological conditions in which such congregations and migrations are observed.

Article 7

With a view to the rational utilization of the stocks of fish in the Black Sea, the Contracting Parties agree to exchange information annually on the results of scientific research in the fields of marine ichthyology, hydrobiology and fishing technique.

The Contracting Parties shall exchange statistical data on catches of fish.

Article 8

With a view to working out and co-ordinating measures for the application of this Convention, a Mixed Commission shall be established.

Within one month after the entry into force of the Convention, each Contracting Party shall appoint one representative to the said Commission and shall communicate the name of its representative to the other Contracting Parties.

The Mixed Commission shall meet at least once

a year in the territory of each of the Contracting Parties in turn.

The Mixed Commission shall function under a statute drafted by it at its first meeting and approved by the Contracting Parties.

Article 9

The Mixed Commission shall have the following functions:

1. It shall work out agreed measures to regulate fishing, with a view to the conservation and augmentation of the stocks of fish in the Black Sea, and to develop industrial fishing technique;

2. It shall introduce amendments to article 5 of the Convention concerning the species and dimensions of fish caught in the Black Sea. Proposals for such amendments must be communicated to the representatives of the Contracting Parties on the Mixed Commission not later than three months before the opening of the Commission's regular session;

3. It shall co-ordinate the planning of scientific research projects on matters relating to fishing in the Black Sea, to be conducted by the competent authorities of the Contracting Parties;

4. It shal determine the nature and extent of the statistical and other data which each Contracting Party shall furnish to the Mixed Commission for the purpose of implementing this Convention;

5. It shall exchange information concerning the application of this Convention;

6. It shall examine such other matters as the Contracting Parties may refer to it.

Article 10

The Mixed Commission shall make recommendations to the Contracting Parties on the matters referred to in article 9 with the exception of paragraph 2 of that article, on which the Commission may take decisions.

Recommendations and decisions shall be deemed to be adopted by the Mixed Commission if they receive the favourable votes of the representatives of all the Contracting Parties.

The recommendations of the Mixed Commission shall be submitted to the Contracting Parties for approval and may be given effect if none of the Parties raises objections within four months.

Article 11

This Convention shall not impede the conclusion of bilateral agreements on matters relating to fishing in the Black Sea between any two Contracting Parties or between a Contracting Party and any other Black Sea State, so long as such agreements do not conflict with the terms of this Convention.

Article 12

This Convention shall be ratified and shall enter into force on the date of deposit of the last instrument of ratification with the Government of the People's Republic of Bulgaria, in whose archives the original of the Convention shall be kept.

The Government of the People's Republic of Bulgaria shall notify the Governments of all Contracting Parties of the date of deposit of the last instrument of ratification.

Certified true copies of this Convention shall be transmitted by the Government of the People's Republic of Bulgaria to the other Contracting Parties.

Article 13

This Convention is concluded for a term of five years. It shall remain in force for successive terms of five years for those Contracting Parties which do not inform the Government of the People's Republic of Bulgaria, six months before the expiry of the current five-year term, that they wish to terminate the Convention.

Article 14

Other Black Sea States may accede to this Convention.

Article 15

The Government of the People's Republic of Bulgaria shall take the necessary action to register this Convention with the Secretariat of the United Nations.

Done at Varna, on 7 July 1959, in one copy in the Bulgarian, Romanian and Russian languages, all texts being equally authentic.

AGREEMENT FOR THE ESTABLISHMENT ON A PERMANENT BASIS OF A LATIN-AMERICAN FOREST RESEARCH AND TRAINING INSTITUTE [20]

Rome, 18 November 1959

PREAMBLE

The Food and Agriculture Organization of the United Nations (hereinafter referred to as "the Organization"),

The Government of the Republic of Venezuela (hereinafter referred to as "the Government of Venezuela"), and such other Member Nations and Associate Members of the Organization as become parties to this Agreement in accordance with the provisions of Articles II and XV of this Agreement.

Considering

the establishment in 1956 on a temporary basis for an initial period of two years of the Latin-American Forest Research and Training Institute by an agreement concluded between the Government of Venezuela and the Organization on 3 May 1956 in pursuance of Resolution No. 33/55 of the Conference of the Organization and extended first until 31 December 1958 in pursuance of Resolution No. 50/57 of the Conference of the Organization and again till 31 December 1959 by an exchange of notes of 1 and 8 December 1958 in pursuance of Resolution No. 3/29 of the Council of the Organization,

the purpose of the Institute which was created under the auspices of the Organization to assist in promoting the implementation of the program of the Organization in the field of forestry in Latin America and to pursue the objectives set forth in the preamble of the provisional agreement of 3 May 1956,

the desirability of establishing the Institute on a permanent basis in pursuance of the above-mentioned Resolutions of the Conference of the Organization, and

In conformity with

the provisions of Article XV of the Constitution of the Organization regarding the conclusion of agreements between the Organization and Member Nations for the establishment of international institutions dealing with questions relating to food and agriculture,

Have agreed as follows:

Article I

ESTABLISHMENT OF THE INSTITUTE

1. The Organization, the Government of Venezuela and the other Member Nations and Associate Members of the Organization that are parties to this agreement hereby establish on a permanent basis the Latin-American Forest Research and Training Institute (hereinafter referred to as "the Institute"), which is placed under the auspices of the Organization and the above mentioned nations, and whose objectives and structure shall be those stated in the following articles.

2. The seat of the Institute shall be the Forestry School of the University of Los Andes, Merida, in the State of Mérida, Republic of Venezuela.

Article II

PARTICIPATION

Participation in this agreement shall be open to:

— the Organization

— Member Nations or Associate Members of the Organization.

Article III

AIMS AND FUNCTIONS

1. The aims and functions of the Institute shall be:

a) to conduct research, especially applied research, which may effectively contribute to proper conservation, utilization and development of the forest resources of Latin America and which is of prime interest to as great a number as possible of Member Nations or Associate Members that are parties to this agreement;

b) to give courses of instruction for the specialized training of forestry technicians, with due regard to the educational needs and facilities of the Latin-American region;

c) to gather, classify and distribute such scientific material as may be forwarded to it by other institutes or national forestry departments within the scope of its own functions;

d) to keep contracting governments abreast of the theoretical and practical work being done in forest and forest products research by other competent agencies in the area with a view to promoting regional co-operation in this field.

2. The aforementioned activities shall be carried out in co-operation with the Forestry School of the University of Los Andes.

Article IV

ORGANS

The organs of the Institute shall be:

— the Governing Council

— the Executive Committee

— the President

— the Director.

Article V

THE GOVERNING COUNCIL

1. The Governing Council shall consist of:

— one representative of the Government of Venezuela;

— one representative of each of the other contracting Member Nations or Associate Members of the Organization;

— the President of the Institute;

— the Director-General of the Organization or his representative, serving in an advisory capacity.

2. The representative of the Government of Venezuela and the other Member Nations and

Associate Members that are parties to this agreement shall each have one vote. The President shall vote in the case of tie only. The Governing Council shall elect three Vice-Presidents from amongst its members and shall adopt its own rules of procedure. The Director of the Institute shall act as Secretary of the Governing Council.

3. The Governing Council shall meet at least once every two years, preferably in conjunction with the Latin-American Forestry Commission of the Organization, and at the place where the Commission holds its session.

4. The Governing Council shall at the first session following the entry into force of this agreement approve the broad guiding lines for a long-term program of work of the Institute.

5. The Governing Council shall also have the following functions:

—consideration and approval of the reports of the activities of the Institute submitted to it by the Executive Committee:

—consideration and approval of the budget of the Institute for the ensuing two years;

—consideration approval of any other proposal which may be submitted by the Executive Committee;

—appointment of the President of the Institute;

—appointment of the Director of the Institute;

—consideration of any other matter, in conformity with the objectives and functions of the Institute, which has not been delegated to any other organ of the Institute.

6. The program of work and budget of the Institute, shall, after having been approved by the Governing Council, be transmitted to the Regional Committee of Forestry Research of the Latin-American Forestry Commission for any comments that the Regional Committee may consider pertinent and which may serve as guidance with respect to future programs of work and budgets.

Article VI

THE EXECUTIVE COMMITTEE

1. The Executive Committee shall be composed of the President, the three Vice-Presidents of the Governing Council, the representative of the Government of Venezuela or his alternate, and the Director-General of the Organization or his representative acting in an advisory capacity. The representative of the Government of Venezuela, and each Vice-President, except when acting as President, shall have one vote. The Director of the Institute shall act as the Secretary of the Executive Committee.

2. The Executive Committee shall hold at least one session every year at the seat of the Institute on the date provided for in the Rules of Procedure. Furthermore, the Executive Committee may hold special sessions elsewhere when necessary.

3. The functions of the Executive Committee shall be as follows:

—consideration and approval of the reports on the activities of the Institute, to be submitted to the Governing Council;

—preparation of the program of work and any other related proposals regarding the following two years which are considered desirable for submission to the Governing Council for approval;

—preparation of the budget for the above-mentioned two years, for submission to the Governing Council for approval;

—preparation, adoption and application of any rules necessary for the carrying out of the activities of the Institute, which rules shall be submitted to the Governing Council for confirmation;

—permanent supervision of all activities of the Institute;

—solving any problems which may arise in the performance of the activities of the Institute and generally taking any other measures which are considered desirable or necessary for the carrying out of said activities, subject to reporting to the Governing Council on these measures and on the reasons therefor.

In case of an emergency arising between two sessions of the Executive Committee, the President shall take appropriate measures with respect to the foregoing functions and shall report thereon to the next session of the Executive Committee.

Article VII

THE PRESIDENT OF THE INSTITUTE

1. The President of the Institute shall be appointed by the Governing Council for a period of four years on the basis of a nomination submitted by the Government of Venezuela in consultation with the Director-General. The President of the Institute shall be the President of the Governing Council and the President of the Executive Committee. He shall be the legal representative of the Institute in all its transactions.

2. The President shall be responsible for the relations between the Institute and the Forestry Science Faculty of the University of Los Andes, bearing in mind the needs of both bodies.

3. Subject to the provisions of Article XXV of this agreement, the President shall be responsible for all official relations between the Institute and the research centres in Venezuela or abroad, as well as for the relations with Governments and International Organizations.

4. The President shall appoint and terminate the technical and administrative staff of the Institute on the basis of proposals made by the Director.

5. The President shall convene the sessions of the Governing Council and of the Executive Committee, in accordance with the provisions of

the Rules of Procedure of the Institute.

6. In addition to the functions mentioned in this article, the President shall perform such other functions as are provided for in other articles of this agreement.

7. The remuneration of the President and the allowances attached to his office shall be determined by the Governing Council and shall be provided for in the budget of the Institute.

Article VIII

THE DIRECTOR

1. The Governing Council, after consultation with the Director-General of the Organization, shall appoint a Director on a full time basis.

2. The Director shall be under the authority of the President and shall have the following functions:

a) management, organization and administration of the Institute;

b) preparation of all publications to be issued under the name of the Institute and their submission to the President for his clearance in consultation with the Director-General of the Organization.

3. The Director shall be appointed for a term of four years. The conditions of his appointment shall be fixed by the Governing Council on the proposal of the Executive Committee which may approve them provisionally subject to confirmation by the Governing Council at its next session. In cases of absence or inability of the Director to perform his duties, the Executive Committee shall designate an officer of the Institute to replace the Director provisionally. The Executive Committee may suspend the Director if it considers such action indispensable in serious cases. The Executive Committee shall, however, convene a special session of the Governing Council to solve the situation.

Article IX

STAFF

The technical staff of the Institute shall be recruited on as wide a geographical basis as possible. The administrative and technical personnel shall be responsible to the President and shall be under the immediate supervision of the Director. The responsibility of the entire staff, including the Director, in exercising their functions shall be international in character.

Article X

PREMISES AND EQUIPMENT

The Government of Venezuela shall ensure that the University of Los Andes shall continue to make available the lands, buildings, furniture, equipment and public utilities listed in Appendix A to this agreement and assumes responsibility for their maintenance and protection. Any expansion of these facilities which the Institute may propose shall be the object of an agreement between the Faculty and the Executive Committee of the Institute.

Article XI

FINANCING, ASSISTANCE AND MANAGEMENT

1. The Institute shall be financed by annual contributions, paid directly into the account of the Institute with the Central Bank of Venezuela, by the Government of Venezuela and the other Member Nations and Associate Members that are parties to this agreement, in accordance with a scale of contributions to be approved by at least two-thirds of the Member Nations and Associate Members parties to this agreement. For the first five years after this agreement has come into force these contributions shall be in accordance with the scale indicated in Appendix B hereto, which scale takes into account the greater responsibility of the Government of Venezuela as well as the size and importance of the forest resources of the other Member Nations and Associate Members that are parties to this agreement.

2. Contributions to be paid by Member Nations or Associate Members of the Organization which are parties to this agreement but are not listed in Appendix B shall be determined by the Governing Council by a two-thirds majority of the votes cast.

3. The Organization, at the request of the Institute, may offer advice and provide technical guidance on the organization and program of work of the Institute. Assistance may likewise be offered by the Organization in the actual implementation of the program of work of the Institute by making available the services of specialists that might be appointed by the Organization on a regional basis under the Expanded or similar Technical Assistance Programs when such a course of action is deemed appropriate and feasible by the Director-General of the Organization. The Director-General of the Organization may also exceptionally, subject to budgetary approval by the Conference, offer assistance financed out of the regular budget of the Organization.

4. The Executive Committee shall be empowered to accept gifts, legacies and grants from governments, institutions or private persons, provided that these gifts, legacies and grants are for purposes in keeping with the aims and functions of the Institute.

5. The Government of Venezuela and the other contracting Member Nations and Associate Members of the Organization undertake to promote the establishment of a private foundation in conformity with the applicable national laws. The purpose of this foundation shall be to act as sponsor of the Institute and to this effect collect monies from public and private sources and to create with these monies a fund, the income of which will be used exclusively towards financing the activities of the Institute.

6. The Executive Committee shall prepare and submit for the approval of the Governing Council a draft program of work and budget of the Institute for the ensuing financial period, within the limits of the foreseeable resources for that period. Whenever unforeseen budgetary income accrues, the

Executive Committee shall decide what use shall be made of it and shall report its decisions to the next session of the Governing Council.

7. The Financial Regulations shall establish the rules to be followed for disbursing, within the limits of the approved budget, ordinary expenditure for the administration of the Institute, as well as for any requirements which may be deemed necessary in connection with transfers within the budget.

8. The Executive Committee shall make the necessary arrangements for an independent audit of the accounts of the Institute.

Article XII

LEGAL STATUS

1. The Institute shall be recognized as an international institution having the capacity of a legal person to perform any legal act appropriate to its purpose which is not beyond the powers granted it by this agreement.

2. Save for the obligations expressly provided for in this agreement, the Organization, the Government of Venezuela and the other contracting Member Nations or Associate Members and the University of Los Andes shall not be responsible for any civil, financial or other obligations in respect of the Institute.

3. The Government of Venezuela shall accord to the Institute the immunities and facilities which are necessary for the operation of the Institute and the achievement of its objectives, including inviolability of premises and archives, immunity from suit, and, subject to the procedure required by law, exemption from taxation and import duties and from restrictions on articles intented for the exclusive use of the Institute.

4. The Government of Venezuela and each of the other Member Nations and Associate Members of the Organization parties to the agreement shall accord to the members of the Governing Council as well as to the staff of the Institute, other than their own nationals, the privileges and immunities which are necessary for the performance of their duties.

5. Moreover, the Government of Venezuela shall facilitate the entry into and the stay in Venezuela, subject to the observance of the appropriate provisions that may be in force, of representatives of Member Nations and Associate Members of the Organization parties to the agreement to visit the Institute and become acquainted with its activities and facilities.

Article XIII

ANNUAL REPORTS

The President shall each year submit to the Executive Committee technical, adminstrative and financial reports on the work accomplished by the Institute. These reports, together with any comments and recommendations thereon of the Executive Committee and a report by the Executive Committee on any action taken by the Executive Committee shall be submitted to the Governing Council. The report of the Governing Council on the matters dealt with in these reports, together with its own comments, recommendations and decisions, shall be communicated to the Government of Venezuela, to the other contracting Member Nations and Associate Members, and to the Regional Forest Research Committee of the Latin-American Forestry Commission for submission, with its comments, to the Council of the Organization. This report shall also be made available to other interested Member Nations and Associate Members of the Organization on their request.

Article XIV

BYELAWS

The Executive Committee shall prepare and adopt such rules and regulations as may be necessary for the work and functioning of the Institute. They shall comprise rules relating to the functioning of the organs of the Institute (rules of procedure) to the staff (staff regulations) and to the financial management of the Institute (financial regulations). Subject to their adaptation to the special requirements of the Institute, these rules and regulations shall be based on the relevant provisions of the Rules and Regulations of the Organization. They shall be submitted for confirmation to the Governing Council at its next session.

Article XV

ACCEPTANCE

1. Acceptance of this agreement by the Government of Venezuela and the governments of the other contracting Member Nations and Associate Members shall be effected by the deposit by each such government of an instrument of acceptance with the Director-General of the Organization and shall take effect on the receipt of this instrument by the Director-General, who shall inform the President of the Institute, the Government of Venezuela, all the other parties to the agreement, the other Member Nations and Associate Members of the Organization and the Secretary-General of the United Nations.

2. Acceptance of this agreement by the Organization shall be effected by the adoption by the Conference of the Organization of the resolution approving this agreement referred to in the testimonium to this agreement.

3. After acceptance by the Organization this agreement shall enter into force as soon as instruments of acceptance have been received by the Director-General of the Organization from the Government of Venezuela and four other Member Nations, providing such acceptances are received within one year of the date of approval of this agreement by the Conference of the Organization.

Article XVI

AMENDMENTS

1. This agreement may be amended with the approval of two-thirds of the Member Nations and

Associate Members of the Organization which are parties to this agreement, provided that Venezuela is among such nations.

2. Any such amendments shall become effective only with the concurrence of the Council of the Organization, unless the Council considers it desirable to refer the amendment to the Conference for approval, and shall come into force only from the date of the decision of the Council or Conference as the case may be, providing that any amendment involving new obligations for the nations that are parties to this agreement shall come into force in respect of each such nation only on its acceptance of such amendment.

3. Instruments of acceptance of amendments involving new obligations shall be deposited with the Director-General of the Organization who shall inform all Member Nations or Associate Members of the Organization that are parties to this agreement, as well as the Secretary-General of the United Nations, of the receipt of acceptance and the entry into force of amendments. The rights and obligations of any Member Nation or Associate Member of the Organization that is a party to this agreement that has not accepted an amendment involving additional obligations shall continue to be governed by the provisions of the agreement as they stood prior to the amendment.

Article XVII

RESERVATIONS

The acceptance of this agreement may not be made subject to any reservation.

Article XVIII

TERRITORIAL APPLICATION

Member Nations of the Organization that become parties to this agreement shall, at the time of acceptance, state explicity to which territories this agreement shall extend. In the absence of such a declaration, the agreement shall be deemed to apply to all the territories situated in the Latin-American region for the international relations of which the government concerned is responsible. Subject to the provisions of Article XX of this agreement, the scope of the territorial application may be modified by a subsequent declaration.

Article XIX

INTERPRETATION AND SETTLEMENT OF DISPUTES

Any dispute regarding the interpretation or application of this agreement, if not settled by the Governing Council, shall be referred to a committee composed of one member appointed by each of the parties to the dispute, and in addition a chairman chosen by the other members of the committee. The recommendations of such a committee, while not binding in character, shall become the basis for renewed consideration by the parties concerned of the matter out of which the disagreement arose. If as the result of this procedure the dispute is not settled, a solution shall be sought through any of the peaceful means mentioned in the Charter of the United Nations.

Article XX

DENUNCIATION

1. Any party to this agreement may denounce the agreement at any time after the expiration of one year from the date of its acceptance or of the entry into force of the agreement whichever is the later. Such denunciation shall take effect six months after the date of receipt by the Director-General of the Organization of the notification thereof. The Director-General of the Organization shall inform the President of the Institute, the Government of Venezuela, all other parties to the agreement and the other Member Nations an Assocaite Members of the Organization as well as the Secretary-General of the United Nations of the receipt of such notification. The financial obligations of the party having denounced the agreement shall include the entire financial period in which the denunciation takes effect.

2. A Member Nation of the Organization, party to this agreement, that is responsible for the international relations of more than one territory shall, when denouncing this agreement, state to which territory or territories the denunciation is to apply. In the absence of such a declaration, the denunciation shall be deemed to apply to all the territories situated in the Latin-American region for the international relations of which the Member Nation concerned is responsible, with the exception of Associate Members.

3. Any Member Nation or Associate Member of the Organization, party to this agreement, that gives notice of withdrawal from the Organization shall be deemed to have simultaneously denounced this agreement, and this denunciation shall be deemed to apply to all the territories for the international relations of which the Member Nation concerned is responsible.

Article XXI

TERMINATION

1. This agreement shall be terminated if:

a) it is denounced either by the Government of Venezuela or the Organization, or

b) the number of the other contracting Member Nations or Associate Members, as the result of denunciations, drops below four. In this case, the agreement may be maintained if the remaining participants unanimously so decide, with the concurrence of the Organization and the Government of Venezuela.

Termination shall be effective six months after the President of the Institute has been informed by the Director-General of the receipt of the necessary notifications.

2. Upon termination of this agreement and once the above-mentioned period has elapsed, the Executive Committee in consultation with the Government of Venezuela shall return to the Forestry Science Faculty of the University of Los Andes all properties put at the disposal of the Institute by the said Faculty and will liquidate all the remaining assets of the Institute. After all obligations have been met, the balance will be

distributed amongst the Government of Venezuela and the other contracting Member Nations and Associate Members in proportion to the contributions they have paid throughout the period of operation of the Institute both on a provisional and on a permanent basis. Participating governments which at the time this agreement is terminated are in arrears of two annual contributions, even if they are not consecutive, shall not be entitled to receive any share of the assets.

Article XXII

AUTHENTIC LANGUAGES

The English, French and Spanish texts of this agreement shall be equally authentic.

Article XXIII

QUORUM AND MAJORITY AT SESSIONS OF THE GOVERNING COUNCIL OR EXECUTIVE COMMITTEE

1. At sessions of the Governing Council the majority of the representatives of the Member Nations or Associate Members of the Organization that are parties to this agreement shall constitute a quorum. If this figure is not obtained, the quorum shall be constituted by the representatives of four Member Nations or Associate Members that are parties to this agreement, provided that they include the representative of the Government of Venezuela and, in addition, the President or one of the Vice-Presidents of the Governing Council. The presence of any four members of the Executive Committee shall constitute its quorum.

2. Except as otherwise provided by this agreement or the relevant rules or regulations, the required majority for any decision by the Governing Council or the Executive Committee shall be more than half of the votes cast. The phrase "votes cast" shall mean affirmative and negative votes and shall not include abstentions or blank votes.

Article XXIV

EXPENSES RELATING TO ATTENDANCE AT SESSIONS OF THE GOVERNING COUNCIL AND EXECUTIVE COMMITTEE

1. The expenses of the Members of the Governing Council and of the Executive Committee when attending sessions of these bodies shall be borne by the respective governments. The expenses of the staff members of the Institute and of experts acting in an individual capacity who, in the opinion of the Executive Committee, should attend sessions of the Governing Council or the Executive Committee as well as the expenses of the President and the Director shall be borne by the Institute.

2. The Organization shall be responsible for the expenses of the Director-General or his representative in connection with attendance at sessions of the Governing Council or the Executive Committee. Any such expenses, when borne by the regular budget of the Organization, shall be determined and paid within the limits of the relevant item of the budget of the Organization as approved by the Conference.

Article XXV

RELATIONS WITH GOVERNMENTS AND ORGANIZATIONS

1. The provisions relating to the granting of observer status to nations adopted by the Conference of the Organization shall apply mutatis mutandis to meetings of the Institute or those convened under its auspices.

2. In its relations with international organizations, the Institute shall be guided by the principles governing the relations between the Organizations and international organizations.

3. Any arrangements between the Institute and nations that are not parties to this agreement shall be made in consultation with the Government of Venezuela and the Director-General of the Organization.

RULES OF PROCEDURE

Introduction

Under the provisions of Article XIV of the Agreement between the Food and Agriculture Organization of the United Nations (hereinafter referred to as "the Organization") and the Government of the Republic of Venezuela (hereinafter referred to as "the Government of Venezuela") and other Member Nations and Associate Members of the Organization parties to the Agreement for the Establishment on a Permanent Basis of a Latin-American Forestry Research and Training Institute (hereinafter referred to as "the Institute"), the Executive Committee at its First Session approved the following Rules of Procedure to govern the work of the organs of the Institute.

Chapter I

THE GOVERNING COUNCIL

Article I

The Governing Council shall follow its own Regulations (Document IFLAIC/CD/61/2/Rev.2.).

Chapter II

THE EXECUTIVE COMMITTEE

Article I

COMPOSITION OF THE EXECUTIVE COMMITTEE

1. The composition of the Executive Committee shall be as provided in Article VI.1 of the Agreement and its functions shall be as stated in Article VI.3 thereof, as well as in these Rules and other regulations of the Institute.

2. Executive Committee members shall enjoy the rights set forth in Article XII.4 of the Agreement.

Article II

OFFICERS

1. The President of the Institute shall be

Chairman of the Executive Committee. He shall convene sessions, open, adjourn and close meetings, give the floor to speakers, submit for consideration proposals of Committee members and of Member Nations or Associate Members parties to the Agreement; and announce results of the voting. During discussions, and after consultation with other members of the Committee, he may set a time limit for each speaker on any item and may adjourn or close the debate; he may also submit for consideration such other measures as he may deem advisable to expedite proceedings.

2. The Director of the Institute, acting as Secretary to the Committee, shall prepare and submit to it all material which the President may deem necessary for the discussions and fulfil any other tasks entrusted to him by the Executive Committee through the President.

Article III

CONVENING AND HOLDING OF SESSIONS

1. The annual session of the Executive Committee called for by Article VI.2 of the Agreement shall be held during the last quarter of each year at dates set by the President after consultation with the members of the Committee.

2. If a session of the Governing Council is also convened within the last quarter of a year, the session of the Executive Committee may be put either before, after, or at the same time and place, as appropriate.

3. When necessary, the Executive Committee may hold additional sessions at the Institute's headquarters. Special sessions may be held elsewhere when warranted by circumstances.

4. Invitations to sessions of the Executive Committee shall be issued at least one month prior to the date on which the sessions are to be held and shall indicate the place and include the provisional agenda.

5. The President of the Institute shall notify the governments of the Member Nations and Associate Members parties to the Agreement that a session of the Executive Committee is to be held in order to enable them to submit to the Committee any proposals which they deem necessary or useful as regards the organization or work of the Institute.

6. As regards the quorum and majority rules in meetings of the Executive Committee, Articles VI.1 and XXIII of the Agreement shall apply.

Article IV

AGENDA

1. The Secretary of the Executive Committee in consultation with the Chairman shall draw up a provisional agenda for each of its sessions.

2. Any member of the Committee may request the Chairman to include in the provisional agenda items which in his opinion should be considered by the Committee.

3. No item proposed to the Executive Committee by the Director-General of the Organization may be deleted from the agenda.

4. The first item on the provisional agenda shall be the examination and approval of the agenda.

5. The provisional agenda shall be distributed by the Secretary to all members of the Executive Committee at least one month prior to the opening of the session, together with copies of all documents whose consideration appears on the agenda.

Article V

VOTING

1. Voting shall usually be by show of hands. If any member proposes a secret ballot this shall be held, and the votes shall be counted by the Secretary and the proposing member in the presence of the Chairman.

2. Any member of the Committee may request a roll call vote, in which case the vote of each member shall be placed on record.

Article VI

RECORDS OF PROCEEDINGS AND REPORTS

1. The Executive Committee shall at each session approve a report setting forth its views, recommendations and decisions and, if requested, minority opinions.

2. The Committee may also on specific occasions approve the preparation of papers for internal use.

3. The President shall communicate all conclusions and recommendations of the session in conformity with Article XIII of the Agreement.

Article VII

LANGUAGES

1. The official languages of the Executive Committee shall be English, French and Spanish.

2. At the opening of each session the Committee shall decide which official languages shall be used as working languages.

Chapter III

Article I

THE PRESIDENT

1. The basic function of the President shall be to implement and ensure the implementation of the Agreement and rules made thereunder.

2. He shall be responsible for the relations between the Institute and the Forestry Science Faculty of the University of Los Andes bearing in mind the needs of both bodies.

3. Subject to the provisions of Article XXV of the Agreement the President shall also be responsible for all official relations between the Institute and the research centres in Venezuela or abroad, as well as for the relations with government and international organizations.

4. In the performance of these functions, the President shall inform the Director of his decisions so that the latter may adjust the work of the Institute accordingly and express his own views on them.

5. During any absence, the President may, in specific cases, delegate the performance of these

functions to the Director. In such cases, the Director shall act and sign on behalf of the President.

6. In case of doubt regarding the interpretation of any provision of the Agreement or of the rules, the President shall consult the Director-General of the Organization in his capacity as advisor to the Governing Council and Executive Committee.

Article II

THE DIRECTOR

1. The Director shall be under the authority of the President, and shall have the following functions:

a) management, organization and administration of the Institute;

b) preparation of all publications to be issued under the name of the Institute and their submission to the President for his clearance in consultation with the Director-General of the Organization;

c) Any other functions assigned to him by the Agreement and rules.

2. When in the discharge of his functions the Director is required to take any decision on a matter not specifically provided for in the instruments governing the activities of the Institute, he shall first consult the President.

3. The Director shall duly take into account the President's proposals regarding the internal management of the Institute and shall be responsible for giving effect to them.

4. The Director shall keep the President informed at all times of the activities of the Institute for which he is responsible.

5. The Director shall prepare, and submit to the President, bimonthly reports on the Institute's activities. These reports, duly complemented, shall be the basis for the preparation of the annual technical and administrative report which the President is required to submit to the Executive Committee (Article XVIII of the Agreement).

Chapter IV

Article I

AMENDMENTS TO THE RULES OF PROCEDURE

The Executive Committee may approve by majority vote any amendment to these Rules, provided that 24 hours' advance notice of the proposed amendment has been given to the Chairman and other members of the Committee. Amendments shall become effective immediately upon their approval by the Committee, and the Governing Council shall be informed thereof.

Article II

GENERAL PROVISIONS

1. The English, French and Spanish language texts of these Rules shall be considered equally authentic.

2. These Rules shall come into force upon approval by the Executive Committee.

THE ANTARCTIC TREATY [21]

Washington, 1 December 1959

The Governments of Argentina, Australia, Belgium, Chile, the French Republic, Japan, New Zealand, Norway, the Union of South Africa, the Union of Soviet Socialist Republics, the United Kingdom of Great Britain and Northern Ireland, and the United States of America,

Recognizing that it is in the interest of all mankind that Antarctica shall continue forever to be used exclusively for peaceful purposes and shall not become the scene or object of international discord;

Acknowledge the substantial contributions to scientific knowledge resulting from international co-operation in scientific investigation in Antarctica;

Convinced that the establishment of a firm foundation for the continuation and development of such co-operation on the basis of freedom of scientific investigation in Antarctica as applied during the International Geophysical Year accords with the interests of science and the progress of all mankind;

Convinced also that a treaty ensuring the use of Antarctica for peaceful purposes only and the continuance of international harmony in Antarctica will further the purposes and principles embodied in the Charter of the United Nations;

Have agreed as follows:

Article I

1. Antarctica shall be used for peaceful purposes only. There shall be prohibited, *inter alia,* any measures of a military nature, such as the establishment of military bases and fortifications, the carrying out of military maneuvers, as well as the testing of any types of weapons.

2. The present Treaty shall not prevent the use of military personnel or equipment for scientific research or for any other peaceful purpose.

Article II

Freedom of scientific investigation in Antarctica and co-operation toward that end, as applied during the International Geophysical Year, shall continue, subject to the provisions of the present Treaty.

Article III

1. In order to promote international co-operation in scientific investigation in Antarctica, as provided for in Article II of the present Treaty, the Contracting Parties agree that, to the greatest extent feasible and practicable:

a) information regarding plans for scientific programs in Antarctica shall be exchanged to permit maximum economy and efficiency of operations;

b) scientific personnel shall be exchanged in Antarctica between expeditions and stations;

c) scientific observations and results from Antarctica shall be exchanged and made freely available.

2. In implementing this Article, every encouragement shall be given to the establishment of co-operative working relations with those Specialized Agencies of the United Nations and other international organizations having a scientific or technical interest in Antarctica.

Article IV

1. Nothing contained in the present Treaty shall be interpreted as:

a) a renunciation by any Contracting Party of previously asserted rights of or claims to territorial sovereignty in Antarctica;

b) a renunciation or diminution by any Contracting Party of any basis of claim to territorial sovereignty in Antarctica which it may have whether as a result of its activities or those of its nationals in Antarctica, or otherwise;

c) prejudicing the position of any Contracting Party as regards its recognition or non-recognition of any other State's right of or claim or basis of claim to territorial sovereignty in Antarctica.

2. No acts or activities taking place while the present Treaty is in force shall constitute a basis for asserting, supporting or denying a claim to territorial sovereignty in Antarctica or create any rights of sovereignty in Antarctica. No new claim, or enlargement of an existing claim, to territorial sovereignty in Antarctica shall be asserted while the present Treaty is in force.

Article V

1. Any nuclear explosions in Antarctica and the disposal there of radioactive waste material shall be prohibited.

2. In the event of the conclusion of international agreements concerning the use of nuclear energy, including nuclear explosions and the disposal of radioactive waste material, to which all of the Contracting Parties whose representatives are entitled to participate in the meetings provided for under Article IX are parties, the rules established under such agreements shall apply in Antarctica.

Article VI

The provisions of the present Treaty shall apply to the area south of 60° South Latitude, including all ice shelves, but nothing in the present Treaty shall prejudice or in any way affect the rights, or the exercise of the rights, of any State under international law with regard to the high seas within that area.

Article VII

1. In order to promote the objectives and ensure the observance of the provisions of the present Treaty, each Contracting Party whose representatives are entitled to participate in the meetings referred to in Article IX of the Treaty shall have the right to designate observers to carry out any inspection provided for by the present Article. Observers shall be nationals of the Contracting Parties which designate them. The names of observers shall be communicated to every other Contracting Party having the right to designate observers, and like notice shall be given of the termination of their appointment.

2. Each observer designated in accordance with the provisions of paragraph 1 of this Article shall have complete freedom of access at any time to any or all areas of Antarctica.

3. All areas of Antarctica, including all stations, installations and equipment within those areas, and all ships and aircraft at points of discharging or embarking cargoes or personnel in Antarctica, shall be open at all times to inspection by any observers designated in accordance with paragraph 1 of this article.

4. Aerial observation may be carried out at any time over any or all areas of Antarctica by any of the Contracting Parties having the right to designate observers.

5. Each Contracting Party shall, at the time when the present Treaty enters into force for it, inform the other Contracting Parties, and thereafter shall give them notice in advance, of

a) all expeditions to and within Antarctica, on the part of its ships or nationals, and all expeditions to Antarctica organized in or proceeding from its territory;

b) all stations in Antarctica occupied by its nationals; and

c) any military personnel or equipment intended to be introduced by it into Antarctica subject to the conditions prescribed in paragraph 2 of Article I of the present Treaty.

Article VIII

1. In order to facilitate the exercise of their functions under the present Treaty, and without prejudice to the respective positions of the Contracting Parties relating to jurisdiction over all other persons in Antarctica, observers designated under paragraph 1 of Article VII and scientific personnel exchanged under subparagraph 1 (*b*) of Article III of the Treaty, and members of the staffs accompanying any such persons, shall be subject only to the jurisdiction of the Contracting Party of which they are nationals in respect of all acts or omissions occurring while they are in Antarctica for the purpose of exercising their functions.

2. Without prejudice to the provisions of paragraph 1 of this Article, and pending the adoption of measures in pursuance of subparagraph 1 (*e*) of Article IX, the Contracting Parties concerned in any case of dispute with regard to the exercise of jurisdiction in Antarctica shall immediately consult together with a view to reaching a mutually acceptable solution.

Article IX

1. Representatives of the Contracting Parties named in the preamble to the present Treaty shall meet at the City of Canberra within two months after the date of entry into force of the Treaty, and

thereafter at suitable intervals and places, for the purpose of exchanging information, consulting together on matters of common interest pertaining to Antarctica, and formulating and considering, and recommending to their Governments, measures in furtherance of the principles and objectives of the Treaty, including measures regarding:

a) use of Antarctica for peaceful purposes only;

b) facilitation of scientific research in Antarctica;

c) facilitation of international scientific co-operation in Antarctica;

d) facilitation of the exercise of the rights of inspection provided for in Article VII of the Treaty;

e) questions relating to the exercise of jurisdiction in Antarctica;

f) preservation and conservation of living resources in Antarctica.

2. Each Contracting Party which has become a party to the present Treaty by accession under Article XIII shall be entitled to appoint representatives to participate in the meetings referred to in paragraph 1 of the present Article, during such time as that Contracting Party demonstrates its interest in Antarctica by conducting substantial scientific research activity there, such as the establishment of a scientific station or the despatch of a scientific expedition.

3. Reports from the observers referred to in Article VII of the present Treaty shall be transmitted to the representatives of the Contracting Parties participating in the meetings referred to in paragraph 1 of the present Article.

4. The measures referred to in paragraph 1 of this Article shall become effective when approved by all the Contracting Parties whose representatives were entitled to participate in the meetings held to consider those measures.

5. Any or all of the rights established in the present Treaty may be exercised as from the date of entry into force of the Treaty whether or not any measures facilitating the exercise of such rights have been proposed, considered or approved as provided in this Article.

Article X

Each of the Contracting Parties undertakes to exert appropriate efforts, consistent with the Charter of the United Nations, to the end that no one engages in any activity in Antarctica contrary to the principles or purposes of the present Treaty.

Article XI

1. If any dispute arises between two or more of the Contracting Parties concerning the interpretation or application of the present Treaty, those Contracting Parties shall consult among themselves with a view to having the dispute resolved by negotiation, inquiry, mediation, conciliation, arbitration, judicial settlement or other peaceful means of their own choice.

2. Any dispute of this character not so resolved shall, with the consent, in each case, of all parties to the dispute, be referred to the International Court of Justice for settlement; but failure to reach agreement or reference to the International Court shall not absolve parties to the dispute from the responsibility of continuing to seek to resolve it by any of the various peaceful means referred to in paragraph 1 of this Article.

Article XII

1. *a*) The present Treaty may be modified or amended at any time by unanimous agreement of the Contracting Parties whose representatives are entitled to participate in the meeting provided for under Article IX. Any such modification or amendment shall enter into force when the depositary Government has received notice from all such contracting Parties that they have ratified it.

b) Such modification or amendment shall thereafter enter into force as to any other Contracting Policy when notice of ratification by it has been received by the depositary Government. Any such Contracting Party from which no notice of ratification is received within a period of two years from the date of entry into force of the modification or amendment in accordance with the provisions of subparagraph 1 (*a*) of this Article shall be deemed to have withdrawn from the present Treaty on the date of the expiration of such period.

2. *a*) If after the expiration of thirty years from the date of entry into force of the present Treaty, any of the Contracting Parties whose representatives are entitled to participate in the meetings provided for under Article IX so requests by a communication addressed to the depositary Government, a Conference of all the Contracting Parties shall be held as soon as practicable to review the operation of the Treaty.

b) Any modification or amendment to the present Treaty which is approved at such a Conference by a majority of the Contracting Parties there represented, including a majority of those whose representatives are entitled to participate in the meetings provided for under Article IX, shall be communicated by the depositary Government to all the Contracting Parties immediately after the termination of the Conference and shall enter into force in accordance with the provisions of paragraph 1 of the present Article.

c) If any such modification or amendment has not entered into force in accordance with the provisions of subparagraph 1 (*a*) of this Article within a period of two years after the date of its communication to all the Contracting Parties, any Contracting Party may at any time after the expiration of that period give notice to the depositary Government of its withdrawal from the present Treaty; and such withdrawal shall take effect two years after the receipt of the notice by the depositary Government.

Article XIII

1. The present Treaty shall be subject to ratification by the signatory States. It shall be open for accession by any State which is a Member of the United Nations, or by any other State which may be invited to accede to the Treaty with the consent of all the Contracting Parties whose representatives are entitled to participate in the meetings provided for under Article IX of the Treaty.

2. Ratification of or accession to the present Treaty shall be effected by each State in accordance with its constitutional processes.

3. Instruments of ratification and instruments of accession shall be deposited with the Government of the United States of America, hereby designated as the depositary Government.

4. The depositary Government shall inform all signatory and acceding States of the date of each deposit of an instrument of ratification or accession, and the date of entry into force of the Treaty and of any modification or amendment thereto.

5. Upon the deposit of instruments of ratification by all the signatory States, the present Treaty shall enter into force for these States and for States which have deposited instruments of accession. Thereafter the Treaty shall enter into force for any acceding State upon the deposit of its instruments of accession.

6. The present Treaty shall be registered by the depositary Government pursuant to Article 102 of the Charter of the United Nations.

Article XIV

The present Treaty, done in the English, French, Russian and Spanish languages, each version being equally authentic, shall be deposited in the archives of the Government of the United States of America, which shall transmit duly certified copies thereof to the Governments of the signatory and acceding States.

In Witness Whereof, the undersigned Plenipotentiaries, duly authorized, have signed the present Treaty.

Done at Washington this first day of December, one thousand nine hundred and fifty-nine.

AGREEMENT CONCERNING CO-OPERATION IN THE QUARANTINE OF PLANTS AND THEIR PROTECTION AGAINST PESTS AND DISEASES [22]

Sofia, 14 December 1959

The Contracting Parties,

Considering the danger presented by the diseases and pests of agricultural plants and by weeds to the national economy of all countries,

Desirous of expanding co-operation in the quarantine of plants and their protection from pests, diseases and weeds and of co-ordinating measures in regard to quarantine and the control of pests and diseases of agricultural plants and the control of weeds,

With a view to the mutual protection of their territories against the importation of quarantinable pests, diseases and weeds and to developing economic and trade relations between their countries,

Having decided to conclude an Agreement for this purpose, have hereby agreed as follows:

Article I

The Contracting Parties shall take such measures as may be necessary for the control of the plant pests and diseases and weeds specified in the list annexed to the Agreement. The said list may be modified by decision of the international conference on the quarantine and protection of plants convened pursuant to article VIII of this Agreement.

Article II

The Contracting Parties shall regularly exchange information concerning the spread of dangerous plant pests and diseases and the measures being taken for their control. The form and frequency of such exchanges of information shall be determined by the international conference on the quarantine and protection of plants provided for in article VIII of this Agreement.

In the event of the outbreak of especially dangerous quarantinable plant pests and diseases, centres of infection of which are discovered for the first time, the relevant information shall be transmitted immediately.

Article III

The Contracting Parties agree to render one another the requisite technical assistance in the control of pests, diseases and weeds, through sales of machinery, equipment, appliances, chemical weed-killers and pesticides and other materials for the control of plant pests and diseases and by undertaking joint measures for the control of plant pests and diseases, on conditions to be determined in each case by special agreement between the parties concerned.

Article IV

The Contracting Parties shall:

1. Exchange copies of legislative provisions relating to plant quarantine and protection, instructions, directives, specialist literature, information on the methods employed by scientific research institutes, curricula and programmes, and statistical and other material relating to plant quarantine and protection.

2. Notify one another of the most important conferences on questions of plant quarantine and protection and advanced training courses for plant quarantine and protection specialists in course of preparation, so that specialists from the Contracting Parties may be given opportunity to take part in them.

3. Provide for exchanges of professors and teachers, scientists, and plant quarantine and protection specialists, with a view to the study of scientific achievements and the exchange of experience in the work of plant quarantine and protection.

4. Ensure co-operation between scientific institutes in the study of diseases and pests and the improvement of diagnostic methods and means of controlling plant pests and diseases.

5. Dispatch, at the request of any Contracting Party, teams of plant quarantine and protection specialists of one or more Contracting Parties with a view to the study of dangerous plant pests and diseases, research into methods of controlling them and the organization of measures for the quarantine of plants and their protection from pests and diseases.

Article V

The Contracting Parties undertake to apply uniform phytosanitary regulations for the import, export and transit of consignments of vegetable origin dispatched from one country to another. The aforesaid regulations shall be formulated at the international conference provided for in article VIII of this Agreement.

Article VI

The Contracting Parties undertake to apply measures to prevent the introduction from one country into another, in exported consignments of goods or by any other means, of quarantinable plant pests and diseases and weeds specified in lists to be drawn up by agreement between the parties concerned.

To this end the Contracting Parties undertake:

To carry out the necessary measures in the areas adjoining their respective frontiers for the eradication of quarantinable plant pests and diseases and weeds by means of chemical, biological, agro-technical and all other methods;

To establish in their territories specific frontier posts through which consignments of vegetable origin may be imported or exported and to equip the said frontier posts with disinfestation chambers for the disinfection of consignments and with means for carrying out analyses of samples of consignments with a view to testing them for infection by quarantinable plant pests and diseases and weeds;

To carry out careful quarantine inspections of consignments of vegetable origin exported from one country to another and of means of transport, and to furnish consignments with quarantine certificates issued by the State plant quarantine and protection services of the exporting country attesting their freedom from infection by quarantinable plant pests and diseases and weeds.

To avoid the use of straw, leaves and other waste products of agricultural plants as packing material and to substitute for them sawdust, wood shavings, moss and other packing materials, according to the conditions prevailing in the exporting country. In the event of absolute necessity, it shall be permissible to use straw and leaves, after disinfection, as packing material.

Article VII

With a view to co-ordinating their activities in the field of quarantine enforcement and to supervising the application of the measures necessary for the control of quarantinable plant pests and diseases in frontier areas, the Contracting Parties agree to establish, where necessary, special commissions consisting of representatives of the countries concerned, the members of such commissions being granted the right of repeated frontier crossing and of remaining in the territory of other States for such time as may be necessary for the fulfilment of the functions assigned to them.

Article VIII

The Contracting Parties have agreed to convene whenever necessary, and not less than once every three years, international conferences on the quarantine and protection of plants, for the purpose of resolving practical problems connected with the fulfilment of the obligations arising from this Agreement and with a view to the exchange of information and of experience gained in carrying out the measures provided for in this Agreement.

The date and place of meeting of each international conference and the topics to be discussed shall be determined by the Contracting Parties.

Communications between the competent authorities of the Contracting Parties on matters arising from this Agreement shall be effected both directly and through the secretariat of the Standing Commission of the Council for Mutual Economic Assistance for economic, scientific and technical co-operation in agriculture.

With a view to the preparation of proposals on the most urgent questions relating to plant quarantine and protection arising during the intervals between conferences, special working groups consisting of representatives of the countries concerned may be established by agreement between them.

Article IX

Expenses incurred in carrying out the provisions of this Agreement shall be allocated as follows:

1. Expenses incurred in carrying out the measures provided for in article II and article IV, sub-paragraph 1, shall be borne by the Contracting Party sending the information and material referred to in the said articles.
2. Travel and subsistence expenses of persons referred to in article IV, sub-paragraphs 2 and 3, and article VIII shall be borne by the Contracting Party sending these persons.
3. Expenses incurred in carrying out the measures provided for in article IV, sub-paragraphs 4 and 5, and article VII shall be allocated by agreement between the parties concerned.
4. Expenses incurred in the organization and conduct of the international conferences provided for in article VIII shall be borne by the States in whose territories they are held.

Article X

This Agreement shall be open for signature in Moscow until 1 July 1960.

The Agreement shall be subject to ratification.

The instruments of ratification shall be deposited with the Secretariat of the Council for Mutual Economic Assistance, which shall act as the depositary of the Agreement.

The Agreement shall enter into force on the date of the deposit of the fifth instrument of ratification, and notice of its entry into force shall be communicated by the depositary to the States signatories to this Agreement.

Article XI

After its entry into force, the Agreement shall be open to accession by any State.

For each State acceding to this Agreement, and for States depositing their instruments of ratification after the entry into force of the Agreement, the Agreement shall enter into force on the date of the deposit by the State concerned of its instrument of ratification or accession.

Article XII

After the expiry of a five-year period from the date of entry into force of this Agreement, any Contracting Party may denounce it by notice in writing to the depositary.

The Agreement shall cease to take effect in respect of such Party six months after the depositary's receipt of the notice of denunciation.

Article XIII

This Agreement has been drawn up in the Russian language in one copy, which shall be deposited with the Secretariat of the Council for Mutual Economic Assistance.

The Secretariat of the Council for Mutual Economic Assistance shall send the Contracting Parties duly certified copies of the Agreement, and shall notify the States signatories to this Agreement and States acceding thereto of the deposit with it of instruments of ratification, accession or denunciation.

Done at Sofia on 14 December 1959.

In Witness Whereof the undersigned, having been duly authorized by their respective Governments, have signed this Agreement.

ANNEX

LIST OF THE PRINCIPAL QUARANTINABLE PESTS, DISEASES AND NOXIOUS WEEDS

Acalla schalleriana L.
Agrilus mali Mats.
Agrobacterium tumefaciens (E.F.Sm et Towns) Conn
Anthonomus grandis Boh.
Aphelenchoides oryzae Yokoo
Aphelenchoides fragariae (Ritz. Bos) Christie
Xanthomonas citri (Hasse) Dowson
Chalara quercina Henry
Colletotrichum gossypii Southw.
Corynebacterium sepedonicum (Spieck. at Kotth.) Skapt. et Burkh.
Cylas formicarius F.
Dacus doralis Hendel.
Dialeurodes citri **Ashm.**
Diarthronomyia chrysanthemi Ahlb.
Diatraca venosata Wlk.
Ditylenchis angustus **(Butler) Filip. (Anguillulina)**
Ditylenchus dipsaci **(Kiihn) Filip.**
Dueterophoma tracheiphila Petri
Endothia parasitica (Murr.) And. et And.
Epidiaspis leperii Sign.
Eriosoma lanigerum Hausm.
Erwinia amylovora (Burr.) Winslow et al.
Eumerus strigatus Flln.
E. tuberculatus Rond.
E. narcisii Smith.
Exobasidium japonicum Shir
Fusarium bulbigenum Cooke et Mass.
Fusarium oxysporum F. gladioli **(Mass.) Snyder et Hansen**
Gracilaria azalcella **Brants.**
Grapholitha inopinata **Heinr.**
Heterodera rostockiensis **Woll.**
Hyphantria cunea **Drury**
Icerya purchasi **Mask.**
Lampetia equestris Fab.
Laspeyresia molesta Busck.
Leptinotarsa decemlineata Say
Leucaspis japonica Ckll.
Melanconis juglandis (Ellis u. Everh.) Graves
Nectria coccinea (Pers.) Fr.
Numonia pyrivorella Mats.
Ovulinia azaleae **Weisz.**
Pantomorus leucoloma Boh.
Pectinophora gossypiella Saund.
Neu: *Playedra g.* Saund.
Phthorimaea ocellatella Boyd.
Phthorimaea operculella Zell.
Phyllocoptes olievorus Ashm.
Phylloxera vastatrix Planch.

Botrytis tulipae (Lib.) Hopk
Carposina sasakii Mats.
Ceratitis capitata Wied.
Ceroplastes floridensis Comst.
Ceroplastes japonicus Green
Ceroplastes rubens Mask.
Ceroplastes rusci L.
Ceroplastes sinensis Guer.
Neu: *Viteus vitifolii* (Fitch.) Shim
Phymatotrichum omnivorum (Shear) Duggar
Bacterium stewarti (Sm. E.) E.F. Smith
Phytophaga destructor Say
Neu: *Mayetiola d. Say*
Piesma quadrata Fieb.
Plasmodiophora brassicae Woron.
Polyspora lini Peth et Laff f.
Popillia japonica Newm.
Prays olcellus F.
Pseudaulacaspis pentagona Targ.
Pseudococcus gahani Green
Pseudococcus comstocki Kuw.
Pseudomonas hyacinthi (Wakk.) E.F. Smith
Neu: *Xanthomonas hyacinthi* (Wakk.) Dowson
Pseudomonas marginata (Mc. Cull.) Stapp
Pseudomonas syringae f. sp. *populea* (v. Hall) Dowson
Pyroderces rileyi Wals
Diaspidiotus perniciosus Comst.
Rhagoletis cerasi L.
Rhagoletis pomonella Walsh.
Saperda candida F.
Sclerotinia bulborum (Walk.) Rehm.
Sclerotinia gladioli (Mass.) Dray.
Septoria azaleae Vogl.
Septoria linicola (Speg.) Gar.
s. *Mycosphaerella linorum* Woll.
Sphaeronema fimbriatum (*Ceratostomella f.*) (Ell. et Halsted)
Spongospora subterranea (Wallr.) Johnson
Synchytrium endobioticum (Schilb.) Perc.
Tarsonemus fragariae Zimmerm.
Taeniothrips simplex Moris.
Tetradacus citri Chen
Tilletia brevifaciens Fisch.
Tilletia indica Mitra
Tortrix pronubana Hbn.
Unaspis yanonensis Kuw.
Uromyces betae Lev.
Xanthomonas begoniae (Takim) Dowson

CONVENTION CONCERNING THE PROTECTION OF WORKERS AGAINST IONIZING RADIATIONS [23]

Geneva, 22 June 1960

The General Conference of the International Labour Organization,

Having been convened at Geneva by the Governing Body of the International Labour Office, and having met in its Forty-fourth Session on 1 June 1960, and

Having decided upon the adoption of certain proposals with regard to the protection of workers against ionising radiations, which is the fourth item on the agenda of the session, and

Having determined that these proposals shall take the form of an international Convention,

adopts this twenty-second day of June of the year one thousand nine hundred and sixty the following Convention, which may be cited as the Radiation Protection Convention, 1960:

Part I

GENERAL PROVISIONS

Article 1

Each Member of the International Labour Organization which ratifies this Convention undertakes to give effect thereto by means of laws or regulations, codes of practice or other appropriate means. In applying the provisions of the Convention the competent authority shall consult with representatives of employers and workers.

Article 2

1. This Convention applies to all activities involving exposure of workers to ionising radiations in the course of their work.

2. This Convention does not apply to radioactive substances, whether sealed or unsealed, nor to apparatus generating ionising radiations which substances or apparatus, owing to the limited doses of ionising radiations which can be received from them, are exempted from its provisions by one of the methods of giving effect to the Convention mentioned in Article 1.

Article 3

1. In the light of knowledge available at the time, all appropriate steps shall be taken to ensure effective protection of workers, as regards their health and safety, against ionising radiations.

2. Rules and measures necessary for this purpose shall be adopted, and data essential for effective protection shall be made available.

3. With a view to ensuring such effective protection:

a) measures for the protection of workers against ionising radiations adopted after ratification of the Convention by the Member concerned shall comply with the provisions thereof;

b) the Member concerned shall modify, as soon as practicable, measures adopted by it prior to the ratification of the Convention, so as to comply with the provisions thereof, and shall promote such modification of other measures existing at the time of ratification;

c) the Member concerned shall communicate to the Director-General of the International Labour Office, when ratifying the Convention, a statement indicating the manner in which and the categories of workers to which the provisions of the Convention are applied, and shall indicate in its reports on the application of the Convention any further progress made in the matter;

d) at the expiration of three years from the date on which this Convention first enters into force the Governing Body of the International Labour Office shall submit to the Conference a special report concerning the application of sub-paragraph (*b*) of this paragraph and containing such proposals as it may think appropriate for further action in regard to the matter.

Part II

PROTECTIVE MEASURES

Article 4

The activities referred to in Article 2 shall be so arranged and conducted as to afford protection envisaged in this Part of the Convention.

Article 5

Every effort shall be made to restrict the exposure of workers to ionising radiations to the lowest practicable level, and any unnecessary exposure shall be avoided by all parties concerned.

Article 6

1 Maximum permissible doses of ionising radiations which may be received from sources external to or internal to the body and maximum permissible amounts of radioactive substances which can be taken into the body shall be fixed in accordance with Part I of this Convention for various categories of workers.

2. Such maximum permissible doses and amounts shall be kept under constant review in the light of current knowledge.

Article 7

1. Appropriate levels shall be fixed in accordance with Article 6 for workers who are directly engaged in radiation work and are:

a) aged 18 and over;

b) under the age of 18.

2. No worker under the age of 16 shall be engaged in work involving ionising radiations.

Article 8

Appropriate levels shall be fixed in accordance with Article 6 for workers who are not directly engaged in radiation work but who remain or pass where they may be exposed to ionising radiations or radioactive substances.

Article 9

1. Appropriate warnings shall be used to indicate the presence of hazards from ionising radiations. Any information necessary in this connection shall be supplied to the workers.

2. All workers directly engaged in radiation work shall be adequately instructed, before and during such employment, in the precautions to be taken for their protection, as regards their health and safety, and the reasons therefor.

Article 10

Laws or regulations shall require the notification in a manner prescribed thereby of work involving exposure of workers to ionising radiations in the course of their work.

Article 11

Appropriate monitoring of workers and places of work shall be carried out in order to measure the exposure of workers to ionising radiations and radioactive substances, with a view to ascertaining that the applicable levels are respected.

Article 12

All workers directly engaged in radiation work shall undergo an appropriate medical examination prior to or shortly after taking up such work and subsequently undergo further medical examinations at appropriate intervals.

Article 13

Circumstances shall be specified, by one of the methods of giving effect to the Convention mentioned in Article 1, in which, because of the nature or degree of the exposure or a combination of both, the following action shall be taken promptly:

a) the worker shall undergo an appropriate medical examination;

b) the employer shall notify the competent authority in accordance with its requirements;

c) persons competent in radiation protection shall examine the conditions in which the worker's duties are performed;

d) the employer shall take any necessary remedial action on the basis of the technical findings and the medical advice.

Article 14

No worker shall be employed or shall continue to be employed in work by reason of which the worker could be subject to exposure to ionising radiations contrary to qualified medical advice.

Article 15

Each Member which ratifies this Convention undertakes to provide appropriate inspection services for the purpose of supervising the application of its provisions, or to satisfy itself that appropriate inspection is carried out.

Part III

FINAL PROVISIONS

Article 16

The formal ratifications of this Convention shall be communicated to the Director-General of the International Labour Office for registration.

Article 17

1. This Convention shall be binding only upon those Members of the International Labour Organization whose ratifications have been registered with the Director-General.

2. It shall come into force twelve months after the date on which the ratifications of two Members have been registered with the Director-General.

3. Thereafter, this Convention shall come into force for any member twelve months after the date on which its ratification has been registered.

Article 18

1. A Member which has ratified this Convention may denounce it after the expiration of five years from the date on which the Convention first comes into force, by an act communicated to the Director-General of the International Labour Office for registration. Such denunciation shall not take effect until one year after the date on which it is registered.

2. Each Member which has ratified this Convention and which does not, within the year following the expiration of the period of five years mentioned in the preceding paragraph, exercise the right of denunciation provided for in this Article, will be bound for another period of five years and, thereafter, may denounce this Convention at the expiration of each period of five years under the terms provided for in this Article.

Article 19

1. The Director-General of the International Labour Office shall notify all Members of the International Labour Organization of the registration of all ratifications and denunciations communicated to him by the Members of the Organization.

2. When notifying the Members of the Organization of the registration of the second ratification communicated to him, the Director-General shall draw the attention of the Members of the Organization to the date upon which the Convention will come into force.

Article 20

The Director-General of the International Labour Office shall communicate to the Secretary-General of the United Nations for registration in accordance with Article 102 of the Charter of the United Nations full particulars of all ratifications and acts of denunciation registered by him in accordance with the provisions of the preceding Articles.

Article 21

At such times as it may consider necessary the Governing Body of the International Labour Office shall present to the General Conference a report on the working of this Convention and shall examine the desirability of placing on the agenda of the Conference the question of its revision in whole or in part.

Article 22

1. Should the Conference adopt a new Convention revising this Convention in whole or in part, then, unless the new Convention otherwise provides:

a) the ratification by a Member of the new revising Convention shall *ipso jure* involve the immediate denunciation of this Convention, notwithstanding the provisions of Article 18 above, if and when the new revising Convention shall have come into force;

b) as from the date when the new revising Convention comes into force this Convention shall cease to be open to ratification by the Members.

2. This Convention shall in any case remain in force in its actual form and content for those Members which have ratified it but have not ratified the revising Convention.

Article 23

The English and French versions of the text of this Convention are equally authoritative.

CONVENTION ON THIRD PARTY LIABILITY IN THE FIELD OF NUCLEAR ENERGY [24]

Paris, 29 July 1960

Text incorporating the provisions of the Additional Protocol to the Convention on Third Party Liability in the Field of Nuclear Energy signed in Paris on 28 January 1964.

The Governments of the Federal Republic of Germany, the Republic of Austria, the Kingdom of Belgium, the Kingdom of Denmark, Spain, the French Republic, the Kingdom of Greece, the Italian Republic, the Grand Duchy of Luxembourg, the Kingdom of Norway, the Kingdom of the Netherlands, the Portuguese Republic, the United Kingdom of Great Britain and Northern Ireland, the Kingdom of Sweden, the Swiss Confederation and the Turkish Republic;

Considering that the European Nuclear Energy Agency, established within the framework of the Organization for European Economic co-operation (hereinafter referred to as the "Organization"), is charged with encouraging the elaboration and harmonization of legislation relating to nuclear energy in participating countries, in particular with regard to third party liability and insurance against atomic risks;

Desirous of ensuring adequate and equitable compensation for persons who suffer damage caused by nuclear incidents whilst taking the necessary steps to ensure that the development of the production and uses of nuclear energy for peaceful purposes is not thereby hindered;

Convinced of the need for unifying the basic rules applying in the various countries to the liability incurred for such damage, whilst leaving these countries free to take, on a national basis, any additional measures which they deem appropriate, including the application of the provisions of this Convention to damage caused by incidents due to ionizing radiations not covered therein;

Have agreed as follows:

Article 1

a) For the purposes of this Convention:

(i) "A nuclear incident" means any occurence or succession of occurrences having the same origin which causes damage, provided that such occurrence or succession of occurrences, or any of the damage caused, arises out of or results from the radioactive properties, or a combination of radioactive properties with toxic, explosive, or other hazardous properties of nuclear fuel or radioactive products or waste or with any to them.

(ii) "Nuclear installation" means reactors other than those comprised in any means or transport; factories for the manufacture or processing of nuclear substances; factories for the separation of isotopes of nuclear fuel; factories for the reprocessing of irradiated nuclear fuel; facilities for the storage of nuclear substances other than storage incidental to the carriage of such substances; and such other installations in which there are nuclear fuel or radioactive products or waste as the Steering Committee of the European Nuclear Agency (hereinafter referred to as the "Steering Commitee") shall from time to time determine.

(iii) "Nuclear fuel" means fissionable material in the form of uranium metal, alloy, or chemical compound (including natural uranium), plutonium metal, alloy, or compound, and such other fissionable material as the Steering Committee shall from time to time determine.

(iv) "Radioactive products or waste" means any radioactive material produced in or made radioactive by exposure to the radiation incidental to the process of producing or utilizing nuclear fuel, but does not include (1) nuclear fuel, or (2) radioisotopes outside a nuclear installation which are used or intended to be used for any industrial, commercial, agricultural, medical or scientific purpose.

(v) "Nuclear substances" means nuclear fuel (other than natural uranium and other than depleted uranium) and radioactive products or waste.

(vi) "Operator" in relation to a nuclear installation means the person designated or recognized by the competent public authority as the operator of that installation.

b) The Steering Committee may, if in its view the small extent of the risks involved so warrants, exclude any nuclear installation, nuclear fuel, or nuclear substances from the application of this Convention.

Article 2

This Convention does not apply to nuclear incidents occurring in the territory of non-Contracting States or to damage suffered in such territory, unless otherwise provided by the legislation of the Contracting Party in whose territory the nuclear installation of the operator liable is situated, and except in regard to rights referred to in Article 6 (*e*).

Article 3

a) The operator of a nuclear installation shall be liable, in accordance with this Convention, for:

(i) damage to or loss of life of any person; and

(ii) damage to or loss of any property other than

1. the nuclear installation itself and any property on the site of that installation which is used or to be used in connection with that installation;

2. in the cases within Article 4, the means of transport upon which the nuclear substances involved were at the time of the nuclear incident, upon proof that such damage or loss (hereinafter referred to as "damage") was caused by a nuclear incident involving either nuclear fuel or radioactive products or waste in, or nuclear substances coming from such installation, except as otherwise provided for in Article 4.

b) Where the damage or loss is caused jointly by a nuclear incident and by an incident other than a nuclear incident, that part of the damage or loss which is caused by such other incident shall, to the extent that it is not reasonably separable from the damage or loss caused by the nuclear incident, be considered to be damage caused by the nuclear incident. Where the damage or loss is caused jointly by a nuclear incident and by an emission of ionizing radiation not covered by this Convention, nothing in this Convention shall limit or otherwise affect the liability of any person in connection with that emission of ionizing radiation.

c) Any Contracting Party may by legislation provide that the liability of the operator of a nuclear installation situated in its territory shall include liability for damage which arises out of or results from ionizing radiations emitted by any source of radiation inside that installation, other than those referred to in paragraph (*a*) of this Article.

Article 4

In the case of carriage of nuclear substances, including storage incidental thereto, without prejudice to Article 2:

a) The operator of a nuclear installation shall be liable, in accordance with this Convention, for damage upon proof that it was caused by a nuclear incident outside that installation and involving nuclear substances in the course of carriage therefrom, only if the incident occurs:

(i) before liability with regard to nuclear incidents involving the nuclear substances has been assumed, pursuant to the express terms of a contract in writing, by the operator of another nuclear installation;

(ii) in the absence of such express terms, before the operator of another nuclear installation has taken charge of the nuclear substances; or

(iii) where the nuclear substances are intended to be used in a reactor comprised in a means of transport, before the person duly authorized to operate that reactor has taken charge of the nuclear substances; but

(iv) where the nuclear substances have been sent to a person within the territory of a non-Contracting State, before they have been unloaded from the means of transport by which they have arrived in the territory of that non-Contracting State.

b) The operator of a nuclear installation shall be liable, in accordance with this Convention, for damage upon proof that it was caused by a nuclear incident outside that installation and involving nuclear substances in the course of carriage thereto, only if the incident occurs:

(i) after liability with regard to nuclear incidents involving the nuclear substances has been assumed by him, pursuant to the express terms of a contract in writing, from the operator of another nuclear installation;

(ii) in the absence of such express terms, after he has taken charge of the nuclear substances; or

(iii) after he has taken charge of the nuclear substances from a person operating a reactor comprised in a means of transport; but

(iv) where the nuclear substances have, with the written consent of the operator, been sent from a person within the territory of a non-Contracting State, after they have been loaded on the means of transport by which they are to be carried from the territory of that State.

c) The operator liable in accordance with this Convention shall provide the carrier with a certificate issued by or on behalf of the insurer or other financial guarantor furnishing the security required pursuant to Article 10. The certificate shall state the name and address of that operator and the amount, type and duration of the security, and these statements may not be disputed by the person by whom or on whose behalf the certificate was issued. The certificate shall also indicate the nuclear substances and the carriage in respect of which the security applies and shall include a statement by the competent public authority that the person named is an operator within the meaning of this Convention.

d) A Contracting Party may provide by legislation that, under such terms as may be contained therein and upon fulfilment of the requirements of Article 10 (*a*), a carrier may, at his request and with the consent of an operator of a nuclear installation situated in its territory, by decision of the competent public authority, be liable in accordance with this Convention in place of that operator. In such case for all the purposes of this Convention the carrier shall be considered, in respect of nuclear incidents occuring in the course of carriage of nuclear substances, as an operator of a nuclear installation on the territory of the Contracting Party whose legislation so provides.

Article 5

a) If the nuclear fuel or radioactive products or waste involved in a nuclear incident have been in more than one nuclear installation and are in a nuclear installation at the time damage is caused, no operator of any nuclear installation in which they have previously been shall be liable for the damage.

b) Where, however, damage is caused by a nuclear incident occurring in a nuclear installation and involving only nuclear substances stored therein incidentally to their carriage, the operator of the nuclear installation shall not be liable where another operator or person is liable pursuant to Article 4.

c) If the nuclear fuel or radioactive products or waste involved in a nuclear incident have been in more than one nuclear installation and are not in a nuclear installation at the time damage is caused, no operator other than the operator of the last nuclear installation in which they were before the damage was caused or an operator who has subsequently taken them in charge shall be liable for the damage.

d) If damage gives rise to liability of more than one operator in accordance with this Convention, the liability of these operators shall be joint and several: provided that where such liability arises as a result of damage caused by a nuclear incident involving nuclear substances in the course of carriage in one and the same means of transport, or, in the case of storage incidental to the carriage, in one and the same nuclear installation, the maximum total amount for which such operators shall be liable shall be the highest amount established with respect to any of them pursuant to Article 7 and provided that in no case shall any one operator be required, in respect of a nuclear incident, to pay more than the amount established with respect to him pursuant to Article 7.

Article 6

a) The right to compensation for damage caused by a nuclear incident may be exercised only against an operator liable for the damage in accordance with this Convention, or, if a direct right of action against the insurer or other financial guarantor furnishing the security required pursuant to Article 10 is given by national law, against the insurer or other financial guarantor.

b) Except as otherwise provided in this Article, no other person shall be liable for damage caused by a nuclear incident, but this provision shall not affect the application of any international agreement in the field of transport in force or open for signature, ratification or accession at the date of this Convention.

c) (i) Nothing in this Convention shall affect the liability:

1. of any individual for damage caused by a nuclear incident for which the operator, by virtue of Articles 3 (*a*) (ii) (*1*) and (*2*) or Article 9, is not liable under this Convention and which results from an act or omission of that individual done with intent to cause damage;

2. of a person duly authorized to operate a reactor comprised in a means of transport for damage caused by a nuclear incident when an operator is not liable for such damage pursuant to Article 4 (*a*) (iii) or (*b*) (iii).

(ii) The operator shall incur no liability outside this Convention for damage caused by a nuclear incident except where use has not been made of the right provided for in Article 7 (*c*), and then only to the extent that national legislation or the legislation of the Contracting Party in whose territory the nuclear installation of the operator liable is situated has made specific provisions concerning damage to the means of transport.

d) Any person who has paid compensation in respect of damage caused by a nuclear incident under any international agreement referred to in paragraph (*b*) of this Article or under any legislation of a non-Contracting State shall, up to the amount which he has paid, acquire by subrogation the rights under this Convention of the person suffering damage whom he has so compensated.

e) Any person who has his principal place of business in the territory of a Contracting Party or who is the servant of such a person and who has paid compensation in respect of damage caused by a nuclear incident occurring in the territory of a non-Contracting State or in respect of damage suffered in such territory shall, up to the amount which he has paid, acquire the rights which the person so compensated would have had against the operator but for the provisions of Article 2.

f) The operator shall have a right of recourse only:

(i) if the damage caused by a nuclear incident results from an act or omission done with intent to cause damage, against the individual acting or omitting to act with such intent;

(ii) if and to the extent that it is so provided expressly by the contract.

g) If the operator has a right of recourse to any extent pursuant to paragraph (*f*) of this Article against any person, that person shall not, to that extent, have a right against the operator under paragraphs (*d*) or (*e*) of this Article.

h) Where provisions of national or public health insurance, social security, workmen's compensation or occupational disease compensation systems include compensation for damage caused by a nuclear incident, rights of beneficiaries of such systems and rights of recourse by virtue of such systems shall be determined by the law of the Contracting Party or by the regulations of the inter-Governmental organization which has established such systems.

Article 7

a) The aggregate of compensation required to be paid in respect of damage caused by a nuclear incident shall not exceed the maximum liability established in accordance with this Article.

b) The maximum liability of the operator in respect of damage caused by a nuclear incident shall be 15,000,000 European Monetary Agreement units of account as defined at the date of this Convention (hereinafter referred to as "units of account"): provided that any Contracting Party, taking into account the possibilities for the operator of obtaining the insurance or other financial security required pursuant to Article 10, may establish by legislation a greater or less amount, but in no event less than 5,000,000 units of account. The sums mentioned above may be converted into national currency in round figures.

c) Any Contracting Party may by legislation provide that the exception in Article 3 (*a*) (ii) (*2*) shall not apply: provided that in no case shall the inclusion of damage to the means of transport result in reducing the liability of the operator in respect of other damage to an amount less than 5,000,000 units of account.

d) The amount of liability of operators of nuclear installations in the territory of a Contracting Party established in accordance with paragraph (*b*) of this Article as well as the provisions of any legislation of a Contracting Party pursuant to paragraph (c) of this Article shall apply to the liability of such operators wherever the nuclear incident occurs.

e) A Contracting Party may subject the transit of nuclear substances through its territory to the condition that the maximum amount of liability of the foreign operator concerned be increased, if it considers that such amount does not adequately cover the risks of a nuclear incident in the course of the transit: provided that the maximum amount thus increased shall not exceed the maximum amount of liability of operators of nuclear installations situated in its territory.

f) The provisions of paragraph (*e*) of this Article shall not apply:

(i) to carriage by sea where, under international law, there is a right of entry in cases of urgent distress into the ports of such Contracting Party or a right of innocent passage through its territory; or

(ii) to carriage by air where, by agreement or under international law there is a right to fly over or land on the territory of such Contracting Party.

g) Any interest and costs awarded by a court in actions for compensation under this Convention shall not be considered to be compensation for the purposes of this Convention and shall be payable by the operator in addition to any sum for which he is liable in accordance with this Article.

Article 8

a) The right of compensation under this Convention shall be extinguished if an action is not brought within ten years from the date of the nuclear incident. National legislation may, however, establish a period longer than ten years if measures have been taken by the Contracting Party in whose territory the nuclear installation of the operator liable is situated to cover the liability for that operator in respect of any actions for compensation begun after the expiry of the period of ten years and during such longer period: provided that such extension of the extinction period shall in no case affect the right of compensation under this Convention of any person who has brought an action in respect of loss of life or personal injury against the operator before the expiry of the period of ten years.

b) In the case of damage caused by a nuclear incident involving nuclear fuel or radioactive products or waste which, at the time of the incident have been stolen, lost, jettisoned or abandoned and have not yet been recovered, the period established pursuant to paragraph (*a*) of this Article shall be computed from the date of that nuclear incident, but the period shall in no case exceed twenty years from the date of the theft, loss, jettison or abandonment.

c) National legislation may establish a period of not less than two years from the extinction of the right or as a period of limitation either from the date at which the person suffering damage has knowledge or from the date at which he ought reasonably to have known of both the damage and the operator liable: provided that the period established pursuant to paragraph (*a*) and (*b*) of this Article shall not be exceeded.

d) Where the provisions of Article 13(*c*) (ii) are applicable, the right of compensation shall not, however, be extinguished if, within the time provided for in paragraph (*a*) of this Article,

(i) prior to the determination by the Tribunal referred to in Article 17, an action has been brought before any of the courts from which the Tribunal can choose; if the Tribunal determines that the competent court is a court other than that before which such action has already been brought, it may fix a date by which such action has to be brought before the competent court so determined; or

(ii) a request has been made to a Contracting Party concerned to initiate a determination by the Tribunal of the competent court pursuant to Article 13 (c) (ii) and an action is brought subsequent to such determination within such time as may be fixed by the Tribunal.

e) Unless national law provides to the contrary, any person suffering damage caused by a nuclear incident who has brought an action for compensation within the period provided for in this Article may amend his claim in respect of any aggravation of the damage after the expiry of such period provided that final judgment has not been entered by the competent court.

Article 9

The operator shall not be liable for damage caused by a nuclear incident directly due to an act of armed conflict, hostilities, civil war, insurrection or, except in so far as the legislation of the Contracting Party in whose territory his nuclear installation is situated may provide to the contrary, a grave natural disaster of an exceptional character.

Article 10

a) To cover the liability under this Convention, the operator shall be required to have and maintain insurance or other financial security of the amount established pursuant to Article 7 and of such type and terms as the competent public authority shall specify.

b) No insurer or other financial guarantor shall suspend or cancel the insurance or other financial security provided for in parargraph (*a*) of this Article without giving notice in writing of at least two months to the competent public authority or in so far as such insurance or other financial security relates to the carriage of nuclear substances, during the period of the carriage in question.

c) The sums provided as insurance, reinsurance, or other financial security may be drawn upon only for compensation for damage caused by a nuclear incident.

Article 11

The nature, form and extent of the compensation, within the limits of this Convention, as well as the equitable distribution thereof, shall be governed by national law.

Article 12

Compensation payable under this Convention, insurance and reinsurance premiums, sums provided as insurance, reinsurance, or other financial security required pursuant to Article 10, and interest and costs referred to in Article 7 (*g*), shall be freely transferable between the monetary areas of the Contracting Parties.

Article 13

a) Except as otherwise provided in this Article, jurisdiction over actions under Articles 3, 4, 6 (*a*) and 6 (*e*) shall lie only with the courts of the Contracting Party in whose territory the nuclear incident occurred.

b) Where a nuclear incident occurs outside the territory of the Contracting Parties, or where the place of the nuclear incident cannot be determined with certainty, jurisdiction over such actions shall lie with the courts of the Contracting Parties in whose territory the nuclear installation of the operator liable is situated.

c) Where jurisdiction would lie with the courts of more than one Contracting Party by virtue of paragraphs (*a*) or (*b*) of this Article, jurisdiction shall lie,

(i) if the nuclear incident occurred partly outside the territory of any Contracting Party and partly in the territory of a single Contracting Party, with the courts of that Contracting Party; and

(ii) in any other case, with the courts of the Contracting Party determined, at the request of a Contracting Party concerned, by the Tribunal referred to in Article 17 as being the most closely related to the case in question.

d) Judgments entered by the competent court under this Article after trial, or by default, shall, when they have become enforceable under the law applied by that court, become enforceable in the territory of any of the other Contracting Parties as soon as the formalities required by the Contracting Party concerned have been complied with. The merits of the case shall not be the subject of further proceedings. The foregoing provisions shall not apply to interim judgments..

e) If an action is brought against a Contracting Party under this Convention, such Contracting Party may not, except in respect of measures of execution, invoke any jurisdictional immunities before the court competent in accordance with this Article.

Article 14

a) This Convention shall be applied without any discrimination based upon nationality, domicile, or residence.

b) "National law" and "national legislation" mean the national law or the national legislation of the court having jurisdiction under this Convention over claims arising out of a nuclear incident, and that law or legislation shall apply to all matters both substantive and procedural not specifically governed by this Convention.

c) That law and legislation shall be applied without any discrimination based upon nationality, domicile, or residence.

Article 15

a) Any Contracting Party may take such measures as it deems necessary to provide for an increase in the amount of compensation specified in this Convention.

b) In so far as compensation for damage involves public funds and is in excess of the 5,000,000 units of account referred to in Article 7, any such measures in whatever form may be applied under conditions which may derogate from the provisions of this Convention.

Article 16

Decisions taken by the Steering Committee under Article 1 (a) (ii), 1 (*a*) (iii) and 1 (*b*) shall be adopted by mutual agreement of the members representing the Contracting Parties.

Article 17

Any dispute arising between two or more Contracting Parties concerning the interpretation or application of this Convention shall be examined by the Steering Committee and in the absence of friendly settlement shall, upon the request of a Contracting Party concerned, be submitted to the Tribunal established by the Convention of 20 December 1957 on the Establishment of a Security Control in the Field of Nuclear Energy.

Article 18

a) Reservations to one or more of the provisions of this Convention may be made at any time prior to ratification of or accession to this Convention or prior to the time of notification under Article 23 in respect of any territory or territories mentioned in the notification, and shall be admissible only if the terms of these reservations have been expressly accepted by the Signatories.

b) Such acceptance shall not be required from a Signatory which has not itself ratified this Convention within a period of twelve months after the date of notification to it of such reservation by the Secretary-General of the Organization in accordance with Article 24.

c) Any reservation admitted in accordance with this Article may be withdrawn at any time by notification addressed to the Secretary-General of the Organization.

Article 19

a) This Convention shall be ratified. Instruments of ratification shall be deposited with the Secretary-General of the Organization.

b) This Convention shall come into force upon the deposit of instruments of ratification by not less than five of the Signatories. For each Signatory ratifying thereafter, this Convention shall come into force upon the deposit of its instrument of ratification.

Article 20

Amendments to this Convention shall be adopted by mutual agreement of all the Contracting Parties. They shall come into force when ratified or confirmed by two-thirds of the Contracting Parties. For each Contracting Party ratifying or confirming thereafter, they shall come into force at the date of such ratification or confirmation.

Article 21

a) The Government of any Member or Associate country of the Organization which is not a Signatory to this Convention may accede thereto by notification addressed to the Secretary-General of the Organization.

b) The Government of any other country which is not a Signatory to this Convention may accede thereto by notification addressed to the Secretary-General of the Organization and with the unanimous assent of the Contracting Parties. Such accession shall take effect from the date of such assent.

Article 22

a) This Convention shall remain in effect for a period of ten years as from the date of its coming into force. Any Contracting Party may, by giving twelve months' notice to the Secretary-General of the Organization, terminate the application of this Convention to itself at the end of the period of ten years.

b) This Convention shall, after the period of ten years, remain in force for a period of five years for such Contracting Parties as have not terminated its application in accordance with paragraph (*a*) of this Article, and thereafter for successive periods of five years for such Contracting Parties as have not terminated its application at the end of one of such periods of five years by giving twelve months' notice to that effect to the Secretary-General of the Organization.

c) A conference shall be convened by the Secretary-General of the Organization in order to consider revisions to this Convention after a period of five years as from the date of its coming into force or, at any other time, at the request of a Contracting Party, within six months from the date of such request.

Article 23

a) This Convention shall apply to the metropolitan territories of the Contracting Parties.

b) Any Signatory or Contracting Party may, at the time of signature or ratification of or accession to this Convention or at any later time, notify the Secretary-General of the Organization that this Convention shall apply to those of its territories, including the territories for whose international relations it is responsible, to which this Convention is not applicable in accordance with paragraph (*a*) of this Article and which are mentioned in the notification. Any such notification may in respect of any territory or territories mentioned therein be withdrawn by giving twelve months' notice to that effect to the Secretary-General of the Organization.

c) Any territories of a Contracting Party, including the territories for whose international relations it is responsible, to which this Convention does not apply shall be regarded for the purposes of this Convention as being a territory of a non-Contracting State.

Article 24

The Secretary-General of the Oranization shall give notice to all Signatories and acceding Governments of the receipt of any instrument of ratification, accession, withdrawal, notification under Article 23, and decisions of the Steering Committee under Article 1 (*a*) (ii), 1 (*a*) (iii) and 1 (*b*). He shall also notify them of the date on which this Convention comes into force, the text of any amendment thereto and of the date on which such amendment comes into force, and any reservation made in accordance with Article 18.

In Witness Whereof, the undersigned Plenipotentiaries, duly empowered, have signed this Convention.

Done in Paris, this twenty-ninth day of July Nineteen Hundred and Sixty, in the English, French, German, Spanish, Italian and Dutch languages in a single copy which shall remain deposited with the Secretary-General of the Organization for European Economic Co-operation by whom certified copies will be communicated to all Signatories.

Annex 1

The following reservations were accepted either at the time of signature of the Convention or at the time of signature of the Additional Protocol:

1. Article 6 (*a*) and (*c*) (i):

Reservation by the Government of the Federal Republic of Germany, the Government of the Republic of Austria and the Government of the Kingdom of Greece.

Reservation of the right to provide, by national law, that persons other than the operator may continue to be liable for damage caused by a nuclear incident on condition that these persons are fully covered in respect of their liability, including defence against unjustified actions, by insurance or other financial security obtained by the operator or out of State funds.

2. Article 6 (*b*) and (*d*):

Reservation by the Government of the Republic of Austria, the Government of the Kingdom of Greece, the Government of the Kingdom of Norway and the Government of the Kingdom of Sweden.

Reservation of the right to consider their national legislation which includes provisions equivalent to those included in the international agreements referred to in Article 6 (*b*) as being international agreements within the meaning of Article 6 (*b*) and (*d*).

3. Article 8 (*a*):

Reservation by the Government of the Federal Republic of Germany and the Government of the Republic of Austria.

Reservation of the right to establish, in respect of nuclear incidents occurring in the Federal Republic of Germany and in the Republic of Austria respectively, a period longer than ten years if measures have been taken to cover the liability of the operator in respect of any actions for compensation begun after the expiry of the period of ten years and during such longer period.

4. Article 9:

Reservation by the Government of the Federal Republic of Germany and the Government of the Republic of Austria.

Reservation of the right to provide, in respect of nuclear incidents occurring in the Federal Republic of Germany and in the Republic of Austria respectively, that the operator shall be liable for damage caused by a nuclear incident directly due to an act of armed conflict, hostilities, civil war, insurrection or a grave natural disaster of an exceptional character.

5. Article 19:

Reservation by the Government of the Federal Republic of Germany, the Government of the Republic of Austria, and the Government of the Kingdom of Greece.

Reservation of the right to consider ratification of this Convention as constituting an obligation under international law to enact national legislation on third party liability in the field of nuclear energy in accordance with the provisions of this Convention.

Annex II

This Convention shall not be interpreted as depriving a Contracting Party, on whose territory damage was caused by a nuclear incident occurring on the territory of another Contracting Party, of any recourse which might be available to it under international law.

PROTOCOL CONCERNING THE CONSTITUTION OF AN INTERNATIONAL COMMISSION FOR THE PROTECTION OF THE MOSEL AGAINST POLLUTION [25]

Paris, 20 December 1961

The Governments of the Federal Republic of Germany, the French Republic and the Grand-Duchy of Luxembourg

Anxious to determine the means of implementing article 55 of the Convention concerning the canalization of the Mosel, signed in Luxembourg on the 27 October 1956,

Have agreed to the following:

Article 1

The signatory Governments shall institute an International Commission for the Protection of the Mosel against Pollution.

Article 2

The Commission instituted according to article 1 of the present Protocol has as its objective establishing collaboration between the competent authorities of the three signatory Governments in order to assure the protection of the waters of the Mosel against pollution.

To this effect, the Commission may:

a) prepare and carry out all necessary research to determine the nature, importance and origin of pollutions and put the results of such research to use;

b) propose to signatory Governments measures capable of protecting the Mosel against pollution.

The Commission, furthermore, shall be empowered to deal with any other matters which the signatory Governments may, by common agreement, confide to it.

Article 3

The Commission shall be composed of delegations of signatory Governments.

Each Government may appoint at the most four delegates, including a head of delegation.

Each signatory Government may appoint experts; the Commission shall determine the conditions of their participation in its work.

Article 4

The chairmanship of the Commission shall be held for two years by the head of each national delegation in turn.

Article 5

The Commission shall meet in ordinary session once a year at the convocation of its Chairman.

Extraordinary sessions shall be convoked by the Chairman at the request of one of the signatory Governments.

The Chairman shall propose the agenda. Each delegation shall have the right to inscribe upon the agenda those points which it wishes to have considered. The agenda shall be addressed to the national delegations a month before the date of the meeting.

Article 6

Each delegation shall have one vote.

Article 7

Decisions of the Commission shall be taken by unanimity.

Article 8

The Commission may set up working groups for the study of certain subjects. Such groups shall be composed of delegates and experts appointed in conformity with the provisions of article 3 supra.

The Commission shall designate among the delegates the chairman of each working group.

Article 9

The Commission shall establish the relations which it considers as necessary with all the competent organizations in the field of water pollution.

Article 10

Each signatory Government shall bear the expenses of its representation within the Commission as well as of current analyses and research undertaken on its territory.

Expenses of common interest shall be divided among the Federal Republic of Germany, the French Republic and the Grand-Duchy of Luxembourg according to formulas proposed by the Commission and adopted by the Governments.

Article 11

Disputes as to the interpretation or application of this Protocol shall be settled according to the provisions of chapter VII of the Convention of 27 October 1956 concerning the Canalization of the Mosel.

Article 12

The present Protocol will be applied to Berlin, unless the Government of the Federal Republic of Germany issues in this sense a contrary declaration to the Governments of the French Republic and the Grand Duchy of Luxembourg within three months following the entry into force of the present Protocol.

Article 13

The working languages of the Commission shall be French and German.

Article 14

The present Protocol shall enter into force on the date agreed upon by the signatory Governments.

After a period of three years from its entry into force,it may be denounced at any moment with three months' notice by each of the signatory Governments.

Done in Paris, 20 December 1961, in three copies, each of which is drawn up in French and German, both texts being equally authentic.

CONVENTION OF THE AFRICAN MIGRATORY LOCUST ORGANIZATION

[26]

Kano, 25 May 1962

The Governments of:

Cameroon
Central African Republic
Congo (Brazzaville)
Congo (Kinshasa)
Ivory Coast
Dahomey
Gambia
Ghana
Upper Volta
Kenya
Mali
Mauritania
Niger
Nigeria
Uganda
Senegal
Sierra Leone
Sudan
Tanzania
Chad
Togo
Zambia

Determined to continue on as wide an international basis as possible the preventive control of the African Migratory Locust undertaken in Africa in accordance with the Convention of 15 May 1952;

Determined to extend this preventive control to any species of migratory acrididae, other than the African Migratory Locust, likely to appear in the Outbreak area on the Niger River;

Taking note that, in order to facilitate the necessary reorganization, the Governments party to the Convention of 15 May 1952, have declared themselves ready to terminate it on the date of entry into force of this Convention;

Have agreed as follows:

Part I

DEFINITION

Article 1

By this Convention there is established an Organization called:

"International African Migratory Locust Organization"

or in French:

"Organisation Internationale contre le Criquet Migrateur Africain"

O.I.C.M.A.

hereinafter referred to as the "Organization"

Article 2

The Organization established by this Convention succeeds to the assets and assumes the obligations of the Organization set up under the Convention of the 15 May 1952.

Article 3

The seat of the Organization shall be at Bamako. It may be transferred to any other place in the Republic of Mali by a decision of the Administrative Council.

Part II

FUNCTIONS

Article 4

The functions of the Organization shall be as follows:

1. To exercise continuous surveillance and preventive control of the African Migratory Locust in the outbreak area already recognized on the River Niger. Such control operations shall include in particular the destruction of all concentrations of this locust which threaten to develop into incipient bands and swarms.

2. To undertake research on the African Migratory Locust in order to determine the ecological factors involved in its multiplication and behaviour.

3. To devise and develop the most economic and effective methods for its control.

4. The Organization may also be entrusted with surveillance, research and preventive control relating to all other species of migratory Acrididae of which incipient bands or swarms may be found in the outbreak area on the River Niger.

5. The Organization may, subject to approval by the Council, extend its operations to any other outbreak areas of the African Migratory Locust that may be recognized.

Part III

STRUCTURE AND ADMINISTRATION

Article 5

The Organization shall comprise:

— an Administrative Council (hereinafter referred to as the "Council")

— an Executive Committee

— a Directorate

Article 6

1. The Organization shall be administered by an Administrative Council composed of Representatives designated by the Contracting Governments.

2. The Council shall meet once each year in Ordinary Session at a place to be decided at its previous meeting.

3. The Council shall elect a President from among its members. He shall hold office for three years, and may be re-elected.

4. Each Contracting Government shall have one vote on the Council. It may delegate its vote to any other Contracting Government and shall notify such delegation of vote formally to the President of the Council.

5. The decisions of the Council, if taken by vote, will be taken by a simple majority of votes cast.

6. The Council shall adopt its own rules of procedure. It shall nominate an Executive Committee and determine its composition and competence.

7. An extraordinary Session of the Council may be convened by the President at the request of at least one third of the Contracting Governments.

8. The Council at its annual meeting shall examine the report and the accounts of the Organization and shall adopt plans and draft estimates for the operations of the following financial year.

9. The Council shall have the right:

a) to invite any international or regional Organization with an interest in Locust Control to appoint observers to attend the meetings of the Council; and:

b) to invite any individual or representative of an Anti-locust research Organization to attend its meetings as a consultant.

Part IV

DIRECTORATE

Article 7

1. The Council shall appoint the Director of the Organization subject to the approval of the authorities of the State in which its Headquarters are situated.

2. The duties of the Director, in addition to those necessary to ensure the discharge of the Organization's main functions outlined in Article 4, shall include:

a) the transmission by means of periodic reports to Contracting Governments, and to such Organizations as are concerned with anti-locust research, of full information on the nature of the locust infestation, the progress of research and the operation of control measures,

b) the maintenance of permanent contact and co-operation with all other Organizations concerned with the locust problem;

c) Responsibility for the collection of the contributions of Contracting Governments;

d) Responsibility for the maintenance of the accounts of the Organization.

3. The Director shall also submit to the Council a report for the past financial year as well as the programmes of work and estimates for the next year. He shall submit annually to the Council duly audited accounts. He shall transmit copies of these documents to the Contracting Governments not later than one month before the annual meeting of the Council.

4. The Director shall send a report for the preceding year, approved by the Council, to the Food and Agriculture Organization of the United Nations and the Economic Commission for Africa (E.C.A.).

Part V

INSPECTIONS

Article 8

The Council may arrange for inspections to be made of the activities of the Organization. Each Contracting Government may, with the prior approval of the Council, undertake similar inspections at its own expense.

Part VI

OBLIGATIONS OF CONTRACTING GOVERNMENTS

Article 9

Each Contracting Government shall contribute in money, supplies or services to the expenses of the equipment and operations of the Organization on the basis of the proportions indicated in the annex to the present Convention. These proportions may be revised by the Contracting Governments:

a) in the event of new accessions in accordance with paragraph 2 of Article 14;

b) in the event of denunciation or withdrawal from this Convention in accordance with paragraph 3 of Article 15;

c) by a decision of the Administrative Council approved by three-quarters of the Contracting Governments.

Article 10

Each Contracting Government shall facilitate the construction on its own territory of the buildings necessary to the operation of the Organization.

Article 11

The Contracting Governments shall, when necessary, give every possible assistance requested by the Organization for the destruction of incipient swarms.

Article 12

Each Contracting Government shall bear the cost of the attendance of its delegation at the Council except that the Organization will bear the transport expenses of one delegate per country which has fulfilled its financial obligations during the previous financial year.

Article 13

The Contracting Governments shall accord to the staff of the Organization operating in their countries the same privileges and immunities as they accord or would accord to the staff of a Specialized Agency of the United Nations.

Part VII

ADHESIONS, RATIFICATIONS AND DENUNCIATIONS

Article 14

1. This Convention shall be ratified or approved by the Signatory Governments in accordance with

their respective constitutional practice, and the instruments of ratification or approval shall be deposited in the archives of the Government of the Republic of Mali.

2. The Government of any State may accede to the present Convention by depositing an instrument of accession with the Government of the Republic of Mali.

The deposit of this instrument must in all cases be preceded by an agreement between the acceding Government and all the contracting Governments in order to determine a new apportionment of the contributions laid down in Article 9 of this Convention. Subject to the conclusion of such an agreement accession shall take effect from the date of deposit of the instrument of accession with the Government of the Republic of Mali.

3. Each Contracting Government shall if it sees fit, specify in its instrument of ratification, approval or accession, the geographical area to which this Convention shall apply in so far as it is concerned.

Article 15

1. This Convention shall enter into force on the date of deposit of an instrument of ratification or approval by the sixth Signatory Government and shall enter into force in respect of the other signatory Governments on the date of deposit of their instruments of ratification or approval.

2. At the expiration of a period of five years from the 1 July 1962 and every five years thereafter, the Contracting Governments shall consult to decide whether the Convention requires modification.

3. After the expiration of a period of five years from ratification any Contracting Government may denounce the Convention by means of a written notification addressed to the Government of the Republic of Mali. Denunciation shall take effect one year after the date of receipt of the notification by the depositary Government.

4. The Government of the Republic of Mali shall inform all Contracting Governments of the deposit of each instrument of ratification, approval or accession, and of each notification of denunciation made in accordance with paragraph 2 of this Article.

Article 16

In the event that the Organization is dissolved, the distribution of its property shall be effected in the following manner:

The Council shall designate a Board of liquidators who shall have the widest powers to collect the assets, pay off the liabilities, carry out all necessary operations and in particular, distribute the assets among the Contracting Governments to the Organization in proportion to their paid-up contributions.

In the event of deficit, this shall be met by Contracting Governments in proportion to their contribution as assessed for the financial year then current.

Article 17

In the event of litigation, the competent Court shall be the one having jurisdiction over the domicile of the plaintiff, if the said domicile is in the territory of one of the Member States. Failing this the Court having jurisdiction over the Headquarters of the Organization shall be competent.

The Organization shall have the legal competence conferred by internal law in each Member State.

Part VIII

AMENDMENTS

Article 18

1. Any Contracting Government may propose amendments to the present Convention.

2. Any proposal shall be submitted in the two official languages of the Organization to the Council for consideration.

3. Any amendment approved by the Council shall come into force immediately after notice of approval of the amendment by three-quarters of the Contracting Governments.

4. The depositary Government shall inform all the Contracting Governments of the coming into force of the amendments.

Part IX

REGISTRATION

Article 19

The Government of the Republic of Mali shall cause this Convention to be registered with the Secretary-General of the United Nations.

In Witness Whereof the undersigned, duly authorized thereto by their respective Governments, have signed the present Convention.

Done at Kano (Nigeria) on the 25th May 1962 and amended in Accra (Ghana), on the 25th July 1968, in the French and English languages, both texts being equally authentic in a single copy which shall be deposited in the archives of the Republic of Mali which shall transmit duly certified copies thereof to all Signatory and acceding Governments.

AGREEMENT CONCERNING CO-OPERATION IN MARINE FISHING [27]

Warsaw, 28 July 1962

The Governments of the German Democratic Republic, the Polish People's Republic and the Union of Soviet Socialist Republics.

Having a common interest in co-operation in the development of marine fishing, fishing techniques and fish processing technology, as well as in scientific research into the condition of live marine resources,

Have decided to conclude this Agreement and have for this purpose appointed their Plenipotentiaries who, having exchanged their full powers, found in good and due form, have agreed on the following provisions:

Article 1

The Contracting Parties agree to co-operate in the development of fishing in the open sea, to consult on practical matters relating to the organization of fishing, to exchange the results of exploration for new fishing grounds and of research into other marine resources, to co-ordinate their research efforts with regard to the raw-materials base of the open sea, and to exchange experience concerning fishing techniques and the preparation, transport and storage of fish products.

Article 2

With a view to working out, co-ordinating and carrying out measures for the application of this Agreement, a Mixed Commission shall be established.

Within one month after the entry into force of this Agreement, each Contracting Party shall appoint a representative and an alternate to the said Commission and shall communicate their names to the other Côntracting Parties.

The Mixed Commission shall convene at least once a year in the territory of each of the Contracting Parties in turn, the costs of organizing such sessions to be borne by the Party in whose territory the session is held. The place and date of convening of the Mixed Commission shall be determined by the Commission in advance.

The Mixed Commission shall function in accordance with Rules of Procedure to be drafted at its first meeting and approved by the Contracting Parties.

Article 3

The Mixed Commission shall have the following functions:

1. It shall prepare plans for scientific and technical co-operation and mutual assistance in the development of fishing in the open sea;
2. It shall organize the exchange of experience in the operation of fishing fleets, in fishing techniques and in the storage, processing and transport of fish, as well as the exchange of information on the results of fisheries exploration and research into live marine resources conducted by the Contracting Parties;
3. It shall submit proposals for convening scientific and technical conferences and meetings on various fishery problems of common interest to the Contracting Parties and shall organize the exchange of experience in the training of personnel;
4. It shall determine the nature and scope of the statistical and other data which each Contracting Party shall furnish to the Mixed Commission with a view to the implementation of this Agreement.
5. It shall examine such other matters as the Contracting Parties may refer to it.

Article 4

The Mixed Commission shall make recommendations to the Contracting Parties concerning the matters referred to in article 3.

Recommendations and decisions shall be deemed to have been adopted by the Mixed Commission if they receive the fovourable votes of the representatives of all the Contracting Parties.

The recommendations of the Mixed Commission shall be submitted to the Contracting Parties for approval and shall be given effect if none of the Parties raises an objection within two months.

Article 5

This Agreement is subject to approval in accordance with the provisions in force in each of the Contracting Parties.

Notifications of the approval of this Agreement shall be transmitted to the Government of the Polish People's Republic, which shall exercise depositary functions.

This Agreement shall enter into force on the date of receipt of the last notification of its approval.

Article 6

This Agreement is concluded for a term of five years. It shall remain in force for successive terms of five years for those Contracting Parties which do not denounce the Agreement at least six months before the expiry of the current five-year term.

Article 7

The Government of the Polish People's Republic shall take the necesary action to register this Agreement with the Secretariat of the United Nations.

Done at Warsaw on 28 July 1962, in one copy in the German, Polish and Russian languages, all three texts being equally authentic.

CONVENTION SUPPLEMENTARY TO THE PARIS CONVENTION OF 29 JULY 1960 ON THIRD PARTY LIABILITY IN THE FIELD OF NUCLEAR ENERGY [28]

Brussels, 31 January 1963

The Governments of the Federal Republic of Germany, the Republic of Austria, the Kingdom of Belgium, the Kingdom of Denmark, Spain, the French Republic, the Italian Republic, the Grand Duchy of Luxembourg, the Kingdom of Norway, the Kingdom of the Netherlands, the United Kingdom of Great Britain and Northern Ireland, the Kingdom of Sweden and the Swiss Confederation,

Being Parties to the Convention of 29 July 1960 on Third Party Liability in the Field of Nuclear Energy, concluded within the framework of the Organization for European Economic Co-operation and Development (hereinafter referred to as the "Paris Convention"),

Desirous of supplementing the. measures provided in that Convention with a view to increasing the amount of compensation for damage which might result from the use of nuclear energy for peaceful purposes,

Have agreed as follows:

Article 1

The system instituted by this Convention is supplementary to that of the Paris Convention, shall be subject to the provisions of the Paris Convention, and shall be applied in accordance with the following Articles.

Article 2

a) The system of this Convention shall apply to damage caused by nuclear incidents, other than those occurring entirely in the territory of a State which is not a Party to this Convention:

(i) for which an operator of a nuclear installation, used for peaceful purposes, situated in the territory of a Contracting Party to this Convention (hereinafter referred to as a "Contracting Party"), and which appears on the list established and kept up-to-date in accordance with the terms of Article 13, is liable under the Paris Convention;

and

(ii) suffered

1. in the territory of Contracting Party, or

2. on or over the high seas on board a ship or aircraft registered in the territory of a Contracting Party;

3. on or over the high seas by a national of a Contracting Party, provided that, in the case of damage to a ship or an aircraft, the ship or aircraft is registered in the territory of a Contracting Party, provided that the courts of a Contracting Party have jurisdiction pursuant to the Paris Convention.

b) Any Signatory or acceding Government may, at the time of signature of or accession to this Convention or on the deposit of its instrument of ratification, declare that, for the purpose of the application of paragraph (*a*) (ii) of this Article, individuals or certain categories thereof, considered under its law as having their habitual residence in its territory, are assimilated to its own nationals.

c) In this Article, the expression "a national of a contracting Party" shall include a Contracting Party or any of its constituent sub-divisions, or a partnership, or any public or private body whether corporate or not established in the territory of a Contracting Party.

Article 3

a) Under the conditions established by this Convention, the Contracting Parties undertake that compensation in respect of the damage referred to in Article 2 shall be provided up to the amount of 120 million units of account per incident.

b) Such compensation shall be provided:

(i) up to an amount of at least 5 million units of account, out of funds provided by insurance or other financial security, such amount to be established by the legislation of the Contracting Party in whose territory the nuclear installation of the operator liable is situated;

(ii) between this amount and 70 million units of account, out of public funds to be made available by the Contracting Party in whose territory the nuclear installation of the operator liable is situated;

(iii) between 70 million and 120 million units of account, out of public funds to be made available by the Contracting Parties according to the formula for contributions specified in Article 12.

c) For this purpose, each Contracting Party shall either:

(i) establish the maximum liability of the operator, pursuant to Article 7 of the Paris Convention, at 120 million units of account, and provide that such liability shall be covered by all the funds referred to in paragraph (*b*) of this Article; or

(ii) establish the maximum liability of the operator at an amount at least equal to that established pursuant to paragraph (*b*) (i) of this Article and provide that, in excess of such amount and up to 120 million units of account, the public funds referred to in paragraph (*b*) (ii) and (iii) of this Article shall be made available by some means other than as cover for the liability of the operator, provided that the rules of substance and procedure laid down in this Convention are not thereby affected.

d) The obligation of the operator to pay compensation, interest or costs out of public funds made available pursuant to paragraphs (*b*) (ii) and (iii) and (*f*) of this Article shall only be enforceable against the operator as and when such funds are in fact made available.

e) The Contracting Parties, in carrying out this Convention, undertake not to make use of the right provided for in Article 15 (*b*) of the Paris Convention to apply special conditions.

(i) in respect of compensation for damage provided out of the funds referred to in paragraph (*b*) (i) of this Article;

(ii) other than those laid down in this Convention in respect of compensation for damage provided out of the public funds referred to in paragraph (*b*) (ii) and (iii) of this Article.

f) The interest and costs referred to in Article 7 (*g*) of the Paris Convention are payable in addition to the amounts referred to in paragraph (*b*) of this Article and shall be borne in so far as they are awarded in respect of compensation payable out of the funds referred to in:

(i) paragraph (*b*) (i) of this Article, by the operator liable;

(ii) paragraph (*b*) (ii) of this Article, by the Contracting Party in whose territory the nuclear installation of that operator is situated;

(iii) paragraph (*b*) (iii) of this Article by the Contracting Parties together.

g) For the purposes of this Convention, "unit of account" means the unit of account of the European Monetary Agreement as defined at the date of the Paris Convention.

Article 4

a) If a nuclear incident causes damage which gives rise to liability of more than one operator, the aggregate liability provided for in Article 5 (*b*) of the Paris Convention shall not, to the extent that public funds have to be made available pursuant to Article 3 (*b*) (ii) and (iii), exceed 120 million units of account.

b) The total amount of the public funds made available pursuant to Article 3 (*b*) (ii) and (iii) shall not, in such event, exceed the difference between 120 million units of account and the sum of the amounts established with respect to such operators pursuant to Article 3 (*b*) (i) or, in the case of an operator whose nuclear installation is situated in the territory of a State which is not a Party to this Convention, the amount established pursuant to Article 7 of the Paris Convention. If more than one Contracting Party is required to make available public funds pursuant to Article 3 (*b*) (ii), such funds shall be made available by them in proportion to the number of nuclear installations situated in their respective territories, which are involved in the nuclear incident and of which the operators are liable.

Article 5

a) Where the operator liable has a right of recourse pursuant to Article 6 (*f*) of the Paris Convention, the Contracting Party in whose territory the nuclear installation of that operator is situated shall take such legislative measures as are necessary to enable both that Contracting Party and the other Contracting Parties to benefit from this recourse to the extent that public funds have been made available pursuant to Article 3 (*b*) (ii) and (iii) and (*f*).

b) Such legislation may provide for the recovery of public funds made available pursuant to Article 3 *(b)* and (iii), and (*f*) from such operator if the damage results from a fault on his part.

Article 6

In calculating the public funds to be made available pursuant to this Convention, account shall be taken only of those rights to compensation exercised within ten years from the date of the nuclear incident. In the case of damage caused by a nuclear incident involving nuclear fuel or radioactive products or waste which at the time of the incident have been stolen, lost or abandoned and have not yet been recovered, the period shall be ten years from the date of the theft, loss or abandonment. It shall also be extended in the cases and under the conditions laid down in Article 8 (*b*) of the Paris Convention. Amendments made to claims after the expiry of this period, under the conditions laid down in Article 8 (*d*) of the Paris Convention, shall also be taken into account.

Article 7

Where a Contracting Party makes use of the right provided for in Article 8 *(a)* of the Paris Convention, the period which it establishes shall be three years either from the date at which the person suffering damage has knowledge or from the date at which he ought reasonably to have known of both the damage and the operator liable.

Article 8

Any person who is entitled to benefit from the provisions of this Convention shall have the right to full compensation in accordance with national law for damage suffered, provided that, where the amount of damage exceeds or is likely to exceed:

(i) 120 million units of account; or

(ii) if there is aggregate liability under Article 5 *(b)* of the Paris Convention and a higher sum results therefrom, such higher sum,

any Contracting Party may establish equitable criteria for apportionment. Such criteria shall be applied whatever the origin of the funds and, subject to the provisions of Article 2, without discrimination based on the nationality, domicile or residence of the person suffering the damage.

Article 9

a) The system of disbursements by which the public funds required under Article (*b*) (ii) and (iii) and (f) are to be made available shall be that of the Contracting Party whose courts have jurisdiction.

b) Each Contracting Party shall ensure that persons suffering damage may enforce their rights to compensation without having to bring separate proceedings according to the origin of the funds provided for such compensation.

c) No Contracting Party shall be required to make available the public funds referred to in Article 3 (*b*) (ii) and (iii) so long as any of the funds referred to in Article 3 (*b*) (i) remain available.

Article 10

a) The Contracting Party whose courts have jurisdiction shall be required to inform the other Contracting Parties of a nuclear incident and its circumstances as soon as it appears that the damage caused by such incident exceeds, or is likely to exceed, 70 million units of account. The Contracting Parties shall without delay make all the necessary arrangements to settle the procedure for their relations in this connection.

b) Only the Contracting Party whose courts have jurisdiction shall be entitled to request the other Contracting Parties to make available the public funds required under Article 3 (*b*) (iii) and (*f*) and shall have exclusive competence to disburse such funds.

c) Such Contracting Party shall, when the occasion arises, exercise the right of recourse provided for in Article 5 on behalf of the other Contracting Parties who have made available public funds pursuant to Article 3 (*b*) (iii) and (*f*).

d) Settlements effected in respect of the payment of compensation out of the public funds referred to in Article 3 (*b*) (ii) and (iii) in accordance with the conditions established by national legislation shall be recognized by the other Contracting Parties, and judgments entered by the competent courts in respect of such compensation shall become enforceable in the territory of the other Contracting Parties in accordance with the provisions of Article 13 (*e*) of the Paris Convention.

Article 11

a) If the courts having jurisdiction are those of a Contracting Party other than the Contracting Party in whose territory the nuclear installation of the operator liable is situated, the public funds required under Article 3 (*b*) (ii) and (*f*) shall be made available by the first-named Contracting Party. The Contracting Party in whose territory the nuclear installation of the operator liable is situated shall reimburse to the other Contracting Party the sums paid. These two Contracting Parties shall agree on the procedure of reimbursement.

b) In adopting all legislative, regulatory or administrative provisions, after the nuclear incident occurred, concerning the nature, form and extent of the compensation, the procedure for making available the public funds required under Article 3 (*b*) (ii) and, if necessary, the criteria for the apportionment of such funds, the Contracting Party whose courts have jurisdiction shall consult the Contracting Party in whose territory the nuclear installation of the operator liable is situated. It shall further take all measures necessary to enable the latter to intervene in proceedings and to participate in any settlement concerning compensation.

Article 12

a) The formula for contributions according to which the Contracting Parties shall make available the public funds referred to in Article 3 (*b*) (iii) shall be determined as follows:

(i) as to 50% on the basis of the ratio between the gross national product at current prices of each Contracting Party and the total of the gross national product at current prices of all Contracting Parties as shown by the official statistics published by the Organization for Economic Co-operation and Development for the year preceding the year in which the nuclear incident occurs;

(ii) as to 50% on the basis of the ratio between the thermal power of the reactors situated in the territory of each Contracting Party and the total thermal power of the reactors situated in the territories of all the Contracting Parties. This calculation shall be made on the basis of the thermal power of the reactors shown at the date of the nuclear incident in the list referred to in Article 2 (*a*) (i); provided that a reactor shall only be taken into consideration for the purposes of this calculation as from the date when it first reaches criticality.

b) For the purposes of this Convention, "thermal power" means:

(i) before the issue of a final operating licence, the planned thermal power;

(ii) after the issue of such licence, the thermal power authorized by the competent national authorities.

Article 13

a) Each Contracting Party shall ensure that all nuclear installations used for peaceful purposes situated in its territory, and falling within the definition in Article 1 of the Paris Convention, appear on the list referred to in Article 2 (*a*) (i).

b) For this purpose, each Signatory or acceding Government shall, on the deposit of its instrument of ratification or accession communicate to the Belgian Government full particulars of such installations.

c) Such particulars shall indicate:

(i) in the case of all installations not yet completed, the expected date on which the risk of a nuclear incident will exist;

(ii) and further, in the case of reactors, the expected date on which they will first reach criticality, and also their thermal power.

d) Each Contracting Party shall also communicate to the Belgian Government the exact date of the existence of the risk of a nuclear incident and, in the case of reactors, the date on which they first reached criticality.

e) Each Contracting Party shall also communicate to the Belgian Government all modifications to be made to the list. Where such modifications include the addition of a nuclear installation, the communication must be made at least three months before the expected date on which the risk of a nuclear incident will exist.

f) If a Contracting Party is of the opinion that the

particulars, or any modification to be made to the list, communicated by another Contracting Party do not comply with the provisions of Article 2 (*a*) (i) and of this Article, it may raise objections thereto only by addressing them to the Belgian Government within three months from the date on which it has received notice pursuant to paragraph (*h*) of this Article.

g) If a Contracting Party is of the opinion that a communication required in accordance with this Article has not been made within the time prescribed in this Article, it may raise objections only by addressing them to the Belgian Government within three months from the date on which it knew of the facts which, in its opinion, ought to have been communicated.

h) The Belgian Government shall give notice as soon as possible to each Contracting Party of the communications and objections which it has received pursuant to this Article.

i) The list referred to in Article 2 (*a*) (i) shall consist of all the particulars and modifications referred to in paragraphs (*b*), (*c*), (*d*) and (*e*) of this Article, it being understood that objections submitted pursuant to paragraphs (*f*) and (*g*) of this Article shall have effect retrospective to the date on which they were raised, if they are sustained.

j) The Belgian Government shall supply any Contracting Party on demand with an up-to-date statement of the nuclear installations covered by this Convention and the details supplied in respect of them pursuant to this Article.

Article 14

a) Except in so far as this Convention otherwise provides, each Contracting Party may exercise the powers vested in it by virtue of the Paris Convention, and any provisions made thereunder may be invoked against the other Contracting Parties in order that the public funds referred to in Article 3 (*b*) (ii) and (iii) be made available.

b) Any such provisions made by a Contracting Party pursuant to Articles 2, 7 (*c*) and 9 of the Paris Convention as a result of which the public funds referred to in Article 3 (*b*) (ii) and (iii) are required to be made available may not be invoked against any other Contracting Party unless it has consented thereto.

c) Nothing in this Convention shall prevent a Contracting Party from making provisions outside the scope of the Paris Convention and of this Convention, provided that such provisions shall not involve any further obligation on the part of the other Contracting Parties in so far as their public funds are concerned.

Article 15

a) Any Contracting Party may conclude an agreement with a State which is not a Party to this Convention concerning compensation out of public funds for damage caused by a nuclear incident.

b) To the extent that the conditions for payment of compensation under any such agreement are not more favourable than those which result from measures adopted by the Contracting Party concerned for the application of the Paris Convention and of this Convention, the amount of damage caused by a nuclear incident covered by this Convention and for which compensation is payable by virtue of such an agreement may be taken into consideration, where the proviso to Article 8 applies, in calculating the total amount of damage caused by that incident.

c) The provisions of paragraphs (*a*) and (*b*) of this Article shall in no case affect the obligations under Article (*b*) (ii) and (iii) of those Contracting Parties which have not given their consent to such agreement.

d) Any Contracting Party intending to conclude such an agreement shall notify the other Contracting Parties of its intention. Agreements concluded shall be notified to the Belgian Government.

Article 16

a) The Contracting Parties shall consult each other upon all problems of common interest raised by the application of this Convention and of the Paris Convention, especially Articles 20 and 22 (*c*) of the latter Convention.

b) They shall consult each other on the desirability of revising this Convention after a period of five years from the date of its coming into force and at any other time upon the request of a Contracting Party.

Article 17

Any dispute arising between two or more Contracting Parties concerning the interpretation or application of this Convention shall, upon the request of a Contracting Party concerned, be submitted to the European Nuclear Energy Tribunal established by the Convention of 20 December 1957 on the Establishment of a Security Control in the Field of Nuclear Energy.

Article 18

a) Reservations to one or more of the provisions of this Convention may be made at any time prior to ratification of this Convention if the terms of these reservations have been expressly accepted by all Signatories or, at the time of accession or of the application of the provisions of Articles 21 and 24, if the terms of these reservations have been expressly accepted by all Signatories and acceding Governments.

b) Such acceptance shall not be required from a Signatory which has not itself ratified this Convention within a period of twelve months after the date of notification to it of such reservation by the Belgian Government in accordance with Article 25.

c) Any reservation accepted in accordance with the provisions of paragraph (*a*) of this Article may be withdrawn at any time by notification addressed to the Belgian Government.

Article 19

No State may become or continue to be a Contracting Party to this Convention unless it is a Contracting Party to the Paris Convention.

Article 20

a) The Annex to this Convention shall form an integral part thereof.

b) This Convention shall be ratified. Instruments of ratification shall be deposited with the Belgian Government.

c) This Convention shall come into force three months after the deposit of the sixth instrument of ratification.

d) For each Signatory ratifying this Convention after the deposit of the sixth instrument of ratification, it shall come into force three months after the date of the deposit of its instrument of ratification.

Article 21

Amendments to this Convention shall be adopted by agreement among all the Contracting Parties. They shall come into force on the date when all Contracting Parties have ratified or confirmed them.

Article 22

a) After the coming into force of this Convention, any Contracting Party to the Paris Convention which has not signed this Convention may request accession to this Convention by notification addressed to the Belgian Government.

b) Such accession shall require the unanimous assent of the Contracting Parties.

c) Once such assent has been given, the Contracting Party to the Paris Convention requesting accession shall deposit its instrument of accession with the Belgian Government.

d) The accession shall take effect three months from the date of deposit of the instrument of accession.

Article 23

a) This Convention shall remain in force until the expiry of the Paris Convention.

b) Any Contracting Party may, by giving twelve months' notice to the Belgian Government, terminate the application of this Convention to itself after the end of the period of ten years specified in Article 22 (*a*) of the Paris Convention. Within six months after receipt of such notice, any other Contracting Party may, by notice to the Belgian Government, terminate the application of this Convention to itself as from the date when it ceases to have effect in respect of the Contracting Party which first gave notice.

c) The expiry of this Convention or the withdrawal of a Contracting Party shall not terminate the obligations assumed by each Contracting Party under this Convention to pay compensation for damage caused by nuclear incidents occurring before the date of such expiry or withdrawal.

d) The Contracting Parties shall, in good time, consult each other on what measures should be taken after the expiry of this Convention or the withdrawal of one or more of the Contracting Parties, to provide compensation comparable to that accorded by this Convention for damage caused by nuclear incidents occurring after the date of such expiry or withdrawal and for which the operator of a nuclear installation in operation before such date within the territories of the Contracting Parties is liable.

Article 24

a) This Convention shall apply to the metropolitan territories of the Contracting Parties.

b) Any Contracting Party desiring the application of this Convention to one or more of the territories in respect of which, pursuant to Article 23 of the Paris Convention, it has given notification of application of that Convention, shall address a request to the Belgian Government.

c) The application of this Convention to any such territory shall require the unanimous assent of the Contracting Parties.

d) Once such assent has been given, the Contracting Party concerned shall address to the Belgian Government a notification which shall take effect as from the date of its receipt.

e) Such notification may, as regards any territory mentioned therein, be withdrawn by the Contracting Party which has made it by giving twelve months' notice to that effect to the Belgian Government.

f) If the Paris Convention ceases to apply to any such territory, this Convention shall also cease to apply thereto.

Article 25

The Belgian Government shall notify all Signatories and acceding Governments of the receipt of any instrument of ratification, accession or withdrawal, and shall also notify them of the date on which this Convention comes into force, the text of any amendment thereto and the date on which such amendment comes into force, any reservations made in accordance with Article 18, and all notifications which it has received.

In Witness Whereof the undersigned Plenipotentiaries, duly empowered, have signed this Convention.

Done at Brussels, this 31st day of January 1963, in the English, Dutch, French, German, Italian and Spanish languages, the six texts being equally authoritative, in a single copy which shall be deposited with the Belgian Government by whom certified copies shall be communicated to all the other Signatories and acceding Governments.

Annex
to the Convention Supplementary to the Paris Convention of 29 July 1960 on Third Party Liability in the Field of Nuclear Energy

The Governments of the Contracting Parties declare that compensation for damage caused by a nuclear incident not covered by the Supplementary Convention solely by reason of the fact that the relevant nuclear installation, on account of its utilization, is not on the list referred to in Article 2 of the Supplementary Convention, (including the case where such installation considered by one or more but not all of the Governments to be outside the Paris Convention):

— shall be provided without discrimination among the nationals of the Contracting Parties to the Supplementary Convention; and

— shall not be limited to less than 120 million units of account.

In addition, if they have not already done so, they shall endeavour to make the rules for compensation of persons suffering damage caused by such incidents as similar as possible to those established in respect of nuclear incidents occurring in connection with nuclear installations covered by the Supplementary Convention.

AGREEMENT CONCERNING THE INTERNATIONAL COMMISSION FOR THE PROTECTION OF THE RHINE AGAINST POLLUTION [29]

Berne, 29 April 1963*

The Governments of the Federal Republic of Germany, the French Republic, the Grand-Duchy of Luxembourg, the Kingdom of the Netherlands and the Swiss Confederation,

Anxious to assure the quality of the waters of the Rhine by attempting to prevent further pollution and to improve the present state,

Convinced of the urgency of this mission,

Wishing to strengthen the collaboration between the signatory Governments already existing since 1950 in this matter,

Have agreed to the following:

Article 1

The Contracting Parties shall continue to collaborate in the question of the protection of the waters of the Rhine below the lower Lake, within the framework of the International Commission for the protection of the Rhine against pollution.

Article 2

The Commission shall:

a) prepare and carry out all necessary research to determine the nature, importance and origin of pollution of the Rhine and put the results of such research to use;

b) propose to Contracting Parties measures capable of protecting the Rhine against pollution;

c) prepare the basis of possible arrangements between the Contracting Parties concerning the protection of the waters of the Rhine.

2. The Commission, furthermore, shall be empowered to deal with any other matters which the Contracting Parties may, by common agreement, confide to it.

Article 3

1. The Commission shall be composed of delegations of Contracting Parties. Each Party may appoint at the most four delegates, including a head of delegation.

2. Each delegation may be assisted by experts to

* Translation by Peaslee, International Governmental Organization, Part IV, Communication, Transfert, Travel, p. 430.

The Agreement was amended and complemented by an additional Agreement signed at Bonn on 3 December 1976 according to which "The European Economic Community shall become a Contracting Party to the Agreement concerning the International Commission for the Protection of the Rhine against Pollution and the Protocol of Signature attached thereto (hereinafter referred to as "the Agreement"), signed in Berne on 29 April 1963, from the date of the entry into force of this Additional Agreement. (Article i)."

The additional Agreement was to enter into force at the same time as the Convention for the Protection of the Rhine against Chemical Pollution, signed at Bonn on the same day.

examine certain questions. The Commission shall determine the conditions of their participation in its work.

Article 4

1. Details regarding the exercise of the chairmanship of the Commission by the delegation shall be worked out by the Commission and included in its rules of procedure; the delegation assuming the chairmanship shall designate one of its members as chairman of the Commission.

2. As a general rule the chairman shall not intervene in meetings of the Commission as spokesman of his delegation.

Article 5

1. The Commission shall meet in ordinary session once a year at the convocation of its Chairman.

2. Extraordinary session shall be convoked by the Chairman at the request of two delegations.

3. The Chairman shall propose the agenda. Each delegation shall have the right to inscribe upon the agenda those points which it wishes to have considered. The order of the agenda shall be decided by the Commission by a majority vote.

Article 6

1. Each delegation shall have one vote.

2. In those areas coming within its jurisdiction, the European Economic Community shall have the number of votes corresponding to the number of its Member States which are Contracting Parties to this Agreement. The European Economic Community shall not vote in cases where its Member States vote and vice versa.

3. Decisions of the Commission shall, except where otherwise provided in this Agreement, be taken in the presence of all delegations and by unanimity; a written method may be used under conditions to be laid down in the rules of procedure.

4. Unanimity shall not be impeded by the abstention of a single delegation. However, this provision shall not apply to the delegation of the European Economic Community.

Article 7

1. The Commission shall set up a working group for current research and may, if necessary, set up others for special missions.

2. The working groups shall be composed of delegates or experts appointed by each delegation.

3. The Commission shall decide the mission of each working group, fix the maximum number of members and appoint its chairman.

*According to Article 3 of the Supplementary Agreement

"1. The delegation which holds the chair of the Commission at the time of the entry into force of the Additional Agreement shall continue to preside until its three-year period of office expires.

"2. The details of the subsequent exercise of the chairmanship of the Commission by the delegations shall be worked out by the Commission in the light of its new composition and before the expiry of the period of office referred to in paragraph 1."

Article 8

Within the framework of its research and the use to be made of the results thereby obtained, the Commission may serve as a scientific institution giving full guarantees of independence.

Article 9

The Commission may make use of services of competent persons or organizations in order to examine special questions.

Article 10

The Commission shall collaborate with the international commissions for the Rhine and its estuaries and shall decide upon co-operation with other organizations entrusted with the protection of waters.

Article 11

The Commission shall each year furnish the signatory Governments with a report of its activity, including in particular the results of its research and analyses.

Article 12

1. Each Contracting Party shall bear the expenses of its representation within the Commission and its working groups, as well as of current research undertaken on its territory.

2. The remaining cost of the Commission's activities shall be shared out among the Contracting Parties as follows:

Federal Republic of Germany	24.5%
French Republic	24.5%
Grand Duchy of Luxembourg	1.5%
Kingdom of the Netherlands	24.5%
European Economic Community	13 %
Swiss Confederation	12 %
Total	100 %

In certain cases, the Commission may adopt a different distribution.

Article 13

The Commission shall draw up its rules of procedure.

Article 14

The working languages of the Commission shall be German and French.

Article 15

1. Each of the Contracting Parties shall notify the Government of the Swiss Confederation when it has carried out the constitutional procedures required to put this agreement into force; the Government of the Swiss Confederation shall immediately confirm the date of receipt of such notification and shall advise the other Contracting Parties. The Agreement shall enter into force the first day of the month following receipt of the last notification.

2. After a period of three years from its entry into force, this Agreement may at any moment be denounced with six months notice by each of the

Contracting Parties, by a declaration addressed to the Government of the Swiss Confederation.

Article 16

This Agreement, drawn up in a single copy, in the German, French and Dutch languages, each of the three texts being equally authentic, shall be deposited in the archives of the Government of the Swiss Confederation which shall send a certified copy to each of the other signatory Governments.

Done at Berne, 29 April 1963.

PROTOCOL OF SIGNATURE

At the time of signature of the Agreement concerning the International Commission for the protection of the Rhine against pollution, the Contracting Parties agree as follows:

Ad Article 2, paragraph 1 (a):

For all research carried out in accordance with Article 2, paragraph 1 (*a*), the Commission shall decide on the purpose and importance of such research in accordance with the provisions of Article 6. Any such research shall, in principle, be carried out by the appropriate national organizations.

Ad Article 4, paragraph 1:

The term of the first chairman shall expire at the end of the third calendar year beginning after the entry into force of this Agreement.

Ad Article 8:

The Government of the Federal Republic of Germany proposes to the Commission that the scientific institution provided in Article 8 should be an independent technical Secretariat set up at the Federal Institute of Hydrology of Coblenz. This Secretariat would be responsible in its work only to the Commission's authority and would receive the Commission's instructions through the Chairman.

The Secretariat shall, taking into account Article 2 and the addendum to this article, support the working groups provided in Article 7 and the appropriate national organizations in carrying out their research and putting it to use. It shall, in particular, publish the reports of the Commission. Each Contracting Party may at any time send delegates to the Secretariat to report on its activity and eventually to participate in its work.

The Contracting Parties agree that their representatives in the Commission shall, within two months of the entry into force of the Agreement, accept for a period of five years the offer of the Government of the Federal Republic of Germany.

They agree that the Commission may, by resolution, extend the term of the Institute of Coblenz, or choose another organization or take any other decision.

Ad Article 10:

The collaboration provided for in Article 10 shall specifically be instituted with the International Commissions for the protection of the Moselle, the Sarre and the Lake of Constance as well as with the Central Commission for the Navigation of the Rhine; the first objective should be a regular and complete exchange of information.

Ad Article 12, paragraph 2:

The distribution provided in Article 12, paragraph 2, shall not apply to expenses concerning measures proposed, in accordance with Article 2, paragraph 1 (*b*), for the protection of the Rhine.

Done at Berne, 29 April 1963.

VIENNA CONVENTION ON CIVIL LIABILITY FOR NUCLEAR DAMAGE [30]

Vienna, 21 May 1963

The Contracting Parties,

Having recognized the desirability of establishing some minimum standards to provide financial protection against damage resulting from certain peaceful uses of nuclear energy,

Believing that a convention on civil liability for nuclear damage would also contribute to the development of friendly relations among nations, irrespective of their differing constitutional and social systems,

Have decided to conclude a convention for such purposes, and thereto have agreed as follows:

Article I

1. For the purpose of this Convention —

a) "Person" means any individual, partnership, any private or public body whether corporate or not, any international organization enjoying legal personality under the law of the Installation State, and any State or any of its constituent sub-divisions.

b) "National of a Contracting Party" includes a Contracting Party or any of its constituent sub-divisions, a partnership, or any private or public body whether corporate or not established within the territory of a Contracting Party.

c) "Operator", in relation to a nuclear installation, means the person designated or recognized by the Installation State as the operator of that installation.

d) "Installation State", in relation to a nuclear installation, means the Contracting Party within whose territory that installation is situated or, if it is not situated within the territory of any State, the Contracting Party by which or under the authority of which the nuclear installation is operated.

e) "Law of the competent court" means the law of the court having jurisdiction under this Convention, including any rules of such law relating to conflict of laws.

f) "Nuclear fuel" means any material which is capable of producing energy by a self-sustaining chain process of nuclear fission.

g) "Radioactive products or waste" means any radioactive material produced in, or any material made radioactive by exposure to the radiation incidental to, the production or utilization of nuclear fuel, but does not include radioisotopes which have reached the final stage of fabrication so as to be usable for any scientific, medical, agricultural, commercial or industrial purpose.

h) "Nuclear material" means —

(i) nuclear fuel, other than natural uranium and depleted uranium, capable of producing energy by a self-sustaining chain process of nuclear fission outside a nuclear reactor, either alone or in combination with some other material; and

(ii) radioactive products or waste.

i) "Nuclear reactor" means any structure containing nuclear fuel in such an arrangement that a self-sustaining chain process of nuclear fission can occur therein without an additional source of neutrons.

j) "Nuclear installation" means —

(i) any nuclear reactor other than one with which a means of sea or air transport is equipped for use as a source of power, whether for propulsion thereof or for any other purpose;

(ii) any factory using nuclear fuel for the production of nuclear material, or any factory for the processing of nuclear material, including any factory for the re-processing of irradiated nuclear fuel; and

(iii) any facility where nuclear material is stored, other than storage incidental to the carriage of such material;

provided that the Installation State may determine that several nuclear installations of one operator which are located at the same site shall be considered as a single nuclear installation.

k) "Nuclear damage" means —

(i) loss of life, and personal injury or any loss of, or damage to, property which arises out of or results from the radioactive properties or a combination of radioactive properties with toxic, explosive or other hazardous properties of nuclear fuel or radioactive products or waste in, or of nuclear material coming from, originating in, or sent to, a nuclear installation.

(ii) any other loss or damage so arising or resulting if and to the extent that he law of the competent court so provides; and

(iii) if the law of the Installation State so provides, loss of life, any personal injury or any loss of, or damage to, property which arises out of or results from other ionizing radiation emitted by any other source of radiation inside a nuclear installation.

l) "Nuclear incident" means any occurrence or series of occurrences having the same origin which causes nuclear damage.

2. An Installation State may, if the small extent of the risks involved so warrants, exclude any small quantities of nuclear material from the application of this Convention, provided that —

a) maximum limits for the exclusion of such quantities have been established by the Board of Governors of the International Atomic Energy Agency; and

b) any exclusion by an Installation State is within such established limits.

The maximum limits shall be reviewed periodically by the Board of Governors.

Article II

1. The operator of a nuclear installation shall be liable for nuclear damage upon proof that such

damage has been caused by a nuclear incident —

a) in his nuclear installation; or

b) involving nuclear material from or originating in his nuclear installation, and occurring —

(i) before liability with regard to nuclear incidents involving the nuclear material has been assumed, pursuant to the express terms of a contract in writing, by the operator of another nuclear installation;

(ii) in the absence of such express terms, before the operator of another nuclear installation has taken charge of the nuclear material; or

(iii) where the nuclear material is intended to be used in a nuclear reactor with which a means of transport is equipped for use as a source of power, whether for propulsion thereof or for any other purpose, before the person duly authorized to operate such reactor has taken charge of the nuclear material; but

(iv) where the nuclear material has been sent to a person within the territory of a non-Contracting State, before it has been unloaded from the means of transport by which it has arrived in the territory of that non-Contracting State;

c) involving nuclear materials to his nuclear installation, and occuring —

(i) after liability with regard to nuclear incidents involving the nuclear material has been assumed by him, pursuant to the express terms of a contract in writing, from the operator of another nuclear installation;

(ii) in the absence of such express terms, after he has taken charge of the nuclear material; or

(iii) after he has taken charge of the nuclear material from a person operating a nuclear reactor with which a means of transport is equipped for use as a source of power, whether for propulsion thereof or for any other purpose; but

(iv) where the nuclear material has, with the written consent of the operator, been sent from a person within the territory of a Contracting State, only after it has been loaded on the means of transport by which it is to be carried from the territory of that State;

provided that, if nuclear damage is caused by a nuclear incident occurring in a nuclear installation and involving nuclear material stored therein incidentally to the carriage of such material, the provisions of sub-paragraph (*a*) of this paragraph shall not apply where another operator or person is solely liable pursuant to the provisions of sub-paragraph (*b*) or (*c*) of this paragraph.

2. The Installation State may provide by legislation that, in accordance with such terms as may be specified therein, a carrier of nuclear material or a person handling radioactive waste may, at his request and with the consent of the operator concerned, be designated or recognized as operator in the place of that operator in respect of such nuclear material or radioactive waste respectively. In this case such carrier or such person shall be considered, for all the purposes of this Convention, as an operator of a nuclear installation situated within the territory of that State.

3. *a*) Where nuclear damage engages the liability of more than one operator, the operators involved shall, in so far as the damage attributable to each operator is not reasonably separable, be jointly and severally liable.

b) Where a nuclear incident occurs in the course of carriage of nuclear material, either in one and the same means of transport, or, in the case of storage incidental to the carriage, in one and the same nuclear installation, and causes nuclear damage which engages the liability of more than one operator, the total liability shall not exceed the highest amount applicable with respect to any one of them pursuant to Article V.

c) In neither of the cases referred to in sub-paragraphs (*a*) and (*b*) of this paragraph shall the liability of any one operator exceed the amount applicable with respect to him pursuant to Article V.

4. Subject to the provisions of paragraph 3 of this Article, where several nuclear installations of one and the same operator are involved in one nuclear incident, such operator shall be liable in respect of each nuclear installation involved up to the amount applicable with respect to him pursuant to Article V.

5. Except as otherwise provided in this Convention, no person other than the operator shall be liable for nuclear damage. This, however, shall not affect the application of any international convention in the field of transport in force or open for signature, ratification or accession at the date on which this Convention is opened for signature.

6. No person shall be liable for any loss or damage which is not nuclear damage pursuant to sub-paragraph (*k*) of paragraph 1 of Article I but which could have been included as such pursuant to sub-paragraph (*k*) (ii) of that paragraph.

7. Direct action shall lie against the person furnishing financial security pursuant to Article VII, if the law of the competent court so provides.

Article III

The operator liable in accordance with this Convention shall provide the carrier with a certificate issued by or on behalf of the insurer or other financial guarantor furnishing the financial security required pursuant to Article VII. The certificate shall state the name and address of that operator and the amount, type and duration of the security, and these statements may not be disputed by the person by whom or on whose behalf the certificate was issued. The certificate shall also indicate the nuclear material in respect of which the security applies and shall include a statement by the competent public authority of the Installation State that the person named is an operator within the meaning of this Convention.

Article IV

1. The liability of the operator for nuclear damage under this Convention shall be absolute.

2. If the operator proves that the nuclear damage resulted wholly or partly either from the gross negligence of the person suffering the damage or from an act or omission of such person done with intent to cause damage, the competent court may, if its law so provides, relieve the operator wholly or partly from his obligation to pay compensation in respect of the damage suffered by such person.

3. *a*) No liability under this Convention shall attach to an operator for nuclear damage caused by a nuclear incident directly due to an act of armed conflict, hostilities, civil war or insurrection.

b) Except in so far as the law of the Installation State may provide to the contrary, the operator shall not be liable for nuclear damage caused by a nuclear incident directly due to a grave natural disaster of an exceptional character.

4. Whenever both nuclear damage and damage other than nuclear damage have been caused by a nuclear incident or jointly by a nuclear incident and one or more other occurrences, such other damage shall, to the extent that it is not reasonably separable from the nuclear damage, be deemed, for the purposes of this Convention, to be nuclear damage caused by that nuclear incident. Where, however, damage is caused jointly by a nuclear incident covered by this Convention and by an emission of ionizing radiation not covered by it nothing in this Convention shall limit or otherwise affect the liability, either as regards any person suffering nuclear damage or by way of recourse or contribution, of any person who may be held liable in connection with that emission of ionizing radiation.

5. The operator shall not be liable under this Convention for nuclear damage —

a) to the nuclear installation itself or to any property on the site of that installation which is used or to be used in connection with that installation; or

b) to the means of transport upon which the nuclear material involved was at the time of the nuclear incident.

6. Any Installation State may provide by legislation that sub-paragraph (*b*) of paragraph 5 of this Article shall not apply, provided that in no case shall the liability of the operator in respect of nuclear damage, other than nuclear damage to the means of transport, be reduced to less than US$5 million for any one nuclear incident.

7. Nothing in this Convention shall affect —

a) the liability of any individual for nuclear damage for which the operator, by virtue of paragraph 3 or 5 of this Article, is not liable under this Convention and which that individual caused by an act or omission done with intent to cause damage; or

b) the liability outside this Convention of the operator for nuclear damage for which, by virtue of sub-paragraph (*b*) of paragraph 5 of this Article, he is not liable under this Convention.

Article V

1. The liability of the operator may be limited by the Installation State to not less than US$5 million for any one nuclear incident.

2. Any limits of liability which may be established pursuant to this Article shall not include any interest or costs awarded by a court in actions for compensation of nuclear damage.

3. The United States dollar referred to in this Convention is a unit of account equivalent to the value of the United States dollar in terms of gold on 29 April 1963, that is to say US$35 per one troy ounce of fine gold.

4. The sum mentioned in paragraph 6 of Article IV and in paragraph 1 of this Article may be converted into national currency in round figures.

Article VI

1. Rights of compensation under this Convention shall be extinguished if an action is not brought within ten years from the date of the nuclear incident. If, however, under the law of the Installation State the liability of the operator is covered by insurance or other financial security or by State funds for a period longer than ten years, the law of the competent court may provide that rights of compensation against the operator shall only be extinguished after a period which may be longer than ten years, but shall not be longer than the period for which his liability is so covered under the law of the Installation State. Such extension of the extinction period shall in no case affect rights of compensation under this Convention of any person who has brought an action for loss of life or personal injury against the operator before the expiry of the aforesaid period of ten years.

2. Where nuclear damage is caused by a nuclear incident involving nuclear material which at the time of the nuclear incident was stolen, lost, jettisoned or abandoned, the period established pursuant to paragraph 1 of this Article shall be computed from the date of that nuclear incident, but the period shall in no case exceed a period of twenty years from the date of the theft, loss, jettison or abandonment.

3. The law of the competent court may establish a period of extinction or prescription of not less than three years from the date on which the person suffering nuclear damage had knowledge or should have had knowledge of the damage and of the operator liable for the damage, provided that the period established pursuant to paragraphs 1 and 2 of this Article shall not be exceeded.

4. Unless the law of the competent court otherwise provides, any person who claims to have suffered nuclear damage and who has brought an action for compensation within the period applicable pursuant to this Article may amend his claim to take into account any aggravation of the

damage, even after the expiry of that period, provided that final judgment has not been entered.

5. Where jurisdiction is to be determined pursuant to sub-paragraph (*b*) of paragraph 3 of Article XI and a request has been made within the period applicable pursuant to this Article to any one of the Contracting Parties empowered so to determine, but the time remaining after such determination is less than six months, the period within which an action may be brought shall be six months, reckoned from the date of such determination.

Article VII

1. The operator shall be required to maintain insurance or other financial security covering his liability for nuclear damage in such amount, of such type and in such terms as the Installation State shall specify. The Installation State shall ensure the payment of claims for compensation for nuclear damage which have been established against the operator by providing the necessary funds to the extent that the yield of insurance or other financial security is inadequate to satisfy such claims, but not in excess of the limit, if any, established pursuant to Article V.

2. Nothing in paragraph 1 of this Article shall require a Contracting Party or any of its constitutent sub-divisions, such as States or Republics, to maintain insurance or other financial security to cover their liability as operators.

3. The funds provided by insurance, by other financial security or by the Installation State pursuant to paragraph 1 of this Article shall be exclusively available for compensation due under this Convention.

4. No insurer or other financial guarantor shall suspend or cancel the insurance or other financial security provided pursuant to paragraph 1 of this Article without giving notice in writing of at least two months to the competent public authority or, in so far as such insurance or other financial security relates to the carriage of nuclear material, during the period of the carriage in question.

Article VIII

Subject to the provisions of this Convention, the nature, form and extent of the compensation, as well as the equitable distribution thereof, shall be governed by the law of the competent court.

Article IX

1. Where provisions of national or public health insurance, social insurance, social security, workmen's compensation or occupational disease compensation systems include compensation for nuclear damage, rights of beneficiaries of such systems to obtain compensation under this Convention and rights of recourse by virtue of such systems against the operator liable shall be determined, subject to the provisions of this Convention, by the law of the Contracting Party in which such systems have been established, or by the regulations of the intergovernmental organization which established such systems.

2. *a*) If a person who is a national of a Contracting Party, other than the operator, has paid compensation for nuclear damage under an international convention or under the law of a non-Contracting State, such person shall, up to the amount which he has paid, acquire by subrogation the rights under this Convention of the person so compensated. No rights shall be so acquired by any person to the extent that the operator has a right of recourse against such person under this Convention.

b) Nothing in this Convention shall preclude an operator who has paid compensation for nuclear damage out of funds other than those provided pursuant to paragraph 1 of Article VII from recovering from the person providing financial security pursuant to that paragraph or from the Installation State, up to the amount he has paid, the sum which the person so compensated would have obtained under this Convention.

Article X

The operator shall have a right of recourse only —

a) if this is expressly provided for by a contract in writing; or

b) if the nuclear incident results from an act or omission done with intent to cause damage, against the individual who has acted or omitted to act with such intent.

Article XI

1. Except as otherwise provided in this Article, jurisdiction over actions under Article II shall lie only with the courts of the Contracting Party within whose territory the nuclear incident occurred.

2. Where the nuclear incident occurred outside the territory of any Contracting Party, or where the place of the nuclear incident cannot be determined with certainty, jurisdiction over such actions shall lie with the courts of the Installation State of the operator liable.

3. Where under paragraph 1 or 2 of this Article, jurisdiction would lie with the courts of more than one Contracting Party, jurisdiction shall lie —

a) if the nuclear incident occurred partly outside the territory of any Contracting Party, and partly within the territory of a single Contracting Party, with the courts of the latter; and

b) in any other case, with the courts of that Contracting Party which is determined by agreement between the Contracting Parties whose courts would be competent under paragraph 1 or 2 of this Article.

Article XII

1. A final judgment entered by a court having jurisdiction under Article XI shall be recognized within the territory of any other Contracting Party, except —

a) where the judgment was obtained by fraud;

b) where the party against whom the judgment

was pronounced was not given a fair opportunity to present his case; or

c) where the judgment is contrary to the public policy of the Contracting Party within the territory of which recognition is sought, or is not in accord with fundamental standards of justice.

2. A final judgement which is recognized shall, upon being presented for enforcement in accordance with the formalities required by the law of the Contracting Party where enforcement is sought, be enforceable as if it were a judgment of a court of that Contracting Party.

3. The merits of a claim on which the judgment has been given shall not be subject to further proceedings.

Article XIII

This Convention and the national law applicable thereunder shall be applied without any discrimination based upon nationality, domicile or residence.

Article XIV

Except in respect of measures of execution, jurisdictional immunities under rules of national or international law shall not be invoked in actions under this Convention before the courts competent pursuant to Article XI.

Article XV

The Contracting Parties shall take appropriate measures to ensure that compensation for nuclear damage. interest and costs awarded by a court in connection therewith, insurance and reinsurance premiums and funds provided by insurance, reinsurance or other financial security, or funds provided by the Installation State, pursuant to this Convention, shall be freely transferable into the currency of the Contracting Party within whose territory the damage is suffered, and of the Contracting Party within whose territory the claimant is habitually resident, and, as regards insurance or reinsurance premiums and payments, into the currencies specified in the insurance or reinsurance contract.

Article XVI

No person shall be entitled to recover compensation under this Convention to the extent that he has recovered compensation in respect of the same nuclear damage under another international convention on civil liability in the field of nuclear energy.

Article XVII

This Convention shall not, as between the parties to them, affect the application of any international agreements or international conventions on civil liability in the field of nuclear energy in force, or open for signature, ratification or accession at the date on which this Convention is opened for signature.

Article XVIII

This Convention shall not be construed as affecting the rights, if any, of a Contracting Party under the general rules of public international law in respect of nuclear damage.

Article XIX

1. Any Contracting Party entering into an agreement pursuant to sub-paragraph (*b*) of paragraph 3 of Article XI shall furnish without delay to the Director General of the International Atomic Energy Agency for information and dissemination to the other Contracting Parties a copy of such agreement.

2. The Contracting Parties shall furnish to the Director General for information and dissemination to the other Contracting Parties copies of their respective laws and regulations relating to matters covered by this Convention.

Article XX

Notwithstanding the termination of the application of this Convention to any Contracting Party, either by termination pursuant to Article XXV or by denunciation pursuant to Article XXVI, the provisions of this Convention shall continue to apply to any nuclear damage caused by a nuclear incident occurring before such termination.

Article XXI

This Convention shall be open for signature by the States represented at the International Conference on Civil Liability for Nuclear Damage held in Vienna from 29 April to 19 May 1963.

Article XXII

This Convention shall be ratified, and the instruments of ratification shall be deposited with the Director General of the International Atomic Energy Agency.

Article XXIII

This Convention shall come into force three months after the deposit of the fifth instrument of ratification, and, in respect of each State ratifying it thereafter, three months after the deposit of the instrument of ratification by that State.

Article XXIV

1. All States Members of the United Nations, or of any of the specialized agencies or of the International Atomic Energy Agency not represented at the International Conference on Civil Liability for Nuclear Damage, held in Vienna from 29 April to 19 May 1963, may accede to this Convention.

2. The instruments of accession shall be deposited with the Director General of the International Atomic Energy Agency.

3. This Convention shall come into force in respect of the acceding State three months after the date of deposit of the instrument of accession of that State but not before the date of the entry into force of this Convention pursuant to Article XXIII.

Article XXV

1. This Convention shall remain in force for a period of ten years from the date of its entry into force. Any Contracting Party may, by giving before the end of that period at least twelve months' notice to that effect to the Director General of the International Atomic Energy Agency, terminate the application of this Convention to itself at the end of that period of ten years.

2. This Convention shall, after that period of ten years, remain in force for a further period of five years for such Contracting Parties as have not terminated its application pursuant to paragraph 1 of this Article, and thereafter for successive periods of five years each for those Contracting Parties which have not terminated its application at the end of one of such periods, by giving, before the end of one of such periods, at least twelve months' notice to that effect to the Director General of the International Atomic Energy Agency.

Article XXVI

1. A conference shall be convened by the Director General of the International Atomic Energy Agency at any time after the expiry of a period of five years from the date of the entry into force of this Convention in order to consider the revision thereof, if one-third of the Contracting Parties express a desire to that effect.

2. Any Contracting Party may denounce this Convention by notification to the Director-General of the International Atomic Energy Agency within a period of twelve months following the first revision conference held pursuant to paragraph 1 of this Article.

3. Denunciation shall take effect one year after the date on which notification to that effect has been received by the Director General of the International Atomic Energy Agency.

Article XXVII

The Director General of the International Atomic Energy Agency shall notify the States invited to the International Conference on Civil Liability for Nuclear Damage held in Vienna from 29 April to 19 May 1963 and the States which have acceded to this Convention of the following:

a) signatures and instruments of ratification and accession received pursuant to Articles XXI, XXII and XXIV;

b) the date on which this Convention will come into force pursuant to Article XXIII;

c) notifications of termination and denunciation received pursuant to Articles XXV and XXVI;

d) requests for the convening of a revision conference pursuant to Article XXVI.

Article XXVIII

This Convention shall be registered by the Director General of the International Atomic Energy Agency in accordance with Article 102 of the Charter of the United Nations.

Article XXIX

The original of this Convention, of which the English, French, Russian and Spanish texts are equally authentic, shall be deposited with the Director General of the International Atomic Energy Agency, who shall issue certified copies.

In Witness Whereof, the undersigned Plenipotentiaries, duly authorized thereto, have signed this Convention.

Done in Vienna, this twenty-first day of May, one thousand nine hundred and sixty-three.

OPTIONAL PROTOCOL CONCERNING THE COMPULSORY SETTLEMENT OF DISPUTES

Vienna, 21 May 1963

The States Parties to the present Protocol and to the Vienna Convention on Civil Liability for Nuclear Damage hereinafter referred to as "the Convention", adopted by the International Conference held at Vienna from 29 April to 19 May 1963,

Expressing their wish to resort in all matters concerning them in respect of any dispute arising out of the interpretation or application of the Convention to the compulsory jurisdiction of the International Court of Justice, unless some other form of settlement has been agreed upon by the parties within a reasonable period,

Have agreed as follows:

Article I

Disputes arising out of the interpretation or application of the Convention shall lie within the compulsory jurisdiction of the International Court of Justice and may accordingly be brought before the Court by an application made by any party to a dispute being a Party to the present Protocol.

Article II

The parties to a dispute may agree, within a period of two months after one party has notified its opinion to the other that a dispute exists, to resort not to the International Court of Justice but to an arbitral tribunal. After the expiry of the said period, either party may bring the dispute before the Court by an application.

Article III

1. Within the same period of two months, the parties may agree to adopt a conciliation procedure before resorting to the International Court of Justice.

2. The conciliation commission shall make its recommendations within five months after the appointment. If its recommendations are not accepted by the parties to the dispute within two months after they have been delivered, either party may bring the dispute before the Court by an application.

Article IV

The present Protocol shall be open for signature

by all States which may become Parties to the Convention.

Article V

The present Protocol is subject to ratification. The instruments of ratification shall be deposited with the Director General of the International Atomic Energy Agency.

Article VI

The present Protocol shall remain open for accession by all States which may become Parties to the Convention. The instruments of accession shall be deposited with the Director General of the International Atomic Energy Agency.

Article VII

1. The present Protocol shall enter into force on the same day as the Convention or on the thirtieth day following the date of deposit of the second instrument of ratification or accession to the Protocol with the Director General of the International Atomic Energy Agency, whichever date is the later.

2. For each State ratifying or acceding to the present Protocol after its entry into force in accordance with paragraph 1 of this Article, the Protocol shall enter into force on the thirtieth day after deposit by such State of its instrument of ratification or accession.

Article VIII

The Director General of the International Atomic Energy Agency shall inform all States which may become Parties to the Convention:

a) of signatures to the present Protocol and of the deposit of instruments of ratification or accession, in accordance with Articles IV, V and VI;

b) of the date on which the present Protocol will enter into force, in accordance with Article VII.

Article IX

The original of the present Protocol, of which the English, French, Russian and Spanish texts are equally authentic, shall be deposited with the Director General of the International Atomic Energy Agency who shall issue certified copies.

In Witness Whereof the undersigned Plenipotentiaries, duly authorized thereto, have signed this Protocol.

Done in Vienna, this twenty-first day of May, one thousand nine hundred and sixty-three.

TREATY BANNING NUCLEAR WEAPON TESTS IN THE ATMOSPHERE, IN OUTER SPACE AND UNDER WATER [31]

Moscow, 5 August 1963

The Governments of the Union of Soviet Socialist Republics, the United Kingdom of Great Britain and Northern Ireland, and the United States of America, hereinafter referred to as the "Original Parties",

Proclaiming as their principal aim the speediest possible achievement of an agreement on general and complete disarmament under strict international control in accordance with the objectives of the United Nations which would put an end to the armaments race and eliminate the incentive to the production and testing of all kinds of weapons, including nuclear weapons,

Seeking to achieve the discontinuance of all test explosions of nuclear weapons for all time, determined to continue negotiations to this end, and desiring to put an end to the contamination of man's environment by radioactive substances,

Have agreed as follows:

Article I

1. Each of the Parties to this Treaty undertakes to prohibit, to prevent, and not to carry out any nuclear weapon test explosion, or any other nuclear explosion, at any place under its jurisdiction or control:

a) in the atmosphere; beyond its limits, including outer space; or underwater, including territorial waters or high seas; or

b) in any other environment if such explosion causes radioactive debris to be present outside the territorial limits of the State under whose jurisdiction or control such explosion is conducted. It is understood in this connection that the provisions of this sub-paragraph are without prejudice to the conclusion of a treaty resulting in the permanent banning of all nuclear test explosions, including all such explosions underground, the conclusion of which, as the Parties have stated in the Preamble to this Treaty, they seek to achieve.

2. Each of the Parties to this Treaty undertakes furthermore to refrain from causing, encouraging, or in any way participating in, the carrying out of any nuclear weapon test explosion, or any other nuclear explosion, anywhere which would take place in any of the environments described, or have the effect referred to, in paragraph 1 of this Article.

Article II

1. Any Party may propose amendments to this Treaty. The text of any proposed amendment shall be submitted to the Depositary Governments which shall circulate it to all Parties to this Treaty. Thereafter, if requested to do so by one-third or more of the Parties, the Depositary Governments shall convene a conference, to which they shall invite all the Parties, to consider such amendment.

2. Any amendment to this Treaty must be

approved by a majority of the votes of all the Parties to this Treaty, including the votes of all of the Original Parties. The amendment shall enter into force for all Parties upon the deposit of instruments of ratification by a majority of all the Parties, including the instruments of ratification of all of the Original Parties.

Article III

1. This Treaty shall be open to all States for signature. Any State which does not sign this Treaty before its entry into force in accordance with paragraph 3 of this Article may accede to it at any time.

2. This Treaty shall be subject to ratification by signatory States. Instruments of ratification and instruments of accession shall be deposited with the Governments of the Original Parties — the Union of Soviet Socialist Republics, the United Kingdom of Great Britain and Northern Ireland, and the United States of America — which are hereby designated the Depositary Governments.

3. This Treaty shall enter into force after its ratification by all the Original Parties and the deposit of their instruments of ratification.

4. For States whose instruments of ratification or accession are deposited subsequent to the entry into force of this Treaty, it shall enter into force on the date of the deposit of their instruments of ratification or accession.

5. The Depositary Governments shall promptly inform all signatory and acceding States of the date of each signature, the date of deposit of each instrument of ratification and accession of this Treaty, the date of its entry into force, and the date of receipt of any requests for conferences or other notices.

6. This Treaty shall be registered by the Depositary Governments pursuant to Article 102 of the Charter of the United Nations.

Article IV

This Treaty shall be of unlimited duration.

Each Party shall in exercising its national sovereignty have the right to withdraw from the Treaty if it decides that extraordinary events, related to the subject matter of this Treaty, have jeopardized the supreme interests of its country. It shall give notice of such withdrawal to all other Parties to the Treaty three months in advance.

Article V

This Treaty, of which the English and Russsian texts are equally authentic, shall be deposited in the archives of the Depositary Governments. Duly certified copies of this Treaty shall be transmitted by the Depositary Governments to the Governments of the signatory and acceding States.

In Witness Whereof the undersigned, duly authorized, have signed this Treaty.

Done in triplicate at the city of Moscow the fifth day of August, one thousand nine hundred sixty-three.

ACT REGARDING NAVIGATION AND ECONOMIC CO-OPERATION BETWEEN THE STATES OF THE NIGER BASIN [32]

Niamey, 26 October 1963

The Federal Republic of Cameroon, the Republic of Chad, the Republic of the Dahomey, the Republic of Guinea, the Republic of the Ivory Coast, the Republic of Mali, the Republic of Niger, the Federal Republic of Nigeria, the Republic of Upper Volta.

Considering their attainment of independence and the need for regulating by new agreement the question of the utilization of the River Niger its tributaries and sub-tributaries of which they are the riparian States;

Desirous of developing close-co-operation for the judicious exploitation of the resources of the river Niger basin as well as to guarantee the freedom of navigation on the River, its tributaries and to ensure equality of treatment to those who use it;

Considering that, in the wake of technical progress, several of the riparian States have already drawn up plans for hydraulic developments such as irrigation, water supply, hydro-electric installations, civil works, soil and river basin improvement, and also plans for dealing with the problems of water pollution, exploitation of fishery resources, the improvement of agricultural practices and industrial developments of the basin;

Considering that the schemes planned in each State are likely to affect the regime of the River and the use of its water by other riparian States;

Considering the need to establish a joint institution to increase co-operation amongst the States interested in common projects concerned with the basin of the River Niger and to ensure the maintenance and application of the agreed major principles;

Solemnly affirm the following principles which will govern the measures of co-operation for the purpose of achieving the objectives of the present Act and declare that:

Article 1

The General Act of Berlin of 26 February 1885, the General Act and Declaration of Brussels of 2 July 1890, and the Convention of Saint-Germian-en-Laye of 10 September 1919 are and remain abrogated as far as they concern the River Niger, its tributaries and sub-tributaries.

Article 2

The utilization of the River Niger, its tributaries and sub-tributaries, is open to each riparian State in respect of the portion of the River Niger basin lying in its territory and without prejudice to its sovereign rights in accordance with the principles defined in the present Act and in the manner that may be set forth in subsequent special agreements.

The utilization of the said River, its tributaries

and sub-tributaries, shall be taken in a wide sense, to refer in particular to navigation, agricultural and industrial uses, and collection of the products of its fauna and flora.

Article 3

Navigation on the River Niger, its tributaries and sub-tributaries, shall be entirely free for merchant vessels and pleasure craft and for the transportation of goods and passengers. The ships and boats of all nations shall be treated in all respects on a basis of complete equality.

Article 4

The riparian States undertake to establish close co-operation with regard to the study and the execution of any project likely to have an appreciable effect on certain features of the regime of the River, its tributaries and sub-tributaries, their conditions of navigability, agricultural and industrial exploitation, the sanitary conditions of their waters, and the biological characteristics of their fauna and flora.

Article 5

In order to further their co-operation for the attainment of the objectives of this Act, the riparian States undertake to establish an Inter-Governmental Organization which will be entrusted with the task of encouraging, promoting and co-ordinating the studies and programmes concerning the exploitation of the resources of the River Niger basin. The composition, the functions and the procedures of such Inter-Governmental Organization shall be the subject of a subsequent agreement.

Article 6

The Inter-Governmental Organization of the River Niger shall establish appropriate close relations with the competent specialised agencies of the Organization of African Unity and shall also maintain useful relations with the United Nations Organization, its specialized agencies, and other international organizations.

Article 7

Any dispute that may arise between the riparian States regarding the interpretation or application of the present Act shall be amicably settled by direct agreement between them or through the Inter-Governmental Organization referred to in Articles 5 and 6 above.

Failing such settlement, the dispute shall be decided by arbitration, in particular by the Commission of Mediation, Conciliation and Arbitration of the Organization of African Unity, or by judicial settlement by the International Court of Justice.

Article 8

The present Act, the French and English texts of which are equally authentic, shall be submitted for ratification to the signatory States and shall come into force immediately after ratification by all the signatory States.

The instruments of ratification shall be deposited with the Government of the Republic of Niger which shall notify each signatory State of the deposit of the said instruments.

Article 9

The Government of the Republic of Niger shall register the present Act, upon its coming into force, in accordance with Article 102 of the Charter of the United Nations.

In Witness Whereof the plenipotentiaries being duly authorized by their respective Governments have signed the present Act.

Done at Niamey on 26 October 1963, one copy each in English and French to be deposited in the archives of the Government of the Republic of Niger, authentic copies thereof to be distributed to each of the signatory States, and one copy to be deposited with the Secretariat of the Organization of African Unity and one with the Secretariat of the United Nations.

AGREEMENT CONCERNING THE RIVER NIGER COMMISSION AND THE NAVIGATION AND TRANSPORT ON THE RIVER NIGER*

Niamey, 25 November 1964

The Contracting Parties,

Having adopted at the Conference of the Riparian States of the River Niger, its tributaries and sub-tributaries, held at Niamey from 24 to 26 October 1963, an Act regarding the navigation and economic co-operation between the States of the River Niger basin,

Desirous of giving effect to Article 5 of the said Act, by which they have undertaken to establish an Inter-Governmental Organization entrusted with the fostering, the promotion and the co-ordination of studies and programmes relating to the utilization and development of the resources of the River Niger basin,

Desirous of specifying some questions relating to navigation and transportation on the River,

Have agreed as follows:

Chapter I

RIVER NIGER COMMISSION

Article 1

There shall be established an Inter-Governmental Organization as mentioned in Article 5 of the Act of Niamey of 26 October 1963, which shall be called River Niger Commission.

Article 2

The Commission shall have the following functions, in particular:

a) to prepare General Regulations which will permit the full application of the principles set forth in the Act of Niamey, and to ensure their effective application.

The General Regulations and the other decisions of the Commission shall, after approval by the riparian States and after a time-limit fixed by the Commission, have binding force as regards relations among the States as well as their internal regulation.

b) to maintain liaison between the riparian States in order to ensure the most effective use of the waters and resources of the River Niger basin.

c) to collect, evaluate and disseminate basic data on the whole of the basin, to examine the projects prepared by the riparian States, and to recommend to the Governments of the riparian States plans for common studies and works for the judicious utilization and development of the resources of the basin.

d) to follow the progress of the execution of studies and works in the basin and to keep the riparian States informed, at least once a year thereon, through systematic and periodic reports which each State shall submit to it.

e) to draw up General Regulations regarding all forms of navigation on the River.

f) to draw up staff regulations and to ensure their application.

g) to examine complaints and to promote the settlement of disputes and the resolution of differences.

h) generally, to supervise the implementation of the provisions of the Act of Niamey and the present Agreement.

Article 3

The Commission shall consist of nine Commissioners one for each riparian State. The Commissioners may be assisted by experts. The Commission shall establish its own Rules of Procedure.

Article 4

The quorum of the Commission shall be six Commissioners. The decisions of the Commission shall be taken by a majority of two-thirds of the Commissioners present and voting.

Article 5

The Commission shall meet in ordinary session once a year. It may meet in extraordinary session at the joint request of any three riparian States by notification addressed to the Administrative Secretary.

The Headquarters of the Commission shall be at Niamey. The meetings of the Commission may take place in the territory of any of the riparian States.

Article 6

The Commission shall have an Administrative Secretary.

The Commission shall, by a two-thirds majority vote, appoint the Administrative Secretary from among the candidates proposed by the riparian States.

Each riparian State shall be entitled to nominate a candidate for the office of Administrative Secretary.

The Administrative Secretary shall hold office for three years and shall be eligible for re-appointment. The conditions of his service shall be defined in the Staff Regulations.

Article 7

The Administrative Secretary shall be assisted in his duties by such staff as the Commission shall determine. The conditions of employment of the Staff shall be defined in the Staff Regulations.

Article 8

The Administrative Secretary shall be in charge of the Staff. He shall exercise such powers and perform such duties as may be determined by the

* The title of the English version of the Agreement has been modified by a procès-verbal of rectification signed in Niamey, on 3 January 1968.

Commission. He shall be responsible to the Commission.

Article 9

The Commission may, by a two-thirds majority vote, remove the Administrative Secretary from office.

Article 10

The riparian States shall make contributions towards the regular Budget of the Commission in proportions to be determined by the Commission. The Commission shall establish an annual Budget and shall submit it to the riparian States for approval.

Any expenditure incurred in respect of special services rendered to a State by the Commission shall be paid by that State.

Article 11

The Commission shall have for all purposes the status of an international organization. The Commissioners and the Administrative Secretary shall be accorded diplomatic privileges and immunities by the riparian States. The other staff of the Commission shall be accorded such privileges and immunities as are accorded to officials of the Organization of African Unity of equivalent status.

Chapter II

Agricultural And Industrial Utilization And Development

Article 12

In order to achieve maximum co-operation in connection with the matters mentioned in Article 4 of the Act of Niamey, the riparian States undertake to inform the Commission as provided for in Chapter I of the present Agreement, at the earliest stage, of all studies and works upon which they propose to embark. They undertake further to abstain from carrying out on the portion of the River, its tributaries and sub-tributaries subject to their jurisdiction any works likely to pollute the waters, or any modification likely to affect biological characteristics of its fauna and flora, without adequate notice to, and prior consultation with, the Commission.

Chapter III

Navigation And Transport

Article 13

The taxes and duties payable by the vessels and goods using the River, its tributaries and sub-tributaries, and facilities thereof, shall be in proportion to the services rendered to navigation, and shall in no way be discriminatory.

Article 14

The roads, railways and lateral canals that may be constructed for the special purpose of avoiding the non-navigable portions of the River or of improving certain sections of the waterways, shall be considered in their use as means of communications, as integral part of the River Niger, and shall be equally open to international traffic within the framework of specific regulations set up by the Commission and approved by the riparian States.

On these roads, railways and canals only such tolls shall be collected as are calculated on the cost of construction, maintenance and management. As regards such tolls, the nationals of all States shall be treated on the basis of complete equality.

Article 15

The River Niger Commission shall establish general regulations to ensure the safety and control of navigation on the understanding that such regulations shall be designed to facilitate, as much as possible, the movement of vessels and boats.

Chapter IV

General Provisions

Article 16

This Agreement shall form an integral part of the Act of Niamey, and shall enter into force immediately after its ratification by all the signatory States. The instruments of ratification shall be deposited with the Government of the Republic of Niger who shall notify the deposit of these instruments to each riparian State.

Article 17

The Act of Niamey together with this Agreement may be denounced by any one of the riparian States after the expiration of a period of ten years from the date of its coming into force. Denunciation shall take the form of a written notice addressed to the Government of the Republic of Niger who shall acknowledge its receipt and shall inform the other contracting States and the Administrative Secretary of the Commission. It shall take effect one year from the date of acknowledgement of its receipt, if not withdrawn earlier. In the absence of agreement to the contrary it shall not affect obligations relating to any program of studies and works agreed to before such denunciation.

Article 18

The Act of Niamey and this Agreement may be amended upon the written request of one third of the riparian States addressed to the Government of the Republic of Niger. Any proposal for revision shall require the approval of two thirds of the riparian States, and shall take effect six months after the date of its adoption.*

Article 19

Upon the coming into force of the present Agreement, the Government of the Republic of Niger shall register it in accordance with Article 102 of the United Nations Charter.

* In order to bring the English version into line with the text originally adopted and with article 18 of the French version, which is equally authentic, this article has been ratified by a proces-verbal signed at Niamey on 3 January 1968.

In Witness Whereof the plenipotentiaries being duly authorized by their respective Governments have signed the present Agreement.

Done at Niamey on 25th day of November 1964, one copy in English and one in French to be deposited in the archives of the Government of the Republic of Niger and certified copies thereof to be sent to each signatory State, and one copy to be deposited with the Secretariat of the Organization of African Unity and one with the Secretariat of the United Nations.

AGREEMENT FOR THE ESTABLISHMENT OF A COMMISSION FOR CONTROLLING THE DESERT LOCUST IN THE EASTERN REGION OF ITS DISTRIBUTION AREA IN SOUTH-WEST ASIA [33]

Rome, 3 December 1963

PREAMBLE

The Contracting Governments, having regard to the urgent necessity of preventing losses to agriculture in certain countries of central and western Asia caused by the Desert Locust, hereby establish within the framework of the Food and Agriculture Organization of the United Nations (hereinafter referred to as "the Organization") a Commission to be known as the "Commission for Controlling the Desert Locust in the Eastern Region of its Distribution Area in South-West Asia", whose object shall be to promote national and international research and action with respect to the control of the Desert Locust in that Region. The Region is defined as consisting of the territories of Afghanistan, India, Iran and Pakistan and any territories adjacent to the above countries.

Article I

MEMBERSHIP

1. The Members of the Commission for Controlling the Desert Locust in the Eastern Region of its Distribution Area in South-West Asia (hereinafter referred to as "the Commission") shall be such Member Nations and Associate Members of the Organization situated in the Region defined in the Preamble as accept this Agreement in accordance with the provisions of Article XV of this Agreement.

2. The Commission may, by a two-thirds majority of its Members, admit to membership such other States, situated in the Region that are Members of the United Nations, any of its Specialized Agencies or the International Atomic Energy Agency, as have submitted an application for membership of the Commission and a declaration made in a formal instrument that they accept this Agreement as in force at the time of admission.

Article II

OBLIGATIONS OF MEMBERS REGARDING NATIONAL POLICIES AND INTERNATIONAL CO-OPERATION FOR THE CONTROL OF THE DESERT LOCUST

1. Members undertake to maintain through the Secretary of the Commission a regular exchange of information on the current locust situation and the progress of control campaigns within their countries, and also to transmit such information regularly to the Desert Locust Information Service in London, in the light of the Agreement between the Organization and the Anti-Locust Research Center.

2. Members undertake to carry out all possible measures to control plagues of the Desert Locust within their countries and to reduce crop damage by adopting at least the following esential procedures:

a) maintaining a permanent locust information and reporting service;

b) maintaining an adequate permanent locust control service;

c) holding reserves of insecticides and application equipment;

d) encouraging and supporting such training, survey and research work, including where appropriate the maintenance of national research stations for the study of the Desert Locust, as may be considered desirable by the Commission and as are compatible with the resources of the country;

e) participating in the implementation of any common policy of locust control or prevention which may be approved by the Commission;

f) facilitating the storage of any items of anti-locust equipment and insecticides held by the Commission and permitting the duty-free import or export without hindrance of such goods and equipment as well as the free movement within the country of such goods and equipment;

g) providing the Commission with any information it may request to carry out its functions effectively.

3. Members undertake to submit to the Commission periodic reports on the action taken to fulfil the obligations specified in paragraphs 1 and 2 above.

Article III

SEAT OF THE COMMISSION

1. The seat of the Commission shall be determined by the Commission.

2. Sessions of the Commission shall normally be held at its seat. Sessions may, however, be convened elsewhere, in consultation with the Director-General of the Orgainzation, in pursuance of a decision of the Commission at a previous session, or, in exceptional circumstances, of a decision by the Executive Committee.

Article IV

FUNCTIONS OF THE COMMISSION

The following shall be the functions of the Commission:

1. *Joint Action and Assistance*

The Commission shall.

a) plan and implement joint action for the survey and control of the Desert Locust in the Region wherever required and, to this effect, arrange means whereby adequate resources can be made available;

b) assist and promote, in any manner which it considers appropriate, any national, regional or international action relating to the control or survey of the Desert Locust;

c) determine, in consultation with the Members concerned, the nature and extent of assistance needed by such Members for implementing their national programme and for supporting regional programmes;

d) assist, at the request of any Member whose territory is faced with Desert Locust situations beyond the capacity of its national services to control and survey, in any measures jointly agreed to that may become necessary;

e) maintain at strategic localities determined by the Commission, in consultation with the Members concerned, reserves of anti-locust equipment, insecticides and other supplies, to be used in cases of emergency in accordance with decisions of the Executive Committee including supplementing of the national resources of any Member.

2. *Information and Co-ordination*

The Commission shall:

a) ensure that all Members are provided with current information in regard to Desert Locust infestations, and collect and disseminate information on experience gained, research conducted and programs adopted on the national, regional and international levels in connection with the control of the Desert Locust;

b) assist the national research organizations of Members and co-ordinate research in the Region by arranging visits of research and survey units and other appropriate means.

3. *Co-operation*

The Commission may:

a) enter into arrangements or agreements, through the Director-General of the Organization, with nations in the Region that are not Members of the United Nations, for common action in connection with survey and control of locusts in the Region;

b) enter into or encourage arrangements, through the Director-General, with other United Nations Specialized Agencies or other international organizations concerned, for common action on the study and control of locusts and for the mutual exchange of information on problems concerning locusts.

4. *Administrative matters*

The Commission shall:

a) consider and approve the report of the Executive Committee on the activities of the Commission, the Programme and Budget of the Commission for the ensuing financial period, and the annual accounts;

b) keep the Director-General of the Organization fully informed of its activities and transmit to him the accounts, the Programme and the Budget of the Commission, the latter for submission to the Council of the Organization prior to implementation.

c) transmit to the Director-General the reports

and recommendations of the Commission, for such action by the Council or Conference of the Organization as may be appropriate.

Article V

SESSIONS OF THE COMMISSION

1. Each Member of the Commission shall be represented at sessions of the Commission by a delegate who may be accompanied by an alternate and by experts and advisers. Alternates, experts and advisers may take part in the proceedings of the Commission but may not vote unless authorized by the delegate to substitute for him.

2. A majority of the Members of the Commission shall constitute a quorum. Each Member shall have one vote. Decisions of the Commission shall be taken by a majority of the votes cast except as otherwise provided for in this Agreement.

3. A Member which is in arrears in the payment of its financial contributions to the Commission shall have no vote if the amount of its arrears equals or exceeds the amount of the Contributions due from it for the two preceding financial years.

4. The Commission shall elect, at the beginning of each regular session, a Chairman and a Vice-Chairman from amongst the delegates.' These Officers shall hold office until the beginning of the next regular session and shall be eligible for re-election.

5. The Director-General of the Organization in consultation with the Chairman of the Commission shall convene a regular session of the Commission at least once a year. Special sessions may be convened by the Director-General in consultation with the Chairman of the Commission, if so requested by the Commission in regular session or by at least one third of the Members during intervals between regular session.

6. The Director-General of the Organization or a representative designated by him shall have the right to participate without vote in all meetings of the Commission or its subsidiary bodies.

Article VI

OBSERVERS AND CONSULTANTS

1. Participation of international organizations in the work of the Commission and the relations between the Commission and such organizations shall be governed by the relevant provisions of the Constitution and the General Rules of the Organization as well as by the rules on relations with international organizations adopted by the Conference or Council of the Organization. All such relations shall be dealt with by the Director-General of the Organization.

2. Member Nations and Associate Members of the Organization that are not Members of the Commission may, upon their request, be represented by an observer at sessions of the Commission and of its subsidiary bodies.

3. States which, while not Members of the Commission nor Members or Associate Members of the Organization, are Members of the United Nations, any of its Specialized Agencies or the International Atomic Energy Agency may, upon request and subject to the concurrence of the Executive Committee and to the Provisions relating to the granting of observer status to nations adopted by the Conference of the Organization, be invited to attend sessions of the Commission and its subsidiary bodies in an observer capacity.

4. The Commission may invite consultants or experts to attend its sessions.

Article VII

SECRETARIAT

The Director-General of the Organization shall provide the Secretary and staff of the Commission, who, for administrative purposes, shall be responsible to him. They shall be appointed under the same terms and conditions as the staff of the Organization.

Article VIII

THE EXECUTIVE COMMITTEE

1. An Executive Committee shall be established and shall be composed of one representative (preferably a locust specialist) of each of the Members of the Commission. The Chairman and Vice-Chairman of the Executive Committee shall be elected from amongst its Members and shall hold office for one year. They shall be eligible for re-election.

2. The Executive Committee shall meet at least once between any two successive regular Sessions of the Commission. The Chairman of the Executive Committee shall, in consultation with the Director-General of the Organization, convene Sessions of the Committee.

3. The Secretary of the Commission shall act as Secretary of the Executive Committee.

Article IX

FUNCTIONS OF THE EXECUTIVE COMMITTEE

The Executive Committee shall:

a) make proposals to the Commission concerning policy matters and the programme of activities;

b) ensure the implementation of the policies and programmes approved by the Commission;

c) submit draft programmes of work and budget and annual accounts to the Commission;

d) prepare the draft annual report on the activities of the Commission for the approval of the Commission with the view of its transmission to the Director-General of the Organization.

e) carry out such other functions as the Commission may delegate to it.

Article X

RULES OF PROCEDURE AND FINANCIAL REGULATIONS

The Commission may, by a two-thirds majority of its membership, adopt and amend its own Rules of Procedure and Financial Regulations which shall be consistent with the General Rules and the Financial Regulations respectively of the

Organization. The Rules of Procedure and Financial Regulations of the Commission and any amendment thereto shall come into force upon approval by the Director-General of the Organization, and as from the date of such approval, the Financial Regulations and amendments thereto being subject to confirmation by the Council of the Organization.

Article XI

SUBSIDIARY BODIES

1. The Commission may, if necessary, establish sub-commissions, committees or working parties, subject to the availability of the necessary funds in the relevant chapters of the approved budgets of the Commission and of the Organization. The determination of such availability shall be made by the Director-General of the Organization. Before taking any decision involving expenditure in connection with the establishment of subsidiary bodies, the Commission shall have before it a report from the Director-General on the administrative and financial implications thereof.

2. Sessions of sub-commissions, committees and working parties shall be convened by the Chairman of such bodies in consultation with the Director-General of the Organization.

3. Membership in subsidiary bodies shall either be open to all Members of the Commission or shall consist of selected Members of the Commission, or of individuals appointed in their personal capacity, as determined by the Commission.

4. The procedure of subsidiary bodies shall be governed *mutatis mutandis* by the Rules of Procedure of the Commission.

Article XII

FINANCE

1. Each Member of the Commission undertakes to contribute annually its share of the Budget in accordance with a scale of contributions to be adopted by a two-thirds majority of the membership of the Commission. The contributions of the Members of the Commission shall, initially, be calculated on the basis of the financial contributions worked out in respect of the Members in connection with the United Nations Special Fund Desert Locust Project, subject to such modifications as may be determined by the Commission as the result of acceptances of the Agreement in addition to those provided for in Article XX of the Agreement.

2. Contributions by Members may be made partly in cash and partly in kind, the proportion of each being determined by the Commission. For budgetary purposes, the cash value of contributions in kind shall be calculated by such means as the Commission may decide.

3. The Commission may also accept contributions and donations from other sources.

4. Contributions shall be payable in currencies to be determined by the Commission after consultation with each Member and with the concurrence of the Director-General of the Organization.

5. All contributions and donations received shall be placed in a Trust Fund administered by the Director-General of the Organization in conformity with the Financial Regulations of the Organization.

Article XIII

EXPENSES

1. The expenses of the Commission shall be paid out of its Budget except those relating to such staff and facilities which can be made available by the Organization. The expenses to be borne by the Organization shall be determined and paid within the limits of an annual budget prepared by the Director-General and approved by the Conference of the Organization in accordance with the Constitution, General Rules and the Financial Regulations of the Organization.

2. Expenses relating to attendance by one delegate of each Member Government of the Commission at sessions of the Commission or its subsidiary bodies shall be borne by the Commission. Expenses of alternates, advisers and observers, shall be borne by their respective governments or organizations.

3. Expenses of individuals invited in their personal capacity to attend sessions or participate in the work of the Commission or its subsidiary bodies shall be borne by such individuals except when they have been requested to perform a specific task on behalf of the Commission or its subsidiary bodies.

4. The expenses of the Secretariat shall be borne by the Organization.

Article XIV

AMENDMENTS

1. This Agreement may be amended by a two-thirds majority of the membership of the Commission.

2. Proposals for amendments may be made by any Member of the Commission in a communication addressed to the Director-General of the Organization not later than 120 days before the Session of the Commission at which the proposal is to be considered. The Director-General shall inform all Members of the Commission of all proposals for amendment, within 30 days of receipt of such proposals.

3. Any amendment to this Agreement shall require the approval of the Council of the Organization unless the Council considers it desirable to refer the amendment to the Conference of the Organization for approval.

4. Amendments not involving new obligations for Members of the Commission shall take effect from the date of the approval by the Council or Conference, as appropriate.

5. Amendments involving new obligations for Members of the Commission shall, after approval by the Conference or Council of the Organization, come into force in respect of each Member only upon acceptance by it. The instruments of

acceptance of amendments involving new obligations shall be deposited with the Director-General of the Organization. The Director-General shall inform all Members of the Commission and the Secretary-General of the United Nations of such acceptance. The rights and obligations of any Member of the Commission that has not accepted an amendment involving new obligations shall continue to be governed by the provisions of the Agreement in force prior to the amendment.

6. The Director-General of the Organization shall inform all Members of the Commission, all Members and Associate Members of the Organization and the Secretary-General of the United Nations of the entry into force of any amendment.

Article XV

ACCEPTANCE

1. Acceptance of this Agreement by any Members or Associate Members of the Organization shall be effected by the deposit of an instrument of acceptance with the Director-General of the Organization and shall take effect on receipt of such instrument by the Director-General.

2. Acceptance of this Agreement by non-member Nations of this Organization shall become effective on the date on which the Commission approves the application for membership in conformity with the provisions of Article I of this Agreement.

3. The Director-General of the Organization shall inform all Members of the Commission, all Members and Associate Members of the Organization and the Secretary-General of the United Nations of all acceptances that have become effective.

4. Acceptance of this Agreement may be made subject to reservations which shall become effective only upon unanimous approval by the Members of the Commission. The Director-General of the Organization shall notify forthwith all Members of the Commission of any reservations. Members of the Commission not having replied within three months from the date of the notification shall be deemed to have accepted the reservation. Failing such approval, the nation making the reservation shall not become a party to this Agreement.

Article XVI

TERRITORIAL APPLICATION

The Members of the Commission shall, when accepting this Agreement, state explicitly to which territories their participation shall extend. In the absence of such a declaration, participation shall be deemed to apply to all the territories for the international relations of which the Member is responsible. Subject to the provisions of Article XVIII-2, the scope of the territorial application may be modified by a subsequent declaration.

Article XVII

INTERPRETATION AND SETTLEMENT OF DISPUTES

Any dispute regarding the interpretation or application of this Agreement, if not settled by the Commission, shall be referred to a Committee composed of one member appointed by each of the parties to the dispute, and in addition an independent chairman chosen by the members of the Committee. The recommendations of such a Committee, while not binding in character, shall become the basis for renewed consideration by the parties concerned of the matter out of which the disagreement arose. If as the result of this procedure the dispute is not settled, it shall be referred to the International Court of Justice in accordance with the Statute of the Court, unless the parties to the dispute agree to another method of settlement.

Article XVIII

WITHDRAWAL

1. Any Member may withdraw from the Commission at any time after the expiration of one year from the date on which its acceptance took effect or from the date on which the Agreement entered into force, whichever is the later, by giving written notice of withdrawal to the Director-General of the Organization, who shall forthwith inform all Members of the Commission, all Member Nations and Associate Members of the Organization and the Secretary-General of the United Nations. The withdrawal shall become effective one year from the date of receipt of the notification of withdrawal.

2. A Member of the Commission may give notice of withdrawal with respect to one or more of the territories for the international relations of which it is responsible. When a Member gives notice of its own withdrawal from the Commission, it shall state to which territory or territories the withdrawal is to apply. In the absence of such a declaration, the withdrawal shall be deemed to apply to all the territories for the international relations of which the Member of the Commission is responsible, except that such withdrawal shall not be deemed to apply to an Associate Member.

3. Any Member of the Commission that gives notice of withdrawal from the Organization shall be deemed to have simultaneously withdrawn from the Commission, and this withdrawal shall be deemed to apply to all the territories for the international relations of which the Member concerned is responsible, except that such withdrawal shall not be deemed to apply to an Associate Member.

Article XIX

TERMINATION

1. This Agreement shall be considered terminated if and when the number of Members of the Commission falls below three, unless the remaining two Members of the Commission decide

to continue, with the approval of the Conference of the Organization. The Director-General of the Organization shall inform all Members of the Commission, all Members and Associate Members of the Organization and the Secretary-General of the United Nations of such termination.

2. On termination of the Agreement all assets of the Commission shall be liquidated by the Director-General of the Organization and after settlement of the liabilities the balance shall be distributed proportionately amongst Members on the basis of the scale of contributions in force at the time. Nations whose contributions are in arrears for two consecutive years shall not be entitled to a share of the assets.

Article XX

ENTRY INTO FORCE

1. This Agreement shall enter into force as soon as three eligible Members or Associate Members of the Organization have become parties to it by the deposit of an instrument of acceptance in accordance with the provisions of Article XV of this Agreement.

2. The Director-General shall notify all Nations having deposited instruments of acceptance as well as all Member Nations and Associate Members of the Organization and the Secretary-General of the United Nations of the date on which this Agreement comes into force.

Article XXI

AUTHENTIC LANGUAGES

The English, French and Spanish texts of this Agreement shall be equally authentic.

CONVENTION FOR THE INTERNATIONAL COUNCIL FOR THE EXPLORATION OF THE SEA [34]

Copenhagen, 12 September 1964

PREAMBLE

The Governments of the States Parties to this Convention,

Having participated in the work of the International Council for the Exploration of the Sea, which was established at Copenhagen in 1902 as a result of conferences held in Stockholm in 1899 and in Christiania in 1901 and entrusted with the task of carrying out a programme of international investigation of the sea,

Desiring to provide a new constitution for the aforesaid Council with a view to facilitating the implementation of its programme,

Have agreed as follows:

Article 1

It shall be the duty of the International Council for the Exploration of the Sea, hereinafter referred to as the "Council",

a) to promote and encourage research and investigations for the study of the sea particularly those related to the living resources thereof;

b) to draw up programmes required for this purpose and to organize, in agreement with the Contracting Parties, such research and investigation as may appear necessary;

c) to publish or otherwise disseminate the results of research and investigations carried out under its auspices or to encourage the publication thereof.

Article 2

The Council shall be concerned with the Atlantic Ocean and its adjacent seas and primarily concerned with the South Atlantic.

Article 3

1. The Council shall be maintained in accordance with the provisions of this Convention.

2. The seat of the Council shall remain at Copenhagen.

Article 4

The Council shall seek to establish and maintain working arrangements with other international organizations which have related objectives and co-operate, as far as possible, with them, in particular in the supply of scientific information requested.

Article 5

The Contracting Parties undertake to furnish to the Council information which will contribute to the purposes of this Convention and can reasonably be made available and, wherever possible, to assist in carrying out the programmes of research co-ordinated by the Council.

Article 6

1. Each Contracting Party shall be represented at

the Council by not more than two delegates.

2. A delegate who is not present at a meeting of the Council may be replaced by a substitute who shall have all the powers of the delegate for that meeting.

3. Each Contracting Party may appoint such experts and advisers as it may determine to assist in the work of the Council.

Article 7

1. The Council shall meet in ordinary session once a year. This session shall be held in Copenhagen, unless the Council decides otherwise.

2. Extraordinary sessions of the Council may be called by the Bureau at such place and time as it may determine and shall be so called on the request of at least one-third of the Contracting Parties.

Article 8

1. Each Contracting Party shall have one vote in the Council.

2. Decisions of the Council shall, except where otherwise in this Convention specially provided, be taken by a simple majority of the votes cast for or against. If there is an even division of votes on any matter which is subject to a simple majority decision the proposal shall be regarded as rejected.

Article 9

1. Subject to the provisions of this Convention the Council shall draw up its own Rules of Procedure which shall be adopted by a two-thirds majority of the Contracting Parties.

2. English and French shall be the working languages of the Council.

Article 10

1. The Council shall elect from among the delegates its President, a first Vice-President and a further 5 Vice-Presidents. This last number may be augmented by a decision taken by the Council by a two-thirds majority.

2. The President and the Vice-Presidents shall assume office on the first day of November next following their election, for a term of three years. They are eligible for re-election according to the Rules of Procedure.

3. On assuming office the President shall cease forthwith to be a delegate.

Article 11

1. The President and Vice-Presidents shall together constitute the Bureau of the Council.

2. The Bureau shall be the Executive Committee of the Council and shall carry out the decisions of the Council, draw up its agenda and convene its meetings. It shall also prepare the budget. It shall invest the reserve funds and carry out the tasks entrusted to it by the Council. It shall account to the Council for its activities.

Article 12

There shall be a Consultative Committee, a Finance Committee and such other committees as the Council may deem necessary for the discharge of its functions with the duties respectively assigned to them in the Rules of Procedure.

Article 13

1. The Council shall appoint a General Secretary on such terms and to perform such duties as it may determine.

2. Subject to any general directions of the Council the Bureau shall appoint such other staff as may be required for the purposes of the Council on such terms and to perform such duties as it may determine.

Article 14

1. Each Contracting Party shall pay the expenses of the delegates, experts and advisers appointed by it, except in so far as the Council may otherwise determine.

2. The Council shall approve an annual budget of the proposed expenditure of the Council.

3. In the first and second financial years after this Convention enters into force in accordance with Article 16 of this Convention the Contracting Parties shall contribute to the expenses of the Council such sum as they respectively contributed, or undertook to contribute, in respect of the year preceding the entry into force of this Convention.

4. In respect of the third and subsequent financial years the Contracting Parties shall contribute sums calculated in accordance with a scheme to be prepared by the Council and accepted by all the Contracting Parties. This scheme may be modified by the Council with the agreement of all Contracting Parties.

5. A Government acceding to this Convention shall contribute to the expenses of the Council such sum as may be agreed between that Government and the Council in respect of each financial year until the scheme under paragraph 4 provides for contributions from that Government.

6. A Contracting Party which has not paid its contribution for two consecutive years shall not enjoy any rights under this Convention until it has fulfilled its financial obligations.

Article 15

1. The Council shall enjoy, in the territories of the Contracting Parties, such legal capacity as may be agreed between the Council and the Government of the Contracting Party concerned.

2. The Council, delegates and experts, the General Secretary and other officials shall enjoy in the territories of the Contracting Parties such privileges and immunities, necessary for the fulfilment of their functions, as may be agreed between the Council and the Government of the Contracting Party concerned.

Article 16

1. This Convention shall be open until 31 December 1961, for signature on behalf of the

Governments of all states which participate in the work of the Council.

2. This Convention is subject to ratification or approval by the signatory Governments in accordance with their respective constitutional procedures. The instruments of ratification or approval shall be deposited with the Government of Denmark, who will act as the depositary Government.

3. This Convention shall enter into force on the 22 July next following the deposit of the instruments of ratification or approval by all signatory Governments. If, however, on the 1 January 1968, all the signatory Governments have not ratified this Convention, but not less than three quarters of the signatory Governments have deposited instruments of ratification or approval, these latter Governments may agree among themselves by special protocol on the date on which this Convention shall enter into force and on other related matters; and in that case this Convention shall enter into force, with respect to any other signatory Government that ratifies or approves thereafter, on the date of deposit of its instrument of ratification or approval.

4. After the entry into force of this Convention in accordance with paragraph 3 of this Article, the Government of any State may apply to accede to this Convention by addressing a written application to the Government of Denmark. It shall be permitted to deposit an instrument of accession with that Government after the approval of the Governments of three quarters of the states which have already deposited their instruments of ratification, approval or accession, has been notified to the Government of Denmark. For any acceding Government this Convention shall enter into force on the date of deposit of its instrument of accession.

Article 17

At any time after two years from the date on which this Convention has come into force any Contracting Party may denounce the Convention by means of a notice in writing addressed to the Government of Denmark. Any such notice shall take effect twelve months after the date of its receipt.

Article 18

When the present Convention comes into force it shall be registered by the depositary Government with the Secretariat of the United Nations Organization in accordance with Article 102 of its Charter.

FINAL CLAUSE

In Witness Whereof the undersigned being duly authorized have signed the present Convention:

Done at Copenhagen this twelfth day of September 1964, in the English and French languages, both texts being equally authentic, in a single copy which shall be deposited in the archives of the Government of Denmark who shall forward certified true copies to all signatory and acceding Governments.

Protocol
to the Convention for the International Council for the Exploration of the Sea

Copenhagen, 13 August 1970

The Governments of the States Parties to the Convention for the International Council for the Exploration of the Sea, signed at Copenhagen on the twelfth day of September 1964 (hereinafter referred to as "the Convention"),

Desiring to amend certain provisions of the Convention,

Have agreed as follows:

Article I

Paragraph (2) of Article 14 of the Convention shall be amended to read as follows:

"(2) the Council shall by a majority vote of all the Contracting Parties approve an annual budget of the Council".

Article II

1. This Protocol shall be open for signature on behalf of the Governments of all States Parties to the Convention with or without reservation as to ratification or approval.

2. Instruments of ratification or approval shall be deposited with the Government of Denmark.

3. This Protocol shall enter into force on the date on which the Governments of all States Parties to the Convention have become Parties to this Protocol.

4. The Government of Denmark shall inform the Governments of the States Parties to the Convention of each signature ratification or approval of this Protocol and of the date of the entry into force of the Protocol.

In Witness Whereof the undersigned being duly authorized have signed this Protocol.

Done at Copenhagen this thirteenth day of August 1970, in the English and French languages, both texts being equally authentic, in a single copy which shall be deposited in the archives of the Government of Denmark who shall forward certified true copies to the Governments of all States Parties to the Convention.

AGREEMENT FOR THE ESTABLISHMENT OF A COMMISSION FOR CONTROLLING THE DESERT LOCUST IN THE NEAR EAST [35]

Rome, 2 July 1965

as amended by the Commission at its Seventh Session (18-22 October 1976) and approved by the FAO Council at its Seventy-Second Session (8-10 November 1977)

PREAMBLE

The Contracting Governments, having regard to the urgent necessity of preventing losses to agriculture in certain countries in the Near East caused by the Desert Locust, hereby establish within the framework of the Food and Agriculture Organization of the United Nations (hereinafter referred to as "the Organization") a Commission to be known as the "Commission for Controlling the Desert Locust in the Near East", whose object shall be to promote national and international research and action with respect to the control of the Desert Locust in the Near East. The Near East (hereinafter referred to as "the Region") is defined, for the purpose of this Agreement, as consisting of the territories of Iraq, Jordan, Kuwait, Lebanon, Saudi Arabia, Sudan, Syrian Arab Republic, Turkey, United Arab Republic and Yemen and of other territories in the Arabian Peninsula situated south of the latitude 27 degrees north.

Article I

MEMBERSHIP

1. The Members of the Commission for Controlling the Desert Locust in the Near East (hereinafter referred to as "the Commission") shall be such Member Nations and Associate Members of the Organization situated in the Region defined in the Preamble as accept this Agreement in accordance with the provision of this Agreement.

2. The Commission may, by a two-thirds majority of its Members, admit to membership such other States, situated in the Region that are Members of the United Nations, any of its Specialized Agencies or the International Atomic Energy Agency as have submitted an application for membership of the Commission and a declaration made in a formal instrument that they accept this Agreement as in force at the time of admission.

Article II

OBLIGATIONS OF MEMBERS REGARDING NATIONAL POLICIES AND INTERNATIONAL CO-OPERATION FOR THE CONTROL OF THE DESERT LOCUST

1. Members undertake to maintain through the Secretary of the Commission a regular exchange of information on the current locust situation and the progress of control campaigns within their countries, and also to transmit such information regularly to the Desert Locust Information Service in London.

2. Members undertake to carry out all possible measures to control plagues of the Desert Locust within their countries and to reduce crop damage by adopting the following procedures:

a) maintaining a permanent locust reporting and control service;

b) holding reserves of insecticides and application equipment;

c) encouraging and supporting such training, survey and research work, including where appropriate the maintenance of national research stations for the study of the Desert Locust, as may be considered desirable by the Commission and as are compatible with the resources of the country;

d) participating in the implementation of any common policy of locust prevention which may be approved by the Commission.

e) facilitating the storage of any items of anti-locust equipment and insecticides held by the Commission and permitting the duty-free import or export without hindrance of such goods and equipment as well as the free movement within the country of such goods and equipment;

f) providing the Commission with any information it may request to carry out its functions effectively.

3. Members undertake to submit to the Commission periodic reports on the action taken to fulfil the obligations specified in paragraphs 1 and 2 above.

Article III

SEAT OF THE COMMISSION

1. The seat of the Commission shall be determined by the Commission.

2. Sessions of the Commission shall normally be held at its seat. Sessions may, however, be convened elsewhere in consultation with the Director-General of the Organization, in pursuance of a decision of the Commission at a previous session, or in exceptional circumstances, of a decision by the Executive Committee.

Article IV

FUNCTIONS OF THE COMMISSION

The following shall be the functions of the Commission:

1. *Joint Action and Assistance*

The Commission shall:

a) plan and promote joint action for the survey and control of the Desert Locust in the Region wherever required and, to this effect, arrange means whereby adequate resources can be made available;

b) assist and promote, in any manner which it considers appropriate, any national, regional or international action relating to the control or survey of the Desert Locust;

c) determine, in consultation with the Members concerned, the nature and extent of assistance needed by such Members for implementing their national programmes and for supporting regional programmes;

d) assist, at the request of any Member whose territory is faced with Desert Locust situations beyond the capacity of its national services to control and survey, in any measures jointly agreed to that may become necessary;

e) maintain at strategic localities determined by the Commission, in consultation with the Members concerned, reserves of anti-locust equipment, insecticides and other supplies, to be used in cases of emergency in accordance with decisions of the Executive Committee including supplementing of the national resources of any Member.

2. *Information and Co-ordination*

The Commission shall:

1. ensure that all Members are provided with current information in regard to Desert Locust infestations, and collect and disseminate information on experience gained, research conducted and programmes adopted on the national, regional and international levels in connection with the control of the Desert Locust;

b) assist the national research organizations of Members and co-ordinate research in the Region by arranging visits of research and survey units from Members and by other appropriate means.

3. *Co-operation*

The Commission may:

a) enter into arrangements or agreements, through the Director-General of the Organization, with nations in the Region that are not Members of the Commission, for common action in connection with survey and control of locusts in the Region;

b) enter into or encourage arrangements, through the Director-General, with other United Nations Specialized Agencies or other international organizations concerned, for common action on the study and control of locusts and for the mutual exchange of information on problems concerning locusts.

4. *Administrative Matters*

The Commission shall:

a) consider and approve the report of the Executive Committee on the activities of the Commission, the Programme and Budget of the Commission for the ensuing financial period, and the annual accounts;

b) keep the Director-General of the Organization fully informed of its activities and transmit to him the accounts, the Programme and the Budget of the Commission, the latter for submission to the Council of the Organization prior to implementation;

c) transmit to the Director-General the reports and recommendations of the Commission, for such action by the Council or Conference of the Organization as may be appropriate.

Article V

SESSIONS OF THE COMMISSION

1. Each Member of the Commission shall be represented at sessions of the Commission by a delegate who may be accompanied by an alternate and by experts and advisers. Alternates, experts and advisers may take part in the proceedings of the Commission but may not vote unless authorized by the delegate to substitute for him.

2. A majority of the Members of the Commission shall constitute a quorum. Each Member shall have one vote. Decisions of the Commission shall be taken by a majority of the votes cast except as otherwise provided for in this Agreement.

3. A Member which is in arrears in the payment of its financial contributions to the Commission shall have no vote if the amount of its arrears equals or exceeds the amount of the contributions due from it for the two preceding financial years.

4. The Commission shall elect, at the beginning of each regular session, a Chairman and a Vice-Chairman from amongst the delegates. These officers shall hold office until the beginning of the next regular session and shall be eligible for re-election.

5. The Director-General of the Organization in consultation with the Chairman of the Commission shall convene a regular session of the Commission at least once a year. Special sessions may be convened by the Director-General in consultation with the Chairman of the Commission, if so requested by the Commission in regular sessions or by at least one-third of the Members during intervals between regular sessions.

6. The Director-General of the Organization or a representative designated by him shall have the right to participate without vote in all meetings of the Commission and of the Executive Committee.

Article VI

OBSERVERS AND CONSULTANTS

1. Participation of international organizations in the work of the Commission and the relations between the Commission and such organizations shall be governed by the relevant provisions of the Constitution and the General Rules of the Organization as well as by the rules on relations with international organizations adopted by the Conference or Council of the Organization. All such relations shall be dealt with by the Director-General of the Organization.

2. Member Nations and Associate Members of the Organization that are not Members of the Commission may, upon their request, be represented by an observer at sessions of the Commission.

3. States which, while not Members of the Commission, nor Members or Associate Members of the Organization, are Members of the United Nations, any of its Specialized Agencies or the International Atomic Energy Agency may, upon request and subject to the concurrence of the Executive Committee and to the provisions

relating to the granting of observer status to nations adopted by the Conference of the Organization, be invited to attend sessions of the Commission in an observer capacity.

4. The Commission may invite consultants or experts to attend its sessions. The Executive Committee may also invite consultants or experts to attend its sessions or those of the Commission.

Article VII

SECRETARIAT

The Director-General of the Organization shall provide the Secretary and staff of the Commission, who, for administrative purposes, shall be responsible to him. They shall be appointed under the same terms and conditions as the staff of the Organization.

Article VIII

THE EXECUTIVE COMMITTEE

1. There shall be an Executive Committee composed of five Members of the Commission, elected by the Commission at each of its regular sessions. Members of the Executive Committee shall be eligible for re-election. The representative of each Member of the Executive Committee should preferably be a Locust Specialist. The Chairman of the Executive Committee shall be elected by the Commission from amongst the representatives of Members of the Committee. He shall hold office until the next regular session of the Commission and shall be eligible for re-election.

2. The Executive Committee shall meet at least once between any two successive regular sessions of the Commission. The Chairman of the Executive Committee shall, in consultation with the Chairman of the Commission and the Director-General of the Organization, convene sessions of the Committee.

3. The Secretary of the Commission shall act as Secretary of the Executive Committee.

Article IX

FUNCTIONS OF THE EXECUTIVE COMMITTEE

The Executive Committee shall:

a) make proposals to the Commission concerning policy matters and the programme of activities;

b) ensure the implementation of the policies and programmes approved by the Commission;

c) submit draft programmes of work and budget and annual accounts to the Commission;

d) prepare the draft annual report on the activities of the Commission and for transmission to the Director-General of the Organization;

e) carry out such other functions as the Commission may delegate to it.

Article X

The Commission may, by a two-thirds majority of its membership, adopt and amend its own Rule of Procedure which shall be consistent with the General Rules of the Organization. The Rules of Procedure of the Commission and any amendments thereto shall come into force upon approval by the Director-General of the Organization, and as from the date of such approval.

Article XI

FINANCE

1. Each Member of the Commission undertakes to contribute annually its share of the Budget in accordance with a scale of contributions to be adopted by a two-thirds majority of the membership of the Commission. Contributions by Members shall be made in cash.

2. The Commission may also accept contributions and donations from other sources.

3. Contributions shall be payable in currencies to be determined by the Commission after consultation with each Member and with the concurrence of the Director-General of the Organization.

4. All contributions and donations received shall be placed in a Trust Fund administered by the Director-General of the Organization in conformity with the Financial Regulations of the Organization.

Article XII

EXPENSES

1. The expenses of the Commission shall be paid out of its Budget except those relating to such staff and facilities which may be made available by the Organization. The expenses to be borne by the Organization shall be determined and paid within the limits of an annual budget prepared by the Director-General and approved by the Conference of the Organization in accordance with the Constitution, General Rules and the Financial Regulations of the Organization.

2. Expenses incurred by delegates of Members of the Commission and of their alternates and advisers, when attending sessions of the Commission, as well as the expenses incurred by observers, shall be borne by the respective governments or organizations. Expenses incurred by the representative of each Member of the Executive Committee when attending sessions of the Executive Committee shall be borne by the Commission.

3. Expenses of consultants or experts invited to attend sessions or participate in the work of the Commission or the Executive Committee shall be borne by the Commission.

4. The expenses of the Secretariat shall be borne by the Organization.

Article XIII

AMENDMENTS

1. This Agreement may be amended by a two-thirds majority of the membership of the Commission.

2. Proposals for amendments may be made by any Member of the Commission or by the Director-General of the Organization. Proposals made by a Member of the Commission shall be

addressed to both the Chairman of the Commission and the Director-General of the Organization and those made by the Director-General of the Organization shall be addressed to the Chairman of the Commission, not later than 120 days before the Session of the Commission at which the proposal is to be considered. The Director-General shall immediately inform all Members of the Commission of all proposals for amendments.

3. Any amendment to this Agreement shall require the approval of the Council of the Organization unless the Council considers it desirable to refer the amendment to the Conference of the Organization for approval.

4. Amendments not involving new obligations for Members of the Commission shall take effect from the date of the approval by the Council or Conference of the Organization, as appropriate.

5. Amendments involving new obligations for Members of the Commission shall, after approval by the Conference or Council of the Organization, come into force in respect of each Member only upon acceptance by it. The instruments of acceptance of amendments involving new obligations shall be deposited with the Director General of the Organization. The Director General shall inform all Members of the Commission and the Secretary-General of the United Nations of such acceptance. The rights and obligations of any Member of the Commission that has not accepted an amendment involving new obligations shall continue to be governed by the provisions of the Agreement in force prior to the amendment.

6. The Director-General of the Organization shall inform all Members of the Commission, all Members and Associate Members of the Organization and the Secretary-General of the United Nations of the entry into force of any amendment.

Article XIV

ACCEPTANCE

1. Acceptance of this Agreement by any Member or Associate Member of the Organization shall be effected by the deposit of an instrument of acceptance with the Director-General of the Organization and shall take effect on receipt of such instrument by the Director-General.

2. Acceptance of this Agreement by non-Member Nations of the Organization shall become effective on the date on which the Commission approves the application for membership in conformity with the provisions of Article 1 of this Agreement.

3. The Director-General of the Organization shall inform all Members of the Commission, all Members and Associate Members of the Organization and the Secretary-General of the United Nations of all acceptances that have become effective.

4. Acceptance of this Agreement may be made subject to reservations which shall become effective only upon unanimous approval by the Members of the Commission. The Director-General of the Organization shall notify forthwith all Members of the Commission of any reservations. Members of the Commission not having replied within three months from the date of the notification shall be deemed to have accepted the reservation. Failing such approval, the nation making the reservation shall not become a party to this Agreement.

Article XV

TERRITORIAL APPLICATION

The Members of the Commission shall, when accepting this Agreement, state explicity to which territories their participation shall extend. In the absence of such a declaration, participation shall be deemed to apply to all the territories for the international relations of which the Member is responsible. Subject to the provisions of Article XVII-2, the scope of the territorial application may be modified by a subsequent declaration.

Article XVI

INTERPRETATION AND SETTLEMENT OF DISPUTES

Any dispute regarding the interpretation or application of this Agreement, if not settled by the Commission, shall be referred to a Committee composed of one member appointed by each of the parties to the dispute, and in addition an independent chairman chosen by the members of the Committee. The recommendations of such a Committee, while not binding in character, shall become the basis for renewed consideration by the parties concerned of the matter out of which the disagreement arose. If as the result of this procedure the dispute is not settled, it shall be referred to the International Court of Justice in accordance with the Statute of the Court, unless the parties to the dispute agree to another method of settlement.

Article XVII

WITHDRAWAL

1. Any Member may withdraw from the Commission at any time after the expiration of one year from the date on which its acceptance took effect or from the date on which the Agreement entered into force, whichever is the later, by giving written notice of withdrawal to both the Chairman of the Commission and the Director-General of the Organization. The Director-General shall forthwith inform all Members of the Commission, all Member Nations and Associate Members of the Organization and the Secretary-General of the United Nations of the receipt of any notice of withdrawal. The withdrawal shall become effective one year from the date of receipt by the Director-General of the Organization of the notification of withdrawal.

2. A Member of the Commission may give notice of withdrawal with respect to one or more of the territories for the international relations of which it

is responsible. When a Member gives notice of its own withdrawal from the Commission, it shall state to which territory or territories the wirthdrawal is to apply. In the absence of such a declaration, the withdrawal shall be deemed to apply to all the territories for the international relations of which the Member of the Commission is responsible, except that such withdrawal shall not be deemed to apply to an Associate Member.

3. Any Member of the Commission that gives notice of withdrawal from the Organization shall be deemed to apply to all the territories for the international relations of which the Member concerned is responsible, except that such withdrawal shall not be deemed to apply to an Associate Member.

Article XVIII

TERMINATION

1. This Agreement shall be considered terminated if and when the number of Members of the Commission falls below three, unless the remaining two Members of the Commission decide to continue, with the approval of the Conference of the Organization. The Director-General of the Organization shall inform all Members of the Commission, all Members and Associate Members of the Organization and the Secretary-General of the United Nations of such termination.

2. On termination of the Agreement all assests of the Commission shall be liquidated by the Director-General of the Organization and after settlement of the liabilites the balance shall be distributed proportionately amongst Members on the basis of the scale of contributions in force at the time. Nations whose contributions are in arrears for two consecutive years shall not be entitled to a share of the assests.

Article XIX

ENTRY INTO FORCE

1. This Agreement shall enter into force as soon as three eligible Members or Associate Members of the Organization have become parties to it by the deposit of an instrument of acceptance in accordance with the provisions of Article XIV of this Agreement.

2. The Director-General shall notify all Nations having deposited instruments of acceptance as well as all Member Nations and Associate Members of the Organization and the Secretary-General of the United Nations of the date on which this Agreeement comes into force.

Article XX

AUTHENTIC LANGUAGES

The English, French and Spanish texts of this Agreement shall be equally authentic.

INTERNATIONAL CONVENTION FOR THE CONSERVATION OF ATLANTIC TUNAS [36]

Rio de Janeiro, 14 May 1966

The Government whose duly authorized representatives have subscribed hereto, considering their mutual interest in the populations of tuna and tuna-like fishes found in the Atlantic Ocean, and desiring to co-operate in maintaining the populations of these fishes at levels which will permit the maximum sustainable catch for food and other purposes, resolve to conclude a Convention for the coservation of the resources of tuna and tuna-like fishes of the Atlantic Ocean, and to that end agree as follows:

Article I

The area to which this Convention shall apply, hereinafter referred to as the "Convention area" shall be all waters of the Atlantic Ocean, including the adjacent Seas.

Article II

Nothing in this Conventior shall be considered as affecting the rights, claims or view of any Contracting Party in regard to the limits of territorial waters or the extent of jurisdiction over fisheries under international law.

Article III

1. The Contracting Parties hereby agree to establish and maintain a Commission to be known as the International Commission for the Conservation of Atlantic Tunas, hereinafter referred to as "the Commission", which shall carry out the objectives set forth in this Convention.

2. Each of the Contracting Parties shall be represented on the Commission by not more than three Delegates. Such Delegates may be assisted by experts and advisors.

3. Except as may otherwise be provided in this Convention, decisions of the Commission shall be taken by a majority of the Contracting Parties, each Contracting Party having one vote. Two-thirds of the Contracting Parties shall constitute a quorum.

4. The Commission shall hold a regular meeting once every two years. A special meeting may be called at any time at the request of a majority of the Contracting Parties or by decision of the Council as constituted in Article V.

5. At its first meeting, and thereafter at each regular meeting, the Commission shall elect from among its Members a Chairman, a first Vice-Chairman and a second Vice-Chairman who shall not be re-elected for more than one term.

6. The meetings of the Commission and its subsidiary bodies shall be public unless the Commission otherwise decides.

7. **The official languages of the Commission shall be English, French and Spanish.**

8. The Commission shall have authority to adopt such rules of procedure and financial regulations as are necessary to carry out its functions.

9. The Commission shall submit a report to the Contracting Parties every two years on its work and findings and shall also inform any Contracting Party, whenever requested, on any matter relating to the objectives of the Convention.

Article IV

1. In order to carry out the objectives of this Convention the Commission shall be responsible for the study of the populations of tuna and tuna-like fishes (the Scombriformes with the exception of the families Trichiuridae and Gempylidae and the genus *Scomber*) and such other species of fishes exploited in tuna fishing in the Convention area as are not under investigation by another international fishery organization. Such study shall include research on the abundance, biometry and ecology of the fishes; the oceanography of their environment; and the effects of natural and human factors upon their abundance. The Commission, in carrying out these responsibilities shall, insofar as feasible, utilise the technical and scientific services of, and information from, official agencies of the Contracting Parties and their political subdivisions and may, when desirable, utilize the available services and information of any public or private institution, organization or individual, and may undertake within the limits of its budget independent research to supplement the research work being done by governments, national institutions or other international organizations.

2. The carrying out of the provisions in paragraph 1 of this Article shall include:

a) collecting and analysing statistical information relating to the current conditions and trends of the tuna fishery resources of the Convention area;

b) studying and appraising information concerning measures and methods to ensure maintenance of the populations of tuna and tuna-like fishes in the Convention area at levels which will permit the maximum sustainable catch and which will ensure the effective exploitation of these fishes in a manner consistent with this catch;

c) recommending studies and investigations to the Contracting Parties;

d) publishing and otherwise disseminating reports of its findings and statistical, biological and other scientific information relative to the tuna fisheries of the Convention area.

Article V

1. There is established within the Commission a Council which shall consist of the Chairman and the Vice-Chairman of the Commission together with the representatives of not less than four and not more than eight Contracting Parties. The Contracting Parties represented on the Council shall be elected at each regular meeting of the Commission. However, if at any time the number of the Contracting Parties exceeds forty, the Commission may elect an additional two Contracting Parties to be represented on the Council. The Contracting Parties of which the Chairman and Vice-Chairman are nationals shall not be elected to the Council. In elections to the Council the Commission shall give due consideration to the geographic, tuna fishing and tuna processing interests of the Contracting Parties, as well as to the equal right of the Contracting Parties to be represented on the Council.

2. The Council shall perform such functions as are assigned to it by this Convention or are designated by the Commission, and shall meet at least once in the interim between regular meetings of the Commission. Between meetings of the Commission the Council shall make necessary decisions on the duties to be carried out by the staff and shall issue necessary instructions to the Executive Secretary. Decisions of the Council shall be made in accordance with rules to be established by the Commission.

Article VI

To carry out the objectives of this Convention the Commission may establish Panels on the basis of species, group of species, or of geographic areas. Each Panel in such case:

a) shall be responsible for keeping under review the species, group of species, or geographic area under its purview, and for collecting scientific and other information relating thereto;

b) may propose to the Commission, upon the basis of scientific investigations, recommendations for joint action by the Contracting Parties;

c) may recommend to the Commission studies and investigations necessary for obtaining information relating to its species, group of species or geographic area, as well as the co-ordination of programmes of investigation by the Contracting Parties.

Article VII

The Commission shall appoint an Executive Secretary who shall serve at the pleasure of the Commission. The Executive Secretary, subject to such rules and procedures as may be determined by the Commission, shall have authority with respect to the selection and administration of the staff of the Commission. He shall also perform, *inter alia*, the following functions as the Commission may prescribe:

a) co-ordinating the programmes of investigation by the Contracting Parties;

b) preparing budget estimates for review by the Commission;

c) authorising the disbursement of funds in accordance with the Commission's budget;

d) accounting for the funds of the Commission;

e) arranging for co-operation with the organizations referred to in Article XI of this Convention;

f) preparing the collection and analysis of data necessary to accomplish the purposes of the

Convention particularly those data relating to the current and maximum sustainable catch of tuna stocks;

g) preparing for approval by the Commission scientific, administrative and other reports of the Commission and its subsidiary bodies.

Article VIII

1. *a*) The Commission may, on the basis of scientific evidence, make recommendations designed to maintain the populations of tuna and tuna-like fishes that may be taken in the Convention area at levels which will permit the maximum sustainable catch. These recommendations shall be applicable to the Contracting Parties under the conditions laid down in paragraphs 2 and 3 of this Article.

b) The recommendations referred to above shall be made:

(i) at the initiative of the Commission if an appropriate Panel has not been established or with the approval of at least two-thirds of all the Contracting Parties if an appropriate Panel has been established;

(ii) on the proposal of an appropriate Panel if such a Panel has been established;

(iii) on the proposal of the appropriate Panels if the recommendation in question relates to more than one geographic area, species or group of species.

2. Each recommendation made under paragraph 1 of this Article shall become effective for all Contracting Parties six months after the date of the notification from the Commission transmitting the recommendation to the Contracting Parties, except as provided in paragraph 3 of this Article.

3. *a*) If any Contracing Party in the case of a recommendation made under paragraph 1 (*b*) (*i*) above, or any Contracting Party member of a Panel concerned in the case of a recommendation made under paragraph 1 (*b*) (*ii*) or (*iii*) above, presents to the Commission an objection to such recommendation within the six months period provided for in paragraph 2 above, the recommendation shall not become effective for an additional sixty days.

b) Thereupon any other Contracting Party may present an objection prior to the expiration of the additional sixty days period, or within forty-five days of the date of the notification of an objection made by another Contracting Party within such additional sixty days, whichever date shall be the later.

c) The recommendation shall become effective at the end of the extended period or periods for objection, except for those Contracting Parties that have presented an objection.

d) However, if a recommendation has met with an objection presented by only one or less than one-fourth of the Contracting Parties, in accordance with subparagraphs (*a*) and (*b*) above, the Commission shall immediately notify the Contracting Party or Parties having presented such objection that it is to be considered as having no effect.

e) In the case referred to in subparagraph (*d*) above the Contracting Party or Parties concerned shall have an additional period of sixty days from the date of said notification in which to reaffirm their objection. On the expiry of this period the recommendation shall become effective, except with respect to any Contracting Party having presented an objection and reaffirmed it within the delay provided for.

f) If a recommendation has met with objection from more than one-fourth but less than the majority of the Contracting Parties, in accordance with subparagraphs (*a*) and (*b*) above, the recommendation shall become effective for the Contracting Parties that have not presented an objection thereto.

g) If objections have been presented by a majority of the Contracting Parties the recommendation shall not become effective.

4. Any Contracting Party objecting to a recommendation may at any time withdraw that objection, and the recommendation shall become effective with respect to such Contracting Party immediately if the recommendation is already in effect, or at such time as it may become effective under the terms of this Article.

5. The Commission shall notify each Contracting Party immediately upon receipt of each objection and of each withdrawal of an objection, and of the entry into force of any recommendation.

Article IX

1. The Contracting Parties agree to take all action necessary to ensure the enforcement of this Convention. Each Contracting Party shall transmit to the Commission, biennially or at such other times as may be required by the Commission, a statement of the action taken by it for these purposes.

2. The Contracting Parties agree:

a) to furnish, on the request of the Commission, any available statistical, biological and other scientific information the Commission may need for the purposes of this Convention;

b) when their official agencies are unable to obtain and furnish the said information, to allow the Commission, through the Contracting Parties, to obtain it on a voluntary basis direct from companies and individual fishermen.

3. The Contracting Parties undertake to collaborate with each other with a view to the adoption of suitable effective measures to ensure the application of the provisions of this Convention and in particular to set up a system of international enforcement to be applied to the Convention area except the territorial sea and other waters, if any, in which a State is entitled under international law to exercise jurisdiction over fisheries.

Article X

1. The Commission shall adopt a budget for the

joint expenses of the Commission for the biennium following each regular meeting.

2. Each Contracting Party shall contribute annually to the budget of the Commission an amount equal to:

a) U.S. $ 1,000 (one thousand United States dollars) for Commission membership.

b) U.S.$ 1,000 (one thousand United States dollars) for each Panel membership.

c) If the proposed budget for joint expenses for any biennium should exceed the whole amount of contributions to be made by the Contracting Parties under (*a*) and (*b*) of this paragraph, one-third of the amount of such excess shall be contributed by the Contracting Parties in proportion to their contributions made under (*a*) and (*b*) of this paragraph. For the remaining two-thirds the Commission shall determine on the basis of the latest available information:

(i) the total of the round weight of catch of Atlantic tuna and tuna-like fishes and the net weight of canned products of such fishes for each Contracting Party;

(ii) the total of (*i*) for all Contracting Parties. Each Contracting Party shall contribute its share of the remaining two-thirds in the same ratio that its total in (*i*) bears to the total in (*ii*). That part of the budget referred to in this sub-paragraph shall be set by agreement of all the Contracting Parties present and voting.

3. The Council shall review the second half of the biennial budget at its regular meeting between Commission meetings and, on the basis of current and anticipated developments, may authorize reapportionment of amounts in the Commission budget for the second year within the total budget approved by the Commission.

4. The Executive Secretary of the Commission shall notify each Contracting Party of its yearly assessment. The contributions shall be payable on January first of the year for which the assessment was levied. Contributions not received before January first of the succeeding year shall be considered as in arrears.

5. Contributions to the biennial budget shall be payable in such currencies as the Commission may decide.

6. At its first meeting the Commission shall approve a budget for the balance of the first year the Commission functions and for the following biennium. It shall immediately transmit to the Contracting Parties copies of these budgets together with notices of the respective assessments for the first annual contribution.

7. Thereafter, within a period not less than sixty days before the regular meeting of the Commission which precedes the biennium, the Executive Secretary shall submit to each Contracting Party a draft biennial budget together with a schedule of proposed assessments.

8. The Commission may suspend the voting rights of any Contracting Party when its arrears of contributions equal or exceed the amount due from it for the two preceding years.

9. The Commission shall establsih a Working Capital Fund to finance operations of the Commission prior to receiving annual contributions, and for such other purposes as the Commission may determine. The Commission shall determine the level of the Fund, assess advances necessary for its establsihment, and adopt regulations governing the use of the Fund.

10. The Commission shall arrange an annual independent audit of the Commission's accounts. The reports of such audits shall be reviewed and approved by the Commission, or by the Council in years when there is no regular Commission meeting.

11. The Commission may accept contributions, other than provided for in paragraph 2 of this Article, for the prosecution of its work.

Article XI

1. The Contracting Parties agree that there should be a working relationship between the Commission and the Food and Agriculture Organization of the United Nations. To this end the Commision shall enter into negotiations with the Food and Agriculture Organization of the United Nations with a view to concluding an agreement pursuant to Article XIII of the Organization's Constitution. Such agreement should provide, *inter alia*, for the Director-General of the Food and Agriculture Organization of the United Nations to appoint a Representative who would participate in all meetings of the Commission and its subsidiary bodies, but without the right to vote.

2. The Contracting Parties agree that there should be co-operation between the Commission and other international fisheries commissions and scientific organizations which might contribute to the work of the Commission. The Commission may enter into agreements with such commissions and organizations.

3. The Commissions may invite any appropriate international organization and any Government which is a Member of the United Nations or of any Specialized Agency of the United Nations and which is not a member of the Commission, to send observers to meetings of the Commission and its subsidiary bodies.

Article XII

1. The Convention shall remain in force for ten years and thereafter until a majority of Contracting Parties agree to terminate it.

2. At any time after ten years from the date of entry into force of this Convention, any Contracting Party may withdraw from the Convention on December thirty-first of any year including the tenth year by written notification of withdrawal given on or before December thirty-first of the preceding year to the Director-General of the Food and Agriculture Organization of the United Nations.

3. Any other Contracting Party may thereupon withdraw from this Convention with effect from the same December thirty-first by giving written notification of withdrawal to the Director-General of the Food and Agriculture Organization of the United Nations not later than one month from the date of receipt of information from the Director-General of the Food and Agriculture Organization of the United Nations concerning any withdrawal, but not later than April first of that year.

Article XIII

1. Any Contracting Party or the Commission may propose amendments to this Convention. The Director-General of the Food and Agriculture Organization of the United Nations shall transmit a certified copy of the text of any proposed amendment to all the Contracting Parties. Any amendment not involving new obligations shall take effect for all Contracting Parties on the thirtieth day after its acceptance by three-fourths of the Contracting Parties. Any amendment involving new obligations shall take effect for each Contracting Party accepting the amendment on the ninetieth day after its acceptance by three-fourths of the Contracting Parties and thereafter for each remaining Contracting Party upon acceptance by it. Any amendment considered by one or more Contracting Parties to involve new obligations shall be deemed to involve new obligations and shall take effect accordingly. A government which becomes a Contracting Party after an amendment to this Convention has been opened for acceptance pursuant to the provisions of this Article shall be bound by the Convention as amended when the said amendment comes into force.

2. Proposed amendments shall be deposited with the Director-General of the Food and Agriculture Organization of the United Nations. Notifications of acceptance of amendments shall be deposited with the Director-General of the Food and Agriculture Organization of the United Nations.

Article XIV

1. This Convention shall be open for signature by any Government which is a Member of the United Nations or of any Specialized Agency of the United Nations. Any such Government which does not sign this Convention may adhere to it at any time.

2. This Convention shall be subject to ratification or approval by signatory countries in accordance with their constitutions. Instruments of ratification, approval, or adherence shall be deposited with the Director-General of the Food and Agriculture Organization of the United Nations.

3. This Convention shall enter into force upon the deposit of instruments of ratification, approval, or adherence by seven Governments and shall enter into force with respect to each Government which subsequently deposits an instrument of ratification, approval or adherence on the date of such deposit.

Article XV

The Director-General of the Food and Agriculture Organization of the United Nations shall inform all Governments referred to in paragraph 1 of Article XIV of deposits of instruments of ratification approval or adherence, the entry into force of this Convention, proposals for amendments, notifications of acceptance of amendments, entry into force of amendments, and notifications of withdrawal.

Article XVI

The original of this Convention shall be deposited with the Director-General of the Food and Agriculture Organization of the United Nations who shall send certified copies to the Governments referred to in paragraph 1 of Article XIV.

In Witness Whereof the representatives duly authorized by their respective Governments have signed the present Convention. Done at Rio de Janeiro this fourteenth day of May 1966 in a single copy in the English, French and Spanish languages, each version being equally authoritative.

Annex II

RESOLUTION ON THE COLLECTION OF STATISTICS ON THE ATLANTIC TUNA FISHERIES

THE CONFERENCE

Taking note of documents FID: AT/66/4, Annex 6, and FID: AT/66/INF-5 relating to the collection and publication of statistics on Atlantic tuna fisheries; and

Agreeing that it is essential that all countries fishing these Atlantic tuna resources should collect adequate statistics on catch and fishing effort and the necessary biological data, and make available for publication the statistical and related economic data with a view to enabling the International Commission for the Conservation of Atlantic Tunas to fulfil its functions adequately as soon as it is established;

Urges all countries to take steps without delay to create, where they do not already exist, offices within their fisheries administrations suitably staffed and having appropriate financial and legislative support to undertake the collection and the processing of the data to be used by the Commission; and

Suggests that all countries faced with the task of establishing and operating such offices, give priority to requests for assistance in this connection through the United Nations Development Programme and through the regular programme of the Food and Agriculture Organization of the United Nations.

AFRICAN CONVENTION ON THE CONSERVATION OF NATURE AND NATURAL RESOURCES [37]

Algiers, 15 September 1968

PREAMBLE:

We the Heads of State and Government of Independent African States,

Fully conscious that soil, water, flora and faunal resources constitute a capital of vital importance to mankind;

Confirming, as we accepted upon declaring our adherence to the Charter of the Organization of African Unity, that we know that it is our duty "to harness the natural and human resources of our continent for the total advancement of our peoples in spheres of human endeavour";

Fully conscious of the ever-growing importance of natural resources from an economic, nutritional, scientific, educational, cultural and aesthetic point of view;

Conscious of the dangers which threaten some of these irreplaceable assets;

Accepting that the utilization of the natural resources must aim at satisfying the needs of man according to the carrying capacity of the environment;

Desirous of undertaking individual and joint action for the conservation, utilization and development of these assets by establishing and maintaining their rational utilization for the present and future welfare of mankind;

Convinced that one of the most appropriate means of achieving this end is to bring into force a convention;

Have agreed as follows;

Article I

The Contracting States hereby establish an African Convention on the Conservation of Nature and Natural Resources.

Article II

FUNDAMENTAL PRINCIPLE

The Contracting States shall undertake to adopt the measures to ensure conservation, utilization and development of soil, water, flora and faunal resources in accordance with scientific principles and with due regard to the best interests of the people.

Article III

DEFINITIONS

For purposes of the present Convention, the meaning of the following expressions shall be as defined below:

1. "Natural Resources" means renewable resources, that is soil, water, flora and fauna.

2. "Specimen" means an individual example of a species of wild animals or wild plant or part of a wild plant.

3. "Trophy" means any dead animal specimen or part thereof whether included in a manufactured or processed object or otherwise dealt with, unless it has lost its original identity; also nests, eggs and eggshells.

4. "Conservation area" means any protected natural resource area, whether it be a strict natural reserve, a national park or a special reserve;

a) "strict nature reserve" means an area:

(i) under State control and the boundaries of which may not be altered nor any portion alienated except by the competent legislative authority,

(ii) throughout which any form of hunting or fishing, any undertaking connected with forestry, agriculture or mining, any grazing, any excavation or prospecting, drilling, levelling of the ground or construction, any work tending to alter the configuration of the soil or the character of the vegetation, any water pollution and, generally, any act likely to harm or disturb the fauna or flora, including intróduction of zoological or botanical species, whether indigenous or imported, wild or domesticated, are strictly forbidden.

(iii) where it shall be forbidden to reside, enter, traverse or camp, and where it shall be forbidden to fly over at low altitude, without a special written permit from the competent authority, and in which scientific investigations (including removal of animals and plants in order to maintain an ecosystem) may only be undertaken by permission of the competent authority;

b) "national park" means an area:

(i) under State control and the boundaries of which may not be altered or any portion alienated except by the competent legislative authority,

(ii) exclusively set aside for the propagation, protection, conservation and management of vegetation and wild animals as well as for the protection of sites, land-scapes or geological formations of particular scientific or aesthetic value, for the benefit and enjoyment of the general public, and

(iii) in which the killing, hunting and capture of animals and the destruction or collection of plants are prohibited except for scientific and management purposes and on the condition that such measures are taken under the direction or control of the competent authority;

(iv) covering any aquatic environment to which all of the provisions of section (*b*) (i-iii) above are applicable.

The activities prohibited in "strict nature reserve" under the provisions of section (*a*) (ii) of paragraph (4) of this article are equally prohibited in national parks except in so far as they are necessary to enable the park authorities to implement the provisions of section (ii) of this paragraph, by applying, for example, appropriate management practices, and to enable the public to visit these parks; however, sport fishing may be practised with the authorization and under the control of the competent authority;

c) "special reserve" means other protected areas such as:

(i) "game reserve" which shall denote an area

a) set aside for the conservation, management and propagation of wild animal life and the protection and management of its habitat,

b) within which the hunting, killing or capture of fauna shall be prohibited except by or under the direction or control of the reserve authorities,

c) where settlement and other human activities shall be controlled or prohobited:

(ii) "partial reserve" or "sanctuary" which shall denote an area

a) set aside to protect characteristicwildlife and especially bird communities, or to protect particularly threatened animal or plant species and especially those listed in the Annex to this Convention, together with the biotopes essential for their survival.

b) in which all other interests and activities shall be subordinated to this end;

(iii) "soil" "water" or "forest" reserve shall denote areas set aside to protect such resources.

Article IV

SOIL

The Contracting States shall take effective measures for conservation and improvement of the soil and shall in particular combat erosion and misuse of the soil. To this end:

a) they shall establish land-use plans based on scientific investigations (ecological, pedological, economic, and sociological) and, in particular, classification and land-use capability;

b) they shall, when implementing agricultural practices and agarian reforms,

(i) improve soil conservation and introduce improved farming methods, which ensure long-term productivity of the land,

(ii) control erosion caused by various forms of land-use which may lead to loss of vegetation cover.

Article V

WATER

1. The Contracting States shall establish policies for conservation, utilization and development of underground and surface water, and shall endeavour to guarantee for their populations a sufficient and continouos supply of suitable water, taking appropriate measures with due regard to:

(i) the study of water cycles and the investigation of each catchment area,

(ii) the co-ordination and planning of water resources development projects,

(iii) the administration and control of all water utilization, and

(iv) prevention and control of water pollution.

2. Where surface of underground water resources are shared by two or more of the Contracting States, the latter shall act in consultation, and if the need arises, set up inter-State Commissions to study and resolve problems arising from the joint use of these resources, and for the joint development and conservation thereof.

Article VI

FLORA

1. The Contracting States shall take all necessary measures for the protection of flora and to ensure its best utilization and development. To this end the Contracting States shall:

a) adopt scientifically-based conservation, utilization and management plans of forests and rangeland, taking into account the social and economic needs of the States concerned, the importance of the vegetation cover for the maintenance of the water balance of any area, the productivity of soils and the habitat requirements of the fauna;

b) observe section (*a*) above by paying particular attention to controlling bush fires, forest exploitation, land clearing for cultivation, and over-grazing by domestic and wild animals;

c) set aside areas for forest reserves and carry out aforestation programmes where necessary;

d) limitation of forest grazing to season and intensities that will not prevent forest regeneration; and

e) establish botanical gardens to perpetuate plant species of particular interest.

2. The Contracting States also shall undertake the conservation of plant species or communities, which are threatened and/or of special scientific or aesthetic value by ensuring that they are included in conservation areas.

Article VII

FAUNAL RESOURCES

1. The Contracting States shall ensure conservation, wise use and development of faunal resources and their environmental, within the framework of land-use planning and of economic and social development. Management shall be carried out in accordance with plans based on scientific principles, and to that end the Contracting States shall:

a) manage wildlife populations inside designated areas according to the objectives of such areas and also manage exploitable wildllife populations outside such areas for an optimum sustained yield, compatible with the complementary to other land uses; and

b) manage aquatic environments, whether in fresh, brackish or coastal water, with a view to minimise deleterious effects of any water and land use practice which might adversely affect aquatic habitats.

2. The Contracting States shall adopt adequate legislation on hunting, capture and fishing, under which:

a) the issue of permits is properly regulated;

b) unauthorized methods are prohibited;

c) the following methods of hunting, capture and fishing are prohibited:

(i) any method liable to cause a mass destruction of wild animals,

(ii) the use of drugs, poisons, poisoned weapons or poisoned baits,

(iii) the use of explosives;

(iv) the following methods of hunting and capture are particularly prohibited:

(1) the use of mechanically propelled vehicles;

(2) the use of fire;

(3) the use of fire arms capable of firing more than one round at each pull of the trigger;

(4) hunting or capture at night;

(5) the use of missiles containing detonators;

d) the following methods of hunting or capture are as far as possible prohibited:

(i) the use of nets and stockades,

(ii) the use of concealed traps, pits, snares setgun traps, deadfalls, and hunting from a blind or hide;

e) (iii) with a view to as rational use as possible of game meat, the abandonment by hunters of carcasses of animals, which represent a food resource, is prohibited.

Capture of animals with the aid of drugs or mechanically propelled vehicles, or hunting or capture by night if carried out by, or under the control of, the competent authority shall nevertheless be exempted from the prohibitions under (*c*) above.

Article VIII

PROTECTED SPECIES

1. The Contracting States recognize that it is important and urgent to accord a special protection to those animal and plant species that are threatened with extinction, or which may become so, and to the habitat necessary to their survival. Where such a species is represented only in the territory of one Contracting State, that State has a particular responsibility for its protection. These species which are, or may be listed, according to the degree of protection that shall be given to them are placed in Class A or B of the Annex to this Convention, and shall be protected by Contracting States as follows:

(i) species in Class A shall be totally protected throughout the entire territory of the Contracting States; the hunting, killing, capture or collection of specimens shall be permitted only on the authorization in each case of the highest competent authority and only if required in the national interest or for scientific purposes; and

(ii) species in Class B shall be totally protected, but may be hunted, killed, captured or collected under special authorization granted by the competent authority.

2. The competent authority of each Contracting State shall examine the necessity of applying the provisions of this article to species not listed in the annex, in order to conserve the indigenous flora and fauna of their respective countries. Such additional species shall be placed in Class A or B by the state concerned, according to its specific requirements.

Article IX

TRAFFIC IN SPECIMENS AND TROPHIES

1. In the case of animal species to which Article VIII does not apply the Contracting States shall:

a) regulate trade in and transport of specimens and trophies;

b) control the application of these regulations in such a way as to prevent trade in specimens and trophies which have been illegally captured or killed or obtained.

2. In the case of plant and animal species to which Article VIII paragraph (1) applies, the Contracting States shall:

a) take all measures similar to those in paragraph (1);

b) make the export of such specimens and trophies subject to an authorization;

(i) additional to that required for their capture, killing or collection by Article VIII,

(ii) which indicates their destination,

(iii) which shall not be given unless the specimens or trophies have been obtained legally,

(iv) which shall be examined prior to exportation;

(v) which shall be on a standard form, as may be arranged under Article XVI;

c) make the import and transit of such specimens and trophies subject to the presentation of the authorization required under section (*b*) above with due provision for the confiscation of specimens and trophies exported illegally, without prejudice to the application of other penalties.

Article X

CONSERVATION AREAS

1. The Contracting States shall maintain and extend where appropriate, within their territory and where applicable in their territorial waters, the Conservation areas existing at the time of entry into force of the present Convention and, preferably within the framework of land-use planning programmes, assess the necessity of establishing additional conservation areas in order to:

(i) protect those ecosystems which are most representative of and particularly those which are in any respect peculiar to their territories,

(ii) ensure conservation of all species and more particularly of those listed or which may be listed in the annex to this Convention;

2. The Contracting States shall establish, where necessary, around the borders of conservation areas, zones within which the competent authorities shall control activities detrimental to the protected natural resources.

Article XI

CUSTOMARY RIGHTS

The Contracting States shall take all necessary

legislative measures to reconcile customary rights with the provisions of this Convention.

Article XII

RESEARCH

The Contracting States shall encourage and promote research in conservation, utilization and management of natural resources and shall pay particular attention to ecological and sociological factors.

Article XIII

CONSERVATION EDUCATION

1. *a*) The Contracting States shall ensure that their peoples appreciate their close dependence on natural resources and that they understand the need, and rules for, the rational utilization of these resources.

b) For this purpose they shall ensure that the principles indicated in paragraph (1):

(i) are included in educational programmes at all levels,

(ii) form the object of information campaigns capable of acquainting the public with, and winning it over to, the idea of conservation.

2. In order to put into effect paragraph (1) above, the Contracting States shall make maximum use of the educational value of conservation areas.

Article XIV

DEVELOPMENT PLANS

1. The Contracting States shall ensure that conservation and management of natural resources are treated as an integral part of national and/or regional development plans.

2. In the formulation of all development plans, full consideration shall be given to ecological, as well as to economic and social factors.

3. Where any development plan is likely to affect the natural resources of another State, the latter shall be consulted.

Article XV

ORGANIZATION OF NATIONAL CONSERVATION SERVICES

Each Contracting State shall establish, if it has not already done so, a single agency empowered to deal with all matters covered by this Convention, but, where this is not possible a co-ordinating machinery shall be established for this purpose.

Article XVI

INTER-STATE CO-OPERATION

1. The Contracting States shall co-operate:

a) whenever such co-operation is necessary to give effect to the provisions of this Convention and

b) whenever any national measure is likely to affect the natural resources of any other State.

2. The Contracting States shall supply the Organization of African Unity with:

a) the text of laws, decrees, regulations and instructions in force in their territories, which are intended to ensure the implementation of this Convention,

b) reports on the results achieved in applying the provisions of this Convention, and

c) all the information necessary for the complete documentation of matters dealt with by this Convention if requested.

3. If so requested by Contracting States, the Organization of African Unity shall organize any meeting which may be necessary to dispose of any matters covered by this Convention. Requests for such meetings must be made by at least three of the Contracting States and be approved by two-thirds of the States which it is proposed should participate in such meetings.

4. Any expenditure arising from this Convention, which devolves upon the Organization of African Unity shall be included in its regular budget, unless shared by the Contracting States or otherwise defrayed.

Article XVII

PROVISION FOR EXCEPTIONS

1. The provisions of this Convention shall not affect the responsibilities of Contracting States concerning:

(i) the paramount interest of the State,

(ii) "force majeure",

(iii) defence of human life

2. The provisions of this Convention shall not prevent Contracting States:

(i) in time of famine,

(ii) for the protection of public health,

(iii) in defence of property.

to enact measures contrary to the provisions of the Convention, provided their application is precisely defined in respect of aim, time and place.

Article XVIII

SETTLEMENT OF DISPUTES

Any dispute between the Contracting States relating to the interpretation or application of this Convention which cannot be settled by negotiation, shall at the request of any party be submitted to the Commission of Mediation, Conciliation and Arbitration of the Organization of African Unity.

Article XIX

SIGNATURE AND RATIFICATION

1. This Convention shall be open for signature immediately after being approved by the Assembly of Heads of State and Government of the Organization of African Unity.

2. This Convention shall be ratified by each of the Contracting States. The instruments of ratification shall be deposited with the Administrative Secretary General of the Organization of African Unity.

Article XX

RESERVATIONS

1. At the time of signature, ratification or

accession, any State may declare its acceptance of this Convention in part only, provided that such reservation may not apply to the provisions of Articles II-XI.

2. Reservations made in conformity with the preceding paragraph shall be deposited together with the instruments of ratification or accession.

3. Any Contracting State which has formulated a reservation in conformity with the preceding paragraph may at any time withdraw it by notifying the Administrative Secretary-General of the Organization of African Unity.

Article XXI

ENTRY INTO FORCE

1. This Convention shall come into force on the thirtieth day following the date of deposit of the fourth instrument of ratification or accession with the Administrative Secretary-General of the Organization of African Unity, who shall inform participating States accordingly.

2. In the case of a State ratifing or acceding to the Convention after the depositing of the fourth instrument of ratification or accesssion, the Convention shall come into force on the thirtieth day after the deposit by such of its instrument of ratification or accession.

3. The London Convention of 1933 or any other Convention on the conservation of flora and fauna in their natural state shall cease to have effect in States in which this Convention has come into force.

Article XXII

ACCESSION

1. After the date of approval specified in Article XIX paragraph (1), this Convention shall be open to accession by any independent and sovereign African State.

2. The instruments of accession shall be deposited with the Administrative Secretary-General of the Organization of African Unity.

Article XXIII

DENUNCIATION

1. Any Contracting State may denounce this Convention by notification in writing addressed to the Administrative Secretary-General of the Organization of African Unity.

2. Such denunciation shall take effect, for such a State, one year after the date of receipt of its notification by the Administrative Secretary-General of the Organization of African Unity.

3. No denunciation shall, however, be made before the expiry of a period of five years from the date at which for the State concerned this Convention came into force.

Article XXIV

REVISION

1. After the expiry of a period of five years from the date of entry into force of this Convention, any Contracting State may at any time make a request for the revision of part or the whole of this Convention by notification in writing addressed to the Administrative Secretary-General of the Organization of African Unity.

2. In the event of such a request the appropriate organ of the Organization of African Unity shall deal with the matter in accordance with the provisions of section 3 of Article XVI of this Convention.

3.(i) At the request of one or more Contracting States and notwithstanding the provisions of paragraph (1) and (2) of this Article, the annex to this Convention may be revised or added to by the appropriate organ of the Organization of African Unity.

(ii) Such revision or addition shall come into force three months after the approval by the appropriate organ of the Organization of African Unity.

Article XXV

FINAL PROVISIONS

The original of this Convention of which both the English and the French texts are authentic, shall be deposited with the Administrative Secretary-General of the Organization of African Unity.

In Witness Whereof we the Heads of State and Government of Independent African States, assembled at Algiers, Algeria, on 15 September 1968, have signed this Convention.

List of Protected Species
Class A

MAMMALIA	MAMMALS
PRIMATES	PRIMATES
Lemuroidae	All Malagasy lemuroids
Macaca sylvana	Barbary ape
Theropithecus gelada	Gelada baboon
Cercocebus galeritus galeritus	Tana River mangabey
Cercopithecus diana	Diana monkey
Colobus badius kirkii	Zanzibar red colobus
Colobus badius ruformitratus	Tana River red colobus
Colobus badius gordonorum	Uhehe red colobus
Colobus verus	Green colobus
Pan troglodytes	Chimpanzee
Pan paniscus	Pygmy chimpanzee
Gorilla gorilla	Gorilla
RODENTIA	RODENTIA
Epixerus spp.	African palm squirrels
CARNIVORA	CARNIVORA
Canis simensis	Simenian jackal
Osbornictis piscivora	Water civet
Fossa fossa	Malagasy civet
Eupleres spp.	Falanouc
Felis nigripes	Black-footed cat

Felis aurata	African golden cat
Acinonyx jubatus	Cheetah
PINNIPEDIA	PINNIPEDIA
Monachus monachus	Mediterranean monk seal
SIRENIA	SIRENIA
Dugong dugong	Dugong
Trichechis senegalenis	West African manatee
PERISSODACTYLA	PERISSODACTYLA
Equus asinus	Wild ass
Equus zebra zebra	Cape mountain zebra
Certotherium simum	Square-lipped rhinoceros
ARTIODACTYLA	ARTIODACTYLA
Cheoropsis liberiensis	Pygmy hippopotamus
Cervus elaphus barbarus	Barbary stag
Okapia johnstoni	Okapi
Taurotaragus derbianus derbianus	Western giant eland
Cephalophus jentiniki	Jentink's duiker
Hippotragus niger varinai	Giant sable antelope
Alcelaphus buselaphus	Tora Hartebeest
Alcelaphus buselaphus	Swaynei's Hartebeest
Nesotragus moschatus moschatus	Zanzibar suni
Dorcatragus megalotis	Biera antelope
Gazella dorcas neglecta	Algerian dorcas gazelle
Gazella dorcas massaesyla	Moroccan dorcas gazelle
Gazella leptocerus leptocerus	Slender-horned gazelle
Gazella pelzelni	Pelzeln's gazelle
Gazella spekei	Speke's gazelle
Gazella dama mhorr	Mhorr gazelle
Gazella dama lozanoi	Rio de Ora dama gazelle
Capra walie	Walia ibex
AVES	BIRDS
Pelecanidae	All pelicans
Ciconiidae, Scopidae,	All storks, hammerkops, ibises
Ardeidae	spoonbills, herons, egrets and bitterns
Phoenicopteridae	All flamingos
Sagittarius serpentarius	Secretary bird
Aegypius, Gyps, Pseudogyps, Torgos, Trigonoceps, Neophron	All vultures
Gypaetus barbatus	Lammergeyer
Stephanoaetus coronatus	Crowned hawk-eagle
Falco fasciinucha	Teita falcon
Agelastes meleagrides	White-head guineafowl
Afropavo congensis	Congo peacock
Gruidae	All cranes
Bucorvus spp.	All ground hornbills
Picarthates oreas	White-necked rockfowl
Picarthartes gymnocephalus	Grey-necked rockfowl
Warsanglia johannis	Warsangli linnet
REPTILIA	REPTILES
Cheloniidae, Dermochelyidae	All marine turtles
Testudo gigantea	Giant tortoise
Testudo yniphora	Angulated tortoise
Testudo radiata	Testudo radiata
Macroscincus coctei	Cape Verde skink
Gecho uroplates	Leaf-tailed gecko
Casarea dussumieri	Plate Island boa
Boilieria multicarinata	Ronde Island boa
Acrantophis madagascariensi	*Acrantophis madagascariensi*
Acrantophis dumerilii	*Acrantophis dumerilii*
Amphibia	
Bufo superciliaris	
Nectophrynoides occidentalis	
PISCES	FISHES
Caecobarbus Caecomastacembelus, Eilichthys, Typheleotris Pharetichthys, Uegitglanis	Blind fishes
PLANTES	PLANTS
Welwitschia bainesii	Welwitschia
Encephalartos laurentanus	Enc ephalartos
Encephalartos septentrionalis	Encephalartos
Class B	
MAMMALIA	MAMMAL
Insectivora	Insectivora
	All other shrews of the family Potamogalidae
PRIMATES	PRIMATES
Lorisidae	All promisians of the family Lorisidae
	All monkeys except common baboons
PHOLIDOTA	PHOLIDOTA
Manis gigantea	Giant pangolin

Manis temmincki	Cape pangolin
Manis tricuspis	Tree pangolin
Manis longicaudata	Long-tailed tree pangolin
CARNIVORA	CARNIVORA
Lutrinae	All others of the subfamily Lutrinae
Proteles cristatus	Aardwolf
Hyaena hyaena barbara	Barbary hyaena
Felis caracal	Caracal lynx
Felis serval	Serval
Panthera leo	Lion
Panthera pardus	Leopard
Tenrecidae	Madagascar Tenrecs (all species)
Crytoprocto ferox	fossa
Gailidinae	All Malagasy mongooses of the subfamily Gailidinae
TUBULIDENTATA	TUBULIDENTATA
Orycteropus afer	Aardvark
PROBOSCIDEA	PROBOSCIDEA
Loxodonta africana	Elephant
PERISSODACTYLA	PERISSODACTYLA
Equus zebra hartmanne	Hartmann's mountain zebra
Equus burchelli	Burchell's zebra
Equus grevyi	Grevy's zebra
Diceros bicornis	Black rhinoceros
ARTIODACTYLA	ARTIODACTYLA
Hylocherus meinertzhageni	Giant forest hog
Hippopotamus amphibius	Hippopotamus
Hyemoschus aquaticus	Water chevrotain
Girrafa camelopardalis	Giraffe
Tragelaphus angasi	Nyala
Tragelaphus buxtoni	Mountain nyala
Tragelaphus spekei	Situtunga
Tragelaphus imberbis	Lesser kudu
Tregelaphus strepsiceros	Greater kudu
Taurotragus oryx	Eland
Taurotragus derbianus	Giant eland
Boocerus eurycerus	Bongo
Syncerus caffer	Buffalo
Cephalophus adersi	Zanzibar duiker
Cephalophus ogilbyi	Ogilby's duiker

Cephalophus silvicultor	Yellow-backed duiker
Cehpalophus spadix	Abbott's duiker
Cephalophus zebra	Banded duiker
Kobus ellipsiprymnus	Waterbuck
Kobus defassa	Defassa waterbuck
Kobus leche	Lechwe
Kobus magaceros	Nile Lechwe
Adenota kob	Kob
Redunca arundinum	Reedbuck
Redunca fulvorufula	Mountain reedbuck
Redunca redunca	Bohor antelope
Hippotragus equinus	Roan antelope
Hippotragus niger	Sable antelope
Oryx gazella	Oryx
Oryx tao	Scimitar-horned oryx
Addax nasomaculatus	Addax
Damaliscus lunatus	Tsessebe (Sassaby)
Damaliscus korrigum	Top
Damaliscus dorcas dorcas	Bontebok
Damaliscus dorcas phillipsi	Blesbok
Damaliscus hunteri	Hunter's hartebeest
Alcelaphus buselaphus	Hartebeest
Alcelaohus lichtensteini	Lichtenstein's hartebeest
Connochaetes gnou	Black wildebeest
Oreotragus oreotragus	Klipspringer
Ourebia spp.	Oribis (All species)
Neotragus pygmaeus	Royal antelope
Neotragus batesi	Dwarf antelope
Madoqua kirki	Damara dikdik
Aepyceros melampus	Impala
Ammodorcas clarkei	Dibatag
Litocranius walleri	Gerenuk
Gazella dorcas	Dorcas gazelle
Gazella rufifrons	Korin gazelle
Gazella tilonura	Heuglin's gazelle
Gazella dama	Dama gazelle
Gazella soemmerringi	Soemmering's gazelle
Capre ibex nubiana	Nubian ibex
Ammotragus lervia	Barbary sheep (Aoudad)
AVES	BIRDS
Struthio camelus	Ostrich
Falconiformes etc Strigiformers	All birds of prey and all owls not in Class A
Otididae	All bustards
REPTILIA	REPTILES
Crocodilia	All Crocodiles

EUROPEAN AGREEMENT ON THE RESTRICTION OF THE USE OF CERTAIN DETERGENTS IN WASHING AND CLEANING PRODUCTS [38]

Strasbourg, 16 September 1968

The Governments of the Kingdom of Belgium, the Kingdom of Denmark, the French Republic, the Federal Republic of Germany, the Italian Republic, the Grand Duchy of Luxembourg, the Kingdom of the Netherlands, the Swiss Confederation and the United Kingdom of Great Britain and Northern Ireland,

Considering that the Parties to the Brussels Treaty of 17 March 1948, as amended on 23 October 1954, resolved to strengthen the social ties by which they are united and to make every effort in common, both by direct consultation and in specialized Agencies, to raise the standards of living of their peoples and promote the harmonious development of social services in their respective countries;

Considering that the social activities governed by the Brussels Treaty and carried on, until 1959, under the auspices of the Brussels Treaty Organization and the Western European Union are now conducted within the framework of the Council of Europe, in accordance with the decision taken on 21 October 1959 by the Council of Western European Union and with Resolution (59) 23 adopted on 16 November 1959 by the Committee of Ministers of the Council of Europe;

Considering that the Swiss Confederation and the Kingdom of Denmark have participated since 6 May 1964 and 2 April 1968 respectively in activities in the field of public health carried on under the aforesaid resolution;

Whereas the aim of the Council of Europe is to achieve greater unity between its Members, so as to further economic and social progress by Agreements and by common action in economic, social, cultural, scientific, legal and administrative matters;

Whereas the said Governments have striven to encourage progress as far as may be practicable not only in social matters but in the related field of public health, and have undertaken to harmonise their national legislations in pursuance of the action mentioned in the foregoing paragraph;

Whereas it is becoming increasingly necessary to secure harmonisation of the laws on the control of fresh water pollution;

Being convinced that appropriate measures are essential not only from the standpoint of human needs but also to ensure the protection of nature in general, the paramount objectives being to protect effectively;

a) the supply of water for the population, for industry, for agriculture and for other business occupations;

b) the natural aquatic fauna and flora, and in particular so far as they contribute to human well-being;

c) the unhindered enjoyment of places devoted to leisure and sport;

Observing that the general household and industrial use of certain types of detergents might cause considerable prejudice to these interests;

Feeling, therefore, that some restriction must be put on the use of such products,

Have agreed as follows:

Article 1

The Contracting Parties undertake to adopt measures as effective as possible in the light of the available techniques, including legislation if it is necessary, to ensure that:

a) in their respective territories, washing or cleaning products containing one or more synthetic detergents are not put on the market unless the detergents in the product considered are, as a whole, at least 80% susceptible to biological degradation;

b) the appropriate measurement and control procedures are implemented in their respective territories to guarantee compliance with the provisions of sub-paragraph (*a*) of this Article.

Article 2

Compliance with the provisions of paragraph (*a*) of Article 1 of this Agreement must not result in the usage of detergents which, under conditions of normal use, might affect adversely human or animal health.

Article 3

The Contracting Parties shall, every five years, or more frequently if one of the Parties should so request, hold multilateral consultations within the Council of Europe to examine the application of this Agreement, and the advisability of revising it or extending any of its provisions. These consultations shall take place at meetings convened by the Secretary-General of the Council of Europe. The Contracting Parties shall communicate the name of their representative to the Secretary-General of the Council of Europe at least two months before the meetings.

Article 4

1. This Agreement shall be open to signature by member States of the Council of Europe which take part in the activities in the field of public health referred to in Resolution (59) 23 mentioned in the Preamble hereto. They may become Parties to it by either:

a) signature without reservation in respect of ratification or acceptance, or

b) signature with reservation in respect of ratification or acceptance, followed by ratification or acceptance.

2. Instruments of ratification or acceptance shall be deposited with the Secretary-General of the Council of Europe.

Article 5

1. This Agreement shall enter into force one month after the date on which three member States of the Council have become Parties to the Agreement, in accordance with the provisions of Article 4.

2. As regards any member States who shall subsequently sign the Agreement without reservation in respect of ratification or acceptance or who shall ratify or accept it, the Agreement shall enter into force one month after the date of such signature or after the date of deposit of the instrument of ratification or acceptance.

Article 6

1. After the entry into force of this Agreement,

a) any member State of the Council of Europe which does not take part in the activities in the field of public health referred to in Resolution (59) 23 mentioned in the Preamble to this Agreement, may accede thereto;

b) the Committee of Ministers of the Council of Europe may invite any State not a Member of the Council to accede to this Agreement provided that the resolution containing such invitation receives the unanimous agreement by member States of the Council of Europe which take part in the activities in the field of public health referred to in Resolution (59) 23 mentioned in the Preamble to this Agreement.

2. Such accession shall be effected by depositing with the Secretary General of the Council of Europe an instrument of accession which shall take effect one month after the date of its deposit.

Article 7

1. Any Contracting Party may at the time of signature or when depositing its instrument of ratification, acceptance or accession, specify the territory or territories to which this Agreement shall apply.

2. Any Contracting Party may, when depositing its instrument of ratification, acceptance or accession or at any later date, by declaration addressed to the Secretary-General of the Council of Europe, extend this Agreement to any other territory or territories specified in the declaration and for whose international relations it is responsible or on whose behalf it is authorised to give undertakings.

3. Any declaration made in pursuance of the preceding paragraph may, in respect of any territory mentioned in such declaration, be withdrawn according to the procedure laid down in Article 8 of this Agreement.

Article 8

1. This Agreement shall remain in force indefinitely.

2. Any Contracting Party may, in so far as it is concerned, denounce this Agreement by means of a notification to the Secretary-General of the Council of Europe.

3. Such denunciation shall take effect six months after the date of receipt by the Secretary-General of such notification.

Article 9

The Secretary-General of the Council of Europe shall notify the member States of the Council and any State which has acceded to this Agreement, of:

a) any signature without reservation in respect of ratification or acceptance;

b) any signature with reservation in respect of ratification or acceptance;

c) the deposit of any instrument of ratification, acceptance or accession;

d) any date of entry into force of this Agreement in accordance with Article 5 thereof;

e) any declaration received in pursuance of the provisions of paragraphs 2 and 3 of Article 7;

f) any notification received in pursuance of the provisions of Article 8 and the date on which denunciation takes effect.

In Witness Whereof the undersigned, being duly authorized thereto, have signed this Agreement.

Done at Strasbourg, this 16th day of September 1968, in the English and French languages, both texts being equally authoritative, in a single copy which shall remain deposited in the archives of the Council of Europe. The Secretary-General of the Council of Europe shall transmit certified copies to each of the signatory and acceding States.

EUROPEAN CONVENTION FOR THE PROTECTION OF ANIMALS DURING INTERNATIONAL TRANSPORT [39]

Paris, 13 December 1968

The member States of the Council of Europe, signatory hereto,

Considering that the aim of the Council of Europe is to achieve a greater unity between its Members for the purpose of safeguarding and realising the ideals and principles which are their common heritage;

Convinced that the requirements of the international transport of animals are not incompatible with the welfare of the animals;

Animated by the desire to safeguard, as far as possible, animals in transport from suffering;

Considering that progress in this respect may be achieved through the adoption of common provisions regarding the international transport of animals,

Have agreed as follows:

Chapter I

Article 1

1. Each Contracting Party shall apply the provisions governing the international transport of animals contained in this Convention.

2. For the purposes of this Convention international transport is understood to be any movement which involves the crossing of a frontier. Frontier traffic shall, however, be excluded.

3. The competent authorities of the country of dispatch shall decide whether the transport is in conformity with the provisions of this Convention. Nevertheless, the country of destination or intermediate countries may dispute whether any particular transport conforms with the provisions of this Convention. Such a consignment shall, however, be detained only when it is strictly necessary for the welfare of the animals.

4. Each Contracting Party take the necessary measures to avoid or reduce to a minimum the suffering of animals in cases when strikes or other unforeseeable circumstances in its territory impede the strict application of the provisions of this Convention. It will be guided for this purpose by the principles set out in this Convention.

Article 2

This Convention applies to the international transport of:

a) domestic solipeds and domestic animals of the bovine, ovine, caprine and porcine species (Chapter II);

b) domestic birds and domestic rabbits (Chapter III);

c) domestic dogs and domestic cats (Chapter IV);

d) other mammals and birds (Chapter V);

e) cold-blooded animals (Chapter VI).

Chapter II

DOMESTIC SOLIPEDS AND DOMESTIC ANIMALS OF THE BOVINE, OVINE, CAPRINE AND PORCINE SPECIES

A. General Provisions

Article 3

1. Before animals are loaded for international transport they shall be inspected by an authorised veterinary officer of the exporting country who shall satisfy himself that they are fit for transportation. For the purposes of this Convention an authorised veterinary officer is understood to be a veterinary officer nominated by the competent authority.

2. Loading shall be carried out under arrangements approved by an authorised veterinary officer.

3. The authorised veterinary officer shall issue a certificate which identifies the animals, states that they are fit for transportation, and, where possible, records the registration number of the means of transport and the type of vehicle used.

4. In certain cases determined by agreement between the Contracting Parties concerned the provisions of this Article need not apply.

Article 4

Animals likely to give birth during carriage or having given birth during the preceding 48 hours shall not be considered fit for transportation.

Article 5

The authorised veterinary officer of the exporting country, country of transit, or importing country may prescribe a period of rest, at a place determined by him, during which the animals shall receive the necessary care.

Article 6

1. Animals shall be provided with adequate space and, unless special conditions require to the contrary, room to lie down.

2. The means of transport and containers shall be constructed so as to protect animals against inclement weather conditions and marked differences in climate conditions. Ventilation and air space shall be adapted to the conditions of transport and be appropriate for the species of animals carried.

3. Containers in which animals are transported shall be marked with a symbol indicating the presence of live animals and a sign indicating the upright position. Containers shall be easy to clean, escape-proof and shall be so constructed as to ensure the safety of the animals. Containers shall also allow for the inspection and care of the animals and shall be stowed in a way which does not interfere with ventilation. During transport and handling, containers shall always be kept upright and shall not be exposed to severe jolts or shaking.

4. During transport animals shall be offered

water and appropriate food at suitable intervals. Animals shall not be left more than 24 hours without being fed and watered. This period may, however, be extended if the journey to the destination where the animals are unloaded can be completed within a reasonable period.

5. Solipeds shall wear halters during transport. This provision need not apply to unbroken animals.

6. When animals are tied the ropes or other attachments used shall be strong enough not to break during the transport under normal conditions, and long enough to allow the animals, if necessary, to lie down and to eat and drink. Bovines shall not be tied by the horns.

7. Solipeds, unless in individual stalls, shall have their hind feet unshod.

8. Bulls over 18 months should preferably be tied. They shall be fitted with a nose-ring for handling purposes only.

Article 7

1. When animals of various species travel in the same truck, vehicle, vessel, or aircraft, they shall be segregated according to species. Furthermore special measures shall be taken to avoid adverse reactions which might result from the transport in the same consignment of species naturally hostile to each other. When animals of different ages are carried in the same truck, vehicle, vessel, or aircraft adult and young animals shall be kept separate; this restriction shall not, however, apply to females travelling with their young which they suckle. With regard to bovine, soliped and porcine animals, mature uncastrated males shall be separated from females. Adult boars shall also be separated from each other; this shall also apply to stallions.

2. In compartments in which animals are transported goods shall not be loaded which could prejudice the welfare of the animals.

Article 8

Suitable equipment for loading and unloading of animals such as bridges, ramps, or gangways shall be used. The flooring of this equipment shall be constructed so as to prevent slipping, and the equipment shall be provided with lateral protection if necessary. Animals shall not be lifted by the head, horns or legs during loading or unloading.

Article 9

The floor of trucks, vehicles, aircraft, or containers shall be sufficiently strong to bear the weight of the animals being transported, close-boarded, and so constructed as to prevent slipping. The floor shall be covered with an adequate amount of litter to absorb excrements unless these can be dealt with in a different way presenting at least the same advantages.

Article 10

In order to ensure the necessary care of the animals during transport, consignments of livestock shall be accompanied by an attendant, except in the following cases:

a) where livestock is consigned in containers which are secured;

b) where the transporter undertakes to assume the functions of the attendant;

c) where the sender has appointed an agent to care for the animals at appropriate staging points.

Article 11

1. The attendant or sender's agent shall look after the animals, feed and water them, and, if necessary, milk them.

2. Cows in milk shall be milked at intervals of not more than 12 hours.

3. To enable the attendant to provide this care, he shall, if necessary, have available a suitable means of lighting.

Article 12

Animals which become ill or injured during transport shall receive veterinary attention as soon as possible, and if necessary be slaughtered in a way which avoids unnecessary suffering.

Article 13

Animals shall only be loaded into trucks, vehicles, vessels, aircraft, or containers which have been thoroughly cleaned. Dead animals, litter and excrements shall be removed as soon as possible.

Article 14

Animals shall be transported to their destination as soon as possible, and delays, particularly in transhipment and marshalling yards, shall be reduced to a minimum.

Article 15

In order that importation and transit formalities may be completed as quickly as possible, consignments of animals shall be notified as early as possible to control posts. In such formalities priority should be given to consignments of animals.

Article 16

At posts where sanitary control is exercised and animals in significant numbers are regularly transported, facilities shall be provided for resting, feeding and watering.

B. Special Provisions for Transport by Railway

Article 17

Any railway truck in which animals are transported shall be marked with a symbol for the living animals. If no trucks particularly adapted for transport of animals are obtainable, animals shall be carried in covered trucks which are capable of travelling at high speed and are provided with sufficiently large air vents. They shall be constructed so as to prevent animals from escaping and ensure their safety. The interior sides of the trucks shall be of wood or other suitable material completely smooth and fitted with rings or bars at suitable height to which the animals may be attached.

Article 18

Solipeds shall be tied in such a way that they are all facing the same side of the vehicle or tied facing each other. However, young unbroken animals shall not be tied.

Article 19

Large animals shall be loaded in such a way as to allow an attendant to move between them.

Article 20

When, in accordance with the provisions of Article 7, the seperation of animals is required, this may be effected either by tying them in separate parts of the truck, if its space permits, or by means of suitable partitions.

Article 21

When assembling trains and during all other movements of trucks all precautions shall be taken to avoid violent jolting of trucks containing animals.

C. SPECIAL PROVISIONS FOR TRANSPORT BY ROAD

Article 22

Vehicles shall be escape-proof and so constructed as to ensure the safety of the animals and shall also be equipped with a roof which ensures effective protection against the weather.

Article 23

Tying facilities shall be provided in vehicles carrying large animals which normally require to be tied. When vehicles are required to be sub-divided, the partitions shall be of rigid construction.

Article 24

Vehicles shall carry a ramp complying with the requirements of Article 8.

D. SPECIAL PROVISIONS FOR TRANSPORT BY WATER

Article 25

The fittings of vessels shall be such that animals can be transported without injury and unnecessary suffering.

Article 26

Animals shall not be transported on open decks unless in adequately secured containers or substantial structures, approved by the competent authority and giving adequate protection against sea and weather.

Article 27

Animals shall be tied or properly accommodated in pens or containers.

Article 28

There shall be adequate passageways having access to all pens and containers accommodating animals. Lighting facilities shall be available.

Article 29

A sufficient number of attendants shall be provided taking into account the number of animals transported and the duration of the voyage.

Article 30

All parts of the vessel where animals are accommodated shall be provided with drainage and shall be kept in a sanitary condition.

Article 31

A type of instrument approved by the competent authority shall be carried for killing animals if necessary.

Article 32

Vessels used for the transport of animals shall, before sailing, be provisioned with such supplies of drinking water and appropriate foodstuffs as shall be considered sufficient by the competent authority of the sending country, having regard to species and number of animals being transported as well as to the duration of.the voyage.

Article 33

Provisions shall be made for isolating ill or injured animals during the voyage and first-aid treatment rendered when necessary.

Article 34

The provisions of Article 25 to 33 shall not apply to the transport of animals loaded in railway trucks or road vehicles on board ferry boats or similiar vessels.

E.SPECIAL PROVISIONS FOR TRANSPORT BY AIR

Article 35

Animals shall be transported in containers or stalls appropriate for the species. Some modifications of these requirements may be permitted if appropriate arrangements are made for restraining the animals.

Article 36

Precautions shall be taken to avoid extremely high or low temperature on board, having regard to the species of animals. In addition, severe fluctuations of air pressure shall be avoided.

Article 37

In freight aircraft a type of instrument approved by the competent authority shall be carried for killing animals if necessary.

Chapter III

DOMESTIC BIRDS AND DOMESTIC RABBITS

Article 38

The following provisions of Chapter II shall apply mutatis mutandis to the transport of domestic birds and domestic rabbits: Article 6, paragraphs 1 to 3, Articles 7, 13 to 17 inclusive, 21, 22, 25 to 30 inclusive, 32, 34 to 36 inclusive.

Article 39

1. Animals that are ill or injured shall not be considered fit for transport. Any that become ill or injured shall receive first-aid treatment as soon as possible and if necessary be submitted to veterinary examination.
2. When animals are loaded in containers one placed on top of another or in a truck or vehicle with more than one floor the necessary precautions shall be taken to avoid droppings falling on the animals placed underneath.
3. Suitable food and, if necessary, water shall be available in adequate quantities, save in the case of:
a) a journey lasting less than 12 hours;
b) a journey lasting less than 24 hours for chicks of all species, provided that it is completed within 72 hours after hatching.

Chapter IV

DOMESTIC DOGS AND DOMESTIC CATS

Article 40

1. The provisions of this Chapter shall apply to the transport of domestic dogs and domestic cats except those that are accompanied by the owner or his representative.
2. The following provisions of Chapter II shall apply mutatis mutandis to the transport of domestic dogs and domestic cats: Article 4, Article 6, paragraphs 1 to 3 inclusive, Articles 7, 9, 10, Article 11, paragraphs 1 and 3, Articles 12 to 17 inclusive, 20 to 23 inclusive, 25 to 29 inclusive and 31 to 37 inclusive.

Article 41

Animals in transport shall be fed at intervals of not more than 24 hours and given water at intervals of not more than 12 hours. There shall be clear written instructions about feeding and watering. Bitches in oestrus shall be separated from male dogs.

Chapter V

OTHER MAMMALS AND BIRDS

Article 42

1. The provisions of this Chapter apply to the transport of those mammals and birds which are not already covered by the provisions of the preceding Chapters.
2. The following provisions of Chapter II shall apply mutatis mutandis to the transport of the species concerned in this Chapter: Articles 4 and 5, Article 6, paragraph 1 to 3 inclusive, Articles 7 to 10 inclusive, Article 11, paragraphs 1 and 3, Articles 12 to 17 inclusive, 20 to 37 inclusive.

Article 43

Animals shall only be transported in suitably constructed vehicles or containers, on which shall, if necessary, be directions that there are wild animals in them which are nervously timid or dangerous. Moreover, there shall be clear written instructions about feeding and watering and any special care required.

Article 44

Antlered animals shall not be transported while in velvet unless special precautions are taken.

Article 45

Animals covered by this Chapter shall be cared for in accordance with the instructions referred to in Article 43.

Chapter VI

COLD-BLOODED ANIMALS

Article 46

Cold-blooded animals shall be transported in such containers, under such conditions, in particular with regard to space, ventilation and temperature, and with such supply of water and oxygen as are considered appropriate for the species. They shall be transported to their destination as soon as possible.

Chapter VII

SETTLEMENT OF DISPUTES

Article 47

1. In case of a dispute regarding the interpretation or the application of the provisions of this Convention, the competent authorities of the Contracting Parties concerned shall consult with each other. Each Contracting Party shall communicate to the Secretary-General of the Council of Europe the names and address of their competent authorities.
2. If the dispute has not been settled by this means, it shall, at the request of one or other of the parties to the dispute, be referred to arbitration. Each Party shall nominate an arbitrator and the two arbitrators shall nominate a referee. If one of the two parties to the dispute has not nominated its arbitrator within the three months following the request for arbitration, he shall be nominated at the request of the other party to the dispute by the President of the European Court of Human Rights. If the latter should be a national of one of the parties to the dispute, this duty shall be carried out by the Vice-President of the Court or, if the Vice-President is a national of one of the parties to the dispute, by the most senior judge of the Court not being a national of one of the parties to the dispute. The same procedure shall be observed if the arbitrators cannot agree on the choice of referee.

3. The arbitration tribunal shall lay down its own procedure. Its decisions shall be taken by majority vote. Its award which shall be based on this Convention shall be final.

Chapter VIII
FINAL PROVISIONS

Article 48

1. The Convention shall be open to signature by the member States of the Council of Europe. It shall be subject to ratification or acceptance. Instruments of ratification or acceptance shall be deposited with the Secretary-General of the Council of Europe.

2. This Convention shall enter into force six months after the date of the deposit of the fourth instrument of ratification or acceptance.

3. In respect of a signatory State ratifying or accepting subsequently, the Convention shall come into force six months after the date of the deposit of its instrument of ratification or acceptance.

Article 49

1. After the entry into force of this Convention, the Committee of Ministers of the Council of Europe may invite any non-member State to accede thereto.

2. Such accession shall be effected by depositing with the Secretary-General of the Council of Europe an instrument of accession which shall take effect six months after the date of its deposit.

Article 50

1. Any Contracting Party may, at the time of signature or when depositing its instrument of ratification, acceptance or accession, specify the territory or territories to which this Convention shall apply.

2. Any Contracting Party may, when depositing its instrument of ratification, acceptance or accession or at any later date, by declaration addressed to the Secretary-General of the Council of Europe, extend this Convention to any other territory or territories specified in the declaration and for whose international relations it is responsible or on whose behalf it is authorized to give undertakings.

3. Any declarations made in pursuance of the preceding paragraph may, in respect of any territory mentioned in such declaration be withdrawn according to the procedure laid down in Article 51 of this Convention.

Article 51

1. This Convention shall remain in force indefinitely.

2. Any Contracting Party may, in so far as it is concerned, denounce this Convention by means of a notification addressed to the Secretary General of the Council of Europe.

3. Such denunciation shall take effect six months after the date of receipt by the Secretary-General of such notification.

Article 52

The Secretary-General of the Council of Europe shall notify the member States of the Council and any State which has acceded to this Convention of:

a) any signature;

b) any deposit of an instrument of ratification, acceptance or accession;

c) and date of entry into force of this Convention in accordance with Article 48 thereof;

d) any declaration received in pursuance of paragraphs 2 and 3 of Article 50;

e) any notification received in pursuance of the provisions of Article 51 and the date on which denunciation takes effect;

f) any communication received in pursuance of Article 47, paragraph 1.

In Witness Whereof the undersigned, being duly authorized thereto, have signed this Convention.

Done at Paris this 13th day of December 1968 in English and in French, both texts being equally authoritative, in a single copy which shall remain deposited in the archives of the Council of Europe. The Secretary-General of the Council of Europe shall transmit certified copies to each of the signatory and acceding States.

EUROPEAN CONVENTION ON THE PROTECTION OF THE ARCHAEOLOGICAL HERITAGE [40]

London, 6 May 1969

The member States of the Council of Europe, signatory hereto,

Considering that the aim of the Council of Europe is to achieve a greater unity between its Members for the purpose, in particular, of safeguarding and realising the ideals and principals which are their common heritage;

Having regard to the European Cultural Convention, signed at Paris on 19 December 1954, and *inter alia* Article 5 of that Convention;

Affirming that the archaeological heritage is essential to a knowledge of the history of civilizations;

Recognising that while the moral responsibility for protecting the European archaeological heritage, the earliest source of European history, which is seriously threatened with destruction, rests in the first instance with the State directly concerned, it is also the concern of European States jointly;

Considering that the first step towards protecting this heritage should be to apply the most stringent scientific methods to archaeological research or discoveries, in order to preserve their full historical significance and render impossible the irremediable loss of scientific information that may result from illicit excavation;

Considering that the scientific protection thus guaranteed to archaeological objects:

a) would be in the interests, in particular, of public collections, and

b) would promote a much-needed reform of the market in archaeological finds;

Considering that it is necessary to forbid clandestine excavations and to set up a scientific control of archaeological objects as well as to seek through education to give to archaeological excavations their full scientific significance,

Have agreed as follows:

Article 1

For the purpose of this Convention, all remains and objects, or any other traces of human existence, which bear witness to epochs and civilizations for which excavations or discoveries are the main source or one of the main sources of scientific information, shall be considered as archaeological objects.

Article 2

With the object of ensuring the protection of deposits and sites where archaeological objects lie hidden, each Contracting Party undertakes to take such measures as may be possible in order:

a) to delimit and protect sites and areas of archaeological interest;

b) to create reserve zones for the preservation of material evidence to be excavated by later generations of archaeologists.

Article 3

To give full scientific significance to archaeological excavations in the sites, areas and zones designated in accordance with Article 2 of this Convention, each Contracting Party undertakes, as far as possible to:

a) prohibit and restrain illicit excavations;

b) take the necessary measures to ensure that excavations are, by special authorization, entrusted only to qualified persons;

c) ensure the control and conservation of the results obtained.

Article 4

1. Each Contracting Party undertakes, for the purpose of the study and distribution of information on archaeological finds, to take all practicable measures necessary to ensure the most rapid and complete dissemination of information in scientific publications on excavations and discoveries.

2. Moreover, each Contracting Party shall also consider ways and means of:

a) establishing a national inventory of publicly-owned and, where possible, privately-owned archaeological objects;

b) preparing a scientific catalogue of publicly-owned and, where possible, privately-owned archaeological objects.

Article 5

With a view to the scientific, cultural and educational aims of this Convention, each Contracting Party undertakes to:

a) facilitate the circulation of archaeological objects for scientific, cultural and educational purposes;

b) encourage exchanges of information on:

(i) archaeological objects,

(ii) authorised and illicit excavations

between scientific institutions, museums and the competent national departments;

c) do all in its power to assure that the competent authorities in the States of origin, Contracting Parties to this Convention, are informed of any offer suspected of coming either from illicit excavations or unlawfully from official excavations, together with the necessary details thereon;

d) endeavour by educational means to create and develop in public opinion a realisation of the value of archaelogical finds for the knowledge of a history of civilization, and the threat caused to this heritage by uncontrolled excavations.

Article 6

1. Each Contracting Party undertakes to co-operate in the most appropriate manner in order to ensure that the international circulation of archaeological objects shall in no way prejudice the

protection of the cultural and scientific interest attaching to such objects.

2. Each Contracting Party undertakes specifically:

a) as regards museums and other similar institutions whose acquisition policy is under State control, to take the necessary measures to avoid their acquiring archaeological objects suspected, for a specific reason, of having originated from clandestine excavations or of coming unlawfully from official excavations;

b) as regards museums and other similar institutions, situated in the territory of a Contracting Party but enjoying freedom from State control in their acquisition policy:

(i) to transmit the text of this Convention, and

(ii) to spare no effort to obtain the support of the said museums and institutions for the principles set out in the preceding paragraph;

c) to restrict, as far as possible, by education, information, vigilance and co-operation, the movement of archaeological objects suspected, for a specific reason, of having been obtained from illicit excavations or unlawfully from official excavations.

Article 7

In order to ensure the application of the principle of co-operation in the protection of the archaeological heritage which is the basis of this Convention, each Contracting Party undertakes, within the context of the obligations accepted under the terms of this Convention, to give consideration to any questions of identification and authentication raised by any other Contracting Party, and to co-operate actively to the extent permitted by its national legislation.

Article 8

The measures provided for in this Convention cannot restrict lawful trade in or ownership of archaeological objects, nor affect the legal rules governing the transfer of such objects.

Article 9

Each Contracting Party shall notify the Secretary-General of the Council of Europe in due course of measures it may have taken in respect of the application of the provisions of this Convention.

Article 10

1. This Convention shall be open to signature by the member States of the Council of Europe. It shall be subject to ratification or acceptance. Instruments of ratification or acceptance shall be deposited with the Secretary-General of the Council of Europe.

2. This Convention shall enter into force three months after the date of the deposit of the third instrument of ratification or acceptance.

3. In respect of a signatory State ratifying or accepting subsequently, the Convention shall come into force three months after the date of the deposit of its instrument of ratification or acceptance.

Article 11

1. After entry into force of this Convention:

a) any non-member State of the Council of Europe which is a Contracting Party to the European Cultural Convention signed at Paris on 19 December 1954 may accede to this Convention;

b) the Committee of Ministers of the Council of Europe may invite any other non-member State to accede thereto.

2. Such accession shall be effected by depositing with the Secretary-General of the Council of Europe an instrument of accession which shall take effect three months after the date of its deposit.

Article 12

1. Each signatory State, at the time of signature or when depositing its instrument of ratification or acceptance, or each acceding State when depositing its instrument of accession, may specify the territory or territories to which this Convention shall apply.

2. Each signatory State, when depositing its instrument of ratification or acceptance or at any later date, or each acceding State, when depositing its instrument of accession or at any later date, by declaration addressed to the Secretary General of the Council of Europe, may extend this Convention to any other territory or territories specified in the declaration and for whose international relations it is responsible or on whose behalf it is authorised to give undertakings.

3. Any declaration made in pursuance of the preceding paragraph may, in respect of any territory mentioned in such declaration, be withdrawn according to the procedure laid down in Article 13 of this Convention.

Article 13

1. This Convention shall remain in force indefinitely.

2. Any Contracting Party may, in so far as it is concerned, denounce this Convention by means of a notification addressed to the Secretary General of the Council of Europe.

3. Such denunciation shall take effect six months after the date of receipt by the Secretary General of such notification.

Article 14

The Secretary General of the Council of Europe shall notify the member States of the Council and any State which has acceded to this Convention of:

a) any signature;

b) any deposit of an instrument of ratification, acceptance or accession;

c) any date of entry into force of this Convention in accordance with Article 10 thereof;

d) any declaration received in pursuance of the

provisions of paragraphs 2 and 3 of Article 12;

e) any notification received in pursuance of the provisions of Article 13 and the date on which denunciation takes effect.

In Witness Whereof the undersigned, being duly authorized thereto, have signed this Convention.

Done at London, this 6th day of May 1969, in English and French, both texts being equally authoritative, in a single copy which shall remain deposited in the archives of the Council of Europe. The Secretary General of the Council of Europe shall transmit certified copies to each of the signatory and acceding States.

AGREEMENT FOR CO-OPERATION IN DEALING WITH POLLUTION OF THE NORTH SEA BY OIL [41]

Bonn, 9 June 1969

The Government of the Kingdom of Belgium, the Kingdom of Denmark, the French Republic, the Federal Republic of Germany, the Kingdom of the Netherlands, the Kingdom of Norway, the Kingdom of Sweden, the United Kingdom of Great Britain and Northern Ireland,

Recognizing that grave pollution of the sea by oil in the North Sea area involves a danger to the coastal states,

Noting that the Council of the Inter-Governmental Maritime Consultative Organization at its third extraordinary session in May 1967, decided to include among the matters requiring study as a matter of urgency, inter alia, "procedures whereby States, regionally or inter-regionally where applicable, can co-operate at short notice to provide manpower, supplies, equipment and scientific advice to deal with discharge of oil or other noxious or hazardous substances including consideration of the possibility of patrols to ascertain the extent of the discharge and the manner of treating it both on sea and land",

Have agreed on the following:

Article 1

This Agreement shall apply whenever the presence or the prospective presence of oil polluting the sea within the North Sea area, as defined in Article 2 of this Agreement, presents a grave and imminent danger to the coast or related interests of one or more Contracting Parties.

Article 2

For the purposes of this Agreement the North Sea area means the North Sea proper southwards of latitude 61°N together with

a) the Stagerrak, the sourthern limit of which is determined by a line joining Skagen and Pater Noster Shaaren,

b) the English Channnel and its approaches eastwards of a line drawn fifty nautical miles to the west of a line joining the Scilly Isles and Ushant.

Article 3

The Contracting Parties consider that protection against pollution of the kind referred to in Article 1 of this Agreement is a matter which calls for active co-operation between the Contracting Parties.

Article 4

Contracting Parties undertake to inform the other Contracting Parties about:

a) their national organization for dealing with oil pollution;

b) the competent authority responsible for receiving reports of oil pollution and for dealing with questions concerning measures of mutual assistance between Contracting Parties;

c) new ways in which oil pollution may be avoided and about new effective measures to deal with oil pollution.

Article 5

1. Whenever a Contracting Party is aware of a casualty or the presence of oil slicks in the North Sea area likely to constitute a serious threat to the coast or related interests of any other Contracting Party, it shall inform that other Party without delay through its competent authority.

2. The Contracting Parties undertake to request the masters of all ships flying their flags and pilots of aircraft registered in their countries to report without delay through the channels which may be most practicable and adequate in the circumstances:

a) all casualties causing or likely to cause oil pollution of the sea;

b) the presence, nature and extent of oil slicks on the sea likely to constitute a serious threat to the coast or related interests of one or more Contracting Parties.

Article 6

1. For the sole purposes of this Agreement the North Sea area is divided into the zones described in the Annex to this Agreement.

2. The Contracting Party within whose zones a situation of the kind described in Article 1 occurs, shall make the necessary assessments of the nature and extent of any casualty or, as the case may be, of the type and approximate quantity of oil floating on the sea, and the direction and speed of movement of the oil.

3. The Contracting Party concerned shall immediately inform all the other Contracting Parties through their competent authorities of its assessments and of any action which it has taken to deal with the floating oil and shall keep the oil under observation as long as it is drifting in its zone.

4. The obligations of the Contracting Parties under the provisions of this Article with respect to the zones of joint responsibility shall be the subject of special technical arrangements to be concluded between the Parties concerned. These arrangements shall be communicated to the other Contracting Parties.

5. In no case shall the division into zones referred to in this Article be invoked as a precedent or argument in any matter concerning sovereignty of jurisdiction.

Article 7

A Contracting Party requiring assistance to dispose of oil floating on the sea or polluting its coast may call on the help of the other Contracting Parties, starting with those which also seem likely to be affected by the floating oil. Contracting Parties called upon for help in accordance with this Article shall use their best endeavours to bring such assistance as is within their power.

Article 8

Any Contracting Party which has taken action in accordance with Article 7 of this Agreement shall submit a report thereon to the other Contracting Parties and to the Inter-Governmental Maritime Consultative Organization.

Article 9

1. This Agreement shall be open for signature by the Governments mentioned in the preamble from 9 June 1969.

2. These Governments may become parties to this Agreement either by signature without reservation as to ratification or approval or by signature subject to ratification or approval followed by ratification or approval.

3. Instruments of ratification or approval shall be deposited with the Government of the Federal Republic of Germany.

4. This Agreement shall enter into force two months after the date on which six Governments have signed the Agreement without reservation as to ratification or approval, or have deposited an instrument of ratification or approval.

5. For each Government which subsequently signs the Agreement without reservation as to ratification or approval, or ratifies or approves it, it shall enter into force two months after the date of its signature or of the deposit of its instrument of ratification or approval.

Article 10

1. After this Agreement has been in force for five years it my be denounced by any Contracting Party.

2. Denunciation shall be effected by a notification in writing addressed to the Government of the Federal Republic of Germany s which shall notify all the other Contracting Parties of any denunciation received and of the date of its receipt.

3. A denunciation shall take effect one year after its receipt by the Government of the Federal Republic of Germany.

In Witness Whereof the undersigned, being duly authorized by their respective Governments have signed this Agreement.

Done at Bonn on this ninth day of June 1969, in the English and French languages, both texts being equally authoritative, in a single copy which shall be deposited in the Archives of the Government of the Federal Republic of Germany which shall transmit a duly certified copy to each of the other signatory Governments. This Agreement shall be registered with the United Nations in conformity with Article 102 of the Charter of the United Nations.

Annex

DESCRIPTION OF THE ZONES REFERRED TO IN ARTICLE 6 OF THIS AGREEMENT

The zones, with the exception of the zones of joint responsibility, are limited by lines joining the following points;

Denmark

55°03'N 8°22'E
55°10'N 7°30'E
55°10'N 2°15E
57°00N 6°40E
58°10N 10°00E
58°10'N 10°00'E
57°48'N 10°57'E
57°44'N 10°38'E (Skagen)

Netherlands

51°32'N 3°18'E
51°32'N 2°06'E
52°30'N 3°10'E
54°00'N 2°40'E
54°00'N 5°30'E
53°34'N 6°38'E

Sweden

57°54'N 11°28'E
(Pater Noster lighthouse)
57°48' N 10°57'E
58°10' N 10°00'E
58°54,5' N 10°43'E
To be continued along the Norwegian-Swedish border.

Germany

53°34'N 6°38'E
54°00'N 5°30'E
54°00'N 2°40'E
55°10'N 2°15'E
55°10'N 7°30'E
55°03'N 8°22'E

Norway

61°00' N 4°30'E
61°00'N 2°00'E
57°00' N 1°30'E
57°00'N 6°40'E
58°10'N 10°00'E
58°54, 5'N 10°43'E
To be continued along the Norwegian-Swedish border.

United Kingdom

61°00' N 0°50'W
61°00'N 2°00'E
57°00'N 1°30'E
52°30'N 3°10'E
51°32'N 2°06'E

The zones of joint responsibility are as follows:

1. Belgium, France and United Kingdom .

Sea area between parallels 51°32'N and 51°06'N

2. France and United Kingdom

The English Channel south-west of parallel 51°06'N to a line drawn between the points

49°52'N 07°44'W and
48°27'N 06°25'W

CONVENTION ON THE CONSERVATION OF THE LIVING RESOURCES OF THE SOUTHEAST ATLANTIC [42]

Rome, 23 October 1969

PREAMBLE

The Government of the States parties to this Convention, considering their mutual interest in the living resources of the Southeast Atlantic and desiring to co-operate in the conservation and rational exploitation of these resources, have agreed as follows:

Article I

1. The area to which this Convention shall apply, hereinafter referred to as the "Convention Area", shall be all waters bounded by a line drawn as follows:

Beginning at a point of 6°04'36" South latitude and 12°19'48' East longitude, thence in a northwesterly direction along a rhumb line to the point at the intersection of the meridian 12° East with the parallel to the meridian 20° West, thence due south along this meridian to the parallel 150° South, thence due east along this parallel to the meridian 40° East, thence due north along this meridian to the coast of the African continent, thence in a westerly direction along this coast to the original point of departure.

2. The eastern boundary at the meridian 40° East shall be reviewed if a convention for the conservation of the living resources of the sea is established applying to an area immediately adjacent to that boundary.

Article II

Nothing in this Convention shall be considered as affecting the rights, claims or view of any Contracting Party in regard to the limits of the territorial sea or to the extent of jurisdiction over fisheries under international law.

Article III

This Convention shall apply to all fish and other living resources in the Convention Area, with the exception of any such resources as may be excluded pursuant to arrangements or agreements entered into by the Commission in accordance with paragraph 1 of Article XI of this Convention.

Article IV

The Contracting Parties hereby agree to establish and to maintain a Commission to be known as the International Commission for the Southeast Atlantic Fisheries, hereinafter referred to as the "Commission", which shall carry out the functions set forth in this Convention.

Article V

1. The Commission shall hold a regular session at least once every two years. A special session shall be called at any time at the request of one Contracting Party provided that such request is

supported by at least three other Contracting Parties.

2. Each of the Contracting Parties shall be represented on the Commission by not more than three Commissioners who may be accompanied by experts and advisers.

3. Each Contracting Party shall have one vote in the Commission. Except as may be otherwise provided in this Convention, decisions of the Commission shall be taken by a majority of two-thirds of the Contracting Parties present and voting. Two thirds of the Contracting Parties shall constitute a quorum.

4. At each regular session the Commission shall elect from among the Commissioners the following officers: a Chairman, a First Vice-Chairman and a Second Vice-Chairman. These officers shall remain in office until the election of their successors at the next regular session and shall not be eligible to serve for more than two consecutive terms in the same office. A Commissioner, when acting as Chairman, shall not vote.

5. The working languages of the Commission shall be English, French and Spanish.

6. The Commission shall adopt such rules of procedure and other internal adminstrative regulations as are necessary to carry out its functions. The rules of procedure of subsidiary bodies established by the Commission under Article VII may be adopted by such subsidiary bodies, but shall only enter into force upon approval by the Commission.

Article VI

1. In order to achieve the objectives set out in this Convention, the Commission shall be responsible for the study of all fish and other living resources in the Convention Area. Such study shall include research on the abundance, life history, biometry and ecology of these resources and the study of their environment. In undertaking the study of these matters, the Commission shall collect, analyse, publish and disseminate, by all appropriate means, statistical, biological and other scientific information on the said resources.

2. The Commission, in carrying out its responsibilities shall, insofar as feasible, utilize the technical and scientific services of, and information from, official agencies of the Contracting Parties. The Commission may, when necessary, utilize other services and information, and may also undertake, within the limits of its supplementary budget, independent research to supplement the research being done by governments, national institutions or other international organizations.

3. The Contracting Parties shall furnish, on the request of the Commission, any available statistical and other data and information the Commission may need for the purposes of the Convention.

Article VII

1. The Commission may establish a Regional Committee for each of the regions into which the Convention Area may be divided on an ecological basis, and a Stock Committee with respect to any stock to be found in the Convention Area. The Commission may also establish a Scientific Advisory Council, hereinafter referred to as the "Council". The Commission may establish such other subsidiary bodies as are necessary for the performance of its functions, determining their composition and terms of reference in each case.

2. Regional Committees shall have the functions specified in this Article, except with respect to any stock for which a Stock Committee is competent.

3. A Regional or Stock Committee may initiate, on the basis of the results of scientific investigations, proposals regarding measures that are applicable to the region or stock for which it has been established and shall consider any proposals that may be referred to it by the Commission.

4. A Regional or Stock Committee may prepare draft recommendations for consideration by the Commission. The Commission may adopt such draft recommendations, with any amendments it may consider desirable, in accordance with Article VIII of this Convention.

5. The Commission shall designate the Contracting Parties that may be represented on a Regional or Stock Committee. However, when a Regional or Stock Committee is established a Contracting Party shall automatically have the right to be represented thereon if it fishes in the region; or if it exploits the stock concerned or if it has a coastline adjacent to the region concerned or the area where the stock is to be found. If a Contracting Party exploits a stock outside the region covered by a Regional or Stock Committee, it may be eligible to be represented thereon if the Commission so decides.

6. The functions of the Council shall be to advise and assist the Commission and its Regional and Stock Committees with respect to the scientific aspects of their responsibilities.

7. Each Contracting Party may send a delegation of scientists to the Council composed of as many experts as it wishes. The Council may establish subsidiary bodies and determine their composition.

8. The Council may, with the concurrence of the Commission, invite other scientists or experts to participate in its deliberations in an advisory capacity.

9. The Council shall hold regular sessions whose timing shall be determined by the Commission in relation to its regular sessions. The Council may hold special sessions subject to the approval of the Commission.

Article VIII

1. The Commission may make, on its own initiative or on the proposal of a Regional or Stock Committee and on the basis of the results of scientific investigations, recommendations relating to the objectives of this Convention. These recommendations shall become binding on the

Contracting Parties under the conditions laid down in Article IX.

2. The matters with respect to which the Commission may make recommendations shall be:

a) the regulation of the sizes of mesh of fishing nets;

b) the regulation of the size limits of fish that may be retained on board any fishing craft or landed, or exposed or offered for sale;

c) the establishment of open and closed seasons;

d) the establishment of open and closed areas;

e) the regulation of fishing gear and appliances, other than regulation of the size of mesh of fishing nets;

f) the improvement and the increase of living resources, which may include artificial propagation, the transplantation and acclimatization of organisms, the transplantation of young, and predator control;

g) the regulation of the total catch by species, group of species or, if appropriate, by regions; and

h) any other type of measure directly related to the conservation of all fish and other living resource in the Convention Area.

3. *a*) If the Commission makes a recommendation under paragraph 2 (*g*) of this Article, it may invite the Contracting Parties concerned, as determined by the Commission, to elaborate agreements on the allocation of a total catch quota taking into account the fishing interests of all the countries concerned and ensuring, as far as possible, that all the countries concerned abide by the Commission's recommendation for a total catch quota and by any agreed allocation.

b) The terms of any such agreement shall be reported by the Contracting Parties concerned to the Commission as soon as possible. Without prejudice to the binding force of such agreements on the parties thereto, the Commission may thereupon make recommendations, pursuant to paragraph 1 of this Article, on the subject matter of the said agreements.

4. The Commission shall notify all Contracting Parties of recommendations adopted by the Commission.

Article IX

1. Subject to the provisions of this Article, the Contracting Parties undertake to give effect to any recommendation adopted by the Commission in accordance with Article VIII.

2. Any Contracting Party may, within ninety days of notification of a recommendation, present an objection to it to the Commission and in that event shall not be under an obligation to give effect to the recommendation.

3. If an objection is presented within the ninety-day period referred to in the preceding paragraph any other Contracting Party may present an objection at any time within a further period of sixty days or within thirty days after notification of an objection presented by another Contracting Party made within the further sixty-day period.

4. If objections to a recommendation are presented by at least three Contracting Parties, all the other Contracting Parties shall be relieved forthwith of any obligations to give effect to that recommendation; nevertheless, any or all of them may agree among themselves to give effect to it.

5. Any Contracting Party which has presented an objection to a recommendation may at any time withdraw that objection and shall then, subject to the provisions of the preceding paragraph, give effect to the recommendation within ninety days.

6. The Commission shall notify all Contracting Parties of each objection or withdrawal immediately upon receipt thereof.

Article X

1. Without prejudice to the rights of States in the waters in which they are entitled under international law to exercise jurisdiction over fisheries, each Contracting Party shall take appropriate measures, in its territories and in these waters with respect to all persons and vessels, and beyond these waters with respect to its nationals and vessels, to ensure the implementation of the provisions of the present Convention and the recommendations of the Commission which have become binding on that Contracting Party, and to apply sanctions for the violation of such recommendations.

2. The Contracting Parties undertake to collaborate with each other with a view to the adoption of effective measures to ensure the implementation of this Convention and the achievement of its objectives.

3. In addition, the Contracting Parties undertake to collaborate with each other with a view to setting up, upon a recommendation by the Commission, a system of international enforcement of such recommendations as the Commission may select for inclusion under the said system, except in the waters in which a State is entitled under international law to exercise jurisdiction over fisheries. The adoption and implementation of such a recommendation shall be governed by Articles VIII and IX of this Convention.

4. The Contracting Parties shall transmit to the Commission, biennially, or at such times as may be required by the Commission, a statement of the action that they have taken pursuant to this Article.

Article XI

1. The Commission shall seek to conclude agreements and maintain working arrangements with other international organizations which have related objectives, and in particular the Food and Agriculture Organization of the United Nations, to ensure effective collaboration and co-ordination and to avoid duplication with respect to their work.

2. The Commission may invite any appropriate international organization and the Government of

of any State eligible to become a party to this Convention under Article XVII, but which is not a member of the Commission, to be represented in an observer capacity at sessions of the Commission or its subsidiary bodies.

Article XII

1. The Commission shall appoint an Executive Secretary on such conditions as it may determine.

2. The staff of the Commission shall be appointed by the Executive Secretary in accordance with such rules and on such conditions as may be determined by the Commission.

3. The Executive Secretary shall perform such functions as the Commission may prescribe, including the following:

a) receiving and transmitting the Commission's official communications;

b) preparing budget estimates for review by the Commission at its regular sessions;

c) preparing for submission to the Commission at its regular sessions a report on the Commission's activities and the programme of work, and arranging for the subsequent publication of this report and the proceedings of the Commission;

d) arranging for the collection and analysis of statistics and other data necessary to accomplish the purposes of this Convention;

e) preparing for submission to the Commission, and for possible subsequent publication, reports on statistical, biological and other matters;

f) authorizing the disbursement of funds in accordance with the Commission's budget.

g) accounting for the funds of the Commission; and

h) arranging for co-operation with international organizations as provided for under Article XI of this Convention.

Article XIII

1. At each regular session the Commission shall adopt a budget for the following fiscal period and budget estimates for the fiscal period following thereafter. The fiscal period shall be two years. However, should the Commission hold more than one regular session during a fiscal period, it may revise the current budget if required. Subject to the agreement of all Contracting Parties, the Commission may, at any session, adopt a supplementary budget.

2. The contributions to the budget and any supplementary budget to be paid by each Contracting Party shall be payable in such currency or currencies and at such time as the Commission shall decide.

3. The voting rights of any Contracting Party whose arrears of contributions equal or exceed its total contribution falling due in the preceding fiscal period shall be suspended unless the Commission decides otherwise.

4. The Commission may also accept from any private or public sources other contributions for the furtherance of its objectives. Such contributions shall be used and administered in accordance with rules to be adopted by the Commission.

5. The Commission shall arrange for an annual independent audit of its accounts to be made and submitted for review and approval by the Commission.

6. The Commission shall establish a Working Capital Fund to finance operations of the Commission prior to receiving annual contributions, and for such other purposes as the Commission may determine. The Commission shall fix the level of the Fund, assess advances necessary for its establishment and adopt regulations governing its use.

Article XIV

The Commission shall calculate the contributions to be made by the Contracting Parties to the budget including any supplementary budget according to the following formula:

a) One third of the total amount of the budget including any supplementary budget shall be contributed by the Contracting Parties in equal parts;

b) Each Contracting Party shall contribute in respect of each Regional or Stock Committee of which it is a member an amount equivalent to one third of its contribution under sub-paragraph (*a*) above. The proportion shall be reduced, if necessary, in order that the total amount contributed by the Contracting Parties under this sub-paragraph shall not exceed one third of the total budget including any supplementary budget;

c) Any remaining portion of the budget including any supplementary budget shall be contributed by each Contracting Party in the proportion that its nominal catch in the Convention Area bears to the aggregate nominal catch of all Contracting Parties in that Area. In computing this catch the Commission shall take into account all fishes, crustaceans, molluscs and other marine invertebrates, with the exception of such species as may be excluded from the application of this Convention in accordance with Article III. The catch shall be determined on the basis of the average for the last two calendar years for which statistics have been published by the Food and Agriculture Organization of the United Nations.

Article XV

1. The Commission shall determine where its seat shall be situated.

2. The Commission shall have legal personality. It shall, in particular, have capacity to contract, and to acquire and dispose of movable and immovable property.

Article XVI

The provisions of this Convention shall not apply to fishing operations conducted solely for the purpose of scientific investigations, by vessels authorized by a Contracting Party for that purpose, or to fish taken in the course of such operations. However, fish so taken shall not be sold, or exposed or offered for sale in violation of a recommendation of the Commission.

Article XVII

1. This Convention shall be open for signature by the Government of any State represented at the Conference which adopted the Convention, or by the Government of any other State which is a Member of the United Nations or of any specialized agency of the United Nations.

2. Signature of this Convention shall be subject to ratification, acceptance or approval.

3. Once this Convention has entered into force, any State referred to in paragraph 1 of this Article which has not signed the Convention or any State unanimously invited by the Commission to become a party to the Convention may adhere to it.

4. Instruments of ratification, acceptance, approval or adherence shall be deposited with the Director-General of the Food and Agriculture Organization of the United Nations, hereinafter referred to as the "Depositary".

5. Ratification, acceptance, approval or adherence may not be made subject to any reservation.

Article XVIII

1. This Convention shall enter into force on the thirtieth day following the date of deposit of at least four instruments of ratification, acceptance or approval, provided that the weight of the aggregate nominal catch in the Convention Area of the countriess having deposited such instruments amounts to at least seven hundred thousand metric tons on the basis of the statistics published by the Food and Agriculture Organization of the United Nations for the year one thousand nine hundred and sixty-eight.

2. After the entry into force of this Convention in accordance with paragraph 1 of this Article, the Convention shall enter into force for each State whose Government deposits an instrument of ratification, acceptance, approval or adherence on the thirtieth day following the date on which such instrument is received by the Depositary.

Article XIX

1. Any Contracting Party may propose amendments to this Convention which shall be referred to the Commission for approval at a regular or special session. Proposals for the amendments of the Convention shall be communicated to the Depositary who shall inform the Contracting Parties thereof. Any amendment shall take effect for each Contracting Party accepting the amendment on the ninetieth day after its acceptance by three-fourths of the Contracting Parties and thereafter for each remaining Contracting Party on the day on which the Depositary receives the notification of such acceptance.

2. Any State which becomes a Contracting Party after an amendment to this Convention has been proposed for acceptance pursuant to the provisions of this Article shall be bound by the Convention as amended when the said amendment comes into force.

Article XX

At any time after ten years from the date of entry into force of this Convention, any Contracting Party may withdraw from the Convention by giving written notification of withdrawal. Withdrawal shall take effect on December thirty-first of the calendar year following the year in which notification of withdrawal was communicated to the Depositary.

Article XXI

1. The Depositary shall inform the Governments of the States referred to in paragraphs 1 to 3 of Article XVII:

a) of the signature of this Convention and of the deposit of instruments of ratification, acceptance, approval or adherence in accordance with Article XVII:

b) of the date on which the Convention will come into force in accordance with paragraph 1 of Article XVIII.

2. Depositary shall inform all Contracting Parties:

a) of proposals for the amendment of the Convention, notification of acceptance of such amendments and the entry into force of amendments, in accordance with Article XIX;

b) of notification of withdrawal made in accordance with Article XX.

3. The original of this Convention shall be deposited with the Depositary who shall send certified copies thereof to the Government of the States eligible to become parties to this Convention in accordance with Article XVII.

Done at Rome this twenty-third of October one thousand nine hundred and sixty-nine, in a single copy in the English, French and Spanish languages, each version being equally authoritative.

INTERNATIONAL CONVENTION RELATING TO INTERVENTION ON THE HIGH SEAS IN CASES OF OIL POLLUTION CASUALTIES [43]

Brussels, 29 November 1969

The States Parties to the present Convention,

Conscious of the need to protect the interests of their peoples against the grave consequences of a maritime casualty resulting in danger of oil pollution of sea and coastlines,

Convinced that under these circumstances measures of an exceptional character to protect such interests might be necessary on the high seas and that these measures do not affect the principle of freedom of the high seas,

Have agreed as follows:

Article I

1. Parties to the present Convention may take such measures on the high seas as may be necessary to prevent, mitigate or eliminate grave and imminent danger to their coastline or related interests from pollution or threat of pollution of the sea by oil, following upon a maritime casualty or acts related to such a casualty, which may reasonably be expected to result in major harmful consequences.

2. However, no measures shall be taken under the present Convention against any. warship or other ship owned or operated by a State and used, for the time being, only on government non-commercial service.

Article II

For the purposes of the present Convention:

1. "maritime casualty" means a collision of ships, stranding or incident of navigation, or other occurrence on board a ship or external to it resulting in material damage or imminent threat of material damage to a ship or cargo;

2. "ship" means:

a) any sea-going vessel of any type whatsoever, and

b) any floating craft with the exception of an installation or device engaged in the exploration and exploitation of the resources of the sea-bed and the ocean floor and the subsoil thereof;

3. "oil" means crude oil, fuel oil, diesel oil and lubricating oil;

4. "related interests" means the interests of a coastal State directly affected or threatened by the maritime casualty, such as:

a) maritime coastal, port or estuarine activities including fisheries activities, constituting an essential means of livelihood of the persons concerned;

b) tourist attractions of the area concerned;

c) the health of the coastal population and the well-being of the area concerned, including conservation of living marine resources and of wildlife;

5. "Organization" means the Inter-Governmental Maritime Consultative Organization.

Article III

When a coastal State is exercising the right to take measures in accordance with Article 1, the following provisions shall apply:

a) before taking any measures, a coastal State shall proceed to consultations with other States affected by the maritime casualty, particularly with the flag State or States;

b) the coastal State shall notify without delay the proposed measures to any persons physical or corporate known to the coastal State, or made known to it during the consultations, to have interests which can reasonably be expected to be affected by those measures. The coastal State shall take into account any views they may submit;

c) before any measure is taken, the coastal State may proceed to a consultation with independent experts, whose names shall be chosen from a list maintained by the Organization;

d) in cases of extreme urgency requiring measures to be taken immediately, the coastal State may take measures rendered necessary by the urgency of the situation, without prior notification or consultation or without continuing consultations already begun;

e) a coastal State shall, before taking such measures and during their course, use its best endeavours to avoid any risk to human life, and to afford persons in distress any assistance of which they may stand in need, and in appropriate cases to facilitate the repatriation of ship's crews, and to raise no obstacle thereto;

f) measures which have been taken in application of Article 1 shall be notified without delay to the States and to the known physical or corporate persons concerned, as well as the Secretary-General of the Organization.

Article IV

1. Under the supervision of the Organization, there shall be set up and maintained the list of experts contemplated by Article III of the present Convention, and the Organization shall make necessary and appropriate regulations in connexion therewith, including the determination of the required qualifications.

2. Nominations to the list may be made by Member States of the Organization and by Parties to this Convention. The experts shall be paid on the basis of services rendered by the States utilizing those services.

Article V

1. Measures taken by the coastal State in accordance with Article 1 shall be proportionate to the damage actual or threatened to it.

2. Such measures shall not go beyond what is reasonably necessary to achieve the end mentioned in Article 1 and shall cease as soon as that end has been achieved; they shall not unnecessarily

interfere with the rights and interests of the flag State, third States and of any persons, physical or corporate, concerned.

3. In considering whether the measures are proportionate to the damage, account shall be taken of:

a) the extent and probability of imminent damage if those measures are not taken; and

b) the likelihood of those measures being effective; and

c) the extent of the damage which may be caused by such measures.

Article VI

Any Party which has taken measures in contravention of the provisions of the present Convention causing damage to others, shall be obliged to pay compensation to the extent of the damage caused by measures which exceed those reasonably necessary to achieve the end mentioned in Article I.

Article VII

Except as specifically provided, nothing in the present Convention shall prejudice any otherwise applicable right, duty, privilege or immunity or deprive any of the Parties or any interested physical or corporate person of any remedy otherwise applicable.

Article VIII

1. Any controversy between the Parties as to whether measures taken under Article I were in contravention of the provisions of the present Convention, to whether compensation is obliged to be paid under Article VI, and to the amount of such compensation, shall, if settlement by negotiation between the Parties involved or between the Party which took the measures and the physical or corporate claimants has not been possible, and if the Parties do not otherwise agree, be submitted upon request of any of the Parties concerned to conciliation or, if conciliation does not succeed, to arbitration, as set out in the Annex to the present Convention.

2. The party which took the measures shall not be entitled to refuse a request for conciliation or arbitration under provisions of the preceding paragraph solely on the grounds that any remedies under municipal law in its own courts have not been exhausted.

Article IX

1. The present Convention shall remain open for signature until 31 December 1970 and shall thereafter remain open for accession.

2. States Members of the United Nations or any of the Specialized Agencies or of the International Atomic Energy Agency or Parties to the Statute of the International Court of Justice may become Parties to this Convention by:

a) signature without reservation as to ratification, acceptance or approval;

b) signature subject to ratification, acceptance or approval followed by ratification, acceptance or approval;

or

c) accession

Article X

1. Ratification, acceptance, approval or accession shall be effected by the deposit of a formal instrument to that effect with the Secretary-General of the Organization.

2. Any instrument of ratification, acceptance, approval or accession deposited after the entry into force of an amendment to the present Convention with respect to all existing Parties or after the completion of all measures required for the entry into force of the amendment with respect to those Parties shall be deemed to apply to the Convention as modified by the amendment.

Article XI

1. The present Convention shall enter into force on the ninetieth day following the date on which Governments of fifteen States have either signed it without reservation as to ratification, acceptance or approval or have deposited intruments of ratification, acceptance, approval or accession with the Secretary-General of the Organization.

2. For each State which subsequently ratifies, accepts, approves or accedes to it the present Convention shall come into force on the ninetieth day after deposit by such State of the appropriate instrument.

Article XII

1. The present Convention may be denounced by any Party at any time after the date on which the Convention comes into force for that State.

2. Denunciation shall be effected by the deposit of an instrument with the Secretary-General of the Organization.

3. A denunciation shall take effect one year, or such longer period as may be specified in the instrument of denunciation, after its deposit with the Secretary-General of the Organization.

Article XIII

1. The United Nations where it is the administering authority for a territory, or any State Party to the present Convention responsible for the international relations of a territory, shall as soon as possible consult with the appropriate authorities of such territories or take such other measures as may be appropriate, in order to extend the present Convention to that territory and may at any time by notification in writing to the Secretary-General of the Organization declare that the present Convention shall extend to such territory.

2. The present Convention shall, from the date of receipt of the notification or from such other date as may be specified in the notification, extend to the territory named therein.

3. The United Nations, or any Party which has

made a declaration under paragraph 1 of this Article may at any time after the date on which the Convention has been so extended to any territory declare by notification in writing to the Secretary-General of the Organization that the present Convention shall cease to extend to any such territory named in the notification.

4. The present Convention shall cease to extend to any territory mentioned in such notification one year, or such longer period as may be specified therein, after the date of receipt of the notificaion by the Secretary-General of the Organization.

Article XIV

1. A Conference for the purpose of revising or amending the present Convention may be convened by the Organization.

2. The Organization shall convene a Conference of the States Parties to the present Convention for revising or amending the present Convention at the request of not less than one-third of the Parties.

Article XV

1. The present Convention shall be deposited with the Secretary-General of the Organization.

2. The Secretary-General of the Organization shall:

a) inform all States which have signed or acceded to the Convention of:

(i) each new signature or deposit of instrument together with the date thereof;

(ii) the deposit of any instrument of denunciation of this Convention together with the date of the deposit;

(iii) the extension of the present Convention to any territory under paragraph 1 of Article XIII and of the termination of any such extension under the provisions of paragraph 4 of that Article stating in each case the date on which the present Convention has been or will cease to be so extended.

b) transmit certified true copies of the present Convention to all Signatory States and to all States which accede to the present Convention.

Article XVI

As soon as the present Convention comes into force, the text shall be transmitted by the Secretary-General of the Organization to the Secretariat of the United Nations for registration and publication in accordance with Article 102 of the Charter of the United Nations.

Article XVII

The present Convention is established in a single copy in the English and French languages, both texts being equally authentic. Official translations in the Russian and Spanish languages shall be prepared and deposited with the signed original.

In Witness Whereof the undersigned being duly authorized by their respective Governments for that purpose have signed the present Convention.

Done at Brussels this twenty-ninth day of November 1969.

ANNEX

Chapter I

CONCILIATION

Article 1

Provided the Parties concerned do not decide otherwise, the procedure for conciliation shall be in accordance with the rules set out in this Chapter.

Article 2

1. A Conciliation Commission shall be established upon the request of one Party addressed to another in application of Article VIII of the Convention.

2. The request for conciliation submitted by a Party shall consist of a statement of the case together with any supporting documents.

3. If a procedure has been initiated between two Parties, any other Party the nationals or property of which have been affected by the same measures, or which is a coastal State having taken similar measures, may join in the conciliation procedure by giving written notice to the Parties which have originally initiated the procedure unless either of the latter Parties object to such joinder.

Article 3

1. The Conciliation Commission shall be composed of three members: one nominated by the coastal State which took the measures, one nominated by the State the nationals or property of which have been affected by those measures and a third, who shall preside over the Commission and shall be nominated by agreement between the two original members.

2. The Conciliations shall be selected from a list previously drawn up in accordance with the procedure set out in Article 4 below.

3. If within a period of 60 days from the date of receipt of the request for conciliation, the Party to which such request is made has not given notice to the other Party to the controversy of the nomination of the Conciliator for whose selection it is responsible, or if, within a period of 30 days from the date of nomination of the second of the members of the Commission to be designated by the Parties, the first two Conciliators have not been able to designate by common agreement the Chairman of the Commission, the Secretary-General of the Organization shall upon request of either Party and within a period of 30 days, proceed to the required nomination. The members of the Commission thus nominated shall be selected from the list prescribed in the preceding paragraph.

4. In no case shall the Chairman of the Commission be or have been a national of one of the original Parties to the procedure, whatever the method of his nomination.

Article 4

1. The list prescribed in Article 3 above shall consist of qualified persons designated by the Parties and shall be kept up to date by the Organization. Each Party may designate for inclusion on the list four persons, who shall not necessarily be its nationals. The nominations shall be for periods of six years each and shall be renewable.

2. In the case of the decease or resignation of a person whose name appears on the list, the Party which nominated such person shall be permitted to nominate a replacement for the remainder of the team of office.

Article 5

1. Provided the Parties do not agree otherwise, the Conciliation Commission shall establish its own procedures, which shall in all cases permit a fair hearing. As regards examination, the Commission, unless it unanimously decides otherwise, shall conform with the provisions of Chapter III of the Hague Convention for the Peaceful Settlement of International Disputes of 18 October 1907.

2. The Parties shall be represented before the Conciliation Commission by agents whose duty shall be to act as intermediaries between the Parties and the Commission. Each of the Parties may seek also the assistance of advisers and experts nominated by it for this purpose and may request the hearing of all Parties as well as from any persons whom, with the consent of their Governments, it may deem useful to call.

3. The commission shall have the right to request explanations from agents, advisers and experts of the Parties as well as from any person whom, with the consent of their Governments, it may deem useful to call.

Article 6

Provided the Parties do not agree otherwise, decisions of the Conciliations Commission shall be taken by a majority vote and the Commissions shall not pronounce on the substance of the controversy unless all its members are present.

Article 7

The Parties shall facilitate the work of the Conciliation Commission and in particular, in accordance with their legislation, and using all means at their disposal:

a) provide the Commission with the necessary documents and information;

b) enable the Commission to enter their territory, to hear witnesses or experts, and to visit the scene.

Article 8

The task of the Conciliation Commission will be to clarify the matters under dispute, to assemble for this purpose all relevant information by means of examination or other means, and to endeavour to reconcile the Parties. After examining the case, the Commission shall communicate to the Parties, a recommendation which appears to the Commission to be appropriate to the matter and shall fix a period of not more than 90 days within which the Parties are called upon to state whether or not they accept the recommendation.

Article 9

The recommendation shall be accompanied by a statement of reasons. If the recommendation does not represent in whole or in part the unanimous opinion of the Commission, any Conciliator shall be entitled to deliver a separate opinion.

Article 10

A conciliation shall be deemed unsuccessful if, 90 days after the Parties have been notified of the recommendation, either Party shall not have notified the other Party of its acceptance of the secommendation. Conciliation shall likewise be deemed unsuccessful if the Commission shall not have been established within the period prescribed in the third paragraph of Article 3 above, or provided the Parties have not agreed otherwise, if the Commission shall not have issued its recommendation within one year from the date on which the Chairman of the Commission was nominated.

Article 11

1. Each member of the Commission shall receive remuneration for his work, such remuneration to be fixed by agreement between the Parties which shall each contribute an equal proportion.

2. Contributions for miscellaneous expenditure incureed by the work of the Commission shall be apportioned in the same manner.

Article 12

The parties to the controversy may at any time during the conciliation procedure decide in agreement to have recourse to a different procedure for settlement of disputes.

Chapter II

ARBITRATION

Article 13

1. Arbitration procedure, unless the Parties decide otherwise, shall be in accordance with the rules set out in this Chapter.

2. Where conciliation is unsuccessful, a request for arbitration may only be made within a period of 180 days following the failure of conciliation.

Article 14

The Arbitration Tribunal shall consist of three members: one Arbitrator nominated by the coastal State which took the measures, one Arbitrator nominated by the State the nationals or property of which have been affected by those measures, and another Arbitrator who shall be nominated by agreement between the two first-named, and shall act as its Chairman.

Article 15

1. If, at the end of a period of 60 days from the nomination of the second Arbitrator, the Chairman of the Tribunal shall not have been nominated, the Secretary-General of the Organization upon request of either Party shall within a further period of 60 days proceed to such nomination, selecting from a list of qualified persons previously drawn up in accordance with the provisions of Article 4 above. This list shall be separate from the list of experts prescribed in Article IV of the Convention and from the list of Conciliations prescribed in Article 4 of the present Annex, the name of the same person may, however, appear both on the list of Conciliators and on the list of Arbitrators in the same matter.

2. If, within a period of 60 days from the date of the receipt of the request, one of the Parties shall not have nominated the member of the Tribunal for whose designation it is responsible, the other Party may directly inform the Secretary-General of the Organization who shall nominate the Chairman of the Tribunal within a period of 60 days, selecting him from the list prescribed in paragraph 1 of the present Article.

3. The Chairman of the Tribunal shall, upon nomination, request the Party which has not provided an Arbitrator, to do so in the same manner and under the same conditions. If the Party does not make the required nomination, the Chairman of the Tribunal shall request the Secretary-General of the Organization to make the nomination in the form and conditions prescribed in the preceding paragraph.

4. The Chairman of the Tribunal, if nominated under the provisions of the present Article, shall not be or have been a national of one of the Parties concerned, except with the consent of the other Party or Parties.

5. In the case of the decease or default of an Arbitrator for whose nomination one of the Parties is responsible, the said Party shall nominate a replacement within a period of 60 days from the date of decease or default. Should the said Party not make the nomination, the arbitration shall proceed under the remaining Arbitrators. In the case of decease or default of the Chairman of the Tribunal, a replacement shall be nominated in accordance with the provisions of Article 14 above, or in the absence of agreement between the members of the Tribunal within a period of 60 days of the decease or default, according to the provisions of the present Article.

Article 16

If a procedure has been initiated between two Parties, any other Party, the nationals or property of which have been affected by the same measures or which is a coastal State having taken similar measures, may join in the arbitration procedure by giving written notice to the Parties which have originally initiated the procedure unless either of the latter Parties object to such joinder.

Article 17

Any Arbitration Tribunal established under the provisions of the present Annex shall decide its own rules of procedure.

Article 18

1. Decisions of the Tribunal both as to its procedure and its place of meeting and as to any controversy laid before it, shall be taken by majority vote of its members; the absence or abstention of one of the members of the Tribunal for whose nomination the Parties were responsible shall not constitute an impediment to the Tribunal reaching a decision. In cases of equal voting, the Chairman shall cast the deciding vote.

2. The Parties shall facilitate the work of the Tribunal and in particular, in accordance with their legislation, and using all means at their disposal:

a) provide the Tribunal with the necessary documents and information;

b) enable the Tribunal to enter their territory, to hear witnesses or experts, and to visit the scene.

3. Absence or default of one Party shall not consititute an impediment to the procedure.

Article 19

1. The award of the Tribunal shall be accompanied by a statement of reasons. It shall be final and without appeal. The Parties shall immediately comply with the award.

2. Any controversy which may arise between the Parties as regards interpretation and execution of the award may be submitted by either Party for judgement to the Tribunal which made the award, or, if it is not available, to another Tribunal constituted for this purpose in the same manner as the original Tribunal.

INTERNATIONAL CONVENTION ON CIVIL LIABILITY FOR OIL POLLUTION DAMAGE [44]

Brussels, 29 November 1969

The States Parties to the present Convention,

Conscious of the dangers of pollution posed by the worldwide maritime carriage of oil in bulk,

Convinced of the need to ensure that adequate compensation is available to persons who suffer damage caused by pollution resulting from the escape or discharge of oil from ships,

Desiring to adopt uniform international rules and procedures for determining questions of liability and providing adequate compensation in such cases,

Have agreed as follows:

Article I

For the purposes of this Convention:

1. "Ship" means any sea-going vessel and any seaborne craft of any type whatsoever, actually carrying oil in bulk as cargo.
2. "Person" means any individual or partnership or any public or private body, whether corporate or not, including a State or any of its constituent subdivisions.
3. "Owner" means the person or persons registered as the owner of the ship or, in the absence of registration, the person or persons owning the ship. However in the case of a ship owned by a State and operated by a company which in that State is registered as the ship's operator, "owner" shall mean such company.
4. "State of the ship's registry" means in relation to registered ships the State of registration of the ship, and in relation to unregistered ships the State whose flag the ship is flying.
5. "Oil" means any persistent oil such as crude oil, fuel oil, heavy diesel oil, lubricating oil and whale oil, whether carried or in the bunkers of such a ship.
6. "Pollution damage" means loss or damage caused outside the ship carrying oil by contamination resulting from the escape or discharge of oil from the ship, wherever such escape or discharge may occur, and includes the costs of preventive measures and further loss or damage caused by preventive measures.
7. "Preventive measures" means any reasonable measures taken by any person after an incident had occurred to prevent or minimize pollution damage.
8. "Incident" means any occurrence, or series of occurrences having the same origin, which causes pollution damage.
9. "Organization" means the Inter-Governmental Maritime Cosultative Organization.

Article II

This Convention shall apply exclusively to pollution damage caused on the territory including the territorial sea of a Contracting State and to preventive measures taken to prevent or minimize such damage.

Article III

1. Except as provided in paragraphs 2 and 3 of this Article, the owner of a ship at the time of an incident, or where the incident consists of a series of occurrences at the time of the first such occurrence, shall be liable for any pollution damage caused by oil which has escaped or been discharged from the ship as a result of the incident.

2. No liability for pollution damage shall attach to the owner if he proves that the damage:

a) resulted from an act of war, hostilities, civil war, insurrection or a natural phenomenon of an exceptional, inevitable and irresistible character, or

b) was wholly caused by an act or omission done with intent to cause damage by a third party, or

c) was wholly caused by the negligence or other wrongful act of any Government or other authority responsible for the maintenance of lights or other navigational aids in the exercise of that function.

3. If the owner proves that the pollution damage resulted wholly or partially either from an act or omission done with intent to cause damage by the person who suffered the damage or from the negligence of that person, the owner may be exonerated wholly or partially from his liability to such person.

4. No claim for compensation for pollution damage shall be made against the owner otherwise than in accordance with this Convention. No claim for pollution damage under this Convention or otherwise may be made against the servants or agents of the owner.

5. Nothing in this Convention shall prejudice any right of recourse of the owner against third parties.

Article IV

When oil has escaped or has been discharged from two or more ships, and pollution damage results therefrom, the owners of all the ships concerned, unless exonerated under Article III, shall be jointly and severally liable for all such damage which is not reasonably reparable.

Article V

1. The owner of a ship shall be entitled to limit his liability under this Convention in respect of any one incident to an aggregate amount of 2,000 francs for each ton of the ship's tonnage. However, this aggregate amount shall not in any event exceed 210 million francs.

2. If the incident occurred as a result of the actual fault or privity of the owner, he shall not be entitled to avail himself of the limitation provided in paragraph 1 of this Article.

3. For the purpose of availing himself of the benefit of limitation provided for in paragraph 1 of this Article the owner shall constitute a fund for the total sum representing the limit of liability with the

Court or other competent authority of any one of the Contracting States in which action is brought under Article IX. The fund can be constituted either by depositing the sum or by producing a bank guarantee or other guarantee, acceptable under the legislation of the Contracting State where the fund is constituted, and considered to be adequate by the Court or another competent authority.

4. The fund shall be distributed among the claimants in proportion to the amounts of their established claims.

5. If before the fund is distributed the owner or any of his servants or agents or any person providing him insurance or other financial security has as a result of the incident in question, paid compensation for pollution damage, such person shall up to the amount he has paid, acquire by subrogation the rights which the person so compensated would have enjoyed under this Convention.

6. The right of subrogation provided for in paragraph 5 of this Article may also be exercised by a person other than those mentioned therein in respect of any amount of compensation for pollution damage which he may have paid but only to the extent that such subrogation is permitted under the applicable national law.

7. Where the owner or any other person establishes that he may be compelled to pay at a later date in whole or in part any such amount of compensation, with regard to which such person would have enjoyed a right of subrogation under paragraphs 5 or 6 of this Article, had the compensation been paid before the fund was distributed, the Court or other competent authority of the State where the fund has been constituted may order that a sufficient sum shall be provisionally set aside to enable such person at such later date to enforce his claim against the fund.

8. Claims in respect of expenses reasonably incurred or sacrifices reasonably made by the owner voluntarily to prevent or minimize pollution damage shall rank equally with other claims against the fund.

9. The franc mentioned in this Article shall be a unit consisting of sixty-five and a half milligrams of gold of millesimal fineness nine hundred. The amount mentioned in paragraph 1 of this Article shall be converted into the national currency of the State in which the fund is being constituted on the basis of the official value of that currency by reference to the unit defined above on the date of the constitution of the fund.

10. For the purpose of this Article the ship's tonnage shall be the net tonnage of the ship with the addition of the amount deducted from the gross tonnage on account of engine room space for the purpose of ascertaining the net tonnage. In the case of a ship which cannot be measured in accordance with the normal rules of tonnage measurement, the ship's tonnage shall be deemed to be 40 per cent of the weight in tons (of 2240 lbs) of oil which the ship is capable of carrying.

11. The insurer or other person providing financial security shall be entitled to constitute a fund in accordance with this Article on the same conditions and having the same effect as if it were constituted by the owner. Such a fund may be constituted even in the event of the actual fault or privity of the owner but its constitution shall in that case not prejudice the rights of any claimant against the owner.

Article VI

1. Where the owner, after an incident, has constituted a fund in accordance with Article V, and is entitled to limit his liability,

a) no person having a claim for pollution damage arising out of that incident shall be entitled to exercise any right against any other assets of the owner in respect of such claim;

b) The Court or other competent authority of any Contracting State shall order the release of any ship or other property belonging to the owner which has been arrested in respect of a claim for pollution damage arising out of that incident, and shall similarly release any bail or other security furnished to avoid such arrest.

2. The foregoing shall, however, only apply if the claimant has access to the Court administering the fund and the fund is actually available in respect of his claim.

Article VII

1. The owner of a ship registered in a Contracting State and carrying more than 2,000 tons of oil in bulk as cargo shall be required to maintain insurance or other financial security, such as the guarantee of a bank or a certificate delivered by an international compensation fund in the sums fixed by applying the limits of liability prescribed in Article V, paragraph 1 to cover his liability for pollution damage under this Convention.

2. A certificate attesting that insurance or other financial security is in force in accordance with the provisions of this Convention shall be issued to each ship. It shall be issued or certified by the appropriate authority of the State of the ship's registry after determining that the requirements of paragraph 1 of this Article have been complied with. This certificate shall be in the form of the annexed model and shall contain the following particulars:

a) name of ship and port of registration;

b) name and principal place of business of owner;

c) type of security;

d) name and principal place of business of insurer or other person giving security and, where appropriate, place of business where the insurance or security is established;

e) period of validity of certificate which shall not be longer than the period of validity of the insurance or other security.

3. The certificate shall be in the official language or languages of the issuing State. If the language used is neither English nor French, the text shall

include a translation into one of these languages.

4. The certificate shall be carried on board the ship and a copy shall be deposited with the authorities who keep the record of the ship's registry.

5. An insurance or other financial security shall not satisfy the requirements of this Article if it can cease, for reasons other than the expiry of the period of validity of the insurance or security specified in the certificate under paragraph 2 of this Article, before three months have elapsed from the date on which notice of its termination is given to the authorities referred to in paragraph 4 of this Article, unless the certificate has been surrendered to these authorities or a new certificate has been issued within the said period. The foregoing provisions shall similarly apply to any modification which results in the insurance or security no longer satisfying the requirements of this Article.

6. The State of registry shall, subject to the provisions of this Article, determine the conditions of issue and validity of the certificate.

7. Certificates issued or certified under the authority of a Contracting State shall be accepted by other Contracting States for the purposes of this Convention and shall be regarded by other Contracting States as having the same force as certificates issued or certified by them. A Contracting State may at any time request consultation with the State of a ship's registry should it believe that the insurer or guarantor named in the certificate is not financially capable of meeting the obligations imposed by this Convention.

8. Any claim for compensation for pollution damage may be brought directly against the insurer or other person providing financial security for the owner's liability for pollution damage. In such case the defendant may, irrespective of the actual fault or privity of the owner, avail himself of the limits of liability prescribed in Article V, paragraph 1. He may further avail himself of the defences (other than the bankruptcy or winding up of the owner) which the owner himself would have been entitled to invoke. Furthermore, the defendant may avail himself of the defence that the pollution damage resulted from the wilful misconduct of the owner himself, but the defendant shall not avail himself of any other defence which he might have been entitled to invoke in proceedings brought by the owner against him. The defendant shall in any event have the right to require the owner to be joined in the proceedings.

9. Any sums provided by insurance or by other financial security maintained in accordance with paragraph 1 of this Article shall be available exclusively for the satisfaction of claims under this Convention.

10. A Contracting State shall not permit a ship under its flag to which this Article applies to trade unless a certificate has been issued under paragraph 2 or 12 of this Article.

11. Subject to the provisions of this Article, each Contracting State shall ensure, under its national legislation, that insurance or other security to the extent specified in paragraph 1 of this Article is in force in respect of any ship, wherever registered, entering or leaving a port in its territory, or arriving at or leaving an off-shore terminal in its territorial sea, if the ship actually carries more than 2,000 tons of oil in bulk as cargo.

12. If insurance or other financial security is not maintained in respect of a ship owned by a Contracting State, the provisions of this Article relating thereto shall not be applicable to such ship, but the ship shall carry a certificate issued by the appropriate authorities of the State of the ship's registry stating that the ship is owned by that State and that the ship's liability is covered within the limits prescribed by Article V, paragrpah 1. Such a certificate shall follow as closely as practicable the model prescribed by paragraph 2 of this Article.

Article VIII

Rights of compensation under this Convention shall be extinguished unless an action is brought thereunder within three years from the date when the damage occurred. However, in no case shall an action be brought after six years from the date of the incident which caused the damage. Where this incident consists of a series of occurrences, the six years' period shall run from the date of the first such occurrence.

Article IX

1. Where an incident has caused pollution damage in the territory including the territorial sea of one or more Contracting States, or preventive measures have been taken to prevent or minimize pollution damage in such territory including the territorial sea, actions for compensation may only be brought in the Courts of any such Contracting State or States. Reasonable notice of such action shall be given to the defendant.

2. Each Contracting State shall ensure that its Courts possess the necessary jurisdiction to entertain such actions for compensation.

3. After the fund has been constituted in accordance with Article V the Courts of the State in which the fund is constituted shall be exclusively competent to determine all matters relating to the apportionment and distribution of the fund.

Article X

1. Any judgement given by a Court with jurisdiction in accordance with Article IX which is enforceable in the State of origin where it is no longer subject to ordinary forms of review, shall be recognized in any Contracting State, except;

a) where the judgement was obtained by fraud; or

b) where the defendant was given reasonable notice and a fair opportunity to present his case.

2. A judgement recognized under paragraph 1 of this Article shall be enforceable in each

Contracting State as soon as the formalities required in that State have been complied with. The formalities shall not permit the merits of the case to be re-opened.

Article XI

1. The provisions of this Convention shall not apply to warships or other ships owned or operated by a State and used, for the time being, only on Government non-commercial service.

2. With respect to ships owned by a Contracting State and used for commercial purposes, each State shall be subject to suit in the jurisdictions set forth in Article IX and shall waive all defences based on its status as a sovereign State.

Article XII

This Convention shall supersede any International Conventions in force or open for signature, ratification or accession at the date in which the Convention is opened for signature, but only to the extent that such Conventions would be in conflict with it; however, nothing in this Article shall affect the obligations of Contracting States to non-Contracting States arising under such International Conventions.

Article XIII

1. The present Convention shall remain open for signature until 31 December 1970 and shall thereafter remain open for accession.

2. States Members of the United Nations or any of the Specialized Agencies or of the International Atomic Energy Agency or Parties to the Statute of the International Court of Justice may become Parties to this Convention by:

a) signature without reservation as to ratification, acceptance or approval;

b) signature subject to ratification, acceptance or approval followed by ratifications, acceptance or approval;

or

c) accession

Article XIV

1. Ratification, acceptance, approval or accession shall be effected by the deposit of a formal instrument to that effect with the Secretary-General of the Organization.

2. Any instrument of ratification, acceptance, approval or accession deposited after the entry into force of an amendment to the present Convention with respect to all existing Contracting States, or after the completion of all measures required for the entry into force of the amendment with respect to those Contracting States shall be deemed to apply to the Convention as notified by the amendment.

Article XV

1. The present Convention shall enter into force on the ninetieth day following the date on which Governments of eight States including five States each with not less than 1,000,000 gross tons of tanker tonnage have either signed it without reservation as to ratification, acceptance or approval or have deposited instruments of ratification, acceptance, approval or accession with the Secretary-General of the Organization.

2. For each State which subsequently ratifies, accepts, approves or accedes to it the present Convention shall come into force on the ninetieth day after deposit by such State of the appropriate instrument.

Article XVI

1. The present Convention may be denounced by any Contracting State at any time after the date on which the Convention comes into force for that State.

2. Denunciation shall be effected by the deposit of an instrument with the Secretary-General of the Organization.

3. A denunciation shall take effect one year, or such longer period as may be specified in the instrument of denunciation, after its deposit with the Secretary-General of the Organization.

Article XVII

1. The United Nations, where it is the administering authority for a territory, or any Contracting State responsible for the international relations of a territory, shall as soon as possible consult with the appropriate authorities of such territory or take such other measures as may be appropriate, in order to extend the present Convention to that territory and may at any time by notification in writing to the Secretary-General of the Organization declare that the present Convention shall extend to such territory.

2. The present Convention shall, from the date of receipt of the notification or from such other date as may be specified in the notification, extend to the territory named therein.

3. The United Nations, or any Contracting State which has made a declaration under paragraph 1 of this Article may at any time after the date on which the Convention has been so extended to any territory declare by notification in writing to the Secretary-General of the Organization that the present Convention shall cease to extend to any such territory named in the notification.

4. The present Convention shall cease to extend to any territory mentioned in such notification one year, or such longer period as may be specified therein after the date of receipt of the notification by the Secretary-General of the Organization.

Article XVIII

1. A Conference for the purpose of revising or amending the present Convention may be convened by the Organization.

2. The Organization shall convene a Conference of the Contracting States for revising or amending the present Convention at the request of not less than one-third of the Contracting States.

Article XIX

1. The present Convention shall be deposited with the Secretary-General of the Organization.

2. The Secretary-General of the Organization shall:

a) inform all States which have signed or acceded to the Convention of

(i) each new signature or deposit of instrument together with the date thereof;

(ii) the deposit of any instruments of denunciation of this Convention together with the date of the deposit;

(iii) the extension of the present Convention to any territory under paragraph 1 of Article XVII and of the termination of any such extension under the provisions of paragraph 4 of that Article stating in each case the date on which to be so extended.

b) transmit certified true copies of the present Convention to all Signatory States and to all States which accede to the present Convention.

Article XX

As soon as the present Convention comes into force, the text shall be transmitted by the Secretary-General of the Organization to the Secretariat of the United Nations for registration and publication in accordance with Article 102 of the Charter of the United Nations.

Article XXI

The present Convention is established in a single copy in the English and French languages, both texts being equally authentic. Official translations in the Russian and Spanish languages shall be prepared and deposited with the signed original.

In Witness Whereof the undersigned being duly authorized by their respective Governments for that purpose have signed the present Convention.

Done at Brussels this twenty-ninth day of November 1969.

BENELUX CONVENTION CONCERNING HUNTING AND THE PROTECTION OF BIRDS [45]

Brussels, 10 June 1970

The Government of the Kingdom of Belgium, the Government of the Grand Duchy of Luxembourg, the Government of the Kingdom of the Netherlands.

Having regard to article 6 of the Treaty instituting the Benelux Economic Union, signed at The Hague on 3 February 1958,

Having regard to the International Convention for the protection of birds, signed at Paris on 18 October 1950, to which the three Benelux countries are parties;

Being desirous of harmonizing the principles governing their laws and regulations on the subject of hunting and the protection of birds in the wild state, which were established in the interests of land-holders, agriculture and the efficient protection of nature;

Considering that such harmonization will make for greater uniformity in the laws relating to the transport of game and birds in the wild state and thereby facilitate the elimination of formalities and inspection measures at the frontiers between the benelux countries;

Having regard to the advice of the Benelux Consultative Interparliamentary Council of 25 April 1970;

Have agreed on the following provisions:

Part I
HUNTING

Article 1

1. Each of the three Governments undertakes to classify game in its national laws according to the following categories: large game, small game, wild fowl and other game.

2. For the purposes of this Convention, these terms shall have the following meaning:

a) large game: European red deer (*Cervus elaphus*), roe deer (*roebuck*) (*Capreolus capreolus*), fallow deer (*Dama dama,*) Sardinian and Corsican mouflon (*Ovis musimon*), European wild boar (*Sus scrofa*);

b) small game: common hare (*Lepus europaeus*), pheasant (*Phasianus colchicus*), black grouse (*Lyryrys tetrix*), Hungarian (European) partridge (*Perdix perdix*), European woodcock (*Scolopax rusticola*);

c) wild fowl, all species of goose and duck (*Anatidae*), Eurasian golden plover (*Pluvialis*) *appricarius*), common snipe (*Gallinago gallinago*) great snipe (*Gallinago media*), jacksnipe (*Lymnocryptes minimus*), European coot (*Fulica atra*);

d) other game: wood-pigeon (*Colomba palumbus*), carrion-crow and hooded crow (*Corvus corone corone and Corvus corone cornix*), rook (*Corvus frugilegus*), jackdaw (*Corvus monedula*), common jay (*Garrulus glandarius*), black-billed magpie (*Pica pica*), European rabbit (*Orvctolagus cuniculus*), common red fox (*Vulpes vulpes*), European wildcat (*Felis catus*), polecat (*Putorius putorius*), stoat (*Mustela erminea*), common weasel (*Mustela nivalis*), pine marten and beech (stone) marten (*Martes martes and Martes fiona*), Eurasian badger (*Meles meles*), Eurasian otter (*Lutra lutra*)[and seal (*Phoca vitulina* and *Halichoerus grypus*).

3. The Committee of Ministers, established under article 15 of the Treaty instituting the Benelux Economic Union, may change or supplement any of the Categories specified in paragraph 2 by decisions taken in conformity with article 19 (*a*) of the Treaty for the Union.

4. Pending harmonization of the categories of game, each of the Contracting Parties may add other species of animal to the aforementioned categories.

Article 2

The three Governments shall consult each other concerning the dates for the opening and closing of the hunting season.

Article 3

Land used for shooting must have minimum dimensions. The dimensions shall conform to the hunting requirements of each country, it being understood that:

a) The minimum area of a single unit may not be less than 25 hectares in the Netherlands, and north and west of the Sambre-Meuse line in Belgium, and may not be less than 50 hectares south of that line in Belgium and also in Luxembourg;

b) Wild fowl may be hunted over a smaller area, provided that, at the time when hunting takes place each single unit of land includes a stretch of water of at least one hectare.

None of the three countries may, however, prescribe minimum areas smaller than those specified in the legal provisions or national regulations at present in force.

Article 4

The three Governments shall consult each other concerning the arms, ammunition, projectiles, tackle, apparatus, procedures and methods permitted for hunting.

Article 5

1. Subject to national health provisions, the transport and marketing of live or dead game shall be authorized from the day of commencement of the hunting season for that particular game until the tenth day after the close of the season.

2. From the eleventh day after the close of the season until commencement of the following season, the transport and marketing of live or dead game shall be authorized only in conformity with the regulations of the Government in whose territory the transport or marketing takes place.

Article 6

In the case of traffic with third countries, the import, export and transit of live or dead game shall be governed by the regulations in force in the partner countries in which such operations take place.

Part II

PROTECTION OF BIRDS

Article 7

The three Governments undertake to protect the species of birds living in the wild state in the Benelux countries, other than the species considered to be game under article 1; to this end, and without prejudice to the provisions of article 8, the Committee of Ministers shall determine, by decisions taken in conformity with article 19 (*a*) of the Treaty of the Union, the protective measures, and the species of birds to which such measures apply.

Article 8

1. Each of the three Governments undertake to adjust its national laws to ensure that it is prohibited, at all times and in all places, to hold for sale, to sell, to purchase or to supply birds belonging to the species determined in accordance with article 7, as well as their eggs, including blown eggs and their young; this prohibition shall also apply to any mounted bird of these species unless prior dispensation has been granted by the competent national authorities.

2. The transport of the birds referred to in paragraph 1, and of their eggs and young, shall be authorized only in conformity with the regulations in force in the country in whose territory the transport takes place.

Article 9

In the case of traffic with third countries, the import, export and transit of all live or dead birds, and of their eggs and young, shall be permitted only with prior authorization from the partner countries in which such operations take place.

Part III

GENERAL PROVISIONS

Article 10

Inspection in pursuance of articles 5, 6, 8 and 9 shall be carried out within each of the countries and at the external frontiers of Benelux, but not in connexion with the crossing of frontiers between the Benelux countries.

Article 11

The Committee of Ministers shall determine by decisions taken in conformity with article 19 (*a*) of the Treaty for the Union, the measures which, notwithstanding the provisions of article 5, paragraph 2, article 6, article 8, paragraph 2, and article 9, need to be taken in one or more countries to avoid any detriment to the interests of partner countries.

Article 12

Each of the three countries retains the right to maintain or to introduce legislative provisions for the regulation of matters not covered by this Convention, provided that such provisions are not incompatible with the Convention.

Article 13

1. Each of the three Governments retains the right, subject to the prior approval of the Committee of Ministers, recorded in a decision taken in conformity with article 19 (*a*) of the Treaty for the Union, to authorize departures from the provisions of this Convention in the interest of science or nature conservation or for the purpose of preventing damage.

2. In cases of emergency, however, each of the Governments may adopt and apply measures which depart from the provisions of this Convention, over a maximum period of three months, pending decision by the Committee of Ministers. The other Governments shall be informed of such provisional application through the Secretary-General of the Benelux Economic Union.

Article 14

In pursuance of article 1, paragraph 2, of the Treaty relating to the institution and statute of a Benelux Court of Justice, the provisions of this Convention shall be designated as common legal rules for the application of chapters III and IV of the aforesaid Treaty.

Article 15

In the case of the Kingdom of the Netherlands, this Convention shall apply only to territory in Europe.

Article 16

1. This Convention shall be subject to ratification. The instruments of ratification shall be deposited with the Secretary-General of the Benelux Economic Union, who shall inform the Contracting Parties of the deposit of such instruments.

2. It shall enter into force on the first day of the second month following the date of deposit of the third instrument of ratification.

3. It shall remain in force for the same period as the Treaty instituting the Benelux Economic Union.

In Witness Whereof the undersigned, duly authorized for the purpose, have signed this Convention.

Done at Brussels on 10 June 1970, in triplicate, in the Dutch and French languages, both texts being equally authentic.

Declarations

"1. The Royal Ministry of Justice and Police is designated as the Central Authority with reference to article 2 and as the Competent Authority with reference to articles 15, 16 and17.

"II. With reference to article 4, paragraphs 3, the Kingdom of Norway declares that letters in the Danish or Swedish languages can be sent to the Central Authority.

"III. By accepting Letters of Request in another language than the Norwegian, the Kingdom of Norway does not undertake to execute the request, or transmit the evidence thus obtained in this other language, nor to have translated the documents which establish the execution of the letter of request.

"IV. By virtue of article 15, evidence can be taken by diplomatic officers or consular agents only if, upon application, prior permission to that effect has been granted.

"V. By virtue of article 23, the Kingdom of Norway declares that it will not execute Letters of Request issued for the purpose of obtaining pre-trial discovery of documents as known in Common Law countries."

AGREEMENT FOR THE ESTABLISHMENT OF A COMMISSION FOR CONTROLLING THE DESERT LOCUST IN NORTHWEST AFRICA [46]

as amended by the Commission at its Sixth Session (4-6 April 1977) and approved by the FAO Council at its Seventy-Second Session (8-10 November 1977)

Rome, November 1970

PREAMBLE

The Contracting Governments, having regard to the urgent necessity of preventing losses to agriculture in certain countries in Northwest Africa caused by the Desert Locust, hereby establish within the framework of the Food and Agriculture Organization of the United Nations (hereinafter referred to as "the Organization") a Commission to be known as the "Commission for Controlling the Desert Locust in Northwest Africa", whose object shall be to promote national and international research and action with respect to the control of the Desert Locust in Northwest Africa. Northwest Africa (hereinafter referred to as "the Region") is defined, for the purpose of this Agreement, as consisting of the territories of Algeria, Libya, Morocco and Tunisia, and the countries adjacent hereto.

Article I

MEMBERSHIP

1. The Members of the Commission for Controlling the Desert Locust in Northwest Africa, (hereinafter referred to as "the Commission"), shall be such Member Nations and Associate Members of the Organizations situated in the Region defined in the Preamble as accept this Agreement in accordance with the provisions of Article XIV of this Agreement.

2. The Commission may, by a two-thirds majority of its membership, admit to membership any other Nations situated in the Region that are part of the United Nations, of any of the specialized agencies, or of the International Atomic Energy Agency and that have submitted an application to this effect together with a declaration made in a formal instrument that they accept this Agreement as in force at the time of admission.

Article II

OBLIGATIONS OF MEMBERS REGARDING NATIONAL POLICIES AND INTERNATIONAL CO-OPERATION FOR THE CONTROL OF THE DESERT LOCUST

1. Members undertake to maintain directly and through the Secretary of the Commission a regular exchange of information on the current locust situation and the progress of control campaigns within their countries, and also to transmit such information regularly to the Organization and to the Desert Locust Information Service in London.

2. Members undertake to carry out all possible measures to control plagues of the Desert Locust within their countries and to reduce crop damage by adopting the following procedures:

a) maintaining a permanent locust reporting and control service;

b) holding reserves of insecticides and application equipment;

c) encouraging and supporting such training, survey and researh work, including where appropriate the maintenance of national research stations for the study of the Desert Locust, as may be considered desirable by the Commission and as are compatible with the resources of the country;

d) participating in the implementation of any common policy of locust control or prevention which may be approved by the Commission;

e) facilitating the storage of any items of anti-locust equipment and insecticides that might be held by the Commission and permitting the duty-free import or export without hindrance of such goods and equipment as well as the free movement within the country of such goods and equipments;

f) providing the Commission with any information it may request to carry out its functions effectively.

3. Members undertake to submit to the Commission periodic reports on the action taken to fulfil the obligations specified in paragraphs 1 and 2 above.

Article III

SEAT OF THE COMMISSION

1. The seat of the Commission shall be determined by the Commission.

2. Sessions of the Commission shall normally be held at its seat. Sessions may, however, be convened elsewhere in consultation with the Director-General of the Organization, in pursuance of a decision of the Commission at a previous session, or in exceptional circumstances of a decision by the Executive Committee.

Article IV

FUNCTIONS OF THE COMMISSION

The following shall be the functions of the Commission:

1. *Joint action and assistance*

The Commission shall:

a) plan and promote joint action for the survey and control of the Desert Locust in the Region wherever required and, to this effect, arrange means whereby adequate resources can be made available;

b) assist and promote, in any manner which it considers appropriate, any national, regional or international action relating to the control or survey of the Desert Locust;

c) determine, in consultation with the Members concerned, the nature and extent of assistance needed by such Members for implementing their national programmes and for supporting regional programmes;

d) assist, at the request of any Member whose territory is faced with Desert Locust situations beyond the capacity of its national services to control and survey, in any measures jointly agreed to that may become necessary;

e) maintain at strategic localities determined by the Commission, in consultation with the Members concerned, reserves of anti-locust equipment, insecticides and other supplies, to be used in cases of emergency in accordance with decisions of the Executive Committee including supplementing of the national resources of any Member.

2. *Information and co-ordination*

The Commission shall:

a) ensure that all Members are provided with current information in regard to Desert Locust infestations, and collect and disseminate information on experience gained, research conducted and programmes adopted on the national, regional and international levels in connexion with the control of the Desert Locust;

b) assist the national research organizations of Members and co-ordinate research in the Region by arranging visits of research and survey units from Members and by other appropriate means.

3. *Co-operation*

The Commission may:

a) enter into arrangements or agreements, through the Director-General of the Organization, with nations in the Region that are not Members in the Commission, for common action in connection with the survey and control of locusts in the Region;

b) enter into or encourage arrangements, through the Director-General of the Organization, with other United Nations Specialized Agencies or other international organizations concerned, for common action in the study and control of locusts and for the mutual exchange of information on problems concerning locusts.

4. *Administrative matters*

The Commission shall:

a) consider and approve the report of the Executive Committee on the activities of the Commission, the Programme and Budget of the Commission for the ensuing financial period, and the annual accounts;

b) keep the Director-General of the Organization fully informed of its activities and transmit to him the accounts, the Programme and the Budget of the Commission, the latter for submission to the Council of the Organization prior to implementation;

c) transmit to the Director-General of the Organization the reports and recommendations of the Commission, for such action by the Council or Conference of the Organization as may be appropriate.

Article V

SESSIONS OF THE COMMISSION

1. Each Member of the Commission shall be represented at sessions of the Commission by a delegate who may be accompanied by alternates or by experts and advisers. Alternates, experts and advisers may take part in the proceedings of the Commission but may not vote unless authorized by the delegate to substitute for him.

2. A majority of the Members of the Commission shall constitute a quorum. Each Member shall have one vote. Decisions of the Commission shall be taken by a majority of the votes cast except as otherwise provided for in this Agreement.

3. A Member which is in arrears in the payment of its financial contributions to the Commission shall have no vote. if the amount of its arrears equals or exceeds the amount of the contributions due from it for the two preceding financial years.

4. The Commission shall elect, at the beginning of each regular session, a Chairman and a Vice-Chairman from amongst the delegates. These officers shall hold office until the beginning of the next regular session and shall be eligible for re-election.

5. The Director-General of the Organization, in consultation with the Chairman of the Commission, shall convene a regular session of the Commission at least once a year. Special sessions may be convened by the Director-General of the Organization in consultation with the Chairman of the Commission, if so requested by the Commission in regular session or by at least one-third of the Members during intervals between regular sessions.

6. The Director-General of the Organization or a representative designated by him shall have the right to participate without vote in all meetings of the Commission and of the Executive Committee.

Article VI

OBSERVERS AND CONSULTANTS

1. Participation of international organizations in the work of the Commission and the relations between the Commission and such organizations shall be governed by the relevant provisions of the Constitution and the General Rules of the Organization as well as by the rules on relations with international organizations adopted by the Conference or Council of the Organization. All such relations shall be dealt with by the Director-General of the Organization.

2. Member Nations and Associate members of the Organization that are not such Members of the Commission may, upon their request, be represented by an observer at sessions of the Commission.

3. Nations which, while not members of the Commission, nor Members or Associate Members of the Organization but which are part of the United Nations, any of the Specialized Agencies, or the International Atomic Energy Agency may, upon request and subject to the concurrence of the Executive Committee and to the provisions

relating to the granting of observer status to nations adopted by the Conference of FAO, be invited to attend sessions of the Commission in an observer capacity.

4. The Commission may invite consultants or experts to attend its sessions. The Executive Committee may also invite consultants or experts to attend its sessions or those of the Commission.

Article VII

SECRETARIAT

The Director-General of the Organization shall provide the Secretary and staff of the Commission, who, for administrative purposes shall be responsible to him. They shall be appointed under the same terms and conditions as the staff of the Organization.

Article VIII

THE EXECUTIVE COMMITTEE

1. There shall be an Executive Committee composed of one representative (preferably a locust specialist) of each of the Members of the Commission. The Executive Committee shall elect its Chairman and Vice-Chairman from amongst the representatives of Members of the Committee. The Chairman and Vice-Chairman of the Executive Committee shall hold office for one year and shall be eligible for re-election.

2. The Executive Committee shall meet at least once between any two successive regular sessions of the Commission. The Chairman of the Executive Committee shall, in consultation with the Chairman of the Commission and the Director-General of the Organization, convene sessions of the Committee.

3. The Secretary of the Commission shall act as Secretary of the Executive Committee.

Article IX

FUNCTIONS OF THE EXECUTIVE COMMITTEE

The Executive Committee shall:

a) make proposals to the Commission with respect to the general policy of the Commission;

b) submit draft programmes of work and budget and annual accounts to the Commission;

c) ensure the implementation of the policies and programmes approved by the Commission;

d) prepare the draft annual report on the activities of the Commission for the approval of the Commission and for transmission to the Director-General of the Organization;

e) carry out such other functions as the Commission may delegate to it.

Article X

RULES OF PROCEDURE

The Commission may, by a two-thirds majority of its membership, adopt and amend its own Rules of Procedure which shall be consistent with the General Rules of the Organization. The Rules of Procedure of the Commission and any amendments that may be made thereto shall come into force upon approval by the Director-General of the Organization, and as from the date of such approval.

Article XI

FINANCE

1. Each Member of the Commission undertakes to contribute annually its share of the Budget in accordance with a scale of contributions to be adopted by a two-thirds majority of the membership of the Commission. Contributions by Members shall be made in cash.

2. The Commission may also accept contributions and donations from other sources.

3. Contributions shall be payable in currencies to be determined by the Commissions after consultation with each Member and with the concurrence of the Director-General of the Organization.

4. All contributions and donations received shall be placed in the Trust Fund administered by the Director-General of the Organization in conformity with the Financial Regulations of the Organization.

Article XII

EXPENSES

1. The expenses of the Commission shall be paid out of its Budget except those relating to such staff and facilities as may be made available by the Organization. The expenses to be borne by the Organization shall be determined and paid within the limits of annual budget prepared by the Director-General of the Organization and approved by the Conference of the Organization in accordance with the Constitution, General Rules and the Financial Regulations of the Organization.

2. Expenses incurred by delegates of Members of the Commission and by their alternates, experts and advisers, when attending sessions of the Commission, as well as the expenses incurred by observers, shall be borne by the respective governments or organizations. Expenses incurred by the representative of each Member of the Commission when attending sessions of the Executive Committee shall be borne by the Commission.

3. Expenses of consultants or experts invited to attend sessions or participate in the work of the Commission or the Ececutive Committee shall be borne by the Commission.

4. The expenses of the Secretariat shall be borne by the Organization.

Article XIII

AMENDMENTS

1. This Agreement may be amended by a two-thirds majority of the membership of the Commission.

2. Proposals for amendments may be made by any Member of the Commission or by the Director-General of the Organization. Proposals made by a Member of the Commission shall be addressed to both the Chairman of the Commission and the Director-General of the

Organization and those made by the Director-General of the Organization shall be addressed to the Chairman of the Commission, not later than 120 days before the Session of the Commission at which the proposal is to be considered. The Director-General of the Organization shall immediately inform all Members of the Commission of all proposals for amendments.

3. Any amendment to this Agreement shall require the approval of the Council of the Organization unless the Council considers it desirable to refer the amendment to the Conference of the Organization for approval.

4. Amendments not involving new obligations for Members of the Commission shall take effect from the date of the approval by the Council or Conference of the Organization, as appropriate.

5. Amendments involving new obligations for Members of the Commission shall after approval by the Conference or Council of the Organization, come into force in respect of each Member only upon acceptance by it. The instruments of acceptance of amendments involving new obligations shall be deposited with the Director-General of the Organization. The Director-General of the Organization shall inform all Members of the Commission and the Secretary-General of the United Nations of such acceptance. The rights and obligations of any Member of the Commission that has not accepted an amendment involving new obligations shall continue to be governed by the provisions of the Agreement in force prior to the amendment.

6. The Director-General of the Organization shall inform all Members of the Commission, all Members and Associate Members of the Organization and the Secretary-General of the United Nations of the entry into force of any amendment.

Article XIV

ACCEPTANCE

1. Acceptance of this Agreement by any Member or Associate Member of the Organization shall be effected by the deposit of an instrument of acceptance with the Director-General of the Organization and shall take effect on receipt of such instrument by the Director-General of the Organization.

2. Acceptance of this Agreement by non-Member Nations of the Organization shall become effective on the date on which the Commission approves the application for membership in conformity with the provisions of Article 1 of this Agreement.

3. The Director-General of the Organization shall inform all Members of the Commission, all Members and Associate Members of the Organization and the Secretary-General of the United Nations of all acceptances that have become effective.

4. Acceptance of this Agreement may be made subject to reservations which shall become effective only upon unanimous approval by the Members of the Commission. The Director-General of the Organization shall notify forthwith all Members of the Commission of any reservations. Members of the Commission not having replied within three months from the date of the notification shall be deemed to have accepted the reservation. Failing such approval, the nation making the reservation shall not become a party to this Agreement.

Article XV

TERRITORIAL APPLICATION

The Members of the Commission shall, when accepting this Agreement, state explicitly to which territories their participation shall extend. In the absence of such a declaration, participation shall be deemed to apply to all the territories for the international relations of which the Member is responsible. Subject to the provisions of Article XVII-2, the scope of the territorial application may be modified by a subsequent declaration.

Article XVI

INTERPRETATION AND SETTLEMENT OF DISPUTES

Any dispute regarding the interpretation or application of this Agreement, if not settled by the Commission, shall be referred to a Committee composed of one member appointed by each of the parties to the dispute, and in addition an independent chairman chosen by the members of the Committee. The recommendations of such a Committee, while not binding in character, shall become concerned of the matter out of which the disagreement arose. If as the result of this procedure the dispute is not settled, it shall be referred to the International Court of Justice in accordance with the Statute of the Court, unless the parties to the dispute agree to another method of settlement.

Article XVII

WITHDRAWAL

1. Any member may withdraw from the Commission at any time after the expiration of one year from the date on which its acceptance took effect or form the date on which the Agreement entered into force, whichever is the later, by giving written notice of withdrawal to both the Chairman of the Commission and the Director-General of the Organization. The Director-General of the Organization shall forthwith inform all Members of the Commission, all Member Nations and Associate Members of the Organization and the Secretary-General of the United Nations of the receipt of any notice of withdrawal. The withdrawal shall become effective one year from the date of receipt by the Director-General of the Organization of the notification of withdrawal.

2. A Member of the Commission may give notice of withdrawal with respect to one more of the territories for the international relations of which it is responsible. When a Member gives notice of its

own withdrawal from the Commission, it shall state to which territory or territories the withdrawal is to apply. In the absence of such a declaration, the withdrawal shall be deemed to apply to all the territories for the international relations of which the Member of the Commission is responsible, except that such withdrawal shall not be deemed to apply to an Associate Member of the Organization.

3. Any Member of the Commission that gives notice of withdrawal from the Organization shall be deemed to have simultaneously withdrawn from the Commission, and this territories for the international relations of which the Member concerned is responsible, except that such withdrawal shall not be deemed to apply to an Associate Member of the Organization.

Article XVIII

TERMINATION

1. This Agreement shall be considered terminated if and when the number of Members of the Commission falls below three, unless the two remaining Members of the Commission decide, with the approval of the Conference of the Organization, to maintain the Agreement in force. The Director-General of the Organization shall inform all Members of the Commission, all Members and Associate Members of the Organization and the Secretary-General of the United Nations of such termination.

2. On termination of the Agreement all assests of the Commission shall be liquidated by the Director-General of the Organization and after settlement of the liabilities the balance shall be distributed proportionately amongst Members on the basis of the scale of contributions in force at the time. Nations whose contributions are in arrears for two consecutive years shall not be entitled to a share of the assets.

Article XIX

ENTRY INTO FORCE

1. This Agreement shall enter into force as soon as three eligible Members or Associate Members of the Organization have become parties to it by the deposit of an instrument of acceptance in accordance with the provisions of Article XIV of this Agreement.

2. The Director-General of the Organization shall notify all Nations having deposited instruments of acceptance as well as all Member Nations and Associate Members of the Organization and the Secretary-General of the United Nations of the date on which this Agreement comes into force.

Article XX

AUTHENTIC LANGUAGES

The English, French and Spanish texts of this Agreement shall be equally authentic.

CONVENTION ON WETLANDS OF INTERNATIONAL IMPORTANCE ESPECIALLY AS WATERFOWL HABITAT [47]

Ramser, 2 February 1971

The Contracting Parties.

Recognizing the interdependence of man and his environment;

Considering the fundamental ecological functions of wetlands as regulations of water regimes and as habitats supporting a characteristic flora and fauna, especially waterfowl;

Being convinced that wetlands constitute a resource of great economic, cultural, scientific and recreational value, the loss of which would be irreparable;

Desiring to stem the progressive encroachment on and loss of wetlands now and in the future;

Recognizing that waterfowl in their seasonal migrations may transcend frontiers and so should be regarded as an international resource;

Being confident that the conservation of wetlands and their flora and fauna can be ensured by combining far-sighted national policies with co-ordinated international action.

Article 1

1. For the purpose of this Convention wetlands are areas of marsh, fen, peatland or water, whether natural or artificial, permanent or temporary, with water that is static or flowing, fresh, brakish or salt, including areas of marine water the depth of which at low tide does not exceed six metres.

2. For the purpose of this Convention waterfowl are birds ecologically dependent on wetlands.

Article 2

1. Each Contracting Party shall designate suitable wetlands within its territory for inclusion in a List of Wetlands of International Importance, hereinafter referred to as the "the List" which is maintained by the bureau established under Article 8. The boundaries of each wetland shall be and they may incorporate riparian and coastal zones adjacent to the wetlands, and islands or bodies of marine water deeper than six metres at low tide lying within the wetlands, especially where these have importance as waterfowl habitat.

2. Wetlands should be elected for the List on account of their international significance in terms of ecology, botany, zoology, limnology or hydrology. In the first instance wetlands of international importance to waterfowl at any season should be included.

3. The inclusion of a wetland in the List does not prejudice the exclusive sovereign rights of the Contracting Party in whose territory the wetland is situated.

4. Each Contracting Party shall designate at least one wetland to be included in the List when signing this Convention or when depositing its instrument

of ratification or accession, as provided in Article 9.

5. Any Contracting Party shall have the right to add to the List further wetlands situated within its territory, to extend the boundaries of those wetlands already included by it in the List, or, because of its urgent national interests, to delete or restrict the boundaries of wetlands already included by it in the List and shall, at the earliest possible time, inform the organization or government responsible for the continuing bureau duties specified in Article 8 of any such changes.

6. Each Contracting Party shall consider its international responsibilities for the conservation, management and wise use of migratory stocks of waterfowl, both when designating entries for the List and when exercising its right to change entries in the List relating to wetlands within its territory.

Article 3

1. The Contracting Parties shall formulate and implement their planning so as to promote the conservation of the wetlands included in the List, and as far as possible the wise use of wetlands in their territory.

2. Each Contracting Party shall arrange to be informed at the earliest possible time if the ecological character of any wetland in its territory and included in the List has changed, is changing or is likely to change as a result of technological developments, pollution or other human interference. Information on such changes shall be passed without delay to the organization or government responsible for the continuing bureau duties specified in Article 8.

Article 4

1. Each Contracting Party shall promote the conservation of wetlands and waterfowl by establishing nature reserves in wetlands, whether they are included in the List or not, and provide adequately for their wardening.

2. Where a Contracting Party in its urgent national interest, deletes or restricts the boundaries of a wetland included in the List, it should as far as possible compensate for any loss of wetland resources, and in particular it should create additional nature reserves for waterfowl and for the protection, either in the same area or elsewhere, of an adequate portion of the original habitat.

3. The Contracting Parties shall encourage research and the exchange of data and publications regarding wetlands and their flora and fauna.

4. The Contracting Parties shall endeavour through management to increase waterfowl populations on appropriate wetlands.

5. The Contracting Parties shall promote the training of personnel competent in the fields of wetland research, management and wardening.

Article 5

The Contracting Parties shall consult with each other about implementing obligations arising from the Convention especially in the case of a wetland extending over the territories of more than one Contracting Party or where a water system is shared by Contracting Parties.

They shall at the same time endeavour to co-ordinate and support present and future policies and regulations concerning the conservation of wetlands and their flora and fauna.

Article 6

1. The Contracting Parties shall, as the necessity arises, convene Conferences on the Conservation of Wetlands and Waterfowl.

2. These Conferences shall have an advisory character and shall be competent inter alia:

a) to discuss the implementation of this Convention;

b) to discuss additions to and changes in the List;

c) to consider information regarding changes in the ecological character of wetlands included in the List provided in accordance with paragraph 2 of Article 3;

d) to make general or specific recommendations to the Contracting Parties regarding the conservation, management and wise use of wetlands and their flora and fauna;

e) to request relevent international bodies to prepare reports and statistics on matters which are essentially international in character affecting wetlands.

3. The Contracting Parties shall ensure that those responsible at all levels for wetlands management shall be informed of, and take into consideration, recommendations of such Conferences concerning the conservation, management and wise use of wetlands and their flora and fauna.

Article 7

1. The representatives of the Contracting Parties at such Conferences should include persons who are experts on wetlands or waterfowl by reason of knowledge and experience gained in scientific, administrative or other appropriate capacities.

2. Each of the Contracting Parties represented at a Conference shall have one vote, recommendations being adopted by a simple majority of the votes cast, provided that not less than half the Contracting Parties cast votes.

Article 8

1. The International Union for the Conservation of Nature and Natural Resources shall perform the continuing bureau duties under this Convention until such time as another organization or government is appointed by a majority of two-thirds of all Contracting Parties.

2. The continuing bureau duties shall be, inter alia:

a) to assist in the convening and organizing of Conferences specified in Article 6;

b) to maintain the List of Wetlands of

International Importance and to be informed by the Contracting Parties of any additions, extensions, deletions or restrictions concerning wetlands included in the List provided in accordance with paragraph 5 of Article 2;

c) to be informed by the Contracting Parties of any changes in the ecological character of wetlands included in the List provided in accordance with paragraph 2 of Article 3;

d) to forward notification of any alterations to the List, or changes in character of wetlands included therein, to all Contracting Parties and to arrange for these matters to be discussed at the next Conference;

e) to make known to the Contracting Party concerned, the recommendations of the Conferences in respect of such alterations to the List or of changes in the character of wetlands included therein.

Article 9

1. This Convention shall remain open for signature indefinitely.

2. Any member of the United Nations or of one of the Specialized Agencies or of the International Atomic Energy or Party to the Statute of the International Court of Justice may become a party to this Convention by:

a) signature without reservation as to ratifications;

b) signature subject to ratification followed by ratification;

c) accession.

3. Ratification or accession shall be effected by the deposit of an instrument of ratification or accession with the Director-General of the United Nations Educational, Scientific and Cultural Organization, (hereinafter referred to as "the Depositary")

Article 10

1. This Convention shall enter into force four months after seven States have become Parties to this Convention in accordance with paragraph 2 of Article 9.

2. Thereafter this Convention shall enter into force for each Contracting Party four months after the day of its signature without reservation as to ratification, or its deposit of an instrument of ratification or accession.

Article 11

1. This Convention shall continue in force for an indefinite period.

2. Any Contracting Party may denounce this Convention after a period of five years from the date on which it entered into force for that Party by giving written notice thereof to the Depositary. Denunciation shall take effect four months after the day on which notice thereof is received by the Depositary.

Article 12

1. The Depositary shall inform all States that have signed and acceded to this Convention as soon as possible of:

a) signatures of the Convention;

b) deposits of instruments of ratification of this Convention;

c) deposits of instruments of accession to this Convention;

d) the date of entry into force of this Convention;

e) notifications of denunciation of this Convention.

2. When this Convention has entered into force, the Depositary shall have it registered with the Secretariat of the United Nations in accordance with Article 102 of the Charter.

In Witness Whereof, the undersigned, being duly authorized to that effect, have signed this Convention.

Done at Ramsar this 2nd day of February 1971, in a single original in the English, French, German and Russian languages, in any case of divergency the English text prevailing, which shall be deposited with the Depositary which shall send true copies thereof to all Contracting Parties.

TREATY ON THE PROHIBITION OF THE EMPLACEMENT OF NUCLEAR WEAPONS AND OTHER WEAPONS OF MASS DESTRUCTION ON THE SEA-BED AND THE OCEAN FLOOR AND IN THE SUBSOIL THEREOF [48]

London, Moscow, Washington, 11 February 1971

The States Parties to this Treaty,

Recognizing the common interest of mankind in the progress of the exploration and use of the sea-bed and the ocean floor for peaceful purposes,

Considering that the prevention of a nuclear arms race on the sea-bed and the ocean floor serves the interests of maintaining world peace, reduces international tensions and strengthens friendly relations among States.

Convinced that this Treaty constitutes a step towards the exclusion of the sea-bed, the ocean floor and the subsoil thereof from the arms race,

Convinced that this Treaty constitutes a step towards a treaty on general and complete disarmament under strict and effective international control, and determined to continue negotiations to this end,

Convinced that this Treaty will further the purposes and principles of the Charter of the United Nations in a manner consistent with the principles of international law and without infringing the freedoms of the high seas.

Have agreed as follows:

Article I

1. The States Parties to this Treaty undertake not to emplant or emplace on the sea-bed and the ocean floor and in the subsoil thereof beyond the outer limit of a sea-bed zone, as defined in Article II, any nuclear weapons or any other types of weapons of mass destruction as well as structures, launching installations or any other facilities specifically designed for storing, testing or using such weapons.

2. The undertakings of paragraph 1 of this Article shall also apply to the sea-bed zone referred to in the same paragraph, except that within such sea-bed zone, they shall not apply either to the coastal States or to the sea-bed beneath its territorial waters.

3. The States Parties to this Treaty undertake not to assist; encourage or induce any State to carry out activities referred to in paragraph 1 of this Article and not to participate in any other way in such actions.

Article II

For the purpose of this Treaty, the outer limit of the sea-bed zone referred to in Article I shall be coterminous with the twelve-mile outer limit of the zone referred to in Part II of the Convention on the Territorial Sea and the Contiguous Zone, signed at Geneva on 29 April 1958, and shall be measured in accordance with the provisions of Part I, Section II of that Convention and in accordance with international law.

Article III

1. In order to promote the objectives of and ensure compliance with the provisions of this Treaty, each State Party to the Treaty shall have the right to verify through observation the activities of other State Parties to the Treaty on the sea-bed and the ocean floor and in the subsoil thereof beyond the zone referred to in Article I, provided that observation does not interfere with such activities.

2. If after observation reasonable doubts remain concerning the fulfilment of the obligations assumed under the Treaty, the State Party having such doubts and the State Party that is responsible for the activities giving rise to the doubts shall consult with a view to removing the doubts. If the doubts persist, the State Party having such doubts shall notify the other States Parties, and the Parties conerned shall co-operate on such further prcedures for verification as may be agreed, including appropriate inspection of objects, structures, installations or other facilities that reasonably may be expected to be of a kind described in Article I. The Parties in the region of the activities, including any coastal State, and any other Party so requesting, shall be entitled to participate in such consultation and co-operation. After completion of the further procedures for verification, an appropriate report shall be circulated to other parties by the Party that initiated such procedures.

3. If the State responsible for the activities giving rise to the reasonable doubts is not identifiable by observation of the object, structure, installation or other facility, the State Party having such doubts shall notify and make appropriate inquiries of States Parties in the region of the activities and of any other State Party. If it is ascertained through these inquiries that a particular State Party is responsible for the activities, that State Party shall consult and co-operate with other Parties as provided in paragraph 2 of this Article. If the identify of the State responsible for the activities cannot be ascertained through these inquiries, then further verification procedures, including inspection, may be undertaken by the inquiring State Party, which shall invite the participation of the Parties in the region of the activities, including any coastal State, and of any other Party desiring to co-operate.

4. If consultation and co-operation pursuant to paragraphs 2 and 3 of this Article have not removed the doubts concerning the activities and there remains a serious question concerning fulfilment of the obligations assumed under this Treaty, a State Party may, in accordance with the provisions of the Charter of the United Nations, refer the matter to the Security Council, which may take action in accordance with the Charter.

5. Verification pursuant to this Article may be undertaken by any State Party using its own means, or with the full or partial assistance of any

other State Party, or through appropriate international procedures within the framework of the United Nations and in accordance with its Charter.

6. Verification activities pursuant to this Treaty shall not interfere with activities of other States Parties and shall be conducted with due regard for rights recognized under international law, including the freedoms of the high seas and the rights of coastal States with respect to the exploration and exploitation of their continental shelves.

Article IV

Nothing in this Treaty shall be interpreted as supporting or prejudicing the position of any State Party with respect to existing international conventions, including the 1958 Convention on the Territorial Sea and the Contiguous Zone, or with respect to rights or claims which such State Party may assert, or with respect to recognition or non-recognition of rights or claims asserted by any other State, related to waters off its coasts, including, *inter alia*, territorial seas and contiguous zones, or to the sea-bed and the ocean floor, including continental shelves.

Article V

The Parties to this Treaty undertake to continue negotiations in good faith concerning further measures in the field of disarmament for the prevention of an arms race on the sea-bed, the ocean floor and the subsoil thereof.

Article VI

Any State Party may propose amendments to this Treaty. Amendments shall enter into force for each State Party accepting the amendments upon their acceptance by a majority of the States Parties to the Treaty and, thereafter, for each remaining State Party on the date of acceptance by it.

Article VII

Five years after the entry into force of this Treaty, a conference of Parties to the Treaty shall be held at Geneva, Switzerland, in order to review the operation of this Treaty with a view to assuring that the purposes of the preamble and the provisions of the Treaty are being realized. Such review shall take into account any relevant technological developments. The review conference shall determine, in accordance with the views of a majority of those Parties attending, whether and when an additional review conference shall be convened.

Article VIII

Each State party to this Treaty shall in exercising its national sovereignty have the right to withdraw from this Treaty if it decides that extraordinary events related to the subject-matter of this Treaty have jeopardized the supreme interests of its country. It shall give notice of such withdrawal to all other States Parties to the Treaty and to the United Nations Security Council three months in advance. Such notice shall include a statement of the extraordinary events it considers to have jeopardized its supreme interests.

Article IX

The provisions of this Treaty shall in no way affect the obligations assumed by States Parties to the Treaty under international instruments establishing zones free from nuclear weapons.

Article X

1. This Treaty shall be open for signature to all States. Any State which does not sign the Treaty before its entry into force in accordance with paragraph 3 of this Article may accede to it at any time.

2. This Treaty shall be subject to ratification by signatory States. Instruments of ratification and of accession shall be deposited with the Governments of the United Kingdom of Great Britain and Northern Ireland, the Union of Soviet Socialist Republics and the United States of America, which are hereby designated the Depositary Governments.

3. This Treaty shall enter into force after the deposit of instruments of ratification by twenty-two Governments, including the Governments designated as Depositary Governments of this Treaty.

4. For States whose instruments of ratification or and accession are deposited after the entry into force of this Treaty, it shall enter into force on the date of the deposit of their instruments of ratification or accesstion.

5. The Depositary Government shall promptly inform the Governments of all signatory and acceding States of the date of each signature, of the date of deposit of each instrument of ratification or of accession, of the date of the entry into force of this Treaty, and of the receipts of other notices.

6. This Treaty shall be registered by the Depositary Governments pursuant to Article 102 of the Charter of the United Nations.

Article XI

This Treaty, the English, Russian, French, Spanish and Chinese texts of which are equally authentic, shall be deposited in the archives of the Depositary Governments. Duly certified copies of this Treaty shall be transmitted by the Depositary Governments to the Governments of the States signatory and acceding thereto.

CONVENTION CONCERNING PROTECTION AGAINST HAZARDS OF POISONING ARISING FROM BENZENE [49]

Geneva, 23 June 1971

The General Conference of the International Labour Organisation,

Having been convened at Geneva by the Governing Body of the International Labour Office, and having met in its Fifty-sixth Session on 2 June 1971, and

Having decided upon the adoption of certain proposals with regard to protection against hazards arising from benzene, which is the sixth item on the agenda of the session, and

Having determined that these proposals shall take the form of an international Convention,

Adopts this twenty-third day of June of the year one thousand nine hundred and seventy-one the following Convention, which may be cited as the Benzene Convention, 1971:

Article 1

This Convention applies to all activities involving exposure of workers to:

a) the aromatic hydrocarbon benzene C_6H_6 hereinafter referred to as "benzene";

b) products the benzene content of which exceeds 1 per cent by volume, hereinafter referred to as "products containing benzene".

Article 2

1. Whenever harmless or less harmful substitute products are available, they shall be used instead of benzene or products containing benzene.

2. Paragraph 1 of this Article does not apply to:

a) the production of benzene;

b) the use of benzene for chemical synthesis;

c) the use of benzene in motor fuel;

d) analytical or research work carried out in laboratories.

Article 3

1. The competent authority in a country may permit temporary derogations from the percentage laid down in Article 1, subparagraph (*b*), and from the provisions of Article 2, paragraph 1, of this Convention under conditions and within limits of time to be determined after consultation with the most representative organizations of employers and workers concerned, where such exist.

2. In such cases the Member in question shall indicate in its reports on the application of this Convention submitted under article 22 of the Constitution of the International Labour Organization the position of its law and practice as regards the derogations and any progress made towards complete application of the terms of the Convention.

3. At the expiration of three years from the date on which this Convention first entered into force, the Governing Body of the International Labour Office shall submit to the Conference a special report concerning the application of paragraphs 1 and 2 of this Article and containing such proposals as it may think appropriate for further action in regard to the matter.

Article 4

1. The use of benzene and of products containing benzene shall be prohibited in certain work processes to be specified by national laws or regulations.

2. This prohibition shall at least include the use of benzene and of products containing benzene as a solvent or dilutent, except where the process is carried out in an enclosed system or where there are other equally safe methods of work.

Article 5

Occupational hygiene and technical measures shall be taken to ensure effective protection of workers exposed to benzene or to products containing benzene.

Article 6

1. In premises where benzene or products containing benzene are manufactured, handled or used, all necessary measures shall be taken to prevent the escape of benzene vapour into the air of places of employment.

2. Where workers are exposed to benzene or to products containing benzene, the employer shall ensure that the concentration of benzene in the air of the places of employment does not exceed a maximum which shall be fixed by the competent authority at a level not exceeding a ceiling value of 25 parts per million (80 mg/m^3).

3. The competent authority shall issue directions on carrying out the measurement of the concentration of benzene in the air of places of employment.

Article 7

1. Work processes involving the use of benzene or of products containing benzene shall as far as practicable be carried out in an enclosed system.

2. Where it is not practicable for the work processes to be carried out in an enclosed system, places of work in which benzene or products containing benzene are used shall be equipped with effective means to ensure the removal of benzene vapour to the extent necessary for the protection of the health of the workers.

Article 8

1. Workers who may have skin contact with liquid benzene or liquid products containing benzene shall be provided with adequate means of personal protection against the risk of absorbing benzene through the skin.

2. Workers who for special reasons may be exposed to concentrations of benzene in the air of places of employment which exceed the maximum referred to in Article 6, paragraph 2, of this

Convention shall be provided with adequate means of personal protection against the risk of inhaling benzene vapour. The duration of exposure shall be limited as far as possible.

Article 9

1. Workers who are to be employed in work processes involving exposure to benzene or to products containing benzene shall undergo:

a) a thorough pre-employment medical examination for fitness for employment which shall include a blood-test;

b) periodic re-examinations, which shall include biological tests including a blood-test, at intervals fixed by national laws or regulations.

2. The competent authority in a country may,after consultation with the most representative organizations of employers and workers concerned, where such exist, permit exceptions from the obligations of paragraph 1 of this Article in respect of specified categories of workers.

Article 10

1. The medical examinations provided for in Article 9, paragraph 1, of this Convention shall be:

a) carried out under the responsibility of a qualified physician, approved by the competent authority, and with the assistance, as appropriate, of a competent laboratory;

b) certified in an appropriate manner.

2. These medical examinations shall not involve the workers in any expense.

Article 11

1. Women medically certified as pregnant, and nursing mothers, shall not be employed in work processes involving exposure to benzene or products containing benzene.

2. Young persons under 18 years of age shall not be employed in work processes involving exposure to benzene or products containing benzene: Provided that this prohibition need not apply to young persons undergoing education or training who are under adequate technical and medical supervision.

Article 12

The word "Benzene" and the necessary danger symbols shall be clearly visible on any container holding benzene or products containing benzene.

Article 13

Each Member shall take appropriate steps to provide that any worker exposed to benzene or products containing benzene receives appropriate instructions on measures to safeguard health and prevent accidents, as well as on the appropriate action if there is any evidence of poisoning.

Article 14

Each Member which ratifies this Convnetion:

a) shall, by laws or regulations or any other method consistent with national practice and conditions take such steps as may be necessary to give effect to the provisions of this Convention:

b) shall, in accordance with national practice, specify the person or persons on whom the obligations of compliance with the provisions of this Convention rests;

c) undertakes to provide appropriate inspection services for the purpose of supervising the application of the provisions of this Convention, or to satisfy itself that appropriate inspection is carried out.

Article 15

The formal ratifications of this Convention shall be communicated to the Director-General of the International Labour Office for registration.

Article 16

1. This Convention shall be binding only upon those Members of the International Labour Organization whose ratifications have been registered with the Director-General.

2. It shall come into force twelve months after the date on which the ratifications of two Members have been registered with the Director-General.

3. Thereafter, this Convention shall come into force for any Member twelve months after the date on which its ratification has been registered.

Article 17

1. A Member which has ratified this Convention may denounce it after the expiration of ten years from the date on which the Convention first comes into force, by an act communicated to the Director-General of the International Labour Office for registration. Such denunciation shall not take effect until one year after the date on which it is registered.

2. Each Member which has ratified this Convention and which does not, within the year following the expiration of the period of ten years mentioned in the preceding paragraph, exercise the right of denunciation provided for in this Article, will be bound for another period of ten years and, thereafter, may denounce this Convention at the expiration of each period of ten years under the terms provided for in this Article.

Article 18

1. The Director-General of the International Labour Office shall notify all Members of the International Labour Organization of the registration of all ratifications and denunciations communicated to him by the Members of the Organization.

2. When notifying the Members of the Organization of the registration of the second ratification communicated to him, the Director-General shall draw the attention of the Members of the Organization to the date upon which the Convention will come into force.

Article 19

The Director-General of the International Labour Office shall communicate to the Secretary-General of the United Nations for registration in accordance with Article 102 of the Charter of the United Nations full particulars of all ratifications and acts of denunciation registered by him in accordance with the provisions of the preceding Articles.

Article 20

At such times as it may consider necessary the Governing Body of the International Labour Office shall present to the General Conference a report on the working of this Convention and shall examine the desirability of placing on the agenda of the Conference the question of its revision in whole or in part.

Article 21

1. Should the Conference adopt a new Convention revising this Convention in whole or in part, then, unless the new Convention otherwise provides;

a) the ratification by a Member of the new revising Convention shall ipso jure involve the immediate denunciation of this Convention, notwithstanding the provisions of Article 17 above, if and when the new revising Convention shall have come into force;

b) as from the date when the new revising Convention comes into force this Convention shall cease to be open to ratification by the Members.

2. This Convention shall in any case remain in force in its actual form and content for those Members which have ratified it but have not ratified the revising Convention.

Article 22

The English and French versions of the text of this Convention are equally authoritative.

CONVENTION RELATING TO CIVIL LIABILITY IN THE FIELD OF MARITIME CARRIAGE OF NUCLEAR MATERIAL [50]

Brussels, 17 December 1971

The High Contracting Parties,

Considering that the Paris Convention of 29 July 1960 on Third Party Liability in the Field of Nuclear Energy and its Additional Protocol of 28 January 1964 (hereinafter referred to as "the Paris Convention ") and the Vienna Convention of 21 May 1963 on Civil Liability for Nuclear Damage (hereinafter referred to as "the Vienna Convention") provide that, in the case of damage caused by a nuclear incident occurring in the course of maritime carriage of nuclear material covered by such Conventions, the operator of a nuclear installation is the person liable for such damage,

Considering that similar provisions exist in the national law in force in certain States,

Considering that the application of any preceding international Convention in the field of maritime transport is however maintained,

Desirous of ensuring that the operator of a nuclear installation will be exclusively liable for damage caused by a nuclear incident occurring in the course of maritime carriage of nuclear material,

Have agreed as follows:

Article 1

Any person who by virtue of an international convention or national law applicable in the field or maritime transport might be held liable for damage caused by a nuclear incident shall be exonerated from such liability:

a) if the operator of a nuclear installation is liable for such damage under either the Paris or the Vienna Convention, or

b) if the operator of a nuclear installation is liable for such damage by virtue of a national law governing the liability for such damage, provided that such law is in all respects as favourable to persons who may suffer damage as either the Paris or the Vienna Convention.

Article 2

1. The exoneration provided for in Article I shall also apply in respect of damage caused by a nuclear incident:

a) to the nuclear installation itself or to any property on the site of that installation which is used or to be used in connexion with that installation, or

b) to the means of transport upon which the nuclear material involved was at the time of the nuclear incident,

for which the operator of the nuclear installations is not liable because his liability for such damage has been excluded pursuant to the provisions of either the Paris or the Vienna Convention, or, in cases referred to in Article (*b*), by equivalent provisions of the national law referred to therein.

2. The provisions of paragraph 1 shall not, however, affect the liability of any individual who has caused the damage by an act or omission done with intent to cause damage.

Article 3

No provisions of the present Convention shall affect the liability of the operator of a nuclear ship in respect of damage caused by a nuclear incident involving the nuclear fuel of or radioactive products or waste produced in such ship.

Article 4

The present Convention shall supersede any international Conventions in the field of maritime transport which, at the date on which the present Convention is opened of signature, are in force or open for signature, ratification or accession but only to the extent that such Conventions would be in conflict with it; however, nothing in this Article shall affect the obligations of the Contracting Parties to the present Convention to non-Contracting States arising under such international Conventions.

Article 5

1. The present Convention shall be opened for signature in Brussels and shall remain open for signature in London at the Headquarters of the Inter-Governmental Maritime Consultative Organization (hereinafter referred to as "the Organizations") until 31 December 1972 and shall thereafter remain open for accession.

2. States Members of the United Nations or any of the Specialized Agencies or of the International Atomic Energy or Parties to the Statute of the International Court of Justice may become Parties to the present Convention by:

a) signature without reservation as to ratification, acceptance or approval;

b) signature subject to ratification, acceptance or approval followed by ratification, acceptance or approval; or

c) accession.

3. Ratification, acceptance, approval or accession shall be effected by the deposit of a formal instrument to that effect with the Secretary-General of the Organization.

Article 6

1. The present Conventions shall enter into force on the ninetieth day following the date on which five States have either signed it without reservation as to ratification, acceptance or approval or have deposited instruments of ratification, acceptance, approval or accession with the Secretary-General of the Organization.

2. For any State which subsequently signs the present Convention without reservation as to ratification, acceptance or approval, or deposits its instrument of ratification, acceptance, approval or accession, the Convention shall come into force on the ninetieth day after the date of such signature or deposit.

Article 7

1. The present Convention may be denounced by any Contracting Party to it at any time after the date on which the Convention comes into force for that State.

2. Denunciation shall be effected by a notification in writing delivered to the Secretary-General of the Organization.

3. A denunciation shall take effect one year, or such longer period as may be specified in the notification, after its receipt by the Secretary-General of the Organization.

4. Notwithstanding a denunciation by a Contracting Party pursuant to this Article the provisons of the present Convention shall continue to apply to any damage caused by a nuclear incident occurring before the denunciation takes effect.

Article 8

1. The United Nations where it is the administering authority for a territory, or any Contracting Party to the present Convention responsible for the international relations of a territory, may at any time by notification in writing to the Secretary-General of the Organization declare that the present Convention shall extend to such territory.

2. The present Convention shall, from the date of receipt of the notification or from such other date as may be specified in the notification, extend to the territory named therein.

3. The United Nations, or any Contracting Party which had made a declaration under paragraph 1 of this Article may at any time after the date on which the Convention has been so extended to any territory declare by notification in writing to the Secretary-General of the Organization that the present Convention shall cease to extend to any such territory named in the notification.

4. The present Convention shall cease to extend to any territory mentioned in such notification one year, or such longer period as may be specified therein, after the date of receipt of the notification by the Secretary-General of the Organization.

Article 9

1. A Conference for the purpose of revising or amending the present Convention may be convened by the Organization.

2. The Organization shall convene a Conference of the Contracting Parties to the present Convention for revising or amending it at the request of not less than one-third of the Contracting Parties.

Article 10

A Contracting Party may make reservations corresponding to those which it has validly made to the Paris or Vienna Convention. A reservation may be made at the time of signature, ratification, acceptance, approval or accession.

Article 11

1. The present Convention shall be deposited with the Secretary-General of the Organization.

2. The Secretary-General of the Organization shall:

a) inform all States which have signed or acceded to the present Convention of:

(i) each new signature and each deposit of an instrument together with the date thereof;

(ii) any reservation made in conformity with the present Convention;

(iii) the date of entry into force of the present Convention;

(iv) any denunciation of the present Convention and the date on which it takes effect;

(v) the extension of the present Convention to any territory under paragraph 1 of Article 8 and of the termination of any such extension under the provisions of paragraph 4 of that Article stating in each case the date on which the present Convention has been or will cease to be so extended;

b) transmit certified copies of the present Convention to all Signatory States and to all States which have acceded to the present Convention.

3. As soon as the present Convention comes into force, a certified, true copy thereof shall be transmitted by the Secretary-General of the Organization to the Secretariat of the United Nations for registration and publication in accordance with Article 102 of the Charter of the United Nations.

Article 12

The present Convention is established in a single original in the English and French languages, both texts being equally authentic. Official translations in the Russian and Spanish languages shall be prepared by the Secretariat of the Organization and deposited with the signed original.

In Witness Whereof the undersigned being duly authorized by their respective Governments for that purpose have signed the present Convention.

Done at Brussels this seventeenth day of December 1971.

INTERNATIONAL CONVENTION ON THE ESTABLISHMENT OF AN INTERNATIONAL FUND FOR COMPENSATION FOR OIL POLLUTION DAMAGE [51]

Brussels, 18 December 1971

The States Parties to the present Convention,

Being Parties to the International Convention on Civil Liability for Oil Pollution Damage, adopted at Brussels on 29 November 1969,

Conscious of the dangers of pollution posed by the world-wide maritime carriage of oil in bulk,

Convinced of the need to ensure that adequate compensation is available to persons who suffer damage caused by pollution resulting from the escape or discharge of oil from ships,

Considering that the International Convention of 29 November 1969, on Civil Liability for Oil Pollution Damage, by providing a regime for compensation for pollution damage in Contracting States and for the costs of measures, wherever taken, to prevent or minimize such damage, represents a considerable progress towards the achievement of this aim,

Considering however that this regime does not afford full compensation for victims of oil pollution damage in all cases while it imposes an additional financial burden on shipowners,

Considering further that the economic consequences of oil pollution damage resulting from the escape or discharge of oil carried in bulk at sea by ships should not exclusively be borne by the shipping industry but should in part be borne by the oil cargo interests,

Convinced of the need to elaborate a compensation and indemnification system supplementary to the International Convention on Civil Liability for Oil Pollution Damage with a view to ensuring that full compensation will be available to victims of oil pollution incidents and that the shipowners are at the same time given relief in respect of the additional financial burdens imposed on them by the said Convention,

Taking note of the Resolution on the Establishment of an International Compensation Fund for Oil Pollution Damage which was adopted on 29 November 1969 by the International Legal Conference on Marine Pollution Damage,

Have agreed as follows:

GENERAL PROVISIONS

Article 1

For the purposes of this Convention:

1. "Liability Convention" means the International Convention on Civil Liability for Oil Pollution Damage, adopted at Brussels on 29 November 1969.

2. "Ship", "Person", "Owner", "Oil", "Pollution Damage", "Preventive Measures", "Incident" and "Organization", have the same meaning as in

Article I of the Liability Convention, provided however that, for the purposes of these terms, "oil" shall be confined to persistent hydrocarbon mineral oils.

3. "Contributing Oil" means crude oil and fuel oil as defined in sub-paragraphs (*a*) and (*b*) below:

a) "Crude Oil" means any liquid hydrocarbon mixture occurring naturally in the earth whether or not treated to render it suitable for transportation. It also includes crude oils from which certain distillate fractions have been removed (sometimes referred to as "topped crudes") or to which certain distillate fractions have been added (sometimes referred to as "spiked" or "reconstituted" crudes).

b) "Fuel Oil" means heavy distillates or residues from crude oil or blends of such materials intended for use as a fuel for the production of heat or power of quality equivalent to the "American Society for Testing and Materials" Specification for Number Four Fuel Oil (Designation D 396-69), or heavier.

4. "Franc" means the unit referred to in Article V, paragraph 9, of the Liability Convention.

5. "Ship's tonnage" has the same meaning as in Article V, paragraph 10, of the Liability Convention.

6. "Ton", in relation to oil, means a metric ton.

7. "Guarantor" means any person providing insurance or other financial security to cover an owner's liability in pursuance of Article VII, paragraph 1, of the Liability Convention.

8. "Terminal installation" means any site for the storage of oil in bulk which is capable of receiving oil from waterborne transportation, including any facility situated off-shore and linked to such site.

9. Where an incident consists of a series of occurrences, it shall be treated as having occurred on the date of the first such occurrence.

Article 2

1. An International Fund for compensation for pollution damage, to be named "The International Oil Pollution Compensation Fund" and hereinafter referred to as "The Fund", is hereby established with the following aims:

a) to provide compensation for pollution damage to the extent that the protection afforded by the Liability Convention is inadequate;

b) to give relief to shipowners in respect of the additional financial burden imposed on them by the Liability Convention, such relief being subject to conditions designed to insure compliance with safety at sea and other conventions;

c) to give effect to the related purposes set out in this Convention.

2. The fund shall in each Contracting State be recognized as a legal person capable under the laws of that State of assuming rights and obligations and of being a party in legal proceedings before the courts of that State. Each Contracting State shall recognize the Director of the Fund (hereinafter referred to as "The Director") as the legal representative of the Fund.

Article 3

This Convention shall apply:

1. with regard to compensation according to Article 4, exclusively to pollution damage caused on the territory including the territorial sea of a Contracting State, and to preventive measures taken to prevent or minimize such damage;

2. with regard to indemnification of shipowners and their guarantors according to Article 5, exclusively in respect of pollution damage caused on the territory including the territorial sea of a State party to the Liability Convention, by a ship registered in or flying the flag of a Contracting State and in respect of preventive measures taken to prevent or minimize such damage.

COMPENSATION AND INDEMNIFICATION

Article 4

1. For the purpose of fulfilling its function under Article 2, paragraph 2 (*a*), the Fund shall pay compensation to any person suffering pollution damage if such person has been unable to obtain full and adequate compensation for the damage under the terms of the Liability Convention,

a) because no liability for the damage arises under the Liability Convention;

b) because the owner liable for the damage under the Liability Convention is financially incapable of meeting his obligations in full and any financial security that may be provided under Article VII of that Convention does not cover or is insufficient to satisfy the claims for compensation for the damage; an owner being treated as financially incapable of meeting his obligations and a financial security being treated as insufficient if the person suffering the damage has been unable to obtain full satisfaction of the amount of compensation due under the Liability Convention after having taken all reasonable steps to pursue the legal remedies available to him;

c) because the damage exceeds the owner's liability under the Liability Convention as limited pursuant to Article V, paragraph 1, of that Convention or under the terms of any other international Convention in force or open for signature, ratification or accession at the date of this Convention.

Expenses reasonably incurred or sacrifices reasonably made by the owner voluntarily to prevent or minimize pollution damage shall be treated as pollution damage for the purposes of this Article.

2. The Fund shall incur no obligation under the preceding paragraph if:

a) it proves that the pollution damage resulted from an act of war, hostilities, civil war or insurrection or was caused by oil which has escaped or been discharged from a warship or other ship owned or operated by a State and used, at the time of the incident, only on Government non-commercial service; or

b) the claimant cannot prove that the damage

resulted from an incident involving one or more ships.

3. If the Fund proves that the pollution damage resulted wholly or partially either from an act or omission done with intent to cause damage by the person who suffered the damage or from the negligence of that person, the Fund may be exonerated wholly or partially from its obligation to pay compensation to such person provided, however, that there shall be no such exoneration with regard to such preventive measures which are compensated under paragraph 1. The Fund shall in any event be exonerated to the extent that the shipowner may have been exonerated under Article III, paragraph 3, of the Liability Convention.

4. *a*) Except as otherwise provided in sub-paragraph (*b*) of this paragraph, the aggregate amount of compensation payable by the Fund under this Article shall in respect of any one incident be limited, so that the total sum of that amount and the amount of compensation actually paid under the Liability Convention for pollution damage caused in the territory of the Contracting States, including any sums in respect of which the Fund is under an obligation to indemnify the owner pursuant to Article 5, paragraph 1, of this Convention, shall not exceed 450 million francs.

b) The aggregate amount of compensation payable by the Fund under this Article for pollution damage resulting from a natural phenomenon of an exceptional, inevitable and irresistible character shall not exceed 450 million francs.

5. Where the amount of established claims against the fund exceeds the aggregate amount of compensation payable under paragraph 4, the amount available shall be distributed in such a manner that the proportion between any established claim and the amount of compensation actually recovered by the claimant under the Liability Convention and this Convention shall be the same for all claimants.

6. The Assembly of the Fund (hereinafter referred to as "the Assembly") may, having regard to the experience of incidents which have occurred and in particular the amount of damage resulting therefrom and to changes in the monetary values, decide that the amount of 450 million francs referred to in paragraph 4, sub-paragraphs (*a*) and (*b*), shall be changed; provided, however, that this amount shall in no case exceed 900 million francs or be lower than 450 million francs. The changed amount shall apply to incidents which occur after the date of the decision effecting the change.

7. The Fund shall, at the request of a Contracting State, use its good offices as necessary to assist that State to secure promptly such personnel, material and services as are necessary to enable the State to take measures to prevent or mitigate pollution damage arising from an incident in respect of which the Fund may be called upon to pay compensation under this Convention.

8. The Fund may on conditions to be laid down in the Internal Regulations provide credit facilities with a view to the taking of preventive measures against pollution damage arising from a particular incident in respect of which the Fund may be called to pay compensation under this Convention.

Article 5

1. For the purpose of fulfilling its function under Article 2, paragraph 1 (*b*), the Fund shall indemnify the owner and his guarantor for that portion of the aggregate amount of liability under the Liability Convention which:

a) is in excess of an amount equivalent to 1,500 francs for each ton of the ship's tonnage or of an amount of 125 million francs, whichever is the less, and

b) is not in excess of an amount equivalent to 2,000 francs for each ton of the said tonnage or an amount of 210 million francs, whichever is the less,

provided, however, that the Fund shall incur no obligation under this paragraph where the pollution damage resulted from the wilful misconduct of the owner himself.

2. The Assembly may decide that the Fund shall, on conditions to be laid down in the Internal Regulations, assume the obligations of a guarantor in respect of ships referred to in Article 3, paragraph 2, with regard to the portion of liability referred to in paragraph 1 of this Article. However, the Fund shall assume such obligations only if the owner so requests and if he maintains adequate insurance or other financial security covering the owner's liability under the Liability Convention up to an amount equivalent to 1,500 francs for each ton of the ship's tonnage or an amount of 125 million francs, whichever is the less. If the Fund assumes such obligations, the owner shall in each Contracting State be considered to have complied with Article VII of the Liability Convention in respect of the portion of his liability mentioned above.

3. The Fund may be exonerated wholly or partially from its obligations under paragraph 1 towards the owner and his guarantor if the Fund proves that as a result of the actual fault or privity of the owner:

a) the ship from which the oil causing the pollution damage escaped did not comply with the requirements laid down in:

(i) the International Convention for the Prevention of Pollution of the Sea by Oil, 1954, as amended in 1962; or

(ii) the International Convention for the Safety of Life at Sea, 1969; or

(iii) the International Convention on Load Lines, 1966; or

(iv) the International Regulations for Preventing Collisions at Sea, 1960; or

(v) any amendments to the above mentioned Conventions which have been determined as being of an important nature in accordance with Article XVI (5) of the Convention mentioned under (i), Article IX (*e*) of the Convention mentioned under

(ii) or Article 29 (3) (*d*) of the Convention mentioned under (iii), provided, however, that such amendments had been in force at least twelve months at the time of the incident;
and

b) the incident or damage was caused wholly or partially by such non-compliance.

The provisions of this paragraph shall apply irrespective of whether the Contracting State in which the ship was registered or whose flag it was flying is a Party to the relevant Instrument.

4. Upon the entry into force of a new Convention designed to replace, in whole or in part, any of the Instruments specified in paragraph 3, the Assembly may decide at least six months in advance a date on which the new Convention will replace such Instrument or part thereof for the purpose of paragraph 3. However, any State Party to this Convention may declare to the Director before that date that it does not accept such replacement; in which case the decision of the Assembly shall have no effect in respect of a ship registered in, or flying the flag of, that State at the time of the incident. Such a declaration may be withdrawn at any later date and shall in any event cease to have effect when the State in question becomes a party to such new Convention.

5. A ship complying with the requirements in an amendment to an Instrument specified in paragraph 3 or with requirements in a new Convention, where the amendment or Convention is designed to replace in whole or in part such Instrument, shall be considered as complying with the requirements in the said Instrument for the purposes of paragraph 3.

6. Where the Fund, acting as a guarantor by virtue of paragraph 2 has paid compensation for pollution damage in accordance with the Liability Convention, it shall have a right of recovery from the owner if and to the extent that the Fund would have been exonerated pursuant to paragraph 3 from its obligations under paragraph 1 to indemnify the owner.

7. Expenses reasonably incurred and sacrifices reasonably made by the owner voluntarily to prevent or minimize pollution damage shall be treated as included in the owner's liability for the purposes of this Article.

Article 6

1. Rights to compensation under Article 4 or indemnification under Article 5 shall be extinguished unless an action is brought thereunder or a notification has been made pursuant to Article 7, paragraph 6, within three years from the date when the damage occurred. However, in no case shall an action be brought after six years from the date of the incident which caused the damage.

2. Notwithstanding paragraph 1, the right of the owner or his guarantor to seek indemnification from the Fund pursuant to Article 5, paragraph 1, shall in no case be extinguished before the expiry of a period of six months as from the date on which the owner or his guarantor acquired knowledge of the bringing of an action against him under the Liability Convention.

Article 7

1. Subject to the subsequent provisions of this Article, any action against the Fund for compensation under Article 4 or indemnification under Article 5 of this Convention shall be brought only before a court competent under Article IX of the Liability Convention in respect of actions against the owner who is or who would, but for the provisions of Article III, paragraph 2, of that Convention, have been liable for pollution damage caused by the relevant incident.

2. Each Contracting State shall ensure that its courts possess the necessary jurisdiction to entertain such actions against the Fund as are referred to in paragraph 1.

3. Where an action for compensation for pollution damage has been brought before a court competent under Article IX of the Liability Convention against the owner of a ship or his guarantor, such court shall have exclusive jurisdictional competence over any action against the Fund for compensation or indemnification under the provisions of Article 4 or 5 of this Convention in respect of the same damage. However, where an action for compensation for pollution damage under the Liability Convention has been brought before a court in a State Party to the Liability Convention but not to this Convention, any action against the Fund under Article 4 or under Article 5, paragraph 1, of this Convention shall at the option of the claimant be brought either before a court of the State where the Fund has its headquarters or before any court of a State Party to this Convention competent under Article IX of the Liability Convention.

4. Each Contracting State shall ensure that the Fund shall have the right to intervene as a party to any legal proceedings instituted in accordance with Article IX of the Liability Convention before a competent court of that State against the owner of a ship or his guarantor.

5. Except as otherwise provided in paragraph 6, the Fund shall not be bound by any judgment or decision in proceedings to which it has not been a party or by any settlement to which it is not a party.

6. Without prejudice to the provisions of paragraph 4, where an action under the Liability Convention for compensation for pollution damage has been brought against an owner or his guarantor before a competent court in a Contracting State, each party to the proceedings shall be entitled under the national law of that State to notify the Fund of the proceedings. Where such notification has been made in accordance with the formalities required by the law of the court seized and in such time and in such a manner that the fund has in fact been in a position effectively to intervene as a party to the proceedings, any judgement rendered by the court in such proceedings shall, after it has become final and enforceable in the State where the judgement was

given, become binding upon the Fund in the sense that the facts and findings in that judgment may not be disputed by the Fund even if the Fund has not actually intervened in the proceedings.

Article 8

Subject to any decision concerning the distribution referred to in Article 4, paragraph 5, any judgment given against the Fund by a court having jurisdiction in accordance with Article 7, paragraphs 1 and 3, shall, when it has become enforceable in the State of origin and is in that State no longer subject to ordinary forms of review, be recognized and enforceable in each Contracting State on the same conditions as are prescribed in Article X of the Liability Convention.

Article 9

1. Subject to the provisions of Article 5, the Fund shall, in respect of any amount of compensation for pollution damage paid by the Fund in accordance with Article 4, paragraph 1, of this Convention, acquire by subrogation the rights that the person so compensated may enjoy under the Liability Convention against the owner or his guarantor.

2. Nothing in the Convention shall prejudice any right of recourse or subrogation of the Fund against persons other than those referred to in the preceding paragraph. In any event the right of the Fund to subrogation against such person shall not be less favourable than that of an insurer of the person to whom compensation or indemnification has been paid.

3. Without prejudice to any other rights of subrogation or recourse against the Fund which may exist, a Contracting State or agency thereof which has been paid compensation for pollution damage in accordance with provisions of national law shall acquire by subrogation the rights which the person so compensated would have enjoyed under this Convention.

CONTRIBUTIONS

Article 10

1. Contributions to the Fund shall be made in respect of each Contracting State by any person who, in the calendar year referred to in Article 11, paragraph 1, as regards initial contributions and in Article 12, paragraph 2 (*a*) or (*b*), as regards annual contributions, has received in total quantities exceeding 150,000 tons:

a) in the ports or terminal installations in the territory of that State contributing oil carried by sea to such ports or terminal installations; and

b) in any installations situated in the territory of that Contracting State contributing oil which has been carried by sea and discharged in a port or terminal installation of a non-Contracting State, provided that contributing oil shall only be taken into account by virtue of this sub-paragraph on first receipt in a Contracting State after its discharge in that non-Contracting State.

2. *a*) For the purposes of paragraph 1, where the quantity of contributing oil received in the territory of a Contracting State by any person in a calendar year when aggregated with the quantity of contributing oil received in the same Contracting State in that year by any associated person or persons exceeds 150,000 tons, such person shall pay contributions in respect of the actual quantity received by him notwithstanding that quantity did not exceed 150,000 tons.

b) "Associated person" means any subsidiary or commonly controlled entity. The question whether a person comes within this definition shall be determined by the national law of the State concerned.

Artiele 11

1. In respect of each Contracting State initial contributions shall be made of an amount which shall for each person referred to in Article 10 be calculated on the basis of a fixed sum for each ton of contributing oil received by him during the calendar year preceding that in which this Convention entered into force for that State.

2. The sum referred to in paragraph 1 shall be determined by the Assembly within two months after the entry into force of this Convention. In performing this function the Assembly shall, to the extent possible, fix the sum in such a way that the total amount of initial contributions would, if contributions were to be made in respect of 90 per cent of the quantities of contribution oil carried by sea in the world, equal 75 million francs.

3. The initial contributions shall in respect of each Contracting State be paid within three months following the date at which the Convention entered into force for that State.

Article 12

1. With a view to assessing for each person referred to in Article 10 the amount of annual contributions due, if any, and taking account of the necessity to maintain sufficient liquid funds, the Assembly shall for each calendar year make an estimate in the form of a budget of:

(i) Expenditure

a) costs and expenses of the administration of the Fund in the relevant year and any deficit from operations in preceding years;

b) payments to be made by the Fund in the relevant year for the satisfaction of claims against the Fund due under Article 4 or 5, including repayment on loans previously taken by the Fund for the satisfaction of such claims, to the extent that the aggregate amount of such claims in respect of any one incident does not exceed 15 million francs;

c) payments to be made by the Fund in the relevant year for the satisfaction of claims against the Fund due under Article 4 or 5, including repayments on loans previously taken by the Fund for the satisfaction of such claims, to the extent that the aggregate amount of such claims in respect of any one incident is in excess of 15 million francs;

(ii) Income

a) surplus funds from operations in preceding

years, including any interest;

b) initial contributions to be paid in the course of the year;

c) annual contributions, if required to balance the budget;

d) any other income.

2. For each person referred to in Article 10 the amount of his annual contribution shall be determined by the Assembly and shall be calculated in respect of each Contracting State:

a) in so far as the contribution is for the satisfaction of payments referred to in paragraph 1(i) (*a*) and (*b*) on the basis of a fixed sum for each ton of contributing oil received in the relevant State by such persons during the preceding calendar year; and

b) in so far as the contribution is for the satisfaction of payments referred to in paragraph 1 (i) (*c*) of this Article on the basis of a fixed sum for each ton of contributing oil received by such person during the calendar year preceding that in which the incident in question occured, provided that State was a party to this Convention at the date of the incident.

3. The sums referred to paragraph 2 above shall be arrived at by dividing the relevant total amount of contributions required by the total amount of contribution oil received in all Contracting States in the relevant year.

4. The Assembly shall decide the portion of the annual contribution which shall be immediately paid in cash and decide on the date of payment. The remaining part of each annual contribution shall be paid upon notification by the Director.

5. The Director may, in cases and in accordance with conditions to be laid down in the Internal Regulations of the Fund, require a contributor to provide financial security for the sum due from him.

6. Any demand for payments made under paragraph 4 shall be called rateably from all individual contributors.

Article 13

1. The amount of any contribution due under Article 12 and which is in arrears shall bear interest at a rate which shall be determined by the Assembly for each calendar year provided that different rates may be fixed for different circumstances.

2. Each Contracting State shall ensure that any obligation to contribute to the Fund arising under this Convention in respect of oil received within the territory of that State is fulfilled and shall take any appropriate measures under its law, including the imposing of such sanctions as it may deem necessary, with a view to the effective execution of any such obligation; provided, however, that such measures shall only be directed against those persons who are under an obligation to contibute to the Fund.

3. Where a person who is liable in accordance with the provisions of Articles 10 and 11 to make contributions to the fund does not fulfil his obligations in respect of any such contributions or any part thereof and is in arrears for a period exceeding three months, the Director shall take all appropriate action against such person on behalf of the Fund with a view to the recovery of the amount due. However, where the defaulting contributor is manifestly insolvent or the circumstances otherwise so warrant, the Assembly may, upon recommendation of the Director, decide that no action shall be taken or continued against the contributor.

Article 14

1. Each Contracting State may at the time when it deposits its instrument of ratification or accession or at any time thereafter declare that it assumes itself obligations that are incumbent under this Convention on any person who is liable to contribute to the Fund in accordance with Article 10, paragraph 1, in respect of oil received within the territory of that State. Such declaration shall be made in writing and shall specify which obligations are assumed.

2. Where a declaration under paragraph 1 is made prior to the entry into force of this Convention in accordance with Article 40, it shall be deposited with the Secretary-General of the Organization who shall after the entry into force of the Convention communicate the declaration to the Director.

3. A declaration under paragraph 1 which is made after the entry into force of this Convention shall be deposited with the Director.

4. A declaration made in accordance with this Article may be withdrawn by the relevant State giving notice thereof in writing to the Director. Such notification shall take effect three months after the Director's receipt thereof.

5. Any state which is bound by a declaration made under this Article shall, in any proceedings brought against it before a competent court in respect of any obligation specified in the declaration, waive any immunity that it would otherwise be entitled to invoke.

Article 15

1. Each Contracting State shall ensure that any person who receives contributing oil within its territory in such quantities that he is liable to contribute to the Fund appears on a list to be established and kept up to date by the Director in accordance with the subsequent provisions of this Article.

2. For the purposes set out in paragraph 1, each Contracting State shall communicate, at a time and in the manner to be prescribed in the Internal Regulations, to the Director the name and address of any person who in respect of that State is liable to contribute to the Fund pursuant to Article 10, as well as data on the relevent quantities of contributing oil received by any such person during the preceding calender year.

3. For the purposes of ascertaining who are, at any given time, persons liable to contribute to the Fund in accordance with Article 10, paragraph 1,

and of establishing, where applicable, the quantities of oil to be taken into account for any such person when determining the amount of his contribution, the list shall be prima facie evidence of the facts stated therein.

ORGANIZATION AND ADMINISTRATION

Article 16

The Fund shall have an Assembly, a Secretariat headed by a Director and, in accordance with the provisions of Article 21, an Executive Committee.

ASSEMBLY

Article 17

The Assembly shall consist of all Contracting States to this Convention.

Article 18

The functions of the Assembly shall, subject to the provisions of Article 26, be:

1. to elect at each regular session its Chairman and two Vice-Chairmen who shall hold office until the next regular session;

2. to determine its own rules of procedure, subject to the provisions of this Convention;

3. to adopt Internal Regulations necessary for the proper functioning of the Fund;

4. to appoint the Director and make provisions for the appointment of such other personnel as may be necessary and determine the terms and conditions of service of the Director and other personnel;

5. to adopt the annual budget and fix the annual contributions;

6. to appoint auditors and approve the accounts of the Fund;

7. to approve settlements of claims against the Fund, to take decisions in respect of the distribution among claimants of the available amount of compensation in accordance with Article 4, paragraph 5 and to determine the terms and conditions according to which provisional payments in respect of claims shall be made with a view to ensuring that victims of pollution damage are compensated as promptly as possible;

8. to elect the members of the Assembly to be represented on the Executive Committee, as provided in Articles 21, 22 and 23;

9. to establish any temporary or permanent subsidiary body it may consider to be necessary;

10. to determine which non-Contracting States and which inter-governmental and international non-governmental organizations shall be admitted to take part, without voting rights, in meetings of the Assembly, the Executive Committee, and the subsidiary bodies;

11. to give instructions concerning the administration of the Fund to the Director, the Executive Committee and subsidiary bodies;

12. to review and approve the reports and activities of the Executive Committee;

13. to supervise the proper execution of the Convention and of its own decisions;

14. to perform such other functions as are allocated to it under the Convention or are otherwise necessary for the proper operation of the Fund.

Article 19

1. Regular sessions of the Assembly shall take place once every calendar year upon convocation by the Director; provided, however, that if the Assembly allocates to the Executive Committee the functions specified in Article 18, paragraph 5, regular sessions of the Assembly shall be held once every two years.

2. Extraordinary sessions of the Assembly shall be convened by the Director at the request of the Executive Committee or of at least one-third of the members of the Assembly and may be convened on the Director's own initiative after consultation with the Chairman of the Assembly. The Director shall give members at least thirty day's notice of such sessions.

Article 20

A majority of the members of the Assembly shall constitute a quorum for its meetings.

EXECUTIVE COMMITTEE

Article 21

The Executive Committee shall be established at the first regular session of the Assembly after the date on which the number of Contracting States reaches fifteen.

Article 22

1. The Executive Committee shall consist of one-third of the members of the Assembly but of not less than seven or more than fifteen members. Where the number of members of the Assembly is not divisible by three, the one-third referred to shall be calculated on the next higher number which is divisible by three.

2. When electing the members of the Executive Committee the Assembly shall:

a) secure an equitable geographical distribution of the seats on the Committee on the basis of an adequate representation of Contracting States particularly exposed to the risks of oil pollution and of Contracting States having large tanker fleets; and

b) elect one half of the members of the Committee, or in case the total number of members to be elected is uneven, such number of the members as is equivalent to one half of the total number less one, among those Contracting States in the territory of which the largest quantities of oil to be taken into account under Article 10 were received during the preceding calendar year, provided that the number of States eligible under this sub-paragraph shall be limited as shown in the table below:

Total number of Members on the Committee	Number of States eligible under sub-paragraph (b)	Number of States to be elected under sub-paragraph (b)
7	5	3
8	6	4
9	6	4
10	8	5
11	8	5
12	9	6
13	9	6
14	11	7
15	11	7

3. A member of the Assembly which was eligible but was not elected under sub-paragraph (*b*) shall not be eligible to be elected for any remaining seat on the Executive Committee.

Article 23

1. Members of the Executive Committee shall hold office until the end of the next regular session of the Assembly.

2. Except to the extent that may be necessary for complying with the requirements of Article 22, no State Member of the Assembly may serve on the Executive Committee for more than two consecutive terms.

Article 24

The Executive Committee shall meet at least once every calendar year at thirty days' notice upon convocation by the Director, either on his own initiative or at the request of its Chairman or of at least one-third of its members. It shall meet at such places as may be convenient.

Article 25

At least two-thirds of the members of the Executive Committee shall constitute a quorum for its meetings.

Article 26

1. The functions of the Executive Committee shall be:

a) to elect its Chairman and adopt its own rules of procedure, except as otherwise provided in this Convention;

b) to assume and exercise in place of the Assembly the following functions:

(i) making provisions for the appointment of such personnel, other than the Director, as may be necessary and determining the terms and conditions of service of such personnel,

(ii) approving settlements of claims against the Fund and taking all other steps envisaged in relation to such claims in Article 18, paragraph 7;

(iii) giving instructions to the Director concerning the administration of the Fund and supervising the proper execution, by him, of the Convention, of the decisions of the Assembly and of the Committee's own decisions; and

c) to perform such other functions as are allocated to it by the Assembly.

2. The Executive Committee shall each year prepare and publish a report of the activities of the Fund during the previous calendar year.

Article 27

Members of the Assembly who are not members of the Executive Committee shall have the right to attend its meetings as observers.

SECRETARIAT

Article 28

1. The Secretariat shall comprise the Director and such staff as the administration of the Fund may require.

2. The Director shall be the legal representative of the Fund.

Article 29

1. The Director shall be the chief administrative officer of the Fund and shall, subject to the instructions given to him by the Assembly and by the Executive Committee, perform those functions which are assigned to him by the Convention, the Internal Regulations, the Assembly and the Executive Committee.

2. The Director shall in particular:

a) appoint the personnel required for the administration of the Fund;

b) take all appropriate measures with a view to the proper administration of the Fund's assets;

c) collect the contributions due under this Convention while observing in particular the provisions of Article 13, paragraph 3;

d) to the extent necessary to deal with claims against the Fund and carry out the other functions of the Fund, employ the services of legal, financial and other experts;

e) take all appropriate measures for dealing with claims against the Fund within the limits and on conditions to be laid down in the Internal Regulations, including the final settlement of claims without the prior approval of the Assembly for the Executive Committee where these Regulations so provide;

f) prepare and submit to the Assembly or to the Executive Committee, as the case may be, the financial statements and budget estimates for each calendar year;

g) assist the Executive Committee in the preparation of the report referred to in Article 26, paragraph 2;

h) prepare, collect and circulate the papers, documents, agenda, minutes and information that may be required for the work of the Assembly, the Executive Committee and subsidiary bodies.

Article 30

In the performance of their duties the Director and the staff and experts appointed by him shall not seek or receive instructions from any Government or from any authority external to the Fund. They shall refrain from any action which might reflect on their position as international officials. Each Contracting State on its part undertakes to respect the exclusively international character of the responsibilities of the Director and the staff and experts appointed by him, and not to seek to influence them in the discharge of their duties.

FINANCES

Article 31

1. Each Contracting State shall bear the salary, travel and other expenses of its own delegation to the Assembly and of its representatives on the Executive Committee and on subsidiary bodies.

2. Any other expenses incurred in the operation of the Fund shall be borne by the Fund.

VOTING

Article 32

The following provisions shall apply to voting in the Assembly and the Executive Committee:

a) each member shall have one vote;

b) except as otherwise provided in Article 33, decisions of the Assembly and the Executive Committee shall be by a majority vote of the members present and voting;

c) decisions where a three-fourths or a two-thirds majority is required shall be by a three-fourths or two-thirds majority vote, as the case may be, of those present;

d) for the purpose of this Article the phrase "members present" means "members present at the meeting at the time of the vote", and the phrase "members present and voting" means "members present and casting an affirmative or negative vote". Members who abstain from voting shall be considered as not voting.

Article 33

1. The following decisions of the Assembly shall require a three-fourths majority:

a) an increase in accordance with Article 4, paragraph 6, in the maximum amount of compensation payable by the Fund;

b) a determination, under Article 5, paragraph 4, relating to the replacement of the Instruments referred to in that paragraph;

c) the allocation to the Executive Committee of the functions specified in Article 18, paragraph 5.

2. The following decisions of the Assembly shall require a two-thirds majority:

a) a decision under Article 13, paragraph 3, not to take or continue action against a contributor;

b) the appointment of the Director under Article 18, paragraph 4;

c) the establishment of subsidiary bodies, under Article 18, paragraph 9.

Article 34

1. The Fund, its assets, income, including contributions, and other property shall enjoy in all Contracting States exemption from all direct taxation.

2. When the Fund makes substantial purchases of movable or immovable property, or has important work carried out which is necessary for the exercise of its official activities and the cost of which includes indirect taxes or sales taxes, the Governments of Member States shall take, whenever possible, appropriate measures for the remission or refund of the amount of such duties and taxes.

3. No exemption shall be accorded in the case of duties, taxes or dues which merely constitute payment for public utility services.

4. The Fund shall enjoy exemption from all customs duties, taxes and other related taxes on articles imported or exported by it or on its behalf for its official use. Articles thus imported shall not be transferred either for consideration or gratis on the territory of the country into which they have been imported except on conditions agreed by the government of that country.

5. Persons contributing to the Fund and victims and owners of ships receiving compensation from the Fund shall be subject to the fiscal legislation of the State where they are taxable, no special exemption or other benefits being conferred on them in this respect.

6. Information relating to individual contributors supplied for the purpose of this Convention shall not be divulged outside the Fund except in so far as it may be strictly necessary to enable the Fund to carry out its functions including the bringing and defending of legal proceedings.

7. Independently of existing or future regulations concerning currency or transfers, Contracting States shall authorize the transfer and payment of any contribution to the Fund and of any compensation paid by the Fund without any restriction.

TRANSITIONAL PROVISIONS

Article 35

1. The Fund shall incur no obligation whatsoever under Article 4 or 5 in respect of incidents occurring within a period of one hundred and twenty days after the entry into force of this Convention.

2. Claims for compensation under Article 4 and claims for indemnification under Article 5, arising from incidents occurring later than one hundred and twenty days but not later than two hundred and forty days after the entry into force of this Convention may not be brought against the Fund prior to the elapse of the two hundred and fortieth day after the entry into force of this Convention.

Article 36

The Secretary-General of the Organization shall convene the first session of the Assembly. This session shall take place as soon as possible after entry into force of this Convention and, in any case, not more than thirty days after such entry into force.

FINAL CLAUSES

Article 37

1. This Convention shall be open for signature by the States which have signed or which accede to the Liability Convention, and by any State represented at the Conference on the Establishment of an International Fund for Compensation for Oil Pollution Damage, 1971. The Convention shall remain open for signature until 31 December 1972.

2. Subject to paragraph 4, this Convention shall be ratified, accepted or approved by the States which have signed it.

3. Subject to paragraph 4, this Convention is open for accession by States which did not sign it.

4. This Convention may be ratified, accepted, approved or acceded to, only by States which have ratified, accepted, approved or acceded to the Liability Convention.

Article 38

1. Ratification, acceptance, approval or accession shall be effected by the deposit of a formal instrument to that effect with the Secretary-General of the Organization.

2. Any instrument of ratification, acceptance, approval or accession deposited after the entry into force of an amendment to this Convention with respect to all existing Contracting States or after the completion of all measures required for the entry into force of the amendment with respect to those Parties shall be deemed to apply to the Convention as modified by the amendment.

Article 39

Before this Convention comes into force a State shall, when depositing an instrument referred to in Article 38, paragraph 1, and annually thereafter at a date to be determined by a Secretary-General of the Organization, communicate to him the name and address of any person who in respect of that State would be liable to contribute to that Fund pursuant to Article 10 as well as data on the relevant quantities of contributing oil received by any such person in the territory of that State during the preceding calendar year.

Article 40

1. This Convention shall enter into force on the ninetieth day following the date on which the following requirements are fulfilled:

a) at least eight States have deposited instruments of ratification, acceptance approval or accession with the Secretary-General of the Organization, and

b) the Secretary-General of the Organization has received information in accordance with Article 39 that those persons in such States who would be liable to contribute pursuant to Article 10 have received during the preceding calendar year a total quantity of at least 750 million tons of contributing oil.

2. However, this Convention shall not enter into force before the Liability Convention has entered into force.

3. For each State which subsequently ratifies, accepts, approves or accedes to it, this Convention shall enter into force on the ninetieth day after deposit by such State of the appropriate instrument.

Article 41

1. This Convention may be denounced by any Contracting State at any time after the date on which the Convention comes into force for that State.

2. Denunciation shall be effected by the deposit of an instrument with the Secretary-General of the Organization.

3. A denunciation shall take effect one year, or such longer period as may be specified in the instrument of denunciation, after its deposit with the Secretary-General of the Organization.

4. Denunciation of the Liability Convention shall be deemed to be a denunciation of this Convention. Such denunciation shall take effect on the same date as the denunciation of the Liability Convention takes effect according to paragraph 3 of Article XVI of that Convention.

5. Notwithstanding a denunciation by a Contracting State pursuant to this Article, any provisions of this Convention relating to the obligations to make contributions under Article 10 with respect to an incident referred to in Article 12, paragraph 2 (b) and occurring before the denunciation takes effect shall continue to apply.

Article 42

1. Any Contracting State may, within ninety days after the deposit of an instrument of denunciation the result of which it considers will significantly increase the level of contributions for remaining Contracting States, request the Director to convene an extraordinary session of the Assembly. The director shall convene the Assembly to meet not later than sixty days after receipt of the request.

2. The Director may convene, on his own initiative, an extraordinary session of the Assembly to meet within sixty days after the deposit of any instrument of denunciation, if he considers that such denunciations will result in a significant increase in the level of contributions for the remaining Contracting States.

3. If the Assembly at an extraordinary session convened in accordance with paragraph 1 and 2 decides that the denunciation will result in a significant increase in the level of contributions for the remaining Contracting States, any such State may, not later than one hundred and twenty days before the date on which that denunciation takes effect, denounce this Convention with effect from the same date.

Article 43

1. This Convention shall cease to be in force on the date when the number of Contracting States falls below three.

2. Contracting States which are bound by this Convention on the date before the day it ceases to be in force, shall enable the Fund to exercise its functions as described under Article 44 and shall, for that purpose only, remain bound by this Convention.

Article 44

1. If this Convention ceases to be in force, the Fund shall nevertheless:

a) meet its obligations in respect of any incident occurring before the Convention ceased to be in force;

b) be entitled to exercise its rights to contributions to the extent that these contributions are necessary to meet the obligations under sub-paragraph (*a*), including expenses for the administration of the fund necessary for this purpose.

2. The Assembly shall take all appropriate measures to complete the winding up of the Fund, including the distribution in an equitable manner of any remaining assets among those persons who have contributed to the Fund.

3. For the purposes of this Article the Fund shall remain a legal person.

Article 45

1. A Conference for the purpose of revising or amending this Convention may be convened by the Organization.

2. The Organization shall convene a Conference of the Contracting States for the purpose of revising or amending this Convention at the request of not less than one-third of all Contracting States.

Article 46

1. This Convention shall be deposited with the Secretary-General of the Organization.

2. The Secretary-General of the Organization shall:

a) inform all States which have signed or acceded to this Convention of:

(i) each new signature or deposit of instrument and the date thereof;

(ii) the date of entry into force of the Convention;

(iii) any denunciation of the Convention and the date on which it takes effect;

b) transmit certified true copies of this Convention to all Signatory States and to all States which accede to the Convention.

Article 47

As soon as this Convention enters into force, a certified true copy thereof shall be transmitted by the Secretary-General of the Organization to the Secretariat of the United Nations for registration and publication in accordance with Article 102 of the Charter of the United Nations.

Article 48

This Convention is established in a single original in the English and French languages, both texts being equally authentic. Official translations in the Russian and Spanish languages shall be prepared by the Secretariat of the Organization and deposited with the signed original.

In Witness Whereof the undersigned plenipotentiaries being duly authorized for that purpose have signed the present Convention.

Done at Brussels this eighteenth day of December one thousand nine hundred and seventy-one.

CONVENTION FOR THE PREVENTION OF MARINE POLLUTION BY DUMPING FROM SHIPS AND AIRCRAFT [52]

Oslo, 15 February 1972

The Contracting Parties

Recognizing that the marine environment and the living resources which it supports are of vital importance to all nations;

Mindful that the ecological equilibrium and the legitimate uses of the sea are increasingly threatened by pollution;

Recognizing that concerted action by Governments at national, regional and global levels is essential to prevent and combat marine pollution;

Noting that this Pollution has many sources, including dumping from ships and aircraft and discharges through rivers, estuaries, outfalls and pipelines within national jurisdiction, that it is important that states use the best practicable means to prevent such pollution, and that products and processes which will minimize the amount of harmful waste requiring disposal should be developed;

Being convinced that international action to control the pollution of the sea by the dumping of harmful substances from ships and aircraft can and should be taken without delay, but that this action should not preclude discussion of measures to control other sources of marine pollution as soon as possible;

Considering that the states bordering the North-East Atlantic have a peculiar responsibility to protect that waters of this region;

Have agreed as follows:

Article 1

The Contracting Parties pledge themselves to take all possible steps to prevent the pollution of the sea by substances that are liable to create hazards to human health, to harm living resources and marine life, to damage amenities or to interfere with other legitimate uses of the sea.

Article 2

The area to which the Convention applies shall be the high seas and the territorial sea which are situated:

a) within those parts of the Atlantic and Arctic Oceans and their dependent seas which lie north of 36° north latitude and between 42° west longitude and 51° east longitude, but excluding

(i) the Baltic Sea and Belts lying to the south and east of lines drawn from Hasenore head to Gniben Point, from Korshage to Spodsbierg and from Gilbierg Head to the Kullen, and

(ii) the Mediterranean Sea and its dependent seas as far as the point of intersection of the parallel of 36° north latitude and the meridian of 5°36′ west longitude.

b) within that part of Atlantic Ocean north of 59° north latitude and between 44° west longitude and 42° west longitude.

Article 3

The Contracting Parties agree to apply measures which they adopt in such a way as to prevent the diversion of dumping of harmful substances into seas outside the area to which this Convention applies.

Article 4

The Contracting Parties shall harmonize their policies and introduce, individually and in common, measures to prevent the pollution of the sea by dumping by or from ships and aircraft.

Article 5

The dumping of the substances listed in Annex I of this Convention is prohibited.

Article 6

No waste containing such quantities of the substances and materials listed in Annex II to this Convention as the Commission established under the provisions of Article 16, hereinafter referred to as "the Commission", shall define as significant, shall be dumped without a specific permit in each case from the appropriate national authority or authorities. When such permits are issued, the provisions of Annexes II and III of this Convention shall be applied.

Article 7

No substance or material shall be dumped without the approval of the appropriate national authority or authorities. When such approval is granted, the provision of Annex III to this Convention shall be applied.

Article 8

1. The provisions of Articles 5.6 and 7 shall not apply in case of force majeure due to stress of weather or any other cause when the safety of human life or of a ship or aircraft is threatened. Such dumping shall immediately be reported to the Commission, together with full details of the circumstances and of the nature and quantities of the substances and materials dumped.

2. The provisions of Article 5 shall not apply where these substances occur as trace contaminants in waste to which they have not been added for the purpose of being dumped. However, such dumping shall remain subject to Article 6 and 7.

Article 9

If a Contracting Party in an emergency considers that a substance listed in Annex I to this Convention cannot be disposed of on land without unacceptable danger or damage, the Contracting Party concerned shall forthwith consult the Commission. The Commission shall recommend methods of storage or the most satisfactory means of destruction or disposal under the prevailing circumstances. The Contracting Party shall inform the Commission of the steps adopted in pursuance of its recommendation. The Contracting Parties pledge themselves to assist one another in such situations.

Article 10

The composition of the waste shall be ascertained by the appropriate national authority or authorities in accordance with the provisions of Annex III to this Convention before any permit or approval for the dumping of waste at sea is issued.

Article 11

Each Contracting Party shall keep, and transmit to the Commission, according to a standard procedure, records of the nature and the quantities of the substances and materials dumped under permits or approvals issued by that Contracting Party, and of the dates, places and methods of dumping.

Article 12

The Contracting Parties agree to establish complementary or joint programmes of scientific and technical research, including research on alternative methods of disposal of harmful substances, and to transmit to each other the information so obtained. In doing so they will have regard to the work carried out by the appropriate international organizations and agencies.

Article 13

The Contracting Parties agree to institute, in co-operation with appropriate international organizations and agencies, complementary or joint programmes for monitoring the distribution and effects of pollutants in the area to which this Convention applies.

Article 14

The Contracting Parties pledge themselves to promote, within the competent specialized agencies and other international bodies, measures concerning the protection of the marine environment against pollution caused by oil and oil wastes, other noxious or hazardous cargoes, and radioactive materials.

Article 15

1. Each Contracting Party undertakes to ensure compliance with the provisions of this Convention:

a) by ships and aircrafts registered in its territory;

b) by ships and aircraft loading in its territory the substances and materials which are to be dumped;

c) by ships and aircraft believed to be engaged in dumping within its territorial sea.

2. Each Contracting Party undertakes to issue instructions to its maritime inspection vessels and aircraft and to other appropriate services to report to its authorities any incidents or conditions on the high seas which give rise to suspicions that dumping in contravention of the provisions of the present Convention has occurred or is about to occur. That Contracting Party shall, if it considers it appropriate, report accordingly to any other Contracting Party concerned.

3. Each Contracting Party shall take in its territory appropriate measures to prevent and punish conduct in contravention of the provisions of this Convention.

4. The Contracting Parties undertake to assist one another as appropriate in dealing with pollution incidents involving dumping at sea, and to exchange information on methods of dealing with such incidents.

5. The Contracting Parties further agree to work together in the development of co-operative procedures for the application of the Convention, particularly on the high seas.

6. Nothing in this Convention shall abridge sovereign immunity to which certain vessels are entitled under international law.

Article 16

A Commission, made up of representatives of each of the Contracting Parties, is hereby established. The Commission shall meet at regular intervals and at any time when, due to special circumstances, it is so decided in accordance with the Rules of Procedure.

Article 17

It shall be the duty of the Commission:

a) To exercise overall supervision over the implementation of this Convention;

b) To receive and consider the records of permits and approvals issued and of dumping which has taken place, as provided for in Articles 8, 9 and 11 of this Convention, and to define the standard procedure to be adopted for this purpose;

c) To review generally the condition of the seas within the area to which this Convention applies, the efficacy of the control measures being adopted, and the need for any additional or different measures;

d) To keep under review the contents of the Annexes to this Convention, and to recommend such amendments, additions or deletions as may be agreed;

e) To discharge such other functions as may be appropriate under the terms of this Convention.

Article 18

1. The Commission shall draw up its own Rules of Procedure which shall be adopted by unanimous vote. The Government of Norway shall call the first meeting of the Commission as soon as practicable after the coming into force of this Convention.

2. Recommendations for modification of the Annexes to this Convention in accordance with Article 17 (*d*) shall be adopted by a unanimous vote in the Commission, and the modification contained therein shall enter into force after unanimous approval by the Governments of the Contracting Parties.

Article 19

For the purpose of this Convention:

1. "Dumping" means any deliberate disposal of substances and materials into the sea by or from ships or aircraft other than:

a) any discharge incidental to or derived from the normal operation of ships and aircraft and their equipment;

b) the placing of substances and materials for a purpose other than mere disposal thereof, is not contrary to the aim of this Convention.

2. "Ships and aircraft" means seagoing vessels and air-borne craft, floating craft whether self-propelled or not, and fixed or floating platforms.

Article 20

This Convention shall be open for signature at Oslo until 15 August 1972 by the States invited to participate in the Conference on Marine Pollution, held there from 19 to 22 October 1971.

Article 21

This Convention shall be subject to ratification. The instruments of ratification shall be deposited with the Government of Norway.

Article 22

This Convention shall be open for accession by any State referred to in Article 20. The Contracting Parties may unanimously invite other States to accede to the Convention. The instruments of accession shall be deposited with the Government of Norway.

Article 23

1. This Convention shall enter into force on the thirtieth day following the date of deposit of the seventh instrument of ratification or accession.

2. For each State ratifying or acceding to the Convention after the deposit of the seventh instrument of ratification or accession, the Convention shall enter into force on the thirtieth day after deposit by such State of its instrument of ratification or accession.

Article 24

At any time after two years from the date on which this Convention has come into force with respect to a Contracting Party, that Party may withdraw from the Convention by means of a notice in writing addressed to the depositary Government. Any such withdrawal shall take effect twelve months after the date of its receipt.

Article 25

A conference for the purpose of revising or amending this Convention may be convened by the depositary Government at the request of the Commission adopted by a two-thirds majority.

Article 26

The depositary Government shall inform the Contracting Parties and the States referred to in Article 20:

a) of signatures to this Convention, of the deposit of instruments of ratification or accesion, and of the receipt of a notice of withdrawal, in accordance with Articles 20, 21 , 22 and 24.

b) of the date on which this Convention will come into force in accordance with Article 23;

c) of the receipt of notification of approval relating to modifications of the Annexes to this Convention and of the entry into force of such modifications in accordance with Article 18.

Article 27

The original of this Convention, of which the English and French texts are equally authentic, shall be deposited with the Government of Norway, which shall send certified copies thereof to the Contracting Parties and to the States referred to in Article 20, and which shall transmit a certified copy to the Secretary-General of the United Nations for registration and publication in accordance with Article 102 of the Charter of the United Nations.

In Witness Whereof the undersigned, being duly authorized by their respective Governments, have signed this Convention.

Done at Oslo, the fifteenth day of February 1972.

Annex I

The following substances are listed for the purposes of Article 5 of the Convention:

1. Organohalogen compounds and compounds which may form such substances in the marine environment, excluding those which are non-toxic, or which are rapidly converted in the sea into substances which are biologically harmless;

2. Organosilicon compounds and compounds which may form such substances in the marine environment, excluding those whih are non-toxic,or which are rapidly converted in the sea substances which are biologically harmless;

3. Substances which have been agreed between the Contracting Parties as likely to be carcinogenic under the conditions of disposal;

4. Mercury and mercury compounds;

5. Cadmium and cadmium compounds;

6. Persistent plastics and other persistent synthetic materials which may float or remain in suspension in the sea, and which may seriously interfere with fishing or navigation, reduce amenities, or interfere with other legitimate uses of the sea.

Annex II

1. The following substances and materials requiring special care are listed for the purposes of Article 6:

a) Arsenic, lead, copper, zinc and their compounds, cyanides and fluorides, and pesticides and their by-products not covered by the provisions of Annex I;

b) Containers, scrap metal, tar-like substances liable to sink to the sea bottom and other bulky wastes which may present a serious obstacle to fishing or navigation;

c) Substances which, though of a non-toxic nature, may become harmful due to the quantities in which they are dumped, or which are liable to seriously reduce amenities.

2. The substances and materials listed under

paragraph 1 (*b*) above should always be deposited in deep water.

3. In the issuance of permits or approvals for the dumping of large quantities of acids and alkalis, consideration should be given to the possible presence in such wastes of the substances listed in paragraph 1 above.

4. When, in the application of the provisions of Annexes II and III, it is considered necessary to deposit waste in deep water, this should be done only when the following two conditions are both fulfilled:

a) that the depth is not less than 2000 metres,

b) that the distance from the nearest land is not less than 150 nautical miles.

Annex III

Provisions governing the issue of permits and approvals for the dumping of wastes at sea.

1. *Characteristics of the waste*

a) Amount and composition;

b) Amount of substances and materials to be deposited per day (per week, per month);

c) Form in which it is presented for dumping, i.e. whether as a solid, sludge or liquid;

d) Physical (especially solubility and specific gravity), chemical, bio-chemical (oxygen demand, nutrient production) and biological properties (presence of viruses, bacteria, yeasts, parasites, etc.);

e) Toxicity;

f) Persistence;

g) Accumulation in biological materials or sediments;

h) Chemical and physical changes of the waste after release, including possible formation of new compounds;

i) Probability of production of taints reducing marketability of resources (fish, shellfish, etc.)

2. *Characteristics of dumping site and method of deposit*

a) Geographical position, depth and distance from coast;

b) Location in relation to living resources in adult or juvenile phases;

c) Location in relation to amenity areas;

d) Methods of packing, if any;

e) Initial dilution achieved by proposed method of release;

f) Dispersal, horizontal transport and vertical mixing characteristics;

g) Existence and effects of current and previous discharges and dumping in the area (including accumulative effects).

3. *General considerations and conditions*

a) Interference with shipping, fishing, recreation, mineral extraction, desalination, fish and shellfish culture, areas of special scientific importance and other legitimate use of the sea;

b) In applying these principles the practical availability of alternative means of disposal or elimination will be taken into consideration.

CONVENTION ON THE PROHIBITION OF THE DEVELOPMENT, PRODUCTION AND STOCKPILING OF BACTERIOLOGICAL (BIOLOGICAL) AND TOXIN WEAPONS AND ON THEIR DESTRUCTION [53]

London, Moscow, Washington, 10 April 1972

The States Parties to this Convention,

Determined to act with a view to achieving effective progress towards general and complete disarmament including the prohibition and elimination of all types of weapons of mass destruction, and convinced that the prohibition of the development, production and stockpiling of chemical and bacteriological (biological) weapons and their elimination, through effective measures, will facilitate the achievement of general and complete disarmament under strict and effective international control,

Recognizing the important significance of the Protocol for the Prohibition of the Use in War of Asphyxiating, Poisonous or Other Gases, and of Bacteriological Methods of Warfare signed at Geneva on 17 June 1925 and conscious also of the contribution which the said Protocol has already made, and continues to make, to mitigating the horrors of war,

Reaffirming their adherence to the principles and objectives of that Protocol and calling upon all States to comply strictly with them.

Recalling that the General Assembly of the United Nations has repeatedly condemned all actions contrary to the principles and objectives of the Geneva Protocol of 17 June 1925,

Desiring to contribute to the strengthening of confidence between peoples and the general improvement of the international atmosphere,

Desiring also to contribute to the realization of the purposes and principles of the Charter of the United Nations,

Convinced of the importance and urgency of eliminating from the arsenals of states, through effective measures, such dangerous weapons of mass destruction as those using chemical or bacteriological (biological) agents,

Recognizing that an agreement on the prohibition of bacteriological (biological) and toxin weapons represents a first possible step towards the achievement of agreement on effective measures also for prohibition of the development, production and stockpiling of chemical weapons, and determined to continue negotiations to that end,

Determined, for the sake of all mankind, to exclude completely the possibility of bacteriological (biological) agents and toxins being used as weapons,

Convinced that such use would be repugnant to the conscience of mankind and that no effort should be spared to minimize the risk,

Have agreed as follows:

Article I

Each State Party to this Convention undertakes never in any circumstances to develop, produce, stockpile or otherwise acquire or retain:

1. Microbial or other biological agents, or toxins whatever their origin or method of production, of types and in quantites that have no justification for prophylactic, protective or other peaceful purposes:
2. Weapons, equipment or means of delivery designed to use such agents or toxins for hostile purposes or in armed conflict.

Article II

Each State Party to this Convention undertakes to destroy or to divert to peaceful purposes, as soon as possible but not later than nine months after the entry into force of the Convention all agents, toxins, weapons, equipment and means of delivery specified in Article I of the Convention, which are in its possession or under its jurisdiction or control. In implementing the provisions of this Article all necessary safety precautions shall be observed to protect populations and the environment.

Article III

Each State Party to this Convention undertakes not to transfer to any recipient whatsoever, directly or indirectly, and not in any way to assist, encourage, or induce any State, group of States or international organizations to manufacture or otherwise acquire any of the agents, toxins, weapons, equipment or means of delivery specified in Article I of the Convention.

Article IV

Each State Party to this Convention shall, in accordance with its constitutional processes, take any necessary measures to prohibit and prevent development, production, stockpiling, acquisition or retention of the agents, toxins, weapons, equipment and means of delivery specified in Article I of the Convention, within the territory of such State, under its jurisdiction or under its control anywhere.

Article V

The States Parties to the Convention undertake to consult one another and to co-operate in solving the problems which may arise in relation to the objective of, or in the application of the provisions of, the Convention. Consultation and co-operation pursuant to this Article may also be undertaken through appropriate international procedures within the framework of the United Nations and in accordance with its Charter.

Article VI

1. Any State Party to the Convention which finds that any other State Party is acting in breach of obligations deriving from the provisions of the Convention may lodge a complaint with the Security Council of the United Nations. Such a complaint should include all possible evidence confirming its validity, as well as a request for its consideration by the Security Council.
2. Each State Party to this Convention undertakes to co-operate in carrying out any investigation which the Security Council may initiate, in accordance with the provisions of the Charter of the United Nations, on the basis of the complaint received by the Council. The Security Council shall inform the States Parties to the Convention of the results of the investigation.

Article VII

Each State Party to the Convention undertakes to provide or support assistance, in accordance with the United Nations Charter, to any Party to the Convention which so requests, if the Security Council decides that such Party has been exposed to danger as a result of violation of this Convention.

Article VIII

Nothing in this Convention shall be interpreted as in any way limiting or detracting from the obligations assumed by any State under the Protocol for the Prohibition of the Use in War of Asphyxiating, Poisonous or Other Gases, and of Bacteriological Methods of Warfare signed at Geneva on 17 June 1925.

Article IX

Each State Party to this Convention affirms the recognized objective of effective prohibition of chemical weapons and, to this end, undertakes to continue negotiations in good faith with a view to reaching early agreement on effective measures for the prohibition of their development, production and stockpiling and for their destruction, and on appropriate measures concerning equipment and means of delivery specifically designed for the production or use of chemical agents for weapons purposes.

Article X

1. The States parties to the Convention undertake to facilitate and have the right to participate in, the fullest possible exchange of equipment, materials and the scientific and technological information for the use of bacteriological (biological) agents and toxins for peaceful purposes. Parties to the Convention in a position to do so shall also co-operate in contributing individually or together with other States or international organizations to the further development and application of scientific discoveries in the field of bacteriology (biology) for prevention of disease, or for other peaceful purposes.
2. This Convention shall be implemented in a manner designed to avoid hampering the economic or technological development of States Parties to the Convention or international co-operation in the field of peaceful bacteriological (biological) agents and toxins and equipment for the processing, use or production of bacteriological (biological) agents and toxins for peaceful purposes in accordance with the provisions of the Convention.

Article XI

Any State Party may propose amendments to this Convention. Amendments shall enter into force for each State Party accepting the amendments upon their acceptance by a majority of the States Parties to the Convention and thereafter for each remaining State Party on the date of acceptance by it.

Article XII

Five years after the entry into force of this Convention, or earlier if it is requested by a majority of Parties to the Convention by submitting a proposal to this effect to the Depositary Governments, a conference of States Parties to the Convention shall be held at Geneva, Switzerland, to review the operation of the Convention, with a view to assuring that the purposes of the preamble and the provisions of the Convention, including the provisions concerning negotiations on chemical weapons, are being realized. Such review shall take into account any new scientific and technological developments relevant to this Convention.

Article XIII

1. This Convention shall be of unlimited duration.

2. Each State Party to this Convention shall in exercising its national sovereignty have the right to withdraw from the Convention if it decides that extraordinary events, related to the subject matter of the Convention, have jeopardized the supreme interests of its country. It shall give notice of such withdrawal to all other States Parties to the Convention and to the United Nations Security Council three months in advance. Such notice shall include a statement of the extraordinary events it regards as having jeopardized its supreme interests.

Article XIV

1. This Convention shall be open to all States for signature. Any State which does not sign the Convention before its entry into force in accordance with paragraph 3 of this Article may accede to it at any time.

2. This Convention shall be subject to ratification by signatory States. Instruments of ratification and instruments of accession shall be deposited with the Governments of the Union of Soviet Socialist Republics, the United Kingdom of Great Britain and Northern Ireland and the United States of America which are hereby designated the Depositary Governments.

3. This Convention shall enter into force after the deposit of instruments of ratification by twenty-two Governments, including the Governments designated as Depositaries of the Convention.

4. For States whose instruments of ratification or accession are deposited subsequent to the entry into force of this Convention, it shall enter into force on the date of the deposit of their instruments of ratification or accession.

5. The Depositary Government shall promptly inform all signatory and acceding States of the date of each signature, the date of deposit of each instrument of ratification or of accession and the date of the entry into force of this Convention, and of the receipt of other notices.

6. This Convention shall be registered by the Depositary Governments pursuant to Article 102 of the Charter of the United Nations.

Article XV

This Convention, the Russian, English, Spanish, Chinese and French texts of which are equally authentic, shall be deposited in the archives of the Depositary Governments. Duly certified copies of this Convention shall be transmitted by the Depositary Governments to the Governments of the signatory and acceding States.

CONVENTION FOR THE CONSERVATION OF ANTARCTIC SEALS [54]

London, 1 June 1972

The Contracting Parties,

Recalling the Agreed Measures for the Conservation of Antarctic Fauna and Flora, adopted under the Antarctic Treaty signed at Washington on 1 December 1959:

Recognizing the general concern about the vulnerability of Antarctic seals to commercial exploitation and the consequent need for effective conservation measures:

Recognizing that the stocks of Antarctic seals are an important living resource in the marine environment which requires an international agreement for its effective conservation;

Recognizing that this resource should not be depleted by over-exploitation, and hence that any harvesting should be regulated so as not to exceed the levels of the optimum sustainable yield;

Recognizing that in order to improve scientific knowledge and so place exploitation on a rational basis, every effort should be made both to encourage biological and other research on Antarctic seal populations and to gain information from such research and from the statistics of future sealing operations, so that further suitable regulations may be formulated;

Noting that the Scientific Committee on Antarctic Research of the International Council of Scientific Unions (SCAR) is willing to carry out the tasks requested of it in this Convention.

Desiring to promote and achieve the objectives of protection, scientific study and rational use of Antarctic seals, and to maintain a satisfactory balance within the ecological system,

Have agreed as follows:

Article 1

SCOPE

1. This Convention applies to the sea south of 60° South Latitude, in respect of which the Contracting Parties affirm the provisions of Article IV of the Antarctic Treaty.

2. This Convention may be applicable to any or all of the following species:

Southern elephant seal *Mirounga leonina,*

Leopard seal *Hydrurga leptonyx,*

Weddell seal *Leptonychotes weddelli,*

Crabeater seal *Lobodon carcinophagus,*

Ross seal *Ommatophoca rossi,*

Southern fur seals *Arctocephalus* sp.

3. The Annex to this Convention forms an integral part thereof.

Article 2

IMPLEMENTATION

1. The Contracting Parties agree that the species of seals enumerated in Article 1 shall not be killed or captured within the Convention area by their nationals or vessels under their respective flags except in accordance with the provisions of this Convention.

2. Each Contracting Party shall adopt for its nationals and for vessels under its flag such laws, regulations and other measures, including a permit system as appropriate, as may be necessary to implement this Convention.

Article 3

ANNEXED MEASURES

1. This Convention includes an Annex specifying measures which the Contracting Parties hereby adopt. Contracting Parties may from time to time in the future adopt other measures with respect to the conservation, scientific study and rational and humane use of seal resources, prescribing *inter alia*:

a) permissible catch;

b) protected and unprotected species;

c) open and closed seasons;

d) open and closed areas, including the designation of reserves;

e) the designation of special areas where there shall be no disturbance of seals;

f) limits relating to sex, size, or age for each species;

g) restrictions relating to time of day and duration, limitations of effort and methods of sealing;

h) types and specifications of gear and apparatus and appliances which may be used;

i) catch returns and other statistical and biological records;

j) procedures for facilitating the review and assessment of scientific information:

k) other regulatory measures including an effective system of inspection.

2. The measures adopted under paragraph (1) of this Article shall be based upon the best scientific and technical evidence available.

3. The Annex may from time to time be amended in accordance with the procedures provided for in Article 9.

Article 4

SPECIAL PERMITS

1. Notwithstanding the provisions of this Convention, any Contracting Party may issue permits to kill or capture seals in limited quantities and in conformity with the objectives and principles of this Convention for the following purposes:

a) to provide indispensable food for men or dogs;

b) to provide for scientific research; or

c) to provide specimens for museums, educational or cultural institutions.

2. Each Contracting Party shall, as soon as possible, inform the other Contracting Parties and SCAR of the purpose and content of all permits issued under paragraph (1) of this Article and

subsequently of the numbers of seals killed or captured under these permits.

Article 5

EXCHANGE OF INFORMATION AND SCIENTIFIC ADVICE

1. Each Contracting Party shall provide to the other Contracting Parties and to SCAR the information specified in the Annex within the period indicated therein.

2. Each Contracting Party shall also provide to the other Contracting Parties and to SCAR before 31 October each year information on any steps it has taken in accordance with Article 2 of this Convention during the preceding period of 1 July to 30 June.

3. Contracting Parties which have no information report under the two preceding paragraphs shall indicate this formally before 31 October each year.

4. SCAR is invited:

a) to assess information received pursuant to this Article; encourage exchange of scientific data and information among the Contracting Parties; recommend programmes for scientific research; recommend statistical and biological data to be collected by sealing expeditions within the Convention area; and suggest amendments to the Annex; and

b) to report on the basis of the statistical, biological and other evidence available when the harvest of any species of seal in the Convention area is having a significantly harmful effect on the total stocks of such species or on the ecological system in any particular locality.

5. SCAR is invited to notify the Depositary which shall report to the Contracting Parties when SCAR estimates in any sealing season that the permissible catch limits for any species are likely to be exceeded and, in that case, to provide an estimate of the date upon which the permissible catch limits will be reached. Each Contracting party shall then take appropriate measures to prevent its nationals and vessels under its flag from killing or capturing seals of that species after the estimated date until the Contracting Parties decide otherwise.

6. SCAR may if necessary seek the technical assistance of the Food and Agriculture Organization of the United Nations in making its assessments.

7. Notwithstanding the provisions of paragraph (1) of Article 1 the Contracting Parties shall, in accordance with their internal law, report to each other and to SCAR, for consideration, statistics relating to the Antarctic seals listed in paragraph (2) of Article 1 which have been killed or captured by their nationals and vessels under their respective flags in the area of floating sea ice north of 60° South latitude.

Article 6

CONSULTATIONS BETWEEN CONTRACTING PARTIES

1. At any time after commercial sealing has begun a Contracting Party may propose through the Depositary that a meeting of Contracting Parties be convened with a view to:

a) establishing by a two-thirds majority of the Contracting Parties, including the concurring votes of all States signatory to this Convention present at the meeting, an effective system of control, including inspection, over the implementation of the provisions of this Convention;

b) establishing a commission to perform such functions under this Convention as the Contracting Parties may deem necessary; or

c) considering other proposals, including:

(i) the provision of independent scientific advice;

(ii) the establishment, by a two-thirds majority, of a scientific advisory committee which may be assigned some or all of the functions requested of SCAR under this Convention, if commercial sealing reaches significant proportions;

(iii) the carrying out of scientific programmes with the participation of the Contracting Parties; and

(iv) the provision of further regulatory measures, including moratoria.

2. if one-third of the Contracting Parties indicate agreement the Depositary shall convene such a meeting, as soon as possible.

3. A meeting shall be held at the request of any Contracting Party, if SCAR reports that the harvest of any species of Antarctic seal in the area to which this Convention applies is having a significantly harmful effect on the total stocks or the ecological system in any particular locality.

Article 7

REVIEW OF OPERATIONS

The Contracting Parties shall meet within five years after the entry into force of this Convention and at least every five years thereafter to review the operation of the Convention.

Article 8

AMENDMENTS TO THE CONVENTION

1. This Convention may be amended at any time.The text of any amendment proposed by a Contracting Party shall be submitted to the Depositary, which shall transmit it to all the Contracting Parties.

2. If one-third of the Contracting Parties request a meeting to discuss the proposed amendment the Depositary shall call such a meeting.

3. An amendment shall enter into force when the Depositary has received instruments of ratification or acceptance thereof from all the Contracting Parties.

Article 9

AMENDMENTS TO THE ANNEX

1. Any Contracting Party may propose amendments to the Annex to this Convention. The text of any such proposed amendment shall be submitted to the Depositary which shall transmit it to all Contracting Parties.

2. Each such proposed amendment shall become effective for all Contracting Parties six months after the date appearing on the notification from the Depositary to the Contracting Parties, if within 120 days of the notification date, no objection has been received and two-thirds of the Contracting Parties have notified the Depositary in writing of their approval.

3. If an objection is received from any Contracting Party within 120 days of the notification date, the matter shall be considered by the Contracting Parties at their next meeting. If unanimity on the matter is not reached at the meeting, the Contracting Parties shall notify the Depositary within 120 days from the date of the closure, of the meeting of their approval or rejection of the original amendment or of any new amendment proposed by the meeting. If, by the end of this period, two-thirds of the Contracting Parties have approved such amendment, it shall become effective six months from the date of the closure of the meeting for those Contracting Parties which have by then notified their approval.

4. Any Contracting Party which has objected to a proposed amendment may at any time withdraw that objection, and the proposed amendment shall become effective with respect to such Party immediately if the amendment is already in effect, or at such time as it becomes effective under the terms of this Article.

5. The Depositary shall notify each Contracting Party immediately upon receipt of each approval or objection, of each withdrawal of objection, and of the entry into force of any amendment.

6. Any State which becomes a party to this Convention after an amendment to the Annex has entered into force shall be bound by the Annex as so amended. Any State which becomes a Party to this Convention during the period when a proposed amendment is pending may approve or object to such an amendment within the time limits applicable to other Contracting Parties.

Article 10

SIGNATURE

This Convention shall be open for signature at London from 1 June to 31 December 1972 by States participating in the Conference on the Conservation of Antarctic Seals held at London from 3 to 11 February 1972.

Article 11

RATIFICATION

This Convention is subject to ratification or acceptance. Instruments of ratification or acceptance shall be deposited with the Government of the United Kingdom of Great Britain and Northern Ireland, hereby designated as the Depositary.

Article 12

ACCESSION

This Convention shall be open for accession by any State which may be invited to accede to this Convention with the consent of all the Contracting Parties.

Article 13

ENTRY INTO FORCE

1. This Convention shall enter into force on the thirtieth day following the date of deposit of the seventh instrument of ratification or acceptance.

2. Thereafter this Convention shall enter into force for each ratifying, accepting or acceding State on the thirtieth day after deposit by such State of its instrument of ratification, acceptance or accession.

Article 14

WITHDRAWAL

Any Contracting Party may withdraw from this Convention on 30 June of any year by giving notice on or before 1 January of the same year to the Depositary, which upon receipt of such a notice shall at once communicate it to the other Contracting Parties. Any other Contracting Party may, in like manner, within one month of the receipt of a copy of such a notice from the Depositary, give notice of withdrawal, so that the Convention shall cease to be in force on 30 June of the same year with respect to the Contracting Party giving such notice.

Article 15

NOTIFICATION BY THE DEPOSITARY

The Depositary shall notify all signatory and acceding States of the following:

a) signatures of this Convention, the deposit of instruments of ratification, acceptance or accession and notices of withdrawal;

b) the date of entry into force of this Convention and of any amendments to it or its Annex.

Article 16

CERTIFIED COPIES AND REGISTRATION

1. This Convention, done in the English, French, Russian and Spanish languages, each version being equally authentic, shall be deposited in the archives of the Government of the United Kingdom of Great Britain and Northern Ireland, which shall transmit duly certified copies thereof to all signatory and acceding States.

2. This Convention shall be registered by the Depositary pursuant to Article 102 of the Charter of the United Nations.

In Witness Whereof, the undersigned, duly authorized, have signed the Convention.

Done at London, this 1st day of June 1972.

Annex

1. *Permissible Catch*

The Contracting Parties in any one year, which shall run from 1 July to 30 June inclusive, restrict the total number of seals of each species killed or captured to the numbers specified below. These numbers are subject to review in the light of scientific assessments:

a) in the case of Crabeater seals *Lobodon carcinophagus*, 175,000;

b) in the case of Leopard seals *Hydrurga leptonyx*, 12,000;

c) in the case of Weddell seals *Leptonychotes weddelli*, 5,000.

2. *Protected Species*

a) It is forbidden to kill or capture Ross seals *Ommatophoca rossi*, Southern elephant seals *Mirounga leonina*, or fur seals of the genus *Arctocephalus*.

b) In order to protect the adult breeding stock when it it is most concentrated and vulnerable, it is forbidden to kill or capture any Weddell seal *Leptonychotes weddelli* one year old or older between 1 September and 31 January inclusive.

3. *Closed Season and Sealing Season*

The period between 1 March and 31 August inclusive is a Closed Season, during which the killing or capturing of seals is forbidden. The period 1 September to the last day in February constitutes a Sealing Season.

4. *Sealing Zones*

Each of the sealing zones listed in this paragraph shall be closed in numerical sequence to all sealing operations for the seal species listed in paragraph 1 of this Annex for the period 1 September to the last day of February inclusive. Such closures shall begin with the same zone as is closed under paragraph 2 of Annex B to Annex 1 of the Report of the Fifth Antarctic Treaty Consultative Meeting at the moment the Convention enters into force. Upon the expiration of each closed period, the affected zone shall reopen:

Zone 1 — between 60° and 120° West Longitude

Zone 2 — between 0° and 60° West Longitude, together with that part of the Weddell Sea lying westward of 60° West Longitude

Zone 3 — between 0° and 70° East Longitude

Zone 4 — between 70° and 130° East Longitude

Zone 5 — between 130° East Longitude and 170° West Longitude

Zone 6 — between 120° and 170° West Longitude.

5. *Seal Reserves*

It is forbidden to kill or capture seals in the following reserves, which are seal breeding areas or the site of long-term scientific research:

a) The area around the South Orkney Islands between 60° 20′ and 60° 56′ South Latitude and 44° 05′ and 46° 25′ West Longitude.

b) The area of the southwestern Ross Sea south of 76° South Latitude and west of 170° East Longitude.

c) The area of Edisto Inlet south and west of a line drawn between Cape Hallett at 72° 19′ South Latitude, 170° 18′ East Longitude, and Helm Point, at 72° 11′ South Latitude, 170° 00′ East Longitude.

6. *Exchange of Information*

a) Contracting Parties shall provide before 31 October each year to other Contracting Parties and to SCAR a summary of statistical information on all seals killed or captured by their nationals and vessels under their respective flags in the Convention area, in respect of the preceding period 1 July to 30 June. This information shall include by zones and months:

(i) The gross and nett tonnage, brake horse-power, number of crew, and number of days' operation of vessels under the flag of the Contracting Party;

(ii) The number of adult individuals and pups of each species taken.

When specially requested, this information shall be provided in respect of each ship, together with its daily position at noon each operating day and the catch on that day.

b) When an industry has started, reports of the number of seals of each species killed or captured in each zone shall be made to SCAR in the form and at the intervals (not shorter than one week) requested by that body.

c) Contracting Parties shall provide to SCAR biological information, in particular:

(i) Sex

(ii) Reproductive condition

(iii) Age

SCAR may request additional information or material with the approval of the Contracting Parties.

d) Contracting Parties shall provide to other Contracting Parties and to SCAR at least 30 days in advance of departure from their home ports, information on proposed sealing expeditions.

7. *Sealing Methods*

a) SCAR is invited to report on methods of sealing and to make recommendations with a view to ensuring that the killing or capturing of seals is quick, painless and efficient. Contracting Parties, as appropriate, shall adopt rules for their nationals and vessels under their respective flags engaged in the killing and capturing of seals, giving due consideration to the views of SCAR.

b) In the light of the available scientific and technical data, Contracting Parties agree to take appropriate steps to ensure that their nationals and vessels under their respective flags refrain from killing or capturing seals in the water, except in limited quantities to provide for scientific research in conformity with the objectives and principles of this Convention. Such research shall include studies as to the effectiveness of methods of sealing from the viewpoint of the management and humane and rational utilization of the Antarctic seal resources for conservation purposes. The undertaking and the results of any such scientific research programme shall be communicated to SCAR and the Depositary which shall transmit them to the Contracting Parties.

Addendum

At the signature, the following statement was made by the Representative of Chile:

"The Delegation of Chile states that the reference to Article IV of the Antarctic Treaty contained in Article 1 of the present Convention signifies that nothing specified therein shall confirm, deny or impair the rights of the Contracting Parties as regards their maritime jurisdictions and their declared juridical position on this matter."

The following statement was made by the Representative of the United States of America:

"The Delegation of the United States of America believes that the Convention should contain stronger provisions for the observation of operations and enforcement of regulations, especially with regard to the use of observers of the Contracting Parties with each others' sealing expeditions. Opposition to stronger provisions has chiefly arisen not from commercial but from juridical interests.

"Nevertheless, the Convention is a new and valuable International Agreement, achieved in advance of the development of commercial sealing in the Antarctic, that contains many provisions important to the conservation of seals and their protection against over-exploitation. We understand exploratory commercial sealing ventures may be imminent.

"In order not to diminish the progress achieved by this Conference in international co-operation effective conservation in the Antarctic, the delegation of the United States of America has decided to sign the Final Act and will submit the Convention for its Government's consideration."

CONVENTION FOR THE PROTECTION OF THE WORLD CULTURAL AND NATURAL HERITAGE [55]

Paris, 23 November 1972

The General Conference of the United Nations Educational, Scientific and Cultural Organization meeting in Paris from 17 October to 21 November 1972, at its seventeenth session,

Noting that the cultural heritage and the natural heritage are increasingly threatened with destruction not only by the traditional causes of decay, but also by changing social and economic conditions which aggravate the situation with even more formidable phenomena of damage or destruction,

Considering that deterioration or disappearance of any item of the cultural or natural heritage constitutes a harmful impoverishment of the heritage of all the nations of the world,

Considering that protection of this heritage at the national level often remains incomplete because of the scale of the resources which it requires and of the insufficient economic, scientific and technical resources of the country where the property to be protected is situated,

Recalling that the Constitution of the Organization proves that it will maintain, increase and diffuse knowledge, by assuring the conservation and protection of the world's heritage, and recommending to the nations concerned the necessary international conventions,

Considering that the existing international conventions, recommendations and resolutions concerning cultural and natural property demonstrate the importance, for all the peoples of the world, of safeguarding this unique and irreplaceable property, to whatever people it may belong,

Considering that parts of the cultural or natural heritage are of outstanding interest and therefore need to be preserved as part of the world heritage of mankind as a whole,

Considering that, in view of the magnitude and gravity of the new dangers threatening them, it is incumbent on the international community as a whole to participate in the protection of the cultural and natural heritage of outstanding universal value, by the granting of collective assistance which, although not taking the place of action by the State concerned, will serve as an effective complement thereto,

Considering that it is essential for this purpose to adopt new provisions in the form of a convention establishing an effective system of collective protection of the cultural and natural heritage of outstanding universal value, organized on a permanent basis and in accordance with modern scientific methods,

Having decided, at its sixteenth session, that this question should be made the subject of an international convention,

Adopts this sixteenth day of November 1972 this Convention.

I. Definitions of the Cultural and the Natural Heritage

Article 1

For the purposes of this Convention, the following shall be considered as "cultural heritage":

monuments: architectural works, works of monumental sculpture and painting, elements or structures of an archaeological nature, inscriptions, cave dwellings and combinations of features, which are of outstanding universal value from the point of view of history, art or science;

groups of buildings: groups of separate or connected buildings which, because of their architecture, their homogeneity or their place in the landscape, are of outstanding universal value from the point of view of history, art or science;

sites: works of man or the combined works of nature and of man, and areas including archeological sites which are of outstanding universal value from the historical, aesthetic, ethnological or anthropological points of view.

Article 2

For the purposes of this Convention, the following shall be considered as "natural heritage";

natural features consisting of physical and biological formations or groups of such formations, which are of outstanding universal value from the aesthetic or scientific point of view;

geological and physiographical formations and precisely delineated areas which constitute the habitat of threatened species of animals and plants of outstanding universal value from the point of view of science or conservation;

natural sites or precisely delineated areas of outstanding universal value from the point of view of science, conservation or natural beauty.

Article 3

It is for each State Party to this Convention to identify and delineate the different properties situated on its territory mentioned in Articles 1 and 2 above.

II. National Protection and International Protection of the Cultural and Natural Heritage

Article 4

Each State Party to this Convention recognizes that the duty of ensuring the identifications, protection, conservation, presentation and transmission to future generations of the cultural and natural heritage referred to in Article 1 and 2 and situated on its territory, belongs primarily to that State. It will do all it can to this end, to the utmost of its own resources and, where appropriate, with any international assistance and co-operation, in particular, financial, artistic, scientific and technical, which it may be able to obtain.

Article 5

To ensure that effective and active measures are taken for the protection, conservation and presentation of the cultural and natural heritage situated on its territory, each State Party to this Convention shall endeavour, in so far as possible, and as appropriate for each country:

a) to adopt a general policy which aims to give the cultural and natural heritage a function in the life of the community and to integrate the protection of that heritage into comprehensive planning programmes;

b) to set up within its territories, where such services do not exist, one or more services for the protection, conservation and presentation of the cultural and natural heritage with an appropriate staff and possessing the means to discharge their functions;

c) to develop scientific and technical studies and research and to work out such operating methods as will make the State capable of counteracting the dangers that threaten its cultural or natural heritage;

d) to take the appropriate legal, scientific, technical, administrative and financial measures necessary for the identification, protection, conservation, presentation and rehabilitation of this heritage; and

e) to foster the establishment or development of national or regional centres for training in the protection, conservation and presentation of the cultural and natural heritage and to encourage scientific research in this field.

Article 6

1. Whilst fully respecting the sovereignty of the States on whose territory the cultural and natural heritage mentioned in Articles 1 and 2 is situated, and without prejudice to property rights provided by national legislation, the States Parties to this Convention recognize that such heritage constitutes a world heritage for whose protection it is the duty of the international community as a whole to co-operate.

2. The States Parties undertake, in accordance with the provisions of this Convention, to give their help in the identification, protection, conservation and preservation of the cultural and natural heritage referred to in paragraphs 2 and 4 of Article 11 if the States on whose territory it is situated so request.

3. Each State Party to this Convention undertakes not to take any deliberate measures which might damage directly or indirectly the cultural and natural heritage referred to in Articles 1 and 2 situated on the territory of other States Parties to this Convention.

Article 7

For the purpose of this Convention, international protection of the world cultural and natural heritage shall be understood to mean the establishment of a system of international co-operation and assistance designed to support States Parties to the Convention in their efforts to conserve and identify that heritage.

III. Intergovernmental Committee for the Protection of the World Cultural and Natural Heritage

Article 8

1. An Intergovermental Committee for the Protection of the Cultural and Natural Heritage of Outstanding Universal Value, called "the World Heritage Committee", is hereby established within

the United Nations Educational, Scientific and Cultural Organization. It shall be composed of 15 States Parties to the Convention, elected by States Parties to the Convention meeting in general assembly during the ordinary session of the General Conference of the United Nations Educational, Scientific and Cultural Organization. The number of States members of the Committee shall be increased to 21 as from the date of the ordinary session of the General Conference following the entry into force of this Convention for at least 40 States.

2. Election of members of the Committee shall ensure an equitable representation of the different regions and cultures of the world.

3. A representative of the International Centre for the Study of the Preservation and Restoration of Cultural Property (Rome Centre), a representative of the International Council of Monuments and Sites (ICOMOS) and a representative of the International Union for Conservation of Nature and Natural Resources (IUCN), to whom may be added, at the request of States Parties to the Convention meeting in general assembly during the ordinary sessions of the General Conference of the United Nations Educational, Scientific and Cultural Organization, representatives of other intergovernmental or non-governmental organizations, with similar objective, may attend the meetings of the Committee in an advisory capacity.

Article 9

1. The term of office of States members of the World Heritage Committee shall extend from the end of the ordinary session of the General Conference during which they are elected until the end of its third subsequent ordinary session.

2. The term of office of one-third of the members designated at the time of the first election shall, however, cease at the end of the first ordinary session of the General Conference following that at which they were elected; and the term of office of a further third of the members designated at the same time shall cease at the end of the second ordinary session of the General Conference following that at which they were elected. The names of these members shall be chosen by lot by the President of the General Conference of the United Nations Educational, Scientific and Cultural Organization after the first election.

3. States members of the Committee shall choose as their representatives persons qualified in the field of the cultural or natural heritage.

Article 10

1. The World Heritage Committee shall adopt its Rules of Procedure.

2. The Committee may at any time invite public or private organizations or individuals to participate in its meetings for consultation or particular problems.

3. The Committee may create such consultative bodies as it deems necessary for the performance of its functions.

Article 11

1. Every State Party to this Convention shall, in so far as possible, submit to the World Heritage Committe an inventory of property forming part of the cultural and natural heritage, situated in its territory and suitable for inclusion in the list provided for in paragraph 2 of this Article. This inventory, which shall not be considered exhaustive, shall include documentation about the location of the property in question and its significance.

2. On the basis of the inventories submitted by States in accordance with paragraph 1, the Committee shall establish, keep up to date and publish, under the title of "World Heritage List", a list of properties forming part of the cultural heritage and natural heritage, as defined in Articles 1 and 2 of this Convention, which it considers as having outstanding universal value in terms of such criteria as it shall have established. An updated list shall be distributed at least every two years.

3. The inclusion of a property in the World Heritage List requires the consent of the State concerned. The inclusion of a property situated in a territory, sovereignty or jurisdiction over which is claimed by more than one State shall in no way prejudice the rights of the parties to the dispute.

4. The Committee shall establish, keep up to date and publish, whenever circumstances shall so require, under the title of "List of World Heritage in Danger", a list of the property appearing in the World Heritage List for the conservation of which major operations are necessary and for which assistance has been requested under this Convention. This list shall contain an estimate of the cost of such operations. The list may include only such property forming part of the cultural and natural heritage as is threatened by serious and specific dangers, such as the threat of disappearance caused by accelerated deterioration, large-scale public or private projects or rapid urban or tourist development projects; destruction caused by changes in the use or ownership of the land; major alterations due to unknown causes; abandonment for any reason whatsoever; the outbreak or the threat of an armed conflict; calamities and cataclysms; serious fires, earthquakes, landslides; volcanic eruptions; changes in water level, floods, and tidal waves. The Committee may at any time, in case of urgent need, make a new entry in the List of World Heritage in Danger and publicize such entry immediately.

5. The Committee shall define the criteria on the basis of which a property belonging to the cultural or natural heritage may be included in either of the lists mentioned in paragraphs 2 and 4 of this article.

6. Before refusing a request for inclusion in one of the two lists mentioned in paragraphs 2 and 4 of this article, the Committee shall consult the State Party in whose territory the cultural or natural

property in question is situated.

7. The Committee shall, with the agreement of the States concerned, co-ordinate and encourage the studies and research needed for the drawing up of the lists referred to in paragraph 2 and 4 of this article.

Article 12

The fact that a property belonging to the cultural or natural heritage has not been included in either of the two lists metioned in paragraphs 2 and 4 of Article 11 shall in no way be construed to mean that it does not have an outstanding universal value for purposes other than those resulting from inclusion in these lists.

Article 13

1. The World Heritage Committee shall receive and study requests for international assistance formulated by States Parties to this Convention with respect to property forming part of the cultural or natural heritage, situated in their territories, and included or potentially suitable for inclusion in the lists refered to in paragraphs 2 and 4 of Article 11. The purpose of such requests may be to secure the protection, conservation, presentation or rehabilitation of such property.

2. Requests for internal assistance under paragraph 1 of this article may also be concerned with identification of cultural or natural property defined in Articles 1 and 2, when preliminary investigations have shown that further inquiries would be justified.

3. The Committee shall decide on the action to be taken with regard to these requests, determine where appropriate, the nature and extent of its assistance, and authorize the conclusion, on its behalf, of the necessary arrangements with the government concerned.

4. The Committee shall determine an order of priorities for its operations. It shall in so doing bear in mind the respective importance for the world cultural and natural heritage of the property requiring protection, the need to give international assistance to the property most representative of a natural environment or of the genius and the history of the peoples of the world, the urgency of the work to be done, the resources available to the States on whose territory the threatened property is situate and in particular the extent to which they are able to safeguard such property by their own means.

5. The Committee shall draw up, keep up to date and publicize a list of property for which international assistance has been granted.

6. The Committee shall decide on the use of the resources of the Fund established under Article 15 of this Convention. It shall seek ways of increasing these resources and shall take all useful steps to this end.

7. The Committee shall co-operate with international and national governmental and non-governmental organizations having objectives similar to those of this Convention. For the implementation of its programmes and projects, the Committee may call on such organization, particularly the International Centre for the Study of the Preservation and Restoration of Cultural Property (the Rome Centre), the International Council of Monuments and Sites (ICOMOS) and the International Union for Conservation of Nature and Natural resources (IUCN), as well as on public and private bodies and individuals.

8. Decisions of the Committee shall be taken by a majority of two-thirds of its members present and voting. A majority of the members of the Committee shall constitute a quorum.

Article 14

1. The World Heritage Committee shall be assisted by a Secretariat appointed by the Director-General of the United Nations Educational, Scientific and Cultural Organization.

2. The Director-General of the United Nations Educational, Scientific and Cultural Organization, utilizing to the fullest extent possible the service of the International Centre for the Study of the Preservation and the Restoration of Cultural Property (the Rome Centre), the International Council of Monuments and Sites (ICOMOS) and the International Union for Conservation of Nature and Natural Resources (IUCN) in their respective areas of competence and capability, shall prepare the Committee's documentation and the agenda of its meetings and shall have the responsibility for the implementation of its decisions.

IV. Fund for the Protection of the World Cultural and Natural Heritage

Article 15

1. A Fund for the Protection of the World Cultural and Natural Heritage of Outstanding Universal Value, called "the World Heritage Fund", is hereby established.

2. The Fund shall constitute a trust fund, in conformity with the provisions of the Financial Regulations of the United Nations Educational, Scientific and Cultural Organization.

3. The resources of the Fund shall consist of:

a) compulsory and voluntary contributions made by the States Parties to this Convention,

b) contributions, gifts or bequests which may be made by:

(i) other States;

(ii) the United Nations Educational, Scientific and Cultural organizations, other organizations of the United Nations system, particularly the United Nations Development Programme or other intergovernmental organizations.

(iii) public or private bodies or individuals;

c) any interest due on the resources of the Fund;

d) funds raised by collections and receipts from events organized for the benefit of the Fund; and

e) all other resources authorized by the Fund's regulations, as drawn up by the World heritage Committee.

4. Contributions to the Fund and other forms of assistance made available to the Committee may be used only for such purposes as the Committee shall define. The Committee may accept contributions to be used only for a certain programme or project, provided that the Committee shall have decided on the implementation of such programme or project. No political conditions may be attached to contributions made to the Fund.

Article 16

1. Without prejudice to any supplementary voluntary contribution, the States Parties to this Convention undertake to pay regularly, every two years, to the World Heritage Fund, contributions, the amount of which, in the form of a uniform percentage applicable to all States, shall be determined by the General Assembly of States Parties to the Convention, meeting during the sessions of the General Conference of the United Nations Educational, Scientific and Cultural Organization. This decision of the General Assembly requires the majority of the States Parties present and voting, which have not made the declaration referred to in paragraph 2 of this Article. In no case shall the compulsory contribution of States Parties to the Convention exceed 1% of the contribution to the Regular Budget of the United Nations Educational, Scientific and Cultural Organization.

2. However, each State referred to in Article 31 or in Article 32 of this Convention may declare, at the time of the deposit of its instruments of ratification, acceptance or accession, that it shall not be bound by the provisions of paragraph 1 of this Article.

3. A State Party to the Convention which has made the declaration referred to in paragraph 2 of this Article may at any time withdraw the said declaration by notifying the Director-General of the United Nations Educational, Scientific and Cultural Organization. However, the withdrawal of the declaration shall not take effect in regard to the compulsory contribution due by the State until the date of the subsequent General Assembly of States Parties to the Convention.

4. In order that the Committee may be able to plan its operations effectively, the contributions of States Parties to this Convention which have made the declaration referred to in paragraph 2 of this Article, shall be paid on a regular basis, at least every two years, and should not be less than the contributions which they should have paid if they had been bound by the provisions of paragraph 1 of this Article.

5. Any State Party to the Convention which is in arrears with the payment of its compulsory or voluntary contributions for the current year and the calendar year immediately preceding it shall not be eligible as a Member of the World Heritage Committee, although this provision shall not apply to the first election.

The terms of office of any such State which is already a member of the Committee shall terminate at the time of the elections provided for in Article 8, paragraph 1 of this Convention.

Article 17

The States Parties to this Convention shall consider or encourage the establishment of national, public and private foundations or associations whose purpose is to invite donations for the protection of the cultural and natural heritage as defined in Articles 1 and 2 of this Convention.

Article 18

The States Parties to this Convention shall give their assistance to international fund-raising campaigns organized for the World Heritage Fund under the auspices of the United Nations Educational, Scientific and Cultural Organization. They shall facilitate collections made by the bodies mentioned in paragraph 3 of Article 15 for this purpose.

V. CONDITIONS AND ARRANGEMENTS FOR INTERNATIONAL ASSISTANCE

Article 19

Any State Party to this Convention may request international assistance for property forming part of the cultural or natural heritage of outstanding universal value situated within its territory. It shall submit with its request such information and documentation provided for in Article 21 as it has in its possession and as will enable the Committee to come to a decision.

Article 20

Subject to the provisions of paragraph 2 of Article 13, sub-paragraph (*c*) of Article 22 and Article 23, international assistance provided for by this Convention may be granted only to property forming part of the cultural and natural heritage which the World Heritage Committee has decided, or may decide, to enter in one of the lists mentioned in paragraphs 2 and 4 of Article 11.

Article 21

1. The World Heritage Committee shall define the procedure by which requests to it for international assistance shall be considered and shall specify the content of the request, which should define the operation contemplated, the work that is necessary, the expected cost thereof the degree of urgency and the reasons why the resources of the State requesting assistance do not allow it to meet all the expenses. Such requests must be supported by experts' reports whenever possible.

2. Requests based upon disasters or natural calamities should, by reasons of the urgent work which they may involve, be given immediate, priority consideration by the Committee, which should have a reserve fund at its disposal against such contingencies.

3. Before coming to a decision, the Committee shall carry out such studies and consultations as it deems necessary.

Article 22

Assistance granted by the World Heritage Committee may take the following forms:

a) studies concerning the artistic, scientific and technical problems raised by the protection, conservation, presentation and rehabilitation of the cultural and natural heritage, as defined in paragraph 2 and 4 of Article 11 of this Convention;

b) provision of experts, technicians and skilled labour to ensure that the approved work is correctly carried out;

c) training of staff and specialists at all levels in the field of identification, protection, conservation, presentation and rehabilitation of the cultural and natural heritage;

d) supply of equipment which the State concerned does not possess or is not in a position to acquire;

e) low-interest or interest-free loans which might be repayable on a longer-term basis;

f) the granting, in exceptional cases and for special reasons, of non-payable subsidies.

Article 23

The World Heritage Committee may also provide international assistance to national or regional centres for the training of staff and specialists at all levels in the field of identification, protection, conservation, presentation and rehabilitation of the cultural and natural heritage.

Article 24

International assistance on a large scale shall be preceded by detailed scientific, economic and technical studies. These studies shall draw upon the most advanced techniques for the protection, conservation, presentation and rehabilitation of the natural and cultural heritage and shall be consistent with the objectives of this Convention. The studies shall also seek means of making rational use of the resources available in the State concerned.

Article 25

As a general rule, only part of the cost of work necessary shall be borne by the international community. The contribution of the State benefiting from international assistance shall constitute a substantial share of the resources devoted to each programme or project, unless its resources do not permit this.

Article 26

The World Heritage Committee and the recipient State shall define in the agreement they conclude the conditions in which a programme or project for which international assistance under the terms of this Convention is provided shall be carried out. It shall be the responsibility of the State receiving such international assistance to continue to protect, conserve and present the property so safeguarded, in observance of the conditions laid down by the agreement.

VI. Educational Programmes

Article 27

1. The States Parties to this Convention shall endeavour by all appropriate means, and in particular by educational and information programmes, to strengthen appreciation and respect by their peoples of the cultural and natural heritage defined in Articles 1 and 2 of the Convention.

2. They shall undertake to keep the public broadly informed of the dangers threatening this heritage and of activities carried on in pursuance of this Convention.

Article 28

States Parties to this Convention which receive international assistance under the Convention shall take appropriate measures to make known the importance of the property for which assistance has been received and the role played by such assistance.

VII. Reports

Article 29

1. The States Parties to this Convention shall, in the reports which they submit to the General Conference of the United Nations Educational, Scientific and Cultural Organization on dates and in a manner to be determined by it, give information on the legislative and administrative provisions which they have adopted and other action which they have taken for the application of this Convention, together with details of the experience acquired in this field.

2. These reports shall be brought to the attention of the World Heritage Committee.

3. The Committee shall submit a report on its activities at each of the ordinary sessions of the General Conference of the United Nations Educational, Scientific and Cultural Organization.

VIII. Final Clauses

Article 30

This Convention is drawn up in Arabic, English, French, Russian and Spanish, the five texts being equally authoritative.

Article 31

1. This Convention shall be subject to ratification or acceptance by States members of the United Nations Educational, Scientific and Cultural Organization in accordance with their respective constitutional procedures.

2. The instruments of ratification or acceptance shall be deposited with the Director-General of the United Nations Educational, Scientific and Cultural Organization

Article 32

1. This Convention shall be open to accession by all States not members of the United Nations Educational, Scientific and Cultural Organization which are invited by the General Conference of the Organization to accede to it.

2. Accession shall be effected by the deposit of an instrument of accession with the Director-General of the United Nations Educational, Scientific and Cultural Organization.

Article 33

This Convention shall enter into force three months after the date of the deposit of the twentieth instrument of ratification, acceptance or accession, but only with respect to those States which have deposited their respective instruments of ratification, acceptance or accession on or before that date. It shall enter into force with respect to any other State three months after the deposit of its instrument of ratification, acceptance or accession.

Article 34

The following provisions shall apply to those States Parties to this Convention which have a federal or non-unitary constitutional system.

a) with regard to the provisions of this Convention, the implementation of which comes under the legal jurisdiction of the federal or central legislative power, the obligations of the federal or central government shall be the same as for those States Parties which are not federal States;

b) with regard to the provisions of this Convention, the implementation of which comes under the legal jurisdiction of individual constituent States, countries, provinces or cantons that are not obliged by the constitutional system of the federation to take legislative measures, the federal government shall inform the competent authorities of such States, countries, provinces or cantons of the said provisions, with its recommendation for their adoption.

Article 35

1. Each State Party to this Convention may denounce the Convention.

2. The denunciation shall be notified by an instrument in writing, deposited with the Director-General of the United Nations Educational, Scientific and Cultural Organization.

3. The denunciation shall take effect twelve months after the receipt of the instrument of denunciation. It shall not affect the financial obligations of the denouncing State until the date on which the withdrawal takes effect.

Article 36

The Director-General of the United Nations Educational, Scientific and Cultural Organization shall inform the States members of the Organization, the States not members of the Organization which are referred to in Article 32, as well as the United Nations, of the deposit of all the instruments of ratification, acceptance, or accession provided for in Articles 31 and 32, and of the denunciations provided for in Article 35.

Article 37

1. This Convention may be revised by the General Conference of the United Nations Educational, Scientific and Cultural Organization. Any such revision shall, however, bind only the States which shall become Parties to the revising convention.

2. If the General Conference should adopt a new convention revising this Convention in whole or in part, then, unless the new convention otherwise provides, this Convention shall cease to be open to ratification, acceptance or accession, as from the date on which the new revising convention enters into force.

Article 38

In conformity with Article 102 of the Charter of the United Nations, this Convention shall be registered with the Secretariat of the United Nations at the request of the Director-General of the United Nations Educational, Scientific and Cultural Organization.

Done at Paris, this twenty-third day of November 1972, in two authentic copies bearing the signature of the President of the seventeenth session of the General Conference and of the Director-General of the United Nations Educational, Scientific and Cultural Organization, and certified true copies of which shall be delivered to all the States referred to in Articles 31 and 32 as well as to the United Nations.

CONVENTION ON THE PREVENTION OF MARINE POLLUTION BY DUMPING OF WASTES AND OTHER MATTER [56]

London, Mexico City, Moscow, Washington, 29 December 1972

The Contracting Parties to this Convention,

Recognizing that the marine environment and the living organisms which it supports are of vital importance to humanity, and all people have an interest in assuring that it is so managed that its quality and resources are not impaired;

Recognizing that the capacity of the sea to assimilate wastes and render them harmless, and its ability to regenerate natural resources, is not unlimited;

Recognizing that States have, in accordance with the Charter of the United Nations and the principles of international law, the sovereign right to exploit their own resources pursuant to their own environmental policies, and the responsibility to ensure that activities within their jurisdiction or control do not cause damage to the environment of other States or of areas beyond the limits of national jurisdiction;

Recalling Resolution 2749 (XXV) of the General Assembly of the United Nations on the principles governing the sea-bed and the ocean floor and the subsoil thereof, beyond the limits of national jurisdiction;

Noting that marine pollution originates in many sources, such as dumping and discharges through the atmosphere, rivers, estuaries, outfalls and pipelines, and that it is important that States use the best practicable means to prevent such pollution and develop products and processes which will reduce the amount of harmful wastes to be disposed of;

Being convinced that international action to control the pollution of the sea by dumping can and must be taken without delay but that this action should not preclude discussion of measures to control other sources of marine pollution as soon as possible; and

Wishing to improve protection of the marine environment by encouraging States with a common interest in particular geographical areas to enter into appropriate agreements supplementary to this Convention;

Have agreed as follows:

Article I

Contracting Parties shall individually and collectively promote the effective control of all sources of pollution of the marine environment, and pledge themselves especially to take all practicable steps to prevent the pollution of the sea by the dumping of waste and other matter that is liable to create hazards to human health, to harm living resources and marine life, to damage amenities or to interfere with other legitimate uses of the sea.

Article II

Contracting Parties shall, as provided for in the following Articles, take effective measures individually, according to their scientific, technical and economic capabilities, and collectively, to prevent marine pollution caused by dumping and shall harmonize their policies in this regard.

Article III

For the purpose of this Convention:

1. *a*) "Dumping" means:

(i) any deliberate disposal at sea of wastes or other matter from vessels, aircraft, platforms or other man-made structures at sea;

(ii) any deliberate disposal at sea of vessels, aircraft, platforms or other man-made structures at sea.

b) "Dumping" does not include:

(i) the disposal at sea of wastes or other matter incidental to, or derived from the normal operations of vessels, aircraft, platforms or other man-made structures at sea and their equipment, other than wastes or other matter transported by or to vessels, aircraft, platforms or other man-made structures at sea, operating for the purpose of disposal of such matter or derived from the treatment of such wastes or other matter on such vessels, aircraft, platforms or structures;

(ii) placement of matter for a purpose other than the mere disposal thereof, provided that such placement is not contrary to the aims of this Convention.

c) The disposal of wastes or other matter directly arising from, or related to the exploration, exploitation and associated off-shore processing of sea-bed mineral resources will not be covered by the provisions of this Convention.

2. "Vessels and aircraft" means waterborne or airborne craft of any type whatsoever. This expression includes air cushioned craft and floating craft, whether self-propelled or not.

3. "Sea" means all marine waters other than the internal waters of States.

4. "Wastes or other matter" means material and substance of any kind, form or description.

5. "Special permit" means permission granted specifically on application in advance and in accordance with Annex II and Annex III.

6. "General permit" means permission granted in advance and in accordance with Annex III.

7. "The Organisation" means the Organisation designated by the Contracting Parties in accordance with Article XIV (2).

Article IV

1. In accordance with the provisions of this Convention Contracting Parties shall prohibit the dumping of any wastes or other matter in whatever form or condition except as otherwise specified below:

a) the dumping of wastes or other matter listed in

Annex I is prohibited;

b) the dumping of wastes or other material listed in Annex II requires a prior special permit;

c) the dumping of all other wastes or matter requires a prior general permit.

2. Any permit shall be issued only after careful consideration of all the factors set forth in Annex III, including prior studies of the characteristics of the dumping site as set forth in Sections B and C of that Annex.

3. No provision of this Convention is to be interpreted as preventing a Contracting Party from prohibiting, insofar as that Party is concerned, the dumping of wastes or other matter not mentioned in Annex I. That Party shall notify such measures to the Organisation.

Article V

1. The provisions of Article IV shall not apply when it is necessary to secure the safety of human life or of vessels, aircraft, platforms or other man-made structures at sea in cases of *force majeure* caused by stress of weather, or in any case which constitutes a danger to human life or a real threat to vessels, aircraft, platforms or other man-made structures at sea, if dumping appears to be the only way of averting the threat and if there is every probability that the damage consequent upon such dumping will be less than would otherwise occur. Such dumping shall be so conducted as to minimise the likelihood of damage to human or marine life and shall be reported forthwith to the Organisation.

2. A Contracting Party may issue a special permit as an exception to Article IV (1) (*a*), in emergencies, posing unacceptable risk relating to human health and admitting no other feasible solution. Before doing so the Party shall consult any other country or countries that are likely to be affected and the Organisation which, after consulting other Parties, and international organisations as appropriate, shall in accordance with Article XIV promptly recommend to the party the most appropriate procedures to adopt. The Party shall follow these recommendations to the maximum extent feasible consistent with the time within which action must be taken and with the general obligation to avoid damage to the marine environment and shall inform the Organisation of the action it takes. The Parties pledge themselves to assist one another in such situations.

3. Any Contracting Party may waive its rights under paragraph (2) at the time of, or subsequent to ratification of, or accession to this Convention.

Article VI

1. Each Contracting Party shall designate an appropriate authority or authorities to:

a) issue special permits which shall be required prior to, and for, the dumping of matter listed in Annex II and in the circumstances provided for in Article V (2).

b) issue general permits which shall be required prior to, and for, the dumping of all other matter;

c) keep records of the nature and quantities of all matter permitted to be dumped and the location, time and method of dumping;

d) monitor individually, or in collaboration with other Parties and competent International Organisations, the condition of the seas for the purposes of this Convention.

2. The appropriate authority or authorities of a Contracting Party shall issue prior special or general permits in accordance with paragraph (1) in respect of matter intended for dumping:

a) loaded in its territory;

b) loaded by a vessel or aircraft registered in its territory or flying its flag, when the loading occurs in the territory of a State not party to this Convention.

3. In issuing permits under sub-paragraphs (1) (*a*) and (*b*) above, the appropriate authority or authorities shall comply with Annex III, together with such additional criteria, measures and requirements as they may consider relevant.

4. Each Contracting Party, directly or through a Secretariat established under a regional agreement, shall report to the Organisation, and where appropriate to other Parties, the information specified in sub-paragraphs (*c*) and (*d*) of paragraph (1) above, and the criteria, measures and requirements it adopts in accordance with paragraph (3) above. The procedure to be followed and the nature of such reports shall be agreed by the Parties in consultation.

Article VII

1. Each Contracting Party shall apply the measures required to implement the present Convention to all:

a) vessels and aircraft registered in its territory or flying its flag;

b) vessels and aircraft loading in its territory or territorial seas matter which is to be dumped;

c) vessels and aircraft and fixed or floating platforms under its jurisdiction believed to be engaged in dumping.

2. Each Party shall take in its territory appropriate measures to prevent and punish conduct in contravention of the provisions of this Convention.

3. The Parties agree to co-operate in the development of procedures for the effective application of this Convention particularly on the high seas, including procedures for the reporting of vessels and aircraft observed dumping in contravention of the Convention.

4. This Convention shall not apply to those vessels and aircraft entitled to sovereign immunity under international law. However each Party shall ensure by the adoption of appropriate measures that such vessels and aircraft owned or operated by it act in a manner consistent with the object and purpose of this Convention, and shall inform the Organisation accordingly.

5. Nothing in this Convention shall affect the right of each Party to adopt other measures, in accordance with the principles of international law, to prevent dumping at sea.

Article VIII

In order to further the objectives of this Convention, the Contracting Parties with common interests to protect in the marine environment in a given geographical area shall endeavour, taking into account characteristic regional features, to enter into regional agreements consistent with this Convention for the prevention of pollution, especially by dumping. The Contracting Parties to the present Convention shall endeavour to act consistently with the objectives and provisions of such regional agreements, which shall be notified to them by the Organisation. Contracting Parties shall seek to co-operate with the Parties to regional agreements in order to develop harmonized procedures to be followed by Contracting Parties to the different conventions concerned. Special attention shall be given to co-operation in the field of monitoring and scientific research.

Article IX

The Contracting Parties shall promote, through collaboration within the Organisation and other international bodies, support for those Parties which request it for:

a) the training of scientific and technical personnel;

b) the supply of necessary equipment and facilities for research and monitoring;

c) the disposal and treatment of waste and other measures to prevent or mitigate pollution caused by dumping;

preferably within the countries concerned, so furthering the aims and purposes of this Convention.

Article X

In accordance with the principles of international law regarding State responsibility for damage to the environment of other States or to any other area of the environment, caused by dumping of wastes and other matter of all kinds, the Contracting Parties undertake to develop procedures for the assessment of liability and the settlement of disputes regarding dumping.

Article XI

The Contracting Parties shall at their first consultative meeting consider procedures for the settlement of disputes concerning the interpretation and application of this Convention.

Article XII

The Contracting Parties pledge themselves to promote, within the competent specialised agencies and other international bodies, measures to protect the marine environment against pollution caused by:

a) hydrocarbons, including oil, and their wastes;

b) other noxious or hazardous matter transported by vessels for purposes other than dumping;

c) wastes generated in the course of operation of vessels, aircraft, platforms and other man-made structures at sea;

d) radio-active pollutants from all sources, including vessels;

e) agents of chemical and biological warfare;

f) wastes or other matter directly arising from, or related to the exploration, exploitation and associated off-shore processing of sea-bed mineral resources.

The Parties will also promote, within the appropriate international organisation, the codification of signals to be used by vessels engaged in dumping.

Article XIII

Nothing in this Convention shall prejudice the codification and development of the law of the sea by the United Nations Conference on the Law of the Sea convened pursuant to Resolution 2750 C (XXV) of the General Assembly of the United Nations nor the present or future claims and legal views of any State concerning the law of the sea and the nature and extent of coastal and flag State jurisdiction. The Contracting Parties agree to consult at a meeting to be convened by the Organisation after the Law of the Sea Conference, and in any case not later than 1976, with a view to defining the nature and extent of the right and the responsibility of a coastal State to apply the Convention in a zone adjacent to its coast.

Article XIV

1. The Government of the United Kingdom of Great Britain and Northern Ireland as a depositary shall call a meeting of the Contracting Parties not later than three months after the entry into force of this Convention to decide on organisational matters.

2. The Contracting Parties shall designate a competent Organisation existing at the time of that meeting to be responsible for Secretariat duties in relation to this Convention. Any Party to this Convention not being a member of this Organisation shall make an appropriate contribution to the expenses incurred by the Organisation in performing these duties.

3. The Secretariat duties of the Organisation shall include:

a) the convening of consultative meetings of the Contracting Parties not less frequently than once every two years and of special meetings of the Parties at any time on the request of two-thirds of the Parties;

b) preparing and assisting, in consultation with the Contracting Parties and appropriate International Organisations, in the development and implementation of procedures referred to in sub-paragraph (4) (*e*) of this Article;

c) considering enquiries by, and information from the Contracting Parties, consulting with them and with the appropriate International

Organisations, and providing recommendations to the Parties on questions related to, but not specifically covered by the Convention;

d) conveying to the Parties concerned all notifications received by the Organisation in accordance with Articles IV (3), V (1) and (2), VI (4), XV, XX and XXI.

Prior to the designation of the Organisation these functions shall, as necessary, be performed by the depositary, who for this purpose shall be the Government of the United Kingdom of Great Britain and Northern Ireland.

4. Consultative or special meetings of the Contracting Parties shall keep under continuing review the implementation of this Convention and may, *inter alia*:

a) review and adopt amendments to this Convention and its Annexes in accordance with Article XV;

b) invite the appropriate scientific body or bodies to collaborate with and to advise the Parties or the Organisation on any scientific or technical aspect relevant to this Convention, including particularly the content of the Annexes;

c) receive and consider reports made pursuant to Article VI (4);

d) promote co-operation with and between regional organisations concerned with the prevention of marine pollution;

e) develop or adopt, in consultation with appropriate International Organisations, procedures referred to in Article V (2) including basic criteria for determining exceptional and emergency situations, and procedures for consultative advice and the safe disposal of matter in such circumstances, including the designation of appropriate dumping areas, and recommend accordingly;

f) consider any additional action that may be required.

5. The Contracting Parties at their first consultative meeting shall establish rules of procedure as necessary.

Article XV

1. *a*) At meetings of the Contracting Parties called in accordance with Article XIV amendments to this Convention may be adopted by a two-thirds majority of those present. An amendment shall enter into force for the Parties which have accepted it on the sixtieth day after two-thirds of the Parties shall have deposited an instrument of acceptance of the amendment with the Organisation. Thereafter the amendment shall enter into force for any other Party 30 days after that Party deposits its instrument of acceptance of the amendment.

b) The Organisation shall inform all Contracting Parties of any request made for a special meeting under Article XIV and of any amendments adopted at meetings of the Parties and of the date on which each such amendment enters into force for each Party.

2. Amendments to the Annexes will be based on scientific or technical considerations. Amendments to the Annexes approved by a two-thirds majority of those present at a meeting called in accordance with Article XIV shall enter into force for each Contracting Party immediately on notification of its acceptance to the Organisation and 100 days after approval by the meeting for all other Parties except for those which before the end of the 100 days make a declaration that they are not able to accept the amendment at that time. Parties should endeavour to signify their acceptance of an amendment to the Organisation as soon as possible after approval at a meeting. A Party may at any time substitute an acceptance for a previous declaration of objection and the amendment previously objected to shall thereupon enter into force for that Party.

3. An acceptance or declaration of objection under this Article shall be made by the deposit of an instrument with the Organisation. The Organisation shall notify all Contracting Parties of the receipt of such instruments.

4. Prior to the delegation of the Organisation, the Secretarial functions herein attributed to it, shall be performed temporarily by the Government of the United Kingdom of Great Britain and Northern Ireland, as one of the depositaries of this Convention.

Article XVI

This Convention shall be open for signature by any State at London, Mexico City, Moscow and Washington from 29 December 1972 until 31 December 1973.

Article XVII

This Convention shall be subject to ratification. The instruments of ratification shall be deposited with the Governments of Mexico, the Union of Soviet Socialist Republics, the United Kingdom of Great Britain and Northern Ireland, and the United States of America.

Article XVIII

After 31 December 1973, this Convention shall be open for accession by any State. The instruments of accession shall be deposited with the Governments of Mexico, the Union of Soviet Socialist Republics, the United Kingdom of Great Britain and Northern Ireland, and the United States of America.

Article XIX

1. This Convention shall enter into force on the thirtieth day following the date of deposit of the fifteenth instrument of ratification or accession.

2. For each Contracting Party ratifying or acceding to the Convention after the deposit of the fifteenth instrument of ratification or accession, the Convention shall enter into force on the thirtieth day after deposit by such Party of its instrument of ratification or accession.

Article XX

The depositaries shall inform Contracting Parties:

a) of signatures to this Convention and of the

deposit of instruments of ratification, accession or withdrawal, in accordance with Articles XVI, XVII, XVIII and XXI, and

b) of the date on which this Convention will enter into force, in accordance with Article XIX.

Article XXI

Any Contracting Party may withdraw from this Convention by giving six months' notice in writing to a depositary which shall promptly inform all Parties of such notice.

Article XXII

The original of this Convention of which the English, French, Russian and Spanish texts are equally authentic, shall be deposited with the Governments of Mexico, the Union of Soviet Socialist Republics, the United Kingdom of Great Britain and Northern Ireland and the United States of America who shall send certified copies thereof to all States.

In Witness Whereof the undersigned Plenipotentiaries, being duly authorised thereto by their respective Governments have signed the present Convention.

Done in quadruplicate at London, Mexico City, Moscow and Washington, this twenty-ninth day of December, 1972.

Annex I

1. Organohalogen compounds.
2. Mercury and mercury compounds.
3. Cadmium and cadmium compounds.
4. Persistent plastics and other persistent synthetic materials, for example, netting and ropes, which may float or may remain in suspension in the sea in such a manner as to interfere materially with fishing, navigation or other legitimate uses of the sea.
5. Crude oil, fuel oil, heavy diesel oil and lubricating oil, hydraulic fluids, and any mixtures containing any of these, taken on board for the purpose of dumping.
6. High-level radio-active wastes or other high-level radio-active matter, defined on public health, biological or other grounds, by the competent international body in this field, at present the International Atomic Energy Agency, as unsuitable for dumping at sea.
7. Materials in whatever form (e.g. solids, liquids, semi-liquids, gases or in a living state) produced for biological and chemical warfare.
8. The preceding paragraphs of this Annex do not apply to substances which are rapidly rendered harmless by physical, chemical or biological processes in the sea provided they do not:

(i) make edible marine organisms unpalatable, or

(ii) endanger human health or that of domestic animals.

The consultative procedure provided for under Article XIV should be followed by a Party if there is doubt about the harmlessness of the substance.

9. This Annex does not apply to wastes or other materials (e.g. sewage sludges and dredged spoils) containing the matters referred to in paragraphs 1-5 above as trace contaminants. Such wastes shall be subject to the provisions of Annexes II and III as appropriate.

Annex II

The following substances and materials requiring special care are listed for the purpose of Article VI (1) (*a*).

A. Wastes containing significant amounts of the matters listed below:

arsenic)
lead) and their compounds
copper)
zinc)

organosilicon compounds

cyanides

fluorides

pesticides and their by-products not covered in Annex I.

B. In the issue of permits for the dumping of large quantities of acids and alkalis, consideration shall be given to the possible presence in such wastes of the substances listed in paragraph A and to the following additional substances:

beryllium)
chromium) and their compounds
nickel)
vanadium)

C. Containers, scrap metal and other bulky wastes liable to sink to the sea bottom which may present a serious obstacle to fishing or navigation.

D Radio-active wastes or other radio-active matter not included in Annex I. In the issue of permits for the dumping of this matter, the Contracting Parties should take full account of the recommendations of the competent international body in this field, at present the International Atomic Energy Agency.

Annex III

Provisions to be considered in establishing criteria governing the issue of permits for the dumping of matter at sea, taking into account Article IV (2), include:

A. *Characteristics and composition of the matter*

1. Total amount and average composition of matter dumped (e.g. per year).
2. Form, e.g. solid, sludge, liquid or gaseous.
3. Properties: physical (e.g. solubility and density), chemical and biochemical (e.g. oxygen demand, nutrients) and biological (e.g. presence of viruses, bacteria, yeasts, parasites).

4. Toxicity.

5. Persistence: physical, chemical and biological.

6. Accumulation and biotransformation in biological materials or sediments.

7. Susceptibility to physical, chemical and biochemical changes and interaction in the aquatic environment with other dissolved organic and inorganic materials.

8. Probability of production of taints or other changes reducing marketability of resources (fish, shellfish, etc.).

B. *Characteristics of dumping site and method of deposit*

1. Location (e.g. co-ordinates of the dumping area, depth and distance from the coast), location in relation to other areas (e.g. amenity areas, spawning, nursery and fishing areas and exploitable resources).

2. Rate of disposal per specific period (e.g. quantity per day, per week, per month).

3. Methods of packaging and containment, if any.

4. Initial dilution achieved by proposed method of release.

5. Dispersal characteristics (e.g. effects of currents, tides and wind on horizontal transport and vertical mixing).

6. Water characteristics (e.g. temperature, pH, salinity, stratification, oxygen indices of pollution — dissolved oxygen (DO), chemical oxygen demand (COD), biochemical oxygen demand (BOD) — nitrogen present in organic and mineral form including ammonia, suspended matter, other nutrients and productivity).

7. Bottom characteristics (e.g. topography, geochemical and geological characteristics and biological productivity).

8. Existence and effects of other dumpings which have been made in the dumping area (e.g. heavy metal background reading and organic carbon content).

9. In issuing a permit for dumping, Contracting Parties should consider whether an adequate scientific basis exists for assessing the consequences of such dumping, as outlined in this Annex, taking into account seasonal variations.

C. *General considerations and conditions*

1. Possible effects on amenities (e.g. presence of floating or stranded material, turbidity, objectionable odour, discolouration and foaming).

2. Possible effects on marine life, fish and shellfish culture, fish stocks and fisheries, seaweed harvesting and culture.

3. Possible effects on other uses of the sea (e.g. impairment of water quality for industrial use, underwater corrosion of structures, interference with ship operations from floating materials, interference with fishing or navigation through deposit of waste or solid objects on the sea floor and protection of areas of special importance for scientific or conservation purposes).

4. The practical availability of alternative land-based methods of treatment, disposal or elimination, or of treatment to render the matter less harmful for dumping at sea.

CONVENTION ON INTERNATIONAL TRADE IN ENDANGERED SPECIES OF WILD FAUNA AND FLORA [57]

Washington, 3 March 1973

The Contracting States,

Recognizing that wild fauna and flora in their many beautiful and varied forms are an irreplaceable part of the natural systems of the earth which must be protected for this and the generations to come;

Conscious of the ever-growing value of wild fauna and flora from aesthetic, scientific, cultural, recreational and economic points of view;

Recognizing that peoples and States are and should be the best protectors of their own wild fauna and flora;

Recognizing, in addition that international co-operation is essential for the protection of certain species of wild fauna and flora against over-exploitation through international trade;

Convinced of the urgency of taking appropriate measures to this end;

Have agreed as follows:

Article I

DEFINITIONS

For the purpose of the present Convention, unles the context otherwise requires:

a) "Species" means any species, sub-species, or geographically separate population there of;

b) "Specimen" means:

(i) an animal or plant, whether alive or dead;

(ii) in the case of an animal: for species included in Appendices I and II, any readily recognizable part or derivative therof; and for species included in Appendix III, any readily recognizable part or derivative thereof specified in Appendix III in relation to the species; and

(iii) in the case of a plant: for species included in Appendix I, any readily recognizable part or derivative thereof; and for species included in Appendices II and III, any readily recognizable part or derivative thereof specified in Appendices II and III in relation to the species;

c) "Trade" means export, re-export, import and introduction from the sea;

d) "Re-export" means export of any specimen that has previously been imported;

e) "Introduction from the sea" means transportation into a State of specimens of any species which were taken in the marine environment not under the jurisdiction of any State;

f) "Scientific Authority" means a national scientific authority designated in accordance with Article IX;

g) "Management Authority" means a national scientific authority designated in accordance with Article IX;

h) "Party" means a State for which the present Convention has entered into force.

Article II

FUNDAMENTAL PRINCIPLES

1. Appendix I shall include all species threatened with extinction which are or may be affected by trade. Trade in specimens of these species must be subject to particularly strict regulation in order not to endanger further their survival and must only be authorized in exceptional circumstances.

2. Appendix II shall include:

a) all species which although not necessarily now threatened with extinction may become so unless trade in specimens of such species is subject to strict regulation in order to avoid utilization incompatible with their survival; and

b) other species which must be subject to regulation in order that trade in specimens of certain species referred to in sub-paragraph (*a*) of this paragraph may be brought under effective control.

3. Appendix III shall include all species which any Party identifies as being subject to regulation within its jurisdiction for the purposes of preventing or restricting exploitation, and as needing the co-operation of other parts in the control of trade.

4. The Parties shall not allow trade in specimens of species included in Appendices I, II and III except in accordance with the provisions of the present Convention.

Article III

REGULATION OF TRADE IN SPECIMENS OF SPECIES INCLUDED IN APPENDIX I

1. All trade in specimens of species included in Appendix I shall be in accordance with the provisions of this Article.

2. The export of any specimen of a species included in Appendix I shall require the prior grant and presentation of an export permit. An export permit shall only be granted when the following conditions have been met:

a) a Scientific Authority of the State of export has advised that such export will not be detrimental to the survival of the species;

b) a Management Authority of the State of export is satisfied that the specimen was not obtained in contravention of the laws of that State for the protection of fauna and flora;

c) a Management Authority of the State of export is satisfied that any living specimen will be so prepared and shipped as to minimize the risk of injury, damage to health or cruel treatment; and

d) a Management Authority of the State of export is satisfied that an import permit has been granted for the specimen.

3. The import of any specimen of a species included in Appendix I shall require the prior grant and presentation of an import permit and either an export permit or a re-export certificate. An import permit shall only be granted when the following conditions have been met:

a) a Scientific Authority of the State of import has advised that the import will be for purposes which are not detrimental to the survival of the species involved;

b) a Scientific Authority of the State of import is satisfied that the proposed recipient of a living specimen is suitably equipped to house and care for it; and

c) a Management Authority of the State of re-export is satisfied that the specimen is not to be used for primarily commercial purposes.

4. The re-export of any specimen of a species included in Appendix I shall require the prior grant and presentation of a re-export certificate. A re-export certificate shall only be granted when the following conditions have been met:

a) a Management Authority of the State of re-export is satisfied that the specimen was imported into that State in accordance with the provisions of the present Convention;

b) a Management Authority of the State of re-export is satisfied that any living specimen will be so prepared and shipped as to minimize the risk of injury, damage to health or cruel treatment; and

c) a Management Authority of the State of re-export is satisfied that an import permit has been granted for any living specimen.

5. The introduction from the sea of any specimen of a species included in Appendix I shall require the prior grant of a certificate from a Management Authority of the State of introduction. A certificate shall only be granted when the following conditions have been met:

a) a Scientific Authority of the State of introduction advises that the introduction will not be detrimental to the survival of the species involved;

b) a Management Authority of the State of introduction is satisfied that the proposed recipient of a living specimen is suitably equipped to house and care for it; and

c) a Management Authority of the State of introduction is satisfied that the specimen is not to be used for primarily commerical purposes.

Article IV

REGULATION OF TRADE IN SPECIMENS OF SPECIES INCLUDED IN APPENDIX II

1. All trade in specimens of species included in Appendix II shall be in accordance with the provisions of this Article.

2. The export of any specimen of a species included in Appendix II shall require the prior grant and presentation of an export permit. An export permit shall only be granted when the following conditions have been met:

a) a Scientific Authority of the State of export has advised that such export will not be detrimental to the survival of that species;

b) a Management Authority of the State of export is satisfied that the specimen was not obtained in contravention of the laws of that State of the protection of fauna and flora; and

c) a Management Authority of the State of export is satisfied that any living specimen will be so prepared and shipped as to minimize the risk of injury, damage to health or cruel treatment.

3. A Scientific Authority in each Party shall monitor both the export permits granted by that State for specimens of species included in Appendix II and the actual exports of such specimens. Whenever a Scientific Authority determines that the export of specimens of any such species should be limited in order to maintain that species throughout its range at a level consistent with its role in the ecosystems in which it occurs and well above the level at which that species might become eligible for inclusion in Appendix I, the Scientific Authority shall advise the appropriate Management Authority of suitable measures to be taken to limit the grant of export permits for specimens of that species.

4. The import of any specimen of a species included in Appendix II shall require the prior presentation of either an export permit or a re-export certificate.

5. The re-export of any specimen of a species included in Appendix II shall require the prior grant and presentation of a re-export certificate. A re-export certificate shall only be granted when the following conditions have been met:

a) a Managment Authority of the State of re-export is satisfied that the specimen was imported into that State in accordance with the provisions of the present Convention; and

b) a Management Authority of the State of re-export is satisfied that any living specimen will be so prepared and shipped as to minimize the risk of injury, damage to health or cruel treatment.

6. The introduction from the sea of any specimen of a species included in Appendix II shall require the prior grant of a certificate from a Management Authority of the State of introduction. A certificate shall only be granted when the following conditions have been met:

a) a Scientific Authority of the State of introduction advises that the introduction will not be detrimental to the survival of the species involved; and

b) a Management Authority of the State of introduction is satisfied that any living specimen will be so handled as to minimize the risk of injury, damage to health or cruel treatment.

7. Certificates referred to in paragraph 6 of this Article may be granted on the advice of a scientific Authority, in consultation with other national scientific authorities or, when appropriate, international scientific authorities, in respect of periods not exceeding one year for total numbers of specimens to be introduced in such periods.

Article V

REGULATION OF TRADE IN SPECIMENS OF SPECIES INCLUDED IN APPENDIX III

1. All trade in specimens of species included in

Appendix III shall be in accordance with the provisions of this Article.

2. The export of any specimen of a species included in Appendix III from any State which has included that species in Appendix III shall require the prior grant and presentation of an export permit. An export permit shall only be granted when the following conditions have been met:

(a) a Scientific Authority of the State of export has advised that such export not be detrimental to the survival of that species;

(b) a Management Authority of the State of export is satisfied that the specimen was not obtained in contravention of the laws of that State for the protection of fauna and flora; and

(c) a Management Authority of the State of export is satisfied that any living specimen will be so prepared and shipped as to minimize the risk of injury, damage to health or cruel treatment.

3. The import of any specimen of a species included in Appendix III shall require, except in circumstances to which paragraph 4 of this Article applies, the prior presentation of a cerificate of origin and, where the import is from a State which has included that species in Appedix III, an export permit.

4. In the case of re-export, a certificate granted by the Management Authority of the State of re-export that the specimen was processed in that State or is being re-exported shall be accepted by the State of import as evidence that the provisions of the present Convention have been complied with in respect of the specimen concerned.

Article VI

PERMITS AND CERTIFICATES

1. Permits and certificates granted under the provisions of Articles III, IV and V shall be in accordance with the provisions of this Article.

2. An export permit shall contain the information specified in the model set forth in Appendix IV, and may only be used for export within a period of six months from the date on which it was granted.

3. Each permit or certificate shall contain the title of the present Convention, the name and any identifying stamp of the Management Authority granting it and a control number assigned by the Management Authority.

4. Any copies of a permit or cerificates issued by a Management Authority shall be clearly marked as copies only and no such copy may be used in place of the original, except to the extent endorsed thereon.

5. A separate permit or certificate shall be required for each consignment of specimens.

6. A Management Authority of the State of import of any specimen shall cancel and retain the export permit or re-export certificate and any corresponding import permit presented in respect of the import of that specimen.

7. When appropriate and feasible a Management Authority may affix a mark upon any specimen to assist in identifying the specimen. For these purposes "mark" means any indelible imprint, lead seal or other suitable means of identifiying a specimen, designed in such a way as to render its imitation by unathorized persons as difficult as possible.

Article VII

EXEMPTIONS AND OTHER SPECIAL PROVISIONS RELATING TO TRADE

1. The provisions of Articles III, IV and V shall not apply to the transit or trans-shipment of specimens through or in the territory of a Party while the specimens remain in Customs control.

2. Where a Management Authority of the State of export or re-export is satisfied that a specimen was acquired before the provisions of the present Convention applied to that specimen, the provisions of Articles III, IV and V shall not apply to that specimen where the Management Authority issues a certificate to that effect.

3. The provisions of Articles III, IV and V shall not apply to specimens that are personal or household effects. This exemption shall not apply where:

a) in the case of specimens of a species included in Appendix I, they were acquired by the owner outside his State of usual residence, and are being imported into that State; or

b) in the case of specimens of species included in Appendix II:

(i) they were acquired by the owner outside his State of usual residence and in a State where removal from the wild occured;

(ii) they are being imported into the owner's State of usual residence; and

(iii) the State where removal from the wild occurred requires the prior grant of export permits before any export of such specimens;

unless a Management Authority is satisfied that the specimens were acquired before the provisions of the present Convention applied to such specimens.

4. Specimens of an animal species included in Appendix I bred in captivity for commercial purposes, or of a plant species included in Appendix I artificially propagated for commericial purposes, shall be deemed to be specimens of species included in Appendix II.

5. Where a Management Authority of the State of export is satisfied that any specimen of an animal species was bred in captivity or any specimen of a plant species was artificially propagated, or is a part of such an animal or plant or was derived therefrom, a certificate by that Management Authority to that effect shall be accepted in lieu of any of the permits or certificates

required under provisions of Articles III, IV or V.

6. The provisions of Articles III, IV and V shall not apply to the non-commercial loan, donation or exchange between scientists or scientific institutions registered by a Management Authority of their State, of herbarium specimens, other preserved, dried or embedded museum specimens, and live plant material which carry a label issued or approved by a Management Authority.

7. A Management Authority of any State may waive the requirements of Articles III, IV and V and allow the movement without permits or certificates of specimens which form part of a travelling zoo, circus, menagerie, plant exhibition or other travelling exhibition provided that:

a) the exporter or importer registers full details of such specimens with that management Authority;

b) the specimens are in either of the categories specified in paragraphs 2 and 5 of this Article; and

c) the Management Authority is satisfied that any living specimen will be so transported and cared for as to minimize the risk of injury, damage to health or cruel treatment.

Article VIII

MEASURES TO BE TAKEN BY THE PARTIES

1. The Parties shall take appropriate measures to enforce the provisions of the present Convention and to prohibit trade in specimens in violation thereof. These shall include measures:

a) to penalize trade in, or possession of such specimens, or both; and

b) to provide for the confiscation or return to the State of export of such specimens.

2. In addition to the measures taken under paragraph 1 of this Article a party may, when it deems it necessary, provide for any method of internal reimbursement for expenses incurred as a result of the confiscation of a specimen traded in violation of the measures taken in the application of the provisions of the present Convention.

3. As far as possible, the Parties shall ensure that specimens shall pass through any formalities required for trade with a minimum of delay. To facilitate such passage, a Party may designate ports of exit and ports of entry at which specimens must be presented for clearance. The Parties shall ensure further that all living specimens, during any period of transit, holding or shipment, are properly cared for so as to minimize the risk of injury, damage to health or cruel treatment.

4. Where a living specimen is confiscated as a result of measures referred to in paragraph 1 of this Article.

a) the specimen shall be entrusted to a Management Authority of the State of confiscation;

b) the Management Authority shall, after consultation with the State of export, return the specimen to that State at the expense of that State, or to a rescue centre or such other place as the Management Authority deems appropriate and consistent with the purposes of the present Convention; and

c) the Management Authority may obtain the advice of a Scientific Authority, or may, wherever it considers it desirable, consult the Secretariat in order to facilitate the decision under sub-paragraph (*b*) of this paragraph, including the choice of a rescue or other place.

5. A rescue centre as referred to in paragraph 4 of this Article means an institution designated by a Management Authority to look after the welfare of living specimens, particularly those that have been confiscated.

6. Each party shall maintain records of trade in specimens of species included in Appendices I, II and III which shall cover:

a) the names and addresses of exporters and importers; and

b) the number and type if permits and certificates granted; the State with which such trade occured; the numbers of quantities and types of specimens, names of species as included in Appendices, I, II and III, where applicable, the size and sex of the specimens in question.

7. Each Party shall prepare periodic reports on its implementation of the present Convention and shall transmit to the Secretariat:

a) an annual report containing a summary of the information specified in sub-paragraph (*b*) of paragraph 6 of this Article; and

b) a biennial report on legislative, regulatory and administrative measures taken to enforce the provisions of the present Convention.

8. The information referred to in paragraph 7 of this Article shall be available to the public where this is not inconsistent with the law of the Party concerned.

Article IX

MANAGEMENT AND SCIENTIFIC AUTHORITIES

1. Each Party shall designate for the purposes of the present Convention:

a) one or more Management Authorities competent to grant permits or certificates on behalf of that Party; and

b) one or more Scientific Authorities.

2. A State depositing an instrument of ratification, acceptance, approval or accession shall at that time inform the Depositary Government of the name and address of the Management Authority authorized to communicate with other Parties and with the Secretariat.

3. Any changes in the designations or authorizations under the provisions of this Article shall be comunicated by the Party concerned to the Secretariat for transmission to all other Parties.

4. Any Management Authority referred to in paragraph 2 of this Article shall if so requested by the Secretariat or the Management Authority of another Party, communicate to it impression of stamps, seals or other devices used to authenticate permits or certificates.

Article X

TRADE WITH STATES NOT PARTY TO THE CONVENTION

Where export or re-export is to, or import is from, a State not a Party to the present Convention, comparable documentation issued by the competent authorities in that State which substantially conforms with the requirements of the present Convention for permits and certificates may be accepted in lieu thereof by any Party.

Article XI

CONFERENCE OF THE PARTIES

1. The Secretariat shall call a meeting of the Conference of the Parties not later than two years after the entry into force of the present Convention.

2. Thereafter the Secretariat shall convene regular meetings at least once every two years, unless the Conference decides otherwise, and extraordinary meetings at any time on the written request of a least one-third of the Parties.

3. At meetings, whether regular or extraordinary the Parties shall review the implementation of the present Convention and may:

a) make such provision as may be necessary to enable the Secretariat to carry out its duties;

b) consider and adopt amendments to Appendices I and II in accordance with Article XV;

c) review the progress made towards the restoration and conservation of the species included in Appendices I, II and III;

d) receive and consider any reports presented by the Secretariat or bv any Party; and

e) where appropriate, make recommendations for improving the effectiveness of the present Convention.

4. At each regular meeting, the Parties may determine the time and venue of the next regular meeting to be held in accordance with the provisions of paragraph 2 of this Article.

5. At any meeting, the Parties may determine and adopt rules of procedure for the meeting.

6. The United Nations, its Specialized Agencies and the International Atomic Energy Agency, as well as any State not a Party to the present Convention, may be observers, who shall have the right to participate but not to vote.

7. Any body or agency technically qualified in protection, conservation or management of wild fauna and flora, in the following categories, which has informed the Secretariat of its desire to be represented at meetings of the Conference by observers, shall be admitted unless at least one-third of the Parties present object:

a) international agencies or bodies either governmental or non-governmental, and national governmental agencies and bodies; and

b) national non-governmental agencies or bodies which have been approved for this purpose by the State in which they are located.

Once admitted, these observers shall have the right to participate but not to vote.

Article XII

THE SECRETARIAT

1. Upon entry into force of the present Convention, a Secretariat shall be provided by the Executive Director of the United Nations Environment Programme. To the extent and in the manner he considers appropriate, he may be assisted by suitable inter-governmental or non-governmental international or national agencies and bodies technically qualified in protection, conservation and management of wild fauna and flora.

2. The functions of the Secretariat shall be:

a) to arrange for and service meetings of the Parties;

b) to perform the functions entrusted to it under the provisions of Articles XV and XVI of the present Convention;

c) to undertake scientific and technical studies in accordance with programmes authorized by the Conference of the Parties as will contribute to the implementation of the present Convention, including studies concerning standards for appropriate preparation and shipment of living specimens and the means of identifying specimens;

d) to study the reports of Parties and to request from Parties such further information with respect thereto as it deems necessary to ensure implementation of the present Convention.

e) to invite the attention of the Parties to any matter pertaining to the aims of the present Convention;

f) to publish periodically and distribute to the Parties current editions of Appendices I, II and III together with any information which will facilitate identification of specimens of species included in those Appendices.

g) to prepare annual reports to the Parties in its work and on the implementation of the present Convention and such other reports as meetings of the Parties may request.

h) to make recommendations for the implementation of the aims and provisions of the present Convention, including the exchange of information of a scientific or technical nature;

i) to perform any other function as may be entrusted to it by the Parties.

Article XIII

INTERNATIONAL MEASURES

1. When the Secretariat in the light of information received is satisfied that any species

included in Appendices I or II is being affected adversely by trade in specimens of that species or that the provisions of the present Convention are not being effectively implemented, it shall communicate such information to the authorized Management Authority of the Party or Parties concerned.

2. When any Party receives a communication as indicated in paragraph 1 of this Article, it shall, as soon as possible, inform the Secretariat of any relevant facts insofar as its laws permit and, where appropriate, propose remedial action. Where the Party considers that an inquiry is desirable, such inquiry may be carried out by one or more persons expressly authorized by the Party.

3. The information provided by the Party or resulting from any inquiry as specified in paragraph 2 of this Article shall be reviewed by the next Conference of the Parties which may take whatever recommendations it deems appropriate.

Article XIV

EFFECT ON DOMESTIC LEGISLATION AND INTERNATIONAL CONVENTIONS

1. The provisions of the present Convention shall in no way affect the right of Parties to adopt:

a) stricter domestic measures regarding the conditions for trade, taking possession or transport of specimens of species included in Appendices I, II and III, or the complete prohibition thereof; or

b) domestic measures restricting or prohibiting trade, taking possession, or transport of species not included in Appendices I, II or III.

2. The provisions of the present Convention shall in no way affect the provisions of any domestic measures or the obligations of Parties deriving from any treaty, convention, or international agreement relating to other aspects of trade, taking possession, or transport of specimens which is in force or subsequently may enter into force for any Party including any measure pertaining to the Customs, public health, veterinary or plant quarantine fields.

3. The provisions of the present Convention shall in no way affect the provisions of, or the obligations deriving from, any treaty, convention or international agreement concluded or which may be concluded between States creating a union or regional trade agreement establishing or maintaining a common external customs control and removing customs controls between the parties thereto insofar as they relate to trade among the States members of that union or agreement.

4. A State Party to the present Convention, which is also a Party to any other treaty, convention or international agreement which is in force at the time of the coming into force of the present Convention and under the provisions of which protection is afforded to marine species included in Appendix II. shall be relieved of the obligations imposed on it under the provisions of the present Convention with respect to trade in specimens of species included in Appendix II that are taken by ships registered in that State and in accordance with the provisions of such other treaty, convention or international agreement.

5. Notwithstanding the provisions of Articles III, IV and V, any export of a specimen taken in accordance with paragraph 4 of this Article shall only require a certificate from a Management Authority of the State of introduction to the effect that the specimen was taken in accordance with the provisions of the other treaty, convention or international agreement in question.

6. Nothing in the present Convention shall prejudice the codification and development of the law of the sea by the United Nations Conference on the Law of the Sea convened pursuant to Resolution 2750C(XXV) of the General Assembly of the United Nations nor the present or future claims and legal view of any State concerning the law of the sea and the nature and extent of coastal and flag State jurisdiction.

Article XV

AMENDMENTS TO APPENDICES I AND II

1. The following provisions shall apply in relation to amendments to Appendices I and II at meetings of the Conference of the Parties:

a) Any Party may propose an amendment to Appendix I or II for consideration at the next meeting. The text of the proposed amendment shall be communicated to the Secretariat at least 150 days before the meeting. The Secretariat shall consult the other Parties and interested bodies on the amendment in accordance with the provisions of sub-paragraphs (*b*) and (*c*) of paragraph 2 of this Article and shall communicate the response to all Parties not later than 30 days before the meeting.

b) Amendments shall be adopted by a two-thirds majority of Parties present and voting. For these purposes "Parties present and voting" means Parties present and casting an affirmative or negative vote. Parties abstaining from voting shall not be counted among the two-thirds required for adopting an amendment.

c) Amendments adopted at a meeting shall enter into force 90 days after that meeting for all Parties except those which make a reservation in accordance with paragraph 3 of this Article.

2. The following provisions shall apply in relation to amendments to Appendices I and II between meetings of the Conference of the Parties:

a) Any Party may propose an amendment to Appendix I and II for consideration between meetings by the postal procedures set forth in this paragraph.

b) For marine species, the Secretariat shall, upon receiving the text of the proposed amendment, immediately communicate it to the Parties. It shall also consult inter-governmental bodies having a function in relation to those species especially with a view to obtaining scientific data these bodies may be able to provide and to ensuring co-ordination with any conservation measures enforced by such bodies. The Secretariat shall communicate the view expressed and data provided by these bodies and its own findings and recommendations to the Parties as soon as possible.

c) For species other than marine species, the Secretariat shall, upon receiving the text of the proposed amendments, immediately communicate it to the Parties, and, as soon as possible thereafter, its own recommendations.

d) Any party may, within 60 days of the date on which the Secretariat communicated its recommendations to the Parties under sub-paragraphs (*b*) or (*c*) of this paragraph, transmit to the Secretariat any comments on the proposed amendment together with any relevant scientific data and information.

e) The Secretariat shall communicate the replies received together with its own recommendations to the Parties as soon as possible.

f) If no objection to the proposed amendment is received by the Secretariat within 30 days of the date the replies and recommendations were communicated under the provisions of sub-paragraph (*e*) of this paragraph, the amendment shall enter into force 90 days later for all Parties except those which make a reservation in accordance with paragraph 3 of this Article.

g) If an objection by any Party is received by the Secretariat, the proposed amendment shall be submitted to a postal vote in accordance with the provisions of sub-paragraphs (*h*), (*i*) and (*j*) of this paragraph.

h) The Secretariat shall notify the Parties that notification of objection has been received.

i) Unless the Secretariat receives the votes for, against or in abstention from at least one-half of the Parties within 60 days of the date of notification under sub-paragraph (*h*) of this paragraph, the proposed amendment shall be referred to the next meeting of the Conference for further consideration.

j) Provided that votes are received from one-half of the Parties, the amendment shall be adopted by a two-thirds majority of Parties casting an affirmative or negative vote.

k) The Secretariat shall notify all Parties of the result of the vote.

l) If the proposed amendment is adopted it shall enter into force 90 days after the date of the notification by the Secretariat of its acceptance for all Parties except those which make a reservation in accordance with paragraph 3 of this Article.

3. During the period of 90 days provided for by sub-paragraph (*c*) of paragraph 1 of sub-paragraph (*l*) or paragraph 2 of this Article any Party may by notification in writing to the Depositary Government make a reservation with respect to the amendment. Until such reservation is withdrawn the Party shall be treated as a State not a Party to the present Convention with respect to trade in the species concerned.

Article XVI

APPENDIX III AND AMENDMENTS THERETO

1. Any Party may at any time submit to the Secretariat a list of species which it identifies as being subject to regulation within its jurisdiction for the purpose mentioned in paragraph 3 of Article II. Appendix III shall include the names of the Parties submitting the species for inclusion therein, the scientific names of the species so submitted, and any parts or derivatives of the animals or plants concerned that are specified in relation to the species for the purposes of sub-paragraph (*b*) of Article I.

2. Each list submitted under the provisions of paragraph 1 of this Article shall be communicated to the Parties by the Secretariat as soon as possible after receiving it. The list shall take effect as part of Appendix III 90 days after the date of such communication. At any time after the communication of such list, any Party may by notification in writing to the Depositary Government enter a reservation with respect to any species or any parts or derivatives, and until such reservation is withdrawn, the State shall be treated as a State not a Party to the present Convention with respect to trade in the species or part or derivative concerned.

3. A Party which has submitted a species for inclusion in Appendix III may withdraw it at any time by notification to the Secretariat which shall communicate the withdrawal to all Parties. The withdrawal shall take effect 30 days after the date of such communication.

4. Any Party submitting a list under the provisions of paragraph 1 of this Article shall submit to the Secretariat a copy of all domestic laws and regulations applicable to the protection of such species, together with any interpretations which the Party may deem appropriate or the Secretariat may request. The Party shall, for as long as the species in question is included in Appendix III, submit any amendments of such laws and regulations or any new interpretations as they are adopted.

Article XVII

AMENDMENT OF THE CONVENTION

1. An extraordinary meeting of the Conference of the Parties shall be convened by the Secretariat on the written request of at least one-third of the Parties to consider and adopt amendments to the present Convention. Such amendments shall be adopted by a two-thirds majority of Parties present and voting. For these purposes "Parties present and voting" means Parties present and casting an affirmative or negative vote. Parties abstaining from voting shall not be counted among the two-thirds required for adopting an amendment.

2. The text of any proposed amendment shall be communicated by the Secretariat to all Parties at least 90 days before the meeting.

3. An amendment shall enter into force for the Parties which have accepted it 60 days after two-

thirds of the Parties have deposited an instrument of acceptance of the amendment with the Depositary Government. Thereafter, the amendment shall enter into force for any other Party 60 days after that Party deposits its instrument of acceptance of the amendment.

Article XVIII

RESOLUTION OF DISPUTES

1. Any dispute which may arise between two or more Parties with respect to the interpretation or application of the provisions of the present Convention shall be subject to negotiation between the Parties involved in the dispute.

2. If the dispute cannot be resolved in accordance with paragraph 1 of this Article, the Parties may, by mutual consent, submit the dispute to arbitration, in particular that of the Permanent Court of Arbitration at The Hague, and the Parties submitting the dispute shall be bound by the arbitral decision.

Article XIX

SIGNATURE

The present Convention shall be open for signature at Washington until 30 April 1973 and thereafter at Berne until 31 December 1974.

Article XX

RATIFICATION, ACCEPTANCE, APPROVAL

The present Convention shall be subject to ratification, acceptance or approval. Instruments of ratification, acceptance or approval shall be deposited with the Government of the Swiss Confederation which shall be the Depositary Government.

Article XXI

ACCESSION

The present Convention shall be open indefinitely for accession. Instruments of accession shall be deposited with the Depositary Government.

Article XXII

ENTRY INTO FORCE

1. The present Convention shall enter into force 90 days after the date of deposit of the tenth instrument of ratification, acceptance, approval or accession, with the Depositary Government.

2. For each State which ratifies, accepts or approves the present Convention or accedes thereto after the deposit of the tenth instrument of ratification, acceptance, approval or accession, the present Convention shall enter into force 90 days after the deposit by such State of its instrument of ratification, acceptance, approval or accession.

Article XXIII

RESERVATIONS

1. The provisions of the present Convention shall not be subject to general reservations. Specific reservations may be entered in accordance with the provisions of this Article and Articles XV and XVI.

2. Any State may, on depositing its instrument of ratification, acceptance, approval or accession, enter a specific reservation with regard to:

a) any species included in Appendix I, II, III; or

b) any parts or derivatives specified in relation to a species included in Appendix III.

3. Until a Party withdraws its reservation entered under the provisions of this Article, it shall be treated as a State not a Party to the present Convention with respect to trade in the particular species or parts or derivatives specified in such reservation.

Article XXIV

DENUNCIATION

Any Party may denounce the present Convention by written notification to the Depositary Government at any time. The denunciation shall take effect twelve months after the Depositary Government has received the notification.

Article XXV

DEPOSITARY

1. The original of the present Convention, in the Chinese, English, French, Russian and Spanish languages, each version being equally authentic, shall be deposited with the Depositary Government, which shall transmit certified copies thereof to all States that have signed it or deposited instruments of accession to it.

2. The Depositary Government shall inform all signatory and acceding States and Secretariat of signatures, deposit of instruments of ratification, acceptance, approval or accession, entry into force of the present Convention, amendments thereto, entry and withdrawal of reservations and notifications of denunciation.

3. As soon as the present Convention enters into force, a certified copy thereof shall be transmitted by the Depositary Government to the Secretariat of the United Nations for registration and publication in accordance with Article 102 of the Charter of the United Nations.

In Witness Whereof the undersigned Plenipotentiaries, being duly authorized to that effect, have signed the present Convention.

Done at Washington this third day of March, One Thousand Nine Hundred and Seventy-three.

APPENDICES I AND II
as at 28 June 1979

INTERPRETATIONS:

1. Species included in these appendices are referred to:

a) by the name of the species; or

b) as being all of the species included in higher taxon or designated part thereof.

2. The abbrevation "ssp". is used to denote all species of a higher taxon.

3. Other references to taxa higher than species are for the purposes of information or classification only.

4. The abbreviation "p.e." is used to denote species which are possibly extinct.

5. An asterisk (*) placed against the name of a species or higher taxon indicates that one or more geographically separate populations, subspecies or species of that species or taxon are included in Appendix I and that these populations, sub-species or species are excluded from Appendix II.

6. Two asterisks (**) placed against a name of a species or higher taxon indicate that one or more geographically separate populations, sub-species or species of that species or taxon are included in Appendix II and that these populations, subspecies or species are excluded from Appendix I.

7. The symbol (+) followed by a number placed against the name of a species or higher taxon denotes that only designated geographically separate populations, subspecies or species of that species or taxon are included in the appendix concerned, as follows:

+ 201 Population of South Africa

+ 202 (A) North Pacific stock
(B) Stock in area from 0 degree longitude to 70 degrees east longitude, from the equator to the Antarctic Continent.

+ 203 Populations of Bhutan, India, Nepal and Pakistan

+ 204 Italian population

+ 205 All North American subspecies

+ 206 Asian population

+ 207 Indian population

+ 208 Australian population

+ 209 Himalayan population

+ 210 Population of the United States of America

+ 211 All New Zealand species

+ 212 Population of Chile

+ 213 All species of the family in the Americas

+ 214 Australian populations

8. The symbol (—) followed by a number placed against the name of a species or higher taxon denotes that designated geographically separate populations, subspecies, species, groups of species or families of that species or taxon are excluded from the appendix concerned, as follows:

— 101 (A) Stock in North Atlantic off Iceland
(B) Stock in North Atlantic off Newfoundland
(C) Stock in area from 40 degrees south latitude to Antarctic Continent, from 120 degrees west longitude to 60 degrees west longitude

— 102 Populations of Bhutan, India, Nepal and Pakistan

— 103 *Panthera tigris altaica (amurensis)*

— 104 Australian population

— 105 Cathartidae

— 106 Population of the United States of America

— 107 Australian population

— 108 Population of Papua New Guinea

— 109 Population of Chile

— 110 All species which are not succulent

9. Any plant, whether alive or dead, as well as any readily recognizable part or derivative of a plant of a species or higher taxon included in Appendix II are covered by the provisions of the Convention, unless the symbol (†) followed by a number is placed against the name of that species or taxon. In such a case, only the plant whether alive or dead, and the parts or derivatives designated as follows are concerned:

† 1 designates roots

† 2 designates timber

† 3 designates trunks

	Appendix I	Appendix II
FAUNA		
MAMMALIA		
Monotremata		
Tachyglossidae	*Zaglossus* spp.	
Marsupialia		
Macropodidae	*Bettongia* spp.	
		Dendrolagus benettianus *Dendrolagus lumholtzi*
	Caloprymus campestris p.e.	
		Dendrolagus inustus *Dendrolagus ursinus*
	Lagorchestes hirsutus *Lagostrophus fasciatus* *Onychogalea frenata* *Onychogalea lunata*	
Phalangeridae		*Phalanger macalatus* *Phalanger orientalis*

Burramyidae		*Burramys parvus*
Vombatidae	*Lasiothinus krefftii*	
Permelidae	*Chaeropus ecaudatus* p.e.	
	Macrotis lagotis	
	Macrotis leucura	
	Permeles bougainville	
Dasyuridae	*Sminthopsis longicaudata*	
	Sminthopsis psammophila	
Thylacinidae	*Thylacinus cynocephalus* p.e.	
Insectivora		
Erinaceidae		*Erinaceus frontalis*
Primates		Primates spp.
Lemuridae	*Allocebus* spp.	
		Cheirogaleus spp.
		Hapalemus spp.
		Lemur spp.
		Lepilemur spp.
	Microcebus spp.	
	Phaner spp.	
	Microcebus spp.	
	Phaner spp.	
Indriidae	*Avahi* spp.	
	Indri spp.	
	Propithecus spp.	
Daubentoniidae	*Daubentonia madagascariensis*	
Calithricidae	*Callimico goeldii*	
	Callitbrix aurita	
	Callithrix flaviceps	
	Leontopithecus (Leontideus) spp.	
	Saguinus bicolor	
	Saguinus leucopus	
	Saguinus eodipus	
Cebidae	*Alouatta palliata (villosa)*	
	Ateles geoffroyi frontatus	
	Ateles geoffroyis panamensis	
	Brachlyteles arachnoides	
	Cacajao spp.	
	Chiropotes albinasus	
	Saimiri oerstedii	
Cercopithecidae	*Cercocebus galertus galeritus*	
	Colobus badius kirkii	
	Colobus badius rufomitratus	
	Macasa silenus	
	Nasalis larvatus	
	Presbytis entellus	
	Presbythis geei	
	Presbytis pileatus	
	Presbytis potenziani	
	Pygathrix nemaeus	
	Simias concolor	
Hylobatidae	*Hylobates* sp.	
	Symphalangus syndactylus	
Pongidae	*Pongidae* spp.	
Edentata		
Myrmeco phagidae		*Myrmechaphaga tridactyla*
		Tamandua tetradactyla chapandensis

Bradypodidae		*Bradypus boliviensis*
Dasypodidae	*Pridontes giganteus* (= maximus)	
Pholidota		*Manis crassicaudata*
Manidae	*Manis pentadactyla* *Manis temmincki*	*Manis javanica*
Lagomorpha		
Leporidae	*Caprolagus·hispidus* *Romerolagus diazi*	*Nesolagus netscheri*
Rhodentia		
Sciuridae	*Cynomys mexicanus*	*Larisus hosei* *Ratuia* spp.
Heteromyidae		*Dipodomys phillipsii phillipsii*
Muridae	*Leporillus conditor* *Pseudomys fumeus* *Pseudomys preaconis* *Xeromys myoides* *Zyzomys pedunculatus*	*Notomys* spp. *Pseudomys shortridgei*
Chinchiliidae	*Chinchilla* spp. + 201	
Cetacea		*Cetacea* spp.
Platanistidae	*Lipoles vexillifer* *Platanista gangetica* *Platanista minor*	
Delphinidae	*Sotalia* spp. *Sousa* spp.	
Phocaenidae	*Neophocaena phocaenoides* *Phocaena sinus*	
Eschrichtidae	*Eschrichtius robustus (glaucus)*	
Balaenopteridae	*Balaenoptera borealis"* + 202 *Balaenoptera musculus* *Balaenoptera physalus"* - 101 *Megaptera novaeangliae*	
Balaenidae	*Balaena mysticetus* *Eubalaena* spp.	
Carnivora		
Canidae	*Canis lupus"* + 203 *Spethos venaticus* *Vulpes velox hebes*	Canis lupus - 102 *Chrysocyon brachyurus* *Cuon alpinus* *Dusicyon culpaeus* *Dusicyon fulripes* *Dusicyon griseus* *Vulpes cana*
Ursidae	*Helarctos malavanus* *Selenarctos thibetanus* *Tremarctos ornatus* *Ursus arctos"* + 204 *Ursus arctos isabellinus* *Ursus arctos nelsoni* *Ursus arctos pruinosus*	*Ursus arctos"* + 205 *Ursus (Thalarctos) maritimus*

Procyonidae		*Ailurus fulgens*
Mustelidae	*Aonyx microdon* *Enhydra lutris nereis* *Lutra felina* *Lutra longicaudis (platensis/ annectens)* *Lutra lutra* *Lutra provocax* *Mustela nigripes* *Pteronura brasilliensis*	*Conepatus humboldti* *Lutrinae* spp.
Viverridae	*Prionodon pardicolor*	*Cryptoprocta ferox* *Cynogale bennetti* *Eupleres goudotii* *Eupleres major* *Fossa fossa* *Hemigalus derbyanus* *Prionodon linsang*
Hyaenidae	*Hyaena brunnea*	
Felidae	*Acinonyx jubatus* *Felis bengalensis bengalensis* *Felis caracal* + 206 *Felis concolor coryi* *Felis concolor costaricensis* *Felis concolor cougar* *Felis jacobita* *Felis marmorata* *Felis nigripes* *Felis pardalis mearnsi* *Felis pardalis mitis* *Felis planiceps* *Felis rubiginosa* + 207 *Felis (Lynx) rufa escuinapae* *Felis temmincki* *Felis tigrina oncilla* *Felis wiedii nicaraguae* *Felis weidii salvinia* *Felis yaguoaroundi cacomilli* *Felis yagouaroundi fossata* *Felis yagouaroundi panamensis* *Felis yagouaroundi tolteca* *Neofelis nebulosa* *Panthera leo persica* *Panthera onca* *Panthera pardus* *Panthera tigris* - 103 *Panthera uncia*	Felidae spp.
Pinnipedia		
Otariidae	*Arctocephalus townsendi*	*Arctocephalus* spp.
Phocidae	*Monachus* spp.	*Mirounga angustirostris* *Mirounga leonina*
Tubulidentata		
Orycteropodidae		*Orycletopus afer*
Proboseidea		
Elephantidae	*Elaphas maximus*	*Loxodonta africana*

Sirenia		
Dugongida	*Dugong dugong* - 104	*Dugong dugong* + 208
Trichechidae	*Trichechus inunguis* *Trichechus manatus*	*Trichechus senegalensis*
Perisodactyla		
Equidae	*Equus grevyi* *Equus heminous heminous* *Equus heminous khur* *Equus przewalskii* *Equus zebra zebra*	*Equus heminous* *Equus zebra harimannae*
Tapiridae	*Tapirus bairdii* *Tapirus indicus* *Tapirus indicus* *Tapirus pinchague*	*Tapirus terrestris*
Rhinocerotidae	*Rhinocerotidae* spp.	
Artiodaetyla		
Suidae	*Babyrousa babyrossa* *Sus salvanius*	
Hippopotamidae		*Cheoropsis liberiensis*
Camelidae	*Vicugna vicugna*	*Lama guanicoe*
Cervidae	*Axis (Hyelaphus) calamianensis* *Axis (Hyelaphus) Kuhli* *Axis (Hyelaphus) porcinus annamiticus* *Blastocerus dichotomus* *Cervus duvauceli* *Cervus elaphus banglu* *Cervus eldi* *Dama mesopotamica* *Hippocamelus antisensis* *Hippocamelus bisulcus* *Moschus moschilerus* + 209 *Ozotoceros bezoarticus* *Pudu pudu*	*Cervus elaphus bactrianus* *Moschus* spp. *Pudu mephistophiles*
Antilocapridae	*Antilocapra american peninsularis* *Antilocapra american sonoriensis*	*Antilocapra american mexicana*
Bovidae	*Bison bison athabascae* *Bos gaurus* *Bos (grunniens)*	*Addax nasomaculatus*

	mutus	
	Bubalus (Anoa) depressicornis	
	Bubalus (Anoa) mindorensis	
	Bubalus (Anoa) guarlesi	
		Capra falconeri
	Capra falconeri chiltanensis	
	Capra falconeri jerdoni	
	Capra falconeri megaceros	
	Capricornis sumatraensis	
		Cephalophus monticola
	Damaliscus forcas dorcas	
	Hippotragus niger variani	
		Kobus leche
	Nemorthaedus goral	
	Novibos (Bos) sauveli	
	Oryx leucoryx	*Oryx (Lao) dammah*
	Ovis ammon hodgsoni	
	Ovis orientalis aphion	*Ovis canadensis*
	Ovis vignei	
	Pantholops hodgsoni	
	Rupicapra rupicapra ornata	
AVES		
Rheiformes		
Rheidae	*Pterocnemia pennala*	
		Rhea american albescens
Tinamiformes	*Tinamus solitarius*	*Rhyncholus rufescens maculicollis*
		Rhyncholus rufescens pallescens
		Rhyncholus rufescens rufescens
Sphenisciformes		
Spheniscidae		*Spheniscus demersus*
Podicipediformes		
Podicpedidae	*Podilymbus gigas*	
Procellariformes		
Diomedeidae	*Diomedea albatrus*	
Pelecaniformes		
Pelecanidae		*Pelecanus crispus*
Sulidae	*Sula abbotii*	
Fregatidae	*Fregata andrewsi*	

Ciconiformes		
Ciconiidae	*Ciconia ciconia boyciana*	
		Ciconia nigra
Threskiornithidae	*Geronticus eremita*	*Geronticus calvus*
	Nippona nippon	*Platalea leucorodia*
Phoenicopteridae		*Phoenicoparrus andinus*
		Phoenicoparrus jamesi
		Phoenicopterus ruber chilensi
		Phoenicopterus ruber ruber
Anseriformes		
Anatidae	*Anas aucklandica nesiotis*	*Anas aucklandica aucklandica*
	Anas laysanensis	*Anas aucklandica cholorotis*
	Anas oustaleti	
	Branta canadensis leucopreia	*Anas bernieri*
		Anser albifrons gambelli
	Branta sandvicensis	*Branta ruficollis*
		Coscoroba coscoroba
	Carina scutulata	*Cygnus bewickii jankowskii*
	Rhodenessa caryophyllacea	*Cygnus melancoryphus*
		Dendrocygna arborea
		Sarkidiornis melanotos
Falconiformes		Falconiformes spp. - 105
Cathartidae	*Vultur gryphus*	
	Gymnogypas californianus	
Accipitridae	*Aquila heliaca*	
	Chondrohierax wilsonii	
	Haliaeelus albicilla	
	Haliaeetus leucocephalus	
	Harpia harpyja	
	Phithecophaga jefferyi	
Falconidae	*Falco araea*	
	Falco newtoni aldabranus	
	Falco pregrinus (pelegrinoides/ babylonicus)	
	Falco panciatus	
	Falco rusticolus	
Galliformes		
Megapodiidae	*Macrocephalon maleo*	
		Megapodius feycinee abbotii
		Megapodius freycinel

		nicobariensis
Cracidae	*Crax blumenbachii* *Nitu mitu mitu* *Creophasis derbianus* *Pipile jacutinga* *Pipile pipile pipile*	
Tetraonidae	*Tymphanuchus cupido attwateri attwateri*	*Lyrurus mlokosiewiczi*
Phasianidae	*Catreus wallichii* *Colinus virginianus ridgway* *Crossoptilon crossoptilon* *Crossoptilon mantchuricum* *Lophophorus impejanus* *Lophophorus ihuysii* *Lophophorous sclateri* *Lophura edwardsi* *Lophophorus scalteri* *Lophura edwardsi* *Lophura imperialis* *Lophura swinheii* *Polyplectronemphanum* *Syrmaticus ellioti* *Syrmaticus humiae* *Syrmaticus mikado* *Tetraogaleus caspius* *Tetraogallus tibetanus* *Tragopan blythii* *Tragopan caboti* *Tragopan melanocephalus*	*Argusianus argus* *Cyrtonyx montezumre mearnsi* - 106 *Cyrtonyx montezumae montezumae* *Francolinus ochropectus* *Francolinus swierstrai* *Gallus sonneratii* *Ithaginis cruentus* *Pavo muticus* *Ithaginis cruentus* *Pavo muticus* *Polyplectron bicalaralum* *Polyplectron germaini* *Polyplectron malacense*
Gruiformes		
Turnicidae		*Turnix melanogaster*
Pedionomidae		*Pedionomus torquatus*
Gruidae	*Grus american* *Grus canadensis nesiotes* *Grus canadensis pulla* *Grus japonensis* *Grus leucogeranus* *Grus monacha* *Grus nigricollis* *Grus vipio*	*Balearica regulorum* *Grus canadensis pratensis*
Rallidae	*Tricholimnas sylvestris*	*Gallirallus australis hectori*
Rhynochetidae	*Rhynochetos jubatus*	
Otididae	*Chlamydotis undulata* *Choriotis nigriceps* *Eupodotis bengalensis*	*Otis tarda*

Charadriiformes		
Scolopacidae	*Numenius borealis*	*Numenius minatus*
	Tringa guttifer	*Numenius tenuirostris*
Laridae	*Larus relietus*	*Larus brunneicephalus*
Columbiformes		
Columbidae	*Caloenas nicobarica*	*Callicolumba luzonica*
	Ducala dindorensis	*Goura cristata*
	Goura scheepmakeri	
		Goura victoria
Psittaciformes		
Psittacidae	*Amazona guildingii*	*Cacatua (Kakatoe) tenairostris*
	Amazona imperialis	*Calyptorhynchus lathami*
	Amazona pretrei pretrei	*Cyanoliseus patagonus byrani*
	Amazona rhodocorytha	*Cyanoramphus matherbi*
	Amazona versicolor	*Cyanoramphus unicolor*
	Amazona vinacea	*Eunymphicus cornutus.*
	Amazona vittata	
	Anodorhynchus glaucus	
	Anodorhynchus leari	
	Aratinga guaruba	
	Cyanopsitta spixii	
	Cyanoramphus auriceps forbesi	
	Cyanoramphus novaezelandiae	
	Geopsittacus occidentalis p.e.	
	Neophema chrysogaster	
	Pezoporus wallicus	*Neophema splendida*
	Pionopsitta pileatea	*Opopsitta diophtalma coxeni*
	Psephotus chrysopteryguis	*Poicephalus robustus*
	Psephotus pulcherrimus p.e.	*Polytelis alexandrae*
	Psittacula krameri-echo	*Probosciger alerrimus*
	Psittaycus erithacus princeps	*Prosopeia personata*
	Pyrrhura cruentata	*Psephotus (Northiella) haemalogaster*
	Rhynchopsitta pachyrhyncha	*Tanygnathus lucionensis*
	Strigops habroptilus	
Cuculiformes		
Musophagidae		*Gallirex porphyreolophus*
		Tauraco corythaix
Strigiformes		*Strigiformes* spp.

Tytonidae	*Tyto soumagnei*	
	Athene blewitti	
Strigidae	*Ninox novaeseelandiae royana* *Ninox squamipila natalis* *Olus gurrneyi*	
Apodiformes		
Trochilidae	*Ramphodan dohrnii*	
Trogoniformes		
Trogonidae	*Pharomachrus mocinno costaricensis* *Pharomachrus mocinno mocinno*	
Coraciiformes		
Bucerotidae	*Buceros bicornis homrai* *Rhinoplax vigil*	*Aceros narcondami* *Buceros bicornis* *Buceros hydrocorax hydrocorax* *Buceros rhinoceros rhinoceros*
Piciformes		
Picidae	*Campephilus imperialis* *Dryocopus javensis richardsi*	*Picus squamatus flavirostris*
Passeriformes		
Pattidae	*Pitta kochi*	*Pitta brachyura nympha*
Cotingidae	*Cotinga maculata* *Xipholena atropurpurea*	*Rupicola peruviana* *Rupicola rupicola*
Atrichornithidae	*Atrichornis clamosa*	
Hirundinidae		*Pseudochelidon sirintarae*
Muscicapidae	*Dasyornis brachypterus longirostris* *Dasyornic broadbenti| littoralis* p.e. *Picathartes gymnocephalus* *Picathartes oreas*	*Muscicapa ruecki* *Psophodes nigrogularis*
Zosteropidae	*Zosterops albogularis*	
Meliphagidae	*Meliphaga cassidix*	
Fringillidae	*Spinus cucullatus*	*Spinus yarrellii*
Estriidae		*Emblema oculata*
Sturnidae	*Leucopsar rothschildi*	

Paradisaeidae		Paradissaeidae spp.
AMPHIBIA		
Urodela		
Cryptobranchidae	*Andrias (= Megalobatrachus) davidianus* *Andrias (= Megalobatrachus) japonicus*	
Ambystomidae		*Ambystoma dumerilli* *Ambystoma lermaensis* *Ambystoma mexicanum*
Salienta		
Bufonidae	*Bufo periglenes* *Bufo superciliaris* *Nectophrynoides* spp.	*Bufo retiformis*
Atelopodidae	*Atelopus varius zeteki*	
REPTILIA		
Testudinata		
Emydidae	*Balagar baska* *Geoclemys (= Demonia) hamiltonii* *Geoemyda (= Nicoria) tricarinata* *Kachuga tecta tecta* *Morenia oceliata* *Terrapene coahuila*	*Clemmys muhlenbergii*
Testudinidae	*Geochelone (= Testudo) elephantopus* *Geochelone (= Testudo) radiata* *Geochelone (= Testudo) yniphora* *Geopherus flavomarginatus* *Psammobates geometrica*	Testudinidae spp.
Cheloniidae	*Caretta caretta* *Chelonia mydas* - 107 *Eretmochelys imbricata* *Lepidochelys kempii* *Lepidochelys olivacea*	Cheloniidae spp.*
Dermocheylidae	*Dermochelys coriacea*	
Trionychidae	*Lissemys punctata*	

Welchschidkroten	*punctata*	
	Trionyx ater	
	Trionyx gangeticus	
	Trionyx hurum	
	Trinoyx nigricans	
Pelomedusidae		*Podocnemis* spp.
Chelidae	*Pseudemydura umbrina*	
Crocodylia		
Alligatoridae		*Alligatoridae spp.*
	Alligator sinensis	
	Carman crocodilus apaporiensis	
	Caiman latirostris	
	Melanosuchus niger	
Crocodylidae	*Crocodylus acutus*** + 210	Crocodylidae spp.*
	Crocodylus cataphractus	
	Crocodylus intermedius	
	Crocodylus moreletii	
	Crocodylus niloticus	
	Crocodylus novaeguineae mindorensis	
	Crocodylus palustris	
	Crocodylus rhombifer	
	Crocodylus siamensis	
	Ostealaemus tetraspis	
	Tamistoma schlegelii	
Gavialidae	*Gavialis gangeticus*	
Rhynochocephalia		
Sphenodentidae	*Sphenodon punclatus*	
Sauria		
Gekkonidae		*Crytodoctylus serpensinsula*
		Phelsuma spp.
		Paradelma orientalis
Pygopodidae		*Uromastyx* spp.
Agamidae		*Chamaeleo* spp.
Chamaeleonidae		*Conolophus* spp.
Iguanidae		*Amblyrhynchus cristatus*
		Cyclura spp.
		Iguana spp.
		Phrynosoma coronatum blainvillei
Teiidae		*Cnemidophorus hyperythrus*
		Crocodilurus lacertinus
		Dracaena guianensis

		Tupinambis spp.
Helodermatidae		*Heloderma* spp.
Varandiae	*Varanus bengalensis* *Varanus flavescens* *Varanus griseus* *Varanus komodoensis*	*Varanus* spp.
Serpentes		
Boidae	*Acrantophis* spp. *Bolyeria* spp. *Casarea* spp. *Epicrates inornatus* *Epicrates subflavus* *Python molurus molurus* *Sanzinia madagascariensis*	*Boidae* spp.
Colubridae		*Cyclagras gigas* *Elachistodon westermanni* *Pseudoboa cloelia* *Thamnophis elegans hammondi*
PISCES		
Acipenseriformes		
Acipenseridae	*Acipenser brevirostrum*	*Acipenser fulvescens* *Acipenser oxyrhynchus* *Acipenser sturio*
Osteoglossiformes		
Osteoglossidae Salmoniformes	*Scleropages formosus*	*Arapaima gigas*
Salmonidae	*Coregonus alpenae*	*Salmo chrysogaster* *Stenodus leucichthys leucichihys*
Cypriniformes		
Castostomidae	*Chasmistes cujus*	
Cyprinidae	*Probarbus jullieni*	*Plagopterus argentissimus* *Ptychocheilus lucius*
Siluriformes		
Schilbeidae	*Pangasianodon gigas*	
Atheriniformes		
Cyprinodontidae		*Cynolebias constanciae* *Cynolebias marmoratus* *Cynolebias minimus* *Cynolebias opalescens* *Cynolebias splendens*
Poeciliidae		*Xiphophorus couchianus*

Perciformes		
Percidae	*Stizostedion vitreum glaucum*	
Sciaenidae	*Cynoscion macdonaldi*	
Coelacanthiformes		
Coelacanthidae		*Latimeria chalimnae*
Ceratodiformes		
Ceratodidae		*Neoceratodus forsteri*
MOLLUSCA		
Anisomyaria		
Mrytilidae		*Mytilus chorus*
Naiadoida		
Unionidae	*Conradilla caelata Dromus dromas Epioblasma (= Dysnomia) florentina curtisi Epioblasma (= Dysnomia) Epiobhrama (= Dysnomia) sampsoni Epiolasma (= Dysnomia) sulcata perobliqua Epioblasma (= Dysnomia) torulosa gubernaculum Epioblasma (= Dynsomia) torulosa torulosa Epioblasma (= Dysnomia) turgidula Epioblasma (= Dysnomia) walkeri Fusconaia cuneolus Fusconaia edgariana Lampsilis higginsi Lampsilis orbiculata orbiculata Lampsilis satura Lampsils virescens Plethobasis cicatricosus plethobasis cooperianus Pleurobema plenum Potamilus (= Proptera) capax Quadrula intermedia Quadrula sparsa Toxoplasma (= Carunculino) cyiindrella*	*Cyprogenia aberti Epioblasma (= Dysnomia) torulosa rangiana Fusconia subtotunba Lampsilis brevicula Lexingtonia dolabelloides Plerobema clava*

	Unio (Megalonaias/?/) nickliniana *Unio (Lampsilis/?/) tampicoensis tecomatensis* *Viliosa (= Micromya) trabalis*	
Stylommatophora		
Camaenidae		*Papustyla (= Papuina) pulcherrima*
Paraphantidae		*Paraphanta* spp. + 211
Prosobranchia		
Hydrobidae		*Coabuilix hubbsi* *Coachilippira milleri* *Durangonella coahuilae* *Mexipyrgus cavanzae* *Mexipyrgus clurinceanus* *Mexipyrgus escobedae* *Mexipyrgus fugoi* *Mexipyrgus mojarralis* *Mexipyrgus multilineatus* *Mexithauma quadripaludium* *Nymphophilus minckleyi* *Paludiscala caramba*
INSECTA		
Lepidoptera		
Papilionidae		*Ornithoptera* spp *Trongonoptera* spp. *Troides* spp. *Parnassius apollo*
FLORA		
Apocynacae		*Pachypodium* spp.
Araceae	*Alocasia sanderana* *Alocasia zebrina*	
Araliaceae		*Panax quinauelchus* > 1
Araucariaceae	*Araucaria araucana* ** + 212	*Araucaria araucana** - 109 > 2
Asclepiadaceae		*Ceropegia* spp.
Byblidaceae		*Byblis* spp.

Cactaceae		*Cactaceae* spp. + 213 *Rhipsalis* spp.
Caryocaraceae	*Caryocar costaricense*	
Caryophyllaceae	*Gymnocarpos prezewalskii* *Melandrium mongolicus* *Silene mongolica* *Stellaria pulvinata*	
Cephalotaceae		*Cephalotus follicularis*
Chloarithaceae		
Compositae		*Sasurea lappa* > 1
Cupressaceae	*Fitzroya cupressoides* *Pilgerodendron uviferum*	
Cyathaeceae		*Cyatheaceae* spp. > 3
Cycadaceae	*Microycas calocama*	*Cycadaceae* spp. *
Dicksoniaceae		*Dicksoniaceae* spp. > 3
Didiereaceae		*Didiereaceae* spp.
Dioscoreaceae		*Dioscorea deltoidea* > 1
Euphorbiaceae		*Euphorbia* spp. - 110
Fagaceae		*Quercus copeyensis* > 2
Gentianaceae	*Prepusa hookeriana*	
Haemodoraceae		*Anigozanihos* spp. *Macropidia filinginosa*
Humriaceae	*Vantenea barbourii*	
Juglandaceae	*Engelhardtia pterocarpa*	
Leguminosae	*Ammopiptanthis mongolicum* *Cynometra hemilomophylla* *Platymiscium pleiostachyum* *Tachigalia versicolor*	*Thermopsis mongolica*
Liliaceae	*Aloe albida* *Aloe pilansii* *Aloe polyphylla* *Aloe thorncroftii* *Aloe vossii*	*Aloe* spp.*
Melastomataceae	*Lavoisiera itambana*	

Meliaceae	*Guarea longipetiola*	*Swientenia humilis* > 2
Moraceae	*Balocarpus costaricensis*	
Myrtaceae		*Verticordia* spp.
Orchildeaceae	*Cattleya skinneri* *Cattleya trianae* *Didiciea cunninghamii* *Laelia jongheana* *Laelia lobata* *Lycaste virginalis* var *alba* *Peristeria elata* *Renanthera imschootiana*	*Orchidaceae* spp.
Palmae		*Areca ipot* *Chrysalidocarpus* decipiens *Chrysalidocarpus lutescens* *Neodypsis decaryi* *Phoenli hancaena* var *philippmensis* *Zalacca clemensiana*
Pinaceae	*Abies guatemalensis* *Abies nebrodensis*	
Podocarpaceae	*Podocarpus costalis* *Podocarpus parlatorei*	
Portulacaceae		*Anacampseros* spp.
Primulaceae		*Cyclamen* spp.
Proteaceae	*Orothamnus zeyheri* . *Protea odorata*	*Banksia* spp. *Conosperum* spp. *Dryandra formosa* *Dryandra polycephala* *Xylomelum* spp.
Rubiaceae	*Balmea stormae*	
Rutaceae		*Boronia* spp. *Crowea* spp. *Geleznowia vettucosa*
Saxifragaceae (Grossulariaceae)	*Ribes sardoum*	
Solanaceae		*Solanum sylvestre*
Strangeriaceae	*Stungeria eriopus*	*Stangeriaceae* spp.*
Steruliaceae		*Basiloxylon excelsum* > 2
Thymelaeceae		*Pimelea physodes*
Ulmaceae	*Celtis aetnensis*	
Verbenaceae		*Caryopteris mongolica*
Welwitschiaceae	*Welwitschiabianesii*	*Welwitschiaceae* spp.
Zamiaceae	*Encephalartos* spp.	*Zamiaceae* spp.

Zygophyllaceae	*Hedychium philippinense*	
Zygophyllaceae		*Guaiacum sanctum* > 2.

APPENDIX III

as at 28 June 1979

Interpretation:

1. Species included in this appendix are referred to:

a) by the name of species; or

b) as being all of the species included in a higher taxon or designated part thereof.

2. The abbreviation "spp." is used to denote all species of a higher taxon.

3. Other references to taxa higher than species are for the purpose of information or classification only.

4. An asterisk (*) placed against, the named of a species or higher taxon indicates that one or more geographically separate populations, subspecies or species of that species or taxon are included in Appendix I and that these populations, subspecies or species are excluded from Appendix III.

5. Two asterisks (**) placed against the name of a species or higher taxon indicate that one or more geographically separate populations, subspecies or species of that species or taxon are included in Appendix II and that these populations, subspecies or species are excluded from Appendix III.

6. The name of the countries placed against the names of species or other taxa are those of the Parties submitting these species or taxa for inclusion in this appendix.

7. Any animal or plant, whether live or dead, of a species or other taxon listed in this appendix, is covered by the provisions of the Convention, as is any readily recognizable part or derivate thereof.

	Appendix I	**Appendix II**
FAUNA		
MAMMALIA		
Chiroptera		
Phyllostomatidae	*Vampyrops lineatus*	Uruguay
Edentata		
Bradypodidae	*Bradypus griseus*	Costa Rica
	Choleopus hoffmanni	Costa Rica
Dasypodidae	*Cabassous centralis*	Costa Rica
	Cabassous gymunurus (tatoucy)	Uruguay
Pholidota		
Manidae	*Manis gigantea*	Ghana
	Manis longicaudata	Ghana
	Manis tricuspis	Ghana
Rodentia		
Sciuridae	*Epixerus ebii*	Ghana
	Sciurus deppei	Costa Rica
Anomaluridae	*Anomalurus* spp.	Ghana
	Idiurus spp.	Ghana
Hystricidae	*Hystrix* spp.	Ghana
Erethisontidae	*Coendou spinosus*	Uruguay
Carnivora		
Canidae	*Fennecus Zerda*	Tunisia
Procyonidae	*Bassaricyon gabii*	Costa Rica

	Bassariscus sumichrasti	Costa Rica
	Nasua nasua solitaria	Uruguay
Mustelidae	*Galictis allamandi*	Costa Rica
	Mellivora capensis	Ghana, Botswana
Viverridae	*Vierra civetta*	Botswana
Hyaenidae	*Proteles cristatus*	Botswana
Pinnipedia		
Odobenidae	*Odobenus rosmarus*	Canada
Artiodactyla		
Hippopotamidae	*Hippotatomus amphibius*	Ghana
Tragulidae	*Hyemoschus aquaticus*	Ghana
Cervidae	*Cervus elaphus barbarus*	Tunisia
Bovidae	*Ammotragus lervia*	Tunisia
	Antilope cervicapra	Nepal
	Boocercus (Taurotragus) euryceros	Ghana
	Bubalus bubalis	Nepal
	Damaliscus linatus	Ghana
	Gazella dorcas	Tunisia
	Gazella gazella cuvieri	Tunisia
	Gazella leptoceros	Tunisia
	Hippotragus equinus	Ghana
	Tetracerus guadricornis	Nepal
	Tragelaphus spekei	Ghana
AVES		
Rheiformes		
Rheidae	*Rhea americana***	Uruguay
Ciconiiformes		
Ardeidae	*Ardea goliath*	Ghana
	Bubulcus ibis	Ghana
	Casmerodius albus	Ghana
	Egretta gargetta	Ghana
Ciconiidae	*Ephippiorhynchus senegalensis*	Ghana
	Leptoptilos crumeniterus	Ghana
Threskiornithidae	*Hagedashia hagedash*	Ghana
	Lampribis rara	Ghana
	Threskiornis aethiopica	Ghana
Anseriformes		
Anatidae	*Anatidae* spp.***	Ghana
Galliformes		
Cracidae	*Crax rubra*	Costa Rica

Phasianidae	*Agelastes meleagrides*	Ghana
	Tragopan satyra	Nepal
Columbiformes		
Columbidae	*Columbidae* spp.***	Ghana
	Nesoenas mayeri	Mauritius
Psittaciformes		
Psittacidae	*Psittacidae* spp.***	Ghana
	Ara ambigue	Costa Rica
	Ara macao	Costa Rica
Cuculiformes		
Musophagidae	Musophagidae spp.	Ghana
Passeriformes		
Muscicapidae	*Bebrornis rodericanus*	Mauritius
	Tchitrea (Terpsiphone) bourbonnensis	
Emberizidae	*Gubernatrix cristata*	Uruguay
Icteridae	*Xanthopsar flavus*	Uruguay
Fringillidae	*Fringillidae* spp.***	Ghana
Ploceidae	*Ploceidae* spp.	Ghana
REPTILIA		
Testudinata		
Trionychidae	*Trionyx triunguis*	Ghana
Pelomedusidae	*Pelumedusa subrufa*	Ghana
	Pelusios spp.	Ghana
FLORA		
Gnetaceae	*Gnetum montanum*	Nepal
Magnoliaceae	*Talauma hodgsonii*	Nepal
Papaveraceae	*Meconopsis regia*	Nepal
Podocarpaceae	*Podocarpus nerifolius*	Nepal
Tetracentraceae	*Tetracentron* spp.	Nepal

CONVENTION ON FISHING AND CONSERVATION OF THE LIVING RESOURCES IN THE BALTIC SEA AND THE BELTS [58]

Gdansk, 13 September 1973

The States Parties to this Convention,

bearing in mind that maximum and stable productivity of the living resources of the Baltic Sea and the Belts is of great importance to the States of the Baltic Sea basin,

recognizing their joint responsibility for the conservation of the living resources and their rational exploitation.

being convinced that the conservation of the living resources of the Baltic Sea and the Belts calls for closer and more expanded co-operation in this region,

have agreed as follows:

Article I

The Contracting States shall:

— co-operate with a view to preserving and increasing the living resources of the Baltic Sea and the Belts and obtaining the optimum yield, and, in particular to expanding and co-ordinating studies towards these ends,

— prepare and put into effect organizational and technical projects on conservation and growth of the living resources, including measures of artificial reproduction of valuable fish species and/or contribute financially to such measures, on a just and equitable basis, as well as take other steps towards rational and effective exploitation of the living resources.

Article II

1. The area to which this Convention applies, hereinafter referred to as "the Convention area", shall be all waters of the Baltic Sea and the Belts, excluding internal waters, bounded in the west by a line as from Hasenore Head to Gniben Point, from Korshage to Spodsbierg and from Gilbierg Head to the Kullen.

2. This Convention shall apply to all fish species and other living marine resources in the Convention Area.

Article III

Nothing in this Convention shall be deemed to affect the rights, claims or view of any Contracting State in regard to the limits of territorial waters and to the extent of jurisdiction over fisheries, according to international law.

Article IV

For the purpose of this Convention the term "vessel" means any vessel or boat in catching or treating fish or other living marine organisms and which is registered or owned in the territory of, or which flies the flag of, any Contracting State.

Article V

1. An International Baltic Sea Fishery Commission, hereinafter referred to as "the Commission", is hereby established for the purposes of this Convention.

2. Each Contracting State may appoint not more than two representatives as members of the Commission and such experts and advisers to assist them as that State may determine.

3. The Commission shall elect a Chairman and a Vice-Chairman from amongst its members who shall serve for a period of four years and who shall be eligible for re-election, but not for two consecutive terms of office.

The Chairman and the Vice-Chairman shall be elected from the representatives of different Contracting States.

4. A member of the Commission elected as its Chairman shall forthwith cease to act as a representative of a State and shall not vote. The State concerned shall have the right to appoint another representative to serve in the Chairman's place.

Article VI

1. The Office of the Commission shall be in Warsaw.

2. The Commission shall appoint its Secretary and as it may require appropriate staff to assist him.

3. The Commission shall adopt its rules of procedure and other provisions which the Commission shall consider necessary for its work.

Article VII

1. The Commission shall adopt its financial rules.

2. The Commission shall adopt a two years budget of proposed expenditures and budget estimates for the period following thereafter.

3. The total amount of the buget including any supplementary budget shall be contributed by the Contracting States in equal parts.

4. Each Contracting State shall pay the expenses related to the participation in the Commission of its representatives, experts and advisers.

Article VIII

1. Except where the Commission decides otherwise, it shall hold its sessions every two years in Warsaw at such time as it shall deem suitable. Upon the request of the representative of a Contracting State in the Commission, provided it is endorsed by a representative of another Contracting State, the Chairman of the Commission shall, as soon as possible, summon an extraordinary session at such time and place as he determines, however not later than three months from the date of the submission of the request.

2. The first session of the Commission shall be called by the Depositary Government of this Convention and shall take place within a period of ninety days from the date following the entry into force of this Convention.

3. Each Contracting State shall have one vote in

the Commission. Decisions and recommendations of the Commission shall be taken by a two-thirds majority of votes of the Contracting States, present and voting at the meeting.

4. English shall be the working language of the Commission. The languages of the Signatory States are the official languages of the Commission. Only recommendations, decisions and resolutions of the Commission shall be made in these languages.

At meetings of the Commission any Contracting State has the right to have all the proceedings translated into its own language. All the costs related to such translations shall be borne by that State.

Article IX

1. It shall be the duty of the Commission:

a) to keep under review the living resources and the fisheries in the Convention area by collecting, aggregating, analysing and disseminating statistical data, for example concerning catch, fishing effort, and other information,

b) to work out proposals with regard to co-ordination of scientific research in the Convention area,

c) to prepare and submit recommendations based as far as practicable on results of the scientific research and concerning measures referred to in Article X for consideration of the Contracting States.

2. In implementing its functions, the Commission shall, when appropriate, seek the services of the International Council for the Exploration of the Sea (ICES) and of other international technical and scientific organizations and shall make use of information provided by the official bodies of the Contracting States.

3. To perform its functions the Commission may set up working groups or other subsidiary bodies and determine their composition and terms of reference.

Article X

Measures relating to the purposes of this Convention which the Commission may consider and in regard of which it may make recommendations to the Contracting States are:

a) any measures for the regulation of fishing gear, appliances and catching methods,

b) any measures regulating the size limits of fish that may be retained on board vessels or landed, exposed or offered for sale,

c) any measures establishing closed seasons,

d) any measures establishing closed areas,

e) any measures improving and increasing the living marine resources, including artificial reproduction and transplantation of fish and other organisms,

f) any measures regulating and/or allocating between the Contracting States the amount of total catch or the amount of fishing effort according to objects, kinds, regions and fishing periods,

g) any measures of control over the implementation of recommendations binding on the Contracting States,

h) any other measures related to the conservation and rational exploitation of the living marine resources.

Article XI

1. Subject to the provisions of this Article, the Contracting States undertake to give effect to any recommendation made by the Commission under Article X of this Convention from the date determined by the Commission, which shall not be before the period for objection provided for in this Article has elapsed.

2. Any Contracting State may within ninety days from the date of notification of a recommendation object to it and in that event shall not be under obligation to give effect to that recommendation.

A Contracting State may also at any time withdraw its objection and give effect to a recommendation.

In the event of an objection being made within the ninety-days period, any other Contracting State may similarly object at any time within a further period of sixty days.

3. If objection to a recommendation are made by three or more Contracting States, the other Contracting States shall be relieved forthwith of any obligation to give effect to that recommendation.

4. The Commission shall notify each Contracting State immediately upon receipt of each objection or withdrawal.

Article XII

1. Each Contracting State shall take in regard to its nationals and its vessels appropriate measurses to ensure the application of the provisions of this Convention and of the recommendations of the Commission which have become binding for the Contracting State and in case of their infringement shall take appropriate action.

2. Without prejudice to the sovereign rights of the Contracting States in regard to their territorial sea and to the rights in their fishing zones, each Contracting State shall implement recommendations of the Commission binding on that State through its national authorities, within its territorial sea and in the waters under its fisheries jurisdiction.

3. Each Contracting State shall furnish to the Commission at such time and in such form as may be required by the Commission, the available statistical data and information referred to in Article IX paragraph 1 (*a*), as well as information on all actions taken by it in accordance with paragraphs 1 and 2 of this Article.

Article XIII

The Commission shall draw the attention of any

State which is not a party to this Convention to such fishing operations, undertaken by its national or vessels in the Convention area, which might affect negatively the activities of the Commission or the implementation of the purposes of this Convention.

Article XIV

The provisions of this Convention shall not apply to operations conducted solely for the purpose of scientific investigations by vessels authorized by a Contracting State for that purpose, or to fish and other marine organisms taken in the course of such operations. Catch so taken shall not be sold, exposed or offered for sale.

Article XV

1. The Commission shall co-operate with other international organizations having related objectives.

2. The Commission may extend an invitation to any international organization concerned or to the Government of any State, not a party to this Convention, to participate as an observer in the sessions of the Commission or meetings of its subsidiary bodies.

Article XVI

1. Each Contracting State may propose amendments to this Convention. Any such proposed amendment shall be submitted to the Depositary Government and communicated by it to all Contracting States, which shall inform the Depositary Government about either their acceptance or rejection of the amendment as soon as possible after the receipt of the communication.

The amendment shall enter into force ninety days after the Depositary Government has received notifications of acceptance of that amendment from all Contracting States.

2. Each State which shall become a party to this Convention after the entry into force of an amendment in accordance with the provisions of paragraph 1 of this Article, is obliged to apply the Convention as amended.

Article XVII

1. This Convention shall be subject to ratification or approval by the Signatory States. Instruments of ratification or instruments of approval shall be deposited with the Government of the Polish People's Republic which shall perform the functions of the Depositary Government.

2. This Convention shall be open for accession to any State interested in preservation and rational exploitation of living resources in the Baltic Sea and the Belts, provided that this State is invited by the Contracting States. Instruments of accession shall be deposited with the Depositary Government.

Article XVIII

1. This Convention shall enter into force on the ninetieth day following the date of the deposit of the fourth instrument of ratification or approval.

2. After entry into force of this Convention in accordance with paragraph 1 of this Article, the Convention shall enter into force for any other State, the Government of which has deposited an instrument of ratification, approval or accession, on the thirtieth day following the date of deposit of such instrument with the Depositary Government.

Article XIX

At any time after the expiration of five years from the date of entry into force of this Convention any Contracting State may, by giving written notice to the Depositary Government, withdraw from this Convention.

The withdrawal shall take effect for such Contracting State on the thirty-first of December of the year which follows the year in which the Depositary Government was notified of the withdrawal.

Article XX

1. The Depositary Government shall inform all Signatory and Acceding States:

a) of signatures of this Convention and deposit of each instrument of ratification, approval or accession, as well as of submitted declarations,

b) of the date of entry into force of this Convention,

c) of proposals relating to amendments to the Convention, notifications of acceptance and of the entry into force of such amendments,

d) of notifications of withdrawal.

2. The original of this Convention shall be deposited with the Government of the Polish People's Republic which shall transmit certified copies thereof to the Government of all Signatory States and of all States which accede to this Convention.

3. The Depositary Governments shall register this Convention with the Secretariat of the United Nations.

In Witness Whereof the undersigned Plenipotentiaries, being duly authorized thereto, have signed this Convention.

Done at Gdansk this thirteenth day of September, one thousand nine hundred and seventy three, in a single copy drawn up in the Danish, Finnish, German, Polish, Russian, Swedish and English languages, each text being equally authentic.

INTERNATIONAL CONVENTION FOR THE PREVENTION OF POLLUTION FROM SHIPS, 1973 [59]

London, 2 November 1973

The Parties to the Convention,

Being conscious of the need to preserve the human environment in general and the marine environment in particular,

Recognizing that deliberate, negligent or accidental release of oil and other harmful substances from ships constitutes a serious source of pollution,

Recognizing also the importance of the International Convention for the Prevention of Polution of the Sea by Oil, 1954, as being the first multilateral instrument to be concluded with the prime objective of protecting the environment, and appreciating the significant contribution which that Convention has made in preserving the seas and coastal environment from pollution,

Desiring to achieve the complete elimination of intentional pollution of the marine environment by oil and other harmful substances and the minimization of accidental discharge of such substances,

Considering that this object may best be achieved by establishing rules not limited to oil pollution having a universal purport,

Have agreed as follows:

Article 1

GENERAL OBLIGATIONS UNDER THE CONVENTION

1. The Parties to the Convention undertake to give effect to the provisions of the present Convention and those Annexes thereto by which they are bound, in order to prevent the pollution of the marine environment by the discharge of harmful substances or effluents containing such substances in contravention of the Convention.

2. Unless expressly provided otherwise, a reference to the present Convention constitutes at the same time a reference to its Protocol and to the Annexes.

Article 2

DEFINITIONS

For the purposes of the present Convention, unless expressly provided otherwise:

1. "Regulations" means the Regulations contained in the Annexes to the present Convention.

2. "Harmful substance" means any substance which, if introduced into the sea, is liable to create hazards to human health, to harm living resources and marine life, to damage amenities or to interfere with other legitimate uses of the sea, and includes any substance subject to control by the present Convention.

3. *a*) "Discharge", in relation to harmful substances or effluents containing such substances, means any release howsoever caused from a ship and includes any escape, disposal, spilling, leaking, pumping, emitting or emptying;

b) "Discharge" does not include:

(i) dumping within the meaning of the Convention on the Prevention of Marine Pollution by Dumping of Wastes and Other Matter, done at London on 13 November 1972; or

(ii) release of harmful substances directly arising from the exploration, exploitation and associated off-shore processing of sea-bed mineral resources; or

(iii) release of harmful substances for purpose of legitimate scientific research into pollution abatement or control.

4. "Ship" means a vessel of any type whatsoever operating in the marine environment and includes hydrofoil boats, air-cushion vehicles, submersibles, floating craft and fixed or floating platforms.

5. "Administration" means the Government of the State under whose authority the ship is operating. With respect to a ship entitled to fly a flag of any State, the Administration is the Government of that State. With respect to fixed or floating platforms engaged in exploration and exploitation of the sea-bed and subsoil thereof adjacent to the coast over which the coastal State exercises sovereign rights for the purposes of exploration and exploitation of their natural resources, the Administration is the Government of the coastal State concerned.

6. "Incident" means an event involving the actual or probable discharge into the sea of a harmful substance, or effluents containing such a substance.

7. "Organization" means the Inter-Governmental Maritime Consultative Organization.

Article 3

APPLICATION

1. The present Convention shall apply to:

a) ships entitled to fly the flag of a Party to the Convention; and

b) ships not entitled to fly the flag of a Party but which operate under the authority of a Party.

2. Nothing in the present Article shall be construed as derogating from or extending the sovereign rights of the Parties under international law over the sea-bed and subsoil thereof adjacent to their coasts for the purposes of exploration and exploitation of their natural resources.

3. The present Convention shall not apply to any warship, naval auxiliary or other ship owned or operated by a State and used, for the time being only on government non-commercial service. However, each Party shall ensure by the adoption of appropriate measures not impairing the operations or operational capabilities of such ships owned or operated by it, that such ships act in a manner consistent, so far as is reasonable and

practiable, with the present Convention.

Article 4

VIOLATION

1. Any violation of the requirements of the present Convention shall be prohibited and sanctions shall be established therefor under the law of the Administration of the ship concerned wherever the violation occurs. If the Adminsitration is informed of such a violation and is satisfied that sufficient evidence is available to enable proceedings to be brought in respect of the alleged violation, it shall cause such proceedings to be taken as soon as possible, in accordance with its law.

2. Any violation of the requirements of the present Convention within the jurisdiction of any Party to the Convention shall be prohibited and sanctions shall be established therefore under the law of that Party. Whenever and violation occurs, the Party shall either:

a) cause proceedings to be taken in accordance with its law; or

b) furnish to the Administration of the ship such information and evidence as may be in its possession that a violation has occurred.

3. Where information or evidence with respect to any violation of the present Convention by a ship is furnished to the Administration of that ship, the Administration shall promptly inform the Party which has furnished the information or evidence, and the Organization, of the action taken.

4. The penalties specified under the law of a Party pursuant to the present Article shall be adequate in severity to discharge violations of the present Convention and shall be equally severe irrespective of where the violations occur.

Article 5

CERTIFICATES AND SPECIAL RULES ON INSPECTION OF SHIPS

1. Subject to the provisions of paragraph (2) of the present Article a certificate issued under the authority of a Party to the Convention in accordance with the provisions of the Regulations shall be accepted by the other Parties and regarded for all purposes covered by the present Convention as having the same validity as a certificate issued by them.

2. A ship required to hold a certificate in accordance with the provisions of the Regulations is subject, while in the ports or off-shore terminals under the jurisdiction of a Party, to inspection by officers duly authorized by that Party. Any such inspection shall be limited to verfying that there is on board a valid certificate, unless there are clear grounds for believing that the condition of the ship or its equipment does not correspond substantially with the particulars of that certificate. In that case, or if the ship does not carry a valid certificate the Party carrying out the inspection shall take such steps as will ensure that the ship shall not sail until it can proceed to sea without presenting an unreasonable threat of harm to the marine environment. That Party may, however, grant such a ship permission to leave the port or off-shore terminal for the purpose of proceedings to the nearest appropriate repair yard available.

3. If a Party denies a foreign ship entry to the ports or off-shore terminals under its jurisdiction or takes any action against such a ship for the reason that the ship does not comply with the provisions of the present Convention, the Party shall immediately inform the consul or diplomatic representative of the Party whose flag the ship is entitled to fly, or if this is not possible, the Administration of the ship concerned. Before denying entry or taking such action the Party may request consultation with the Administration of the ship concerned. Information shall also be given to the Administration when a ship does not carry a valid certificate in accordance with the provisions of the Regulations.

4. With respect to the ships of non-Parties to the Convention, Parties shall apply the requirements of the present Convention as may be necessary to ensure that no more favourable treatment is given to such ships.

Article 6

DETECTION OF VIOLATIONS AND ENFORCEMENT OF THE CONVENTION

1. Parties to the Convention shall co-operate in the detection of violations and the enforcement of the provisions of the present Convention, using all appropriate and practicable measures of detection and environmental monitoring, adequate procedures for reporting and accumulation of evidence.

2. A ship to which the present Convention applies may, in any port or off-shore terminal of a Party, be subject to inspection by officers appointed or authorized by that Party for the purpose of verifying whether the ship has discharged any harmful substances in violation of the provisions of the Regulations. If an inspection indicates a violation of the Convention, a report shall be forwarded to the Administration for any appropriate action.

3. Any Party shall furnish to the Administration evidence, if any, that the ship had discharged harmful substances in violation of the provisions of the Regulations. If it is practicable to do so, the competent authority of the former Party shall notify the Master of the ship of the alleged violation.

4. Upon receiving such evidence, the Administration so informed shall investigate the matter, and may request the other Party to furnish further or better evidence of the alleged contravention. If the Administration is satisfied that sufficient evidence is available to enable proceedings to be brought in respect of the alleged violation, it shall cause such proceedings to be taken in accordance with its law as soon as possible. The Administration shall promptly inform the Party which has reported the alleged

violation, as well as the Organization, of the action taken.

5. A Party may also inspect a ship to which the present Convention applies when it enters the ports or off-shore terminals under its jurisdiction, if a request for an investigation is received from any Party together with sufficient evidence that the ship has discharged harmful substances or effluents containing such substances in any place. The report of such investigation shall be sent to the Party requesting it and to the Administration so that the appropriate action may be taken under the present Convention.

Article 7

UNDUE DELAY TO SHIPS

1. All possible efforts shall be made to avoid a ship being unduly detained or delayed under Article 4, 5, or 6 of the present Convention.

2. When a ship is unduly detained or delayed under Article 4, 5, 6 of the present Convention, it shall be entitled to compensation for any loss or damage suffered.

Article 8

REPORTS ON INCIDENTS INVOLVING HARMFUL SUBSTANCES

1. A report of an incident shall be made without delay to the fullest extent possible in accordance with the provisions of Protocol I to the present Convention.

2. Each Party to the Convention shall:

a) make all arrangements necessary for an appropriate officer or agency to receive and process all reports on incidents; and

b) notify the Organization with complete details of such arrangements for circulation to other Parties and Member States of the Organization.

3. Whenever a Party receives a report under the provisions of the present Article, the Party shall relay the report without delay to:

a) the Administration of the ship involved; and

b) any other State which may be affected.

4. Each Party to the Convention undertakes to issue instructions to its maritime inspection vessels and aircraft and to other appropriate services to report to its authorities any incident referred to in Protocol I to the present Convention. That Party shall, if it considers it apporpriate, report accordingly to the Organization and to any other party concerned.

Article 9

OTHER TREATIES AND INTERPRETATION

1. Upon its entry into force, the present Convention supersedes the International Convention for the Prevention of Pollution of the Sea by Oil, 1954, as amended, as between Parties to that Convention.

2. Nothing in the present Convention shall prejudice the codification and development of the law of the sea by the United Nations Conference on the Law of the Sea convened pursuant to Resolution 2750 C (XXV) of the General Assembly of the United Nations nor the present or future claims and legal views of any State concerning the law of the sea and the nature and extent of coastal and flag State jurisdiction.

3. The term "jurisdiction" in the present Convention shall be construed in the light of international law in force at the time of application or interpretation of the present Convention.

Article 10

SETTLEMENT OF DISPUTES

Any dispute between two or more Parties to the Convention concerning the interpretation or application of the present Convention shall, if settlement by negotiation between the Parties involved has not been possible, and if these Parties do not otherwise agree, be submitted upon request of any of them to arbitration as set out in Protocol II to the present Convention.

Article 11

COMMUNICATION OF INFORMATION

1. The Parties to the Convention undertake to communicate to the Organization:

a) the text of laws, orders, decrees and regulations and other instruments which have been promulgated on the various matters within the scope of the present Convention;

b) a list of non-governmental agencies which are authorized to act on their behalf in matters relating to the design, construction and equipment of ships carrying harmful substances in accordance with the provisions of the Regulations;

c) a sufficient number of specimens of their certificates issued under the provisions of the Regulations;

d) a list of reception facilities including their location, capacity and available facilities and other characteristics;

e) official reports or summaries of official reports in so far as they show the results of the application of the present Convention; and

f) an annual statistical report, in a form standardized by the Organization, of penalties actually imposed for infringement of the present Convention.

2. The Organization shall notify Parties of the receipt of any communications under the present Article and circulate to all Parties any information communicated to it under sub-paragraphs (1) (*b*) to (*f*) of the present Article.

Article 12

CASUALTIES TO SHIPS

1. Each Administration undertakes to conduct an investigation of any casualty occuring to any of its ships subject to the provisions of the Regulations if such casualty has produced a major deleterious effect upon the marine environment.

2. Each Party to the Convention undertakes to supply the Organization with information concerning the findings of such investigation,

when it judges that such information may assist in determining what changes in the present Convention might be desirable.

Article 13

SIGNATURES, RATIFICATION, ACCEPTANCE, APPROVAL AND ACCESSION

1. The present Convention shall remain open for signature at the Headquarters of the Organization from 15 January 1974 until 31 December 1974 and shall thereafter remain open for accession. States may become Parties to the present Convention by:

a) signature without reservation as to ratification, acceptance or approval; or

b) signature subject to ratification, acceptance or approval, followed by ratification, acceptance or approval; or

c) accession.

2. Ratification, acceptance, approval or accession shall be effected by the deposit of an instrument to that effect with the Secretary-General of the Organization.

3. The Secretary-General of the Organization shall inform all States which have signed the present Convention or acceded to it of any signature or of the deposit of any new instrument of ratification, acceptance, approval or accession and the date of its deposit.

Article 14

OPTIONAL ANNEXES

1. A State may at the time of signing, ratifying, accepting, approving or acceding to the present Convention declare that it does not accept any one or all of Annexes III, IV, and V (hereinafter referred to as "Optional Annexes") of the present Convention. Subject to the above, Parties to the Convention shall be bound by any Annex in its entirety.

2. A State which has declared that it is not bound by an Optional Annex may at any time accept such Annex by depositing with the Organization an instrument of the kind referred to in Article 13 (2).

3. A State which makes a declaration under paragraph (1) of the present Article in respect of an Optional Annex and which has not subsequently accepted that Annex in accordance with paragraph (2) of the present Article shall not be under any obligation nor entitled to claim any privileges under the present Convention in respect of matters related to such Annex and all reference to Parties in the present Convention shall include that State in so far as matters related to such Annex are concerned.

4. The Organization shall inform the States which have signed or acceded to the present Convention of any declaration under the present Article as well as the receipt of any instrument deposited in accordance with the provisions of paragraph (2) of the present Article.

Article 15

ENTRY INTO FORCE

1. The Convention shall enter into force twelve months after the date on which not less than 15 States, the combined merchant fleets of which constitute not less than fifty per cent of the gross tonnage of the world's merchant shipping, have become parties to it in accordance with Article 13.

2. An Optional Annex shall enter into force twelve months after the date on which the conditions stipulated in paragraph (1) of the present Article have been satisfied in relation to that Annex.

3. The Organization shall inform the States which have signed the present Convention or acceded to it of the date on which it enters into force and of the date on which the Optional Annex enters into force in accordance with paragraph (2) of the present Article.

4. For States which have deposited an instrument of ratification, acceptance, approval or accession in respect of the present Convention or any Optional Annex after the requirements for entry into force thereof have been met but prior to the date of entry into force, the ratification, acceptance, approval or accession shall take effect on the date of entry into force of the Convention or such Annex or three months after the date of deposit of the instrument whichever is the later date.

5. For States which have deposited an instrument of ratification, acceptance, approval or accession after the date on which the Convention or an Optional Annex entered into force, the Convention or the Optional Annex shall become effective three months after the date of deposit of the instrument.

6. After the date on which all the conditions required under Article 16 to bring an amendment to the present Convention or an Optional Annex into force have been fulfilled, any instrument of ratification, acceptance, approval or accession deposited shall apply to the Convention or Annex as amended.

Article 16

AMENDMENTS

1. The present Convention may be amended by any of the procedures specified in the following paragraphs.

2. Amendments after consideration by the Organization:

a) any amendment proposed by a Party to the Convention shall be submitted to the Organization and circulated by its Secretary-General to all Members of the Organization and all Parties at least six months prior to its consideration;

b) any amendment proposed and circulated as above shall be submitted to an appropriate body by the Organization for consideration;

c) Parties to the Convention, whether or not Members of the Organization, shall be entitled to participate in the proceedings of the appropriate body;

d) amendments shall be adopted by a two-thirds majority of only the Parties to the Convention present and voting;

e) if adopted in accordance with sub-paragraph *c*) above, amendments shall be communicated by the Secretary-General of the Organization to all the Parties to the Convention for acceptance;

f) an amendment shall be deemed to have been accepted in the following circumstances:

(i) an amendment to an Article of the Convention shall be deemed to have been accepted on the date on which it is accepted by two-thirds of the Parties, the combined merchant fleets of which constitute not less than fifty per cent of the gross tonnage of the world's merchant fleet;

(ii) an amendment to an Annex to the Convention shall be deemed to have been accepted in accordance with the procedure specified in sub-paragraph (*f*) (iii) unless the appropriate body, at the time of its adoption, determines that the amendment shall be deemed to have been accepted on the date on which it is accepted by two-thirds of the Parties, the combined merchant fleets of which constitute not less than fifty per cent of the gross tonnage of the world's merchant fleet. Nevertheless, at any time before the entry into force of an amendment to an Annex to the Convention, a Party may notify the Secretary-General of the Organization that its express approval will be necessary before the amendment enters into force for it. The latter shall bring such notification and the date of its receipt to the notice of Parties.

(iii) an amendment to an Appendix to an Annex to the Convention shall be deemed to have been accepted at the end of a period to be determined by the appropriate body at the time of its adoption, which period shall be not less than ten months, unless within that period an objection is communicated to the Organization by not less than one-third of the Parties or by the Parties the combined merchant fleets of which constitute not less than fifty per cent of the gross tonnage of the world's merchant fleet whichever condition is fulfilled;

(iv) an amendment to Protocol I to the Convention shall be subject to the same procedures as for the amendments to the Annexes to the Convention, as provided for in sub-paragraphs (*f*) (ii) or (*f*) (iii), above;

(v) an amendment to Protocol II to the Convention shall be subject to the same procedures as for the amendments to an Article of the Convention, as provided for in sub-paragraph (*f*) (i) above;

g) the amendment shall enter into force under the following conditions:

(i) in the case of an amendment to an Article of the Convention, to Protocol II, or to Protocol I or to an Annex to the Convention not under the procedure specified in sub-paragraph (*f*) (iii), the amendment accepted in conformity with the foregoing provisions shall enter into force six months after the date of its acceptance with respect to the Parties which have declared that they have accepted it;

(ii) in the case of an amendment to Protocol I, to an Appendix to an Annex or to an Annex to the Convention under the procedure specified in sub-paragraph (*f*) (iii), the amendment deemed to have been accepted in accordance with the foregoing conditions shall enter into force six months after its acceptance for all the Parties with the exception of those which, before that date, have made a declaration that they do not accept it or a declaration under sub-paragraph (*f*) (ii), that their express approval is necessary.

3. Amendment by a Conference.

a) Upon the request of a Party, concurred in by at least one-third of the Parties, the Organization shall convene a Conference of Parties to the Convention to consider amendments to the present Convention.

b) Every amendment by such a Conference by a two-thirds majority of those present and voting of the Parties shall be communicated by the Secretary-General of the Organization to all Contracting Parties for their acceptance.

c) Unless the Conference decides otherwise, the amendment shall be deemed to have been accepted and to have entered into force in accordance with the procedures specified for that purpose in paragraph (2) (*f*) and (*g*) above.

4. *a*) In the case of an amendment to an Optional Annex, a reference in the present Article to a "Party to the Convention" shall be deemed to mean a reference to a Party bound by that Annex.

b) Any Party which has declined to accept an amendment to an Annex shall be treated as a non-Party only for the purpose of application of that Amendment.

5. The adoption and entry into force of a new Annex shall be subject to the same procedures as for the adoption and entry into force of an Article of the Convention.

6. Unless expressly provided otherwise, any amendment to the present Convention made under this Article, which relates to the structure of a ship, shall apply only to ships for which the building contract is placed, or in the absence of a building contract, the keel of which is laid, on or after the date on which the amendment comes into force.

7. Any amendment to a Protocol or to an Annex shall relate to the substance of that Protocol or Annex and shall be consistent with the Articles of the present Convention.

8. The Secretary-General of the Organization shall inform all Parties of any amendments which enter into force under the present Article, together with the date on which each such amendment enters into force.

9. Any declaration of acceptance or of objection to an amendment under the present Article shall be notified in writing to the Secretary-General of the Organization. The latter shall bring such notification and the date of its receipt to the notice of the Parties to the Convention.

Article 17

PROMOTION OF TECHNICAL CO-OPERATION

The Parties to the Convention shall promote, in consultation with the Organization and other international bodies, with assistance and co-ordination by the Executive Director of the United Nations Environment Programme, support for those Parties which request technical assistance for:

a) the training of scientific and technical personnel;

b) the supply of necessary equipment and facilities for reception and monitoring;

c) the facilitation of other measures and arrangements to prevent or mitigate pollution of the marine environment by ships; and

d) the encouragement of research;

preferably within the countries concerned, so furthering the aims and purposes of the present Convention.

Article 18

DENUNCIATION

1. The present Convention or any Optional Annex may be denounced by any Party to the Convention at any time after the expiry of five years from the date on which the Convention or such Annex enters into force for that Party.

2. Denunciation shall be effected by notification in writing to the Secretary-General of the Organization who shall inform all the other Parties of any such notification received and of the date of its receipt as well as the date on which such denunciation takes effect.

3. A denunciation shall take effect twelve months after receipt of the notification of denunciation by the Secretary-General of the Organization or after the expiry of any other longer period which may be indicated in the notification.

Article 19

DEPOSIT AND REGISTRATION

1. The present Convention shall be deposited with the Secretary-General of the Organization who shall transmit certified true copies thereof to all States which have signed the present Convention or acceded to it.

2. As soon as the present Convention enters into force, the text shall be transmitted by the Secretary-General of the Organization to the Secretary-General of the United Nations for registration and publication, in accordance with Article 102 of the Charter of the United Nations.

Article 20

LANGUAGES

The present Convention is established in a single copy in the English, French, Russian and Spanish languages, each text being equally authentic. Official translations in the Arabic, German, Italian and Japanese languages shall be prepared and deposited with the signed original.

In Witness Whereof the undersigned * being duly authorized by their respective Governments for that purpose have signed the present Convention.

Done at London this second day of November, one thousand nine hundred and seventy-three.

* Signatures omitted.

PROTOCOL I

Provisions Concerning Reports on Incidents Involving Harmful Substances (in accordance with Article 8 of the Convention)

Article I

DUTY TO REPORT

1. The Master of a ship involved in an incident referred to in Article III of this Protocol, or other person having charge of the ship, shall report the particulars of such incident without delay and to the fullest extent possible in accordance with the provisions of this Protocol.

2. In the event of the ship referred to in paragraph (1) of the present Article being abandoned, or in the event of a report from such ship being incomplete or unobtainable, the owner, charterer, manager or operator of the ship, or their agents shall, to the fullest extent possible assume the obligations placed upon the Master under the provisions of this Protocol.

Article II

METHODS OF REPORTING

1. Each report shall be made by radio whenever possible, but in any case by the fastest channels available at the time the report is made. Reports made by radio shall be given the highest possible priority.

2. Reports shall be directed to the appropriate officer or agency specified in paragraph (2)(*a*) of Article 8 of the Convention.

Article III

WHEN TO MAKE REPORTS

The report shall be made whenever an incident involves:

a) a discharge other than as permitted under the present Convention; or

b) a discharge permitted under the present Convention by virtue of the fact that:

(i) it is for the purpose of securing the safety of a ship or saving life at sea; or

(ii) it results from damage to the ship or its equipment; or

c) a discharge of a harmful substance for the purpose of combating a specific pollution incident or for purposes of legitimate scientific research into pollution abatement or control; or

d) the probability of a discharge referred to in sub-paragraphs (*a*), (*b*) or (*c*) of this Article.

Article IV

CONTENTS OF REPORT

1. Each report shall contain in general:

a) the identity of the ship;

b) the time and date of the occurence of the incident;

c) the geographic position of the ship when the incident occurred;

d) the wind and sea conditions prevailing at the time of the incident; and

2. Each report shall contain, in particular:

a) a clear indication or description of the harmful substances involved, including, if possible, the correct technical names of such substances (trade names should not be used in place of the correct technical names);

b) a statement or estimate of quantities, concentrations and likely conditions of harmful substances discharged or likely to be discharged into the sea;

c) where relevant, a description of the packaging and identifying marks; and

d) if possible the name of the consignor, consignee or manufacturer.

3. Each report shall clearly indicate whether the harmful substance discharged, or likely to be discharged is oil, a noxious liquid substance, a noxious solid substance or a noxious gaseous substance and whether such substance was or is carried in bulk or contained in packaged form, freight containers, portable tanks, or road and rail tank wagons.

4. Each report shall be supplemented as necessary by any other relevant information requested by a recipient of the report or which the person sending the report deems appropriate.

Article V

SUPPLEMENTARY REPORT

Any person who is obliged under the provisions of this Protocol to send a report shall, when possible:

a) supplement the initial report, as necessary, with information concerning further developments; and

b) comply as fully as possible with requests from affected States for additional information concerning the incident.

PROTOCOL II

Arbitration
(in accordance with Article 10 of the Convention)

Article I

Arbitration procedure, unless the Parties to the dispute decide otherwise, shall be in accordance with the rules set out in this Protocol.

Article II

1. An Arbitration Tribunal shall be established upon the request of one Party to the Convention addressed to another in application of Article 10 of the present Convention. The request for arbitration shall consist of a statement of the case together with any supporting documents.

2. The requesting Party shall inform the Secretary-General of the Organization of the fact that it has applied for the establishment of a Tribunal, of the names of the Parties to the dispute, and of the Articles of the Convention or Regulations over which there is in its opinion disagreement concerning their interpretation or application. The Secretary-General shall transmit this information to all Parties.

Article III

The Tribunal shall consist of three members: one Arbitrator nominated by each Party to the dispute and a third Arbitrator who shall be nominated by agreement between the two first named, and shall act as its Chairman.

Article IV

1. If, at the end of a period of sixty days from the nomination of the second Arbitrator, the Chairman of the Tribunal shall not have been nominated, the Secretary-General of the Organization upon request of either Party shall within a furhter period of sixty days proceed to such nomination, selecting him from a list of qualified persons previously drawn up by the Council of the Organization.

2. If, within a period of sixty days from the date of the receipt of the request, one of the Parties shall not have nominated the member of the Tribunal for whose designation it is responsible, the other Party may directly inform the Secretary-General of the Organization who shall nominate the Chairman of the Tribunal within a period of sixty days, selecting him from the list prescribed in paragraph (1) of the present Article.

3. The Chairman of the Tribunal shall, upon nomination, request the Party which has not provided an Arbitrator, to do so in the same manner and under the same conditions. If the Party does not make the required nomination, the Chairman of the Tribunal shall request the Secretary-General of the Organization to make the nomination in the form and conditions prescribed in the preceding paragraph.

4. The Chairman of the Tribunal, if nominated under the provisions of the present Article, shall not be or have been a national of one of the Parties concerned, except with the consent of the other Party.

5. In the case of the decease or default of an Arbitrator for whose nomination one of the Parties is responsible, the said Party shall nominate a replacement within a period of sixty days from the date of decease or default. Should the said Party not make the nomination, the arbitration shall proceed under the remaining Arbitrators. In case of the decease or default of the Chairman of the Tribunal, a replacement shall be nominated in accordance with the provisions of Article III above, or in the absence of agreement between the members of the Tribunal within a period of sixty days of the decease or default, according to the provisions of the present Article.

Article V

The Tribunal may hear and determine counter-claims arising directly out of the subject matter of this dispute.

Article VI

Each Party shall be responsible for the remuneration of its Arbitrator and connected costs and for the costs entailed by the preparation of its own case. The remuneration of the Chairman of the Tribunal and of all general expenses incurred by the Arbitration shall be borne equally by the Parties. The Tribunal shall keep a record of all its expenses and shall furnish a final statement thereof.

Article VII

Any Party to the Convention which has an interest of a legal nature and which may be affected by the decision in the case may, after giving written notice to the Parties which have originally initiated the procedure, join in the arbitration procedure with the consent of the Tribunal.

Article VIII

Any Arbitration Tribunal established under the provision of the present Protocol shall decide its own rules of procedure.

Article IX

1. Decisions of the Tribunal both as to its procedure and its place of meeting and as to any question laid before it, shall be taken by majority votes of its members; the absence or abstention of one of the members of the Tribunal for whose nomination the Parties were responsible, shall not constitute an impediment to the Tribunal reaching a decision. In cases of equal voting, the vote of the Chairman shall be decisive.

2. The Parties shall facilitate the work of the Tribunal and in particular, in accordance with their legislation, and using all means at their disposal:

a) provide the Tribunal with the necessary documents and information;

b) enable the Tribunal to enter their territory, to hear witnesses or experts, and to visit the scene.

3. Absence or default of one Party shall not constitute an impediment to the procedure.

Article X

1. The Tribunal shall render its award within a period of five months from the time it is established unless it decides, in the case of necessity, to extend the time limit for a further period but not exceeding three months. The award of the Tribunal shall be accompanied by a statement of reasons. It shall be final and without appeal and shall be communicated to the Secretary-General of the Organization. The Parties shall immediately comply with the award.

2. Any controversy which may arise between the Parties as regards interpretation or execution of the award may be submitted by either Party for judgement to the Tribunal which made the award, or, if it is not available to another Tribunal constituted for this purpose, in the same manner as the original Tribunal.

ANNEX I

REGULATIONS FOR THE PREVENTION OF POLLUTION BY OIL

Chapter I — General

Regulation 1

DEFINITIONS

For the purposes of this Annex:

1. "Oil" means petroleum in any form including crude oil, fuel oil, sludge, oil refuse and refined products (other than petrochemicals which are subject to the provisions of Annex II of the present Convention) and, without limiting the generality of the foregoing, includes the substances listed in Appendix I to this Annex.

2. "Oily mixture" means a mixture with any oil content.

3. "Oil fuel" means any oil used as fuel in connexion with the propulsion and auxiliary machinery of the ship in which such oil is carried.

4. "Oil tanker" means a ship constructed or adapted primarily to carry oil in bulk in its cargo spaces and includes combination carriers and any "chemical tanker" as defined in Annex II of the present Convention when it is carrying a cargo or part cargo of oil in bulk.

5. "Combination carrier" means a ship designed to carry either oil or solid cargoes in bulk.

6. "New ship" means a ship:

a) for which the building contract is placed after 31 December 1975; or

b) in the absence of a building contract, the keel of which is laid or which is at a similar stage of construction after 30 June 1976; or

c) the delivery of which is after 31 December 1979; or

d) which has undergone a major conversion:

(i) for which the contract is placed after 31 December 1975; or

(ii) in the absence of a contract, the construction work of which is begun after 30 June 1976; or

(iii) which is completed after 31 December 1979.

7. "Existing ship" means a ship which is not a new ship.

8. "Major conversion" means a conversion of an existing ship:

a) which substantially alters the dimensions or carrying capacity of the ship; or

b) which changes the type of the ship; or

c) the intent of which in the opinion of the Administration is substantially to prolong its life; or

d) which otherwise so alters the ship that if it were

a new ship, it would become subject to relevant provisions of the present Convention not applicable to it as an existing ship.

9. "Nearest land". The term "from the nearest land" means from the baseline from which the territorial sea of the territory in question is established in accordance with international law, except that for the purposes of the present Convention "from the nearest land" off the north eastern coast of Australia shall mean from a line drawn from a point on the coast of Australia in latitude 11°00′ South, longitude 142°08′ East to a point in latitude 10°35′ South,

longitude 141°55′ East — thence to a point latitude 10°00′ South,

longitude 142°00' East, thence to a point latitude 9°10′ South,

longitude 143°52′ East, thence to a point latitude 9°00' South,

longitude 144°00′ East, thence to a point latitude 15°′ South,

longitude 147°00′ East, thence to a point latitude 21°00′ South,

longitude 153°00′ East, thence to a point on the coast of Australia in latitude 24° 42° South, longitude 153°15′ East.

10. "Special area" means a sea where for recognized technical reasons in relation to its oceanographical and ecological condition and to the particular character of its traffic the adoption of special mandatory methods for the prevention of sea pollution by oil is required. Special areas shall include those listed in Regulation 10 of this Annex.

11. "Instantaneous rate of discharge of oil content" means the rate of discharge of oil litres per hour at any instant divided by the speed of the ship in knots at the same instant.

12. "Tank" means an enclosed space which is formed by the permanent structure of a ship and which is designed for the carriage of liquid in bulk.

13. "Wing tank" means any tank adjacent to the side shell plating.

14. "Centre tank" means any tank inboard of a longitudinal bulkhead.

15. "Slop tank" means a tank specifically designated for the collection of tank drainings, tank washings and other oily mixtures.

16. "Clean ballast" means the ballast in a tank which since oil was last carried therein, has been so cleaned that effluent therefrom if it were discharged from a ship which is stationary into clean calm water on a clear day would not produce visible traces of oil on the surface of the water or upon adjoining shorelines or cause a sludge or emulsion to be deposited beneath the surface of the water or upon adjoining shorelines. If the ballast is discharged through an oil discharge monitoring and control system approved by the Administration, evidence based on such a system to the effect that the oil content of the effluent did not exceed 15 parts per million shall be determinative that the ballast was clean, notwithstanding the presence of visible traces.

17. "Segregated ballast" means the ballast water introduced into a tank which is completely separated from the cargo oil and oil fuel system and which is permanently allocated to the carriage of ballast or to the carriage of ballast or cargoes other than oil or noxious substances as variously defined in the Annexes of the present Convention.

18. "Length" (*L*) means 96 per cent of the total length on a waterline at 85 per cent of the least moulded depth measured from the top of the keel, or the length from the foreside of the stem to the axis of the rudder stock on that waterline, if that be greater. In ships designed with a rake of keel the waterline on which this length is measured shall be parallel to the designed waterline. The length (*L*) shall be measured in meters.

19. "Forward and after perpendiculars" shall be taken at the forward and after ends of the length (*L*). The forward perpendicular shall coincide with the foreside of the stem on the waterline on which the length is measured.

20. "Amidships" is at the middle of the length (*L*).

21. "Breadth" (*B*) means the maximum breadth of the ship, measured amidships to the moulded line of the frame in a ship with a metal shell and to the outer surface of the hull in a ship with a shell of any other material. The breadth (*B*) shall be measured in meters.

22. "Deadweight" (*DW*) means the difference in metric tons between the displacement of a ship in water of specific gravity of 1.025 at the load waterline corresponding to the assigned number freeboard and the lightweight of the ship.

23. "Lightweight" means the displacement of a ship in metric tons without cargo, oil fuel, lubricating oil, ballast water, fresh water and feedwater in tanks, consumable stores, passengers and their effects.

24. "Permeability" of a space means the ratio of the volume within that space which is assumed to be occupied by water to the total volume of that space.

25. "Volumes" and "areas" in a ship shall be calculated in all cases to moulded lines.

Regulation 2

APPLICATION

1. Unless expressly provided otherwise, the provisions of this Annex shall apply to all ships.

2. In ships other than oil tankers fitted with cargo spaces which are constructed and utilized to carry oil in bulk of an aggregate capacity of 200 cubic meters or more, the requirements of Regulations 9, 10, 14, 15 (1), (2) and (3), 18, 20 and 24 (4) of this Annex for oil tankers shall apply to the construction and operation of those spaces, except that where such aggregate capacity is less than 1,000 cubic metres the requirements of Regulation 15(4) of this Annex may apply in lieu of Regulation 15(1), (2) and (3).

3. Where a cargo subject to the provisions of Annex II of the present Convention is carried in a cargo space of an oil tanker, the appropriate requirements of Annex II of the present Convention shall also apply.

4. *a*) Any hydrofoil, air-cushion vehicle and other new type of vessel (near-surface craft, submarine craft, etc) whose constructional features are such as to render the application of any of the provisions of Chapters II and III of this Annex relating to construction and equipment unreasonable or impracticable may be exempted by the Administration from such provisions, provided that the construction and equipment of that ship provides equivalent protection against pollution by oil, having regard to the service for which it is intended.

b) Particulars of any such exemption granted by the Administration shall be indicated in the Certificate referred to in Regulation 5 of this Annex.

c) The Administration which allows any such exemption shall, as soon as possible, but not more than ninety days thereafter, communicate to the Organization particulars of same and the reasons therefor, which the Organization shall circulate to the Parties to the Convention for their information and appropriate action, if any.

Regulation 3

EQUIVALENTS

1. The Administration may allow any fitting, material, appliance or apparatus to be fitted in a ship as an alternative to that required by this Annex if such fitting, material, appliance or apparatus is at least as effective as that required by this Annex. This authority of the Administration shall not extend to subsitution of operational methods to effect the control of discharge of oil as equivalent to those design and construction features which are prescribed by Regulations in this Annex.

2. The Administration which allows a fitting, material, appliance or apparatus, as an alternative to that required by this Annex shall communicate to the Organization for circulation to the Parties to the Convention particulars thereof, for their information and appropriate action, if any.

Article 4

SURVEYS

1. Every oil tanker of 150 tons gross tonnage and above, and every other ship of 400 tons gross tonnage and above shall be subject to the surveys specified below:

a) An initial survey before the ship is put in service or before the Certificate required under Regulation 5 of this Annex is issued for the first time, which shall include a complete survey of its structure, equipment, fittings, arrangements and material in so far as the ship is covered by this Annex. This survey shall be such as to ensure that the structure, equipment, fittings, arrangements and material fully comply with the applicable requirements of this Annex.

b) Periodical surveys at intervals specified by the Administration, but not exceeding five years, which shall be such as to ensure that the structure, equipment, fittings, arrangements and material fully comply with the applicable requirements of this Annex. However, where the duration of the International Oil Pollution Certificate (1973) is extended as specified in Regulation 8 (3) or (4) of this Annex, the interval of the periodical survey may be extended correspondingly.

c) Intermediate surveys at intervals specified by the Administration but not exceeding thirty months, which shall be such as to ensure that the equipment and associated pump and piping systems, including oil discharge monitoring and control systems, oily-water separating equipment and oil filtering systems, fully comply with the applicable requirements of this Annex and are in good working order. Such intermediate surveys shall be endorsed on the International Oil Pollution Prevention Certificate (1973) issued under Regulation 5 of this Annex .

2. The Administration shall establish appropriate measures for ships which are not subject to the provisions of paragraph (1) of this Regulation in order to ensure that the applicable provisions of this Annex are complied with.

3. Surveys of the ship as regards enforcement of the provisions of this Annex shall be carried out by officers of the Administration. The Administration may, however, entrust the surveys either to surveyors nominated for the purpose or to organizations recognized by it. In every case the Administration concerned fully guarantees the completeness and efficiency of the surveys.

4. After any survey of the ship under this Regulation has been completed, no significant change shall be made in the structure, equipment, fittings, arrangements or material covered by the survey without the sanction of the Administration, except the direct replacement of such equipment or fittings.

Regulation 5

ISSUE OF CERTIFICATE

1. An International Oil Pollution Certificate (1973) shall be issued, after survey in accordance with the provisions of Regulation 4 of this Annex, to any oil tanker of 150 tons gross tonnage and above and any other ships of 400 tons gross tonnage and above which are engaged in voyages to ports or off-shore terminals under the jurisdiction of other Parties to the Convention. In the case of existing ships this requirement shall apply twelve months after the date of entry into force of the present Convention.

2. Such Certificate shall be issued either by the Administration or by any persons or organization duly authorized by it. In every case the Administration assumes full responsibility for the Certificate.

Regulation 6

ISSUE OF A CERTIFICATE BY ANOTHER GOVERNMENT

1. The Government of a Party to the Convention may, at the request of the Administration, cause a ship to be surveyed and, if satisfied that the provisions of this Annex are complied with, shall issue or authorize the issue of an International Oil Pollution Prevention Certificate (1973) to the ship in accordance with this Annex.

2. A copy of the Certificate and a copy of the survey report shall be transmitted as soon as possible to the requesting Administration.

3. A Certificate so issued shall contain a statement to the effect that it has been issued at the request of the Administration and it shall have the same force and receive the same force and receive the same recogimition as the Certificate issued under Regulation 5 of this Annex.

4. No International Oil Pollution Prevention Certificate (1973) shall be issued to a ship which is entitled to fly the flag of a State which is not a Party.

Regulation 7

FORM OF CERTIFICATE

The International Oil Pollution Prevention Certificate (1973) shall be drawn up in an official language of the issuing country in the form corresponding to the model given in Appendix II to this Annex. If the language used is neither English nor French, the text shall include a translation into one of these languages.

Regulation 8

DURATION OF CERTIFICATE

1. An International Oil Pollution Prevention Certificate (1973) shall be issued for a period specified by the Administration, which shall not exceed five years from the date of issue, except as provided in paragraphs (2), (3) and (4) of this Regulation.

2. If a ship at the time when the Certificate expires is not in a port or off-shore terminal under the jurisdiction of the Party to the Convention whose flag the ship is entitled to fly, the Certificate may be extended by the Administration, but such extension shall be granted only for the purpose of allowing the ship to complete its voyage to the State whose flag the ship is entitled to fly or in which it is to be surveyed and then only in cases where it appears proper and reasonable to do so.

3. No Certificate shall be thus extended for a period longer than five months and a ship to which such extension is granted shall not on its arrival in the State whose flag it is entitled to fly or the port in which it is to be surveyed, be entitled by virtue of such extension to leave that port or State without having obtained a new Certificate.

4. A Certificate which has not been extended under the provisions of paragraph (2) of this Regulation may be extended by the Administration for a period of grace of up to one month from the date of expiry stated on it.

5. A Certificate shall cease to be valid if significant alterations have taken place in the construction, equipment, fittings, arrangements, or material required without the sanction of the Administration, except the direct replacement of such equipment or fittings, or if intermediate surveys as specified by the Administration under Regulation 4(1)(c) of this Annex are not carried out.

6. A Certificate issued to a ship shall cease to be valid upon transfer of such a ship to the flag of another State, except as provided in paragraph (7) of this Regulation.

7. Upon transfer of a ship to the flag of another Party, the Certificate shall remain in force for a period not exceeding five months provided that it would not have expired before the end of that period, or until the Administration issues a replacement Certificate, whichever is earlier. As soon as possible after the transfer has taken place the Government of the Party whose flag the ship was formerly entitled to fly shall transmit to the Administration a copy of the Certificate carried by the ship before the transfer and, if availbale, a copy of the relevant survey report.

Chapter II

REQUIREMENTS FOR CONTROL OF OPERATIONAL POLLUTION

Regulation 9

CONTROL OF DISCHARGE OF OIL

1. Subject to the provisions of Regulations 10 and 11 of this Annex and paragraph (2) of this Regulation, any discharge into the sea of oil or oily mixtures from ships to which this Annex applies shall be prohibited except when all the following conditions are satisfied:

a) for an oil tanker, except as provided for in sub-paragraph (*b*) of this paragraph:

(i) the tanker is not within a special area;

(ii) the tanker is more than 50 nautical miles from the nearest land;

(iii) the tanker is proceeding en route;

(iv) the instantaneous rate of discharge of oil content does not exceed 60 litres per nautical mile;

(v) the total quantity of oil discharged into the sea does not exceed for existing tankers 1/15,000 of the total quantity of the particular cargo of which the residue formed a part, and for new tankers 1/30,000 of the total quantity of the particular cargo of which the residue formed a part; and

(vi) the tanker has in operation, except as provided for in Regulation 15(3) of this Annex, an oil discharge monitoring and control system and a slop tank arrangements as required by Regulation 15 of this Annex;

b) from a ship of 400 tons gross tonnage and above other than an oil tanker and from machinery space bilges excluding cargo pump room bilges of an oil tanker unless mixed with oil cargo residue:

(i) the ship is not within a special area;

(ii) the ship is more than 12 nautical miles from the nearest land;

(iii) the ship is proceeding en route;

(iv) the oil content of the effluent is less than 100 parts per million; and

(v) the ship has in operation an oil discharge monitoring and control system, oily-water separating equipment, oil filtering system or other installation as required by Regulation 16 of this Annex.

2. In the case of a ship of less than 400 tons gross tonnage other than oil tanker whilst outside the special area, the Administration shall ensure that it is equipped as far as practicable and reasonable with installations to ensure the storage of oil residues on board and their discharge to reception facilities or into the sea in compliance with the requirements of paragraph (1) (*b*) of this Regulation.

3. Whenever visible traces of oil are observed on or below the surface of the water in the immediate vicinity of a ship or its wake, Governments of Parties to the Convention should, to the extent they are reasonably able to do so, promptly investigate the facts bearing on the issue of whether there has been a violation of the provisions of this Regulation or Regulation 10 of this Annex. The investigation should include, in particular, the wind and sea conditions, the track and speed of the ship, other possible sources of visible traces in the vicinity, and any relevant oil discharge records.

4. The provisions of paragraph (1) of this Regulation shall not apply to the discharge of clean or segregated ballast. The provisions of sub-paragraph (1)(*b*) of this Regulation shall not apply to the discharge of oily mixture which without dilution has an oil content not exceeding 15 parts per million.

5. No discharge into the sea shall contain chemicals or other substances in quantities or concentrations which are hazardous to the marine environment or chemicals or other substances introduced for the purpose of circumventing the conditions of discharge specified in this Regulation.

6. The oil residues which cannot be discharged into the sea in compliance with paragraphs (1), (2) and (4) of this Regulation shall be retained on board or discharged to reception facilities.

Regulation 10

METHODS FOR THE PREVENTION OF OIL POLLUTION FROM SHIPS WHILE OPERATING IN SPECIAL AREAS

1. For the purposes of this Annex the special areas are the Mediterranean Sea area, the Baltic Sea area, the Black Sea area and the "Gulfs area" which are defined as follows:

a) The Mediterranean Sea area means the Mediterranean Sea proper including the gulfs and seas therein with the boundary between the Mediterranean and the Black Sea constituted by the 41°N parallel and bounded to the west by the Straits of Gibraltar at the meridian of 5°36′ W.

b) The Baltic Sea area means the Baltic Sea proper with the Gulf of Bothnia, the Gulf of Finland and the entrance to the Baltic Sea bounded by the parallel of the Skaw in the Skagerrak at 57°44.8′ N.

c) The Black Sea area means the Black Sea proper with the boundary between the Mediterranean and the Black Sea constituted by the parallel 41° N.

d) The Red Sea area means the Red Sea proper including the Gulfs of Suez and Aqaba bounded at the South by the rhumb line between Ras si Ane (12° 8.5′ N, 43° 19.6′ E) and Husn Murad (12° 40.4′ N, 43° 30.2′ E).

e) The Gulfs area means the sea area located north west of the rhumb line between Ras al Hadd (22°30′ N, 59°48′ E) and RAs Al Fasteh (25°04′ N, 61°25′ E).

2. *a*) Subject to the provisions of Regulation 11 of this Annex, any discharge into the sea of oil or oily mixture from any oil tanker and any ship or 400 tons gross tonnage and above other than an oil tanker shall be prohibited, while in a special area.

b) Such ships while in a special area shall retain on board all oil drainage and sludge, dirty ballast and tank washing waters and discharge them only to reception facilities.

3. *a*) Subject to the provisions of Regulation 11 of this Annex, any discharge into the sea of oil or mixture from a ship of less than 400 tons gross tonnage, other than oil tanker, shall be prohibited while in a special area, except when the oil content of the effluent without dilution does not exceed 15 parts per million or alternatively when all of the following conditions are satisfied:

(i) the ship is proceeding en route;

(ii) the oil content of the effluent is less than 100 parts per million; and

(iii) the discharge is made as far as practicable from the land, but in no case less than 12 nautical miles from the nearest land.

b) No discharge into the sea shall contain chemicals or other substances in quantities or concentrations which are hazardous to the marine environment or chemicals or other substances introduced for the purpose of circumventing the conditions of discharge specified in this Regulation.

c) The oil residues which cannot be discharged into the sea in compliance with sub-paragraph (*a*) of this paragraph shall be retained on board or discharged to reception facilities.

4. The provisions of this Regulation shall not apply to the discharge of clean or segregated ballast.

5. Nothing in this Regulation shall prohibit a ship on a voyage only part of which is in a special area from discharging outside the special area in accordance with Regulation 9 of this Annex.

6. Whenever visible traces of oil are observed on or below the surface of the water in the immediate vicinity of a ship or its wake, the Governments of Parties to the Convention should, to the extent

they are reasonably able to do so, promptly investigate the facts bearing on the issue of whether there has been a violation of the provisions of this Regulation or Regulation 9 of this Annex. The investigation should include, in particular, the wind and sea conditions, the track and speed of the ship, other possible sources of the visible traces in the vicinity,and any relevant oil discharge records.

7. Reception facilities within special areas:

a) Mediterranean Sea, Black Sea and Baltic Sea areas:

(i) The Government of each Party to the Convention, the coastline of which borders on any given special area undertakes to ensure that not later than 1 January 1977 all oil loading terminals and repair ports within the special area are provided with facilities adequate for the reception and treatment of all the dirty ballast and tank washing water from oil tankers. In addition all ports within the special area shall be provided with adequate reception facilities for other residues and oily mixtures from all ships. Such facilities shall have adequate capacity to meet the needs of the ships using them without causing undue delay.

(ii) The Government of each Party having under its jurisdiction entrances to seawater courses with low depth contour which might require a reduction of draught by the discharge of ballast undertakes to ensure the provision of the facilities referred to in sub-paragraph (*a*)(i) of this paragraph but with the proviso that ships required to discharge slops or dirty ballast could be subject to some delay.

(iii) During the period between the entry into force of the present Convention (if earlier than 1 January 1977) and 1 January 1977 ships while navigating in the special areas shall comply with the requirements of Regulation 9 of this Annex. However, the Governments of Parties the coastlines of which border any of the special areas under this sub-paragraph may establish a date earlier than 1 January 1977, but after the date of entry into force of the present Convention, from which the requirements of this Regulation in respect of the special areas in question shall take effect:

(1) if all the reception facilities required have been provided by the date so established, and

(2) provided that the Parties concerned notify the Organization of the date so established at least six months in advance, for circulation to other Parties.

(iv) After 1 January 1977, or the date established in accordance with sub-paragraph (*a*)(iii) of this paragraph if earlier, each Party shall notify the Organization for transmission to the Contracting Governments concerned of all cases where the facilities are alleged to be inadequate.

b) Red Sea area and Gulfs area:

(i) The Government of each Party the coastline of which borders on the special areas undertakes to ensure that as soon as possible all oil loading terminals and repair ports within these special areas are provided with facilities adequate for the reception and treatment of all the dirty ballast and tank washing water from tankers. In addition all ports within the special area shall be provided with adequate reception facilities for other residues and oily mixtures from all ships. Such facilities shall have adequate capacity to meet the needs of the ships using them without causing undue delay.

(ii) The Government of each Party having under its jurisdiction entrances to seawater courses with low depth contour which might require a reduction of draught by the discharge of ballast in sub-paragraphs (*a*)(i) of this paragraph but with the proviso that ships required to discharge slops or dirty ballast could be subject to some delay.

(iii) Each Party concerned shall notify the Organization of the measures taken pursuant to provisions of sub-paragraph (*b*)(i) and (ii) of this paragraph. Upon receipt of sufficient notifications the Organization shall establish a date from which the requirements of this Regulation in respect of the area in question shall take effect. The Organization shall notify all Parties of the date so established no less than twelve months in advance of that date.

(iv) During the period between the entry into force of the present Convention and the date so established, ships while navigating in the special area shall comply with the requirements of Regulation 9 of this Annex.

(v) After such date oil tankers loading in ports in these special areas where such facilities are not yet available shall also fully comply with the requirements of this Regulation. However, oil tankers entering these special areas for the purpose of loading shall make every effort to enter the area with only clean ballast on board.

(vi) After the date on which the requirements for the special area in question take effect, each Party shall notify the Organization for transmission to the Parties concerned of all cases where the facilities are alleged to be inadequate.

(vii) At least the reception facilities as prescribed in Regulation 12 of this Annex shall be provided by 1 January 1977 or one year after the date of entry into force of the present Convention whichever occurs later.

Regulation 11

EXCEPTIONS

Regulations 9 and 10 of this Annex shall not apply to:

a) the discharge into the sea of oil or oily mixture necessary for the purpose of securing the safety of a ship or saving life at sea; or

b) the discharge into the sea of oil or oily mixture resulting from damage to a ship or its equipment:

(i) provided that all reasonable precautions have been taken after the occurrence of the damage or discovery of the discharge for the purpose of preventing or minimizing the discharge; and

(ii) except if the owner or the Master acted either with intent to cause damage, or recklessly and with knowledge that damage would probably result; or

c) the discharge into the sea of substances containing oil, approved by the Administration, when being used for the purpose of combating specific pollution incidents in order to minimize the damage from pollution. Any such discharge shall be subject to the approval of any Government in whose jurisdiction it is contemplated the discharge will occur.

Regulation 12

RECEPTION FACILITIES

1. Subject to the provisions of Regulation 10 of this Annex, the Government of each Party undertakes to ensure the provision at oil loading terminals, repair ports, and in other ports in which ships have oily residues to discharge, of facilities for the reception of such residues and oily mixtures as remain from oil tankers and other ships adequate to meet the needs of the ships using them without causing undue delay to ships.

2. Reception facilities in accordance with paragraph (1) of this Regulation shall be provided in:

a) all ports and terminals in which crude oil is loaded into oil tankers where such tankers have immediately prior to arrival completed a ballast voyage of not more than 72 hours or not more than 1,200 nautical miles;

b) all ports and terminals in which oil other than crude oil in bulk is loaded at an average quantity of more than 1,000 metric tons per day;

c) all ports having ship repair yards or tank cleaning facilities;

d) all ports and terminals which handle ships provided with the sludge tank(s) required by Regulation 17 of this Annex:

e) all ports in respect of oily bilge waters and other residues, which cannot be discharged in accordance with Regulation 9 of this Annex; and

f) all loading ports for bulk cargoes in respect of oil residues from combination carriers which cannot be discharged in accordance with Regulation 9 of this Annex.

3. The capacity for the reception facilities shall be as follows:

a) Crude oil loading terminals shall have sufficient reception facilities to receive oil and oily mixtures which cannot be discharged in accordance with the provisions of Regulation 9(1)(*a*) of this Annex from all oil tankers on voyages as described in paragraph (2) (*a*) of this Regulation.

b) Loading ports and terminals referred to in paragraph (2)(*b*) of this Regulation shall have sufficient reception facilities to receive oil and oily mixtures which cannot be discharged in accordacne with the provisions of Regulation 9(1) (*a*) of this Annex from oil tankers which load oil other than crude oil in bulk.

c) All ports having ship repair yards or tank cleaning facilities shall have sufficient reception facilities to receive all residues and oily mixtures which remain on board for disposal from ships prior to entering such yards or facilities.

d) All facilities provided in ports and terminals under paragraph (2)(*d*) of this Regulation shall be sufficient to receive all residues retained according to Regulation 17 of this Annex from all ships that may reasonably be expected to call at such ports and terminals.

e) All facilities provided in ports and terminals under this Regulation shall be sufficient to receive oily bilge waters and other residues which cannot be discharged in accordance with Regulation 9 of this Annex.

f) The facilities provided in loading ports for bulk cargoes shall take into account the special problems of combination carriers as appropriate.

4. The reception facilities prescribed in paragraphs (2) and (3) of this Regulation shall be made available no later than one year from the date of entry into force of the present Convention or by 1 January 1977, whichever occurs later.

5. Each Party shall notify the Organization for transmission to the Parties concerned of all cases where the facilities provided under this Regulation are alleged to be inadequate.

Regulation 13

SEGREGATED BALLAST OIL TANKERS

1. Every new oil tanker of 70,000 tons deadweight and above shall be provided with segregated ballast tanks and shall comply with the requirements of this Regulation.

2. The capacity of the segregated ballast tanks shall be so determined that the ship may operate safely on ballast voyages without recourse to the use of oil tanks for water ballast except as provided for in paragraph (3) of this Regulation. In all cases, however, the capacity of segregated ballast tanks shall be at least such that in any ballast condition at any part of the voyage, including the conditions consisting of lightweight plus segregated ballast only, the ship's draughts and trim can meet each of the following requirements:

a) the moulded draught amidships (dm) in metres (without taking into account any ship's deformation) shall not be les than:

$$dm = 2.0 + 0.02L;$$

b) the draughts at the forward and after perpendiculars shall correspond to those determined by the draught amidships (*dm*), as specified in sub-paragraph (*a*) of this paragraph, in association with the trim by the stern of not greater than $0.015L$; and

c) in any case the draught at the after perpendicular shall not be less than that which is necessary to obtain full immersion of the propeller(s).

3. In no case shall ballast water be carried in oil tanks except in weather conditions so severe that, in the opinion of the Master, it is necessary to carry additional ballast water in oil tanks for the safety of the ship. Such additional ballast water shall be processed and discharged in compliance with Regulation 9 and in accordance with the requirements of Regulation 15 of this Annex, and entry shall be made in the Oil Record Book

referred to in Regulation 20 of this Annex.

4. Any oil tanker which is not required to be provided with segregated ballast tanks in accordance with paragraph (1) of this Regulation may, however, be qualified as a segregated ballast tanker, provided that in the case of an oil tanker of 150 metres in length and above it fully complies with the requirements of paragraphs (2) and (3) of this Regulation and in the case of an oil tanker of less than 150 metres in length the segregated ballast conditions shall be to the satisfaction of the Administration.

Regulation 14

SEGREGATION OF OIL AND WATER BALLAST

1. Except as provided in paragraph (2) of this Regulation, in new ships of 4,000 tons gross tonnage and above other than oil tankers, and in new oil tankers of 150 tons gross tonnage and above, no ballast water shall be carried in any oil fuel tank.

2. Where abnormal conditions or the need to carry large quantities of oil fuel render it necessary to carry ballast water which is not a clean ballast in any oil fuel tank, such ballast water shall be discharged to reception facilities or into the sea in compliance with Regulation 9 using the equipment specified in Regulation 16 (2) of this Annex, and an entry shall be made in the Oil Record Book to this effect.

3. All other ships shall comply with the requirements of paragraph (1) of this Regulation as far as reasonable and practicable.

Regulation 15

RETENTION OF OIL ON BOARD

1. Subject to the provisions of paragraphs (5) and (6) of this Regulation, oil tankers of 150 tons gross tonnage and above shall be provided with arrangements in accordance with the requirements of paragraphs (2) and (3) of this Regulation, provided that in the case of existing tankers the requirements for oil discharge monitoring and control systems and slop tank arrangements shall apply three years after the date of entry into force of the present Convention.

2. *a*) Adequate means shall be provided for cleaning the cargo tanks and transferring the dirty ballast residue and tank washings from the cargo tanks into a slop tank approved by the Administration. In existing oil tankers, any cargo tank may be designated as a slop tank.

b) In this system arrangements shall be provided to transfer the oily waste into a slop tank or combination of slop tanks in such a way that any effluent discharged into the sea will be such as to comply with the provisions of Regulation 9 of this Annex.

c) The arrangements of the slop tank or combination of slop tanks shall have a capacity necessary to retain the slops generated by tank washing, oil residues and dirty ballast residues but the total shall be not less than 3 per cent of the oil carrying capacity of the ship, except that, where segregated ballast tanks are provided in accordance with Regulation 13 of this Annex, or where arrangements such as eductors involving the use of water additional to the washing water are not fitted, the Administration may accept 2 per cent. New oil tankers over 70,000 tons deadweight shall be provided with at least two slop tanks.

d) Slop tanks shall be designed particularly in respect of the position of inlets, outlets, baffles or where fitted, so as to avoid excessive turbulence and entrainment of oil or emulsion with the water.

3. *a*) An oil discharge monitoring and control system approved by the Administration shall be fitted. In considering the design of the oil content meter to be incorporated in the system, the Administration shall have regard to the specification recommended by the Organization.* The system shall be fitted with a recording device to provide a continuous record of the discharge in litres per nautical mile and total quantity discharged, or the oil content and rate of discharge. This record shall be identifiable as to time and date and shall be kept for at least three years. The oil discharge monitor and control system shall come into operation when there is any discharge of effluent into the sea and shall be such as will ensure that any discharge of oily mixture is automatically stopped when the instantaneous rate of discharge of oil exceeds that permitted by Regulation 9(1)(*a*) of this Annex. Any failure of this monitoring and control system shall stop the discharge and be noted in the Oil Record Book. A manually operated alternative method shall be provided and may be used in the event of such failure, but the defective unit shall be made operable before the oil tanker commences its next ballast voyage unless it is proceeding to a repair port. Existing oil tankers shall comply with all of the provisions specified above except that the stopping of the discharge may be performed manually and the rate of discharge may be estimated from the pump characteristic.

b) Effective oil/water interface detectors approved by the Administration shall be provided for a rapid and accurate determination of the oil/water interface in slop tanks and shall be available for use in other tanks where the separation of oil and water is effected and from which it is intended to discharge effluent direct to the sea.

c) Instructions as to the operation of system shall be in accordance with an operational manual approved by the Administration. They shall cover manual as well as automatic operations and shall be intended to ensure that at no time shall oil be discharged except in compliance with the conditions specified in Regulation 9 of this Annex*

* Reference is made to "Clean Seas Guide for Oil Tankers", published by the International Chamber of Shipping and the Oil Companies International Marine Forum.

* Reference is made to the Recommendation on International Performance Specifications for Oily-Water Separating Equipment and Oil Content Meters adopted by the Organization by Resolution A.233 (VII).

4. The requirements of paragraphs (1), (2) and (3) of this Regulation shall not apply to oil tankers of less than 150 tons gross tonnage, for which the control of discharge of oil under Regulation 9 of this Annex shall be effected by the retention of oil on board with subsequent discharge of all contaminated washings to reception facilities. The total quantity of oil and water used for washing and returned to a storage tank shall be recorded in the Oil Record Book. This total quantity shall be discharged to reception facilities unless adequate arrangements are made to ensure that any effluent which is allowed to be discharged into the sea is effectively monitored to ensure that the provision of Regulation 9 of this Annex are complied with.

5. The Administration may waive the requirements of paragraphs (1), (2) and (3) of this Regulation for any oil tanker which engages exclusively on voyages both of 72 hours or less in duration and within 50 miles from the nearest land, provided that the oil tanker is not required to hold and does not hold an International Oil Pollution Prevention Certificate (1973). Any such waiver shall be subject to the requirements that the oil tanker shall retain on board all oily mixtures for subsequent discharge to reception facilities and to the determination by the Administration that facilities available to receive such oily mixtures are adequate.

6. Where in the view of the Organization equipment required by Regulation 9(1)(*a*)(vi) of this Annex and specified in sub-paragraph (3)(a) of this Regulation is not obtainable for the monitoring of discharge of light refined products (white oils), the Administration may waive compliance with such procedures established by the Organization which shall satisfy the conditions of Regulation 9(1)(*a*) of this Annex except the obligation to have an oil discharge monitoring and control system in operation. The Organization shall review the availability of equipment at intervals not exceeding twelve months.

7. The requirements of paragraphs (1), (2) and (3) of this Regulation shall not apply to oil tankers carrying asphalt, for which the control of discharge of asphalt under Regulation 9 of this Annex shall be effected by the retention of asphalt residues on board with discharge of all contaminated washings to reception facilities.

Regulation 16

OIL DISCHARGE MONITORING AND CONTROL SYSTEM AND OILY-WATER SEPARATING EQUIPMENT

1. Any ship of 400 tons gross tonnage and above shall be fitted with an oily-water separating equipment or filtering system complying with the provisions of paragraph (6) of this Regulation. Any such ship which carries large quantities of oil fuel shall comply with paragraph 2 of this Regulation or paragraph (1) of Regulation 14.

2. Any ship of 10,000 tons gross tonnage and above shall be fitted:

a) in addition to the requirements of paragraph (1) of this Regulation with an oil discharge monitoring and control system complying with paragraph (5) of this Regulation; or

b) as an alternative to the requirements of paragraph (1) and sub-paragraph (2)(*a*) of this Regulation, with an oily-water separating equipment complying with paragraph (6) of this Regulation and an effective filtering system, complying with paragraph (7) of this Regulation.

3. The Administration shall ensure that ships of less 400 tons gross tonnage are equipped, as far as practicable, to retain on board oil or oily mixtures or discharge them in accordance with the requirements of Regulation 9(1)(*b*) of this Annex.

4. For existing ships the requirements of paragraphs (1),(2) and (3) of this Regulation shall apply three years after the date of entry into force of the present Convention.

5. An oil discharge monitoring and control system shall be of a design approved by the Administration. In considering the design of the oil content meter to be incorporated into the system, the Administration shall have regard to the specification recommended by the Organization.* The system shall be fitted with a recording device to provide a continuous record of the oil content in parts per million. This record shall be identifiable as to time and date and shall be kept for at least three years. The monitoring and control system shall come into operation when there is any discharge of effluent into the sea and shall be such as will ensure that any discharge of oily mixture is automatically stopped when the oil content of effluent exceeds that permitted by Regulation 9(1)(*b*) of this Annex. Any failure of this monitoring and control system shall stop the discharge and be noted in the Oil Record Book. The defective unit shall be made operable before the ship commences its next voyage unless it is proceeding to a repair port. Existing ships shall comply with all of the provisions specified above except that the stopping of the discharge may be performed manually.

6. Only-water separating equipment or an oil filtering system shall be of a design approved by the Administration and shall be such as will ensure that any oily mixture discharged into the sea after passing through the separator or filtering systems shall have an oil content of not more than 100 parts per million. In considering the design of such equipment, the Administration shall have regard to the specification recommended by the Organization.*

7. The oil filtering system referred to in paragraph (2)(*b*) of this Regulation shall be of a design approved by the Administration and shall be such that it will accept the discharge from the separating system and produce an effluent the oil content of which does not exceed 15 parts per million. It shall be provided with alarm arrangements to indicate when this level cannot be maintained.

Regulation 17

TANKS FOR OIL RESIDUES (SLUDGE)

1. Every ship of 400 tons gross tonnage and above shall be provided with a tank or tanks of adequate capacity, having regard to the type of machinery and length of voyage, to receive the oily residues (sludges) which cannot be dealt with otherwise in accordance with the requirements of this Annex, such as those resulting from the purification of fuel and lubricating oils and oil leakages in the machinery spaces.

2. In new ships, such tanks shall be designed and constructed so as to facilitate their cleaning and the discharge of residues to reception facilities. Existing ships shall comply with this requirement as far as is reasonable and practicable.

Regulation 18

PUMPING, PIPING AND DISCHARGE ARRANGEMENTS OF OIL TANKERS

1. In every oil tanker, a discharge manifold for connexion to reception facilities for the discharge of dirty ballast water or oil contaminated water shall be located on the open deck on both sides of the ship.

2. In every oil tanker, pipelines for the discharge to the sea of effluent which may be permitted under Regulation 9 of this Annex shall be led to the open deck or to the ship's side above the waterline in the deepest ballast condition. Different piping arrangements to permit operation in the manner permitted in sub-paragraphs (4)(*a*) and (*b*) of this Regulation may be accepted.

3. In new oil tankers means shall be provided for stopping the discharge of effluent into the sea from a position on upper deck or above located so that the manifold in use referred to in paragraph (1) of this Regulation and the effluent from the pipelines referred to in paragraph (2) of this Regulation may be visually observed. Means for stopping the discharge need not be provided at the observation position if a positive communication system such as telephone or radio system is provided between the observation position and the discharge control position.

4. All discharges shall take place above the waterline except as follows:

a) Segregated ballast and clean ballast may be discharged below the waterline in ports or at offshore terminals.

b) Existing ships which, without modification, are not capable of discharging segregated ballast above the waterline may discharge segregated ballast below the waterline provided that an examination of the tank immediately before the discharge has established that no contamination with oil has taken place.

Regulation 19

STANDARD DISCHARGE CONNECTION

To enable pipes of reception facilities to be connected with the ship's discharge pipeline for residues from machinery bilges, both lines shall be fitted with a standard discharge connection in accordance with the following table:

Standard Dimensions of Flanges for Discharge Connections

Description	Dimension
Outside diameter	215 mm
Inner diameter	According to pipe outside diameter
Bolt circle diameter	183 mm
Slots in flange	6 holes 22 mm in diameter equidistantly placed on a bolt circle of the above diameter, slotted to the flange periphery. The slot width to be 22 mm
Flange thickness	20 mm
Bolts and nuts: quantity, diameter	6, each of 20 mm in diameter and of suitable length
The flange is designed to accept pipes up to a maximum internal diameter of 125 mm and shall be of steel or other equivalent material having a flat face. This flange, together with a gasket of oilproof material, shall be suitable for a service pressure of 6 kg/cm[1].	

Regulation 20

OIL RECORD BOOK

1. Every oil tanker of 150 tons gross tonnage and above and every ship of 400 tons gross tonnage and above other than oil tanker shall be provided with an Oil Record Book, whether as part of the ship's official log book or otherwise, in the form specified in Appendix III to this Annex.

2. The Oil Record Book shall be completed on each occasion, on a tank-to-tank basis, whenever any of the following operations take place in the ship:

a) For oil tankers

(i) loading of oil cargo;

(ii) internal transfer of oil cargo during voyage;

(iii) opening or closing before and after loading and unloading operations of valves or similar devices which inter-connect cargo tanks;

(iv) opening or closing of means of communication between cargo piping and seawater ballast piping;

(v) opening or closing of ship's side valves before, during and after loading and unloading operations;

(vi) unloading of oil cargo;

(vii) ballasting of cargo tanks;

(viii) cleaning of cargo tanks;

(ix) discharge of ballast except from segregated ballast tanks;

(x) discharge of water from slop tanks;

(xi) disposal of residues;

(xii) discharge overboard of bilge water which has accumulated in machinery spaces whilst in port and the routine discharge at sea of bilge water which has accumulated in machinery spaces.

b) For ships other than oil tankers

(i) ballasting or cleaning of fuel oil tanks or oil cargo spaces;

(ii) discharge of ballast or cleaning water from tanks referred to under (i) of this sub-paragraph;

(iii) disposal of residues;

(iv) discharge overboard of bilge water which has accumulated in machinery spaces whilst in port, and the routine discharge at sea of bilge water which has accumulated in machinery spaces.

3. In the event of such discharge of oil or oily mixture as is referred to in Regulation 11 of this

Annex or in the event of accidental or other exceptional discharge of oil not expected by that Regulation, a statement shall be made in the Oil Record Book of the circumstances of, and the reasons for, the discharge.

4. Each operation described in paragraph (2) of this Regulation shall be fully recorded without delay in the Oil Record Book so that all the entries in the book appropriate to that operation are completed. Each section of the book shall be signed by the officer or officers in charge of the operations concerned and shall be countersigned by the Master of the ship. The entries in the Oil Record Book shall be in an official language of the State whose flag the ship is entitled to fly, and, for ships holding an International Oil Pollution Prevention Certificate (1973), in English or French. The entries in an official national language of the State whose flag the ship is entitled to fly shall prevail in case of a dispute or discrepancy.

5. The Oil Record Book shall be kept in such a place as to be readily available for inspection at all reasonable times and, except in the case of unmanned ships under tow, shall be kept on board the ship. It shall be preserved for a period of three years after the last entry has been made.

6. The competent authority of the Government of a party to the Convention may inspect the Oil Record Book on board any ship to which this Annex applies while the ship is in its port or offshore terminals and may take a copy of any entry in that book and may require the Master of the ship to certify that the copy is a true copy of such entry. Any copy so made which has been certified by the Master of the ship as a true copy of an entry in the ship's Oil Record Book shall be made admissible in any judicial proceedings as evidence of the facts stated in the entry. The inspection of an Oil Record Book and the taking of a certified copy of the competent authority under this paragraph shall be performed as expeditiously as possible without causing the ship to be unduly delayed.

Regulation 21

SPECIAL REQUIREMENTS FOR DRILLING RIGS AND OTHER PLATFORMS

Fixed and floating drilling rigs when engaged in the exploration, exploitation and associated offshore processing of sea-bed mineral resources and other platforms shall comply with the requirements of this Annex applicable to ships of 400 tons gross tonnage and above other than oil tankers, except that:

a) they shall be equipped as far as practicable with the installations required in Regulations 16 and 17 of this Annex;

b) they shall keep a record of all operations involving oil or oily mixture discharges, in a form approved by the Administration; and

c) in any special area and subject to the provisions of Regulation 11 of this Annex, the discharge into the sea of oil or oily mixture shall be prohibited except when the oil content of the discharge without dilution does not exceed 15 parts per million.

Chapter III

REQUIREMENTS FOR MINIMIZING OIL POLLUTION FROM OIL TANKERS DUE TO SIDE AND BOTTOM DAMAGES

Regulation 22

DAMAGE ASSUMPTIONS

1. For the purpose of calculating hypothetical oil outflow from oil tankers, three dimensions of the extent of damage of a parallelepiped on the side and bottom of the ship are assumed as follows. In the case of bottom damages two conditions are set forth to be applied individually to the stated portions of the oil tanker.

a) *Side damage*

(i)	Longitudinal extent (l_c);	$\frac{1}{3} L^{\frac{2}{3}}$ or 14.5 metres, whichever is less
(ii)	Transverse extent (l_c): (inboard from the ship's side at right angles to the centre-line at the level corresponding to the assigned summer freeboard)	$\frac{B}{5}$ or 11.5 metres, whichever is less
(iii)	Vertical extent (v_c):	from the base line upwards without limit

b) Bottom damage

		For 0.3L from the forward perpendicular of the ship	Any other part of the ship
(i)	Longitudinal extent (l_s)	$\frac{L}{10}$	$\frac{L}{10}$ or 5 metres, whichever is less
(ii)	Transverse extent (t_s)	$\frac{B}{6}$ or 10 metres, whichever is less but not less than 5 metres	5 metres
(iii)	Vertical extent from the base line (v_s):	$\frac{B}{15}$ or 6 metres, whichever is less	

2. Whenever the symbols given in this Regulation appear in this Chapter, they have the meaning as defined in this Regulation.

Regulation 23

HYPOTHETICAL OUTFLOW OF OIL

1. The hypothetical outflow of oil in the case of side damage (O_c) and bottom damage (O_s) shall be calculated by the following formulae with

respect to compartments breached by damage to all conceivable locations along the length of the ship to the extent as defined in Regulation 22 of this Annex.

a) for side damages:

$$O_c = \Sigma W_i + \Sigma K_i C_i \qquad (I)$$

b) for bottom damages:

$$O_s = \frac{1}{3}(\Sigma Z_i W_i + \Sigma Z_i C_i) \qquad (II)$$

where:

W_i = volume of a wing tank in cubic metres assumed to be breached by the damage as specified in Regulation 22 of this Annex; W_i for a segregated ballast tank may be taken equal to zero.

C_i = volume of a centre tank in cubic metres assumed to be breached by the damage as specified in Regulation 22 of this Annex; C_i for a segregated ballast tank may be taken equal to zero.

$K_i = 1 - \frac{b_i}{t_c}$ when b_i is equal to or greater than t_c, K_i shall be taken equal to zero,

$Z_i = 1 - \frac{h_i}{v_s}$ when h_i is equal to or greater than v_s, Z_i shall be taken equal to zero,

b_i = width of wing tank in metres under consideration measured inboard from the ship's side at right angles to the centreline at the level corresponding to the assigned summer freeboard,

h_i = minimum depth of the double bottom in metres under consideration; where no double bottom is fitted h_i shall be taken to be equal to zero.

Whenever symbols given in this paragraph appear in the Chapter, they have the meaning as defined in this Regulation.

2. If a void space or segregated ballast tank of a length less than l_c as defined in Regulation 22 of this Annex is located between wing oil tanks, O_c in formula (1) may be calculated on the basis of volume W_i being the actual volume of one such tank (where they are of equal capacity) or the smaller of the two tanks (if they differ in capacity) adjacent to such space, multiplied by S_i as defined below and taking for all other wing tanks involved in such a collision the value of the actual full volume.

$$S_i = 1 - \frac{l_i}{l_c}$$

where l_i = length in metres of void space or segregated ballast tank under consideration.

3. *a*) Credit shall only be given in respect of double bottom tanks which are either empty or carrying clean water when cargo is carried in the tanks above.

b) Where the double bottom does not extent for the full length and width of the tank involved, the double bottom is considered non-existent and the volume of the tanks above the area of the bottom damage shall be included in formula (II) even if the tank is not considered breached because of the installation of such a partial double bottom.

c) Suction wells may be neglected in the determination of the value h_i provided such wells are not excessive in area and extend below the tank for a minimum distance and in no case more than half the height of the double bottom. If the depth of such a well exceeds half the height of the double bottom, h_i shall be taken equal to the double bottom height minus the well height.

Piping serving such wells if installed within the double bottom shall be fitted with valves or other closing arrangements located at the point of connexion to the tank served to prevent oil outflow in the event of damage to the piping. Such piping shall be installed as high from the bottom shell as possible. These valves shall be kept closed at sea at any time when the tank contains oil cargo, except that they may be opened only for cargo transfer needed for the purpose of trimming of the ship.

4. In the case where bottom damage simultaneously involves four centre tanks, the value of O_s may be calculated according to the formula

$$O_s = \tfrac{1}{4}(\Sigma Z_i W_i + \Sigma Z_i C_i) \qquad (III)$$

5. An Administration may credit as reducing oil outflow in case of bottom damage, an installed cargo transfer system having an emergency high suction in each cargo oil tank, capable of transferring from a breached tank or tanks to segregated ballast tanks or to available cargo tankage if it can be assured that such tanks will have sufficient ullage. Credit for such a system would be governed by ability to transfer in two hours of operation oil equal to one half of the largest of the breached tanks involved and by availability of equivalent receiving capacity in ballast or cargo tanks. The credit shall be confined to permitting calculation of O_s according to formula (III). The pipes for such suctions shall be installed at least at a height not less than the vertical extent of the bottom damage v_s. The Administration shall supply the Organization with the information concerning the arrangements accepted by it, for circulation to other Parties to the Convention.

Regulation 24

LIMITATION OF SIZE AND ARRANGEMENT OF CARGO TANKS

1. Every new oil tanker shall comply with the provision of this Regulation. Every existing oil tanker shall be required, within two years after the date of entry into force of the present Convention, to comply with the provisions of this Regulation if such a tanker falls into either of the following categories:

a) a tanker, the delivery of which is after 1 January 1977; or

b) a tanker to which both the following conditions apply:

(i) delivery is not later than 1 January 1977; and

(ii) the building contract is placed after 1 January 1974, or in cases where no building contract has previously been placed, the keel is laid or the tanker is at a similar stage of construction after 30 January 1974.

2. Cargo tanks of oil tankers shall be of such size and arrangements that the hypothetical outflow O_c or O_s calculated in accordance with the provisions of Regulation 23 of this Annex anywhere in the length of the ship does not exceed 30,000 cubic metres or 400 $\sqrt[3]{DW}$, whichever is the greater, but subject to a maximum of 40,000 cubic metres.

3. The volume of any one wing cargo oil tank of an oil tanker shall not exceed seventy-five per cent of the limits of the hypothetical oil outflow referred to in paragraph (2) of this Regulation. The volume of any one centre cargo oil tank shall not exceed 50,000 cubic metres. However, in segregated ballast oil tankers as defined in Regulation 13 of this Annex, the permitted volume of a wing cargo oil tank situated between two segregated ballast tanks, each exceeding l_c in length, may be increased to the maximum limit of hypothetical oil outflow provided that the width of the wing tanks exceeds t_c.

4. The length of each cargo tank shall not exceed 10 metres or one of the following values, whichever is the greater:

a) where no longitudinal bulkhead is provided: $0.1L$

b) where a longitudinal bulkhead is provided at the centreline only: $0.15L$

c) where two or more longitudinal bulkheads are provided:

(i) for wing tanks: $0.2L$

(ii) for centre tanks:

(1) if $\frac{b_i}{B}$ is equal to or greater than $\frac{1}{5}$: $0.2L$

(2) if $\frac{b_i}{B}$ is less than $\frac{1}{5}$:

— where no centreline longitudinal bulkhead is provided:

$$\left(0.5\frac{b_i}{B} + 0.1\right)L$$

—where a centreline longitudinal bulkhead is provided:

$$\left(0.25\frac{b_i}{B} + 0.15\right)L$$

5. In order not to exceed the volume limits established by paragraphs (2), (3) and (4) of this Regulation and irrespective of the accepted type of cargo transfer system installed, when such a system inter-connects two or more cargo tanks, valves or other similar closing devices shall be provided for separating the tanks from each other. These valves or devices shall be closed when the tanker is at sea.

6. Lines of piping which run through cargo tanks in a position less than t_c from the ship's side or less than v_c from the ship's bottom shall be fitted with valves or similar closing devices at the point at which they open into any cargo tank. These valves shall be kept closed at sea at any time when the tanks contain cargo oil, except that they may be opened only for cargo transfer needed for the purpose of trimming of the ship.

Regulation 25

SUBDIVISION AND STABILITY

1. Every new oil tanker shall comply with thc subdivision and damage stability criteria as specified in paragraph (3) of this Regulation, after the assumed side or bottom damage as specified in paragraph (2) of this Regualtion, for any operating draught reflecting actual partial or full load conditions consistent with trim and strength of the ship as well as specific gravities of the cargo. Such damage shall be applied to all conceivable locations along the length of the ship as follows:

a) in tankers of more than 225 metres in length, anywhere in the ship's length;

b) in tankers of more than 150 metres, but not exceeding 225 metres in length, anywhere in the ship's length except involving either after or forward bulkhead bounding the machinery space located aft. The machinery space shall be treated as a single floodable compartment;

c) in tankers not exceeding 150 metres in length, anywhere in the ship's length between adjacent transverse bulkheads with the exception of the machinery space. For tankers of 100 metres or less in length where all requirements of paragraph (3) of this Regulation cannot be fulfilled without materially impairing the operational qualities of the ship, Administrations may allow relaxations from these requirements.

Ballast conditions where the tanker is not carrying oil in cargo tanks excluding any oil residues, shall not be considered.

2. The following provisions regarding the extent and the character of the assumed damage shall apply:

a) The extent of side or bottom damage shall be as specified in Regulation 22 of this Annex, except that the longitudinal extent of the bottom damage within $0.3L$ from the forward perpendicular shall be the same as for side damage, as specified in Regulation 22 (1)(*a*)(i) of this Annex. If any damage of lesser extent results in a more severe condition such damage shall be assumed.

b) Where the damage involving transverse bulkheads is envisaged as specified in sub-paragraphs (1)(*a*) and (*b*) of this Regulation, transverse watertight bulkheads shall be spaced at least at a distance equal to the longitudinal extent of assumed damage specified in sub-paragraph (*a*) of this paragraph in order to be considered effective. Where transverse bulkheads are spaced at a lesser distance, one or more of these bulkheads within such extent of damage shall be assumed as non-existent for the purpose of determining flooded compartments.

c) Where the damage between adjacent transverse watertight bulkheads is envisaged as specified in sub-paragraph (1)(*c*) of this Regulation, no main transverse bulkhead or a transverse bulkhead bounding side tanks or double bottom tanks shall be assumed damaged, unless:

(i) the spacing of the adjacent bulkheads is less than the longitudinal extent of assumed damage specified in sub-paragraph (*a*) of this paragraph; or

(ii) there is a step or a recess in a transverse bulkhead of more than 3.05 metres in length, located within the extent of penetration of assumed damage. The step forward by the after peak bulkhead and after peak tank top shall not be regarded as a step for the purpose of this Regulation.

d) If pipes, ducts or tunnels are situated within the assumed extent of damage, arrangements shall be made so that progressive flooding cannot thereby extend to compartments other than those assumed to be floodable for each case of damage.

3. Oil tankers shall be regarded as complying with the damage stability criteria if the following requirements are met:

a) The final waterline, taking into account sinkage, heel and trim, shall be below the lower edge of any opening through which progressive flooding may take place. Such openings shall include air pipes and those which are closed by means of weathertight doors or hatch covers and may exclude those openings closed by means of watertight manhole covers and flush scuttles, small watertight cargo tank hatch covers which maintain the high integrity of the deck, remotely operated watertight sliding doors, and side scuttles of the non-opening type.

b) In the final stage of flooding, the angle of heel due to unsymmetrical flooding shall not exceed 25 degrees, provided that this angle may be increased up to 30 degrees if no deck edge immersion occurs.

c) The stability in the final stage of flooding shall be investigated and may be regarded as sufficient if the righting lever curve has at least a range of 20 degrees beyond the position of equilibrium in association with a maximum residual righting lever of at least 0.1 metre. The Administration shall give consideration to the potential hazard presented by protected or unprotected openings which may become temporarily immersed within the range of residual stability.

d) The Administration shall be satisfied that the stability is sufficient during intermediate stages of flooding.

4. The requirements of paragraph (1) of this Regulation shall be confirmed by calculations which take into consideration the design characteristics of the ship, the arrangements, configuration and contents of the damaged compartments; and the distribution, specific gravities and the free surface effect of liquids. The calculations shall be based on the following:

a) Account shall be taken of any empty or partially filled tank, the specific gravity of cargoes carried, as well as any outflow of liquids from damaged compartments.

b) The permeabilities are assumed as follows:

Spaces	*Permeability*
Appropriated to stores	0.60
Occupied by accommodation	0.95
Occupied by machinery	0.85
Voids	0.95
Intended for consumable liquids	0 to 0.95*
Intended for other liquids	0 to 0.95**

* Whichever results in the more severe requirements.

** The permeability of partially filled compartments shall be consistent with the amount of liquid carried.

c) The buoyancy of any superstructure directly above the side damage shall be disregarded. The unflooded parts of superstructures beyond the extent of damage, however, may be taken into consideration provided that they are separated from the damaged space by watertight bulkheads and the requirements of sub-paragraph (3)(*a*) of this Regulation in respect of these intact spaces are complied with. Hinged watertight doors may be acceptable in watertight bulkheads in the superstructure.

d) The free surface effect shall be calculated at an angle of heel of 5 degrees for each individual compartment. The Administration may require or allow the free surface corrections to be calculated at an angle of heel greater than 5 degrees for partially filled tanks.

e) In calculating the effect of free surfaces of consumable liquids it shall be assumed that, for each type of liquid at least one transverse pair or a single centreline tank has a free surface and the tank or combination of tanks to be taken into account shall be those where the effect of free surfaces is the greatest.

5. The Master of every oil tanker and the person in charge of a non-self-propelled oil tanker to which this Annex applies shall be supplied in an approved form with:

a) information relative to loading and distribution of cargo necessary to ensure compliance with the provisions of this Regulation; and

b) data on the ability of the ship to comply with damage stability criteria as determined by this Regulation, including the effect of relaxations that may have been allowed under sub-paragraph (1)(*c*) of this Regulation.

APPENDIX I

LIST OF OILS*

Asphalt solutions
Blending Stocks
Roofers Flux
Straight Run Residue

Oils
Clarified
Crude Oil
Mixtures containing crude oil
Diesel Oil
Fuel Oil No. 4
Fuel Oil No. 5
Fuel Oil No. 6
Road Oil
Transformer Oil
Aromatic Oil (excluding vegetable oil)
Lubricating Oils and Blending Stocks
Mineral Oil
Motor Oil
Penetrating Oil
Spindle Oil
Turbine Oil

Distillates
Straight Run
Flashed Feed Stocks

Gas Oil
Cracked

Gasoline Blending Stocks
Aklylates — fuel
Reformates
Polymer — fuel

Gasolines
Casinghead (natural)
Automotive
Aviation
Straight Run
Fuel Oil No. 1 (Kerosene)
Fuel Oil No. 1-D
Fuel Oil No. 2
Fuel Oil No. 2-D

Jet Fuels
JP-1 (Kerosene)
JP-3
JP-4
JP-5 (Kerosene, Heavy)
Turbo Fuel
Kerosene
Mineral Spirit

Naphtha
Solvent
Petroleum
Heartcut Distillate Oil

* The list of oils shall not necessarily be considered as comprehensive.

APPENDIX II
Form of Certificate

INTERNATIONAL OIL PREVENTION CERTIFICATE (1973)

Issued under the Provisions of the International Convention for the Prevention of Pollution from Ships, 1973, under the Authority of the Government of

....

(full designation of the country)

by ....

(full designation of the competent person or organization authorized under the provisions of the International Convention for the Prevention of Pollution from Ships, 1973)

Name of Ship	Number or Distinctive Letter	Port of Registry	Gross Tonnage

Type of ship:

Oil tanker, including combination carrier*

Asphalt carrier*

Ship other than oil tanker with cargo tanks coming under Regulation 2(2) of Annex I of the Convention*
Ship other than any of the above*

New/existing ship*

Date of building or major conversion contract ....

Date on which keel was laid or ship was at a similar stage of construction or on which major conversion was commenced ....

Date of delivery or completion of major conversion ....

* Delete as appropriate

PART A

ALL SHIPS

The ship is equipped with:

for ships of 400 tons gross tonnage and above:

a) oily-water separating equipment* (capable of producing the effluent with an oil content not exceeding 100 parts per million) or

b) an oil filtering system* (capable of producing the effluent with an oil content not exceeding 100 parts per million)

for ships of 10,000 tons gross tonnage and above:

c) an oil discharge monitoring and control system* (additional to *(a)* or *(b)* above) or

d) oil-water separating equipment and an oil filtering system* (capable of producing the effluent with an oil content not exceeding 15 pars per million) in lieu of *(a)* or *(b)* above.

Particulars of requirement from which exemption is granted under Regulation 2(2) and 2(4) (*a*) of Annex I of the Convention:

....

....

Remarks:

* Delete as appropriate

PART B

OIL TANKER

Deadweight .... metric tons. Length of ship.................................. metres.

It is certified that this ship is:

a) required to be constructed according to and complies with

b) not required to be constructed according to

c) nor required to be constructed according to, but complies with the requirements of Regulation 24 of Annex I of the Convention.

The capacity of segregated ballast tanks is.. cubic metres and complies with the requirements of Regulation 24 of Annex I of the Convention

The segregated ballast is distributed as follows:

Tank	Quantity	Tank	Quantity

This Part should be completed for oil tankers including combination carriers and asphalt carriers, and those entries which are applicable should be completed for ships other than oil tankers which are constructed and utilized to carry oil in bulk of an aggregate capacity of 200 cubic metres or above.

[2] This page need not be reproduced on a Certificate issued to any ship other than those referred to in footnote.[1]

[3] Delete as appropriate

THIS IS TO CERTIFY:

That the ship has been surveyed in accordance with Regulation 4 of Annex I of the International Covention for the Prevention of Pollution from Ships, 1973, concerning the prevention of pollution of oil; and

That the survey shows that the structure, equipment, fittings, arrangements and material of the ship and the condition thereof are in all respects, satisfactory and that the ship complies with the applicable requirements of Annex I of the Convention.

This Certificate is valid until ....

subject to intermediate survey(s) at intervals of ....

Issued at ....

(place of issue of Certificate)

....19 ....

(Signature of duly authorized official issuing the Certificate)

(Seal or stamp of the issuing Authority, as appropriate)

Endorsement for existing ships[4]

This is to certify that this ship has been so equipped as to comply with the requirements of the International Convention for the Prevention of Pollution from Ships, 1973 as relating to existing ships three years.from the date of entry into force of the Convention.

signed ....

signed ....
(Signature of duly authorized official)

Place of endorsement ....

Date of endorsement ....

(Seal or stamp of the Authority, as appropriate)

[4] This entry need not be reproduced on a Certificate other than the first Certificate issued to any ship.

Intermediate survey

This is to certify that at an intermediate survey required by Regulation 4(1)(*c*) of Annex I of the Convention, this ship and the condition thereof are found to comply with the relevant provisions of the Convention.

Signed ....
(Signature of duly authorized official)

Place ....

Date ....

(Seal or stamp of the Authority, as appropriate)

Signed ....

(Signature of duly authorized official)

Place ....

Date ....

(Seal or stamp of the Authority, as appropriate)

Under the provisions of Regulation 8(2) and (4) of Annex I of the Convention the validity of this Certificate is extended until

....

Signed ....
(Signature of duly authorized official)

Place ....

Date ....

(Seal or stamp of the Authority, as appropriate)

APPENDIX III

FORM OF OIL RECORD BOOK

OIL RECORD BOOK

I — FOR OIL TANKERS[1]

Name of ship ....

Total cargo carrying capacity of ship in cubic metres ....

Voyage .... (date) .... to .... (date) ....

a) Loading of oil cargo

1. Date and place of loading			
2. Types of oil loaded			
3. Identity of tank(s) loaded			
4. Closing of applicable cargo tank valves and applicable line cut-off valves on completion of loading[2]			

The undersigned certifies that in addition to the above, all sea valves, overboard discharges valves, cargo tank and pipeline connections and inter-connections, were secured on completion of loading oil cargo.

Date of entry .... Officer in charge ....

Master ....

b) Internal transfer of oil cargo during voyage

5. Date of internal transfer				
6. Identity of tank(s)	(i)	From		
	(ii)	To		
7. Was(were) tank(s) in 6(i) emptied?				

[1] This Part should be completed for oil tankers including combination carriers and asphalt carriers, and those entries which are applicable shall be completed for ships other than oil tankers which are constructed and utilized to carry oil in bulk of an aggregate capacity of 200 cubic metres or above. This Part need not be reproduced on an Oil Record Book issued to any ship other than those referred to above.

[2] Applicable valves and similar devices are those referred to in Regulations 20(2)(a)(iii), 23 and 24 of Annex I of the Convention.

The undertsigned certifies that in addition to the above, all sea valves overboard discharge valves, cargo tank and pipeline connections and inter-connections, were secured on completion of internal transfer of oil cargo.

Date of entry .... Officer in charge ....

Master ....

c) Unloading of oil cargo

8. Date and place of unloading			
9. Identity of tank(s) unloaded			
10. Was(were) tank(s) emptied?			
11. Opening of applicable cargo tank valves and applicable line cut-off valves on completion of unloading[2]			
12. Closing of applicable cargo tank valves and applicable line cut off valves on completion of un-loading[2]			

The tank certifies that in addition to the above, all sea valves, overboard discharge valves, cargo tank and pipeline connections and inter-connections, were secured on completion of unloading of oil cargo.

Date of entry .... Officer in charge ....

Master ....

d) Ballasting of cargo tanks

13. Identity of tank(s) ballasted			
14. Date and position of ship at start of ballasting			
15. If valves connecting cargo lines and segregated ballast lines were used give time, date and position of ship when valves were (a) opened, and (b) closed			

The undersigned certifies that in addition to the above, all sea valves, overboard discharge valves, cargo tank and pipeline connections and inter-connections, were secured on completion of unloading of oil cargo.

Date of entry .... Officer in charge ....

Master ....

[2] Applicable valves and similar devices are those referred to in Regulation 20(2)(*a*)(iii), 23 and 24 of Annex I of the Convention.

e) Cleaning of cargo tanks

16. Identity of tank(s) cleaned			
17. Date and duration of cleaning			
18. Methods of cleaning[3]			

Date of entry .... Officer in charge ....

Master ....

f) Discharge of dirty ballast

19. Identity of tank(s)			
20. Date and position of ship at start of discharge to sea			
21. Date and position of ship at finish of discharge to sea			
22. Ship's speed(s) during discharge			
23. Quantity discharged to sea			
24. Quantity of polluted water transferred to slop tank(s) (identify slop tank(s)			
25. Date and port of discharge into shore reception facilities (if applicable)			
26. Was any part of the discharge conducted during darkness, if so, for how long?			
27. Was a regular check kept on the effluent and the surface of the water in the locality of the discharge?			
28. Was any oil observed on the surface of the water in the locality of the discharge?			

Date of entry .... Officer in charge ....

Master ....

[3] Hand hosing, machine washing and/or chemical cleaning. Where chemically cleaned, the chemical concerned and the amount used should be stated.

g) Discharge of water from slop tanks

29. Identity of slop tank(s)			
30. Time of settling from last entry of residues, or			
31. Time of settling from last discharge			
32. Date, time and position of ship at start of discharge			
33. Sounding of total contents at start of discharge			
34. Sounding of oil/water interface at start of discharge			
35. Bulk quantity discharged and rate of discharge			
36. Final quantity discharged and rate of discharge			
37. Date, time and position of ship at end of discharge			
38. Ship's speed(s) during discharge			
39. Sounding of oil/water interface at end of discharge			
40. Was any part of the discharge conducted during darkness, if so, for how long?			
41. Was a regular check kept on the effluent and surface of the water in the locality of the discharge?			
42. Was any oil observed on the surface of the water in the locality of the discharge?			

Date of entry .... Officer in charge ....

Master ....

h) Disposal of residues

43. Identity of tank(s)			
44. Quantity disposed from each tank			
45. Method of disposal of residue: (a) Reception of facilities (b) Mixed with cargo (c) Transferred to another (other) tank(s) (identify tank(s) (d) Other method (state which)			
46. Date and port of disposal of residue			

Date of entry .... Officer in charge ....

Master ....

i) Discharge of clean ballast contained in cargo tanks

47. Date and position of ship at commencement of discharge of clean ballast			
48. Identity of tank(s) discharged			
49. Was(were) the tank(s) empty on completion?			
50. Position of vessel on completion if different from 47			
51. Was any part of the discharge conducted during darkness, if so, for how long?			
52. Was a regular check kept on the effluent and the surface of the water in the locality of the discharge?			
53. Was any oil observed on the surface of the water in the locality of the discharge?			

Date of entry .... Officer in charge ....

Master ....

j) Discharge overboard of bilge water containing oil which has accumulated in machinery spaces whilst in port[4]

54. Port			
55. Duration of stay			
56. Quantity disposed			
57. Date and place of disposal			
58. Method of disposal (state whether a separator was used)			

Date of entry.. Officer in charge ....

Master..

k) Accidental or other exceptional discharges of oil

59. Date and time of occurrence			
60. Place or position of ship at time of occurrence			
61. Approximate quantity and type of oil			
62. Circumstances of discharge or escape, the reasons therefor and general remarks			

Date of entry.. Officer in charge ....

Master..

1. Has the oil monitoring and control system been out of operation at any time when discharging overboard? If so, give time and date of failure and time and date of restoration and confirm that this was due to equipment failure and state reason if known..

....

....

Date of entry.. Officer in charge ....

Master..

(m) Additional operational procedures and general remarks ....

....

....

....

[4] Where the pump starts automatically and discharges through a separator at all times it will be sufficient to enter each day "Automatic discharge from bilges through a separator".

For oil tankers of less than 150 tons gross tonnage operating in accordance with Regulation 15(4) of Annex I of the Convention, an appropriate oil record book should be developed by the Administration.

For asphalt carriers, a separate oil record book may be developed by the Administration utilizing sections (*a*), (*b*), (*c*), (*e*), (*h*), (*j*), (*k*) and (*m*) of this form of oil record book.

II — FOR SHIPS OTHER THAN OIL TANKERS

Name of ship ....

Operations from .... (date), to .... (date)

a) Ballasting or cleaning of oil fuel tanks

1. Identity of tank(s) ballasted			
2. Whether cleaned since they last contained oil, and if not, type of oil previously carried			
3. Date and position of ship at start of cleaning			
4. Date and position of ship at start of ballasting			

Date of entry .... Officer in charge ....

Master ....

b) Discharge of dirty ballast or cleaning water from tanks referred to under section (a)

5. Identity of tank(s)			
6. Date and position of ship at start of discharge			
7. Date and position of ship at finish of discharge			
8. Ship's speed(s) during discharge			
9. Method of discharge (state whether to reception facility or through installed equipment)			
10. Quantity discharged			

Date of entry .... Officer in charge ....

Master ....

c) Disposal of residues

11. Quantity of residue retained on board			
12. Methods of disposal of residue: (a) reception facilities (b) mixed with next bunkering (c) transferred to another (other) tank (d) other method (state which).			
13. Date and port of disposal of residue			

Date of entry.. Officer in charge ....

Master..

d) Discharge overboard of bilge water containing oil which has accumulated in machinery spaces whilst in port[5]

14. Port			
15. Duration of stay			
16. Quantity disharged			
17. Date and place of discharge			
18. Method of discharge: (a) through oily-water separating equipment; (b) through oil filtering system; (c) through oily-water separating equipment and an oil filtering system; (d) to reception facilities			

Date of entry.. Officer in charge ....

Master..

[5] Where the pump starts automtically and discharges through a separator at all times it will be sufficient to enter each day "Automatic discharge from bilges through a separator".

e) Accidental or other exceptional discharges of oil

19. Date and time of occurrence			
20. Place or position of ship at time of occurrence			
21. Approximate quantity and type of oil			
22. Circumstances of discharge or escape, the reasons therefor and general remarks			

Date of entry .... Officer in charge ....

Master ....

f) Has the required oil monitoring and control system been out of operation at any time when discharging overboard? If so, state time and date of failure and time and date of restoration, and confirm that this was due to equipment failure, and state reason if known.

Date of entry .... Officer in charge ....

Master ....

g) New ships of 4,000 tons gross tonnage and above has dirty ballast been carried in oil fuel tanks?

Yes/No ....

If so, state which tanks were so ballasted and method of discharge of the dirty ballast ....

....

....

Date of entry .... Officer in charge ....

Master ....

h) Additional operational procedures and general remarks ....

....

....

....

Date of entry .... Officer in charge ....

Master ....

ANNEX II

REGULATIONS FOR THE CONTROL OF POLLUTION BY NOXIOUS LIQUID IN BULK

Regulation 1

DEFINITIONS

For the purposes of this Annex:

1. "Chemical tanker" means a ship constructed or adapted primarily to carry a cargo of noxious liquid substances in bulk and includes an "oil tanker" as defined in Annex I of the present Convention when carrying a cargo or part cargo of noxious liquid substances in bulk.

2. "Clean ballast" means ballast carried in a tank which, since it was last used to carry a cargo containing a substance in Category A, B, C or D has been thoroughly cleaned and the residues resulting therefrom have been discharged and the tank emptied in accordance with the appropriate requirements of this Annex.

3. "Segregated ballast" means ballast water introduced into a tank permanently allocated to the carriage of ballast or to the carriage of ballast or cargoes other than oil or noxious liquid substances as variously defined in the Annexes of the present Convention, and which is completely separated from the cargo and oil fuel system.

4. "Nearest land" is as defined in Regulation 1 (9) of Annex I of the present Convention.

5. "Liquid substances" are those having a vapour pressure not exceeding 2.8 kp/cm^1 at a temperature of 37.8°C.

6. "Noxious liquid substance" means any substance designated in Appendix II to this Annex or provisionally assessed under the provisions of Regulation 3 (4) as falling into Category A, B, C or D.

7. "Special area" means a sea area where for recognized technical reasons in relation to its oceanographic and ecological condition and to its peculiar transportation traffic the adoption of special mandatory methods for the prevention of sea pollution by noxious liquid substances is required.

Special areas shall be:

a) The Baltic Sea Area, and

b) The Black Sea Area.

8. "Baltic Sea Area" is as defined in Regulation 10(1)(*b*) of Annex I of the present Convention.

9. "Black Sea Area" is as defined in Regulation 10(1)(*c*) of Annex I of the present Convention.

Regulation 2

APPLICATION

1. Unless expressly provided otherwise the provisions of this Annex shall apply to all ships carrying noxious liquid substances in bulk.

2. Where a cargo subject to the provisions of Annex I of the present Convention is carried in a cargo space of a chemical tanker, the appropriate requirements of Annex I of the present Convention shall also apply.

3. Regulation 13 of this Annex shall apply only to ships carrying substances which are categorized for discharge control purposes in Category A, B or C.

Regulation 3

CATEGORIZATION AND LISTING OF NOXIOUS LIQUID SUBSTANCES

1. For the purpose of the Regulation of this Annex, except Regulation 13, noxious liquid substances shall be divided into four categories as follows:

a) Category A — Noxious liquid substances which if discharged into the sea from tank cleaning or deballasting operations would present a major hazard to either marine resources or human health or cause serious harm to amenities or other legitimate uses of the sea and therefore justify the application of stringent anti-pollution measures.

b) Category B — Noxious liquid substances which if discharged into the sea from tank cleaning or deballasting operations would present a hazard to either marine resources or human health or cause harm to amenities or other legitimate uses of the sea and therefore justify the application of special anti-pollution measures.

c) Category C — Noxious liquid substances which if discharged into the sea from tank cleaning or deballasting operations would present a minor hazard to either marine resources or human health or cause minor harm to amenities or other legitimate uses of the sea and therefore require special operational conditions.

d) Category D — Noxious liquid substances which if discharged into the sea from tank cleaning or deballasting operations would present a recognizable hazard to either marine resources or human health or cause minimal harm to amenities or other legitimate uses of the sea and therefore require some attention in operational conditions.

2. Guidelines for use in the categorization of noxious liquid substances are given in Appendix I to this Annex.

3. The list of noxious liquid substances carried in bulk and presently categorized which are subject to the provisions of this Annex is set out in Appendix II to this Annex.

4. Where it is proposed to carry a liquid substance in bulk which has not been categorized under paragraph (1) of this Regulation or evaluated as referred to in Regulation 4(1) of this Annex, the Governments of Parties to the Convention involved in the proposed operation shall establish and agree on a provisional assessment for the proposed operation on the basis of the guidelines referred to in paragraph (2) of this Regulation. Until full agreement between the Governments involved has been reached, the substance shall be carried under the most severe conditions proposed. As soon as possible, but not later than ninety days after its first carriage, the Administration concerned shall notify the Organization and provide details of the substance and the provisional assessment for prompt circulation to all Parties for their information and

consideration. The Government of each Party shall have a period of ninety days in which to forward its comments to the Organization, with a view to the assessment of the substance.

Regulation 4

OTHER LIQUID SUBSTANCES

1. The substances listed in Appendix III to this Annex have been evaluated and found to fall outside the Categories A, B, C and D, as defined in Regulation 3(1) of this Annex because they are presently considered to present no harm to human health, marine resources, amenities or other legitimate uses of the sea, when discharged into the sea from tank cleaning or deballasting operations.

2. The discharge of bilge or ballast water or other residues or mixtures containing only substances listed in Appendix III to this Annex shall not be subject to any requirement of this Annex.

3. The discharge into the sea of clean ballast or segregated ballast shall not be subject to any requirement of this Annex.

Regulation 5

DISCHARGE OF NOXIOUS LIQUID SUBSTANCES

Categories A, B and C Substances outside Special Areas and Category D Substances in all Areas

Subject to the provisions of Regulation 6 of this Annex,

1. The discharge into the sea of substances in Category A as defined in Regulation 3(1)(*a*) of this Annex or of those provisionally assessed as such or ballast water, tank washings, or other residues or mixtures containing such substances shall be prohibited. If tanks containing such substances or mixtures are to be washed, the resulting residues shall be discharged to a reception facility until the concentration of the substance in the effluent to such facility is at or below the residual concentration prescribed for that substance in column III of Appendix II to this Annex and until the tank is empty. Provided that the residue then remaining in the tank is subsequently diluted by the addition of a volume of water of not less than 5 per cent of the total volume of the tank, it may be discharged into the sea when all the following conditions are also satisfied:

a) the ship is proceeding en route at a speed of at least 7 knots in the case of self-propelled ships or at least 4 knots in the case of ships which are not self-propelled;

b) the discharge is made below the waterline, taking into account the location of the seawater intakes; and

c) the discharge is made at a distance of not less than 12 nautical miles from the nearest land and in a depth of water of not less than 25 metres.

2. The discharge into the sea of substances in Category B as defined in Regulation 3(1)(*b*) of this Annex or of those provisionally assessed as such, or ballast water, tank washings, or other residues or mixtures containing such substances shall be prohibited except when all the following conditions are satisfied:

a) the ship is proceeding en route at a speed of at least 7 knots in the case of self-propelled ships or at least 4 knots in the case of ships which are not self-propelled;

b) the procedures and arrangements for discharge are approved by the Administration. Such procedures and arrangements shall be based upon standards developed by the Organization and shall ensure that the concentration and rate of discharge of the effluent is such that the concentration of the substance in the wake astern of the ship does not exceed 1 part per million;

c) the maximum quantity of cargo discharged from each tank and its associated piping system does not exceed the maximum quantity approved in accordance with the procedures referred to in sub-paragraph (*b*) of this paragraph, which shall in no case exceed the greater of 1 cubic metre or 1/3,000 of the tank capacity in cubic metres;

d) the discharge is made below the waterline, taking into account the location of the seawater intakes; and

e) the discharge is made at a distance of not less than 12 nautical miles from the nearest land and in a depth of water of not less than 25 metres.

3. The discharge into the sea of substances in Category C as defined in Regulation 3(1)(*c*) of this Annex or of those provisionally assessed as such, or ballast water, tank washings, or other residues or mixtures containing such substances shall be prohibited except when all the following conditions are satisfied:

a) the ship is proceeding en route at a speed of at least 7 knots in the case of self-propelled ships or at least 4 knots in the case of ships which are not self-propelled;

b) the procedures and arrangements for discharge are approved by the Administration. Such procedures and arrangements shall be based upon standards developed by the Organization and shall ensure that the concentration and rate of discharge of the effluent is such that the concentration of the substance in the wake astern of the ship does not exceed 10 parts per million;

c) the maximum quantity of cargo discharged from each tank and its associated piping system does not exceed the maximum quantity approved in accordance with the procedures referred to in sub-paragraph (*b*) of this paragraph, which shall in no case exceed the greater of 3 cubic metres or 1/1,000 of the tank capacity in cubic metres.

d) the discharge is made below the waterline, taking into account the location of the seawater intakes; and

e) the discharge is made at a distance of not less than 12 nautical miles from the nearest land and in a depth of water of not less than 25 meters.

4. The discharge into the sea of substances in Category D as defined in Regulation 3(1)(*d*) of this Annex, or of those provisionally assessed as such, or ballast water, tank washings, or other residues or mixtures containing such substances

shall be prohibited except when all the following conditions are satisfied:

a) the ship is proceeding en route at a speed of at least 7 knots in the case of self-propelled ships or at least 4 knots in the case of ships which are not self-propelled;

b) such mixtures are of a concentration not greater than one part of the substance in ten parts of water; and

c) the discharge is made at a distance of not less than 12 nautical miles from the nearest land.

5. Ventilation procedures approved by the Administration may be used to remove cargo residues from a tank. Such procedures shall be based upon standards developed by the Organization. If subsequent washing of the tank is necessary, the discharge into the sea of the resulting tank washings shall be made in accordance with paragraph (1), (2), (3) or (4) of this Regulation, whichever is applicable.

6. The discharge into the sea of substances which have not been categorized, provisionally assessed, or evaluated or referred to in Regulation 4(1) of this Annex, or of ballast water, tank washings, or other residues or mixtures containing such substances shall be prohibited.

Categories A, B and C Substances within Special Areas

Subject to the provisions of Regulation 6 of this Annex,

7. The discharge into the sea of substances in Category A as defined in regulation 3(1)(*a*) of this Annex or of those provisionally assessed as such, or ballast water, tank washings, or other residues or mixtures containing such substances shall be prohibited. If tanks containing such substances or mixtures are to be washed the resulting residues shall be discharged to a reception facility which the States bordering the special area shall provide in accordance with Regulation 7 of this Annex, until the concentration of the substance in the effluent to such facility is at or below the residual concentration prescribed for that substance in column IV of Appendix II to this Annex and until the tank is empty. Provided that the residue then remaining in the tank is subsequently diluted by the addition of a volume of water of not less than 5 per cent of the total volume of the tank, it may be discharged into the sea when all the following conditions are also satisfied:

a) the ship is proceeding en route at a speed of at least 7 knots in the case of self-propelled ships or a least 4 knots in the case of ships which are not self-propelled;

b) the discharge is made below the waterline, taking into acount the location of the seawater intakes; and

c) the discharge is made at a distance of not less than 12 nautical miles from the nearest land and in a depth of water of not less than 25 meters.

8. The discharge into the sea of substances in category B as defined in Regulation 3(1)(*b*) of this Annex or of those provisionally assessed as such, or ballast water, ballast tank, washings, or other residues or mixtures containing such substances shall be prohibited except when all the following conditions are satisfied:

a) the tank has been washed after unloading with a volume of water of not less than 0.5 per cent of the total volume of the tank, and resulting residues have been discharged to a reception facility until the tank is empty;

b) the ship is proceeding en route at a speed of at least 7 knots in the case of self-propelled ships or at least 4 knots in the case of ships which are not self-propelled;

c) the procedures and arrangements for discharge and washings are approved by the Administration. Such procedures and arrangements shall be based upon standards developed by the Organization and shall ensure that the concentration and rate of discharge of the effluent is such that the concentration of the substance in the wake astern of the ship does not exceed 1 part per million;

d) the discharge is made below the waterline, taking into account the location of the seawater intakes; and

e) the discharge is made at a distance of not less than 12 nautical miles from the nearest land and in a depth of water of not less than 25 metres.

9. The discharge into the sea of substances in Category C as defined in Reulation 3(1)(*c*) of this Annex or of those provisionally assessed as such, or ballast water, tank washings, or other residues or mixtures containing such substances shall be prohibited except when all the following conditions are satisfied:

a) the ship is proceeding en route at a speed of at least 7 knots in the case of self-propelled ships or at least 4 knots in the case of ships which are not self-propelled;

b) the procedures and arangements for discharge are approved by the Administration. Such procedures and arrangements shall be based upon standards developed by the Organization and shall ensure that the concentration and rate of discharge of the effluent is such that the concentration of the substance in the wake astern of the ship does not exceed 1 part per million;

c) the maximum quantity of cargo discharged from each tank and its associated piping system does not exceed the maximum quantity approved in accordance with the procedures referred to in sub-paragraph (*b*) of this paragraph which shall in no case exceed the greater of 1 cubic metre or 1/3,000 of the tank capacity in cubic metres;

d) the discharge is made below the waterline, taking into account the location of the seawater intakes; and

e) the discharge is made at a distance of not less than 12 nautical miles from the nearest land and in a depth of water of not less than 25 metres.

10. Ventilation procedures approved by the Administation may be used to remove cargo residues from a tank. Such procedures shall be

based upon standards developed by the Organization. If subsequent washing of the tank is necessary, the discharge into the sea of the resulting tank washings shall be made in accordance with paragraph (7), (8) or (9) of this Regulation, whichever is applicable.

11. The discharge into the sea of substances which have not been categorized, provisionally assessed or evaluated as referred to in Regulation 4(1) of this Annex, or of ballast water, tank washings, or other residues or mixtures containing such substances shall be prohibited.

12. Nothing in this Regulation shall prohibit a ship from retaining on board the residues from a Category B or C cargo and discharging such residues into the sea outside a special area in accordance with paragraph (2) or (3) of this Regulation, respectively.

13. *a*) The Governments of Parties to the Convention, the coastlines of which border on any given special area, shall collectively agree and establish a date by which time the requirement of Regulation 7(1) of this Annex will be fulfilled and from which the requirements of paragraphs (7), (8), (9) and (10) of this Regulation in respect of that area shall take effect and notify the Organization of the date so established at least six months in advance of that date. The Organization shall then promptly notify all Parties of that date.

b) If the date of entry into force of the present Convention is earlier than the date established in accordance with sub-paragraph (*a*) of this paragraph, the requirements of paragraphs (1), (2) and (3) of this Regulation shall apply during the interim period.

Regulation 6

EXCEPTIONS

Regulation 5 of this Annex shall not apply to:

a) the discharge into the sea of noxious liquid substances or mixtures containing such substances necessary for the purpose of securing the safety of a ship or saving life at sea; or

b) the discharge into the sea of noxious liquid substances or mixtures containing such substances resulting from damage to a ship or its equipment:

(i) provided that all reasonable precautions have been taken after the occurrence of the damage or discovery of the discharge for the purpose of preventing or minimizing the discharge; and

(ii) except if the owner or the Master acted either with intent to cause damage, or recklessly and with knowledge that damage would probably result; or

c) the discharge into the sea of noxious liquid substances or mixtures containing such substances, approved by the Administration, when being used for the purpose of combating specific pollution incidents in order to minimize the damage from pollution. Any such discharge shall be subject to the approval of any Government in whose jurisdiction it is contemplated the discharge will occur.

Regulation 7

RECEPTION FACILITIES

1. The Government of each Party to the Convention undertakes to ensure the provision of reception facilities according to the needs of ships using its ports, terminals or ports as follows:

a) cargo loading and unloading ports and terminals shall have facilities adequate for reception without undue delay to ships of such residues and mixtures containing noxious liquid substances as would remain for disposal from ships carrying them as a consequence of the application of this Annex; and

b) ship repair ports undertaking repairs to chemical tanks shall have facilities adequate for the reception of residues and mixtures containing noxious liquid substances.

2. The Government of each Party shall determine the types of facilities provided for the purpose of paragraph (1) of this Regulation at each cargo loading and unloading port, terminal and ship repair in its territories and notify the Organization thereof.

3. Each Party shall notify the Organization, for transmission to the Parties concerned, of any case where facilities required under paragraph (1) of this Regulation are alleged to be inadequate.

Regulation 8

MEASURES OF CONTROL

1. The Government of each Party to the Convention shall appoint or authorize surveyors for the purpose of implementing this Regulation.

Category A Substances in all Areas

2. *a*) If a tank is partially unloaded or unloaded but not cleaned, an appropriate entry shall be made in the Cargo Record Book.

b) Until that tank is cleaned every subsequent pumping or transfer operation carried out in connexion with that tank shall also be entered in the Cargo Record Book.

3. If the tank is to be washed:

a) the effluent from the tank washing operations shall be discharged from the ship to a reception facility at least until the concentration of the substance in the discharge, as indicated by analyses of samples of the effluent taken by the surveyor, has fallen to the residual concentration specified for that substance in Appendix II to this Annex. When the required residual concentration has been achieved, remaining tank washings shall continue to be discharged to the reception facility until the tank is empty. Appropriate entries of these operations shall be made in the Cargo Record Book and certified by the surveyor; and

b) after diluting the residue then remaining in the tank with at least 5 per cent of the tank capacity of water, this mixture may be discharged into the sea in accordance with the provisions of sub-paragraphs (1)(*a*), (*b*) and (*c*) or 7(*a*), (*b*) and (*c*), whichever is applicable, of Regulation 5 of this Annex. Appropriate entries of these operations shall be made in the Cargo Record Book.

4. Where the Government of the receiving Party is satisfied that it is impracticable to measure the concentration of the substance in the effluent without causing undue delay to the ship, that Party may accept an alternative procedure as being equivalent to sub-paragraph (3)(*a*) provided that:

a) a precleaning procedure for that tank and that substance, based on standards developed by the Organization, is approved by the Administration and that Party is satisfied that such procedure will fulfil the requirements of paragraph (1) or (7), whichever is applicable, of Regulation 5 of this Annex with respect to the attainment of the prescribed residual concentrations;

b) a surveyor duly authorized by that Party shall certify in the Cargo Record Book that:

(i) the tank, its pump and piping system have been emptied, and that the quantity of cargo remaining in the tank is at or below the quantity on which the approved precleaning procedure referred to in sub-paragraph (ii) of this paragraph has been based;

(ii) precleaning has been carried out in accordance with the precleaning procedure approved by the Administration for that tank and that substance; and

(iii) the tank washings resulting from such precleaning have been discharged to a reception facility and the tank is empty;

c) the discharge into the sea of any remaining residues shall be in accordance with the provisions of paragraph (3)(*b*) of this Regulation and an appropriate entry is made in the Cargo Record Book.

Category B Substances outside Special Areas and Category C Substances in all Areas.

5. Subject to such surveillance and approval by the authorized or appointed surveyor as may be deemed necessary by the Government of the Party, the Master of a ship shall, with respect to a Category B substance outside a special area or a Category C substance in all areas, ensure compliance with the following:

a) If a tank is partially unloaded but not cleaned, an appropriate entry shall be made in the Cargo Record Book.

b) If the tank is to be cleaned at sea:

(i) the cargo piping system serving that tank shall be drained and an appropriate entry made in the Cargo Record Book;

(ii) the quantity of substance remaining in the tank shall not exceed the maximum quantity which may be discharged into the sea for that substance under Regulation 5(2)(*c*) of this Annex outside special areas in the case of Category B substances, or under Regulations 5(3)(*c*) and 5(9)(*c*) outside and within special areas respectively in the case of Category C substances. An appropriate entry shall be made in the Cargo Record Book;

(iii) where it is intended to discharge the quantity of substance remaining into the sea the approved procedures shall be complied with, and the necessary dilution of the substance satisfactory for such a discharge shall be achieved. An appropriate entry shall be made in the Cargo Record Book; or

(iv) where the tank washings are not discharged into the sea, if any internal transfer of tank washings takes place from that tank an appropriate entry shall be made in the Cargo Record Book; and

(v) any subsequent discharge into the sea of such tank washings shall be made in accordance with the requirements of Regulation 5 of this Annex for the appropriate area and Category of substance involved.

c) If the tank is to be cleaned in port:

(i) the tank washings shall be discharged to a reception facility and an appropriate entry shall be made in the Cargo Record Book; or

(ii) the tank washings shall be retained on board the ship and appropriate entry shall be made in the Cargo Record Book indicating the location and disposition of the tank washings.

d) If after unloading a Category C substance within a special area, any residues or tank washings are to be retained on board until the ship is outside the special area, the Master shall so indicate by an appropriate entry in the Cargo Record Book and in this case the procedures set out in Regulation 5(3) of this Annex shall be applicable.

Category B Substances within Special Areas

6. Subject to such surveillance and approval by the authorized or appointed surveyor as may be deemed necessary by the Government of the Party, the master of a ship shall, with respect to a Category B substance within a special area, ensure compliance with the following:

a) If a tank is partially loaded or unloaded but not cleaned, an appropriate entry shall be made in the Cargo Record Book.

b) Until that tank is cleaned every subsequent pumping or transfer operation carried out in connexion with that tank shall also be entered in the Cargo Record Book.

c) If the tank is to be washed, the effluent from the tank washing operation, which shall contain a volume of water not less than 0.5 per cent of the total volume of the tank, shall be discharged from the ship to a reception facility until the tank, its pump and piping system are empty. An appropriate entry shall be made in the Cargo Record Book.

d) If the tank is to be further cleaned and emptied at sea, the Master shall:

(i) ensure that the approved procedures referred to in Regulation 5(8)(*c*) of this Annex are complied with and that the appropriate entry is made in the Cargo Record Book.

(ii) ensure that any discharge into the sea is made in accordance with the requirements of Regulation 5(8) of this Annex and an appropriate entry is made in the Cargo Record Book.

e) If after unloading a Category B substance within a special area, any residues or tank washings are to be retained on board until the ship is outside the special area, the Master shall so indicate by an appropriate entry in the Cargo Record Book and in this case the procedures set out in Regulation 5(2) of this Annex shall be applicable.

Category D Substances in all Areas

7. The Master of a ship shall, with respect to a Category D substance, ensure compliance with the following:

a) If a tank is partially unloaded or unloaded but not cleaned, an appropriate entry shall be made in the Cargo Record Book.

b) If the tank is to be cleaned at sea:

(i) the cargo piping system serving that tank shall be drained and an appropriate entry made in the Cargo Record Book;

(ii) where it is intended to discharge the quantity of substance remaining into the sea, the necessary dilution of the substance satisfactory for such a discharge shall be achieved. An appropriate entry shall be made in the Cargo Record Book; or

(iii) where the tank washings are not discharged into the sea, if any internal transfer of tank washings takes place from that tank an appropriate entry shall be made in the Cargo Record Book; and

(iv) any subsequent discharge into the sea of such tank washings shall be made in accordance with the requirements of Regulation 5(4) of this Annex.

c) If the tank is to be cleaned in port:

(i) the tank washings shall be discharged to a reception facility and an appropriate entry shall be made in the Cargo Record Book; or

(ii) the tank washings shall be retained on board the ship and an appropriate entry shall be made in the Cargo Record Book indicating the location and disposition of the tank washings.

Discharge from a Slop Tank

8. Any residues retained on board in a slop tank, including those from pump room bilges, which contain a Category A substance, or within a special area either a Category A or a Category B substance, shall be discharged to a reception facility in accordance with the provisions of Regulation 5(1), (7) or (8) of this Annex, whichever is applicable. An appropriate entry shall be made in the Cargo Record Book.

9. Any residues retained on board in a slop tank, including those from pump room bilges, which contain a quantity of a Category B substance outside a special area of a Category C substance in all areas in excess of the aggregate of the maximum quantities specified in Regulation 5(2)(*c*), (3)(*c*) or (9)(*c*) of this Annex, whichever is applicable, shall be discharged to a reception facility. An appropriate entry shall be made in the Cargo Record Book.

Regulation 9

CARGO RECORD BOOK

1. Every ship to which this Annex applies shall be provided with a Cargo Record Book, whether as part of the ship's official log book or otherwise, in the form specified in Appendix IV to this Annex.

2. The Cargo Record Book shall be completed, on a tank-to-tank basis, whenever any of the following operations with respect to a noxious liquid substance take place in the ship:

(i) loading of cargo;

(ii) unloading of cargo;

(iii) transfer of cargo;

(iv) transfer of cargo, cargo residues or mixtures containing cargo to a slop tank;

(v) cleaning of cargo tanks;

(vi) transfer from slop tanks;

(vii) ballasting of cargo tanks;

(viii) transfer of dirty ballast water;

(ix) discharge into the sea in accordance with Regulation 5 of this Annex.

3. In the event of any discharge of the kind referred to in Article 7 of the present Convention and Regulation 6 of this Annex of any noxious liquid substance or mixture containing such substances, whether intentional or accidental, an entry shall be made in the Cargo Record Book stating the circumstances of, and the reason for, the discharge.

4. When a surveyor appointed or authorized by the Government of the Party to the Convention to supervise any operations under this Annex has inspected a ship, then that surveyor shall make appropriate entry in the Cargo Record Book.

5. Each operation referred to in paragraph (2) and (3) of this Regulation shall be fully recorded without delay in the Cargo Record Book so that all the entries in the Book appropriate to that operation are completed. Each entry shall be signed by the officer or officers in charge of the operation concerned and, when the ship is manned, each page shall be signed by the Master of the ship. The entries in the Cargo Record Book shall be in an official language of the State whose flag the ship is entitled to fly, and, for ships holding an International Pollution Prevention Certificate for the carriage of Noxious Liquid Substances in Bulk (1973) in English or French. The entries in an official national language of the State whose flag the ship is entitled to fly shall prevail in case of a dispute or discrepancy.

6. The Cargo Record Book shall be kept in such a place as to be readily available for inspection and, except in the case of unmanned ships under tow, shall be kept on board the ship. It shall be retained for a period of two years after the last entry has been made.

7. The competent authority of the Government of a Party may inspect the Cargo Record Book on board any ship to which this Annex applies while the ship is in its port, and may make a copy of any entry in that book and may require the Master of the ship to certify that the copy is a true copy of such entry. Any copy so made which has been certified by the Master of the ship as a true copy of an entry in the ship's Cargo Record Book shall be made admissible in any judicial proceedings as

evidence of the facts stated in the entry. The inspection of a Cargo Record Book and the taking of a certified copy by the competent authority under this paragraph shall be performed as expeditiously as possible without causing the ship to be unduly delayed.

Regulation 10

SURVEYS

1. Ships which are subject to the provisions of this Annex and which carry noxious liquid substances in bulk shall be surveyed as follows:

a) An initial survey before a ship is put into service or before the certificate required by Regulation 11 of this Annex is issued for the first time, which shall include a complete inspection of its structure, equipment, fittings, arrangements and material in so far as the ship is covered by this Annex. The survey shall be such as to ensure full compliance with the applicable requirements of this Annex.

b) Periodical surveys at intervals specified by the Administration which shall not exceed five years and which shall be such as to ensure that the structure, equipment, fittings, arrangements and material fully comply with the applicable requirements of this Annex. However, where the duration of the International Pollution Prevention Certificate for the Carriage of Noxious Liquid Substances in Bulk (1973) is extended as specified in Regulation 12(2) or (4) of this Annex, the interval of the periodical survey may be extended correspondingly.

c) Intermediate surveys at intervals specified by the Administration which shall not exceed thirty months and which shall be such as to ensure that the equipment and associated pump and piping system, fully comply with the applicable requirements of this Annex and are in good working order. The survey shall be endorsed on the International Pollution Prevention Certificate for the Carriage of Noxious Liquid Substances in Bulk (1973) issued under Regulation 11 of this Annex.

2. Surveys of a ship with respect to the enforcement of the provisions of this Annex shall be carried out by officers of the Administration. The Administration may, however, entrust the surveys either to surveyors nominated for the purpose or to organizations recognized by it. In every case the Administration concerned shall fully guarantee the completeness and efficiency of the surveys.

3. After any survey of a ship under this Regulation has been completed, no significant change shall be made in the structure, equipment, fittings, arrangements or material, covered by the survey without the sanction of the Administration, except the direct replacement of such equipment and fittings for the purpose of repair or maintenance.

Regulation 11

ISSUE OF CERTIFICATE

1. An International Pollution Prevention Certificate for the Carriage of Noxious Liquid Substances in Bulk (1973) shall be issued to any ship carrying noxious liquid substances which is engaged in voyages to ports or offshore terminals under the jurisdiction of other Parties to the Convention after survey of such ship in accordance with the provisions of Regulation 10 of this Annex.

2. Such Certificate shall be issued either by the Administration or by a person or organization duly authorized by it. In every case the Administration shall assume full responsibility for the Certificate.

3. *a*) The Government of a Party may, at the request of the Administration, cause a ship to be surveyed and if satisfied that the provisions of this Annex are complied with shall issue or authorize the issue of a Certificate to the ship in accordance with this Annex.

b) A copy of the Certificate and a copy of the survey report shall be transmitted as soon as possible to the requesting Administration.

c) A Certificate so issued shall contain a statement to the effect that it has been issued at the request of the Administration and shall have the same force and receive the same recognition as a certificate issued under paragraph (1) of this Regulation

d) No International Pollution Prevention Certificate for the Carriage of Noxious Liquid Substances in Bulk (1973) shall be issued to any ship which is entitled to fly the flag of a State which is not a Party.

4. The Certificate shall be drawn up in an official language of the issuing country in a form corresponding to the model given in Appendix V of this Annex. If the language used is neither English nor French, the text shall include a translation into one of these languages.

Regulation 12

DURATION OF CERTIFICATE

1. An International Pollution Prevention Certificate for the Carriage of Noxious Liquid Substances in Bulk (1973) shall be issued for a period specified by the Administration, which shall not exceed five years from the date of issue, except as provided in paragraphs (2) and (4) of this Regulation.

2. If a ship at the time when the Certificate expires is not in a port or offshore terminal under the jurisdiction of the Party to the Convention whose flag the ship is entitled to fly, the Certificate may be extended by the Administration, but such extension shall be granted only for the purpose of allowing the ship to complete its voyage to the State whose flag the ship is entitled to fly or in which it is to be surveyed and then only in cases where it appears proper and reasonable to do so.

3. No Certificate shall be thus extended for a period longer than five months and a ship to which such extension is granted shall not on its arrival in the State whose flag it is entitled to fly or the port in which it is to be surveyed, be entitled by virtue of such extension to leave that port or State without

having obtained a new Certificate.

4. A Certificate which has not been extended under the provisions of paragraph (2) of this Regulation may be extended by the Administration for a period of grace of up to one month from the date of expiry stated on it.

5. A Certificate shall cease to be valid if significant alterations have taken place in the structure, equipment, fittings, arrangements and material required by this Annex without sanction of the Administration, except the direct replacement of such equipment or fitting for the purpose of repair or maintenance or if intermediate surveys as specified by the Administration under Regulation 10(1)(*c*) of this Annex are not carried out.

6. A Certificate issued to a ship shall cease to be valid upon transfer of such a ship to the flag of another State, except as provided in paragraph (7) of this Regulation.

7. Upon transfer of a ship to the flag of another Party, the Certificate shall remain in force for a period not exceeding five months provided that it would have expired before the end of that period, or until the Administration issues a replacement Certificate, whichever is earlier. As soon as possible after the transfer has taken place the Government of the Party whose flag the ship was formerly entitled to fly shall transmit to the Administration a copy of the Certificate carried by the ship before the transfer and, if available, a copy of the relevant survey report.

Regulation 13

REQUIREMENTS FOR MINIMIZING ACCIDENTAL POLLUTION

1. The design, construction, equipment and operation of ships carrying noxious liquid substances in bulk which are subject to the provisions of this Annex shall be such as to minimize the uncontrolled discharge into the sea of such substances.

2. Pursuant to the provisions of paragraph (1) of this Regulation, the Government of each Party shall issue, or cause to be issued, detailed requirements on the design, construction, equipment and operation of such ships.

3. In respect of chemical tankers, the requirements referred to in paragraph (2) of this Regulation shall contain at least all the provisions given in the Code for the Construction and Equipment of Ships carrying Dangerous Chemicals in Bulk adopted by the Assembly of the Organization in Resolution A.212 (VII) and as may be amended by the Organization, provided that the amendments to that Code are adopted and brought into force in accordance with the provisions of Article 16 of the present Convention for amendment procedures to an Appendix to an Annex.

APPENDIX I

GUIDELINES FOR THE CATEGORIZATION OF NOXIOUS LIQUID SUBSTANCES

Category A

Substances which are bioaccumulated and liable to produce a hazard to aquatic life or human health; or which are highly toxic to aquatic life (as expressed by a Hazard Rating 4, defined by a TLm less than 1 ppm); and additionally certain substances which are moderately toxic to aquatic life (as expressed by a Hazard Rating 3, defined by a TLm of 1 or more, but less than 10 ppm) when particular weight is given to additional factors in the hazard profile or to special characteristics of the substances.

Category B

Substances which are bioaccumulated with a short retention of the order of one week or less; or which are liable to produce tainting of the sea food; or which are moderately toxic to aquatic life (as expressed by a Hazard Rating 3, defined by a TLm of 1 ppm or more, but less than 10 ppm); and additionally certain substances which are slightly toxic to aquatic life (as expressed by a Hazard Rating 2, defined by a TLm of 10 ppm or more, but not less than 100 ppm) when particular weight is given to additional factors in the hazard profile or to special characteristics of the substance.

Category C

Substances which are slightly toxic to aquatic life (as expressed by a Hazard Rating 2, defined by a TLm of 10 or more, but less than 100 ppm); and additionally certain substances which are particularly non-toxic to aquatic life (as expressed by a Hazard Rating 2, defined by a TLm of 100 ppm or more, but not less than 1,000 ppm) when particular weight is given to additional factors in the hazard profile or to special characteristics of the substance.

Category D

Substances which are practically non-toxic to aquatic life, (as expressed by a Hazard Rating 1, defined by a TLm of 100 ppm or more, but less than 1,000 ppm); or causing deposits blanketing the seafloor with a high biochemical oxygen demand (BOD); or highly hazardous to human health, with an LD_{50} of less than 5 mg/kg; or produce moderate reduction of amenities because of persistency, smell or poisonous or irritant characteristics, possibly interfering with use of beaches; or moderately hazardous to human health, with an LD_{50} of 5 mg/kg or more, but less than 50 mg/kg and produce slight reduction of amenities.

Other Liquid Substances (for the purposes of Regulation 4 of this Annex)

Substances other than those categorized in Categories A, B, C and D above.

APPENDIX II

LIST OF NOXIOUS LIQUID SUBSTANCES CARRIED IN BULK

Substance	UN Number	Pollution Category for operational discharge (Paragraph B of Regulation 5)	Residual concentration (per cent by weight)	Paragraph D(1) of Regulation 5)
	I	II	III	IV *Within the Baltic Sea Area*
Acetaldehyde	1089	C		
Acetic acid	1842	C		
Acetic anhydride	1715	C		
Acetone	1090	D		
Acetone cyanohydrin	1541	A	0.1	0.05
Acetyl chloride	1717	C		
Acrolein	1092	A	0.1	0.05
Acrylic acid*	—	C		
Acrylonitrile	1093	B		
Adiponitrile	—	D		
Alkylbenzene sulfonate				
(straight chain)	—	C		
(branched chain)	—	B		
Allyl alcohol	1098	B		
Allyl chloride	1100	C		
Alum (15% solution)	—	D		
Aminoethylethanolamine (Hydroxyethyl-ethylenediamine)*	—	D		
Ammonia (28% aqueous)	1005	B		
iso-Amyl acetate	1104	C		
n-Amyl acetate	1104	C		
n-Amyl alcohol	—	D		
Aniline	1547	C		
Benzene	1114	C		
Benzyl alcohol	—	D		
Benzyl chloride	1738	B		
n-Butyl acetate	1123	D		

* Asterisk indicates that the substance has been provisionally included in this list and that further data are necessary in order to complete the evaluation of its environmental hazards, particularly in relation to living resources.

Substance	I	II	III	IV
sec-Butyl acetate	1124	D		
n-Butyl acrylate	—	D		
Butyl butyrate*	—	B		
Butylene glycol(s)	—	D		
Butyl methacrylate	—	D		
n-Butyraldehyde	1129	B		
Butyric acid	—	B		
Calcium hydroxide (solution)	—	D		
Camphor oil	1130	B		
Carbon disulphide	1131	A	0.1	0.005
Carbon tetrachloride	1846	B		
Caustic potash (Potassium hydroxide)	1814	C		
Cloroacetic acid	1750	C		
Chloroform	1888	B		
Chlorohydrins (crude)*	—	D		
Chloroprene*	1991	C		
Chlorosulphonic acid	1754	C		
para-Chlorotoluene	—	B		
Citric acid (10—25%)	—	D		
Creosote	1334	A	0.1	0.05
Cresols	2076	A	0.1	0.05
Cresylic acid	2022	A	0.1	0.05
Crotonaldehyde	1143	B		
Cumene	1918	C		
Cyclohexane	1145	C		
Cyclohexanol	—	D		
Cyclohexanone	1915	D		
Cyclohexylamine*	—	D		
para-Cymene (Isopropyltoluene)*	2046	D		
Decahydronaphthalene	1147	D		
Decane*	—	D		
Diacetone alcohol*	1148	D		
Dibenzyl ether*	—	C		
Dichlorobenzenes	1591	A	0.1	0.05
Dichloroethyl ether	1916	B		
Dichloropropene — Dichloropropane mixture (D.D. Soil fumigant)	2047	B		
Diethylamine	1154	C		
Diethylbenzene (mixed isomers)	2049	C		
Diethyl ether	1155	D		
Diethylene triamine*	2079	C		
Diethylene glycol monocthyl ether	—	C		
Diethylketone (3-Pentanone)	1156	D		
Diisobutylene*	2050	D		
Diisobutyl ketone	1157	D		
Diisopropanolamine	—	C		
Diisopropylamine	1158	C		
Diisopropyl ether*	1159	D		

* Asterisk indicates that the substance has been provisionally included in this list and that further data are necessary in order to complete the evaluation of its environmental hazards, particularly in relation to living resources.

Substance	I	II	III	IV
Dimethylamine (40% aqueous)	1160	C		
Dimethylethanolamine (2-Dimethylaminoethanol)*	2051	C		
Dimethylformamide	—	D		
1, 4-Dioxane*	1165	C		
Diphenyl/Diphenyloxide mixtures*	—	D		
Dodecylbenzene	—	C		
Epichlorohydrin	2023	B		
2-Ethoxyethyl acetate*	1172	D		
Ethyl acetate	1173	D		
Ethyl acrylate	1917	D		
Ethyl amyl ketone*	—	C		
Ethylbenzene	1175	C		
Ethyl cyclohexane	—	D		
Ethylene chlorohydrin (2-Chloro-ethanol)	1135	D		
Ethylene cyanohydrin*	—	D		
Ethylenediamine	1604	C		
Ethylene dibromide	1605	B		
Ethylene dichloride	1184	B		
Ethylene glycol monethyl ether (Methyl cellosolve)	1171	D		
2-Ethylhexyl acrylate*	—	D		
2-Ethylhexyl alcohol	—	C		
Ethyl lactate*	1192	D		
2-Ethyl 3-propylacrolein*	—	B		
Formaldehyde (37—50% solution)	1198	C		
Formic acid	1779	D		
Furfuryl alcohol	—	C		
Heptanoic acid*	—	D		
Hexamethylenediamine*	1783	C		
Hydrochloric acid	1789	D		
Hyrdofluoric acid (40% aqueous)	1790	B		
Hydrogen peroxide (greater than 60%)	2015	C		
Isobutyl acrylate	—	D		
Isobutyl alcohol	1212	D		
Isobutyl methacrylate	—	D		
Isobutyraldehyde	2045	C		
Isooctane*	—	D		
Isopentane	—	D		
Isophorone	—	D		
Isoprophylamine	1221	C		
Isopropyl cyclohexane	—	D		
Isoprene	1218	D		
Lactic acid	—	D		
Nesityl oxide*	1229	C		
Methyl acetate	1231	D		
Methyl acrylate	1919	C		
Methylamyl alcohol	—	D		

* Asterisk indicates that the substance has been provisionally included in this list and that further data are necessary in order to complete the evaluation of its environmental hazards, particularly in relation to living resources.

SUBSTANCE	I	II	III	IV
Methylene Chloride	1593	B		
2-Methyl-5-Ethylpyridine*	—	B		
Methyl methacrylate	1247	D		
2-Methypentene*	—	D		
alpha-Methylstyrene*	—	D		
Monochlorobenzene	1134	B		
Monoethanolamine	—	D		
Monoisopropanolamine	—	C		
Monomethyl ethanolamine	—	C		
Mononitrobenzene	—	C		
Monoisopropylamine	—	C		
Morpholine*	2054	C		
Naphthalene (molten)	1334	A	0.1	0.05
Naphthenic acids*	—	A	0.1	0.05
Nitric acid (90%)	2031/2032	C		
2-Nitropropane	—	D		
ortho-Nitrotoluene	1664	C		
Nonyl alcohol*	—	C		
Nonylphenol	—	C		
n-Octanol	—	C		
Oleum	1831	C		
Oxalic acid ((10—25%)	—	D		
Pentachloroethane	1669	B		
n-Pentane	1265	C		
Perchlorocthylene (Tetrachloroethylene)	1897	B		
Phenol	1671	B		
Phosphoric acid	1805	D		
Phosphorus (elemental)	1338	A	0.1	0.005
Phthalic Anhydride (molten)	—	C		
beta-Propiolactone*	—	B		
Propionaldehyde	1275	D		
Propionic acid	1848	D		
Propionic anhydride	—	D		
n-Propyl acetate*	1276	C		
n-Propyl alcohol	1274	D		
n-Propylamine	1277	C		
Pyridine	1282	B		
Silicon tetrachloride	1818	D		
Sodium bichromate (solution)	—	C		
Sodium hydroxide	1824	C		
Sodium pentachlorophenate (solution)	—	A	0.1	0.05
Styrene monomer	2055	C		
Sulphuric acid	1830/1831/ 1832	C		
Tallow	—	D		
Tetraethyl Lead	1649	A	0.1	0.05
Tetrahydrofuran	2056	D		
Tetrahydronaphthalene	1540	C		

* Asterisk indicates that the substance has been provisionally included in this list and that further data are necessary in order to complete the evaluation of its environmental hazards, particularly in relation to living resources.

Substance	I	II	III	IV
Tetramethylbenzene	—	D		
Tetramethyl Lead	1649	A	0.1	0.05
Titranium tetrachloride	1838	D		
Toluene	1294	C		
Toluene diisocyanate*	2078	B		
Trichloroethane	—	C		
Trichloroethylene	1710	B		
Triethanolamine	—	D		
Triethylamine	1296	C		
Trimethylbenzene*	—	C		
Tritoly phosphate (Tricresyl phosphate)*	—	B		
Turpentine (wood)	1299	B		
Vinyl acetate	1301	C		
Vinylidene chloride*	1303	B		
Xylenes (mixed isomers)	1307	C		

APPENDIX III

LIST OF OTHER LIQUID SUBSTANCES CARRIED IN BULK

Acetonitrile (Methyl cyanide)
tert-Amyl alcohol
n-Butyl alcohol
Butyrolactone
Calcium chloride (solution)
Castor oil
Citic juices
Coconut oil
Cod liver oil
iso-Decyl alcohol
n-Decyl alcohol
Deycl octyl alcohol
Dibutyl ether
Diethanolamine
Diethylene glycol
Dipentene
Dipropylene glycol
Ethyl alcohol
Ethylene glycol
Fatty alcohols (C_{12}—C_{20})
Glycerine
n-Heptane
Heptene (mixed isomers)
n-Hexane
Ligroin
Methyl alcohol
Methylamyl acetate
Methyl ethyl ketone (2-butanone)
Milk
Molasses
Olive Oil
Polypropylene glycol
iso-Propyl acetate
iso-Propyl alcohol
Propylene glycol
Propylene oxide
Propylene tetramer
Propylene trimer
Sorbitol
Sulphur (liquid)
Tridecanol
Triethylene glycol
Triethylenetetramine
Tripropylene glycol
Water
Wine

APPENDIX IV

CARGO RECORD BOOK FOR SHIPS CARRYING NOXIOUS LIQUID SUBSTANCES IN BULK

Name of ship ....

Cargo carrying capacity of each tank in cubic metres ....

Voyage from ....

to ....

a) Loading of cargo

1. Date and place of loading
2. Name and category of cargo(es) loaded
3. Identity of tank(s) loaded

* Asterisk indicates that the substance has been provisionally included in this list and that further data are necessary to complete the evaluation of its environmental hazards, particularly in relation to living resources.

b) *Transfer of cargo*
4. Date of transfer
5. Identity of tank(s) (i) From
   (ii) To
6. Was(were) tank(s) in 5 (i) emptied?
7. If not, quantity remaining

c) *Unloading of cargo*
8. Date and place of unloading
9. Identity of tank(s) unloaded
10. Was(were) tank(s) emptied?
11. If not, quantity remaining in tank(s)
12. Is(are) tank(s) to be cleaned?
13. Amount transferred to slop tank
14. Identity of slop tank

d) *Ballasting of cargo tanks*
15. Identity of tank(s) ballasted
16. Date and position of ship at start of ballasting

....Signature of Master

e) *Cleaning of cargo tanks*

Category A Substances
17. Identity of tank(s) cleaned
18. Date and location of cleaning
19. Method(s) of cleaning
20. Location of reception facility used
21. Concentration of effluent when discharge to reception facility stopped
22. Quantity remaining in tank
23. Procedure and amount of water introduced into tank in final cleaning
24. Location, date of discharge into sea
25. Procedure and equipment used in discharge into the sea

Category B, C and D substances
26. Washing procedure used
27. Quantity of water used
28. Date, location of discharge into sea
29. Procedure and equipment used in discharge into the sea

f) *Transfer of dirty ballast water*
30. Identity of tank(s)
31. Date and position of ship at start of discharge into sea
32. Date and position of ship at finish of discharge into sea
33. Ship's speed(s) during discharge
34. Quantity discharged into sea
35. Quantity of polluted water transferred to slop tank(s) (identify slop tank(s))
36. date and port of discharge to shore reception facilities (if applicable)

....Signature of Master

g) *Transfer from slop tank/disposal of residue*
37. Identity of slop tank(s)
38. Quantity disposed from each tank
39. Method of disposal of residue:
   a) Reception facilities
   b) Mixed with cargo
   c) Transferred to another(other) tank(s) (identify tank(s))
40. Date and port of disposal of residue

h) *Accidental or other exceptional discharge*
41. Date and time of occurrence
42. Place or position of ship at time of occurrence
43. Approximate quantity, name and category of substance
44. Circumstances of discharge or escape and general remarks

....Signature of Master

APPENDIX V

Form of Certificate

INTERNATIONAL POLLUTION PREVENTION CERTIFICATE FOR THE CARRIAGE OF NOXIOUS LIQUID SUBSTANCES IN BULK (1973)

(Note: This Certificate shall be supplemented in the case of a chemical tanker by the certificate required pursuant to the provisions of Regulation 13 (3) of Annex II of the Convention)

(Official Seal)

Issued under the provisions of the International Convention for the Prevention of Pollution from Ships, 1973, under the authority of the Government of

....

(full official designation of the country)

by ....

(full official designation of the competent person or organization authorized under the provisions of the International Convention for the Prevention of Pollution from Ships, 1973)

Name of Ship	Distinctive Number or Letter	Port of Registry	Gross Tonnage

THIS IS TO CERTIFY:

1. That the ship has been surveyed in accordance with the provisions of Regulation 10 of Annex II of the Convention.

2. That the survey showed that the design, construction and equipment of the ship are such as to minimize the uncontrolled discharge into the sea of noxious liquid substances.

3. That the following arrangements and procedures have been approved by the Administration in connexion with the implementation of Regulation 5 of Annex II of the Convention.

....

(Continued on the annexed signed and dated sheet(s))

....

This certificate is valid, until ....

subject to intermediate survey(s) at intervals of ....

Issued at ....
(place of issue of Certificate)

.... 19 .....

....
(Signature of duly authorized official issuing the Certificate)

(Seal or stamp of the issuing Authority, as appropriate)

Intermediate surveys

This is to certify that at an intermediate survey required by Regulation 10 (1) (*c*) of Annex II of the Convention, this ship and the condition thereof are found to comply with the relevant provisions of the Convention.

Signed...
(Signature of duly authorized Officer)

Place ....

Date ....

(Seal or stamp of the Authority, as appropriate)

Under the provisions of Regulation 12 (2) and (4) of Annex II of the Convention the validity of this Certificate is extended until

....

Signed...
(Signature of duly authorized official)

Place ....

Date ....

(Seal or stamp of the Authority, as appropriate)

ANNEX III

Regulations for the Prevention of Pollution by Harmful Substances Carried by Sea in Packaged Forms or in Freight Containers, Portable Tanks or Road and Rail Tank Wagons

Regulation 1

APPLICATION

1. Unless expressly provided otherwise, the Regulations of this Annex apply to all ships carrying harmful substances in packaged forms, or in freight containers, portable tanks or road and rail tank wagons.

2. Such carriage of harmful substances is prohibited except in accordance with the provisions of this Annex.

3. To supplement the provisions of this Annex the Government of each Party to the Convention shall issue, or cause to be issued, detailed requirements on packaging, marking and labelling, documentation, stowage, quantity limitations, exceptions and notification, for preventing or minimizing pollution of the marine environment by harmful substances.

4. For the purpose of this Annex, empty receptacles, freight containers, portable tanks and road and rail tank wagons which have been used previously for the carriage of harmful substances shall themselves be treated as harmful substances unless adequate precautions have been taken to ensure that they contain no residue that is hazardous to the marine environment.

Regulation 2

PACKAGING

Packagings, freight containers, portable tanks and road and rail tank wagons shall be adequate to minimize the hazard to the marine environment having regard to their specific contents.

Regulation 3

MARKING AND LABELLING

Packages, whether shipped individually or in units or in freight containers, portable tanks or road and rail tank wagons containing a harmful substance, shall be durably marked with the correct technical name (trade names shall not be used as the correct technical name), and further marked with a distinctive label or stencil of label, indicating that the contents are harmful. Such identification shall be supplemented where possible by any other means, for example by the use of the United Nations number.

Regulation 4

DOCUMENTATION

1. In all documents relating to the carriage of harmful substances by sea where such substances are named, the correct technical name of the substances shall be used (trade names shall not be used).

2. The shipping documents supplied by the shipper shall include a certificate or declaration that the shipment offered for carriage is properly packed, marked and labelled and in proper condition for carriage to minimize the hazard to the marine environment.

3. Each ship carrying harmful substances shall have a special list or manifest setting forth the harmful substances on board and the location thereof. A detailed stowage plan which sets out the location of all harmful substances on board may be used in place of such special list or manifest. Copies of such documents shall also be retained on shore by the owner of the ship or his representative until the harmful substances are unloaded.

4. In a case where the ship carries a special list or manifest or a detailed stowage plan, required for the carriage of dangerous goods by the International Convention for the Safety of Life at Sea in force, the documents required for the purpose of this Annex may be combined with those for dangerous goods. Where documents are combined, a clear distinction shall be made between dangerous goods and other harmful substances.

Regulation 5

STOWAGE

Harmful substances shall be both properly stowed and secured so as to minimize the hazards to the marine environment without impairing the safety of ship and persons on board.

Regulation 6

QUANTITY LIMITATIONS

Certain harmful substances which are very hazardous to the marine environment may, for sound scientific and technical reasons, need to be prohibited for carriage or be limited as to the quantity which may be carried aboard any one ship. In limiting the quantity due consideration shall be given to size, construction and equipment of the ship as well as the packaging and the inherent nature of the substance.

Regulation 7

EXCEPTIONS

1. Discharge by jettisoning of harmful substances carried in packaged forms, freight containers, portable tanks or road and rail tank wagons shall be prohibtied except where necessary for the purpose of securing the safety of the ship or saving life at sea.

2. Subject to the provisions of the present Convention, appropriate measures based on the physical, chemical and biological properties of harmful substances shall be taken to regulate the washing of leakages overboard provided that compliance with such measures would not impair the safety of the ship and persons on board.

Regulation 8

NOTIFICATION

With respect of certain harmful substances, as may be designated by the Government of a Party to the Convention, the master or owner of the ship or his representative shall notify the appropriate port authority of the intent to load or unload such substances at least 24 hours prior to such action.

ANNEX IV

Regulations for the Prevention of Pollution by Sewage from Ships

Regulation 1

DEFINITIONS

For the purposes of the present Annex:

1. "New ship" means a ship:

a) for which the building contract is placed, or in the absence of a building contract, the keel of which is laid, or which is at a similar stage of construction, on or after the date of entry into force of this Annex; or

b) the delivery of which is three years or more after the date of entry into force of this Annex.

2. "Existing ship" means a ship which is not a new ship.

3. "Sewage" means:

a) drainage and other wastes from any form of toilets, urinals, and WC scuppers;

b) drainage from medical premises (dispensary, sick bay, etc.) via wash basins, wash tubs and scuppers located in such premises;

c) drainage from spaces containing living animals; or

d) other waste waters when mixed with the drainages defined above.

4. "Holding tank" means a tank used for the collection and storage of sewage.

5. "Nearest land". The term "from the nearest land" means from the baseline from which the territorial sea of the territory in question is established in accordance with international law except that, for the purposes of the present Convention "from the nearest land" off the north eastern coast of Australia shall mean from a line drawn from a point on the coast of Australia in latitude 11° 00′ South, longitude 142° 08′ East to a point in latitude 10° 35′ South,

longitude 141′ 55′ East — thence to a point latitude 10° 00′ South,

longitude 142° 00′ East, thence to a point latitude 9° 00′ South,

longitude 143° 52′ East, thence to a point latitude 0° 00′ South,

longitude 144° 30′ East, thence to a point latitude 13° 00′ South

longitude 144° 00′ East, thence to a point latitude 15° 00′ South,

longitude 146° 00′ East, thence to a point latitude 18° 00′ South,

longitude 147° 00′ East, thence to a point latitude 21° 00′ South,

longitude 153° 00′ East, thence to a point on the coast of Australia in latitude 24° 42′ South, longitude 153° 15′ East.

Regulation 2

APPLICATION

The provisions of this Annex shall apply to:

a) (i) new ships of 200 tons gross tonnage and above;

(ii) new ships of less than 200 tons gross tonnage which are certified to carry more than 10 persons;

(iii) new ships which do not have a measured gross tonnage and are certified to carry more than 10 persons; and

b) (i) existing ships of 200 tons gross tonnage and above, 10 years after the date of entry into force of this Annex;

(ii) existing ships less than 200 tons gross tonnage which are certified to carry more than 10 persons, 10 years after the date of entry into force of this Annex; and

(iii) existing ships which do not have a measured gross tonnage and are certified to carry more than 10 persons, 10 years after the date of entry into force of this Annex.

Regulation 3

SURVEYS

1. Every ship which is required to comply with the provisions of this Annex and which is engaged in voyages to ports or offshore terminals under the jurisdiction of other Parties to the Convention shall be subject to the surveys specified below:

a) An initial survey before the ship is put in service or before the Certificate required under Regulation 4 of this Annex is issued for the first time, which shall include a survey of the ship which shall be such as to ensure:

(i) when the ship is equipped with a sewage treatment plant the plant shall meet operational requirements based on standards and the test methods developed by the Organization;

(ii) when the ship is fitted with a system to comminute and disinfect the sewage, such a system shall be of a type approved by the Administration;

(iii) when the ship is equipped with a holding tank the capacity of such a tank shall be to the satisfaction of the Administration for the retention of all sewage having regard to the operation of the ship, the number of persons on board and other relevant factors. The holding tank shall have a means to indicate visually the amount of its contents; and

(iv) that the ship is equipped with a pipeline leading to the exterior convenient for the discharge of sewage to a reception facility and that such a pipeline is fitted with a standard shore connection in compliance with Regulation 11 of this Annex.

This survey shall be such as to ensure that the equipment, fittings, arrangements and material fully comply with the applicable requirements of this Annex.

b) Periodical surveys at intervals specified by the Administration but not exceeding five years which shall be such as to ensure that the equipment, fittings, arrangements and material fully comply with the applicable requirements of this Annex. However, where the duration of the International Sewage Pollution Prevention Certificate (1973) is extended as specified in Regulation 7(2) or (4) of this Annex, the interval of the periodical survey may be extended correspondingly.

2. The Administration shall establish appropriate measures for ships which are not subject to the provisions of paragraph (1) of this Regulation in order to ensure that the provisions of this Annex are complied with.

3. Surveys of the ship as regards enforcement of the provisions of this Annex shall be carried out by officers of the Administration. The Administration may, however, entrust the surveys either to surveyors nominated for the purpose or to organizations recognized by it. In every case the Administration concerned fully guarantees the completeness and efficiency of the surveys.

4. After any survey of the ship under this Regulation has been completed, no significant change shall be made in the equipment, fittings, arrangements, or material covered by the survey without the approval of the Administration, except the direct replacement of such equipment or fittings.

Regulation 4

ISSUE OF CERTIFICATE

1. An International Sewage Pollution Certificate (1973) shall be issued, after survey in accordance with the provisions of Regulation 3 of this Annex, to any ship which is engaged in voyages to ports or offshore terminals under the jurisdiction of other Parties to the Convention.

2. Such Certificate shall be issued either by the Administration or by any persons or organization duly authorized by it. In every case the Administration assumes full responsibility for the Certificate.

Regulation 5

ISSUE OF A CERTIFICATE BY ANOTHER GOVERNMENT

1. The Government of a Party to the Convention, may, at the request of the Administration, cause a ship to be surveyed and if satisfied that the provisions of this Annex are complied with, shall issue or authorize the issue of an International Sewage Pollution Prevention Certificate (1973) to the ship in accordance with this Annex.

2. A copy of the Certificate and a copy of the survey report shall be transmitted as early as possible to the Administration requesting the survey.

3. A Certificate so issued shall contain a statement to the effect that it has been issued at the request of the Administration and it shall have the same force and receive the same recognition as the Certificate issued under Regulation 4 of this Annex.

4. No International Sewage Pollution Prevention Certificate (1973) shall be issued to a ship which is entitled to fly the flag of a State, which is not a Party.

Regulation 6

FORM OF CERTIFICATE

The International Sewage Pollution Certificate (1973) shall be drawn up in an official language of the issuing country in the form corresponding to the model given in the Appendix to this Annex. If the language used is neither English nor French, the text shall include a translation into one of these languages.

Regulation 7

DURATION OF CERTIFICATE

1. An International Sewage Pollution Certificate (1973) shall be issued for a period specified by the Administration, which shall not exceed five years from the date of issue, except as provided in paragraphs (2), (3) and (4) of this Regulation.

2. If a ship at the time when the Certificate expires is not in a port or offshore terminal under the jurisdiction of the Party to the Convention whose flag the ship is entitled to fly, the Certificate may be extended by the Administration, but such extension shall be granted only for the purpose of allowing the ship to complete its voyage to the State whose flag the ship is entitled to fly or in which it is to be surveyed and only in cases where it appears proper and reasonable to do so.

3. No Certificate shall be thus extended for a period longer than five months and a ship to which such extension is granted shall not on its arrival in the State whose flag it is entitled to fly or the port in which it is to be surveyed, be entitled by virtue of such extension to leave that port or State without having obtained a new Certificate.

4. A Certificate which has not been extended under the provisions of paragraph (2) of this Regulation may be extended by the Administration for a period of grace of up to one month from the date of expiry stated on it.

5. A Certificate shall cease to be valid if significant alterations have taken place in the equipment, fittings, arrangements or material required without the approval of the Administration, except the direct replacement of such equipment or fittings.

6. A Certificate issued to a ship shall cease to be valid upon transfer of such a ship to the flag of another State, except as provided in paragraph (7) of this Regulation.

7. Upon transfer of a ship to the flag of another Party, the Certificate shall remain in force for a period not exceeding five months provided that it would not have expired before the end of that period, or until the Administration issues a replacement Certificate, whichever is earlier. As soon as possible after the transfer has taken place the Government of the Party whose flag the ship was formerly entitled to fly shall transmit to the Administration a copy of the Certificate carried by the ship before the transfer and, if available, a copy of the relevant survey report.

Regulation 8

DISCHARGE OF SEWAGE

1. Subject to the provisions of Regulation 9 of this Annex, the discharge of sewage into the sea is prohibited, except when:

a) the ship is discharged comminuted and disinfected sewage using a system approved by the Administration in accordance with Regulation 3(1)(*a*) at a distance of more than four nautical miles from the nearest land, or sewage which is not comminuted or disinfected at a distance of more than 12 nautical miles from the nearest land, provided that in any case, the sewage that has been stored in holding tanks shall not be discharged instantaneouly but at a moderate rate when the ship is en route and proceeding at not less than 4 knots; the rate of discharge shall be approved by the Administration based upon standards developed by the Organization; or

b) the ship has in operation an approved sewage treatment plant which has been certified by the Administration to meet the operational requirements referred to in Regulation 3(1)(*a*)(i) of this Annex, and

(i) the text results of the plant are laid down in the ship's International Sewage Pollution Prevention Certificate (1973);

(ii) additionally, the effluent shall not produce visible floating solids in, nor cause the discolouration of, the surrounding water; or

c) the ship is situated in the waters under the jurisdiction of a State and is discharged sewage in accordance with such less stringent requirements as may be imposed by such State.

2. When the sewage is mixed with wastes or waste water having different discharge requirements, the more stringent requirements shall apply.

Regulation 9

EXCEPTIONS

a) the discharge of sewage from a ship necessary for the purpose of securing the safety of a ship and those on board or saving life at sea; or

b) the discharge of sewage resulting from damage to a ship or its equipment if all reasonable precautions have been taken before and after the occurrence of the damage, for the purpose of preventing or minimizing the discharge.

Regulation 10

RECEPTION FACILITIES

1. The Government of each Party to the Convention undertakes to ensure the provision of facilities at ports and terminals for the reception of sewage, without causing undue delay to ships, adequate to meet the needs of the ships using them.

2. The Government of each Party shall notify the Organization for transmission to the Contracting Governments concerned of all cases where the facilities provided under this Regulation are alleged to be inadequate.

Regulation 11

STANDARD DISCHARGE CONNECTIONS

To enable pipes of reception facilities to be connected with the ship's discharge pipeline, both lines shall be fitted with a standard discharge connection in accordance with the following table:

Standard Dimensions of Flanges for Discharge Connections

Dimension	Description
Outside diameter	210 mm
Inner diameter	According to pipe outside diameter
Bolt circle diameter	170 mm
Slots in flange	4 holes 18 mm diameter equidistantly placed on a bolt circle of the above diameter, slotted to the flange periphery. The slot width to be 18 mm.
Flange thickness	16 mm
Bolts and nuts: quantity and diameter	4, each of 16 mm in diameter and of suitable length
The flange is designed to accept pipes up to a maximum internal diameter of 100 mm and shall be of steel or other equivalent material having a flat face. This flange, together with a suitable gasket, shall be suitable for a service pressure of 6 kg/cm^2.	

For ships having a moulded depth of 5 metres and less, the inner diameter of the discharge connection may be 38 millimetres.

APPENDIX

FORM OF CERTIFICATE

INTERNATIONAL SEWAGE POLLUTION PREVENTION CERTIFICATE (1973)

Issued under the Provisions of the International Convention for the Prevention of Pollution from Ships, 1973, under the Authority of the Government of

....

(full designation of the country)

by ....

(full designation of the competent person or organization authorized under the provisions of the International Convention for the Prevention of Pollution from Ships, 1973)

Name of ship	Distinctive Number or Letters	Port of Registry	Gross Tonnage	Number of persons which the ship is certified to carry

New/existing ship*

Date of building contract ....

Date on which keel was laid or ship was at a similar stage of construction ....

Date of delivery ....

*Delete as appropriate

THIS IS TO CERTIFY THAT:

1. The ship is equipped with a sewage treatment plant/comminuter/holding tank* and a discharge pipeline in compliance with Regulation 3(1)(*a*)(i) to (iv) of Annex IV of the Convention as follows:

**a*) Description of the sewage treatment plant:

Type of sewage treatment plant ....

Name of manufacturer ....

The sewage treatment plant is certified by the Administration to meet the following effluent standards:** ....

**b*) Description of comminuter:

Type of comminuter ....

Name of manufacturer ....

Standard of sewage after disinfection ....

**c*) Description of holding tank equipment:

Total capacity of the holding tank .... m^3

Location ....

d) A pipeline for the discharge of sewage to a reception facility, fitted with a standard shore connection.

2. The ship has been surveyed in accordance with Regulation 3 of Annex IV of the International Convention for the Prevention of Pollution from Ships, 1973, concerning the prevention of pollution by sewage and the survey showed that the equipment of the ship and the condition thereof are in all respects satisfactory and the ship complies with the applicable requirements of Annex IV of the Convention.

This Certificate is valid until ....

Issued at ....

(place of issue of Certificate)

....19 ....

(Signature of official issuing the Certificate)

(Seal or stamp of the Issuing Authority, as appropriate)

Under the provisions of Regulation 7(2) and (4) of Annex IV of the Convention the validity of this Certificate is extended until

....

Signed ....

(Signature of duly authorized official)

Place ....

Date ....

(Seal or stamp of the Authority, as appropriate)

* Delete as appropriate

** Parameters should be incorporated

ANNEX V

REGULATIONS FOR THE PREVENTION OF POLLUTION BY GARBAGE FROM SHIPS

Regulation 1

DEFINITIONS

For the purposes of this Annex:

1. "Garbage" means all kinds of victual, domestic and operational waste excluding fresh fish and parts thereof, generated during the normal operation of the ship and liable to be disposed of continuously or periodically except those substances which are defined or listed in other Annexes to the present Convention.

2. "Nearest land". The term "from the nearest land" means from the baseline from which the territorial sea of the territory in question is established in accordance with international law except that, for the purposes of the present Convention "from the nearest land" off the north eastern coast of Australia shall mean from a line drawn from a point on the coast of Australia in latitude of 11° 00′ South, longitude 142° 08′ East to a point in latitude 10° 35′ South,

longitude 141‡ 55′ East, thence to a point latitude 10° 00′ South,

longitude 142° 00′ East, thence to a point latitude 9° 00′ South,

longitude 143° 52′ East, thence to a point latitude 9° 00′ South,

longitude 144° 30′ East, thence to a point latitude 13° 00′ South,

longitude 144° 00′ East, thence to a point latitude 15° 00′ South,

longitude 146° 00′ East, thence to a point latitude 18° 00′ South,

longitude 147° 00′ East, thence to a point latitude 21° 00′ South,

longitude 153° 00′ East, thence to a point on the coast of Australia in latitude 24° 42′ South, longitude 153° 15′ East.

3. "Special Area" means a sea area where for recognized technical reasons in relation to its oceanographical and ecological condition and to the particular character of its traffic the adoption of special mandatory methods for the prevention of sea pollution by garbage is required. Special areas shall include those listed in Regulation 5 of this Annex.

Regulation 2

APPLICATION

The provisions of this Annex shall apply to all ships.

Regulation 3

DISPOSAL OF GARBAGE OUTSIDE SPECIAL AREAS

1. Subject to the provisions of Regulations 4, 5 and 6 of this Annex:

a) the disposal into the sea of all plastics, including but not limited to synthetic ropes, synthetic fishing nets and plastic garbage bags is prohibited;

b) the disposal into the sea of the following garbage shall be made as far as practicable from the nearest land but in any case is prohibited if the distance from the nearest land is less than:

(i) 25 nautical miles for dunnage, lining and packing material which will float;

(ii) 12 nautical miles for food wastes and all other garbage including paper products, rags, glass, metal, bottles, crockery and similar refuse;

c) disposal into the sea of garbage specified in sub-paragraph (*b*)(ii) of this Regulation may be permitted when it has passed through a comminute or grinder and made as far as practicable from the nearest land but in any case is prohibited if the distance from the nearest land is less than 3 nautical miles. Such comminuted or ground garbage shall be capable of passing through a screen with openings no greater than 25 millimetres.

2. When the garbage is mixed with other discharges having different disposal or discharge requirements the more stringent requirements shall apply.

Regulation 4

SPECIAL REQUIREMENTS FOR DISPOSAL OF GARBAGE

1. Subject to the provisions of paragraph (2) of this Regulation, the disposal of any materials regulated by this Annex is prohibited from fixed or floating platforms engaged in the exploration, exploitation and associated offshore processing of seabed mineral resources, and from all other ships when alongside or within 500 metres of such platforms.

2. The disposal into the sea of food wastes may be permitted when they have been passed through a comminuter or grinder from such fixed or floating platforms located more than 12 nautical miles from land and all other ships when alongside or within 500 metres of such platforms. Such comminuted or ground food wastes shall be capable of passing through a screen with openings no greater than 25 millimetres.

Regulation 5

DISPOSAL OF GARBAGE WITHIN SPECIAL AREAS

1. For the purposes of this Annex the special areas are the Mediterranean Sea area, the Baltic Sea area, the Black Sea area, the Red Sea area and the "Gulfs area" which are defined as follows:

a) The Mediterranean Sea area means the Mediterranean Sea proper including the gulfs and seas therein with the boundary between the Mediterranean and the Black Sea constituted by the 41° N parallel and bounded to the west by the Gibraltar at the meridian of 5° 36′ W.

b) The Baltic Sea area means the Baltic Sea proper with the Gulf of Bothnia and the Gulf of Finland and the entrance to the Baltic Sea bounded by the parallel of the Skaw in the Skagerrak at 57° 44.8′ N.

c) The Black Sea area means the Black Sea proper with the boundary between the Mediterranean and the Black Sea constituted by the parallel 41° N.

d) The Read Sea area means the Red Sea proper including the Gulfs of Suez and Aqaba bounded at the south of the rhumb line between Ras si Ane (12° 8.5′ N, 43° 19.6′ E) and Husn Murad (12° 40.4′ N, 43° 30.2′ E).

e) The "Gulfs area" means the sea area located north west of the rhumb line between Ras al Hadd (22° 30′ N, 59° 48′ E) and Ras el Fasteh (25° 04′N, 61° 25′E).

2. Subject to the provisions of Regulation 6 of this Annex:

a) disposal into the sea of the following is prohibited:

(i) all plastics, including but not limited to synthetic ropes, synthetic fishing nets and plastic garbage bags; and

(ii) all other garbage, including paper products, rags, glass, metal, bottles, crockery, dunnage, lining and packing materials;

b) disposal into the sea of food wastes shall be made as far as practicable from land, but in any case not less than 12 nautical miles from the nearest land.

3. When the garbage is mixed with other discharges having different disposal or discharge requirements the more stringent requirements shall apply.

4. Reception facilities within special areas:

a) The Government of each Party to the Convention. the coastline of which borders a special area undertakes to ensure that as soon as possible in all ports within a special area, adequate reception facilities are provided in accordance with Regulation 7 of this Annex, taking into account the special needs of ships operating in these areas.

b) The Government of each Party concerned shall notify the Organization of the measures taken pursuant to sub-paragraph (*a*) of this Regulation. Upon receipt of sufficient notifications the Organization shall establish a date from which the requirements of this Regulation in respect of the area in question shall take effect. The Organization shall notify the Parties of the date so established no less than twelve months in advance of that date.

c) After the date so established, ships calling also at ports in these special areas where such facilities are not yet available, shall fully comply with the requirements of this Regulation.

Regulation 6

EXCEPTIONS

Regulations 3, 4 and 5 of this Annex shall not apply to:

a) the disposal of garbage from a ship necessary for the purpose of securing the safety of a ship and those on board or saving life at sea; or

b) the escape of garbage resulting from damage to a ship or its equipment provided all reasonable precautions have been taken before and after the occurrence of the damage, for the purpose of preventing or minimizing the escape; or

c) the accidental loss of synthetic fishing or synthetic material incidental to the repair of such nets, provided that all reasonable precautions have been taken to prevent such loss.

Regulation 7

RECEPTION FACILITIES

1. The Government of each Party to the Convention undertakes to ensure the provision of facilities at ports and terminals for the reception of garbage, without causing undue delay to ships, and according to the needs of the ships using them.

2. The Government of each Party shall notify the Organization for transmission to the Parties of all cases where the facilities provided under this Regulation are alleged to be inadequate.

PROTOCOL OF 1978 RELATING TO THE INTERNATINAL CONVENTION FOR THE PREVENTION OF POLLUTION FROM SHIPS, 1973

London, 17 February 1978

The Parties to the present Protocol,

Recognizing the signficiant contribution which can be made by the International Convention for the Prevention of Pollution from Ships, 1973, to the protection of the marine environment from pollution from ships,

Recognizing also the need to improve further the prevention and control of marine pollution from ships, particularly oil tankers,

Recognizing further the need for implementing the Regulation for the Prevention of Pollution by Oil contained in Annex I of that Convention as early and as widely as possible,

Acknowledging however the need to defer the application of Annex II of that Convention until certain technical problems have been satisfactorily resolved.

Considering that these objections may best be achieved by the conclusion of a Protocol relating to the International Convention for the Prevention of Pollution from Ships, 1973,

Have agreed as follows:

Article I

GENERAL OBLIGATIONS

1. The Parties to the present Protocol undertake to give effect to the provisions of:

a) the present Protocol and the Annex hereto which shall constitute an integral part of the present Protocol; and

b) the International Convention for the Prevention of Pollution from Ships, 1973 (hereinafter referred to as "the Convention"), subject to the modifications and additions set out in the present Protocol.

2. The provisions of the Convention and the present Protocol shall be read and interpreted together as one single instrument.

3. Every reference to the present Protocol constitutes at the same time a reference to the Annex hereto.

Article II

IMPLEMENTATION OF ANNEX II OF THE CONVENTION

1. Notwithstanding the provisions of Article 14(1) of the Convention, the Parties to the present Protocol agree that they shall not be bound by the provisions of Annex II of the Convention for a period of three years from the date of entry into force of the present Protocol or for such longer period as may be decided by a two-thirds majority of the Parties to the present Protoçol in the Marine Environment Protection Committee (hereinafter referred to as "the Committee") of the Inter-Governmental Maritime Consultative Organization (hereinafter referred to as "the Organization").

2. During the period specified in paragraph 1 of this Article, the Parties to the present Protocol shall not be under any obligations nor entitled to claim any privileges under the Convention in respect of matters relating to Annex II of the Convention and all reference to Parties in the Convention shall not include the Parties to the present Protocol in so far as matters relating to that Annex are concerned.

Article III

COMMUNICATION OF INFORMATION

The text of Article 11(1)(*b*) of the Convention is replaced by the following:

"a list of nominated surveyors or recognized organizations which are authorized to act on their behalf in the administration of matters relating to the design, construction, equipment and operation of ships carrying harmful substances in accordance with the provisions of the Regulations for circulation to the Parties for information of their officers. The Administration shall therefore notify the Organization of the specific responsibilities and conditions of the authority delegated to nominated surveyors or recognized organizations."

Article IV

SIGNATURE, RATIFICATION, ACCEPTANCE, APPROVAL AND ACCESSION

1. The present Protocol shall be open for signature at the Headquarters of the Organization from 1 June 1978 to 31 May 1979 and shall thereafter remain open for accession. States may become Parties to the present Protocol by:

a) signature without reservation as to ratification, acceptance or approval; or

b) signature, subject to ratification, acceptance or approval, followed by ratification, acceptance or approval; or

c) accession.

2. Ratification, acceptance, approval or accession shall be effected by the deposit of an instrument to that effect with the Secretary-General of the Organization.

Article V

ENTRY INTO FORCE

1. The present Protocol shall enter into force twelve months after the date on which not less than fifteen States, the combined merchant fleets of which constitute not less than fifty per cent of the gross tonnage of the world's merchant shipping, have become Parties to it in accordance with Article IV of the present Protocol.

2. Any instrument of ratification, acceptance, approval or accession deposited after the date on which the present Protocol enters into force shall take effect three months after the date of deposit.

3. After the date on which an amendment to the present Protocol is deemed to have been accepted in accordance with Article 16 of the Convention,

any instrument of ratification, acceptance, approval or accession deposited shall apply to the present Protocol as amended.

Article VI

AMENDMENTS

The procedures set out in Article 16 of the Convention in respect of amendments to the Articles, an Annex and an Appendix to an Annex of the Convention shall apply respectively to amendments to the Articles, the Annex and an Appendix to the Annex of the present Protocol.

Article VII

DENUNCIATION

1. The present Protocol may be denounced by any Party to the present Protocol at any time after the expiry of five years from the date on which the Protocol enters into force for that Party.

2. Denunciation shall be effected by the deposit of an instrument of denunciation with the Secretary-General of the Organization.

3. A denunciation shall take effect twelve months after receipt of the notification by the Secretary-General of the Organization or after the expiry of any other longer period which may be indicated in the notification.

Article VIII

DEPOSITARY

1. The present Protocol shall be deposited with the Secretary-General of the Organization (hereinafter referred to as "the Depositary").

2. The Depositary shall:

a) inform all States which have signed the present Protocol or acceded thereto of:

(i) each new signature or deposit of an instrument of ratification, acceptance, approval or accession, together with the date thereof;

(ii) the date of entry into force of the present Protocol;

(iii) the deposit of any instrument of denunciation of the present Protocol together with the date on which it is received and the date on which the denunciation takes effect.

(iv) any decisions made in accordance with Article II(1) of the present Protocol;

b) transmit certified true copies of the present Protocol to all States which have signed the present Protocol or acceded thereto.

3. As soon as the present Protocol enters into force, a certified true copy thereof shall be transmitted by the Depositary to the Secretariat of the United Nations for registration and publication in accordance with Article 102 of the Charter of the United Nations.

Article IX

LANGUAGE

The present Protocol is established in a single original in the English, French, Russian and Spanish language, each text being equally authentic. Official translations in the Arabic, German, Italian and Japanese languages shall be prepared and deposited with the signed original.

In Witness Whereof the undersigned being duly authorized by their respective Governments for that purpose have signed the present Protocol.

Done at London this seventeenth day of February one thousand nine hundred and seventy-eight.

ANNEX

MODIFICATIONS AND ADDITIONS TO THE INTERNATIONAL CONVENTION FOR THE PREVENTION OF POLLUTION FROM SHIPS, 1973

ANNEX I

REGULATIONS FOR THE PREVENTION OF POLLUTION BY OIL

Regulation 1

DEFINITIONS

Paragraphs (1) to (7) - No change

The existing text of paragraph (8) is replaced by the following:

8. *a*) 'Major conversion' means a conversion of an existing ship:

(i) which substantially alters the dimensions or carrying capacity of the ship; or

(ii) which changes the type of the ship; or

(iii) the intent of which in the opinion of the Administration is substantially to prolong its life; or

(iv) which otherwise so alters the ship that, if it were a new ship, it would become subject to relevant provisions of the present Protocol not applicable to it as an existing ship.

b) Notwithstanding the provisions of sub-paragraph (*a*) of this paragraph, conversion of an existing oil tanker of 20,000 tons deadweight and above to meet the requirements of Regulation 13 of this Annex shall not be deemed to constitute a major conversion for the purpose of this Annex.

Paragraph (9) to (22) — No change

The existing text of paragraph (23) is replaced by the following:

(23) 'Lightweight' means the displacement of a ship in metric tons without cargo, fuel, lubricating oil, ballast water, fresh water and feed water in tanks, consumable stores, and passengers and crew and their effects.

Paragraphs (24) and (25) — No change

The following paragraphs are added to the existing text:

(26) Notwithstanding the provisions of paragraph (6) of this Regulation, for the purposes of Regualtion 13, 13B, 13E and 18 (5) of this Annex, "new oil tanker" means an oil tanker:

a) for which the building contract is placed after 1 June 1979; or *b*) in the absence of a building contract, the keel of which is laid, or which is at a similar stage of construction after 1 January 1979; or

c) the delivery of which is after 1 June 1982; or

d) which has undergone a major conversion:

(i) for which the contract is placed after 1 June 1979; or

(ii) in the absence of a contract, the construction work of which is begun after 1 January 1980; or

(iii) which is completed after 1 June 1982, except that, for oil tankers of 70,000 tons deadweight and above, the definition in paragraph (6) of this Regulation shall apply for the purposes of Regulation 13(1) of this Annex.

(27) Notwithstanding the provisions of paragraph (7) of this Regulation, for the purposes of Regulations 13, 13A, 13B, 13C, 13D and 18(6) of this Annex, "existing oil tanker" means an oil tanker which is not a new oil tanker as defined in paragraph (26) of this Regulation.

(28) "Crude Oil" means any liquid hydrocarbon mixture occuring naturally in the earth whether or not treated to render it suitable for transportaction and includes:

a) crude oil from which certain distillate fractions may have been removed; and

b) crude oil to which certain distillate fractions may have been added.

(29) "Crude oil tanker" means an oil tanker engaged in the trade of carrying crude oil.

(30) "Product carrier" means an oil tanker engaged in the trade of carrying oil other than crude oil.

Regulations 2 and 3 — No change

The existing text of Regulation 4 is replaced by the following:

Surveys and Inspections

(1) Every oil tanker of 150 tons gross tonnage and above, and every other ship of 400 tons gross tonnage and above shall be subject to the surveys specified below:

a) An initial survey before the ship is put in service or before the Certificate required under Regulation 5 of this Annex is issued for the first time, which shall include a complete survey of its structure, equipment, systems, fittings, arrangements and material in so far as the ship is covered by this Annex. This survey shall be such as to ensure that the structure, equipment, system fittings, arrangements and material fully comply with the applicable requirements of this Annex.

b) Periodical surveys at intervals specified by the Administration, but not exceeding five years, which shall be such as to ensure that the structure, equipment, systems, fittings, arrangements and material fully comply with the requirements of this Annex.

c) A minimum of one intermediate survey during the period of validity of the Certificate which shall be such as to ensure that the equipment and associated pump and piping systems, including oil discharge monitoring and control systems, crude oil washing systems, oily-water separating equipment and oil filtering systems, fully comply with the applicable requirements of this Annex and are in good working order. In cases where only one such intermediate survey is carried out in any one Certificate validity period, it shall be held not before six months prior to, nor later than six months after the half-way date of the Certificate's period of validity. Such intermediate surveys shall be endorsed on the Certificate issued under Registration 5 of this Annex.

2. The Adminsitration shall establish appropriate measures for ships which are not subject to the provisions of paragraph (1) of this Regulation in order to ensure that the applicable provisions of this Annex are complied with.

3. *a*) Surveys of ships as regards the enforcement of the provisions of this Annex shall be carried out by officers of the Administration. The Administration may, however, entrust the surveys either to surveyors nominated for the purpose or to organizations recognized by it.

b) The Administration shall institute arrangments for unscheduled inspections to be carried out during the period of validity of the Certificate. Such inspections shall ensure that the ship and its equipment remain in all respects satisfactory for the services for which the ship is intended. These inspections may be carried out by their own inspection services, or by nominated surveyors or by recognized organizations, or by other Parties upon request of the Administration. Where the Administration, under the provisions of paragraph (1) of this Regulation, establishes mandatory annual surveys, the above unscheduled inspections shall not be obligatory.

c) An Administration nominating surveyors or recognizing orgnizations to conduct surveys and inspections as set forth in sub-paragraphs (*a*) and (*b*) of this paragraph, shall as a minimum empower any nominated surveyor or recognized organization to:

(i) require repairs to a ship; and

(ii) carry out surveys and inspections if requested by the appropriate authorities of a Port State.

The Administration shall notify the Organization of the specific responsibilities and conditions of the authority delegated to the nominated surveyors or recognized organizations, for circulation to Parties to the present Protocol for the information of their officers.

d) When a nominated surveyor or recognized organization determines that the condition of the ship or its equipment does not correspond substantially with the particulars of the Certificate or is and there the ship is not fit to proceed to sea without presenting an unreasonable threat of harm to the marine environment, such survey or organization shall immediately ensure that corrective action is taken and shall in due course notify the Administration. If such corrective action is not taken the Certificate should be withdrawn and the Administration shall be notified immediately; and if the ship is in a port of another Party, the appropriate authorities of the Port State shall also be notified immediately. When an officer of the Administration, a nominated surveyor or recognized organization has notified the appropriate authorites of the Port State, the Government of the Port State concerned shall give such officer, surveyor or organization any necessary assistance to carry out their obligations under this Regulation. When applicable, the Government of the Port State concerned shall take such steps as will ensure that the ship shall not sail until it can proceed to sea or leave the port for the purpose of proceeding to the nearest appropriate repair yard available without presenting an unreasonable threat of harm to the marine environment.

e) In every case, the Administration concerned shall fully guarantee the completeness and efficiency of the survey and inspection and shall undertake to ensure the necessary arrangements to satisfy this obligation.

4. *a*) The condition of the ship and its equipment shall be maintained with the provisions of the present Protocol to ensure that the ship in all respects will remain fit to proceed to sea without presenting an unreasonable threat of harm to the marine environment.

b) After any survey of the ship under paragraph (1) of this Regulation has been completed, no change shall be made in the structure, equipment, fittings, arrangements or material covered by the survey, without the sanction of the Adminsitration, except the direct replacement of such equipment and fittings.

c) Whenever an accident occurs to a ship or a defect is discovered which substantially affects the integrity of the ship or the efficiency or completeness of its equipment covered by this Annex the master or owner of the ship shall report at the earliest opportunity to the Administration the recognized organization of the nominated surveyor responsible for issuing the relevant Certificate, who shall cause investigations to be initiated to determine whether a survey as required by paragraph (i) of this Regulation is necessary. If the ship is in port of another Party, the master or owner shall also report immediately to the appropriate authorities of the Port State and the nominated surveyor or recognized organization shall ascertain that such report has been made.

Regulations 5, 6 and 7

In the existing text of these Regulations, delete all reference to "(1973)" in relation to the International Oil Pollution Prevention Certificate.

Regulation 8

DURATION OF CERTIFICATE

The existing text of Regulation 8 is replaced by the following:

1. An International Oil Pollution Prevention Certificate shall be issued for a period specified by the Administration, which shall not exceed five years from the date of issue, provided that in the case of an oil tanker operating with dedicated clean ballast tanks for a limited period specified in Regulation 13(9) of this Annex, the period of validity of the Certificate shall not exceed such specified period.

2. A Certificate shall cease to be valid if significant alterations have taken place in the construction, equipment, systems, fittings, arrangements or material required without the sanction of the Administration, except the direct replacement of such equipment or fittings, or of intermediate surveys as specified by the Adminsitration under Regulation 4(1)(*c*) of this Annex are not carried out.

3. A Certificate issued to a ship shall also cease to be valid upon transfer of the ship to the flag of another State. A newCertificateshall only be issued when the Governments issuing the new Certificate is fully satisfied that the ship is in full compliance with the requirements of Regulation 4(4)(*a*) and (*b*) of this Annex. In the case of a transfer between Parties, if requested within three months after the transfer has taken place, the Government of the Party whose flag the ship was formerly entitled to fly shall transmit as soon as possible to the Administration a copy of the Certificate carried by the ship before the transfer and, if available, a copy of the relevant survey report.

Regulations 9 to 12 — No change

the existing text to Regulation 13 is replaced by the following Regulations:

Regulation 13

SEGREGATED BALLAST TANKS, DEDICATED CLEAN BALLAST TANKS AND CRUDE OIL WASHING

Subject to the provisions of Regulation 13C and 13D of this Annex, oil tanker shall comply with the requirements of this Regulation.

New oil tankers 20,000 tons deadweight and above

1. Every new crude oil tanker of 20,000 tons deadweight and above and every new product carrier of 30,000 tons deadweight and above shall be provided with segregated ballast tanks and shall comply with paragraphs (2), (3) and (4), or paragraph (5) as appropriate, of this Regulation.

2. The capacity of the segregated ballast tanks shall be so determined that the ship may operate safely on ballast voyages without recourse to the use of cargo tanks for water ballast except as provided for in paragraph (3) or (4) of this Regulation. In all cases, however, the capacity of segregated ballast tanks shall be at least such that, in any ballast condition at any part of the voyage, including conditions consisting of lightweight plus segregated ballast only, the ship's draughts and trim can meet each of the following requirements:

a) the moulded draught amidships (dm) in

meters (without taking into account any ship's deformation) shall not be less than:

dm = 2.0 + 0.02L;

b) the draughts at the forward and after perpendiculars shall correspond to those determined by the draught aimdships (dm) as specified in sub-paragraphs (*a*) of this paragraph, in association with the trim by the stern of not greater than 0.015L; and

c) in any case the draught at the after perpendicular shall not be less than that which is necessary to obtain full immersion of the propeller(s).

3. In no case shall ballast water be carried in cargo tanks except on those rare voyages when wheather conditions are so severe that, in the opinion of the master, it is necessary to carry additional ballast water in cargo tanks for the safety of the ship. Such additional ballast water shall be processed and discharged in compliance with Regulation 9 of this Annex and in accordance with the requirements of Regulation 15 of this Annex and entry shall be made in the Oil Record Book referred to in Regulation 20 of this Annex.

4. In the case of new crude oil tankers, the additional ballast permitted in paragraph (3) of this Regulation shall be carried in cargo tanks only if such tanks have been crude oil washed in accordance with Regulation 13B of this Annex before departure from an oil unloading port or terminal.

5. Notwithstanding the provisions of paragraph (2) of this Regulation, the segregated ballast conditions for oil tankers less than 150 meters in length shall be to the satisfaction of the Administration.

6. Every new crude oil tanker of 20,000 tons deadweight and above shall be fitted with cargo tank cleaning system using crude oil washing. The Administration shall undertake to ensure that the system fully complies with the requirements of Regulation 13B of this Annex within one year after the tanker was first engaged in the trade of carrying crude oil or by the end of the third voyage carrying crude oil suitable for crude oil washing, whichever occurs later. Unless such oil tanker carries crude oil which is not suitable for crude oil washing, the oil tanker shall operate the system in accordance with the requirements of that Regulation.

Existing crude oil tankers of 40,000 tons deadweight and above

7. Subject to the provisions of paragraphs (8) and (9) of this Regulation every existing crude oil tanker of 40,000 tons deadweight and above shall be provided with segregated ballast tanks and shall comply with the requirements of paragraphs (2) and (3) of this Regulation from the date of entry into force of the present Protocol.

8. Existing crude oil tankers referred to in paragraph (7) of this Regulation may, in lieu of being provided with segregated ballast tanks, operate with a cargo tank cleaning procedure using crude oil washing in accordance with Regulation 13B of this Annex unless the crude oil tanker is intended to carry crude oil which is not suitable for crude oil washing.

9. Existing crude oil tankers referred to in paragraphs (7) and (8) of this Regulation may, in lieu of being provided with segregated ballast tanks or operating with a cargo tank cleaning procedure using crude oil washing, operate with dedicated clean ballast tanks in accordance with the provisions of Regulation 13A of this Annex for the following period:

a) for crude oil tankers of 70,000 tons deadweight and above, until two years after the date of entry into force of the present Protocol; and

b) for crude oil tankers of 40,000 tons deadweight and above but below 70,000 tons deadweight, until four years after the date of entry into force of the present Protocol.

Existing product carriers of 40,000 tons deadweight and above

(10) From the date of entry into force of the present Protocol, every existing product carrier of 40,000 tons deadweight and above shall be provided with segregated ballast tanks and shall comply with the requirements of paragaphs (2) and (3) of this Regulation, or, alternatively, operate with dedicated clean ballast tanks in accordance with the provisions of Regulation 13A of this Annex.

An oil tanker qualified as a segregated ballast oil tanker

(11) Any oil tanker which is not required to be provided with segregated ballast tanks in accordance with paragraph (1), (7) or (10) of this Regulation may, however, be qualified as a segregated ballast tanker, provided that it complies with the requirements of paragraphs (2) and (3), or paragraph (5) as appropriate, of this Regulation.

Regulation 13A

REQUIREMENTS FOR OIL TANKERS WITH DEDICATED CLEAN BALLAST TANKS

1. An oil tanker operating with dedicated clean ballast tanks in accordance with the provisions of Regulation 13(9) or (10) of this Annex, shall have adequate tank capacity, dedicated solely to the carriage of clean ballast as defined in Regulation 1(16) of this Annex, to meet the requirements of Regulations 13(2) and (3) of this Annex.

2. The arrangements and operational procedures for dedicated clean ballast tanks shall comply with the requirements established by the Administration. Such requirements shall contain at least all the provisions of the Specifications for Oil Tankers with Dedicated Clean Ballast Tanks adopted by the International Conference on Tanker Safety and Pollution Prevention, 1978, in Resolution 14 and as may be revised by the Organization.

3. An oil tanker operating with dedicated clean ballast tanks shall be equipped with an oil content meter, approved by the Administration on the basis of specification recommended by the

Organization*, to enable supervision of the oil content in ballast water being discharged. The oil content meter shall be installed no later than at the first scheduled shipyard visit of the tanker following the entry into force of the present Protocol. Until such time as the content meter is installed, it shall immediately before discharge of ballast be established by examination of the ballast water from dedicated tanks that no contamination with the oil has taken place.

4. Every oil tanker operating with dedicated clean ballast tanks shall be provided with:

a) a Dedicated Clean Ballast Tank Operations Manual detailing the system and specifying operational procedures. Such a Manual shall be to the satisfaction of the Administration and shall contain all the information set out in the Specifications referred to in paragraph (2) of this Regulation. If an alteration affecting the dedicated clean ballast tank system is made, the Operation Manual shall be revised accordingly: and

b) a Supplement to the Oil Record Book referred to in Regulation 20 of this Annex as set out in Supplement 1 to Appendix III of this Annex. The Supplement shall be permanently attached to the Oil Record Book.

Regulation 13B

REQUIREMENTS FOR CRUDE OIL WASHING

1. Every crude oil washing system required to be provided in accordance with Regulation 13(6) and (8) of this Annex shall comply with the requirements of this Regulation.

2. The crude oil washing installation and associated equipment and arrangements shall comply with the requirements established by the Administration. Such requirements shall contain at least all the provisions of the Specifications for the Design, Operation and Control of Crude Oil Washing Systems adopted by the International Conference on Tanker Safety and Pollution Prevention, 1978, in Resolution 15 and as may be revised by the Organization.

3. An inert gas system shall be provided in every cargo tank and slop tank in accordance with the appropriate Regulations of Chapter II-2 of the International Convention for the Safety of Life at Sea, 1974, as modified and added to by the Protocol of 1978 Relating to the International Convention for the Safety of Life at Sea, 1974.

4. With respect to the ballasting of cargo tanks, sufficient cargo tanks shall be crude oil washed prior to each ballast voyage in order that, taking into account the tanker's trading pattern and expected wheather conditions, ballast water is put only into cargo tanks which have been crude oil washed.

5. Every oil tanker operating with crude oil washing systems shall be provided with:

a) an Operations and Equipment Manual detailing the system and equipment and specifying an operational procedure. Such a Manual shall be to the satisfaction of the Administration and shall contain all the information set out in the Specifications referred to in paragraph (2) of this Regulation. If an alteration affecting the crude oil washing system is made, the Operations and Equipment Manual shall be revised accordingly; and

b) a Supplement to the Oil Record Book referred to in Regulation 20 of this Annex as set out in Supplement 2 of Appendix III of this Annex. The Supplement shall be permanently attached to the Oil Record Book.

Regulation 13C

EXISTING TANKERS ENGAGED IN SPECIFIC TRADES.

1. Subject to the provisions of paragraphs (2) and (3) of this Regulation, Regulation 13(7) to (10) of this Annex shall not apply to an existing oil tanker solely engaged in specific trades between:

a) ports or terminals within a State Party to the present Protocols; or

b) ports or terminals of States Parties to the present Protocol, where:

(i) the voyage is entirely within a Special Area as defined in Regulation 10(1) of this Annex; or

(ii) the voyage is entirely within other limits designated by the Organization.

2. The provisions of paragraph (1) of this Regulation shall only apply when the ports or terminals where cargo is loaded on such voyages are provided with reception facilities adequate for the reception and treatment of all the ballast and tank washing water from oil tankers using them and all the following conditions are complied with:

a) subject to the exceptions provided for in Regulation 11 of this Annex, all ballast water, including clean ballast water, and tank washing residues are retained on board and transferred to the reception facilities and the entry in the appropriate Sections of the Supplement to the Oil Record Book referred to in paragraph (3) of this Regulation is endorsed by the competent Port State authority;

b) agreement has been reached between the Administration and the Governments of the Port States referred to in sub-paragraph (1)(*a*) or (*b*) of this Regulation concerning the use of an existing oil tanker for a specific trade;

c) the adequacy of the reception facilities in accordance with the relevant provisions of this Annex at the ports or terminals referred to above,

d) The International oil pollution prevention certificate is endorsed to the effect that the oil tanker is solely engaged in such specific trade,

* Reference is made to the Recommendations on International Performance and Test Specifications for Oily-Water separating Equipment and Oil content meters adopted by the organization by Resolution A. 393 (x)

3. Every oil tanker engaged in a specific trade shall be provided with a Supplement to the Oil Record Book referred to in Regulation 20 of this Annex as set out in Supplement 3 to Appendix III of this Annex. The Supplement shall be permanently attached to the Oil Record Book.

Regulation 13D

EXISTING OIL TANKERS HAVING SPECIAL BALLAST ARRANGEMENTS

1. Where an existing oil tanker is so constructed or operates in such a manner that it complies at all times with the draught and trim requirements set out in Regulation 13(2) of this Annex without recourse to the use of ballast water, it shall be deemed to comply with the segregated ballast tank requirements referred to in Regulation 13(7) of this Annex, provided that all of the following conditions are complied with:

a) operational procedures and ballast arrangements are approved by the Administration;

b) agreement is reached between the Administration and the Governments of the Port States Parties to the present Protocol concerned when the draught and trim requirements are achieved through an operational procedure; and

c) the International Oil Pollution Prevention Certificate is endorsed to the effect that the oil tanker is operating with special ballast arrangements.

2. In no case shall ballast water be carried in oil tanks except on those rare voyages when weather conditions are so severe that, in the opinion of the master, it is necessary to carry additional ballast water in cargo tanks for the safety of the ship. Such additional ballast water shall be processed and discharged in compliance with Regulation 9 of this Annex and in accordance with the requirements of Regulation 15 of this Annex, and entry shall be made in the Oil Record Book referred to in Regulation 20 of this Annex.

3. An Administration which has endorsed a Certificate in accordance with sub-paragraph (1)(*c*) of this Regulation shall communicate to the Organization the particulars thereof for circulation to the Parties to the present Protocol.

Regulation 13E

PROTECTIVE LOCATION OF SEGREGATED BALLAST SPACES

1. In every new crude oil tanker of 20,000 tons deadweight and above and every new product carrier of 30,000 tons deadweight and above, the segregated ballast tanks required to provide the capacity to comply with the requirements of Regulation 13 of this Annex which are located within the cargo tank length, shall be arranged in accordance with the requirements of paragraphs (2), (3) and (4) of this Regulation to provide a measure of protection against oil outflow in the event of grounding or collision.

2. Segregated ballast tanks and spaces other than oil tanks within the cargo tank length (L_t) shall be so arranged as to comply with the following requirement:

$$PA_c + \quad PA_s \quad J[L_T + 2D)]$$

where:

PA_c = the side shell area in square metres for each segregated ballast tank or space other than an oil tank based on projected moulded dimensions,

PA_s = the bottom shell area in square metres for each such tank or space based on projected moulded dimensions,

L_t = length in metres between the forward and after extremities of the cargo tanks,

B = maximum breadth of the ship in metres as defined in Regulation 1(21) of this Annex,

D = moulded depth in metres measured vertically from the top of the keel to the top of the freeboard deck beam at side amidships. In ships having rounded gunwales, the moulded depth shall be measured to the point of intersection of the moulded lines of the deck and side shell plating, the lines extending as though the gunwale were of angular design,

J = 0.45 for oil tankers of 20,000 tons deadweight 0.03 for oil tankers of 200,000 tons deadweight and above, subject to the provisions of paragraph (3) of this Regulation.

For intermediate values of deadweight the value of J shall be determined by linear interpolation.

Whenever symbols given in this paragraph appear in this Regulation, they have the meaning as defined in this paragraph.

3. For tankers of 200,000 tons deadweight and above the value of J may be reduced as follows:

$$J \text{ reduced} = [J — (a — \quad O_c + O_s)] \text{ or } 0.2$$
$$4 \quad 0_A$$

. whichever is greater

where:

a = 0.25 for oil tankers of 200,000 tons deadweight

a = 0.40 for oil tankers of 300,000 tons deadweight

a = 0.50 for oil tankers of 420,000 tons deadweight and above,

For intermediate values of deadweight the a shall be determined by linear interpolation. interpolation.

O_c = as defined in Regulation 23(1)(a) of this Annex,

O_s = as defined in Regulation 23(1)(b) of this Annex,

O_a = the allowable oil outflow as required by Regulation 24(2) of this Annex.

4. In the determination of PA_c and PA_s for segregated ballast tanks and spaces and other than oil tanks the following shall apply:

a) the mainimum width of each wing tank or space either of which extends for the full depth of the ship's side or from the deck to the top of the double bottom shall be not less than 2 metres. The width shall be measured inboard from the ship's side at right angles to the centre line. Where a lesser width is provided the wing tank or space shall not be tàken into account when calculating the protecting area PA_c ; and

b) the minimum vertical depth of each double bottom tank or space shall be B/15 or 2 metres, whichever is the lesser. Where a lesser depth is provided the bottom tank or space shall not be taken into account when calculating the protecting area PA_s .

The minimum width and depth of wing tanks and double bottom tanks shall be measured clear of the bilge area and, in the case of minimum width, shall be measured clear of any rounded gunwale area.

Regulation 14 — No change

Regulation 15

In the existing text of this Regulation, delete reference to "(1973)" in relation to the International Oil Pollution Prevention Certificate.

Regulation 16 and 17 — No change

Regulation 18

PUMPING, PIPING AND DISCHARGE ARRANGEMENTS OF OIL TANKERS

Paragraphs (1) to (4) — No change

The following paragraphs are added to the existing text:

5. Every new oil tanker required to be provided with segregated ballast tanks, or fitted with a crude oil washing system shall comply with the following requirements:

a) it shall be equipped with oil piping so designed and installed such that oil retention in the lines is minimized; and

b) means shall be provided to drain all cargo pumps and all oil lines at the completion of cargo discharge, where necessary by connexion to a striping device. The line and pump drainings shall be capable of being discharged both ashore and to a cargo tank or a slop tank. For discharge ashore a special small diameter line shall be provided for that purpose and connected outboard of the ship's manifold valves.

6. Every existing crude carrier required to be provided with segregated ballast tanks, or fitted with a crude oil washing system or operated with dedicated clean ballast tanks, shall comply with the provisions of paragraph (5)(b) of this Regulation.

Regulation 19 — No change

Regulation 20

In the existing text of this Regulation, delete reference to "(1973)" in relation to the International Oil Pollution Prevention Certificate.

Regulation 21 to 25 — No change

APPENDIX I — List of Oils

No change

APPENDIX II — FORM OF CERTIFICATE

The existing form of Certificate is replaced by the following form:

INTERNATIONAL OIL POLLUTION PREVENTION CERTIFICATE

Issued under the provision of the Protocol of 1978 Relating to the International Convention for the Prevention of Pollution from Ships, 1973, under the Authority of the Government of

....

(full designation of the country)

by ....

(full designation of the competent person or organization authorized under the provision of the Protocol of 1978 Relating to the International Convention for the Prevention of Pollution from Ships, 1973)

Name of Ship	Distinctive Number or Letters		Port of Registry	Gross Tonnage

Type of ship:

Crude oil tanker*

Product carrier*

Crude oil/product carrier*

Ship other than an oil tanker with cargo tanks coming under Regulation 2 (2) of Annex I of the Protocol*

Ship other than any of the above*

Date of building or major conversion contract ....

Date on which keel was laid or ship was at a similar stage of construction or on which major conversion was commenced ....

Date of delivery or completion of major conversion ....

PART A ALL SHIPS

The ship is equipped with:

for ships of 400 tons gross tonnage and above:

a) oily-water separating equipment* (capable of producing effluent with an oil content not exceeding 100 parts per million)

b) an oil filtering system* (capable of producing effluent with an oil content not exceeding 100 parts per million)

for ships of 10,000 tons gross tonnage and above:

c) an oil discharge monitoring and control system* (additional) to (*a*) or (*b*) above) or

d) oily-water separating equipment and an oil filtering system* (capable of producing effluent with an content not exceeding 15 parts per million) in lieu of (*a*) or (*b*) above.

Particulars of requirements from which exemption is granted under Regulations 2 (2) and 2 (4) of Annex I of the Protocol:

....

....

Remarks:

* Delete as appropriate.

Endorsement for existing ships (1)

This is to certify that this ship has now been so equipped as to comply with the requirements of the Protocol of 1978 Relating to the International Convention for the Prevention of Pollution from Ships, 1973, as relating to existing ships (2)

Signed...
(Signature of duly authorized official)

Place ....

Date ....
(Seal or stamp of the Authority, as appropriate)

PART B OIL TANKERS(3)

Carrying Capacity of Ship (m^2)	Deadweight of Ship (metric tons)	Length of Ship (m)

It is certified that this ship is constructed and equipped, and must operate, in accordance with the following:

1. This ship is:

a) required to be constructed to and complies with (4)

b) not required to be constructed according to (4)

c) not required to be constructed according to, but complies with (4)

the requirements of Regulation 24 of Annex I of the Protocol.

2. The ship is:

a) required to be constructed according to and complies with (4)

b) not required to be constructed according to (4)

the requirements of Regulation 13E of Annex I of the Protocol.

3. This ship is:

a) required to be provided with segregated ballast tanks according to, and complies with (4)

b) not required to be provided with segregated ballast tanks according to[4]

c) not required to be provided with segregated ballast tanks according to, but complies with[4])

d) in accordance with Regulation 13C or 13D of Annex I of the Protocol, and as specified in Part C of this Certificate, exempted from (4)

the requirements of Regulation 13 of Annex I of the Protocol.

e) fitted with a cargo tank cleaning system using crude oil washing in accordance with the provisions of Regulation 13B of Annex I of the Protocol, in lieu of being provided with segregated ballast tanks (4)

f) provided with dedicated clean ballast tanks in accordance with the provisions of Regulation 13A of Annex I of the Protocol, in lieu of being either provided with segregated ballast tanks or fitted with a cargo tank cleaning system using crude oil washing (4)

(1) This entry need not be reproduced on a Certificate other than the first Certificate issued to any ship.

(2) The period after the entry into force of the Protocol within which oily-water separating equipment, oil discharge control systems, oil filtering systems and/or slop tank arrangements must be provided is set out in Regulations 13A(3), 15(1) and 16(4) of Annex I of the Protocol.

(3) This Part should be completed for oil tankers including combination carriers, and those entries which are applicable should be completed for ships other than oil tankers which are constructed and utilized to carry oil in bulk of an aggregate capacity of 200 cubic metres or above.

(4) Delete as appropriate.

4. This ship is:

a) required to be fitted with a cargo tank cleaning system using crude oil washing according to, and complies with*

b) not required to be fitted with a cargo tank cleaning system using crude oil washing according to*

the requirements of Regulation 13(6) of Annex I of the Protocol.

*Segregated ballast tanks***

The segregated ballast tanks are distributed as follows:

Tank	Volume (m^2)	Tank	Volume (m^2)

*Dedicated Clean Ballast Tanks***

This ship is operating with dedicated clean ballast tanks until ....
(date)

in accordance with the requirements of Regulation 13A of Annex I of the Protocol.

The dedicated clean ballast tanks are designated as follows:

Tank	Volume (m^2)	Tank	Volume (m^2)

*Manual***

This is to certify that this ship has been supplied with:

a) a valid Dedicated Clean Ballast Tank Operation Manual in accordance with Regulation 13A of Annex I of the Protocol*

b) a valid Operations and Equipment Manual for Crude Oil Washing in accordance with Regulation 13B of Annex I of the Protocol*

Identification of the valid Manual ....

Signed..
(Signature of duly authorized official)

Place ....

Date ....

(Seal or stamp of the Authority, as appropriate)

Identification of the valid Manual ....

Signed..
(Signature of duly authorized official)

Place ....

Date ....

(Seal or stamp of the Authority, as appropriate)

* Delete as appropriate.

** Delete if not applicable.

PART C EXEMPTIONS*

This is to certify that this ship is:

a) solely engaged in trade between .... and ....

in accordance with Regulation of 13C of Annex I of the Protocol**; or

b) operating with special ballast arrangements in accordance with Regulation 13D of Annex I of the Protocol**

and is therefor exempted from the requirements of Regulation 13 of Annex I of the Protocol.

Signed ....
(Signature of duly authorized official)

Place ....

Date ....

(Seal or stamp of the Authority, as appropriate)

THIS IS TO CERTIFY:

That the ship has been surveyed in accordance with Regulation 4 of Annex I of the Protocol of 1978 Relating to the International Convention for the Prevention of Pollution from Ships, 1973, concerning the prevention of pollution by oil; and

that the survey shows that the structure, equipment, systems, fittings, arrangement and material of the ship and the condition thereof are in all respects satisfactory and that the ship complies with the applicable requirements of Annex I of that Protocol.

This Certificate is valid until ....

subject to intermediate
survey(s) at intervals of ....

Issued at ....
(Place of issue of Certificate)

.... 19 .....

....
(Signature of duly authorized official)

(Seal or stamp of the Authority, as appropriate)

* Delete if not applicable.

** Delete as appropriate.

Intermediate Survey

This is to certify that at an intermediate survey required by Regulation 4 (1) (*c*) of Annex I of the Protocol 1978 Relating to the International Convention for the Prevention of Pollution from Ships, 1973, this ship and the condition thereof were found to comply with the relevant provisions of that Protocol.

Signed ....
(Signature of duly authorized official)

Place ....

Date ....

Next intermediate survey due ....

(Seal or stamp of the Authority, as appropriate)

Signed ....
(Signature of duly authorized official)

Place ....

Date ....

Next intermediate survey due ....

(Seal or stamp of the Authority, as appropriate)

Signed ....
(Signature of duly authorized official)

Place ....

Date ....

Next intermediate survey due ....

(Seal or stamp of the Authority, as appropriate)

Signed ....

(Signature of duly authorized official)

Place ....

Date ....

(Seal or stamp of the Authority, as appropriate)

APPENDIX III

Form of Oil Record Book

The following forms of Supplements to the Oil Record Book are added to the existing form:

Supplement I

FORM OF SUPPLEMENT TO OIL RECORD BOOK FOR OIL TANKERS
OPERATED WITH DEDICATED CLEAN BALLAST TANKS*

Name of ship ....

Distinctive number or letters ....

Total cargo carrying capacity .... cubic metres

Total dedicated clean ballast capacity .... cubic metres

The following tanks are designated as dedicated clean ballast tanks:

Tank	Volume (m^2)	Tank	Volume (m^2)

NOTE: The periods covered by the Supplement should be consistent with the periods covered by the Oil Record Book.

* This Supplement should be attached to the Oil Record Book for oil tankers operating with dedicated clean ballast tanks in accordance with Regulation 13A of Annex I of the Protocol of 1978 Relating to the International Convention for the Prevention of Pollution from Ships, 1973. Other information as required should be entered in the Oil Record Book.

(A) *Ballasting of dedicated clean ballast tanks*

101.	Identity of tank(s) ballasted			
102.	Date and position of ship when water intended for flushing, or port ballast was taken to dedicated clean ballast tank(s)			
103.	Date and position of ship when pump(s) and lines were flushed to slop tank			
104.	Date and position of ship when additional ballast water was taken to dedicated clean ballast tank(s)			
105.	Date, time and position of ship when (a) valves to slop tank, (b) valves to cargo tanks, (c) other valves affecting the clean ballast system were closed			
106.	Quantity of clean ballast taken on board			

The undersigned certifies that, in addition to the above, all sea valves, cargo tanks and pipeline connexions and connexions between tanks or inter-tank connexions, were secured on the completion of ballasting tanks.

Date of entry .... Officer in charge ....

Master ....

(B) *Discharge of clean ballast*

107.	Identity of tank(s)			
108.	Date, time and position of ship at start of discharge of clean ballast (a) to sea, or (b) into reception facility			
109.	Date, time and position of ship upon completion of discharge to sea			
110.	Quantity discharged (a) to sea, or (b) into reception facility			
111.	Was the ballast water checked for oil contamination before discharge?			
112.	Was the discharge monitored during discharge by an oil content meter?			
113.	Was there any indication of oil contamination of the ballast water before or during discharge?			
114.	Date and position of ship when pump and lines were flushed after loading			
115.	Date, time and position of ship when (a) valves to slop tank, (b) valves to cargo tanks, (c) other valves affecting the clean ballast system were closed			
116.	Quantity of polluted water transferred to slop tank(s). (Identity slop tank(s))			

The undersigned certifies that, in addition to the above, all sea valves overboard discharge valves, cargo tank and pipeline connexions and connexions between tanks or inter-tank connexions, were secured on completion of discharge of clean ballast and that the pump(s) and pipes designated for clean ballast operations were properly cleaned upon completion of discharge of clean ballast.

Date of entry .... Officer in charge ....

Master ....

Supplement 2

FORM OF SUPPLEMENT TO OIL RECORD BOOK FOR CRUDE OIL TANKERS OPERATING WITH A CARGO TANK CLEANING PROCEDURE USING CRUDE OIL WASHING*

Name of ship ....

Distinctive number of letters ....

Total cargo carrying capacity .... cubic metres

Voyage from .... (Port(s)) .... (date) to .... (Port(s)) .... (date)

NOTES:

The periods covered by the supplement should be consistent with the periods covered by the Oil Record Book.

The cargo tanks crude oil washed should be those laid down in the Operations and Equipment Manual required by Regulation 13B (5) (a) of the Protocol.

A separate column should be used for each tank washed or water rinsed.

(A) *Crude oil washing*

201.	Date when and port where crude oil washing was carried out or ship's position if carried out between two discharge ports				
202.	Identity of tank(s) washed (see Note 1)				
203.	Number of machines in use				
204.	Commenced washing (a) date and time (b) ullage				
205.	Washing pattern employed (see Note 2)				
206.	Washing line pressure				
207.	Completed or stopped washing (a) date and time (b) ullage				
208.	Remarks				

The tanks were washed in accordance with programmes given in the Operations and Equipment Manual (see Note 3) and confirmed dry on completion.

Date of entry .... Officer in charge ....

Master ....

* This Supplement should be attached to the Oil Record Book for crude oil tankers operating with a cargo tank cleaning procedure using crude oil washing in accordance with Regulation 13B of Annex I of the Protocol of 1978 Relating to the International Convention for the Prevention of Pollution from Ships, 1973, and is intended to replace Section (e) of the Oil Record Book. Details of ballasting and deballasting and other information required should be entered in the Oil Record Book.

Note 1 **When an individual tank has more machines than can be operated simultaneously, as described in the Operations and Equipment Manual, then the section being crude oil washed should be identified, e.g. No. 2 centre, forward section.**

Note 2 In accordance with the Operations and Equipment Manual, enter whether single-stage or multi-stage method of washing is employed. If multi-stage method is used, give the vertical arc covered by the machines and the number of times that arc is covered for that particular stage of the programme.

Note 3 If the programmes given in the Operations and Equipment Manual are not followed, then details must be given under Remarks.

(B) *Water rinsing or flushing of tank bottom*

209.	Date and position of ship when rinsing or flushing was carried out				
210.	Identity of tank(s) and date				
211.	Volume of water used				
212.	Transferred to: (a) reception facilities (b) slop tank(s) (identify slop tank(s))				

Date of entry .... Officer in charge ....

Master ....

Supplement 3

FORM OF SUPPLEMENT TO OIL RECORD BOOK FOR OIL TANKERS ENGAGED IN SPECIFIC TRADES*

Name of ship ....

Distinctive number or letters ....

Total cargo carrying capacity .... cubic metres

Total ballast water capacity required for compliance with Regulation 13(2) and (3) of Annex I of the Protocol .... cubic metres

Voyages from .... to ....
(Port(s)) (Port(s))

NOTE: The periods covered by the Supplement should be consistent with the periods covered by the Oil Record Book.

* This Supplement should be attached to the Oil Record Book for crude oil tankers operating with a cargo tank cleaning procedure using crude oil washing in accordance with Regulation 13B of Annex I of the Protocol of 1978 Relating to the International Convention for the Prevention of Pollution from Ships, 1973, and is intended to replace Section (e) of the Oil Record Book. Details of ballasting and deballasting and other information required should be entered in the Oil Record Book.

(A) *Loading of ballast water*

301.	Identity of tank(s) ballasted				
302.	Date and position of ship when ballasted				
303.	Total quantity of ballast loaded in cubic metres				
304.	Method of calculting ballast quantity				
305.	Remarks				
306.	Date and signature of officer in charge				
307.	Date and signature of Master				

(B) *Re-allocation of ballast water within the ship*

308.	Reason for re-allocation				
309.	Date and signature of officer in charge				
310.	Date and signature of Master				

(C) *Ballast water discharge to reception facility*

311.	Date and port(s) where ballast water was discharged				
312.	Name or designation of reception facility				
313.	Total quantity of ballast water discharged in cubic metres				
314.	Method of calculating ballasting quantity				
315.	Date and signature of officer in charge				
316.	Date and signature of Master				
317.	Date, signature and stamp of port authority official				

*** This Supplement should be attached to the Oil Record Book for oil tankers engaged in specific traders in accordance with Regulation 13C of Annex I of the Protocol of 1978 Relating to the International Convention for the Prevention of Pollution from Ships, 1973, and is intended to replace Sections (d), (f), (g) and (i) of the Oil Record Book. Other information required should be entered in the Oil Record Book.**

PROTOCOL RELATING TO INTERVENTION ON THE HIGH SEAS IN CASES OF MARINE POLLUTION BY SUBSTANCES OTHER THAN OIL [60]

London, 2 November 1973

The Parties to the present Protocol,

Being Parties to the International Convention relating to Intervention on the High Seas in Cases of Oil Pollution Casualties, done at Brussels on 29 November 1969,

Taking into account the Resolution on International Co-operation Concerning Pollutants other than Oil adopted by the International Legal Conference on Marine Pollution Damage, 1969,

Further taking into account that pursuant to the Resolution, the Inter-Govermental Maritime Consultative Organization has intensified its work, in collaboration with all interested organizations, on all aspects of pollution by substances other than oil,

Have agreed as follows:

Article I

1. Parties to the present Protocol may take such measures on the high seas as may be necessary to prevent, mitigate or eliminate grav e and imminent danger to their coastline or related interests from pollution or threat of pollution by substances other than oil following upon a maritime casualty or acts related to such a casualty, which may reasonably be expected to result in major harmful consequences.

2. "Substances other than oil" as referred to in paragraph 1 shall be:

a) those substances enumerated in a list which shall be established by an appropriate body designated by the Organization and which shall be annexed to the present Protocol, and

b) those other substances which are liable to create hazards to human health, to harm living resources and marine life, to damage amenities or to interfere with other legitimate uses of the sea.

3. Whenever an intervening Party takes action with regard to a substance referred to in paragraph 2(*b*) above that Party shall have the burden of establishing that the substance, under the circumstances present at the time of the intervention, could reasonably pose a grave and imminent danger analogous to that posed by any of the subtannces enumerated in the list referred to in paragraph 2(*a*) above.

Article II

1. The provisions of paragraph 2 of Article I and of Articles II to VIII of the Convention Relating to Intervention on the High Seas in Cases of Oil Pollution Casualties, 1969, and the Annex thereto as they relate to oil, shall be applicable with regard to the substances referred to in Article I of the present Protocol.

2. For the purpose of the present Protocol the list of experts referred to in Articles III (*c*) and IV of the Convention shall be extended to include experts qualified to give advice in relation to substances other than oil. Nominations to the List may be made by Member States of the Organization and by Parties to the present Protocol.

Article III

1. The list referred to in paragraph 2(*a*) of Article I shall be maintained by the appropriate body designated by the Organization.

2. Any amendment to the list proposed by a Party to the present Protocol shall be submitted to the Organizations and circulated by it to all Members of the Organization and all Parties to the present Protocol at least three months prior to its consideration by the appropriate body.

3. Parties to the present Protocol whether or not Members of the Organization shall be entitled to participate in the proceedings of the appropriate body.

4. Amendments shall be adopted by a two-thirds majority of only the Parties to the present Protocol present and voting.

5. If adopted, in accordance with paragraph 4 above, the amendment shall be communicated by the Organization to all Parties to the present Protocol for acceptance.

6. The amendment shall be deemed to have been accepted at the end of a period of six months after it has been communicated, unless within that period an objection to the amendment had been communicated to the Organization by not less than one-third of the Parties to the present Protocol.

7. An amendment deemed to have been accepted in accordance with paragraph 6 above shall enter into force three months after its acceptance for all Parties to the present Protocol, with the exception of those which before that date have made a declaration of non-acceptance of the said amendment.

Article IV

1. The present Protocol shall be open for signature by the States which have signed the Convention referred to in Article II or acceded thereto, and by any State invited to be represented at the International Conference on Marine Pollution 1973. The Protocol shall remain open for signature from 15 January 1974 until 31 December 1974 at the Headquarters of the Organization.

2. Subject to paragraph 4 of this Article, the present Protocol shall be subject to ratification, acceptance or approval by the States which have signed it.

3. Subject to paragraph 4, this protocol shall be open for accession by States which did not sign it.

4. The present Protocol may be ratified, accepted approved or acceded to only by States which have ratified, accepted, aproved or acceded to the Convention referred to in Article II.

Article V

1. Ratification, acceptance, approval or

accession shall be effected by the deposit of a formal instrument to that effect with the Secretary-General of the Organization.

2. Any instrument of ratification, acceptance, approval or accession deposited after the entry into force of an amendment to the present Protocol with respect to all existing Parties or after the completion of all measures required for the entry into force of the amendment with respect to all existing Parties shall be deemed to apply to the Protocol as modified by the amendment.

Article VI

1. The present Protocol shall enter into force on the ninetieth day following the date on which fifteen States have deposited instruments of ratification, acceptance, approval or accession with the Secretary-General of the Organization, provided however that the present Protocol shall not enter into force before the Convention referred to in Article II has entered into force.

2. For each State which subsequently ratifies, accepts, approves or accedes to it, the present Protocol shall enter into force on the ninetieth day after the deposit by such State of the appropriate instrument.

Article VII

1. The present Protocol may be denounced by any Party at any time after the date on which the Protocol enters into force for that Party.

2. Denunciation shall be effected by the deposit of an instrument to that effect with the Secretary-General of the Organization.

3. Denunciation shall take effect one year, or such longer period as may be specified in the instrument of denunciation, after its deposit with the Secretary-General of the Organization.

4. Denunciation of the Convention referred to in Article II by a Party shall be deemed to be a denunciation of the present Protocol by that Party. Such denunciation shall take effect on the same day as the denunciation of the Convention takes effect in accordance with paragraph 3 of Article XII of that Convention.

Article VIII

1. A conference for the purpose of revising or amending the present Protocol may be convened by the Organization.

2. The Organization shall convene a conference of Parties to the present Protocol for the purpose of revising or amending it at the request of not less than one- third of the Parties.

Article IX

1. The present Protocol shall be deposited with the Secretary-General of the Organization.

2. The Secretary-General of the Organization shall:

a) inform all States which have signed the present protocol or acceded thereto of:

(i) each new signature or deposit of an instrument together with the date thereof;

(ii) the date of entry into force of the present Protocol;

(iii) the deposit of any instrument of denunciation of the present Protocol together with the date on which the denunciation takes effect;

(iv) any amendments to the present Protocol or its Annex and any objection or declaration of non-acceptance of the said amendment.

b) transmit certified true copies of the present Protocol to all States which have signed the present Protocol or acceded thereto.

Article X

As soon as the present Protocol enters into force, a certified true copy thereof shall be transmitted by the Secretary-General of the Organization to the Secretariat of the United Nations for registration and publication in accordance with Article 102 of the Charter or the United Nations.

Article XI

The present Protocol is established in a single original in the English, French, Russian and Spanish languages, all four texts being equally authentic.

In Witness Whereof the undersigned being duly authorized for that purpose have signed the present Protocol.

Done at London this second day of November one thousand nine hundred and seventy-three.

AGREEMENT ON CONSERVATION OF POLAR BEARS [61]

Oslo, 15 November 1973

The Governments of Canada, Denmark Norway, the Union of Soviet Socialist Republics, and the United States of America,

Recognizing the special responsibilities and special interests of the States of the Arctic Region in relation to the protection of the fauna and flora of the Arctic Region;

Recognizing that the polar bear is a significant resource of the Arctic Region which requires additional protection;

Having decided that such protection should be achieved through co-ordinated national measures taken by the States of the Arctic Region;

Desiring to take immediate action to bring further conservation and management measures into effect;

Having agreed as follows:

Article I

1. The taking of polar bears shall be prohibited except as provided in Article III.

2. For the purposes of this Agreement, the term "taking" includes hunting, killing and capturing.

Article II

Each Contracting Party shall take appropriate action to protect the ecosystems of which polar bears are a part, with special attention to habitat components such as denning and feeding sites and migration patterns, and shall manage polar bear populations in accordance with sound conservation practices based on the best available scientific data.

Article III

1. Subject to the provisions of Articles II and IV, any Contracting Party may allow the taking of polar bears when such taking is carried out:

a) for *bona fide* scientific purposes; or

b) by that Party for conservation purposes; or

c) to prevent serious disturbance of the management of other living resources, subject to forfeiture to that Party of the skins and other items of value resulting from such taking; or

d) by local people using traditional methods in the exercise of their traditional rights and in accordance with the laws of that Party; or

e) wherever polar bears have or might have been subject to taking by traditional means by its nationals.

2. The skins and other items of value resulting from taking under sub-paragraph (*b*) and (*c*) of paragraph 1 of this Article shall not be available for commercial purposes.

Article IV

The use of aircraft and large motorized vessels for the purpose of taking polar bears shall be prohibited, except where the application of such prohibition would be inconsistent with domestic laws.

Article V

A Contracting Party shall prohibit the exportation from, the importation and delivery into, and traffic within, its territory of polar bears or any part or product thereof taken in violation of this Agreement.

Article VI

1. Each Contracting Party shall enact and enforce such legislation and other measures as may be necessary for the purpose of giving effect to this Agreement.

2. Nothing in this Agreement shall prevent a Contracting Party from maintaining or amending existing legislation or other measures or establishing new measures on the taking of polar bears so as to provide more stringent controls than those required under the provisions of this Agreement.

Article VII

The Contracting Parties shall conduct national research programmes on polar bears, particularly research relating to the conservation and management of the species. They shall as appropriate co-ordinate such research with research carried out by other Parties, consult with with other Parties on the management of migrating polar bear populations, and exchange information on research and management programmes, research results and data on bears taken.

Article VIII

Each Contracting Party shall take action as appropriate to promote compliance with the provisions of this Agreement by nationals of States not party to this Agreement.

Article IX

The Contracting Parties shall continue to consult with one another with the object of giving further protection to polar bears.

Article X

1. This Agreement shall be open for signature at Oslo by the Governments of Canada, Denmark, Norway, the Union of Soviet Socialist Republics and the United States of America until 31st March 1974.

2. This Agreement shall be subject to ratification or approval by the signatory Governments. Instruments of ratification or approval shall be deposited with the Government of Norway as soon as possible.

3. This Agreement shall be open for accession by the Governments referred to in paragraph I of this Article. Instruments of accession shall be deposited with the Depositary Government.

4. This Agreement shall enter into force ninety days after the deposit of the third instrument of ratification, approval or accession. Thereafter, it shall enter into force for a signatory or acceding Government on the date of deposit of its instrument of ratification, approval or accession.

5. This Agreement shall remain in force initially for a period of five years from its date of entry into force, and unless any Contracting Party during that period requests the termination of the Agreement at the end of that period, it shall continue in force thereafter.

6. On the request addressed to the Depositary Government by any of the Governments referred to in paragraph 1 of this Article, consultations shall be conducted with a view to convening a meeting of representatives of the five Governments to consider the revision or amendment of this Agreement.

7. Any Party may denounce this Agreement by written notification to the Depositary Government at any time after five years from the date of entry into force of this Agreement. The denunciation shall take effect twelve months after the Depositary Government has received the notification.

8. The Depositary Government shall notify the Governments referred to in paragraph 1 of this Article of the deposit of instruments of ratification, approval or accession, of the entry into force of this Agreement and of the receipt of notifications of denunciation and any other communications from a Contracting Party specifically provided for in this Agreement.

9. The original of this Agreement shall be deposited with the Government of Norway which shall deliver certified copies thereof to each of the Governments referred to in paragraph 1 of this Article.

10. The Depositary Government shall transmit certified copies of this Agreement to the Secretary-General of the United Nations for registration and publication in accordance with Article 102 of the Charter of the United Nations.

In Witness Whereof the undersigned, being duly authorized by their Governments, have signed this Agreement.

Done at Oslo, in the English and Russian languages, each text being equally authentic, this fifteenth day of November, 1973.

THE NORDIC ENVIRONMENTAL PROTECTION CONVENTION [62]

Stockholm, 19 February 1974

Convention on the Protection of the Environment between Denmark, Finland, Norway and Sweden

The Governments of Denmark, Finland, Norway and Sweden, convinced of the urgent need to protect and improve the environment, have agreed as follows:

Article 1

For the purpose of this Convention, environmentally harmful activities shall mean the discharge from the soil or from buildings or installations of solid or liquid waste, gas or any other substance into water courses, lakes or the sea and the use of land, the seabed, buildings or installations in any other way which entails or may entail environmental nuisance by water pollution or any other effect on water conditions, sand drift, air pollution, noise, vibration, changes in temperature, ionizing radiation, light etc.

The Convention shall not apply insofar as environmentally harmful activities are regulated by a special agreement between two or more of the Contracting States.

Article 2

In considering the permissibility of environmentally harmful activities, the nuisance which such activities entail or may entail in another Contracting States shall be equated with a nuisance in the States where the activities are carried out.

Article 3

Any person who is affected or may be affected by a nuisance caused by environmentally harmful activities in another Contracting State shall have the right to bring before the appropriate Court or Administrative Authority of that State the question of the permissibility of such activities, including the question of measures to prevent damage, and to appeal against the decision of the Court or the Administrative Authority to the same extent and on the same terms as a legal entity of the State in which the activities are being carried out.

The provisions of the first paragraph of this Article shall be equally applicable in the case of proceedings concerning compensation for damage caused by environmentally harmful activities. The question of compensation shall not be judged by rules which are less favourable to the injured party than the rules of compensation of the State in which the activities are being carried out.

Article 4

Each State shall appoint a special authority (supervisory authority) to be entrusted with the task of safeguarding general environmental interests insofar as regards nuisances arising out of environmentally harmful activities in another Contracting State.

For the purpose of safeguarding such interests, the supervisory authority shall have the right to institute proceedings before or be heard by the competent Court or Administrative Authority of another Contracting State regarding the permissibility of the environmentally harmful activities if an authority or other representative of general environmental interests in that State can institute proceedings or be heard in matters of this kind, as well as the right to appeal against the decision of the Court or the Administrative Authority in accordance with the procedures and rules of appeal applicable to such cases in the State concerned.

Article 5

If the Court or the Administrative Authority examining the permissibility of environmentally harmful activities (examining authority) finds that the activities entail or may entail nuisance of significance in another Contracting State, the examining authority shall, if proclamation or publication is required in cases of that nature, send as soon as possible a copy of the documents of the case to the supervisory authority of the other State, and afford it the opportunity of giving its opinion. Notification of the date and place of a meeting or inspection shall, where appropriate, be given well in advance to the supervisory authority which, moreover, shall be kept informed of any developments that may be of interest to it.

Article 6

Upon the request of the supervisory authority, the examining authority shall, insofar as compatible with the procedural rules of the States in which the activities are being carried out, require the applicant for a permit to carry out environmentally harmful activities to submit such additional particulars, drawings and technical specifications as the examining authority deems necessary for evaluating the effects in the other State.

Article 7

The supervisory authority, if it finds it necessary on account of public or private interests, shall publish communications from the examining authority in the local newspaper or in some other suitable manner. The supervisory authority shall also institute such investigations of the effects in its own State as it deems necessary.

Article 8

Each State shall defray the cost of the activities of its supervisory authority.

Article 9

If, in a particular case, the supervisory authority has informed the appropriate Court of Administrative authority of the State in which the activities are being carried out that in the case concerned the duties of the supervisory authority shall be discharged by another authority, the provisions of this Convention relating to supervisory activities shall, where appropriate, apply to that authority.

Article 10

If necessary for determining the damage caused in another State by environmentally harmful activities, the supervisory authority of that other State shall upon request of the examining authority of the State in which the activities are being carried out make arrangements for on-site inspection. The examining authority or an expert appointed by it may be present at such an inspection.

Where necessary, more detailed instructions concerning inspections such as referred to in the preceding paragraph shall be drawn up in consultation between the countries concerned.

Article 11

Where the permissibility of environmentally harmful activities which entail considerable nuisance in another Contracting State is being examined by the Government or by the appropriate Minister or Ministry of the State in which the activities are being carried out, consultations shall take place between the States concerned if the Government of the former State so requests.

Article 12

In cases such as those referred to in Article 11, the Government of each State concerned may demand that an opinion be given by a Commission which, unless otherwise agreed, shall consist of a chairman from another Contracting State to be appointed jointly by the parties and three members from each of the States concerned. Where such a Commission has been appointed, the case cannot be decided upon until the Commision has given its opinion.

Each State shall remunerate the members it has appointed. Fees or other remuneration of the Chairman as well as any other costs incidental to the activities of the Commission which are not manifestly the responsibility of one or the other State, shall be equally shared by the States concerned.

Article 13

This Convention shall also apply to the continental shelf areas of the Contracting States.

Article 14

This Convention shall enter into force six months from the date on which all the Contracting States have notified the Swedish Ministry for Foreign Affairs that the constitutional measures necessary for the entry into force of the Convention have been implemented. The Swedish Ministry of Foreign Affairs shall notify the other Contracting States of the receipt of such communications.

Article 15

Actions or cases relevant to this Convention, which are pending before a Court or an Administrative Authority on the date when this Convention enters into force, shall be dealt with and judged according to provisions previously in force.

Article 16

Any Contracting State wishing to denounce this Convention shall give notice of its intention in writing to the Swedish Government, which shall forthwith inform the other Contracting States of the denunciation and of the date on which notice was received.

The denunciation shall take effect twelve months from the date on which the Swedish Government received such notification or on such later date as may be indicated in the notice of denunciation.

This Convention shall be deposited with the Swedish Ministry for Foreign Affairs, which shall send certified copies thereof to the Government of each Contracting State.

In witness whereof the undersigned, representative of the Contracting States, being duly authorized thereto by their respective Governments, have signed this Convention.

Done at Stockholm, this 19th day of February 1974 in a single copy in the Danish, Finnish, Norwegian and Swedish languages, all texts being equally authoritative.

PROTOCOL

In connection with the signing today of the Nordic Environmental Protection Convention the duly authorized signatories agreed that the following comments on its application shall be appended to the Convention.

In the applications of Article I discharge from the soil, or from buildings or installations of solid or liquid waste, gases or other substances into watercourses, lakes or the sea shall be regarded as environmentally harmful activities only if the discharge entails or may entail a nuisance to the surroundings.

The right established in Article 3 for anyone who suffers injury as result of environmentally harmful activities in a neighbouring State to institute proceedings for compensation before a court or administrative authority of that State shall, in principle, be regarded as including the right to demand the purchase of his real property.

Article 5 shall be regarded as applying also to application for permits where such applications are referred to certain authorities and organizations for their opinion but not in conjunction with proclamation or publication procedures.

The Contracting States shall require officials of the supervisory authority to observe professional secrecy as regards trade secrets, operational devices or business conditions of which they have become cognizant in dealing with cases concerning environmentally harmful activities in another State.

Stockholm, 19th February, 1974.

CONVENTION ON THE PROTECTION OF THE MARINE ENVIRONMENT OF THE BALTIC SEA AREA [63]

Helsinki, 22 March 1974

The States Parties to this Convention,

Conscious of the indispensable economic, social and cultural values of the marine environment of the Baltic Sea Area and its living resources for the peoples of the Contracting Parties;

Bearing in mind the exceptional hydrographic and ecological characteristics of the Baltic Sea Area and the sensitivity of its living resources to changes in the environment;

Noting the rapid development of human activities at the Baltic Sea Area, the considerable population living within its catchment area and the highly urbanized and industrialized state of the Contracting Parties as well as their intensive agriculture and forestry;

Noting with deep concern the increasing pollution of the Baltic Sea or Area, orginating from many sources such as discharges through rivers, estuaries, outfalls and pipelines, dumping and normal operations of vessels as well as through airborne pollutants;

Conscious of the responsibility of the Contracting Parties to protect and enhance the values of the marine environment of the Baltic Sea Area for the benefit of their peoples;

Recognizing that the protection and enhancement of the marine environment of the Baltic Sea Area are tasks that cannot effectively be accomplished by national efforts only but that also close regional co-operation and other appropriate international measures aiming at fulfilling these tasks are urgently needed;

Noting that the relevant recent international conventions even after having entered into force for the respective Contracting Parties do not cover all special requirements to protect and enhance the marine environment of the Baltic Sea Area;

Noting the importance of scientific and technological co-operation in the protection and enhancement of the marine environment of the Baltic Sea Area, particularly between the Contracting Parties;

Desiring to develop further regional co-operation in the Baltic Sea Area, the possibilities and requirements of which were confirmed by the signing of the Convention on Fishing and Conservation of the Living Resources in the Baltic Sea and the Belts, Gdansk 1973;

Conscious of the importance of regional inter-governmental co-operation in the protection of the marine environment of the Baltic Sea Area as an integral part of the peaceful co-operation and mutual understanding between all European States;

Have agreed as follows:

Article 1

CONVENTION AREA

For the purposes of the present Convention "the Baltic Sea Area" shall be the Baltic Sea proper with the Gulf of Bothnia, the Gulf of Finland and the entrance to the Baltic Sea bounded by the parallel of the Skaw in the Skagerrak at 57° 44'8" N. It does not include internal waters of the Contracting Parties.

Article 2

DEFINITIONS

For the purposes of the present Convention:

1. "Pollution" means introduction by man, directly or indirectly, of substances or energy into the marine environment, including estuaries, resulting in such deleterious effects as hazard to human health, harm to living resources and marine life, hindrance to legitimate uses of the sea including fishing, impairment of the quality for use of sea water, and reduction of amenities;

2. "land-based pollution" means pollution of the sea caused by discharges from land reaching the sea waterborne, airborne or directly from the coast, including outfalls from pipelines;

3. *a*) "Dumping" means:

(i) any deliberate disposal at sea of wastes or other matter from vessels, aircraft, platforms or other man-made structures at sea;

(ii) any deliberate disposal at sea of vessels, aircraft, platforms or other man-made structures at sea;

b) "Dumping" does not include:

(i) the disposal at sea of wastes or other matter incidental to, or derived from the normal operations of vessels, aircraft, platforms or other man-made structures at sea and their equipment, other than wastes or other matter transported by or to vessels, aircraft, platforms or other man-made structures at sea, operating for the purpose of disposal of such matter or derived from the treatment of such wastes or other matter or such vessels, aircraft, platforms or structures;

disposal of such matter or derived from the treatment of such wastes or other matter or such vessels, aircraft, platforms or structures;

(ii) placement or matter for a purpose other than the mere disposal thereof, provided that such placement is not contrary to the aims of the present Convention;

4. "Vessels and aircraft" means waterborne or airborne craft of any type whatsoever. This expression includes hydrofoil boats, air-cushion vehicles, submersibles, floating craft whether self-propelled or not, and fixed or floating platforms;

5. "Oil" means petroleum in any from including crude oil, fuel oil, sludge, oil refuse and refined products;

6. "Harmful substances" means any hazardous, noxious or other substances, which, if introduced into the sea, is liable to cause pollution;

7. "Incident" means and event involving the actual or probable discharge into the sea of a harmful substance, or effluents containing such a substance.

Article 3

FUNDAMENTAL PRINCIPLES AND OBLIGATIONS

1. The Contracting Parties shall individually or jointly take all appropriate legislative, admininstr-tive or other relevant measures in order to prevent and abate pollution and to protect and enhance the marine environment of the Baltic Sea Area.

2. The Contracting Parties shall use their best endeavours to ensure that the implementation of the present Convention shall not cause an increase in the pollution of sea areas outside the Baltic Sea Area.

Article 4

APPLICATION

1. The present Convention shall apply to the protection of the marine environment of the Baltic Sea Area which comprises the water-body and the sea-bed including their living resources and other forms of marine life.

2. Without prejudice to the sovereign rights in regard to their territorial sea, each Contracting Party shall implement the provisions of the present Convention within its territorial sea through its national authorities.

3. While the provisions of the present Convention do not apply to internal waters which are under the sovereignty of each Contracting Party, they undertake, without prejudice to their sovereign rights, to ensure that the purposes of the present Convention will be obtained in these waters.

4. The present Convention shall not apply to any warship, naval auxiliary, military aircraft or other ship and aircraft owned or operated by a State and used, for the time being, only on governmental non-commercial service.

However, each Contracting Party shall ensure, by the adoption of appropriate measures not impairing the operations or operational capabilities of such ships and aircraft owned or operated by it, that such ships and aircraft act in a manner consistent, so far as is reasonable and practicable, with the present Convention.

Article 5

HAZARDOUS SUBSTANCES

The Contracting Parties undertake to counteract the introduction, waterborne or otherwise, into the Baltic Sea Area of hazardous substances as specified in Annex I of the present Convention.

Article 6

PRINCIPLES AND OBLIGATIONS CONCERNING LAND-BASED POLLUTION

1. The Contracting Parties shall take all appropriate measures to control and minimize land-based pollution of the marine environment of the Baltic Sea Area.

2. In particular, the Contracting Parties shall take all appropriate measures to control and strictly limit pollution by noxious substances and materials in accordance with Annex II of the present Convention. To this end they shall, inter-alia, as appropriate co-operate in the development and adoption of specific programmes, guidelines, standards or regulations concerning discharges, environmental quality, and products containing such substances and materials and their use.

3. The substances and materials listed in Annex II of the present Convention shall not be introduced into the marine environment of the Baltic Sea in significant quantities without a prior special permit, which may be periodically reviewed, by the appropriate national authority.

4. The appropriate national authority will inform the Commission referred to in Article 12 of the present Convention of the quantity, quality and way of discharge if it considers that significant quantities of substances and materials listed in Annex II of the present Convention were discharged.

5. The Contracting Parties shall endeavour to establish and adopt common criteria for issuing permits for discharges.

6. To control and minimize pollution of the Baltic Sea Area by harmful substances the Contracting Parties shall, in addition to the provisions of Article 5 of the present Convention, aim at attaining the goals and applying the criteria enumerated in Annex III of the present Convention.

7. If the discharge from a watercourse, flowing through the territories of two or more Contracting Parties or forming a boundary between them, is liable to cause pollution of the marine environment of the Baltic Sea Area, the Contracting Parties concerned shall in common take appropriate measures in order to prevent and abate such pollution.

8. The Contracting Parties shall endeavour to use best practicable means in order to minimize the airborne pollution of the Baltic Sea Area by noxious substances.

Article 7

PREVENTION OF POLLUTION FROM SHIPS

1. In order to protect the Baltic Sea Area from pollution by deliberate, negligent or accidental release of oil, harmful substances other than oil, and by the discharge of sewage and garbage from ships, the Contracting Parties shall take measures as set out in Annex IV of the present Convention.

2. The Contracting Parties shall develop and apply uniform requirements for the capacity and location of facilities for the reception of residues of oil, harmful substances other than oil, including sewage and garbage, taking into account inter alia the special needs of passenger ships and combination carriers.

Article 8

PLEASURE CRAFT

The Contracting Parties shall, in addition to implementing those provisions of the present Convention which can appropriately be applied to pleasure craft, take special measures in order to abate harmful effects on the marine environment of the Baltic Sea Area of pleasure craft activities. The measures shall inter alia deal with adequate reception facilities of wastes from pleasure craft.

Article 9

PREVENTION OF DUMPING

1. The Contracting Parties shall, subject to Paragraphs 2 and 4 of this Article, prohibit dumping in the Baltic Sea Area.

2. Dumping of dredged spoils shall be subject to a prior special permit by the appropriate national authority in accordance with the provisions of Annex V of the present Convention.

3. Each Contracting Party undertakes to ensure compliance wih the provisions of this Article by vessels and aircraft:

a) registered in its territory or flying its flag;

b) loading, within its territory or territorial sea, matter which is to be dumped; or

c) believed to be engaged in dumping within its territorial sea.

4. The provisions of this Article shall not apply when the safety of human life or of a vessel or aircraft at sea is threatened by the complete destruction or total loss of the vessel or aircraft, or in any case which constitutes a danger to human life, if dumping appears to be the only way of averting the threat and if there is every probability that the damage consequent upon such dumping will be less than would otherwise occur. Such dumping shall be so conducted as to minimize the likelihood of damage to human or marine life.

5. Dumping made under the provisions of Paragraph 4 of this Article shall be reported and dealt with in accordance with Annex VI of the present Convention and shall also be reported forthwith to the Commission referred to in Article 12 of the present Convention in accordance with the provisions of Regulation 4 of Annex V of the present Convention.

6. In case of dumping suspected to be in contravention of the provisions of this Article the Contracting Parties shall co-operate in investigating the matter in accordance with Regulation 2 of Annex IV of the present Convention.

Article 10

EXPLORATION AND EXPLOITATION OF THE SEA-BED AND ITS SUBSOIL

Each Contracting Party shall take all appropriate measures in order to prevent pollution of the marine environment of the Baltic Sea Area resulting from exploration or exploitation of its part of the sea-bed and its subsoil or from any associated activities thereon. It shall also ensure that adequate equipment is at hand to start an immediate abatement of pollution in that area.

Article 11

CO-OPERATION IN COMBATING MARINE POLLUTION

The Contracting Parties shall take measures and co-operate as set out in Annex VI of the present Convention in order to eliminate or minimize pollution of the Baltic Sea Area by oil or other harmful substances.

Article 12

INSTITUTIONAL AND ORGANIZATIONAL FRAMEWORK

1. The Baltic Marine Environment Protection Commission, hereinafter referred to as "the Commission", is hereby established for the purposes of the present Convention.

2. The chairmanship of the Commission shall be given to each Contracting Party in turn in alphabetical order of the names of the States in the English language.

The Chairman shall serve for a period of two years, and cannot during the period of his chairmanship serve as representative of his country.

Should the chairmanship fall vacant, the Contracting Party chairing the Commission shall nominate a successor to remain in office until the term of chairmanship of that Contracting Party expires.

3. Meetings of the Commission shall be held at least once a year upon convocation by the Chairman. Upon the request of a Contracting Party, provided it is endorsed by another Contracting Party, the Chairman shall, as soon as possible, summon an extraordinary meeting at such time and place as the Chairman determines, however, not later than ninety days from the date of the submission of the request.

4. The first meeting of the Commission shall be called by the Depositary Government and shall take place within a period of ninety days from the

date following the entry into force of the present Convention.

5. Each Contracting Party shall have one vote in the Commission. Unless otherwise provided under the present Convention, the Commission shall take its decisions unanimously.

Article 13

THE DUTIES OF THE COMMISSION

The duties of the Commission shall be:

a) To keep the implementation of the present Convention under continuous observation;

b) To make recommendations on measures relating to the purposes of the present Convention;

c) To keep under review the contents of the present Convention including its Annexes and to recommend to the Contracting Parties such amendments to the present Convention including its Annexes as may be required including changes in the lists of substances and materials as well as the adoption of new Annexes;

d) To define pollution control criteria, objectives for the reduction of pollution, and objectives concerning measures, particularly according to Annex III of the present Convention;

e) To promote in close co-operation with appropriate governmental bodies, taking into consideration Sub-Paragraph (*f*) of this Article, additional measures to protect the marine environment of the Baltic Sea Area and for this purpose:

(i) to receive, process, summarize and disseminate from available sources relevant scientific, technological and statistical information; and

(ii) to promote scientific and technological research;

f) To seek, when appropriate, the services of competent regional and other international organizations to collaborate in scientific and technological research as well as other relevant activities pertinent to the objectives of the present Convention;

g) To assume such other functions as may be appropriate under the terms of the present Convention.

Article 14

ADMINISTRATIVE PROVISIONS FOR THE COMMISSION

1. The working language of the Commission shall be English.

2. The Commission shall adopt its Rules of Procedure.

3. The office of the Commission, hereafter referred to as the "Secretariat", shall be in Helsinki.

4. The Commission shall appoint an Executive Secretary and make provisions for the appointment of such other personnel as may be necessary, and determine the duties, terms and conditions of the Executive Secretary.

5. The Executive Secretary shall be the chief administrative official of the Commission and shall perform the functions that are necessary for the administration of the present Convention, the work of the Commission and other tasks entrusted to the Executive Secretary by the Commission and its Rules of Procedure.

Article 15

FINANCIAL PROVISIONS FOR THE COMMISSION

1. The Commission shall adopt its Financial Rules.

2. The Commission shall adopt an annual or biennial budget of proposed expenditures and budget estimates for the fiscal period following thereafter.

3. The total amount of the budget, including any supplementary budget adopted by the Commission, shall be contributed by the Contracting Parties in equal parts, unless the Commission unanimously decides otherwise.

4. Each Contracting Party shall pay the expenses related to the participation in the Commission of its representatives, experts and advisers.

Article 16

SCIENTIFIC AND TECHNOLOGICAL CO-OPERATION

1. The Contracting Parties undertake directly, or when appropriate through competent regional and other international organizations, to co-operate in the fields of science, technology and other research, and to exchange data as well as other scientific information for the purposes of the present Convention.

2. Without prejudice to Paragraphs 1, 2 and 3 of Article 4 of the present Convention the Contracting Parties undertake directly, or when appropriate through competent regional or other international organizations, to promote studies, undertake, support or contribute to programmes aimed at developing ways and means for the assessment of the nature and extent of pollution, pathways, exposures, risks and remedies in the Baltic Sea Area, and particularly to develop alternative methods of treatment, disposal and eliminations of such matter and substances that are likely to cause pollution of the marine environment of the Baltic Sea Area.

3. The Contracting Parties undertake, directly, or when appropriate through competent or other international organizations, and, on the basis of the information and data acquired pursuant to Paragraphs 1 and 2 of this Article, to co-operate in developing inter-comparable observation methods in performing baseline studies and in establishing complementary or joint programmes for monitoring.

4. The organizations and scope of work connected with the implementation of tasks referred to in the preceding Paragraphs should primarily be outlined by the Commission.

Article 17

RESPONSIBILITY FOR DAMAGE

The Contracting Parties undertake, as soon as possible, jointly to develop and accept rules concerning responsibility for damage resulting from acts or omissions in contravention of the present Convention, including inter alia, limits of responsibility, criteria and procedures for the determination of liability and available remedies.

Article 18

1. In case of a dispute between Contracting Parties as to the interpretation or application of the present Convention, they should seek a solution by negotiation. If the Parties concerned cannot reach agreement they should seek the good offices of or jointly request the mediation by a third Contracting Party, a qualified international organization or a qualified person.

2. If the Parties concerned have not been able to resolve their dispute through negotiation or have been unable to agree on measures as described above, such disputes shall be, upon common agreement, submitted to an ad-hoc arbitration tribunal, to a permanent arbitration tribunal, or to the International Court of Justice.

Article 19

SAFEGUARD OF CERTAIN FREEDOMS

Nothing in the present Convention shall be construed as infringing upon the freedom of navigation, fishing, marine scientific research and other legitimate uses of the high seas, as well as upon the right of innocent passage through the territorial sea.

Article 20

STATUS OF ANNEXES

The Annexes attached to the present Convention form an integral part of the Convention.

Article 21

RELATION TO OTHER CONVENTIONS

The provisions of the present Convention shall be without prejudice to the rights and obligations of the Contracting Parties under treaties concluded previously as well as under treaties which may be concluded in the future, furthering and developing the general principles of the Law of the Sea that the present Convention is based upon and in particular provisions concerning the prevention of pollution of the marine environment.

Article 22

REVISION OF THE CONVENTION

A conference for the purpose of a general revision of the present Convention may be convened with the consent of the Contracting Parties or at the request of the Commission.

Article 23

AMENDMENTS TO THE ARTICLES OF THE CONVENTION

1. Each Contracting Party may propose amendments to the Articles of the present Convention. Any such proposed amendments shall be submitted to the Depositary Government and communicated by it to all Contracting Parties, which shall inform the Depositary Government of either their acceptance or rejection of the amendment as soon as possible after the receipt of the communication.

The amendment shall enter into force ninety days after the Depositary Government has received notifications of acceptance of that amendment from all Contracting Parties.

2. With the consent of the Contracting Parties or at the request of the Commission a conference may be convened for the purpose of amending the present Convention.

Article 24

AMENDMENTS TO THE ANNEXES AND THE ADOPTION OF ANNEXES

1. Any amendment to the Annexes proposed by a Contracting Party shall be communicated to the other Contracting Parties by the Depositary Government and considered in the Commission. If adopted by the Commission, the amendment shall be communicated to the Contracting Parties and recommended for acceptance.

2. Such amendment shall be deemed to have been accepted at the end of a period determined by the Commission unless within that period any one of the Contracting Parties has objected to the amendment. The accepted amendment shall enter into force on a date determined by the Commission.

The period determined by the Commission shall be prolonged for an additional period of six months and the date of entry into force of the amendment postponed accordingly, if, in exceptional cases, any Contracting Party before the expiry of the period determined by the Commission informs the Depositary Government, that, although it intends to accept the proposal, the constitutional requirements for such an acceptance are not yet fulfilled in its State.

3. An Annex to the present Convention may be adopted in accordance with the provisions of this Article.

4. The Depositary Government shall inform all Contracting Parties of any amendments or the adoption of a new Annex which enter into force under this Article and of the date on which such amendment or new Annex enters into force.

5. Any objection under this Article shall be made by notification in writing to the Depositary Government which shall notify all Contracting Parties and the Executive Secretary of any such notification and the date of its receipt.

Article 25

RESERVATIONS

1. The provisions of the present Convention shall not be subject to reservations.

2. The provisions of Paragraph 1 of this Article does not prevent a Contracting Party from suspending for a period not exceeding one year the

application of an Annex of the present Convention or part thereof or an amendment thereof after the Annex in question or the amendment thereto has entered into force.

3. If after the entry into force of the present Convention a Contracting Party invokes the provisions of Paragraph 2 of this Article it shall inform the other Contracting Parties, at the time of the adoption by the Commission of an amendment to an Annex or a new Annex, of those provisions which will be suspended in accordance with Paragraphs 2 of this Article.

Article 26

SIGNATURE, RATIFICATION, APPROVAL AND ACCESSION

1. The present Convention shall be open for signature in Helsinki on 22 March 1974 by the Baltic Sea Area States participating in the Diplomatic Conference on the Protection of the Marine Environment of the Baltic Sea Area, held in Helsinki from 18 to 22 March 1974. The present Convention shall be open for accession to any other State interested in fulfilling the aims and purposes of the present Convention, provided that this State is invited by all the Contracting Parties.

2. The present Convention shall be subject to ratification or approval by the States which have signed it.

3. The instruments of ratification, approval, or accession shall be deposited with the Government of Finland, which will perform the duties of the Depositary Government.

Article 27

ENTRY INTO FORCE

The present Convention shall enter into force two months after the deposit of the seventh instrument of ratification or approval.

Article 28

WITHDRAWAL

1. At any time after the expiry of five years from the date of entry into force of the present Convention any Contracting Party may, by giving written notification to the Depositary Government, withdraw from the present Convention. The withdrawal shall take effect for such Contracting Party on the thirty-first day of December of the year which follows the year in which the Depositary Government was notified of the withdrawal.

2. In case of notification of withdrawal by a Contracting Party the Depositary Government shall convene a meeting of the Contracting Parties for the purpose of considering the effects of the withdrawal.

Article 29

LANGUAGE

The present Convention has been drawn up in a single copy in the English language. Official translations into the Danish, Finnish, German, Polish, Russian, and Swedish languages shall be prepared and deposited with the signed original.

In Witness Whereof the undersigned Plenipotentiaries, being duly authorized thereto, have signed the present Convention.

Done at Helsinki, this twenty-second day of March one thousand nine hundred and seventy-four.

ANNEX I

HAZARDOUS SUBSTANCES

The protection of the Baltic Sea Area from pollution by the substances listed below can involve the use of appropriate technical means, prohibitions and regulations of the transport, trade, handling application, and final deposition of products containing such substances.

1. DDT (1,1,1-trichloro-2,2-bis-(chlorophenyl)-ethane) and its derivatives DDE and DDD.

2. PCB's (polychlorinated biphenyls).

ANNEX II

NOXIOUS SUBSTANCES AND MATERIALS

The following substances and materials are listed for the purposes of Article 6 of the present Convention.

The list is valid for substances and materials introduced as waterborne into the marine environment. The Contracting Parties shall also endeavour to use best practicable means to prevent harmful substances and materials from being introduced as airborne into the Baltic Sea Area.

A. For urgent consideration

1. Mercury, cadmium, and their compounds.

B. 2. Antimony, arsenic, beryllium, chromium, copper, lead, molybdenum, nickel, selemium, tin, vanadium, zinc, and their compounds, as well as elemental phosphorus.

3. Phenols and their derivatives.

4. Phthalic acid and its derivatives.

5. Cyanides.

6. Persistent halogenated hydrocarbons.

7. Polycyclic aromatic hydrocarbons and their derivatives.

8. Persistent toxic organosilicic compounds.

9. Persistent pesticides, including organophosophoric and organostannic pesticides, herbicides, slimicides and chemicals used for the preservation of wood, timber, wood pulp, cellulose, paper, hides and textiles, not covered by the provisions of Annex I of the present Convention.

10. Radioactive materials.

11. Acids, alkalis and surface active agents in high concentrations or big quantities.

12. Oil and wastes of petrochemical and other industries containing lipid-soluble substances.

13. Substances having adverse effects on the taste and/or smell or products for human consumption from the sea, or effects on taste, smell, colour, transparency or other characteristics of the water

seriously reducing its amenity values.

14. Materials and substances which may float, remain in suspension or sink, and which may seriously interfere with any legitimate use of the sea.

15. Lignin substances contained in industrial waste waters.

16. The chelators EDTA (ethylenedinitrilotetraacetic acid or ethylenediaminetetraacetic acid) and DPTA (diethylenetriaminopentaacetic acid).

ANNEX III

GOALS, CRITERIA AND MEASURES CONCERNING THE PREVENTION OF LAND-BASED POLLUTION

In accordance with the provisions of Article 6 of the present Convention the Contracting Parties shall endeavour to attain the goals and apply the criteria and measures enumerated in this Annex in order to control and minimize land-based pollution of the marine environment of the Baltic Sea Area.

1. Municipal sewage shall be treated in an appropriate way so that the amount of organic matter does not cause harmful changes in the oxygen content of the Baltic Sea Area and the amount of nutrients does not cause harmful eutrophication of the Baltic Sea Area.

2. Municipal sewage shall also be treated in an appropriate way to ensure that the hygienic quality, and in particular epidemiological and texiocological safety, of the receiving sea area is maintained at a level which does not cause harm to human health, and in a way that under the given composition of the sewage no significant amount of such harmful substances as are listed in Annexes I and II of the present Convention is formed.

3. The polluting load of industrial wastes shall be minimized in an appropriate way in order to reduce the amount of harmful substances, organic matter and nutrients.

4. The means referred to in Paragraphs 3 of this Annex shall in particular include minimization of production of wastes by processing techniques, re-circulation and re-use of processing water, developing of water economy and improvement of qualifications for water treatment. In the treatment of waste water mechanical, chemical, biological and other measures, according to the quality of the waste water, and as required to maintain or improve the quality of the recipient water, shall be applied.

5. The discharge of cooling water from nuclear power plants or other kinds of industries using large amounts of water shall be effected in a way which minimizes the pollution of the marine environment of the Baltic Sea Area.

6. The Commission will define pollution control criteria, objectives for reduction of pollution and objectives concerning measures, including processing techniques and waste treatment, to reduce pollution of the Baltic Sea Area.

ANNEX IV

PREVENTION OF POLUTION FROM SHIPS

Regulation 1

The Contracting Parties shall as appropriate co-operate and assist each other in initiating action by the Inter-Governmental Maritime Consultative Organization to develop:

a) international rules for navigation of deep draught ships in narrow and shallow waters in international waters of the Baltic Sea Area and in the entrances to the Baltic Sea for the prevention of collisions, strandings and groundings;

b) an international radio reporting system for large ships en route within the Baltic Sea Area as well as for ships carrying a significant amount of a harmful substance.

Regulation 2

The Contracting Parties shall, without prejudice to Paragraph 4 of Article 4 of the present Convention, as appropriate assist each other in investigating violations of the existing legislation on antipollution measures, which have occurred or are suspected to have occurred within the Baltic Sea Area. This assistance may include but is not limited to inspection by the competent authorities of oil record books, cargo record books, log books and engine log books and taking oil samples for analytical identification purposes and in respect of the system of tagging oil residues.

Regulation 3

DEFINITIONS

For the purposes of this Annex:

1. "Ship" means a vessel of any type whatsoever operating in the marine environment and includes hydrofoil boats, air-cushion vehicles, submersibles, floating craft and fixed or floating platforms.

2. "Administration" means the Government of the State under whose authority the ship is operating. With respect to a ship entitled to fly a flag of any State, the Administration is the Government of that State. With respect of fixed or floating platforms engaged in exploration and exploitation of the sea-bed and subsoil thereof adjacent to the coast over which the coastal State exercises sovereign rights for the purposes of exploration and exploitation of their natural resources, the Administration is the Government of the coastal State concerned.

3. *a*) "Discharge", in relation to harmful substances or effluents containing such substances, means any release howsoever caused from a ship and includes any escape, disposal, spilling, leaking, pumping, emitting or emptying;

b) "Discharge" does nto include:

(i) dumping within the meaning of the Convention on the Prevention of Marine Pollution by Dumping of Wastes and Other Matter done at London on 29 December 1972; or

(ii) release of harmful substances directly arising

from the exploration, exploitation and associated off-shore processing of sea-bed mineral resources; or

(iii) release of harmful substances for purposes of legitimate scientific research into pollution abatement or control.

4. "Nearest land". The term "from the nearest land" means from the baseline from which the territorial sea of the territory in question is established in accordance with international law.

5. The term "jurisdiction" shall be interpreted in accordance with international law in force at the time of application or interpretation of this Annex.

Regulation 4

OIL

The Contracting Parties shall as soon as possible but not later than 1 January 1977 or on the date of entry into force of the present Convention, whichever occurs later, apply the provisions of Paragraph A to D of this Regulation on methods for the prevention of pollution by oil from ships while operating in the Baltic Sea Area.

A. DEFINITIONS

For the purposes of this Regulation:

1. "Oil" means petroleum in any form including crude oil, fuel oil, sludge, oil refuse and refined products (other than petrochemicals which are subject to the provisions of Regulation 5 of this Annex) and, without limiting the generality of the foregoing, includes the substances listed in Appendix I to this Annex.

2. "Oily mixture" means a mixture with any oil content.

3. "Oil fuel" means any oil used as fuel in connection with the propulsion and auxiliary machinery of the ship in which such oil is carried.

4. "Oil tanker" means a ship constructed or adapted primarily to carry oil in bulk in its cargo space and includes combination carriers and any "chemical tanker" as defined in Regulation 5 of this Annex when it is carrying a cargo or part cargo of oil in bulk.

5. "Combination carrier" means a ship designed to carry either oil or solid cargoes in bulk.

6. "Clean ballast" means the ballast in a tank which since oil was last carried therein has been so cleaned that effluent therefrom if it were discharged from a ship which is stationery into clean water on a clear day would not produce visible traces of oil on the surface of the water or on adjoining shore lines or cause a sludge or emulsion to be deposited beneath the surface of the water or upon adjoining shore lines. If the ballast is discharged through an oil discharge monitoring and control system approved by the Administration, evidence based on such a system to the effect that the oil content of the effluent did not exceed 15 parts per million shall be determinative that the ballast was clean, notwithstanding the presence of visible trace.

7. "Segregated ballast" means the ballast water introduced into a tank which is completely separated from the cargo oil and oil fuel system and which is permanently allocated to the carriage of ballast or to the carriage of ballast or cargoes other than oil or noxious substances as variously defined in the Regulations of this Annex.

B. CONTROL OF DISCHARGE OF OIL

1. *a*) Subject to the provisions of Paragraph C of this Regulation, any discharge into the sea of oil or oily mixtures from any oil tanker and any ship of 400 tons gross tonnage and above other than an oil tanker shall be prohibited, while in the Baltic Sea Area;

b) such ships while in the Baltic Sea Area shall retain on board all oil drainage and sludge, dirty ballast and tank washings waters and discharge them only to reception facilities.

2. *a*) Subject to the provisions of Paragraph C of this Regulation, any discharge into the sea of oil or oily mixtures from a ship of less than 400 tons gross tonnage, other than an oil tanker, shall be prohibited while in the Baltic Sea Area, except when the oil content of the effluent without dilution does not exceed 15 parts per million or alternatively when all of the following conditions are satisfied:

(i) the ship is proceeding en route;

(ii) the oil content of the effluent is less than 100 parts per million; and

(iii) the discharge is made as far as practicable from the land, but in no case less than 12 nautical miles from the nearest land;

b) no discharge into the sea shall contain chemicals or other substances in quantities or concentrations which are hazardous to the marine environment or chemicals or other substances introduced for the purpose of circumventing the conditions of discharge specified in this Regulation;

c) the oil residues which cannot be discharged into the sea in compliance with Sub-Paragraph 2 (*a*) of this Paragraph shall be retained on board or discharged to reception facilities.

3. The provisions of this Paragraph shall not apply to the discharge of clean or segregated ballast.

4. Whenever visible traces of oil are observed on or below the surface of the water in the immediate vicinity of a ship or its wake, the Contracting Parties should, to the extent they are reasonably able to do so, promptly investigate the facts bearing on the issue of whether there has been a violation of the provisions of this Regulation. The investigation should include, in particular, the wind and sea conditions, the track and speed of the ship, other possible sources of the visible traces in the vicinity, and any relevant oil discharge records.

C. EXCEPTIONS

Paragraph B of this Regulation shall not apply to:

a) the discharge into the sea of oil or oily mixtures necessary for the purpose of securing the safety of a ship or saving life at sea; or

b) the discharge into the sea of oil or oily mixtures resulting from damage to a ship or its equipment:

(i) provided that all reasonable precautions have been taken after the occurrence of the damage or discovery of the discharge for the purpose of preventing or minimizing the dishcarge; and

(ii) except if the owner or the Master acted either with intent to cause damage, or recklessly and with knowledge that damage would probably result; or

c) the discharge into the sea of substances containing oil, approved by the Administration, when being used for the purpose of combating specific pollution incidents in order to minimize the damage from pollution. Any such discharge shall be subject to the approval of any Contracting Party in whose jurisdiction it is contemplated the discharge will occur.

D. SPECIAL REQUIREMENTS FOR DRILLING RIGS AND OTHER PLATFORMS

Fixed and floating drilling rigs when engaged in the exploration, exploitation and associated offshore processing of sea-bed mineral resources and other platforms shall comply with the requirements of this Regulation applicable to ships of 400 tons gross tonnage and above other than oil tankers, except that:

a) they shall keep a record of all operations involving oil or oily mixture discharges, in a form approved by the Administration; and

b) subject to the provisions of Paragraph C of this Regulation, the discharge into the sea of oil or oily mixture shall be prohibited except when the oil content of the discharge without dilution does not exceed 15 parts per million.

E. RECEPTION FACILITIES OF THE BALTIC SEA AREA

The Contracting Parties undertake to ensure that not later than 1 Janaury 1977 all oil loading terminals and repair ports of the Baltic Sea Area are provided with facilities adequate for the reception and treatment of all the dirty ballast and tank washing waters from oil tankers. In addition all ports of the area shall be provided with adequate reception facilities for other residues and oily mixtures from all ships. Such facilities shall have adequate capacity to meet the needs of the ships using them without causing undue delay.

Regulation 5

NOXIOUS LIQUID SUBSTANCES IN BULK

The Contracting Parties shall as soon as possible, but not later than 1 January 1977 or at a date not later than one year after the date of the entry into force of the present Convention, whichever occurs later, decide upon a date from which the provisions of Paragraphs A to D of this Regulation on the discharge of noxious liquid substances in bulk from ships while operating in Baltic Sea Area shall apply.

A. DEFINITIONS

For the purpose of this Regulation:

1. "Chemical tanker" means a ship constructed or adapted primarily to carry a cargo of noxious liquid substances in bulk and includes an "oil tanker" as defined in Regulation 4 of this Annex when carrying a cargo or part cargo of noxious liquid substances in bulk.

2. "Clean ballast" means ballast carried in a tank which, since it was last used to carry a cargo containing a substance in Category A, B, C or D has been thoroughly cleaned and the residues resulting therefrom have been discharged and the tank emptied in accordance with the appropriate requirements of this Regulation.

3. "Segregated ballast" means ballast water introduced into a tank permanently allocated to the carriage of ballast or to the carriage of ballast or cargoes other than oil or noxious liquid substances as variously defined in the Regulations of this Annex, and which is completely separated from the cargo and oil fuel system.

4. "Liquid substances" are those having a vapour pressure not exceeding 2.8 kp/cm^2 at a temperature of 37.8° C.

5. "Noxious liquid substance" means any substance designated in Appendix III to this Annex or provisionally assessed under the provisions of Sub-Paragraph 4 of Paragraph B of this Regulation as falling into Category A, B, C, or D.

B. CATEGORIZATION AND LISTING OF NOXIOUS LIQUID SUBSTANCES

1. For the purposes of this Regulation noxious liquid substances shall be divided into four categories as follows:

a) Category A — noxious liquid substances which if discharged into the sea from tank cleaning or deballasting operations would present a major hazard to either marine resources or human health or cause serious harm to amenities or other legitimate uses of the sea and therefore justify the application of stringent anti-pollution measures;

b) Category B — noxious liquid substances which if discharged into the sea from tank cleaning or deballasting operations would present a hazard to either marine resources or human health or cause harm to amenities or other legitimate uses of the sea and therefore justify the application of special anti-pollution measures;

c) Category C — noxious liquid substances which if discharged into the sea from tank cleaning or deballasting operations would present a minor hazard to either marine resources or human health or cause minor harm to amenities or other legitimate uses of the sea and therefore require special operational conditions;

d) Category D — noxious liquid substances which if discharged into the sea from tank cleaning or deballasting operations would present a recognizable hazard to either marine resources or human health or cause minimal harm to amenities or other legitimate uses of the sea and therefore require some attention in operational conditions.

2. Guidelines for use in the categorization of

noxious liquid substances are given in Appendix II to this Annex.

3. The list of noxious liquid substances carried in bulk and presently categorized which are subject to the provisions of this Regulation is set out in Appendix II to this Annex

4. Where it is proposed to carry a liquid substance in bulk which has not been categorized under paragraph (i) of this Regulation or evaluated as referred to in Regulation 4(1) of this Annex, the Governments of Parties to the Convention involved in the proposed operation shall establish and agree on a provisional assessment for the proposed operation on the basis of the guidelines referred to in paragraph (2) of this Regulation. Until full agreement between the Governments involved has been reached, the substance shall be carried under the most severe conditions proposed. As soon as possible, but not later than ninety days after its first carriage, the Administration concerned shall notify the Organization and provide details of the substance and the provisional assessment for prompt circulation to all Parties for their information and consideration. The Government of each Party shall have a period of ninety days in which to forward its comments to the Organization, with a view to the assessment of the substance.

C. OTHER LIQUID SUBSTANCES

1. The substances listed in Appendix III to this Annex have been evaluated and found to fall outside the Categories A, B, C and D, as defined in Regulation 3(1) of this Annex because they are presently considered to present no harm to human health, marine resources, amenities or other legitimate uses of the sea, when discharged into the sea from tank cleaning or deballasting operations.

2. The discharge of bilge or ballast water or other residues or mixtures containing only substances listed in Appendix III to this Annex shall not be subject to any requirements of this Annex.

3. The discharge into the sea of clean ballast or segregated ballast shall 'not be subject to any requirement of this Annex.

D. DISCHARGE OF NOXIOUS LIQUID SUBSTANCES

Subject to the provisions of Regulation E of this Regulation:

1. The discharge into the sea of substances in Category A as defined in Regulation 3(1)(a) of this annex or of those provisionally assesed as such or ballast water, tank washings, or other residues or mixtures containing such substances shall be prohibited. If tanks containing such substances or mixtures are to be washed, the resulting residues shall be disharged to a reception facility until the concentration of the substance in the effluent to such facility is at or below the residual concentration prescribed for that substance in column III of Appendix II of this Annex and until the tank is empty. Provided that the residue then remaining in the tank is subsequently diluted by the addition of a volume of water of not less than 5 per cent of the total volume of the tank, it may be discharged into the sea when all the following conditions are also satisfied:

a) the ship is proceeding en route at a speed of at least 7 knots in the case of self-propelled ships or at least 4 knots in the case of ships which are not self-propelled;

b) the discharge is made below the waterline, taking into account the location of the seawater intakes; and

c) the discharge is made at a distance of not less than 12 nautical miles from the nearest land and in a depth of water of not less than 25 metres.

2. The discharge into the sea of substances in Category B as defined in Sub-Paragraph 1 b) of this Regulation or of those provisionally assessed as such or ballast water, tank washings, or other residues or mixtures containing such substances shall be prohibited except when all the following conditions are satisfied:

a) the tank has been washed after unloading with a volume of water of not less than 0.5 per cent of the total volume or the tank and the resulting residues have been discharged to a reception facility until the tank is empty;

b) the ship is proceeding en route at a speed of at least 7 knots in the case of self-propelled ships or at least 4 knots in the case of ships which are not self-propelled;

c) the procedures and arrangements for discharge and washings are approved by the Administration and shall ensure that the concentration and rate of discharge of the effluent is such that the concentration of the substance in the wake astern if the ship does not exceed 1 part per million;

d) the discharge is made below the waterline, taking into account the location of the seawater intakes; and

e) the discharge is made at a distance of not less than 12 nautical miles from the nearest land and in a depth of water of not less than 25 metres.

3. The discharge into the sea of substances in Category C as defined in Sub-Paragraphs 1 (*c*) of Paragraph B of this Regulation or of those provisionally assessed as such or ballast water, tank washings, or other residues or mixtures containing such substances shall be prohibited except when all the following conditions are satisfied:

a) the ship is proceeding en route at a speed of at least 7 knots in the case of self-propelled ships or at least 4 knots in the case of ships which are not self-propelled;

b) the procedures and arrangements for discharge are approved by the Administration and shall ensure that the concentration and rate of discharge of the effluent is such that the concentration of the substance in the wake astern of the ship does not exceed 1 part per million;

c) the maximum quantity of cargo discharged from each tank and its associated piping system does not exceed the maximum quantity approved in accordacne with the procedures referred to in Sub-Paragraphs 3 (*b*) of this Paragraph which shall in no case exceed the greater of 1 cubic metre or 1/3,000 of the tank capacity in cubic metres;

d) the discharge is made below the waterline, taking into account the location of the seawater intakes; and

e) the discharge is made at a distance of not less than 12 nautical miles from the nearest land and in a depth of water of not less than 24 metres.

4. The discharge into the sea of substances in Category D as defined in Regulation 3(1)(d) of this Annex, or of those provisionally assessed as such, or ballast water, tank washings, or other residues or mixtures containing such substances shall be prohibited except when all the following conditions are satisfied:

a) the ship is proceeding en route at a speed of at least 7 knots in the case of self-propelled ships or at least 4 knots in the case of ships which are not self-propelled;

b) such mixtures are of a concentration not greater than one part of the substance in ten parts of water; and

c) the discharge is made at a distance of not less than 12 nautical miles from the nearest land.

5. Ventilation procedures approved by the Administration may be used to remove cargo residues from a tank. Such procedures shall be based upon standards developed by the Organization. If subsequent washing of the tank is necessary, the discharge into the sea of the resulting tank washings shall be made in accordance with paragraphs (1), (2), (3) or (4) of this Regulation, whichever is applicable.

6. The discharge into the sea of substances which have not been categorized, provisionally assessed, or evalutated as referred to in Regulation 4(1) of this Annex, or of ballast water, tank washings, or other residues or mixtures containing such substances shall be prohibited.

E. EXCEPTIONS

Paragraph D of this Regulation shall not apply to:

a) the discharge into the sea of noxious liquid substances or mixtures containing such substances necessary for the purpose of securing the safety of a ship or saving life at sea; or

b) the discharge into the sea of noxious liquid substances or mixtures containing such substances resulting from damage to a ship or its equipment.

(i) provided that all reasonable precautions have been taken after the occurrence of the damage or discovery of the discharge for the purpose of preventing or minimizing the discharge; and

(ii) except if the owner or the Master acted with intent to cause damage, or recklessly and with knowledge that damage would probably result; or

c) the discharge into the sea of noxious liquid substances or mixtures containing such substances, approved by the Adminsitration, when being used for the purpose of combating specific position incidents in order to minimize the damage from pollution. Any such discharge shall be subject to the approval of any Contracting Party in whose jurisdiction it is contemplated the discharge will occur.

F. MEASURES OF CONTROL

1. The Contracting Parties shall appoint or authorize surveyors for the purpose of implementing this Paragraph.

Category A Substances

2. *a*) If a tank is partially unloaded or unloaded but not cleaned, an appropriate entry shall be made in the Cargo Record Book:

b) until that tank is cleaned every subsequent pumping or transfer operation carried out in connection with that tank shall also be entered in the Cargo Record Book.

3. If the tank is to be washed:

a) the effluent from the tank washing operation shall be discharged from the ship to a reception facility at least until the concentration of the substance in the discharge, as indicated by analysis of samples of the effluent taken by the surveyor, has fallen to the residual concentration specified for that substance in Appendix III to this Annex. When the required residual concentration has been achieved, remaining tank washings shall continue to be discharged to the reception facility until the tank is empty. Appropriate entries of these operations shall be made in the Cargo Record Book and certified by the surveyor; and

b) after diluting the residue then remaining in the tank with at least 5 per cent of the tank capacity of water, this mixture may be discharged into the sea in accordance with the provisions of Sub-Paragraph 1 (*a*), (*b*), and (*c*) of Paragraph D of this Regulation. Appropriate entrie of these operations shall be made in the Cargo Record Book.

4. Where the Government of the receiving Party is satisfied that it is impracticable to measure the concentration of the substance in the effluent without causing undue delay to the ship, that Party may accept an alternative procedure as being equivalent to Sub-Paragraph 3 (*a*) of this Paragraph provided that:

a) a precleaning procedure for that tank and that substance is approved by the Administration and that Party is satisfied that such procedure will fulfil the requirements of Sub-Paragraph 1 of Paragraph D of this Regulation with respect to the attainment of the prescribed residual concentrations;

b) a surveyor duly authorized by that Party shall certify in the Cargo Record Book that:

(i) the tank, its pump and piping system have been emptied, and that the quantity of cargo remaining in the tank is at or below the quantity on which the approved precleaning procedure referred to in Sub-Paragraph (ii) of this Sub-Paragraph has been based;

(ii) precleaning has been carried out in accordacne with the precleaning procedure approved by the Administration for that tank and that substance; and

(iii) the tank washings resulting from such precleaning have been discharged to a reception facility and the tank is empty;

c) the discharge into the sea of any remaining residues shall be in accordance with the provisions of Sub-Paragraph 3 (*b*) of this Paragraph and an appropriate entry is made in the Cargo Record Book.

Category B Substances

5. Subject to such surveillance and approval by the authorized or appointed surveyor as may be deemed necessary by the Contracting Party, the Master of a ship shall, with respect to a Category B substance, ensure compliance with the following:

a) if a tank is partially unloaded or unloaded but not cleaned, an appropriate entry shall be made in the Cargo Record Book;

b) until that tank is cleaned every subsequent pumping or transfer operation carried out in connection with that tank shall also be entered in the Cargo Record;

c) if the tank is to be washed, the effluent from the tank washing operation, which shall contain a volume of water not less than 0.5 per cent of the total volume of the tank, shall be discharged from the ship to a reception facility until the tank, its pump and piping system are empty. An appropriate entry shall be made in the Cargo Record Book;

d) if the tank is to be further cleaned and emptied at sea, the Master shall:

(i) ensure that the approved procedures referred to in Sub-Paragraph 2 (*c*) of Paragraph D of this Regulation are complied with and that the appropriate entries are made in the Cargo Record Book; and

(ii) ensure that any discharge into the sea is made in accordance with the requirements of Sub-Paragraph 2 of Paragraph D of this Regulation and an appropriate entry is made in the Cargo Record Book;

e) if after unloading a Category B substance any residues of tank washing are to be retained on board until the ship is outside the Baltic Sea Area, the Master shall so indicate by an appropriate entry in the Cargo Record Book;

Category C Substances

6. Subject to such surveillance and approval by the authorized or appointed surveyor as may be deemed necessary by the Contracting Party, the Master of a ship shall with respect to a Category C substance, ensure compliance with the following:

a) if a tank is partially unloaded or onloaded but not cleaned, an appropriate entry shall be made in the Cargo Record Book;

b) if the tank is to be cleaned at sea:

(i) the cargo piping system serving that tank shall be drained and an appropriate entry made in the Cargo Record Book;

(ii) the quantity of substance remaining in the tank shall not exceed the maximum quantity which may be discharged into the sea for that substance under Sub-Paragraph 3 (*c*) of Paragraph D of this Regulation. An appropriate entry shall be made in the Cargo Record Book;

(iii) where it is intended to discharge the quantity of substance remaining into the sea the approved procedures shall be complied with, and the necessary dilution of the substance satisfactory for such a discharge shall be achieved. An appropriate entry shall be made in the Cargo Record Book; or

(iv) where the tank washings are not discharged into the sea, if any internal transfer of tank washings takes place from that tank an appropriate entry shall be made in the Cargo Record Book; and

(v) any subsequent discharge into the sea of such tank washings shall be made in accordance with the requirements of Sub-Paragraph 3 of Paragraph D of this Regulation;

c) if the tank is to be cleaned in port;

(i) the tank washings shall be discharged to a reception facility and an appropriate entry shall be made in the Cargo Record Book; or

(ii) the tank washings shall be retained on board the ship and an appropriate entry shall be made in the Cargo Record Book indicating the location and disposition of the tank washings;

d) if after loading a Category C substance within the Baltic Sea Area, any residues or tank washings are to be retained on board until the ship is outside the area, the Master shall so indicate by an appropriate entry in the Cargo Record Book.

Category D Substances

7. The Master of a ship shall, with respect to a Category D substance, ensure compliance with the following:

a) if a tank is partiallly unloaded or loaded but not cleaned, an appropriate entry shall be made in the Cargo Record Book;

b) if the tank is to be cleaned at sea:

(i) the cargo piping system serving that tank shall be drained and an appropriate entry made in the Cargo Record Book;

(ii) where it is intended to discharge the quantity of substance remaining into the sea, the necessary dilution of the substance satisfactory for such a discharge shall be achieved. An appropriate entry shall be made in the Cargo Record Book;

(iii) where the tank washings are not discharged into the sea, if any internal transfer of tank washings takes place from that tank an appropriate entry shall be made in the Cargo Record Book; and

(iv) any subsequent discharge into the sea of such tank washings shall be made in accordance with the requirements of Sub-Paragraph 4 of Paragraph D of this Regulation;

c) if the tank is to be cleaned in port:

(i) the tank washings shall be discharged to a reception facility and an appropriate entry shall be made in the Cargo Record Book; or

(ii) the tank washings shall be retained on board the ship and an appropriate entry shall be made in the Cargo Record Book indicating the location and disposition of the tank washings.

Discharge from a Slop Tank

8. Any residues on board in a slop tank, including those from pump room bilges, which contain a Category A or a Category B substance, shall be discharged to a reception facility in accordance with the provisions of Sub-Paragraph 1 or 2 of Paragraph D of this Regulation, whichever is applicable. An appropriate entry shall be made in the Cargo Record Book.

9. Any residues retained on board in a slop tank, including those from pump room bilges, which contain a Category C substance in excess of the aggregate of the maximum quantities specified in Sub-Paragraph 3 (*c*) of Paragraph D of this Regulation shall be discharged to a reception facility. An appropriate entry shall be made in the Cargo Record Book.

G. CARGO RECORD BOOK

1. Every ship to which this Regulation applies shall be provided with a Cargo Record Book, whether as part of the ship's official log book or otherwise, in the form specified in Appendix V to this Annex.

2. The Cargo Record Book shall be completed, on a tank-to-thank basis, whenever any of the following operations with respect to a noxious liquid substance takes place in the ship:

(i) loading of cargo;
(ii) unloading of cargo;
(iii) transfer of cargo;
(iv) transfer of cargo, cargo residues or mixtures containing cargo to a slop tank;
(v) cleaning of cargo tanks;
(vi) transfer from slop tanks;
(vii) ballasting of cargo tanks;
(viii) transfer of dirty ballast water;
(ix) discharge into the sea in accordance with Paragraph D of this Regulation.

3. In the event of any discharge of the kind referred to in Annex VI of the present Convention and Paragraph E of this Regulation of any noxious liquid substance or mixture containing such substances, whether intentional or accidental, an entry shall be made in the Cargo Record Book stating the circumstances of, and the reason for, the discharge.

4. When a surveyor appointed or authorized by a Contracting Party to supervise any operations under this Regulation has inspected a ship, then that surveyor shall make an appropriate entry in the Cargo Record Book.

5. Each operation referred to in Sub-Paragraphs 2 and 3 of this Paragraph shall be fully recorded without delay in the Cargo Record Book so that all the entries in the Book appropriate to that operation are completed. Each entry shall be signed by the officer or officers in charge of the operation concerned and, when the ship is manned, each page shall be signed by the Master of the ship. The entries in the Cargo Record Book shall be in an official language of the State whose flag the ship is entitled to fly, and, except when the ship is engaged in domestic voyages, in English or French. The entries in an official national language or the State whose flag the ship is entitled to fly shall prevail in case of a dispute or discrepancy.

6. The Cargo Record Book shall be kept in such a place as to be readily available for inspection and, except in the case of unmanned ships under two, shall be kept on board the ship. It shall be retained for a period of two years after the last entry has been made.

7. The competent authority of a Contracting Party may inspect the Cargo Record Book on board any ship to which this Regulation applies while the ship is in its port, and may make a copy of any entry in that Book and may require the Master of the ship to certify that the copy is a true copy of such entry. Any copy so made which has been certified by the Master of the ship as a true copy of an entry in the ship's Cargo Record Book shall be made admissible in any judicial proceedings as evidence of the facts stated in the entry. The inspection of a Cargo Record Book and the taking of a certified copy by the competent authority under this Paragraph shall be performed as expeditiously as possible without causing the ship to be unduly delayed.

H. RECEPTION FACILITIES

1. The Contracting Parties undertake to ensure the provisions of reception facilities according to the needs of ships using their ports, terminals or repair ports of the Baltic Sea Area as follows:

a) cargo loading and unloading ports and terminals shall have facilities adequate for reception without undue delay to ships of such residues and mixtures containing noxious liquid substances as would remain for disposal from ships carrying them as a consequence of the application of this Regulation; and

b) ship repair ports undertaking repairs to chemical tankers shall have facilities adequate for the reception of residues and mixtures containing noxious liquid substances.

2. Each Contracting Party shall determine the types of facilities provided for the purpose of Sub-Paragraph 1 of this Paragraph at its cargo loading and unloading ports, terminals and ship repair ports of the Baltic Sea Area.

Regulation 6

HARMFUL SUBSTANCES IN PACKAGED FORMS

A. The Contracting Parties shall as soon as possible apply suitable uniform rules for the carriage of harmful substances in packaged forms or in freight containers, portable tanks or road and rail tank wagons.

B. With respect to certain harmful substances, as may be designated by the Commission, the Master or owner of the ship or his representative shall notify the appropriate port authority of the intent to load or unload such substances at least 24 hours prior to such action.

C. A report of an incident involving harmful substances shall be made in accordance with the provisions of Annex VI of the present Convention.

Regulation 7

SEWAGE

The Contracting Parties shall apply the provisions of Paragraphs A to D of this Regulation on discharge of sewage from ship while operating in the Baltic Sea Area.

A. Definitions

For the purpose of this Regulation:

1. "New ship" means a ship:

a) for which the building contract is placed, or in the absence of a building contract, the keel of which is laid, or which is at a similar stage of construction, on or after the date of entry into force of the present Convention; or

b) the delivery of which is three years or more after the date of entry into force of the present Convention.

2. "Existing ship" means a ship which is not a new ship.

3. "Sewage means"

a) drainage and wastes from any form of toilets, urinals, and WC scuppers;

b) drainage from medical premises (dispensary), sick bay, etc.) via wash basins wash tubs and scuppers located in such premises;

c) drainage from spaces containing living animals; or

d) other waste waters when mixed with the drainages defined above.

4. "Holding tank" means a tank used for the collection and storage of sewage.

B. Application

1. The provisions of this Regulation shall apply to:

a) new ships certified to carry more than 100 persons from a date not later than 1 January 1977;

b) existing ships certified to carry more than 400 persons from a date not later than 1 January 1978; and

c) other ships, as specified in Sub-Paragraphs (i), (ii), and (iii), from dates decided by the Contracting Parties on recommendations by the Commission:

(i) ships of 200 tons gross tonnage and above;

(ii) ships of less than 200 tons gross tonnage which are certified to carry more than 10 persons;

(iii) ships which do not have a measured gross tonnage and are certified to carry more than 10 persons.

In the case of new ships the date shall be not later than 1 January 1979. In the case of existing such ships the date shall be not later than ten years after the date decided for new ships.

2. A Contracting Party may, if it is satisfied that the application of the provisions of Sub-Paragraph 1(*b*) of this Paragraph with respect to a certain ship would necessitate contructional alterations which would be unreasonable, exempt the ship from the application until the date not later than ten years after the date of entry into force of the present Convention.

C. Discharge of Sewage

1. Subject to the provisions of Paragraph D of this Regulation, the discharge of sewage into the sea is prohibited, except when;

a) the ship is discharging comminuted and disinfected sewage using a system approved by the Administration at a distance of more than 4 nautical miles from the nearest land, or sewage which is not comminuted or disinfected at a distance of more than 12 nautical miles from the nearest land, provided that in any case the sewage that has been stored in holding tanks shall not be discharged instantaneously but at a moderate rate when the ship is en route and proceeding at not less than 4 knots; or

b) the ship has in operation a sewage treatment plant which has been approved by the Adminsitration, and

(i) the test results of the plant are laid down in a document carried by the ship;

(ii) additionally, the effluent shall not produce visible floating solids in, nor cause discolouration of the surrounding water; or

c) the ship is situated in the waters under the jurisdiction of a State and is discharging sewage in accordance with such less stringent requirements as may be imposed by such State.

2. When the sewage is mixed with wastes or waste water having different discharge requirements, the more stringent requirements shall apply.

D. Exceptions

Paragraph C of this Regulation shall not apply to:

a) the discharge of sewage from a ship and for the purpose of securing the safety of a ship and those on board or saving life at sea; or

b) the discharge of sewage resulting from damage to a ship or its equipment if all reasonable precautions have been taken before and after the occurrence of the damage for the purpose of preventing or minimizing the discharge.

E. Reception Facilities

1. Each Contracting Party undertakes to ensure the provisions of facilities at its ports and terminals of the Baltic Sea Area for the reception of sewage, without causing undue delay to ships using them.

2. To enable pipes of reception facilities to be connected with the ship's discharge pipeline, both lines shall be fitted with a standard discharge connection in accordance with the following table:

Standard Dimensions of Flanges for Discharge Connections

Description	Dimension
Outside diameter	210 mm
Inner diameter	According to pipe outside diameter
Bolt circle diameter	170 mm
Slots in flange	4 holes 18 mm in diameter equidistantly placed on a bolt circle of the above diameter, slotted to the flange periphery. The slot width to be 18 mm.
Flange thickness	16 mm
Bolts and nuts: quantity and diameter	4, each of 16 mm in diameter and of suitable length
The flange is designed to accept pipes up to a maximum internal diameter of 100 mm and shall be of steel or other equivalent material having a flat face. This flange, together with a suitable gasket, shall be suitable for a service pressure of 6 kg/cm^2.	

For ships having a moulded depth of 5 metres and less, the inner diameter of the discharge connection may be 38 millimetres.

Regulation 8

GARBAGE

The Contracting Parties shall as soon as possible but not later than 1 January 1976 or on the date of entry into force of the present Convention, whichever occurs later, apply the provisions of Paragraphs A to D of this Regulation on the disposal of garbage from ships while operating in the Baltic Sea Area.

A. Definition

For the purposes of this Regulation:

"Garbage" means all kinds of victual, domestic and operational waste excluding fresh fish and parts thereof, generated during the normal operation of the ship and liable to be disposed of continuously or periodically except those substances which are defined or listed in other Regulations of this Annex.

B. Disposal of Garbage

1. Subject to the provisions of Paragraphs C and D of this Regulation:

a) disposal into the sea of the following is prohibited:

(i) all plastics, including but not limited to synthetic ropes, synthetic fishing nets and plastic garbage bags; and

(ii) all other garbage, including paper products, rags, glass, metal, bottles, crockery, dunnage, lining and packing materials;

b) disposal into the sea of food wastes shall be made as far as possible from land, but in any case not less than 12 nautical miles from the nearest land.

2. When the garbage is mixed with other discharges having different disposal or discharge requirements the more stringent requirements shall apply.

C. Special Requirements for Fixed and Floating Platforms

1. Subject to the provisions of Sub-Paragraph 2 of this Paragraph, the disposal of any materials regulated by this Regulation is prohibited from fixed or floating platforms engaged in the exploration, exploitation and associated offshore processing of sea-bed mineral resources, and all other ships when alongside or within 500 metres of such platforms.

2. The disposal into the sea of food wastes may be permitted when they have passed through a comminuter or grinder from such fixed or floating platforms located more than 12 nautical miles from land and all other ships when alongside or within 500 metres of such platforms. Such comminuted or ground food wastes shall be capable of passing through a screen with openings no greater than 25 millimetres.

D. Exceptions

Paragraph B and C of this Regulation shall not apply to:

a) the disposal of garbage from a ship necessary for the purpose of securing the safety of a ship and those on board or saving life at sea; or

b) the escape of garbage resulting from damage to a ship or its equipment provided all reasonable precautions have been taken before and after the occurrence of the damage, for the purpose of preventing or minimizing the escape; or

c) the accidental loss of synthetic fishing nets or synthetic material incidental to the repair of such nets, provided that all reasonable precautions have been taken to prevent such loss.

E. Reception Facilities

Each Contracting Party undertakes to ensure the provision of facilities at its ports and terminals of the Baltic Sea Area for the reception of garbage, without causing undue delay to ships, and according to the needs of the ships using them.

ANNEX IV
APPENDIX I

List of Oils*

Asphalt solutions	*Gasolene Blending Stocks*
Blending Stocks	Alkylates — fuel
Roofers Flux	Reformates
Straight Run Residue	Polymer — fuel
Oils	*Gasolenes*
Clarified	Casinghead (natural)
Crude Oil	Automotive
Mixtures containing crude oil	Aviation
Diesel Oil	Straight Run
Fuel Oil No. 4	Fuel Oil No. 1 (Kerosene)
Fuel Oil No. 5	Fuel Oi No. 1 — D
Fuel Oil No. 6	Fuel Oil No. 2
Residual Fuel Oil	Fuel Oil No. 2 — D
Road Oil	
Transformer Oil	*Jet Fuels*
Aromatic Oil (excluding vegetable oil)	JP—1 (Kerosene)
Lubricating Oils and	JP—3
Blending Stocks	JP—4
	JP—5 (Kerosene, Heavy)
Mineral Oil	Turbo Fuel
Motor Oil	Kerosene
Penetrating Oil	Mineral Spirit
Spindle Oil	
Turbine Oil	
Distillates	*Naptha*
Straight Run	Solvent
Flashed Feed Stocks	Petroleum
	Heartcut Distillate Oil
Gas Oil	
Cracked	

* The list of oils shall not necessarily be considered as comprehensive.

ANNEX IV
APPENDIX II

GUIDELINES FOR THE CATEGORIZATION OF NOXIOUS LIQUID SUBSTANCES

Category A

Substances which are bioaccumulated and liable to produce a hazard to aquatic life or human health; or which are highly toxic to aquatic life (as expressed by a Hazard Rating 4, defined by a TLm less than 1 ppm); and additionally certain substances which are moderately toxic to aquatic life (as expressed by a Hazard Rating 3, defined by a TLm of 1 or more, but less than 10 ppm) when particular weight is given to additional factors in the hazard profile or to special characteristics of the substance.

Category B

Substances which are bioaccumulated with a short retention of the order of one week or less; or which are liable to produce tainting of the sea food; or which are moderately toxic to aquatic life (as expressed by a Hazard Rating 3, defined by a TLm of 1 ppm or more, but less than 10 ppm); and additionally certain substances which are slightly toxic to aquatic life (as expressed by a Hazard Rating 2, defined by a TLm of 10 ppm or more, but less than 100 ppm) when particular weight is given to additional factors in the hazard profile or to special characteristics of the substance.

Category C

Substances which are slightly toxic to aquatic life (as expressed by a Hazard Rating 2, defined by a TLm of 10 or more, but less than 100 ppm); and additionally certain substances which are practically non-toxic to aquatic life (as expressed by a Hazard Rating 1, defined by a TLm of 100 ppm or more, but less than 1.000 ppm) when particular weight is given to additional factors in the hazard profile or to special characteristics of the substance.

Category D

Substances which are practically non-toxic to aquatic life, (as expressed by a Hazard Rating 1, defined by a TLm of 100 ppm or more, but less than 1.000 ppm); or causing deposits blanketing the seafloor with a high biochemical oxygen demand (BOD); or highly hazardous to human health, with an LD_{50} of less than 5 mg/kg; or produce moderate reduction of amenities because of persistency, smell or poisonous or irritant characteristics, possibly interfering with use of beaches; or moderately hazardous to human health, with an LD_{50} of 5 mg/kg or more, but less than 50 mg/kg and produce slight reduction of amenities.

Other Liquid Substances (for the purpose of Paragraph C of Regulation 5)

Substances other than those categorized in Categories A, B, C, and D above.

ANNEX IV
APPENDIX III

APPENDIX III

LIST OF NOXIOUS LIQUID SUBSTANCES CARRIED IN BULK

Substance	UN Number	Pollution Category for operational discharge (Paragraph B of Regulation 5)	Residual concentration (per cent by weight)	Residual concentration (per cent by weight) Paragraph D(1) of Regulation 5)
	I	II	III	IV *Within the Baltic Sea Area*
Acetaldehyde	1089	C		
Acetic acid	1842	C		
Acetic anhydride	1715	C		
Acetone	1090	D		
Acetone cyanohydrin	1541	A		0.05
Acetyl chloride	1717	C		
Acrolein	1092	A		0.05
Acrylic acid*	—	C		
Acrylonitrile	1093	B		
Adiponitrile	—	D		
Alkylbenzene sulfonate				
(straight chain)	—	C		
(branched chain)	—	B		
Allyl alcohol	1098	B		
Allyl chloride	1100	C		
Alum (15% solution)	—	D		
Aminoethylethanolamine (Hydroxyethyl-ethylenediamine)*	—	D		
Ammonia (28% aqueous)	1005	B		
iso-Amyl acetate	1104	C		
n-Amyl acetate	1104	C		
n-Amyl alcohol	—	D		
Aniline	1547	C		
Benzene	1114	C		
Benzyl alcohol	—	D		
Benzyl chloride	1738	B		
n-Butyl acetate	1123	D		

*Asterisk indicates that the substance has been provisionally included in this list and that further data are necessary in order to complete the evaluation of its environmental hazards, particularly in relation to living resources.

Substance	I	II	III	IV
sec-Butyl acetate	1124	D		
n-Butyl acrylatc	—	D		
Butyl butyrate*	—	B		
Butylene glycol(s)	—	D		
Butyl methacrylate	—	D		
n-Butyraldehyde	1129	B		
Butyric acid	—	B		
Calcium hydroxide (solution)	—	D		
Camphor oil	1130	B		
Carbon disulphide	1131	A		0.005
Carbon tetrachloride	1846	B		
Caustic potash (Potassium hydroxide)	1814	C		
Cloroacetic acid	1750	C		
Chloroform	1888	B		
Chlorohydrins (crudc)*	—	D		
Chloroprene*	1991	C		
Chlorosulphonic acid	1754	C		
para-Chlorotoluene	—	B		
Citric acid (10—25%)	—	D		
Creosote	1334	A		0.05
Cresols	2076	A		0.05
Cresylic acid	2022	A		0.05
Crotonaldehyde	1143	B		
Cumene	1918	C		
Cyclohexane	1145	C		
Cyclohexanol	—	D		
Cyclohexanone	1915	D		
Cyclohexylamine*	—	D		
para-Cymene (Isopropyltoluene)*	2046	D		
Decahydronaphthalene	1147	D		
Decane*	—	D		
Diacetone alcohol*	1148	D		
Dibenzyl ether*	—	C		
Dichlorobenzenes	1591	A		0.05
Dichloroethyl ether	1916	B		
Dichloropropene — Dichloropropane mixture (D.D. Soil fumigant)	2047	B		
Diethylamine	1154	C		
Diethylbenzene (mixed isomers)	2049	C		
Diethyl ether	1155	D		
Diethylene triamine*	2079	C		
Diethylene glycol monoethyl ether	—	C		
Diethylketone (3-Pentanone)	1156	D		
Diisobutylene*	2050	D		
Diisobutyl ketone	1157	D		
Diisopropanolamine	—	C		
Diisopropylamine	1158	C		
Diisopropyl ether*	1159	D		

* Asterisk indicates that the substance has been provisionally included in this list and that further data are necessary in order to complete the evaluation of its environmental hazards, particularly in relation to living resources.

Substance	I	II	III	IV
Dimethylamine (40% aqueous)	1160	C		
Dimethylethanolamine (2-Dimethylaminoethanol)*	2051	C		
Dimethylformamide	—	D		
1, 4-Dioxane*	1165	C		
Diphenyl/Diphenyloxide mixtures*	—	D		
Dodecylbenzene	—	C		
Epichlorohydrin	2023	B		
2-Ethoxyethyl acetate*	1172	D		
Ethyl acetate	1173	D		
Ethyl acrylate	1917	D		
Ethyl amyl ketone*	—	C		
Ethylbenzene	1175	C		
Ethyl cyclohexane	—	D		
Ethylene chlorohydrin (2-Chloro-ethanol)	1135	D		
Ethylene cyanohydrin*	—	D		
Ethylenediamine	1604	C		
Ethylene dibromide	1605	B		
Ethylene dichloride	1184	B		
Ethylene glycol monethyl ether (Methyl cellosolve)	1171	D		
2-Ethylhexyl acrylate*	—	D		
2-Ethylhexyl alcohol	—	C		
Ethyl lactate*	1192	D		
2-Ethyl 3-propylacrolein*	—	B		
Formaldehyde (37—50% solution)	1198	C		
Formic acid	1779	D		
Furfuryl alcohol	—	C		
Heptanoic acid*	—	D		
Hexamethylenediamine*	1783	C		
Hydrochloric acid	1789	D		
Hydrofluoric acid (40% aqueous)	1790	B		
Hydrogen peroxide (greater than 60%)	2015	C		
Isobutyl acrylate	—	D		
Isobutyl alcohol	1212	D		
Isobutyl methacrylate	—	D		
Isobutyraldehyde	2045	C		
Isooctane*	—	D		
Isopentane	—	D		
Isophorone	—	D		
Isoprophylamine	1221	C		
Isopropyl cyclohexane	—	D		
Isoprene	1218	D		
Lactic acid	—	D		
Mesityl oxide*	1229	C		
Methyl acetate	1231	D		
Methyl acrylate	1919	C		
Methylamyl alcohol	—	D		

* Asterisk indicates that the substance has been provisionally included in this list and that further data are necessary in order to complete the evaluation of its environmental hazards, particularly in relation to living resources.

SUBSTANCE	I	II		IV
Methylene ehloride	1593	B		
2-Methyl-5-Ethylpyridine*	—	B		
Methyl methacrylate	1247	D		
2-Methypentene*	—	D		
alpha-Methylstyrene*	—	D		
Monochlorobenzene	1134	B		
Monoethanolamine	—	D		
Monoisopropanolamine	—	C		
Monomethyl ethanolamine	—	C		
Mononitrobenzene	—	C		
Monoisoproplamine	—	C		
Morpholine*	2054	C		
Naphthalene (molten)	1334	A		0.05
Naphthenic acids*	—	A		0.05
Nitric acid (90%)	2031/2032	C		
2-Nitropropane	—	D		
ortho-Nitrotoluene	1664	C		
Nonyl alcohol*	—	C		
Nonylphenol	—	C		
n-Octanol	—	C		
Oleum	1831	C		
Oxalic acid ((10—25%)	—	D		
Pentachloroethane	1669	B		
n-Pentane	1265	C		
Perchlorocthylene (Tetrachloroethylene)	1897	B		
Phenol	1671	B		
Phosphoric acid	1805	D		
Phosphorus (elemental)	1338	A		0.005
Phthalic Anhydride (molten)	—	C		
beta-Propiolactone*	—	B		
Propionaldehyde	1275	D		
Propionic acid	1848	D		
Propionic anhydride	—	D		
n-Propyl acetate*	1276	C		
n-Propyl alcohol	1274	D		
n-Propylamine	1277	C		
Pyridine	1282	B		
Silicon tetrachloride	1818	D		
Sodium bichromate (solution)	—	C		
Sodium hydroxide	1824	C		
Sodium pentachlorophenate (solution)	—	A		0.05
Styrene monomer	2055	C		
Sulphuric acid	1830/1831/ 1832	C		
Tallow	—	D		
Tetraethyllead	1649	A		0.05
Tetrahydrofuran	2056	D		
Tetrahydronaphthalene	1540	C		

* Asterisk indicates that the substance has been provisionally included in this list and that further data are necessary in order to complate the evaluation of its environmental hazards, particularly in relation to living resources.

Substance	I	II	III	IV
Tetramethylbenzene	—	D		0.05
Tetramethyllead	1649	A		
Titranium tetrachloride	—	D		
Toluene	1294	C		
Toluene diisocyanate*	2078	B		
Trichloroethane	—	C		
Trichloroethylene	1710	B		
Triethanolamine	—	D		
Triethylamine	1296	C		
Trimethylbenzene*	—	C		
Tritolyl phosphate (Tricresyl phosphate)*	—	B		
Turpentine (wood)	1299	B		
Vinyl acetate	1301	C		
Vinylidene chloride*	1303	B		
Xylenes (mixed isomers)	1307	C		

ANNEX IV
APPENDIX IV

LIST OF OTHER LIQUID SUBSTANCES CARRIED IN BULK

Acetonitrile (Methyl cyanide)
tert-Amyl alcohol
n-Butyl alcohol
Butyrolactone
Calcium chloride (solution)
Castor oil
Citric Juices
Coconut oil
Cod liver oil
iso-Decyl alcohol
n-Decyl alcohol
Decyl octyl alcohol
Dibutyl ether
Diethanolamine
Diethylene glycol
Dipentene
Dipropylene glycol
Ethyl alcohol
Ethylene glycol
Fatty alcohols (C_{12}—C_{20})
Glycerine
n-Heptane
Heptene (mixed isomers)
n-Hexane
Ligroin
Methyl alcohol
Methylamyl acetate
Methyl ethyl ketone (2-butanone)
Milk
Molasses
Olive Oil
Polypropylene glycol
iso-Propyl acetate
iso-Propyl alcohol
Propylene glycol
Propylene oxide
Propylene tetramer
Propylene trimer
Sorbitol
Sulphur (liquid)
Tridecanol
Triethylene glycol
Triethylenetetramine
Tripropylene glycol
Water
Wine

ANNEX IV
APPENDIX V

CARGO RECORD BOOK FOR SHIPS CARRYING NOXIOUS LIQUID SUBSTANCES IN BULK

Name of ship ....

Cargo carrying capacity of each tank in cubic

metres ....

Voyage from ....

to ....

a) *Loading of cargo*

1. Date and place of loading
2. Name and category of cargo(es) loaded
3. Identity of tank(s) loaded

b) *Transfer of cargo*

4. Date of transfer

* Asterisk indicates that the surface has been provisionally included in this list and that further data are necessary to complete the evaluation of its environmental hazards, particularly in relation to living resources.

5. Identity of tank(s)
(i) From
(ii) To
6. Was (were) tank(s) in 5 (i) emptied?
7. If not, quantity remaining

c) Unloading of cargo

8. Date and place of unloading
9. Identity of tank(s) unloaded
10. Was (were) tank(s) emptied?
11. If not, quantity remaining in tank(s)
12. Is (are) tank(s) to be cleaned?
13. Amount transferred to slop tank
14. Identity of slop tank

d) Ballasting of cargo tanks

15. Identity of tank(s) ballasted
16. Date and position of ship at start of ballasting

e) Cleaning of cargo tanks

Category A substances

17. Identity of tank(s) cleaned
18. Date and location of cleaning

.... Signature of Master

19. Method(s) of cleaning
20. Location of reception facility used
21. Concentration of effluent when discharge reception facility stopped
22. Quantity remaining in tank
23. Procedure and amount of water introduced into tank in final cleaning
24. Location, date of discharge into the sea
25. Procedure and equipment used in discharge into the sea

Category B, C, and D substances

26. Washing procedure used
27. Quantity of water used
28. Date, location of discharge into the sea
29. Procedure and equipment used in discharge into the sea

f) Transfer of dirty ballast water

30. Identity of tank(s)
31. Date and position of ship at start of discharge into the sea
32. Date and position of ship at finish of discharge into the sea
33. Ship's speed(s) during discharge
34. Quantity discharged into the sea
35. Quantity of polluted water transferred to slop tank(s) (identity slop tank(s))
36. Date and port of discharge to reception facilities (if applicable)

g) Transfer from slop tank/disposal of residue

37. Identity of slop tank(s)
38. Quantity disposed from each tank
39. Method of disposal of residue:
    (a) Reception facilities
    (b) Mixed with cargo
    (c) Transferred to another (other) tank(s) (identity tank(s))
40. Date and port of disposal of residue

h) Accidental or other exceptional discharge

41. Date and time of occurrence
42. Place or position of ship at time of occurrence
43. Approximate quantity, name and category of substance
44. Circumstances of discharge or escape and general remarks.

.... Signature of Master

ANNEX V

Exceptions from the General Prohibition of Dumping of Waste and Other Matter in the Baltic Sea Area

Regulation 1

In accordance with Paragraph 2 of Article 9 of the present Convention the prohibition of dumping shall not apply to the disposal at sea of dredged spoils provided that:

1. they do not contain significant quantities and concentrations of substances to be defined by the Commission and listed in Annexes I and II of the present Convention; and

2. the dumping is carried out under a prior special permit given by the appropriate national authority, either

a) within the area of the territorial sea of the Contracting Party; or

b) outside the area of the territorial sea, whenever necessary, after prior consultations in the Commission.

When issuing such permits the Contracting Party shall comply with the provisions in Regulation 3 of this Annex.

Regulation 2

1. The appropriate national authority referred to in Paragraph 2 of Article 9 of the present Convention shall:

a) issue special permits provided for in Regulation 1 of this Annex;

b) keep records of the nature and quantities of matter permitted to be dumped and the location, time and method of dumping;

c) collect available information concerning the nature and quantities of matter that has been dumped in the Baltic Sea Area recently and up to the coming into force of the present Convention, provided that the dumped matter in question could be liable to contaminate water or organisms in the Baltic Sea Area, to be caught by fishing equipment, or otherwise to give rise to harm, and the location, time and method of such dumping.

2. The appropriate national authority shall issue special permits in accordance with Regulation 1 of this Annex in respect of matter intended for dumping in the Baltic Sea Area:

a) loaded in its territory;

b) loaded by a vessel or aircraft registered in its territory or flying its flag, when the loading occurs in the territory of a State not Party to the present Convention.

3. When issuing permits under Sub-Paragraph 1 (*a*) above, the appropriate national authority shall comply with Regulation 3 of this Annex, together with such additional criteria, measures and requirements as they may consider relevant.

4. Each Contracting Party shall report to the Commission, and where appropriate to other Contracting Parties, the information specified in Sub-Paragraph 1 (*c*) of Regulation 2 of this Annex. The procedure to be followed and the nature of such reports shall be determined by the Commission.

Regulation 3

When issuing special permits according to Regulation 1 of this Annex the appropriate national authority shall take into account:

1. Quantity of dredged spoils to be dumped.

2. The content of the matter referred to in Annexes I and II of the present Convention.

3. Location (e.g. co-ordinates of the dumping area, depth and distance form coast) and its relation to areas of special interest (e.g. amenity areas, spawning, nursery and fishing areas, etc.)

4. Water characteristics, if dumping is carried out outside the territorial sea, consisting of:

a) hydrographic properties (e.g. temperature, salinity, density, profile);

b) chemical properties (e.g. pH, dissolved oxygen, nutrients);

c) biological properties (e.g. primary production and benthic animals).

5. The existence and effects of other dumping which may have been carried out in the dumping area.

Regulation 4

Reports made in accordance with Paragraph 5 of Article 9 of the present Convention shall include the following information:

1. Location of dumping, characteristics of dumped material, and counter measures taken:

a) location (e.g. co-ordinates of the accidental dumping site, depth and distance from the coast);

b) method of deposit;

c) quantity and composition of dumped matter as well as its physical (e.g. solubility and density), chemical and biochemical (e.g. oxygen demand, nutrients), and biological properties (e.g. presence of viruses, bacteria, yeasts, parasites);

d) toxicity;

e) content of the substances referred to in Annexes I and II of the present Convention;

f) dispersal characteristics (e.g. effects of currents and wind, and horizontal transport and vertical mixing);

g) water characteristics (e.g. temperature, pH, redox conditions, salinity and stratification;

h) bottom characteristics (e.g. topography, geological characteristics and redox conditions);

i) counter measures taken and follow-up operations carried out or planned.

2. General considerations and conditions:

a) possible effects on amenities (e.g. floating or stranded material, turbidity, objectionable odour, discolouration and foaming);

b) possible effect on marine life, fish and shellfish culture, fish stocks and fisheries, seaweed harvesting and cultures; and

c) possible effects on other uses of the sea (e.g. impairment of water quality for industrial use, underwater corrosion of structures, interference with ship operations from floating materials, interference with fishing or navigation and protection of areas of special importance for scientific or conservation purposes).

ANNEX VI

CO-OPERATION IN COMBATING MARINE POLLUTION

Regulation 1

For the purposes of this Annex:

1. "Ship" means a vessel of any type whatsoever operating in the marine environment and includes hydrofoil boats, air-cushion vehicles, submersibles, floating craft and fixed or floating platforms.

2. "Administration" means the Government of the State under whose authority the ship is operating. With respect to a ship entitled to fly a flag of any State, the Administration is the Government of that State. With respect to fixed or floating platforms engaged in exploration and exploitation of the sea-bed and subsoil thereof adjacent to the coast over which the coastal State exercises sovereign rights for the purposes of exploration and exploitation of their natural resources, the Administration is the Government of the coastal State concerned.

3. *a*) "Discharge", in relation to harmful substances or effluents containting such substances, means any release howsoever caused from a ship and includes any escape, disposal, spilling, leaking, pumping, emitting or emptying.

b) "Discharge" does not include:

(i) dumping within the meaning of the Convention on the Prevention of Marine Pollution by Dumping of Wastes and Other Matter done at London on 29 December 1972; or

(ii) release of harmful substances directly arising from the exploration, exploitation and associated off-shore processing of sea-bed mineral resources; or

(iii) release of harmful substances for purposes of legitimate scientific research into pollution abatement or control.

Regulation 2

The Contracting Parties undertake to maintain ability to combat spillages of oil and other harmful substances on the sea. This ability shall include adequate equipment, ships and manpower prepared for operations in coastal waters as well as on the high sea.

Regulation 3

The Contracting Parties shall, without prejudice to Paragraph 4 of Article 4 of the present Convention, develop and apply, individually or in co-operation, surveillance activities covering the Baltic Sea Area, in order to spot and monitor oil and other harmful substances released into the sea.

Regulation 4

In the case of loss overboard of harmful substances in packages, freight containers, portable tanks, or road and rail tank wagons, the Contracting Parties shall co-operate in the salvage and recovery of such packages, containers or tanks so as to minimize the danger to the environment.

Regulation 5

1. The Contracting Parties shall develop and apply a system for receiving, channelling and dispatching reports on significant spillages of oil or other harmful substances observed at sea, as well as any incident causing or likely to cause any kind of significant pollution.

2. The Contracting Parties shall request masters of ships and pilots of aircraft to report without delay in accordance with this system on significant spillages of oil or other harmful substances observed at sea. Such reports should as far as possible contain the following data: time, position, wind and sea conditions, and kind, extent and probable source of the spill observed.

3. The master of a ship involved in an incident referred to in Paragraph 1 of this Regulation, or other person having charge of the ship, shall without delay and to the fullest extent possible report in accordance with this system and with the provisions of the Appendix to the present Annex.

4. Each Contracting Party undertakes to issue instructions to its maritime inspection vessels and aircarft and to other appropriate services, to report to its authorities any observation or incident referred to in Paragraph 1 of this Regulation. Such reports shall as far as possible contain the data referred to in Paragraph 2 and 3 of this Regulation respectively, as well as possible indications on the spreading or drifting tendencies of the spill in question.

5. Whenever a Contracting Party is aware of a casualty or the presence of spillages of oil or other harmful substances in the Baltic Sea Area likely to constitute a serious threat to the marine environment of the Baltic Sea Area or the coast or related interests of any other Contracting Party, it shall without delay transmit all relevant information thereon to the Contracting Party which may be affected by the pollutant and, as regards ship casualty incidents, to the Administration of the ship involved.

Regulation 6

Each Contracting Party shall request masters of ships flying its flag to provide, in case of an incident, on request by the proper authorities, such detailed information about the ship and its cargo which is relevant to actions for preventing or combating pollution of the sea, and to co-operate with these authorities.

Regulation 7

1. *a*) The Contracting Parties shall as soon as possible agree bilaterally or multilaterally on those regions of the Baltic Sea Area in which they will take action for combating or salvage activities whenever a significant spillage of oil or other harmful substances or any incidents causing or likely to cause pollution within the Baltic Sea Area have occurred or are likely to occur. Such agreements shall not prejudice any other agreements concluded between Contracting Parties concerning the same subject. The neighbouring States shall ensure the harmonization of the different agreements. The Contracting Parties shall inform each other about such agreements.

The Contracting Parties may ask the Commission for assistance to reach agreement, if needed.

b) The Contracting Party within whose region a situation as described in Regulation 1 of this Annex occurs shall make the necessary assessments of the situation and take adequate action in order to avoid or minimize subsequent pollution effects and shall keep drifting parts of the spillage under observation until no further action is called for.

2. In the case that such a spillage is drifting or is likely to drift into a region, where another Contracting Party should take action for purposes as defined in Sub-Paragraph 1 (*a*) of this Regulation, that Party shall without delay be informed of the situation and the actions that have been taken.

Regulation 8

A Contracting Party requiring assistance for combatting spillages of oil or other harmful substances at sea is entitled to call for assistance by other Contracting Parties, starting with those who seem likely also to be affected by the spillage. Contracting Parties called upon for assistance in accordance with this Regulation shall use their best endeavours to bring such assistance.

Regulation 9

1. The Contracting Parties shall provide information to the other Contracting Parties and the Commission about

a) their national organization for dealing with spillages at sea of oil and other harmful substances;

b) national regulations and other matters which have a direct bearing on combating pollution at sea by oil and other harmful substances;

c) the competent authority responsible for receiving and dispatching reports of pollution at sea by oil and other harmful substances;

d) the competent authorities for dealing with questions concerning measures of mutual assistance, information and co-operation between the Contracting Parties according to this Annex;

e) actions taken in accordance with Regulation 8 of this Annex.

2. The Contracting Parties shall exchange information of research and development programs and results concerning ways in which pollution by oil and other harmful substances at sea may be dealt with and experiences in combating such pollution.

Regulation 10

The authorities referred to in Sub-Paragraph 1 (*d*) of Regulation 9 of this Annex shall establish direct contact and co-operate in operational matters.

ANNEX VI
APPENDIX

PROVISIONS CONCERNING REPORTS ON INCIDENTS INVOLVING HARMFUL SUBSTANCES

Regulation 1

DUTY TO REPORT

1. The Master of a ship involved in an incident referred to Regulation 3 of this Appendix, or other person having charge of the ship, shall report the particulars of such incident without delay and to the fullest extent possible in accordance with the provisions of this Appendix.

2. In the event of the ship referred to in Paragraph 1 of this Regulation being abandoned, or in the event of a report from such ship being incomplete or unobtainable, the owner, character, manager or operator of the ship, or their agents shall, to the fullest extent possible assume the obligations placed upon the Master under the provisions of this Appendix.

Regulation 2

METHODS OF REPORTING

1. 'Each report shall be made by radio whenever possible, but in any case by the fastest channels available at the time the report is made. Reports made by radio shall be given the highest possible priority.

2. Reports shall be directed to the appropriate officer or agency referred to in Sub-Paragraph 1 (*c*) of Regulation 9 of Annex VI of the present Convention.

Regulation 3

WHEN TO MAKE REPORTS

The report shall be made whenever an incident involves:

a) a discharge other than as permitted under the present Convention; or

b) a discharge permitted under the present Convention by virtue of the fact that:

(i) it is for the purpose of securing the safety of a ship or saving life at sea, or

(ii) it results from damage to the ship or its equipment; or

c) a discharge of a harmful substance for the purpose of combating a specific pollution incident or for purposes of legitimate scientific research into pollution abatement or control; or

d) the probability of a discharge referred to in Sub-Paragraph (*a*), (*b*), or (*c*) of this Regulation.

Regulation 4

CONTENTS OF REPORT

1. Each report shall contain in general:

a) the identity of ship;

b) the time and date of the occurrence of the incident;

c) the geographic position of the ship when the incident occurred;

d) the wind and sea conditions prevailing at the time of the incident; and

e) relevant details respecting the condition of the ship.

2. Each report shall contain, in particular:

a) a clear indication or description of the harmful substances involved, including, if possible, the correct technical names of such substances (trade names should not be used in place of the correct technical names);

b) a statement or estimate of the quantities, concentrations and likely condition of harmful substances discharged or likely to be discharged into the sea;

c) where relevant, a description of the packaging and identifying marks; and

d) if possible the name of the consignor, consignee or manufacturer.

3. Each report shall clearly indicate whether the harmful substance discharged, or likely to be discharged is oil, a noxious liquid substance, a noxious solid substance, or a noxious gaseous substance and whether such substance was or is carried in bulk or contained in packaged form, freight containers, portable tanks, or road and rail tank wagons.

4. Each report shall be supplemented as necessary by any other relevant information requested by a recipient of the report or which the person sending the report deems appropriate.

Regulation 5

SUPPLEMENTARY REPORT

Any person who is obliged under the provisions of this Appendix to send a report shall, when possible:

a) supplement the initial report, as necessary, with information concerning further developments; and

b) comply as fully as possible with requests from affected States for additional information concerning the incident.

CONVENTION FOR THE PREVENTION OF MARINE POLLUTION FROM LAND-BASED SOURCES [64]

Paris, 4 June 1974

The Contracting Parties:

Recognizing that the marine environment and the fauna and flora which it supports are of vital importance to all nations;

Mindful that the ecological equilibrium and the legitimate uses of the sea are increasingly threatened by pollution;

Considering the recommendations of the United Nations Conference on the Human Environment, held in Stockholm in June 1972;

Recognizing that concerted action at national, regional and global levels is essential to prevent and combat marine pollution;

Convinced that international action to control the pollution of the sea from land-based sources can and should be taken without delay, as part of progressive and coherent measures to protect the marine environment from pollution, whatever its origin, including current efforts to combat the pollution of international waterways;

Considering that the common interests of States concerned with the same marine area should induce them to co-operate at regional or sub-regional levels;

Recalling the Convention for the Prevention of Marine Pollution by Dumping from Ships and Aircraft concluded in Oslo on 15 February 1972,

Have agreed as follows:

Article 1

1. The Contracting Parties pledge themselves to take all possible steps to prevent pollution of the sea, by which is meant the introduction by man, directly or indirectly, of substances or energy into the marine environment (including estuaries) resulting in such deleterious effects as hazards to human health, harm to living resources and to marine eco-systems, damage to amenities or interference with other legitimate uses of the sea.

2. The Contracting Parties shall adopt individually and jointly measures to combat marine pollution from land-based sources in accordance with the provisions of the present Convention and shall harmonize their policies in this regard.

Article 2

The present Convention shall apply to the maritime area within the following limits:

a) those parts of the Atlantic and Arctic Oceans and the dependent seas which lie North of 36° north latitude and between 42° west longitude and 51° east longitude, but excluding:

(*i*) the Baltic Sea and Belts lying to the south and east of lines drawn from Hasenore Head to Gniben Point, from Korshage to Spodsbjerg and from Gilbjerg Head to Kullen, and

(*ii*) the Mediterranean Sea and its dependent seas as far as the point of intersection of the parallel of 36° north latitude and the meridian of 5° 36′ west longitude;

b) that part of the Atlantic Ocean north of 59° north latitude and between 44° west longitude and 42° west longitude.

Article 3

For the purpose of the present Convention:

a) "Maritime area" means: the high seas, the territorial seas of Contracting Parties and waters on the landward side of the base lines from which the breadth of the territorial sea is measured and extending in the case of watercourses, unless otherwise decided under article 16 *c* of the present Convention, up to the freshwater limit;

b) "Freshwater limit" means: the place in the watercourse where, at low tide and in a period of low freshwater flow, there is an appreciable increase in salinity due to the presence of seawater;

c) "Pollution from land-based sources" means: the pollution of the maritime area

(i) through watercourses,

(ii) from the coast, including introduction through underwater or other pipelines,

(iii) from man-made structures placed under the jurisdiction of a Contracting Party within the limits of the area to which the present Convention applies.

Article 4

1. The Contracting Parties undertake:

a) to eliminate, if necessary by stages, pollution of the maritime area from land-based sources by substances listed in Part I of Annex A to the present Convention;

b) to limit strictly pollution of the maritime area from land-based sources by substances listed in Part II of Annex A to the present Convention.

2. In order to carry out the undertakings in paragraph 1 of this Article, the Contracting Parties, jointly or individually as appropriate, shall implement programmes and measures:

a) for the elimination, as a matter of urgency, of pollution of the maritime area from land-based sources by substances listed in Part I of Annex A to the present Convention;

b) for the reduction or, as appropriate, elimination of pollution of the maritime area from land-based sources by substances listed in Part II of Annex A to the present Convention. These substances shall be discharged only after approval has been granted by the appropriate authorities within each Contracting State. Such approval shall be periodically reviewed.

3. The programmes and measures adopted under paragraph 2 of this article shall include, as appropriate, specific regulations or standards governing the quality of the environment, discharges into the maritime area, such discharges into watercourses as affect the maritime area, and the composition and use of substances and products. These programmes and measures shall take into account the latest technical developments.

The programmes shall contain time-limits for

their completion.

4. The Contracting Parties may, furthermore, jointly or individually as appropriate, implement programmes or measures to forestall, reduce or eliminate pollution of the maritime area from land-based sources by a substance not then listed in Annex A to the present Convention, if scientific evidence has established that a serious hazard may be created in the maritime area by that substance and if urgent action is necessary.

Article 5

1. The Contracting Parties undertake to adopt measures to forestall and, as appropriate, eliminate pollution of the maritime area from land-based sources by radio-active substances referred to in Part III of Annex A of the present Convention.

2. Without prejudice to their obligations under other treaties and conventions, in implementing this undertaking the Contracting Parties shall:

a) take full account of the recommendations of the appropriate international organizations and agencies;

b) take account of the monitoring procedures recommended by these international organizations and agencies,

c) coordinate their monitoring and study of radio-active substances in accordance with Articles 10 and 11 of the present Convention.

Article 6

1. With a view to preserving and enhancing the quality of the marine environment, the Contracting Parties, without prejudice to the provisions of Article 4, shall endeavour:

a) to reduce existing pollution from land-based sources;

b) to forestall any new pollution from land-based sources, including that which derives from new substances.

2. In implementing this undertaking, the Contracting Parties shall take account of:

a) the nature and quantities of the pollutants under consideration;

b) the level of existing pollution;

c) the quality and absorptive capacity of the receiving waters of the maritime area;

d) the need for an integrated planning policy consistent with the requirement of environmental protection.

Article 7

The Contracting Parties agree to apply the measures they adopt in such a way as to avoid increasing pollution:

— in the seas outside the area to which the present Convention applies;

— in the maritime area covered by the present Convention, originating otherwise than from land-based sources.

Article 8

No provision of the present Convention shall be interpreted as preventing the Contracting Parties from taking more stringent measures to combat marine pollution from land-based sources.

Article 9

1. When pollution from land-based sources originating from the territory of a Contracting Party by substances not listed in Part I of Annex A of the present Convention is likely to prejudice the interests of one or more of the other Parties to the present Convention, the Contracting Parties concerned undertake to enter into consultation, at the request of any one of them, with a view to negotiating a co-operation agreement.

2. At the request of any Contracting Party concerned, the Commission referred to in Article 15 of the present Convention shall consider the question and may make recommendations with a view to reaching a satisfactory solution.

3. The special agreements specified in paragraph 1 of this Article may, among other things, define the areas to which they shall apply, the quality objectives to be achieved, and the methods for achieving these objectives including methods for the application of appropriate standards and the scientific and technical information to be collected.

4. The Contracting Parties signatory to these special agreements shall, through the medium of the Commission, inform the other Contracting Parties of their purport and of the progress made in putting them into effect.

Article 10

The Contracting Parties agree to establish complementary or joint programmes of scientific and technical research, including research into the best methods of eliminating or replacing noxious substances so as to reduce marine pollution from land-based sources, and to transmit to each other the information so obtained. In doing so they shall have regard to the work carried out, in these fields, by the appropriate international organizations and agencies.

Article 11

The Contracting Parties agree to set up progressively and to operate within the area covered by the present Convention a permanent monitoring system allowing:

— the earliest possible assessment of the existing level of marine pollution;

— the assessment of the effectiveness of measures for the reduction of marine pollution from land-based sources taken under the terms of the present Convention.

For this purpose the Contracting Parties shall lay down the ways and means of pursuing individually or jointly systematic and ad hoc monitoring programmes. These programmes shall take into account the deployment of research vessels and other facilities in the monitoring area.

The programmes shall take into account similar programmes pursued in accordance with conventions already in force and by the appropriate international organisations and agencies.

Article 12

1. Each Contracting Party undertakes to ensure

compliance with the provisions of this Convention and to take in its territory appropriate measures to prevent and punish conduct in contravention of the provisions of the present Convention.

2. The Contracting Parties shall inform the Commission of the legislative and administrative measures they have taken to implement the provisions of the preceding paragraph.

Article 13

The Contracting Parties undertake to assist one another as appropriate to prevent incidents which may result in pollution from land-based sources, to minimize and eliminate the consequences of such incidents, and to exchange information to that end.

Article 14

1. The provisions of the present Convention may not be invoked against a Contracting Party to the extent that the latter is prevented, as a result of pollution having its origin in the territory of a non-Contracting State, from ensuring their full application.

2. However, the said Contracting Party shall endeavour to co-operate with the non-Contracting State so as to make possible the full application of the present Convention.

Article 15

A Commission composed of representatives of each of the Contracting Parties is hereby established. The Commission shall meet at regular intervals and at any time when due to special circumstances it is so decided in accordance with its rules of procedure.

Article 16

It shall be the duty of the Commission:

a) to exercise overall supervision over the implementation of the present Convention;

b) to review generally the condition of the seas within the area to which the present Convention applies, the effectiveness of the control measures being adopted and the need for any additional or different measures;

c) to fix, if necessary, on the proposal of the Contracting Party or Parties bordering on the same watercourse and following a standard procedure, the limit to which the maritime area shall extend in that watercourse;

d) to draw up, in accordance with Article 4 of the present Convention, programmes and measures for the elimination or reduction of pollution from land-based sources;

e) to make recommendations in accordance with the provisions of Article 9;

f) to receive and review information and distribute it to the Contracting Parties in accordance with the provisions of Articles 11, 12 and 17 of the present Convention;

g) to make, in accordance with Article 18, recommendations regarding any amendment to the lists of substances included in Annex A to the present Convention;

h) to discharge such other functions, as may be appropriate, under the terms of the present Convention.

Article 17

The Contracting Parties, in accordance with a standard procedure, shall transmit to the Commission:

a) the results of monitoring pursuant to Article 11;

b) the most detailed information available on the substances listed in the Annexes to the present Convention and liable to find their way into the maritime area.

The Contracting Parties shall endeavour to improve progressively techniques for gathering such information which can contribute to the revision of the pollution reduction programmes drawn up in accordance with Article 4 of the present Convention.

Article 18

1. The Commission shall draw up its own Rules of Procedure which shall be adopted by unanimous vote.

2. The Commission shall draw up its own Financial Regulations which shall be adopted by unanimous vote.

3. The Commission shall adopt, by unanimous vote, programmes and measures for the reduction or elimination of pollution from land-based sources as provided for in Article 4, programmes for scientific research and monitoring as provided for in Articles 10 and 11, and decisions under Article 16*c*.

The programmes and measures shall commence for and be applied by all Contracting Parties two hundred days after their adoption, unless the Commission specifies another date.

Should unanimity not be attainable, the Commission may nonetheless adopt a programme or measures by a three quarters majority vote of its members. The programmes or measures shall commence for those Contracting Parties which voted for them two hundred days after their adoption, unless the Commission specifies another date, and for any other Contracting Party after it has explicitly accepted the programme or measures, which it may do at any time.

4. The Commission may adopt recommendations for amendments to Annex A to the present Convention by a three quarters majority vote of its members and shall submit them for the approval of the Governments of the Contracting Parties. Any Government of a Contracting Party that is unable to approve an amendment shall notify the depositary Government in writing within a period of two hundred days after the adoption of the Recommendation of amendment in the Commission. Should no such notification be received, the amendment shall enter into force for all Contracting Parties two hundred and thirty days after the vote in the Commission. The depositary. Government shall notify the Contracting Parties as soon as possible of the receipt of any notification.

Article 19

Within the areas of its competence, the

European Economic Community is entitled to a number of votes equal to the number of its member States which are Contracting Parties to the present Convention.

The European Economic Community shall not exercise its right to vote in cases where its member States exercise theirs and conversely.

Article 20

The depositary Government shall convene the first meeting of the Commission as soon as possible after the coming into force of the present Convention.

Article 21

Any dispute between Contracting Parties relating to the interpretation or application of the present Convention, which cannot be settled otherwise by the Parties concerned, for instance by means of inquiry or conciliation within the Commission, shall, at the request of any of those Parties, be submitted to arbitration under the conditions laid down in Annex B to the present Convention.

Article 22

The present Convention shall be open for signature at Paris, from 4th June 1974 to 30th June 1975, by the States invited to the Diplomatic Conference on the Convention for the Prevention of Marine Pollution from Land-Based Sources, held at Paris, and by the European Economic Community.

Article 23

The present Convention shall be subject to ratification, acceptance or approval. The instruments of ratification, acceptance or approval shall be deposited with the Government of the French Republic.

Article 24

1. After 30th June 1975, the present Convention shall be open for accession by States referred to in Article 22 and by the European Economic Community.

2. The present Convention shall also be open for accession from the same date by any other Contracting Party to the Convention for the Prevention of Marine Pollution by Dumping from Ships and Aircraft, opened for signature at Oslo on 15th February 1972.

3. From the date of its entry into force, the present Convention shall be open for accession by any State not referred to in Article 22, located upstream on watercourses crossing the territory of one or more Contracting Parties to the present Convention and reaching the maritime area defined in Article 2.

4. The Contracting Parties may unanimously invite other States to accede to the present Convention. In that case the maritime area in Article 2 may, if necessary, be amended in accordance with Article 27 of the present Convention.

5. The instruments of accession shall be deposited with the Government of the French Republic.

Article 25

1. The present Convention shall come into force on the thirtieth day following the date of deposit of the seventh instrument of ratification, acceptance, approval or accession.

2. For each Party ratifying, accepting or approving the present Convention or acceding to it after the deposit of the seventh instrument of ratification, acceptance, approval or accession, the present Convention shall enter into force on the thirtieth day after the date of deposit by that Party of its instrument of ratification, approval or accession.

Article 26

At any time after the expiry of two years from the date of coming into force of the present Convention in relation to any Contracting Party such Party may withdraw from the Convention by notice in writing to the depositary Government. Such notice shall take effect one year after the date on which it is received.

Article 27

1. The depositary Government shall, at the request of the Commission on a decision taken by a two-thirds majority of its members, call a Conference for the purpose of revising or amending the present Convention.

2. Upon accession by a State as provided for in paragraphs 2, 3 and 4 of Article 24, the maritime area in Article 2 may be amended upon a proposal by the Commission adopted by a unanimous vote. These amendments shall enter into force after unanimous approval by the Contracting Parties.

Article 28

The depositary Government shall inform the Contracting Parties and those referred to in Article 22:

a) of signatures to the present Convention, of the deposit of instruments of ratification, acceptance, approval or accession, and of notices of withdrawal in accordance with Articles 22, 23, 24 and 26;

b) of the date on which the present Convention comes into force in accordance with Article 25;

c) of the receipt of notifications of approval or objection, and of the entry into force of amendments to the present Convention and its Annexes, in accordance with Articles 18 and 27.

Article 29

The original of the present Convention of which the French and English texts shall be equally authentic, shall be deposited with the Government of the French Republic which shall send certified copies thereof to the Contracting Parties and the States referred to in Article 22 and shall deposit a certified copy with the Secretary General of the United Nations for registration and publication in accordance with Article 102 of the United Nations Charter.

IN WITNESS WHEREOF, the undersigned, duly authorized by their respective Governments, have signed this Convention.

DONE AT PARIS, THIS 4TH DAY OF JUNE 1974

ANNEX A

The allocation of substances to Parts I, II and III below takes account of the following criteria:

a) persistence;

b) toxicity or other noxious properties;

c) tendency to bio-accumulation;

These criteria are not necessarily of equal importance for a particular substance or group of substances, and other factors, such as the location and quantities of the discharge, may need to be considered.

Part I

The following substances are included in this Part

(i) because they are not readily degradable or rendered harmless by natural processes; and

(ii) because they may either:

a) give rise to dangerous accumulation of harmful material in the food chain, or

b) endanger the welfare of living organisms causing undesirable changes in the marine ecosystems, or

c) interfere seriously with the harvesting of sea foods or with other legitimate uses of the sea; and

(iii) because it is considered that pollution by these substances necessitates urgent action:

1. Organohalogen compounds and substances which may form such compounds in the marine environment, excluding those which are biologically harmless, or which are rapidly converted in the sea into substances which are biologically harmless.

2. Mercury and mercury compounds.

3. Cadmium and cadmium compounds.

4. Persistent synthetic materials which may float, remain in suspection or sink, and which may seriously interfere with any legitimate use of the sea.

5. Persistent oils and hydrocarbons of petroleum origin.

Part II

The following substances are included in this Part because, although exhibiting similar characteristics to the substances in Part I and requiring strict control, they seem less noxious or are more readily rendered harmless by natural processes:

1. Organic compounds of phosphorous, silicon, and tin and substances which may form such compounds in the marine environment, excluding those which are biologically harmless, or which are rapidly converted in the sea into substances which are biologically harmless.

2. Elemental phosphorus.

3. Non-persistent oils and hydrocarbons of petroleum origin.

4. The following elements and their compounds:

Arsenic	Lead
Chromium	Nickel
Copper	Zinc

5. Substances which have been agreed by the Commission as having a deleterious effect on the taste and/or smell of products derived from the marine environment for human consumption.

Part III

The following substances are included in this Part because, although they display characteristics similar to those of substances listed in Part I and should be subject to stringent controls with the aim of preventing and, as appropriate, eliminating the pollution which they cause, they are already the subject of research, recommendations and, in some cases, measures under the auspices of several international organisations and institutions; those substances are subject to the provisions of Article 5:

Radioactive substances, including wastes.

ANNEX B

Article 1

Unless the parties to the dispute decide otherwise, the arbitration procedure shall be in accordance with the provisions of this Annex.

Article 2

1. At the request addressed by one Contracting Party in accordance with Article 21 of the Convention, an arbitral tribunal shall be constituted. The request for arbitration shall state the subject matter of the application including in particular the Articles of the Convention, the interpretation or application of which is in dispute.

2. The claimant shall inform the Commission that he has requested the setting up of an arbitral tribunal, stating the name of the other party to the dispute and the Articles of the Convention the interpretation or application of which is in his opinion in dispute. The Commission shall forward the information thus received to all Contracting Parties to the Convention.

Article 3

The arbitral tribunal shall consist of three members: each of the parties to the dispute shall appoint an arbitrator; the two arbitrators so appointed shall designate by common agreement the third arbitrator who shall be the chairman of the tribunal. The latter shall not be a national of one of the parties to the dispute, nor have his usual place of residence in the territory of one of these parties, nor be employed by any of them, nor have dealt with the case in any other capacity.

Article 4

1. If the chairman of the arbitral tribunal has not been designated within two months of the appointment of the second arbitrator, the Secretary General of the United Nations shall, at the request of either party, designate him within a further two months' period.

2. If one of the parties to the dispute does not appoint an arbitrator within two months of receipt of the request, the other party may inform the Secretary General of the United Nations who shall designate the chairman of the arbitral tribunal within a further two months' period. Upon designation, the chairman of the arbitral tribunal

shall request the party which has not appointed an arbitrator to do so within two months. After such period, he shall inform the Secretary General of the United Nations who shall make this appointment within a further two months' period.

Article 5

1. The arbitral tribunal shall decide according to the rules of international law and, in particular, those of this Convention.

2. Any arbitral tribunal constituted under the provisions of this Annex shall draw up its own rules of procedure.

Article 6

1. The decisions of the arbitral tribunal, both on procedure and on substance, shall be taken by majority voting of its members.

2. The tribunal may take all appropriate measures in order to establish the facts. It may, at the request of one of the Parties, recommend essential interim measures of protection.

3. If two or more arbitral tribunals constituted under the provisions of this Annex are seized of request with identical or similar subjects, they may inform themselves of the procedures for establishing the facts and take them into account as far as possible.

4. The parties to the dispute shall provide all facilities necessary for the effective conduct of the proceedings.

5. The absence or default of a party to the dispute shall not constitute an impediment to the proceedings.

Article 7

1. The award of the arbitral tribunal shall be accompanied by a statement of reasons. It shall be final and binding upon the parties to the dispute.

2. Any dispute which may arise between the parties concerning the interpretation or execution of the award may be submitted by either party to the arbitral tribunal which made the award or, if the latter cannot be seized therof, to another arbitral tribunal constituted for this purpose in the same manner as the first.

Article 8

The European Economic Community, like any Contracting Party to the present Convention, has the right to appear as applicant or respondent before the arbitral tribunal.

AGREEMENT ON AN INTERNATIONAL ENERGY PROGRAM [65]

Paris, 18 November 1974

The Governments of the Republic of Austria, the Kingdom of Belgium, Canada, the Kingdom of Denmark, the Federal Republic of Germany, Ireland, the Italian Republic, Japan, the Grand Duchy of Luxembourg, the Kingdom of the Netherlands, Spain, the Kingdom of Sweden, the Swiss Confederation, the Republic of Turkey, the United Kingdom of Great Britain and Northern Ireland, and the United States of America,

Desiring to promote secure oil supplies on reasonable and equitable terms,

Determined to take common effective measures to meet oil supply emergencies by developing an emergency self-sufficiency in oil supplies, restraining demand and allocating available oil among their countries on an equitable basis,

Desiring to promote co-operative relations with oil producing countries and with other oil consuming countries, including those of the developing world, through a purposeful dialogue, as well as through other forms of co-operation, to further the opportunities for a better understanding between consumer and producer countries,

Mindful of the interests of other oil consuming countries, including those of the developing world.

Desiring to play a more active role in relation to the oil industry by establishing a comprehensive international information system and a permanent framework for consultation with oil companies,

Determined to reduce their dependence on imported oil by undertaking long term co-operative efforts on conservation of energy, on accelerated development of alternative sources of energy, on research and development in the energy field and on uranium enrichment,

Convinced that these objectives can only be reached through continued co-operative efforts within effective organs,

Expressing the intention that such organs be created within the framework of the Organisation for Economic Co-operation and Development.

Recognizing that other Member countries of the Organisation for Economic Co-operation and Development may desire to join in their efforts,

Considering the special responsibility of governments for energy supply,

Conclude that it is necessary to establish an International Energy Program to be implemented through an International Energy Agency, and to that end,

Have agreed as follows:

Article 1

1. The Participating Countries shall implement the International Energy Program as provided for in this Agreement through the International Energy Agency, described in Chapter IX,

hereinafter referred to as the "Agency".

2. The term "Participating Countries" means States to which this Agreement applies provisionally and States for which the Agreement has entered into and remains in force.

3. The term "group" means the Participating Countries as a group.

Chapter I

EMERGENCY SELF-SUFFICIENCY

Article 2

1. The Participating Countries shall establish a common emergency self-sufficiency in oil supplies. To this end, each Participating Country shall maintain emergency reserves sufficient to sustain consumption for at least 60 days with no net oil imports. Both consumption and net oil imports shall be reckoned at the average daily level of the preceding calendar year.

2. The Governing Board shall, acting by special majority, not later than 1st July, 1975, decide the date from which the emergency reserve commitment of each Participating Country shall, for the purpose of calculating its supply right referred to in Article 7, be deemed to be raised to a level of 90 days. Each Participating Country shall increase its actual level of emergency reserves to 90 days and shall endeavour to do so by the date so decided.

3. The term "emergency reserve commitment" means the emergency reserves equivalent to 60 days of net oil imports as set out in paragraph 1 and, from the date to be decided according to paragraph 2, to 90 days of net oil imports as set out in paragraph 2.

Article 3

1. The emergency reserve commitment set out in Article 2 may be satisfied by:

— oil stocks,

— fuel switching capacity,

— stand-by oil production,

in accordance with the provisions of the Annex which forms an integral part of this Agreement.

2. The Governing Board shall, acting by majority, not later than 1st July, 1975, decide the extent to which the emergency reserve commitment may be satisfied by the elements mentioned in paragraph 1.

Article 4

1. The Standing Group on Emergency Questions shall, on a continuing basis, review the effectiveness of the measures taken by each Participating Country to meet its emergency reserve commitment.

2. The Standing Group on Emergency Questions shall report to the Management Committee, which shall make proposals, as appropriate, to the Governing Board. The Governing Board may, acting by majority, adopt recommendations to Participating Countries.

Chapter II

DEMAND RESTRAINT

Article 5

1. Each Participating Country shall at all times have ready a program of contingent oil demand restraint measures enabling it to reduce its rate of final consumption in accordance with Chapter IV.

2. The Standing Group on Emergency Questions shall, on a continuing basis, review and assess:

— each Participating Country's program of demand restraint measures,

— the effectiveness of measures actually taken by each Participating Country.

3. The Standing Group on Emergency Questions shall report to the Management Committee, which shall make proposals, as appropriate, to the Governing Board. The Governing Board may, acting by majority, adopt recommendations to Participating Countries.

Chapter III

ALLOCATION

Article 6

1. Each Participating Country shall take the necessary measures in order that allocation of oil will be carried out pursuant to this Chapter and Chapter IV.

2. The Standing Group on Emergency Questions shall, on a continuing basis, review and assess:

— each Participating Country's measures in order that allocation of oil will be carried out pursuant to this Chapter and Chapter IV,

— the effectiveness of measures actually taken by each Participating Country.

3. The Standing Group on Emergency Questions shall report to the Management Committee, which shall make proposals, as appropriate, to the Governing Board. The Governing Board may, acting by majority, adopt recommendations to Participating Countries.

4. The Governing Board shall, acting by majority, decide promptly on the practical procedures for the allocation of oil and on the procedures and modalities for the participation of oil companies therein within the framework of this Agreement.

Article 7

1. When allocation of oil is carried out pursuant to Article 13, 14, or 15, each Participating Country shall have a supply right equal to its permissible consumption less its emergency reserve drawdown obligation.

2. A Participating Country whose supply right exceeds the sum of its normal domestic production and actual net imports available during an emergency shall have an allocation right which entitles it to additional net imports equal to that excess.

3. A Participating Country in which the sum of normal domestic production and actual net

imports available during an emergency exceeds its supply right shall have an allocation obligation which requires it to supply, directly or indirectly, the quantity of oil equal to that excess to other Participating Countries. This would not preclude any Participating Country from maintaining exports of oil to non-participating countries.

4. The term "permissible consumption" means the average daily rate of final consumption allowed when emergency demand restraint at the applicable level has been activated; possible further voluntary demand restraint by any Participating Country shall not affect its allocation right or obligation.

5. The term "emergency reserve drawdown obligation" means the emergency reserve commitment of any Participating Country divided by the total emergency reserve commitment of the group and multiplied by the group supply shortfall.

6. The term "group supply shortfall" means the shortfall for the group as measured by the aggregate permissible consumption for the group minus the daily rate of oil supplies available to the group during an emergency.

7. The term "oil supplies available to the group" means

— all crude oil available to the group,

— all petroleum products imported from outside the group, and

— all finished products and refinery feedstocks which are produced in association with natural gas and crude oil and are available to the group.

8. The term "final consumption" means total domestic consumption of all finished petroleum products.

Article 8

1. When allocation of oil to a Participating Country is carried out pursuant to Article 17, that Participating Country shall

— sustain from its final consumption the reduction in its oil supplies up to a level equal to 7 per cent of its final consumption during the base period.

— have an allocation right equal to the reduction in its oil supplies which results in a reduction of its final consumption over and above that level.

2. The obligation to allocate this amount of oil is shared among the other Participating Countries on the basis of their final consumption during the base period.

3. The Participating Countries may meet their allocation obligations by any measures of their own choosing, including demand restraint measures or use of emergency reserves.

Article 9

1. For purposes of satisfying allocation rights and allocation obligations, the following elements will be included:

— all crude oil,

— all petroleum products

— all refinery feedstocks, and

— all finished products produced in association with natural gas and crude oil.

2. To calculate a Participating Country's allocation right, petroleum products normally imported by that Participating Country, whether from other Participating Countries or from non-participating countries, shall be expressed in crude oil equivalents and treated as though they were imports of crude oil to that Participating Country.

3. Insofar as possible, normal channels of supply will be maintained as well as the normal supply proportions between crude oil and products and among different categories of crude oil and products.

4. When allocation takes place, an objective of the Program shall be that available crude oil and products shall, insofar as possible, be shared within the refining and distributing industries as well as between refining and distributing companies in accordance with historical supply patterns.

Article 10

1. The objectives of the Program shall include ensuring fair treatment for all Participating Countries and basing the price for allocated oil on the price conditions prevailing for comparable commercial transactions.

2. Questions relating to the price of oil allocated during an emergency shall be examined by the Standing Group on Emergency Questions.

Article 11

1. It is not an objective of the Program to seek to increase, in an emergency, the share of world oil supply that the group had under normal market conditions. Historical oil trade patterns should be preserved as far as is reasonable, and due account should be taken of the position of individual non-participating countries.

2. In order to maintain the principles set out in paragraph 1, the Management Committee shall make proposals, as appropriate, to the Governing Board, which, acting by majority, shall decide on such proposals.

Chapter IV

ACTIVATION

Article 12

Whenever the group as a whole or any Participating Country sustains or can reasonably be expected to sustain a reduction in its oil supplies, the emergency measures, which are the mandatory demand restraint referred to in Chapter II and the allocation of available oil referred to in Chapter III, shall be activated in accordance with this Chapter.

Article 13

Whenever the group sustains or can reasonably be expected to sustain a reduction in the daily rate of its oil supplies at least equal to 7 per cent of the average daily rate of its final consumption during the base period, each Participating Country shall implement demand restraint measures sufficient to reduce its final consumption by an amount equal to 7 per cent of its final consumption during the base period, and allocation of available oil among the Participating Countries shall take place in accordance with Articles 7, 9, 10 and 11.

Article 14

Whenever the group sustains or can reasonably be expected to sustain a reduction in the daily rate of its oil supplies at least equal to 12 per cent of the average daily rate of its final consumption during the base period, each Participating Country shall implement demand restraint measures sufficient to reduce its final consumption by an amount equal to 10 per cent of its final consumption during the base period, and allocation of available oil among the Participating Countries shall take place in accordance with Articles 7, 9, 10 and 11.

Article 15

When cumulative daily emergency reserve drawdown obligations as defined in Article 7 have reached 50 per cent of emergency reserve commitments and a decision has been taken in accordance with Article 20, each Participating Country shall take the measures so decided, and allocation of available oil among the Participating Countries shall take place in accordance with Articles 7, 9, 10 and 11.

Article 16

When demand restraint is activated in accordance with this Chapter, a Participating Country may substitute for demand restraint measures use of emergency reserves held in excess of its emergency reserve commitment as provided in the Program.

Article 17

1. Whenever any Participating Country sustains or can reasonably be expected to sustain a reduction in the daily rate of its oil supplies which results in a reduction of the daily rate of its final consumption by an amount exceeding 7 per cent of the average daily rate of its final consumption during the base period, allocation of available oil to that Participating Country shall take place in accordance with Article 8 to 11.

2. Allocation of available oil shall also take place when the conditions in paragraph 1 are fulfilled in a major region of a Participating Country whose oil market is incompletely integrated. In this case, the allocation obligation of other Participating Countries shall be reduced by the theoretical allocation obligation of any other major region or regions of the Participating Country concerned.

Article 18

1. The term "base period" means the most recent four quarters with a delay of one quarter necessary to collect information. While emergency measures are applied with regard to the group or to a Participating Country, the base period shall remain fixed.

2. The Standing Group on Emergency Questions shall examine the base period set out in paragraph 1, taking into account in particular such factors as growth, seasonal variations in consumption and cyclical changes and shall, not later than 1st April, 1975, report to the Management Committee. The Management Committee shall make proposals, as appropriate, to the Governing Board, which, acting by majority, shall decide on these proposals not later than 1st July, 1975.

Article 19

1. The Secretariat shall make a finding when a reduction of oil supplies as mentioned in Article 13, 14 or 17 has occurred or can reasonably be expected to occur, and shall establish the amount of the reduction or expected reduction for each Participating Country and for the group. The Secretariat shall keep the Management Committee informed of its deliberations, and shall immediately report its finding to the members of the Committee and inform the Participating Countries thereof. The report shall include information on the nature of the reduction.

2. Within 48 hours of the Secretariat's reporting a finding, the Committee shall meet to review the accuracy of the data compiled and the information provided. The Committee shall report to the Governing Board within a further 48 hours. The report shall set out the views expressed by the members of the Committee, including any views regarding the handling of the emergency.

3. Within 48 hours of receiving the Management Committee's report, the Governing Board shall meet to review the finding of the Secretariat in the light of that report. The activation of emergency measures shall be considered confirmed and Participating Countries shall implement such measures within 15 days of such confirmation unless the Governing Board, acting by special majority, decides within a further 48 hours not to activate the emergency measures, to activate them only in part or to fix another time limit for their implementation.

4. If, according to the finding of the Secretariat, the conditions of more than one of the Articles 14, 13 and 17 are fulfilled, any decision not to activate emergency measures shall be taken separately for each Article and in the above order. If the conditions in Article 17 are fulfilled with regard to more than one Participating Country any decision not to activate allocation shall be taken separately with respect to each Country.

5. Decisions pursuant to paragraphs 3 and 4 may at any time be reversed by the Governing Board, acting by majority.

6. In making its finding under this Article, the Secretariat shall consult with oil companies to obtain their views regarding the situation and the appropriateness of the measures to be taken.

7. An international advisory board from the oil industry shall be convened, not later than the

activation of emergency measures, to assist the Agency in ensuring the effective operation of such measures.

Article 20

1. The Secretariat shall make a finding when cumulative daily emergency reserve drawdown obligations have reached or can reasonably be expected to reach 50 per cent of emergency reserve commitments. The Secretariat shall immediately report its finding to the members of the Management Committee and inform the Participating Countries thereof. The report shall include information on the oil situation.

2. Within 72 hours of the Secretariat's reporting such a finding, the Management Committee shall meet to review the data compiled and the information provided. On the basis of available information the Committee shall report to the Governing Board within a further 48 hours proposing measures required for meeting the necessities of the situation, including the increase in the level of mandatory demand restraint that may be necessary. The report shall set out the views expressed by the members of the Committee.

3. The Governing Board shall meet within 48 hours of receiving the Committee's report and proposal. The Governing Board shall review the finding of the Secretariat and the report of the Management Committee and shall within a further 48 hours, acting by special majority, decide on the measures required for meeting the necessities of the situation, including the increase in the level of mandatory demand restraint that may be necessary.

Article 21

1. Any Participating Country may request the Secretariat to make a finding under Article 19 or 20.

2. If, within 72 hours of such request, the Secretariat does not make such a finding, the Participating Country may request the Management Committee to meet and consider the situation in accordance with the provisions of this Agreement.

3. The Management Committee shall meet within 48 hours of such request in order to consider the situation. It shall, at the request of any Participating Country, report to the Governing Board within a further 48 hours. The report shall set out the views expressed by the members of the Committee and by the Secretariat, including any views regarding the handling of the situation.

4. The Governing Board shall meet within 48 hours of receiving the Management Committee's report. If it finds, acting by majority, that the conditions set out in Article 13, 14, 15 or 17 are fulfilled, emergency measures shall be activated accordingly.

Article 22

The Governing Board may at any time decide by unanimity to activate any appropriate emergency measures not provided for in this Agreement, if the situation so requires.

DEACTIVATION

Article 23

1. The Secretariat shall make a finding when a reduction of supplies as mentioned in Article 13, 14 or 17 has decreased or can reasonably be expected to decrease below the level referred to in the relevant Article. The Secretariat shall keep the Management Committee informed of its deliberations and shall immediately report its finding to the members of the Committee and inform the Participating Countries thereof.

2. Within 72 hours of the Secretariat's reporting a finding, the Management Committee shall meet to review the data compiled and the information provided. It shall report to the Governing Board within a further 48 hours. The report shall set out the views expressed by the members of the Committee, including any views regarding the handling of the emergency.

3. Within 48 hours of receiving the Committee's report, the Governing Board shall meet to review the finding of the Secretariat in the light of the report from the Management Committee. The deactivation of emergency measures or the applicable reduction of the demand restraint level shall be considered confirmed unless the Governing Board, acting by special majority, decides within a further 48 hours to maintain the emergency measures or to deactivate them only in part.

4. In making its finding under this Article, the Secretariat shall consult with the international advisory board, mentioned in Article 19, paragraph 7, to obtain its views regarding the situation and the appropriateness of the measures to be taken.

5. Any Participating Country may request the Secretariat to make a finding under this Article.

Article 24

When emergency measures are in force, and the Secretariat has not made a finding under Article 23, the Governing Board, acting by special majority, may at any time decide to deactivate the measures either wholly or in part.

Chapter V

INFORMATION SYSTEM ON THE INTERNATIONAL OIL MARKET

Article 25

1. The Participating Countries shall establish an Information System consisting of two sections:

— a General Section on the situation in the international oil market and activities of oil companies.

— a Special Section designed to ensure the efficient operation of the measures described in Chapters I to IV.

2. The System shall be operated on a permanent basis, both under normal conditions and during

emergencies, and in a manner which ensures the confidentiality of the information made available.
3. The Secretariat shall be responsible for the operation of the Information System and shall make the information compiled available to the Participating Countries.

Article 26

The term "oil companies" means international companies, national companies, non-integrated companies and other entities which play a significant role in the international oil industry.

General Section

Article 27

1. Under the General Section of the Information System, the Participating Countries shall, on a regular basis, make available to the Secretariat information on the precise date identified in accordance with Article 29 on the following subjects relating to oil companies operating within their respective jurisdictions:

a) Corporate structure;

b) Financial structure, including balance sheets, profit and loss accounts, and taxes paid;

c) Capital investments realised;

d) Terms of arrangements for access to major sources of crude oil;

e) Current rates of production and anticipated changes therein;

f) Allocation of available crude supplies affiliates and other customers (criteria and realisations);

g) Stocks;

h) Cost of crude oil and oil products;

i) Prices, including transfer price to affiliates;

j) Other subjects, as decided by the Governing Board, acting by unanimity.

2. Each Participating Country shall take appropriate measures to ensure that all oil companies operating within its jurisdiction make such information available to it as is necessary to fulfil its obligations under Paragraph 1, taking into account such relevant information as is already available to the public or to Governments.

3. Each Participating Country shall provide information on a non-proprietary basis and on a company and/or country basis as appropriate, and in such a manner and degree as will not prejudice competition or conflict with the legal requirements of any Participating Country relating to competition.

4. No Participating Country shall be entitled to obtain, through the General Section, any information on the activities of a company operating within its jurisdiction which could not be obtained by it from that company by application of its laws or through its institutions and customs if that company were operating solely within its jurisdiction.

Article 28

Information provided on a "non-proprietary basis" means information which does not constitute or relate to patents, trademarks, scientific or manufacturing processes or developments, individual sales, tax returns, customer lists or geological and geophysical information, including maps.

Article 29

1. Within 60 days of the first day of the provisional application of this Agreement, and as appropriate thereafter, the Standing Group on the Oil Market shall submit a report to the Management Committee identifying the precise date within the list of subjects in Article 27, paragraph 1, which are required for the efficient operation of the General Section, and specifying the procedures for obtaining such data on a regular basis.

2. The Management Committee shall review the report and make proposals to the Governing Board which, within 30 days of the submission of the report to the Management Committee, and acting by majority, shall take the decisions necessary for the establishment and efficient operation of the General Section.

Article 30

In preparing its reports under Article 29, the Standing Group on the Oil Market shall

— consult with oil companies to ensure that the System is compatible with industry operations;

— identify specific problems and issues which are of concern to Participating Countries;

— identify specific data which are useful and necessary to resolve such problems and issues;

— work out precise standards for the harmonization of the required information in order to ensure comparability of the data;

— work out procedures to ensure the confidentiality of the information.

Article 31

1. The Standing Group on the Oil Market shall on a continuing basis review the operation of the General Section.

2. In the event of changes in the conditions of the international oil market, the Standing Group on the Oil Market shall report to the Management Committee. The Committee shall make proposals on appropriate changes to the Governing Board which acting by majority, shall decide on such proposals.

Special Section

Article 32

1. Under the Special Section of the Information System, the Participating Countries shall make available to the Secretariat all information which is necessary to ensure the efficient operation of emergency measures.

2. Each Participating Country shall take

appropriate measures to ensure that all oil companies operating within its jurisdiction make such information available to it as is necessary to enable it to fulfil its obligations under paragraph 1 and under Article 33.

3. The Secretariat shall, onl the basis of this information and other information available, continuosly survey the supply of oil to and the consumption of oil within the group and each Participating Country.

Article 33

Under the Special Section, the Participating Countries, on a regular basis, make available to the Secretariat information on the precise data indentified in accordance with Article 34 on the following subjects:

a) Oil consumption and supply;

b) Demand restraint measures

c) Levels of emergency reserves;

d) Availability and utilisation of transportation facilities;

e) Current and projected levels of international supply and demand;

f) Other subjects, as decided by the Governing Board, acting by unanimity.

Article 34

1. Within 30 days of the first day of the provisional application of this Agreement, the Standing Group on Emergency Questions shall submit a report to the Management Committee identifying the precise date within the list of subjects in Article 33 which are required under the Special Section to ensure the efficient operation of emergency measures and specifying the procedures for obtaining such data on a regular basis, including accelerated procedures in times of emergency.

2. The Management Committee shall review the report and make proposals to the Governing Board which, within 30 days of the submission of the report to the Management Committee, and acting by majority, shall take the decisions necessary for the establishment and efficient operation of the Special Section.

Article 35

In preparing its report under Article 31, the Standing Group on Emergency Questions shall

—consult with oil companies to ensure that the Systems in compatible with industry operations;

— work out precise standards for the harmonization of the required information in order to ensure comparability of the data;

— work out procedures to ensure the confidentiality of the information.

Article 36

The Standing Group on Emergency Questions shall on a continuing basis review the operation of the Special Section and shall, as appropriate, report to the Management Committee. The Committee shall make proposals on appropriate changes to the Government Board, which, acting by majority, shall decide on such proposals.

CHAPTER VI

FRAMEWORK FOR CONSULTATION WITH OIL COMPANIES

Article 37

1. The Participating Countries shall establish within the Agency a permanent framework for consultation within which one or more Participating Countries may, in an appropriate manner, consult with and request information from individual oil companies on all important aspects of the oil industry, and within which the Participating Countries may share among themselves on a co-operative basis the results of such consultations.

2. The framework for consultation shall be established under the auspices of the Standing Group on the Oil Market.

3. Within 60 days of the first day of the provisional application of this Agreement, and as appropriate thereafter, the Standing Group on the Oil Market, after consultation with oil companies, shall submit a report to the Managing Committee on the procedures for such consultations. The Management Committee shall review the report and make proposals to the Governing Board, which, within 30 days of the submission of the report to the Management Committee, and acting by majority, shall decide on such procedures.

Article 38

1. The Standing Group on the Oil Market shall present a report to the Management Committee on consultation held with any oil company within 30 days thereof.

2. The Management Committee shall consider the report and may take proposals on appropriate co-operative action to the Governing Board, which shall decide on such proposals.

Article 39

1. The Standing Group on the Oil Market shall, on a continuing basis, evaluate the results of the consultations with and the information collected from oil companies.

2. On the basis of these evaluations, the Standing Group may examine and assess the international oil situation and the position of the oil industry and shall report to the Management Committee.

3. The Management Comittee shall review such reports and make proposals on appropriate co-operative action to the Governing Board, which shall decide on such proposals.

Article 40

The Standing Group on the Oil Market shall submit annually a general report to the Management Committee on the functioning of the framework for consultation with oil companies.

CHAPTER VII

LONG TERM CO-OPERATION ON ENERGY

Article 41

1. The Participating Countries are determined to reduce over the longer term their dependence on imported oil for meeting their total energy requirements.

2. To this end, the Participating Countries will undertake national programes and promote the adoption of co-operative programs, including, as appropriate, the sharing of means and efforts, while concerting national policies, in the areas set out in Article 42.

Article 42

1. The Standing Group on Long Term Co-operation shall examine and report to the Management Commitee on co-operative action. The following areas shall in particular be considered:

a) Conservation of energy, including co-operative programs on

— exchange of national experiences and information on energy conservation;

— ways and means of reducing the growth of energy consumption through conservation.

b) Development of alternative sources of energy such as domestic oil, coal, natural gas, nuclear energy and hydro-electric power, including co-operative programs on

— exchange of information on such matters as resources, supply and demand, price and taxation;

—ways and means of reducing the growth of consumption of imported oil through the development of alternative sources of energy;

— concrete projects, including jointly financed projects;

—criteria, quality of objectives and standards for

— environmental protection.

c) Energy research and development, including as a matter of priority co-operative programs on

— coal technology;
solar energy;

— radioactive waste management;

— controlled thermonuclear fusion;

— production of hydrogen from water;

— nuclear safety;

— waste heat utilisation;

— conservation of energy;

— municipal and industrial waste utilisation for energy conservation;

— overall energy system analysis and general studies.

d) Uranium enrichment, including co-operative programs

— to monitor developments in natural and enriched uranium supply;

— to facilitate development of natural uranium resources and enrichment services;

— to encourage such consultations as may be required to deal with international issues that may arise in relation to the expansion of enriched uranium supply;

— to arrange for the requisite collection, analysis and dissemination of data related to the planning of enrichment services.

2. In examining the areas of co-operative action, the Standing Group shall take due account of ongoing activities elsewhere.

3. Programs developed under Paragraph 1 may be jointly financed. Such joint financing may take place in accordance with Article 64, paragraph 2.

Article 43

1. The Management Committee shall review the reports of the Standing Group and make appropriate proposals to the Governing Board, which shall decide on these proposals not later than 1st July, 1975.

2. The Governing Board shall take into account possibilities for co-operation within a broader framework.

CHAPTER VIII

RELATIONS WITH PRODUCER COUNTRIES AND WITH OTHER CONSUMER COUNTRIES

Article 44

The Participating Countries will endeavour to promote co-operative relations with oil producing countries and with other oil consuming countries, including developing countries. They will keep under review developments in the energy field with a view to identifying opportunities for and promoting a purposeful dialogue, as well as other forms of co-operation, with producer countries and with other consumer countries.

Article 45

To achieve the objectives set out in Article 44, the Participating Countries will give full consideration to the needs and interests of other oil consuming countries, particularly those of the developing countries.

Article 46

The Participating Countries will, in the context of the Program, exchange views on their relations with oil producing countries. To this end, the Participating Countries should inform each other of co-operative action on their part with producer countries which is relevant to the objectives of the Program.

Article 47

The Participating Countries will, in the context of the Program

— seek, in the light of their continuous review of developments in the international energy situation and its effect on the world economy, opportunities and means of encouraging stable international trade in oil and of promoting secure oil supplies on reasonable and equitable terms for each Participating Country;

— consider, in the light of work going on in other international organisations, other possible fields of co-operation including the prospects for co-operation in accelerated industrialisation and socio-economic development in the principal producing areas and the implications of this for international trade and investment.

— keeping under review the prospects for co-operation with oil producing countries on energy questions of mutual interest, such as conservation of energy, the development of alternative sources, and research and development.

Article 48

1. The Standing Group on Relations with Producer and other Consumer Countries will examine and report to the Management Committee on the matters described in this Chapter.

2. The Management Committee may make proposals on appropriate co-operative action regarding these matters to the Governing Board, which shall decide on such proposals.

CHAPTER IX

INSTITUTIONAL AND GENERAL PROVISIONS

Article 49

1. The Agency shall have the following organs:

— a Governing Board

— a Management Committee

— Standing Groups on
  - — Emergency Questions
  - — The Oil Market
  - — Long Term Co-operation
  - — Relations with Producer and other Consumer Countries.

2. The Governing Board or the Management Committee may, acting by majority, establish any other organ necessary for the implementation of the Program.

3. The Agency shall have a Secretariat to assist the organs mentioned in paragraphs 1 and 2.

GOVERNING BOARD

Article 50

1. The Governing Board shall be composed of one or more ministers or their delegates from each Participating Country.

2. The Governing Board, acting by majority, shall adopt its own rules of procedure. Unless otherwise decided in the rules of procedure, these rules shall also apply to the Management Committee and the Standing Groups.

3. The Governing Board, acting by majority, shall elect its Chairman and Vice-Chairman.

Article 51

1. The Governing Board shall adopt decisions and make recommendations which are necessary for the proper functioning of the Program.

2. The Governing Board shall review periodically and take appropriate action concerning developments in the international energy situation, including problems relating to the oil supplies of any Participating Country or Countries, and the economic and monetary implications of developments in the international energy situation, the Governing Board shall take into account the competence and activities of international institutions responsible for overall economic and monetary questions.

3. The Governing Board, acting by majority, may delegate any of its functions to any other organ of the Agency.

Article 52

1. Subject to Article 61, paragraph 2, and Article 65, decisions adopted pursuant to this Agreement by the Governing Board or by any other organ by delegation from the Board shall be binding on the Participating Countries.

2. Recommendations shall not be binding.

MANAGEMENT COMMITTEE

Article 53

1. The Management Committee shall be composed of one more senior representatives of the Government of each Participating Country.

2. The Management Committee shall carry out the functions assigned to it in this Agreement and any other function delegated to it by the Governing Board.

3. The Management Committee may examine and make proposals to the Governing Board, as appropriate, on any matter within the scope of this Agreement.

4. The Management Committee shall be convened upon the request of any Participating Country.

5. The Management Comittee, acting by majority, shall elect its Chairman and Vice-Chairman.

STANDING GROUPS

Article 54

1. Each Standing Group shall be composed of one or more representatives of the Government of each Participating Country.

2. The Management Committee, acting by majority, shall elect the Chairman and Vice-Chairmen of the Standing Groups.

Article 55

1. The Standing Group on Emergency Questions shall carry out the functions assigned to it in Chapters I to V and the Annex and any other function delegated to it by the Governing Board.

2. The Standing Group may review and report to the Management Committee on any matter within

the scope of Chapters I to V and the Annex.

3. The Standing Group may consult with oil companies on any matter within its competence.

Article 56

1. The Standing Group on the Oil Market shall carry out the functions assigned to it in Chapters V and VI and any other function delegated to it by the Governing Board.

2. The Standing Group may review and report to the Management Committee on any matter within the scope of Chapters V to VI.

3. The Standing Group may consult with oil companies on any matter within its competence.

Article 57

1. The Standing Group on Long Term Co-operating shall carry out the functions assigned to it in Chapter VII and any other function delegated to it by the Governing Board.

2. The Standing Group may review and report to the Management Committee on any matter within the scope of Chapter VII.

Article 58

1. The Standing Group on Relations with Producer and other Consumer Countries shall carry out the functions assigned to it in Chapter VIII and any other function delegated to it by the Governing Board.

2. The Standing Group may review and report to the Management Committee on any matter within the scope of Chapter VIII.

3. The Standing Group may consult with oil companies on any matter within its competence.

SECRETARIAT

Article 59

1. The Secretariat shall be composed of an Executive Director and such staff as is necessary.

2. The Executive Director shall be appointed by the Governing Board.

3. In the performance of their duties under this Agreement the Executive Director and the staff shall be responsible to and report to the organs of the Agency.

4. The Governing Board, acting by majority, shall take all decisions necessary for the establishment and the functioning of the Secretariat.

Article 60

The Secretariat shall carry out the functions assigned to it in this Agreement and any other function assigned to it by the Governing Board.

VOTING

Article 61

1. The Governing Board shall adopt decisions and recommendations for which no express voting provision is made in this Agreement, as follows:

a) by majority:

—decisions on the management of the Program, including decisions on applying provisions of this Agreement which already impose specific obligations on Participating Countries.

— decisions on procedural questions

— recommendations

b) by unanimity:

— all other decisions, including in particular decisions which impose on Participating Countries new obligations not already specified in this Agreement.

2. Decisions mentioned in paragraph 1 (*b*) may provide:

a) that they shall not be binding on one or more Participating Countries;

b) that they shall be binding only under certain conditions.

Article 62

1. Unanimity shall require all of the votes of the Participating Countries present and voting. Countries abstaining shall be considered as not voting.

2. When majority or special majority is required, the Participating Countries shall have the following voting weights:

	General voting weights	Oil consumption voting weights	Combined voting weights
Austria	3	1	4
Belgium	3	2	5
Canada	3	5	8
Denmark	3	1	4
Germany	3	8	11
Ireland	3	0	3
Italy	3	6	9
Japan	3	15	18
Luxembourg	3	0	3
The Netherlands	3	2	5
Spain	3	2	5
Sweden	3	2	5
Switzerland	3	1	4
Turkey	3	1	4
United Kingdom	3	6	9
United States	3	48	51
Totals	48	100	148

3. Majority shall require 60 per cent of the total combined voting weights and 50 per cent of the general voting weights cast.

4. Special majority shall require:

a) 60 percent of the total combined voting weights and 36 general voting weights for:

— the decision under Article 2, paragraph 2, relating to the increase in the emergency reserve commitment;
— decisions under Article 19, paragraph 3, not to activate the emergency measures referred to in Articles 13 and 14;
— decisions under Article 20, paragraphs 3, on the measures required for meeting the necessities of the situation;
— decisions under Article 23, paragraph 3, to maintain the emergency measures referred to in Articles 13 and 14;
— decisions under Article 24 to deactivate the emergency measures referred to in Articles 13 and 14.

b) 42 general voting weights for:

— decisions under Article 19 paragraph 3, not to activate the emergency measures referred to in Article 17;
— decisions under Article 23, paragraph 3, to maintain the emergency measures referred to in Article 17;
—decisions under Article 24 to deactivate the emergency measures referred to in Article 17.

5. The Governing Board, acting by unanimity, shall decide on the necessary increase, decrease, and redistribution of the voting weights referred to in paragraph 2, as well as on amendment of the voting requirements set out in paragraphs 3 and 4 in the event that

— a Country accedes to this Agreement in accordance with Article 71, or
— a Country withdraws from this Agreement in accordance with Article 68, paragraph 2, or Article 69, paragraph 2.

6. The Governing Body shall review annually the number and distribution of voting weights specified in paragraph 2, and, on the basis of such review, acting by unanimity, shall decide whether such voting weights should be increased or decreased, or redistributed, or both, because a change in any Participating Country's share in total oil consumption has occured or for any other reason.

7. Any change in paragraph 2, 3 or 4 shall be based on the concepts underlying those paragraphs and paragraph 6.

RELATIONS WITH OTHER ENTITIES

Article 63

In order to achieve the objectives of the Programme, the Agency may establish appropriate relations with non-participating countries, international organisations, whether governmental or non-governmental, other entities and individuals.

FINANCIAL ARRANGEMENTS

Article 64

1. The expenses of the Secretariat and all other common expenses shall be shared among all Participating countries according to a scale of contributions elaborated according to the principles and rules set out in the Annex to the "OECD Resolution of the Council on Determination of the Scale of Contributions by Member Countries to the Budget of the Organisation" of the 10th December, 1963. After the first year of application of this Agreement, the Governing Board shall review the scale of contribution and, acting by unanimity, shall decide upon any appropriate changes in accordance with Article 73.

2. Special expenses incurred in connection with special activities carried out pursuant to Article 65 shall be shared by the Participating Countries taking part in such special activities in such proportions as shall be determined by unanimous agreement between them.

3. The Executive Director shall, in accordance with the financial regulation adopted by the Governing Board and not later than 1 October of each year, submit to the Governing Board a draft budget including personnel requirements. The Governing Board, acting by majority, shall adopt the budget.

4. The Governing Board, acting by majority, shall take all other necessary decisions regarding the financial administration of the Agency.

5. The financial year shall begin on 1st January and end on 31st December of each year. At the end of each financial year, revenues and expenditures shall be submitted to audit.

SPECIAL ACTIVITIES

Article 65

1. Any two or more Participating Countries may decide to carry out within the scope of this Agreement special activities, other than activities which are required to be carried out by all Participating Countries under Chapters I to V. Participating Countries which do not wish to take part in such special activities shall abstain from taking part in such decisions and shall not be bound by them. Participating Countries carrying out such activites shall keep the Governing Board informed thereof.

2. For the implementation of such special activities, the Participating Coutries concerned may agree upon voting procedures other than thoses provided for in Articles 61 and 62.

IMPLEMENTATION OF THE AGREEMENT

Article 66

Each Participating Country shall take the necessary measures, including any necessary legislative measures, to implement this Agreement and decisions taken by the Governing Board.

Chapter X

FINAL PROVISIONS

Article 67

1. Each signatory State shall, not later than 1st

May, 1975, notify the Government of the Kingdom of .Belgium that, having complied with its constitutional procedures, it consents to be bound by this Agreement.

2. On the tenth day following the day on which at least six States holding at least 60 per cent of the combined voting weight mentioned in Article 62 have deposited a notification of consent to be bound or an instrument of accession, this Agreement shall enter into force for such States.

3. For each Signatory State which deposits its notification thereafter, this Agreement shall enter into force on the tenth day following the day of deposit.

4. The Governing Board, acting by majority, may upon request from any Signatory State decide to extend, with request to that State, the time limit for notification beyond 1st May, 1975.

Article 68

1. Notwithstanding the provisions of Article 67, this Agreement shall be applied provisionally by all Signatory States, to the extent possible not inconsistent with their legislation, as from 18th November, 1974 following the first meeting of the Governing Board.

2. Provisional application of the Agreement shall continue until:

— the Agreement enters into force for the State concerned in accordance with Article 67, or

— 60 days after the Government of the Kingdom of Belgium receives notification that the State concerning will not consent to be bound the Agreement, or

— the time limit for notification of consent by the State concerned referred to in Article 67 expires.

Article 69

1. This Agreement shall remain in force for a period of ten years from the date of its entry into force and shall continue in force thereafter unless and until the Governing Board, acting by majority, decides on its termination.

2. Any Participating Country may terminate the application of this Agreement for its part upon twelve months written notice to the Government of the Kingdom of Belgium to that effect, given not less than three years after the first day of the provisional application of this Agreement.

Article 70

1. Any State may, at the time of signature, notification of consent to be bound in accordance with Article 67, accession or at any later date, declare by notification addressed to the Government of the Kingdom of Belgium that this Agreement shall apply to all or any of the territories for whose international relations it is responsible, or to any territories within its frontiers for whose oil supplies it is legally responsible.

2. Any declaration made pursuant to paragraph 1 may, in respect of any territory mentioned in such declaration, be withdrawn in accordance with the provisions of Article 69, paragraph 2.

Article 71

1. This Agreement shall be open for accession by any Member of the Organisation for Economic Co-operation and Development which is able and willing to meet the requirements of the Program. The Governing Board, acting by majority, shall decide on any request for accession.

2. This Agreement shall enter into force for any State whose request for accession has been granted on the tenth day following the deposit of its instrument of accession with the Government of the Kingdom of Belgium, or on the date of entry into force of the Agreement pursuant to Article 67, paragraph 2, whichever is the later.

3. Until 1st May, 1975, accession may take place on a provisional basis under the conditions set out in Article 68.

Article 72

1. This Agreement shall be open for accession by the European Communities.

2. This Agreement shall not in any way impede the further implementation of the treaties establishing the European Communities.

Article 73

This Agreement may at any time be amended by the Governing Board, acting by unanimity. Such amendment shall come into force in a manner determined by the Governing Board, acting by unanimity and making provisions for Participating Countries to comply with their respective constitutional procedures.

Article 74

This Agreement shall be subject to a general review after 1st May, 1980.

Article 75

The Government of the Kingdom of Belgium shall notify all Participating Countries of the deposit of each notification of consent to be bound in accordance with Article 67, and of each instrument of accession, or the entry into force of this Agreement or any amendment thereto, of any denunciation thereof, and of any other declaration or notification received.

Artile 76

The original of this Agreement, of which the English, French and German texts are equally authentic, shall be deposited with the Government of the Kingdom of Belgium, and a certified copy thereof shall be furnished to each other Participating Country by the Government of the Kingdom of Belgium.

In Witness Whereof the undersigned, being duly authorized thereto by their respective Governments, have signed this Agreement.

Done at Paris this eighteenth day of November, Nineteen Hundred and Seventy-Four.

ANNEX

EMERGENCY RESERVES

Article 1

1. Total oil stocks are measured according to the OECD and EEC definitions, revised as follows:

A. Stocks included:

crude oil, major products and unfinished oil held
- in refinery tanks
- in bulk terminals
- in pipeline tankage
- in barges
- in intercoastal tankers
- in oil tankers in port
- in inland ship bunkers
- in storage tank bottoms
- in working stocks
- by large consumers as required by law or otherwise controlled by Governments.

B. Stocks excluded:

a) crude oil not yet produced

b) crude oil, major products and unfinished oils held
- in pipelines
- in rail tank cars
- in truck tank cars
- in seagoing ships' bunkers
- in service stations and retail stores
- by other consumers
- in tankers at sea
- as military stocks

2. That portion of oil stocks which can be credited toward each Participating Country's emergency reserve commitment is its total oil stocks under the above definition minus those stocks which can be technically determined as being absolutely unavailable in even the most severe emergency. The Standing Group on Emergency Questions shall examine this concept and report on criteria for the measurement of absolutely unavailable stocks.

3. Until a decision has been taken on this matter, each Participating Country shall substract 10 per cent from its total stocks in measuring its emergency reserves.

4. The Standing Group on Emergency Questions shall examine and report to the Management Committee on:

a) the modalities of including naphtha for uses other than motor and aviation gasoline in the consumption against which stocks are measured.

b) the possibility of creating common rules for the treatment of marine bunkers in an emergency, and of including marine bunkers in the consumption against which stocks are measured,

c) the possibility of creating common rules concerning demand restraint for aviation bunkers,

d) the possibility of crediting towards emergency reserve commitments some portion of oil at sea at the time of activation of emergency measures,

e) the possibility of increasing supplies available in an emergency through savings in the distribution system.

Article 2

1. Fuel switching capacity is defined as normal oil consumption that may be replaced by other fuels in an emergency, provided that this capacity is subject to government control in an emergency, can be brought into operation within one month, and that secure supplies of the alternative fuel are available for use.

2. The supply of alternative fuel shall be expressed in terms of oil equivalent.

3. Stocks of an alternative fuel reserved for fuel switching purposes may be credited towards emergency reserve commitments insofar as they can be used during the period of self-sufficiency.

4. Stand-by production of an alternative fuel reserved for fuel switching purposes will be credited towards emergency reserve commitments on the same basis as stand-by oil production, subject to the provisions of Article 4 of this Annex.

5. The Standing Group on Emergency Questions shall examine and report to the Management Committee on

a) the appropriateness of the time limit of one month mentioned in paragraph 1,

b) the basis of accounting for the fuel switching capacity based on stocks of an alternative fuel, subject to the provisions of paragraph 3.

Article 3

A Participating Country may credit towards its emergency reserve commitment oil stocks in another country, provided that the Governemnt of that other country has an agreement with the Government of the Participating Country that it shall impose no impediment to the transfer of those stocks in an emergency to the Participating Country.

Article 4

1. Stand-by production is defined as a Participating Country's potential oil production in excess of normal oil production within its jurisdiction
- which is subject to government control, and
- which can be brought into use during an emergency within the period of self-sufficiency.

2. The Standing Group on Emergency Questions shall examine and report to the Management Committee on

a) the concept of and methods of measurement of stand-by oil production as referred to in paragraph 1,

b) the appropriates of "the period of self-sufficiency" as a time limit,

c) the question of whether a given quantity of stand-by oil production is of greater value for purposes of emergency self-sufficiency than the same quantity of oil stocks, the amount of a possible credit for stand-by production, and the method of its calculation.

Article 5

Stand-by oil production available to a Participating Country within the jurisdiction of another country may be credited towards its emergency reserve commitment on the same basis as stand-by production within its own juridiction, subject to the provisions of Article 4 of this Annex provided that the Government of that other country has an agreement with the Government of the Participating Country that it shall impose no impediment to the supply of oil from that stand-by capacity to the Participating Country in an emergency.

Article 6

The Standing Group Emergency Questions shall examine and report to the Management Committee on the possibility of crediting towards a Participating Country's emergency reserve commitment mentioned in Article 2, paragraph 2, of the Agreement, long term investments which have the effect of reducing the Participating Country's dependence on imported oil.

Article 7

1. The Standing Group on Emergency Questions shall examine and report to the Management Committee regarding the reference period set out in Article 2, paragraph 1, of the Agreement, in particular taking into account such factors as growth, seasonal variations in consumption and cyclical changes.

2. A decision by the Governing Board to change the definition of the reference period mentioned in paragraph 1 shall be taken by unanimity.

Article 8

The Standing Group on Emergency Questions shall examine and report to the Management Committee on all elements of Chapters I to IV of the Agreement to eliminate possible mathematical and statistical anomalies.

Article 9

The reports from the Standing Group on Emergency questions on the matters mentioned in this Annex shall be submitted to the Management Committee by 1st April, 1975. The Management Committee shall make proposals, as appropriate, to the Governing Board, which, acting by majority, not later than 1st July 1975, shall decide on these proposals, except as provided for in Article 7, paragraphs 2, of this Annex.

CONVENTION FOR THE PROTECTION OF THE MEDITERRANEAN SEA AGAINST POLLUTION [66]

Barcelona, 16 February 1976

THE CONTRACTING PARTIES,

Conscious of the economic, social, health and cultural value of the marine environment of the Mediterranean Sea area,

Fully aware of their responsibility to preserve this common heritage for the benefit and enjoyment of present and future generations,

Recognizing the threat posed by pollution to the marine environment, its ecological equilibrium, resources and legitimate uses,

Mindful of the special hydrographic and ecological characteristics of the Mediterranean Sea area and its particular vulnerability to pollution,

Noting that existing international conventions on the subject do not cover, in spite of the progress achieved, all aspects and sources of marine pollution and do not entirely meet the special requirements of the Mediterranean Sea area,

Realizing fully the need for close co-operation among the States and international organizations concerned in a co-ordinated and comprehensive regional approach for the protection and enhancement of the marine environment in the Mediterranean Sea area,

Have agreed as follows:

Article 1

GEOGRAPHICAL COVERAGE

1. For the purposes of this Convention, the Mediterranean Sea area shall mean the maritime waters of the Mediterranean Sea proper, including its gulfs and seas, bounded to the west by the meridian passing through Cape Spartel lighthouse, at the entrance of the Straits of Gibraltar, and to the east by the southern limits of the Straits of the Dardanelles between the Mehmetcik and Kumkale lighthouses.

2. Except as may be otherwise provided in any Protocol to this Convention, the Mediterranean Sea area shall not include internal waters of the Contracting Parties.

Article 2

DEFINITIONS

For the purposes of this Convention:

(*a*) 'Pollution' means the introduction by man, directly or indirectly, of substances or energy into the marine environment resulting in such deleterious effects as harm to living resources, hazards to human health, hindrance to marine activities including fishing, impairment of quality for use of sea water and reduction of amenities.

(*b*) 'Organization' means the body designated as responsible for carrying out secretariat functions pursuant to Article 13 of this Convention.

Article 3

GENERAL PROVISIONS

1. The Contracting Parties may enter into bilateral or multilateral agreements, including regional or sub-regional agreements, for the protection of the marine environment of the Mediterranean Sea against pollution, provided that such agreements are consistent with this Convention and conform to international law. Copies of such agreements between Contracting Parties to this Convention shall be communicated to the Organization.

2. Nothing in this Convention shall prejudice the codification and development of the law of the sea by the United Nations Conference on the Law of the Sea convened pursuant to resolution 2750 C (XXV) of the General Assembly of the United Nations, nor the present or future claims and legal views of any State concerning the law of the sea and the nature and extent of coastal and flag State jurisdiction.

Article 4

GENERAL UNDERTAKINGS

1. The Contracting Parties shall individually or jointly take all appropriate measures in accordance with the provisions of this Convention and those Protocols in force to which they are party, to prevent, abate and combat pollution of the Mediterranean Sea area and to protect and enhance the marine environment in that area.

2. The Contracting Parties shall cooperate in the formulation and adoption of Protocols, in addition to the protocols opened for signature at the same time as this Convention, prescribing agreed measures, procedures and standards for the implementations of this Convention.

3. The Contracting Parties further pledge themselves to promote, within the international bodies considered to be competent by the Contracting Parties, measures concerning the protection of the marine environment in the Mediterranean Sea area from all types and sources of pollution.

Article 5

POLLUTION CAUSED BY DUMPING FROM SHIPS AND AIRCRAFT

The Contracting Parties shall take all appropriate measures to prevent and abate pollution of the Mediterranean Sea area caused by dumping from ships and aircraft.

Article 6

POLLUTION FROM SHIPS

The Contracting Parties shall take all measures in conformity with international law to prevent, abate and combat pollution of the Mediterranean Sea area caused by discharges from ships and to ensure the effective implementation in that area of the rules which are generally recognized at the international level relating to the control of this type of pollution.

Article 7

POLLUTION RESULTING FROM EXPLORATION AND EXPLOITATION OF THE CONTINENTAL SHELF AND THE SEABED AND ITS SUBSOIL

The Contracting Parties shall take all appropriate measures to prevent, abate and combat pollution of the Mediterranean Sea area resulting from exploration and exploitation of the continental shelf and the seabed and its subsoil.

Article 8

POLLUTION FROM LAND-BASED SOURCES

The Contracting Parties shall take all appropriate measures to prevent, abate and combat pollution of the Mediterranean Sea area caused by discharges from rivers, coastal establishments or outfalls, or emanating from any other land-based sources within their territories.

Article 9

COOPERATION IN DEALING WITH POLLUTION EMERGENCIES

1. The Contracting Parties shall co-operate in taking the necessary measures for dealing with pollution emergencies in the Mediterranean Sea area, whatever the causes of such emergencies, and reducing or eliminating damage resulting therefrom.

2. Any Contracting Party which becomes aware of any pollution emergency in the Mediterranean Sea area shall without delay notify the Organization and, either through the Organization or directly, any Contracting Party likely to be affected by such emergency.

Article 10

MONITORING

1. The Contracting Parties shall endeavour to establish, in close co-operation with the international bodies which they consider competent, complementary or joint programmes, including, as appropriate, programmes at the bilateral or multilateral levels, for pollution monitoring in the Mediterranean Sea area and shall endeavour to establish a pollution monitoring system for that area.

2. For this purpose, the Contracting Parties shall designate the competent authorities responsible for pollution monitoring within areas under their national jurisdiction and shall participate as far as practicable in international arrangements for pollution monitoring in areas beyond national jurisdiction.

3. The Contracting Parties undertake to co-operate in the formulation, adoption and implementation of such Annexes to this Convention as may be required to prescribe common procedures and standards for pollution monitoring.

Article 11

SCIENTIFIC AND TECHNOLOGICAL CO-OPERATION

1. The Contracting Parties. undertake as far as possible to co-operate directly, or when

appropriate through competent regional or other international organizations, in the fields of science and technology and to exchange data as well as other scientific information for the purpose of this Convention.

2. The Contracting Parties undertake as far as possible to develop and co-ordinate their national research programmes relating to all types of marine pollution in the Mediterranean Sea area and to co-operate in the establishment and implementation of regional and other international research programmes for the purposes of this Convention.

3. The Contracting Parties undertake to co-operate in the provision of technical and other possible assistance in fields relating to marine pollution, with priority to be given to the special needs of developing countries in the Mediterranean region.

Article 12

LIABILITY AND COMPENSATION

The Contracting Parties undertake to co-operate as soon as possible in the formulation and adoption of appropriate procedures for he determination of liability and compensation for damage resulting from the pollution of the marine environment deriving from violations of the provisions of this Convention and applicable Protocols.

Article 13

INSTITUTIONAL ARRANGEMENTS

The Contracting Parties designate the United Nations Environment Programme as responsible for carrying out the following secretariat functions:

(i) to convene and prepare the meetings of Contracting Parties and conferences provided for in Articles 14, 15 and 16;

(ii) to transmit to the Contracting Parties notifications, reports and other information received in accordance with Articles 3, 9 and 20;

(iii) to consider inquiries by, and information from, the Contracting Parties, and to consult with them on questions relating to this Convention and the Protocols and Annexes thereto;

(iv) to perform the functions assigned to it by the Protocols to this Convention;

(v) to perform such other functions as may be assigned to it by the Contracting Parties;

(vi) to ensure the necessary co-ordination with other international bodies which the Contracting Parties consider competent, and in particular, to enter into such administrative arrangements as may be required for the effective discharge of the secretariat functions.

Article 14

MEETINGS OF THE CONTRACTING PARTIES

1. The Contracting Parties shall hold ordinary meetings once every two years and extraordinary meetings at any other time deemed necessary, upon the request of the Organization or at the request of any Contracting Party, provided that such requests are supported by at least two Contracting Parties;

2. It shall be the function of the meetings of the Contracting Parties to keep under review the implementation of this Convention and the Protocols and, in particular:

(i) to review gradually the inventories carried out by Contracting Parties and competent international organizations on the state of marine pollution and its effects in the Mediterranean Sea area;

(ii) to consider reports submitted by the Contracting Parties under Article 20;

(iii) to adopt, review and amend as required the Annexes to this Convention and to the Protocols, in accordance with the procedure established in Article 17;

(iv) to make recommendations regarding the adoption of any Additional Protocols or any amendments to this Convention or the Protocols in accordance with the provisions of Articles 15 and 16;

(v) to establish working groups as required to consider any matters related to this Convention and the Protocols and Annexes;

(vi) to consider and undertake any additional action that may be required for the achievement of the purposes of this Convention and the Protocols.

Article 15

ADOPTION OF ADDITIONAL PROTOCOLS

1. The Contracting Parties, at a diplomatic conference, may adopt Additional Protocols to this Convention pursuant to paragraph 2 of Article 4.

2. A diplomatic conference for the purpose of adopting Additional Protocols shall be convened by the Organization at the request of two thirds of the Contracting Parties.

3. Pending the entry into force of this Convention the Organization may, after consulting with the signatories to this Convention, convene a diplomatic conference for the purpose of adopting Additional Protocols.

Article 16

AMENDMENT OF THE CONVENTION OR PROTOCOLS

1. Any Contracting Party to this Convention may propose amendments to the Convention. Amendments shall be adopted by a diplomatic conference which shall be convened by the Organization at the request of two thirds of the Contracting Parties.

2. Any Contracting Party to this Convention may propose amendments to any Protocol. Such amendments shall be adopted by a diplomatic conference which shall be convened by the Organization at the request of two thirds of the Contracting Parties to the Protocol concerned.

3. Amendments to this Convention shall be adopted by a three-fourths majority vote of the Contracting Parties to the Convention which are

represented at the diplomatic conference and shall be submitted by the Depositary for acceptance by all Contracting Parties to the Convention. Amendments to any Protocol shall be adopted by a three-fourths majority vote of the Contracting Parties to such Protocol which are represented at the diplomatic conference and shall be submitted by the Depositary for acceptance by all Contracting Parties to such Protocol.

4. Acceptance of amendments shall be notified to the Depositary in writing. Amendments adopted in accordance with paragraph 3 of this Article shall enter into force between Contracting Parties having accepted such amendments on the 30th day following the receipt by the Depositary of notification of their acceptance by at least three-fourths of the Contracting Parties to this Convention or to the Protocol concerned, as the case may be.

5. After the entry into force of an amendment to this Convention or to a Protocol, any new Contracting Party to this Convention or such Protocol shall become a Contracting Party to the instrument as amended.

Article 17

ANNEXES AND AMENDMENTS TO ANNEXES

1. Annexes to this Convention or to any Protocol shall form an integral part of the Convention or such Protocol, as the case may be.

2. Except as may be otherwise provided in any Protocol, the following procedure shall apply to the adoption and entry into force of any amendments to Annexes to this Convention or to any Protocol, with the exception of amendments to the Annex on Arbitration:

(i) any Contracting Party may propose amendments to the Annexes to this Convention or to any Protocols and the meetings referred to in Article 14;

(ii) such amendments shall be adopted by a three-fourths majority vote of the Contracting Parties to the instrument in question;

(iii) the Depositary shall without delay communicate the amendments so adopted to all Contracting Parties;

(iv) any Contracting Party that is unable to approve an amendment to the Annexes to this Convention or to any Protocol shall so notify in writing the Depositary within a period determined by the Contracting Parties concerned when adopting the amendment;

(v) the Depositary shall without delay notify all Contracting Parties of any notification received pursuant to the proceeding subparagraph;

(vi) on expiry of the period referred to in subparagraph (iv) above, the amendment to the Annex shall become effective for all Contracting Parties to this Convention or to the Protocol concerned which have not submitted a notification in accordance with the provisions of that subparagraph.

3. The adoption and entry into force of a new Annex to this Convention or to any Protocol shall be subject to the same procedure as for the adoption and entry into force of an amendment to an Annex in accordance with the provisions of paragraph 2 of this Article, provided that, if any amendment to the Convention or the Protocol concerned is involved, the new Annex shall not enter into force until such time as the amendment to the Convention or the Protocol concerned enters into force.

4. Amendments to the Annex on Arbritation shall be considered to be amendments to this Convention and shall be proposed and adopted in accordance with the procedures set out in Article 16 above.

Article 18

RULES OF PROCEDURE AND FINANCIAL RULES

1. The Contracting Parties shall adopt rules of procedure for their meetings and conferences envisaged in Articles 14, 15 and 16 above.

2. The Contracting Parties shall adopt financial rules, prepared in consultation with the Organization, to determine, in particular, their financial participation.

Article 19

SPECIAL EXERCISE OF VOTING RIGHT

Within the areas of their competence, the European Economic Community and any regional economic grouping referred to in Article 24 of this Convention shall exercise their right to vote with a number of votes equal to the number of their Member States which are Contracting Parties to this Convention and to one or more Protocols; the European Economic Community and any grouping as referred to above shall not exercise their right to vote in cases where the Member States concerned exercise theirs, and conversely.

Article 20

REPORTS

The Contracting Parties shall transmit to the Organization reports on the measures adopted in the implementation of this Convention and of Protocols to which they are Parties, in such form and at such intervals as the meetings of Contracting Parties may determine.

Article 21

COMPLIANCE CONTROL

The Contracting Parties undertake to co-operate in the developing of procedures enabling them to control the application of this Convention and the Protocols.

Article 22

SETTLEMENT OF DISPUTES

1. In case of a dispute between Contracting Parties as to the interpretation or application of this Convention or the Protocols, they shall seek a settlement of the dispute through negotiation or any other peaceful means of their own choice.

2. If the Parties concerned cannot settle their

dispute through the means mentioned in the preceding paragraph, the dispute shall upon common agreement be submitted to arbitration under the conditions laid down in Annex A to this Convention.

3. Nevertheless, the Contracting Parties may at any time declare that they recognize as compulsory *ipso facto* and without special agreement, in relation to any other Party accepting the same obligation, the application of the arbitration procedure in conformity with the provisions of Annex A. Such declaration shall be notified in writing to the Depositary, who shall communicate it to the other Parties.

Article 23

RELATIONSHIP BETWEEN THE CONVENTION AND PROTOCOLS

1. No one may become a Contracting Party to this Convention unless it becomes at the same time a Contracting Party to at least one of the Protocols. No one may become a Contracting Party to a Protocol unless it is, or becomes at the same time, a Contracting Party to this Convention.

2. Any Protocol to this Convention shall be binding only on the Contracting Parties to the Protocol in question.

3. Decisions concerning any Protocol pursuant to Articles 14, 16 and 17 of this Convention shall be taken only by the Parties to the Protocol concerned.

Article 24

SIGNATURE

This Convention, the Protocol for the prevention of pollution of the Mediterranean Sea by dumping from ships and aircraft and the Protocol concerning co-operation in combating pollution of the Mediterranean Sea by oil and other harmful substances in cases of emergency shall be open for signature in Barcelona on 16 February 1976 and in Madrid from 17 February 1976 to 16 February 1977 by any State invited as a participant in the Conference of Plenipotentiaries of the Coastal States of the Mediterranean Region on the Protection of the Mediterranean Sea, held in Barcelona from 2 to 16 February 1976, and by any State entitled to sign any Protocol. They shall also be open until the same date for signature by the European Economic Community and by any similar regional economic grouping at least one member of which is a coastal State of the Mediterranean Sea area and which exercise competences in fields covered by this Convention, as well as by any Protocol affecting them.

Article 25

RATIFICATION, ACCEPTANCE OR APPROVAL

This Convention and any Protocol thereto shall be subject to ratification, acceptance, or approval. Instruments of ratification, acceptance or approval shall be deposited with the Government of Spain, which will assume the functions of Depositary.

Article 26

ACCESSION

1. As from 17 February 1977, the present Convention, the Protocol for the prevention of pollution of the Mediterranean Sea by dumping from ships and aircraft, and the Protocol concerning co-operation in combating pollution of the Mediterranean Sea by oil and other harmful substances in cases of emergency shall be open for accession by the States, by the European Economic Community and by any grouping as referred to in Article 24.

2. After the entry into force of the Convention and of any Protocol, any State not referred to in Article 24 may accede to this Convention and to any Protocol, subject to prior approval by three-fourths of the Contracting Parties to the Protocol concerned.

3. Instruments of accession shall be deposited with the Depositary.

Article 27

ENTRY INTO FORCE

1. The Convention shall enter into force on the same date as the Protocol first entering into force.

2. The Convention shall also enter into force with regard to the States, the European Economic Community and any regional economic grouping referred to in Article 24 if they have complied with the formal requirements for becoming Contracting Parties to any other Protocol not yet entered into force.

3. Any Protocol to this Convention, except as otherwise provided in such Protocol, shall enter into force on the 30th day following the date of deposit of at least six instruments of ratification, acceptance, or approval of, or accession to such Protocol by the Parties referred to in Article 24.

4. Thereafter, this Convention and any Protocol shall enter into force with respect to any State, the European Economic Community and any regional economic grouping referred to in Article 24 on the 30th day following the date of deposit of the instruments of ratification, acceptance, approval or accession.

Article 28

WITHDRAWAL

1. At any time after three years from the date of entry into force of this Convention, any Contracting Party may withdraw from this Convention by giving written notification of withdrawal.

2. Except as may be otherwise provided in any Protocol to this Convention, any Contracting Party may, at any time after three years from the date of entry into force of such Protocol, withdraw from such Protocol by giving written notification of withdrawal.

3. Withdrawal shall take effect 90 days after the date on which notification of withdrawal is received by the Depositary.

4. Any Contracting Party which withdraws from

this Convention shall be considered as also having withdrawn from any Protocol to which it was a Party.

5. Any Contracting Party which, upon its withdrawal from a Protocol, is no longer a Party to any Protocol to this Convention, shall be considered as also having withdrawn from this Convention.

Article 29

RESPONSIBILITIES OF THE DEPOSITARY

1. The Depositary shall inform the Contracting Parties, any other Party referred to in Article 24, and the Organization:

(i) of the signature of this Convention and of any Protocol thereto, and of the deposit of instruments of ratification, acceptance, approval or accession in accordance with Articles 24, 25 and 26;

(ii) of the date on which the Convention and any Protocol will come into force in accordance with the provisions of Article 27;

(iii) of notifications of withdrawal made in accordance with Article 28;

(iv) of the amendments adopted with respect to the Convention and to any Protocol, their acceptance by the Contracting Parties and the date of entry into force of those amendments in accordance with the provisions of Article 16;

(v) of the adoption of new Annexes and of the amendment of any Annex in accordance with Article 17;

(vi) of declarations recognizing as compulsory the application of the arbitration procedure mentioned in paragraph 3 of Article 22.

2. The original of this Convention and of any Protocol thereto shall be deposited with the Depositary, the Government of Spain, which shall send certified copies thereof to the Contracting Parties, to the Organization, and to the Secretary-General of the United Nations for registration and publication in accordance with Article 102 of the United Nations Charter.

In witness whereof the undersigned, being duly authorized by their respective Governments, have signed this Convention.

Done at Barcelona on 16 February 1976 in a single copy in the Arabic, English, French and Spanish languages, the four texts being equally authoritative.

ANNEX A

ARBITRATION

Article 1

Unless the Parties to the dispute otherwise agree, the arbitration procedures shall be conducted in accordance with the provisions of this Annex.

Article 2

1. At the request addressed by one Contracting Party to another Contracting Party in accordance with the provisions of paragraph 2 or paragraph 3 of Article 22 of the Convention, an arbitral tribunal shall be constituted. The request for arbitration shall state the subject matter of the application including, in particular, the articles of the Convention or the Protocols, the interpretation or application of which is in dispute.

2. The claimant party shall inform the Organization that it has requested the setting up of an arbitral tribunal, stating the name of the other Party to the dispute and articles of the Convention or the Protocols the interpretation or application of which is in its opinion in dispute. The Organization shall forward the information thus received to all Contracting Parties to the Convention.

Article 3

The arbitral tribunal shall consist of three members: each of the Parties to the dispute shall appoint an arbitrator; the two arbitrators so appointed shall designate by common agreement the third arbitrator who shall be the chairman of the tribunal. The latter shall not be a national of one of the Parties to the dispute, nor have his usual place of residence in the territory of one of these Parties, nor be employed by any of them, nor have dealt with the case in any other capacity.

Article 4

1. If the chairman of the arbitral tribunal has not been designated within two months of the appointment of the second arbitrator, the Secretary-General of the United Nations shall, at the request ot the most diligent Party, designate him within a further two months' period.

2. If one of the Parties to the disputes does not appoint an arbitrator within two months of receipt of the request, the other Party may inform the Secretary-General of the United Nations who shall designate the chairman of the arbitral tribunal within a further two months' period. Upon designation, the chairman of the arbitral tribunal shall request the Party which has not appointed an arbitrator to do so within two months. After such period, he shall inform the Secretary-General of the United Nations, who shall make this appointment within a further two months's period.

Article 5

1. The arbitral tribunal shall decide according to the rules of international law and, in particular, those of this Convention and the Protocols concerned.

2. Any arbitral tribunal constituted under the provisions of this Annex shall draw up its own rules of procedure.

Article 6

1. The decisions of the arbitral tribunal, both on procedure and on substance, shall be taken by majority vote of its members.

2. The tribunal may take all appropriate measures in order to establish the facts. It may, at the request of one of the Parties, recommend essential interim measures of protection.

3. If two or more arbitral tribunal constituted under the provisions of this Annex are seized of requests with identical or similar subjects, they may inform themselves of the procedures for establishing the facts and take them into account as far as possible.

4. The Parties to the dispute shall provide all facilities necessary for the effective conduct of the proceedings.

5. The absence or default of a Party to the dispute shall not constitute an impediment of the proceedings.

Article 7

1. The award of the arbitral tribunal shall be accompanied by a statement of reasons. It shall be final and binding upon the Parties to the dispute.

2. Any dispute which may arise between the Parties concerning the interpretation or execution of the award may be submitted by the most diligent Party to the arbitral tribunal which made the award or, if the latter cannot be seized thereof, to another arbitral tribunal constituted for this purpose in the same manner as the first.

Article 8

The European Economic Community and any regional economic grouping referred to in Article 24 of the Convention, like any Contracting Party to the Convention, are empowered to appear as complainants or as respondents before the arbitral tribunal.

PROTOCOL FOR THE PREVENTION OF POLLUTION OF THE MEDITERRANEAN SEA BY DUMPING FROM SHIPS AND AIRCRAFT

Barcelona, 16 February 1976

THE CONTRACTING PARTIES TO THE PRESENT PROTOCOL

Being Parties to the Convention for the protection of the Mediterranean Sea against pollution,

Recognizing the danger posed to the marine environment by pollution caused by the dumping or wastes or other matter from ships and aircraft,

Considering that the coastal States of the Mediterranean Sea have a common interest in protecting the marine environment from this danger,

Bearing in mind the Convention on the prevention of marine pollution by dumping of wastes and other matter, adopted in London in 1972,

Have agreed as follows:

Article 1

The Contracting Parties to this Protocol (hereinafter referred to as 'the Parties') shall take all appropriate measures to prevent and abate pollution of the Mediterranean Sea area caused by dumping from ships and aircraft.

Article 2

The area to which this Protocol applies shall be the Mediterranean Sea area as defined in Article 1 of the Convention for the Protection of the Mediterranean Sea against Pollution (hereinafter referred to as 'the Convention').

Article 3

For the purposes of this Protocol:

1. 'ships and aircraft' means waterborne or airborne craft of any type whatsoever. This expression includes air-cushioned craft and floating craft, whether self-propelled or not, and platforms and other man-made structures at sea and their equipment.

2. 'Wastes or other matter' means material and substances of any kind, form or description.

3. 'Dumping' means:

(*a*) any deliberate disposal at sea of wastes or other matter from ships or aircraft;

(*b*) any deliberate disposal at sea of ships or aircraft.

4. 'Dumping' does not include:

(*a*) the disposal at sea of wastes or other matter incidental to, or derived from, the normal operations of vessels, or aircraft and their equipment, other than wastes or other matter transported by or to vessels or aircraft, operating for the purpose of disposal of such matter, or derived from the treatment of such wastes or other matter on such vessels or aircraft;

(*b*) placement of matter for a purpose other than the mere disposal thereof, provided that such placement is not contrary to the aims of this Protocol.

5. 'Organization' means the body referred to in Article 13 of the Convention.

Article 4

The dumping into the Mediterranean Sea area of wastes or other matter listed in Annex 1 to this Protocol is prohibited.

Article 5

The dumping into the Mediterranean Sea area of all wastes or other matter listed in Annex II to this Protocol requires, in each case, a prior special permit from the competent national authorities.

Article 6

The dumping into the Mediterranean Sea of all other wastes or other matter requires a prior general permit from the competent national authorities.

Article 7

The permits referred to in Articles 5 and 6 above

shall be issued only after careful consideration of all the factors set forth in Annex III to this Protocol. The Organization shall receive records of such permits.

Article 8

The provisions of Articles 4, 5 and 6 shall not apply in case of *force majeure* due to stress of weather or any other cause when human life or the safety of a ship or aircraft is threatened. Such dumpings shall immediately be reported to the Organization and either through the Organization or directly, to any Party or Parties likely to be affected, together with full details of the circumstances and of the nature and quantities of the wastes or other matter dumped.

Article 9

If a Party in a critical situation of an exceptional nature considers that wastes or other matter listed in Annex I to this Protocol cannot be disposed of on land without unacceptable danger or damage, above all for the safety of human life, the Party concerned shall forthwith consult the Organization. The Organization, after consulting the Parties to this Protocol, shall recommend methods of storage or the most satisfactory means of destruction or disposal under the prevailing circumstances. The Party shall inform the Organization of the steps adopted in pursuance of these recommendations. The Parties pledge themselves to assist one another in such situations.

Article 10

1. Each Party shall designate one or more competent authorities to:

(*a*) issue the special permits provided for in Article 5;

(*b*) issue the general permits provided for in Article 6;

(*c*) keep records of the nature and quantities of the wastes or other matter permitted to be dumped and of the location, date and method of dumping.

2. The competent authorities of each Party shall issue the permits provided for in Articles 5 and 6 in respect of the wastes or other matter intended for dumping:

(*a*) loaded in its territory;

(*b*) loaded by a ship or aircraft registered in its territory or flying its flag, when the loading occurs in the territory of a State not Party to this Protocol.

Article 11

1. Each Party shall apply the measures required to implement this Protocol to all:

(*a*) ships and aircraft registered in its territory or flying its flag;

(*b*) ships and aircraft loading in its territory wastes or other matter which are to be dumped;

(*c*) ships and aircraft believed to be engaged in dumping in areas under its jurisdiction in this matter.

2. This Protocol shall not apply to any ships or aircraft owned or operated by a State Party to this Protocol and used for the time being only on Government noncommercial service. However, each Party shall ensure by the adoption of appropriate measures not impairing the operations or operational capabilities of such ships or aircraft owned or operated by it, that such ships and aircraft act in a manner consistent, so far as is reasonable and practicable, with this Protocol.

Article 12

Each Party undertakes to issue instructions to its maritime inspection ships and aircraft and to other appropriate services to report to its authorities any incidents or conditions in the Mediterranean Sea area which give rise to suspicions that dumping in contravention of the provisions of this Protocol has occurred or is about to occur. That Party shall, if it considers it appropriate, report accordingly to any other Party concerned.

Article 13

Nothing in this Protocol shall affect the right of each Party to adopt other measures, in accordance with international law, to prevent pollution due to dumping.

Article 14

1. Ordinary meetings of the Parties to this Protocol shall be held in conjunction with ordinary meetings of the Contracting Parties to the Convention held pursuant to Article 14 of the Convention. The Parties to this Protocol may also hold extraordinary meetings in conformity with Article 14 of the Convention.

2. It shall be the function of the meetings of the Parties to this Protocol:

(*a*) to keep under review the implementation of this Protocol, and to consider the efficacy of the measures adopted and the need for any other measures, in particular in the form of Annexes:

(*b*) to study and consider the records of the permits issued in accordance with Articles 5, 6 and 7 and of the dumping which has taken place.

c) to review and amend as required any Annex to this Protocol;

(*d*) to discharge such other functions as may be appropriate for the implementation of this Protocol.

3. The adoption of amendments to the Annexes to this Protocol pursuant to Article 17 of the Convention shall require a three-fourths majority vote of the Parties.

Article 15

1. The provisions of the Convention relating to any Protocol shall apply with respect to the present Protocol.

2. The rules of procedure and the financial rules adopted pursuant to Article 18 of the Convention shall apply with respect to this Protocol, unless the Parties to this Protocol agree otherwise.

In witness whereof the undersigned, being duly authorized by their respective Governments, have signed this Protocol.

Done at Barcelona on 16 February 1976 in a single copy in the Arabic, English, French and Spanish languages, the four texts being equally authoritative.

ANNEX 1

A. The following substances and materials are listed for the purpose of Article 4 of the Protocol.

1. Organohalogen compounds and compounds which may form such substances in the marine environment, excluding those which are non-toxic or which are rapidly converted in the sea into substances which are biologically harmless, provided that they do not make edible marine organisms unpalatable.

2. Organosilicon compounds and compounds which may form such substances in the marine environment, excluding those which are non-toxic or which are rapidly converted in the sea into substances which are biologically harmless, provided that they do not make edible marine organisms unpalatable.

3. Mercury and mercury compounds.

4. Cadmium and cadmium compounds.

5. Persistent plastic and other persistent synthetic materials which may materially interfere with fishing or navigation, reduce amenities, or interfere with other legitimate uses of the sea.

6. Crude oil and hydrocarbons which may be derived from petroleum, and any mixtures containing any of these, taken on board for the purpose of dumping.

7. High-, medium- and low-level radioactive wastes or other high-, medium- and low-level radioactive matter to be defined by the International Atomic Energy Agency.

8. Acid and alkaline compounds of such composition and in such quantity that they may seriously impair the quality of sea water. The composition and quantity to be taken into consideration shall be determined by the Parties in accordance with the procedure laid down in Article 14 (3) of this Protocol.

9. Materials in whatever form (e.g. solids, liquids, semi-liquids, gases, or in a living state) produced for biological and chemical warfare, other than those rapidly rendered harmless by physical, chemical or biological processes in the sea, provided that they do not:

(i) make edible marine organisms unpalatable; or

(ii) endanger human or animal health.

B. This Annex does not apply to wastes or other materials, such as sewage sludge and dredge spoils, containing the substances referred to in paragraphs 1 to 6 above as trace contaminants. The dumping of such wastes shall be subject to the provisions of Annexes II and III as appropriate.

ANNEX II

The following wastes and other matter, the dumping of which requires special care, are listed for the purposes of Article 5.

1. (i) arsenic, lead, copper, zinc, beryllium, chromium, nickel, vanadium, selenium, antimony and their compounds;

(ii) cyanides and fluorides;

(iii) pesticides and their by-products not covered in Annex I;

(iv) synthetic organic chemicals, other than those referred to in Annex I, likely to produce harmful effects on marine organisms or to make edible marine organisms unpalatable;

2. (i) acid and alkaline compounds the composition and quantity of which have not yet been determined in accordance with the procedure referred to in Annex I A (8):

(ii) acid and alkaline compounds not covered by Annex I, excluding compounds to be dumped in quantities below thresholds which shall be determined by the Parties in accordance with the procedure laid down in Article 14 (3) of this Protocol.

3. Containers, scrap metal and other bulky wastes liable to sink to the sea bottom which may present a serious obstacle to fishing or navigation.

4. Substances which, though of a non-toxic nature may become harmful owing to the quantities in which they are dumped, or which are liable to reduce amenities seriously or to endanger human life or marine organisms or to interfere with navigation.

5. Radioactive waste or other radioactive matter which will not be included in Annex I. In the issue of permits for the dumping of this matter, the Parties should take full account of the recommendations of the competent international body in this field, at present the International Atomic Energy Agency.

ANNEX III

The factors to be considered in establishing criteria governing the issue of permits for the dumping of matter at sea taking into account Article 7 include:

A. Characteristics and composition of the matter

1. Total amount and average compositions of matter dumped (e.g. per year).

2. Form (e.g. solid, liquid or gaseous).

3. Properties: physical (e.g solubility and density), chemical and biochemical (e.g. oxygen demand, nutrients) and biological.(e.g. presence of viruses, bacteria, yeasts, parasites).

4. Toxicity.

5. Persistence: physical, chemical and biological.

6. Accumulation and biotransformation in biological materials or sediments.

7. Susceptibility to physical, chemical and biochemical changes and interaction in the aquatic environment with other dissolved organic and inorganic materials.

8. Probability of production of taints or other changes reducing marketability of resources (fish, shellfish, etc.).

B. Characteristics of dumping site and method of deposit

1. Location (e.g. coordinates of the dumping area, depth and distance from the coast), location in relation to other areas (e.g. amenity areas, spawning, nursery and fishing areas and exploitable resources).

2. Rate of disposal per specific period (e.g. quantity per day, per week, per month).

3. Methods of packaging and containment, if any.

4. Initial dilution achieved by proposed method of release, particularly the speed of the ship.

5. Dispersal characteristics (e.g. effects of currents, tides and wind on horizontal transport and vertical mixing).

6. Water characteristics (e.g. temperature, pH, salinity, stratification, oxygen indices of pollution — dissolved oxygen (DO), chemical oxygen demand (COD), biochemical oxygen demand (BOD), nitrogen present in organic and mineral form, including ammonia, suspended matter, other nutrients and productivity).

7. Bottom characteristics (e.g. topography, geochemical and geological characteristics and biological productivity).

8. Existence and effects of other dumpings which have been made in the dumping area (e.g. heavy metal background reading and organic carbon content).

9. When issuing a permit for dumping, the Contracting Parties shall endeavour to determine whether an adequate scientific basis exists for assessing the consequences of such dumping in the area concerned, in accordance with the foregoing provisions and taking into account seasonal variations.

C. General considerations and conditions

1. Possible effects on amenities (e.g. presence of floating or stranded material, turbidity, objectionable odour, discoloration and foaming).

2. Possible effects on marine life, fish and shellfish culture, fish stocks and fisheries, seaweed harvesting and culture.

3. Possible effects on other uses of the sea (e.g. impairment of water quality for industrial use, underwater corrosion, of structures, interference with ship operations from floating materials, interference with fishing or navigation through deposit of waste or solid objects on the sea floor and protection of areas of special importance for scientific or conservation purposes).

4. The practical availability of alternative land-based methods of treatment, disposal or elimination or of treatment to render the matter less harmful for sea dumping.

PROTOCOL CONCERNING CO-OPERATION IN COMBATING POLLUTION OF THE MEDITERRANEAN SEA BY OIL AND OTHER HARMFUL SUBSTANCES IN CASES OF EMERGENCY

Barcelona, 2 February 1976

THE CONTRACTING PARTIES TO THE PRESENT PROTOCOL,

Being Parties to the Convention for the Protection of the Mediterranean Sea against Pollution,

Recognizing that grave pollution of the sea by oil and other harmful substances in the Mediterranean Sea Area involves a danger for the coastal States and the marine eco-system,

Considering that the co-operation of all the coastal States of the Mediterranean is called for to combat this pollution,

Bearing in mind the International Convention for the Prevention of Pollution from Ships, 1973, the International Convention relating to Intervention on the High Seas in Cases of Oil Pollution Casualties, 1969, as well as the Protocol relating to Intervention on the High Seas in Cases of Marine Pollution by Substances Other than Oil, 1973,

Further taking into account the International Convention on Civil Liability for Oil Pollution Damage, 1969 —

Have agreed as follows:

Article 1

The Contracting Parties to this Protocol (hereinafter referred to as "the Parties") shall co-operate in taking the necessary measures in cases of grave and imminent danger to the marine environment, the coast or related interests of one or more of the Parties due to the presence of massive quantities of oil or other harmful substances resulting from accidental causes or an accumulation of small discharges which are polluting or threatening to pollute the sea within the area defined in Article 1 of the Convention for the Protection of the Mediterranean Sea against Pollution, (hereinafter referred to as "the Convention").

Article 2

For the purpose of this Protocol, the term "related interests" means the interests of a costal State directly affected or threatened and concerning, among others:

(*a*) activities in coastal waters, in ports or estuaries, including fishing activities;

(*b*) the historical and tourist appeal to the area in question, including water sports and recreation;

(*c*) the health of the coastal population;

(*d*) the preservation of living resources.

Article 3

The Parties shall endeavour to maintain and promote, either individually or through bilateral or multilateral co-operation, their contingency plans and means for combating pollution of the sea by oil and other harmful substances. These means shall include, in particular, equipment, ships, aircraft and manpower prepared for operations in cases of emergency.

Article 4

The Parties shall develop and apply, either individually or through bilateral or multilateral co-operation, monitoring activities covering the Mediterranean Sea Area in order to have as precise information as possible on the situations referred to in article 1 of this Protocol.

Article 5

In case of release or loss overboard of harmful substances in packages, freight containers, portable tanks or road and rail tank wagons, the Parties shall co-operate as far as practicable in the salvage and recovery of such substances so as to reduce the danger of pollution of the marine environment.

Article 6

1. Each Party undertakes to disseminate to the other Parties information concerning:

(*a*) The competent national organization or authorities responsible for combating pollution of the sea by oil and other harmful substances;

(*b*) The competent national authorities responsible for receiving reports of pollution of the sea by oil and other harmful substances and for dealing with matters concerning measures of assistance between Parties;

(*c*) New ways in which pollution of the sea by oil and other harmful substances may be avoided, new measures of combating pollution and the development of related research programmes.

2. Parties which have agreed to exchange information directly between themselves shall nevertheless communicate such information to the regional centre. The latter shall communicate this information to the other Parties and, on a basis of reciprocity, to coastal States of the Mediterranean Sea Area which are not Parties to this Protocol.

Article 7

The Parties undertake to co-ordinate the utilization of the means of communication at their disposal in order to ensure, with the necessary speed and reliability, the reception, transmission and dissemination of all reports and urgent information which relate to the occurrences and situations referred to in article I. The regional centre shall have the necessary means of communication to enable it to participate in this co-ordinated effort and, in particular, to fulfill the functions assigned to it by paragraph 2 of article 10.

Article 8

1. Each Party shall issue instructions to the masters of ships flying its flag and to the pilots of aircraft registered in its territory requiring them to report by the most rapid and adequate channels in the circumstances, and in accordance with Annex I to this Protocol, either to a Party or to the regional centre:

(*a*) All accidents causing or likely to cause pollution of the sea by oil or other harmful substances;

(*b*) The presence, characteristics and extent of spillages, of oil or other harmful substances observed at sea which are likely to present a serious and imminent threat to the marine environment or to the coast or related interests of one or more of the Parties.

2. The information collected in accordance with paragraph 1 shall be communicated to the other Parties likely to be affected by the pollution;

a) by the Party which has received the information, either directly or preferably, through the regional centre; or

(*b*) by the regional centre.

In case of direct communication between Parties, the regional centre shall be informed of the measures.

3. In consequence of the application of the provisions of paragraph 2, the Parties are not bound by the obligation laid down in article 9, paragraph 2, of the Convention.

Article 9

1. Any Party faced with a situation of the kind defined in article 1 of this Protocol shall:

(*a*) Make the necessary assessments of the nature and extent of the casualty or emergency or, as the case may be, of the type and approximate quantity of oil or other harmful substances and the direction and speed of drift of the spillage;

(*b*) Take every practicable measure to avoid or reduce the effects of pollution:

(*c*) Immediately inform all other Parties, either directly or through the regional centre, of these assessments and of any action which it has taken or which it intends to take to combat the pollution;

(*d*) Continue to observe the situation for as long as possible and report thereon in accordance with article 8.

2. Where action is taken to combat pollution originating from a ship, all possible measures shall be taken to safeguard the persons present on board and, to the extent possible, the ship itself. Any Party which takes such action shall inform the Inter-Governmental Maritime Consultative Organization.

Article 10

1. Any Party requiring assistance for combating pollution by oil or other harmful substances polluting or threatening to pollute its coasts may call for assistance from other Parties, either directly or through the regional centre referred to in article 6, starting with the Parties which appear likely to be affected by the pollution. This assistance may comprise, in particular, expert advice and the supply to or placing at the disposal of the Party concerned of products, equipment and

national facilities. Parties so requested shall use their best endeavours to render this assistance.

2. Where the Parties engaged in an operation to combat pollution cannot agree on the organization of the operation, the regional centre may, with their approval, co-ordinate the activity of the facilities put into operation by these Parties.

Article 11

The application of the relevant provisions of articles 6, 7, 8, 9 and 10 of this Protocol relating to the regional centre shall be extended, as appropriate, to sub-regional centres in the event of their establishment, taking into account their objectives and functions and their relationship with the said regional centre.

Article 12

1. Ordinary meetings of the Parties to this Protocol shall be held in conjunction with ordinary meetings of the Contracting Parties to the Convention, held pursuant to article 14 of the Convention. The Parties to this Protocol may also hold extra-ordinary meetings as provided in article 14 of the Convention.

2. It shall be the function of the meetings of the Parties to this Protocol, in particular:

(*a*) To keep under review the implementation of this Protocol, and to consider the efficacy of the measures adopted and the need for any other measures, in particular in the form of Annexes,

(*b*) To review and amend as required any Annex to this Protocol;

(*c*) To discharge such other functions as may be appropriate for implementation of this Protocol.

Article 13

1. The provisions of the Convention relating to any Protocol shall apply with respect to the present Protocol.

2. The rules of procedure and the financial rules adopted pursuant to article 18 of the Convention shall apply with respect to this Protocol, unless the Parties to this Protocol agree otherwise.

In witness whereof the undersigned, being duly authorized by their respective Governments, have signed this Protocol.

Done at Barcelona on 16 February 1976 in a single copy in the Arabic, English, French and Spanish languages, the four texts being equally authoritative.

ANNEX I

CONTENTS OF THE REPORT TO BE MADE PURSUANT TO ARTICLE 8 TO THIS PROTOCOL

1. Each report shall, as far as possible, contain, in general:

(*a*) The identification of the source of pollution (identity of the ship, where appropriate);

(*b*) The geographic position, time and date of the occurrence of the incident or of the observation;

(*c*) The wind and sea conditions prevailing in the area;

(*d*) Where the pollution originates from a ship, relevant details respecting the conditions of the ship.

2. Each report shall contain, whenever possible, in particular:

(*a*) A clear indication or description of the harmful substances involved, including the correct technical names of such substances (trade names should not be used in place of the correct technical names);

(*b*) A statement or estimate of the quantities, concentrations and likely conditions of harmful substances discharged or likely to be discharged into the sea;

(c) Where relevant, a description of the packaging and identifying marks; and

(*d*) The name of the consignor, consignee or manufacturer.

3. Each report shall clearly indicate whenever possible, whether the harmful substance discharged or likely to be discharged is oil or a noxious liquid, solid or gaseous substance and whether such substance was or is carried in bulk or contained in packaged form, freight containers, portable tanks, or road and a rail tank wagons.

4. Each report shall be supplemented as necessary by any relevant information requested by a recipient of the report or deemed appropriate by the person sending the report.

5. Any of the persons referred to in article 8, paragraph 1, of this Protocol shall:

(*a*) Supplement as far as possible the initial report, as necessary, with information concerning further developments; and

(*b*) Comply as fully as possible with requests from affected States for additional information.

CONVENTION ON CONSERVATION OF NORTH PACIFIC FUR SEALS [67]

Washington, 7 May 1976

The Governments of Canada, Japan, the Union of Soviet Socialist Republics, and the United States of America,

Desiring to take effective measures towards achieving the maximum sustainable productivity of the fur seal resources of the North Pacific Ocean so that the fur seal populations can be brought to and maintained at the levels which will provide the greatest harvest year after year, with due regard to their relation to the productivity of other living marine resources of the area,

Recognizing that in order to determine such measures it is necessary to conduct adequate scientific research on the said resources, and

Desiring to provide for international cooperation in achieving these objectives,

Agree as follows:

Article I

1. The term "pelagic sealing" is hereby defined for the purposes of this Convention as meaning the killing, taking, or hunting in any manner whatsoever of fur seals at sea.

2. The words "each year", "annual" and "annually" as used hereinafter refer to Convention year, that is, the year beginning on the date of entry into force of the Convention.

3. Nothing in this Convention shall be deemed to affect in any way the position of the Parties in regard to the limits of territorial waters or to the jurisdiction over fisheries.

Article II

1. In order to realize the objectives of this Convention, the Parties agree to co-ordinate necessary scientific research programs and to co-operate in investigating the fur seal resources of North Pacific Ocean to determine:

a) what measures may be necessary to make possible the maximum substainable productivity of the fur seal resources so that the fur seal populations can be brought to and maintained at the levels which will provide the greatest harvest year after year; and

b) what the relationship is between fur seals and other living marine resources and whether fur seals have detrimental effects on other living marine resources substantially exploited by any of the Parties and, if so, to what extent.

2. The research referred to in the preceding paragraph shall include studies of the following subjects:

a) size of each fur seal herd and its age and sex composition;

b) natural mortality of the different age groups and recruitment of young to each age or size class at present and subsequent population levels;

c) with regard to each of the herds, the effect upon the magnitude of recruitment of variations in the size and the age and sex composition of the annual kill;

d) migration routes of fur seals and their wintering areas;

e) numbers of seals from each herd found on the migration routes and in wintering areas and their ages and sexes;

f) relationship between fur seals and other living marine resources, including the extent to which fur seals affect commercial fish catches, the damage fur seals inflict on fishing gear, and the effect of commercial fisheries on the fur seals;

g) effectiveness of each method of sealing from the viewpoint of management and rational utilization of fur seal resources for conservation purposes;

h) quality of sealskins by sex, age, and time and method of sealing;

i) effect of man-caused environmental changes on the fur seal populations; and

j) other subjects involved in achieving the objectives of the Convention, as determined by the Commission established under Article V, paragraph 1.

3. In furtherance of the research referred to in this Article, the Parties agree:

a) to continue to mark adequate numbers of pups;

b) to devote to pelagic research an effort which, to the greatest extent possible, should be similar in extent to that expended in recent years, provided that this shall not involve the annual taking by all the Parties combined of more than 2,500 seals in the Eastern and more than 2,200 seals in the Western Pacific Oceans, unless the Commission, pursuant to Article V, paragraph 3, shall decide otherwise, and

c) to carry out the determinations made by the Commission pursuant to Article V, paragraph 3.

4. Each Party agrees to provide the Commission annually with information on:

a) number of black pups tagged for each breeding area;

b) number of fur seals, by sex and estimated age, taken at sea and on each breeding area; and

c) tagged seals recovered on land and at sea;

and, so far as is practicable, other information pertinent to scientific research which the Commission may request.

5. The Parties further agree to provide for the exchange of scientific personnel; each such exchange shall be subject to mutual consent of the Parties directly concerned.

1. The Interim Convention adopted at Washington on February 9, 1957, has been amended by a Protocol adopted at Washington on October 8, 1963, by exchanges of notes which entered into force on September 3, 1969, and by a second Protocol adopted at Washington on May 7, 1976.

6. The Parties agree to use for the scientific pelagic research provided for in this Article only government-owned or government-chartered vessels operating under strict control of their respective authorities. Each Party shall communicate to the other Parties the names and descriptions of vessels which are to be used for pelagic research.

Article III

In order to realize the purposes of the Convention, including the carrying out of the co-ordinated and co-operative research, each Party agrees to prohibit pelagic sealing, except as provided in Article II, paragraph 3 in the Pacific Ocean north of the 30th parallel of north latitude including the seas of Bering, Okhotsk, and Japan by any person or vessel subject to its jurisdiction.

Article IV

Each Party shall bear the expense of its own research. Title to seal-skins taken during the research shall vest in the Party conducting such research.

Article V

1. The Parties agree to establish the North Pacific Fur Seal Commission to be composed of one member from each Party.

2. The duties of the Commission shall be to:

a) formulate and co-ordinate research programs designed to achieve the objectives set forth in Article II, paragraph 1;

b) recommend these co-ordinated research programs to the respective Parties for implementation;

c) study the data obtained from the implementation of such co-ordinated research programs;

d) recommend appropriate measures to the Parties on the basis of the findings obtained from the implementation of such coordinated research programmes, including measures regarding the size and the sex and age composition of the seasonal commercial kill from a herd and regarding a reduction or suspension of the harvest of seals on any island or group of islands in case the total number of seals on that island or group of islands falls below the level of maximum sustainable productivity; provided, however, that due consideration be given to the subsistence needs of Indians, Ainos, Aleuts, or Eskimos who live on the islands where fur seals breed, when it is not possible to provide sufficient seal mat for such persons from the seasonal commercial harvest or research activities; and

e) study whether or not pelagic sealing in conjunction with land sealing could be permitted in certain circumstances without adversely affecting achievement of the objectives of this Convention, and make recommendations thereon to the Parties at the end of the twenty-first year after entry into force of the Convention.

3. In addition to the duties specified in paragraph 2 of this Article, the Commission shall, subject to Article II, paragraph 3, determine from time to time the number of seals to be marked on the rookery islands, and the total number of seals which shall be taken at sea for research purposes, the times at which such seals shall be taken and the areas in which they shall be taken, as well as the number to be taken by each Party, taking into account any recommendations made pursuant to Article V, paragraph 2(d).

4. Each Party shall have one vote. Decisions and recommendations shall be made by unanimous vote. With respect to any recommendations regarding the size and the sex and age composition of the seasonal commercial kill from a herd, only those Parties sharing in the seal-skins from that herd under the provisions of Article IX, paragraph 1 shall vote.

5. The Commission shall elect from its members a Chairman and other necessary officials and shall adopt rules of procedure for the conduct of its work.

6. The Commission shall hold an annual meeting at such time and place as it may decide. Additional meetings shall be held when requested by two or more members of the Commission.

7. The expenses of each member of the Commission shall be paid by his own Government. Such joint expenses as may be incurred by the Commission shall be defrayed by the Parties by equal contributions. Each Party shall also contribute to the Commission annually an amount equivalent to the value of the sealskins it confiscates under the provisions of Article VI, paragraph 5.

8. The Commission shall submit an annual report of its activities to the Parties.

9. The Commission may from time to time make recommendations to the Parties on any matter which relates to the fur seal resources or to the administration of the Commission.

Article VI

In order to implement the provisions of Article III, the Parties agree as follows:

1. When a duly authorized official of any of the Parties has reasonable cause to believe that any vessel outfitted for the harvesting of living marine resources and subject to the jurisdiction of any of the Parties is offending against the prohibition of pelagic sealing as provided for by Article III, he may, except within the territorial waters of another State, board and search such vessel. Such official shall carry a special certificate issued by the competent authorities of his Government and drawn up in the English, Japanese, and Russian languages which shall be exhibited to the master of the vessel upon request.

2. When the official after searching a vessel continues to have reasonable cause to believe that the vessel or any person on board thereof is offending against the prohibition, he may seize or arrest such vessel or person. In that case, the Party

to which the official belongs shall as soon as possible notify the Party having jurisdiction over the vessel or person of such arrest or seizure and shall deliver the vessel or person as promptly as practicable to the authorized officials of the Party having jurisdiction over the vessel or person at a place to be agreed upon by both Parties; provided, however, that when the Party receiving notification cannot immediately accept delivery of the vessel or person, the Party which gives such notification may, upon request of the other Party, keep the vessel or person under surveillance within its own territory, under the conditions agreed upon by both Parties.

3. The authorities of the Party to which such person or vessel belongs alone shall have jurisdiction to try any case arising under Article III and this Article and to impose penalties in connection therewith.

4. The witnesses or their testimony and other proofs necessary to establish the offense, so far as they are under the control of any of the Parties, shall be furnished with all reasonable promptness to the authorities of the Party having jurisdiction to try the case.

5. Sealskins discovered on seized vessels shall be subject to confiscation on the decision of the court or other authorities of the Party under whose jurisdication the trial of a case takes place.

6. Full details of punitive measures applied to offenders against the prohibition shall be communicated to the other Parties not later than three months after the application of the penalty.

Article VII

The provisions of this Convention shall not apply to Indians, Ainos, Aleuts, or Eskimos dwelling on the coast of the waters mentioned in Article III, who carry on pelagic sealing in canoes not transported by or used in connection with other vessels, and propelled entirely by oars, paddles, or sails, and manned by not more than five persons each, in the way hitherto practiced and without the use of firearms; provided that such hunters are not in the employment of other persons or under contract to deliver the skins to any person.

Article VIII

1. Each Party agrees that no person or vessel shall be permitted to use any of its ports or harbors or any part of its territory for any purpose designed to violate the prohibition set forth in Article III.

2. Each Party also agrees to prohibit the importation and delivery into and the traffic within its territories of skins of fur seals taken in the area of the North Pacific Ocean mentioned in Article III, except only those taken by the Union of Soviet Socialist Republics or the United States of America on rookeries, those taken at sea for research purposes in accordance with Article II, paragraph 3, those taken under the provisions of Article VII, those confiscated under the provisions of Article VI, paragraphs 5, and those inadvertently captured which are taken possession of by a Party; provided, however, that all such excepted skins shall be officially marked and duly certified by the authorities of the Party concerned.

Article IX

1. The respective Parties agree that, of the total number of sealskins taken commercially each season on land, there shall at the end of the season be delivered a percentage of the gross in number and value thereof as follows:

By the Union of Soviet Socialist Republics	
To Canada	15 per cent
to Japan	15 per cent
By the United States of America	
to Canada	15 per cent
to Japan	15 per cent

2. Each Party agrees to deliver such sealskins to an authorized agent of the recipient Party at the place of taking, or at some other place mutually agreed upon by such Parties.

3. The respective Parties will seek to ensure the utilization of those methods for the capture and killing and marking of fur seals on land or at sea which will spare the fur seals pain and suffering to the greatest extent practicable.

Article X

1. Each Party agrees to enact and enforce such legislation as may be necessary to guarantee the observance of this Convention and to make effective its provisions with appropriate penalties for violation thereof.

2. The Parties further agree to co-operate with each other in taking such measures as may be appropriate to carry out the purposes of this Convention, including the prohibition of pelagic sealing as provided for by Article III.

Article XI

The Parties agree to meet in the twenty-second year after entry into force of the Convention to consider the recommendations in accordance with Article V, paragraph 2(e) and to determine what further agreements may be desirable in order to achieve the maximum sustainable productivity of the North Pacific fur seal herds.

Article XII

Should any Party consider that the obligations of Article II, paragraphs 3, 4, or 5 or any other obligation undertaken by the Parties is not being carried out and notify the other Parties to that effect, all the Parties shall, within three months of the receipt of such notification, meet to consult together on the need for and nature of remedial measures. In the event that such consultation shall not lead to agreement as to the need for and nature of remedial measures, any Party may give written notice to the other Parties of intention to terminate the Convention and, notwithstanding the provisions of Article XIII, paragraph 4, the Convention shall thereupon terminate as to all the

Parties nine months from the date of such notice.

Article XIII

1. This Convention shall be ratified and the instruments of ratification deposited with the Government of the United States of America as soon as practicable.

2. The Government of the United States of America shall notify the other signatory Governments of ratifications deposited.

3. The Convention shall enter into force on the date of the deposit of the fourth instrument of ratification.

4. The Convention shall continue in force for twenty-two years and thereafter until the entry into force of a new or revised fur seal convention between the Parties, or until the expiration of one year after such period of twenty-two years, whichever may be the earlier; provided, however, that the Convention shall terminate one year from the day on which a Party gives written notice to the other Parties of an intention of terminating the Convention.

5. At the request of any Party, representatives of the Parties will meet at a mutually convenient time within ninety days of such request to consider the desirability of modifications of the Convention.

6. The original of this Convention shall be deposited with the Government of the United States of America, which shall communicate certified copies thereof to each of the Governments signatory to the Convention.

IN WITNESS WHEREOF the undersigned, being duly authorized by their respective Governments, have signed this Convention.

Done in Washington this ninth day of February 1957, in the English, Japanese, and Russian languages, each text equally authentic.

CONVENTION ON CONSERVATION OF NATURE IN THE SOUTH PACIFIC [68]

Apia, 12 June 1976

The Contracting Parties,

Having in mind the Principles set out in the Declaration adopted by the United Nations Conference on the Human Environment at Stockholm in June 1972;

Convinced of the urgency for action inspired by these Principles, especially in relation to the maintenance of the capacity of the earth to produce essential renewable natural resources, the safeguarding of representative samples of natural ecosystems, and the safeguarding of the heritage of wildlife and its habitat;

Conscious of the importance of natural resources from a nutritional, scientific, educational, cultural and aesthetic point of view;

Conscious also of the dangers threatening these irreplaceable resources;

Recognizing the special importance in the South Pacific of indigenous customs and traditional cultural practices and the need to give due consideration to such matters;

Desirous of taking action for the conservation, utilization and development of these resources through careful planning and management for the benefit of present and future generations;

Have agreed as follows:

Article I

For the purpose of this Convention:

a) "Protected area" means national park or national reserve;

b) "National park" means an area established for the protection and conservation of ecosystems, containing animal and plant species, geomorphological sites and habitats of special scientific, educative and recreational interest or a natural landscape of great beauty, which is under the control of the appropriate public authority and open to visits by the public;

c) "National reserve" means an area recognized and controlled by the appropriate public authority and established for protection and conservation of nature, and includes strict nature reserve, managed nature reserve, wilderness reserve, fauna or flora reserve, game reserve, bird sanctuary, geological or forest reserve, archaeological reserve and historical reserve, these being reserves affording various degrees of protection to the natural and cultural heritage according to the purposes for which they are established.

Article II

1. Each Contracting Party shall, to the extent that it is itself involved, encourage the creation of protected areas which together with existing protected areas will safeguard representative samples of the natural ecosystems occurring therein (particular attention being given to endangered species), as well as superlative scenery,

striking geological formations, and regions and objects of aesthetic interest or historic, cultural or scientific value.

2. Each Contracting Party shall notify the body charged with the continuing bureau duties under this Convention of the establishment of any protected area and of the legislation and the methods of administrative control adopted in connection therewith.

Article III

1. The boundaries of national parks shall not be altered so as to reduce their areas, nor shall any portions of such parks be capable of alienation, except after the fullest examination.

2. The resources of national parks shall not be subject to exploitation for commercial profit, except after the fullest examination.

3. The hunting, killing, capture or collection of specimens (including eggs and shells) of the fauna and destruction or collection of specimens of the flora in national parks shall be prohibited, except when carried out by or under the direction or control of the appropriate authorities or for duly authorized scientific investigations.

4. Provision shall be made for visitors to enter and use national parks, under appropriate conditions, for inspirational, educative, cultural and recreative purposes.

Article IV

National reserves shall be maintained inviolate, as far as practicable, it being understood that in addition to such uses as are consistent with the purposes for which a national reserve was established, permission may be given to carry out scientific investigations.

Article V

1. The Contracting Parties shall, in addition to the protection given to indigenous fauna and flora in protected areas, use their best endeavours to protect such fauna and flora (special attention being given to migratory species) so as to safeguard them from unwise exploitation and other threats that may lead to their extinction.

2. Each Contracting Party shall establish and maintain a list of species of its indigenous fauna and flora that are threatened with extinction. Such lists shall be prepared as soon as possible after this Convention has come into force and shall be communicated to the body charged with the continuing bureau duties under this Convention.

3. Each Contracting Party shall protect as completely as possible as a matter of special urgency and importance the species included in the list it has established in accordance with the provisions of the last preceding paragraph. The hunting, killing, capture or collection of specimens (including eggs and shells) of such species shall be allowed only with the permission of the appropriate authority. Such permission shall be granted only under special circumstances, in order to further scientific purposes or when essential for the maintenance of the equilibrium of the ecosystem or for the administration of the area in which the animal or plant is found.

4. Each Contracting Party shall carefully consider the consequences of the deliberate introduction into ecosystems of species which have not previously occurred therein.

Article VI

Notwithstanding the provisions of Articles III, IV and V, a Contracting Party may make appropriate provision for customary use of areas and species in accordance with traditional cultural practices.

Article VII

1. The Contracting Parties shall co-operate amongst themselves in promoting the objectives of this Convention, especially within the framework of the South Pacific Commission.

2. The Contracting Parties shall wherever practicable conduct research relating to the conservation of nature. They shall as appropriate co-ordinate such research with research carried out by other Parties. They shall co-operate in the exchange of information on the results of such research and on the management of protected areas and of protected species.

3. The Contracting Parties shall co-operate in the interchange and training of personnel for the conservation of nature.

4. The Contracting Parties shall work towards harmonization of objectives relating to the conservation of nature.

5. With a view to attaining the objectives of this Convention the Contracting Parties shall examine the possibility of developing programmes of education and public awareness relating to conservation of nature.

Article VIII

1. The Contracting Parties shall maintain consultations with one another with the object of giving effect to the provisions of this Convention.

2. The South Pacific Commission shall provide for the continuing bureau duties under this Convention, including the circulation to the Contracting Parties of information and documents to be provided by the Parties under the provisions of the Convention.

Article IX

A State may at the time of deposit of its instrument of ratification, acceptance, approval or accession declare that the provisions of this Convention on conservation of nature in the South Pacific do not apply to its territories outside the territorial scope of the South Pacific Commission.

Article X

This Convention shall be open for signature at Apia until 31 December 1977 by all States members of the South Pacific Commission or eligible to be invited to become members of that Commission.

Article XI

This Convention shall be subject to ratification, acceptance or approval. Instruments of ratification, acceptance or approval shall be deposited with the Government of the Independent State of Western Samoa which shall be the Depositary.

Article XII

This Convention shall be open indefinitely for accession by the States referred to in Article X and by other States which are unanimously invited by the Contracting Parties to accede to it. Instruments of accession shall be deposited with the Depositary.

Article XIII

1. This Convention shall enter into force ninety days after the date of deposit of the fourth instrument of ratification, acceptance, approval or accession with the Depositary.

2. For each State which ratifies, accepts or approves this Convention or accedes thereto after the deposit of the fourth instrument of ratification, acceptance, approval or accession, the Convention shall enter into force ninety days after the deposit by such State of its instrument of ratification, acceptance, approval or accession.

Article XIV

Any Contracting Party may denounce this Convention by written notification to the Depositary at any time after five years from the date of entry into force of the Convention. The denunciation shall take effect twelve months after the Depositary has received the notification.

Article XV

1. The original of this Convention in the English and French languages, each version being equally authentic, shall be deposited with the Depositary, which shall transmit certified copies thereof to all States that have signed it or deposited instruments of accession to it.

2. The Depositary shall inform all signatory and acceding States of signatures, deposits of instruments of ratification, acceptance, approval or accession, entry into force of this Convention, and notifications of denunciation.

3. The Depositary shall transmit certified copies of this Convention to the Secretary-General of the United Nations for registration and publication in accordance with Article 102 of the Charter of the United Nations.

IN WITNESS WHEREOF the undersigned, being duly authorized by their Governments, have signed this Convention.

Done at Apia this twelfth day of June One Thousand Nine Hundred and Seventy-Six.

CONVENTION ON THE PROTECTION OF THE ARCHAEOLOGICAL, HISTORICAL AND ARTISTIC HERITAGE OF THE AMERICAN NATIONS [69]

(Convention of San Salvador)

Santiago, 16 June 1976

The Governments of the Members States of the Organization of American States,

Having seen the continuous looting and plundering of the native cultural heritage suffered by the countries of the hemisphere, particularly the Latin American countries; and

Considering:

That such acts of pillage have damaged and reduced the archeological, historical and artistic wealth, through which the national character of their people is expressed;

That there is a basic obligation to transmit to coming generations the legacy of their cultural heritage;

That this heritage can only be protected and preserved through mutual appreciation and respect for such properties, within a framework of the soundest inter-American co-operation; and

That the member states have repeatedly demonstrated their willingness to establish standards for the protection and surveillance of the archeological, historical, and artistic heritage,

Declare:

That it is essential to take steps, at both the national and international levels, for the most effective protection and retrieval of cultural treasures, and

Have agreed upon the following:

Article 1

The purpose of this Convention is to identify, register, protect, and safeguard the property making up the cultural heritage of the American nations in order: (a) to prevent illegal exportation or importation of cultural property; and (b) to promote co-operation among the American states for mutual awareness and appreciation of their cultural property.

Article 2

The cultural property referred to in the preceding Article is that included in the following categories:

a) Monuments, objects, fragments of ruined buildings, and archeological materials belonging to American cultures existing prior to contact with European culture, as well as remains of human beings, fauna, and flora related to such cultures;

b) Monuments, buildings, objects of artistic, utilitarian, and ethnological nature, whole or in fragments, from the colonial era and the Nineteenth Century;

c) Libraries and archives; incunabula and manuscripts; books and other publications, iconographies, maps and documents published before 1850;

d) All objects orginating after 1850 that the States Parties have recorded as cultural property, provided that they have given notice of such registration to the other parties to the treaty;

e) All cultural property that any of the State Parties specifically declares to be included within the scope of this convention.

Article 3

The cultural property included in the above article shall receive maximum protection at the international level, and its exportation and importation shall be considered unlawful, except when the state owning it authorizes its exportation for purposes of promoting knowledge of national cultures.

Article 4

Any disagreements between the parties to this Convention, regarding application of the definitions and categories of Article 2 to specific property, shall be resolved definitively by the Inter-American Council for Education, Science, and Culture (CIECC), following an opinion by the Inter-American Committee on Culture.

Article 5

The cultural heritage of each state consists of property mentioned in Article 2, found or created in its territory and legally acquired items of foreign origin.

Article 6

The control exercised by each state over its cultural heritage and any actions that may be taken to reclaim items belonging to it are imprescriptible.

Article 7

Regulations on ownership of cultural property and its transfer within the territory of each state shall be governed by domestic legislation. With a view to preventing unlawful trade in such goods, the following measures shall be encouraged:

a) Registration of collections and of transfer of cultural property subject to protection;

b) Registration of transactions carried out by establishments engaged in the sale and purchase of such property;

c) Prohibition of imports or cultural property from other states without appropriate certificate and authorization.

Article 8

Each state is responsible for identifying, registering, protecting, preserving, and safeguarding its cultural heritage; in fulfilment of these functions each state undertakes to encourage:

a) Preparation, in accordance with its respective constitutional standards, of rules and legislative provisions required for effective protection of this heritage from destruction resulting from neglect or inadequate preservation work;

b) Establishment of technical organs entrusted

specifically with the protection and safeguarding of cultural property;

c) Establishment and maintenance of an inventory and record of cultural property, to make it possible to identify and locate it;

d) The establishment and development of museums, libraries archives, and other centres for the protection and preservation of cultural property;

e) The delimitation and protection of archeological sites and places of historic and artistic interest·

f) Exploration, excavation, investigation, and preservation of archeological sites and objects by scientific institutions, in collaboration with the national agency in charge of the archeological heritage.

Article 9

Each State Party shall prevent by all available means any unlawful excavation in its territory or any removal of cultural property therefrom.

Article 10

Each State Party to this Convention undertakes to take whatever measures it may consider effective to prevent and curb the unlawful exportation, importation, and removal of cultural property, as well as those necessary for the return of such property to the state to which it belongs in the event of its removal.

Article 11

When the government of a State Party becomes aware of the unlawful exportation of an item of cultural property it may address the government of the state to which the property has been removed, requesting that it takes measures for its recovery and return. This shall be done through diplomatic channels. The request shall be accompanied by evidence of the unlawful removal of the property in question, in accordance with the laws of the requesting state. This evidence shall be considered by the state petitioned.

The state petitioned shall employ all available lawful means in order to locate, recover, and return the cultural property claimed and that may have been removed after this Convention has gone into effect.

If the laws of the state petitioned require judicial action for recovery of foreign cultural property unlawfully imported or removed, such judicial action shall be instituted in the appropriate courts by the competent authority of that state.

Article 12

As soon as the state petitioned is in a position to do so, it shall return to the petitioning state the cultural property that has been removed. The cost of returning such property shall be covered by the state petitioned without prejudice to the measures or action it should take in order to be reimbursed for such expenses.

Article 13

No tax or government fee shall be charged for cultural property returned in accordance with the provisions of Article 12.

Article 14

Those responsible for crimes against the integrity of cultural property or for crimes resulting from the illegal exportation or importation thereof are subject to extradition treaties, when appropriate.

Article 15

The States Parties bind themselves to co-operate in the mutual knowledge and appreciation of their cultural values by taking the following measures:

a) Facilitating the circulation, exchange, and exhibition, for educational, scientific, and cultural purposes, of cultural property from other nations and of their own cultural property abroad, when authorized by the pertinent governmental agencies;

b) Promoting the exchange of information on cultural property and on archeological excavations and discoveries.

Article 16

Articles on loan to museums, exhibitions, or scientific institutions that are outside the state to whose cultural heritage they belong shall not be subject to seizure as a result of public or private lawsuits.

Article 17

For the purposes of compliance with the objectives of this Convention, the General Secretariat of the Organization of American States is charged with:

a) Ensuring the enforcement and effectiveness of this Convention;

b) Promoting the adoption of collective measures directed towards the protection and preservation of cultural property belonging to the American States;

c) Establishing an inter-American registry of cultural property, both movable and immovable, that is of special value;

d) Promoting co-ordination of national legislation on this subject;

e) Granting and arranging any technical co-operation the States Parties may request;

f) Disseminating information on the cultural property of the States Parties and the objectives of this convention;

g) Promoting the circulation, exchange, and exhibition of cultural property among the States Parties.

Article 18

None of the provisions of this Convention shall impede the States Parties from entering into bilateral or multilateral agreements relative to their cultural heritage, nor shall they limit the application of any agreements to the same end as may it be in force.

Article 19

The present Convention is open to signature by the member states of the Organization of American States and to adherence by any state.

Article 20

The present Convention shall be ratified by the signatory states in accordance with their respective constitutional procedures.

Article 21

The original instruments, whose Spanish, French, English and Portugese texts are equally authentic, shall be deposited with the General Secretariat of the Organization of American States, which shall send certified copies to the signatory states for purpose of ratification. The instruments of ratification shall be deposited with the General Secretariat of the Organization of American States, which shall notify the signatory governments of the deposit.

Article 22

This Convention shall enter into force among the states ratifying it in the order of deposit of their instruments of ratification.

Article 23

The present Convention shall be in force indefinitely; however, any of the States Parties may denounce it. The denunciation shall be communicated to the General Secretariat of the Organization of American States, which shall inform the other States Parties thereof. One year from the date of denunciation the Convention shall cease to be in force for the state that denounced it and remain in force for the other States Parties.

In Witness whereof, the undersigned Plenipotentiaries, whose powers have been found to be in due and proper form, sign this Convention in the city of Washington D.C., on the dates appearing beside their signatures.

CONVENTION FOR THE PROTECTION OF THE RHINE AGAINST CHEMICAL POLLUTION

Bonn, 3 December 1976

The Government of the Federal Republic of Germany, the Government of the French Republic, the Government of the Grand Duchy of Luxembourg, the Government of the Kingdom of the Netherlands, the Governemnt of the Swiss Confederation, and the European Economic Community,

Having regard to the Agreement of 29 April 1963 and the Additional Agreement of 3 December 1976 Concerning the International Commission for the Protection of the Rhine against Pollution,

Whereas chemical pollution of the Rhine threatens for certain uses of the waters of the Rhine;

Aware of the dangers that may result therefrom from certain uses of the waters of the Rhine;

Desirous of improving the quality of Rhine water for these uses;

Whereas the Rhine is used for other purposes such as navigation and as the receiving medium for waste waters;

Convinced that international action for the protection of the Rhine against chemical pollution must be assessed in conjunction with other efforts to protect the Rhine, particularly efforts to conclude agreements against pollution by chlorides and thermal pollution, and that such action is one of the continuous and coherent measures to protect fresh water and sea water from pollution;

Whereas the European Economic Community has taken measures to protect the aquatic environment particularly within the framework of the Council Directive of 4 May 1976 on pollution caused by certain dangerous substances discharged into the aquatic environment of the Community;

Having regard to the results of the Ministerial Conferences of 25 and 26 October 1972 in the Hague, 4 and 5 December 1973 and 1 April 1976 in Paris on the Protection of the Rhine against Pollution,

Have agreed as follows:

Article 1

1. The Contracting Parties shall, in accordance with the following provisions, take the appropriate measures, with a view to improving the quality of the waters of the Rhine, to:

a) eliminate pollution of the surface waters of the Rhine basin by dangerous substances in the families and groups of substances appearing in Annex I (hereinafter referred to as 'Annex I substances'). The purpose of the measures is to effect substances, taking into account the findings of investigations carried out by experts separately for each one of them and the available technical means;

b) reduce the pollution of the Rhine by the

dangerous substances in the families and groups of substances appearing in Annex II (hereinafter referred to as Annex II substances).

2. The measures referred to in paragraph I above shall take into reasonable account the fact that Rhine water is used for:

a) the production of drinking water for human consumption;

b) comsumption by domestic and wild animals;

c) the conservation and development of the national species of flora and fauna and the preservation of the self-purifying capacity of water;

d) fishing;

e) recreational purposes, bearing in mind hygienic and aesthetic requirements;

f) the direct or indirect supply of fresh water to agricultural lands;

g) the production of water for industrial purposes, and the need to preserve an acceptable quality of sea water.

3. The provisions of this Convention shall constitute only an initial step towards the achievement of the objectives set out in paragragh 1 above.

4. Annex A to this Convention shall determine what the Contracting Parties mean by the word 'Rhine' for the purposes of applying the said Convention.

Article 2

1. The Governments which are Parties to this Convention shall, pursuant to Annex III (1), establish for their own use a national inventory of discharges into the surface waters of the Rhine basin which may contain substances listed in Annex I, which are subject to emission standards.

2. Pursuant to Annex III (2), the Governments shall communicate to the International Commission for the Protection of the Rhine against Pollution (hereinafter referred to as the 'International Commission') the contents of their inventories, which shall be regularly updated at intervals not exceeding three years.

3. The proposals of the International Commission provided for in Article 6 (3) may, if necessary, include an inventory of various substances falling under Annex II.

Article 3

1. Any discharge into the surface waters of the Rhine basin likely to contain a substance referred to in Annex I shall be subject to prior authorization from the responsible authorities of the Government concerned.

2. For discharges of these substances into the surface waters of the Rhine basin and, when necessary for the purpose of applying this Convention, for discharges of these substances into sewers, the authorization shall fix emission standards which may not exceed the limit values laid down in accordance with Article 5.

3. In the case of existing discharges of these substances, the authorization shall fix a time limit within which the conditions laid down in the authorization must be met. This time limit must not exceed the period laid down in accordance with Article 5 (3).

4. The authorization may only be granted for a limited period of time. It may be renewed in the light of any alternations in the limit values referred to in Article 5.

Article 4

1. The emission standards laid down in the authorizations issued pursuant to Article 3 shall establish:

a) the maximum permissible concentration of a substance in discharges. In cases where there is dilution, the limit value provided for in Article 5 (2) (*a*) shall be divided by the dilution factor;

b) the maximum permissible quantity of a substance in discharges during one or more specific periods. If necessary this quantity may also be expressed as a unit of weight of the pollutant per unit of the characteristic element of the polluting activity (e.g. unit of weight per unit of raw material or product unit).

2. If the discharger states that he is unable to conform to the emission standards or if the responsible authorities of the Government concerned establish this, authorization shall be refused.

3. If the emission standards are not observed, the responsible authorities of the Government concerned shall take all necessary measures to ensure that the conditions for the authorization are met and, if necessary that the discharge is prohibited.

Article 5

1. The International Commission shall propose the limit values provided for in Article 3 (2) and if necessary their application to discharges into sewers. These limit values shall be laid down in conformity with the procedure provided for in Article 14. Upon adoption, they shall be included in Annex IV.

2. These limit values are fixed in terms of:

a) the maximum permissible concentration of a substance in discharge and,

b) where appropriate, the maximum permissible quantity of such a substance expressed as a unit of weight of the pollutant per unit of the characteristic element of the polluting activity (e.g unit of weight per unit of raw material or product unit).

Where appropriate, the limit values applicable to industrial effluent shall be laid down individually by sector and by type of product.

The limit values applicable to Annex I substances shall be laid down mainly on the basis of

— toxicity,

— persistence,

— bioaccumulation,

taking into account the best available technical means.

3. The International Commission shall propose to the Contracting Parties the time limits referred to in Article 3 (3), making due allowance for the specific characteristics of the industrial sectors involved and, as appropriate, the types of product. These time limits shall be determined in accordance with the procedure laid down in Article 14.

4. The International Commission shall use the results obtained at international measuring points to determine the extent to which the level of Annex I substances in the Rhine varies following the application of the above provisions.

5. As regards the quality of Rhine water, the International Commission may if necessary propose other measures for reducing the pollution of the Rhine taking into account, *inter alia*, the toxicity, persistence and bioccumulation of the substance under consideration. These proposals shall be adopted in accordance with the procedure laid down in Article 14.

Article 6

1. The discharge of any Annex II substance likely to affect the quality of Rhine water must be regulated by the national authorities with a view to limiting it strictly.

2. The Governments which are Parties to this Convention shall strive to establish, within a period of two years from the entry into force of this Convention, national programmes for the reduction of the pollution of the Rhine by Annex II substances for the implementation of which they shall apply, in particular, the means provided for in paragraphs 1, 4, 5, 6 and 7 of this Article.

3. Before drawing up their national programmes, the Contracting Parties shall consider within the International Commission. To this end, the International Commission shall regularly compare the draft national programmes in order to ensure that their aims and means coincide; it shall submit proposals for achieving, *inter alia*, common goals in reducing pollution of the Rhine. These proposals shall be adapted by applying the procedure laid down in Article 14 of this Convention.

Comparison of draft national programmes should not entail delays in the implementation, at either national or regional level, of measures for reducing the pollution of the Rhine.

4. Any discharge which may contain an Annex I substances shall require prior authorization, laying down emission standards, from the responsible authorities of the Government concerned. These standards shall be fixed in accordance with the quality objectives provided for in paragraph 5.

5. The programmes may also contain specific provision concerning the composition and use of substances or groups of substances and products; they shall include quality objectives for Rhine water.

6. The programmes may also contain specific provisions concerning the composition and use of substances or groups of substances and products; they shall take into account the latest economically feasible technical advice.

7. The programmes shall lay deadlines for their implementation.

8. Summaries of the programmes and the results of their implementation shall be communicated to the International Commission.

Article 7

1. The Contracting Parties shall take all legislative and administrative measures to ensure that the storage and deposit of Annex I and II substances are so carried out as to entail no danger of pollution to the Rhine.

2. If necessary, the International Commission shall propose to the Contracting Parties appropriate measures for protecting underground water in order to prevent pollution of the Rhine by Annex I and II substances.

Article 8

1. The Contracting Parties shall ensure that discharges are monitored in accordance with this Convention.

2. The Contracting Parties shall inform the International Commission annually of the experience gained.

Article 9

Implementation of the measures taken pursuant to this Convention shall in no case result in a direct or indirect increase in the pollution of the Rhine.

Article 10

1. With a view to monitoring levels in the Rhine of Annex I and II substances, each Government concerned shall take responsibility at the agreed measuring stations on the Rhine for installing and operating measuring systems and apparatus for determining the concentrations of such substances.

2. Every Government involved shall regularly inform the International Commission of the results of its monitoring, at least once a year.

3. The International Commission shall draft an annual report summarizing the monitoring results and enabling the progress of the quality of Rhine water to be observed.

Article 11

If a Government which is a Party to this Commission detects a sudden considerable increase in Annex I or II substances, or learns of an accident which could seriously threaten the quality of Rhine water, it shall inform the International Commission and the Contracting Parties which could be affected without delay and in accordance with a procedure to be worked out by the International Commission.

Article 12

1. The Contracting Parties shall regularly inform the International Commission of the experience gained in the course of implementing this Convention.

2. The International Commission shall also make recommendations, as appropriate, designed gradually to improve the implementation of this Convention.

Article 13

The International Commission shall work out draft recommendations for achieving comparable results by the use of appropriate measuring and analysis methods.

Article 14

1. Annexes I to IV inclusive, which shall form an integral part of this Convention, may be amended or added to for the purposes of adapting them to technical or scientific advances of or more effectively combating the chemical pollution of the Rhine.

2. To this end, the International Commission shall recommend the amendments or additions which it considers appropriate.

3. The amended or supplemented texts shall enter into force following unanimous acceptance by the Contracting Parties.

Article 15

Any dispute between the Contracting Parties concerning the interpretation or implementation of this Convention which cannot be settled by negotiation shall be submitted to arbitration unless the parties to the dispute decide otherwise and at the request of one of them, in accordance with the provisions of Annex B which shall form an integral part of this Convention.

Article 16

For the purposes of applying this Convention, the European Economic Community and its Member States shall act in their respective areas of competence.

Article 17

1. Each Signatory Party shall notify the Government of the Swiss Confederation of the completion of their procedures for bringing this Convention into force.

2. Subject to notification by each Contracting Party that the required procedures for the entry into force of the Additional Agreement to the Agreement concerning the International Commission for the Protection of the Rhine against Pollution have been completed, this Convention shall enter into force on the first day of the second month following receipt of the last notification provided for in the preceeding paragraph.

Article 18

Three years after its entry into force, this Convention may be denounced at any time by any of the Contracting Parties by means of a declaration transmitted to the Government of the Swiss Confederation. The denunciation shall become effective for the denouncing Party six months after the receipt by the Government of the Swiss Confederation of the declaration.

Article 19

The Government of the Swiss Confederation will inform the Contracting Parties of the date of receipt of any notification or declaration received in accordance with Articles 14, 17 and 18.

Article 20

1. If the Agreement of 29 April 1963 concerning the International Commission for the Protection of the Rhine against Pollution is denounced by one of its Contracting Parties, the Contracting Parties shall immediately consult with regard to the appropriate measures to be taken to ensure the continued performance of the duties which are encumbent on the International Commission pursuant to this Convention.

2. If agreement is not reached within six months of the opening of these consultations, any Contracting Party may at any time denounce this Convention in accordance with Article 18 without waiting for the expiry of the three-year time limit.

Article 21

This Convention, drawn up in a single original in the Dutch, French and German languages, all three texts being equally authentic, will be deposited in the archives of the Government of the Swiss Confederation, which will transmit a certified copy to each Contracting Party.

ANNEX A

For the purpose of implementing this Convention, the Rhine shall be taken as beginning at its outflow from the Untersee and including the arms, up to the coastline, through which its waters flow freely into the North Sea, inclusive of the Ijssel up to Kampen.

During the drawing-up of the national programmes provided for in Article 6 of the Convention — where quality objectives are concerned — and during the co-ordination of these programmes within the International Commission, a distinction shall be made in each separate case between the fresh water and the salt water of the river.

ANNEX B

ARBITRATION

1. Unless the parties to a dispute decide otherwise, the arbitration procedure shall be conducted in accordance with the provisions of this Annex.

2. The arbitral tribunal shall consist of three members; each of the Parties to the dispute shall appoint an arbitrator, the two arbitrators so appointed shall by common consent designate a third who shall chair the tribunal.

If the chairman has not been appointed within two months of the designation of the second arbitrator, the President of the European Court of Human Rights shall, within a further two months, designate him at the request of the first party to act.

3. If, within two months or receipt of the request provided for in Article 15 of the Convention, one of the parties to the dispute has not designated an arbitrator, the other party may submit the matter to the President of the European Court Human Rights who shall designate the chairman of the arbitral tribunal within a further two months. Once appointed the chairman of the arbitral tribunal shall request the party which has not appointed an arbitrator to do so within two months. Upon expiry of this time limit, he shall submit the matter to the President of the European Court of Human Rights who shall make this appointment within a further two months.

4. If, in one of the cases referred to above, the President of the European Court of Human Rights is prevented from acting, or if he is a national of one of the parties to the dispute, the Vice-President of the Court or the most senior member of the Court who is not prevented from acting and who is not a national of one of the parties to the dispute shall appoint a chairman of the arbitral tribunal or an arbitrator.

5. These provisions shall apply, *mutatis mutandis*, to the filling of posts which have become vacant.

6. The arbitral tribunal shall decide on the basis of the rules of international law and in particular on the basis of the provisions of this Convention.

7. As regards both procedural and substantive matters, the arbitral tribunal shall decide by a majority of its members' votes; the absence or abstention of one of the members of the tribunal appointed by the parties shall not prevent the tribunal from reaching a decision. In the case of parity of votes, the chairman shall have a casting vote. The decisions of the tribunal shall be binding on the parties. Each party shall bear the costs of the arbitrator appointed by it and shall share the other costs equally. For other matters, the arbitral tribunal shall establish its own rules of procedure.

8. In the case of dispute between two Contracting Parties, only one of which is a Member State of the European Economic Community, which is itself a Contracting Party, the other party shall simultaneoulsy transmit its request to that Member State and the Community, which shall jointly notify the party within two months following receipt of the request whether the Member State, the Community or the Member State and the Community together are parties to the dispute. If such notification is not given within the appointed time, both the Member State and the Community shall be regarded as constituting one and the same party to the dispute for the purposes of applying this Annex. The same shall obtain when the Member State and the Community are jointly a party to the dispute.

ANNEX I

FAMILIES AND GROUPS OF SUBSTANCES

Annex I includes certain individual substances from the following families or groups of substances, selected mainly on the basis of toxicity, persistence and bioaccumulation, with the exception of those which are biologically harmless or which are rapidly converted into substances which are biologically harmless.

1. Organohalogen compounds and substances which may form such compounds in the aquatic environment,
2. Organophosphorous compounds,
3. Organotic compounds,
4. Substances in respect of which it has been proved that they possess carcinogenic properties in or via the aquatic environment.
5. Mercury and its compounds,
6. Cadmium and its compounds,
7. Persistent mineral oils and hydrocarbons of petroleum origin.

ANNEX II

Annex II contains:

— substances belonging to the families and groups in Annex I for which the limit values referred to in Article 5 of the Convention have not been determined.

— certain individual substances and categories of substances belonging to the families and groups of substances listed below, and which have a deleterious effect on the aquatic environment, which can, however, be confined to a given area and which depend on the characteristics and location of the water into which they are discharged.

Families and groups of substances referred to in the second indent:

1. The following metalloids and metals and their compounds:

1.	Zinc	11.	Tin
2.	Copper	12.	Barium
3.	Nickel	13.	Beryllium
4.	Chromium	14.	Boron
5.	Lead	15.	Uranium
6.	Selenium	16.	Vanadium
7.	Arsenic	17.	Cobalt
8.	Antimony	18.	Thalium
9.	Nolybdenum	19.	Tellurium
10.	Titanium	20.	Silver

* Where certain substances in Annex II are carcinogenic, they are included in category 4 of this Annex.

2. Biocides and their derivatives not appearing in Annex I.

3. Subtances which have a deleterious effect on the taste and/or smell of the products for human consumption derived from the aquatic environment, and compounds liable to give rise to such subtances in water.

4. Toxic or persistent organic compounds of silicon and substances which may give rise to such compounds in water, excluding those which are biologically harmless or are rapidly converted in water into harmless substances.

5. Inorganic compounds of phosphorus and elemental phosphorus.

6. Non-persistent mineral oils and hydrocarbons of petroleum origin.

7. Cyanides,
Fluorides

8. Substances which have an adverse effect on the oxygen balance, in particular:
Ammonia,
Nitrites.

ANNEX III

1. The national inventory provided for in Article 2 (1) of this Convention shall show discharges, points of discharge, and discharged substances classified according to type and quality.

2. The contents of the inventory referred to in Article 2 (2) of the Convention shall include the total quantities of each of the various substances set out in Annex I, disharges into the waters of the Rhine basin between the measuring points proposed by the International Commission and accepted by all the Contracting Parties.

ANNEX IV

Limit values (Article 5)

Substance or group of substances	Origin	Limit value expressed as maximum quantity of a substance	Time limit for existing disharges	Limit value expressed as maximum concentration of a substance	Comments

CONVENTION ON CIVIL LIABILITY FOR OIL POLLUTION DAMAGE RESULTING FROM EXPLORATION FOR AND EXPLOITATION OF SEABED MINERAL RESOURCES

London, 1 May 1977

The States Parties to this Convention,

Conscious of the dangers of oil pollution posed by the exploration for, and exploitation of, certain seabed mineral resources,

Convinced of the need to ensure that adequate compensation is available to persons who suffer damage caused by such pollution,

Desiring to adopt uniform rules and procedures for determining questions of liability and provide adequate compensation in such cases,

Have agreed as follows:

Article 1

For the purposes of this Convention:

1. *a*) "Oil" means crude oil and natural gas liquids, whether or not such oil or liquids are mixed with or present in other substances; and

b) "crude oil" includes crude oil treated to render it suitable for transmission, for example, by adding or removing certain fractions.

2. "Installation" means:

a) any well or other facility, whether fixed or mobile, which is used for the purpose of exploring for, producing, treating, storing, transmitting or regaining control of the flow of crude oil from the seabed or its subsoil;

b) any well which has been used for the purpose of exploring for, producing or regaining control of the flow of crude oil from the seabed or its subsoil and which has been abandoned after the entry into force of this Convention for the Controlling State concerned;

c) any well which is used for the purpose of exploring for, producing or regaining control of the flow of gas or natural gas liquids from the seabed or its subsoil during the period that any such well is being drilled, including completion, or worked upon except for normal maintenance operations;

d) any well which is used for the purpose of exploring for any mineral resources other than crude oil, gas or natural gas liquids, where such exploration involves the deep penetration of the subsoil of the seabed; and

e) any facility which is normally used for storing crude oil from the seabed or its subsoil; which, or a substantial part of which, is located seaward of the low-water line along the coast as marked on large-scale charts officially recognized by the Controlling State;

provided, however, that

(i) where a well or a number of wells is directly connected to a platform or similar facility, the well or wells together with such platform or facility shall constitute one installation; and

(ii) a ship as defined in the International Convention on Civil Liability for Oil Pollution Damage, done at Brussels on 29 November 1969, shall not be considered to be an installation.

3. "Operator" means the person, whether licensee or not, designated as operator for the purposes of this Convention by the Controlling State, or, in the absence of such designation, the person who is in overall control of the activities carried on at the installation.

4. "Controlling State" means the State Party which exercises sovereign rights for the purpose of exploring for and exploiting the resources of the seabed and its subsoil in the area in or above which the installator is situated. In the case of an installation extending over areas in which two or more States Parties exercise such rights, these States may agree which of them shall be the Controlling State.

5. "Person" means any individual or partnership or any public or private body, whether corporate or not, including a State or any of its constituent subdivisions.

6. "Pollution damage" means loss or damage outside the installation caused by contamination resulting from the escape or discharge of oil from the installation and includes the cost of preventive measures and further loss or damage outside the installation caused by preventive measures.

7. "Preventive measures" means any reasonable measures taken by any person in relation to a particular incident to prevent or minimize pollution damage with the exception of well control measures and measures taken to protect, repair or replace an installation.

8. "Incident" means any occurrence, or series of occurrences having the same origin, which causes pollution damage.

9. "Special Drawing Right" means Special Drawing Right as defined by the International Monetary Fund and used for its own operations and transactions.

Article 2

This Convention shall apply exclusively to pollution damage:

a) resulting from an incident which occurred beyond the coastal low-water line at an installation under the jurisdiction of a Controlling State, and

b) suffered in the territory, including the internal waters and territorial sea, of a State Party or in the areas in which, in accordance with international law, it has sovereign rights over natural resources, and to preventive measures, wherever taken, to prevent or minimize such pollution damage.

Article 3

1. Except as provided in paragraphs 3, 4 and 5 of this Article, the operator of the installation at the time of an incident shall be liable for any pollution damage resulting from the incident. When the incident consists of a series of occurrences, liability for pollution damage arising out of each occurrence shall attach to the operator of the

installation at the time of that occurrence.

2. Where an installation has more than one operator they shall be jointly and severally liable.

3. No liability for pollution damage shall attach to the operator if he proves that the damage resulted from an act of war, hostilities, civil war, insurrection, or a natural phenomenon of an exceptional, inevitable and irresistible character.

4. No liability for pollution damage shall attach to the operator of an abandoned well if he proves that the incident which caused the damage occurred more than five years after the date on which the well was abandoned under the authority and in accordance with the requirements of the Controlling State. Where a well has been abandoned in other circumstances, the liability of the operator shall be governed by the applicable national law.

5. If the operator proves that the pollution damage resulted wholly or partly either from an act of omission done with intent to cause damage by the person who suffered the damage or from the negligence of that person, the operator may be exonerated wholly or partly from his liability to such person.

Article 4

1. No claim for compensation for pollution damage shall be made against the operator otherwise in accordance with this Convention.

2. No claim for compensation for pollution damage under this Convention or otherwise may be made against the servants or agents of the operator.

3. Nothing in this Convention shall prejudice the question whether the operator liable for damage in accordance with its provisions has a right of recourse.

Article 5

1. When oil has escaped or has been discharged from two or more installations, and pollution damage results therefrom, the operators of all the installations concerned, unless exonerated under Article 3, shall be jointly and severally liable for all such damage which is not reasonably separable.

2. When oil has escaped or has been discharged from one installation as a result of an incident, and pollution damage results therefrom, and during the course of the incident there is a change of operator, all operators of the installation, unless exonerated under Article 3, shall be jointly and severally liable for all such damage which is not reasonably separable.

Article 6

1. The operator shall be entitled to limit his liability under this Convention for each installation and each incident to the amount of 30 million Special Drawing Rights until five years have elapsed from the date on which the Convention is opened for signature and to the amount of 40 million Special Drawing Rights thereafter.

2. Where operators of different installations are liable in accordance with paragraph 1 of Article 5, the liability of the operator of any one installation shall not for any one incident exceed any limit which may be applicable to him in accordance with the provisions of this Article and of Article 15.

3. When in the case of any one installation more than one operator is liable under this Convention, the aggregate liability of all of them in respect of any one incident shall not exceed the highest amount that could be awarded against any of them, but none of them shall be liable for an amount in excess of the limit applicable to him.

4. The operator shall not be entitled to limit his liability if it is proved that the pollution damage occurred as a result of an act or omission by the operator himself, done deliberately with actual knowledge that pollution damage would result.

5. For the purpose of availing himself of the benefit of limitation to which he may be entitled under paragraph 1 of this Article, the operator shall constitute a fund for the total sum representing the limit of his liability with the court or other competent authority of any one of the States Parties in which action is brought under Article 11. A fund constituted by one of the operators mentioned in paragraph 2 of Article 3 shall be deemed to be constituted by all of them. The fund can be constituted either by depositing the sum or by producing a bank guarantee or other guarantee, acceptable under the legislation of the State Party where the fund is constituted, and considered to be adequately by the court or other competent liability.

6. The fund shall be distributed among the claimants in proportion to the amounts of their established claims.

7. If before the fund is distributed the operator or any of his servants or agents or any person providing him with insurance or other financial security, has, as a result of the incident in question, paid compensation for pollution damage, such person shall, up to the amount he has paid, acquire by subrogation the rights which the person so compensated would have enjoyed under this Convention.

8. The right of subrogation provided for in paragraph 7 of this Article may also be exercised by a person other than those mentioned therein in respect of any amount of compensation for pollution damage which he may have paid but only to the extent that such subrogation is permitted under the applicable national law.

9. Where the operator or any other person establishes that he may be compelled to pay at a later date in whole or in part any such amount of compensation, with regard to which such person would have enjoyed a right of subrogation under paragraph 7 or 8 of this Article, had the compensation been paid before the fund was distributed, the court or other competent authority of the State Party where the fund has been constituted may order that a sufficient sum shall be provisionally set aside to enable such person at such later date to enforce his claim against the

fund.

10. An operator who has taken preventive measures shall in respect of those measures have the same rights against the fund as any other claimant.

11. The amount referred to in paragraph 1 of this Article shall be converted into the national currency of the State Party in which the fund is constituted on the basis of the value of that currency by reference to the average, during the thirty days immediately preceding the date on which the fund is constituted, of the Special Drawing Rights as published by the International Monetary Fund.

12. The insurer or other person providing financial security shall be entitled, alone or together with the operator, to constitute a fund in accordance with this Article on the same conditions and having the same effect as if it were constituted by the operator. Such a fund may be constituted even where the pollution damage occurred as a result of an act or omission by the operator himself, done deliberately with actual knowledge that pollution damage would result, but the constitution of the fund shall in that case not prejudice the rights of any claimant against the operator.

Article 7

1. Where the operator, after an incident, has constituted a fund in accordance with Article 6 and is entitled to limit his liability:

a) no person having a claim for pollution damage arising out of that incident shall be entitled to exercise any right against any other assets of the operator in respect of such claim;

b) the court or other competent authority of any State Party shall order the release of any property belonging to the operator which has been arrested in respect of a claim for pollution damage arising out of that incident, and shall similarly release any bail or other security furnished to avoid such arrest.

2. Paragraph 1 of this Article shall, however, only apply if the claimant has access to the court administering the fund and the fund is actually available in respect of his claim.

Article 8

1. To cover his liability under this Convention, the operator shall be required to have and maintain insurance or other financial security to such amount, of such type and on such terms as the Controlling State shall specify, provided that the amount shall not be less than 22 million Special Drawing Rights until five years have elapsed from the date on which this Convention is opened for signature and not less than 35 million Special Drawing Rights thereafter. However the Controlling State may exempt the operator wholly or in part from the requirement to have and maintain such insurance or other financial security to cover his liability for pollution damage wholly caused by an act of sabotage or terrorism.

2. An insurance or other financial security shall not satisfy the requirements of this Article if it can cease, for reasons other than the expiry of the period of validity of the insurance or security, before two months have elapsed from the date on which notice of its termination is given to the competent public authority of the Controlling State. The foregoing provision shall similarly apply to any modification which results in the insurance or security no longer satisfying the requirements of this Article.

3. Any claim for compensation for pollution damage may be brought directly against the insurer or other person providing financial security for the operator's liability for pollution damage. In such case the liability of the defendant shall be limited to the amount specified in accordance with paragraph 1 of this Article irrespective of the fact that the pollution damage occurred as a result of an act or omission by the operator himself, done deliberately with actual knowledge that pollution damage would result. The defendant may further avail himself of the defences, other than the bankruptcy or winding-up of the operator, which the operator himself would have been entitled to invoke. Furthermore, the defendant may avail himself of the defence that the pollution damage resulted from the wilful misconduct of the operator himself, but the defendant may not avail himself of any other defence which he might have been entitled to invoke in proceedings brought by the operator against him. The defendant shall in any event have the right to require the operator to be joined in the proceedings.

4. Any sums provided by insurance or by other financial security maintained in accordance with paragraph 1 of this Article shall be available in the first place for the satisfaction of claims under this Convention.

5. Where the operator is a State Party, the operator shall not be required to maintain insurance or other financial security to cover its liability.

Article 9

1. A Committee composed of a representative of each State Party is hereby established.

2. If a State Party considers that any of the amounts currently appliable under Article 6 or 8 is no longer adequate, or is otherwise unrealistic, it may convene a meeting of the Committee to consider the matter. States which have signed this Convention but are not yet Parties will be invited to participate in the work of the Committee as observers. The Committee may recommend to the States Parties an amendment to any of the amounts if representatives of at least three-quarters of the States Parties to this Convention vote in favour of such a recommendation. In making such a recommendation, the Committee shall take into account:

a) any information concerning events causing or likely to cause pollution damage having a bearing on the objects of this Convention;

b) any information on increases and decreases occurring after the entry into force of this

Convention in the costs of goods and services of the kinds involved in the treatment and remedying of marine oil spillages;

c) the availability of reliable insurance cover against the risk of liability for pollution damage.

3. Any amount recommended in accordance with paragraph 2 of this Article shall be notified by the depositary Government to all States Parties. It shall replace the amount currently applicable thirty days after its acceptance by all States Parties. A State Party which has, within six months of such notification or such other period as has been specified in the recommendation, notified the depositary Government that it is unable to accept the recommended amount, shall be deemed to have accepted it.

4. If the recommended amount has not been accepted by all States Parties within six months, or such other period as has been specified in the recommendation, after it has been notified by the depositary Government it shall, thirty days thereafter, replace the amount currently applicable as between those States Parties which have accepted it. Any other State Party may subsequently accept the recommended amount which shall become applicable to it thirty days thereafter.

5. A State acceding to this Convention shall be bound by any recommendation of the Committee which has been unanimously accepted by States Parties. Where a recommendation has not been so accepted, an acceding State shall be deemed to have accepted it unless, at the time of its accession, that State notifies the depositary Government that it does not accept such a recommendation.

Article 10

Rights of compensation under this Convention shall be extinguished unless, within twelve months of the date on which the person suffering the damage knew or ought reasonably to have known of the damage, the claimant has in writing notified the operator of his claim or has brought an action in respect of it. However in no case shall an action be brought after four years from the date of the incident which caused the damage. Where the incident consists of a series of occurrences, the four years' period shall run from the date of the last occurrence.

Article 11

1. Actions for compensation under this Convention may be brought only in the courts of any State Party where pollution damage was suffered as a result of the incident or in the courts of the Controlling State. For the purpose of determining where the damage was suffered, damage suffered in an area in which, in accordance with international law, a State has sovereign rights over natural resources shall be deemed to have been suffered in that State.

2. Each State Party shall ensure that its courts possess the necessary jurisdiction to entertain such actions for compensation.

3. After the fund has been constituted in accordance with Article 6, the courts of the State Party in which the fund is constituted shall be exclusively competent to determine all matters relating to the apportionment and distribution of the fund.

Article 12

1. Any judgement given by a court with jurisdiction in accordance with Article 11, which is enforceable in the State of origin where it is no longer subject to ordinary forms of review, shall be recognized in any State Party, except:

a) where the judgement was obtained by fraud; or

b) where the defendant was not given reasonable notice and a fair opportunity to present his case.

2. A judgement recognized under paragraph 1 of this Article shall be enforceable in each State Party as soon as the formalities required in that State have been complied with. The formalities shall not permit the merits of the case to be re-opened, nor a reconsideration of the applicable law.

Article 13

Where a State Party is the operator, such State shall be subject to suit in the jurisdictions set forth in Article 11 and shall waive all defences based on its status as a sovereign State.

Article 14

No liability shall arise under this Convention for damage caused by a nuclear incident:

a) if the operator of a nuclear installation is liable for such damage under either the Paris Convention of 29 July 1960 on Third Party Liability in the Field of Nuclear Energy or the Vienna Convention of 21 May 1963 on Civil Liability for Nuclear Damage, or if the operator of a nuclear ship is liable for such damage under the Brussels Convention of 25 May 1962 on the Liability of Operators of Nuclear Ships; or

b) if the operator of a nuclear installation or the operator of a nuclear ship is liable for such damage by virtue of a national law governing the liability for such damage, provided that such law is in all respects as favourable to persons who may suffer damage as, in the case of the operator of a nuclear installation, either the Paris or the Vienna Convention or, in the case of the operator of a nuclear ship, the Brussels Convention.

Article 15

1. This Convention shall not prevent a State from providing for unlimited liability or a higher limit of liability than that currently applicable under Article 6 for pollution damage caused by installations for which it is the Controlling State and suffered in that State or in another State Party; provided however that in so doing it shall not discriminate on the basis of nationality. Such provision may be based on the principle of reciprocity.

2. The courts of each State Party shall apply the law of the Controlling State in order to determine

whether the operator is entitled under the provisions of this Article and paragraph 1 of Article 6 to limit his liability and, if so, the amount of such liability.

3. Nothing in this Article shall affect the amount of compensation available for pollution damage suffered in States Parties in respect of which the provision made in accordance with paragraph 1 of this Article does not apply.

4. For the purposes of this Article, pollution damage suffered in a State Party means pollution damage suffered in the territory of that State or in the areas in which, in accordance with international law, it has sovereign rights over natural resources.

Article 16

This Convention shall be open for signature at London from 1 May 1977 until 30 April 1978 by the States invited to participate in the Intergovernmental Conference on the Convention on Civil Liability for Oil Pollution Damage from Offshore Operations, held there from 20 October to 31 October 1975 and from 13 December to 17 December 1976, and shall thereafter be open for accession by such States.

Article 17

This Convention shall be subject to ratification, acceptance or approval.

Article 18

The States Parties may unanimously invite to accede to this Convention other States which have coastlines on the North Sea, the Baltic Sea or that part of the Atlantic Ocean to the north of 36° North latitude.

Article 19

The instruments of ratification, acceptance, approval and accession shall be deposited with the Government of the United Kingdom of Great Britain and Northern Ireland.

Article 20

1. This Convention shall enter into force on the ninetieth day following the date of deposit of the fourth instrument of ratification, acceptance, approval or accession.

2. For each State ratifying, accepting, approving or acceding to the Convention after the deposit of the fourth instrument, the Convention shall enter into force on the ninetieth day after deposit by such State of its instrument.

Article 21

A State Party may denounce this Convention at any time by means of a notice in writing addressed to the depositary Government. Any such denunciation shall take effect twelve months after the date on which the depositary Government has received such notice, or at such later date as may be specified in the notice.

Article 22

1. Any State may, at the time of ratification, acceptance, approval or accession or at any later date, declare by means of a notice in writing addressed to the depositary Government that this Convention shall apply to all or any of the territories for whose international relations it is responsible, provided that they are situated within the area defined in Article 18.

2. Such declaration shall take effect on the ninetieth day after its receipt by the depositary Government or, if on such date the Convention has not yet entered into force, from the date of its entry into force.

3. Each State Party which has made a declaration in accordance with paragraph 1 of this Article may, in accordance with Article 21, denounce this Convention in relation to all or any of the territories concerned.

Article 23

Any State Party may, after having obtained the agreement of at least one-third of the States Parties, convene a Conference of States Parties for the revision or amendment of this Convention.

Article 24

No reservation may be made to this Convention.

Article 25

The depositary Government shall inform the States referred to in Article 16 and the acceding States:

a) of signatures to this Convention, of the deposit of instruments of ratification, acceptance, approval or accession, of the receipt of notices in accordance with Article 22, and of the receipt of notices of denunciation;

b) of the date on which the Convention will enter into force; and

c) of the recommendations of the Committee convened under Article 9, of the acceptances and non-acceptances of such recommendations, and of the dates on which these recommendations take effect.

Article 26

The original of this Convention, of which the English and French texts are equally authentic, shall be deposited with the Government of the United Kingdom of Great Britain and Northern Ireland, which shall send certified copies thereof to the States referred to in Article 16 and the acceding States and which, upon its entry into force, shall transmit a certified copy to the Secretariat of the United Nations for registration and publication in accordance with Article 102 of the Charter of the United Nations.

In witness whereof the undersigned, being duly authorised thereto, have signed this Convention.

Done at London this First Day of May, 1977.

CONVENTION ON THE PROHIBITION OF MILITARY OR ANY OTHR HOSTILE USE OF ENVIRONMENTAL MODIFICATION TECHNIQUES [72]

Geneva, 18 May 1977

The States Parties to this Convention,

Guided by the interest of consolidating peace, and wishing to contribute to the cause of halting the arms race, and of bringing about general and complete disarmament under strict and effective international control, and of saving mankind from the danger of using new means of warfare,

Determined to continue negotiations with a view to achieving effective progress towards further measures in the field of disarmament,

Recognizing that scientific and technical advances may open new possibilities with respect to modification of the environment,

Recalling the Declaration of the United Nations Conference on the Human Evironment, adopted at Stockholm on 16 June 1972,

Realizing that the use of environment modification techniques for peaceful purposes could improve the interrelationship of man and nature and contribute to the preservation and improvement of the environment for the benefit of present and future generations,

Recognizing, however, that military or any other hostile use of such techniques could have effects extremely harmful to human welfare.

Desiring to prohibit effectively military or any other hostile use of environment modification techniques in order to eliminate the dangers to mankind from such use, and affirming their willingness to work towards the achievement of this objective,

Desiring also to contribute to the strengthening of trust among nations and to the further improvement of this international situation in accordance with the purposes and principles of the Charter of the United Nations,

Have agreed as follows

Article I

1. Each State Party to this Convention undertakes not to engage in military or any other hostile use of environmental modification techniques having widespread, long-lasting or severe effects as the means of destruction, damage or injury to any other State Party.

2. Each State Party to this Convention undertakes not to assist, encourage or induce any State, group of States or international organization to engage in activities contrary to the provisions of paragraph 1 of this article.

Article II

As used in Article I, the term "environmental modification techniques" refers to any technique for changing — through the deliberate manipulation of natural processess — the dynamics, composition or structure of the earth, including its biota, lithosphere, hydrosphere and atmosphere, or of outer space.

Article III

1. The provisions of this Convention shall not hinder the use of environmental modification techniques for peaceful purposes and shall be without prejudice to the generally recognized principles and applicable rules of international law concerning such use.

2. The State Parties to this Convention undertake to facilitate, and have the right to participate in, the fullest possible exchange of scientific and technological information on the use of environmental modification techniques for peaceful purposes. States Parties in a position to do so shall contribute, alone or together with other States or international organizations, to international economic and scientific co-operation in the preservation, improvement and peaceful utilization of the environment, with due consideration for the needs of the developing areas of the world.

Article IV

Each State Party to this Convention undertakes to take any measures it considers necessary in accordance with its constitutional processes to prohibit and prevent any activity in violation of the provisions of the Convention anywhere under its jurisdiction or control.

Article V

1. The States Parties to this Convention undertake to consult one another and to co-operate in solving any problems which may arise in relation to the objectives of, or in the application of the provisions of, the Convention. Consultation and co-operation pursuant to this article may also be undertaken through appropriate international procedures within the framework of the United Nations and in accordance with its Charter. These international procedures may include the services of appropriate international organizations, as well as of a Consultative Committee of Experts as provided for in paragraph 2 of this article.

2. For the purpose set forth in paragraph 1 of this article, the Depositary shall, within one month of the receipt of a request from any State Party to this Convention, convene a Consultative Committee of Experts. Any State Party may appoint an expert to the Committee whose functions and rules of procedure are set out in the annex, which constitutes an integral part of this Convention. The Committee shall transmit to the Depositary a summary of its findings of fact, incorporating all view and information presented to the Committee during its proceedings. The Depositary shall distribute the summary to all States Parties.

3. Any State Party to this Convention which has reason to believe that any other State Party is acting in breach of obligations deriving from the provisions of the Convention may lodge a complaint with the Security Council of the United

Nations. Such a complaint should include all relevant information as well as all possible evidence supporting its validity.

4. Each State Party to this Convention undertakes to co-operate in carrying out any investigation which the Security Council may initiate, in accordance with the provisions of the Charter of the United Nations, on the basis of the complaint received by the Council. The Security Council inform the States Parties of the results of the investigation.

5. Each State Party to this Convention undertakes to provide or support assistance, in accordance with the provisions of the Charter of the United Nations, to any State Party which so requests, if the Security Council decides that such Party has been harmed or is likely to be harmed as a result of violation of the Convention.

Article VI

1. Any State Party to this Convention may propose amendments to the Convention. The text of any proposed amendment shall be submitted to the Depositary, who shall promptly circulate it to all States Parties.

2. An amendment shall enter into force for all States Parties to this Convention which have accepted it, upon the deposit with the Depositary of instruments of acceptance by a majority of States Parties. Thereafter it shall enter into force for any remaining State Party on the date of deposit of its instrument of acceptance.

Article VII

This Convention shall be of unlimited duration.

Article VIII

1. Five years after the entry into force of this Convention, a conference of the States Parties to the Convention shall be convened by the Depositary at Geneva, Switzerland. The conference shall review the operation of the Convention with a view to ensuring that its purpsoes and provisions are being realized, and shall in particular examine the effectiveness of the provisions of paragraph 1 of article 1 in eliminating the dangers of military or any other hostile use of environment modification techniques.

2. At intervals of not less than five years thereafter, a majority of the States Parties to this Convention may obtain, by submitting a proposal to this effect to the Depositary, the convening of a conference with the same objectives.

3. If no conference has been convened pursuant to paragraph 2 of this article within ten years following the conclusion of a previous conference, the Depositary shall solicit the views of all States Parties to this Convention, concerning the convening of such a conference, If one third or ten of the States Parties, whichever number is less, respond affirmatively, the Depositary shall take immediate steps to convene the conference.

Article IX

1. This Convention shall be open to all States for signature. Any State which does not sign the Convention before its entry into force in accordance with paragraph 3 of this article may accede to it at any time.

2. This Convention shall be subject to ratification by signatory States. Instruments of ratification or accession shall be deposited with the Secretary-General of the United Nations.

3. This Convention shall enter into force upon the deposit of instruments of ratification by twenty Governments in accordance with paragraph 2 of this article.

4. For those States whose instruments of ratification or accession are deposited after the entry into force of this Convention, it shall enter into force on the date of the deposit of their instruments of ratification or accession.

5. The Depositary shall promptly inform all signatory and acceding States of the date of each signature, and the date of deposit of each instrument of ratification or accession and the date of the entry into force of this Convention and of any amendments thereto, as well as of the receipt of other notices.

6. This Convention shall be registered by the Depositary in accordacne with Article 102 of the Charter of the United Nations.

Article X

This Convention, of which the English, Arabic, Chinese, French, Russian and Spanish texts are equally authentic, shall be deposited with the Secretary-General of the United Nations, who shall send duly certified copies thereof to the Governments of the signatory and acceding States.

In Witness Whereof, the undersigned, being duly authorized thereto by their respective Governments, have signed this Convention, opened for signature at Geneva on the eighteenth day of May, one thousand nine hunderd and seventy-seven.

ANNEX TO THE CONVENTION

CONSULTATIVE COMMITTEE OF EXPERTS

1. The Consultative Committee of Experts shall undertake to make appropriate findings of fact and provide expert views relevant to any problem raised pursuant to paragraph 1 of article V of this Convention by the State Party requesting the convening of the Committee.

2. The work of the Consultative Committee of Experts shall be organized in such a way as to permit it to perform the functions set forth in paragraph 1 of this annex. The Committee shall decide procedural questions relative to the organization of its work, where possible by consensus and voting. There shall be no voting on matters of substance.

3. The Depositary or his representative shall serve as the Chairman of the Committee.

4. Each expert may be assisted at meetings by one or more advisers.

5. Each expert shall have the right, through the Chairman, to request from States, and from international organizations, such information and assistance as the expert considers desirable for the accomplishment of the Committee's work.

CONVENTION CONCERNING THE PROTECTION OF WORKERS AGAINST OCCUPATIONAL HAZARDS IN THE WORKING ENVIRONMENT DUE TO AIR POLLUTION, NOISE AND VIBRATION [73]

Geneva, 20 June 1977

The General Conference of the International Labour Organisation,

Having been convened at Geneva by the Governing Body of the International Labour Office, and having met in its Sixty-third Session on 1 June 1977, and

Noting the terms of existing international labour Conventions and Recommendations which are relevant and, in particular, the Protection of Workers' Health Recommendation, 1953, the Occupational Health Services Recommendation, 1959, the Radiation Protection Convention and Recommendation, 1963, the Employment Injury Benefits Convention, 1964, the Hygiene (Commerce and Offices) Convention and Recommendation, 1964, the Benzene Convention and Recommendation, 1971, and the Occupational Cancer Convention and Recommendation, 1974, and

Having decided upon the adoption of certain proposals with regard to working environment: atmospheric pollution, noise and vibration, which is the fourth item on the agenda of the session, and

Having determined that these proposals shall take the form of an international Convention,

adopts this twentieth day of June of the year one thousand nine hundred and seventy-seven the following Convention, which may be cited as the Working Environment (Air Pollution, Noise and Vibration) Convention, 1977:

PART 1

SCOPE AND DEFINITIONS

Article 1

1. This Convention applies to all branches of economic activity.

2. A Member ratifying this Convention may, after consultation with the representative organisations of employers and workers concerned, where such exist, exclude from the application of the Convention particular branches of economic activity in respect of which special problems of a substantial nature arise.

3. Each Member which ratifies this Convention shall list in the first report on the application of the Convention submitted under article 22 of the Constitution of the International Labour Organisation any branches which may have been excluded in pursuance of paragraph 2 of this Article, giving the reasons for such exclusion, and shall state in subsequent reports the position of its law and practice in respect of the branches excluded, and the extent to which effect has been given or is proposed to be given to the Convention in respect of such branches.

Article 2

1. Each Member, after consultation with the representative organisations of employers and workers, where such exist, may accept the obligations of this Convention separately in respect of —

a) air pollution;

b) noise; and

c) vibration.

2. A Member which does not accept the obligations of the Convention in respect of one or more of the categories of hazards shall specify this in its ratification and shall give reasons in the first report on the application of the Convention submitted under article 22 of the Constitution of the International Labour Organisation; it shall state in subsequent reports the position of its law and practice in respect of the category or categories of hazards excluded and the extent to which effect has been given or is proposed to be given to the Convention in respect of each such category of hazards.

3. Each Member which has not on ratification accepted the obligations of this Convention in respect of all the categories of hazards shall subsequently, when it is satisfied that conditions permit this, notify the Director-General of the International Labour Office that it accepts the obligations of the Convention in respect of a category or categories previously excluded.

Article 3

For the purpose of this Convention —

a) the term "air pollution" covers all air contaminated by substances, whatever their physical state, which are harmful to health or otherwise dangerous;

b) the term "noise" covers all sound which can result in hearing impairment or be harmful to health or otherwise dangerous;

c) the term "vibration" covers any vibration which is transmitted to the human body through solid structures and is harmful to health or otherwise dangerous.

PART II

GENERAL PROVISIONS

Article 4

1. National laws or regulations shall prescribe that measures be taken for the prevention and control of, and protection against, occupational hazards in the working environment due to air pollution, noise and vibration.

2. Provisions concerning the practical implementation of the measures so prescribed may be adopted through technical standards, codes of practice and other appropriate methods.

Article 5

1. In giving effect to the provisions of this Convention, the competent authority shall act in consultation with the most representative

organisations of employers and workers concerned.

2. Representatives of employers and workers shall be associated with the elaboration of provisions concerning the practical implementation of the measures prescribed in pursuance of Article 4.

3. Provision shall be made for as close a collaboration as possible at all levels between employers and workers in the application of the measures prescribed in pursuance of this Convention.

4. Representatives of the employer and representatives of the workers of the undertaking shall have the opportunity to accompany inspectors supervising the application of measures prescribed in pursuance of this Convention, unless the inspectors consider, in the light of the general instructions of the competent authority, that this may be prejudical to the performance of their duties.

Article 6

1. Employers shall be made responsible for compliance with the prescribed measures.

2. Whenever two or more employers undertake activities simultaneously at one workplace, they shall have the duty to collaborate in order to comply with the prescribed measures, without prejudice to the responsibility of each employer for the health and safety of his employees. In appropriate circumstances, the competent authority shall prescribe general procedures for this collaboration.

Article 7

1. Workers shall be required to comply with safety procedures relating to the prevention and control of, and protection against, occupational hazards due to air pollution, noise and vibration in the working environment.

2. Workers or their representatives shall have the right to present proposals, to obtain information and training and to appeal to appropriate bodies so as to ensure protection against occupational hazards due to air pollution, noise and vibration in the working environment.

PART III

Preventive and Protective Measures

Article 8

1. The competent authority shall establish criteria for determining the hazards of exposure to air pollution, noise and vibration in the working environment and, where appropriate, shall specify exposure limits on the basis of these criteria.

2. In the elaboration of the criteria and the determination of the exposure limits the competent authority shall take to account the opinion of technically competent persons designated by the most representative organisations of employers and workers concerned.

3. The criteria and exposure limits shall be established, supplemented and revised regularly in the light of current national and international knowledge and data, taking into account as far as possible any increase in occupational hazards resulting from simultaneous exposure to several harmful factors at the workplace.

Article 9

As far as possible, the working environment shall be kept free from any hazard due to air pollution, noise or vibration —

a) by technical measures applied to new plant or processes in design or installation, or added to existing plant or processes; or, where this is not possible,

b) by supplementary organisational measures.

Article 10

Where the measures taken in pursuance of Article 9 do not bring air pollution, noise and vibration in the working environment within the limits specified in pursuance of Article 8, the employer shall provide and maintain suitable personal protective equipment. The employer shall not require a worker to work without the personal protective equipment provided in pursuance of this Article.

Article 11

1. There shall be supervision at suitable intervals, on conditions and in circumstances determined by the competent authority, of the health of workers exposed or liable to be exposed to occupational hazards due to air pollution, noise or vibration in the working environment. Such supervision shall include a pre-assignment medical examination and periodical examinations, as determined by the competent authority.

2. The supervision provided for in paragraph 1 of this Article shall be free of cost to the worker concerned.

3. Where continued assignment to work involving exposure to air pollution, noise or vibration is found to be medically inadvisable, every effort shall be made, consistent with national practice and conditions, to provide the worker concerned with suitable alternative employment or to maintain his income through social security measures or otherwise.

4. In implementing this Convention, the rights of workers under social security or social insurance legislation shall not be adversely affected.

Article 12

The use of processes, substances, machinery and equipment, to be specified by the competent authority, which involve exposure of workers to occupational hazards in the working environment due to air pollution, noise or vibration, shall be notified to the competent authority and the competent authority, as appropriate, may authorise the use on prescribed conditions or prohibit it.

Article 13

All persons concerned shall be adequately and suitably —

a) informed of potential occupational hazards in the working environment due to air pollution, noise and vibration; and

b) instructed in the measures available for the prevention and control of, and protection against, those hazards.

Article 14

Measures taking account of national conditions and resources shall be taken to promote research in the field of prevention and control of hazards in the working environment due to air pollution, noise and vibration.

PART IV

MEASURES OF APPLICATION

Article 15

On conditions and in circumstances determined by the competent authority, the employer shall be required to appoint a competent person, or use a competent outside service or service common to several undertakings, to deal with matters pertaining to the prevention and control of air pollution, noise and vibration in the working environment.

Article 16

Each Member shall —

a) by laws or regulations or any other method consistent with national practice and conditions take such steps, including the provision of appropriate penalties, as may be necessary to give effect to the provisions of this Convention;

b) provide appropriate inspection services for the purpose of supervising the application of the provisions of this Convention, or satisfy itself that appropriate inspection is carried out.

PART V

FINAL PROVISIONS

Article 17

The formal ratifications of this Convention shall be communicated to the Director-General of the International Labour Office for registration.

Article 18

1. This Convention shall be binding only upon those Members of the International Labour Organisation whose ratifications have been registered with the Director-General.

2. It shall come into force twelve months after the date on which the ratifications of two Members have been registered with the Director-General.

3. Thereafter, this Convention shall come into force for any Member twelve months after the date on which its ratification has been registered.

Article 19

1. A Member which has ratified this Convention may denounce it, in whole or in respect of one or more of the categories of hazards referred to in Article 2 thereof, after the expiration of ten years from the date on which the Convention first comes into force, by an act communicated to the Director-General of the International Labour Office for registration. Such denunciation shall not take effect until one year after the date on which it is registered.

2. Each Member which has ratified this Convention and which does not, within the year following the expiration of the period of ten years mentioned in the preceding paragraph, exercise the right of denunciation provided for in this Article, will be bound for another period of ten years and, thereafter, may denounce this Convention at the expiration of each period of ten years under the terms provided for in this Article.

Article 20

1. The Director-General of the International Labour Office shall notify all Members of the International Labour Organisation of the registration of all ratifications and denunciations communicated to him by the Members of the Organisation.

2. When notifying the Members of the Organisation of the registration of the second ratification communicated to him, the Director-General shall draw the attention of the Members of the Organisation to the date upon which the Convention will come into force.

Article 21

The Director-General of the International Labour Office shall communicate to the Secretary-General of the United Nations for registration in accordance with Article 102 of the Charter of the United Nations full particulars of all ratifications and acts of denunciation registered by him in accordance with the provisions of the preceding Articles.

Article 22

At such times as it may consider necessary the Governing Body of the International Labour Office shall present to the General Conference a report on the working of this Convention and shall examine the desirability of placing on the agenda of the Conference the question of its revision in whole or in part.

Article 23

1. Should the Conference adopt a new Convention revising this Convention in whole or in part, then, unless the new Convention otherwise provides —

a) the ratification by a Member of the new revising Convention shall *ipso jure* involve the immediate denunciation of this Convention, notwithstanding the provisions of Article 19 above, if and when the new revising Convention shall have come into force;

b) as from the date when the new arising Convention comes into force this Convention shall cease to be open to ratification by the Members.

2. This Convention shall in any case remain in force in its actual form and content for those Members which have ratified it but have not ratified the revising Convention.

Article 24

The English and French versions of the text of this Convention are equally authoritative.

KUWAIT REGIONAL CONVENTION FOR CO-OPERATION ON THE PROTECTION OF THE MARINE ENVIRONMENT FROM POLLUTION [74]

Kuwait, 24 April 1978

The Government of the State of Bahrain,

The Imperial Government of Iran,

The Government of the Republic of Iraq,

The Government of the State of Kuwait,

The Government of the Sultanate of Oman,

The Government of the State of Qatar,

The Government of the Kingdom of Saudi Arabia,

The Government of the United Arab Emirates,

Realizing that pollution of the marine environment in the Region shared by Bahrain, Iran, Iraq, Kuwait, Oman, Qatar, Saudi Arabia and the United Arab Emirates, by oil and other harmful or noxious materials arising from human activities on land or at sea, especially through indiscriminate and uncontrolled discharge of these substances, presents a growing threat to marine life, fisheries, human health, recreational uses of beaches and other amenities.

Mindful of the special hydrographic and ecological characteristics of the marine environment of the Region and its particular vulnerability to pollution.

Conscious of the need to ensure that the processes of urban and rural development and resultant land use should be carried out in such a manner as to preserve, as far as possible, marine resources and coastal amenities, and that such development should not lead to deterioration of the marine environment,

Convinced of the need to ensure that the processes of industrial development should not, in any way, cause damage to the marine environment of the Region, jeopardize its living resources or create hazards to human health,

Recognizing the need to develop an integrated management approach to the use of the marine environment and the coastal areas which will allow the achievement of environmental and development goals in a harmonious manner,

Recognizing also the need for a carefully planned research, monitoring and assessment programme in view of the scarcity of scientific information on marine pollution in the Region,

Considering that the States sharing the Region have a special responsibility to protect its marine environment,

Aware of the importance of co-operation and co-ordination of action on a regional basis with the aim of protecting the marine environment of the Region for the benefit of all concerned, including future generations,

Bearing in mind the existing international conventions relevant to the present Convention,

Have agreed as follows:

Article I

DEFINITIONS

For the purpose of the present Convention:

a) marine pollution means the introduction by man, directly or indirectly, of substances or energy into the marine environment resulting or likely to result in such deleterious effects as harm to living resources, hazards to human health, hindrance to marine activities including fishing, impairment of quality for use of sea and reduction of amenities;

b) "National Authority" means the authority designated by each Contracting States as responsible for the co-ordination of national efforts for implementing the Convention and its protocols;

c) "Organization" means the organization established by the Contracting States in accordance with Article XVI;

d) "secretariat" means the organ of the Organization established in accordance with Article XVI;

e) "Action Plan" means the Action Plan for the Development and Protection of the Marine Environment and the Coastal Areas of Bahrain, Iran, Iraq, Kuwait, Oman, Qatar, Saudi Arabia and the United Arab Emirates adopted at the Kuwait Regional Conference of Plenipotentiaries on the Protection and Development of the Marine Environment and the Coastal Areas, convened from 15 to 23 April 1978.

Article II

GEOGRAPHICAL COVERAGE

a) The present Convention shall apply to the sea area in the Region bounded in the south by the following rhumb lines: from Ras Dharbat Ali in (16° 39'N, 35° 3'30"E) then to a position in (16° 00'N, 53° 25'E) then to a position in (17° 00'N, 56° 30'E) then to a position in (20° 30'N, 60° 00'E) then to Ras Al-Fasteh in (25° 04'N, 61° 25'E);

b) The Sea Area shall not include internal waters of the Contracting States unless it is otherwise stated in the present Convention or in any of its protocols.

Article III

GENERAL OBLIGATIONS

a) The Contracting States shall, individually and/or jointly, take all appropriate measures in accordance with the present Convention and those protocols in force to which they are party to prevent, abate and combat pollution of the marine environment in the Sea Area;

b) In addition to the Protocol concerning Regional Co-operation in Combating Pollution by Oil and other Harmful Substances in Cases of Emergency opened for signature at the same time as the present Convention, the Contracting States shall co-operate in the formulation and adoption of other protocols prescribing agreed measures, procedure and standards for the implementation of the Convention;

c) The Contracting States shall establish national

standards, laws and regulations as required for the effective discharge of the obligation prescribed in paragraph (a) of this article, and shall endeavour to harmonise their national policies in this regard and for this purpose appoint the National Authority;

d) The Contracting States shall co-operate with the competent international, regional and sub-regional organizations to establish and adopt regional standards, recommended practices and procedures to prevent, abate and combat pollution from all sources in conformity with the objectives of the present Convention, and to assist each other in fulfilling their obligations under the present Convention;

e) The Contracting Series shall use their best endeavour to ensure that the implementation of the present Convention shall not cause transformation of one type of pollution to another which could be more detrimental to the environment.

Article IV

POLLUTION FROM SHIPS

The Contracting States shall take all appropriate measures in conformity with the present Convention and the applicable rules of international law to prevent, abate and combat pollution in the Sea Area caused by intentional or accidental discharges from ships, and shall ensure effective compliance in the Sea Area with applicable international rules relating to the control of this type of pollution, including load-on-top, segregated ballast and crude oil washing procedures for tankers.

Article V

POLLUTION CAUSED BY DUMPING FROM SHIPS AND AIRCRAFT

The Contracting States shall take all appropriate measures to prevent, abate and combat pollution in the Sea Area caused by dumping of wastes and other matter from ships and aircraft, and shall ensure effective compliance in the Sea Area with applicable international rules relating to the control of this type of pollution as provided for in relevant international conventions.

Article VI

POLLUTION FROM LAND-BASED SOURCES

The Contracting States shall take all appropriate measures to prevent, abate and combat pollution caused by discharges from land reaching the Sea Area whether water-borne, air-borne, or directly from the coast including outfalls and pipelines.

Article VII

POLLUTION RESULTING FROM EXPLORATION AND EXPLOITATION OF THE BED OF THE TERRITORIAL SEA AND ITS SUB-SOIL AND THE CONTINENTAL SHELF

The Contracting States shall take all appropriate measures to prevent, abate and combat pollution in the Sea Area resulting from exploration and exploitation of the bed of the territorial sea and its sub-soil and the continental shelf, including the prevention of accidents and the combating of pollution emergencies resulting in damage to the marine environment.

Article VIII

POLLUTION FROM OTHER HUMAN ACTIVITIES

The Contracting States shall take all appropriate measures to prevent, abate and combat pollution of the Sea Area resulting from land reclamation and associated suction dredging and coastal dredging.

Article IX

CO-OPERATION IN DEALING WITH POLLUTION EMERGENCIES

a) The Contracting States shall, individually and/or jointly, take all necessary measures, including those to ensure that adequate equipment and qualified personnel are readily available, to deal with pollution emergencies in the Sea Area, whatever the cause of such emergencies, and to reduce or eliminate damage resulting therefrom;

b) Any Contracting State which becomes aware of any pollution emergency in the Sea Area shall, without delay, notify the Organization referred to under Article XVI and, through the secretariat, any Contracting State likely to be affected by such emergency.

Article X

SCIENTIFIC AND TECHNOLOGICAL CO-OPERATION

a) The Contracting States shall co-operate directly, or, where appropriate, through competent international and regional organizations, in the field of scientific research, monitoring and assessment concerning pollution in the Sea Area, and shall exchange data as well as other scientific information for the purpose of the present Convention and any of its protocols;

b) The Contracting States shall co-operate further to develop and co-operate national research and monitoring programmes relating to all types of pollution in the Sea Area and to establish in co-operation with competent regional or international organizations, a regional network of such programmes to ensure compatible results. For this purpose, each Contracting State shall designate the National Authority responsible for pollution research and monitoring within the areas under its national jurisdiction. The Contracting States shall participate in international arrangements for pollution research and monitoring in areas beyond their national jurisdiction.

Article XI

ENVIRONMENTAL ASSESSMENT

a) Each Contracting State shall endeavour to include an assessment of the potential environmental effects in any planning activity entailing projects within its territory, particularly in the coastal areas, which may cause significant risks of pollution in the Sea Area;

b) The Contracting States may, in consultation

with the secretariat, develop procedures for dissemination of information of the assessment of the activities referred to in paragraph (a) above;

c) The Contracting States undertake to develop, individually or jointly, technical and other guidelines in accordance with standard scientific practice to assist the planning of their development projects in such a way as to minimize their harmful impact on the marine environment. In this regard international standards may be used where appropriate.

Article XII

TECHNICAL AND OTHER ASSISTANCE

The Contracting States shall co-operate directly or through competent regional or international organizations in the development of programmes of technical and other assistance in fields relating to marine pollution in co-ordinating with the Organization referred to in Article XVI.

Article XIII

LIABILITY AND COMPENSATION

The Contracting States undertake to co-operate in the formulation and adoption of appropriate rules and procedure for the determination of:

a) civil liability and compensation for damage resulting from pollution of the marine environment, bearing in mind applicable international rules and procedures relating to those matters; and

b) liability and compensation for damage resulting from violation of obligations under the present Convention and its protocols.

Article XIV

SOVEREIGN IMMUNITY

Warships or other ships owned or operated by a State, and used only on Government non-commercial service, shall be exempted from the application of the provisions of the present convention. Each Contracting State shall, as far as possible, ensure that its warships or other ships owned or operated by that State, and used only on Government non-commercial service, shall comply with the present Convention in the prevention of pollution to the marine environment.

Article XV

DISCLAIMER

Nothing in the present Convention shall prejudice or affect the rights or claims of any Contracting State in regard to the nature or extent of its maritime jurisdiction which may be established in conformity with international law.

Article XVI

REGIONAL ORGANIZATION FOR THE PROTECTION OF THE MARINE ENVIRONMENT

a) The Contracting States hereby establish a Regional Organization for the Protection of the Marine Environment, the permanent headquarters of which shall be located in Kuwait.

b) The organization shall consist of the following organs:

(i) a Council which shall be comprised of the Contracting States and shall perform the functions set forth in paragraph (d) of Article XVII;

(ii) a secretariat which shall perform the functions set forth in paragraph (a) of Article XVIII; and

(iii) a Judicial Commission for the Settlement of Disputes whose composition, terms of reference and rules of procedure shall be established at the first meeting of the Council.

Article XVII

COUNCIL

a) The meetings of the Council shall be convened in accordance with paragraph (a) of Article XVIII and paragraph (b) of Article XXX. The Council shall hold ordinary meetings once a year. Extra-ordinary meetings of the Council shall be held upon the request of at least one Contracting State endorsed by at least one other Contracting State, or upon the request of the Executive Secretary endorsed by at least two Contracting States. Meeting of the Council shall be convened at the headquarters of the Organization or at any other place agreed upon by consultation amongst the Contracting States. Three-fourths of the Contracting States shall constitute a quorum.

b) The Chairmanship of the Council shall be given to each Contracting State in turn in alphabetical order of the names of the States in the English language. The Chairman shall serve for a period of one year and cannot during the period of chairmanship serve as a representative of his State. Should the chairmanship fall vacant, the Contracting State chairing the Council shall designate a successor to remain in office until the term of chairmanship of that Contracting State expires.

c) The voting procedure in the Council shall be as follows:

(i) each Contracting State shall have one vote;

(ii) decisions on substantive matters shall be taken by a unanimous vote of the Contracting States present and voting;

(iii) decisions on procedural matters shall be taken by three-fourths majority vote of the Contracting States present and voting.

d) The functions of the Council shall be:

(i) to keep under review the implementation of the Convention and its protocols, and the Action Plan referred to in paragraph (e) in Article I;

(ii) to review and evaluate the state of marine pollution and its effects on the Sea Area on the basis of reports provided by the Contracting States and the competent international or regional organizations;

(iii) to adopt, review and amend as required in accordance with procedures established in Article XXI, the annexes to the Convention and to its protocols;

(iv) to receive and to consider reports submitted by

the Contracting States under Articles IX and XXIII;

(v) to consider reports prepared by the secretariat on questions relating to the Convention and to matters relevant to the administration of the Organization;

(vi) to make recommendations regarding the adoption of any additional protocols or any amendments to the Convention or to its protocols in accordance with Articles XIX and XX;

(vii) to establish subsidiary bodies and ad hoc working groups as required to consider any matters related to the Convention and its protocols and annexes to the Convention and its protocols;

(viii) to appoint an Executive Secretary and to make provision for the appointment by the Executive Secretary of such other personnel as may be necessary;

(ix) to review periodically the functions of the secretariat;

(x) to consider and to undertake any additional action that may be required for the achievement of the purposes of the Convention and its protocols.

Article XVIII

SECRETARIAT

a) The secretariat shall be comprised of an Executive Secretary and the personnel necessary to perform the following functions:

(i) to convene and to prepare the meetings of the Council and its subsidiary bodies and ad hoc working groups as referred to in Article XVII, and conferences as referred to in Articles XIX and XX;

(ii) to transmit to the Contracting States notifications, reports and other information received in accordance with Articles IX and XXIII;

(iii) to consider enquiries by, and information from, the Contracting States and to consult with them on questions relating to the Convention and its protocols and annexes thereto;

(iv) to prepare reports on matters relating to the Convention and to the administration of the Organization;

(v) to establish, maintain and disseminate an up-to-date collection of national laws of all States concerned relevant to the protection of the marine treatment;

(vi) to arrange, upon request, for the provision of technical assistance and advice for the drafting of appropriate national legislation for the effective implementation of the Convention and its protocols;

(vii) to arrange for training programmes in areas related to the implementation of the Convention and its protocols;

(viii) to carry out its assignments under the protocols to the Convention;

(ix) to perform such other functions as may be assigned to it by the Council for the implementation of the Convention and its protocols.

b) The Executive Secretary shall be the chief administrative official of the Organization and shall perform the functions that are necessary for the administration of the present Convention, the work of the secretariat and other tasks entrusted to the Executive Secretary by the Council and as provided for in its rules and procedures and financial rules.

Article XIX

ADOPTION OF ADDITIONAL PROTOCOLS

Any Contracting State may propose additional protocols to the present Convention pursuant to paragraph (b) of Article III at a diplomatic conference of the Contracting States to be convened by the secretariat at the request of at least three Contracting States. Additional protocols shall be adopted by a unanimous vote of the Contracting States present and voting.

Article XX

AMENDMENTS TO THE CONVENTION AND ITS PROTOCOLS

a) Any Contracting State to the present Convention or any of its protocols may propose amendments to the Convention or to the protocol concerned at a diplomatic conference to be convened by the secretariat at the request of at least three Contracting States. Amendments to the Convention and its protocols shall be adopted by a unanimous vote of the Contracting States present and voting.

b) Amendments to the Convention or any protocol adopted by a diplomatic conference shall be submitted by the Depositary for acceptance by all Contracting States. Acceptance of amendments to the Convention or to any protocol shall be notified to the Depositary in writing. Amendments adopted in accordance with this article shall enter into force for all Contracting States, except those which have notified the Depositary of a different intention, on the thirtieth day following the receipt by the Depositary of notification of their acceptance by at least three-fourths of the Contracting States to the Convention or any protocol concerned as the case may be.

c) After the entry into force of an amendment to the Convention or to a protocol, any new Contracting State to the Convention or such protocol shall become a Contracting State to the instrument as amended.

Article XXI

ANNEXES AND AMENDMENTS TO ANNEXES

a) Annexes to the Convention or to any protocol shall form an integral part of the Convention or such protocol.

b) Except as may be otherwise provided in any protocol, the following procedure shall apply to the adoption and entry into force of any amendments to annexes to the Convention or to any protocol:

(i) any Contracting State to the Convention or to a protocol may propose amendments to the annexes to the instrument in question at the meetings of the

Council referred to in Article XVII;

(ii) such amendments shall be adopted at such meetings by a unanimous vote;

(iii) the Depositary referred to in Article XXX shall communicate amendments so adopted to all Contracting State without delay;

(iv) any Contracting State which has a different intention with respect to an amendment to the annexes to the Convention or to any protocol shall notify the Depositary in writing within a period determined by the Contracting States concerned when adopting the amendment;

(v) the Depositary shall notify all Contracting States without delay of any notification received pursuant to the preceding sub-paragraph;

(vi) on the expiry of the period referred to in sub-paragraph (iv) above, the amendment to the annex shall become effective for all Contracting States to the Convention or to the protocol concerned which have not submitted a notification in accordance with the provisions of that sub-paragraph.

c) The adoption and entry into force of a new annex to the Convention or to any protocol shall be subject to the same procedure as for the adoption and entry into force of an amendment to an annex in accordance with the provisions of this article, provided that, if any amendment to the Convention or the protocol concerned is involved, the new annex shall not enter into force until such time as the amendment to the Convention or the protocol concerned enters into force.

Article XXII

RULES OF PROCEDURE AND FINANCIAL RULES

a) The Council shall, at the first meeting, adopt its own rules.

b) The Council shall adopt financial rules to determine, in particular, the financial participation of the Contracting States.

Article XXIII

REPORTS

Each Contracting State shall submit to the secretariat reports on measures adopted in implementation of the provisions of the Convention and its protocols in such form and at such intervals as may be determined by the Council.

Article XXIV

COMPLIANCE CONTROL

The Contracting State shall co-operate in the development of procedures for the effective application of the Convention and its protocols, including detection of violations, using all appropriate and practicable measures of detection and environmental monitoring, including adequate procedures for reporting and accumulation of evidence.

Article XXV

SETTLEMENT OF DISPUTES

a) In case of a dispute as to the interpretation or application of this Convention or its protocols, the Contracting States concerned shall seek a settlement of the dispute through negotiation or any other peaceful means of their own choice.

b) If the Contracting States concerned cannot settle the dispute through the means mentioned in paragraph (a) of this article, the dispute shall be submitted to the Judicial Commission for the Settlement of Disputes referred to in paragraph (a) (iii) of Article XVI.

Article XXVI

SIGNATURE

The present Convention together with the Protocol concerning Regional Co-operation in Combating Pollution by Oil and other Harmful Substances in Cases of Emergency shall be open for signature in Kuwait from 24 April to 23 July 1978 by any State invited as a participant in the Kuwait Regional Conference of Plenipotentiaries on the Protection and Development of the Marine Environment and the Coastal Areas, convened from 15 to 23 April 1978 for the purpose of adopting the Convention and the Protocol.

Article XXVII

RATIFICATION, ACCEPTANCE, APPROVAL OR ACCESSION

a) The present Convention together with the Protocol concerning Regional Co-operation in Combating Pollution by Oil and other Harmful Substances in Cases of Emergency and any other protocol thereto shall be subject to ratification, acceptance, or approval by the States referred to in Article XXVI.

b) As from 24 July 1978, this Convention together with the Protocol concerning Regional Co-operation in Combating Pollution by Oil and other Harmful Substances in Cases of Emergency shall be open for accession by the States referred to in Article XXVI.

c) Any State which has ratified, accepted, approved or acceded to the present Convention shall be considered as having ratified, accepted, approved or acceded to the Protocol concerning Regional Co-operation in Combating Pollution by Oil and other Harmful Substances in Cases of Emergency;

d) Instruments of ratification, acceptance, approval or accession shall be deposited with the Government of Kuwait which will assume the functions of Depositary.

Article XXVIII

ENTRY INTO FORCE

a) The present Convention together with the Protocol concerning Regional Co-operation in Combating Pollution by Oil and other Harmful Substances in Cases of Emergency shall enter into force on the nineteenth day following the date of deposit of at least five instruments of ratification, acceptance or approval of, or accession to, the Convention;

b) Any other protocol to this Convention, except as

otherwise provided in such protocol, shall enter into force on the ninetieth day following the date of deposit of at least five instruments of ratification, acceptance or approval of, or accession to, such protocol;

c) After the date of deposit of five instruments of ratification, acceptance or approval of, or accession to, this Convention or any other protocol, this Convention or any such protocol shall enter into force with respect to any State on the ninetieth day following the date of deposit by that State of the instrument of ratification, acceptance, approval or accession.

Article XXIX

WITHDRAWAL

a) At any time after five years from the date of entry into force of this Convention, any Contracting State may withdraw from this Convention by giving written notification of withdrawal to the Depositary;

b) Except as may be otherwise provided in any other protocol to the Convention, any Contracting State may, at any time after five years from the date of entry into force of such Protocol, withdraw from such protocol by giving written notification of withdrawal to the Depositary;

c) Withdrawal shall take effect ninety days after the date on which notification of withdrawal is received by the Depositary;

d) Any Contracting State which withdraws from the Convention shall be considered as also having withdrawn from any protocol to which it was a party;

e) Any Contracting State which withdrawals from the Protocol concerning Regional Co-operation in Combating Pollution by Oil and other Harmful Substances in Cases of Pollution Emergency shall be considered as also having withdrawn from the Convention.

Article XXX

RESPONSIBILITIES OF THE DEPOSITARY

a) The Depositary shall inform the Contracting States and the secretariat of the following:

(i) signature of this Convention and of any protocol thereto, and of the deposit of the instruments of ratification, acceptance, approval or accession in accordance with Article XXVII;

(ii) date on which Convention and any protocol will enter into force in accordance with the provision of Article XXVIII;

(iii) notification of a different intention made in accordance with Articles XX and XXI;

(iv) notification of withdrawal made in accordance with Article XXIX;

(v) amendments adopted with respect to the Convention and to any protocol, their acceptance by the Contracting State and the date of entry into force of those amendments in accordance with the provisions of Article XX;

(vi) adoption of new annexes and of the amendment of any annex in accordance with Article XXI;

b) The Depositary shall call the first meeting of the Council within six months of the date on which the Convention enters into force.

The original of this Convention, of any protocol thereto, of any annex to the Convention or to a protocol, or of any amendment to the Convention, to a protocol or to an annex of the Convention or of a protocol shall be deposited with the Depositary, the Government of Kuwait who shall send copies thereof to all States concerned and shall register all such instruments and all subsequent actions in respect of them with the Secretariat of the United Nations in accordance with article 102 of the Charter of the United Nations.

In witness whereof the undersigned Plenipotentiaries, being duly authorised by their respective Governments, have signed the present Convention.

Done at Kuwait this twenty-fourth day of April, in the year one thousand nine hundred and seventy-eight in the Arabic, English and Persian languages, the three texts being equally authentic. In case of a dispute as to the interpretation or application of the Convention or its protocols, the English text shall be dispositively authorative.

PROTOCOL CONCERNING REGIONAL CO-OPERATION IN COMBATING POLLUTION BY OIL AND OTHER HARMFUL SUBSTANCES IN CASES OF EMERGENCY

Kuwait, 24 April 1978

The Contracting States

Being parties to the Kuwait Regional Convention for Co-operation on the Protection of the Marine Environment from Pollution (hereinafter referred to as "the Convention");

Conscious of the particular urgency to realize the ever present potential emergencies which may result in substantial pollution by oil and other harmful substances and to provide co-operative and effective measures to deal with them;

Being aware that existing measures for responding to pollution emergencies need to be enhanced on a national and regional basis to deal with this problem in a comprehensive manner for the benefit of the Region;

Have agreed as follows:

Article I

For the purposes of this Protocol:

1. "Appropriate Authority" means either the National Authority defined in Article I of the Convention, or the authority or authorities within the Government of a Contracting State, designated by the National Authority and responsible for:

a) combating and otherwise operationally responsible to marine emergencies;

b) receiving and co-ordinating information of particular marine emergencies;

c) co-ordinating available national capabilities, for dealing with marine emergencies in general within its own Government and with other Contracting States.

2. "Marine Emergency" means any casualty, incident, occurrence or situation, however caused, resulting in substantial pollution or imminent threat of substantial pollution to the marine environment by oil or other harmful substances and includes, *inter alia,* collisions, strandings and other incidents involving ships, including tankers, blow-outs arising from petroleum drilling and production activities, and the presence of oil or other harmful substances arising from the failure of industrial installations;

3. "Marine Emergency Contingency Plan" means a plan or plans, prepared on a national, bilateral or multilateral basis, designed to co-ordinate the deployment, allocation and use of personnel, material and equipment for the purpose of responding to marine emergencies;

4. "Marine Emergency Response" means any activity intended to prevent, mitigate or eliminate pollution by oil or other harmful substances or threat of such pollution resulting from marine emergencies;

5. "Related Interests" means the interests of a Contracting State directly or indirectly affected or threatened by a marine emergency, such as:

a) Maritime, coastal, port or estuary activities, including fisheries activities, constituting an essential means of livelihood of the persons concerned;

b) historic and tourist attractions of the area concerned;

c) the health of the coastal population and the well-being of the area concerned, including conservation of living marine resources and of wildlife;

d) industrial activities which rely upon intake of water, including distillation plants, and industrial plants using circulation water;

6. "Convention" means the Kuwait Regional Convention for Co-operation on the Protection of the Marine Environment from Pollution;

7. "Sea Area" means the area specified in paragraph (a) of Article II of the Convention;

8. "Council" means the organ of the Regional Organization for the Protection of the Marine Environment established under Article XVI of the Convention;

9. "Centre" means the Marine Emergency Mutual Aid Centre established under Article III, paragraph 1 of the present Protocol.

Article II

1. The Contracting States shall co-operate in taking the necessary and effective measures to protect the coastline and related interests of one or more of the States from the threat and effects of pollution due to the presence of oil or other harmful substances in the marine environment resulting from marine emergencies.

2. The Contracting States shall endeavour to maintain and promote, either individually or through bilateral or multilateral co-operation, their contingency plans and means for combating pollution in the Sea Area by oil and other harmful substances. These means shall include, in particular, available equipment, ships, aircraft and manpower prepared for operations in cases of emergency.

Article III

1. The Contracting States hereby establish the Marine Emergency Mutual Aid Centre.

2. The objectives of the Centre shall be:

a) to strengthen the capacities of the Contracting States and to facilitate co-operation among them in order to combat pollution by oil and other harmful substances in cases of marine emergencies;

b) to assist Contracting States, which so request, in the development of their own national capabilities to combat pollution by oil and other harmful substances and to co-ordinate and facilitate information exchange, technological co-operation and training.

c) a later objective, namely the possibility of initiating operations to combat pollution by oil and other harmful substances at the regional level, may be considered. This possibility should be submitted for approval by the Council after evaluating the results achieved in the fulfilment of the previous objectives and in the light of financial resources which could be made available for this purpose.

3. The functions of the Centre shall be:

a) to collect and disseminate to the Contracting States information concerning matters covered by this Protocol, including:

(i) laws, regulations and information concerning appropriate authorities of the Contracting States and marine emergency contingency plans referred to in Article V of this Protocol;

(ii) information concerning methods, techniques and research relating to marine emergency response referred to in Article II of this Protocol; and

(iii) list of experts, equipment and materials available for marine emergency responses by the Contracting States;

b) to assist the Contracting States, as requested:

(i) in the preparation of laws and regulations concerning matters covered by this Protocol and in the establishment of appropriate authorities;

(ii) in the preparation of marine emergency contingency plans;

(iii) in the establishment of procedures under which personnel, equipment and materials involved in marine emergency responses may be expeditiously transported into, out of, and through their respective countries;

(iv) in the transmission of reports concerning marine emergencies; and

(v) in promoting and developing training programmes for combating pollution.

c) to co-ordinate training programmes for combating pollution and prepare comprehensive anti-pollution manuals;

d) to develop and maintain a communication/information system appropriate to the needs of the Contracting States and the Centre for the prompt exchange of information concerning marine emergencies required by this Protocol;

e) to prepare inventories of the available personnel, material, vessels, aircraft, and other specialized equipment for marine emergency responses;

f) to establish and maintain liaison with competent regional and international organizations, particularly the Inter-Governmental Maritime Consultative Organization, for the purposes of obtaining and exchanging scientific and technological information and data, particularly in regard of any new innovation which may assist the Centre in the performance of its functions;

g) to prepare periodic reports on marine emergencies for submission to the Council; and

h) to perform any other functions assigned to it either by this Protocol or by the Council.

4. The Centre may fulfill additional functions necessary for initiating operations to combat pollution by oil and other harmful substances on a regional level, when authorized by the Council, in accordance with paragraph 2 (c) above.

Article IV

1. The present Protocol shall apply to the Sea Area specified in paragraph (a) of Article II of the Convention.

2. For the purposes of dealing with a marine emergency, ports, harbours, estuaries, bays and lagoons may be treated as part of the Sea Area if the concerned Contracting State so decides.

Article V

Each Contracting State shall provide the Centre and the other Contracting States with information concerning:

a) its appropriate authority;

b) its laws, regulations, and other legal instruments relating generally to matters addressed in this Protocol, including those concerning the structure and operation of the authority referred to in paragraph (a) above;

c) its national marine emergency contingency plans.

Article VI

Each Contracting State shall provide to other Contracting States and the Centre information concerning:

a) existing and new methods, techniques, materials, and procedures relating to marine emergency response;

b) existing and planned research and developments in the areas referred to in Paragraph (a) above; and

c) results of research and developments referred to in Paragraph (b) above.

Article VII

1. Each Contracting State shall direct its appropriate officials to require masters of ships, pilots of aircraft and persons in charge of offshore platforms and other similar structures operating in the marine environment and under its jurisdiction to report the existence of any marine emergency in the Sea Area to the appropriate national authority and to the Centre.

2. Any Contracting State receiving a report pursuant to paragraph 1 above shall promptly inform the following of the marine emergency;

a) the Centre;

b) all other Contracting States;

c) the flag State of any foreign ship involved in the marine emergency concerned.

3. The content of the reports, including supplementary reports where appropriate, referred to in paragraph 1 above should conform to Appendix A of this Protocol.

4. Any Contracting State which submits a report pursuant to paragraph 2 (a) and (b) above, shall be exempted from the obligations specified in paragraph (b) of Article IX of the Convention.

Article VIII

The Centre shall promptly transmit information and reports which it receives from a Contracting State pursuant to Article V, VI and paragraph 2 of Article VII of this Protocol to all other Contracting States.

Article IX

Any Contracting State which transmits information pursuant to this Protocol may specifically restrict its dissemination. In such a case, any Contracting State or the Centre to whom this information has been transmitted shall not divulge it to any other person, government, or to any public or private organization without the specific authorization of the former Contracting State.

Article X

Any Contracting State faced with a marine emergency situation as defined in Paragraph 2 of Article I of this Protocol shall:

a) take every appropriate measure to combat pollution and/or to rectify the situation;

b) immediately inform all other Contracting States, either directly or through the Centre, or any action which it has taken or intends to take to combat the pollution. The Centre shall promptly transmit any such information to all other Contracting States;

c) make assessment of the nature and extent of the marine emergency, either directly or with the assistance of the Centre;

d) determine the necessary and appropriate action to be taken with respect to the marine emergency, in consultation, where appropriate, with other Contracting States, affected States and the Centre.

Article XI

1. Any Contracting State requiring assistance in a marine emergency response may call for assistance directly from any other Contracting State or through the Centre. Where the services of the Centre are utilized, the Centre shall promptly transmit requests received to all other Contracting States. The Contracting States to whom a request is made pursuant to this paragraph shall use their best endeavours within their capabilities to render the assistance requested.

2. The assistance referred to in paragraph 1 above may include:

a) personnel, material, and equipment, including facilities or methods for the disposal of recovered pollutant;

b) surveillance and monitoring capacity;

c) facilitation of the transfer of personnel, material, and equipment into, out of, and through the territories of the Contracting States.

3. The services of the Centre may be utilized by the Contracting States to co-ordinate any marine emergency response in which assistance is called for pursuant to paragraph 1 above.

4. Any Contracting State calling for assistance pursuant to paragraph 1 above shall report the activities undertaken with this assistance and its results to the Centre. The Centre shall promptly transmit any such report to all other Contracting States.

5. In cases of special emergencies, the Centre may call for the mobilization of resources made available by the Contracting States to combat pollution by oil and other harmful substances.

Article XII

1. Having due regard to the functions assigned to the Centre under this Protocol, each Contracting State shall establish and maintain an appropriate authority to carry out fully its obligations under this Protocol. With the assistance of the Centre, where appropriate, the appropriate authority of each Contracting State shall co-operate and co-ordinate its activities with counterparts in the other Contracting States.

2. Among other matters with respect to which co-operation and co-ordination efforts shall be directed under paragraph 1 above are the following:

a) distribution and allocation of stocks of material and equipment;

b) training of personnel for marine emergency response;

c) marine pollution surveillance and monitoring activities;

d) methods of communication in respect of marine emergencies;

e) facilitation of the transfer of personnel equipment and materials involved in marine emergency responses into, out of, and through the territories of the Contracting States;

f) other matters to which this Protocol applies.

Article XIII

The Council shall:

a) review periodically the activities of the Centre performed under this Protocol;

b) decide on the degree to which, and stages by which, the functions of the Centre set out in Article III will be implemented; and

c) determine the financial, administrative and other support to be provided by the Contracting States to the Centre for the performance of its functions.

In witness whereof the undersigned Plenipotentiaries, being duly authorized by their respective Governments, have signed this Protocol:

Done at Kuwait this twenty-fourth day of April, in the year one thousand nine hundred and seventy-eight in the Arabic, English and Persian languages, the three texts being equally authentic. In case of a dispute as to the interpretation or application of this Protocol, the English text shall be dispositively authoritative.

APPENDIX A

GUIDELINES FOR THE REPORT TO BE MADE PURSUANT TO ARTICLE VII OF THE PROTOCOL

1. Each report shall, as far as possible, contain, in general:

a) the identification of the source of pollution (e.g. identity of the ship), where appropriate;

b) the geographic position, time and date of the occurrence of the incident or of the observation;

c) the marine meteorological conditions prevailing in the area;

d) where the pollution originates from a ship, relevant details respecting the conditions of the ship.

2. Each report shall contain, whenever possible, in particular:

a) a clear indication or description of the harmful substances involved, including the correct technical names of such substances (trade names should not be used in place of the correct technical names);

b) a statement or estimate of the quantities, concentrations and likely conditions of harmful substances discharged or likely to be discharged into the sea;

c) where relevant, a description of the packaging and identifying marks; and

d) the name of the consignor, consignee or producer.

3. Each report shall clearly indicate, whenever possible, whether the harmful substance discharged or likely to be discharged is oil or a noxious liquid, solid or gaseous substance, and whether such substance was or is carried in bulk or contained packaged form, freight containers, portable tanks, or submarine pipelines.

4. Each report shall be supplemented, as necessary, by any relevant information requested by a recipient of the report or deemed appropriate by the person sending the report.

5. Any of the persons referred to in Article VII, paragraph 1 of this Protocol shall:

a) supplement as far as possible the initial report, as necessary, with information concerning further developments; and

b) comply as fully as possible with requests from affected States for additional information.

TREATY FOR AMAZONIAN CO-OPERATION [75]

Brasilia, 3 July 1978

The Republics of Bolivia, Brazil, Colombia, Ecuador, Guyana, Peru, Suriname and Venezuela,

Conscious of the importance of each one of the Parties of their respective Amazonian regions as an integral part of their respective territories,

Inspired by the common aim of pooling the efforts being made, both within their respective territories as well as among themselves, to promote the harmonious development of the Amazon region, to permit an equitable distribution of the benefits of said development among the Contracting Parties so as to raise the standard of living of their peoples and so as to achieve total incorporation of their Amazonian territories into their respective national economies,

Conscious of the usefulness of sharing national experience in matters pertaining to the promotion of regional development,

Considering that, so as to achieve overall development of their respective Amazonian territories, it is necessary to maintain a balance between economic growth and conservation of the environment,

Conscious that both socio-economic development as well as conservation of the environment are responsibilities inherent in the sovereignty of each State, and that co-operation among the Contracting Parties shall facilitate fulfillment of these responsibilities, by continuing and expanding the joint efforts being made for the ecological conservation of the Amazon region,

Confident that co-operation among the Latin American nations, on specific matters which they have in common shall contribute to progress on the road towards the integration and solidarity of all Latin America,

Convinced that this Treaty represents the beginning of a process of co-operation which shall benefit their respective countries and the Amazon region as a whole,

Resolve to sign the following Treaty:

Article I

The Contracting Parties agree to undertake joint actions and efforts to promote the harmonious development of their respective Amazonian territories in such a way that these joint actions produce equitable and mutually beneficial results and achieve also the preservation of the environment, and the conservation and rational utilization of the natural resources of these territories.

Paragraph: To this end, they would exchange information and prepare operational agreements and understandings as well as the pertinent legal instruments which will permit the aims of the present Treaty to be attained.

Article II

This Treaty shall be in force in the territories of the Contracting Parties in the Amazonian Basin as well as in any territory of a Contracting Party which, by virtue of its geographical, ecological or economic characteristics is considered closely connected with that Basin.

Article III

In accordance with and without prejudice to the rights granted by unilateral acts, to the provisions of bilateral treaties among the Parties and to the principles and rules of International Law, the Contracting Parties mutually guarantee on a reciprocal basis that there shall be complete freedom of commercial navigation on the Amazon and other international Amazonian rivers, observing the fiscal and police regulations in force now or in the future within the territory of each. Such regulations should, insofar as possible, be uniform and favour said navigation and trade.

Paragraph: This article shall not apply to cabotage.

Article IV

The Contracting Parties declare that the exclusive use and utilization of natural resources within their respective territories is a right inherent in the sovereignty of each state and that the exercise of this right shall not be subject to any restrictions other than those arising from International Law.

Article V

Taking account of the importance and multiplicity of the functions which the Amazonian rivers have in the process of economic and social development of the region, the Contracting Parties shall make efforts aimed at achieving rational utilization of the hydro resources.

Article VI

In order to enable the Amazonian rivers to become an effective communication link among the Contracting Parties and with the Atlantic Ocean, the riparian states interested in any specific problem affecting free and unimpeded navigation shall, as circumstances may warrant, undertake national, bilateral or multilateral measures aimed at improving and making the said rivers navigable.

Paragraph: For this purpose, they shall carry out studies into the means for eliminating physical obstacles to the said navigation as well as the economic and financial implications so as to put into effect the most appropriate operational measures.

Article VII

Taking into account the need for the exploitation of the flora and fauna of the Amazon region to be rationally planned so as to maintain the ecological balance within the region and preserve the species, the Contracting Parties decide to:

a) Promote scientific research and exchange

information and technical personnel among the competent agencies within the respective countries so as to increase their knowledge of the flora and fauna of their Amazon territories and prevent and control diseases in said territories.

b) Establish a regular system for the proper exchange of information on the convervationist measures adopted or to be adopted by each State in its Amazonian territories; these shall be the subject of an annual report to be presented by each country.

Article VIII

The Contracting Parties decide to promote co-ordination of the present health services in their respective Amazonian territories and to take other appropriate measures to improve the sanitary conditions in the region and perfect methods for preventing and combating epidemics.

Article IX

The Contracting Parties agree to establish close co-operation in the fields of scientific and technological research, for the purpose of creating more suitable conditions for the acceleration of the economic and social development of the region.

Paragraph One: For the purposes of this Treaty, the technical and scientific co-operation among the Contracting Parties may be as follows:

a) Joint or co-ordinated implementation of research and development programmes;

b) Creation and operation of research institutions or centres for improvement and experimental production;

c) Organization of seminars and conferences, exchange of information and documentation, and organization of means for their dissemination.

Paragraph Two: The Contracting Parties may, whensoever they deem it necessary and convenient, request the participation of international agencies in the execution of studies; programmes and projects resulting from the forms of technical and scientific co-operation defined in Paragraph One of this Article.

Article X

The Contracting Parties agree on the advisability of creating a suitable physical infrastructure among their respective countries, especially in relation to transportation and communications. They therefore undertake to study the most harmonious ways of establishing or improving road, river, air and telecommunication links bearing in mind the plans and programmes of each country aimed at attaining the priority goal of fully incorporating those respective Amazonian territories into their respective national economies.

Article XI

In order to increase the rational utilisation of the human and natural resources of their respective Amazonian territories, the Contracting Parties agree to encourage joint studies and measures aimed at promoting the economic and social development of said territories and generating complementary methods for reinforcing the actions envisaged in the national plans of their respective territories

Article XII

The Contracting Parties recognise the benefit to be derived by developing, under equitable and mutually beneficial conditions, retail trade of products for local consumption among the respective Amazonian border populations, by means of suitable bilateral or multilateral agreements.

Article XIII

The Contracting Parties shall co-operate to increase the flow of tourists, both national and from third countries, in their respective Amazonian territories, without prejudice to national regulations for the protection of indigenous cultures and natural resources.

Article XIV

The Contracting Parties shall co-operate in ensuring that measures adopted for the conservation of ethnological, and archeological wealth of the Amazon region are effective.

Article XV

The Contracting Parties shall seek to maintain a permanent exchange of information and co-operation among themselves and with the agencies for Latin American co-operation in the areas pertaining to matters covered by this Treaty.

Article XVI

The decisions and commitments adopted by the Contracting Parties under this Treaty shall not be to the detriment of projects and undertakings executed within their respective territories, according to International Law and fair practice between neighbouring and friendly countries.

Article XVII

The Contracting Parties shall present initiatives for undertaking studies for the elaboration of programmes of common interest for developing their Amazonian territories and in general terms provide for the fulfillment of the actions contemplated in the present Treaty.

Paragraph: The Contracting Parties agree to give special attention to the consideration of initiatives presented by the least developed countries which require joint action and efforts by the Contracting Parties.

Article XVIII

Nothing contained in this Treaty shall in any way limit the rights of the Contracting Parties to conclude bilateral or multilateral agreements on specific or generic matters, provided that these are not contrary to the achievement of the common aims for co-operation in the Amazonian region stated in this instrument.

Article XIX

Neither the signing of this Treaty nor its

execution shall have any effect on any other international treaties in force between the Parties nor on any differences with regard to limits or territorial rights which may exist between the Parties nor shall the signing or implementation of this Treaty be interpreted or invoked to imply acceptance or renunciation, affirmation or modification, direct or indirect, express or tacit, or the position or interpretation that each Contracting Party may hold on these matters.

Article XX

Notwithstanding the fact that more adequate frequency for meetings can be established at a later date, the Ministers of Foreign Affairs of the Contracting Parties shall convene meetings when deemed opportune or advisable, in order to establish the basic guidelines for common policies, for assessing and evaluating the general development or the process of Amazonian co-operation and for taking decisions designed to carry out the aims set out in this document.

Paragraph One: Meetings of Foreign Affairs Ministers shall be convened at the request of any of the Contracting Parties, provided that the request has the support of no fewer than four Member States.

Paragraph Two: The first meeting of Foreign Affairs Ministers shall be held within a period of two years following the date of entry into force of this Treaty. The venue and date of the first meeting shall be established by agreement among the Ministries of Foreign Affairs of the Contracting Parties.

Paragraph Three: Designation of the host country for the meetings shall be by rotation and in alphabetical order.

Article XXI

The Amazonian Co-operation Council comprising of top level diplomatic representatives shall meet once a year. Its duties shall be as follows:

1. To ensure that the aims and objectives of the Treaty are complied with.

2. To be responsible for carrying out the decisions taken at meetings of Foreign Affairs Ministers.

3. To recommend to the Parties the advisability and the appropriateness of convening meetings of Foreign Affairs Ministers and of drawing-up the corresponding Agenda.

4. To take under consideration initiatives and plans presented by the Parties as well as to adopt decisions for undertaking bilateral or multilateral studies and plans, the execution of which as the case may be, shall be the duty of the Permanent National Commissions.

5. To evaluate the implementation of plans of bilateral or multilateral interest.

6. To draw-up the Rules and Regulations for its proper functioning.

Paragraph One: The Council shall hold special meetings through the initiative of any of the Contracting Parties with the support of the majority of the rest.

Paragraph Two: The venue of regular meetings shall be rotated in alphabetical order among the Contracting Parties.

Article XXII

The functions of the Secretariat shall be performed *pro tempore* by the Contracting Party in whose territory the next regular meeting of the Amazonian Co-operation Council is scheduled to be held.

Paragraph Three: The *pro tempore* Secretariat shall send the pertinent documentation to the Parties.

Article XXIII

The Contracting Parties shall create Permanent National Commissions charged with enforcing in their respective territories the provisions set out in this Treaty, as well as carrying out the decisions taken at meetings of Foreign Affairs Ministers and by the Amazonian Co-operation Council, without jeopardizing other tasks assigned them by the State.

Article XXIV

Whenever necessary, the Contracting Parties may set up special Commissions to study specific problems or matters related to the aims of this Treaty.

Article XXV

Decisions at meetings held in accordance with Articles XX and XXI shall always require the unanimous vote of the Member Countries of this Treaty. Decisions made at meetings held in accordance with Article XXIV shall always require the unanimous vote of the participating countries.

Article XXVI

The Contracting Parties agree that the present Treaty shall not be susceptible to interpretative reservation or statements.

Article XXVII

This Treaty shall remain in force for an unlimited period of time, and shall not be open to adherence.

Article XXVIII

This Treaty shall be ratified by all the Contracting Parties and the instruments of ratification shall be deposited with the Government of the Federative Republic of Brazil.

Paragraph One: This Treaty shall become effective thirty days after the last instrument of ratification has been deposited by the Contracting Parties.

Paragraph Two: The intention to denounce this Treaty shall be communicated by a Contracting Party to the remaining Contracting Parties at least ninety days prior to formal delivery of the instrument of denunciation to the Government of the Federative Republic of Brazil. This Treaty shall cease to have effect for the Contracting Party denouncing it one year after the denunciation has been formalized.

Paragraph Three: This Treaty shall be drawn up in English, Dutch, Portuguese and Spanish, all having equal validity.

In witness whereof the undersigned Ministers of Foreign Affairs have signed the present Treaty.

Executed in the city of Brasilia, on July 3, 1978, to be deposited in the archives of the Ministry of Foreign Affairs of Brazil which shall provide the other signatory countries with true copies.

CONVENTION ON THE CONSERVATION OF MIGRATORY SPECIES OF WILD ANIMALS[76]

Bonn, 23 June 1979

The Contracting Parties,

Recognizing that wild animals in their innumerable forms are an irreplaceable part of the earth's natural system which must be conserved for the good of mankind;

Aware that each generation of man holds the resources of the earth for future generations and has an obligation to ensure that this legacy is conserved and, where utilized, is used wisely;

Conscious of the ever-growing value of wild animals from environmental, ecological, genetic, scientific, aesthetic, recreational, cultural, educational, social and economic points of view;

Concerned particularly with those species of wild animals that migrate across or outside national jurisdictional boundaries;

Recognizing that the States are and must be the protectors of the migratory species of wild animals that live within or pass through their national jurisdictional boundaries;

Convinced that conservation and effective management of migratory species of wild animals require the concerted action of all States within the national jurisdictional boundaries of which such species spend any part of their life cycle;

Recalling Recommendation 32 of the Action Plan adopted by the United Nations Conference on the Human Environment (Stockholm, 1972) and note with satisfaction at the Twenty-seventh Session of the General Assembly of the United Nations,

Have agreed as follows:

Article I

INTERPRETATION

1. For the purpose of this Convention:

a) "Migratory species" means the entire population or any geographically separate part of the population of any species or lower taxon of wild animals, a significant proportion of whose members cyclically and predictably cross one or more national jurisdictional boundaries;

b) "Conservation status of a migratory species" means the sum of the influences acting on the migratory species that may affect its long-term distribution and abundance;

c) "Conservation status" will be taken as "favourable" when:

(1) population dynamics data indicate that the migratory species is maintaining itself on a long-term basis as a viable component of its ecosystems;

(2) the range of the migratory species is neither currently being reduced, nor is likely to be reduced, on a long-term basis;

(3) there is, and will be in the foreseeable future, sufficient habitat to maintain the population of the migratory species on a long-term basis; and

(4) the distribution and abundance of the migratory species approach historic coverage and levels to the extent that potentially suitable ecosystems exist and to the extent consistent with wise wildlife management;

d) "Conservation status" will be taken as "unfavourable" if any of the conditions set out in sub-paragraph (c) of this paragraph is not met;

e) "Endangered" in relation to a particular migratory species means that the migratory species is in danger of extinction throughout all or a significant portion of its range;

f) "Range" means all the areas of land or water that a migratory species inhabits, stays in temporarily, crosses or overlies at any time on its normal migration route;

g) "Habitat" means any area in the range of a migratory species which contains suitable living conditions for that species;

h) "Range State" in relation to a particular migratory species means any State (and where appropriate any other Party referred to under sub-paragraph (k) of this paragraph) that exercises jurisdiction over any part of the range of that migratory species, or a State, flag vessels of which are engaged outside national jurisdictional limits in taking that migratory species;

i) "Taking" means taking, hunting, fishing, capturing, harassing, deliberate killing, or attempting to engage in any such conduct;

j) "Agreement" means an international agreement relating to the conservation of one or more migratory species as provided for in Articles IV and V of this Convention; and

k) "Party" means a State or any regional economic integration organization constituted by sovereign States which has competence in respect of the negotiation, conclusion and application of international agreements in matters covered by this Convention for which this Convention is in force.

2. In matters within their competence, the regional economic integration organizations which are Parties to this Convention shall in their own name exercise the rights and fulfil the responsibilities which this Convention attributes to their member States. In such cases the member States of these organizations shall not be entitled to exercise such rights individually.

3. Where this Convention provides for a decision to be taken by either a two-thirds majority or a unanimous decision of "the Parties present and voting" this shall mean "the Parties present and casting an affirmative or negative vote". Those abstaining from voting shall not be counted amongst "the Parties present and voting" in determining the majority.

Article II

FUNDAMENTAL PRINCIPLES

1. The Parties acknowledge the importance of migratory species being conserved and of Range States agreeing to take action to this end whenever

possible and appropriate, paying special attention to migratory species the conservation status of which is unfavourable, and taking individually or in co-operation appropriate and necessary steps to conserve such species and their habitat.

2. The Parties acknowledge the need to take action to avoid any migratory species becoming endangered.

3. In particular, the Parties:

a) should promote, co-operate in and support research relating to migratory species;

b) shall endeavour to provide immediate protection for migratory species included in Appendix I; and

c) shall endeavour to conclude AGREEMENTS covering the conservation and management of migratory species included in Appendix II.

Article III

ENDANGERED MIGRATORY SPECIES: APPENDIX I

1. Appendix I shall list migratory species which are endangered.

2. A migratory species may be listed in Appendix I provided that reliable evidence, including the best scientific evidence available, indicates that the species is endangered.

3. A migratory species may be removed from Appendix I when the Conference of the Parties determines that:

a) reliable evidence, including the best scientific evidence available, indicates that the species is no longer endangered, and

b) the species is not likely to become endangered again because of loss of protection due to its removal from Appendix I.

4. Parties that are Range States of a migratory species listed in Appendix I shall endeavour:

a) to conserve and, where feasible and appropriate, restore those habitats of the species which are of importance in removing the species from danger of extinction;

b) to prevent, remove, compensate for or minimize, as appropriate, the adverse effects of activities or obstacles that seriously impede or prevent the migration of the species; and

c) to the extent feasible and appropriate, to prevent, reduce or control factors that are endangering or are likely to further endanger the species, including strictly controlling the introduction of, or controlling or eliminating, already introduced exotic species.

5. Parties that are Range States of a migratory species listed in Appendix I shall prohibit the taking of animals belonging to such species. Exceptions may be made to this prohibition only if:

a) the taking is for scientific purposes;

b) the taking is for the purpose of enhancing the propagation or survival of the affected species;

c) the taking is to accommodate the needs of traditional subsistence users of such species; or

d) extraordinary circumstances so require;

provided that such exceptions are precise as to content and limited in space and time. Such taking should not operate to the disadvantage of the species.

6. The Conferences of the Parties may recommend to the Parties that are Range State of a migratory species listed in Appendix I that they take further measures considered appropriate to benefit the species.

7. The Parties shall as soon as possible inform the Secretariat of any exceptions made pursuant to paragraph 5 of this Article.

Article IV

MIGRATORY SPECIES TO BE THE SUBJECT TO AGREEMENTS: APPENDIX II

1. Appendix II shall list migratory species which have an unfavourable conservation status and which require international agreements for their conservation and management, as well as those which have a conservation status which would significantly benefit from the international co-operation that could be achieved by an international agreement.

2. If the circumstances so warrant, a migratory species may be listed both in Appendix I and Appendix II.

3. Parties that are Range States of migratory species listed in Appendix II shall endeavour to conclude agreements where these should benefit the species and should give priority to those species in an unfavourable conservation status.

4. Parties are encouraged to take action with a view to concluding agreements for any population or any geographically separate part of the population of any species or lower taxon of wild animals, members of which periodically cross one or more national jurisdiction boundaries.

5. The Secretariat shall be provided with a copy of each agreement concluded pursuant to the provisions of this Article.

Article V

GUIDELINES FOR AGREEMENTS

1. The object of each agreement shall be to restore the migratory species concerned to a favourable conservation status or to maintain it in such a status. Each agreement should deal with those aspects of the conservation and management of the migratory species concerned which serve to achieve that object.

2. Each agreement should cover the whole of the range of the migratory species concerned and should be open to accession by all Range States of that species, whether or not they are Parties to this Convention.

3. An agreement should, wherever possible, deal with more than one migratory species.

4. Each agreement should:

a) identify the migratory species covered;

b) describe the range and migration route of the migratory species;

c) provide for each Party to designate its national authority concerned with the implementation of the agreement.

d) establish, if necessary, appropriate machinery to assist in carrying out the aims of the agreement, to monitor its effectiveness, and to prepare reports for the Conference of the Parties;

e) provide for procedures for the settlement of disputes between Parties to the agreement; and

f) at a minimum, prohibit, in relation to a migratory species of the Order Cetacea, any taking that is not permitted for that migratory species under any other multilateral agreement and provide for accession to the agreement by States that are not Range States of that migratory species.

5. Where appropriate and feasible, each agreement should provide for but not be limited to:

a) periodic review of the conservation status of the migratory species concerned and the identification of the factors which may be harmful to that status;

b) co-ordinated conservation and management plans;

c) research into the ecology and population dynamics of the migratory species concerned, with special regard to migration;

d) the exchange of information on the migratory species concerned, special regard being paid to the exchange of the results of research and of relevant statistics;

e) conservation and, where required and feasible, restoration of the habitats of importance in maintaining a favourable conservation status, and protection of such habitats from disturbances, including strict control of the introduction of, or control of already introduced, exotic species detrimental to the migratory species;

f) maintenance of a network of suitable habitats appropriately disposed in relation to the migration routes;

g) where it appears desirable, the provision of new habitats favourable to the migratory species or reintroduction of the migratory species into favourable habitats;

h) elimination of, to thc maximum extent possible, or compensation for activities and obstacles which hinder or impede migration;

i) prevention, reduction or control of the release into the habitat of the migratory species of substances harmful to that migratory species;

j) measures based on sound ecological principles to control and manage the taking of the migratory species;

k) procedures for co-ordinating action to suppress illegal taking;

l) exchange of information on substantial threats to the migratory species;

m) emergency procedures whereby conservation action would be considerably and rapidly strengthened when the conservation status of the migratory species is seriously affected; and

n) making the general public aware of the contents and aims of the agreement.

Article VI

RANGE STATES

1. A list of the Range States of migratory species listed in Appendices I and II shall be kept up to date by the Secretariat using information it has received from the Parties.

2. The Parties shall keep the Secretariat informed as to which of the migratory species listed in Appendices I and II they consider they are Range States; including provision of information on their flag vessels engaged outside national jurisdictional limits in taking the migratory species concerned and, where possible, future plans in respect of such taking.

3. The Parties which are Range States for migratory species listed in Appendix I or Appendix II should inform the Conference of the Parties through the Secretariat, at least six months prior to each ordinary meeting of the Conference, on measures that they are taking to implement the provisions of this Convention for these species.

Article VII

THE CONFERENCE OF THE PARTIES

1. The Conference of the Parties shall be the decision-making organ of this Convention.

2. The Secretariat shall call a meeting of the Conference of the Parties not later than two years after the entry into force of this Convention.

3. Thereafter the Secretariat shall convene ordinary meetings of the Conference of the Parties at intervals of not more than three years, unless the Conference decides otherwise, and extraordinary meetings at any time on the written request of at least one-third of the Parties.

4. The Conference of the Parties shall establish and keep under review the financial regulations of this Convention. The Conference of the Parties shall, at each of its ordinary meetings, adopt the budget for the next financial period. Each Party shall contribute to this budget according to a scale to be agreed upon by the Conference. Financial regulations, including the provisions on the budget and the scale of contributions as well as their modifications, shall be adopted by unanimous vote of the Parties present and voting.

5. At each of its meetings the Conference of the Parties shall review the implementation of this Convention and may in particular:

a) review and assess the conservation status of migratory species;

b) review the progress made towards the conservation of migratory species, especially those listed in Appendices I and II;

c) make such provision and provide such guidance as may be necessary to enable the

Scientific Council and the Secretariat to carry out their duties;

d) receive and consider any reports presented by the Scientific Council, the Secretariat, any Party or any standing body established pursuant to an agreement;

e) make recommendations to the Parties for improving the conservation status of migratory species and review the progress being made under agreements;

f) in those cases where an agreement has not been concluded, make recommendations for the convening of meetings of the Parties that are Range States of a migratory species or group of migratory species to discuss measures to improve the conservation status of the species;

g) make recommendations to the Parties for improving the effectiveness of this Convention; and

h) decide on any additional measure that should be taken to implement the objectives of this Convention.

6. Each meeting of the Conference of the Parties should determine the time and venue of the next meeting.

7. Any meeting of the Conference of the Parties shall determine and adopt rules of procedure for that meeting. Decisions at a meeting of the Conference of the Parties shall require a two-thirds majority of the Parties present and voting, except where otherwise provided for by this Convention.

8. The United Nations, its Specialized Agencies, the International Atomic Energy Agency, as well as any State not a party to this Convention and, for each agreement, the body designated by the parties to that agreement, may be represented by observers at meetings of the Conference of the Parties.

9. Any agency or body technically qualified in protection, conservation and management of migratory species, in the following categories, which has informed the Secretariat of its desire to be represented at meetings of the Conference of the Parties by observers, shall be admitted unless at least one-third of the Parties present object:

a) international agencies or bodies, either governmental or non-governmental, and national governmental agencies and bodies; and

b) national non-governmental agencies or bodies which have been approved for this purpose by the State in which they are located.

Once admitted, these observers shall have the right to participate but not to vote.

Article VIII

THE SCIENTIFIC COUNCIL

1. At its first meeting, the Conference of the Parties shall establish a Scientific Council to provide advice on scientific matters.

2. Any Party may appoint a qualified expert as a member of the Scientific Council. In addition, the Scientific Council shall include as members qualified experts selected and appointed by the Conference of the Parties; the number of these experts, the criteria for their selection and the terms of their appointments shall be as determined by the Conference of the Parties.

3. The Scientific Council shall meet at the request of the Secretariat as required by the Conference of the Parties.

4. Subject to the approval of the Conference of the Parties, the Scientific Council shall establish its own rules of procedure.

5. The Conference of the Parties shall determine the functions of the Scientific Council, which may include:

a) providing scientific advice to the Conference of the Parties, to the Secretariat, and, if approved by the Conference of the Parties, to any body set up under this Convention or an agreement or to any Party;

b) recommending research and the co-ordination of research on migratory species, evaluating the results of such research in order to ascertain the conservation status of migratory species and reporting to the Conference of the Parties of such status and measures for its improvement;

c) making recommendations to the Conference of the Parties as to the migratory species to be included in Appendices I or II, together with an indication of the range of such migratory species;

d) making recommendations to the Conference of the Parties as to specific conservation and management measures to be included in agreements on migratory species; and

e) recommending to the Conference of the Parties solutions to problems relating to the scientific aspects of the implementation of this Convention, in particular with regard to the habitats of migratory species.

Article IX

THE SECRETARIAT

1. For the purposes of this Convention a Secretariat shall be established.

2. Upon entry into force of this Convention, the Secretariat is provided by the Executive Director of the United Nations Environment Programme. To the extent and in the manner he considers appropriate, he may be assisted by suitable intergovernmental and non-governmental, international or national agencies and bodies technically qualified in protection, conservation and management of wild animals.

3. If the United Nations Environment Programme is no longer able to provide the Secretariat, the Conference of the Parties shall make alternative arrangements for the Secretariat.

4. The functions of the Secretariat shall be:

a) to arrange for and service meetings:

(i) of the Conference of the Parties, and

ii) of the Scientific Council;

b) to maintain liaison with and promote liaison between the Parties, the standing bodies set up under agreements and other international organizations concerned with migratory species;

c) to obtain from any appropriate source reports and other information which will further the objectives and implementation of this Convention and to arrange for the appropriate dissemination of such information;

d) to invite the attention of the Conference of the Parties to any matter pertaining to the objectives of this Convention;

e) to prepare for the Conference of the Parties reports on the work of the Secretariat and on the implementation of this Convention;

f) to maintain and publish a list of Range States of all migratory species included in Appendices I and II;

g) to promote, under the direction of the Conference of the Parties, the conclusion of agreements,

h) to maintain and make available to the Parties a list of agreements and, if so required by the Conference of the Parties, to provide any information on such agreements;

i) to maintain and publish a list of the recommendations made by the Conference of the Parties pursuant to sub-paragraphs (e), (f) and (g) of paragraph 5 of Article VII or of decisions made pursuant to sub-paragraph (h) of that paragraph;

j) to provide for the general public information concerning this Convention and its objectives; and

k) to perform any other function entrusted to it under this Convention or by the Conference of the Parties.

Article X

AMENDMENTS OF THE CONVENTION

1. This Convention may be amended at any ordinary or extraordinary meeting of the Conference of the Parties.

2. Proposals for amendment may be made by any Party.

3. The text of any proposed amendment and the reasons for it shall be communicated to the Secretary at least one hundred and fifty days before the meeting at which it is to be considered and shall promptly be communicated by the Secretary to all Parties. Any comments on the text by the Parties shall be communicated to the Secretariat not less than sixty days before the meeting begins. The Secretariat shall, immediately after the last day for submission of comments, communicate to the Parties all comments submitted by that day.

4. Amendments shall be adopted by a two-thirds majority of Parties present and voting.

5. An amendment adopted shall enter into force for all Parties which have accepted it on the first day of the third month following the date on which two-thirds of the Parties have deposited an instrument of acceptance with the Depositary. For each Party which deposits an instrument of acceptance after the date on which two-thirds of the Parties have deposited an instrument of acceptance, the amendment shall enter into force for that Party on the first day of the third month following the deposit of its instrument of acceptance.

Article XI

AMENDMENT OF THE APPENDICES

1. Appendices I and II may be amended at any ordinary or extraordinary meeting of the Conference of the Parties.

2. Proposals for amendment may be made by any Party.

3. The text of any proposed amendment and the reasons for it, based on the best scientific evidence available, shall be communicated to the Secretariat at least 150 days before the meeting and shall promptly be communicated by the Secretariat to all Parties. Any comments on the text by the Parties shall be communicated to the Secretariat not less than 60 days before the meeting begins. The Secretariat shall, immediately after the last day for submission of comments, communicate to the Parties all comments submitted by that day.

4. Amendments shall be adopted by a two-thirds majority of Parties present and voting.

5. An amendment to the Appendices shall enter into force for all Parties 90 days after the meeting of the Conference of the Parties at which it was adopted, except for those Parties which make a reservation in accordance with paragraph 6 of this Article.

6. During the period of 90 days provided for in paragraph 5 of this Article, any Party may by notification in writing to the Depositary make a reservation with respect to the amendment. A reservation to an amendment may be withdrawn by written notification to the Depositary and thereupon the amendment shall enter into force for that Party 90 days after the reservation is withdrawn.

Article XII

EFFECT ON INTERNATIONAL CONVENTIONS AND OTHER LEGISLATION

1. Nothing in this Convention shall prejudice the codification and development of the law of the sea by the United Nations Conference on the Law of the Sea convened pursuant to Resolution 2750 C (XXV) of the General Assembly of the United Nations nor the present or future claims and legal views of any State concerning the law of the sea and the nature and extent of coastal and flag State jurisdiction.

2. The provisions of this Convention shall in no way affect the right of Parties to adopt stricter domestic measures concerning the conservation of migratory species listed in Appendices I and II or to adopt domestic measures concerning the conservation of species not listed in Appendices I and II.

Article XV

SIGNATURE

This Convention shall be open for signature at Bonn for all States and any regional economic integration organization until the twenty-second day of June 1980.

Article XVI

RATIFICATION, ACCEPTANCE, APPROVAL

This Convention shall be subject to ratification, acceptance or approval. Instruments of ratification, acceptance or approval shall be deposited with the Government of the Federal Republic of Germany, which shall be the Depositary.

Article XVII

ACCESSION

After the twenty-second day of June 1980 this Convention shall be open for accession by all non-signatory States and any regional economic integration organization. Instruments of accession shall be deposited with the Depositary.

Article XVIII

ENTRY INTO FORCE

1. This Convention shall enter into force on the first day of the third month following the date of deposit of the fifteenth instrument of ratification, acceptance, approval or accession with the Depositary.

2. For each State or each regional economic intergration organization which ratifies, accepts or approves this Convention or accedes thereto after the deposit of the fifteenth instrument of ratification, acceptance, approval or accession, this Convention shall enter into force on the first day of the third month following the deposit by such State or such organization of its instrument of ratification, acceptance, approval or accession.

Article XIX

DENUNCIATION

Any Party may denounce this Convention by written notification to the Depositary at any time. The denunciation shall take effect twelve months after the Depositary has received the notification.

Article XX

DEPOSITARY

1. The original of this Convention, in the English, French, German, Russian and Spanish languages, each version being equally authentic, shall be deposited with the Depositary. The Depositary shall transmit certified copies of each of these versions to all States and all regional economic integration organizations that have signed the Convention or deposited instruments of accession to it.

2. The Depositary shall, after consultation with the Governments concerned, prepare official versions of the text of this Convention in the Arabic and Chinese languages.

3. The Depositary shall inform all signatory and acceding States and all signatory and acceding regional economic integration organizations and the Secretariat of signatures, deposit of instruments of ratification, acceptance, approval or accession, entry into force of this Convention, amendments thereto, specific reservations and notifications of denunciation.

4. As soon as this Convention enters into force, a certified copy thereof shall be transmitted by the Depositary to the Secretariat of the United Nations for registration and publication in accordance with Article 102 of the Charter of the United Nations.

In witness whereof the undersigned, being duly authorized thereto, have signed the present Convention.

Done at Bonn, this 23rd day of June 1979.

APPENDIX I

INTERPRETATION

1. Migratory species included in this Appendix are referred to:

a) by the name of the species or subspecies; or

b) as being all of the migratory species included in a higher taxon or designated part thereof.

2. Other references to taxa higher than species are for the purposes of information or classification only.

3. The abbreviation "(s.l.)" is used to denote that the scientific name is used in its extended meaning.

4. The symbol (—) followed by a number placed against the name of a taxon indicates the exclusion from that taxon of designated geographically separate populations as follows:

— 101 Peruvian populations.

5. The symbol (+) followed by a number placed against the name of a species denotes that only designated geographically separate populations of that species are included in this Appendix, as follows:

+ 201 Northwest African populations

+ 202 African populations

+ 203 Upper Amazon populations.

6. An asterisk (*) placed against the name of a species indicates that the species or a separate population of that species or a higher taxon which includes that species, is included in Appendix II.

MAMMALIA	
Chiroptera	
Molossidae	*Tadarida brasiliensis*
Primates	
Pongidae	*Gorilla gorilla beringei*
Cetacea	
Balaenopteridae	*Balaenoptera musculus*
	Megaptera novaeangliae
Balaenidae	*Balaena mysticetus*
	Eubalaena glacialis (s.l.)
Pinnipedia	
Phocidae	*Monachus monachus**
Perissodactyla	
Equidae	*Equus grevyi*
Artiodactyla	
Camelidae	*Lama vicugna** (- 101)
Cervidae	*Cervus elaphus barbarus*
Bovidae	*Bos sauveli*
	Addax nasomaculatus
	Gazella cuvieri
	Gazella dama
	Gazella dorcas (+ 201)
AVES	
Procellariformes	
Diomedeidae	*Diomediea albatrus*
Procellaridae	*Pterodroma cahow*
	Pterodroma phaeopygia
Ciconiiformes	
Ardeidae	*Egretta eulophotes*
Ciconiidae	*Ciconia boyciana*
Threskiornithidae	*Geronticus eremita*
Anseriformes	
Anatidae	*Chloephaga rubidiceps**
Falconiformes	
Accipitridae	*Haliaeetus pelagicus**
Gruiformes	
Gruidae	*Grus japonensis**
	*Grus leucogeranus**
	*Grus nigricollis**
Otididae	*Chlamydotis undulata** (+ 201)
Charadriiformes	
Scolopacidae	*Numenius borealis**
	*Numenius tenuirositris**
Laridae	*Larus audouinii*
	Larus relictus
	Larus saundersi
Alcidae	*Synthliboramphus wumizusume*
Passeriformes	
Parulidae	*Dendroica kirtlandii*
Fringillidae	*Serinus syriacus*

REPTILIA	
Testudines	
Cheloniidae	*Lepiodochelys kempii**
Dermochelidae	*Dermochelys coriacea**
Pelomedusidae	*Podocnemis expansa** (+ 203)
Crocodylia	
Gavialidae	*Gavialis gangeticus*
PISCES	
Siluriformes	
Schiibeidae	*Pangasianodon gigas*

APPENDIX II

Interpretation

1. Migratory species included in this Appendix are referred to:
   (a) by the name of the species or subspecies; or
   (b) as being all of the migratory species included in a higher taxon or designated part thereof.

Unless otherwise indicated, where reference is made to a taxon higher that species, it is understood that all the migratory species within that taxon could significatly benefit from the conclusion of agreements.

2. The abbreviation 'spp.' following the name of a family or genus us used to denote all migratory species within that family or genus.

3. Other references to taxa higher than species are for purposes of information or classification only.

4. The abbreviation '(s.l)' is used to denote that the scientific name is used in its extended meaning.

5. The symbol (+) followed by a number placed against the name of a species or higher taxon denotes that only designated geographically separate populations of that taxon are included in this Appendix as follows:

+ 201 Asian populations.

6. As asterisk (*) placed against the name of a species or higher taxon indicates that the species or a separate population of that species or one or more species included in that higher taxon, are included in Appendix I.

MAMMALIA	
Cetacea	
Monodontidae	*Delphinapterus leucas*
Proboscidae	
Elephantidae	*Loxodonta africana*
Sirenia	
Dugongidae	*Dudong dugon*
Pinnipedia	
Phocidae	*Monachus monachus (*)*
Artiodactyla	
Camelidae	*Vicugna vicugna (*)*
Bovidae	*Oryx dammah* *Gazella gazella* (+ 201)
AVES	
Pelecaniformes	
Pelecanidae	*Pelacanus crispus*
Ciconiiformes	
Ciconiidae	*Ciconia ciconia* *Ciconia nigra*
Theskiornithidae	*Platalea leucorodia*
Poenicopteridae	spp.
Anseriformes	
Anatidae	spp.*
Falconiformes	
Cathartidae	spp.
Pandionidae	*Pandion haliaetus*
Accipitridae	spp.*
Falconidae	spp.
Galliformes	
Phasianidae	*Coturnix coturnix coturnix*

Gruiformes	
Gruidae	*Gruss spp.**
	Anthropoides virgo
Otididae	*Chlamydotis undulata**
	(+ 201)
Charadriiformes	
Charadriidae	spp.
Scolopacidae	spp.*
Recurvirostridae	spp.
Phalaropodidae	spp.
Passeriformes	
Muscicapidae (s.l.)	spp.
REPTILIA	
Testudines	
Cheloniidae	spp.*
Dermochelidae	spp.*
Pelomedusidae	*Podocnemis expansa**
Crocodylia	
Crocodylidae	*Crocodilus porosus*
PISCES	
Acipenseriformes	
Acipenseridae	*Acipenser fulvescens*
INSECTA	
Lepidoptera	
Danaidae	*Danaus plexippus*

Resolution on financial matters

The Conference,

Referring to Article VII and NOTING that Article IX of the Convention on the Conservation of Migratory Species of Wild Animals indicates that the United Nations Environment Programme shall provide a Secretariat upon the entry into force of the Convention;

Recognizing that the Parties to the Convention shall bear responsibility for the financing of the administration of the Convention;

Welcoming the offer by the United Nations Evironment Programme to provide a Secretariat and to make an initial contribution, as appropriate, in order to meet the expenses of the Secretariat during the first four years after the entry into force of the Convention;

Expressing the view that it would be useful for the Secretariat to co-operate closely with the Secretariat of the Convention on International Trade in Endangered Species of Wild Fauna and Flora in order to benefit from the experience already gained by said Secretariat;

Aware of the fact that a final decision on the catalytic role which may be conferred on the United Nations Environment Programme in starting up a Secretariat for the Convention has to be taken by the Governing Council as its eighth session in the spring of 1980,

1. Requests the Depositary to fulfil interim Secretariat functions until the entry into force of the Convention;

2. Requests the Executive Director of the United Nations Environment Programme to consider the inclusion within the frame of the limited initial contribution from the United Nations Environment Programme, and in line with its catalytic role, of the funds required to finance a first meeting of the Conference of the Parties;

3. Decides, in the event that the United Nations Environment Programme cannot provide a Secretariat;

a) to invite the Parties to the Convention to communicate to the Depositary alternative proposals for consideration at the first meeting of the Conference of the Parties;

b) to request the Depositary to transmit to the Parties such alternative proposals at least ninety days in advance of the first meefing of the Conference of the Parties;

c) to invite the Depositary to continue fulfilling interim Secretariat functions pending consideration of this matter at the first meeting of the Conference of the Parties;

4. Decides that the Depositary, in fulfilling interim Secretariat functions, may request the assistance of intergovernmental or non-governmental, international or national agencies and bodies technically qualified in the protection, conservation and management of wild animals.

CONVENTION ON THE CONSERVATION OF EUROPEAN WILDLIFE AND NATURAL HABITATS [77]

Bern, 19 September 1979

PREAMBLE

The Member States of the Council of Europe and the other signatories hereto,

Considering that the aim of the Council of Europe is to achieve a greater unity between its members;

Considering the wish of the Council of Europe to co-operate with other States in the field of nature conservation;

Recognizing that wild flora and fauna consitute an natural heritage of aesthetic, scientific, cultural, recreational, economic and intrinsic value that needs to be preserved and handed on to future generations;

Recognizing the essential role played by wild flora and fauna in maintaining biological balances;

Noting that numerous species of wild flora and fauna are being seriously depleted and that some of them are threatened with extinction;

Aware that the conservation of natural habitats is a vital component of the protection and conservation of wild flora and fauna;

Recognizing that the conservation of wild flora and fauna should be taken into consideration by the governments in their national goals and programmes, and that international co-operation should be established to protect migratory species in particular;

Bearing in mind the widespread requests for common action made by governments or by international bodies, in particular the requests expressed by the United Nations Conference on the Human Environment 1972 and the Consultative Assembly of the Council of Europe;

Desiring particularly to follow, in the field of wildlife conservation, the recommendations of Resolution No. 2 of the Second European Ministerial Conference on the Environment,

Have agreed as follows:

Chapter 1

GENERAL PROVISIONS

Article 1

1. The aims of this Convention are to conserve wild flora and fauna and their natural habitats, especially those species and habitats whose conservation requires the co-operation of several States, and to promote such co-operation.

2. Particular emphasis is given to endangered and vulnerable species, including endangered and vulnerable migratory species.

Article 2

The Contracting Parties shall take requisite measures to maintain the population of wild flora and fauna at, or adapt it to, a level which corresponds in particular to ecological, scientific and cultural requirements, while taking account of economic and recreational requirements and the needs of sub-species, varieties or forms at risk locally.

Article 3

1. Each Contracting Party shall take steps to promote national policies for the conservation of wild flora, wild fauna and natural habitats, with particular attention to endangered and vulnerable species, especially endemic ones, and endangered habitats, in accordance with the provisions of this Convention.

2. Each Contracting Party undertakes, in its planning and development policies and in its measures against pollution, to have regard to the conservation of wild flora and fauna.

3. Each Contracting Party shall promote education and disseminate general information on the need to conserve species of wild flora and fauna and their habitats.

Chapter II

PROTECTION OF HABITATS

Article 4

1. Each Contracting Party shall take appropriate and necessary legislative and administrative measures to ensure the conservation of the habitats of the wild flora and fauna species, especially those specified in the Appendices I and II, and the conservation of endangered natural habitats.

2. The Contracting Parties in their planning and development policies shall have regard to the conservation requirements of the areas protected under the preceding paragraph, so as to avoid or minimise as far as possible any deterioration of such areas.

3. The Contracting Parties undertake to give special attention to the protection of areas that are of importance for the migratory species specified in Appendices II and III and which are appropriately situated in relation to migration routes, as wintering, staging, feeding, breeding or moulting areas.

4. The Contracting Parties undertake to co-ordinate as appropriate their efforts for the protection of the natural habitats referred to in this Article when these are situated in frontier areas.

Chapter III

PROTECTION OF SPECIES

Article 5

Each Contracting Party shall take appropriate and necessary legislative and administrative measures to ensure the special protection of the wild flora species specified in Appendix I. Deliberate picking, collecting, cutting or uprooting of such plants shall be prohibited. Each Contracting Party shall, as apropriate, prohibit the possession or sale of these species.

Article 6

Each Contracting Party shall take appropriate and necessary legislative and administrative measures to ensure the special protection of the wild fauna species specified in Appendix II. The following will in particular be prohibited for these species:

a) all forms of deliberate capture and keeping and deliberate killing;

b) the deliberate damage to or destruction of breeding or resting sites;

c) the deliberate disturbance of wild fauna, particularly during the period of breeding, rearing and hibernation, insofar as disturbance would be significant in relation to the objectives of this Convention;

d) the deliberate destruction or taking of eggs from the wild or keeping these eggs even if empty;

e) the possession of and internal trade in these animals, alive or dead, including stuffed animals and any readily recognizable part or derivative thereof, where this would contribute to the effectiveness of the provisions of this Article.

Article 7

1. Each Contracting Party shall take appropriate and necessary legislative and administrative measures to ensure the protection of the wild fauna species specified in Appendix III.

2. Any exploitation of wild fauna specified in Appendix III shall be regulated in order to keep the populations out of danger, taking into account the requirements of Article 2.

3. Measures to be taken shall include:

a) closed seasons and/or other procedures regulating the exploitation;

b) the temporary or local prohibition of exploitation, as appropriate, in order to restore satisfactory population levels;

c) the regulation as appropriate of sale, keeping for safe, transport for sale or offering for sale of live and dead wild animals.

Article 8

In respect of the capture or killing of wild fauna species specified in Appendix III and in cases where, in accordance with Article 9, exceptions are applied to species specified in Appendix II, Contracting Parties shall prohibit the use of all indiscriminate means of capture and killing and the use of all means capable of causing local disappearance of, or serious disturbance to, populations of a species, and in particular, the means specified in Appendix IV.

Article 9

1. Each Contracting Party may make exceptions from the provisions of Articles 4, 5, 6, 7 and from the prohibition of the use of the means mentioned in Article 8 provided that there is no other satisfactory solution and that the exception will not be detrimental to the survival of the population concerned:

— for the protection of flora and fauna;

— to prevent serious damage to crops, livestock, forests, fisheries, water and other forms of property;

— in the interests of public health and safety, air safety or other overriding public interests;

— for the purposes of research and education, of repopulation, of reintroduction and for the necessary breeding;

— to permit, under strictly supervised conditions, on a selective basis and to a limited extent, the taking, keeping or other judicious exploitation of certain wild animals and plants in small numbers.

2. The Contracting Parties shall report every two years to the Standing Committee on the exceptions made under the preceding paragraph. These reports must specify:

— the populations which are or have been subject to the exceptions and, when practical, the number of specimens involved;

— the means authorised for the killing or capture;

— the conditions of risk and the circumstances of time and place under which such exceptions were granted;

— the authority empowered to declare that these conditions have been fulfilled, and to take decisions in respect of the means that may be used, their limits and the persons instructed to carry them out;

— the controls involved.

Chapter IV

SPECIAL PROVISIONS FOR MIGRATORY SPECIES

Article 10

1. The Contracting Parties undertake, in addition to the measures specified in Articles 4, 6, 7 and 8, to co-ordinate their efforts for the protection of the migratory species specified in Appendices II and III whose range extends into their territories.

2. The Contracting Parties shall take measures to seek to ensure that the closed seasons and/or other procedures regulating the exploitation established under paragraph 3.*a* of Article 7 are adequate and approximately disposed to meet the requirements of the migratory species specified in Appendix III.

Chapter V

SUPPLEMENTARY PROVISIONS

Article 11

1. In carrying out the provisions of this Convention, the Contracting Parties undertake:

a) to co-operate whenever appropriate and in particular where this would enhance the effectiveness of measures taken under other articles of this Convention;

b. to encourage and co-ordinate research related to the purposes of this Convention.

2. Each Contracting Party undertakes:

a) to encourage the reintroduction of native species of wild flora and fauna when this would contribute to the conservation of an endangered species, provided that a study is first made in the light of the experiences of other Contracting Parties to establish that such reintroduction would be effective and acceptable;

b) to strictly control the introduction of non-native species.

3. Each Contracting Party shall inform the Standing Committee of the species receiving complete protection on its territory and not included in Appendices I and II.

Article 12

The Contracting Parties may adopt stricter measures for the conservation of wild flora and fauna and their natural habitats than those provided under this Convention.

Chapter VI

STANDING COMMITTEE

Article 13

1. For the purposes of this Convention, a Standing Committee shall be set up.

2. Any Contracting Party may be represented on the Standing Committee by one or more delegates. Each delegation shall have one vote. Within the areas of its competence, the European Economic Community shall exercise its right to vote with a number of votes equal to the number of its member States which are Contracting Parties to this Convention; the European Economic Community shall not exercise its right to vote in cases where the member States concerned exercise theirs, and conversely.

3. Any member State of the Council of Europe which is not a Contracting Party to the Convention may be represented on the Committee as an observer.

The Standing Committee may, by unanimous decision, invite any non-member State of the Council of Europe which is not a Contracting Party to the Convention to be represented by an observer at one of its meetings.

Any body or agency technically qualified in the protection, conservation or management of wild fauna and flora and their habitats, and belonging to one of the following categories;

a) international agencies or bodies, either governmental or non-governmental, and national governmental agencies or bodies;

b) national non-governmental agencies or bodies which have been approved for this purpose by the State in which they are located,

may inform the Secretary-General of the Council of Europe, at least three months before the meeting of the Committee, of its wish to be represented at that meeting by observers. They shall be admitted unless, at least one month before the meeting, one-third of the Contracting Parties have informed the Secretary General of their objection.

4. The Standing Committee shall be convened by the Secretary General of the Council of Europe. Its first meeting shall be held within one year of the date of the entry into force of the Convention. It shall subsequently meet at least every two years and whenever a majority of the Contracting Parties so request.

5. A majority of the Contracting Parties shall constitute a quorum for holding a meeting of the Standing Committee.

6. Subject to the provisions of this Convention, the Standing Committee shall draw up its own Rules of Procedure.

Article 14

1. The following Committee shall be responsible for following the application of this Convention. It may in particular:

— keep under review the provisions of this Convention, including its Appendices, and examine any modifications necessary;

— make recommendations to the Contracting Parties concerning measures to be taken for the purposes of this Convention;

— recommend the appropriate measures to keep the public informed about the activities undertaken within the framework of this Convention;

— make recommendations to the Committee of Ministers concerning non-member States of the Council of Europe to be invited to accede to this Convention;

— make any proposal for improving the effectiveness of this Convention, including proposals for the conclusion, with the States which are not Contracting Parties to the Convention, of agreements that would enhance the effective conservation of species or groups of species.

2. In order to discharge its functions, the Standing Committee may, on its own initiative, arrange for meetings of groups of experts.

Article 15

After each meeting, the Standing Committee shall forward to the Committee of Ministers of the Council of Europe a report on its work and on the functioning of the Convention.

Chapter VII

AMENDMENTS

Article 16

1. Any amendment to the articles of this Convention proposed by a Contracting Party or the Committee of Ministers shall be communicated to the Secretary General of the Council of Europe and forwarded by him at least two months before the meeting of the Standing Committee to the member States of the Council of Europe, to any signatory, to any Contracting Party, to any State invited to sign this Convention in accordance with the provisions of Article 19 and to any State invited to accede to it in accordance with the provisions of Article 20.

2. Any amendment proposed in accordance with

the provisions of the preceding paragraph shall be examined by the Standing Committee which:

a) for amendments to Articles 1 to 12, shall submit the text adopted by a three-quarters majority of the votes cast of the Contracting Parties for acceptance;

b) for amendments to Articles 13 to 24, shall submit the text adopted by a three-quarters majority of the votes cast to the Committee of Ministers for approval. After its approval, this text shall be forwarded to the Contracting Parties for acceptance.

3. Any amendment shall enter into force on the thirtieth day after all the Contracting Parties have informed the Secretary General that they have accepted it.

4. The provisions of paragraphs 1, 2.*a* and 3 of this Article shall apply to the adoption of new Appendices to this Convention.

Article 17

1. Any amendment to the Appendices of this Convention proposed by a Contracting Party or the Committee of Ministers shall be communicated to the Secretary General of the Council of Europe and forwarded by him at least two months before the meeting of the Standing Committee to the member States of the Council of Europe, to any signatory, to any Contracting Party, to any State invited to sign this Convention in accordance with the provisions of Article 19 and to any State invited to it in accordance with the provisions of Article 20.

2. Any amendment proposed in accordance with the provisions of the preceding paragraph shall be examined by the Standing Committee, which may adopt it by a two-thirds majority of the Contracting Parties. The text adopted shall be forwarded to the Contracting Parties.

3. Three months after its adoption by the Standing Committee and unless one-third of the Contracting Parties have notified objections, any amendment shall enter into force for those Contracting Parties which have not notified objections.

Chapter VIII

SETTLEMENT OF DISPUTES

Article 18

1. The Standing Committee shall use its best endeavours to facilitate a friendly settlement of any difficulty to which the execution of this Convention may give rise.

2. Any dispute between Contracting Parties concerning the interpretation or application of this Convention which has not been settled on the basis of the provisions of the preceding paragraph or by negotiation between the parties concerned shall, unless the said parties agree otherwise, be submitted, at the request of one of them, to arbitration. Each party shall designate an arbitrator and the two arbitrators shall designate a third arbitrator. Subject to the provisions of paragraph 3 of this Article, if one of the parties has not designated its arbitrator within the three months following the request for arbitration, he shall be designated at the request of the other party by the President of the European Court of Human Rights within a further three months' period. The same procedure shall be observed if the arbitrators cannot agree on the choice of the third arbitrator within the three months following the designation of the two first arbitrators.

3. In the event of a dispute between two Contracting Parties one of which is a member State of the European Economic Community, the latter itself being a Contracting Party, the other Contracting Party shall address the request for arbitration both to the member State and to the Community, which jointly, shall notify it, within two months of receipt of the request, whether the member State or the Community, or the member and the Community jointly, shall be party to the dispute. In the absence of such notification within the said time limit, the member State and the Community shall be considered as being one and the same party to the dispute for the purposes of the application of the provisions governing the constitution and procedure of the arbitration tribunal. The same shall apply when the member State and the Community jointly present themselves as party to the dispute.

4. The arbitration tribunal shall draw up its own Rule of Procedure. Its decisions shall be taken by majority vote. Its award shall be final and binding.

5. Each party to the dispute shall bear the expenses of the arbitrator designated by it and the parties shall share equally the expenses of the third arbitrator, as well as other costs entailed by the arbitration.

Chapter IX

FINAL PROVISIONS

Article 19

1. This Convention shall be open for signature by the member States of the Council of Europe and non-member States which have participated in its elaboration and by the European Economic Community.

Up until the date when the Convention enters into force, it shall also be open for signature by any other State so invited by the Committee of Ministers.

The Convention is subject to ratification, acceptance or approval. Instruments of ratification, acceptance or approval shall be deposited with the Secretary General of the Council of Europe.

2. The Convention shall enter into force on the first day of the month following the expiry of a period of three months after the date on which five States, including at least four member States of the Council of Europe, have expressed their consent to be bound by the Convention in accordance with the provisions of the preceding paragraph.

3. In respect of any signatory State or the European

Economic Community which subsequently express their consent to be bound by it, the Convention shall enter into force on the first day of the month following the expiry of a period of three months after the date of the deposit of the instrument of ratification, acceptance or approval.

Article 20

1. After the entry into force of this Convention, the Committee of Ministers of the Council of Europe, after consulting the Contracting Parties, may invite to accede to the Convention any non-member State of the Council which, invited to sign in accordance with the provisions of Article 19, has not yet done so, and any other non-member State.

2. In respect of any acceding State, the Convention shall enter into force on the first day of the month following the expiry of a period of three months after the date of the deposit of the instrument of accession with the Secretary General of the Council of Europe.

Article 21

1. Any State may, at the time of signature or when depositing its instrument of ratification, acceptance, approval or accession, specify the territory or territories to which this Convention shall apply.

2. Any Contracting Party may, when depositing its instrument of ratification, acceptance, approval or accession or at any later date, by declaration addressed to the Secretary General of the Council of Europe, extend the application of this Convention to any other territory specified in the declaration and for whose international relations it is responsible or on whose behalf it is authorized to give undertakings.

3. Any declaration made under the preceding paragraph may, in respect of any territory mentioned in such declaration, be withdrawn by notification addressed to the Secretary General. Such withdrawal shall become effective on the first day of the month following the expiry of a period of six months after the date of receipt of the notification by the Secretary General.

Article 22

1. Any State may, at the time of signature or when depositing its instrument of ratification, acceptance, approval or accession, make one or more reservations regarding certain species specified in Appendices I to III and/or, for certain species mentioned in the reservation or reservations, regarding certain means or methods of killing, capture and other exploitation listed in Appendix IV. No reservations of a general nature may be made.

2. Any Contracting Party which extends the application of this Convention to a territory mentioned in the declaration referred to in paragraph 2 of Article 21 may, in respect of the territory concerned, make one or more reservations in accordance with the provisions of the preceding paragraph.

3. No other reservation may be made.

4. Any Contracting Party which has made a reservation under paragraph 1 and 2 of this Article may wholly or partly withdraw it by means of a notification addressed to the Secretary General of the Council of Europe. Such withdrawal shall take effect as from the date of receipt of the notification by the Secretary General.

Article 23

1. Any Contracting Party may, at any time, denounce this Convention by means of a notification addressed to the Secretary General of the Council of Europe.

2. Such denunciation shall become effective on the first day of the month following the expiry of a period of six months after the date of the notification by the Secretary General.

Article 24

The Secretary General of the Council of Europe shall notify the member States of the Council of Europe, any signatory State, the European Economic Community if a signatory of this Convention and any Contracting Party of:

a) any signature;

b) the deposit of any instrument of ratification, acceptance, approval or accession;

c) any date of entry into force of this Convention in accordance with Articles 19 and 20;

d) any information forwarded under the provisions of paragraph 3 of Article 13;

e) any report established in pursuance of the provisions of Article 15;

f) any amendment or any new Appendix adopted in accordance with Articles 16 and 17 and the date on which the amendment or new Appendix comes into force;

g) any declaration made under the provisions of paragraphs 2 and 3 of Article 21;

h) any reservation made under the provisions of paragraphs 1 and 2 of Article 22;

i) the withdrawal of any reservation carried out under the provisions of paragraph 4 of Article 22;

j) any notification made under the provisions of Article 23 and the date on which the denunciation takes effect.

In witness whereof the undersigned, being duly authorised thereto, have signed this Convention.

Done at Bern, this 19th day of September 1979, in English and French, both texts being equally authentic, in a single copy which shall be deposited in the archives of the Council of Europe. The Secretary General of the Council of Europe shall transmit certified copies to each member State of the Council of Europe, to any signatory State, to the European Economic Community if a signatory and to any State invited to sign this Convention or to accede thereto.

APPENDIX I
Strictly protected flora species

PTERIDOPHYTA
ASPIDIACEAE
Diplazium caudatum (Cav.) Jermy
PTERIDACEAE
Pteris serrulata Forssk.

GYMNOSPERMAE
PINACEAE
Abies nebrodensis (Lojac.) Mattei

ANGIOSPERMAE
ALISMATACEAE
Alisma wahlenbergii (O.R. Holmberg) Juzepezuk
BERBERIDACEAE
Gymnospermium altaicum (Pallas) Spach
BORAGINACEAE
Anchusa crispa Viv.
Myosotis rehsteneri Wartm.
Omphalodes littoralis Lehin.
Onosma caespitosum Kotschy
Onosma troodi Kotschy
Solenanthus albanicus (Degen *et al.*) Degen & Baldacci
Symphytum cycladense Pawl.
CAMPANULACEAE
Campanula sabatia De Not.
CARYOPHYLLACEAE
Arenaria lithops Heywood ex McNeill
Gypsophila papillosa P. Porta
Loeflingia tavaresiana G. Samp.
Silene orphanidis Boiss.
Silene rothmaleri Pinto de Silva
Silene velutina Pourret ex Loisel.
CHENOPODIACEAE
Kochia saxicola Guss.
Salicornia veneta Pignatti & Lausi
CISTACEAE
Tuberaria major (Willk.) Pinto da Silva
COMPOSITAE
Anacyclus alboranensis Esteve Chueca & Varo
Anthemis glaberrima (Rech.f) Greuter
Artemisia granatensis Poiss.
Artemisia laciniata Willd.
Aster pyrenaeus Desf. ex DC.
Aster sibiricus L.
Centaurea balearica J.D. Rodriguez
Centaurea heldreichii Halaosy
Centaurea horrida Badaro
Centaurea kalambakensis Freyn & Sint.
Centaurea lactiflora Halacsy
Centaurea lineresii Lazaro
Centaurea megarensis Halacsy & Hayek
Centaurea niederi Heldr.
Centaurea peucedanifolia Boiss. & Orph.
Centaurea princeps Boiss. & Heldr.
Crepis crocifolia Boiss. & Heldr.
Lamyropsis microcephala (Moris) Dittrich & Greuter
Leontodon siculus (Guss.) Finch & Sell
Logfia neglecta (Soy. Will.) Holub
Senecio alboranicus Maire
CONVOLVULACEAE
Convolvulus argyrothamnos Greuter
CRUCIFERAE
Alyssum akamasicum B.L. Burtt
Alyssum fastigiatum Heywood
Arabis kennedyae Meikle
Biscutella neustriaca Bonnet
Brassica hilarionis Post
Brassica macrocarpa Guss
Braya purpurascens (R. Br.) Bunge
Coronopus navasii Pau
Diplotaxis siettiana Maire
Enarthrocarpus pterocarpus DC.
Hutera rupestris P. Porta
Iberis arbuscula Runemark
Ionopsidium acaule (Desf.) Reichenb.
Ptilotrichum pyrenaicum (Lapeyr.) Boiss.
Rhynchosinapis johnstonii (G. Samp.) Heywood
Sisymbrium matritense P.W. Ball & Heywood
EUPHORBIACEAE
Euphorbia ruscinonensis Boiss.
GRAMINEAE
Stipa bavarica Martinovsky & H. Scholz
GROSSULARIACEAE
Ribes sardoum Martelli
HYPERICACEAE
Hypericum aciferum (Greuter) N.K.B. Robson
IRIDACEAE
Crocus cyprius Boiss. & Kotschy
Crocus hartmannianus Holmboe
LABIATAE
Amaracus cordifolium Montr. & Auch.
Micromeria taygetea P.H. Davis
Nepeta sphaciotica P.H. Davis
Phlomis brevibracteata Turrill
Phlomis cypria Post
Salvia crassifolia Sibth. & Smith
Sideritis cypria Post
Thymus camphoratus Hoffmann's & Link
Thymus carnosus Boiss.
Thymus cephalotos L.
LEGUMINOSEAE
Astragalus algarbiensis Coss. ex Bunge
Astragalus aquilinus Anzalone
Astragalus maritimus Moris
Astragalus verrucosus Moris
Cytisus aeolicus Guss. ex Lindi.
Ononis maweana Ball
Oxytropis deflexa (Pallas) DC.
LENTIBULARIACEAE
Pinguicula crystallina Sibth & Smith
LILIACEAE
Androcymbium rechingeri Greuter
Chionodoxa lochiae Meikle
Muscari gussonei (Pari.) Tod.
Scilla morrisii Meikle
ORCHIDACEAE
Ophyrys kotschyi Fleisch. & Soo
PAPAVERACEAE
Rupicapnos africana (Lam.) Pomel

PLUMBAGINACEAE
Armeria rouyana Daveau
Limonium paradoxum Pugsley
Limonium recurvum C.E. Salmon
POLYGONACEAE
Rheum rhaponticum L.
PRIMULACEAE
Primula apennina Widmer
Primula egaliksensis Wormsk.
RANUNCULACEAE
Aquilegia cazorlensis Heywood
Aquilegia kitaibelii Schott
Consolida samia P.H. Davis
Delphinium caseyi B.L. Burtt
Ranunculus kykkoensis Miekle
Ranunculus weyleri Mares
RUBIACEAE
Galium litorale Guss.
SCROPHULARIACEAE
Antirrhinum charidemi Lange
Euphrasia marchesetti Wettst. ex Marches.
Linaria algarviana Chav.
Linaria ficalhoana Rouy
SELAGINACEAE
Globularia stygia Orph. ex Boiss.
SOLANACEAE
Atropa baetica Willk.
THYMELAEACEAE
Daphne rodriguezii Texidor
UMBELLIFERAE
Angelica heterocarpa Lloyd
Angelica palustris (Besser) Hoffman
Bupleurum kakiskalac Greuter
Ferula cypria Post
Laserpitium longiradium Boiss.
Oenanthe conioides Lange
VALERIANACEAE
Valeriana longiflora Willk.
VIOLACEAE
Viola hispida Lam.
Viola jaubertiana Mares & Vigineix

APPENDIX II

Strictly protected fauna species

Mammals

INSECTIVORA
Talpidae
Desmana pyrenaica
(Galemys pyrenaicus)
MICROCHIROPTERA
all species except
Pipistrellus pipistrellus
RODENTIA
Sciuridae
Citellus citellus
Cricetidae
Cricetus criceus
Hystricidae
Hystrix cristata
CARNIVORA
Canidae
Canis lupus
Alopex lagopus
Ursidae
all species
Mustelidae
Lutreola (Mustela) lutreola
Lutra lutra
Gulo gulo
Felidae
Lynx pardina (pardellus)
Panthera pardus
Panthera tigris
Odobenidae
Odobenus rosmarus
Phocidae
Monachus monachus
ARTIODACTYLA
Bovidae
Capra aegagrus
Rupicapra rupicapra ornata
Ovibos moschatus
ODONTOCETI
Delphinidae
Delphinus delphis
Tursiops truncatus (tursio)
Phocaenidae
Phocaena phocaena
MYSTACOCETI
Balaenopteridae
Sibbaldus (Balaenoptera) musculus
Megaptera novaengliae (longimana, nodosa)
Balaenidae
Eubalaena glacialis
Balaena mysticetus

Birds

GAVIIFORMES
Gaviidae
all species
PODICIPEDIFORMES
Podicipedidae
Podiceps griseigena
Podiceps auritus
Podiceps nigricollis (caspicus)
Podiceps ruficollis
PROCELLARIIFORMES
Hydrobatidae
all species
Procellariidae
Puffinus puffinus
Procellaria diomedea
PELECANIFORMES
Phalacrocoracidae
Phalocrocorax pygmaeus
Pelecanidae
all species
CICONIIFORMES
Ardeidae
Ardea purpurea
Casmerodius albus (Egretta alba)

Egretta garzetta
Ardeola ralloides
Bulbucus (Ardeola) ibis
Nycticorax nycticorax
Ixobrychus minutus
Botaurus stellaris
Ciconiidae
all species
Threskiornithidae
all species
Phoenicopteridae
Phoenicopterus ruber
ANSERIFORMES
Anatidae
Cygnus cygnus
Cygnus bewickii (columbianus)
Anser erythropus
Branta leucopsis
Branta ruficollis
Tadorna tadorna
Tadorna ferruginea
Marmaronetta (Anas) angustirostris
Somateria spectabilis
Polysticta stelleri
Histrionicus histrionicus
Bucephala islandica
Mergus albellus
Oxyura leucocephala
FALCONIFORMES
all species
GRUIFORMES
Turnicidae
Turnix sylvatica
Gruidae
all species
Rallidae
Porzana porzana
Porzana pusilla
Porzana parva
Crex crex
Porphyrio porphyrio
Fulica cristata
Ottidae
all species
CHARADRIIFORMES
Charadriidae
Hoplopterus spinosus
Charadrius hiaticula
Charadrius dubius
Charadrius alexandrinus
Charadrius leschenaulti
Eudromias morinellus
Arenaria interpres
Scolopacidae
Gallinago media
Numenius tenuirostris
Tringa stagnatilis
Tringa ochropus
Tringa glareola
Tringa hypoleucos
Tringa cinerea
Calidris minuta
Calidris temminckii
Calidris maritima
Calidris alpina
Calidris ferruginea
Calidris alba
Limicola falcinellus
Recurvirostridae
all species
Phalaropodidae
all species
Burhinidae
Burhinus oedicnemus
Glareolidae
all species
Laridae
Pagophila eburnea
Larus audouinii
Larus melanocephalus
Larus genei
Larus minutus
Larus (Xenia) sabini
Chalidonias niger
Chlidonias leucopterus
Chlidonias hybrida
Gelochelidon nilotica
Hydroprogne caspia
Sterna hirundo
Sterna paradisaea (macrura)
Sterna dougallii
Sterna albifrons
Sterna sandvicensis
COLUMBIFORMES
Pteroclididae
all species
CUCULIFORMES
Cuculidae
Clamator glandarius
STRIGIFORMES
all species
CAPRIMULGIFORMES
Caprimulgidae
all species
APODIFORMES
Apodidae
Apus pallidus
Apus melba
Apus caffer
CORACIIFORMES
Alcedinidae
Alcedo atthis
Meropidae
Merops apiaster
Coraciidae
Coracias garrulus
Upopidae
Upopa epops
PICIFORMES
all species
PASSERIFORMES

Aludidae
Calandrella brachydactyla
Calandrella rufescens
Melanocorypha calandra
Melanocorypha leucoptera
Melanocorypha yeltoniensis
Galerida theklae
Eremophila alpestris
Hirundinidae
all species
Motacillidae
all species
Laniidae
all species
Bombycillidae
Bombycilla garrulus
Cinclidae
Cinclus cinclus
Troglodytidae
Troglodytes troglodytes
Prunellidae
all species
Muscicapidae
Turdinae
Saxicola rubetra
Saxicola torquata
Oenanthe oenanthe
Oenanthe pleschanka (leucomela)
Oenanthe hispanica
Oenanthe isabellina
Oenanthe leucura
Cercotrichas galactotes
Monticola saxatilis
Monticola solitarius
Phoenicurus ochruros
Phoenicurus phoenicurus
Erithacus rubecula
Luscinia megarhynchos
Luscinia luscinia
Luscinia (Cyanosylvia) svecica
Tarsiger cyanurus
Sylviinae
all species
Regulinae
all species
Muscicapinae
all species
Timaliinae
Panurus biarmicus
Paridae
all species
Sittidae
all species
Certhiidae
all species
Emberizidae
Emberiza citrinella
Emberiza leucophala
Emberiza cirluce
Emberiza cineracea
Emberiza caesia
Emberiza cia
Emberiza schoeniclus
Emberiza melanocephala
Emberiza aureola
Emberiza pusilla
Emberiza rustica
Plectrophenax nivalis
Calcarius lapponicus
Fringillidae
Carduelis chloris
Carduelis carduelis
Carduelis spinus
Carduelis flavirostris
Carduelis cannabina
Carduelis flammea
Carduelis hornemanni
Serinus citrinella
Serinus serinus
Loxia curvirostra
Loxia pityopsittacus
Loxia leucoptera
Pinicola enucleator
Carpodacus erythrinus
Rhodopechys githaginea
Coccothraustes coccothraustes
Ploceidae
Petronia petronia
Montrifringilla nivalis
Sturnidae
Sturnus unicolor
Sturnus roseus
Oriolidae
Oriolus oriolus
Corvidae
Perisoreus infaustus
Cyanopica cyanus
Nucifraga caryocatactes
Pyrrhocorax pyrrhocorax
Pyrrhocorax graculus

Reptiles

TESTUDINES
Testudinidae
Testudo hermanni
Testudo graeca
Testudo marginata
Emydidae
Emys orbicularis
Mauremys caspica
Dermochelyidae
Dermochelys coriacea
Cheloniidae
Caretta caretta
Lepidochelys kempii
Chelonia mydas
Eretmochelys imbricata
SAURIA
Gekkonidae
Cyrtodactylus kotschyi
Chamaeleontidae
Chamaeleon chamaeleon
Lacertidae
Algyroides marchi
Lacerta lepida
Lacerta parva
Lacerta simonyi
Lacerta princeps
Lacerta viridis
Podarcis muralis
Podarcis lilfordi
Podarcis sicula

Podarcis filfolensis
Scincidae
Ablepharus kitaibelii

OPHIDIA

Colubridae
Coluber hippocrepis
Elaphe situla
Elaphe quatuorlineata
Elaphe longissima
Coronella austriaca

Viperidae
Vipera ursinii
Vipera latasti
Vipera ammodytes
Vipera xanthina
Vipera lebetina
Vipera kaznakovi

Amphibians

CAUDATA
Salamandridae
Salamandra (Mertensiella) luschani
Salamandrina terdigitata
Chioglossa lusitanica
Triturus cristatus
Proteidae
Proteus anguinus

ANURA
Discoglossidae
Bombina variegata
Bombina bombina
Alytes obstetricans
Alytes cisternasii
Pelobatidae
Pelobates cultripes
Pelobates fuscus
Bufonidae
Bufo calamita
Bufo viridis
Hylidae
Hyla arborea
Ranidae
Rana arvalis
Rana dalmatina
Rana latastei

APPENDIX III
Protected fauna species
Mammals

INSECTIVORA

Erinaceidae
Erinaceus europaeus
Soricidae
all species

MICROCHIROPTERA

Vespertilionidae
Pipistrellus pipistrellus

DUPLICIDENTATA
Leporidae
Lepus timidus
Lepus capensis (europaeus)

RODENTIA
Sciuridae
Sciurus vulgaris
Marmota marmota
Castoridae
Castor fiber
Gliridae
all species

Microtidae
Microtus ratticeps (oeconomus)
Microtus nivalis (lebrunii)

CETACEA
all species not mentioned in Appendix II
CARNIVORA
Mustelidae
Meles meles
Mustela erminea
Mustela nivalis
Putorius (Mustela) putorius
Martes martes
Martes foina
Viverridae
all species
Felidae
Felis catus (silvestris)
Lynx lynx
Phocidae
Phoca vitulina
Pusa (Phoca) hispida
Pagophilus groenlandicus (Phoca groenlandica)
Erignathus barbatus
Halichoerus grypus
Cystophora cristata

ARTIODACTYLA
Suidae
Sus scrofa meridionalis
Cervidae
all species
Bovidae
Ovis aries (musimon, ammon)
Capra ibex
Capra pyrenaica
Rupicapra rupicapra

Birds

all species not included in Appendix II with the exception of:
Larus marinus
Larus fuscus
Larus agentatus
Columba palumbus
Passer domesticus
Sturnus vulgaris
Garrulus glandarius
Pica pica
Corvus monedula

Corvus frugilegus
Corvus corone (coronet and cornix)

Amphibians

All species not included in Appendix II

Reptiles

All species not included in Appendix II

APPENDIX IV

Prohibited means and methods of killing, capture and other forms of exploitation

MAMMALS

Snares
Live animals used as decoys which are blind or mutilated
Tape recorders
Electrical devices capable of killing and stunning
Artificial light sources
Mirrors and other dazzling devices
Devices for illuminating targets
Sighting devices for night shooting comprising an electronic image magnifier or image converter
Explosives[1]
Nets[2]
Traps[2]
Poison and poisoned or anaesthetic bait
Gassing or smoking out
Semi-automatic or automatic weapons with a magazine capable of holding more than two rounds of ammunition
Aircraft
Motor vehicles in motion

BIRDS

Snares[3]
Limes
Hooks
Live birds used as decoys which are blind or mutilated
Tape recorders
Electrical devices capable of killing and stunning
Artificial light sources
Mirrors and other dazzling devices
Devices for illuminating targets
Sighting devices for night shooting comprising an electronic image magnifier or image converter
Explosives
Nets
Traps
Poison and poisoned or anaesthetic bait
Semi-automatic or automatic weapons with a magazine capable of holding more than two rounds of ammunition
Aircraft
Motor vehicles in motion

1. Except for whale hunting
2. If applied for large scale or non-selective capture or killing.
3. Except Lagopus north of latitude 58° N.

CONVENTION ON LONG-RANGE TRANSBOUNDARY AIR POLLUTION[78]

Geneva, 13 November 1979

The Parties to the present Convention,

Determined to promote relations and co-operation in the field of environmental protection,

Aware of the significance of the activities of the United Nations Economic Commission for Europe in strengthening such relations and co-operation, particularly in the field of air pollution including long-range transport of air pollutants,

Recognizing the contribution of the Economic Commission for Europe to the multilateral implementation of the pertinent provisions of the Final Act of the Conference on Security and Co-operating in Europe,

Cognizant of the references in the chapter on environment of the Final Act of the Conference on Security and Co-operation in Europe calling for co-operation to control air pollution and its effects, including long-range transport of air pollutants, and to the development through international co-operation of an extensive programme for the monitoring and evaluation of long-range transport of air pollutants, starting with sulphur dioxide and with possible extension to other pollutants,

Considering the pertinent provisions of the Declaration of the United Nations Conference on the Human Environment, and in particular principle 21, which expresses the comon conviction that States have, in accordance with the Charter of the United Nations and the principles of international law, the sovereign right to exploit their own resources pursuant to their own environmental policies, and the responsibility to ensure that activities within their jurisdiction or control do not cause damage to the environment of other States or of areas beyond the limits of national jurisdiction,

Recognizing the existence of possible adverse effects, in the short and long term, of air pollution including transboundary air pollution,

Concerned that a rise in the level of emission of air pollutants within the region as forecast may increase such adverse effects,

Recognizing the need to study the implications of the long-range transport of air pollutants and the need to seek solutions for the problems identified,

Affirming their willingness to reinforce active international co-operation to develop appropriate national policies and by means of exchange of information, consultation, research and monitoring, to co-ordinate national action for combating air pollution including long-range transboundary air pollution,

Have agreed as follows:

DEFINITIONS

Article 1

For the purpose of the present Convention:

a) "air pollution" means the introduction by man, directly or indirectly, of substances or energy into the air resulting in deleterious effects of such a nature as to endanger human, harm living resources and ecosystems and material property and impair or interfere with amenities and other legitimate uses of the environment, and "air pollutants" shall be construed accordingly;

b) "long-range transboundary air pollution" means air pollution whose physical origin is situated wholly or in part within the area under the national jurisdiction of one State and which has adverse effects in the area under the jurisdiction of another State at such a distance that it is not generally possible to distinguish the contribution of individual emission sources or groups of sources.

FUNDAMENTAL PRINCIPLES

Article 2

The Contracting Parties, taking due account of the facts and problems involved, are determined to protect man and his environment against air pollution and shall endeavour to limit and, as far as possible, gradually reduce and prevent air pollution including long-range transboundary pollution.

Article 3

The Contracting Parties, within the framework of the present Convention, shall be means of exchanges of information, consultation, research and monitoring, develop without undue delay policies and strategies which shall serve as a means of combating the discharge of air pollutants, taking into account efforts already made at national and international levels.

Article 4

The Contracting Parties shall exchange information on and review their policies, scientific activities and technical measures aimed at combating, as far as possible, the discharge of air pollutants, which may have adverse effects, thereby contributing to the reduction of air pollution including long-range transboundary air pollution.

Article 5

Consultations shall be held, upon request, at an early stage between, on the one hand, Contracting Parties which are actually affected by or exposed to a significant risk of long-range transboundary air pollution and, on the other hand, Contracting Parties within which and subject to whose jurisdiction a significant contribution to long-range transboundary air pollution originates, or could orginate, in connexion with activities carried on or contemplated therein.

Footnote to the Convention:

i) The present Convention does not contain a rule on State Liability as to damage

AIR QUALITY MANAGEMENT

Article 6

Taking into account articles 2 to 5, the ongoing research, exchange of information and monitoring and the results thereof, the cost and effectiveness of local and other remedies and, in order to combat air pollution in particular that originating from new or rebuilt installations, each Contracting Party undertakes to develop the best policies and strategies including air quality management systems, and, as part of them, control measures compatible with balanced development, in particular by using the best available technoloy which is economically feasible and low-and non-waste technology.

RESEARCH AND DEVELOPMENT

Article 7

The Contracting Parties, as appropriate to their needs, shall initiate and co-operate in the conduct of research into and/or development of:

a) existing and proposed technologies for reducing emissions of sulphur compounds and other major air pollutants, including technical and economic feasibility, and evironmental consequences;

b) instrumentation and other techniques for monitoring and measuring emission rates and ambient concentrations of air pollutants;

c) improved models for a better understanding of the transmission of long-range transboundary air pollutants;

d) the effects of sulphur compounds and other major air pollutants on human health and the environment, including agriculture, forestry, materials, aquatic and other natural ecosystems and visibility, with a view to establishing a scientific basis for dose/effect relationships designed to protect the environment;

e) the economic, social and evironmental assessent of alternative measures for attaining environmental objectives including the reduction of long-range transboundary air pollution;

f) education and training programmes related to the environmental aspects of pollution by sulphur compounds and other major air pollutants.

EXCHANGE OF INFORMATION

Article 8

The Contracting Parties, within the framwork of the Executive Body referred to in article 10 and bilaterally, shall, in their common interests, exchange available information on:

a) data on emission at periods of time to be agreed upon, of agreed air pollutants, starting with sulphur dioxide, coming from grid-units of agreed size; or on the fluxes of agreed air pollutants, starting with sulphur dioxide, across national borders, at distances and at periods of time to be agreed upon;

b) major changes in national policies and in

general industrial development, and their potential impact, which would be likely to cause significant changes in long-range transbounary air pollution;

c) control teachnologies for reducing air pollution relevant to long-range transboundary air pollution;

d) the projected cost of the emission control or sulphur compounds and other major air pollutants on a national scale;

e) meteorological and physico-chemical data relating to the processes during transmission;

f) physico-chemical and biological data relating to the effects of long-range transboundary air pollution and the extent of the damage 1 which these data indicate can be attributed to long-range transboundary air pollution;

g) national, subregional and regional policies and strategies for the control of sulphur compounds and other major oil pollutants.

IMPLEMENTATION AND FURTHER DEVELOPMENT OF THE CO-OPERATIVE PROGRAMME FOR THE MONITORING AND EVALUATION OF THE LONG-RANGE TRANSMISSION OF AIR POLLUTANTS IN EUROPE

Article 9

The Contracting Parties stress the need for the implementation of the existing "Co- operative programme for the monitoring and evaluation of the long-range transmission of air pollutants in Europe" (hereinafter referred to as EMEP) and, with regard to the further development of this programme, agree to emphasize:

a) the desirability of Contracting Parties joining in and fully implementing EMEP which, as a first step, is based on the monitoring of sulphur dioxide and related substances;

b) the need to use comparable or standardized procedures for monitoring whenever possible;

c) the desirability of basing the monitoring programme on the framework of both national and international programmes. The establishment of monitoring stations and the collection of data shall be carried out under the national jurisdiction of the country in which the monitoring stations are located;

d) the desirability of establishing a framework for a co-operative environmental monitoring programme, based on and taking into account present and future national, subregional regional and other international programmes;

e) the need to exchange data on emissions at periods of time to be agreed upon, of agreed air pollutants, starting with sulphur dioxide, coming from grid-units of agreed size; or on the fluxes of agreed air pollutants, starting with sulphur dioxide, across national borders, at distances and at periods of time to be agreed upon. The method including the model, used to determine the fluxes, as well as the method, including the model, used to determine the transmission of air pollutants, based on the emissions per grid-unit, shall be made available and periodically reviewed, in order to improve the methods and the models;

f) their willingness to continue the exchange and periodic updating of national data on total emissions of agreed air pollutants, starting with sulphur dioxide;

g) the need to provide meteorological and physico-chemical data relating to processes during transmission;

h) the need to monitor chemical components in other media such as water, soil and vegetation, as well as a similar monitoring programme to record effects on health and environment;

i) the desirability of extending the national EMEP networks to make them operational for control and surveillance purposes.

EXECUTIVE BODY

Article 10

1. The representatives of the Contracting Parties shall, within the framework of the Senior Advisers to ECE Governments on Environmental Problems, constitute the Executive Body of the present Convention, and shall meet at least annually in that capacity.

2. The Executive Body shall:

a) review the implementation of the present Convention;

b) establish, as appropriate, working groups to consider matters related to the implementation and development of the present Convention and to this end to prepare appropriate studies and other documentation and to submit recommendations to be considered by the Executive Body;

c) fulfil such other functions as may be appropriate under the provisions of the present Convention.

3. The Executive Body shall utilize the Steering Body for the EMEP to play an integral part in the operation of the present Convention, in particular with regard to data collection and scientific co-operation.

4. The Executive Body, in discharging its functions, shall, when it deems appropriate, also make use of information from other relevant international organizations.

SECRETARIAT

Article 11

The Executive Secretary of the Economic Commission for Europe shall carry out, for the Executive Body, the following secretariat functions -

a) to convene and prepare the meetings of the Executive Body;

b) to transmit to the Contracting Parties reports and other information received in accordance with the provisions of the present Convention;

c) to discharge the functions assigned by the Executive Body.

AMENDMENTS TO THE CONVENTION

Article 12

1. Any Contracting Party may propose amendments to the present convention.

2. The text of proposed amendments shall be submitted in writing to the Executive Secretary of the Economic Commission for Europe, who shall communicate them to all Contracting Parties. The Executive Body shall discuss proposed amendments at its next annual meeting provided that such proposals have been circulated by the Executive Secretary of the Economic Commission for Europe to the Contracting Parties at least ninety days in advance.

3. An amendment to the present Convention shall be adopted by consensus of the representatives of the Contracting Parties, and shall enter into force for the Contracting Parties which have accepted it on the ninetieth day after the date on which two-thirds of the Contracting Parties have deposited their instruments of acceptance with the depositary. Thereafter, the amendment shall enter into force for any other Contracting Party on the ninetieth day after the date on which that Contracting Party deposits its instrument of acceptance of the amendment.

SETTLEMENT OF DISPUTES

Article 13

If a dispute arises between two or more Contracting Parties to the present Convention as to the interpretation or application of the Convention, they shall seek a solution by negotiation or by any other method of dispute settlement acceptable to the parties to the dispute.

SIGNATURE

Article 14

1. The present Convention shall be open for signature at the United Nations Office at Geneva from 13 to 16 November 1979 on the occassion of the High-level Meeting within the framework of the Economic Commission for Europe on the Protection of the Environment, by the member States of the Economic Commission for Europe as well as States having consultative status with the Economic Commission for Europe, pursuant to paragraph 8 of Economic and Social Council resolution 36 (IV) of 28 March 1947, and by regional economic intergration organizations, constituted by sovereign States members of the Economic Commission for Europe, which have competence in respect of the negotiation, conclusion and application of international agreements in matters covered by the present Convention.

2. In matters within their competence, such regional economic integration organizations shall, on their own behalf, exercise the rights and fulfil the responsibilities which the present Convention attributes to their member States. In such cases, the member States of these organizations shall not be entitled to exercise such rights individully.

RATIFICATION, ACCEPTANCE, APPROVAL AND ACCESSION

Article 15

1. The present Convention shall be subject to ratification, acceptance or approval.

2. The present Convention shall be open for accession as from 17 November 1979 by the States and organizations referred to in article 14, paragraph 1.

3. The instruments of ratification, acceptance, approval or accession shall be deposited with the Secretary-General of the United Nations, who will perform the functions of the depositary.

ENTRY INTO FORCE

Article 16

1. The present Convention shall enter into force on the ninetieth day after the date of deposit of the twenty-fourth instrument of ratification, acceptance, approval or accession.

2. For each Contracting Party which ratifies, accepts or approves the present Convention or accedes thereto after the deposit of the twenty-fourth instrument of ratification, acceptance, approval or accession, the Convention shall enter into force on the ninetieth day after the date of deposit by such Contracting Party of its instrument of ratification, acceptance, approval or accession.

WITHDRAWAL

Article 17

At any time after five years from the date on which the present Convention has come into force with respect to a Contracting Party, that Contracting Party may withdraw from the Convention by giving written notification to the depositary. Any such withdrawal shall take effect on the ninetieth day after the date of its receipt by the depositary.

AUTHENTIC TEXTS

Article 18

The original of the present Convention, of which the English, French and Russian texts are equally authentic, shall be deposited with the Secretary-General of the United Nations.

In witness whereof the undersigned, being duly authorized thereto, have signed the present Convention.

Done at Geneva, this thirteenth day of November, one thousand nine hundred and seventy nine.

Index